FULLY REVISED 4th EDITION

PISTOLS of the WORLD

Ian V. Hogg & John Walter

©2004 by Ian V. Hogg, John Weeks and John Walter

Published by

krause publications
An imprint of F+W Publications, Inc.

700 East State Street • Iola, WI 54990-0001
715-445-2214 • 888-457-2873
www.krause.com

Our toll-free number to place an order or obtain a free catalog is 800-258-0929.

Library of Congress Catalog Number: 2002107614

ISBN: 0-87349-460-1

Interior designed by Sandy Kent

Edited by Joel Marvin

Printed in the United States of America

ABOUT OUR
Covers

New for 2004 from Heckler & Koch is the P2000 SK Sub-Compact pistol. Identical in almost every respect to the P2000 US Compact, this new version is destined to become an instant favorite for shooters needing a smaller-framed gun for lighter weight, particularly in concealed-carry situations. Built on a rugged corrosion-proof fiber-reinforced frame, both models feature a robust dual-recoil assembly and HK's patented pre-cocked hammer system, which combines the advantages of a constant level of trigger pull with a shorter trigger travel for each round fired. This unique system offers the crisp trigger pull of a single action with the rock-solid reliability of a double-action pistol. Other shared features include an innovative trigger-guard design that perfectly guides your finger to the trigger or further back to engage the ambidextrous magazine release. Standard equipment exclusive to P2000 pistols include HK's new modular grip. Fitted with interchangeable back straps (four for the US and two for the SK Sub-Compact), the P2000 SK Sub-Compact pistols are able to accommodate almost any hand size comfortably. Also included is an industry-standard mounting rail, so your P2000 SK Sub-Compact is ready to carry a complete line-up of accessories. The new P2000 SK Sub-Compact is lightweight, rugged, accurate and reliable – everything a compact pistol should be!

For more information on the P2000 SK Sub-Compact and other HK products, please contact Heckler & Koch at 21480 Pacific Blvd, Sterling, VA 20166. They can be reached by phone at 703-450-1900, FAX at 703-450-0721 or on the Internet at *www.hk-usa.com*.

TABLE OF Contents

PART ONE: INTRODUCTION

INTRODUCTION 7

THE DIRECTORY 8

PART TWO: THE DIRECTORY

A.A. ARMS 9

ABADIE 9

ACCU-TEK 9

ACHA BROTHERS /
    DOMINGO ACHA & CO. 9

JOHN ADAMS.......................10

ADLERWAFFENFABRIK 10

FRED ADOLPH 11

ADVANTAGE ARMS CO. 11

AETNA ARMS CO. 11

AGNER-SAXHØJ PRODUCTS 11

AGUIRRE & CO. 11

ALDAY & GABILONDO 11

A. ALDAZABAL 11

JOSE ALDAZABAL SONS.........11

ALDAZABAL, LETURIONDO
    & CO. 11

ALKARTASUNA 11

ALLEN & WHEELOCK..............12

AMERICAN ARMS 12

AMERICAN ARMS &
    AMMUNITION CO. 12

AMERICAN ARMS CO. 12

AMERICAN ARMS, INC. 12

AMERICAN DERRINGER 13

AMERICAN FIRE ARMS
    MFG CO. 14

AMERICAN FRONTIER
    FIREARMS CO....................14

AMERICAN GUN CO. 14

AMERICAN STANDARD
    TOOL CO. 14

AMES SWORD CO...................14

AMTEC...............................14

L. ANCION-MARX 15

J.G. ANSCHÜTZ 15

UDO ANSCHÜTZ....................15

APAOLOZO BROTHERS 15

A & R SALES 16

ARAÑA & CO. 16

ARCADIA MACHINE &
    TOOL CO. 16

F. ARIZAGA SONS 16

GASPAR ARIZAGA 16

FRANCISCO ARIZMENDI 17

ARIZMENDI & GOENAGA 18

ARIZMENDI, ZULAICA
    & CO 18

ARMAMENT SYSTEMS &
    PROCEDURES 18

ARMAS DE FUEGO 19

ARMAS DE TIRO Y CASA SA 19

ARMERO ESPECIALISTAS 19

ARMI-JAGER 19

ARMINEX LTD 19

ARMSCOR...........................19

EULOGIO AROSTEGUI 20

SALVATOR AROSTEGUI 20

ARRIOLA BROTHERS 20

CALIXTO ARRIZABALAGA
    SONS 20

ASCASO 21

ASERMA MANUFACTURING
    CO. 21

ASTRA–UNCETA & CO. 21

ATLAS ARMS 25

AUTAUGA ARMS 25

AUTO-MAG CORPORATION 25

AUTO-ORDNANCE CO. 25

AZANZA & ARRIZABALAGA 26

ANTONIO AZPIRI 26

AZPIRI & CO. 26

BACON ARMS CO. 27

LES BAER CUSTOM, INC...........27

BAFORD ARMS, INC. 28

BALLARD.............................28

BARRENECHEA &
    GALLASTEGUI....................28

JORGE BASCARAN SONS 28

MARTIN A. BASCARAN 28

KARL BAUER.........................29

BAUER FIREARMS CORP. 29

BAYONNE 29

EDUARD DE BEAUMONT 29

BECKER & HOLLANDER 29

BEEMAN PRECISION ARMS 29

BEISTEGUI BROTHERS..............29

BENELLI ARMI 30

PIETRO BERETTA 31

LOUIS BERGERON..................41

THEODOR BERGMANN.............41

BERISTAIN & CO....................43

BERLIN-SUHLER WERKE...........43

BERN ARMS FACTORY 43

BERNADON-MARTIN 45

VINCENZO BERNARDELLI 45

VINCENZO BERNEDO & CO. 47

BERSA...............................47

BERASALUZE, ARIETO-AURTENA
    & CO. 48

JULES BERTRAND 49

BIG HORN ARMS CO. 49

GUSTAV BITTNER 49

BLAND 49

BLISS & GOODYEAR 49

JOHN BLISSETT & SONS 49

BODEO...............................49

GREGORIO BOLUMBURU 50

BOND ARMS, INC 50

JAMES BOWN & SON 51

BRAENDLIN ARMOURY............51

BRESCIA ARMS FACTORY 51

BRILEY 51

BRITARMS 51

BROLIN ARMS 51

BROOKLYN ARMS CO. 52

E. ARTHUR BROWN CO., INC 52

ED BROWN 52

BROWN MFG CO. 52

BROWNING ARMS CO...............52

BRYCO ARMS 53

BSA GUNS LTD......................54

ERNST FRIEDRICH BÜCHEL......54

BÜCHSENMACHER HANDWERK-
    GENOSSENSCHAFT AG 55

KARL BURGSMÜLLER 55

CALICO 56

CARTUCHOES DEPORTIVOS DE
    MEXICO 56

CASPIAN ARMS 56

CASULL ARMS, INC. 56

CENTURY GUN
    DISTRIBUTORS, INC. 56

CENTURY INTERNATIONAL
    ARMS....................56

CESKÁ ZBROJOVKA 56

CESKOSLOVENSKÁ
    ZBROJOVKA......................61

CHAMELOT-DELVIGNE 62

CHAPUIS ARMES 62

ÉTABLISSEMENTS CHARLIER....62

ISIDOR CHAROLA 62

CHAROLA & ANITUA 62

CHARTER 2000, INC. 63

CHARTER ARMS CORP. 63

CHÂTELLERAULT ARMS
    FACTORY 65

CHICAGO FIREARMS
    COMPANY 65

CHINESE STATE FACTORIES 65

CHIPMUNK MFG., INC. 65

LOUIS CHOBERT 65

CHUCHU..............................66

WYTOLD CHYLEWSKI 66

CIMARRON FIRE ARMS MFG
    CO. 66

CLAIR BROTHERS 67

CLARIDGE............................67

CHARLES PH. CLÉMENT 67

CLERKE 68

COBRAY INDUSTRIES...............68

CODY MFG CO. 68

COLT 68

COLUMBIA ARMORY 90

COMPETITION ARMS 91

COMPETITOR CORP., INC........91

CONNECTICUT ARMS &
    MFG CO. 91

COONAN ARMS......................91

COOPERATIVA OBRERA 91

FRANK COPELAND...................91

CRESCENT FIREARMS CO. 91

CROWN CITY ARMS, INC. 91

CRUCELEGUI BROTHERS 91

CRVENA ZASTAVA 92

DAEWOO PRECISION
    INDUSTRIES LTD 93

CHARLES DALY 93

DANSK REKYLRIFFEL
   SYNDIKAT 93
DARDICK CORP. 94
DAVIS INDUSTRIES 94
DAVIS-WARNER 94
D. DEBOUXTAY 95
WILHELM DECKER 95
F. DELU 95
DEMON 95
DENEL 95
DERINGER RIFLE &
   PISTOL WORKS 96
ÉTABLISSEMENTS
   DERKENNE 96
DESERT INDUSTRIES 96
DETONICS 96
DEUTSCHE WAFFEN-
   & MUNITIONSFABRIKEN 97
DEUTSCHE-WERKE AG 101
DICKINSON 101
D-MAX, INC. 101
DOLNE 102
DORNHEIM 102
DORNAUS & DIXON 102
DOWNSIZER
   CORPORATION 102
FRANZ VON DREYSE 102
DRULOV 102
DUMOULIN 103
DUSEK 103

EAGLE ARMS CO. 104
EASTERN ARMS CO. 104
JAVIER ECHANIZ 104
ECHAVE Y ARIZMENDI 104
BONIFACIO ECHEVERRIA 104
EGYPTIAN STATE FACTORY 105
EIG 105
ELY & WRAY 105
EMF CO. 105
EMPIRE ARMS CO. 106
ENFIELD (ROYAL SMALL ARMS
   FACTORY) 107
ENTERPRISE GUN WORKS 107
ENTRÉPRISE ARMS 107
ENVALL 107
ERFURT RIFLE FACTORY 107
ERMA 107
ERMA (-WERKE) 108
ERQUIAGA 109
ANTONIO ERRASTI 110

MANUEL ESCODIN 110
ESPERANZA Y CIA 110
ESPERANZA & UNCETA 111
ESPRIN BROTHERS 113
EUROPEAN-AMERICAN
   ARMORY 113
EXCEL INDUSTRIES 113
EXTEGARRA 113

FABBRICA ARMI SPORTIVE 114
FABRICA DE ARMAS
   GARANTIZADA 114
FABRICATION FRANÇAISE 114
FABRIQUE FRANÇAISE
   D'ARMES DE GUERRE 114
FABRIQUE NATIONALE D'ARMES
   DE GUERRE 114
FAGNUS 123
FALCON FIREARMS
   MFG. CO. 123
FABRICACIONES MILITARES
   DEL EJERCITO 123
FEATHER INDUSTRIES 123
FEDERAL ARMS COMPANY 123
FEDERAL ORDNANCE, INC. 123
FEGYVER ÉS GÁZKESZUELEK-
   GYÁRA 123
FELK, INC. 125
FÉMÁRU FEGYVER ÉS
   GÉPGYÁR 125
FÉMÁRU ÉS
   SZERSZÁMGEPGYÁR NV 127
FIALA ARMS &
   EQUIPMENT CO. 127
GUILIO FIOCCHI SPA 127
FIREARMS IMPORT
   & EXPORT CO. 127
F.M.E./F.M.G. 127
FOEHL & WEEKS FIREARMS
   MFG. CO. 127
FOREHAND & WADSWORTH 128
FORT WORTH FIREARMS 128
LUIGI FRANCHI 128
AUGUSTE FRANCOTTE 128
ADOLPH FRANK 129
FREEDOM ARMS CO. 129
ANDREW FYRBERG 130

GABILONDO 131
GALAND 135
GALEF 136

GALESI 136
GAMBA 137
GARANTAZADA 137
GARATE BROTHERS 138
GARATE & ANITUA 138
GARBI, MORETTI Y CIA 139
GASSER 139
GATLING ARMS &
   AMMUNITION CO. LTD 140
GAUCHER ARMES 140
GAVAGE 140
GAZTAÑAGA 140
GAZTAÑAGA, TROCAOLA
   & IBARZABAL 141
GENERAL MOTORS 141
GENSCHOW 141
GERING 142
GERSTENBERGER &
   EBERWEIN 142
GIACOSA 142
GLISENTI 142
GLOCK AG 143
GRÄBNER 145
FABRIQUE D'ARMES
   DE GRANDE PRÉCISION 145
GREAT WESTERN ARMS CO. 146
GREEN 146
GRENDEL 147
GRUSONWERKE AG 147
GUISASOLA 147
GUISASOLA BROTHERS 147
GUSTLOFF-WERKE 147

HAENEL 149
HÆRENS TØJHUS 149
HAMAL 149
HÄMMERLI 149
HAMMOND 153
HARRINGTON &
   RICHARDSON, INC. 153
HARRIS GUNWORKS, INC. 157
HARTFORD ARMS & EQUIPMENT
   COMPANY 157
HAWES FIREARMS 157
HEBSACKER GESELLSCHAFT 157
HECKLER & KOCH GMBH 157
HEINZELMANN 163
HELLENIC ARMS 163
HELLFRITZSCH 163
HEMBRUG ARMS FACTORY 163

HENRION, DASSY
   & HEUSCHEN 163
HERITAGE MFG INC. 164
HERMAN 164
HERTER'S, INC. 164
HEYM 164
HIGGINS 165
HIGH STANDARD 165
HIGH-STANDARD MFG
   CO. INC. 169
HI-POINT 169
HISPANO-ARGENTINA FABRICAS
   DE AUTOMOVILES SA 169
HJS ARMS, INC. 170
HOLLY MFG. CO. 170
HOOD FIRE ARMS CO. 170
HOPKINS & ALLEN 171
HOURAT & VIE 172
H&R 1871, INC. 173
HUNTER 173
HUSQVARNA ARMS
   FACTORY 173

IAI 174
IAR, INC. 174
TEODORO IBARZABAL 174
ILLINOIS ARMS COMPANY 174
IMPERIAL ARMS COMPANY 174
INAGAKI 174
INDIAN ARMS CORP. 174
INDIAN SALES COMPANY 174
INDUSTRIA ARGENTINA 174
INDUSTRIA ARMERA 174
INDUSTRIÁ DO MATERIEL
   BELICÓ DE BRASIL 175
INDUSTRIA NACIONAL
   DE ARMAS 175
JOHN INGLIS & CO. 175
INTERARMS 176
INTERDYNAMICS OF
   AMERICA 176
INTRATEC 176
IRAOLA Y SALAVERRIA 176
WILLIAM IRVING 176
ISRAEL MILITARY
   INDUSTRIES 176
ITALGUNS INTERNATIONAL 178
ITHACA GUN COMPANY 178
INDUSTRIAL TECHNOLOGY
   & MACHINES AG 178

IZHEVSK ENGINEERING FACTORY 179

JAQUEMART......182
JAEGER 182
JAMES 182
JANSSEN SONS......182
JAPAN GUN CO. LTD......183
JENNINGS 183
IVER JOHNSON 183
J.H. JOHNSON 185
JOHNSON, BYE & COMPANY ..185
JYVÄSKYLÄ ARMS FACTORY ..186

KAHR ARMS 188
K.B.I., INC. 188
KEL-TEC CNC INDUSTRIES, INC. 188
F.W. KESSLER 188
KIMBALL ARMS COMPANY 189
KIMBER MFG, INC. 189
ALBRECHT KIND......190
A. KLESESEWSKI 190
KOHOUT 190
KOISHIKAWA ARMS FACTORY 190
KOKURA ARMS FACTORY 192
HENRY M. KOLB 192
THEODOR KOMMER 192
KOMURO ARMS FACTORY 193
KONGSBERG ARMS FACTORY....193
KORTH......193
KORRIPHILA......194
ALFRED KRAUSER 194
HEINRICH KRIEGHOFF......195
KAREL KRNKA 195
KRONBORG ARMS FACTORY ..195
KYNOCH 196

CHARLES LANCASTER 197
LANDSTAD 197
LANGENHAN 197
LAR MANUFACTURING, INC. 198
LARRANAGA Y ELARTZA 198
LASAGABASTER HERMANOS ..198
LASERAIM TECHNOLOGIES, INC. 198
JOSEF LAUMANN 198
LEE ARMS COMPANY 198
EUGÈNE LEFAUCHEUX 198

LE PAGE 199
LERCKER 199
LES, INC. 199
LIGNOSE 199
LITTLE ALL RIGHT FIREARMS COMPANY 200
LLAMA–GABILONDO 200
LUDWIG LOEWE 200
LORCIN ENGINEERING 201
LOWELL ARMS COMPANY 201

MACCHINE TERMO BALLISTICHE......202
MAGNUM RESEARCH, INC. 202
MAKÍNA VE KIMYA ENDÜSTRÍSÍ 203
MALTBY, CURTIS & CO......203
MANN 203
MANUFACTURE D'ARMES À FEU 203
MANUFACTURE D'ARMES DE BAYONNE......203
MANUFACTURE D'ARMES DES PYRÉNÉES 205
MANUFACTURE DE MACHINES DU HAUT RHIN 208
MANUFACTURE FRANÇAISE DES ARMES ET CYCLES......210
MANUFACTURE LIÉGEOISE D'ARMES À FEU 212
MARGA 212
MARGOLIN 212
MARLIN 212
MARS 213
MARSTON 213
T. MARTIN......213
MARTZ......213
MAUSER......214
MAUSER-JAGDWAFFEN GMBH 222
MAXIM GUN & AMMUNITION CO. 225
MAYOR......225
MB ASSOCIATES 225
MENDOZA 226
MENZ......226
MERIDEN 227
MERRILL 227
MERRIMAC......227
MERWIN 227

METALLURGICA BRESCIANA GIA TEMPINI 228
MEXICO CITY ARMS FACTORY 228
MIEG 229
MIKKENGER......229
MIROKU 229
MITCHELL 229
MKS 230
MOLGORA 230
MOA CORPORATION 230
MOHAWK ARMS COMPANY 230
MOORE 230
MORAIN 230
MORINI 230
MORITZ......230
MOSSBERG 231
MUGICA 231
MÜLLER 231
MUSGRAVE 231

NAGANT 232
NAGOYA ARMS FACTORY 233
NAMBU 233
NATIONAL ARMS CO......234
NAVY ARMS CO. 234
NEUMANN 234
NEW ENGLAND FIREARMS CO......235
NORDHEIM 235
NORTH AMERICAN ARMS CO. LTD......235
NORTH AMERICAN ARMS CORP. 235
NORTH AMERICAN ARMS CO. 235
NORTH CHINA INDUSTRIES CORP. 236
NORTH KOREAN ARMS FACTORIES......237
NORTON 237
NORWICH FALLS PISTOL CO......237
NORWICH PISTOL CO......237

OESTERREICHISCHE WAFFENFABRIKS-GESELLSCHAFT 238
OESTERREICHISCHE WERKE ANSTALT......242
OJANGUREN Y MARCAIDO 242

OJANGUREN Y VIDOSA 242
ORBEA 243
LA INDUSTRIAL ORBEA 244
FERNANDO ORMACHEA......244
ORTEGA......244
HEINRICH ORTGIES & CO. 244
ORUETA......244
OSGOOD 245
OVIEDO ARMS FACTORY 245
OYEZ ARMS COMPANY 245

PACIFIC INTERNATIONAL 246
PAGÈS......246
PARA ORDNANCE 246
PARDINI 247
PARKER-HALE 247
PASSLER & SEIDL 247
PATRO 247
PAVLICEK 247
PETERS STAHL 247
PFANNL 248
PHELPS 248
PHILLIPS & RODGERS, INC. 248
PHOENIX ARMS......248
PICKERT 248
HENRI PIEPER 249
NICOLAS PIEPER 251
PIETTA 251
PINDAD ARMS FACTORY......251
PIRLOT......251
PITTSTON ARMS COMPANY ..252
PLANT 252
PLZEN 252
POND 252
POWERS 252
POSZUMAVSKÁ ZBROJOVKA KDYNE 252
PRAGA 252
PRECISE IMPORTS CORP. 253
PRESCOTT 253
PRETORIA ARMS FACTORY......253
PRYSE 253
PYRÉNÉES 253

RADOM ARMS FACTORY......254
RAICK 255
RANDALL 255
RAST & GASSER 256
RAVEN ARMS 256
RECK 256
REID 256

REIGER 257
REISING.........................257
REMINGTON 257
REPUBLIC ARMS, INC. 260
REPUBLIC ARMS PTY 260
RETOLAZA BROTHERS.............260
FABRIQUE D'ARMES
   RÉUNIES.....................261
RH-ALAN 261
RHEINISCHE METALLWAAREN-
   & MASCHINENFABRIK 262
RHEINISCHE WAFFEN- &
   MUNITIONSFABRIK 264
RHÖNER 264
RIGARMI 264
ROBAR 265
ROCK RIVER ARMS.............265
ROCKY MOUNTAIN ARMS
   CORP. 266
RÖHM 266
RÖMERWERKE.................267
RONGÉ.........................268
ROSSI 268
ROTH 271
RPM 271
RUPERTUS.....................271
RYAN MFG CO.................271
THOMAS J. RYAN.............271

SABATTI & TANFOGLIO...........272
SAFARI ARMS/SCHUETZEN
   PISTOL WORKS 272
SAINT-ÉTIENNE ARMS
   FACTORY 272
SAKO 273
SALABERRIN....................273
SALAVERRIA 274
SAN PAOLO 274
CASIMIR SANTOS 274
MODESTO SANTOS.................274
SAUER 274
SAVAGE ARMS CO..................277
SAVAGE ARMS, INC. 278
SCHALL 278
SCHILLING 278
SCHMIDT 279
SCHÜLER 279
SCHULHOF......................279
SCHUTZ & LARSEN..............279
SCHWARZLOSE 279

SCHWEIZERISCHE INDUSTRIE
   GESELLSCHAFT 280
SCOTT 284
SECURITY INDUSTRIES
   OF AMERICA 284
SEDGELY 284
SEECAMP 284
SEMMERLING CORP. 284
SEYTRES 284
SHARPS 285
SHATUCK 285
SHERIDAN 285
SHIN CHUO KOGYO KK 285
SIMSON 285
SIRKIS 286
SKODA 286
SLOUGH 286
SMITH 286
SMITH & WESSON 287
SOCIEDAD ESPAÑOL DE
   ARMAS Y MUNICIONES 315
SOCIÉTÉ ALSACIENNE DES
   CONSTRUCTIONS
   MECANIQUES 315
SOCIÉTÉ FRANÇAISE D' ARMES
   AUTOMATIQUES 315
SOCIÉTÉ FRANÇAISE
   DES MUNITIONS 315
SOKOLOVSKY CORP.................315
SPANDAU ARMS FACTORY 316
SPANGENBERG & SAUER 316
SPESCO CORPORATION 316
SPHINX AG 316
SPREEWERKE GMBH 317
SPRINGFIELD, INC. 317
SPRINGFIELD ARMORY 321
SQUIRES, BINGHAM
   MFG CO. 322
STAR–BONIFACIO
   ECHEVERRIA SA 322
STEEL CITY ARMS.................325
STENDAWERKE GMBH 326
STERLING ARMAMENT
   CO. LTD 326
STERLING ARMS CORP. 326
J. STEVENS ARMS &
   TOOL CO. 327
STEYR-MANNLICHER GMBH ..328
STOCK 329
A.F. STOEGER/STOEGER
   ARMS............................329

STURM, RUGER & CO. 329
SUINAGA Y ARAMPERRI 337
SUPER SIX LTD 337
SWIFT RIFLE COMPANY 337

TALLERES DE ARMAS LIVIANAS
   ARGENTINAS.....................338
TANFOGLIO BROTHERS 338
GIUSEPPE TANFOGLIO 338
TAURUS 339
TEXAS LONGHORN 345
THÄLMANN 346
THAMES 346
THAYER, ROBERSTON
   & CAREY 346
THIEME & EDELER 346
THOMPSON/CENTER ARMS....346
THORSSIN 346
TIPPING & LAWDEN.................347
TOKYO GAS &
   ELECTRIC CO. 347
TOMISKA........................347
TRANSMARK 347
TRANTER 347
TREJO...........................348
TRIBUZIO 348
TROCAOLA 348
TSINNTOCHMASH 348
TTIBAR 349
TULA ARMS FACTORY 349
TULLE ARMS FACTORY 350
TURBIAUX 351

ALDO UBERTI 352
ULTRA-LIGHT ARMS, INC. 353
UNATTRIBUTABLE DESIGNS ..353
UNCETA Y CIA 355
UNIES..........................356
UNION ARMERA
   EIBARENSE.......................357
UNION FIREARMS
   COMPANY 357
MANUFACTURE D'ARMES
   "UNIQUE" 357
UNITED STATES ARMS
   CORPORATION...................357
UNITED STATES PATENT
   FIRE-ARMS MFG CO. 357
TÓMAS DE URIZAR 357
URREJOLA Y CIA 358
U.S. ARMS CO. 358

VALENCIA ARMS FACTORY......359
VALTRO 359
VENUS-WAFFENWERK(E) 359
MANUFACTURE D'ARMES
   VERNEY-CARRON 359
VICTORY ARMS CO. 359
VOERE GMBH 359

WAHL 360
CARL WALTHER
   WAFFENFABRIK 360
CARL WALTHER
   SPORTWAFFENFABRIK 366
WAMO MFG CO. 372
WARNANT 372
WARNER ARMS CO. 372
JAMES WARNER 372
WEATHERBY, INC.................373
WEBLEY (& SCOTT) 373
WEIHRAUCH 383
DAN WESSON FIREARMS 385
WESSON FIREARMS CORP. 386
FRANK WESSON 387
WESTINGER &
   ALTENBURGER 387
WHITE 387
WHITE-MERRILL 387
WHITNEY ARMS COMPANY....387
WHITNEY FIREARMS, INC. 388
WICHITA 388
WIENER WAFFENFABRIK 388
WILDEY 388
WILKINSON 389
WILL 389
WILSON COMBAT 390
WINCHESTER 390
WINFIELD 390
WORTHER.......................390
WYATT-IMTHURN 390

ZARAGOZA ARMS FACTORY ..391
ZASTAVA ARMS 391
ZEHNER........................392
ZOLI 392
ZULAICA 392

PART THREE: APPENDICES
DATABANK 394
GLOSSARY 427
BIBLIOGRAPHY 431

Introduction

When John Weeks and I sat down to write the first edition of *Pistols of the World*, we little knew how much work we had created for ourselves; the passing years dimmed the memory, and when I began to re-write this edition, the size of the task came as a shock. In the intervening years, there has been an explosion in development. The original edition contained nothing of the current Berettas; Smith & Wesson had but one modern automatic; and a score of other designs were merely lines on paper.

So not only has there been a great deal to add, but to keep the book within manageable bounds, there has had to be some shaving of the existing material. This has led to the removal of occasional comments and minor details to make space for the new entries. It would be idle to suggest that every pistol in the world is within these pages; try as I might, there will be some that have eluded me or, in some cases, have been consciously excluded.

There is little mention, for example, of the multitude of single-shot pocket pistols, commonplace in the second half of the 19th century; of the legions of cheap Spanish guns with no identifying mark other than "Automatic Pistol" on the slide; of the many custom-built free pistols; of the currently-fashionable "semi-auto-only" cut-down submachine guns; of the countless reproductions of Colt, Remington and Deringer cap-locks; or, of course, of the innumerable European blank-firing, tear-gas and starting pistols.

Illustrations are divided between those furnished by manufacturers, for which they have my sincere thanks, and those taken especially for the book. It is impossible to include a picture of every gun, so I have had to be selective. It would be pointless, for example, to illustrate every "Eibar"-type automatic — "seen one, seen them all," you might say, though I have endeavored to show some of the unusual variations on the theme. In some cases, I have had to use old catalogue engravings, which add visual interest in addition to being important documentary evidence.

Lastly, I must thank the many people who have provided information that has been assimilated into the text. The list of people who have written to draw my attention to particular pistols, to add some piece of information or to argue my conclusions (invariably in the most good-natured way) would run to several pages ... as would the list of manufacturers who have been kind enough to supply me with information, allow me to visit their factories and fire their pistols, provide photographs, and answer questions with the utmost patience.

Instead of listing everyone individually, I must take refuge in offering my sincere thanks to all of you, for without your help, this book would be a mere shadow of its present self.

— Ian Hogg, 2002

Publisher's Note

Sadly, Ian Hogg died in March 2002 before this edition of *Pistols of the World* had progressed past the draft stage. It was subsequently agreed that the work be completed by John Walter, author of *The Luger Story* and *Rifles of the World*, who gives this appreciation of Britain's best-known author of firearms books:

" ... I first became aware of Ian Hogg when I joined Arms & Armour Press in 1969, just as *Military Pistols and Revolvers* was making its way through the proofs stage. Ian was then still serving in the Royal Artillery, having joined the British Army at the end of World War II, and had had his first book published just a year previously.

I eventually began work on *German Pistols & Revolvers 1871-1945* and was given access to the author. I arrived to meet Ian (then lecturing at the Royal Military College of Science) far later than had been agreed, but he had a knack of putting people at their ease and we immediately became friends — even though, theoretically at least, we should have been professional enemies!

Ian was exceptionally prolific, producing about 150 books on small arms, ammunition, artillery, fortification and military history; editing *Jane's Infantry Weapons* (1972-94); contributing articles to a variety of journals; and enjoying a fruitful collaboration with artist John Batchelor. Ian's books have been translated into a dozen languages, selling well in excess of a million copies.

Military Small Arms of the Twentieth Century, published in 1972 and now in its seventh edition, is undoubtedly the best-selling encyclopedia of its type. Ian continued work after the unexpected death of his co-author Colonel John Weeks (one-time British military attaché in Washington) on the first day of 1983, and I sincerely hope that *Military Small Arms* will continue to act as a memorial to its creators in the twenty-first century. *Pistols of the World* — first published in 1977, and again in 1992 — has proved to be another long-lived project.

However, the breathtaking complexity of his output often obscured the real Ian Hogg. He was a very private man in many ways, and after 27 years in the Army, many of them spent giving orders, could give the impression that he didn't suffer fools gladly. Yet he could be incredibly generous and was always quick to give encouragement. I have no idea how many photographs he gave me over the years, and I know from personal experience that he could pass projects to others simply to help them through bad times. But the best things, for me at least, were his lack of pomposity and his dry sense of humor.

Even during his last illness, Ian could restore my flagging spirits with a self-deprecating joke. It's hard to realize that I cannot ask him for another photograph or telephone for a half-hour pep talk. It is a measure of Ian the person that the lives not only of his family, but also of his friends, will never be the same again ..."

— John Walter, 2004

Books of this type are notoriously awkward to compile, as it is very difficult — indeed, almost impossible — to devise a listing that is simultaneously comprehensive, easy to use, consistent and non-repetitive.

The format adopted for this edition is similar to that of the 1992 version, except that separate entries devoted to individual brand names have been put back into "main entries" based primarily on the name of the manufacturer.

Experience suggests that this is usually the best starting point, even though it can have drawbacks if guns are marked with nothing other than a brand name or if they have been made by several manufacturers concurrently. The former is true of many US-made "Suicide Special" revolvers or Spanish blowbacks; the latter is common with military weapons such as the Parabellum ("Luger") or even the M1911A1 Colt-Browning. In addition, many gunmaking businesses have histories stretching back a hundred years or more in which changes of corporate structure have been common. Colt and Mauser are particularly good examples of this fragmentation, and it is not always easy to decide where (if at all) these entries should be split.

In addition, the involvement of intermediaries, especially in the USA, presents particular difficulties. For example, "Western-style" cartridge revolvers made in Italy by Uberti may be encountered with the marks of distributors such as Cimarron Arms, EAA, EMF or the United States Patent Fire-Arms Co. The lists would be straightforward but for the tendency to invent specific brand names for the US market. It is easy to understand that these are needed to distinguish essentially similar products that are being sold by different people in the same marketplace, but they can hinder precise identification. Consequently, some of the most important distributors have been given entries of their own, allowing their brand names to be listed in the directory instead of being relegated to an index or becoming part of an over-elaborate cross-reference system.

Most entries begin with a keyword (or words) in the form of a name. This will usually be the fore- and surnames of individual gunmakers or reflect corporate structure (partnership, company, corporation, etc.). Foreign-language terms are not always recognized in the Anglo-American collecting world, and it may not be clear where in the sequence a name such as "Hijos de Calixto Arrizabalaga" may be found. Hijo is Spanish for "son", so this particular name could be written in English as "C. Arrizabalaga Sons" — and would clearly be listed under "A" instead of "H". To keep confusion to a minimum, all terms such as "sons", "brothers", "successors" and "cousins" have been translated into English for the headings, and an ampersand ("&") is usually substituted for "and", "et" (French), "e" (Portuguese), "i" (Italian), "und" (German) and "y" (Spanish).

Government-owned arms factories, which often have convoluted titles that changed with politics (i.e., the French *Manufacture impériale* became *Manufacture nationale* after the Franco-Prussian War), are listed by their geographical locations: "Enfield small-arms factory", "Springfield Armory", "Tokyo artillery arsenal".

Where the name of a manufacturer and the designer/patentee has not been established, the guns have been entered under "Unattributed."

Prototypes and guns of unknown manufacture, but established origin, may be listed under the name of the designer/patentee. However, the name of manufacturer is considered to be primary, even though the story of the Parabellum (Luger) or the Nambu, for example, may be split over several entries. The information path is clearly indicated whenever appropriate.

The keywords are followed by details of original name, changes of name, the location of the business (if known) and a brief summary of operations. Then come the lists of individual guns, within the subgroups "Single-shot pistol", "Repeating pistol", "Revolver" and "Automatic pistol". The use of "automatic" is accepted as idiomatic, at the expense of the more accurate "semi-automatic".

The gun-by-gun entries are usually organized on the basis of alphabetical order (usually by brand names) or as a simple numeric progression based on model dates, calibers … or manufacturers' whims. However, a few complex large-scale listings — e.g., Smith & Wesson, Webley — are based on chronological development or groups of related designs. These deviations from normal are noted in the individual entries.

The stories of some manufacturers have been split into several components, particularly if there is an obvious chronological break (e.g., Mauser at the end of World War II) or a large-scale change of corporate structure has been established with certainty. In addition, where organization on the basis of dates of introduction has been attempted, it should be remembered that published sources often create as much confusion as they provide information because the dates of conception, patenting, announcement, "first display", pre-production and full-scale commercial availability may differ considerably. In extreme cases, the spread may be 10 years. Unless stated otherwise, therefore, we have tried to standardize on the basis of commercial availability.

The use of dual imperial/metric designators for cartridges and chamberings can create unnecessary duplication. Consequently, these are given in imperial measure for Anglo-American designs and in metric measure for those that originally emanated from Europe and Asia. The 30 Luger and 9mm Luger cartridges are listed here as 7.65mm Parabellum and 9mm Parabellum, and "11.25mm Colt" as 45 ACP. But the same cartridge may still have two names. This is particularly true of the Browning-designed rounds exploited both by Colt and in Europe prior to the First World War. Those that are listed in North America as "25 ACP", "32 ACP" and "380 ACP" are known in Europe as "6.35mm Auto", "7.65mm Auto" and "9mm Short", respectively.

Problems can also be created by legislation such as the assault-rifle bill passed in 1994, which limited handguns to 10 rounds at a time when manufacturers were competing with each other to offer the highest-capacity magazine. Gunmakers solved the problem simply by changing the design of the magazine and magazine-well to comply with the legislation, but some gave the 10-shot guns new designations and others did not. Similarly designated guns may be found with different magazines, and, as this is regarded here as a fundamental change, they are listed in the directory as if they were separate patterns. However, the 1994 Act runs its term in 2004, and another wholesale change of plan may yet be ordered!

A.A. ARMS

A.A. Arms, Inc., Monroe, North Carolina, USA.
Possibly an offshoot of Kimel Industries, listed in the 1990s as the manufacturer of the guns, this company distributed the AP-9 and its derivatives until 2001.

AP-9 Resembling a cut-down submachine gun, with a ventilated barrel shroud, a detachable 20-round magazine ahead of the trigger and a cocking handle protruding from the left side of the tubular receiver, the AP-9 appeared in 1988. Chambered for the 9mm Parabellum cartridge, the basic version had an overall length of 11.8 inches with a 5-inch barrel, and weighed 3.5 lbs. It fired automatically from the closed-bolt position, and had a safety that blocked the trigger and sear simultaneously. The rear sight was fixed, but the front sight post could be adjusted within its hood. Finish was either matted blue-black or electroless nickel. Pistols made after the implementation of the Gun Control Act of 1994 had magazines holding just 10 rounds.

• *AP-9 Target* Distinguished by a 12-inch barrel (subsequently reduced to 11 inches and sometimes listed as "AP-9/11"), this version also had a separate fore-end with longitudinal flutes. Finish was restricted to blue.

• *AP-9 Mini/3 and AT-9 Mini/5* These were similar to the standard AP-9, but are said to have had refinements to their contours that reduced size and weight. However, published data seems to be contradictory. The barrels, as the designations suggest, were 3 inches and 5 inches respectively.

ABADIE

Liége, Belgium.
This gunsmith was reputedly the original patentee of the common system for revolvers in which an ejector rod housed within a hollow cylinder axis pin was pulled forward and then swung sideways to eject cases singly through a loading gate. However, his name is normally found in connection with a loading gate safety arrangement used on numerous European service revolvers from 1878 to 1900. In this device, the usual loading gate was connected to the hammer by way of a cam, so that when the gate was opened for loading, the pistol hammer was drawn back to half-cock and secured there, preventing it from falling forward during the loading process. At the same time, the hammer was freed from the trigger, so that pulling the trigger would revolve the cylinder, a chamber at a time, for unloading and loading.

Although this device was quite widely adopted, only the two Portuguese service revolvers noted below ever used Abadie's name. Both these pistols were actually of Belgian design, originally made by L. Soleil of Liége, and used the double-action Nagant M1878 lock mechanism together with the Abadie loading gate. The Soleil name will be found stamped on the frame.

M1878 "Système Abadie" Issued to officers, this was a 9.1mm centerfire six-shot revolver, solid framed with a rod ejector permanently aligned with the right-side loading gate. The barrel was octagonal and the lock was double or single action.

M1886 "Système Abadie" This was of the same caliber and general description but was the "trooper's model" and was therefore larger and heavier. Again, the rod ejector was permanently aligned, but it was simpler than the preceding pattern.

ACCU-TEK

Chino, California, USA.
This gunmaking business began operations in the late 1980s, producing a variety of sturdy, inexpensive pistols. Virtually all are made of stainless steel. It was acquired by Excel Industries (q.v.) in 2001.

AT-9 Announced in 1992, chambered for the 9mm Parabellum cartridge, this was a compact, chunky, locked-breech design embodying the usual dropping-barrel mechanism. The lockwork was double-action-only, with an enclosed hammer, and safety arrangements were confined to an internal firing-block; no external manual safety was provided. The AT-9 was 6.3 inches long, had a 3.2-inch barrel and weighed 28 oz. The base of the seven-round magazine had a short, spurred extension to improve grip.

AT-25SS In 1991, the range was expanded by adding a seven-shot 25 ACP model to the AT series, though this was comparatively short-lived and had been abandoned by 2000. A few guns were made with an aluminum-alloy slide in the mid 1990s, reducing weight to merely 11 oz.

• *AT-25SSB* A variant of the basic gun with a blacked finish, though still made of stainless steel. It dates from 1992.

AT-32SS Dating from in 1990, this 32 ACP blowback offered "satin stainless" finish.

AT-40SS This was a short-lived variant of the AT-9 chambered for the 40 S&W cartridge. Introduced in 1992, it was initially accompanied by a blacked version designated A*T-40SSB* or simply "AT-40B".

AT-380SS Chambered for the 380 Auto cartridge, this gun appeared in 1992. An unusually compact design, resembling the Walther TPH externally, it has a five-round magazine and measures just 5.6 inches overall; the barrel is a mere 2.75 inches, and the weight (empty) is 20 oz. The base of the magazine is extended to provide a better grip, the hammer has a ring-tip and a radial safety lever may be found on the left side of the slide beneath the rear sight. Internally, the AT-380 has a firing-pin block and an additional safety that ensures that the gun cannot be fired if the magazine is removed.

• *AT-380SSB* A 1991-vintage introduction, with blackened stainless-steel components.

• *ATL-380* (later renamed *Lady 380*) A more elegant version of the AT-380 with chrome finish and gray bleached-oak grips instead of the blued finish and plastic grips of the standard models.

• *AT-380HC* (now known as HC-380) The existence of this "High Capacity" AT-380 derivative was announced in 1993. The original version—made only in small numbers—had an extended grip and enlarged magazine holding 12 rounds. In 1994, however, a new Gun Control Act restricted magazine capacity to 10 rounds, and the AT-380HC was modified accordingly.

BL-9 Introduced in 1997, chambered for the 9mm Parabellum cartridge and offered only in black finish, this has much squarer contours than the earlier Accu-Tek pistols. The slide-retraction grooves are broad and vertical, and the sights are fixed. An extension is provided on the base of the five-round magazine to improve grip, as the gun is just 5.6 inches long, has a 3-inch barrel, and weighs 22 oz empty. The trigger system is double-action-only.

XL-9 Introduced in 1999, this variant of the BL-9 offers adjustable three-dot sights and stainless-steel construction.

ACHA BROTHERS
DOMINGO ACHA & CO.

Acha Hermanos y Cia ("Acha Brothers"),
Domingo Acha, and Domingo Acha & Co. ("y Cia"),
all of Ermua, Vitoria, Spain.
The Acha brothers began by manufacturing the Ruby (q.v.) automatic under license some time during World War I, helping to satisfy French Army contracts. When these ended, Domingo Acha continued trading alone until the mid-1920s — after which a company was formed, remaining in business until the Spanish Civil War began in 1936.

Acha A 7.65mm auto blowback of Eibar type, made c. 1916-22, this had no distinguishing mechanical features and was marked "F de Acha Hrs C 7.65" on the slide — sometimes with an additional "Model 1916". Although these guns were reputedly made for the French Army, it seems that most were made for the commercial market after the end of World War I.

Atlas This was a 6.35mm auto pistol loosely based on the Browning 1906 design and manufactured by Domingo Acha. Generally found marked "Pistolet Automatique 6.35 ATLAS", its appearance suggested that it was the first commercial design after the original "Acha" pistol, and some of the smaller parts appeared to have been made on the same machinery.

Colonial Two pistols bear this name, a 6.35mm blowback of the usual "Eibar" type and a 7.65mm blowback that resembles the FN-Browning of 1910 externally but is a standard "Eibar" beneath the skin. The small-caliber guns take a variety of forms with the manual safety catch above the trigger or on the rear of the frame and radial or vertical grooves on the slide. One gun has been seen marked "MODEL 1920 PATENT No 12586". The markings on the 7.65mm version include reference to "PATENT DEPOSE 39391". Both have the "COLONIAL" on the grips, and may display "EC" monograms associated with Fabrique d'Armes de Guerre de Grande Précision (q.v.) instead of the "DAC" of Domingo Acha.

Helvece This is the same pistol as a 6.35mm Colonial, with the full company name and "Helvece Patent" on the slide. The grips have the word "Patent" at the top and a "DAC" monogram in the center.

Looking Glass Another 6.35mm auto model based on the Browning 1906 design, this offered a better finish than the Atlas. The sole marking on the slide was "LOOKING GLASS" while the grips were either embossed "Patent" or had the registered Acha trademark of a female head in a surround suggesting a hand mirror. Differing versions of this pistol have been seen; the usual type duplicated the Browning in size, with a 2-inch barrel concealed within the slide, and could be found in blued or nickel-plated finish. Advertisements also noted "Special" and "Target Special" models, with adjustable rear sights and long barrels protruding from the slide.

JOHN ADAMS

Adams Patent Small Arms Company, London, England.

Adams and his brother Robert had been involved in the production of caplock revolvers, patenting a solid-frame design in 1851. In 1864, he formed the Adams Patent Small Arms Company, which appears to have been little more than a syndicate for licensing patents, the actual manufacture of pistols being done elsewhere (probably by Adams & Company of Finsbury, which may well have been related to the other two). A most detailed examination of the various Adams and their affairs will be found in A.W.F. Taylerson's *The Revolver, 1865-1888*.

Adams revolver The British Army had adopted a Beaumont-Adams caplock revolver in 1855, as the "Deane & Adams Revolver Pistol". John Adams subsequently perfected a conversion system cover-

ing a new cylinder, rammer and loading gate, adapting the weapon to breech loading. The conversion was accepted for naval service as the "Deane & Adams Revolver Pistol, Converted to BL, by Mr. J. Adams" on November 20, 1868. This appears to have been an interim measure pending the adoption of a fresh design of breech-loading revolver, as the British *United Services Magazine* of October 1869 noted: "The introduction of Adams' BL revolver into the service having been decided upon, the Deane and Adams pistols already in use are now being converted by Mr. Adams. The converted pistol differs from the revolver in having five chambers instead of six."

The new design was introduced as "Pistol, Adams, Centre-fire, BL, Mark 2" on February 22, 1872, and the differences between it and the Mark 1 (as the conversion was now known) were relatively small. Six months later, on August 24, 1872, the Mark 3 appeared, the only difference from the Mark 2 being the adoption of an improved extractor. Finally, on December 24, 1872, the Mark 4 was approved; this was "the alteration of all converted ML Pistols Mark 1" and was described as "differing in minor features to overcome the tendency to non-revolution of the cylinder and the liability of the screw of the ejector spring cover to come out."

Adams revolvers were adopted by several British Colonial governments and foreign countries, but in British service, they were superseded by the Enfield in 1880. Probably because of the military demand, few of them seem to have reached the commercial market.

ADLERWAFFENFABRIK

Adlerwaffenfabrik Max Hermsdorff, Zella St Blasii, Germany.

This metalworking business was responsible for a 7mm-caliber automatic pistol, designed by a patentee named Häussler whose name always appears on the pistol in that context. However, Max Hermsdorff took out German Patent 176909 on August 22, 1905 — making improvements to the Häussler design — and it is this patent that, strictly speaking, covers the Adler pistol.

The third party in the story was Engelbrecht & Wolff, presumably the manufacturers, whose name also appears on the pistol. "Adlerwaffenfabrik Max Hermsdorff" was purely a sales organization, though it is the origin of the Adler name. Relatively few pistols were made; the design was poor, and could not compete in the marketplace against the FN-Brownings.

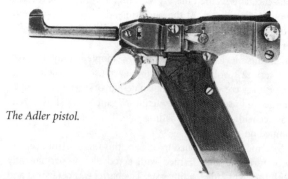

The Adler pistol.

Adler Made in 1905-7, this was a blowback design with a bolt reciprocating inside a square-section receiver. A prominent cocking knob protruded from a slot in the top. The grip was well raked, but excessive rearward overhang made the gun awkward to hold. It chambered the 7mm Adler cartridge, a bottlenecked rimless round that was never adopted by any other maker.

The principal novelty of the design lay in the construction of the receiver; the rear and top were in one piece, hinged at the bottom rear and locked by a transverse pin. By removing the pin and hinging this cover up, it was possible to remove the bolt and gain access for cleaning.

The British Adams 450-caliber revolver, 1872.

The pistol was striker fired and had a safety catch on the left of the frame. A slot in the receiver sidewall allowed the face of the bolt to be inspected and enabled the user to see if a cartridge occupied the chamber.

FRED ADOLPH
Genoa, New York, USA.
Active c. 1900-24, Adolph specialized in the development of "wildcat" cartridges to meet his own ballistic requirements, chambering long-range rifles accordingly. He reportedly spent time in 1913-15 designing an automatic rifle, but it never reached production. Adolph apparently lost interest in firearms in the early 1920s and retired to devote the rest of his life to music.

Target pistols A few single-shot pistols, mating a modified Martini lever action with a 10-inch barrel, were made shortly before World War I began. They chambered a special cartridge made by loading a 22 Savage Hi-Power bullet into a cut-down and necked 28-30-120 Stevens case.

ADVANTAGE ARMS CO.
St Paul, Minnesota, USA.
This gunmaking business introduced the *Advantage 422 Derringer* in 1983. This four-shot repeating pistol, similar in principle to the Sharps, had four barrels in a block and a sequencing firing pin operated by a double-action trigger. It was offered in 22 LR or 22 WMR chamberings and in various grades and types of finish.

AETNA ARMS CO.
New York, USA.
Active c. 1875-90, this is said to have been one of the many small revolver-making businesses that sprang into action when the Rollin White patents expired. The guns were virtual copies of Smith & Wesson designs and were of that class now generally called "Suicide Specials" — rimfire, sheathed-trigger, solid-frame or tip-barrel examples, made as cheaply as possible. Two production models are known:

22 caliber An imitation Smith & Wesson Model 1, this had a 3-inch tipping barrel, a seven-chamber cylinder and a brass frame. It accepted 22 Short rimfire ammunition.

32 caliber Chambered for rimfire ammunition, this five-shot gun had a 2.4-inch tip-up octagonal barrel and a brass frame. It was another imitation of the Smith & Wesson Model 1.

The 22LR Agner M80 target pistol.

AGNER-SAXHØJ PRODUCTS
Copenhagen, Denmark.
Agner M80 This target pistol appeared in 1981 and was made in small quantities for about five years. It was a 22 rimfire automatic, largely made of stainless steel, and designed expressly for target and competitive shooting. It had a fully adjustable trigger, an unusual safety catch-cum-locking key and an internal dry-firing mechanism. The grips were anatomical, with an adjustable hand rest. Some guns will be found with the marks of Beeman Arms of Santa Rosa, California, the principal US distributor.

AGUIRRE & CO.
Aguirre y Cia, Eibar, Spain.
The connection between Aguirre & Co. and Aguirre, Zamacolas & Co. is no longer clear. The confusion is not helped by the presence of a third firm, Aguirre & Aranzabal ("AyA"), which specialized in long arms. Aguirre & Co. traded during the 1920s but appears to have left the pistol field by 1933.

Basculant A 6.35mm auto blowback of the usual Browning 1906 pattern; made in the 1920s but of no particular merit. Note that "Basculant" was also used by Pieper of Liége and that there is no resemblance to, or connection with, the Aguirre product.

Le Dragon Virtually the same as the Basculant but renamed for sale in Belgium and France, owing to the prior use of the same name by Pieper. Guns were invariably found with Liége proof marks and often assumed to be Belgian. The slide was marked "Cal 6.35 Automatic Pistol Le Dragon" and the grips had a molded stylized-dragon trademark.

ALDAY & GABILONDO
Alday y Gabilondo, Placencia, Spain.
Manufacturers of cheap Smith & Wesson-pattern revolvers in the 1920s. The business was liquidated and re-formed as "Alday y Cia" in 1932 but was wiped out by the Spanish Civil War.

A. ALDAZABAL
Eibar, Spain.
A.A.A. This was a 7.65mm Eibar-style automatic manufactured c. 1918-23. It had a seven-cartridge magazine and was rifled with six grooves, left-handed. The slide was marked "AAA Manufactura de Armas Eibar 1919 MCA 35761". The five-digit number referred to the patent covering the registered trademark, and there was a knight's helmet above the "AAA" found on the slide and grips. The same pistol was also sold as the *Benemerita*.

JOSE ALDAZABAL SONS
Hijos de Jose Aldazabal, Eibar, Spain.
This gunmaking business made cheap, solid-frame, double-action, hand-ejecting revolvers in the 1920s based on the 38 S&W Military & Police pattern. They were offered in 32 S&W, 38 S&W and 38 Special chamberings. Aldazabal also marketed the *Sharp-Shooter* automatic pistol manufactured by Arrizabalaga (q.v.) for some years in the 1920s.

Imperial A 7.65mm Eibar automatic marked "Imperial No 2 'Union' Mod 1915 Cal 7,65 Eibar" and with a "JA" monogram on the grips. The monogram suggested manufacture by Jose Aldazabal, but the word "Union" could have meant that the pistol was sold by Union Armera Eibarense, a little-known marketing co-operative.

ALDAZABAL, LETURIONDO & CO.
Aldazabal, Leturiondo y Cia, Eibar, Spain.
This gunmaking business manufactured a 7.65mm auto Eibar-type pistol in the early 1920s. Of standard type, it differed from the general run only in having a deeper butt and a greater cartridge capacity. It displayed the maker's full name, "AL" in an oval on the rear of the frame and had plain grips.

ALKARTASUNA
SA Alkartasuna Fábrica de Armas, Eibar, Spain.
This gunmaking business was formed during World War I by a group of ex-employees of Esperanza y Unceta. The original intention was to make "Ruby" pistols as subcontractors to Gabilondo y Urresti.

Alkar This will be found on a number of different automatic pistols, though never as part of the name. Instead, it may appear as part of a trademark formed by an angular "S" surmounted by the word ALKAR and with "Mca. Regisda." (*Marca Registrada,* "registered trademark") beneath. Alternatively, the word may be superimposed on the "S" as a grip motif, or simply molded into the grip.

The slide of the wartime guns bore the company name and the Alkar trademark. When the contract was completed, production continued for the commercial market. Some minor variants appeared — e.g., with seven-round magazines instead of nine, or a modified trademark omitting "Alkar" — until, probably in 1919, the front of the slide was rounded so that (externally at least) the pistol resembled the Browning M1910. On stripping, however, it became apparent that the recoil spring still lay beneath the barrel, just like any other Eibar-type gun, instead of being wrapped around the barrel as in the Browning. This pistol was marked "STANDARD AUTOMATIC PISTOL SA ALKARTASUNA" and had the Alkar trademark molded into the grip.

In 1920 the factory burned down, and what happened next is far from clear. The company was formally dissolved in 1922, but in 1924, a 6.35mm auto pistol, broadly based on the Browning 1906 but without grip safety and with a peculiarly notched backstrap, appeared with the Alkar name molded into the grip but with the name of an entirely new company on the slide: "Manufactura de Armas de Fuego–Guernica". This pistol had some unusual features: the safety catch is a push-through bolt at the top of the grip, and the left grip plate was perforated so as to reveal an indicator, part of the magazine platform, and thus show the contents of the magazine.

No other pistols by this firm are known, and it seems probable that Manufactura de Armas de Fuego had purchased the trademark and goodwill from the moribund Alkartasuna business, intending to continue trading. A version of the earlier Alkar marked "ALKATASUNA" (note the subtle change in spelling!) has been reported with Armas de Fuego markings, but confirmation is still lacking. The same remark applies to an identically marked revolver.

Kapitain A 7.65mm Eibar-type pistol made in the early 1920s. The slide was marked "Pistolet Automatique Kapitain Caliber 7,65m/m (32) Alkar Patent".

A 36 rimfire Allen & Co. "Navy" revolver.

ALLEN & WHEELOCK

Worcester, Massachusetts, USA.

Ethan Allen (1806-71) established himself as a millwright before he was 20 and in 1837 perfected a double-action caplock revolver. In collaboration with his brother-in-law, Charles Thurber, he created Allen & Thurber to make pistols. The partners moved from Grafton, Massachusetts, to Norwich, Connecticut, in 1842, and then to Worcester, Massachusetts, in 1847. The trading style became "Allen, Thurber & Co."

Thurber resigned in 1855, his place being taken by Thomas Wheelock — another brother-in-law of Allen — and the company became "Allen & Wheelock". They manufactured caplock pepperboxes and revolvers from 1856 onwards, in calibers from 25 to 44. Wheelock died in 1863, and the trading name reverted to "Allen & Co". Ethan Allen, having outlived his brothers-in-law, now enlisted sons-in-law Sullivan Forehand and Henry Wadsworth. And finally, on Allen's death in 1871, the company became Forehand & Wadsworth (q.v.).

~ PISTOLS ~

These single-shot guns offered 22, 32 and 41 RF chamberings; all had

octagonal barrels, square butts and sheathed triggers. The breech swung to the right to permit loading.

~ REVOLVERS ~

Introduced in the mid-1860s, these distinctive side-hammer rimfire designs ranged from seven-chamber 22 Short and 25 Short, by way of 32, 36 and 38, to 44. The six-chamber solid-frame guns all had sheathed triggers and squared butts.

AMERICAN ARMS

Garden Grove, California, USA.

This short-lived business was responsible for the *American Eagle 380*, a 380 ACP double-action six-shot pistol based on the Walther PPK. Though the exterior contours were much squarer than the original, the slide-mounted radial safety lever and external ring-tip hammer were retained. The guns were 6.25 inches long, had 2.5-inch barrels and weighed about 20 oz. Their grips were usually checkered walnut, though black rubber could be requested; construction was stainless steel. A few guns were finished in black Teflon, the rubber grips being regarded as standard. Production began in 1984, but the gamble soon failed and the guns that remained in stock were sold in 1985 to the Wilkerson Firearms Corporation of Westminster, California.

AMERICAN ARMS & AMMUNITION CO.

Miami, Florida, USA.

This company, a successor to the Norton Armament Corp. (q.v.), operated briefly in 1978-81. It marketed the German Korriphila TP-70 pistol in 22 and 25 calibers.

AMERICAN ARMS CO. ("A.A.CO.")

Boston and Chicopee Falls, Massachusetts,
and Milwaukee, Wisconsin, USA.

This gunmaking business began making revolvers in 1882, supervising work in a factory in Chicopee Falls from an office in Boston. A move to Milwaukee took place in 1897, but trading ceased in 1904. The revolvers were made under patents assigned by various inventors, one of the more significant being a grant in 1890 to Henry F. Wheeler (US Pat 430243) to protect a revolver lock mechanism that allowed the hammer to be cocked by pressure on the trigger, after which a second pressure released it to fire the cartridge.

A selector on the left side of the frame allowed this mode of operation to be selected, or the lock to function in the usual double-action fashion. However, only the newest examples used the Wheeler lock, the earlier models being much less distinctive; however, most had a ribbed barrel, a hinged frame and a removable cylinder.

The earliest guns had sheathed triggers, whereas later examples were fitted with conventional trigger guards. The grips were small and rounded with the side-plates forming an ornate "AAC" monogram.

Excepting the 38 S&W *Baby Russian* of the early 1890s (a five-chamber single-action top-break revolver with a spur trigger), few AACo. products were distinguished by any form of model name or number. The "model numbers" listed in the data table are purely for convenience.

AMERICAN ARMS, INC.

North Kansas City, Missouri, USA.

Apparently unrelated to American Arms of Garden Grove, California, which had failed some years previously, this business began in the 1980s by importing Spanish shotguns and rifles made in Yugoslavia. Handguns were soon being imported from Italy and Germany, and the company was claiming to be a "manufacturer" by 1990. However, it seems more likely that little other than assembly was undertaken, as some of the pistols clearly have Erma connections, and the Spectre originated in Italy. From 1995 onwards, American Arms also distributed the Italian Mateba (q.v.) "auto-revolver" in North America. However, the business was sold to Tristar Ltd Sporting Arms in 2001 and its current status is unclear.

∼ REVOLVERS ∼

Regulator A single-action Western-style revolver (in 357 Magnum, 44-40 WCF or 45 Long Colt) with walnut grips, a case-hardened frame, brass trigger guard and backstrap, and blued cylinder and barrel. The guns are made in Italy by Uberti (q.v.).

• *Regulator Deluxe* A variant of the standard Regulator with trigger guards and backstraps of steel instead of brass; available only in 45 Long Colt.

∼ AUTOMATIC PISTOLS ∼

Aussie Model Named in honor of its designer, an Australian, this handgun was apparently made in Spain. It chambers the 9mm or 40 S&W rounds, has a 10-round magazine complying with the Gun Control Act of 1994, and has a polymer frame. The steel slide has an electroless nickel finish.

CX-22 DA Announced in 1989, this was a 22 LR blowback based loosely on the Walther PPK. About 6.3 inches long, with a 3.3-inch barrel, it weighed 22 oz and had a matted blue-black finish. The lockwork was double action, with an exposed ring-tip hammer and a hammer-blocking radial safety lever set into the left side of the slide.

EP-380 A seven-shot 380 ACP Erma (q.v.) pistol imported from Germany, 1988-91.

Escort This was a double-action-only personal-defense pistol introduced in 1995 but made only in small numbers. Made largely of stainless steel and chambered only for the 380 ACP cartridge, it was about 6.1 inches long and weighed 19 oz. Features included a loaded-chamber indicator, a laterally-adjustable rear sight and a soft-polymer wrap-around grip. The magazine held seven rounds.

P-98 Introduced in 1989, this was a 22 LR rimfire blowback based externally on the Walther P38, with a ring-tip hammer, grooved polymer grips and a radial hammer-blocking safety lever on the left side of the slide. An additional safety system was fitted in the frame, preventing the gun from firing if the magazine had been removed. The P-98 was 8.1 inches long with a 5-inch barrel, weighed 25 oz and had an eight-round single-column magazine.

PK-22 DA Chambered for the 22 LR rimfire cartridge, this pistol was similar to the CX-22 (above), excepting for lines that were based more on the M1911A1 Colt-browning than the Walther PPK. However, it retained the slide-mounted radial safety lever.

PX-22 Externally similar to the Walther TPH (q.v.), this 1989-vintage 22 LR blowback pistol was 5.4 inches long with its 2.9-inch barrel, weighed 15 oz and had fixed sights. The magazine held seven rounds. Finish was customarily blue.

Spectre Little more than a cut-down submachine gun, originating in Italy, this was advertised as a "triple-action blowback"—meaning that it could fire single shots from a closed breech with a simple pull on the trigger, or the hammer could be dropped by means of a de-cocking lever. The controls were ambidextrous. The basis gun was 13.8 inches long, with a 6-inch barrel, and weighed 4.5 lbs empty. The grips were black nylon; finish could be blue or nickel. The height of the front-sight post could be adjusted within its hood, and the rear sight, though nominally fixed, could be driven laterally in its dovetail to adjust the point of impact. The magazines originally held 30 9mm Parabellum or 45 ACP rounds but were restricted to 10 after the Gun Control Act of 1994 was activated.

ZC-380 A Yugoslavian-made 380 ACP (9mm Short) pistol imported from Zastava Arms (q.v.) for a few years from 1988 onward. It was essentially a shortened Tokarev adapted to blowback operation, known to the manufacturer as the "Model 70k".

AMERICAN DERRINGER
American Derringer Corporation, Waco, Texas, USA.
Established in the early 1980s, this gunmaking business has offered an extensive range of two-shot derringers based on the Remington Double Derringer (q.v.) as well as the latest incarnation of the Semmerling series.

∼ SINGLE-SHOT PISTOLS ∼

Model 2 Pen-Pistol Made only for a few years, beginning in 1993, this was a simple tapered-cylinder design resembling a pen. Chamberings were restricted to three low-power cartridges: 22 LR rimfire, 25 ACP and 32 ACP. The gun (about 5.5 inches long with a two-inch barrel) weighed 5-6 oz. It had to be pulled apart and the "grip" turned downward through about 80 degrees before it could be fired.

Model 3 This was a single-barrel "tip up" derringer, based loosely on the Model 1. Made largely of stainless steel, it was about 5 inches long and weighed 8 oz. Chamberings were restricted to 32 Magnum and 38 Special.

∼ MULTI-SHOT PISTOLS ∼

COP 4 Shot Resembling a small automatic pistol, this interesting design has four barrels in a cluster, fired sequentially by a striker concealed in the rear of the frame. The trigger is a sliding double-action pattern. Chambering is restricted to 357 Magnum.

DA-38 Introduced in 1989, this was an improved version of the High Standard (q.v.) 22 rimfire Double Derringer, which American Derringer acquired after the collapse of the original manufacturer. Offered in 357 Magnum, 9mm Parabellum, 38 Special or 40 S&W, it had a double-action trigger, a flush-milled steel barrel cluster, an aluminum frame and wood grips. The DA-38 is heavier than its rimfire predecessor and has a much more streamlined appearance.

LM-4 This is a revival of the manually-operated repeating pistol originally manufactured by the Semmerling Corporation (q.v.). Sometimes mistakenly identified as a modern adaptation of the blow-forward principle, the gun is actually loaded by pushing the barrel-block forward (ejecting a spent case if applicable) and then releasing the block to run back and chamber a new round. Firing is done simply by pulling through on the double-action trigger. The LM-4 is chambered for the 45 ACP cartridge and has a detachable five-round magazine in the butt. The gun is 5.2 inches long, weighs about 22 oz and may be obtained in blue or hard-chrome finish. The appearance is most distinctive. Though resembling a small automatic pistol, the barrel block is grooved directly above the trigger and the front of the trigger guard sweeps upward in a graceful arc to join the frame beneath the muzzle.

LM-5 A small-caliber variant of the LM-4, this is offered only in 25 ACP or 32 Magnum. It has a four-round magazine and is made largely of stainless steel. Overall length is about 4 inches with a 2.25-inch barrel; weight averages 15 oz.

Mini-COP 4-Shot This is similar to the centerfire gun, but chambers the 22 Magnum rimfire cartridge.

Model 1 Based on the Remington (q.v.) over/under design patented by William Elliott in December 1865, this has been offered in a bewildering variety of chamberings, ranging from 22 LR rimfire to 45-70 Government. The frame and barrel-block are stainless steel, though the finish may be high-polish or satin-matte. Some guns have been supplied with the barrels chambered differently and with grips that can range from exotic wood to stag-horn, mother-of-pearl or ivory. The guns, also available in "Deluxe engraved", are usually about 4.75 inches long, with 3-inch barrels, and weigh 14-17 oz depending on chambering.

• *Model 1 Anniversary Commemorative* Made in 1991 to celebrate the 125th anniversary of the patenting of the original Remington derringer. Offered only in 38 Special, 44-40 WCF and 45 Long Colt, the guns had brass frames, stainless steel barrels, and bore the patent date of December 12, 1865, on the right side of the barrel block.

- *Model 1 Lady Derringer* Offered in "Deluxe" and "Deluxe Engraved" patterns, with scrimshawed ivory grips and (in the latter case only) floral-scroll decoration, this was chambered only for 32 Magnum, 38 Special, 357 Magnum or 45 Long Colt.
- *Model 1 NRA* A limited edition finished in gold or blue over stainless steel.
- *Model 1 Texas Commemorative* Five hundred of these were made in 1987-8 in each of three chamberings (38 Special, 44-40 WCF, 45 Long Colt) to commemorate the 150th anniversary of the declaration of Texan independence. They have brass frames, stainless steel barrels, grips of stag-horn or rosewood and "MADE IN THE 150TH YEAR OF TEXAS FREEDOM" on the barrel-top.

Model 4 Introduced in 1985, this is a long-barreled Model 1 chambered for the 357 Magnum, 41 Magnum or 45 Long Colt centerfire rounds or, alternatively, 410 shotshells. The guns are 6.5 inches long, have 4.75-inch barrels and weigh 16-17 oz, depending on chambering.

- *Model 4 Alaskan Survival Model* Distinguished by its over-size grips, this was chambered for 44 Magnum or 45 Long Colt (both barrels) or, alternatively, 45-70 Government (upper barrel) and 410 shotshell or 45 Long Colt (lower barrel).

Model 6 This derringer was distinguished by 6-inch barrels in a flush-sided block and oversize rosewood or rubber grips. Chamberings were usually 410 shotshell or 45 Long Colt, but 357 Magnum and 45 ACP versions have been supplied to order.

Model 7 "Ultra-Lightweight" Introduced in 1986 for use as a concealed "back-up" weapon, this has a frame and barrel assembly made of gray-matte aluminum alloy, which reduces weight to 7.5 oz. Chamberings range from 22 LR rimfire to 32 S&W Long and 44 Special.

Model 8 "Target" Distinguished by its 8-inch barrels in a conventional contoured block, this has a single-action trigger system and a manual safety that disengages automatically as the hammer is thumbed back. Chamberings have been restricted to 45 Long Colt and 410 shotshell.

Model 10 "Lightweight" This is little more than a gray-finished Model 1 with an alloy frame and a stainless steel barrel-block, offered only in 38 Special, 45 ACP or 45 Long Colt. Wood grips are standard.

Model 11 A variant of the Model 10, with an aluminum frame and steel barrel-block, offered in chamberings ranging from 22 LR rimfire to 380 Auto.

Millenium Series 2000 Announced in 1999, these guns are short-barrel derivatives of the Model 8 with a single-action trigger and differentiated largely by decoration. The chamberings are customarily restricted to 38 Special, 44-40 WCF and 45 Long Colt. The basic "Millenium 2000" has scrimshaw grips with the yellow rose of Texas on one side and the Lone Star flag on the other.

- *Cowboy Model* This is identical with the standard pattern, except for rosewood grips etched with the Lone Star flag and a "COWBOY SERIES 2000" inscription on the barrel-block.
- *Gambler Model* This was simply the Cowboy pattern without the inscription.
- *Women of Texas Model* Identical with the Millennium pattern, except for "WOMEN OF TEXAS SERIES 2000" on the barrel-block.

AMERICAN FIRE ARMS MFG CO.
San Antonio, Texas, USA.
This company operated between 1972 and 1974, marketing a Remington "Double Derringer" reproduction in 38 Special and the *AFM Mark X* or *American Mark X*, a 25 ACP automatic pistol of conventional blowback type. These 2-inch-barreled guns were made of blued or stainless steel and had seven-round magazines. Sales literature claimed that the Mark X was also available in "250 Magnum", but the identity of this cartridge remains unknown. A handful of essentially similar pistols in 380 Auto chambering also existed with a 3.5-inch barrel and an eight-round magazine.

AMERICAN FRONTIER FIREARMS CO.
Aguanga, California, USA.
Originally an importer of "Old Timers", customarily replica caplock and early cartridge revolvers made in Italy by Uberti (q.v.) and others, this business had progressed to assembly and finishing Italian-made guns by 1996.

The *Regulator*, *Silverado* and *Storekeeper* (introduced in the USA in 1992) were copies of the Colt Peacemaker. An 1851-type Navy Colt 36-caliber caplock and a "Richards & Mason" cartridge transformation of the Pocket Navy appeared in 1996 alongside an "1851 Navy Conversion", an "1871-1872 Pocket Model" and an "1871-1872 Open Top". A "Richards 1860 Army" — a cartridge transformation of the 44-caliber Army-type caplock — followed in 1997. These guns were all based on Colt designs, but AFC has also marketed a New Model Remington caplock (1996) and a "Remington New Model Cavalry" (1997).

AMERICAN GUN CO.
Norwich, Connecticut, USA.
This name was used on revolvers made in 1892-3 by the Crescent Arms Co. (q.v.) for supply to the H & D Folsom Company, retailers of sporting goods. Folsom actually bought Crescent Arms in 1893, after which the production of revolvers ceased and the company concentrated on shotgun manufacture — under a myriad brand names — until taken over by Davis-Warner in 1930. The revolvers were the usual 32 S&W, five-shot, top-break, double-action models with ribbed barrels that typified the period. They were essentially similar to those pioneered by Smith & Wesson.

AMERICAN STANDARD TOOL CO.
Newark, New Jersey, USA.
This firm operated briefly, in 1865-70, as successors to the Manhattan Firearms Co. It continued to manufacture a "Manhattan design" in the form of a 22 RF tip-up revolver with a seven-chamber cylinder, a sheathed trigger, and wood or ivory grips. This was very similar to the contemporary Smith & Wesson models.

AMES SWORD CO.
Chicopee Falls, Massachusetts, USA.
Best known for edged weapons, cutlery and tools, Ames entered the handgun business as contractors. An American company, the Minneapolis Firearms Co., had purchased the right to make and sell the French "Turbiaux" (q.v.) palm-squeezer pistol under the name "Protector". These rights were then taken over by one Peter Finnegan, an agent of the company, who not only created the Chicago Firearms Co. (q.v.) but also contracted with Ames to make the pistols.

Ames made sundry improvements to the original design, but production fell short of the quantity demanded by Finnegan and, in 1896-7, a series of lawsuits left Ames saddled with rights to the Protector. Attempts to market the guns were made for a few years, but the 1882-patent design was obsolescent by 1900 and could not compete with more modern rivals. By about 1910, the Ames company had given up the struggle and abandoned production.

AMTEC
This was the name of a collaborative 1995 sales venture between Erma of Germany and Harrington & Richardson of the USA. The five-shot, solid-frame, double-action *Amtec 2000* revolver, with side-opening cylinder, seems to have been an Erma Model 443 with different butt-grips. The 38 Special Amtec was offered in blued or stainless steel, with an optional cylinder chambered for 9mm Parabellum ammunition.

L. ANCION-MARX
Liége, Belgium.
Beginning in the 1860s with a variety of open-frame Lefaucheux-type pinfires and later moving to the smaller centerfire patterns, Ancion-Marx was one of the more prolific Belgian distributors of cheap revolvers. These latter models were all solid-frame revolvers of Velo-Dog type, in 5.5mm or 6.35mm Auto chamberings. They were advertised under a variety of names, probably for sale through different outlets, and may have been purchased elsewhere in Liége. Unfortunately, few of the names were registered, and similar weapons with the same names could be made by other companies in Belgium and elsewhere.

Cobolt This was a 450-caliber revolver of very similar pattern to the Cobold (see "Henrion, Dassy & Heuschen"), dating from the 1880s and probably named to tap the popularity of the original gun.

Extracteur A name given to a break-open S&W-type auto-ejecting revolver dating from the 1890s.

Le Novo A five-chamber 6.35mm pocket revolver with butt that folded up around the trigger and frame, customarily identified with Ancion-Marx. However, the gun was actually made by Derkenne (q.v.) and distributed to the trade by Dumoulin. Ancion-Marx would have been acting as a retailer. Marks of Bertrand of Liége and Galand of Paris have also been found on guns of this type.

Lincoln This particular name was very popular among Liége gunmakers, who applied it to a wide variety of revolvers made in 1880-1914. Most were of the folding-trigger pocket variety, hammer and "hammerless" types, in chamberings ranging from 22RF and 5.5mm Velo-Dog to 380CF. Other gunmakers linked with "Lincoln" included Bertrand, Debouxtay, Dumoulin, Jannsen Fils & Cie, Le Page, Neumann Frères and Raick Frères, all of Liége, and Albrecht Kind in Germany. It is suspected that most (or, indeed, all) the guns were the work of Manufacture Liégeoise d'Armes à Feu, and that most will bear appropriate crowned "ML" trademarks.

Milady A name given to pocket revolvers advertised by both Ancion-Marx and Jannsen Fils of Liége. They were either of the hammerless Velo-Dog type, in 5.5mm caliber, or folding-trigger hammer revolvers in 6.35mm or 7.65mm Auto. Manufacture extended from about 1895 to 1914.

J.G. ANSCHÜTZ ("JGA")
J.G. Anschütz "Germania Waffenfabrik", Mehlis (to 1919) and Zella-Mehlis (1919-45); J.G. Anschütz GmbH, Ulm/Donau, Germany.
Founded by Johann Gottfried Anschütz in 1856, this gunmaking business rapidly attained a high reputation for the quality of its sporting guns. By 1900, the company was specializing in "Flobert pistols, muzzle loaders, Lefaucheux [pinfires], centerfire guns, pocket pistols, revolvers …" Target pistols were being made in quantity prior to World War One — some are shown in the 1911 ALFA catalog — and by 1925, Anschütz was making "Flobert-, target and other pistols, revolvers of all types …" Catalogs published in the early 1930s suggest that this was a period of distribution rather than manufacture. Trading ceased at the end of the Second World War.

Operations were rebuilt in the early 1950s in Ulm, when shooting galleries were made for amusement arcades. The introduction of the improved "Model 64" 22 RF bolt-action then allowed the company to make great success of its firearms-making business. Anschütz is best known for rifles and airguns. However, the company also makes a long-range 22-caliber competition pistol.

∼ PISTOLS ∼
Exemplar Introduced in 1987 for silhouette shooting and built on the basis of a left-hand Model 64 match-rifle action, this is generally chambered for the 22 Long Rifle rimfire cartridge. The rear sight and the trigger are adjustable, a detachable five-round magazine lies ahead of the trigger guard, and a 10-inch barrel was standard. A few single-shot guns have been made together with a few chambered for 22 WMR ammunition. The Exemplar series was replaced by the Model 64P in 1998.

• *Exemplar Kurz* (or "Court", "Short") This is a short version of the standard 22-caliber gun, with a 7-inch barrel.

• *Exemplar Hornet* A designation that distinguishes the optional 22 Hornet centerfire chambering. Guns of this type are usually supplied without sights.

• *Exemplar XIV* Identical to the standard gun except for a 14-inch barrel, this was announced in 1988.

Model 64P Seen as a replacement for the Exemplar and also built on a Model 64 action, this five-shot competition pistol appeared in 1998. Chambered only for the 22LR rimfire cartridge, it has a synthetic Choate Rynite stock and a 10-inch barrel that gives an overall length of about 18.5 inches; empty weight is about 3.5 lb. Unlike the Exemplar, a conventional right-hand action is used and iron sights are customarily omitted.

• *Model 64P Mag* This is identical with the standard pattern, but in 22 WMR instead of 22 LR rimfire.

∼ REVOLVER ∼
J.G.A. This was a "hammerless" solid-frame, non-ejecting, folding-trigger revolver chambered for the 7.65mm Auto semi-rim cartridge. Apart from an unusual safety catch mounted high on the frame, locking the hammer when applied, it was comparable to contemporaneous Velo-Dog models. The mark of a double-encircled "JGA" was granted to "J.G. Anschütz Germania-Waffenwerk" in March 1915, supplementing the head of Germania (a female personification of Germany) that had been used from the late 1890s.

UDO ANSCHÜTZ ("UAZ")
Zella-Mehlis, Germany.
This gunmaking business specialized in single-shot "free" target pistols between 1927 and 1939. Although made to a basic design, they were invariably highly customized to the demands of individuals and nominally identical models often exhibit startling differences. Udo Anchütz purchased the business of Ernst Friedrich Büchel in 1934, continuing to make the Luna (and probably also the Tell) pistol until the beginning of the Second World War.

Rekord The "Rekord-Match 1933" and "Rekord-Match 210" both used Martini hinged-block actions and were chambered for the 22 Long Rifle round. Target sights of various patterns were fitted and the stocks and grips were to individual requirements.

UAZ This was essentially the Büchel "Tell" pistol under another name, embodying the same type of swinging block actuated by a lever set into the backstrap. A single trigger was customarily "set" with a radial lever on the left side of the frame.

APAOLOZO BROTHERS
Apaolozo Hermanos, Zumorraga, Spain.
Little is known of these brothers, other than that they manufactured pistols from the early 1920s until the Spanish Civil War (1936-9). Their name never appears on their products, and identification is only possible from a trademark of a swooping bird, resembling a dove, impressed in the butt grips of the various models.

They were also fond of stamping "ACIER COMPRIME" on the guns, which means no more than "compressed steel" in French (indicating the intended market for Apaolozo products), but it has sometimes been quoted as a maker's or model name.

∼ REVOLVER ∼
Apaolozo A 38-caliber revolver based upon the Colt Police Positive model.

∼ AUTOMATIC PISTOLS ∼
Paramount This name has obviously been popular in Spain, since a number of Eibar-type blowbacks in both 6.35mm and 7.65mm calibers

were made in 1920-35. The 6.35mm examples were also made by Beistegui Hermanos and the 7.65mm guns by Retolaza Hermanos. In addition, there are at least two known distinct 6.35mm models by unidentified makers. There are no notable features about any of them.

The Apaolozo version is a 6.35mm automatic based on the Browning 1906 that is marked "Paramount Cal .25" on the slide and "Cal 6.35" on the grips. The flying bird trademark also appears on the grips.

Triomphe A 6.35mm pistol, identical with the Paramount except for the slide inscription "Pistolet Automatique Triomphe Acier Comprimé". The butt grips are the same as those on the Paramount. The Triomphe was probably made for sale in France and Belgium.

A & R SALES
South El Monte, California, USA.
This company existed briefly in the latter 1970s, marketing a copy of the 45-caliber Colt M1911 with a light alloy frame.

ARANA & CO.
Arana y Cia, Eibar, Spain.
El Cano A 32-caliber, six-shot, solid-frame revolver with a 6-inch barrel and a side-opening cylinder, this was based on the Smith & Wesson Military & Police model (though lacking support for the tip of the ejector rod). It dated from the 1920s.

ARCADIA MACHINE & TOOL CO. ("AMT")
Covina, California, USA.
AMT began by customizing the Colt 45 M1911A1 Government Model, and from this, developed modifications of its own. Part of the business was sold to Galena Industries, Inc. in the late 1990s (leaving AMT only with the Back-Up series) but Galena ceased trading in 2002 and the current status of the Hardballer and Automag ranges is uncertain.

Automag II AMT began making the original Automag (q.v.) in 1985, and then modified the design to fire the 22 WMR cartridge. The "Automag II" of 1986 was made of stainless steel and retained a degree of gas assistance in the operating system. However, in the process of modification, the distinctive outline of the original was lost and the "II" became just another rectangular all-enveloping slide design (albeit with an abnormally long frame and slide) with a radial hammer-dropping safety catch on the left side. The Automag II was about 9.4 inches long with the standard 6-inch barrel and weighed 23 oz. The single-column magazine usually held nine rounds, though the shortest of the barrel options, 3.4 inches, was paired with a seven-round magazine.

Automag III This variant of the Automag II, chambered for the 30 M1 Carbine or 9mm Win Mag cartridges, appeared in 1989. It was 10.5 inches long with a 6.4-inch barrel and weighed 43 oz. Unlike the Automag II, which had the top surface of the slide partially cut away to reveal the barrel-top, the "III" had a conventional all-enveloping slide broken only by the ejection port. An eight-round, single-column magazine was standard.

Automag IV Introduced in 1990, this accepted either the 10mm Magnum or the 45 Win Mag rounds with the standard barrel lengths being 6.5 and 8.6 inches respectively. Magazines held six rounds, loaded weight being 46-51 oz depending on barrel length and chambering.

Automag V Those with nerves of steel could choose this version of the basic Automag chambered for the 50 Action Express round. Guns of this type can be recognized by the large gas ports in the front end of the slide top, an endeavor to keep the muzzle somewhere near the line of fire after the trigger was pulled.

Back-Up This "pocket automatic" apparently originated in the 1960s with the TDE Marketing Corporation as a 380 blowback. The 1980s AMT version, however, became a smaller 22 RF blowback. Made largely of stainless steel, the Back-Up had manual and grip safeties and an eight-cartridge magazine. A new 380 Auto version subsequently appeared. Both AMT pistols had concealed hammers and recessed "no-snag" sights, facilitating a quick draw. Minor changes were made to the design in 1992, creating the "Back-Up II", and a double-action-only version (*Back-Up DAO*) appeared at much the same time.

Hardballer Built of stainless steel, this pistol had an elongated grip and manual safeties, a loaded-chamber indicator, an adjustable trigger, a chamfered magazine aperture and a matt-finished slide rib. Minor changes advanced the designation to "Hardballer II" in 1993. The *Hardballer Long Slide* version is 2 inches longer (10.5 inches overall), allowing slightly greater velocity to be generated from the standard 45 ACP round. This caused the original short-barrel gun to be renamed "Hardballer Government". Other variants have included the *Commando* and the *400 Accelerator*.

Javelina Introduced in 1989 but abandoned in 1992, this was little more than a Hardballer Long Slide (see above) chambering the 10mm Auto cartridge. The magazine held eight rounds.

Lightning Introduced in 1984, this combined a modified Ruger Target frame with an AMT receiver and barrel unit of stainless steel. The Clark trigger had adjustable stops and the trigger guard was modified to suit a two-handed grip. Options ranged from a 5-inch "bull" barrel to 6.5-, 8.5-, 10.5- and 12.5-inch barrels that may be either the regular tapered pattern or heavy cylindrical type. The *Bullseye* had a 6.5-inch barrel with a ventilated rib and mounts for an optical sight.

On Duty DA Introduced in 1991 and resembling an amalgam of SIG and Beretta designs externally, this was a conventional, good-quality, double-action pistol with a stainless steel barrel, a steel slide and an aluminum frame with a steel recoil-shoulder insert. Guns were chambered for the 9mm Parabellum (15-round magazine), 40 S&W (11 rounds) and 45 ACP (8 rounds). The length was 7.8 inches with a 4.5-inch barrel; the weight averaged 32 oz. but depended on chambering. Three-dot sights were standard, and an additional safety system ensured that the gun could not be fired if the magazine had been removed. An *On Duty De-Cocker* was also available.

F. ARIZAGA SONS
Hijos de F. Arizaga ("Sons of F. Arizaga"), Eibar, Spain.
Kolibri This 6.35mm Eibar-type pistol is said to have been made in the early 1920s, though confirmation is still lacking.

GASPAR ARIZAGA
Eibar, Spain.
Arizaga produced automatic pistols that, while unremarkable, were as reliable as could be expected. Thus they achieved worthwhile sales from the early 1920s until the Spanish Civil War (1936-9).

Arizaga The least common of the products, this was a 7.65mm automatic pistol of Eibar type; marked "GASPAR ARIZAGA EIBAR Cal 7.65" on the slide.

Mondial A 6.35mm automatic of unusual appearance, this appeared, externally at least, to be a copy of the Savage (q.v.).

A 6.35mm example of the Arizaga "Mondial" pistol.

However, the resemblance was only skin-deep; internally, it was nothing but a Browning-derived blowback. Two versions of this pistol are said to have been made: a *Model 1*, with grip, applied and magazine safeties, and a cheaper *Model 2* with only the applied safety. Only guns of the second pattern have been traced for examination, but they bore no model number and existence of the first type still lacks confirmation. Identification is aided by the trademark of an owl in a circle, surmounted by the word "Mondial", that will be found on the butt.

Pinkerton Perhaps the most common Arizaga product, this was made in two types. One was a copy of the 6.35mm Browning 1906, distinguished by holes in the right-hand grip that allow the contents of the magazine to be checked. The second model, also derived from the Browning 1906 mechanically, showed affinities with the Mondial. The slide had large vertical grooves resembling those of the Mondial and Savage, and the safety catch was not only the same component but also fitted in the same fashion. Neither gun displayed the Arizaga trademark, being marked only "Pinkerton Automatic 6.35mm" on the slides. A 7.65mm variant of the first model is also claimed to exist.

Warwinck This was simply a 7.65mm version of the Mondial, differing only in dimensions. The top of the slide was marked "Automatic Pistol 7.65 Warwinck" and the grips carried the Arizaga owl mark surmounted by "Warwinck".

FRANCISCO ARIZMENDI

Eibar, Spain.

Arizmendi succeeded to the Arizmendi y Goenaga (below) in 1914 and had soon undertaken development of most of the automatic pistols associated with the name. Most are readily identified by their incorporation of Arizmendi's patented loaded-chamber indicator. In this device, a groove in the top of the slide is marked with an axial line, and a movable unit in the center of the groove continues this line. When the chamber is empty, the line is continuous; when the chamber is loaded, the movable section is displaced laterally to give a "step" in the line. Production ceased during the Spanish Civil War (1936-9).

∼ REVOLVERS ∼

Arizmendi Two revolvers classified as "Arizmendi" are known, though the only identification is Arizmendi's trademark, a circle with a five-pointed star surmounted by "FA" in a tablet. Both were simple five-shot solid-frame folding-trigger guns that were similar to the Velo-Dog type. No extracting mechanism was fitted; they were gate-loaded, and spent cases were simply ejected by an ejector rod carried on a crane attached to the cylinder axis pin. The first model chambered the 7.65mm Auto cartridge. The rear of the frame was high and only the tip of the hammer protruded. The second model, in 32 S&W, had a lower frame, exposing the entire hammerhead, and a sliding safety catch lay on the backstrap.

Puppy This name was popular with Spanish gunmakers, at least five of whom used it. The Arizmendi "Puppy" was a hammerless 5.5mm Velo-Dog revolver with a solid frame, a folding trigger, and a five-chamber cylinder. The barrel was marked "Puppy", and the "FA" trademark lay on the frame.

Velomith Artian Little is known of this model, identifiable only by Francisco Arizmendi's mark. It was a "Velo-mith", a revolver designed to look as much like an automatic as possible. Top-break construction and a barrel formed into a slab-sided deep unit, with a groove in the side, was intended to duplicate the appearance of the 1900-pattern FN-Browning pistol. The butt was straight, terminating in a simulated "magazine", and the frame rose high and square at the rear to end in what was actually a frame latch instead of a hammer-tip. The hammer was internal, the trigger folded, and, unusually, a cam-actuated self-extracting mechanism was fitted into the five-chamber cylinder. Pressing a button under the front end of the barrel isolated the cam, allowing the pistol to be opened without ejecting.

∼ AUTOMATIC PISTOLS ∼

Boltun Two different guns bore this name. The first, in 6.35mm caliber, was very similar in appearance to the Pieper of 1907. Close examination showed that it was simpler, lacking the hinged barrel of the Pieper, though a separate bolt moving in the receiver had a Pieper-like thumb grip above the receiver top. This gun is generally attributed to Arizmendi, though there is no firm confirmation and the slide marking "Automatic Pistol Boltun Patent" omits the patent number usually found on Arizmendi's products. The only specimen seen had no proofmarks and could not be conclusively identified as being Spanish … excepting on the basis of comparatively poor quality.

The second model, in 7.65mm caliber, was based on the 1919-pattern FN-Browning 1910 and was thus practically the same as the 9mm Walman. The slide inscription read "Automatic Pistol Boltun Patent Marca Registrada 7375 Cal 7,65".

Kaba Spezial Made for Karl Bauer (q.v.) of Berlin in the 1920s, these succeeded the pre-1914 pattern made by Arizmendi y Goenaga. The post-1920 version was similar to its predecessor, being little more than a 6.35mm Eibar-type copy of the Browning, but the design was "squared off" and better-looking. The slide inscription was the same, but stamped more neatly and accompanied by the "FA" trademark. The grips had a motif in the center — a circle with the words "Kaba Spezial" — that was all but identical with the markings on the original. A 7.65mm variant was also made in Eibar in small numbers, but Bauer (apparently from 1927 onward) then substituted the Menz Liliput pistol instead of Spanish products.

Pistolet Automatique Arizmendi failed to find a model name for this 6.35mm Eibar-type gun, the slide bearing nothing but "Pistolet Automatique" and the "FA" trademark.

Roland This Eibar-type pistol was made in the early 1920s in 6.35mm and 7.65mm versions and was a little above average in the quality of its finish. Arizmendi had by this time changed his trademark to a circle with a star and a crescent, and "Marca Registrada" was first seen impressed into the Roland butt grips.

Singer Francisco Arizmendi abandoned the Arizmendi y Goenaga "Singer" (below) in favor of the "Victor", a design of his own. Goodwill attached to the Singer name apparently persuaded him to re-name the "Victor" in 1918, registering a new trademark in the form of an oval with a human figure, arms akimbo, beneath a radiant sun. This appeared on the grips of the new Singer pistols. These were made in 6.35mm and 7.65mm but were simply standard Eibar-type Browning copies with slides bearing Patent Number 25389 (protecting the new trademark).

Victor The original name for the 1915-vintage pistols that became the "Singer".

Walman Francisco Arizmendi continued to produce this Arizmendi y Goenaga design until the late 1920s, abandoning the unique construction of the 6.35mm variant in favor of the plainer 7.65mm form. The later examples can also be distinguished by a change in the mark-

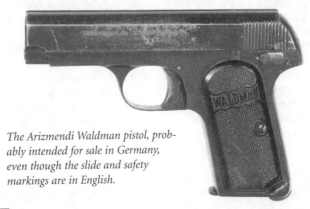

The Arizmendi Waldman pistol, probably intended for sale in Germany, even though the slide and safety markings are in English.

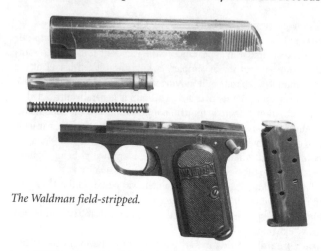

The Waldman field-stripped.

ings: "Walman" on the slide, and the same word on the grips, running diagonally down to the rear across the center, whereas A&G guns had the diagonal running up to the rear. In addition, Francisco Arizmendi grips were squared off, instead of rounded at the top.

The rarest of the Walman family was the 9mm Short (380 ACP) version introduced in the mid-1920s. Based on the 1910 FN-Browning, it had the return spring around the barrel, an automatic grip safety, and retained the patented cartridge indicator. The slide was marked "Automatic Pistol Walman Patent Marca Registrada 7375 9m/m".

Ydeal This name was applied to 6.35mm or 7.65mm Eibar-type pistols that offered lower standards of manufacture than other Arizmendi products. Markings were confined to "Pistolet Automatique Ydeal" and the "FA" trademark on the slide with "Ydeal" embossed on the grips. They appear to date from about 1916 and use the patented loaded indicator. The existence of guns chambered for the 9mm Short cartridge has been reported.

ARIZMENDI & GOENAGA ("FAG")
F. Arizmendi y Goenaga, Eibar, Spain.
This gunmaking business, trading 1886-1914, began producing "Velo-Dog" revolvers in the 1890s. In the early years of the twentieth century, A&G began to develop automatic pistols, eventually producing a varied line. In 1914, however, the business was reorganized as Francisco Arizmendi (above).

∼ REVOLVER ∼
F.A.G. Arizmendi y Goenaga made two different revolvers marked with these initials. The first was chambered for the 8mm Lebel cartridge, being a virtual copy of the French M1892 service weapon. The other was in 7.62mm Nagant, essentially the Russian M1895 Nagant revolver without the gas seal feature. They are assumed to date from 1897-1905, but both are extremely rare.

∼ AUTOMATIC PISTOLS ∼
Continental A 6.35mm Eibar-type copy of the Browning 1906 without grip safety, this was the work of Arizmendi y Goenaga of Eibar in the 1920s. The only marking is "6.35" on the butt grip and "Continental Patent 16137" on the slide.
Ideal A 7.65mm "Eibar" automatic by Arizmendi y Goenaga of Eibar, it carries the firm's name and "Pistolet Automatique Ideal", with the safety catch markings in French, suggesting an export model.
Kaba Spezial This name was a trademark of Karl Bauer (q.v.), a German gun dealer, who ordered guns from Spain shortly before the First World War began. The Arizmendi y Goenaga trademark lay on the slide, together with "Pistolet Automatique Kaba Spezial" and the word "Kaba" across the grips. The weapon itself was a 6.35mm "Eibar" based on the Browning 1906. However, relatively few had been made when Francisco Arizmendi (above) took over operations. The post-1920 deliveries took a different form.

Singer Two versions of the A&G "Singer" existed, a 6.35mm Browning 1906 type and a 7.65mm gun derived from the 1910 FN-Browning. They apparently dated from 1913 and bore "Pistola Automatica 7,65" (or "…6,35") on the slide, together with a trademark of a crown surmounting "AG" above a crescent. The butt apparently represented a diva in an opera house. A different gun of the same name was subsequently made by Francisco Arizmendi.
Teuf-Teuf Another successful brand name appropriated in Spain, the original 6.35mm guns were made in Belgium in about 1907. The Spanish version was a 7.65mm-caliber "Eibar", probably made in 1912-13, and bears no resemblance to its Belgian prototype. The slide was marked "Automatic Teuf-Teuf Pistol 7,65mm" and had the A&G trademark.
Walman This is probably the most common of the A&G pistols. These standard striker-fired "Eibar" blowbacks were made in 6.35mm and 7.65mm Auto chamberings and displayed "American Automatic Pistol Walman Patent" on the slide (though "American" was dropped towards the end of the production run). "Walman" and the A&G trademark appeared on the grips. The muzzle of the 6.35mm gun was formed into a lump carrying the front sight, requiring a rectangular cut to be made in the top of the slide. The 7.65mm pattern had an uncut slide with the front-sight blade mounted on it. Post-1914 guns were made by Francisco Arizmendi (q.v.).

ARIZMENDI, ZULAICA & CO.
Arizmendi, Zulaica y Cia, Eibar, Spain.
The relationship of this gunmaking business to other "Arizmendi" companies is still unresolved. It was created in 1916 to make the "Ruby" pistol for the French government, acting as a sub-contractor to Gabilondo y Urresti. Like many of the lesser manufactories involved with the Ruby, Arizmendi, Zulaica y Cia continued to commercially exploit the design after World War I had ended. Trading ceased in about 1925.

The 38-caliber Cebra revolver, made by Zrizmendi, Zulaica & Co.

∼ REVOLVER ∼
Cebra A 38-caliber solid-frame revolver based on S&W practice.
∼ AUTOMATIC PISTOL ∼
Cebra A 7.65mm M1916 "Ruby" pistol made under license in the early 1920s. The notable feature was the depth of the butt, accommodating a nine-cartridge magazine, but there were numerous differences in the shape of the grips, the number and design of the slide grooves, and the machining of the safety catch. The guns were all marked "Pistolet Automatique 'Cebra' Arizmendi Zulaica y Cia Eibar (Espana)".

ARMAMENT SYSTEMS & PROCEDURES ("ASP")
Appleton, Wisconsin, USA.
This business marketed the Asp conversion of the 9mm Smith & Wesson Model 39 pistol from the mid-1970s to 1987. The goal was to provide law-enforcement personnel with a concealable but powerful pistol of high reliability. The exterior of the M39 was welded up and ground smooth, the working surfaces were ground and polished, a new

recoil spring was fitted, and the trigger components were honed. The magazine was given a slot in the side and clear plastic grips allowed the ammunition to be seen. A "Guttersnipe" sight was fitted, which allowed very rapid aiming. The Asp was made in limited quantities to special order only and was never available to the general public.

ARMAS DE FUEGO

Manufactura de Armas de Fuego, Guernica, Spain.

Little is known of this gunmaking business except that it apparently inherited the brand names associated with Alkartasuna (q.v.) and may simply have been a reorganization of the original company for legal or financial reasons. Support for this belief is provided by the appearance of an identical trademark on Alkartasuna and Armas de Fuego products. Trading seems to have been confined to 1920-4, producing only the *Alkar* and *Alkatasuna* pistols.

ARMAS DE TIRO Y CASA SA ("ATCSA")

Barcelona, Spain.

This company was formed in the early 1930s to make a single-shot target pistol chambered for the 4mm Übungspatrone saloon cartridge, the barrel being carried on a vertical pivot in front of the chamber and swung to one side to expose the chamber for loading. This was followed in 1934 by a six-shot solid-frame side-opening revolver in 38 Special. This latter weapon was reputedly of high quality, using stainless steel for the cylinder, and had an unusual quick-release on the crane that allowed the cylinder to be replaced with a pre-loaded one. The gun had an unusual arc-shaped cutaway on the front lower edge of the butt, forming a rest for the little finger, but was otherwise based broadly on the Colt Police Positive. The only marking is on the left of the frame below the hammer: "ATCSA Pat 130395".

Contemporary reports spoke favorably about these revolvers, but the Spanish Civil War brought work to a stop and ATCSA closed down. Consequently, the pistols are now uncommon.

ARMERO ESPECIALISTAS

Armero Especialistas Reunidas ("United Arms Specialists"), Eibar, Spain.

This group of workmen from the Spanish gun trade set themselves up in business in the early 1920s to manufacture an automatic pistol. They then acted as marketing agents for a line of revolvers made by Orueta Hermanos (q.v.) until they were in a position to manufacture guns of their own, which were well received in contemporaneous reports. Trading continued until the Spanish Civil War (1936-9).

～ REVOLVER ～

Alfa Several revolvers of this name were made. The first, made by Orueta Hermanos, were copies of the Smith & Wesson No 2 hinged-frame models in 32, 38 and 44 caliber. They can be readily identified by the "Alfa" mark on the grips. Armero Especialistas subsequently began to make guns of their own, electing to base work on the 38-caliber Colt Police Positive and the Smith & Wesson Military & Police patterns. These also bore "Alfa" trademarks and were followed by 22 LR

Made by Armero Especialistas, the 38-caliber "Alfa" was a Smith & Wesson copy.

and 32 S&W variants. Production continued until the Civil War, and guns were exported in large numbers. (Note that "ALFA" was also the trademark of Adolph Frank [q.v.] of Hamburg.)

～ AUTOMATIC PISTOL ～

Omega Aptly named, as the last in the line, these pistols were simple 6.35mm and 7.65mm Eibar-type automatics. They were marked "Omega" on slide and butt, and have a triangular trademark at the right rear of the frame.

ARMI-JAGER

Armi-Jager di Armando Piscetta Srl, Milan, Italy.

Armi-Jager is best known for its numerous look-alike 22 RF automatic rifles, including near-replicas of the Kalashnikov, the AR15/M16 and the FA MAS. The company has also made rimfire revolvers based upon the Colt Peacemaker.

Frontier series *The Baby Frontier, Frontier* and *Super Frontier* rimfires differed largely in barrel length and general finish. The Frontier and Super Frontier were also offered in 357 Magnum and 44 Magnum centerfire.

ARMINEX LTD

Scottsdale, Arizona, USA.

This small gunmaking business, operated by James Mongello, made a modernized version of the US Government M1911A1 in 1981-5.

The Arminex Trifire is one of many 1911-type Colt-Browning clones.

Trifire This combined the proven advantages of the original Browning design with the improvements that added to the efficiency. The safety catch was moved to the slide, where it was rather easier to use and where it could also actuate a positive firing-pin lock; the grip safety was removed; and the extractor and ejector were on pivoted mountings, improving both handling and reliability.

Changes were also made to the recoil-spring guide, and the butt frame was re-shaped to give a better hold. An ambidextrous safety catch was available to order, and while the pistol was fitted with the original US Government-pattern 45-caliber barrel, interchangeable barrels in 9mm Parabellum or 38 Super (with appropriate magazines) were also available. However, although the pistol was well made and reliable, sales were so disappointing that manufacture soon ceased. A long-barreled "Target" model with an adjustable rear sight was also made in small numbers.

ARMSCOR

Arms Corporation of the Philippines, Quezon City.

Previously trading as Squires Bingham (q.v.), or "Squibman", this company has manufactured various firearms including a series of 38-caliber revolvers. (Note that this firm should not be confused with the South African armaments consortium of the same name.)

～ REVOLVERS ～

M100 Dating from the 1980s, this conventional double-action revolver with a yoke-mounted cylinder, derived from Colt practice, had a 4-inch barrel with a ventilated rib and an adjustable rear sight. Chamberings were confined to 22 LR rimfire, 22 WRM and 38 Special.

M200 series These were solid-frame side-opening double-action types with Colt pull-back thumb catches, safety transfer bars and floating firing pins.

- *M200P "Police"* This had a six-chamber cylinder, fixed sights, a half-length ejector rod shroud, rubber or wood grips, and a 4-inch barrel.
- *M200TC "Thunder Chief"* Basically the same as the Police model, this had a full length ejector-rod shroud, an adjustable rear sight and wood grips.
- *M200 DC "Detective Chief"* Reintroduced in 1996, this is a compact version of the series with a 2.5-inch barrel with a full-length ejector rod shroud, fixed sights, and rubber grips with finger grooving.
- *M201S "Stainless"* This was simply the M200P made of stainless (instead of blued) steel.

∼ AUTOMATIC PISTOLS ∼

M1911 Armscor began making a near facsimile of the 45 ACP Colt Government Model in 1995, which has since led to a number of variants.

- *M1911-A1* The basic 45 ACP gun, with a 5-inch barrel, has a single-column magazine holding seven rounds. Blue finish is standard. Most guns have skeleton triggers, cut-out hammers, and elongated "beavertail" grip-safety levers. The slide release and the manual safety-catch head are also enlarged compared with the US service-pattern originals.
- *M1911-A1P* A Parkerized version of the "A1", available with a magazine holding seven or 10 rounds.
- *M1911-A2* A short-lived variant, deemed illegal by the Gun Control Act of 1994, this originally had a double-column magazine holding 13 rounds. Post-1994 guns are restricted to 10 rounds.

EULOGIO AROSTEGUI

Eibar, Spain.

Arostegui operated a small gunmaking company from the mid-1920s until the Spanish Civil War (1936-9). His products included Eibar automatics, Velo-Dog revolvers and copies of the Smith & Wesson M&P.

∼ REVOLVERS ∼

E.A. A 380-caliber S&W-type swing-cylinder revolver.

Oscillant Azul Similar to the E.A., this was another of the Smith & Wesson-inspired guns.

∼ AUTOMATIC PISTOLS ∼

Azul This name initially appeared on a 6.35mm Eibar-type automatic based on the Browning 1906, dating from the early 1920s. It was then applied to a 7.65mm gun based on the Browning 1903, another typical "Eibar". Then came another 7.65mm pattern, with an external hammer and a lanyard loop on the butt, suggesting that it was aimed at the military or police markets. Finally, the name was attached to Mauser C/96-pattern pistols made by Bestegui (q.v.) that were sold by Arostegui in the early 1930s.

E.A. Another 6.35mm Eibar-type pistol, this was hard to distinguish from the Azul. The frame is marked with "EA" in a circle, and a motif of a dog retrieving game is molded into the grips.

Super Azul Arostegui also marketed the Royal selective-fire pistol, a similar weapon to the better-known Mauser "Schnellfeuerpistole," which in fact pre-dated the Mauser machine pistol design by several years. This was manufactured by Bestegui Hermanos, but many were distributed by Arostegui to China and South America by way of agents in Germany.

SALVATOR AROSTEGUI

Eibar, Spain.

Browreduit Another example of the "Brow" family of Velo-Dog revolvers, this five-shot 6.35mm gun offered the usual hammerless solid-frame folding-trigger construction. The fondness of using the prefix "Brow" in these Velo-Dogs arises from their use of "Browning" cartridges.

ARRIOLA BROTHERS

Arriola Hermanos, Eibar, Spain.

Little is known about the affairs of this small gunmaking business, which produced a 38-caliber revolver copied from the Colt Police Positive in the mid-1920s. The barrel is marked "Arriola Eibar [date] .38 Long Ctg", and the left side of the frame usually displays "Made in Spain".

CALIXTO ARRIZABALAGA SONS

Hijos de Calixto Arrizabalaga ("Sons of Calixto Arrizabalaga"), Eibar, Spain.

This business appears to have begun trading during World War I, helping to make 7.65mm "Ruby" pistols for the French Army. Thereafter, it continued to manufacture the same type of pistol in various forms until the Spanish Civil War (1936-9) brought an end to activities. Some of the guns were Eibar-type blowbacks, derived from the FN-Brownings, but Arrizabalaga also made an original design under the names Jo-Lo-Ar and Sharp-Shooter.

Arrizabalaga This was the original 7.65mm-caliber "Eibar", offering average quality. It was apparently sold with official use in mind, as it was provided with a lanyard ring and the frame was large enough to take a 9-round magazine. The slides bore the company name and "Pistola Automatica 32 ACP". See also "Azanza & Arrizabalaga", below.

Campeon This name appears on two automatics, one chambered for the 6.35mm Auto cartridge and the other for the 7.65mm Auto type. The former was based on the Browning 1906 design, and the latter on the Browning 1903. Both were identified by the name "Campeon" on the grips and "Automatic Pistol Campeon for … cartridge" on the slide. The 7.65mm version also had "7.65 1919" embossed above the name, together with the initials "CH" in a diamond on the lower rear of the butt (representing Crucelegui Hermanos, who sold the pistol under their own name). The 6.35mm gun was subsequently produced under the name "Terrible".

The slides are cut away on both sides of the top surface immediately behind the breech face, leaving a central ridge into which a transverse striker-retaining pin was driven. This ridge appears on one or two other Eibar automatics, but there seems to be no valid reason for it; it was probably no more than a styling feature to distinguish the guns from their rivals.

Crucelegui A 7.65mm Eibar-type blowback sold by Crucelegui Hermanos, probably because the latter business was not geared to the production of automatic pistols.

Especial A 7.65mm "Eibar" pistol dating from the 1920s; it was simply the standard "Arrizabalaga" model under a different name.

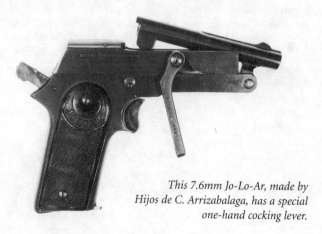

This 7.6mm Jo-Lo-Ar, made by Hijos de C. Arrizabalaga, has a special one-hand cocking lever.

Jo-Lo-Ar This name was derived from the name of José López Arnaíz, patentee of the extractor added to the Sharp-Shooter (q.v.) in 1919. Most guns were to be found with a peculiar hand-cocking lever attached by screw to the right side of the frame, patented by Sr Arnaíz in 1923. The Jo-Lo-Ar was made in the same calibers, plus 9mm Bergmann-Bayard (for Peru) and even 45 ACP, though these must have been somewhat close to the safety margin for blowback weapons. The slide was marked "Pistola Jo-Lo-Ar Eibar (Espana) Patent Nos 68027, 70235". Like the Sharp-Shooter, the Jo-Lo-Ar was also sold by Ojanguren y Vidosa (q.v.), distinguished by small white-metal "OV" monogram grip medallions. Work seems to have ceased about 1930.

Sharp-Shooter Often misspelled "Sharp-Sooter" on the pistols, this appeared in 1918 and was based on Spanish Patent 68027 of 1917. Its unusual features make a welcome change from the ubiquitous "Eibars" of the time. The slide was open-topped in front of the breech face, the upper surface of the barrel being exposed. There were two lugs under the barrel, one at the muzzle, pinned to the front of the frame, and another below the chamber to engage a cutaway section of the safety-catch shaft.

A small coil spring lay under the front lug. When the safety catch was rotated completely to the rear, past the "safe" position, the back lug was freed and the barrel could tip around the front pivot so that the breech could rise. The barrel could then be examined, cleaned, or loaded with a single cartridge, closed, and then locked by rotating the safety catch back to its initial position. The hammer could then be thumb-cocked and the trigger pressed to fire one shot. The guns notably lacked a trigger guard, the trigger simply being sheathed in a frame extension.

The Sharp-Shooter lacked an extractor, relying instead on residual chamber pressure to eject the spent case —a system that fails when confronted with extracting an unfired cartridge. However, an extractor was added in 1919. Sharp-Shooters were made in 6.35mm, 7.65mm and 9mm Short chamberings with the slide being marked "Sharp-Shooter Patent No 68027".

Terrible This is merely the 6.35mm Campeon with a new sales name. The choice of name has been questioned many times, but it was bestowed in honor of a large British protected cruiser, HMS *Terrible*, that (together with sister-ship *Powerful*) had attained prominence during the South African or "Anglo-Boer" war of 1899-1902 by landing marines and unshipping some large-caliber guns to help the land campaign.

ASCASO

Francisco Ascaso was a noted revolutionary firebrand whose name was linked with a number of political murders in Spain during the late 1920s. Deported in 1931, he returned to Spain in 1935 to take up the political cudgels and was killed on 20 July 1936, three days after the start of the Civil War.

How his name comes to be attached to a pistol is far from clear, but it was probably in commemoration of his activities (cf., "Gustloff"). Ascaso could have had no hand in the project, as production did not begin until 1937 and was simply a rapid response to a shortage of pistols among the Republican forces. The gun was an exact copy of the contemporary army-issue M1921 (Astra 400), differing only in markings and finish.

The Ascaso has an oval engraving in the forward portion of the barrel casing containing the words "F. Ascaso Tarassa" (Tarassa in Catalonia is assumed to have been the site of the factory), and the general finish is inferior to an issue Astra. However, work on the Ascaso pistol is highly creditable, particularly as innumerable simpler designs could have been copied in such trying circumstances. Production appears to have continued through 1937 and 1938, but it is doubtful if more than a few thousand were made.

ASERMA MANUFACTURING CO.

New Germany, South Africa

This engineering business entered the gunmaking field in the mid-1990s with the ADP Mark II. Chambered for the 9mm Parabellum cartridge, this is an extremely compact gas-retarded blowback.

ASTRA–UNCETA & CO

Astra–Unceta y Cia SA, Guernica, Spain.

This gunmaking business makes a variety of handguns. The company was founded in Eibar in 1908 as Esperanza y Unceta (q.v.), registered the Astra trademark in 1914, moved to Guernica in 1913, and became "Unceta y Cia" in 1925. The company was one of only four gunmakers permitted to continue trading after the Spanish Civil War ended in 1939, and the current trading name was officially adopted in 1955. Brief details of the guns that had been introduced before this date will be found in the sections devoted to "Esperanza & Unceta" and "Unceta & Co."

However, it must be remembered that guns introduced prior to 1955 (in this particular case) were often still being made many years afterward with nothing more than a change of manufacturer's name — and sometimes also designation — to distinguish them from their predecessors.

The business collapsed at the end of 1997 only a few months after Star–Bonifacio Echeveria SA (q.v.) and during a severe recession in the Spanish gunmaking industry. A workforce numbering 103 was dispersed as a result. Some of the assets were acquired by Guerniquesa de Mecanizado, Tratamiento y Montaje de Armas SAL, registered in Vizcaya, but the current status of the handguns is unclear. They were available for some years after the collapse of Astra, but it is likely that these were being assembled from pre-1997 components.

∼ REVOLVERS ∼

Astra did not enter the revolver field until 1958 when the Cadix range was announced. The popularity of these guns allowed the development of several larger guns under the same brand name.

Astra Cadix Confined to 1959-68, this was a Smith & Wesson-type double-action revolver with the cylinder mounted on a side-swinging yoke. The most distinctive feature was the trigger guard, which had a slightly spurred rear web that has become a characteristic of Astra

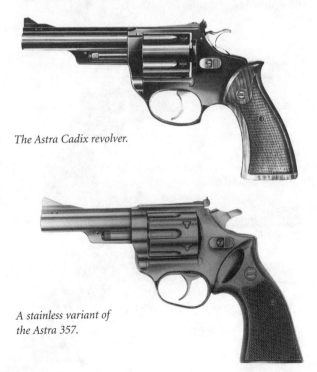

The Astra Cadix revolver.

A stainless variant of the Astra 357.

revolvers. The Cadix was offered as a nine-shot in 22 LR rimfire or a five-shot in 38 Special with barrels measuring 4 or 6 inches.

Astra 357 Derived from the Cadix range in 1972, this was the first Astra revolver to adopt the transfer-bar safety system of connecting the hammer and the firing pin, doubtless to comply with American regulations inspired by the 1968 Gun Control Act. It was also the first to adopt a cartridge powerful enough to compete with US designs. Barrels varied from 3 to 6 inches, finish was either blued or stainless steel and various degrees of embellishment were available.

The 357 Magnum Astra Police revolver, with exchangeable 9mm Parabellum cylinder and loading clip.

Astra 357 Police Intended as a police or military weapon, this six-shot solid-frame swing-cylinder revolver was available in 357 Magnum, 38 Special or 9mm Parabellum chamberings, and a 9mm Steyr cylinder could be provided as a replacement in 9mm caliber. Cylinders accepting rimless cartridges were supplied with loading clips.

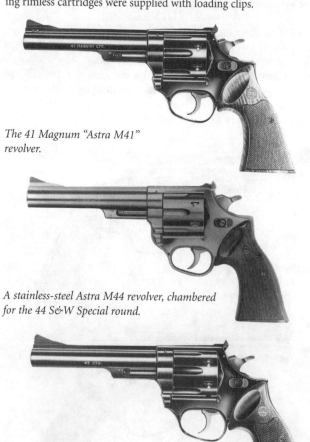

The 41 Magnum "Astra M41" revolver.

A stainless-steel Astra M44 revolver, chambered for the 44 S&W Special round.

The Astra M45 for the 45 Long Colt cartridge.

Astra 41, 44, 45 The numbers indicated the caliber of these six-shot solid-frame revolvers with swing-out cylinders, barrel ribs, and shrouded ejector rods. Rear sights were fully adjustable, and barrels measured 6 or 8.5 inches. Chamberings were 41 Magnum, 44 Magnum and 45 Colt cartridges, respectively.

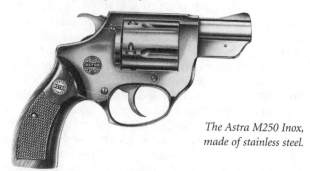

The Astra M250 Inox, made of stainless steel.

Astra 250 A smaller version of the Astra 960 (below), this had a short barrel and a rear sight that was merely a groove in the frame top. It could be had in 22 LR, 22 WMRF, 38 Long or 38 Special chamberings. Finish was usually blue, but a stainless-steel variant has been offered under the designation *250 Inox*.

The 38-caliber Astra M680.

Astra 680 Introduced in 1981, this variation of the Model 250 had minor changes in the shaping of the frame and recoil shield, probably in order to facilitate manufacture.

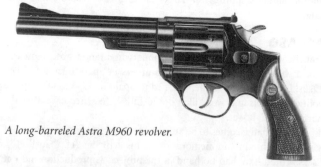

A long-barreled Astra M960 revolver.

Astra 960 This six-shot solid-frame swing-cylinder revolver had a prominent barrel rib and a shrouded ejector.

~ AUTOMATIC PISTOLS ~

Astra 800 (or "Condor") Introduced in 1958, this could be considered as an Astra 600 with an external hammer and a loaded-chamber indicator. Chambered for 9mm Parabellum, it was 207mm long with an eight-cartridge magazine and a butt-tip that curved to improve hold. The grips had the word "Condor" molded in, and the safety catch was moved from behind the trigger to the left rear of the frame. Production ended in 1969 after 11,400 had been made.

Astra 4000 (or "Falcon") This 1956-vintage introduction was little more than the Astra 3000 with an external hammer and was offered in

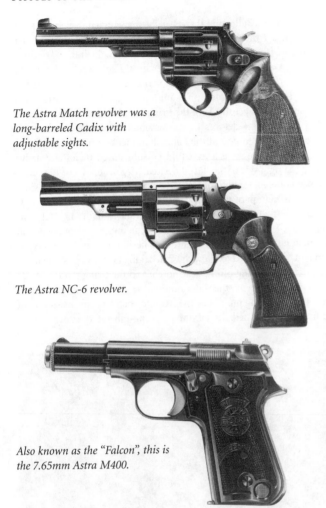

The Astra Match revolver was a long-barreled Cadix with adjustable sights.

The Astra Constable Sport was a version of the standard gun with a long barrel and adjustable competition-type sights.

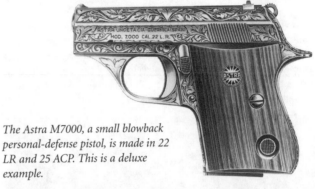

The Astra NC-6 revolver.

The Astra M7000, a small blowback personal-defense pistol, is made in 22 LR and 25 ACP. This is a deluxe example.

Astra 7000 This was a slightly enlarged Astra 2000 chambered for the 22 LR cartridge. The barrel was 59mm long and the magazine held seven rounds.

Also known as the "Falcon", this is the 7.65mm Astra M400.

22 LR, 7.65mm Auto or 9mm Short chamberings. The heel of the butt was rounded to improve handling characteristics, and the grip safety was discarded. The grip is marked with "Mod 4000" and "Falcon" in addition to the Astra trademark.

Astra 5000 (or "Constable") Announced in 1969, this marked a major design change. The streamlined shape was reminiscent of the Walther PP, a resemblance that was heightened by the adoption of a double-action lock with external hammer and a slide-mounted safety catch. The catch locked the firing pin when applied and dropped the hammer. The method of removing the slide differed from Walther practice, however, as a separate catch was set in the frame above the trigger guard.

Guns have been chambered for 22 LR, 7.65mm Auto and 9mm Short. There has also been a *Constable Sport* (22 LR only) with a micro-adjustable rear sight and an extended barrel carrying a ramped front sight at the muzzle.

The Astra A-50, shown here in "Sport" guide, is little more than a Constable without the de-cocking/safety system.

Astra A-50 A single-action version of the Model 5000, this lacked the slide-release catch and had the safety catch on the left rear of the frame instead of the slide.

Astra A-60 Based on the Model 5000, this was updated with a large capacity staggered-row magazine holding 13 9mm Short rounds and an ambidextrous safety catch on the slide. It was introduced in 1987.

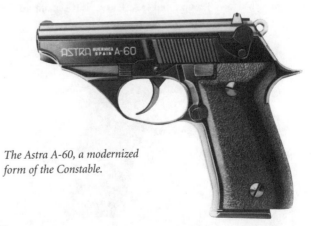

The Astra Constable II, a typical Walther-inspired blowback pistol.

The Astra A-60, a modernized form of the Constable.

The Astra A-70 has a decidedly military look, but remains a blow-back.

Astra A-70 Dating from 1992, this is a lightweight single-action pistol offered in 9mm Parabellum or 40 S&W with magazine capacities of 8 and 7 rounds, respectively. Three-dot combat sights, blue finish and plastic grips are standard, though nickel plating can be obtained to order. A typical gun measures about 7.2 inches overall with a 3.5-inch barrel and weighs about 29 oz.

The double-cocking version of the A-70, the A-75 also has a simplified slide.

Astra A-75 (De-cocker) Introduced in 1993, this is essentially similar to the A-70. However, it has a double-action trigger and a de-cocking system inspired by the SIG-Sauer designs. Available in 9mm Parabellum, 40 S&W or 45 ACP, it may be finished in blue or nickel. Steel-frame versions weigh 31-35 oz, depending on caliber, but the "Featherweight" alloy-frame pattern (9mm Parabellum only) weighs merely 23 oz.

Astra A-80 Dating from 1982, this had a distinct resemblance to contemporaneous SIG-Sauers. It originally chambered the 9mm Parabellum cartridge — 38 Super and 45 ACP have also been offered —

The Astra A-80 is a military-style pistol with a tipping-barrel lock.

and was locked by allowing the specially-shaped chamber area of the barrel to engage the ejection port cut in the slide. The barrel was freed when a cam below the breech acted against a pin in the frame. The double-action A-80 had a de-cocking lever on the left side, which could drop the hammer on to a notch in the sear before it could strike the firing pin. There was an additional automatic safety in the form of a spring-loaded plunger that kept the firing pin locked at all times except during the last few degrees of movement of the trigger, when the plunger withdrew to permit the falling hammer to drive the firing pin forward. The de-cocking lever could be substituted by an alternative lever on the right side of the slide if desired. Magazines of 9 or 15 rounds have been offered, though the latter has not been seen in the USA since the implementation of the Gun Control Act of 1994.

Astra A-90 Offered only in 9mm Parabellum or 45 ACP, this improved A-80 appeared in 1985, featuring an improved double-action system, adjustable sights and slightly smaller dimensions. The mechanism had been adapted to allow the de-cocking lever to arrest the hammer instead of relying on the sear notch, and the firing pin was made in two pieces. Applying the slide-mounted safety catch moved the rear portion of the firing pin out of the hammer-path. The front section of the firing pin retained the automatic firing-pin safety system as the A-80.

Offered with a large-capacity magazine, the Astra A-100 is an improved version of the A-80

Astra A-100 Introduced in 1993, this is a refined version of the A-80. The double-action trigger system is accompanied by a de-cocking lever, finish may be blue or nickel, and the grips are generally plastic. Chamberings are restricted to 9mm Parabellum (17-round magazine), 40 S&W (13 rounds) and 45 ACP (9 rounds) with weight being 33-35 oz, depending on caliber. Overall length with the standard 3.8-inch barrel is about 7.5 inches. An alloy-frame "Featherweight" variant is offered in 9mm Parabellum only, weighing merely 26 oz, and the magazine capacities of the 9mm and 40-caliber guns can be restricted to comply with the Gun Control Act of 1994.

- *Astra A-100 Carry Comp* Distinguished by a 4.3-inch barrel and a prominent compensator to improve recovery in timed competition shooting, this has been offered in 9mm Parabellum (10- or 17-round magazine), 40 S&W and 45 ACP (10-round magazines apiece); finish is exclusively blue and weight averages 38 oz.

Astra TS-22 A comparatively cheap but eminently satisfactory pistol for competition use, this 22 LR target pistol was derived from the A-50 by the substitution of a longer barrel and an extension that dovetailed into the standard slide. The extension also carried a full-length sight ramp and was weighted at the muzzle to improve balance. The elongated grip had a thumb-rest and a finger-rest was added on the magazine floor-plate.

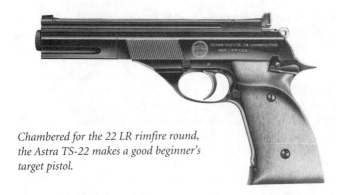

Chambered for the 22 LR rimfire round, the Astra TS-22 makes a good beginner's target pistol.

The Auto-Mag — this is an M180 chambering the 44 AMP round — was a large and powerful gun that attracted a great deal of publicity.

ATLAS ARMS

Chicago, Illinois, USA.

Operating in 1960-72, this company, principally concerned with the distribution of shotguns, produced two "Derringer" pistols. These had superposed barrels chambered for the 22 LR or 38 Special cartridges.

AUTAUGA ARMS

Autauga Arms, Inc, Prattville, Alabama, USA.

Promoters of the Autauga 32 pistol, a stainless steel 32 ACP personal-defense design with a double-action-only trigger system and a six-round detachable magazine in the butt. Overall length is just 4.3 inches with a 2-inch barrel, and weight is a mere 11 oz.

AUTO-MAG CORPORATION

Pasadena, California, USA.

This business was formed to promote a powerful automatic pistol that had been developed around the 44 Auto Magnum wildcat cartridge, which was essentially a 44-caliber revolver bullet in a cut-down 308 Winchester case. The round was first seen in the mid-1950s and, by 1962, Max Gera of Sanford Arms had designed the pistol that came to be called the "Auto-Mag".

Auto-Mag Placed on the commercial market in 1970, this recoil-operated pistol was locked by a rotating bolt head controlled by cam tracks in the frame. A 240-grain 44-caliber bullet propelled by a 25-grain powder charge gave a velocity of 1640 ft/sec and a muzzle energy of 1455 ft-lb, the recoil force being claimed to be 11.7 ft-lb.

Soon after the first announcement came news that the pistol was to be made by the Auto-Mag Corporation and would be available in October 1970 for $200. At that time, of course, anyone purchasing the gun was committed to making his own ammunition, though the interest of commercial ammunition manufacturers was growing.

Delivery of guns began as promised, but the developmental burden proved too great for the finances of the Auto-Mag Corporation and bankruptcy was declared in 1972. The patents, stock and machinery had soon been bought by the Thomas Oil Company, which formed a subsidiary called TDE Corporation to make Auto-Mags. TDE opened a factory in North Hollywood and Harry Sanford, originator of the Sanford Arms Co and "father" of the pistol, became chief engineer.

Production recommenced, offering the *Model 160* in 357 Auto-Mag and the *Model 180* in 44 Auto-Mag, the 357 round also being based on an adapted 308 Winchester case. The High Standard Company (q.v.) assumed responsibility for the Auto-Mag in mid-1974, leaving manufacture to TDE but guaranteeing the necessary sales outlets and financial backing. The 44-caliber ammunition became available commercially, first from Cartouches Deportivo de Mexico and later from Norma, but 357 owners still had to make their own.

High Standard withdrew support in 1977, and work on the Auto-Mag ceased. The design reverted to Sanford, who announced in 1979 that five hundred *Model B* pistols would be made and that production would end only when all the components had been used. Despite this

claim, however, it is suspected that less than a hundred "Model B" Auto-Mags had been completed when a halt was finally called in 1980. The price of a Model B had climbed to around $1000, which was far too expensive to compete with rival designs.

The AMT Corporation (q.v.) acquired the rights and introduced the Auto-Mag *Model C*, differing from its predecessors in having a Behlert adjustable rear sight. Fewer than a hundred guns were made before the new owners gave up the struggle in 1981. AMT attempted to revive the design in 22 caliber, but this was equally unsuccessful. The basic design eventually evolved into a more conventional form described in the AMT entry.

Variations in the Auto-Mag are numerous, as details were altered during production runs almost as the ideas suggested themselves. The original 44-caliber model had a 6-inch barrel. The TDE 44 had a 6-inch barrel, and the 357 barrel was either 6 or 8 inches, the latter lacking the otherwise-standard ventilated rib. "Customized" versions with special grips, known as *Lee Jurras Specials* in honor of their originator, were sold under names such as "Bicentennial", "Backpacker", "International", "Grizzly", "Condor", "Alaskan" and "Silhouette". Most of them were supplied to order and could be found with special barrels chambering the 41 JMP ("Jurras Mag Pistol") cartridge, another modification of the original 44 cartridge developed by Jurras for silhouette shooting. Then came interchangeable barrel-conversion units that allowed a 357-caliber barrel to be fitted to a 44 frame.

The Model B of 1979 was similar to the original gun, but a change in bolt design made it stronger and optional 8-inch or 10-inch heavy target barrels were offered. These barrels can be identified by "Silhouette" engraved on the side.

The original pistols were marked "Auto Mag .44 AMP Model 180 Pasadena California Pat Pending" on the slide, together with an AM monogram in a circle. Under the TDE regime, this changed to "Auto Mag .44 AMP Model 280 El Monte California Patented" and TDE in a circle. This then changed to "High Standard Auto Mag .44 AMP Model 180 El Monte California Patented" with the High Standard symbol.

It is believed that the Model B bore either TDE or High Standard markings, as Sanford's production was based on existing components. The AMT models carried similar markings but with a circle and AMT; they also had "C"-prefix serial numbers.

AUTO-ORDNANCE CO.

West Hurley, New York, USA.

The original Auto-Ordnance Company was formed in the 1920s to market the Thompson submachine gun with the actual manufacture being done by other firms. The patents and rights have passed through several hands since then, and the present Auto-Ordnance Company has no direct connection with the original other than to promote a semi-automatic version of the Thompson. Auto-Ordnance was purchased by High Standard (q.v.) in 2001, but then sold to Kahr Arms. Only the standard and deluxe variants of the M1911A1 are currently being offered.

M1911A1 Auto-Ordnance has also made a copy of the 45-caliber Government Model Colt, indistinguishable from the original excepting for Auto-Ordnance markings and trademark on the slide.

The *M41 Action Express* has been made in 41 AE chambering, and the *AOC M1911A1 Competition Model* was a carefully selected standard gun with a hand-finished trigger unit and an efficient muzzle compensator. The *ZG-51 Pit Bull* (41 AE or 45 ACP) was simply another variation on the basic theme, being somewhat more compact than the M1911A1.

AZANZA & ARRIZABALAGA
Azanza y Arrizabalaga y Cia, Eibar, Spain.
The connection between this gunmaking business and Hijos de Calixto Arrizabalaga has never been properly explored, though it is suspected that this Arrizabalaga was the father of the "Hijos". Azanza y Arrizabalaga operated briefly during World War I, making the usual Eibar-type automatic pistols of average quality.

A.A. Chambered for the 7.65mm Auto cartridge, this was originally made in accordance with a sub-contract for French Army orders placed in 1915-16 and, consequently, was larger than usual with a nine-cartridge magazine. Slides were marked "Azanza & Arrizabalaga Modelo 1916 Eibar (Espana)", and an "AA"-in-an-oval trademark lay on the left rear of the frame.

Reims This was made in 6.35mm and 7.65mm calibers. Both types were blowback automatics, copies of the Browning 1906 model, with small butts and five- or six-round magazines. They were marked "1914 Model Automatic Reims Patent" and display a trademark in the form of a crowned circle containing "AA". It is thought that these pistols were produced for export to France in 1914-15 (when soldiers were buying every pistol that could be found), but before the French government issued official contracts to Spanish gunmakers.

ANTONIO AZPIRI
Eibar, Spain.
Little is known about this gunmaker or the pistols he made in 1912-17, aimed largely at the French market. It is assumed that Antonio Azpiri was the original proprietor, and thus that the "y Cia" style came later.

Avion This was a good-quality 6.35mm-caliber copy of the Browning of 1906. The slide was marked "Pistolet Automatique Avion Brevete", which suggested manufacture for export to France. The frame had the usual "Made in Spain" mark, in the smallest lettering possible, and the butt grips are embossed with a Blériot-type monoplane.

AZPIRI & CO.
Azpiri y Cia, Eibar, Spain.
Possibly a successor to Antonio Azpiri (above), this gunmaking business remained active virtually until the start of the Spanish Civil War in 1936.

Colon Apparently dating from 1919-30, these 6.35mm and 7.65mm Eibar-type pistols were made in two patterns within each caliber group, all based on either the FN-Browning M1903 or M1906.

One of the 6.35mm guns had a grip safety, and the first 7.65mm pattern model was not only smaller but also had a smaller magazine capacity than its replacement. However, distinguishing marks were confined to the standardized "Automatic Pistol 'Colon'..." and caliber identifier on the left side of the slide. Some guns also had the "AA" monogram on the grips.

The 6.35mm Colon offered much poorer quality than the Avion and was apparently intended solely for domestic consumption. [Note: the name "Colon" — *Cristobal Colón* being the Spanish version of "Christopher Columbus" — was also used by Orbea Hermanos for a revolver.]

BACON ARMS CO.

Or "Bacon Mfg. Co.", Norwich, Connecticut, USA.
The small town of Norwich became a prominent pistol-making community in the second half of the nineteenth century, and the interrelationship of the gunmakers can be difficult to disentangle. The affairs of the Bacon Arms Company were typical. Founded by Thomas K. Bacon about 1862, the business initially made single-shot 32 RF pistols and 36-caliber caplock revolvers before progressing to solid-frame rimfire revolvers, made under license from Smith & Wesson. The principal post-1870 products were those cheap solid-frame revolvers usually classed as "Suicide Specials", and, as most were made to sell for no more than a dollar, nothing in the way of outstanding quality or originality was expected. Bacon went out of business in 1891.

Bacon Gem This seems to have been the only gun to incorporate the Bacon name. It was a tiny 22 RF five-shot solid-frame revolver with sheathed trigger.

Bang-Up Although lacking distinguishing marks, this 32 RF revolver was sufficiently like the "Guardian" either to suggest it as a Bacon product or that someone had taken the Guardian as a model. Excepting a small change in the location of a pin, there were no particular differences; both guns were solid-frame, non-ejecting, stud-trigger designs with octagonal barrels.

Big Bonanza A seven-shot 22 Short RF solid frame single-action revolver with a spur trigger, made about 1880.

Bonanza Patented in 1878, this 22 RF solid-frame revolver had a seven-chamber cylinder and a sheathed trigger. The patent referred to a cylinder-release catch in front of the trigger, which allowed the arbor pin to be withdrawn and the cylinder removed from the frame. Spent cases were then extracted by punching them out of the chambers with the arbor pin.

Conqueror Patented in 1878, this appeared in 22 RF and 32 RF versions. Both were solid-frame models with 2.5-inch round barrels and a cylinder release operated by two spring catches in the frame. The guns were loaded through a gate on the right side of the frame but lacked ejectors. The 22-caliber cylinder had seven chambers, whereas the 32 had five. Conqueror revolvers are said to have been made in 38 RF and 41 RF, five-shot in each case, but none have been examined.

Daisy Dating from the 1880s, this was a 22 RF seven-shot solid-frame stud-trigger revolver with a bird's-head grip. It had an unusual pincer-type cylinder arbor catch and a brass front sight blade but was otherwise standard for its time.

Express A 22-caliber seven-shot solid-frame revolver with a sheathed trigger made to the 1878 patent, the Express resembled the Conqueror except for its 2-inch octagonal barrel. It used the same double-spring catch to allow removal of the cylinder. Though gate-loaded, spent cases could be extracted only by removing the cylinder and driving them clear with the cylinder axis pin.

Governor Yet another cheap rimfire revolver, this was chambered for 22 Short RF ammunition, had a seven-chamber cylinder and was fitted with a 2-inch round barrel. The solid frame differed from Conqueror and Express designs, owing to a removable sideplate covering the lockwork that formed half the trigger-sheath. The arbor pin extended about an inch beneath the barrel and was retained by a push-in catch on the right side of the frame. There was no ejector.

Guardian Made in 22 RF and 32 RF, this was another solid-frame sheathed-trigger revolver. The rear of the frame was unusually high-set, concealing most of the hammer, and the butt was of bird's-head form. The 22-caliber version had the usual seven-shot chamber cylinder, whereas the 32 version was five-shot; both had 2.75-inch octagonal barrels.

Little Giant Resembling the Express and Conqueror models, this was distinguished by a large circular plate on the left of the frame — slotted for a turnscrew — which acted both as a cover plate for the action and a pivot for the hammer. The gun was otherwise the usual Bacon mixture— a non-ejecting seven-shot 22 RF with a 2-inch or 2.5-inch round barrel and a bird's-head grip.

LES BAER CUSTOM, INC.

Hillsdale, Illinois, USA.
Baer is basically a maker of variations on the M1911 Colt-Browning theme, but also a prolific innovator. Most of the guns embody features such as forged-steel frames, full-length recoil rods and retraction grips at the muzzle end of the slide as well as the rear. The magazine wells are chamfered, the grip-safety and the slide-release lever are extended to facilitate operation, and the front strap of the butt is customarily checkered to improve grip. Most guns have Bo-Mar sights, speed triggers, greatly refined lockwork, elongated ejectors and (unless stated otherwise) 5-inch barrels.

Bullseye Wadcutter A target-shooting derivative suited only to 45 ACP Wadcutter (flat nose) ammunition, this is distinguished by a Bo-Mar rear sight set into a detachable full-length top rib. Alternatively, an optical sight rail may be fitted to order.

Concept series These guns offer a variety of "semi-custom" features at a lower price than the other Baer Colt-Browning derivatives. Except for 4.25-inch-barreled "Commander" type guns, the Concepts all have full-length slides with retraction grooves duplicated at the muzzle.

• *Concept I* A standard blued-steel 45 ACP gun with adjustable Bo-Mar sights and a 5-inch barrel. A single-column seven-round magazine is fitted.

• *Concept II* Similar to Concept I, this has a Baer-type rear sight that can be adjusted only by drifting it laterally across the slide.

• *Concept III* A variant of Concept I with adjustable Bo-Mar sights and a stainless steel frame. The slide remains blued-steel.

• *Concept IV* A version of Concept III with Baer-type sights.

• *Concept V* Offered with 5-inch or 6-inch barrels, this is made largely of stainless steel. A Bo-Mar adjustable rear sight is standard.

• *Concept VI* As Concept V, but with Baer-type sights. The "Concept VI LW" has a blacked aluminum frame and a National Match barrel.

• *Concept VII* This gun has a blued steel slide and frame, Baer-type sights and a short 4.25-inch barrel/slide combination. These guns are about 7.75 inches long and weigh 27-28 oz.

• *Concept VIII* A variant of Concept VII made of stainless steel.

• *Concept IX* Also similar to Concept VI with the same fixed Baer-type sights, this has an aluminum frame and a blued-steel slide.

• *Concept X* A minor variant of Concept VI, with a stainless-steel slide and an aluminum frame.

Custom Carry Usually distinguished by 4.25-inch "Commanche" barrels, these guns had fixed sights with three-dot Tritium inserts fitted as standard after 2000. The slides and frames may be blued or stainless steel, or, alternatively, a blued or stainless steel slide may be paired with a blacked aluminum-alloy frame.

• *Custom Carry-5* A minor variant of the standard gun, this has a 5-inch barrel and a slide with retraction grips duplicated at the muzzle.

IPSC Action Pistol (or "1911 IPSC Action Pistol") This is simply a variant of the standard Baer Colt-Browning derivative with blued finish on the slide and frame.

Lightweight 22 These are simple fixed-barrel derivations of the standard centerfire guns, made with 4.5-inch barrels and fixed sights; a

5-inch barrel and fixed sights; or a 5-inch barrel and an adjustable Bo-Mar rear sight.

National Match Hardball Intended for competition shooting undertaken under Director of Civilian Marksmanship (DCM) rules, this is a comparatively standard gun with a solid trigger shoe and an adjustable rear sight. It is chambered only for 45 ACP and has a seven-round magazine.

PPC Distinguished Match Usually encountered in blue, with an Aristocrat rear sight instead of a Bo-Mar, this was introduced in 1999 for Practical Pistol Competition shooting. The ejection port has been lowered and chamfered, or "flared", to reduce the possibility of a spent case fouling the return of the slide, and an elongated ambidextrous safety is used. The 5-inch-barreled guns are available in 9mm Parabellum and 45 ACP.

• *PPC Open Class* Essentially similar to the Distinguished Match pistol but fitted with a 6-inch barrel.

Premier II Supplied in blued steel, in 9mm Largo (9x23), 38 Super, 400 Cor-Bon or 45 ACP, this had a 5-inch barrel and an adjustable Bo-Mar rear sight. A few guns have been made in stainless steel in addition to a handful with the alternative 6-inch barrel/slide combination. Most are built on the standard Baer frame and supplied with seven-round magazines. However, a few Premiers have used the long-grip Para-Ordnance (q.v.) frame, increasing magazine capacity to 10.

• *Premier II LW* The "lightweight" version of the Premier has an aluminum-alloy frame. It has been supplied with an adjustable LCB rear sight ("LW1") or with fixed combat sights ("LW2").

Prowler III Made only in 45 ACP, this is a variant of the Premier with an auxiliary tapered-cone stub weight and a full-length recoil rod. The 6-inch slide/barrel unit is standard, and the finish is usually blue.

• *Prowler IV* Similar to the Prowler III, but offered in 38 Super in addition to 45 ACP, this is built on a Para-Ordnance (q.v.) large-grip frame. Barrels may measure 5 or 6 inches.

Super-Tac Similar to the Premier II, this has a low-mount adjustable rear sight and "Baer Ultra-Coat" finish. Chamberings are customarily 40 S&W, 400 Cor-Bon or 45 ACP.

Swift Response Pistol ("SRP") Introduced in 1996, this specially "tuned" plain-finish gun (based on those supplied to the FBI) is also usually built on an enlarged Para-Ordnance frame and has a 10-round magazine. However, a few have used the smaller Baer frame, and a handful have been made with the 4.5-inch "Commando" barrel and slide. The guns have Trijicon sights, Wolff springs and Magnafluxed parts to ensure reliability.

Target Master Intended for centerfire competition shooting under National Rifle Association (NRA) rules, this is available exclusively in 45 ACP.

Thunder Ranch Special Available only in 45 ACP, this all-steel pistol has a fixed rear sight with Tritium "night light" inserts. The frontstrap of the butt is checkered, the "slimline" wooden grips bear a "Thunder Ranch" logo and a seven-round magazine is standard. A special engraved version is available to order.

Ultimate Master Combat Offered in a variety of chamberings, including 9mm Largo (9x23) 38 Super, 400 Cor-Bon and 45 ACP, this may be obtained with a 5- or 6-inch barrel and a 10-round magazine.

• *Ultimate Master Compensator* Chambered for the 45 ACP cartridge, this gun also has a three-port compensator attached to the muzzle.

• *Ultimate Master Para* Designed for ISPC competition shooting and offered in two versions: "Limited", with open sights, and "Unlimited" with a three-port compensator and provision for optical sights. Chamberings are restricted to 9mm Largo (9x23), 38 Super and 45 ACP.

• *Ultimate Master Steel Special* Specifically intended for competitions involving the use of steel targets, this 38 Super derivative is adjusted to work with comparatively weakly loaded ammunition.

BAFORD ARMS, INC.

Bristol, Tennessee, USA.

Beginning in 1988, this company made small quantities of *Thunder* derringers — a single-barrel "tip-up" design chambered for cartridges ranging from 22 LR rimfire to 44 Special. Made of blued steel, with walnut or rosewood grips, the derringers could be fitted with a long barrel and an optical sight.

The *Firepower* pistol, also known as the "Model 35", was a 9mm Parabellum automatic supplied with adjustable Millett sights, Pachmayr grips and a 14-round staggered-column magazine. Neither design seems to have been made in quantity.

BALLARD

C.H. Ballard, Worcester, Massachusetts, USA.

Charles Ballard was much better known for his single-shot dropping-block rifle, made by a variety of gunmakers during and immediately after the American Civil War but exploited with far greater effect by Marlin from 1875 onward. However, Ballard also made (or, perhaps, commissioned the production of) a small number of 38 and 41 rimfire single-shot derringers patented in June 1869. Probably dating from 1871-3, these had barrels that tipped downward after a catch on the left side of the barrel block had been disengaged from the standing breech. The sheath trigger frame was customarily iron, often nickel or even silver plated, and the grips were walnut or gutta-percha.

BARRENECHEA & GALLASTEGUI

Barrenechea y Gallastegui, Eibar, Spain.

The only product bearing the name of this company, a copy of the S&W Military & Police revolver in 38 Special, bore "Fdo por Barrenechea y Gallastegui, Eibar, Spain" on the barrel. This suggested that B&E were distributors and thus that the guns were made elsewhere. Comparison with other makes suggests Manuel Escodin as the likely source and 1925-35 as the probable date.

JORGE BASCARAN SONS

Hijos de ("sons of") Jorge Bascaran, Eibar, Spain.

Although information on this firm is scant, it seems that when Martin Bascaran brought his brothers into the business, "Hijos de Jorge Bascaran" was the result. The new partnership made unremarkable Eibar-type pistols in 1922-7, the 7.65mm *Marke* and the 6.35mm/7.65mm *Martigny*. None could be traced for examination.

MARTIN A. BASCARAN

Eibar, Spain.

Bascaran began his gunmaking business during World War I, producing a weapon of original design and good quality instead of the ubiquitous French-ordered Ruby (q.v.). However, he seems to have included his brothers in his operations in post-war years: see "Jorge Bascaran Sons", above.

A catalog engraving of a 7.65mm Bascaran Martian pistol.

Martian This first of two variants appeared early in 1915 in 6.53mm and 7.65mm. An original blowback design, well made and finished, it discarded the usual Browning-inspired method of attaching the barrel to the frame by means of lugs beneath the breech. Instead, the squared-off Martian barrel, with a ridge on top and shoulders beneath, was held in the frame by a catch operated by pulling the rear end of the trigger guard down and away from the butt. The slide was shaped internally to ride on the squared sides and ridge of the barrel, keeping the working parts securely aligned during recoil.

The pistols were striker-fired and had an unusual safety catch on the left side in front of the grip that moved vertically to disconnect the sear from the trigger—a considerable improvement on the usual Eibar-pattern radial latch. The slides were usually marked "Automatic Pistol Martian Cal x.xx" and display an encircled "MAB" monogram; "Martian" is usually embossed across the grips.

The unusually complex design of the earliest Martians, incompatible with wartime mass-production, was abandoned in 1916. The name was transferred to a run-of-the-mill 7.65mm Eibar-type copy of the Browning M1903. Marked "Fa de Martin A Bascaran Eibar Martian Cal 7.65", it was produced to satisfy military contracts placed during World War I. Work continued after 1918 alongside a 6.35mm pistol based on the Browning 1906, both types being known as *Martian Commercial*. The grips bore encircled "MAB" trademarks surrounded by "Martian Commercial". Work continued until Bascaran ceased independent trading.

Thunder While Bascaran was quite content to make second-model Martians for his bread-and-butter, he seems to have realized that a market still existed for something better. In 1919, therefore, this gun appeared. It was little more than a 6.35mm version of the original Martian. The quality was much higher than the Martian Commercials, but identifying marks were confined to "Thunder" embossed across the grips. Guns of this type remained available until the late 1920s.

KARL BAUER
Berlin, Germany.
Kaba, Ka-Ba Applied to 4.25mm Liliput pistols made by Menz but sold by Karl Bauer of Berlin.
Kaba Spezial This gun existed in two patterns. The first was a 6.35mm Eibar-type pistol made by Arizmendi y Goenaga and then Francisco Arizmendi. It appears that Bauer acquired these guns shortly after the end of World War I, then dropped them in favor of the Menz product in about 1928. The slides were marked "Pistolet Automatique Kaba Spezial", while the grips bore an encircled "Kaba Spezial" — subsequently used on the Menz products.

The second Kaba Spezial was a 6.35mm blowback automatic similar to the Mauser 6.35mm with the slide cut away to expose the barrel. Made by August Menz of Suhl and merely sold by Bauer, it was marked "Kaba Kal 6,35 Spezial" on the slide and grips.

BAUER FIREARMS CORP.
Fraser, Michigan, USA.
Operating from 1972 to 1984, Bauer made a high-quality 6.35mm blowback automatic pistol derived from the Baby Browning. Guns were available in two models with 2.5-inch barrels and detachable six-round box magazines in their butts: *SS* (Satin Stainless) and *SB* (Stainless Blued), with walnut or simulated pearl grips. The Bauer was among the best of the several 6.35mm designs that appeared contemporaneously in the US to fill the gap in the market caused by the restrictions on imports imposed by the Gun Control Act of 1968. The pistol was subsequently marketed by R.B. Industries, Ltd. under the brandname "Fraser" after Bauer's business failed. However, work seems to have stopped entirely by 1990.

BAYONNE (MAB)
See "Manufacture d'Armes de Bayonne", under "M".

EDUARD DE BEAUMONT
Maastricht, The Netherlands.
This gunmaker's sole venture into the handgun-making business concerned the supply of service revolvers to the Dutch government, few of which were ever offered commercially. When the Dutch adopted the FN-Browning and Parabellum (Luger) automatic pistols shortly before World War I, de Beaumont left the business, though the revolvers remained in reserve service until 1940.
Model 1873 ("Dutch Service") These are often called "Chamelot-Delvigne" designs, but they bear no resemblance to others bearing that name excepting general features. The original M1873 revolver was eventually known as the 1873 OM ("Old Model") and was typical of its era — a solid-framed gate-loading design that relied on a rod carried in the holster to eject spent cartridge cases. Chambered for the 9.4mm Dutch Service cartridge, the "OM" weighed 43.7 oz with an octagonal 6.3-inch barrel and had a double-action lock. It was followed by the *1873 NM* ("New Model") with a lightweight cylindrical barrel and the *1873 Kl.M* ("Small Model") with a short octagonal barrel and five chambers in the cylinder instead of six.

BECKER & HOLLANDER
Suhl, Germany.
This gunmaking partnership, renowned for shotguns and sporting rifles, made a 7.65mm pistol designed by Leopold Stenda during World War I. The design was also made for the military as the *Stenda* and *Menta* (q.v.) and subsequently appeared commercially as the *Leonhardt* (q.v.).
Beholla The only unusual feature of these guns was the method of retaining the barrel in the frame. A lump beneath the chamber was formed into a dovetail that slid into a matching seat in the frame, where it was retained by a pin. The pin had to be punched-out before the pistol was dismantled, two holes being provided in the slide to allow it to be removed. The slide could then be pulled back, locked by turning the safety catch upward, and the barrel could then be driven back until it came free from the seat in the frame. This allowed the slide and barrel to be removed. The slides displayed "Selbstlade Pistole "Beholla" Cal. 7.65" on the left and "Becker u Hollander Waffenbau Suhl" on the right. The guns were all supplied to the German War Department and customarily bear inspectors' stamps.

BEEMAN PRECISION ARMS
Santa Rosa, California, USA.
Best known as a distributor of airguns, Beeman has marketed a variety of handguns in the USA, including the Danish-made Agner (q.v.) and German Rhöner (q.v.) 22-caliber target pistols. The *Beeman Model P '08* and the *Beeman Mini-P '08* were the Erma KGP-69 and KGP-68A toggle-type blowbacks, described in detail in the appropriate entry.

BEISTEGUI BROTHERS
Beistegui Hermanos, Eibar, Spain.
In addition to making and selling their own pistols, the Beistegui brothers made pistols for other distributors and acted as sales agents for pistols made elsewhere. Consequently, it can be difficult to unravel the parentage of some guns, and it is clear that Fábrica de Armas de Grand Precision (q.v.) distributed many Beistegui-made products. Beistegui Hermanos, like so many others, obtained a foothold in the pistol business as sub-contractors to Gabilondo y Urresti for the Ruby automatics being made for France and Italy. They continued to make handguns until the business was forcibly closed during the Spanish Civil War.

∼ REVOLVER ∼

B.H. This was a copy of the Smith & Wesson Military & Police Model in 38 S&W Long chambering with resemblance being emphasized by a florid "B&H" monogram engraved on the left side of the frame in the same place the familiar "S&W" mark that it was intended to duplicate was found. Similar monograms on white metal medallions were let into the top of the grips in Smith & Wesson style.

∼ AUTOMATIC PISTOLS ∼

Beistegui This was the original Ruby copy, doubtless made on the machinery installed for the French contract work. It was misleadingly marketed as the "1914 Model" but was little more than a standard (if generously sized) 7.65mm Eibar-type blowback with a lanyard ring on the butt. The slide was marked "1914 Model Automatic Pistol Beistegui Hermanos Eibar (Espana)" and the grips were the usual plain-checkered pattern.

B.H. Pistols bearing these marks have been reported in 6.35mm and 7.65mm, but none could be found for examination. If they existed, it is probable that they were commercial versions of the Beistegui produced immediately after World War I. Identified only by plastic grips with a "BH" monogram.

Bulwark (1) This pistol apparently spanned the gap between Beistegui and the Grand Precision company. The first version, a rarely seen fixed-barrel external-hammer 6.35mm (rare) or 7.65mm (common) blowback, bore no markings other than the "B&H" monogram on the grips. The slide was split at the front to expose the whole length of the barrel, perhaps influenced by the first Echeverria "Star" that, in its turn, had drawn inspiration from the Mannlicher of 1901. Copying foreign designs was an acceptable old Spanish custom, but copying Spanish designs was less successful and (perhaps owing to objections from Echeverria) the first Bulwark was soon a thing of the past.

Bulwark (2) A simple 6.35mm or 7.65mm copy of the 1906-pattern FN-Browning, complete with grip safety, this replaced the earlier Bulwark. However, though bearing the Beistegui monogram on the grips, the slide was marked "Fabrique de Armes de Guerre de Grand Precision Bulwark Patent Depose No 67259".

Libia All but identical with the Bulwark, this had "Libia" substituted for "Bulwark" in the slide inscription. Guns of this type invariably had "Spain" stamped in minute letters somewhere on the frame, indicating production for export.

Paramount This name has obviously been popular in Spain, where a variety of Eibar-type blowback automatics were made in both 6.35mm and 7.65mm calibers in 1920-35. In fact, 6.35mm "Paramount" pistols were also made by Apaolozo Hermanos of Eibar, and Retolaza Hermanos made 7.65mm examples. There were also at least two other 6.35mm designs of unknown provenance. None of these guns had any features of note.

BENELLI ARMI

Benelli Armi SpA, Urbino, Italy.

An old-established gunmaking company noted for its shotguns, purchased by Beretta in 2000, Benelli introduced an interesting 9mm Parabellum pistol in 1976.

B-76 This was intended for military use and embodied an ingenious delayed blowback system. The barrel was fixed, and the slide contained a separate breechblock linked to the slide by a toggle joint. Pressure from the usual type of return spring held the slide forward, pushing on the breechblock by way of the toggle to drive the rear end of the block down into a recess in the frame. When the gun was fired, chamber pressure attempted to drive the bolt backward out of the recess, but movement was slowed by the angle of the toggle and the bullet was clear of the muzzle before the block rose far enough to drive the slide back. The double-action trigger operated an external hammer, a manual safety catch on the frame locked the hammer and trigger in either cocked or

The 9mm Benelli B-76 had distinctly sloped grips.

uncocked positions and a loaded-chamber indicator was set into the slide.

The B-76 was moderately successful and is said to have been used in small quantities by US Navy SEALs. But sales were not enough to justify keeping it in production and it was terminated in 1989. Some guns are said to have been made to special order in 9x18mm Police and 9mm Largo (9x23) chamberings, but confirmation is lacking. A blowback 22 RF version was made for training, dispensing with the toggle joint and separate bolt.

- *B-76S* A target-shooting version of the standard B-76, this had a 5.5-inch barrel instead of the standard 4.3-inch version, an adjustable rear sight and thumb-rest grips.

B-77 This designation was applied to a small quantity of B-76 pistols — possibly 400 — that had been converted to blowback operation by removing the toggle mechanism, though they retained the separate bolt. Chambered for the 32 ACP cartridge, they were distributed in the USA in the late 1970s.

B-80 This was another target-shooting version of the B-76; made for a short time for the 7.65mm Parabellum cartridge, with a long barrel, a balance weight at the muzzle and fully adjustable sights.

MP-90S World Cup A blowback competition pistol chambered for 22 LR RF or 32 S&W Wadcutter ammunition, this has a 4.4-inch barrel, an adjustable rear sight, optical-sight grooves on the top of the frame and slab-type walnut grips with an adjustable palm-shelf. The trigger mechanism is a single-action pattern adjustable for pressure, rake and angle. The fixed slab-side frame/grip unit contains a reciprocating breech-bolt, with the cocking grips extended forward to allow the gun to lie as low as possible in the hand. A detachable box magazine in the frame ahead of the trigger aperture holds five rounds, and counterweights can be hung beneath the frame to adjust the balance. Finish was burnished black.

MP-95E (sometimes known as "MP-95E Atlanta") Similar to the MP-90S, dating from 1994, this low-set target pistol is offered in 22 LR rimfire (6-round magazine) or 32 S&W Wadcutter (five rounds). The distinguishing characteristic is usually provided by the standard grip, an anatomical pattern that lacks the palm shelf of the MP-90S. Finish may be black or satin-chrome. A nine-round 22-caliber magazine and a palm-rest grip can be obtained to order. And an optical sight such as a Tasco Pro-Point can be fitted above the front of the frame. The trigger mechanism, usually factory-set at 1000gm (22 LR) or 1360gm (32 S&W), can be exchanged when required.

PIETRO BERETTA

Pietro Beretta SpA (also known as "Armi Beretta"),
Gardone Val Trompia (Brescia), Italy.

The first member of the Beretta dynasty began trading as a barrel-maker in 1526, and the family has since created an enviable record of excellence in the manufacture of sporting shoulder arms. The first pistols were made in 1915, under the pressure of war, but by the end of the 20th century, Beretta had become one of the world's major handgun manufacturers.

The adoption of the Model 92 by the US armed forces was conditional on the establishment of manufacturing facilities in the USA, and a factory was built in Accokeek, Maryland. Beretta USA Corporation has a degree of autonomy and has been responsible for the development of the U22 NEOS pistol.

A variety of subsidiary companies exist. They include Beretta Australia Pty Ltd of Dandenong, Victoria; Beretta Hallas srl of Athens, Greece; and Beretta-Benelli Iberica SA of Vitoria, Spain. Itself partly owned by FN Herstal SA (q.v.), Beretta also has links with Sako Oy and Sako Sweden.

Alley Cat Dating from 2001, and really little more than a promotional tool, this is essentially an M3032 Tomcat (q.v.) with an AO Big Dot low-light sight.

Model 9 The US Army designation for the Model 92F and 92FS pistols. The *Model 9 Limited Edition*, apparently exclusive to the North American market, appeared in 1995 to mark the 10th anniversary of official adoption. Ten thousand guns were made, with the legend "U.S. 9mm M9 – BERETTA U.S.A. – 65490" and the "PB" trademark on the left side of the slide. A few "deluxe" guns were offered with walnut grips and gold plating on the hammer and grip screws.

Model 20 Discontinued in 1985. The first Beretta to incorporate double-action lockwork, this 6.35mm (25 ACP) gun retained the open-topped slide and tipping barrel. After chambering a round in the usual way, applying the safety catch dropped the hammer safely. When firing became necessary, the safety was released and a pull on the trigger operated the hammer. Alternatively, the hammer could simply be thumb-cocked. Generally encountered in blue, it had walnut or black plastic grips.

Model 21 Introduced in 1985 in 22 LR rimfire (7-round magazine) and 25 ACP (eight rounds), this is similar to the Model 950BS. A double-action design with a tipping barrel, it may be found with blue or nickel finish; grips can be plastic or wood. It is known in the USA as the "Bobcat".

- *Model 21EL* A designation applied to a deluxe variant with walnut grips and a gold-line designation panel on the slide.
- *Model 21 Inox* Introduced in 2000, this pairs a satin-finish stainless-steel slide with a bright-anodized alloy frame. The grips are usually black rubber.

Model 70 (1958-85) Introduced to replace the Model 948, this embodied a streamlined form of the usual Beretta shape and had a through-bolt safety, a mechanical hold-open and a push-button magazine release. The standard gun chambered the 7.65mm Auto cartridge and had either a steel or light alloy slide. Barrels usually measured 3.5 inches. Some guns were chromed, others had been silver-plated and a few had been decoratively engraved.

- *Model 70S* was offered in 22 LR, 7.65mm Auto or 9mm Short and had a magazine safety. The 22-caliber version was usually fitted with an adjustable rear sight and large thumbrest-style grips. Magazine capacity was eight rounds in all three chamberings, though legal restrictions ensured that the 380 version could only be sold outside Italy.
- *Model 70T* had a 6-inch barrel and an adjustable rear sight.
- *Model 71*, chambered for the 22 LR rimfire cartridge, had an anodized alloy frame and a 3.5-inch barrel. The magazines held

A typical Beretta M70S, in 22 LR rimfire.

eight rounds. Guns sold in the USA after the implementation of the Gun Control Act of 1968 usually had 5.9-inch barrels, though the original 3.5-inch type remained standard elsewhere. Those distributed after 1970 were customarily advertised as "M101", or the "New Jaguar".

- *Model 72* (or "Jaguar") This was basically an M71 supplied with two sets of barrels and return springs.
- *Model 73* A variant of the 22 rimfire M71 with a 5.9-inch barrel carrying both the sights. The magazine held 10 rounds instead of eight, owing to the elongated grip.
- *Model 74* Similar to the Model 73, this had an adjustable rear sight on the barrel instead of a fixed standing notch.
- *Model 75* A variant of the M72 with a 5.9-inch barrel only. The rear sight lay on the frame, immediately ahead of the hammer.

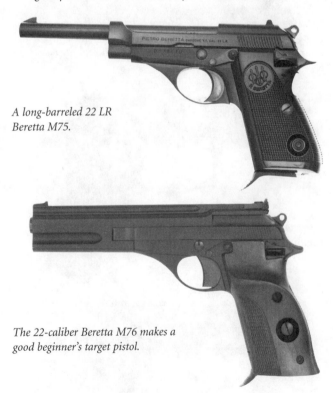

A long-barreled 22 LR Beretta M75.

The 22-caliber Beretta M76 makes a good beginner's target pistol.

Model 76 This external-hammer 22 LR target pistol had a special slab-sided alloy shroud around the barrel, extended back to support the adjustable rear sight. The bolt reciprocated in a slot at the rear. Visually, the effect was that of a combat pistol, except for the adjustable competition-style sights. The original M76 was sometimes advertised as the "Sable" in the USA. After c. 1968, the designation and name were altered to "Model 102" and "New Sable".

Model 80 series The design of automatic pistols took a sudden leap forward in the 1970s, owing to demands made by military and police forces for guns with faster lock times, better safety arrangements and larger magazine capacities. Beretta read the signs very early and began developing a completely new range of guns, introducing the first gun, the Model 81, in 1976. Many of the guns sold in the USA, especially the Models 84, 85, 86 and 87, have been known indiscriminately as the "Cheetah".

- *Model 81* This 7.65mm-caliber pistol retained the familiar open-topped Beretta slide, well-shaped wooden grips, external hammer and double-action lockwork. However, a 12-round double-row magazine was adopted and the safety catch became ambidextrous (being duplicated on both sides of the frame). The magazine-release catch ran through the frame immediately behind the trigger guard and could be switched from left to right side if desired. A new type of stripping catch was fitted in the frame, and a magazine safety was optional.

- *Model 81BB* This was an improved 81 with a new chamber-loaded indicator that moved laterally in the slide and a new firing-pin safety system in which the pin was positively locked except during the final movement of the trigger as it released the hammer.

The 7.6mm Beretta M82B is one of the "80 Series" of blowbacks with double-action lockwork and high-capacity magazines.

A Beretta M83F, chambered for the 380 ACP round (9mm Short).

The Beretta M84F, in 380 ACP/9mm Short.

- *Model 82BB* Little more than an "81BB" with a slimmer butt, this had a single-column eight-round magazine.
- *Model 84* Dating from 1977, this gun resembled the Model 81 in all respects except chambering (9mm Short), magazine capacity (13 rounds) and weight. Available in blue or nickel, the guns had grips of black plastic or walnut.
- *Model 84BB* Discontinued in 1983, this was an improved 380 ACP Model 84 with "BB" features — an eight-round magazine, a loaded-chamber indicator and a firing-pin safety system.
- *Model 84F* Identifiable by the shape of the trigger guard, which was adapted for a two-handed grip, this also had a hammer de-cocking capability incorporated into the safety-catch mechanism.

A nickeled Beretta M85BB, in 380 ACP.

- *Model 85BB* This was similar to the 84BB but had the slim butt and eight-round magazine.
- *Model 85F* Similar to the Model 84F, excepting for its small-capacity magazine, this could also be described as an 85BB with a hammer de-cocking system.
- *Model 86* Introduced in 1987, this updated Model 950 retained the tipping barrel of its predecessor. It had an external hammer, double-action lockwork, a hammer de-cocking system, a loaded-chamber indicator, an ambidextrous safety catch and a light anodized-alloy frame. Offered only in 380 ACP, the Model 86 had a 4.4-inch barrel and weighed about 23 oz. It was customarily blued and had walnut grips.

A long-barrel 22 LR Beretta 87BB, with a single-action trigger.

- *Model 87BB* Similar to the Model 84BB, this gun was chambered for 22 LR ammunition and had an eight-round magazine. It dates from 1986. Barrels may be 3.8 or 5.9 inches long, and an adjustable rear sight lies on top of the slide ahead of the hammer.
- *Model 87BB/LB* A "Long Barrel" version (5.9 inches) of the standard 87BB.
- *Model 87 Target* Introduced in 2000, this has a heavy squared barrel shroud and an aluminum-alloy frame, giving a weight of about 41 oz. The rear sight is adjustable and an integral optical-sight base is a standard fitting.

Seen as a replacement for the M76, the M89 is a 22-caliber target pistol.

Model 89 (also known in the USA as "Model 89 Gold Standard") An updated version of the 22 LR Model 76, configured in slab-sided combat pistol form, this was promoted as a military training and competition pistol bearing some resemblance to service weapons. It had an external hammer, an ambidextrous safety catch, a fully adjustable rear sight, a trigger stop and a magazine safety. There are also distinctive longitudinal flutes on the barrel shroud and auxiliary under-muzzle weight.

The Beretta M90, made in Rome.

Model 90 (1969-83) Made in a factory in Rome, alongside Garand-type rifles, this extended the double-action system to 7.65mm caliber and also forsook the familiar open-topped slide for a conventional solid-topped version. The gun presented a streamlined modernistic appearance. With a 3.5-inch barrel and an eight-round magazine, the M90 was a successful personal-defense pistol.

Model 92 The third 1976 introduction was this 9mm Parabellum combat pistol, essentially the Model 951 brought up to date. The proven locking wedge was retained; but the lock was double-action, the extractor was adapted to serve as a loaded-chamber indicator (as did in the Models 81 and 84) and a 15-round staggered-row magazine was fitted. The Model 92 was adopted by the Italian forces in the late 1970s and subsequently not only equipped many other armies but also provided the basis for many licensed copies (see "Denel", "Taurus").

The 92-series guns have been made in made in five patterns: S (discontinued), D, DS, FS and G. Guns in the "**S**" series were distinguished by a safety catch on the slide instead of the frame, acting as a de-cocking lever in addition to its primary role. Applying the catch when the pistol is cocked would deflect the firing pin, drop the hammer and break the connection between trigger and sear.

The standard "**D**" guns (introduced in 1992) are self-cocking "DAO" patterns, entirely lacking manual safety and de-cocking devices and, therefore, with plain-sided slides and a hammer that is flush with the rear face of the slide. A firing-pin lock ensures that they cannot fire when dropped. "**DS**" guns are similar, but have an ambidextrous safety catch on the slide.

The "**FS**" group, the most numerous, contains traditional double-action/single-action patterns with an ambidextrous dual-purpose safety/de-cocking lever, a firing-pin lock, a trigger-bar disconnector and an external hammer. The rear part of the striker is tipped down out of the hammer path when the safety catch is applied. "**G**" guns are similar to the FS type, but the lever on the slide lacks the auxiliary safety feature and functions solely as a de-cocker. It springs back to its "up" position after the de-cocking motion is complete.

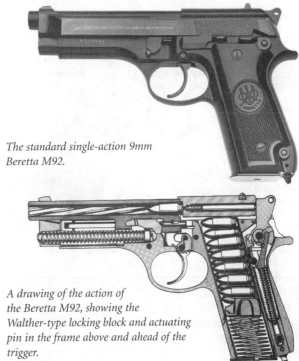

The standard single-action 9mm Beretta M92.

A drawing of the action of the Beretta M92, showing the Walther-type locking block and actuating pin in the frame above and ahead of the trigger.

- *Model 92* (1976-92) These 9mm-caliber guns had distinctive open-topped slides, said to reduce jamming and also allow the firer to insert single cartridges directly into the chamber if the magazine is lost or damaged. Except for special patterns, the grips were checkered black plastic with the Beretta rings-and-arrows trademark. The stripping catch and the hold-open lay on the left side of the frame, and the magazine catch (reversible in later variants) ran laterally through the grip behind the rear of the trigger guard.

  Markings customarily included "PIETRO BERETTA" ahead of "GARDONE V.T. — MADE IN ITALY" and "PB" in an oval, all on the left side of the slide. The caliber, the designation of the gun and patent-protection claims usually appeared on the right, though some guns also have the Accokeek address in this location.

  Made with an alloy frame and a steel slide—the guns originally had a blue finish (subsequently superseded by matte-black "Bruniton")—the Model 92 was about 8.5 inches long, had a 4.9-inch barrel and weighed about 33 oz without its 15-round double-column magazine.

- *Model 92 Billennium* (2001) Only 2000 of these guns were made. They were finished in nickel alloy and had very distinctive linear engraving on both sides of the slide (including "billennium"). The retraction grips have a checkerboard appearance. The trigger mechanism was restricted to single action, the grips were carbon fiber and the sights were adjustable.

- *Model 92D* (1992 to date) The basic gun in the range, this is double-action-only and has no manual safety catch or de-cocking mechanism. The hammer lies flush with the rear of the slide, but, apart from an unusually neat appearance, the gun was otherwise similar to the 92F.

- *Model 92D Compact Inox* (2000 to date) This offers stainless steel construction.
- *Model 92D-C Type M* ("92D Compact M" or "92DCM") This was a shortened gun with a 4.3-inch barrel, an abbreviated grip and an eight-round single-column magazine.
- *Model 92DS* This self-cocking (or "double-action-only") version of the Model 92F had a hammer that followed the slide home after each shot and came to rest in the double-action position. The hammer spur was removed, allowing the hammer to be flush with the rear end of the slide, and a manual safety lever was fitted.

A 9mm Beretta 9mm M92F.

- *Model 92F* The American testing authority requested changes in the 92S before the Beretta could be approved for issue. These included reshaping the trigger guard for a two-handed grip; curving the front butt strap inward; fitting a special base to the magazine to enhance grip; fitting new grip plates; adding a lanyard ring; chromium-plating the bore; and protecting the exterior surfaces with Bruniton, a Teflon-type coating. The resulting "92F" was adopted by the US forces in 1985 as the "US Pistol 9mm M9" and has subsequently been adopted by police, security agencies and several other armies.
- *Model 92F Compact* (or "Model 92FC") This is a smaller version of the 92F, with a 4.3-inch barrel and a 13-round magazine. Discontinued in 2000.

- *Model 92F Compact Type M* (or "Model 92FCM") Another compact 92F, this had a slimmer grip and an eight-round single-column magazine.
- *Model 92F Inox* (1992-2000) A stainless steel variant of the basic "F" model.
- *Model 92FS* (1990 to date) Introduced to replace the Model 92F, in response to complaints from the USA that over-loading caused the slide to crack, this has an extended hammer axis pin and grooves cut along most of the length of the slide. Should the pistol be fired with an excessive load, any tendency for the slide to over-travel would be stopped as the ends of the pin strike the solid portion of the slide at the end of the grooves. The guns have 4.9-inch barrels and weigh 34-35 oz. A three-dot high-definition sighting system is standard. The slide is usually blacked steel, the frame being sand-blasted black-anodized aluminum alloy. Guns made after 2001 have their extractors adapted so that a red-painted head projects laterally from the slide when a round is in the chamber.
- *Model 92[FS] Border Marshal* (2000 only) Based on guns supplied to the US Immigration and Naturalization Service, this short-lived variant had a 4.7-inch barrel and a steel slide allied with the "FS" safety features. It also had Tritium night sights and rubber grips. The mark "Border Marshal" and "BRIGADIER • MADE IN THE USA" appeared on the right side of the slide.
- *Model 92[FS] Brigadier* (1999 to date) This is a heavy-slide version of the M92FS, originally developed in 40 S&W — see "Model 96 Brigadier" below. The 9mm Parabellum version weighs about 34 oz without its 15-round magazine.
- *Model 92[FS] Brigadier Inox* (2000 to date) This has a stainless steel slide and frame.
- *Model 92FS-C* A smaller "Compact" version of the standard 92FS with a 4.3-inch barrel and a 13-round magazine, dating from 1998.
- *Model 92FS-C Inox* (2000 to date) This is a stainless steel variant of the 92FS-C. The original versions had bright stainless steel slides and bright-anodized alloy frames, but post-2001 examples are blacked.

The Beretta M92FS Compact "Type M", with a single-column magazine.

A typical compact example of the Beretta M92F, with a short barrel and a short butt.

A Beretta 92FS with a target-shooting conversion kit, consisting of a long barrel, a frame extension and adjustable sights.

A 9mm Parabellum double-action-only Beretta M92 Centurion.

- *Model 92FS-C Type M* Introduced in 1990, discontinued in 1993 and reintroduced in 1998, this is a 92FSC with an eight-round single-column "Type M" magazine.
- *Model 92FS Centurion* Dating from 1992, this combines the frame and 15-round magazine capacity of the standard Model 92FS with the 4.3-inch barrel and slide of the Compact versions. Special Centurion variants have been sold into particular markets, amalgamating the basic standard frame/short slide characteristics with the particular features of "D", "DS" and "G" patterns listed previously.
- *Model 92FS CO_2* This "lookalike" trainer for the standard guns, powered by a carbon-dioxide bulb inserted in the butt, is an alternative to the traditional replacement 22 rimfire blowback barrel/slide unit. It is made under license from Beretta by Umarex of Germany. Offered in blue or nickel, it may be seen as short-barreled "combat" or long-barreled "Match" patterns. The eight-chamber disk magazine holds eight 177-caliber pellets.
- *Model 92[FS] Custom Carry* This is basically a standard 92FS-C with a 4.3-inch barrel, a short grip and low-profile controls with the safety lever confined to the left side of the gun. The magazine capacity is restricted to 10 rounds to comply with the 1994 gun-control act.
- *Model 92FS Deluxe* A few guns of this type have been offered with light scroll engraving on the slide and frame and select walnut grips with a gold plate to receive the purchaser's initials. Finish may be high-polish blue, silver or gold.
- *Model 92FS Enduring Freedom* Announced shortly after the terrorist attack of September 11, 2002, this is basically a standard "92FS" with a Crimson Trace laser designator attached beneath the frame.
- *Model 92FS Inox* A 2000-vintage stainless steel variant of the standard 92FS. The original versions had bright stainless steel slides and bright-anodized alloy frames, but some post-2001 examples have been blacked. The current version has a bright anodized-alloy frame, a slide made of satin finish stainless steel and stippled rubber grips with the rings-and-arrows logo. The grips are retained by hex-head screws.
- *Model 92FS Inox Tactical* (1999 to date) This is an otherwise standard full-length "92FS" with a satin-matte finish on the stainless steel slide and anodized aluminum-alloy frame. Black rubber grips and Tritium night-sight inserts are standard fittings.
- *Model 92FS Limited Editions* Several different guns have been made in this category. The most commonly encountered is the Beretta 470th-year pattern, 470 being made in 1999 to celebrate the manufacturer's anniversary — though a very odd number to commemorate! They had high-polish finish and gold-plated Beretta trademark medallions set in plain walnut grips. An anniversary logo was cut in the top of the slide and also on the chrome-plated magazine. Serial numbers (" ... of 470") were also filled in gold. The guns being offered in 2003, totaling just ten Model 92 FS and ten Model 98 FS, are hand-engraved overall and have grips of "fossil ivory". The company name and address on the left side of the slide are filled in tooled gold wire.
- *Model 92FS Vertec* (2002 to date) Designed in the USA, this combines a frame with a parallel-sided butt and slender dual-texture grips with a short-reach trigger that is suited to comparatively small hands. An accessory rail has been added beneath the squared foreend, the front sight is exchangeable and the magazine well is beveled to accelerate reloading. The angle between the grip and the bore has been adjusted to duplicate that of the M1911 Colt-Browning.
- *Model 92FS Vertec Inox* This is simply the 92 FS Vertec (above) with a satin-matte finished stainless steel slide and an anodized-aluminum frame.
- *Model 92G* "G" is for "Gendarmerie", signifying adoption by the French Gendarmerie Nationale. The pistol resembles the Model 92F

The M92G Beretta pistol.

externally but has a de-cocking lever instead of the combined safety catch/de-cocking lever of its predecessor. When the lever was released, after the hammer had been lowered, it sprang up to the ready position. The Gendarmerie pistol was subsequently adopted by the army and air force and is being manufactured in France as the "PA-MAS-G1".
- *Model 92G Elite* (1999 to date) Built on a heavy frame (see "Model 96 FS Brigadier"), this has a 4.7-inch stainless steel barrel and a "de-cock-only" trigger system. The retraction grips are duplicated behind the muzzle, the magazine well is beveled to assist reloading, the hammer is a skeleton pattern instead of the more usual ring type and the frontstrap is ribbed. The sights are an exchangeable white dot at the front and a two-dot Novak Lo-Mount Carry at the rear. The original pattern had a steel slide with a Bruniton finish, but the Elite II of 2002 combines a satin-finish stainless steel slide with a blacked alloy frame. Markings usually include an "ELITE" logo above the Accokeek address on the left side of the slide between the two sets of retraction grips.
- *Model 92S* An otherwise conventional member of the "92" series, this gun has a combination safety catch/de-cocking lever on the slide instead of the frame. Applying the catch when the action is cocked moves the firing pin out of the way of the dropping hammer and breaks the connection between trigger and sear.

The 9x19mm (9mm Parabellum) Beretta M92SB.

- *Model 92SB* This was developed for the US Army pistol trials of 1979-80. In accordance with the specifications, an ambidextrous safety catch was fitted and the magazine-release catch (which could be easily switched from left to right as required) was moved to the front edge of the butt below the trigger guard. In addition, the firing-pin lock that had originated in the Model 81BB was used and the butt straps were grooved to improve the grip. The 92SB was subsequently adopted by the Italian Special Forces and several police forces, but, although victorious in US Army trials, it required minor changes to satisfy the Americans. These created the 92F (above).
- *Model 92SB-C* A compact version of the 92SB, this was smaller, lighter and fitted with a 13-round magazine.

A Beretta M92SB Compact pistol, in 9mm Parabellum.

- *Model 92SB-C Type M* This was little more than a 92SB-C with an eight-round single-column magazine. The base of the magazine was shaped to form a rest for the shooter's little finger, and the forward butt strap was curved inward to improve grip.
- *Model 92SB-P (1980-5)* A designation applied to standard full-length guns with a high-polish blue finish.
- *Model 92 Stock* Sharing the Brigadier slide (see "Model 92FS Brigadier") and the standard "FS" trigger system, with the combination safety catch/de-cocking lever, this offers a 4.9-inch barrel with a special "accurizing bushing" to eliminate the play between barrel and slide. The retraction grips are duplicated and a Bruniton finish is standard.

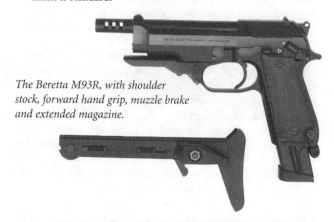

The Beretta M93R, with shoulder stock, forward hand grip, muzzle brake and extended magazine.

Model 93R ("R", *Raffica*, "squall") This was the Model 951R improved in much the same way as the Model 92 was derived from the Model 951. The 93R was essentially a 92 with a longer barrel, ported at the muzzle to form a compensator, and a three-round burst capability that could be activated by a thumb-switch. The three-round mechanism gave a reasonable chance of keeping the burst on target and gave better accuracy than the Model 951R.

Control during burst-firing was helped by allowing the shooter to hook his thumb into the extended trigger guard while simultaneously holding the folding metal grip attached to the front of the frame. A folding metal stock could be attached to the butt, turning the pistol into a carbine, and a 20-round magazine was supplied (though the standard 15-round magazine of the Model 92 could also be used). The Model 93R has been adopted by Italian and other Special Forces and by the anti-terrorist units of the Carabinieri.

Model 96 series Introduced in 1992, this consisted of several different guns, all based on the similarly designated "92FS" patterns, except that they chamber the 40 Smith & Wesson cartridge and have 11-round magazines (currently restricted to 10 in the USA).

- *Model 96 [FS] Border Marshal* This is identical with the M92 [FS] Border Marshal (q.v.) but chambers the 10mm S&W cartridge instead of 9mm Parabellum.
- *Model 96 [FS] Brigadier (1999 to date)* Prolonged service experience with the 9mm M9 US service pistol revealed a weakness in the

construction of the slide, which was corrected by altering the machining. This was undetectable externally. However, a visibly-altered slide has been offered commercially on the Brigadier, Elite and Stock derivatives of the 92/96/98 series. This arose from requests made by the US Immigration & Naturalization Service (INS), which wanted an M9 chambered for the 40 S&W round. The standard slide has its top edge beveled virtually from the muzzle to the enlargement designed to facilitate ejection; on the Brigadier, however, the beveling tapers off to create a noticeable "flat" on the slide in line with the locking-lug recesses. Markings on the left side of the slide have been changed so that the "PB" mark, within its oval cartouche, appears beneath the wording. Most guns have exchangeable front sights, allowing Tritium or similar night sights to be fitted, and the grips may be wrap-round rubber retained by hex-head screws.

- *Model 96 [FS] Brigadier Inox* A minor variant of the 96 [FS] Brigadier, this has a stainless steel slide and an anodized aluminum frame.
- *Model 96 Combat Combo* Developed for IPSC competition shooting, this has a strengthened Brigadier-type slide and an adjustable single-action trigger. The barrel may be a standard 5.9-inch pattern with a bushing to enhance accuracy and an aluminum counterweight, or a 4.9-inch version intended for use in the "Standard" competition category. Match-type sights are fitted. A typical gun is 9.5 inches long with a 5.9-inch barrel and weighs about 40 oz without its 11-round magazine.
- *Model 96C (Compact)* A 10mm S&W version of the Model 92FS-C with a 4.3-inch barrel and a 13-round magazine.

A Beretta M96 Centurian.

- *Model 96 Centurion* Introduced in 1993, this offers a full-length grip (and 10-round magazine) allied with a 4.3-inch barrel.
- *Model 96 Combat (1997-2001)* This is actually intended for practical pistol shooting. The barrel is 5.9 inches long, an integral muzzle weight is standard, the rear sight is adjustable and the trigger mechanism is restricted to single action. The guns weigh about 40 oz. Magazines are usually restricted to nine rounds to ensure that they feed efficiently.
- *Model 96C Type M* A 10mm S&W short-barrel "compact" with a single-column eight-round magazine.
- *Model 96 [FS] Custom Carry* Introduced in 1999, this is a 10mm version of the 9mm M92 [FS] Custom Carry.
- *Model 96D* A 10mm-caliber variant of the Model 92D, with a double-action trigger mechanism.
- *Model 96DS* A 10mm version of the 9mm Model 92DS with a double-action trigger and an additional manual safety catch.
- *Model 96FS Deluxe* This offers light scroll engraving on the slide and frame and select walnut grips with a gold plate to receive the purchaser's initials. Finish may be high-polish blue, silver or gold.
- *Model 96G* A 10mm S&W version of the Model 92G (q.v.).
- *Model 96G Elite* Dating from 1999, this is a 10mm S&W variant of the 9mm Model 92G Elite. The 96G Elite II (2002 to date) combines a satin-finish stainless steel slide with a blacked alloy frame.

- *Model 96 Inox* This was simply the standard 96 with a stainless steel slide.
- *Model 96 Stock* Introduced in 1997, this has the standard double-action and a half-cock notch in the trigger system. It has the standard 4.9-inch barrel and fixed sights, though three different front sight options can be fitted interchangeably.
- *Model 96 Target* An alternative designation for the "96 Combat" described above.
- *Model 96 Vertec* A 10mm S&W variant of the 9mm Model 92[FS] Vertec (q.v.), this shares the re-shaped grip, short-reach trigger and slender grips.
- *Model 96 Vertec Inox* A variant of the standard 96 Vertec, with a satin-finish stainless steel slide and an anodized-aluminum frame.

Model 98 series Originally a 7.65mm Parabellum 92SB-C, this was used by the police forces that were already wedded to this particular chambering. Sales were small, however, and the original Model 98 was superseded in 1988 by a 9x21mm IMI version, to be sold commercially in countries where 9mm Parabellum was restricted to military use. The full-length magazines all hold 15 rounds, though they are currently restricted to 10 when sold commercially in the USA.

- *Model 98F* This was the same as the Model 98 but is available in either 7.65mm Parabellum or 9x21mm IMI chambering.
- *Model 98FS* This was an "FS" version of the basic Model 98, chambered for the 9x21mm IMI cartridge, with an extended hammer-axis pin and grooves in the slide to prevent over-travel.
- *Model 98[FS] Brigadier* (1999 to date) Introduced in 1999, this is a heavy-slide version of the 9x21mm M98FS. See "Model 96 Brigadier", above.
- *Model 98[FS] Brigadier Inox* (2000 to date) This has a stainless steel slide and frame.
- *Model 98FS Deluxe* Distinguished by light scroll engraving on the slide and frame, this has select walnut grips with a gold plate to receive the purchaser's initials. Finish may be high-polish blue, silver or gold.
- *Model 98FS Inox* A derivative of the 98FS with a stainless steel slide and an anodized-aluminum frame.
- *Model 98FS Limited Edition* Details of this "super deluxe" variant will be found under "Model 92FS Limited Edition", above.

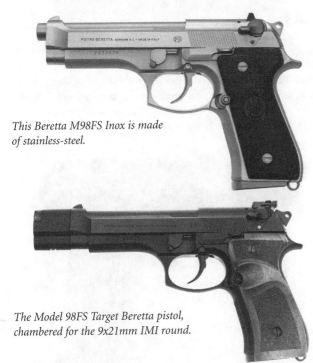

This Beretta M98FS Inox is made of stainless-steel.

The Model 98FS Target Beretta pistol, chambered for the 9x21mm IMI round.

- *Model 98FS Target* A target-shooting derivative of the 98FS, this originally had an extended hammer axis pin and grooves in the slide. The current version, however, is simply an adaptation of the M98 FS with a 5.9-inch barrel, an aluminum counterweight-sleeve at the muzzle, match-quality sights and stippled walnut semi-anatomical grips. It is 9.5 inches long with the standard 5.9-inch barrel and weighs about 37 oz empty.
- *Model 98 Vertec* A 9x21mm IMI variant of the 9mm Model 92[FS] Vertec, sharing the re-shaped grip, short-reach trigger and slender grips.
- *Model 98 Vertec Inox* A variant of the previous gun, with a satin-finish stainless steel slide and an anodized-aluminum frame.
- *Model 98F Target* A variant of the 98F with a 5.9-inch/15cm barrel, muzzle counterweight and adjustable target sights.
- *Model 98G Elite II* (2002 to date) Essentially similar to the 92G Elite II (q.v.) but chambered for the 9x21mm IMI round instead of 9mm Parabellum, this combines a satin-finish stainless steel slide with a blacked alloy frame.
- *Model 98 Stock* Sharing the Brigadier-type heavy slide and the "FS" trigger system, with the combination safety catch/de-cocking lever, this offers a 4.9-inch barrel with a special "accurizing bushing" to eliminate the play between barrel and slide. The retraction grips are duplicated and a Bruniton finish is standard. Three types of sight can be fitted.

Model 99 Intended for police use, this was a 92SB-C Type M chambered for the 7.65mm Parabellum cartridge. Production ceased in 1988, owing to lack of demand.

Model 101 Also called the "New Jaguar", this was simply a new name for the 22-caliber Model 71 fitted with a 6-inch barrel and new adjustable rear sight.

Model 102 An American sales designation applied in the 1960s to the Model 76.

Model 104 A similar designation for the Model 951.

Model 318 Introduced in 1935 and little more than an improved 25 ACP M1919, this had a 2.5-inch barrel and a butt that was contoured to give a better grip. Production continued until 1946. Post-war guns, often sold in the USA as the *Panther*, could be supplied in finishes ranging from browned steel to gold plating.

Model 418 The M318 was replaced in 1947 by this slightly improved version, offering a rounded plastic grip, a more elegant grip safety and a loaded-chamber indicator pin in the slide. It was called the "25 ACP Bantam" in the USA during the 1950s.

- *Model 420* An engraved chrome-plated version of the Model 418.
- *Model 421* The variant with engraving, gold plating and tortoise-shell grips.

Model 948 ("Featherweight" or "Plinker") This was the Model 1934 chambered for the 22 Long Rifle rimfire cartridge, sold with barrels of 3.3 inches (standard) or 5.9 inches. The grip displayed an embossed "Beretta" instead of the previous "PB" monogram.

Model 949 "Tipo Olimpionico" Designed for Olympic-quality target shooting, chambered for 22 Short or LR rimfire ammunition, this shared the general open-top slide arrangement of the M1915. The barrel measured 8.75 inches, a muzzle brake/compensator was a standard fitting, the grips were anatomical and fully adjustable target sights were

A 22-caliber Beretta M949 "Tipo Olimpionico".

supplied. Balance weights could be attached beneath the barrel when required. Production was confined to 1959-64.

Model 950 (or "Jetfire") This 22-caliber pistol presented an interesting departure from the line of development that had begun in 1915. Though the external appearance resembled a modernized M1915, the barrel was pinned to the front of the frame so that it could be released by rotating the safety catch. The breech could then be raised clear of the slide, allowing the barrel to be cleaned, or the chamber loaded, the barrel closed and the gun fired. This gave the pistol an additional single-shot capability absent from its Beretta predecessors (but not from rivals such as the Le Français). The standard Model 950 had a 2.35-inch 22 LR barrel and a distinctive stamped-strip trigger guard (cf., M3032 Tomcat). Guns of this type have been widely advertised in the USA under the name "Minx".

- *Model 950 Special* A variant of the M950 with a 3.75-inch 22 LR barrel.
- *Model 950B* An M950 chambered for the 22 Short rimfire cartridge.

The 22 Short rimfire Beretta M950BS pistol.

- *Model 950B Special* This was offered with a 3.3-inch barrel in 22 Short RF.
- *Model 950 Inox* Introduced in 2000, this has a stainless steel slide and an anodized-aluminum-alloy frame.

Model 951 (or "Brigadier") Developed in response to a demand by the Italian army for a 9mm Parabellum service pistol, this not only marked Beretta's rehabilitation in military circles but was also the company's first successful locked-breech handgun design. The lock was a minor adaptation of the wedge pioneered in the Walther P.38, though the open-topped slide and external hammer recalled the Model 1934 Beretta. The safety bolt running laterally through the frame was convenient to push to "fire", if less easy to return to "safe".

Series-production guns did not appear in quantity until 1957, owing to problems with the weight-saving light-alloy frame. Prolonged testing showed that this could not withstand the battering it took from the slide, and the frame was replaced by a steel equivalent before production began. The M951 was initially adopted by the Italian forces, then, amongst others, by the Egyptian and Israeli armies.

A version of the M951 made for Egypt in the mid-1950s.

- *Model 951R* Supplied to the Italian Special Forces and police in small numbers, this was a specialized machine-pistol variant of the 951 with a selector switch on the left side of the slide and adaptations in the trigger system to allow 1200 rds/min to be fired when required. Control was improved by a wooden handgrip, fitted to the front of the frame ahead of the trigger, and a special 10-round magazine protruded from the bottom of the butt.
- *Model 951 Target* Apparently manufactured specially for the Egyptian army, this was virtually a Model 952 Special (below) chambering the 9mm Parabellum cartridge. However, the rear sight differed and the magazine catch lay on the heel of the butt.

The Beretta M952 Special was usually restricted to the 7.65mm Parabellum round.

Model 952 A variant of the Model 951 chambered for the 7.65mm Parabellum cartridge.
- *Model 952 Special* This was a target adaptation of the 7.65mm Model 952 with a longer barrel, revised sights and anatomical grips.

Model 1915 The first Beretta pistol was a wartime project and, as a result, quality fell below the customarily exemplary standards. The gun was a 7.65mm blowback with the slide cut to form two arms lying alongside the barrel, which was a separate unit pinned to the frame.

An early 9mm Beretta M951 Brigadier.

The 7.65mm (32 ACP) Beretta M1915 pistol.

A 9mm Short (380 ACP) example of the Beretta M1915, with slide markings that show it was sold commercially.

Extracted cases were ejected by the tip of the firing pin, which had been moved forward in the breech-block during the recoil stroke by the internal hammer. A separate ejection port was provided in the solid-topped portion of the slide. The slide inscription read "Pietro Beretta Brescia Casa Fondata nel 1680 Cal XXmm Brevetto 1915".

A few guns were made in 9mm Short and others for the 9mm Glisenti cartridge. The latter group incorporated stronger return springs, buffer springs to soften the slide return and positive ejectors. Both models had a prominent safety catch on the left side of the frame, which could also engage recesses in the slide to assist in dismantling. Some M1915 pistols have been reported with a second safety catch on the frame, under the rear end of the slide, but the reasons for this are still unclear.

Model 1915/1919 The most obvious change made in this improved M1915 was the elongation of the cut-out portion of the slide to include the ejection port. A lump on the barrel beneath the chamber slid horizontally into its seat, instead of dropping vertically into a hole, and a smaller and neater safety catch was fitted. The 15/19 was made only in 7.65mm caliber.

Model 1919 Beretta's first commercial pistol, this 6.35mm version of the M1915/19 had an additional grip safety set in the rear of the butt. It was introduced in 1920 and remained in production until 1939.

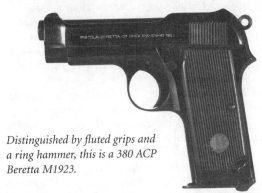

Distinguished by fluted grips and a ring hammer, this is a 380 ACP Beretta M1923.

Model 1923 This was basically a 15/19 with an external hammer, chambering the 9mm Glisenti cartridge. Only a few were ever made, originally for military service and subsequently for commercial sale. The slides were marked "Brev 1915-1919 Mlo 1923", but the most obvious feature was the long butt with metal grip plates ending half an inch above the bottom of the frame. Some frames are slotted in this area to allow a holster-stock to be attached.

Model 1931 Another improvement of the basic design, this 7.65mm model reverted to the size of the 1915 pattern but had a streamlined appearance and an external hammer. The majority of these pistols went to the Italian navy, with the naval emblem "RM" divided by an anchor on small medallions let into the wooden grips. The few guns sold commercially had "PB" embossed on their black plastic grips.

A typical Beretta M1931 7.65mm (32-caliber) pistol.

The "9mm Corto" (380 ACP) Beretta M1934 was made during Mussolini's Fascist regime.

The right side of a typical Beretta M1934.

This M1934 Beretta pistol was made in 1967, virtually unchanged from the original pre-war type (apart from the design of the grips and the marks on the slide).

Model 1934 Probably the most common of all pre-1945 Beretta pistols and little more than a 9mm Short version of the M1931, this served throughout World War II and was eventually discontinued in 1959. The slides were marked "P.Beretta Cal 9 Corto - Mo 1934 Brevet Gardone VT" followed by the date of manufacture in the Christian calendar — e.g. "1942" — followed by Roman numerals indicating the year of a

Fascist calendar commencing in 1922. Thus a date might be marked "1937 XV" or "1942 XX". Military weapons were also marked "RE" (*Regio Esercito*, "Royal Army"), "RA" (*Regia Aeronautica*) or "RM" (*Regia Marina*); police weapons displayed "PS" (*Publica Sicurezza*) on the left rear of the frame. A few M1934 pistols were sold commercially, but distribution was limited by the demands of the Italian armed forces. However, a few guns were sold to the Romanian army in the 1930s, distinguished by a "9mm Scurt" caliber mark on the left side of the frame instead of "9mm Corto".

Model 1935 This is simply the 1934 pistol in 7.65mm caliber. Most guns of this type were issued to the air force and the navy and will be found with "RA" or "RM" on the frame. Production continued after the end of World War II for commercial sale, becoming the *Model 935*.

Model 3032 Tomcat Introduced in 1996, this 32 ACP double-action blowback is an enlargement of the Model 950 (q.v.) with the trigger guard formed integrally with the frame. The exposed hammer and tip-barrel construction has been retained. The M3032 is about 5 inches long, has a 2.4-inch barrel and weighs 14-15 oz. The magazine is a seven-round single-column box, and finish is blue or matte black.

- *Model 3032 Tomcat Inox* Introduced in 2000, this version of the basic gun has a stainless steel finish.
- *Model 3032 Tomcat Titanium* Dating from 2001, this has a titanium-finished steel slide and black plastic grips. Weight is about 16.5 oz.

Model 8000 (Cougar) series (1994 to date) Introduced as the "Beretta Compact Frame Pistol Family", these guns have an all-enveloping slide and a rotating-barrel locking system that probably drew inspiration from the Steyr-Hahn pistol (Österreichische Waffenfabriks-Gesellschaft, q.v.). Lugs on the barrel lock the barrel and slide together, relying on a separate lug moving in a helical groove in the frame to rotate the barrel out of engagement.

Cougars are made only in "D" and "F" patterns, the former being double-action-only and the latter being comparable with the "FS"-series Model 92. Most of them have plastic grips with ring-and-arrow trademarks and trigger guards that are shaped for a two-hand or "combat" hand-grasp. The frames are light alloy, anodized black, while the steel slides have Bruniton finish. Barrels are chrome-plated carbon-steel.

- *Model 8000 Cougar D Inox* The designation applied to the standard 9mm Parabellum or 9x21 IMI (to special order) double-action-only pistol, 7 inches long with a 3.6-inch barrel and weighing about 33 oz. The magazine holds 15 rounds. The finish is a combination of satin finish on the stainless steel slide and a bright anodized-alloy frame. Grips are usually walnut.
- *Model 8000 Cougar D L* This is a lightweight version of the basic Cougar design, with a slimmer barrel, a "step-beveled" slide and a butt that is about 0.6 inches shorter than normal. This restricts magazine capacity to 13 rounds (10 in the USA). The guns are 7 inches long, have 3.6-inch barrels and weigh 28 oz empty.
- *Model 8000 Cougar D L Type P* This is a variant of the "L" patterns, sharing the lightweight slide and barrel but with a full-length butt. It weighs about 30 oz without the standard 15-round magazine.
- *Model 8000 Cougar F Inox* This was introduced specifically in 41 AE chambering. However, the cartridge failed to gain widespread acceptance and 9mm Parabellum (9x19) and 9x21 IMI chamberings were soon being offered instead.
- *Model 8000 Cougar F L.* A lightweight version of the F Inox, this has the same constructional features and restricted magazine capacity as the D L. The differences lie in the trigger system and the presence of a safety catch/de-cocking lever.
- *Model 8000 Cougar F L Type P.* This combines the lightweight construction of the F L with a full-length butt.
- *Model 8000 Mini-Cougar F* (1997 to date) The first of these appeared in 1997 but are little more than compact versions of the full-length guns with grips that were about an inch shorter than normal. A typical 9mm Parabellum example is 7 inches long, has a 3.6-inch barrel and weighs 27.5 oz without its 10-round magazine. The depth from the top of the slide to the base of the butt is about 4.5 inches, though the 15-round Model 92 magazine (fitted with a synthetic grip extension or "sleeve") can be used if required. A 9x21 IMI chambering is optional.

- *Model 8000 Mini-Cougar F Inox* This is simply a version of the Mini-Cougar F with a stainless steel slide and a bright-finish aluminum-alloy frame.
- *Model 8040 Cougar D* A variant of the M8000 in 10mm S&W (11-round magazine, 10 in the USA), this has a double-action-only trigger system.
- *Model 8040 Cougar F* Also chambered for the 40 S&W round, this has a conventional double-action trigger system with a de-cocking lever.
- *Model 8040 Cougar F Inox* A variant of the 8040 Cougar F with a stainless steel slide and bright-finish aluminum-alloy frame.
- *Model 8040 Mini-Cougar F* A short-grip version of the basic 40 S&W Cougar, this has a double-action trigger system. The standard magazines hold eight rounds.
- *Model 8040 Mini-Cougar F Inox* This is simply a variant of the preceding gun with a stainless steel slide and an aluminum-alloy frame.
- *Model 8045 Cougar D* Introduced in 1998, this is chambered for the 45 ACP cartridge. It is 7.2 inches long with a 3.7-inch barrel and weighs about 32 oz without its 8-round magazine.
- *Model 8045 Cougar F* The standard 45-caliber version of the Cougar, this has a double-action trigger mechanism that incorporates a de-cocking lever.
- *Model 8045 Mini-Cougar F* Derived from the 8045 Cougar F, this is a compact version with a short butt that restricts the magazine capacity to six rounds (though the full-length eight-round version can be substituted if required).
- *Model 8045 Mini-Cougar F Inox* This is a variant of the preceding gun with a stainless steel slide and the standard lightweight aluminum-alloy frame.
- *Model 8357 Cougar D* Chambering the comparatively new 357 SIG pistol cartridge, this has an 11-round magazine (currently restricted to 10 in the USA). Its dimensions duplicate the 8000 model.
- *Model 8357 Cougar F* The standard 357 SIG pistol, this has a conventional double-action trigger system incorporating a dual-purpose de-cocking lever/safety catch.

Model 9000S series (2000 to date) Offered only in "D" (double-action-only) and "F" (traditional double-action) guise, these guns represent Beretta's first foray into the currently fashionable synthetic frame/grip design. However, unlike guns such as the Glock and the Walther P99, which tend towards squared contours and chunky controls, the 9000 owes its flowing ergonomics and faired controls to the Giugiaro industrial-design house. Chambered for the 9mm Parabellum, 9x21 IMI or 40 S&W rounds, the guns are surprisingly compact. They have traditional Beretta open-topped steel slides, chrome-lined carbon-steel barrels and fiberglass-reinforced polymer frames. Finish is usually Bruniton on the slide and a natural gray/black coloring to the frame/grip unit. The butt is comparatively short, accepting double-column magazines holding 12 9mm or 10 40-caliber cartridges. However, the standard 15-round Model 92 magazine can be used if it has been fitted with a grip-extension sleeve.

The tilting-barrel lock is clearly inspired by the Colt-Browning, but the lugs lie on the side of the barrel and are tipped to engage directly in the slide without requiring any actuators or other intermediate parts. This is claimed to be simpler, sturdier and more reliable than many rival designs but requires alloy-steel inserts in the frame. Firing-pin and manual safety systems are fitted, and the sights are usually three-dot.

An optional key-operated "B-Lok" security feature (introduced in 2002), which cannot be cut or "picked", intercepts the movement of the hammer.

- *Model 9000S Type D* This has a double-action-only trigger system, lacking the projecting hammer spur of the "F" pattern. It is about 6.6 inches long with a 3.5-inch barrel and weighs about 26 oz.
- *Model 9000S Type F* A variant of the 9000D with a conventional double-action trigger system, embodying a combination safety/decocking lever, this has a hammer with a projecting ring-type head.

U22 Neos (2002 to date) Styled by Giugiaro but designed and made in the Beretta factory in the USA, this is intended as a basic 22 LR rimfire blowback target pistol or "plinker". Distinguished by its ultra-modern lines, it is 10.2 inches long with the 5.9-inch barrel and weighs about 35 oz without its 10-round magazine. The Neos is designed to dismantle into five basic components, without tools, and has exchangeable sights and a lightweight optical-sight mounting rail above the barrel shroud. The sculpted plain synthetic grip/frame units may be blue, black or red; those with rubber inlay grips are black with pale blue, sky blue or gray. The magazine-release catch lies on the right side of the frame above the trigger.

Alternative names

- *Bantam* See "Model 418".
- *Bobcat* See "Model 21".
- *Brigadier* See "Model 951", "Model 92" and "Model 96".
- *Centurion* See "Model 92" and "Model 96".
- *Cougar* See "Model 8000 series".
- *Featherweight* See "Model 948".
- *Jetfire* See "Model 950".
- *Jaguar* See "Model 72".
- *Plinker* See "Model 948".
- *Tomcat* See "Model 3032".

LOUIS BERGERON

Saint-Étienne, France.

Little is currently known about this French gunmaker. His only pistol appears to have been the 6.35mm *Le Steph*, a blowback resembling the 1906-type FN-Browning that was made for a few years prior to World War I.

THEODOR BERGMANN

Waffenfabrik Th. Bergmann, Suhl, Germany.

Bergmann's name remains prominent in the history of modern firearms, though recent research indicates that he was more entrepreneur than engineer and that credit for the design of "Bergmann" guns was due to employees such as Louis Schmeisser. There has been some doubt over the location of the manufactory, and claims have been made that "Werk Gaggenau" was actually sited in Suhl. These seem to have arisen simply on the basis that Gaggenau was not included in the 1906 Baedeker guide to Germany (the implication being that it did not then exist). However, a map printed on the back of the manual *Description of the Bergmann Pistol (Selfloader)* makes it clear beyond doubt that operations were well-established in Gaggenau by 1896. However, the guns were being made in Suhl by V.C. Schilling.

Bergmann's first handgun patent was taken out in conjunction with Otto Brauswetter, a watchmaker of Szegedin, Hungary, in June 1892 and related to a long-recoil automatic pistol that was made only as a prototype. The first pistol to appear under the name Bergmann had a bolt that engaged with an inclined face in the receiver to delay the opening of the breech. One of these Schmeisser-type delayed blowbacks was supplied to the Swiss army for trial in 1893, but none are known to survive.

M1894 (Bergmann-Schmeisser) Louis Schmeisser simplified his pistol during the lengthy trials undertaken in Switzerland, discarding the dubious delayed-action system in favor of simple blowback. One of the most remarkable features of the resulting "Model 1894" or "Bergmann-Schmeisser" was the absence of an extractor, empty cases being blown from the chamber by residual pressure striking a protrusion in the bolt-way that doubled as an ejector. Thus the cartridge cases had neither rims nor grooves. Unfortunately, though the gas-extraction system usually worked satisfactorily, the empty cases could not be guaranteed to strike the ejector protrusion cleanly and frequently jammed in the bolt-way. The 8mm Model 1894 was extensively tested in Switzerland and elsewhere, but relatively few were made. An exceptionally compact 5mm-caliber version had a folding trigger, common on the pocket revolvers of the time but rarely encountered on automatic pistols. So little enthusiasm was generated commercially that the pistols had soon been superseded by the Model 1896

M1896 (Bergmann-Schmeisser) A greatly refined version of the 1894 guns, this was a simple blowback with a revolver-type butt and the return spring inside the hollow bolt instead of beneath the barrel. The magazine case was contained in the frame ahead of the trigger. A hinged cover, with two diagonal slots, could be pivoted down to allow a five-round clip to be dropped into the magazine well. Closing the

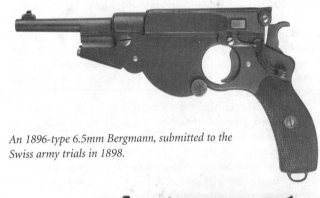

An 1896-type 6.5mm Bergmann, submitted to the Swiss army trials in 1898.

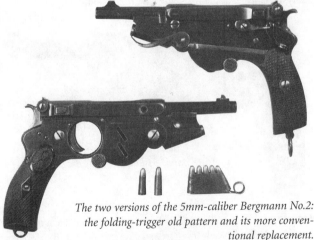

The two versions of the 5mm-caliber Bergmann No.2: the folding-trigger old pattern and its more conventional replacement.

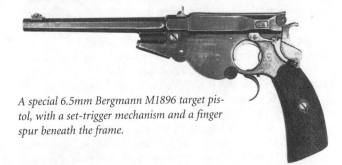

A special 6.5mm Bergmann M1896 target pistol, with a set-trigger mechanism and a finger spur beneath the frame.

cover engaged a spring-loaded follower arm with the bottom round, forcing the rounds upwards into the bolt-way. The clip could be left in place, or the ring that protruded below the magazine could pull the clip free once the magazine cover was closed. The pistol was supposed to work equally well with the clip removed, but contemporary reports suggest that this left too much between the cartridges and the frame walls and that jamming occurred.

The M1896 was originally offered in 5mm and 6.5mm calibers, retaining the gas-powered extraction system and the rimless/grooveless cartridge cases. The 5mm pistol, which had a folding trigger, was identified as the *Bergmann No. 2*; the more conventional 6.5mm version was the *Bergmann No. 3*.

Dissatisfaction with the erratic ejection of rimless/grooveless cases, and the difficulty of extracting an unfired round that was obvious to everyone (excepting Bergmann and Schmeisser), forced the substitution of a conventional extractor and a rimless cartridge case. This occurred when the serial numbers of the 5mm and 6.5mm pistols had reached about 500 and 1000, respectively. The folding trigger feature was abandoned at this time, and the "New Model" Bergmann No. 2 had a conventional trigger within a circular aperture in the frame.

The enthusiasm with which Bergmann was willing to adapt pistols to individual requests has left a legacy in the form of guns with long barrels, adjustable sights and finger spurs beneath their frames. Chamberings are said to have included non-Bergmann cartridges, but too few pistols have been examined to allow confirmation. Perhaps individual gunsmiths had simply made non-standard alterations once Bergmann ammunition (especially the rimless/grooveless type) ceased to be widely available.

An enlargement of the 6.5mm No. 3, the 8mm-caliber *Bergmann No. 4* was offered for military service. The conventional rimless cartridge shared the length and base diameter of the 6.5mm round, and the pistol was identical with the No. 3 except for the barrel and the dimensions of the magazine. Unfortunately, the 8mm guns were numbered in the same series as the No. 3, and it is difficult to judge how many were made. There may only have been a handful.

The 7.8mm "Military Model" Bergmann of 1897.

M1897 (or "No. 5 Military Model") Schmeisser patented a method of retaining the breech bolt by a screwed plug in 1895, but the Borchardt and Mauser pistols were reaching the market, other designs were being developed, and it had become apparent that the ambition of all handgun designers — a lucrative military contract — could be gained only with the help of a locked breech and a powerful cartridge.

The blowback Bergmann-Schmeisser was abandoned in favor of an 1897 patent that used short-recoil principles to tip the rear of the bolt laterally into the frame. A detachable box magazine replaced the clip-loaded pattern, and a stripper-clip loading system was copied from the Mauser C/96. The cartridge was similar to the 7.63mm Mauser type (which had been copied from the 7.65mm Borchardt) but had a longer neck. Though the caliber was also 7.63mm, the Bergmann cartridge was called "7.8mm Bergmann No. 5" to avoid confusion. The pistol

became the "M1897 No. 5" or *Militärisches-Modell*. The layout of the No. 5 was similar to that of the previous Bergmanns, with the magazine ahead of the trigger guard and fragile-looking construction that seemed to owe much to revolver design. However, the box magazine was detachable and the whole weapon was clearly aimed at the military market. It proved to be much too fragile and was speedily superseded by the "Mars" pattern described below.

M1899 (or "No. 6") This combined the locking system of the No. 5 with the old clip-loading magazine. Initially offered in 8mm caliber, another Bergmann-inspired cartridge that later became the 8mm Simplex (and bore no similarity to the earlier 8mm No 4), it was then chambered for cartridges such as the 7.5mm No. 4A, 7.5mm No. 7A and 7.65mm No. 8. Production was meager, as the No. 6, a poor design, was rejected by military and commercial customers alike. A solitary No. 6 rebuilt to incorporate the No. 5 box magazine, chambered for an odd 10mm cartridge (for many years wrongly identified as the "10mm Hirst"), was rejected by the British army in 1902.

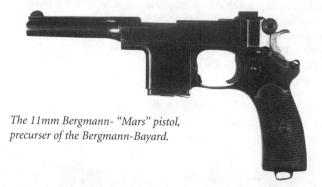

The 11mm Bergmann- "Mars" pistol, precurser of the Bergmann-Bayard.

Mars-Pistole (or "Bergmann-Mars") In 1901, Hugo Schmeisser and Bergmann patented a machinegun in which a vertically-moving locking piece engaged the breech-block. The idea was soon combined with the "magazine-forward" layout of the No. 5 pistol top, resulting in the Mars. Prototypes were made in various calibers, but the series-made guns were chambered for the new 9mm Bergmann No. 6 cartridge, later to achieve fame as the 9mm Bergmann-Bayard or (in Spain) 9mm Largo.

The pistol brought Bergmann his first military success when it was adopted as the "Model 1903" by the Spanish army. But the moment of success presaged disaster. The guns were being made for Bergmann by V.Chr. Schilling of Suhl, but Schilling's facilities are said to have been purchased by Heinrich Krieghoff in 1904 and, in 1905, in circumstances that cannot now be resolved, the Spanish order was declined. Bergmann unsuccessfully tried to organize production in his own small factory in Suhl, but then elected to abandon the pistol business entirely.

Production of the "Mars" was licensed to Anciens Établissements Pieper (q.v.) of Herstal-lèz-Liége, which completed the Spanish order, went on to market the "Mars" under its own name, then made some modifications to create the "Bergmann-Bayard" in 1908. The layout of the guns was clearly inspired by the No. 5 of 1897 (see above), with the magazine ahead of the trigger guard, but the construction was much sturdier and the locking system was more efficient. Bergmann-made guns had a much larger near-rectangular trigger-aperture than the near-circular design found on Pieper-made examples.

Simplex Unmistakably Bergmann in outline, this had a box magazine ahead of the trigger guard, a revolver lock and butt and a lightweight bolt. It was apparently designed in 1902 as a cheap blowback version of the Bergmann-Mars. The earliest examples were probably made in Germany by V.Chr. Schilling, but the Simplex was still being listed in Bergmann factory catalogues in 1906 and the later guns were made in Belgium. The 8mm cartridge subsequently became the "Bergmann No. 6", but was only ever used in the Simplex and soon lost

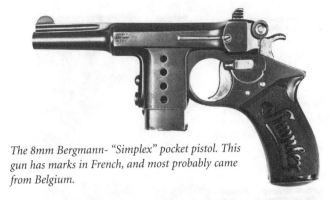

The 8mm Bergmann- "Simplex" pocket pistol. This gun has marks in French, and most probably came from Belgium.

its Bergmann title. Production has been estimated at little more than 3000, with only the most minor changes in design. The Bergmann-Simplex was marketed in England by the Wilkinson Sword Company.

Taschenmodell Theodor Bergmann died during World War I, though the Bergmann company continued to make machineguns and, towards the end of hostilities, the first true submachine guns. Louis Schmeisser had left Bergmann for Rheinische Metallwaaren- & Maschinenfabrik in 1905, and his son Hugo left in 1921 to work for Haenel. The Bergmann factory in Suhl and rights to the surviving patents were then sold to the Actien-Gesellschaft Lignose, a consortium led by Pulverfabrik Lignose.

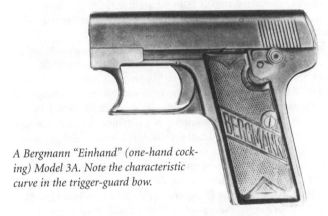

A Bergmann "Einhand" (one-hand cocking) Model 3A. Note the characteristic curve in the trigger-guard bow.

Prior to 1918, however, the Bergmann company had acquired rights to a small automatic pistol that could be cocked by the fingers of the trigger hand. Designed in 1913-16 by Wytold Chylewski (q.v.), this had been made in small numbers by Schewizerische Industrie-Gesellschaft. Guns of this type had been promoted under the Bergmann name shortly before the sale to Lignose, but the guns are better known under the latter name and described in detail in the appropriate entry.

However, perhaps as a safeguard should the "one-hand" system fail, a conventional internal-hammer blowback design based on the FN-Browning of 1906 was produced as the "Taschenmodell" ("Pocket model"). *Models 2 and 3* were 6.35mm-caliber, with six- and nine-round magazines, respectively. The slides were marked "Theodor Bergmann Gaggenau Waffenfabrik Suhl Cal 6,35 DRGM" and the grips were embossed with the word "Bergmann". A 7.65mm *Model 4* and a 9mm Short *Model 6* were proposed but never produced in quantity before Lignose took over.

Bergmann-Erben AG Lignose acquired the Menz of Suhl in 1937, and from then until the beginning of World War II marketed guns marked "Theodor Bergmann Erben" (*Erben*, "heirs", "successors"). The name was little more than an attempt to profit from the goodwill extant in the Bergmann name.

The first 7.65mm pistol was simply the Menz "PB Spezial" with different markings. The 6.35mm "Model II" was based on an earlier Menz design, though slight changes were made in the slide contours. It is

probable that these guns were assembled from stocks of parts in existence in 1937 and that the totals involved were very small.

BERISTAIN & CO.

Armeria Beristain y Cia, Barcelona, Spain.

The pistols attributed to this distributor were made in 1919-25 by Gabilondo y Cia of Vitoria but display "BC" monograms molded into their grips. Beristain had patented a grip safety, a loaded-chamber indicator and other items applicable to automatic pistols, the safety mechanism being used in the Bufalo range. Production ceased on the expiry of Beristain's patents, after which pistols continued to be made under the name "Danton".

Bufalo The smallest gun in the series was a 6.35mm Eibar-type, copied, as usual, from the FN-Browning of 1906. The slide is marked "Automatica Pistola Espana Pats 62004 y 67577 Bufalo 6,35 (.25 Cal)". The larger models, in 7.65mm Auto and 9mm Short, were copied from the FN-Browning 1910, with a recoil spring that was concentric with the barrel, but substituting an internal hammer for the original striker and fitted with a Beristain grip safety instead of the Browning type. The slide markings repeated those of the 6.35mm model, except for the caliber and the omission of "Pistola". "Made in Spain" was usually present on the right side of the slide.

BERLIN-SUHLER WERKE ("BSW")

Berlin-Suhler Waffen- und Fahrzeugfabrik, Suhl, Germany.

BSW succeeded to the business of Simson & Co. (q.v.) of Suhl in 1934, Simson having the misfortune of being under Jewish ownership. Sporting rifles and shotguns were made alongside bicycles and vehicle components, and a double-action automatic pistol was offered for military service. The business was then enveloped in the "Wilhelm-Gustloff Stiftung", Herman Goering's private munitions consortium, and ceased trading at the end of World War II. See also "Gustloff".

BSW (1936-7) Though attempts have been made to date this gun as early as 1933, the BSW name was not adopted until the enforced change of ownership had been completed. Unlike the competing Walther and Mauser designs, which relied on recoil operation, the BSW design tapped gas from a port in the underside of the muzzle to push the head of a pivoting locking bar out of engagement with a transom in the slide. This allowed the slide to run back, returning to strip a new round into the chamber, ride over a lug in the locking bar and cam the bar back into engagement with the transom. The trigger was a double-action design with an enclosed hammer, and the box magazine was placed conventionally within the butt.

The German army preferred the Walther Heeres-Pistole, subsequently adopted as the P.38, and so the complicated and probably fragile BSW was rejected. No more was heard of the gas-operated pistol, and only two 9mm Parabellum specimens survive.

BERN ARMS FACTORY

Eidgenössische Waffenfabrik, Bern, Switzerland (until 1995);
W+F Bern, Switzerland (1995 to date).

Founded in 1871 as the Eidgenössische Montierwerkstätte ("state-owned assembly workshops"), the Swiss government arsenal began to make Vetterli rifles in 1875. It has since been involved in the manufacture of machineguns, rifles and a variety of handguns, particularly during the directorships of Louis von Stürler (1894-1920) and Adolf Fürrer (1921-40).

∼ REVOLVERS ∼

M1878 (Ordonnanzrevolver) This solid-frame six-shot rod-ejecting weapon chambered a 10.4mm centerfire cartridge. It is sometimes called the "Schmidt", acknowledging the part played in its design by Rudolf Schmidt, Director of the arsenal. The trigger was double-action and a hinged plate on the left side of the frame could be swung forward to give access to the lockwork. The guns could be identified by the Swiss cross embossed on the grips and by their excellent quality.

The preceding M1872 revolver, a Chamelot-Delvigne design modified by Schmidt, had chambered a 10.4mm rimfire round. About a thousand survivors made in Belgium by Pirlot Frères of Liége were subsequently converted to centerfire as the *Ordonnanzrevolver M1872/78*.

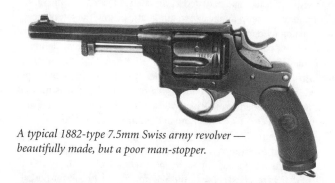

A typical 1882-type 7.5mm Swiss army revolver — beautifully made, but a poor man-stopper.

M1882 (Ordonnanzrevolver) In 1880, the Swiss army requested a lighter revolver to arm infantry officers, and Schmidt responded with a 7.5mm design that introduced the concept of small caliber and high velocity instead of the large caliber/low velocity combination that had previously been standard. The experimental small-caliber revolver was so well received that it was adopted for all services in 1882. Except for its size and weight, it was little different from its predecessors — remaining a solid-frame double-action rod-ejecting weapon with an Abadie-style loading-gate lock. Alterations were made in 1887 to prevent the hammer being cocked if the loading gate was open or, if the mechanism was already cocked, preventing the hammer from falling. A jacketed bullet replaced the original patched lead bullet at much the same time. More changes were made in 1889 when the angle of the butt was altered and the locking of the hinged side-plate changed. The resulting *M1882/89* remained the standard universal-issue service pistol until the 7.65mm Parabellum was introduced for officers, senior NCOs and some specialized units.

The simplified Swiss 7.5mm M1882/29 ordnance revolver.

M82/29 (Ordonnanzrevolver) The design of the 1882/89 revolver was modernized in 1928-30, when the frame was lightened and the lockwork was simplified. About 18,000 new guns were then made for issue to junior NCOs and men throughout the army. A cyclists' variant was made with a large fixed lanyard loop on the butt.

∼ AUTOMATIC PISTOLS ∼

Pistole 1906 W+F The Bern factory was initially responsible for the assembly and marking of the perfected *M1900* and *M1906* pistols, the parts being supplied by DWM from Germany between 1903 and 1914. Supplies were stopped by the outbreak of World War I, but by 1917, the Swiss were in dire need of pistols and began preparing a production line. This was completed in 1918 and the first Swiss-made Parabellums were delivered to the army in 1919. Production of the *Ordonnanzpistole*

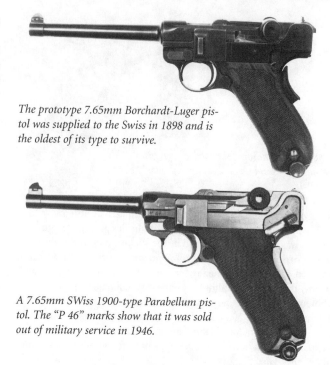

The prototype 7.65mm Borchardt-Luger pistol was supplied to the Swiss in 1898 and is the oldest of its type to survive.

A 7.65mm SWiss 1900-type Parabellum pistol. The "P 46" marks show that it was sold out of military service in 1946.

1906 W+F continued until 1928, by which time 12,385 had been made. Apart from its markings, it was identical to the original German-made pattern.

Pistole 06/29 W+F One benefit of Swiss manufacture was to reduce the price to the army from 400 to 225 Francs, but minor modifications continued to be made in an endeavor to lower costs still further, including the adoption of plastic grips and supplying two magazines per pistol instead of three. This produced the so-called "Pistole 1906/24" (1928-33), but the changes saved just ten francs. A more thorough overhaul of the design produced the *Ordonnanzpistole 06/29 W+F*, with a straight frontstrap to the grip, a vertically ridged trigger cover-plate, a flat safety-catch that moved upward to "safe", smooth toggle grips and a grip safety that was almost twice the normal size. After testing 20 pre-production examples (numbered V1–V21), the Swiss adopted the 06/29 Parabellum on November 30, 1929, and the first supplies were delivered in August 1933. A total of 27,931 guns had been made when

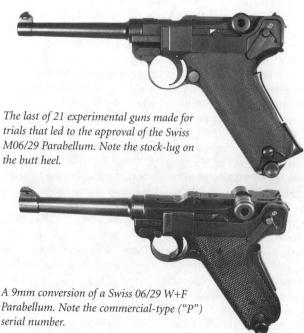

The last of 21 experimental guns made for trials that led to the approval of the Swiss M06/29 Parabellum. Note the stock-lug on the butt heel.

A 9mm conversion of a Swiss 06/29 W+F Parabellum. Note the commercial-type ("P") serial number.

military production ceased in 1946; there had also been sporadic production for the commercial market, but this totaled no more than about 2000 pistols. The last guns were assembled in the spring of 1947.

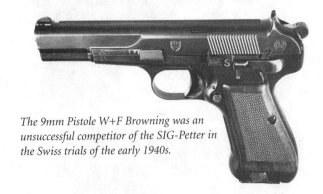

The 9mm Pistole W+F Browning was an unsuccessful competitor of the SIG-Petter in the Swiss trials of the early 1940s.

Pistole 43 W+F Browning The Swiss military authorities concluded just as World War II began that the Parabellum pistol was not only too expensive a manufacturing proposition but was also past its prime. Work began on a new pistol, based loosely on the FN-Browning GP35, and about a dozen variants were made under the general designation "W+F 43 Browning". The guns all used a cam to drop the barrel out of engagement with the slide, differences between individual guns being confined to magazine capacity, grip angle, triggers and safety systems.

The experimental Pistole W+F 47 superseded the M43 Browning, without success.

Pistole 47 W+F Trials showed the W+F 43 to be inferior to the SIG-Petter SP 44, and the Eidgenössische Waffenfabrik staff concentrated instead on the "W+F 47 Gaskolbensreaktion" design, which relied on gas diverted from the barrel into an expansion chamber in the slide to keep the breech closed until the bullet had left the barrel. Approximately 10 prototypes were made, but the SIG submission was ultimately victorious.

BERNADON-MARTIN

Établissments Bernadon-Martin et Cie, Saint-Étienne, France.
This small gunmaking business, active 1906-12, was a partnership of the financier Bernadon and designer Martin. Patents were obtained in 1905-7 to protect small details of bolt and trigger design, and manufacture of the "1907/8 Model" began late in 1906.
Bernadon-Martin The 7.65mm-caliber pistol was a simple generously-proportioned blowback with its fixed barrel fully exposed above the divided front arms of the slide. An unusual and distinctive spring catch in the front web of the trigger guard locked the slide open to facilitate cleaning. Late in 1908, a variant, the "1908/9 Model", added the grip safety that had also been a feature of the patents.

Martin obtained a new patent in 1910 to protect a method of attaching the barrel by a dovetail and a spring catch, but the sales had

been so poor that the new design was never introduced. In late 1912, in dire financial straits, the company went into liquidation.
Hermetic This was simply the 1907/8 model under another name, but it is not known whether it was used Bernadon-Martin or whether stock remaining after the collapse of the business had been sold to a new distributor. The latter course was more likely, as the stamping of the slide-mark "Hermetic Cal 7.65mm St Etienne" was aligned badly enough to suggest that it had been added some time after manufacture.

VINCENZO BERNARDELLI

Vincenzo Bernardelli SpA, Gardone Val Trompia, Italy.
This long-established gunmaking business began making gun barrels in 1865 and had soon moved to the manufacture of shotguns and sporting rifles. Bernardelli made 10.4mm M1889 (Bodeo) service revolvers in 1929-33, but did not seriously enter the handgun business until World War II had ended.

A typical long-barreled Bernardelli revolver, based on Smith & Wesson practice.

～ REVOLVERS ～

Bernardelli revolvers, made from the early 1950s until 1962, are generally based upon Smith & Wesson practice, with side-opening cylinders. Some later models dispense with the ejector rod lug beneath the barrel.
Martial Built on the same frame as the Pocket model, this had a 5-inch barrel and grips that extended about half an inch below the butt frame to provide a better hold. Individual examples will chamber 22 LR or 32 S&W Long cartridges.

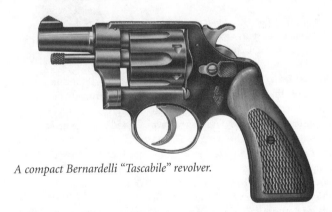

A compact Bernardelli "Tascabile" revolver.

New Pocket Model Also called the "VB Tascabile", this was the original Pocket Model altered by the omission of the ejector-rod lug beneath the 2.5-inch tapered barrel. It was available in 22 LR or 32 S&W Long.
Pocket (or VB Model) Introduced in 22 RF or 32 CF, this had a 2-inch barrel and an ejector-support lug beneath the muzzle.
Special (or VB MR) Announced as the "Special" and offering the same frame and butt as the Martial, this had a 7-inch barrel and fully adjustable target sights. Made only in 22 LR chambering, it was later renamed the VB MR (*mira regolabile*, "adjustable sights") and given a barrel rib.

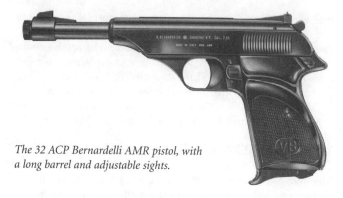

The 32 ACP Bernardelli AMR pistol, with a long barrel and adjustable sights.

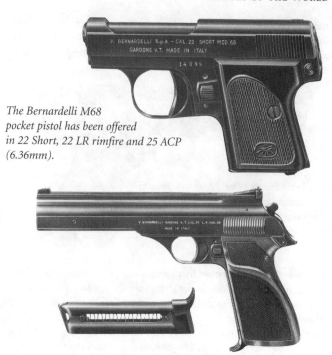

The Bernardelli M68 pocket pistol has been offered in 22 Short, 22 LR rimfire and 25 ACP (6.36mm).

∼ AUTOMATIC PISTOLS ∼

AMR A variant of the USA Model with a 5.9-inch barrel, carrying the front sight on a distinctive muzzle collar.

Baby Model This, the first Bernardelli rimfire pistol, appeared in 1949. It was no more than the VP with the alterations necessary to handle 22 Short or 22 LR cartridges. It was discontinued in 1968.

• *Baby Model 68* As the name suggests, this was simply the Baby with the 1968-vintage cosmetic improvements.

Elite Aimed largely at the Italian "Practical Pistol" market and chambered only for the 9x21 IMI cartridge, this was another adaptation of the P-018. The elongated barrel had a muzzle compensator and telescope-sight mounts on the slide above the barrel. The pawl of the frame and the hammer spur were extended, the trigger was fully adjustable and even the direction of ejection could be varied to suit individual preferences.

Another of the "beginner-class" target pistols dating from the 1960s and 1970s, the 22-caliber M69 was Bernardelli's entry in the field.

Model 69 Target This was identical to the standard gun except for higher standards of finish, wooden grips and the addition of a ramp that could accept optical sights.

Model 80 A name for an improved version of the "Model USA" distributed by Interarms, 1968-88.

P-1, P-One (officially known as "P-One") This is an improved form of the P-018, offered in 9mm Parabellum and 40 S&W. It has a conventional double-action trigger, a 4.75-inch barrel and a magazine holding 10 rounds. Finish may be black or chrome; grips are checkered plastic with integrally moulded Bernadelli trademarks. The P-One, which weighs about 34 oz, can be recognized by its flat-side slide with the retraction grips duplicated ahead of the ejection port.

• *P-One Compact* A shortened version of the standard gun, this has a 4-inch barrel and weighs 31 oz. A few guns have been made in 380 ACP, but most handle either 9mm Parabellum or 40 S&W ammunition.

Bernardelli's P010 is a modern slab-side target pistol with the sights on a non-reciprocating rib extending back above the slide.

Model 010 Introduced in 1989 to replace the 69 TS, this target pistol shared the full-length sight rib and general construction of its predecessor but has an improved trigger, retraction grips that run diagonally (instead of vertically) and an improved "saddle" or U-shape counterweight beneath the muzzle. Chamberings are restricted to 22 LR rimfire. Finished in matte black with stippled walnut grips, the M010 weighs about 40 oz.

Model 60 Offered in 22 LR rimfire, 7.65mm Auto and 9mm Short, this updated Pocket Model was introduced in Europe in 1959. It displayed a streamlined slide and a modified frame that gave a better angle to the grip. Unusually, twin return springs were used to soften the opening stroke of the slide.

Model 68 A replacement for the VP Model with a variety of cosmetic changes, this had a rounded slide and a better-angled grip. A loaded-chamber indicator pin protruded from the rear of the slide, and an extended magazine with an auxiliary grip was also available. Production ceased in 1970.

Model 69 Tiro Standard ("TS 69") Adapted from the Model 60, this was designed to meet the ISU regulations for competition shooting. The barrel and slide were extended, the latter acting as a muzzle counterweight, and micro-adjustable sights were fitted.

• *P-One Practical* Introduced in 1994, this is intended for "Practical Pistol" competition shooting. The safety and magazine-release catches could be fitted on either side, micro-adjustable sights were available, and 9x21 IMI and 40 S&W chamberings were available in addition to the more familiar 9mm Parabellum. Magazine capacities were customarily 16 rounds in 9mm and 10 rounds in 40 S&W.

P-018 Bernardelli's first locked-breech design was announced in 1982, though full production was not reached until 1985. The appearance was somewhat angular but compact, the familiar Browning cam was used to disengage barrel lugs from the slide, and the lock was double-

A Bernardelli P-018-9, chambered for the 9mm Parabellum round, had a nine-round single-column magazine.

action. The P-018 had the usual type of firing-pin lock, released only during the final movement of the trigger. It also had a 15-round double-row magazine. The standard chambering was always 9mm Parabellum, but guns have been made in small quantities in 7.65mm Parabellum and 9mm Largo.

• *P-018-9* Also called "P-018 Compact", this was smaller in all dimensions and had a 14-round magazine.

P-060A Introduced in the mid-1980s, this double-action blowback pistol (an updated and re-christened Model 60) was equipped with a hammer-drop safety and chambered for the 22 LR, 7.65mm Auto or 9mm Short cartridges.

Pocket Model Dating from 1947, this 7.65mm blowback was an enlargement of the VP, retaining the dismantling system. However, the barrel was screwed into a lump formed in the frame to allow differing barrel-length options, and the design was soon refined so that a 9mm Short version could be marketed. The standard barrel was 3.35 inches long, but lengths up to 9.85 inches were available. The longest barrels had front sights fitted to collars that slipped over the muzzle and were locked in place by a screw, allowing the sight to be removed when the slide needed to be slipped over the barrel during the dismantling process.

Practical VB (sometimes known as "Practical VB Custom" in the USA) A modified form of the P-018, this is intended for IPSC practical pistol competition shooting. Though retaining the distinctively contoured frame of the P-018, it has a 5.4-inch barrel and an exchangeable two- or four-port compensator at the muzzle. The retraction grips are duplicated on the front of the slide, the rear of the frame is extended above the thumb-web in a graceful curve (a "full beavertail") and the controls have been enlarged. The magazine-release catch behind the trigger can be reversed for left-handed shooters. The grips are normally black plastic with Bernardelli trademarks, but walnut can be obtained to order. The finish is blue or matte chrome, though the forged-steel slide and frame can be matched to give contrasting frame/slide finished. The Practical VB is 11.1 inches long (4-port compensator), weighs about 39 oz and has full-length rails supporting the slide. The magazine mouth is chamfered or "flared", the trigger system is restricted to single action and a micro-adjustable rear sight is provided. The chamberings are usually either 9mm Parabellum (16-round magazine) or 40 S&W (12 rounds), but 9x21 IMI can also be obtained.

• *Practical VB Target* This is identical with the preceding gun but has a fixed two-port compensator.

Standard Model Also dating from 1949, this was the Pocket Model adapted for 22 LR ammunition. The normal barrel was 3.55 inches long, but others up to 9.9 inches were available to order. The detachable collar-mounted front sight was retained.

Super Match Introduced concurrently with the P-One, this has only been made in small numbers. It is essentially a Practical VB, and thus a modified P-018, conforming to the requirements of ISU "Sport Pistol" competition. It was made in single-action-only form with micrometer sights and a fully adjustable trigger. Particular attention was paid to the finishing and fitting of the barrel.

UB Model (or "New Pocket Model") This was an enlargement of the Pocket Model, chambering 9mm Browning Long or even 9mm Parabellum cartridges, and was developed in both hammer and striker-fired versions. Few of these guns seem to have been made, which is probably a valid commentary on the undesirability of a compact blowback system handling ammunition of such power.

USA Model Designed to satisfy the requirements of the US 1968 Gun Control Act, this was a modification of the Model 60 with a Walther-style slide-mounted safety catch — which locked the firing pin — in addition to the standard frame-mounted and magazine safeties of the Model 60. Chamberings were restricted to 22 LR rimfire, 32 ACP and 380 ACP.

The 32 ACP (7.65mm Auto) Bernardelli "Model USA".

VP Model Introduced late in 1945, this was a small 6.35mm blowback similar to the Walther Model 9. The barrel was forged integrally with the frame, and the slide was retained by a dumbbell-shaped locking piece that formed part of the frame. Releasing a small spring catch allowed the locking piece to be forced out by the firing-pin spring, and the slide could then be removed. The standard five-round magazine gave a small grip and a poor hold, and so an extended eight-round magazine (with the extension sheathed in plastic) was offered as an optional extra. Production continued until 1970.

VINCENZO BERNEDO & CO.

Vincenzo Bernedo y Cia, Eibar, Spain.

Little is known of this firm other than that it entered the pistol business during World War I and lasted until the end of the 1920s. The first Bernedo handgun was the usual Eibar pattern in 7.65mm, but after the war came a pistol of their own design.

Bernedo (or "B.C.") This was a 6.35mm automatic with a short slide/breech-block that ran half the length of the frame behind a completely exposed fixed barrel. Held in the frame by a transverse pin held by a spring catch, the barrel could easily be removed for cleaning without the aid of tools. The slide was marked "Pistolet Automatique Bernedo Patent No 69952", and a circular motif with "V Bernedo Co" embossed around it appeared on the grips. The pistol did not sell in large numbers and specimens are rarely seen today.

BERSA

Fábrica de Armas Bersa SA, Ramos Mejia, Buenos Aires, Argentina.

This gunmaking business is not widely known outside Argentina, although it has successfully marketed its pistols throughout the Americas for many years. There they have attained a reputation for good quality and sensible prices. Many of the Bersa pistols have borne a vague resemblance to the Beretta and Bernardelli designs of the 1960/70s. Bersa's influence waned in the 1990s, perhaps in the face of competition in South America from Taurus and (to a lesser extent) Rossi. By 2003, only the "Thunder 380" and "Thunder Deluxe" were still being offered in the USA.

Model 23 Offered from 1988 only in 22 LR rimfire, with a 3.3-inch barrel and a 10-round magazine, this was an updated version of the Model 223 with minor changes in the action and styling. The front of the trigger guard was fashionably squared (the so-called "combat guard") and the safety catch was mounted, Walther fashion, on the left side of the slide ahead of the hammer. Finish was blue or satin nickel, and the grips were usually walnut. The *Model 24, Model 25* and *Model 26* were similar, differing only in the length of the barrel: 4, 5 and 6 inches, respectively.

Model 83 Introduced in 1988 and chambered only for the 380 ACP cartridge, this was an improved version of the Model 383 with neater contours and simplified controls. Only the head of the magazine-release catch protruded from the side of the frame. The magazine was a single-row pattern holding seven rounds.

A 380 ACP Bersa M85 DA. The position of the trigger indicates that this has a double-action trigger system.

The Bersa Piccola pistol, in 22 Short rimfire.

Model 85 This was similar to the Model 83, but had a 13-round double-column magazine.

Model 86 Derived from the Model 85, and thus ultimately from the Model 83, this offered matte-blue or satin-nickel finish, wraparound rubber grips and three-dot sights. It retained the two-row large-capacity magazine.

Model 97 Another variant of the Model 644, this personal-defense pistol was enlarged to handle the 9mm Short cartridge.

Model 223 Confined to 1984-8, this 22 LR blowback pistol marked the adoption of double-action lockwork. Presenting a more modern appearance than its predecessors, it also had an 11-round magazine and black polymer grips. The Model 223 had a 3-inch barrel, but the same basic gun was offered with 4-, 5- or 6-inch barrels as the *Model 224*, *Model 225* and *Model 226*, respectively. The M225 was discontinued in 1986, the M226 in 1988, and the others in 1990. They were replaced by the Models 23-26 (above).

Model 323 Chambered for the 32 ACP cartridge, with a slide mounted safety catch and fixed sights, this was a large-caliber version of the Model 223. A 3.3-inch barrel and a seven-round single-column magazine were standard. The grips were usually checkered black plastic.

Model 383 Introduced in 1984, this 380 ACP personal-defense pistol was little more than a modernized version of the 9mm Short Model 97, with double-action lockwork and a seven-round magazine. About 6.6 inches long with a 3.3-inch barrel and weighing about 24 oz, it was abandoned in favor of the Model 83 in 1988.

• *Model 383A* A deluxe version of the basic design, this had a high-polish blue or nickel-plated finish and walnut grips.

Model 622 This was generally similar to the 644, except for an extended barrel that carried the front sight. It was intended as an inexpensive target pistol.

Model 644 A single-action blowback pocket automatic in 22 LR with an external hammer, this might be called the bedrock of the Bersa line. Its affinity with the early Bernardelli pistols may be no more than coincidental.

The Bersa M644, in 22 rimfire.

Picolla This was simply a smaller 644, chambered for the 22 Short cartridge.

Series 95 Dating from 1992, this was a 380 ACP double-action blowback with firing-pin and magazine safety systems, fixed sights, an exposed hammer and a fashionably recurved trigger guard. It had a 3.5-inch barrel and a seven-round magazine. Finish was matte blue or satin nickel. The Thunder 380 (below) was essentially the same gun under another name.

Thunder 9 The first of these locked-breech "combat pistols" was introduced in 1993. Though conventionally shaped, the pistol had a style of its own; it could not be labeled merely as a copy of something else and showed evidence of original thought in its design. The safety, magazine-release catch and the slide stop were ambidextrous, and an automatic firing-pin safety system was included in the lockwork. Chambered for the 9mm Parabellum cartridge, the Thunder 9 was a serious contender in the South American marketplace. The earliest guns had a 15-round staggered-column magazine, but a single-row 10-round version was introduced to comply with the US Gun Control Act of 1994.

Thunder 22 Introduced in 1995, this was simply a redesigned 22 rimfire Model 23 with the trigger guard shaped for a two-hand grip and the controls made slightly more robust. It bore no resemblance to the Thunder 9.

Thunder 380 (also known as "Thunder 380 Lite") Contemporaneous with the Thunder 22, this combined the "20 series" style with the revised "two-hand grip" trigger guard and modified controls. It chambered the 380 ACP (9mm Short) cartridge.

• *Thunder 380 Plus* A 1996 introduction, this had a nine-round magazine instead of the customary seven-round type.

• *Thunder 380 Deluxe* ("Thunder 380 DLX") A post-2001 name for the Thunder 380 Plus.

BERASALUZE, ARIETO-AURTENA & CO.

Fábrica de Armas de Berasaluze Arieto-Aurtena y Cia, Eibar, Spain (sometimes listed as "Bersaluze", "Bersaluce").

Allies This 7.65mm Eibar-type pistol, made in the early 1920s, appears to have originated as a result of one of the many wartime French contracts. Some reports list it "Model 1916", though such a marking could easily be a spurious attempt to suggest a long-established production run. The usual marking was "MODEL AUTOMATIC PISTOL CAL 7.65 ALLIES EIBAR 1924" with ALLIES and a crowned "BA" monogram molded into the grips. Some guns, however, had "CA de BERASALUZE ARIETO AURTENA y CIA Cal 7.65 ALLIES" and plain grips.

A 6.35mm "MODEL 1924", smaller but otherwise identical to the 7.65mm version, was made in small numbers. Then came two "vest pocket" models, in 6.35mm and 7.65mm calibers, which are somewhat smaller than comparable Model 1924 versions and may lack the company name on the slide. They will, however, have "ALLIES" and the crowned "BA" monogram molded into the grips. Work seems to have ceased prior to 1930.

JULES BERTRAND

Manufacture Générale d'Armes et Munitions
Jules Bertrand, Liége, Belgium.

Despite the grandiose title of his business, Bertrand was just one of many small manufacturers operating in Liége prior to 1914, turning out cheap revolvers in the 1890s and graduating to equally cheap automatic pistols at the turn of the century. The German occupation then brought trading to an end. Bertrand also distributed guns made elsewhere, including "Le Novo" (made by Derkenne) and "Lincoln" (probably the work of Manufacture Liégeoise d'Armes à Feu). Those handled by Bertrand often bore a "JB" monogram on the grips.

∼ REVOLVER ∼

Lincoln A popular name among Liége gunmakers, this was applied to a wide variety of revolvers produced from 1880 to 1914. Most were of the folding-trigger pocket variety, including hammer and "hammerless" types, in chamberings ranging from 22 RF and 5.5mm Velo-Dog to 380 CF. Among the gunmakers using "Lincoln" were Ancion Marx, Debouxtay, Dumoulin, Jannsen Fils et Cie, Le Page, Neumann Frères and Raick Frères, all of Liége, and Albrecht Kind of Germany. However, many of these were distributors, and it is likely that most (or, indeed all) of the guns were made by Manufacture Liégeoise d'Armes à Feu.

∼ AUTOMATIC PISTOLS ∼

Continental This 6.35mm blowback was Bertrand's principal design, differing slightly from his earlier "Le Rapide" due to small changes in the trigger mechanism. The barrel was forged with the frame, and a separate breech-block was controlled by a return spring in a tunnel above the barrel. The pistol was marked "Continental" on the slide, but the grips were those of the "Le Rapide", and thus the new pistol may simply have been the old pattern with a few minor changes. (The name "Continental" was also used by many other makers.)

Le Rapide This was the original 6.35mm Bertrand pistol. The slide was marked "Manre. Grl d'Armes et Munitions Cal Browning 6,35 Le Rapide", and the grips displayed a "JB" monogram with "Le Rapide".

BIG HORN ARMS CO.

Watertown, South Dakota, USA.

This company produced a futuristic-style 22-caliber single-shot pistol in the 1960s. The mechanism was simple: a hand-actuated sliding bolt was set in a tubular receiver, and the receiver/barrel unit was in turn set in an ornate plastic stock with a decorated fore-end and an anatomical-style palm-rest grip. A rib on the barrel carried the fixed sights.

GUSTAV BITTNER

Gebrüder Bittner, Weipert, Bohemia, Austria-Hungary.

Bittner's family had been gun makers since the early 17th century. By the 1880s, he was associated with his brother Raimund and Wenzel Fuckert, another gunsmith, as "Gebrüder Bittner". The business was renowned for its sporting guns but also repaired military arms for the Austrian army and Landwehr (reserve forces).

Bittner began work on a mechanical repeating pistol about 1880 and, after producing many prototypes, began series production of the "Model 1893". Most survivors display proofmarks dated 1897 or later, which suggests that Bittner's pistol reached the market contemporaneously with semi-automatics such as the Borchardt, the Mauser C/96 and the first Bergmanns.

Like many others of this class, the Bittner was locked by a rotating bolt that was operated by a ring-type actuator. The rear surface of this actuator was slotted to admit the trigger blade. The forefinger was inserted into the ring and pushed forward, opening the bolt, cocking the striker (inside the bolt) and allowing a cartridge to rise from a five-shot magazine in the front of the frame. Pulling the actuator-ring backward closed and locked the bolt; additional backward movement then allowed the shooter's finger to press the trigger, which had protruded

from the slot in the back of the ring. The trigger then activated the sear to release the striker.

The magazine was loaded by a clip and used a spring-loaded follower arm to force the cartridges up to the bolt-way. The hexagonal barrel was 5.4 inches long and was chambered for the 7.7mm Bittner cartridge, a rimmed round using an 85-grain bullet.

The Bittner was as good as any of its type, but arrived on the market at the same time as the first true semi-automatic pistols and failed to prosper. Nevertheless, it seems to have been made in quantity — perhaps as many as 1000 before work stopped about 1900 — and it is the most common mechanical repeater to be found today.

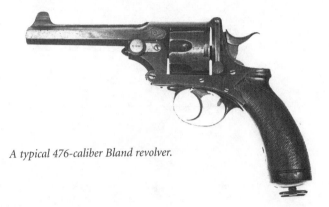

A typical 476-caliber Bland revolver.

BLAND

Thomas Bland & Sons, Birmingham and London, England.

This gunmaker commenced operations in 1862 and was mainly concerned with sporting guns. After a few years, he began selling large-caliber military-style revolvers, though the actual maker of these guns remains in doubt. In 1887, in conjunction with Frank Cashmore, another Birmingham gun maker, Bland patented a four-barreled drop-down pistol similar to that of Lancaster (q.v.). A rotating firing pin struck by a self-cocking hammer fired the four barrels in succession. These pistols were made in 455 caliber, with the military market in mind, but competition from the double-action revolvers of the day makes it unlikely that many were sold.

BLISS & GOODYEAR

America Manufactured in 1878 by a short-lived partnership, this was a simple solid-frame sheathed-trigger seven-shot revolver in 22 RF. Little is known of the makers, but William H. Bliss was the superintendent of the Norwich Falls Pistol Company (q.v.) in the same era. Bliss & Goodyear may have been a sideshow, producing designs in which the Norwich owners showed no interest.

American Boy This revolver was very similar to the gun described previously but in 32 Short RF; it was made in 1878/79 for sale by the Townley Hardware Company.

JOHN BLISSETT & SONS

London, England.

Excelsior This was a 380-caliber revolver, modeled on the Rast & Gasser (q.v.), sold in Britain in 1867-75. The maker cannot be identified but was probably Belgian.

BODEO

The "Pistola a Rotazione, Systema Bodeo, Modello 1889" became the Italian service revolver in 1891 and remained the principal handgun until supplanted by the Glisenti automatic (issued largely as a weapon to officers and senior NCOs) in 1910. However, the revolver continued to serve rank-and-file, police and colonial units until the end of World War II.

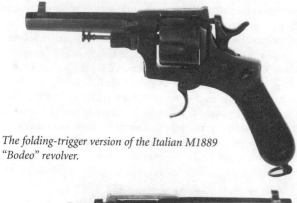

The folding-trigger version of the Italian M1889 "Bodeo" revolver.

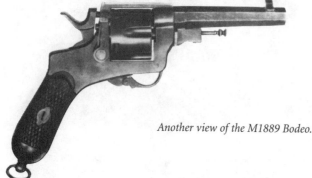

Another view of the M1889 Bodeo.

Made by a variety of gunmaking businesses in Italy, it was a solid-frame six-shot double-action revolver in 10.4mm caliber, loaded through a gate — on the right rear of the frame behind the cylinder — connected to the hammer on the Abadie system. An ejector rod was provided beneath the barrel. There were few original features in the design, and the name of Bodeo was attached merely because he had headed the development commission. The only unusual mechanical feature (at least for the 1890s) was the hammer block, which prevented the hammer from falling far enough to fire the cartridge unless the trigger was pulled fully back.

One type of M1889, for rank-and-file, had an octagonal barrel and a folding trigger without a guard; the other, for officers and NCOs, had a cylindrical barrel and a conventionally guarded trigger. Consequently, though a few of the "trigger guard" guns were sold commercially, the folding-trigger pattern was more common prior to 1914. Production continued until about 1931.

Among the manufacturers identified with the M1889 were Castelli of Brescia, Fabbrica d'Armi of Brescia, Metallurgica Bresciana gia Tempini of Brescia, Società Siderurgica Glisenti of Turin, Real Fabbrica d'Armi of Brescia and Vincenzo Bernardelli of Gardone. Errasti and Arrostegui of Eibar are both known to have made guns on contract to the Italian government during World War I, and it is possible that there were other Spanish participants — Francisco Arizmendi, for example.

GREGORIO BOLUMBURU

Eibar, Spain.

Bolumburu was an industrious producer of automatic pistols under several names who, like many others, made his start by pirating the 1906-type Browning. He remained in business until the Spanish Civil War began in 1936.

Bufalo (1919-25) This was made for a distributor, Armeria Beristain y Cia of Barcelona, and has a "BC" monogram molded into the grips. Beristain had patented a grip safety, a chamber-loaded indicator and various other features for automatic pistols, but only the grip safety was used in the Bufalo design. The agreement appears to have lapsed because of the expiry of Beristain's patent; thereafter, the pistols continued to be made but under different names.

- **6.35mm type** This was a copy of the 1906 FN-Browning, and was marked "AUTOMATICA ESPAÑOLA PAT'D 62004 Y 67577" over "… "BUFALO" CAL 6,35" on the left side of the slide. The grips bore a "GB" monogram and an encircled buffalo-head motif.
- **7.65mm and 9mm Short type** The larger models, in 7.65mm and 9mm Short, were copies of the Browning 1910, with concentric recoil spring but using an internal hammer instead of a striker. The Beristain grip safety also differed internally from the Browning type. The marking was apparently similar to that of the 6.35mm gun, excepting changes in the caliber notation.

Bristol This was a conventional Eibar-style blowback automatic in 7.65mm caliber, identifiable by the name on the slide.

A typical 7.65mm (32ACP) Giralda pistol, made by Gregorio Bolumburu.

Giralda Another routine 7.65mm "Eibar", except that the safety catch lay at the rear of the frame (instead of midway), this gun was marked "7.65 1915 Model Automatic Pistol Giralda Patent". The grips carried a trademark of a charging bull.

Gloria The "Gloria Model of 1913" was one of Bolumburu's first products, a 6.35mm blowback copied from the Browning 1906. It was followed by a 7.65mm pistol based on the FN-Browning of 1903 that was probably the result of French Army contracts. The inscription on the slide read "7.65mm 1915 Model Automatic Pistol Gloria Patent".

Marina A 6.35mm Eibar-type gun of no particular merit, this was identified by "Pistolet Automatique Marina Brevete SGDG (Cal 6,35)" on the slide and a fouled anchor above "Marina" on the grips.

Regent Except for the name on the slide and the rear of the frame being slightly more rounded, there was no significant difference between this and the Marina.

Regina This modified Regent was made in two versions. The 6.35mm guns had their slide-tops relieved at both sides similarly to the Campeon (q.v.) and were of the worst quality. The slide was marked "American Automatic Pistol Regina" beneath a crown with "GB" stamped somewhere on the slide or frame. The 7.65mm Regina offered better quality, omitted "American" from the inscription and carried a floral design across the grip instead of the name. The grip was elongated to hold a nine-round magazine.

Rex Top of the Bolumburu line, this was a well-finished copy of the 1910-pattern FN-Browning in 6.35mm Auto, 7.65mm Auto and 9mm Short chamberings. It shared the design of the return spring with the Browning — concentric with the barrel, retained by a knurled collar — but the sides of the slide-top were relieved over the breech area similarly to the Regina. The slide was marked "Manufacture d'Armes a Feu "Rex" Patent", but the grips carried the "GB" monogram and the letters "GB" were stamped on the frame. (Note: The Regina has been identified elsewhere as Belgian, but no record of the "Rex" firm has been found. The name is most likely to have been simply to impress the export market.)

BOND ARMS, INC.

Grandbury, Texas, USA.

Promoters of the *Texas Defender* (introduced in 1997) and *Century 2000 Defender* (1999), two-shot Remington-type derringers in chamberings ranging from 357 Magnum to 45 Long Colt. The interchangeable stainless steel barrel-blocks are usually 3 inches long, the grips are usually ash or rosewood (including laminates) and the sheath-type trigger has a guard of a type rarely found on derringers of this type.

JAMES BOWN & SON

Enterprise Gun Works, Pittsburgh, Pennsylvania, USA.
This company made a single-shot rimfire derringer called the *Eclipse*. It then marketed a line of cheap *Enterprise* revolvers in 1870-80, though these may have been made elsewhere. The revolvers were all solid-frame designs with stud triggers, bird's-head butts and loading gates on the right side of their frames. Ejection relied on each case being punched backward through the gate with a suitable tool (no ejector rod being fitted) or, alternatively, simply removing the cylinder. Guns were made in 22, 32, 38 and 41 RF chamberings, all but the seven-shot 22-caliber version offering five shots.

BRAENDLIN ARMOURY

The Braendlin Armoury Co. Ltd, Birmingham and London, England.
Formed in 1871, this company manufactured a "Mitrailleuse Pistol" at the end of the 19th century. London gunmaker Joseph Marres may have had a financial stake in the pistol and may even have been employed by the Braendlin Armoury from 1884 until the business was liquidated in 1888. Rights to the Braendlin name were acquired by Charles Greener, and a four-barreled Mitrailleuse pistol — apparently based on a patent granted in 1885 to Francotte of Liége — was offered in the 1890s. This gun was clearly as unsuccessful as its predecessor, as none could be traced for examination. The reconstituted Braendlin Armoury closed its doors for the last time in 1915.

Martini-Marres-Braendlin This 450-caliber multi-barreled repeating pistol was patented in 1880 by Alexander Martini, son of the better-known engineer renowned for the dropping-block rifle of the same name. The gun had eight barrels arranged in a monoblock in a double vertical row, the block being hinged to the frame to drop downward for loading. The trigger controlled a vertical rod carrying the cams that cocked and released the firing pins of the barrels sequentially as the trigger was pulled. The cartridges were mounted in a perforated metal plate (similar to the loading plate of the original French *Mitrailleuse*), allowing the barrels to be loaded simultaneously with one stroke. However, the handgun was never popular, and survivors are exceptionally rare.

BRESCIA ARMS FACTORY

Fabbrica Nationale d'Armi Brescia ("FNAB").
Giuilio Sosso of Turin patented a series of remarkable automatic pistols in 1934-7, and a very small number were manufactured in Brescia between 1935 and 1941.

Sosso The pistol was a delayed blowback, relying on the recoil of barrel to drive a rack-and-pinion mechanism that accelerated the slide away from the breech. However, the endless-chain magazine was the most remarkable feature of the design. Propelled by the recoiling slide, it moved around sprockets in the butt to replenish the chamber.

Three models were apparently made: *Model 1* had a 21-round magazine, *Model 2* a 20-round magazine and the *Sosso-FNA* also a 20-round magazine. It is believed that the Models 1 and 2 were prototypes and thus that the *Sosso-FNA* was intended as the production version. All were chambered for the 9mm Glisenti cartridge.

BRILEY

Briley Manufacturing, Inc., Houston, Texas, USA.
This gunmaking business makes a variety of 1911-type Colt-Browning pistols, amalgamating frames purchased from elsewhere with a variety of extra features.

Carry Comp Model ("Defense") Distinguished by a 5-inch barrel and a dual-port compensator, this is available only in 45 ACP.

El Presidente Available in "Unlimited" form and built to any appropriate chambering the purchaser requests, this offers rails for optical-sight mounts, an extended beavertail grip safety, a multi-port compensator, a chamfered ejection port, a squared trigger guard and many other features commonly associated with the guns intended for practical pistol shooting.

Lightning Model ("Action Pistol") Built on a standard 1911-type frame, this is offered only in 9mm Parabellum and 38 Super. A titanium compensator is attached to the muzzle.

Versatility Model This is the simplest of the series, available in 9mm Parabellum, 40 S&W and 45 ACP, with an adjustable Bo-Mar rear sight and features such as an enlarged ejection port and a refined trigger mechanism.

- *Versatility Plus* Similar to the standard version, this has extensively checkered grip straps and a square-front "combat" trigger guard.

BRITARMS

This business promoted a target pistol of a type that has become popular in recent years: a slab-sided blowback semi-automatic with a steeply raked anatomical grip that places the barrel low in the hand to counteract recoil-climb. The bolt-retracting grips lay ahead of the ejection port, and a hold-open catch was set into the top of the left grip. The integral magazine was loaded through the open action.

The first Britarms pistols appeared in the 1970s, and the perfected 22 LR rimfire *Mark III* and 32 CF *Model 3000* were soon achieving success in international shooting competitions. Unfortunately, teething troubles undermined progress and the ability to compete effectively against better-funded and better-backed projects. The project passed through the hands of several manufacturers, including the Berdan Group and Westlake Engineering, before being ended by draconian (if ineffectual) legislation banning the use of handguns in Britain.

BROLIN ARMS

La Verne and Pomona, California, USA.
Operating from 1995 to 1999, Brolin began making pistols derived from the 1911-type Colt-Browning in 1996.

Legend Series Also known as "L45", these came in a variety of patterns but only in a single chambering — 45 ACP. However, common features included fixed sights, enlarged ejection ports, chamfered magazine well and a throated match barrel with a hand-honed feed ramp. Skeleton triggers, matte-blue finish and wooden grips were standard.

- *L45* (or "L45 Standard") This had a 5-inch barrel and a seven-round single-column magazine; it weighed 36 oz..
- *L45 Compact* Identical mechanically with the standard gun, this had a 4.5-inch barrel and a short grip that reduced magazine capacity by one round.
- *L45T* Introduced in 1997, this was a hybrid that paired the compact slide and barrel with a full-depth frame. Consequently, the magazine capacity was restored to seven rounds.

Patriot Series These were essentially deluxe versions of the Legend-series guns with compensators built into the slides, extended beavertail grip-safety levers, and adjustable triggers. The finish was usually matte blue on the flat-top slides and satin-nickel on the frames, but all-blue and all-nickel guns were also made.

- *P45 Comp* ("Standard Carry Comp") Dating from 1996, this was the same length as the L45, though the barrel was reduced to 4 inches to accept the compensator.
- *P45C Comp* ("Compact Carry Comp") Identical with the P45 Comp, except barrel length was 3.25 inches.
- *P45T* This was a 1997-vintage hybrid with the short "Compact" barrel/slide assembly on a shortened full-grip frame.

Pro-Series This contained the competition-shooting pistols, with full-length recoil spring guides, extended "beavertail" grip-safety levers, ambidextrous controls and adjustable rear sights.

- *Pro-Stock* The standard gun with a 5-inch barrel and matte-blue or two-tone finish. The checkered walnut grips usually displayed the Brolin dragon logo on a large plain diamond-shaped panel.
- *Pro-Comp* Though the same length as the Pro-Stock pattern, this had a 4-inch barrel to allow a compensator to be formed integrally with the slide at the muzzle.

Tactical Series Introduced in 1997, this included a single-action gun and a range of double-action guns derived from the Colt-Browning.

- *M40* This was a variant of the M45 chambered for the 40 S&W cartridge. The magazine held 10 rounds.
- *MB40* A "super compact" version of the M40, in 40 S&W chambering, this had a short barrel and a short butt, restricting magazine capacity to six rounds. The hammer was flush with the rear of the slide.
- *MC40* A compact version of the M40, chambering the 40 S&W round. Magazine capacity remained 10 rounds.
- *M45* The standard double-action gun, with a 5-inch barrel, this had three-dot sights. The standard finish was matte blue, but a high-polish blue could be obtained on request.
- *MS45* A variant of the M45, this had a 6-inch barrel.
- *M90* A version of the M45 chambered for the 9mm Parabellum cartridge. The 10-round magazine remained standard in the USA.
- *MB90* A "super compact" version of the M90 with a six-round magazine.
- *MC90* A compact version of the M90, chambering the 9mm Parabellum cartridge and retaining the same 10-round magazine.
- *TAC-11* This was little more than a standard L45 Legend (q.v.) with a special coned match barrel, Novak low-profile sights and black rubber grips. Three-dot and Tritium night sights were optional extras. Chambered for the 45 ACP round, the TAC-11 was supplied with an eight-round magazine.

BROOKLYN ARMS CO.

Also known as the "Brooklyn Fire Arms Co.", Brooklyn, New York, USA.
This gunmaking business was responsible for about 10,000 32 RF sheath-trigger revolvers made in 1863-4 in accordance with patents granted to Frank Slocum. The guns had brass frames, 3-inch round barrels and a cylinder containing five individual sliding tubes with ribbed thumb-pieces. This was seen as a way of evading the Rollin White patent controlled by Smith & Wesson but was an unsatisfactory answer to the basic problem. Most of the guns had fluted cylinders, though a few hundred were made with plain-surface cylinders in 22 and 32 RF. The frame was often silver-plated, disguising its brass construction, and displayed light scroll engraving. The barrel and cylinder were blued or plated steel. A "B.A. CO." mark appeared on the barrel, accompanied by the April 14, 1863, patent date.

E. ARTHUR BROWN CO., INC.

Akron, Ohio, USA.
Also known as "E.A. Brown Mfg. Co.", this gunmaking business introduced the *BF* single-shot falling-block pistol in 1988. A 15-inch barrel is regarded as standard, though other lengths may be obtained to order. Chamberings, however, can be virtually anything from 17 Ackley to 45-70 Government. Derivatives such as the *BF Ultimate Silhouette* (also dating from 1988) and the *Classic BF Hunting Pistol* (2001) have also been offered.

ED BROWN

Ed Brown Products Inc, Perry, Missouri, USA.
Best known for "semi-custom" rifles, Brown has also made variations of the M1911A1 Colt-Browning.

Class A Limited Made only to individual order with a 4.25-inch "Commander"-length barrel, this may chamber cartridges ranging from 9mm Parabellum to 45 ACP. It has a skeletonized hammer and trigger, an extended "beavertail" grip safety and fixed sights.

Classic Custom Supplied only in 45 ACP, this has a Videki trigger, an enlarged manual safety-lever head and an adjustable Bo-Mar rear sight. The barrel measures 5 inches.

Commander Bobtail Fitted with a 4.25-inch barrel, this has exotic Hogue hardwood grips and a variety of special features. Chamberings include 9mm Parabellum, 9x23, 38 Super, 400 Cor-Bon, 40 S&W and 45 ACP.

BROWN MFG CO.

Newburyport, Massachusetts, USA.
This gunmaking business made the *Southerner*, a 41 RF single-shot swing-barrel sheath-trigger derringer, succeeding the Merrimack Arms & Mfg Co. (q.v.). Production was confined to 1869-73.

BROWNING ARMS COMPANY

Morgan, Utah, USA.
This was the descendant of the original Browning gunmaking business formed in 1880 as "J.M. Browning & Bro." to make single-shot dropping-block rifles. It originally had no link with Fabrique Nationale, excepting the distribution of FN products in the USA. These have included the GP-35/High-Power and BDA-380, marked with the appropriate trademark and name, but also a short-lived "BDA" (imported in 1977-80 only) that was little more than a SIG-Sauer P220!

Among the Belgian-made guns being sold in 1997 were the BDA/BDAO; the BDM; the BDA-380; and the "Hi-Power" in 9mm and 40 S&W, the latter dating from 1993. The 1991-vintage "Hi-Power Practical" was also being offered. By 2003, however, this range had contracted to the standard and Mk 3 Hi-Power and the Hi-Power Practical.

Browning has also distributed 22 RF blowback target/sport pistols of the type made in Belgium from 1962 until 1974 (see "Fabrique Nationale d'Armes de Guerre") but eventually graduated to making guns in the USA, beginning with the Challenger II of 1976. The importation of Japanese Miroku shotguns conflicted with FN-made Browning rivals, and so FN Herstal SA and Miroku together acquired a majority holding in the Browning Arms Company in 1977.

Buck Mark series These 22 LR rimfire target/sport pistols were derived from the FN designs, which were the work of Bruce Browning. They all had a fixed barrel/frame group with a separate half-length slide at the rear — similar to the Colt Woodsman, or many High Standard designs. The first of a series of carbines appeared in 2001. These are little more than a pistol action with 18-inch barrels, walnut butts attached to the existing frame (the pistol grip is retained) and short walnut fore-ends.

- *Buck Mark Standard* (or "Buck Mark 22", 1985 to date) Combining a steel breech-block/slide assembly, a steel barrel and a frame milled from an aluminum billet, this gun has a 5.5-inch heavy barrel (with distinctively flattened sides) and retraction grooves that were confined to a small panel on the half-slide beneath the adjustable rear sight. The finish was usually blue-black, while the synthetic grips originally had skip-line checkering and small circular deer's-head (the "buck mark") medallions. Overall length was 9.5 inches; weight with an empty magazine being about 34 oz. A manual safety catch protrudes above the grip on the left side of the frame, and a cross-bolt-type magazine-release catch runs through the frame behind the trigger aperture. The current guns have Pro-Target rear sights, matte finish and checkered thumbrest-style composite grips. The 10-round magazines rely on coil springs to improve feed.
- *Buck Mark Bullseye* (1996 to date) Destined for metallic-silhouette competition shooting, its features include an adjustable rear sight

mounted on a half-length top-rib and a 7.25-inch cylindrical barrel with three flutes on each side. The trigger can be adjusted and the barrel is exchangeable. Finish is usually blue, and the standard grips (laminated wood or composite) can be replaced with target-style walnut or rosewood if desired. The guns are about 11.3 inches long and weigh 36 oz without their magazines.

- *Buck Mark Camper* (1999 to date) This is essentially a "Buck Mark Challenge" (q.v.) with a cylindrical 5.5-inch heavy barrel, matte-blue finish and plastic grips. A variant is available in a rust-resistant satin-nickel finish.
- *Buck Mark Challenge* (1999 to date) The first of a series of revised designs, this is a refinement of the standard 1985-type Buck Mark with a lightly tapered 5.5-inch barrel and a 10-round magazine. The rear sight lies on a half-length top-rib that protrudes over the rear of the barrel block. The guns weigh about 25 oz. The standard finish is matte blue, and the grips are usually wooden. The shape of the grip is the easiest way of distinguishing the 1985-type guns from the 1999 refinements; the former is "swamped" (swelling towards the base), but the latter, doubtless inspired by the ubiquitous 1911-type Colt-Browning, is virtually parallel-sided as far as the inward curve at the base of the backstrap. This small-frame/small-grip design is intended for shooters with small hands. The grips are usually finely checkered walnut.
- *Buck Mark Classic Plus* (2001 to date) A deluxe version of the standard gun, this is distinguished by a Truglo/Marble front sight and rosewood-laminate grips.
- *Buck Mark Commemorative* (or "Buck Mark Limited Edition", 2001) A thousand of these guns were made to celebrate the 25th anniversary of the commencement of US 22 RF handgun production. They have 6.75-inch barrels, matte-blue finish on the barrel and frame, and ivory grips etched in pseudo-scrimshaw style.
- *Buck Mark Field* (or "5.5 Field", 1991 to date) This is a variant of the Target 5.5 without the hooded sights. Some of the earliest guns had enlarged grips with grasping grooves on the front edge, but these have now been replaced by conventional thumb-rest-style grips. The current version also has a Pro-Target rear sight.
- *Buck Mark Micro* (or "Buck Mark 22 Micro", 1992-9) This has a 4-inch heavyweight ("bull") barrel with flattened sides and an adjustable rear sight on a ramp that extends from the rear of the slide over the rear of the barrel. The finish may be polished or matte blue, the standard grips being plastic thumb-rest styles. The "Buck Mark Micro Plus" is identical mechanically but has walnut grips, and the "Buck Mark Micro Plus Nickel" (introduced in 1996) has a satin-nickel finish on the barrel and slide and a black-anodized frame.
- *Buck Mark Micro* (1999 to date) This is a refinement of the original Micro with a lightweight 4-inch barrel, adjustable rear sight on a half-length top-rib and the new parallel-side grip. It is available in blue or nickel.
- *Buck Mark Plus* (1987 to date) A version of the Buck Mark Standard, this had blue finish and plain wood grips. A "Buck Mark Plus Nickel", with a rust-resisting satin-nickel finish on the slide and barrel, appeared in 1991. The current version has a Truglo/Marble front sight.
- *Buck Mark Silhouette* (1987-95?) Intended for metallic-target competition shooting, this gun shares the 9.75-inch heavy barrel of the Varmint model but has grips with finger grooves on the leading edge, a heavy wooden fore-end with a single longitudinal flute and hooded adjustable sights. The guns are 14 inches long and weigh about 53 oz.
- *Buck Mark Target* (or "Buck Mark 5.5 Target" 1990 to date) This has a 5.5-inch heavy barrel, adjustable target-type hooded sights on a full-length rib that will accept optical-sight mounts and walnut "anatomi-

cal" grips. Weight averages 36 oz. The "5.5 Blued Target" was joined in 1991 by the "5.5 Gold Target" with a gold anodized frame/rib and a blued slide, but this was made only in small numbers.
- *Buck Mark Unlimited Match* (1989-95?) Essentially similar to the Buck Mark Silhouette (q.v.), intended for metallic-silhouette target shooting, this had a 14-inch heavyweight barrel with a full-length rib and a fluted wooden fore-end. Hooded sights were fitted, though the front sight lay far enough back from the muzzle to comply with the 15-inch maximum sight-radius rule. The guns weighed about 64 oz.
- *Buck Mark Varmint* (1987-95?) This had a 9.75-inch heavy barrel, giving an overall length of 14 inches and a weight of about 48 oz with an empty 10-round magazine. No open sights were provided, as the full-length ramp was designed to accept optical-sight mounts. The walnut grips took sculpted or "anatomical" form.

Challenger series (c. 1976-85) These guns were derived from the FN-made Challenger (q.v.), which was discontinued in 1974. The first US-made guns left the Salt Lake City factory in 1976. They were so similar to their predecessors that it is concluded that the FN production line had been transferred. The only major differences concerned the frame and grips, as the angle between the bore axis and the grip had been increased to improve feed from the magazine. Consequently, the "US Challenger" has a grip that is noticeably squarer to the bore. It was ultimately replaced by the Buck Mark described above.
- *Challenger II* Made from 1976 until 1982, this had a 6.75-inch barrel and hardwood grips, impregnated with high-gloss phenolic resin, that displayed small "B" medallions. The metal parts, including the alloy frame, were finished in blue.
- *Challenger III* Dating from 1982-4, this had a 5.5-inch heavyweight barrel, with characteristic flattened sides, and an adjustable rear sight.
- *Sporter* This was simply a Challenger III, sharing the sights, with a 6.75-inch tapered barrel. Few of these guns seem to have been made.

Medalist series (1962-80) "Medalist" was the name given by the Browning Arms Company to the standard FN-made Target Model, 1962-74. Details will be found in the Fabrique Nationale entry.
- *Gold Line Medalist* Distinguished, as the name suggests, by delicate linear engraving filled with gold, only a few hundred of these were sold in the USA in 1962-74.
- *Renaissance Medalist* A variant of the standard gun, this had delicate engraving overall, a silver or nickeled finish and special one-piece walnut wraparound grips. A handful was sold in the USA in the early 1970s.
- *International Medalist* The US name for the FN-made Target 150 Model, distributed in the USA in 1977-80 only.
- *International Medalist II* (or "Second Model") This name was attached to the modernized FN-made International pattern, dating from the late 1970s.

BRYCO ARMS
Carson City, Nevada, and Irvine, California, USA.

This business was responsible for the *Bryco 38* and *Bryco 48* pistols, single-action blowbacks in 22 LR rimfire, 32 ACP or 380 ACP with fixed sights and detachable six-round box magazines in the butt. The Model 38 was 5.3 inches long with a 2.8-inch barrel and a weight of about 15 oz; comparable dimensions for the Model 48 were 6.7 inches, 4 inches, and 19-20 oz. The guns had polished wood grips with a matted phenolic resin impregnation, distinguished by eight widely spaced horizontal flutes and an impressed "BRYCO" name; finish could be satin nickel, bright chrome or black Teflon. Bryco guns were distributed by Jennings Firearms (q.v.), which is sometimes regarded as the actual manufacturer.

BSA GUNS LTD

Small Heath, Birmingham, England.
Renowned for its rifles and sporting guns, BSA was persuaded to enter the handgun field immediately after World War I had ended. The revolver appeared to be in decline, whereas the automatic pistol was "on the way up".

A 34-caliber BSA pistol.

BSA pistol One of the few public mentions of this gun came in H.B.C. Pollard's book Automatic Pistols, published in 1920. "A new range of .400 automatics are now being tried for military purposes", he wrote, "and the postwar models are obviously better than existing types, as they embody the latest ideas and practise on the subject … An entirely new set of automatic pistol cartridges are now in preparation. These will have a belt around the case designed to prevent any possible jams caused by interlocking of the rim flanges. The calibers are 7, 9 and probably 11mm".

The BSA cartridges were developed by Explosives Trades Ltd (formed by Kynoch, Eley and Nobel) immediately after the end of the First World War, though they may have had pre-1914 Eley origins. The three belted rimless rounds were offered to (but rejected by) Webley & Scott before BSA became interested. They were originally known as ".275 BSA", ".335 BSA" and ".393 BSA", but the designations were soon changed to ".28", ".34", and ".39".

A few pistols were made in this era, though details are unclear. The gun pictured here is claimed to be a 40-caliber blowback, but the ballistics of the 39 BSA round, firing a 140-grain bullet at 1400 ft/sec, would suggest that some form of breech lock would have been needed.

Several pistols are said to have been tested by the British Small Arms Committee in 1920-2, but the army was determined to have a 38-caliber revolver and doubted that any automatic pistol was suitable for military service. The trial guns were presumably returned to BSA, and the company lost interest in the project.

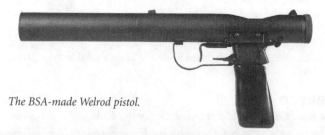

The BSA-made Welrod pistol.

Welrod This repeating pistol, with an integral silencer, fell into the class of strange weapons that creep out of the shadows during a war and disappear into obscurity once the affray is over. It was intended for the Special Operations Executive (SOE), the British organization responsible for directing and fomenting underground warfare by resistance groups in German-occupied Europe but was ultimately adopted by other clandestine organizations and special forces. The "Wel" prefix arose from the SOE workshop in Welwyn Garden City, north of London, where development took place; "rod" was conferred from the contemporary popularity of the humorous short stories

of Damon Runyon, whose gangsters habitually referred to their pistols in such a way.

The entire weapon was contained in a cylinder about a foot long with a rotating bolt at the rear. Turning a knurled knob at the end of the cylinder released the bolt, which could then be drawn back to allow a cartridge to rise from the magazine into the feed-way. Pushing the bolt back cocked the striker and propelled the new round into the chamber. Several holes were drilled into the short barrel, which was concealed inside the mid-section of the cylinder, and there were circular baffles between the end of the barrel and the front end of the cylinder.

The magazine was contained in the pistol grip, though the entire grip unit had to be removed before the magazine could be reloaded. The trigger was a simple rod, a grip safety lay behind the pistol grip, an ejection port appeared on the top of the cylindrical breech and the fixed sights were regulated for a range of 25 yards.

When the Welrod was fired, the bullet set off down the barrel and some of the propellant gas escaped through the holes into the space between the barrel and cylinder. The bullet then left the barrel, passed through the central hole in the baffles and emerged from the muzzle. However, the gas that followed the bullet was delayed and re-directed by the baffles until it left the muzzle of the cylinder at a temperature and velocity low enough to give neither flash nor sound.

There were several versions, culminating in the Welrod Mark 2A, though the differences are minor. A 22 LR rimfire version is said to have been made in small numbers but has never been found.

ERNST FRIEDRICH BÜCHEL

Mehlis (prior to 1919) and Zella Mehlis (after 1919), Germany.
Büchel specialized in the construction of "Free pistols", intended for international pistol-shooting competitions. Most of these guns were single-shot designs with dropping-block breech systems and barrels that could be as long as 12 inches. However, Büchel was adept at customizing his guns to suit each individual purchaser, and so the grips, sights and decoration (in particular) were subject to variation. Most of the post-1920 pistols chambered 22 rimfire ammunition, but other chamberings are known (e.g., 8.1x24, 5.6x35 Vierling). The business was sold in 1934 to Udo Anschütz (q.v.), though production of Tell and Luna pistols continued until World War II began.

Büchel Among the hinged-barrel guns made under this name were the pre-1914 *Model B I*, which had a simple trigger and an external hammer, and the more sophisticated *Model B II*, with a more sophisticated trigger and an internal hammer and a locking lever on the side of the breech. Several chamberings were available.

Ideal Embodying the customary radial-block locking system, this single-shot pistol was intended for competitions that were limited by time. Cartridges that had not been pushed fully forward were seated automatically as the breech was closed, and, unlike most other Büchel pistols, spent cases were ejected as the action opened.

Luna Usually regarded as a replacement for the Tell, this had its grip set at a more conventional angle and a breech-block that was operated by a ring-tipped lever inside the grip. This allowed the breech to be actuated without disturbing the precise grip of the firing hand. Most guns were provided with set triggers and were cocked by pressing a thumb-lever protruding from the lower left side of the breech.

Meisterschaftpistole This was another of the "Büchel block" designs operated by a back-strap lever. An internal hammer was linked with the double set-trigger mechanism, which cocked as the action closed and released automatically as the breech opened. Chambering was customarily 22 LR rimfire.

Müllner Also listed as "Möllner" or "Müller", made in 22 LR rimfire and other chamberings, this had a compact tipping-block mechanism inspired by the old Bavarian Werder (q.v.). The breech was opened by simultaneously pressing the trigger and pushing forward on the hammer extension. A cartridge was inserted in the chamber, the hammer extension was retracted to close the breech and the trigger system could be set by pressing a cocking lever in the trigger guard.

Stern Locked by a vertically moving block controlled by a lever on the side of the breech, this 22-caliber pistol had an exposed hammer.

Tell This had a locking block that moved radially, patented by Cuno Buchel in 1887. The *Model I* and *Model II* both had the hammer contained in the breech-block, but the former had a simple set-trigger with the setting lever contained within the trigger guard; whereas the latter had a more complicated mechanism "set" by a lever protruding from the lower left side of the action. The breech was opened by pulling up on a lever set in the backstrap (inspired by the Schulhof design, q.v.), and the grip was set at an acute angle that was fashionable with the European pistol shooters of the time.

W.B. Chambered for the 22 LR rimfire cartridge, this embodied a Roux lock and a concealed hammer. Released by pushing down on an under-lever that followed the contours of the trigger guard, the barrel tipped downward to load.

Zimmerpistole ("saloon pistol") Also known as the *Übungspistole* or "practice pistol", this was a simple single-shot design in 22 Short RF or 4mm Übungspatrone. The breech was a simple "Warnant type", pivoted ahead of the chamber, which lifted to expose the chamber.

BÜCHSENMACHER HANDWERKGENOSSENSCHAFT AG ("BÜHAG")

In the days of the German Democratic Republic (East Germany), this gunmaking co-operative was one of the few companies maintaining the gunmaking tradition of Suhl.

⟿ SINGLE-SHOT PISTOL ⟿

Zentrum This was a single-shot 22-caliber Free Pistol, inspired by pre-war Büchel (q.v.) "Tell" and "Luna" designs, with a Martini-type dropping-block action.

⟿ AUTOMATIC PISTOLS ⟿

Olimpiamodell Products included this 22 Short RF target pistol, which was apparently based on the pre-war Walther design (q.v.). It had a long fixed barrel, an open-topped slide and an internal hammer. Sophisticated sights, muzzle weights and a variety of grips were among the optional extras.

Ziegenhahn IV A 22 Short rimfire exposed-hammer competition pistol very similar to the Unique DES-69, this also had ports bored into the barrel. These could be closed at will to balance the venting effect of the muzzle-lift experienced with different brands of ammunition.

KARL BURGSMÜLLER

Kreiensen, Germany.

This distributor of sporting guns, ammunition and accessories has handled a variety of pistols and revolvers. They have included the *Burgo*, the 22-caliber Röhm RG-10 and the *Regent*, a double-action 22 LR rimfire gun resembling the Colt Police Positive. These date from 1955-70.

CALICO

Californian Instrument Co., Inc., Bakersfield, California, USA.

Formerly distributed by American Industries in Cleveland, Ohio, the 22 LR rimfire M-100P (1986, also known as "M-110") and 9mm Parabellum M-950 (1988) pistols derive from the Calico selective-fire carbine — a 1986-vintage blowback design distinguished by futuristic lines, extensive use of synthetic components in an attempt to reduce weight and a high-capacity helical-feed magazine placed horizontally above the breech. Both guns have 6-inch barrels, but magazine capacities are usually 100 rounds in 22-caliber and only 50 rounds in 9mm. The distinctive appearance of the Calico pistols ensures that they cannot be mistaken for any other design.

CARTUCHOES DEPORTIVOS DE MEXICO ("CDM")

An aluminum-framed 22 LR six-shot double-action revolver was marketed briefly in the USA in the 1970s as the *CDM*. However, though claimed as "American manufacture" in advertising literature, it is more likely to have been made in Mexico. Best known for ammunition, CDM has ventured into gunmaking in recent years even though a chance remains that production was actually undertaken elsewhere.

CASPIAN ARMS

Hardwick, Vermont, USA.

Beginning in 1986, this gunmaking business has produced variations on the popular Colt-Browning M1911 theme. They have included a 45 ACP *Government Model*, with interchangeable 9mm Parabellum and 38 Super options. Made of blued carbon or bright-finish stainless steel, this gun has high-profile sights, an adjustable trigger and walnut grips. The *Model 110* (introduced in 1988) is a version of the Government Model, with skeleton trigger and hammer, an extended "beavertail" grip-safety, adjustable sights, enlarged ejection port, chamfered magazine well and other "custom" features. A thousand *Viet Nam Commemoratives* were made in 1986-7, featuring nickel-plated engraving and a commemorative medallion, showing the purchaser's arm-of-service, let into the walnut grips.

CASULL ARMS, INC

Afton, Wyoming, USA.

Best known for his cartridge designs, Dick Casull has also made handguns. These have included the fine double-action *CA 2000* revolver, similar to those that were popular in Europe prior to World War II (e.g., the "Arminius" series made by Frierich Pickert). Chambered only for the 22 LR rimfire cartridge, the five-shot CA 2000 has a folding trigger and is small enough to be concealed within the palm. It is made of stainless steel and has a radial safety lever on the rear right side of the frame behind the cyclinder. The *CA 3800* is a variant of the Colt-Browning M1911, chambering the 38 Casull cartridge. Offered with a 6-inch match barrel and an eight-round magazine, the guns have checkering on the gripstrap and main-spring housing, extended "beavertail" grip safeties, match-grade triggers and adjustable rear sights.

CENTURY GUN DISTRIBUTORS, INC.

Greenfield, Indiana, USA.

Formed in Evansville, Indiana, in 1975 (as "Century Mfg., Inc."), this manufacturing company underwent a change of ownership and name in 1986.

Model 100 Announced in 1975 and originally largely handmade, this was a large single-action weapon in the Peacemaker mold that

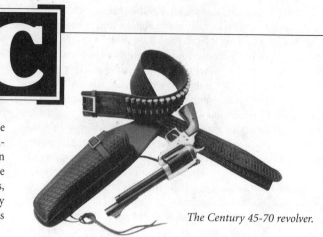

The Century 45-70 revolver.

originally chambered the 45-70 Government cartridge. Made only to order; it was subsequently offered in 30-30 WCF, 375 Winchester, 444 Marlin and 50-70 Government rounds. The Model 100 has a safety bolt running laterally through the manganese-bronze alloy frame and a steel cylinder holding six rounds. Barrel length can vary from 6.5 to 15 inches, making a large and heavy handgun that demands great skill to shoot accurately. Production in Evansville ceased after only a little over 500 guns had been made; it recommenced after the change of corporate structure, in 1986, but only about 600 had been made by 2000.

CENTURY INTERNATIONAL ARMS

St Albans, Vermont, USA.

Best known as the importer of European-made shotguns and for the conversion of countless military rifles (e.g., Mauser 98, Lee-Enfield, FAL) to sporting form, Century International has also acquired rifles and handguns in what was formerly the Soviet bloc. FÉG pistols (q.v.) were first distributed in the 1990s, and the company now also handles M1911A1-type guns made by Armscor (q.v.) in the Philippines. These Colt-Browning clones are currently offered in the *Blue Thunder* and the *Commodore*.

ČESKÁ ZBROJOVKA

Jihočeská Zbrojovka, Pilsen and Strakonice (1919-21); Česká Zbrojovka, Prague, Strakonice (1921-48); Narodní podnik "Přesné strojírentsví", Uherský Brod (1948-92); Česká Zbrojovka a.s., Uherský Brod (1992 to date).

Česká Zbrojovka was founded in 1919 in Pilsen and began production of handguns with the "Fox". The business was moved to Strakonice in 1921 and in 1923 obtained a contract to produce pistols for the Czechoslovakian army. Production expanded in the 1920s and 1930s to cover rifles, machineguns, submachine guns, bicycles, artillery, motorcycles and machine tools. In 1949, under Communist rule, it became the Česká Zbrojovka Narodní Podník ("national enterprise") and by 1955 the amount of non-firearms work was reflected in a change of name, the firm becoming the Česke Závody Motocyklové (Czech Motorcycle Corporation).

ČZ1922 Little more than an improved "Fox", with simpler sights than its predecessor (a groove in the slide-top sufficed), this also had a conventional trigger and guard. The gun remained in production until 1936, many being exported.

ČZ1924 (or "vz. 24") Production of the vz. 22 (see "Československá Zbrojovka", below) passed to the Strakonice factory in 1923, though production must have been small; no pistol of this type with Strakonice markings has ever been recorded. František Myška set about re-designing the vz. 22 to simplify production, owing to the inability of the Brno factory to meet production schedules. Most of the changes made in the

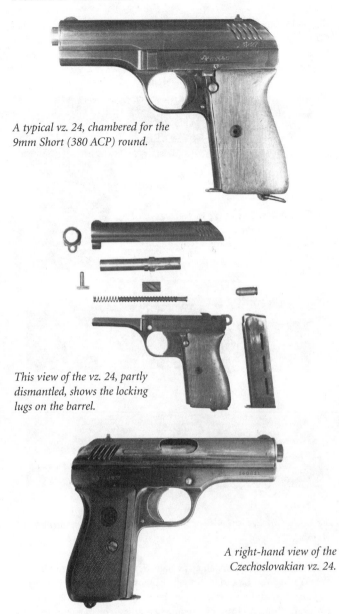

A typical vz. 24, chambered for the 9mm Short (380 ACP) round.

This view of the vz. 24, partly dismantled, shows the locking lugs on the barrel.

A right-hand view of the Czechoslovakian vz. 24.

The vz. 27, chambered for the 32 ACP (7.65mm Auto) cartridge, was a simplified blowback version of the vz. 24. This gun was made during the German occupation of Czechoslovakia.

A partly dismantled vz. 27, showing the plain barrel.

ČZ1924 were minor, such as the addition of a magazine safety and the adoption of hard rubber for the grips instead of wood. The marking was changed to "ČESKÁ ZBROJOVKA A.S. v PRAZE", impressed in the top rib of the slide ahead of the serial number, which was repeated on the front right side of the frame. Most guns also displayed the concentric "encircled CZ" trademark and inspectors' marks in the form "J [Lion of Bohemia] 37"; others received German inspectors' marks prior to issue to the Wehrmacht. Factory records claim that a 9mm Parabellum version, fitted for a shoulder stock, was made for the Turkish army. However, no gun of this type survives.

ČZ1927 (or "vz. 27") Myška was still not satisfied with the 1924 model, largely because he could see no good reason for retaining a locked breech for a chambering as weak as 9mm Short. He had soon substituted a simple 7.65mm-caliber blowback, similar externally to the earlier locked-breech pattern except for slide-retraction grooves that were milled vertically.

The ČZ1927 remained in production for the Czechoslovakian army until the German occupation in 1939. From then until 1945, guns were made as "Pistolen 27 (t)" and were marked "BÖHMISCHE WAFFEN-FABRIK A.G. IN PRAG", a literal German translation of the original Czechoslovakian marking. Most of the pistols made under German supervision had vertical retraction grooves instead of the diagonal pat-

tern associated with pre-1940 output. "Pistole Modell 27 [space] Kal. 7,65" appeared on the left side of the slide. In 1941, however, the slide-top marking was abandoned in favor of the manufacturer's code "fnh" ahead of the designation/caliber mark. Production resumed after the war, continuing until 1951. About half a million guns had been made.

A few guns will be found with the muzzle extended to accept a silencer, but their origins are unclear. It has been suggested that they were produced under German supervision, or for the "secret police" after the communist takeover of Czechoslovakia, but neither case is proven.

ČZ1936 The ČZ1922 was replaced by this new design, with a self-cocking action that had been patented in 1927-34. Pulling back the slide loaded the chamber in the normal way, but the hammer did not remain cocked; as the slide returned, the hammer fell on to a blocking bar. When the trigger was pulled, the hammer was cocked, the blocking bar moved away, and the hammer was then released. The blocking bar was restored by the disconnector after every shot. The ČZ1936 was undoubtedly Myška's trial run for the vz. 38. A trigger system of this type was acceptable in a pocket pistol, and so the ČZ1936 sold well until work stopped in 1940.

ČZ1937 and ČZ1938 ("vz. 38") These were essentially adaptations of the 6.35mm ČZ1936. Myška subsequently incorporated a similar self-cocking action in a larger 9mm Short pistol intended for military service with the cavalry. The "vz. 37" was made in small numbers to allow field trials to be undertaken. A few small changes were made, the most obvious being a change to the dismantling catch and the left side of the frame. The perfected design was adopted by the Czechoslovakian army in April 1938 as the "vz. 38", but this is now considered to have been a mistake. Although firing the comparatively weak 9mm Short cartridge, the ČZ38 was as large as most pistols chambering 9mm Parabellum; and the stiffness of the self-cocking action made accurate

The Czechoslovakian 9mm vz. 38 was a quirky double-action design.

shooting impossible without long and arduous practice. The only virtue was the ease of dismantling; a catch at the side released the slide/barrel unit to tip on a transverse pivot in the front of the frame. This allowed the slide to be slipped from the rear of the barrel, and a sideplate could be slid off to expose the lockwork.

An order for 41,000 guns was placed in June 1938, but no issues had been made when the Germans occupied the Strakonice factory. The pistols were immediately assimilated into German service as "Pistolen 39 (t)" with all but the 3000 Luftwaffe-issued guns going to the army. The 1937-type guns displayed the manufacturer's name "ČESKÁ ZBROJOVKA A.S. v PRAZE" on the left side of the frame, while the vz. 38 were marked "ČESKÁ ZBROJOVKA AKC. SPOL. V PRAZE" on the slide beneath the ejection port. Most have Czechoslovakian inspectors' marks in the form "F8 [Lion of Bohemia] 39", the final digits giving the date ("39" = 1939). German displayed-eagle inspectors' marks may also be present.

ČZ448 Designed during World War II and made for a few years after 1945, this 22 RF automatic pistol had a detachable 10-round box magazine in the butt. It was designed by Myška and Lacina and used only by Czech competition shooters.

ČZ45 Production of an improved version of the 1936-type pocket pistol, credited to Jan Kratochvíl, began again after World War II. Post-war guns were identical externally with their predecessors except for the removal of the safety catch (felt to be redundant with such a trigger mechanism). Work continued until 1951.

ČZ47 This was an experimental 9mm Parabellum service pistol with an eight-round box magazine and a butt-shape inspired by the Walther P. 38. Developed by František Myška shortly after World War II, it was rejected by the Czechoslovakian army principally because it lacked a manual safety catch. Only a few were ever made.

ČZ50 Not surprisingly, few people wanted much to do with the ČZ38 after World War II, and so Jan and Jaroslav Kratochvíl developed a new 7.65mm design in 1947-8. This leaned heavily on the Walther PP for its inspiration, though the safety catch was to be found on the frame instead of the slide, the loaded-chamber indicator protruded from the side of the slide (instead of the end), the trigger guard was an integral part of the frame and dismantling was controlled by a catch in the frame-side. The ČZ50 was serviceable enough, but 7.65mm-caliber

Influenced by the Walther PP, the ČZ50 was popular with Czechoslovakian police.

was inadequate for military use and weaknesses in the trigger mechanism were never entirely overcome. Though it was widely adopted by the police, and a few were sold commercially, production ended in 1969. It was replaced by the ČZ70 (below).

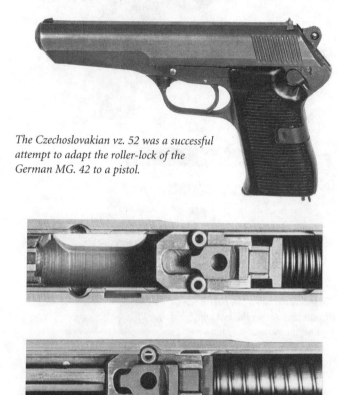

The Czechoslovakian vz. 52 was a successful attempt to adapt the roller-lock of the German MG. 42 to a pistol.

The locking mechanism of the vz. 52, engaged (top) and disengaged (bottom).

ČZ52 The Czechoslovakian army had been "Sovietized" immediately after World War II and eventually accepted Warsaw Pact-standard weapons such as the Kalashnikov at the expense of indigenous designs. However, though Tokarev pistols were issued in quantity, the Czechoslovakian authorities steadfastly refused to accept that it was good enough. Development of a new gun began in 1947-9, when prototypes based on the Browning GP-35 were tested against a roller-locked rival. The roller-locked ČZ482 was preferred, developing into the double-action ČZ491 and the single-action ČZ513. The latter was tested against the ZKP 524 (modified Colt-Browning) and the ČZ531 (modified Tokarev) and finally approved for service as the "vz. 52".

The 7.62mm Soviet pistol cartridge was retained, although the Czechoslovakian version developed a higher muzzle velocity and demanded that a breechlock be retained. The ČZ52 relied on two rollers that engaged in the slide under the control of cams and cam-tracks in the frame, clearly inspired by the MG. 42 and thus to a patent granted in Poland in the 1930s. This was among the most complex systems ever incorporated in a mass-produced handgun, though the ČZ52 had remarkably light recoil considering the power of the cartridge. Production ended in about 1956, and those that survive are held in reserve.

ČZ70 By the late 1960s, the ČZ50 had acquired such a poor reputation for reliability that improvements were sought. These resulted in the ČZ70, made until 1983, though external appearance had scarcely changed. Only the markings and the design of the grips distinguished the two guns.

ČZ75 Probably the best pistol ever to appear from Czechoslovakia, and one of the outstanding designs of the post-1945 period, this has attained wide popularity outside its country of origin and has been widely imitated (e.g. licensed to ITM and simply copied by Tanfoglio and others). TheČZ75 was intended for export, as the 9mm Parabellum chambering precluded adoption by any Warsaw Pact forces.

Designed by František Koucký for what was then Narodní podník "Přesné strojírentsví" ("Precision Engineering National Enterprise") in Uherský Brod, in 1975-6, the pistol bears no relationship to previous Czechoslovakian designs. The standard of manufacture was excellent and handling qualities were exactly right. Series production began in Czechoslovakia in 1980, with an initial pre-production run of 2000 guns, but the manufacturer was unprepared for the response that led to a demand for 20,000 guns annually. The ČZ75 offered nothing revolutionary but was simply the sound application of proven design features. The locking system was pure Browning, relying on a cam to drop the breech end of the barrel from engagement with the slide. Doubtless inspired by the SIG-Petter, the slide rode on internal rails in the frame to offer better support and finer accuracy than the customary exterior rails. The magazine held 15 rounds, and the double-action trigger operated an external hammer. ČZ MODEL 75 CAL. 9 PARA" ("9 LUGER" on many guns destined for English-speaking markets) appeared on the left side of the slide behind the trademark, with "MADE IN CZECHOSLOVAKIA" in a single line on the frame. Guns "made in the Czech Republic" post-date the partition of Czechoslovakia.

Originally made with a spurred hammer and a conventionally rounded trigger guard, the pistols are 8.1 inches long, have 4.7-inch barrels and weigh 35 oz with an empty magazine. Options have been restricted to 9mm Parabellum, 9x21 IMI and 40 S&W with magazine capacities ranging from 10 to 15 rounds, depending on chambering. Production was initially confined to the standard pistol, with baked-on black epoxy paint finish, and to highly decorative examples that were equally unacceptable in most Western markets. Waffen Frankonia of Wurzburg, Germany, initially altered many Czech-made pistols, adding adjustable sights and walnut grips. Subsequently, however, the manufacturer offered matte and gloss blue, nickel-plating and a combination of blue and nickel finishes. A ring-head hammer replaced the spur variety in the early 1990s, and the original hold-open latches and safety catches, which had slender heads and rounded contours, have been replaced with enlarged-head, squared components.

- *ČZ75 Automatic* This rarely seen ČZ75 derivative, capable of firing fully automatically, had the frame adapted ahead of the trigger guard to accept either a laser-spot projector or (perhaps more practically) an inverted loaded magazine to double as a forward grip. This also added muzzle weight to prevent the weapon leaping in the air when fired at 1000 rds/min. The basic model shared the appearance of the ČZ75; the other had a longer barrel and muzzle-brake/compensator slots cut in the slide extension. An extended 25-round magazine has also been made.

A nickeled ČZ75B.

- *ČZ75B* Announced in 1992, but not made in quantity until 1994, this is a "product improved" ČZ75 with an additional firing-pin safety system, the front sight pinned in the slide, a "Commander" (ring-type) hammer that was subsequently fitted to the standard ČZ75 and a ribbed-top non-reflective slide. The safety lever and hold-open/stripping latch were enlarged and squared-off. Chamberings are customarily 9mm Parabellum and 40 S&W; finish may be baked-on black epoxy paint, matte blue, gloss blue, nickel-plating or a "duotone" combination.

- *ČZ75BD* Dating from 1995, this is a minor variant of the ČZ75B with a de-cocking feature built into the safety-lever mechanism. The catch on the left rear of the frame rotates clockwise instead of counterclockwise. It retains the standard 4.7-inch barrel and accepts a 15-round staggered-column magazine (currently restricted to 10 for the US market).

- *ČZ75BD Compact* Introduced in 2001, this is a smaller version of the 75BD, with a 3.9-inch barrel and a short grip. The standard magazine holds 10 9mm Parabellum or 40 S&W rounds.

- *ČZ75BD Compact Carry* Also introduced in 2001, this is a minor variant of the preceding gun. Care has been taken to round the edges of the slide and frame, to prevent snagging, and the squared "combat" trigger guard has been replaced with a traditional rounded design.

- *ČZ75B SA* Introduced in 2000, this is a variant of the standard ČZ75 with a trigger system restricted to single action. The trigger lever is straight, and the sights are usually fixed.

- *ČZ75 Champion* (or "Champion Competition") Introduced in 1995/6 for 9mm Parabellum (15-round magazine) or 40 S&W (11-round magazine), this has an adjustable single-action trigger system. The trigger lever is straight, an adjustable LPA rear sight is fitted and the grips are contoured walnut. The slide is extended to form an integral three-port compensator, and the retraction grips are duplicated. The slide is usually blued, but the frame has a matte nickel finish. The guns are typically 9.4 inches long, have 4.5-inch barrels and weigh about 36 oz.

The short-barreled ČZ75 Compact pistol, in 9mm Parabellum.

- *ČZ75[B] Compact* Introduced in 1992, this "B"-series pistol, with a firing-pin safety, is distinguished by a 3.9-inch barrel and a grip shortened to accept a 12-round double-row magazine. The guns are about 7.3 inches long and weigh 32 oz.

- *ČZ75D* This is an improved form of the ČZ75B, with a de-cocking feature built into the trigger system that is actuated by a radial lever on the left rear of the frame that rotates clockwise. The rear sight was a three-dot pattern, within angular protectors; wraparound rubber grips were fitted, and the retraction grips were duplicated on the front of the slide behind the muzzle. A lightweight aluminum-alloy frame reduced weight to 28 oz, but the "D" variant does not seem to have been successful and may have been discontinued.

- *ČZ75[B] DAO* The trigger mechanism of this 1995-vintage "B"-series gun is restricted to double-action-only. The radial safety lever is absent, and the hammer is a spurless pattern that lies flush with the rear of the frame/slide when down. The sights are usually Tru-Dot patterns with Tritium inserts.

- *ČZ75D Compact* A variant of the full-length gun, this has a 3.8-inch barrel, a full grip holding a 15-round magazine and weighs about 24 oz. Production is believed to have been restricted to about a hundred.
- *ČZ75D PCR Compact* Said to have been developed for the Czechoslovakian police forces, this is a "concealment" variant of the ČZ75D with a de-cocking double-action trigger system, low-profile sights and flutes on the grip straps to improve handling. The grip is shortened to accept a 10-round magazine.
- *ČZ75 Kadet* Usually known as "Cadet" in English-speaking markets, though usually marked "KADET" on the slide, this was introduced in 1995. It resembles the normal ČZ75 at first glance, but is actually a 22-caliber blowback trainer supplied either as a complete gun or as an accessory kit. The barrel, the frame and what appears to be most of the slide were a single solid forging. The retraction grips may be pulled back to reveal a separate "side-arm" breechblock unit, similar in design to many target pistols. The left side-arm displayed "ČZ75 KADET".
- *ČZ75M ISPC* Essentially similar to the ČZ75 Standard IPSC pistol described below, this is intended for use with red-dot sights mounted on a bracket attached to the extended frame. The guns have two-port compensators made integrally with the slide, which is fitted with an auxiliary racker (a top-rib that flares at the rear to provide retraction grips) and a transverse blast shield to protect the sight. The 75M appeared in 2001.
- *ČZ75[B] Police* Introduced in 1995, this is a variant of the de-cocking "75BD", with the firing-pin safety system. It has ambidextrous controls, checkered butt straps, rubber grips, Tru-Dot sights and a lanyard eye on the heel of the butt. One of the most distinctive features, however, is the presence of a loaded-chamber indicator pin on top of the slide ahead of the ejection port.
- *ČZ75[B] SC (Semi-Compact)* Introduced in 1994, with the firing-pin safety system, this 9mm Parabellum variant combines the 3.9-inch barrel with a full-size frame that accepts the standard 15-round magazine. It is 7.3 inches long and weighs 34 oz.
- *ČZ75 Silver Anniversary Model* A thousand of these guns were made in 2000-1 to celebrate the 25th anniversary of the announcement (though not series production) of the basic pistol. The slide and frame display photo-etched leaf-and-tendril "engraving", the metal parts have a gloss nickel finish and the walnut grips have both an incised leaf design and a "25" medallion.
- *ČZ75 Standard IPSC* Introduced in 1999, this is a distinctive-looking gun with a blued slide that runs back on a squared full-length nickel-finish frame. The low-profile grips are checkered walnut, the rear sight is adjustable and the retraction grips are duplicated.

ČZ82 and ČZ83
Comparatively conventional fixed-barrel pistols, known to the manufacturer as the "Model 033", these could be considered as an improved ČZ70 with an ambidextrous safety catch and a magazine catch — behind the trigger guard — that can be operated from both sides. An automatic safety device in the double-action lockwork prevented the hammer from reaching the firing pin except when the trigger was fully squeezed. The trigger guard, controlled by a spring catch, could be swung downward to release the slide. An interlock ensured that the guard could not open if a magazine was still in the butt; conversely, a magazine could not be inserted if the trigger guard had not been closed satisfactorily.

- *ČZ82* The military version of the basic design, this was chambered for the 9mm Soviet-bloc Makarov cartridge or the Czechoslovakian "vz. 82" equivalent. The guns had polygonal bores, holes drilled laterally through the heel of the butt (behind the magazine well) for a lanyard, and had a matte military finish. The slide is customarily unmarked.

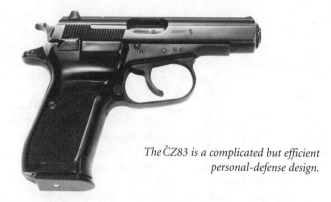

The ČZ83 is a complicated but efficient personal-defense design.

- *ČZ83* The commercial version has been chambered for the 32 ACP (15-round magazine) and 380 ACP (12 rounds) cartridges. The bore is rifled conventionally, and the finish is customarily a deeply polished blue-black. Some of the internal parts are plated with cadmium to prolong their life. Some guns will be encountered with extensive decoration, usually in the form of photo-etched "engraving". The first slides were marked "ČZ 033 CAL 7,65mm" on the left side, above "MOD. 83" and ahead of "MADE IN" above "CZECHO-SLOVAKIA". Later examples, however, display the company trademark ahead of "CZ83" and "CAL. … BROWNING" above "MADE IN CZECH REPUBLIC".
- *ČZ83B* Introduced in 1986 (but possibly not a factory-recognized designation), this is an improved form of the standard Model 83 with a squared "combat" guard.

The Czech ČZ85 is an improved version of the ČZ75.

ČZ85
First made in quantity in 1984, this was an updated ČZ75, retaining the size, shape and general design of its predecessor. The manual safety and the slide stop became ambidextrous, new anatomical grips were fitted, the top rib of the slide was grooved to reduce reflections, the striker was improved to increase the certainty of ignition, and the movement safety and slide-stop catches were limited mechanically.

- *ČZ85B* Dating from 1986, this was an improved form of the ČZ85 with a new firing-pin safety system. Externally, the hammer became a ring-head pattern instead of a spur, and the controls were squared.
- *ČZ85 Combat.* Introduced in 1985 and updated in 1986, this was simply an 85 or 85B with an adjustable rear sight, a squared "combat" trigger guard (subsequently extended to virtually every other variant), walnut grips instead of plastic and an extended magazine-release cross-bolt. The magazine-retaining spring or "brake" was removed to ensure that a spent magazine simply dropped free when released. Chamberings have been restricted to 9mm Parabellum and 9x21, each being accompanied by a 15-round magazine (restricted to 10 in the USA).
- *ČZ85 Kadet* Introduced in 1995, this is a 22 LR rimfire blowback version of the locked-breech ČZ85B, similar to the ČZ75 equivalent (q.v.).

ČZ92
Introduced commercially in 1994, this is a modernized version

A ČZ92 pocket pistol, in 25 ACP.

of the 25 ACP ČZ45 pocket pistol described previously. The trigger system is double-action-only, without any form of applied safety except for a block that prevents the gun from firing if the magazine has been removed. The gun is 5 inches long, has a 2.5-inch barrel and weighs about 15 oz; the magazine holds 8 rounds. Finish may be blue or matte nickel, and the grips are usually black polymer.

ČZ97B Announced in 1997, but not made until 1999, this is a 45 ACP version of the basic ČZ75, with a conventional double-action trigger system. It can be identified by the flat-side frame, extending to the muzzle, by the duplicated retraction grips and by the slide mark: "CZ97 B CAL ..45 ACP", behind the trademark on the left side. The finish is blue, the magazine holds 10 rounds and the guns have 4.75-inch barrels.

ČZ100 Introduced in 1995 and now available in 9mm Parabellum (13-

The ČZ100, with a polymer frame, is the latest service-pistol design to come out of the Czech Republic.

round magazine) or 40 S&W (11 rounds), this chunky pistol — locked by a Browning-type cam lifting the squared chamber-top into the ejection port — introduced synthetic materials to ČZ construction. Plastic and steel are used in the slide and the frame, giving a weight of only 24 oz, and the design of the self-cocking "DAO" firing system ensures that it is under tension only when the trigger is being pulled. The controls are ambidextrous, an automatic firing-pin safety device is fitted and a laser-spot projector can be fitted into rails provided in the front of the frame. An unusual protrusion on top of the slide, behind the ejection port, allows the pistol to be cocked one-handed. The protrusion is pressed against a hard surface and the grip is pushed forward, forcing the slide to load the first round. The ČZ100 is 7 inches long, has a 3.7-inch barrel and weighs 24 oz with an empty magazine.

• *ČZ101* Similar to the ČZ100, this compact variation had a smaller magazine capacity: seven 9mm or six 40-caliber rounds.

Fox This 6.35mm blowback appeared in 1920. It had an odd appearance—the slide being almost tubular—with the recoil spring retained around the barrel by a knurled ring at the muzzle. The trigger folded beneath the frame and there was no trigger guard. The gun was made until 1926.

Model Z This was a "Duo" under another name. Shortly after the

Communist takeover, the gunmaking business of František Dušek (q.v.) was nationalized. The Duo was put back into production in the ČZ factory in Strakonice and marked "Z Auto Pistol R 6,35 Made in Czechoslovakia".

P. 38 This was the standard German military-issue Walther pistol made during World War II in what was then the Reichsprotektorat Böhmen-Mahren. Official procurement figures show that a hundred guns were accepted in May and June 1942, but none thereafter. No explanation for this is possible, but a decision may have been taken to concentrate ČZ production on the vz. 27 ("Pistole 27 [t]") and allow Spreewerke (q.v.) to make P.38 pistols in Grottau. Neither is it known if the ČZ P.38 bore the "fnh" code or any other identifying marks on the slides. A gun of this type, if genuine, would be a tremendous find.

The Mauser-made Nickl-Pistole 'N' provided the prototype for the post-war Czechoslovakian vz. 22 and vz. 24.

ČESKOSLOVENSKÁ ZBROJOVKA

Brno, Czechoslovakia.

This company owed its origins to Státní zbrojovka a strojírna v Brně ("State armament and engineering works in Brno"), founded by the Czechoslovakian government immediately after the end of World War I in a former Austro-Hungarian artillery arsenal in Brno-Zábrdovice. On February 1, 1919, the state-owned business was renamed "Československé Statní Závody na Výrobu Zbraní" and was ultimately reorganized as the privately-owned Československá Zbrojovka AS in June 1924 to permit unfettered export trade. Its primary role was to make Mauser rifles, but production of the Pistol "N" for the Czechoslovakian army began in 1922. However, no sooner had work got underway than the government decided that logistics were better served by concentrating manufacture of military handguns in one factory. Thus the "N" was passed to Česká Zbrojovka of Strakonice (see previous entry) and Československá Zbrojovka concentrated on rifles and machineguns until the first post-World War II pistols were introduced.

∼ SINGLE-SHOT PISTOL ∼

ZKP 493-S This was a single-shot 22 LR rimfire target pistol with a hinged barrel and an external hammer, very similar in outline to a revolver. Designed in 1949-50 by Augustin Nečas, it was marketed as the "Champion" but has rarely been seen outside Czechoslovakia.

∼ REVOLVERS ∼

ZKR 551 This was a single-action, solid-frame, gate-loaded revolver developed specifically for international competition shooting. Designed by the Koucký brothers in 1955-6, but not made in quantity for some years, this was chambered for the 38 Special cartridge. The heavy slab-sided barrel had a prominent rib and an interchangeable front sight, the rear sight being a micro-adjustable design. The ZKR 551 was extensively used by Czech shooters but was rarely seen outside the country.

ZKR 590 (or "Grand") This title covers a range of six-shot revolvers designed by Augustin Nečas and made in the Brno factory from the 1950s. They are all based on the same pattern of solid-frame, swing-out cylinder based largely upon Smith & Wesson practice. They were available chambered for either 38 Special or 357 Magnum, in barrel lengths from 2 to 6 inches. Various sight and grip options were available. A 22-caliber version, intended for sport and target shooting, was sold as the *Major* (though still designated "ZKR 590").

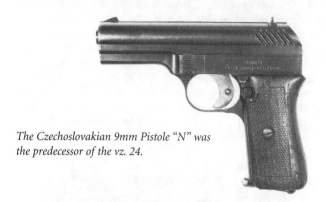

The Czechoslovakian 9mm Pistole "N" was the predecessor of the vz. 24.

∾ AUTOMATIC PISTOLS ∾

VZ. 1922 (or Pistole "N") This was the work of Josef Nickl (also known by the German form of "Nickel"), an ex-Mauser engineer who had assisted in organizing production of Mauser rifles in the Brno factory in 1921. Nickl was a frustrated pistol designer who had offered a variety of designs to the Mauser management during World War I. The Germans rejected them all, including a modification of the 7.65mm 1910-type Mauser M1910, locked by rotating the barrel, but the Czechoslovaks were more accommodating. Nickl had submitted a prototype in 1921, and after trials against Tomiška and Zbrojovka Praga rivals, the Pistol "N" was officially adopted on July 19, 1922, and rights to exploit the Nickl patents were sought from Mauser. Owing to the time taken to transfer the project to Strakonice, about 18,000 1922-type guns were made in Brno alongside the Mauser rifles.

The mechanism was complicated, considering the power of the 9mm Short cartridge. A lug on each side of the barrel engaged slots in the slide walls, and an additional helical lug under the barrel engaged in a groove in the frame. When the gun was fired, the barrel and slide moved backward until, as the helical lug was being pulled through the fixed groove, the barrel rotated about 20 degrees to release the side lugs. The barrel then stopped, allowing the slide to reciprocate to complete the extraction/reloading cycle. As the slide closed, the barrel was driven forward and turned back into engagement with the slide by the helical lug. An external hammer replaced the internal striker of the original Nickl design.

The beautifully made VZ. 22 had an odd appearance, with virtually no overhang at the rear; the back of the slide was virtually flush with the backstrap. The slide swelled into a tubular upper part, and the retracting ribs were diagonal. The marking "9.mm.N." above "Čs. st. zbrojovka, Brno." appeared on the lock-cover plate above the left grip.

ZKP 501 This was a 22-caliber automatic target pistol, with a box magazine in the butt and a ring hammer. The barrel unit could be pivoted upward around a transverse pivot in the tip of the frame.

ZKP 521 Often described as an "army pistol", this was a 22-caliber blowback with a slide-tip/muzzle design resembling the Sauer Behörden Modell (q.v.), squared grips, a ring hammer and a single-action trigger system. It was apparently intended as a trainer, but was made only in small numbers.

ZKP 524 This was a 7.62mm automatic pistol designed by František and Josef Koucký, drawing inspiration from the M1911 Colt-Browning, using the swinging-link barrel-locking system. It fired by an external hammer and had a slide stop and a safety catch copied from the Colt. No grip safety was fitted, and the butt was more wedge-shaped and rounded than that of its prototype. Chambered for the

7.62mm Soviet cartridge, it had an eight-round magazine and could be stripped without tools. It was apparently intended as a military weapon, but only a handful were made. In retrospect, it seems probable that this was a step on the way to the ČZ75.

ZKP 541 A "Universal" target pistol, designed by Nečas, this bore a resemblance to the Colt Woodsman (q.v.). It was made in several patterns.

- *Precision (22 LR)* A variant with a single-slot muzzle-brake/compensator.
- *Sport model (22 LR)* This had a plain barrel.
- *Super Rapid (22 Short only)* Intended for rapid-fire competitions, this had a heavy slab-sided barrel and a faired rear sight.

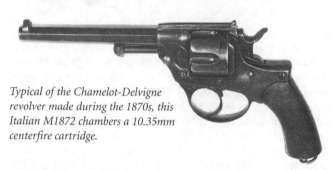

Typical of the Chamelot-Delvigne revolver made during the 1870s, this Italian M1872 chambers a 10.35mm centerfire cartridge.

CHAMELOT-DELVIGNE

This designation, popularly attached to a variety of 19th-century revolvers, is that of the designers. See "Pirlot".

CHAPUIS ARMES

Saint-Bonnet-la-Château, France.

This business was founded in the early 1900s, in Saint-Étienne, by André Chapuis. The gunmaker was initially content to be an "outworker" of the local government arms factory, but his son Jean subsequently began trading independently. Now run by the grandson of the founder, Chapuis Armes has always specialized in shortguns and sporting rifles. However, in the late 1990s, it acquired the handgun-making operations of Manurhin (Manufacture de Machines du Haut-Rhin, q.v.) and now makes the MR73, MR88 and MR96 revolvers.

ÉTABLISSEMENTS CHARLIER

Hognée, Belgium.

Wegria-Charlier This odd little 6.35mm-caliber blowback pistol is uncommon, and very little is known about it. A patent was granted in 1908, but Charlier vanished during World War I and the pistol was never revived; even less is known of "Wegria", who was presumably the designer. The most unusual feature was the empty trigger guard, which was simply there to locate a finger; squeezing the hand around the grip depressed what looked like a grip safety (in the butt backstrap) to release the sear. The barrel was fixed and the slide, unusual for its day, ran inside the frame.

ISIDOR CHAROLA

Eibar, Spain.

Chanticler This was a simple 7.65mm Eibar-type automatic pistol, dating from the early 1920s.

CHAROLA & ANITUA

Eibar, Spain.

Automatic Pistol (c. 1899-1904) Among the earliest successful designs, this was patented in Spain in 1897 by gunmaker Ignacio Charola and promoted with the assistance of financier Gregorio Anitua. It has the dubious distinction of being the smallest-caliber locked-breech pistol ever made, chambering a unique bottlenecked

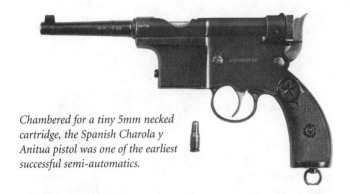

Chambered for a tiny 5mm necked cartridge, the Spanish Charola y Anitua pistol was one of the earliest successful semi-automatics.

rimless cartridge that later became better known as the "5mm Clément". Some Charolas were also made after c. 1900 in 7mm caliber (DWM 501), some apparently with detachable magazines. However, this cartridge does not seem to have been marketed commercially with any vigor, and it is assumed that the guns were little more than an experiment.

The breech is locked by a swinging wedge, pinned to the frame, that engages in a lug on the bolt. The barrel, barrel extension and bolt all recoil together for about 5mm when the gun is fired, until the wedge disengages to allow the bolt to run back and cock the external hammer. A spring returns the bolt, stripping a new round out of the magazine, until the wedge re-engages and the parts return to battery. The butt and trigger are based on revolver practice, the magazine is a detachable box, but the remainder of the design clearly owes a debt to the Mauser C/96.

Some Charolas were also made in 7mm caliber after 1900, with fixed or detachable magazines. Markings include "PISTOLA AUTOMATICA PATENTE CHAROLA Y ANITUA EIBAR" on top of the barrel and a winged-bullet trademark on the left side of the frame above the trigger. The motif may be accompanied either by "MARCA REGIST^DA" or "TRADE MARK" on a scroll. Spanish production was meager, and it is believed that a license was eventually granted to an unidentified gunmaker in Liége. Belgian examples, with short safety levers and Liége proof marks, often displayed "STANDART" on the left side of the frame. Production is unlikely to have exceeded 5000, and work had ceased by 1904. The guns are said to have been popular in Russia, where much of the Belgian production was presumably sent at the time of the Russo-Japanese War (1904-5) or the 1905 revolution. They are rarely seen today.

CHARTER 2000, INC.

Shelton, Connecticut, USA.

This business was formed to salvage something from the wreckage of Charter Arms, which, under increasing pressure from imports, had ceased trading with insuperable debts. Charter 2000 has continued to market the *Bulldog* and *Undercover* revolvers and has introduced one new gun of its own.

Mag Pug This is based on the original Bulldog Pug (see "Charter Arms" below) but has a stainless-steel frame and a 2.25-inch barrel with ports to reduce the tendency for the muzzle to jump upward on firing. It is chambered only for the 357 Magnum cartridge.

CHARTER ARMS CORP.

Stratford, Connecticut, USA.

This company was founded in 1964 by Douglas McClenahan, an engineer with experience in firearms manufacture who had worked for Colt, High Standard and Sturm Ruger. He saw a market for a short-barreled pocket revolver and, unable to interest his employers, began a business of his own to make what had become the "Undercover". After struggling initially against better-established rivals such as Colt and Smith & Wesson, Charter Arms became a well-respected producer of

high-quality arms. A move to Ansonia occurred in the 1990s, but by the end of the decade, the company found competition offered by imports (particularly from South America) too great to bear and collapsed in 1999. Charter 2000, Inc. (above), is a lineal successor.

◦◦ REVOLVERS ◦◦

Note: An interesting detail is the beryllium-copper firing pin, unconditionally guaranteed against breakage. Virtually all Charter Arms products could be obtained with a satin stainless-steel finish. This was customarily indicated by an "S" suffix to catalog numbers; consequently, the guns are not listed here separately.

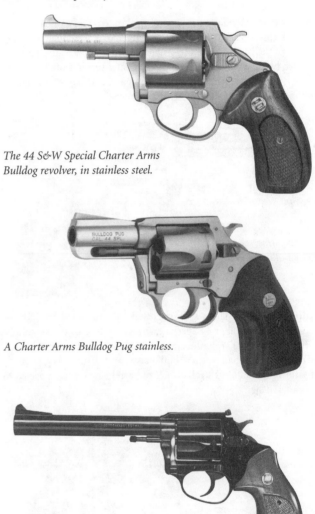

The 44 S&W Special Charter Arms Bulldog revolver, in stainless steel.

A Charter Arms Bulldog Pug stainless.

A typical 5-shot 357 Magnum Bulldog Tracker.

Bulldog This was an enlarged Undercover chambered for the 44 Special cartridge, with a five-chamber cylinder, a 2.5- or 3-inch barrel and an empty weight of 19 oz. Finish was blue or stainless steel, and a "pocket hammer" (lacking a spur) was optional.

- *Bulldog Pug* Introduced in 1986 in 44 Special only, this had a shrouded ejector rod, a wide trigger, a wide hammer spur (the "pocket hammer" was optional) and a 2.5-inch barrel. Finish was blue or matte stainless steel; grips were neoprene or walnut.
- *Bulldog Tracker* Chambered for the 357 Magnum cartridge, this offered adjustable sights, bigger grips and 2.5-inch, 4-inch or 6-inch barrels.

Off-Duty Dating from 1984, this was a 22 LR rimfire or 38 Special Undercover with a 2-inch barrel that gave an overall length of merely 5.75 inches. The usual choice of finish and hammer style was offered.

The Pathfinder is a 22-rimfire "sport" revolver by Charter Arms.

Pathfinder Intended as a "kit gun" for hunters, and as a recreational pistol, this replaced the 22-caliber Undercover. Essentially another variant of the basic design, the original six-shot 22 LR Pathfinder had a 3-inch barrel and a ramped front sight. Later versions offered 2-inch or 6-inch barrels (the latter being accompanied by adjustable sights), optional large grips and 22 WMR chambering.

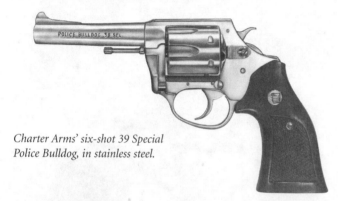

Charter Arms' six-shot 39 Special Police Bulldog, in stainless steel.

Police Bulldog This was a small Bulldog chambered for 32 H&R Magnum, 38 Special or 44 Special cartridges instead of the Magnums. Various forms have been offered: the "P" models had the "pocket hammer"; "B" models had a heavy "bull" barrel; and "S" models were made of satin-finish stainless steel. Choice of barrel length was restricted to 3.5 and 4 inches.

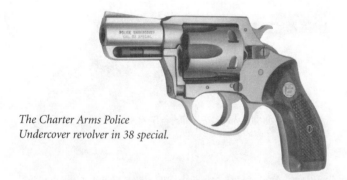

The Charter Arms Police Undercover revolver in 38 special.

Police Undercover Introduced in 1984, this was an Undercover with 2-inch barrel chambered either for the 32 H&R Magnum (rarely seen, as the cartridge was never made in quantity) or for the 38 Special cartridge. A "pocket hammer" was available as an option. The 32-caliber guns had a six-chamber cylinder; the 38 examples were five-shot. Offered with blue or stainless steel finish, the guns had checkered neoprene or walnut grips.

Target Bulldog Made only in 1986-8, available in 357 or 44 Magnum, this had a heavy barrel, adjustable sights and a square butt. As the name implies, it was intended for competition shooting.

Undercover The company's first product was a 38 Special five-shot double-action revolver with a solid frame and a swing-out cylinder. A 2-inch barrel was standard. The frame was chrome-molybdenum steel,

The Charter Arms Target Bulldog revolver, in 44S&W Special, has adjustable sights.

A 38 Special Undercover revolver by Charter Arms, with a spurless "pocket hammer".

relying on the aluminum-alloy frame of the butt and trigger guard to reduce empty weight to exactly one pound.

Undercover revolvers have been made in several variants, including a 3-inch barrel in 38 Special, in 22 LR, 22 WMR or 32 S&W Long — all with six-chamber cylinders instead of the customary five — or with enlarged hand-filling grips. The sights were sturdy, and a transfer block was included in the firing mechanism to prevent accidental discharge. The block relayed the blow of the hammer to the firing pin only if the trigger had been pulled correctly.

Undercoverette A six-shot Undercover in 32 S&W Long chambering with a 2-inch barrel and a slender butt, this was specifically developed for female police officers. It replaced the 32-caliber Undercover until 1982.

∼ AUTOMATIC PISTOLS ∼

Explorer II This was a 22 LR rimfire "recreational pistol" derived from the AR-7 survival rifle, which Charter Arms also made in large numbers. An uncomplicated blowback, with a reciprocating bolt in a tubular receiver, the Explorer was discontinued in 1986. The barrels, which measured 6, 8 or 10 inches, were retained by a large collar, and a detachable 10-round box magazine lay in front of the trigger. Finish could be black, silver, gold or even a camouflage pattern. The grips were plastic.

Model 40 Assembled from parts supplied by Erma (q.v.) in Germany, this was a conventional double-action blowback design in 22 LR rimfire. The guns were made of stainless steel, had black checkered-plastic grips and barrels of 3.5 inches. The detachable box magazines held eight rounds. Work ceased in the late 1980s. See also "Erma EP-452".

Model 42T Made only in 1984-5 and intended for plinking and casual target shooting, this was a single-action pistol with a 6-inch barrel and adjustable sights. The finish was almost always blue, and the grips were checkered walnut. See "Erma ESP-85A".

Model 79K Similar to the M40, sharing the finish and general constructional features, this was offered in 32 ACP or 380 ACP. The magazines held seven rounds. See also "Erma EP-457, EP-459".

CHÂTELLERAULT ARMS FACTORY

Manufacture d'Armes de Châtellerault ("MAC"),
Département de Vienne, France.
Founded in 1819 and closed in 1968, this French small-arms and ordnance factory also made (or perhaps simply assembled) 7.65mm Petter-type Model 1935S pistols immediately after World War II. Details of the MAS 35S will be found in the "Saint-Étienne" section.

A French 9mm M1950 pistol, made in Châtellerault.

MAC-50 Made in Châtellerault for about 10 years, beginning in 1953, this was an improved version of the 7.65mm MAS 35S chambered for the 9mm Parabellum round. Externally similar to the 35S, it had a radial hammer-blocking safety lever on the top left side of the slide immediately ahead of the ring-head hammer and a slide stop on the left side of the frame above the trigger. The magazine catch was a cross bolt through the frame. The butt was extended to hold a 9-round single-column magazine, and the grips were usually plastic (though the guns assembled by Saint-Étienne in 1963, after production in Châtellerault had ceased, had wood grips that were grooved horizontally). The factory initials "M A C" ("M A S" for Saint-Étienne) will be found on the left side of the slide, with the designation on the right. The serial number is usually on the right side of the frame ahead of the trigger. MAC-50 pistols are 7.6 inches long, have 4.4-inch barrels and weigh about 33.5 oz.

CHICAGO FIREARMS COMPANY

Chicago, Illinois, USA.
This promotional agency was organized by P.H. Finnegan to sell a US-made version of the Turbiaux (q.v.) disc-pistol, which was sold as the *Protector* or *Chicago Protector*. Finnegan then approached the Ames Sword Company and redesigned the Protector, with the help of an Ames engineer, to incorporate a grip safety over the barrel. This resembled a trigger and had to be kept pressed to permit firing. A few other small changes were made in accordance with Finnegan's 1893 patent, and Ames began work on an order for 25,000 pistols identifiable by "Chicago Firearms Co. Chicago Ill." on the body. But only 1500 were delivered, and even they were late. Finnegan sued Ames; Ames counter-sued and other interested parties joined in. Finally, the unfortunate manufacturer gained rights to a pistol it didn't want. Ames unsuccessfully tried to market the Protector for some years, and then abandoned the project entirely.

CHINESE STATE FACTORIES

Any attempt to tabulate the handguns emanating from China in the 20th century would be doomed before it started, since they often defy classification. The expression "Chinese Copy" is no mere figure of speech when applied to pistols. Apart from some "official" patterns — such as the well-known 45 ACP Mauser C/96 made in the Shensi and Shantung arsenals in the 1930s — most were produced by the handful in backyard workshops. The 1900-type FN-Browning was particularly favored, but virtually all the Chinese variants shared a fine crop of spu-

rious markings. Some of these were incomprehensible strings of letters, but others were facsimiles of prized trademarks such as the Mauser banner.

Consequently, this section records only those pistols that served the Chinese military forces prior to the emergence of Norinco (North China Industries Corp., q.v.) in the 1960s. Most of the earliest guns were supplied by the Soviet Union, reflecting the Sovietization of the army of the People's Republic of China in the 1950s. These were then copied in China, with modifications that have gradually increased as the gap between Soviet/Russian and Chinese political viewpoints widened.

Type 51 This copy of the Tokarev TT-33 could be distinguished by the finer retraction grooves on the slide and Chinese-character markings. It chambered the Soviet 7.62mm pistol cartridge, also known as the "Type 51" in China.

Type 59 A Chinese-made 9mm Makarov, this was identical with its Soviet prototype except for a slight difference in weight. The cartridge was also designated "Type 59".

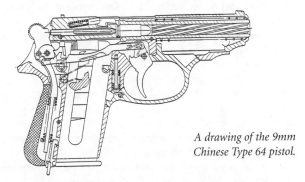

A drawing of the 9mm Chinese Type 64 pistol.

Type 64 Basically little more than a simple blowback, this unusual weapon had a built-in silencer. It chambered a special *rimless* 32-caliber cartridge known as the Type 64, made only in China; the standard 32 ACP round will not fit, as it is semi-rimmed.

The silencer was formed in a bulbous casing around the barrel. Escaping gas was trapped by a series of rubber discs and directed into an expansion chamber filled with wire gauze. In the normal course of events, silent discharge would be followed by the clatter of the slide as it blew back and extracted the spent case, then ran forward to reload. Though the Type 64 will work in this way, if absolute silence is required, the slide can be locked to the barrel to prevent movement. The shooter could then depart the scene, manually opening the breech when the opportunity presented itself.

Type 67 This was simply an improved Type 64 with a near-tubular silencer that was noticeably more slender than its predecessor; operation remained the same.

CHIPMUNK MFG, INC.

Medford and Prospect, Oregon, USA.
Chipmunk and its predecessor, Oregon Arms, have made a few single-shot 22 LR rimfire target pistols, built on what was designed as a bolt-action rifle. Introduced in 1985 for metallic-target shooting under IHMSA rules, the "Silhouette" had a 14.9-inch barrel and was 20 inches long. It had open sights and a plain pistol-grip butt.

LOUIS CHOBERT

Paris, France.
Chobert, of 16 rue Lafayette, described himself as an "arquebusier", an old-fashioned term for "gunsmith". Yet he was no more than a salesman, dealing largely in imported Belgian revolvers of the cheaper kind. The usual weapons found with his name are hammerless small-caliber Velo-Dog revolvers with folding triggers. These were popular as home

and personal defense weapons in the 1880s and were made by any of a dozen small Liége companies.

CHUCHU

Best known for a block-action carbine issued in the 1870s to gendarmerie in Brazil, Athanäse Chuchu also patented a four-barreled 22 RF folding pistol in 1884. It embodied a rotating firing pin, driven by a self-cocking hammer that struck the four cartridges in succession. A hinge allowed the barrels to be folded beneath the frame, making the gun easier to pocket, and a latch prevented the cartridges falling out of the chambers. Pushing on the head of the rod that passed down the center of the barrel cluster ejected all four cases. It is assumed that small numbers of the Chuchu pistol were made (perhaps in Liége as the carbines had been), but survivors are few and far between.

WYTOLD CHYLEWSKI

Basle, Switzerland.

In the early days of the automatic pistol, promoters often made much of the fact that a revolver could be fired one-handed, whereas the autoloader required both hands to cock and load before firing. Chylewski, born in Poland but resident in Switzerland, was one of many inventors who tried to develop a pistol that could also be operated with one hand.

Many attempts failed simply because a complexity of levers was rarely compatible with powerful military cartridges, but Chylewski had the sense to restrict his intentions to a 25-caliber blowback pocket pistol with a weak recoil spring and a short slide travel. A connection between the front edge of the trigger guard and the slide enabled the shooter, by pulling back on the guard with the forefinger, to cock and load. It was then a simple move to transfer the forefinger to the trigger. Some designs even released the slide automatically and then allowed additional pressure on the trigger guard to push back on the trigger and fire the gun.

Chylewski received several patents in 1910-18, and a few guns—probably no more than 200 or so—were made by Schweizerische Industrie-Gesellschaft (SIG). These bore "BREVET" above "Chylewski" on the left side of the retraction-spur block. Unfortunately, SIG no longer has any record of the exact number.

What happened next is not clear. Many surviving Chylewski pistols have had the one-hand feature disabled, and it has been suggested that this may have arisen from conflict with one-hand cocking patents granted to Ole Krag. Assuming they had not simply expired, ownership of Chylewski's patents and designs may have passed to Bergmann (q.v.) and then Lignose. Similar guns were produced as the *Einhand* in the late 1920s.

More remarkably, the design re-appeared in China in the early 1980s. It was called simply the "Type 77" and marketed by the North China Industries Company ("Norinco", q.v.). This pistol is almost identical to the Einhand version of the Chylewski, though chambered for the Chinese 7.62mm Type 64 cartridge.

CIMARRON FIREARMS MFG CO.

Fredericksburg, Texas, USA.

Founded in 1984, this business is primarily a distributor of Italian-made caplock and cartridge revolvers, customarily purchased from Pietta, San Marco and Uberti (q.v.). They have been sold in the USA under a variety of names.

Colt patterns These are usually made by Uberti.

• *Richards Conversions* These are essentially caplock revolvers adapted to accept cartridges, details being found in the Colt section. Cimarron has offered Model 1851 and Model 1861 (Navy) and Model 1860 (Army) patterns in chamberings ranging from 38 Special to 45 Long Colt. Finish may be blue or nickel, with grips of

walnut or ivory. The barrels will measure 5 inches (all three), 7 inches (Navy guns only) or 7.5 inches (Army guns only).

• *Model 1872 Open-Top* A copy of the immediate predecessor of the Peacemaker, this reflects the influence of the Colt caplocks and lacks the strengthening strap above the cylinder. The frame may be brass or steel, the barrels are 5.5 or 7 inches long and chambering may be 38 Colt, 38 S&W Special, 44 S&W Russian or 44 S&W Schofield.

• *Colt Peacemaker* The basic "Frontier Six Shooter", or "Model 1873 Frontier", has been offered in several distinctive patterns. Barrels can measure 4.75, 5.5 or 7.5 inches, and the chamberings can be 357 Magnum, 38-40 WCF, 44-40 WCF, 45 Long Colt or 45 ACP. A charcoal-blue finish is an optional extra.

A "New Model P", offered in Old Model or New Model ("prewar") styles, has a variety of barrels—4.75 to 7.5 inches—and may be chambered for cartridges ranging from 32-20 WCF to 45 Long Colt. The Model P has been offered as the "A.P. Casey Model" and "Rinaldo A. Carr Model", the names referring to the reproduction US Army inspector's cartouches that are pressed into the grips. The former has a 5.5-inch "Artillery" barrel, and the latter has the 7.5-inch "Cavalry" type. Chamberings are restricted to 45 Long Colt.

The "Model P Junior" is a reduced-scale version of the standard Model P, approximately one-fifth smaller. Chambered only for the 38 Special cartridge, it may be obtained with barrels of 3.5 or 4.75 inches.

The "Sheriff's Model", confined to 44 WCF or 45 Long Colt and built on an Old Model frame, has a 3-inch barrel that lacks the ejector case. The "New Sheriff's Model" is similar but built on a New Model frame and fitted with a 3.5-inch ejector-case barrel. It is available in 357 Magnum, 44 S&W Special, 44-40 WCF and 45 Long Colt.

The "US Cavalry Model" (sometimes known as the "General Custer 7th Cavalry Model") has replica US military markings, a 7.5-inch barrel, a cylinder chambered for 45 Long Colt only and an "Old Model" frame. The "Rough Rider Artillery Model" is similar, but has a 5.5-inch barrel.

A "Frontier Flat Top Model" (or "1880 Frontier Flat Top"), introduced in 1998 in either of the two frame styles, has adjustable sights—back for windage, front for elevation. The barrel measures 4.75, 5.5 or 7.5 inches, chamberings being 357 Magnum, 44-40 WCF, 45 S&W Schofield and 45 Long Colt.

The "Bisley Model", also added to Cimarron's list in 1998, duplicates the original cramped-looking "high-grip" style. Barrels and chambering options duplicate those of the Flat Top, and the finish is usually rich blue with a color case-hardened frame. A "Bisley Flat Top" is also made, with sights that are adjustable for windage (back) and elevation (front).

Introduced in 1993, the "New Thunderer" is a standard single-action gun, built on an Old Model frame, with ejector-case 3.5-, 4.75- or 5.5-inch barrels. A "Thunderer Long Tom" has the full-length 7.5-inch "Cavalry" barrel. The plates of the bird's-head grip may be plain or checkered walnut. Chamberings range from 357 Magnum to 45 Long Colt. The "Lightning" is similar to the Thunderer but has a lighter frame and chambers the 38 Special cartridge; its barrels measure 3.5 to 5.5 inches. The finish of these guns is usually a rich blue with a color case-hardened frame.

Dating from 1997, "El Pistolero" is an inexpensive derivation of the Frontier Six Shooter, with brass straps and trigger guard. The grips are plain walnut, and the finish is overall blue. Offered in the three standard barrel lengths (4.75, 5.5 and 7.5 inches), the gun chambers only 357 Magnum or 45 Long Colt.

S&W Schofield patterns Made by Armi San Marco and introduced to the Cimarron catalog in 1999, the basic *Model No. 3 Schofield* (or "1875 Schofield") has a 7-inch barrel and a six-round cylinder chambered for the 44 S&W Russian, 44 S&W Special, 44-40 WCF, 45

S&W Schofield or 45 Long Colt cartridges. The "Civilian" and "Military" patterns differ only in their markings. The *Schofield Wells Fargo Model* is similar, but the barrel is merely 5 inches long and weight is reduced accordingly.

CLAIR BROTHERS

Saint-Étienne, France.

It has often been claimed, especially by the French, that the Clair Brothers — Benoît, Jean-Baptiste and Victor — produced the first practical automatic pistol, but this has equally often been contested. R.K. Wilson, author of *Automatic Pistols* (1943), wrote that "It is said that the brothers were just simple-minded mechanics who shunned publicity and who were apparently too ingenuous to patent their ideas. If this is so, they were indeed unusual inventors and quite unlike any other of the breed ever seen in the gun trade ... " However, Wilson was something of a xenophobe who was reluctant to look at evidence anywhere other than in the English-speaking world.

The Clairs were granted a variety of European patents, beginning in France in 1887, and undoubtedly made some gas-operated shotguns (called "L'Éclair") at the beginning of the 1890s. The actual production date of weapons is in some doubt.

Michel Josserand, in *Pistols, Revolvers & Ammunition*, claims that a five-shot pistol was made in this period, but Lelu (in *L'Exposition Universelle de 1900 à Paris*) prefers 1895. The phrasing of the 1893 patent may suggest that nothing more than a model had been made at that time, but much more research is needed.

The Clair pistol included in a patent granted in Britain in 1893 had a circular tube magazine in the butt, curling round to meet the frame, and chambers what seems to be the standard French rimmed 8mm revolver cartridge. Later drawings show rimless arounds in the magazine, the proportions of which suggest the 9mm Steyr or Bergmann-Bayard rounds, but the suspicion exists that these were added by promoters who were anxious to depict the Clair system to best advantage. Surviving guns have conventional tube magazines beneath the barrel.

There is no doubt that Clair pistols were offered commercially. Pollard (Automatic Pistols, 1920) describes one as "large and clumsy compared to the French revolver, with a folding trigger and no trigger guard. Its ballistics are, however, an improvement on the revolver ... ", and he gave the following comparison: Clair velocity 850 ft/sec, penetration 120mm; French revolver velocity 752 ft/sec, penetration 85mm.

But any claim for the Clair Brothers to have produced the first automatic pistol has to be questioned. Paulson, Brauswetter (Bergmann), Laumann (Schönberger), Schmeisser (Bergmann) and Borchardt had all produced designs by 1893, and an Orbea gas-operated revolver had been made in Eibar as early as 1863.

CLARIDGE

Claridge Hi-Tech, Inc., Northridge, California, USA.

This gunmaking business, which operated briefly in the early 1990s, offered a single type of pistol. Work seems to have ceased in 1995.

Hi-Tec This handgun, little more than a cut-down submachine gun restricted to semi-automatic operation, was offered in "S" (short) and "L" (long) patterns, with barrels measuring 5.5 and 9 inches respectively. The latter was 15 inches overall and weighed about 50 oz with an empty magazine. Chamberings were restricted to 9mm Parabellum and 45 ACP, with magazines that held 18 (9mm) or 10 (45 ACP) rounds.

Features included a telescoping bolt, keeping overall length to a minimum, and a floating firing pin that could be locked by the manual safety. The sights were adjustable for windage (back) and elevation (front). The pistols had ventilated barrel shrouds, a cocking lever that protruded from the left side of the blued tubular receiver above the trigger and molded plastic grips on the aluminum-alloy or stainless steel frame unit.

A "T" variant was offered for target shooting, with a heavyweight 9.5-inch barrel, more sophisticated sights and sculpted wooden grips; a "ZL" pattern (7.5- or 9.5-inch barrel) had a laser sight beneath the fore-end.

CHARLES PH. CLÉMENT

Subsequently trading as "C. Clément, Neumann Frères", Liége, Belgium.

Clément is best known for an ingenious automatic pistol made prior to World War I, though he was also responsible for auto-loading carbines and a variety of sporting guns. See also "Arva", in the section devoted to "Unidentified guns".

∼ REVOLVERS ∼

Clément made a variety of guns of Bulldog, Constabulary and Velo-Dog patterns, before graduating to a copy of the Colt Police Positive (q.v.) that was promoted as the "Modèle Americain" or "American Model". The chambering appears to have been 38 Special. Most of the guns were sold by Neumann Frères (c. 1912-14) but retained the Clément monogram ("CC" linked back-to-back) molded into their grips.

∼ AUTOMATIC PISTOLS ∼

Clement-Fulgor Very little is known of this pistol, its only appearance being in advertisements of Neumann Frères in the 1913-14 period. It was a 32 ACP blowback based on the FN-Browning M1903 and has no Clément features at all, though it could be seen as the 32 ACP equivalent of the Clément 1912 model. Manufacture is said to have begun in 1913, and in view of the imminent beginning of World War I, production probably never reached any sizeable quantity.

M1903 This was a simple blowback design, with a fixed barrel and moving bolt. The barrel and return spring were concealed in a fixed housing attached to the frame by two screws engaged in a pillar formed by the rear end of the frame. The bolt was slightly offset to clear this pillar and recoiled from the concealment of the housing. The guns were chambered for the 5mm Charola & Anitua cartridge, but the ammunition was made in Belgium and, as the Clément pistol survived the Charola & Anitua pistol by some years, the cartridge also became known as "5mm Clément".

M1907 Clément soon overhauled the design, making the retaining pillar more robust and in the center of the frame and slotting the bolt to pass around it. An extension at the front of the bolt engaged the

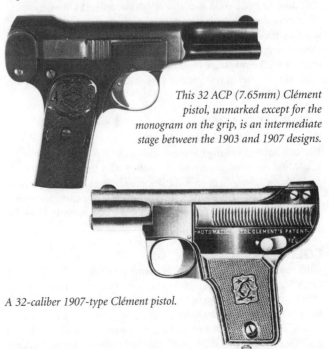

This 32 ACP (7.65mm) Clément pistol, unmarked except for the monogram on the grip, is an intermediate stage between the 1903 and 1907 designs.

A 32-caliber 1907-type Clément pistol.

return spring, which was in the housing above. The pistol was now chambered for 25 or 32 ACP cartridges.

M1908 A new model soon appeared, the main changes being in the shape of the grip, parallel sided instead of tapered, and the relocation of the magazine catch. On earlier models this had been a button recessed in the butt backstrap, but it now became a more conventional button in the side of the grip.

M1910 A fresh design patented in Belgium in 1910, this was a rationalization of the older design. The barrel housing and barrel were now a single unit, pinned to the same central pillar but retained by a catch controlled by the trigger guard; springing the guard free from the butt, and pulling it forward, unlocked the barrel unit to be pivoted upwards. This allowed the bolt to be removed and the barrel cleaned.

M1912 Clément's final product abandoned his patented designs and introduced a conventional 25 ACP blowback similar to the Browning 1906, though without a grip safety. Few were made, and there are many detail differences among surviving guns. One type has the barrel retained by a collar attached to the muzzle and screwed to the frame; another has the more usual slide but with the top recessed over the breech area, while a third (the newest) has a flush-topped slide. Some are marked "AUTOMATIC PISTOL CLEMENT'S PATENT", usually on the right side of the slide. The mark "MODELE 1912 BREVET 246878" (sometimes listed as "243849") lies above "– LIEGE – ACIER – GARANTI –" on the left. It is believed that by the time this pistol was ready for production, Clément had retired, and Neumann Frères had taken over the firm. But the company did not survive the German occupation of Liége in August 1914.

CLERKE

The Clerke Company, Santa Monica, California, USA.

This promoter advertised two revolvers in the mid-1970s. Both were nickel-plated solid-frame models, double-action, with swing-out five-chamber cylinders. One was in 32 S&W, the other in 22 LR rimfire chambering. Other reports speak of two blowback automatic pistols, in 22LR and 380 Auto. None of the guns appear to have remained on the market for very long.

COBRAY INDUSTRIES

Atlanta, Georgia, USA.

This company and SWD, Inc., also of Atlanta, are best known for manufacturing the Ingram submachine gun. Semi-automatic "handgun" versions, the 9mm Parabellum *M-11 Pistol* and 380 ACP *M-12 Pistol*, were also made in small numbers. Distinguished by their box-like shape, with the magazine protruding beneath a pistol grip placed virtually at the center of gravity, they were made largely of steel stampings and were usually parkerized.

CODY MFG. CORP.

Chicopee Falls, Massachusetts, USA.

This curious weapon might be considered the 1960s equivalent of the Velo-Mith and similar weapons, a revolver with the barrel shaped to resemble the front end of an automatic pistol. It was a hinged-frame 6-shot weapon in 22 LR, with a respectably-sized frame that gave a comfortable grip. However, it failed to attract many customers and had disappeared by the mid-1960s.

COLT

Colt's Patent Firearms Mfg. Co., Colt's Firearms Company (1847-1947); Colt's Manufacturing Co., (1947- 55); Colt's Patent Firearms Mfg Co. (1955-64); Firearms Division, Colt Industries (1964-89); Colt Firearms, Inc. (1989-91); Colt's Manufacturing Co., Inc. (1991 to date).

Among the most famous of all firearms inventors, Samuel Colt was born into an affluent family in 1814. Blessed with an adventurous spir-

it, he determined to make a name for himself, and after a short period selling patent medicine, spent most of his life inventing and manufacturing firearms.

The first Colt long arms were made in Baltimore in 1832-5, working well enough to encourage Colt to seek patents in the USA, Britain and France. A factory was founded in Paterson, New Jersey, but the venture failed in the early 1840s after a variety of caplock guns had been made. Success awaited cooperation with Eli Whitney and the production of the so-called "Walker Colt" and "Dragoon Colt" revolvers of the late 1840s. These in turn led to the creation of the factory in Hartford, Connecticut, and to the highly successful 36-caliber Navy Revolver of 1851. This was followed by many others, including the 44-caliber Army Model of 1860, until Colt died suddenly in 1862 during the Civil War.

The war made a huge fortune for the company, which was controlled by directors who were skillful enough to retain a substantial lead in the arms field. Even though the first metallic-cartridge Colts were inferior to their Smith & Wesson rivals, the adoption of the Single Action Army (SAA) revolver by the US Army (in 1873) clawed back the lead. Smith & Wesson was so committed to export orders in this period, most notably for Russia, that the US commercial market remained virtually at Colt's mercy.

The SAA has since dominated the legend and myth of the cowboy and the Wild West, allowing "Colt" to become synonymous with "revolver". The adoption of the perfected 38-caliber Colt revolver by the US Army, in 1892, was another landmark even though the choice of caliber was subsequently rescinded in favor of 45. Colt revolvers have also been supplied in huge quantities to police forces not just in North America, but also throughout the world.

The development of automatic pistols followed a similar pattern. Though Colt rejected the original 1897-patent blowback, which was initially exploited in Europe by Fabrique Nationale d'Armes de Guerre (q.v.), development of the locked-breech Brownings allowed a pistol incorporating the perfected "one link" depressor to be adopted by the US Army in March 1911. This particular gun, perhaps the most influential of all military handguns, not only remained service issue until the adoption of the 9mm Beretta M9 in 1985 (a decision that still rankles with many people) but has also laid the basis for countless copies, clones and customizations.

Despite the success of the AR-15/M16 Armalite rifle series, the recent history of the company has included great financial difficulties. Strikes, lock-outs and acrimonious mergers followed, until a management buyout finally restored an independence. The present operations have slowly regained strength by returning to the virtues that made Colt's name—good quality, careful manufacture and sound design.

Note: No attempt has been made to catalog the commemorative issues that have become popular since the 1960s. A comprehensive list of these will be found in the latest edition of the Standard Catalog of Firearms.

～ SINGLE-SHOT PISTOLS ～

Breechloading pocket derringers became popular in the mid-1860s, when the 41 rimfire chambering became standard. Many designs were exploited, but Colt entered what had become a crowded field simply by purchasing the National Arms Company (q.v.) of Brooklyn in 1870. This gunmaking business was promoting the guns that were to become the First and Second Model Colts. All Colt derringers are loaded by pivoting the barrel, the National models by swinging the barrel sideways about a pin beneath the breech—so that the barrel dropped to the left—and the Third Model by swinging the barrel horizontally so that the breech moves to the right.

First Model Derringer (1870-90) This was almost identical with the National equivalent, but bore the Colt name and address. The barrel swung sideways and down to reload, and the butt was a small curled pattern forged integrally with the frame. The barrel was 2.5 inches long,

The Colt No. 1 derringer.

the front sight was a semicircular blade and a rear-sight notch was cut in the hammer spur. Two notches gave the hammer half- and full-cock positions, and a spring-loaded sheath on the right of the breech locked the barrel in place. The First Model was 4.9 inches long and weighed just under 7 oz; finish could be blue, nickeled or silver-plated, usually with light scroll engraving on the frame.

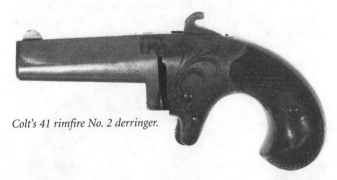

Colt's 41 rimfire No. 2 derringer.

Second Model Derringer (1870-90) This was identical with the First Model except that separate walnut grips replaced grips that had been forged integrally with the butt. Production is generally agreed to have amounted to about 6500.

The 41-caliber Colt No. 3 ('Thuer') derringer.

Third Model Derringer (1871-1912) Patented by F. Alexander Thuer, this was a considerable departure from the National patterns. It looked more like a pistol than its predecessors, with a conventionally shaped butt, walnut grips and a bronze frame that was customarily nickel- or silver-plated. The barrel was still 2.5 inches long and the overall length a fraction under 5 inches, but the weight dropped to 6.5 oz. The frame ran forward under the barrel, carrying a vertical barrel-pivot screw. This allowed the barrel to swing laterally for loading, an ejector pin pushing the empty case out of the chamber at the end of the opening movement. The earliest guns had a prominent bolster around the barrel-pivot screw, and the sheath that protected the trigger was vertical instead of angled forward. It has been estimated that about

45,000 Third Model derringers were made, although, as they were contemporaneous with National-type guns, the precise quantity is difficult to determine.

Camp Perry Model (1920) Named after the NRA range in Ohio, this 22-caliber single-shot pistol was Colt's first attempt to enter the specialized target-shooting market. Prototypes were tested in the Camp Perry matches as early as 1920, but the guns were not marketed commercially until the beginning of 1927. The frame of the Officer's Model Target revolver (q.v.) was fitted with a special flattened "chamber block" instead of the cylinder. The barrel ran back into the block, and the entire unit could be swung out to the left for reloading. The gun weighed about 35 oz, which was claimed to accustom the shooter to the weight of the full-bore Officer's Model. However, few purchasers were convinced of these merits, and sales of the target pistol, which bore "CAMP PERRY MODEL" on the left side of the chamber block, were restricted to 2525 pieces. The manufacture of parts stopped in February 1939, but new guns were still being offered when World War II began. Most guns were blued, with walnut "Colt medallion" grips. The earliest examples had 10-inch barrels, but an improved version, introduced in 1934, had a 10-inch barrel and a recessed-head chamber to allow high-power ammunition to be used. The firing mechanism was improved, gaining a straighter trigger lever and a faster lock-time.

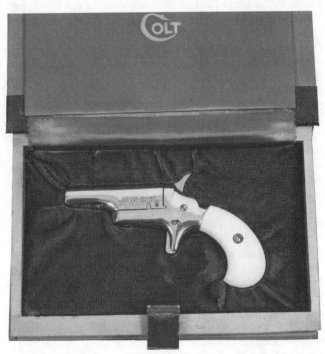

A limited-edition stainless-steel Colt "No. 4" derringer in 22 Short, sold in a case disguised as a book.

Fourth Model Derringer (1959-1963) At the same time as the Colt Single Action Army was revived, so was this derringer, intended largely for collectors. To allow them to be fired for amusement, they were in 22RF Short caliber and some 112,000 were sold. It was a copy of the Third Model except for caliber and finish, as many were elaborately engraved and finished with wood, ivory or mother-of-pearl grips.

Lord and Lady Model Derringers (1970) The success of the Fourth Model led to the production of these, a fancy pair of what was actually the Fourth Model. The Lord Derringer had a gold-plated frame, blued barrel and walnut grips. The Lady model had a gold frame and barrel, blued hammer and trigger and simulated pearl grips. Both were in 22RF Short chambering.

～ REVOLVERS ～

These are treated approximately chronologically in order of introduction. However, as guns such as the Single Action Army remained in production for many years, sub-variants introduced are entered under the date of the original pattern. Hence the Bisley version of the SAA, dating from 1894, precedes the double-action Colt "Lightning" of 1878 in the directory.

Colt-Thuer (or "Thuer Transformation") Patented in September 1868 by F. Alexander Thuer, this was a complicated and comparatively unsuccessful metallic-cartridge conversion of the open-frame caplock revolvers that had made Colt's name during the Civil War. About 5000 revolvers were altered in 1869-70, including the 31-caliber 1849 Pocket, 36-caliber 1851 and 1861 Navy, 44-caliber 1860 Army, and 36-caliber 1862 Pocket and Police patterns. The cylinders were shortened to allow an auxiliary ring (containing a separate rebounding firing pin) to be placed between the cylinder and the recoil shield. Though the chambers were bored entirely through the cylinders, they were loaded from the front with a unique tapered-case cartridge necessary to avoid infringing the Rollin White patent controlled by Smith & Wesson.

Colt-Richards (or "Richards Transformation") The expiry of the Rollin White patent allowed Colt to introduce a conventional metallic-cartridge conversion that relied on the simple substitution of a bored-through cylinder for the caplock pattern. Patented in July 1871 by Charles B. Richards, a "Conversion Plate" (a circular disk containing a firing pin and a pivoted loading gate) was placed behind a shortened cylinder, and an ejector rod sliding in a tubular case was attached to the right side of the barrel. About 9000-10,000 Richards Transformations were made on the basis of a number of the old caplock designs, including the 44-caliber M1860 revolver, 1153 being converted for the US Army in 1871, and the 36-caliber M1851 and M1861 with 368 38-caliber rimfire adaptations going to the US Navy in 1873.

Colt-Richards & Mason (or "Richards-Mason Transformation") This was an improved form of the Richards Transformation, with an ejector patented in July 1872 by William Mason, a talented designer who is credited with work not only on the Single Action Army Model but also the double-action trigger mechanism of the Lightning revolver—not counted among Colt's better achievements. However, Mason was also responsible for the first of the Colt swing-out-cylinder designs.

Many of the 30,000 Richards & Mason transformations had newly forged barrels, and it is clear that they were not initially intended simply as a stop-gap. The 38-caliber adaptations of the 1862 Police and Pocket revolvers were the most numerous, identifiable not only by the Mason ejector rod, with a case-mouth that lay much closer to the cylinder than the Richards type, but also by the extended nose of the hammer. The separate firing-pin disk/short-cylinder combination had been eliminated in favor of a full-length cylinder.

House Model (first pattern, 1871-4) This was the first Colt revolver specifically made for metallic cartridges. A small, light, solid-frame 41 RF design with a short curved butt and a sheathed trigger, it had a barrel measuring 1.5 or 3 inches and weighed 14.5 oz (3-inch barrel). The

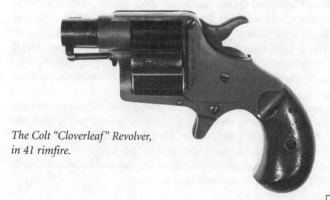

The Colt "Cloverleaf" Revolver, in 41 rimfire.

four-chamber cylinder gave rise to the nickname "Cloverleaf", owing to the deep flutes between the chambers. Each chamber was recessed to conceal the cartridge rim and was loaded from the right side simply by manually rotating the cylinder until it was clear of the frame. A sheath kept the cartridges in place as the cylinder rotated and could be swung aside for loading. Alternatively, the cylinder could be removed from the frame and the empty cases poked out by an ejector rod housed inside the cylinder arbor pin.

First-model guns had brass frames, often nickel-plated, and steel barrels that could be finished in blue or nickel. Grips were usually rosewood, although walnut examples are known. Markings included "PAT. SEPT, 19, 1871" on the topstrap of the frame. The earliest hammers had a high spur, but this was later changed to one less likely to catch in the pocket. Total production is estimated as 7500 guns.

• *Second Model* (1874-6) Made from serial number 6100, initially interspersed with the original Cloverleaf, this had a conventionally flat-surfaced five-chamber cylinder. The barrel length was standardized at 2.875 inches, and the ejector rod was discarded. Loading could still be done through the side groove, but unloading had to be done by removing the cylinder. Only about 2500 revolvers of this type are said to have been made.

The Colt 22 rimfire Open Top Pocket revolver.

Open-Top Pocket Model (1871-7) Anachronistic for its day, this sold well enough to retain popularity into the 1880s; total production is estimated as 114,000. The seven-shot 22 RF revolver had barrels measuring 2.4 or 2.9 inches, an open brass frame (usually nickel-plated) and a plain cylinder. The butt was of bird's-head form, with separate rosewood grips, and the usual sheath trigger was employed. Loading could be done with the help of a groove cut in the rear right side of the frame, behind the cylinder. The earliest guns had an ejector rod on the right side of the barrel, but this was abandoned in 1874 and the cylinder had to be removed to expel its contents.

Open Top Rimfire Model ("New Model Army Revolver", "New Model Holster Revolver" or "Model 1872") Though the US Army had decided as early as 1868 to adopt only a solid-frame revolver design, Colt offered yet another open-top weapon in the hope of gaining a military contract. Chambering a special 44-23-200 cartridge (not the 44 Henry rimfire, as so often claimed), it was speedily rejected. The M1872 had a six-chamber cylinder, a small Navy-style grip, a maritime scene rolled into the cylinder and a flat-side frame lug grooved to receive the ejector case. It remained in production for four years to satisfy the commercial market, while the Single Action Army Model was being perfected, but total production probably amounted to merely 7000-7500. Many of these were sold in Mexico after the introduction of better designs, often plated with nickel and fitted with ornate pressed-metal or carved ivory grips. Uniquely for a cartridge Colt, the rear sight lay on the rear end of the barrel-block ahead of the cylinder.

Single Action Army Model ("SAA" or "Model 1873") This was the successor to the Open Top, developed in 1871-2 from all the Colt revolvers that had gone before. It was developed specifically to met the requirements of the US Army and incorporate the latest metallic-cartridge technology.

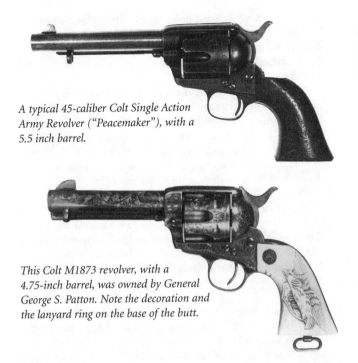

A typical 45-caliber Colt Single Action Army Revolver ("Peacemaker"), with a 5.5 inch barrel.

This Colt M1873 revolver, with a 4.75-inch barrel, was owned by General George S. Patton. Note the decoration and the lanyard ring on the base of the butt.

The solid frame is designed with economy of line, the flat underside sloping down and carrying a flattened oval trigger guard of relatively small dimensions. The standing breech is of a distinctive hemispherical shape, with a loading gate on the right side. The butt is set low, giving the pistol a high sight line above the hand, and is well flared to give an excellent grip. The rounded contours of the hammer shank match the curve of the breech, and the hammer spur is large, well curved for the thumb and deeply checkered to improve grip.

The barrel is a plain cylinder, and an ejector rod is carried in a slotted housing or "case" pinned to the right lower side of the barrel and brazed into a receiver in the frame. The front sight, brazed to the muzzle, is a plain flat blade. A simple rear-sight groove running the length of the topstrap, above the cylinder, was suggested by the US Army Board of Officers convened in December 1872 under the Presidency of Captain John Eadie; the first few hundred guns had the rear of the frame "pinched" upward to form a small open "V"-notch.

It is usually claimed that the so-called "Old Model" SAA, chambered for blackpowder ammunition, had a cylinder axis-pin that was retained by a screw; the later "New Model", strengthened for smokeless propellant, had a spring-button axis-pin retained. However, the retainer had been patented by William Mason as far back as September 1874 and had been introduced to the SAA in 1893; virtually every gun made after 1896 was so fitted. However, as the first smokeless-propellant chamberings were offered only in 1900, the distinction being drawn between the "Old" and "New" models on the basis of propellant may be misleading.

- *Single Action Army Revolver, military patterns* (1873-91) Beginning with an order for 8000 guns placed on July 23, 1873, a total of 37,063 revolvers were acquired by the US Army. They had a "military finish" blue on the barrel and cylinder, less lustrous than the commercial equivalent, color case-hardened frames and plain oil-finished walnut grips. Inspector's initials (e.g., "DAL" for David A. Lyle) will be found in a cartouche impressed in the grips, often accompanied by the date of inspection.

  Military-service guns originally had 7.5-inch barrels. They were initially issued to mounted units, and full-length guns (of any type) are now often known as "Cavalry Models". However, after the introduction of the 38-caliber M1892 and M1894 revolvers, most of the SAAs were withdrawn. The first batches of nearly 17,000 survivors were recalled in 1893, about 6400 being altered in Springfield Armory in 1895-1903 to emerge with barrels that had been cut to 5.5 inches. The guns were refinished, inspected once again and then reissued to men of the light artillery batteries. Consequently, this short-barreled pattern has acquired the sobriquet "Artillery Model". Surviving unaltered long-barrel guns were given to state militiamen.

- *Single Action Army Revolver, commercial patterns* (1873-1940) The SAA was always regarded as a tool, and although many ornate presentation or "commemorative-issues" examples have been made, the standard revolver was plain and unadorned.

  The SAA usually had a polished blue finish on its metal parts, excepting the color case-hardened frame. The barrel-top mark on the earliest examples was a cursive ("script") form, but this was eventually replaced by simpler "block" lettering. The grips were invariably walnut, often varnished, until checkered rubber patterns bearing an eagle-and-shield motif were introduced in c. 1882. These lasted until 1897, when the "rampant colt" design was substituted. However, purchasers could request deluxe grips, ranging from mother-of-pearl to ivory; barrel lengths from 2.5 to 16 inches (the most popular were 4.75, 5.5 and 7.5), often with German-silver front sights; and finishes that included nickel, silver or gold plating. A few guns intended for presentation or exhibition were decorated by the leading gun-engravers of all time.

However, although initially produced for the army, the success of the SAA was so great that it became the symbol of the Old West: the immortal cowboy's gun. Production began in 1873 and continued until 1940, by which time 310,386 guns (excluding Flat Top and Bisley patterns) had been made. A few guns were assembled from existing parts during World War II, but work then ceased until popular demand persuaded Colt to recommence manufacture in 1955 (see below).

The SAA revolvers made prior to World War II were offered in thirty chamberings, from 22 Short rimfire to 476 Eley, though the popularity of each varied. By far the most common was 45 Long Colt, amounting to 150,683 examples—nearly half the total. The popularity of Winchester rifles "Out West" persuaded Colt to chamber revolvers for the most popular WCF ("Winchester Central Fire") cartridges. These included 32-20 WCF, 38-40 WCF and 44-40 WCF, the total numbers of SAA in each category amounting to 29,812, 38,240 and 64,489 respectively. The only other chambering to be applied to more than 10,000 guns was 41 centerfire (16,402).

At the other extreme, there were only nine in 38 S&W, four 45-caliber smoothbores, two each in 32-44 and 38-44 and only a single factory-original SAA in 32 RF and 380 Eley. However, it must be remembered that not only have guns been rebarreled and re-chambered down the years, but there is also a healthy market for fakes!

Few guns have had such an extended production run, and few revolvers have exceeded the total numbers of the SAA. In addition to Colt's own production, reduced almost to nothing in recent years, there have been many copies. A few guns were made in Spain prior to the Spanish Civil War, often showing important differences in detail, but nostalgia and the "fast-draw" craze created such a demand for single-action Western-style revolvers that they have been made in huge quantities—particularly in Italy by Armi San Marco and Uberti. Others have been made by in Switzerland by Hämmerli (subsequently passed to Interarms in the USA) and in Germany by Sauer and Schmidt. The SAA has also provided the inspiration for a legion of adaptations.

This SAA is not particularly unusual in either design or construction and is simply a solid embodiment of a single-action operating system that became obsolete within a few years of its introduction. It was based on patents granted to Charles Richards and William Mason in 1871-2 and on a third granted to Mason in 1875. The form of the patent markings, therefore, depends on the age of the gun.

The earliest guns lacked caliber marks, but, owing to a steady increase in options, these were added to the barrel or frame after c. 1880.

Among the most desirable are survivors of a few thousand 44-40 WCF revolvers dating from 1878-82, found in a variety of finishes, that bore "COLT'S FRONTIER SIX-SHOOTER" on the left side of the barrel. However, the mark was applied by an acid-etching process and was not particularly durable. Equally noteworthy are pre-1891 guns marked by the Colt agency in London, which display "COLT'S PT. F.A. MFG. CO. HARTFORD, CT. U.S.A. DEPOT 14 PALL MALL LONDON" on the barrel. The agency moved to Glasshouse Street, London, in 1892. British guns are often (though not exclusively) also chambered for British cartridges, particularly 450 Boxer (total production of 729 examples), 450 Eley (2697), 455 Eley (1150) and 476 Eley (161); many were also decoratively cased and accompanied by a variety of accessories.

The "Sheriff's" or "Storekeeper's" pattern, introduced in the early 1880s and offered in a variety of chamberings, had a short barrel—most commonly 4 inches long—and a special frame that lacked provision for the ejector rod/rod-case assembly. Nickel plating was popular (though blue finish predominated) and the front sight, which could snag in a pocket or waistband, was often absent.

The "Long-Flute Cylinder" SAA is another recognizable variant, made in 1913-15 to rid Colt of unwanted parts that had been in store for many years. The components in question were M1878 or "Double Action Army Model" cylinders, which, with care, could be altered to fit the SAA frame. Production amounted to 1478 guns, in 32-20 WCF, 38-40 WCF, 41 CF, 44 S&W Special and 45 Long Colt.

The SAA in its heyday was inexpensive and reliable, though only a fool carried the hammer (which had a fixed firing pin) down on a loaded chamber. The mechanism was so simple that there was comparatively little to break, and anything that did fail could be repaired by even the most inexperienced gunsmith. The only accessory offered with the gun was a turnscrew, and even that was not essential.

• *Single Action Army Revolver, rimfire type* (1875-80) Only about 2000 of these were ever made, supposedly to capitalize on the popularity of the 1866-type rimfire Winchester rifle. Unfortunately, the success of centerfire ammunition soon showed the weakness of the 44 Henry RF and so the guns—virtually all 2000 of them—were dumped in Central and South America. They included a high proportion of nickel-plated examples, some with eagle-and-snake grips, but were generally badly treated. Many of the original 7.5-inch barrels were shortened, and the ejector/rod-case unit, one of the weakest parts of an otherwise sturdy design, was removed. About 90 44-caliber revolvers were converted to 22 RF for sale in the USA, and a single example was made in 32 RF.

• *Single Action Army Revolver, Flat Top Target Model* (1888-95) This variant of the SAA was a specialized target-shooting version, made in very limited numbers. It was little more than a standard SAA with flattened topstrap on the frame, above the cylinder, instead of the normal grooved design. The rear sight was dovetailed into the flat strap, and the factory-fitted front sight became a thin German-silver blade pinned into a rectangular slotted block. However, sights could be replaced with their owner's particular fancy, and many variations will be seen. The ejector rod and its case were also frequently removed, the owners preferring to remove the cylinder to reload.

Barrel lengths ranged from 4.25 to 9 inches, though the 7.5-inch pattern was preferred. Factory records list 21 different chamberings in a total of merely 914 revolvers, the most popular being 38 Long Colt (122 examples), 45 Long Colt (100), 22 RF (93), 41 CF (91), 450 Boxer (89) and 450 Eley (84); only a single gun was ever chambered for the 44 S&W Special.

• *Single Action Army Revolver, Bisley Model* (1894-1915) Named after the premier British rifle range, at Bisley Camp in Surrey, England, this was a direct derivative of the Flat Top Target. It was built with British target shooters in mind, but, interestingly, most of the 44,350 guns were sold in the USA.

The Bisley butt has a distinctive hump-backed appearance, designed to lower the axis of the bore in relation to the shooter's hand and give a better hold in the manner that had become fashionable. The hammer had a low "dished" spur, and, internally, the hammer was hooked to the main spring by a stirrup in an attempt to reduce friction and improve the pull-off. The trigger is longer than that of the SAA, checkered and markedly curved.

Colt records confirm that 18 chamberings had been made prior to World War I, with barrels that ranged in length from 3.5 to 7.5 inches. Most guns were blued, with color case-hardened frames and checkered rubber grips. The most popular cartridge-option was 32-20 WCF (13,291 guns), followed closely by 38-40 WCF (12,163). There were also 8005 in 45 Long Colt and 6803 in 44-40 WCF. Only three guns, one in 44-caliber and two in 45-caliber, were smooth-bored.

• *Single Action Army Revolver, Bisley Flat Top Target Model* (1894-1913) Produced concurrently with the standard Bisley pattern, this could be identified by the design of its flattop frame and improved sights, which duplicated those of the 1888-vintage Target Model described above. The barrel length was standardized at 7.5 inches, and few, if any, alternatives were offered. Only 976 examples were made, but there were 14 chamberings ranging in popularity from 455 Eley (196 examples) and 32-20 WCF (131) to 32 Colt and 32 S&W (17 apiece) and 38 S&W (5).

New Line Pocket Models (1873-84) These were little more than the Open-Top rebuilt to have a topstrap over the grooved cylinder. When it appeared, the Open-Top became known as the "Old Model". In addition, the frame was lightened and refined. Loading was still by the groove, unloading by cylinder removal.

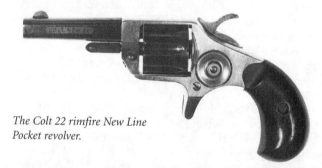

The Colt 22 rimfire New Line Pocket revolver.

• *22-caliber version* (1873-7) The barrel was originally cylindrical, but was later changed to flattened sides. There were two distinct models during the period of manufacture. The first had short cylinder flutes and locking recesses just behind them, while the second (1876) had the locking recesses on the rear face of the cylinder and lengthened the flutes accordingly. Both had 7-chamber cylinders and 2.25-inch octagonal barrels marked "COLT NEW .22". The frames were nickeled brass, the barrel and cylinder were either blued or nickel-plated, and the grips were rosewood. Total production is estimated at about 55,000. They are sometimes listed as the "Baby Colt", a promotional name coined by the well-known distributor of guns and ammunition, Benjamin Kittredge of Cincinnati, Ohio.

• *30-caliber version* (1874-6) Known to Kittredge as the "Pony Colt", this was simply an enlargement of the 22-caliber version with a five-chamber cylinder that accepted 30 RF Short or Long cartridges indiscriminately. The frame was steel, often color case-hardened, and the barrel and cylinder were blued. A few guns were engraved, but are the exception to the general rule. Only about 11,000 were made.

A Colt 32-caliber New Line Pocket revolver.

- *32-caliber version* (1873-84) Similar in construction to the 30-caliber New Line revolver, this was adapted for the 32 RF or 32 CF rounds and could accept long- or short-case ammunition. The cylinders had five chambers, and the barrel could measure 2.25 inches (common) or 4 inches (rare). Known to Kittredge as the "Lady Colt", about 11,000 of these guns were made.

The 38-caliber Colt New Line revolver.

- *38-caliber version* (1874-80) Only about 5500 of these guns were made, chambered originally for the 38 RF Short and Long cartridges and later for the 38 Short Colt centerfire round. With a 2.25-inch barrel, the 38-caliber New Line or "Pet Colt" (the latter being its Kittredge name) weighed merely 13.5 oz. A 4-inch barrel was an uncommon option.
- *41-caliber version* (1874-9) Little more than an enlargement of the 38-caliber guns and chambering the 41 RF round, the "Big Colt" was the largest of the series. After c. 1877, it was also offered in 41 Long Colt centerfire. The barrel measured 2.25 or 4 inches, the latter being comparatively rare, and the cylinder had five chambers. The short-barreled gun weighed about 12 oz. Only about 7000 were made.

Double Action Model (or "Model 1877") Samuel Colt was a life-long opponent of double-action trigger mechanisms. Stung by criticism of his designs, particularly from Britain, Colt had often stated publicly that the extra trigger pull required to cock the trigger and rotate the cylinder prevented a steady aim being taken. This was true of many of the designs of the 1850s, but the Beaumont-Adams was just one of the efficient double-action revolvers being made during the life of Colt's London factory and it might have been expected that the principles would be adopted in the USA. Colt himself died in 1862, scarcely time enough to witness the emergence in the USA of revolvers such as the Cooper, made in quantity in Philadelphia, which fitted a double-action trigger within external lines that were (no doubt deliberately) surprisingly similar to the Colt "Pocket Model" caplocks.

Eventually, the success of rival designs convinced the Colt management that a double-action design was necessary to retain a hold on the commercial market in North America. Designs that had been prepared by William Mason, dating back to 1871, were hurriedly perfected and the new double-action Colt was advertised for the first time on January 1, 1877. Chamberings were initially restricted to 38 and 41 Colt centerfire.

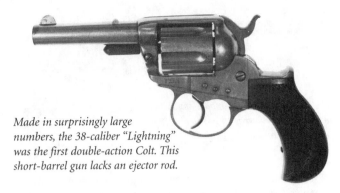

Made in surprisingly large numbers, the 38-caliber "Lightning" was the first double-action Colt. This short-barrel gun lacks an ejector rod.

"Soon known as the "Lightning" (38-caliber) and "Thunderer" (41-caliber), the names being bestowed by Kittredge of Cincinnati to boost sales, the first double-action Colt remained in production until 1909. It was based on the Single Action Army revolver, using what was effectively a scaled-down SAA frame, but had a slender bird's-head grip and a trigger that was set almost centrally within the guard. Barrel length varied from 1.5 inches to 10 inches, the most popular options being 2.5, 4.5 and 6 inches. Barrels measuring less than 4 inches—and some longer examples supplied to order—lacked the ejector rod and rod-case assembly.

The standard finish was originally blue, with a color case-hardened frame, and rosewood grips. Checkered rubber grips were introduced c. 1882, and a variety of individual finishes (including nickel plating) were offered. Individual guns may exhibit grips of mother-of-pearl or ivory, extensive decoration and precious-metal plating.

Individual cartridges were inserted in the cylinder through a pivoting gate on the rear right side of the frame and expelled by using the ejector (if fitted) on the right side of the barrel to push them back out through the gate. The short-barreled ejectorless "Sheriff's" or "Storekeeper's" guns had a removable cylinder arbor.

The action of the double-action Colts was complicated, and some of the individual components were only marginally strong enough to withstand continual use. However, there is no real evidence that gunsmiths found them unrepairable, and the manufacture of 166,849 in 1877-1909 shows that they were virtually as popular as the Single Action Army Revolver. The ease with which they could be fired commended the Double Action Models to discerning gunmen such as William Bonney ("Billy the Kid") and John Wesley Hardin; and, with Colt's hold on the US domestic market prior to 1900, it is not difficult to see why they survived for so long. Almost all of the guns chambered the 38 or 41 Colt cartridges, being marked "COLT. D.A.38" (or "41") in a panel on the left side of the barrel, though about two hundred were made for the 32-20 WCF round prior to 1897. Others will be found with the pre-1891 London address (14 Pall Mall) on top of the barrel.

DA Army & Frontier Model (or "Model 1878") The 38-caliber and 41-caliber double-action revolvers were aimed squarely at commercial markets and had little hope of attracting the attention of an army that was firmly wedded to 45-caliber handguns. The Army & Frontier Model was the immediate result, incorporating improvements in the trigger system that were ultimately patented by William Mason in 1881.

Although heavier and stronger than its predecessors, the Army & Frontier Model had a weak main spring—needed to allow self-cocking—and was prone to misfires and accidental discharges, the reasons behind its rejection by the US Army when first offered in 1879. Yet it was a better combat weapon than the Lightning and Thunderer, easier to repair and more resistant to misuse and dirt.

The Army & Frontier Model resembled the preceding models, with a bird's-head grip, but the shape of the frame behind the hammer followed a sinuous curve instead of the original SAA-like design. The bar-

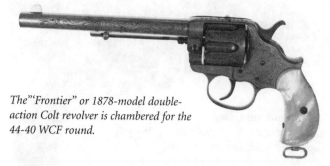

The "Frontier" or 1878-model double-action Colt revolver is chambered for the 44-40 WCF round.

rel was usually 4.75, 5.5 or 7.5 inches long, giving the revolver a weight of about 39 oz (7.5-inch type). Barrels from 2 to 12 inches were available on request with those measuring less than 4 inches being the ejectorless 44-40 WCF and 45 Long Colt "Sheriff's" or "Storekeeper's" patterns. Chamberings varied from 22 rimfire to 476 Eley, though 32-20 WCF, 38-40 WCF, 41 Colt, 44-40 WCF and 45 Long Colt were the most popular. Some guns were marked "OMNIPOTENT" on the barrel—another of the many names bestowed by Kittredge of Cincinnati.

When work ceased in 1905, 51,210 guns had been made. Among them were about 4200 45-caliber "Model 1902" guns, also known as the "Alaska Model", with blued finish, a lanyard ring on the butt, a 6-inch barrel, "U.S." on the frame and army inspector's marks on the grip. Among the most obvious features is the ungainly-looking trigger guard, which was deepened to admit a gloved trigger finger. A very few "hammerless" Army & Frontier revolvers were also made, with the hammer hidden by a separate shroud.

The 38-caliber Colt New House revolver.

New House Model (1880-6) This was an improvement of the New Line, with a square-heel butt. The five-chamber cylinders had long flutes, with the locking notches on the rear face, and the cylinder axis-pin was held by a lock screw that passed laterally through the frame. The sheathed trigger was retained, the topstrap was forged as part of the frame and the standard barrel measured 2.25 inches. Some guns were nickel-plated, though most were blued with color case-hardened frames; grips were rosewood or checkered rubber with "COLT" in an oval panel. Chamberings were restricted to 32, 38 and 41 centerfire. Demand, however, was not great and only about 4000 guns were made.

New Police Model (1882-6) Made in quantities similar to the New House Model, this was offered with barrels of 2.25 to 6 inches. Chambering was usually 38 Colt, though 32 CF and 41 Colt were also

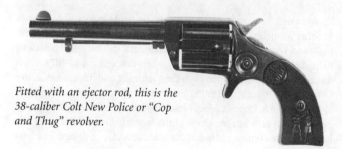

Fitted with an ejector rod, this is the 38-caliber Colt New Police or "Cop and Thug" revolver.

available. All but the shortest barrel options had an ejector rod. The molded rubber grips depicted a policeman arresting a thief, giving the popular name of the "Cop and Thug", although most of the guns exported to Britain had plain wooden grips.

Navy Model (1889-94) The advent of efficient auto-extracting revolvers, actively promoted by Smith & Wesson, slowly eroded markets that had previously been dominated by Colt. A search for a design that combined ease of use with strength of construction resulted in the introduction of a cylinder mounted on a yoke that could be swung laterally outward when the recoil shield on the left side of the frame was pulled backward to disengage the lock.

William Mason had filed a patent as early as 1881, though he was by no means first in the field. Stephen Wood, working for the Winchester Arms Company, had obtained protection for swinging-cylinder designs as early as 1876. Colt investigated features patented in 1884 by Horace Lord and Carl Ehbets, including a cylinder that swung on the topstrap and a trigger guard that swung down, forwards, and then clockwise to open the action and eject the cases. In fact, few avenues were left untouched by Colt's engineers in a most comprehensive exploration of exploitable designs. Finally, in November 1888, a patent protecting the finalized yoke-mounted cylinder design was obtained.

The "1889" or Navy-model Colt embodied features contributed by William Mason, Jean Warnant, Horace Lord, Carl Ehbets and other leading engineers. From then on, the improvements flowed steadily from the Colt drawing office and almost every year brought a new modification.

The cylinder was carried on a crane or yoke set into the left side of the frame, retained by a spring latch, doubling as a recoil shield, which slid forward to lock the cylinder by pushing a bolt into a recess in the cylinder arbor. Pressing back on the cylinder axis pin once the yoke had been opened allowed a star-shape extractor plate set in the rear of the cylinder to slide back and expel spent cases.

The 1889-type cylinder was revolved counter-clockwise and locked by a pawl engaging notches in its rear face. The frame was deepened at the front and the lower run beneath the cylinder—almost flat—was squared at the front edge, giving an appearance of solidity and strength. However, the method of locking the cylinder during the firing cycle was poor. It was substantially revised before the improved New Army & Navy Revolver appeared in 1892.

- *Navy purchases* The US Navy ordered 5000 38-caliber revolvers in 1889, with 6-inch barrels, blue finish and wooden grips. They could be identified by markings: "U.S.N." and an anchor on the buttstrap, accompanied by the caliber, the serial number, inspector's initials and the year of acceptance. A typical example reads "38 DA", "No. 2289", "P" over "WWK", and "1889". Very few of these survive in their original condition, as all but a handful were recalled in 1895 to be upgraded to approximate the Army M1892.
- *Commercial patterns* (1889-94) About 31,000 of these guns were made, with barrels measuring from 3 to 6 inches. Chamberings were confined to 38 and 41 Colt centerfire cartridges. Most of the revolvers were blued, with checkered rubber "rampant colt" grips, but nickel-plating was a popular option. M1889 revolvers can be identified by the design of the cylinders, which have long flutes and lack the locking or stop-notches, and by patent dates in the barrel inscriptions that extend only to 1888. The cylinders rotate counter-clockwise when viewed from the rear.

New Army & Navy Models (1892-1908) Trials undertaken in 1890-1 by the US Army revealed the weakness of the 1889-type locking system, which allowed the cylinder to rotate when the gun was holstered or even if the shooter attempted to turn the cylinder as the trigger was being pulled. The problem was addressed by combining the trigger with the cylinder-rotating pawl and adding a double-locking bolt, necessitating an extra set of bolt-stop notches in the periphery of

The 38-caliber M1894 US Army revolver, made by Colt.

the cylinder. The locking bolt dropped clear as soon as the hammer lifted to cock, and the pawl engaged the ratchet on the rear of the cylinder to commence rotation.

- *Military purchases* Satisfied with the changes that had been made, the US Army adopted the 38-caliber M1892 revolver, built on a robust "41-caliber" frame, to replace the 45-caliber M1873 (Single Action Army Model) in April 1892. Colt was given an initial order for 5000 guns, with 6-inch barrels and blued finish. Their markings included "COLT'S PT. F. A. MFG. CO. HARTFORD CT. U.S.A. PATENTED AUG. 5, 1884, NOV. 6, '88" on top of the barrel, with "COLT. D.A.38" on the left side. The bottom of the buttstrap bears the property mark, model-date and serial number in six lines. Inspectors' initials will be found on the frame and grips, one of the latter usually also bearing the date of inspection.

Service soon showed that the 1892-type Colt had serious weaknesses. The cylinder still revolved counterclockwise, which, as the mechanism opened to the left, tended to push the yoke/cylinder unit out of the frame as the trigger was pressed. Wear eventually prevented the chamber aligning properly with the bore, and the shooting became progressively less accurate. Changes were soon made, though there is still some doubt if the model-designation was changed. This arises because the marks on the butt, which are separated into short lines, can be read as either "U.S. ARMY MODEL 1896" (for example) or "U.S. ARMY MODEL", "1896". The first instance would suggest that the date is part of the designation, whereas the second could simply be a generic "army model" description with a separate date of acceptance. There is no doubt that the M1894 was a separate pattern, but the status of others is less clear.

The principal changes included the addition in 1894 of an interlock that prevented the gun firing before the yoke was fully closed, the improvement being credited to a Colt engineer named Frank Felton, and an additional patent acknowledgement of March 5, 1895, will often be found in the barrel inscription. Eight thousand original 1892-type revolvers were rebuilt to "1894" standards in Springfield Armory in 1897 and unaltered examples are now exceptionally rare.

Changes were made internally in 1896 after experience had been gained with smokeless ammunition. A lanyard ring was added to the heel of the butt in 1901, when the thickness of the grips was reduced, and the diameter of the bore was reduced in 1903 to improve accuracy. It has been claimed that cylinders rotated clockwise after 1901, but it seems that this improvement (though introduced commercially in 1893) was introduced, so far as the US Army was concerned, with the New Service Model of 1909.

- *Navy purchases* A few "Model of 1895" guns were acquired in 1895-7, incorporating the improvements made by Felton. They are distinguished by the markings on the backstrap, which parallel those of the M1889 Navy revolver (q.v.) excepting for the designation and the patent dates on the barrel.
- *Marine Corps purchases* About 800 "M1905" double-action revolvers were delivered to the US Marine Corps in 1905-9. Distinguished by round-heel butts, walnut grips and lanyard rings

on the butt-bottom, these also bear "U.S." over "M.C." markings on the buttstraps, differentiating them from 126 otherwise similar examples made for the commercial market, which had blue or nickel finish and checkered rubber grips.

- *Commercial patterns* Sales were brisk. When production ended in 1907, more than 291,000 had been made, and the reputation of Colt DA revolvers was secure. Most of the guns were blued, with checkered rubber grips, but nickel plating was popular and a few highly decorative examples were made to order. Chamberings were restricted to 32-20 WCF, 38 Long Colt, 38 Special and 41 Long Colt, the "non-Colt" options being comparatively rare. The manufacturer's marks will include reference to patent-protection granted in 1884, 1888 and 1895, which helps to date individual guns if the other indicators (e.g., serial number) are unclear. The New Army & Navy Model was superseded by the New Service Model (q.v.) in 1908.
- *Officer's Model* (1903-8) Intended for target shooting, offered only in 38 Long Colt and 38 Special, this was built on a slightly modified New Army frame. The sights had fine adjustments, controlled by lock-screws, and the checkered walnut grip lacked the customary medallions. Production was meager.

New Pocket Model (1895-1905) A reduced-scale personal-defense version of the 1892-type army revolver built on the Model "A" frame, this was offered in 32 Short Colt, 32 Long Colt or 32 Colt New Police/32 S&W Long chamberings. Barrels measured 2.5 inches to 6 inches, the finish was blued steel or nickel plating and the grips were usually checkered rubber with "COLT" in an oval. The most obvious improvement was the introduction of a clockwise-rotating cylinder, which tended to push into the frame as the trigger was pressed. Readily identified by a "COLT'S NEW POCKET" mark on the frame, the compact revolver was not only an instant success but also began an entire line of similar Colts. About 30,000 were made before the Pocket Positive (q.v.) was substituted.

A 32-caliber Colt New Police Revolver.

New Police Model (1896-1907) This is said to have been developed to satisfy the New York Police Department, purchaser of 4500 appropriately-marked guns in a special 32 New Police/32 S&W Long chambering. Guns were also offered commercially in 32 Short Colt and 32 Long Colt, with blue or nickel finishes and checkered-rubber "COLT" grips. The shape of the frame was a throwback to the 1889 Colt Navy revolver, with a straight underside, but the cylinder and locking mechanism duplicated those of the New Pocket Model. Distinguished by "NEW POLICE" on the frame, the gun remained in production until 49,500 had been made.

- *Target Model* About 5000 of these were made in the late 1890s. It was identical to the standard New Police Model except for a standardized 6-inch barrel and an adjustable rear sight set in a flattop frame.

New Service Model (1897-1944) Built on a "45-caliber frame", this, the largest of the swing-cylinder Colts, was intended as a military weapon from the outset and faced considerable competition from rival

A 455-caliber Colt New Service revolver, made for sale in Britain in World War I.

manufacturers seeking the same sort of contract. The guns did not initially sell in large numbers, but owing to large-scale purchases in 1917-18, 356,000 had been delivered when work finally stopped.

Initially available only in 45 Long Colt, the New Service was eventually available in 11 chamberings ranging from 357 Magnum to 476 Eley. Barrel lengths ran from 2 inches to 7.5 inches with a typical 4.4-inch-barreled 45-caliber example weighing about 40 oz. The general design was little different from the New Pocket Model of 1893, with essentially the same clockwise-rotating-cylinder mechanism, but minor changes improved the robustness and reliability. Additional alterations were made in the early 1900s prior to the M1909, including the introduction of a positive hammer-lock and a pivoted firing pin. This is acknowledged by the addition of the patent date, "JULY 4 1905", in the barrel-top inscription. Another patent (October 1926) was added after World War I.

Commercial New Service Model revolvers had blue or nickel finish. Their grips were checkered rubber until 1928, when medallions were let into checkered walnut. A few were made for target shooting, with long barrels and adjustable rear sights set in flattop frames. Among the rarest variants is a "Marine Corps" gun, destined for commercial sale, which had the characteristically small round-heel butt.

• *Model 1909* The failure of the regulation 38-caliber revolvers to stop fanatical opponents during the Philippine insurrection, coupled with the delay in perfecting the 45-caliber Colt M1911 pistol, persuaded the authorities to purchase New Service Model revolvers for the armed forces. The quantities were not particularly large, owing to the approval of the M1911, and surviving examples are comparatively scarce. Army-issue guns are marked "U.S. ARMY", "MODEL" and "1909" on the backstrap; those issued in the Navy and the Marines substitute "U.S.N." and "U.S." over "M.C." respectively. The grips of army and navy revolvers are plain oil-finished walnut, but the Marine Corps preferred checkering. All three types had lanyard rings on the butt-bottom.

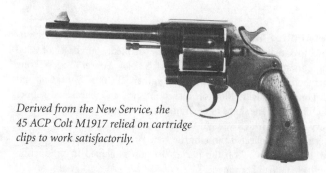

Derived from the New Service, the 45 ACP Colt M1917 relied on cartridge clips to work satisfactorily.

• *Model 1917* The "U.S. Revolver, Colt, Caliber .45-inch, Model of 1917" was chambered for the 45 ACP rimless cartridge. To position these cartridges in the cylinder and enable them to be ejected, they were fitted into two spring half-moon clips and then loaded in two clusters of three rounds into the cylinder; the clip ensured the correct headspace and it also gave the ejector something to push against. After 50,000 revolvers had been delivered, a shoulder was

added within each chamber to allow loose cartridges to be used; previously, these had often entered too far to be struck by the firing pin. About 151,700 Colts were acquired in 1917-18, and about a thousand were assembled after hostilities had finished for the commercial market. These lack "UNITED STATES PROPERTY" under the barrel; "U.S.", "ARMY", "MODEL", "1917" and the serial number on the backstrap; and the inspectors' marks that characterize military issues.

• *Shooting Master* Known to the Colt factory as "Model J", this was introduced in August 1900 and made in small numbers until World War II began. Distinguished by a 6-inch or 7.5-inch barrel, the Shooting Master was restricted to 357 Magnum, 38 Special, 44 Special, 45 Long Colt, 45 ACP and 455 Eley. Most guns had checkered Colt-medallion walnut grips, checkered butt straps, a hand-honed action, an adjustable rear sight in a flattop frame and a prominent front sight with the blade pinned in its seat. A "COLT SHOOTING MASTER" inscription appeared on top of the barrel. The earliest guns had broad-grip butts, but a narrow pattern subsequently became standard; the original pattern was then reduced to the status of an option.

Officer's Model Target (1908-40) Introduced to replace the "Officer's Model" version of the New Army & Navy Model, this was always a rather special revolver, intended for target shooting rather than general purposes. Built on the standard "41-caliber frame", the guns had 6-inch barrels, hand-finished actions and adjustable rear sights. They were customarily blued and had checkered walnut grips. Chamberings were restricted to 22 LR rimfire (introduced in February 1930) and 32 Colt Police Positive/32 S&W Long (from August 1932) in addition to 38 Special.

Pocket Positive Model (1905-45) Built on either the 32-caliber or 38-caliber frames (factory models "B" and "C", respectively), this gun owed its introduction to the development of the "Positive Lock" mechanism—patented in July 1905 by George Tansley—which ensured that the firing pin could not strike the cartridge unless the hammer had been drawn back to full cock. Apart from the incorporation of this feature, there was little change from the New Pocket Model. Production of the small-frame guns, introduced in 1908, continued until 1941, in 22 LR rimfire, 32 Colt Police Positive/32 S&W Long or 32 Long Colt; 1905-type large-frame guns (22 LR, 32 Colt PP, 38 Colt PP) were still being assembled in 1945-6. Most guns were blued, though a few nickel-plated examples were made; the grips were customarily checkered "COLT"-marked rubber. A few Pocket Positives were made with spurless hammers, allowing them to be carried in a pocket in greater safety, but it is not known whether this alteration was undertaken in the Hartford factory.

Police Positive Model (1905-43) Developed in answer to a demand for a more powerful version of the 32-caliber Police Positive, firing a heavier bullet with better ballistics, this 38-caliber gun was scarcely larger than its predecessor. Offered in blue and nickel, with barrels of 2-6 inches chambering 32 Colt, 32 S&W, 32 New Police, 38 New Police or 38 Special, it proved to be popular—more than 200,000 had been sold when production ceased. Police Positive revolvers were sold to many police forces, especially in the Americas, and others were acquired by European military purchasing commissions (including the British) in 1938-41. It was also widely copied by many Spanish makers, quality varying from good to terrible.

• *Police Positive Model* (32-caliber, 1907) This was essentially the New Police Model (q.v.) incorporating the Positive Lock mechanism, and was made in parallel with its predecessor for some months. Work continued until 1939, by which time about 200,000 had been made.

• *Pequeño or "Pequano" Model Police Positive* (1933) About 11,000 of these second-grade revolvers were made with left-over parts and poor-quality stocks on hand at the factory. They were dispersed throughout South America, in Puerto Rico and in the Philippines, and some survived to be bought by the British Purchasing Commission in 1940. The name derives from "El Pequeño" (Spanish: "The Little One"), but the guns were outwardly identical with the standard Police Positive.

• *Police Positive Target Model* Introduced in 1905 and made until 1925 as factory models "G" (centerfire) and "H" (rimfire), these guns had 6-inch barrels and adjustable rear sights. In October 1925, the original patterns were replaced by factory model "C", which was made until 1943. Offered in 22 LR rimfire, 22 WRF and 32 Colt Police Positive chamberings, these guns had narrow butts that were subsequently widened. Triggers were checkered, the topstrap was matted, and after 1934, the chambers were recessed to protect the case rims. About 28,000 target-type Police Positives were made.

Police Positive Special Model (1907-73) Also known as factory model "D", this was the first small-frame swing cylinder revolver to be made for a powerful cartridge and became a very popular police weapon. It could be chambered for 32 Colt New Police/32 S&W Long, 32-20 WCF or 38 Special cartridges, the cylinder being 0.25 inch longer than the standard Police Positive model to accommodate the longer rounds. Barrel lengths vary from 1.25 to 6 inches, the 4-inch version being most common, and more than 750,000 had been made when work stopped.

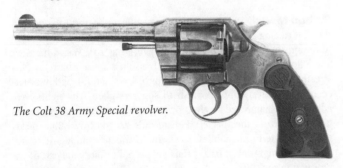

The Colt 38 Army Special revolver.

Army Special Model (1908-28) A modernization of the New Army & Navy Model (q.v.), built on the same "41-caliber frame", this incorporated several improvements. The shape of the frame was modernized, the front face being sloped back and the lower run deeply curved over the trigger guard. More of the trigger was exposed, and the cylinder rotation was changed to clockwise, thus pushing the cylinder into the frame. The hammer was given a loosely pivoting firing pin, and barrel lengths were restricted to 4.5 and 6 inches. Chamberings were restricted to 32-20 WCF, 38 Special and 41 Long Colt; finish was blue, or optional nickel plating; and the grips were successively checkered hard rubber with a rampant-colt motif, checkered walnut with a medallion, and checkered plastic. The butt was widened towards the end of production, the topstrap was matted, the trigger was checkered and a square-notch Patridge rear sight was fitted. Production, which continued until March 1928, totaled about 240,000.

Banker's Special Model (1926-43) Designed for "easy carrying and quick access ... primarily for bank employees", this 2-inch barreled variant of the Police Positive was restricted to 38 Special. Colt advertising made much of the fact that the full-size butt was retained, thus giving a good handgrip, and a few guns were made with spurless hammers. The US Postal Service equipped its railroad-mail clerks with this revolver and it was also used by some police forces. About 35,000 were made before production ended. Virtually all of them had been blued, though a few nickel-plated examples were made.

Detective Special Model (1926-73) This resembles the Banker's Special but was simply a 2-inch barreled Police Positive Special. It retained the long cylinder and was offered only in 32 and 38 New Police

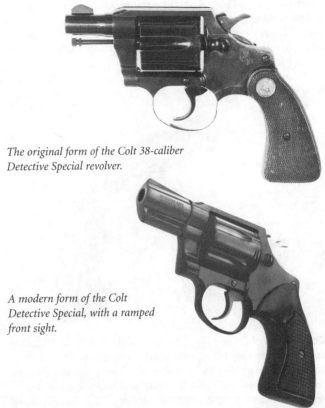

The original form of the Colt 38-caliber Detective Special revolver.

A modern form of the Colt Detective Special, with a ramped front sight.

(both discontinued in the 1930s). First-pattern guns were made until they were superseded by an improved "Second version", listed separately. Most were blued, with checkered wood or plastic grips. A few had even been made with a shrouded hammer, giving them the usual "hammerless" appearance.

Official Police Model (1927-69) Made on the basis of the "41-caliber frame", this was no more than the Army Special of 1908 under a new name. Few purchases were being made by the military in the mid-1920s, but, as large numbers of pistols were being bought by police forces, a change in name improved marketing potential. The revolvers were available in blue or nickel, with squared butts and checkered walnut or plastic grips. Barrels measured from 2 inches to 6 inches, the 2-inch option being offered with a slender round-heel butt. Chamberings were restricted to 22 LR rimfire (introduced in November 1930), 32-20 WCF (discontinued in 1942), 38 Special and 41 Long Colt (abandoned in 1930). The rear-sight notch was a broad Patridge-type square notch, the topstrap was matted, the trigger was checkered during production, and the chambers of post-1934 guns were recessed to protect the cartridge-case rims. Work continued until more than 400,000 guns had been made.

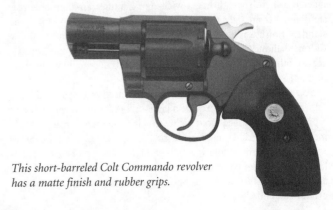

This short-barreled Colt Commando revolver has a matte finish and rubber grips.

Commando (1942-5) A special wartime order for factory guards and other security forces, placed by the US Government in November 1942, this was the 38-caliber Official Police revolver with a 4-inch barrel (a few 6-inch examples are known), a matte-blue sandblasted finish and checkered hardwood or plastic grips. The guns can be identified by the "COLT COMMANDO" marking on the barrel; about 50,000 had been made when World War II ended.

A 38 Special-chambered Colt Cobra.

Cobra Model (1950-73 - "first issue") This was really the Detective Special with an alloy frame, reducing the weight from 22 oz to 15 oz. Offered in blue or nickel, with checkered walnut grips, the Cobra had barrels of 2 inches or 4 inches. The butts were generally round-heeled, though a squared version could be supplied with the longer barrel. Chamberings were restricted to 22 LR rimfire, 32 and 38 Special. The "second issue", made into the 1980s, had wraparound grips and a streamlined ejector-rod shroud beneath the barrel.

Aircrewman (1951) About 1200 revolvers of this type, with an alloy frame and an alloy cylinder that reduced weight to just 11 oz, were made for the US Air Force. Chambered exclusively for the 38 Special round, they had 2-inch barrels, walnut grips and blue finish. They are believed to have been marked "U.S." over "A.F." on the buttstrap. None were sold commercially.

Border Patrol Model (1952) Only 400 of these revolvers were made. Little more than an ordinary Police Special with a heavy-duty 4-inch barrel, they were designed to be exceptionally strong and resistant to rough treatment. Chambering was restricted to 38 Special.

357 Magnum Model (1953-61) This was a deluxe version of the Trooper, fitted with a wide-spur hammer, target sights and an enlarged walnut grip. Chambering 357 Magnum or 38 Special cartridges, the guns had 4-inch or 6-inch barrels. Only about 15,000 had been made when the "Magnum Model" was absorbed into the Trooper production run.

Officer's Model Match (1953-1972) The "O.M.M." as it was usually called, carried on from the "Special" when that was discontinued in 1952. Offered only in 22 LR rimfire and 38 Special, with a heavy tapered 6-inch barrel, it had a wide-spur hammer, an adjustable rear sight and a front sight that was mounted on a prominent ramp. The standard finish was blue, and the grips were checkered walnut with the Colt medallion. There was virtually no change between it and its predecessor other than a change of frame metal and consequent numbering in the "J"-frame series.

Trooper Model (1953-69) This was introduced as a separate design, rather than a variant, to provide a large-caliber holster revolver. It had a prominently ramped front sight, an adjustable target rear sight, 4-inch or 6-inch barrels, and could be had in 22, 357 Magnum or 38 Special chamberings. Finish was blue or nickel, grips being "medallion"-type checkered walnut. The frame and general design were almost identical to the Police Special, and sales remained good until production ended.

Marshall Model (1954-6) This was the Official Police revolver marketed under another name. Offered in 38 Special with barrels of 2 or 4 inches, with blue finish and walnut grips, the Marshall had a round-heel butt, an "M"-suffix serial number and "COLT MARSHALL" on the left side of the barrel. Only 2500 were sold.

Agent Model (1955-73 - "first issue") This was basically a short-butt version of the Cobra (q.v.), intended to facilitate concealment. A "second issue" (1973-86) could be identified by a shroud around the ejector rod, most of the guns made after 1981 also displaying a matte instead of polished-blue finish.

Courier Model (1955-7) Made for only two years, this was a variant of the Cobra with a 3-inch barrel and a shorter butt. It was offered in 22 LR rimfire and 32 caliber only and production amounted to less than 3000 guns.

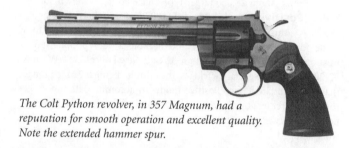

The Colt Python revolver, in 357 Magnum, had a reputation for smooth operation and excellent quality. Note the extended hammer spur.

Python Model (1955-90) This became one of the prime weapons in the Colt catalog and was the first revolver to show a substantial change in design since the early 1900s. The Python has a flat-faced hammer and a floating firing pin in the frame. It also has a heavy barrel, with a streamlined shroud covering the ejector rod, and a full-length ventilated top-rib with a stippled finish to suppress glare. The sights were adjustable. Chambered for the 357 Magnum cartridge, the Python was heavy at 41 oz (4-inch barrel). Finish could be Colt Royal Blue, nickel plate or matte-finish stainless steel. An "Ultimate" stainless-steel version with a high-polish bright finish appeared towards the end of the production run.

• *Python 38* (1955-6) A few of these guns were made early in the production run, chambered specifically for 38 Special ammunition and so marked, but were unsuccessful.

• *Python Hunter* (1981) Offered only for a single year, these guns had neoprene "Gripper" grips and 8-inch barrels that had been drilled and tapped for optical-sight mounts. A 2x Leupold long-eye-relief sight was supplied as part of the "Hunter Kit" contained in an aluminum case.

Single Action Army Model (1956-75 - "Second Generation") The enduring popularity of the SAA eventually persuaded Colt to resume manufacture. Much of the original tooling remained at the factory, and the first guns are said to have incorporated original pre-war parts even though small changes had been made internally. The variations between pre-and post-war models are so slight that only the serial numbers can be relied upon to positively identify the difference—post-war guns have "SA" suffixes. However, the multiplicity of chamberings, no longer economic, was reduced to 357 Magnum, 38 Special (scarce), 44 Special and 45 Long Colt. Some catalogs, particularly those produced in the 1980s and 1990s, refer to "European Models" in 9mm

Modern variants of the Colt Single Action Army revolver or Peacemaker include the "150th Anniversary Commemorative".

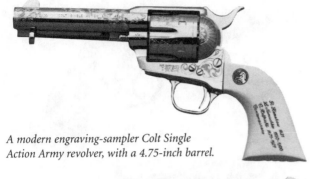

A modern engraving-sampler Colt Single Action Army revolver, with a 4.75-inch barrel.

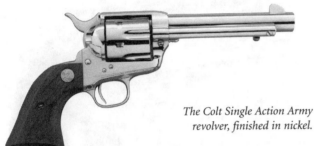

The Colt Single Action Army revolver, finished in nickel.

(actually in 357 Magnum) and a "U.S. Model" in 45 Long Colt. Barrel lengths were 4.75, 5.5 and 7.5 inches; finish was a rich blue, with a color case-hardened frame. The grips were usually walnut, though checkered rubber can be found. Some guns were nickel-plated, a few were extensively decorated, and ivory grips may be found. "Third Generation" or "Third Issue" guns (1976-81) had additional changes in the action but continued the numbering series until, at 99999SA, the suffix became a prefix. A few guns were made in 4-40 WCF, with "Black Powder" frames (cylinders were retained by a screw). In 1982, faced with legions of Italian, German and similar "re-creations" of the SAA, Colt elected to reduce the project to "custom" status. Guns were then offered only through the Custom Shop, with barrels of 3-10 inches, several finish/engraving options and chamberings restricted to 357 Magnum, 38-40 and 44-40 WCF, 44 Special and 45 Long Colt. Standard commercial guns then reappeared in 1992 in 44-40 WCF and 45 Colt.

• *Sheriff's Model* (1960-75 - "Second Generation") This designation was restricted to about 500 guns with special frames and 3-inch barrels that lacked the ejector assembly. All except 25 nickel-plated examples were blued, with color case-hardened frames, and chambering was restricted to 45 Long Colt. Serial numbers had an "SM" suffix. A few "Third Generation" guns were apparently made in 1976-81 but may have been numbered in the regular "SA" series.

Buntline Model (or "Buntline Special", 1957-74 - "Second Generation") The Buntline has acquired a reputation far in excess of its importance, numbers or usefulness. The name attaches to a variety of long-barreled SAA revolvers. Guns of this type were exhibited at the Centennial Exhibition in Philadelphia in 1876 but were "Buggy Rifles" with folding rear sights and skeleton stocks.

It is probable that others were made for the 1878 St. Louis Exposition, but legend says that five such guns were purchased by Edward Judson, a writer of Western novels under the pseudonym "Ned Buntline", for presentation to lawmen Bat Masterson, Wyatt Earp, Charlie Bassett, Neal Brown and Bill Tilghman. This is supposed to have occurred in the early 1900s, but supporting evidence has never been provided by factory records. It is possible, of course, that Judson acquired them elsewhere or commissioned the work from an independent gunsmith.

The barrels of these guns measured 10, 12 and 16 inches. Colt records note the manufacture of only 18 long-barreled guns (apparently numbered in the 28800-28030 block), and it is believed that some

were cut to more manageable proportions within a few years of purchase. However, so remarkable was the mystique attached to the "Buntline Special" that about 4000 12-inch-barreled guns have been made in 45 Long Colt. All but a few nickel-plated examples have been blued, with walnut or checkered rubber grips. They are marked "COLT BUNTLINE SPECIAL .45" on the left side of the barrel.

A few "Third Generation" guns were made in the late 1970s but are difficult to distinguish externally from their predecessors. The revisions were primarily internal.

Frontier Scout Model (light-frame or "Q" type, 1957-71) To meet the demand for an SAA replica that was smaller and lighter than the standard gun, this alloy-frame model was produced in 22 LR rimfire (introduced in 1957) and 22 WMR (1959), simplifying construction and reducing costs. Produced by modern precision casting methods, the Frontier Scout was about 8 oz lighter than the standard SAA. The earliest guns had a duotone finish — bright frame, blued barrel and cylinder — but this was soon reduced to the status of an option when overall bluing was introduced and was abandoned in 1961. The standard barrel lengths were 4.25 and 4.75 inches, but a 9.5-inch "Buntline" was made in small numbers. A few of these Frontier Scouts had "F" suffix numbers instead of "Q".

• *Frontier Scout Model* (heavy-frame or "K" type, 1960-70) Identical with the "Q" type apart from the heavier frame, which gave an overall weight 6 oz greater than its predecessor, this was sometimes nickel-plated and almost always had walnut grips. It can be distinguished by the serial-number prefix.

The Colt New Frontier Model, with a 5.5-inch barrel and adjustable sights.

New Frontier Model (Single Action Army Revolver, 1961-75 - "Second Generation") This was the "target model" of the post-war SAA, capitalizing upon the presidential campaign slogan of John F. Kennedy in 1960. The principal features were the adjustable rear sight and flattop frame. Most of the guns were blued, with a color case-hardened frame, but nickel plating and "full blue" were supplied on request. The grips were usually walnut, serial numbers had an "NF" suffix and the barrels (4.75-7.5 inches long) displayed "COLT NEW FRONTIER S.A.A." on the left side. Chamberings were restricted to 357 Magnum, 38 Special (very scarce), 44-40 WCF (very rare), 44 Special (scarce) and 45 Long Colt. Total production amounted to about 4250, including about 70 45-caliber "Buntlines" with 12-inch barrels. A few "Third Generation" New Frontier revolvers were made in 1976-81, with internal changes that are identified by five-digit serial numbers. Options were restricted to 44-40 WCF (rare), 44 Special and 45 Long Colt.

Scout Model (SAA, 1962-71) This was a reduced-scale version of the Single Action Army revolver, chambered only for the 22 LR rimfire round. The barrels measured 4.75, 6 and 7 inches. The earliest examples were blued with color case-hardening on the frame, but this was abandoned in 1971 in favor of all-blue. The original walnut grips were replaced by checkered rubber grips at about the same time. Revolvers of this later type are said to have remained on sale into the mid-1980s.

Peacemaker Scout (SAA, c. 1964-82) Made exclusively in 22LR and 22 WM rimfire, with interchangeable cylinders, this had a steel frame that was often color case-hardened instead of over-all blue. The grips were usually checkered plastic with a molded-in eagle motif. Most of the guns had 4.5 or 6-inch barrels, though a few "Buntlines" were made with 7.5-inch barrels. Serial numbers had a "G" (or occasionally "L") suffix.

- *Peacemaker Scout New Frontier Model* Dating from 1982-6, this had adjustable sights, a safety bolt running laterally through the frame and "GS"-suffix serial numbers. It is suspected that comparatively few were ever made.

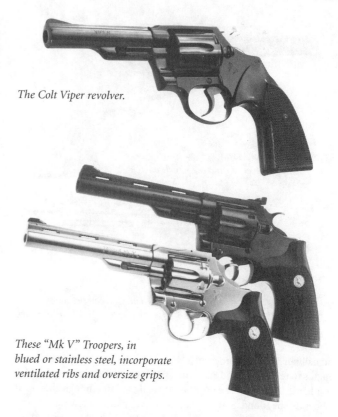

The Colt Viper revolver.

A Colt Diamondback revolver.

Diamondback Model (1966-86) This is a combination of the Detective Special and the Python, amalgamating the short-grip medium frame of the Detective Special with the ventilated rib, shrouded ejector rod, target hammer and sights of the Python. Heavy for its size, chambering either 22 LR rimfire of 38 Special, it had barrels measuring 2.5-6 inches. Finish was blue or nickel, grips being checkered walnut with inset Colt medallions.

Mark III Series (1969-83) These guns were designed to replace many of the existing Colt revolvers, introducing features such as stainless-steel springs, surface-hardening of all major parts, and a general improvement in manufacture and finish.

- *Police Mark III* Chambered for 38 Special only, with 4-, 5- or 6-inch barrels.
- *Lawman Mark III* (1969-82) Chambered for 357 Magnum only, with a 2- or 4-inch barrel, this could be obtained in blue or nickel. The grips were checkered walnut.
- *Metropolitan Mark III* (1969-72) Offered only in blue, with walnut grips, this was an updated Official Police Model. It chambered 38 Special ammunition and had a heavy 4-inch barrel.

These "Mk V" Troopers, in blued or stainless steel, incorporate ventilated ribs and oversize grips.

Mark V Series (1982-5) This designation referred to revised versions of the Mark III Trooper and Lawman models. The principal changes included an improved trigger mechanism, a shorter lock time and a redesigned grip.

Boa (1985) This was a special version of the Trooper Mark V, with a high-polish blue finish, made exclusively for the Lew Horton Distributing Co. of Southboro, Massachusetts.

Peacekeeper (1985-7) Introduced to replace the Lawman Mark V, this was similar to the King Cobra but had a half-length ejector-rod shroud and a distinctive matte-blue finish. The same "Gripper" neoprene grip was fitted. Sights were adjustable, barrels measured 4 or 6 inches and chambering was restricted to 357 Magnum.

A member of the "Mk III" series, the Trooper was a basic form of the Python.

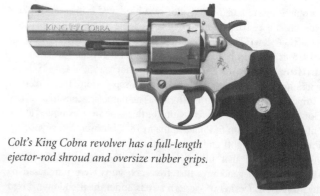

Colt's King Cobra revolver has a full-length ejector-rod shroud and oversize rubber grips.

- *Trooper Mark III* (1969-83) This version of the Mark III series, intended as the target-shooting pattern, had a barrel that was shrouded and ribbed in the same manner as the Python. It was offered in 22 LR and 22 WM rimfire, 357 Magnum and 38 Special, with barrels of 4-8 inches. The guns had adjustable sights and walnut grips and were available in blue or nickel finish.

Viper (1977-84) This 38 Special revolver was little more than an updated version of the Police Positive (q.v.), with a 4-inch barrel and an alloy frame. Finish was restricted to blue, grips being checkered walnut.

King Cobra (1986-9) This was a stainless steel model of Python pattern with a forged-steel frame, a full-length ejector-rod shroud, a solid barrel-rib and ultra-short hammer fall. The grips were wraparound neoprene "combat" pattern with finger grooves in the front edge, and the adjustable sights had red and white inserts to assist rapid aiming. Barrels measured 4-8 inches, compensating ports being offered on the longest options in 1997-9. The finish was originally blue or stainless steel, but bluing was abandoned in the early 1990s.

The Colt Anaconda.

Anaconda (1990-9) The latest variation in the "snake" line, the Anaconda is a large-frame revolver in 44 Magnum, 44 Remington Magnum (introduced in 1997) or 45 Long Colt (1993) chamberings, with the ventilated rib and full-length ejector shroud of the King Cobra and a hand-filling contoured wraparound grip. The entire pistol is machined from stainless steel, with a matte finish, and is intended to satisfy hunters and silhouette shooters. Barrels measure 4-8 inches, many being drilled and tapped for optical sight mounts (after 1998) or ported (1997-9 only) to reduce muzzle jump.

• *Anaconda Realtree* Made in small numbers in 1996, only in 44 Magnum, this had a distinctive all-over camouflage pattern.

Police Positive Special Mark V (1994-7) This is an updated version of the original revolver, with a streamlined ejector-rod shroud, fixed sights and a round-heel butt with a checkered rubber grip. Offered only with a 4-inch barrel, giving an overall length of about 9 inches, it can chamber 38 Special and "+P" ammunition.

SF-VI (1995-9) This is really little more than a matte stainless-steel version of the Detective Special but incorporates a transfer-bar safety system and has a wraparound rubber "medallion" grip. Chambered only for 38 Special ammunition, it can be obtained with a 2-inch (standard) or 4-inch (optional) barrel.

• *SF-VI Special Lady* (1996) A variant of the standard pattern with bright finish and a spurless "bobbed" hammer.

Detective Special II (DS-II, 1997-8) Similar to the SF-VI, this shares the transfer-bar safety system. It was offered only in 38 Special, with rubber "combat" grips, until the introduction of a 357 Magnum option in 1998. The name was almost immediately changed to "Magnum Carry".

Cowboy Single Action ("CSA", 1998 to date) This is a variant of the Single Action Army Model incorporating a transfer-bar safety system. Available exclusively in 45 Long Colt, with a 5.5-inch barrel, it is invariably blued with a color case-hardened frame. The grips are plain walnut.

Magnum Carry (1998-2000) A new name for what was previously the "Detective Special II" (above).

Python Elite (1998-2000) This was a short-lived revision of the original 1950s Python (q.v.), chambered only for the 357 Magnum round. It had a 6-inch ventilated-rib barrel, a transfer-bar safety system and adjustable sights. The grips were checkered walnut with an inset Colt medallion.

Survivor (or "Multi-Caliber", 1999-2000) This short-lived revolver, made of stainless steel, was based on a Phillips & Rodgers chambering design that allowed the cylinder to accommodate a variety of rimmed and rimless cartridges interchangeably: 9x18, 9mm Parabellum (9x19), 9mm Largo (9x23), 9mm Ruger, 380 ACP, 38 Super, 38 Special (and "+P") and 357 Magnum. The five-shot guns had 3-inch barrels and textured rubber "combat" grips.

∿ AUTOMATIC PISTOLS, PRE-1945 ∿

The advent of the automatic pistol in Europe in the 1890s was largely ignored by American manufacturers who were then preoccupied with revolvers. Colt was the exception, realizing that the pistol could easily rival the revolver if it could be made to operate reliably. The company took an interest in the development of automatic pistols from the start, gaining a lead over its leading American gunmaking rivals that lasted until the 1950s.

Among the earliest designs was a strange blow-forward design patented in 1895 by Carl Ehbets, but the first to show genuine promise was a small Browning blowback demonstrated in the summer of 1895. This was successful enough to encourage the inventor to deliver three additional guns early in 1896 — each operating in a different way. Eventually, John Browning received a variety of patents in April 1897. Ironically, the original small-caliber blowback, which had no future as a military weapon, was abandoned in favor of a recoil-operated locked-breech design. Exploitation of the blowback was left to Fabrique Nationale d'Armes de Guerre (q.v.), though Colt's management ultimately had a change of heart and began production of adapted FN-style guns in 1903.

The recoil-operated gun originally chambered a rimmed 38-caliber revolver cartridge, but it was soon adapted to semi-rim ammunition loaded with smokeless propellant. Demonstrated to the US Army towards the end of 1898, it was developed to become the "Model 1900". This eventually led to the 45 ACP Model 1911, which has enjoyed the longest production run of any automatic pistol in history.

A 1900-type Colt-Browning pistol, used by the US Army for trials. Note the position of the retraction grips and the spur-type hammer.

A commercial version of the M1900 Colt-Browning, with conventional slide-retraction grips.

Model 1900 (1900-3) This was little more than a development model, as only 3500 were made. The US Army bought 200 for field trials (1900-2), and the US Navy bought about 50; the rest were sold commercially.

Patented by John Browning on April 20, 1897, the action could be locked by two transverse ribs on the upper surface of the barrel engaging in two grooves machined in the upper surface of the slide. The barrel was held to the frame by two links — one at the front, one at the rear — until recoil moved it back and down, parallel with the frame, until the lugs disengaged from the grooves. This left the slide free to move back, extracting the empty case, and to chamber a fresh round on the return stroke. Shortly before the forward movement ended, the links raised the barrel until the lugs once again engaged the slide recesses.

The 38-caliber Model 1900 had a 6-inch barrel and a detachable magazine containing seven rounds. It was blued, with a color case-hardened hammer and rear sight/safety assembly, and the retraction grips lay conventionally at the rear of the slide on all but a few guns made for military trial. These had the grips at the front of the slide to facilitate charging the gun with the left hand by pushing instead of pulling. The hammer had a flat cocking spur. The combination of rear sight and safety catch proved to be too delicate, so most of the guns made after 1902 had a plain rear sight; the safety mechanism was simply eliminated. Most of the military trials guns had plain wooden grips, held to the butt with short threaded bolts, but those sold on the commercial market had grips of checkered walnut or molded rubber.

The first 38 Colt-Browning "pocket pistol" was a large and heavy gun.

A 38-caliber military M1902 Colt-Browning.

The 32-caliber M1903 Colt-Browning was the first of the blowback pocket pistols.

Model 1902 (Sporting, 1902-8) This was an improved version of the M1900 with the most notable changes being the introduction of an inertial firing pin and a hold-open latch that slid vertically in a channel in the left side of the frame. These changes were patented by Browning in September 1902. The 1900-type firing pin was long enough to rest on the primer as the slide closed and represented a source of potential danger if an accidental discharge occurred. Shortening the pin ensured that it only passed through its bush to strike the cap when propelled by the hammer. The grips were molded rubber (with the rampant-colt motif) and the hammer was rounded, but otherwise the mechanical arrangements were the same as those of the 1900 model. The slides bore patent marks to 1902. The first guns also had checkered or "diced" retraction grips at the front of the slide, but these were subsequently replaced by the more familiar rear-of-slide grooves. The tip of the hammer spur was usually rounded, and the rear sight was dovetailed into the slide. About 7500 Sporting Model guns were made.

• *Model 1902, Military* This was a little larger and heavier than the Sporting M1902 and had an eight-round magazine. The front of the slide was checkered, and the squared-off butt had a lanyard ring. Two hundred guns were purchased by the US Army for field trials, in January 1902, but the caliber was judged to be too small and the cavalrymen, in particular, expressed a strong preference for revolvers.

Model 1903 (Pocket Pistol, 1903-29) This was really the 1902-type Sporting Model with a short barrel and slide. "New" guns were still being sold from stock in the late 1920s, though it is assumed that production had stopped long before World War I. When promotion eventually ceased, about 26,000 had been made. The barrel was 4.5 inches long, but the 38-caliber M1903 was really far too big to be a "pocket" weapon.

Model 1903 Hammerless (Pocket Pistol (32 caliber), 1903-45) This was much more successful than the 38-caliber "pocket" model of the same date. Colt had observed the runaway sales of the Browning pistols being made in Europe by Fabrique Nationale d'Armes de Guerre and approached John Browning for a blowback design. Essentially a reduced-scale version of the 9mm FN-Browning M1903, which was intended for military use, the Model 1903 Colt chambered for the 32 ACP semi-rimmed cartridge. It had a detachable box magazine in the butt and, though called "hammerless", had a hammer concealed within the slide.

The guns had a slide stop, a grip safety, and the 4-inch barrel was shortened to 3.75 inches in 1910 after about 70,000 had been made. This was due to the elimination of the separate barrel bush. The finish was blue or, more rarely, nickel plate; the grips were rubber with the rampant-colt motif, until these gave way in 1924 to checkered walnut with an inlaid medallion. About 572,215 of these pistols had been sold commercially, and another 200,000 had been purchased on behalf of the US armed forces. Military guns are usually marked "U.S. PROPERTY" on the right side of the frame and have a matte-blue sandblasted or "parkerized" finish.

The M1905 Colt-Browning was the first of the 45-caliber guns.

Model 1905 (45 caliber, 1905-11) The Philippine Insurrection convinced the US Army of the need for a minimum caliber of .45-inch for any future sidearm, persuading Colt to begin work on an adaptation of the existing 38-caliber M1902. The new 45 "Rimless Smokeless" cartridge proved to be weaker than the US Army requested, but eventually led to the legendary 45 ACP.

The 1905-type military pistol retained the inertia-type firing pin and the two-link barrel-depressing system that swung the barrel down and back, parallel to the axis of the bore. It was tested extensively against guns such as the Luger and the Savage, performing well enough to become the favorite in "run-off" trials with the Savage after DWM had withdrawn the 45-caliber Luger from the competition.

However, the US Army took only 200 1905-type Colt-Brownings for evaluation, delivered in March 1908, and the production line that Colt had set up had produced only 6250 when work stopped. The guns had 5-inch barrels, seven-round detachable box magazines, and weighed about 33 oz empty. Military-trials guns also had a grip safety mechanism and a loaded-chamber indicator, the subject of patents granted to Peard, Ehbets and Tansley in 1908-9. The trials guns had spur hammers with full- and half-cock positions, enlarged ejection ports and long extractors that cut through the retraction grips.

Those that were sold commercially were blued, had walnut grips and color case-hardened hammers with a rounded spur. Approximately midway through production, after the military trials guns had been delivered, the hammer acquired an elongated pointed spur to facilitate thumb-cocking. Some of the pistols sold commercially after the advent of the M1909 (below) are said to have chambered the 45 ACP round. They had 4.9-inch barrels.

A small number of M1905 military-type guns (probably less than 100) also had the backstrap of the butt slotted to take a special leather and metal holster, so converting it into a carbine. However, the absence of any sort of safety device was an unattractive feature that caused such great problems in trials held in Britain that Colt was forced to seek a solution.

Model 1908 Hammerless (Pocket Pistol (38 caliber) 1908-45) This was little more than an enlargement of the 32-caliber M1903, chambered for a cartridge specifically designed for this pistol that subsequently became widely known as the "380 Auto" or "380 ACP" ("Automatic Colt Pistol"). Work continued until the end of World War II, but the 380 ACP guns were much less popular than their smaller cousins and only about 138,000 were made for the commercial market. Small, but unknown, numbers were also acquired militarily.

Model 1908 Hammerless (Pocket Pistol (25 caliber) 1908-41) This was the Colt version of the 6.35mm FN-Browning Model 1906 or "Baby Browning", which had proved to be exceptionally popular in Europe before Colt was persuaded to start production in the USA. This was truly a pocket pistol, 4.5 inches long with a 2-inch barrel, and weighed only 13 oz. The short butt was difficult to hold satisfactorily, but the recoil of the 25 ACP cartridge was light and the pistol was easily controlled. It was amply provided with safety devices, the original grip and manual locks being joined after gun No. 141000 (1916) by a magazine safety system designed by George Tansley. The standard finish was a rich blue, but substantial quantities of nickel-plated guns were sold and some highly decorative examples are known. The grips were either hard rubber, with "COLT" and a "rampant colt and C" motif. Markings included "COLT AUTOMATIC" above "CALIBER .25" on the right side of the slide beneath the ejection port. Production amounted to about 409,000.

Model 1909 (45 caliber, 1909-10) Though a lineal successor to the M1905, this was the first of the Colt-Brownings to incorporate the improved depressor system patented by John Browning in February 1911, though protection had actually been sought 18 months previously.

Browning replaced the cumbersome parallel-motion depressor of the M1905 with a single link beneath the breech and guided the movement of the barrel by inserting a barrel-bushing in the front end of the slide.

When the pistol is ready to fire, two lugs on the top of the barrel above the chamber engage recesses cut in the under-surface of the slide. The front of the barrel is supported in the bushing at the muzzle, and the rear of the barrel is held up by a pivoting link, attached to the barrel at the top and the slide-stop pin at the bottom.

When the gun fires, recoil moves the barrel and slide backwards. As the barrel runs back, it begins to pivot the actuating link around the slide-stop pin and the top of the link, which describes an arc, pulls the rear of the barrel down until the locking lugs disengage the slide. The barrel then comes to a halt, but the slide continues to move back, allowing the extractor to pull the empty case from the chamber, the spent case to be ejected, and the hammer to be cocked.

At the end of the recoil stroke, a return spring beneath the barrel, compressed during the opening movement, expands to drive the slide forward. This action strips a fresh cartridge out of the magazine and into the chamber, allows the link to swing the rear of the barrel back up and into engagement with the slide, and runs the locked parts back into battery. The hammer remains cocked and the pistol is ready to fire again.

A manual safety catch lies on the frame, and a grip safety (in the form of a movable plate) is let into the rear of the butt. Unless the hand grips the butt securely enough to release the grip safety, the weapon cannot be fired.

The system soon proved to be sturdy and reliable, although, because the barrel began to tilt before the bullet left the muzzle, there were concerns that the accuracy would fall short of the original "parallel motion" system. However, as with many firearms theories, practical experience showed that there was no noticeable difference.

The M1909 shares the external appearance of the M1905, with the grip almost square to the bore axis, but has a variety of refinements. In addition to the new method of depressing the barrel, these included revisions to the grip-safety mechanism and the replacement of the butt-heel magazine catch with a cross-bolt through the frame behind the trigger. The guns were 8 inches long, had 5-inch barrels and weighed about 43 oz empty. Their detachable box magazines held seven rounds.

Model 1910 (45 caliber, 1910 only) Only a handful of these guns were made. They were essentially modifications of the M1909 with the grip raked backward. The prototype was demonstrated to the army in February 1910. Eight guns were acquired for trials, and a perfected version, with an additional manual safety catch, performed well enough to allow the basic design to be adopted.

A Colt-Browning M1911 pistol, fitted with a modern Squires Bingham stock and drum magazine.

Model 1911 (45 caliber, 1911-26) Formally adopted on March 29, 1911, the perfected version of the M1910 had a new slide stop and manual safety catch linked by plungers actuated by a single coil spring in a tunnel above the left grip. A patent protecting the plunger system was eventually granted to John Browning in August 1913.

The Model 1911 is one of Colt's great contributions to the history of firearms. It served the US Armed Forces for 75 years, and the basic design is still being exploited not only by Colt but also by a host of other gunmaking businesses.

• *US military patterns* The first order, for about 31,000 guns, was given to Colt's Patent Fire Arms Mfg Co. in May 1911. However, as part of the agreement with Colt, the US Government acquired the right to make 50,000 guns of its own, and a production line was duly created in Springfield Armory (q.v.). The first Colt-made pistols were delivered in 1912, followed in 1914 by the first batches from Springfield; however, the guns were all numbered in a single sequence that had begun at "1", blocks of serial numbers being allocated in advance. By the end of 1916, about 137,400 M1911 pistols had been made for the US Army, Navy and Marine Corps. The guns were about 8 inches long, had 5-inch barrels and weighed about 40 oz empty. Their magazines held seven 45 ACP rounds. The grips were checkered walnut, with plain lozenge-shape panels around each grip-retaining bolt. Finish was invariably blue.

The marks on the Colt-made pistols included the company name on the left side of the slide, behind a separate block containing patent dates. On the earliest deliveries, these ran from "APR. 20, 1897" (for the basic recoil-operated action) to "FEB. 14, 1911" (for the single-link depressor). An additional mark, "AUG. 19, 1913", was subsequently added to acknowledge protection for the hold-open spring-plunger and manual safety catch arrangement. "UNITED STATES PROPERTY" was rolled into the left side of the frame, with "MODEL OF 1911. U.S. ARMY" on the right side of the slide. US Navy guns were marked differently, but the comparatively small numbers acquired by the Marines bore standard army-type markings

When World War I began, handguns were in short supply. Colt and Springfield Armory were too busy with more important work to concentrate on the M1911, and so the government elected to recruit additional contractors. Orders were placed with companies such as the Remington Arms–Union Metallic Cartridge Co. (q.v.), and other metalworking businesses, such as Lanston Monotype, with no prior experience of gunmaking. However, only Remington delivered any significant quantities of 1911-type pistols; the North American Arms Co., based in Montreal, Canada, completed only about 100 guns after the First World War had finished.

Remington guns were numbered in a separate series, beginning from "1". Winchester was granted numbers in the 629501-700000 group, though no guns were ever made, and there is no evidence that Colt completed the 594001-629500 block allotted in 1919. Work ceased in the Hartford factory shortly after World War I had ended and did not recommence until 1924.

- *Commercial patterns* The military success of the M1911 was mirrored in commercial sales. The first 5000 guns had an exquisite "fire blue" finish, blued barrels and the mark "GOVERNMENT MODEL" on the front right side of the frame. The bluing process was then altered, giving a much less intense color; the barrel was left bright, and the frame mark was moved back above the trigger. All commercial M1911 pistols had "C"-prefix numbers. They were succeeded in the 1920s by the M1911A1 version, though the distinguishing features were added gradually and transitional examples will be found in the C130000-C140000 group.
- *Export patterns* Several batches of 1911-type pistols were exported prior to World War I, including about 100 "m/1912" pistols sent to Norway for field trials. These were the predecessors of the perfected "m/1914", which was made under license in the Kongsberg (q.v.) factory. Argentina purchased the first of many Colts in 1914, continuing to buy guns until the M1927 (1911A1-type) pistol was approved in 1927. Work then continued in the Argentine small-arms factory in Rosario, Santa Fé (see "FMAP").

Orders were also accepted during World War I from Britain and from a British purchasing commission acting on behalf of the Russian government. Purchased in 1915-18, the British guns were chambered for the 455 Webley & Scott cartridge and had "W" suffix serial numbers in a separate sequence from the regular commercial production runs. Most of them went to the Royal Flying Corps (renamed "Royal Air Force" in 1918) and remained in use until 1945. The Russian guns, in 45 ACP, can be distinguished by the Cyrillic frame-mark "АНГ л. 3AKA3." for *Angliskii Zakazivat* or "English order".

This Colt 22 sport/target pistol was a prototype of the Woodsman.

Woodsman (22 pistol, 1915) This pistol, the first of a long series, was designed by John Browning for Colt, though the name "Woodsman" was not adopted until 1927. It was intended as a general target and hunting weapon, firing the 22 Long Rifle cartridge. It has a long fixed barrel with a short slide behind and operates in the simple blowback mode, with a concealed hammer beneath the slide. The grip was well raked and the proportions made it a handsome weapon with good balance. It soon acquired a good reputation for low-cost accuracy and reliability and by 1932 84,000 had been made. Minor changes were then made to the design and it was continued, in two slightly different versions, until 1943 when production finally ceased. Barrel lengths came in 4.5- and 6.5-inch sizes and there were a variety of finishes, trigger pulls and sights.

A comparison of the M1911 (left) and M1911A1 (right). Note the difference in the shape of the backstrap.

M1911A1 Combat experience during World War I suggested a number of changes to the 1911-type "Government Model", though none of them affected the single-link locking mechanism or general construction. The improved "A1" version was developed in 1923-4 and had the nomenclature "M1911A1" approved in 1926, though series production did not commence until more than a decade later. The rear of the butt was more curved; the front edge of the butt was chamfered behind the trigger; the hammer spur was shortened; and the trigger was made slightly smaller and grooved for a better grip. The M1911A1 served the US Army until replaced in 1985 by the 9mm Pistol M9 (Beretta 92F), though there were — and still are — many shooters to champion the older design.

- *Military production* Work was confined to Colt until the US Army entered the Second World War in 1941, when the problems that had been evident in 1917 recurred. The solution was identical: recruit new manufacturers. The principal participants were Remington-Rand, the Ithaca Gun Co. and Union Switch & Signal Co. These guns can all be identified by their markings.

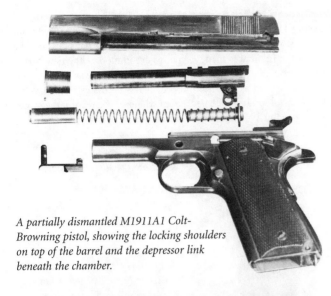

A partially dismantled M1911A1 Colt-Browning pistol, showing the locking shoulders on top of the barrel and the depressor link beneath the chamber.

An M1911A1 Colt-Browning pistol made during World War II by the Union Switch & Signal Company.

- *Commercial production* The first guns of this type appeared in 1926, but, owing to the need to use existing 1911-type parts, some time elapsed before the design features were stabilized. A few thousand were even made in the 1930s with an additional safety device patented by William Swartz. Work continued until 1942, when, in the region of serial number C215000, war-work took priority. Assembly recommenced when World War II had finished. By 1950, the prefix had become a suffix. The original bright blue finish gave way to matte blue on some parts of the slide and frame, and checkered walnut grips gave way to plastic. All but a handful of the guns made until work stopped in 1969 (at about 336000-C) bore "GOVERNMENT MODEL" on the frame. The last batches also had a modified barrel-bushing system and were marked "B B" beneath the serial numbers. The original commercial M1911A1 pistol designs were replaced by the "Series 70" guns (q.v.).
- *Export patterns* Colt sold substantial quantities of M1911A1 pistols to Argentina (as the "Modelo 1927"), Brazil and Mexico. These can usually be identified by national markings on the slide or frame. Similar guns have also been made in Argentina, Brazil, Cambodia, the Philippines and the People's Republic of China. Most of these variants can be identified by their slide markings.

Super Model (1929) A successor to the long-obsolete Model 1902, this was simply a smaller-caliber version of the M1911. It used as many of the 1911-type parts as possible but was chambered for the 38 Super cartridge and had a 9-round magazine. The slide markings, which include the caliber, provide an instant identification feature.

Ace Model (1931) Realizing that the 45 ACP cartridge was expensive, Colt produced this 22 rimfire M1911 look-alike. Size and weight were identical with the Government Model, but the barrel was fixed, the operation was pure blowback and an "Improved Ace Adjustable Target [Rear] Sight" was fitted. Criticism of a lack of power in the action was made, probably due to the inertia of the full-sized slide, but the Ace shot very well once the right brand of ammunition had been

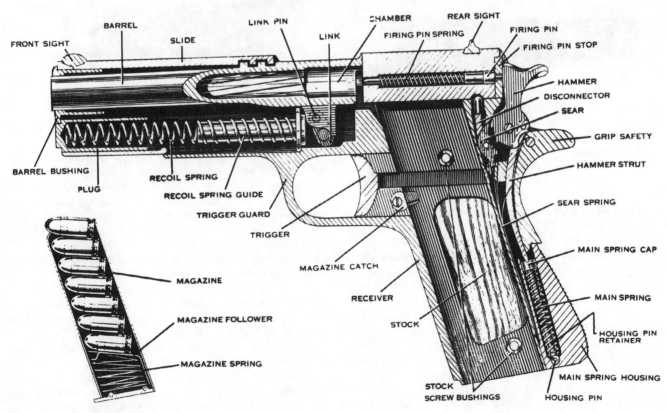

A sectional drawing of the M1911A1.

found. Production continued until 1941 and limited assembly began again in 1945. About 11,000 guns had been made when work ceased, including 206 purchased by the US Army in the 1930s.

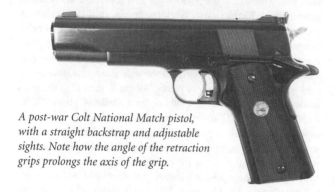

A post-war Colt National Match pistol, with a straight backstrap and adjustable sights. Note how the angle of the retraction grips prolongs the axis of the grip.

National Match Model (first pattern, 1933) The M1911 was popular with target shooters, most of whom "tuned" their pistols to produce the trigger pull they preferred and to remove excess play between components. Colt decided they could probably do this better and produced the National Match model, a proper factory-prepared target version of the M1911 using selected components, carefully hand-fitted and finished. Special sights were also fitted, and the result was a remarkably accurate pistol.

Super Match Model (1935) Another of guns chambered for the 38 Super cartridge, this was only made in small numbers — about 5000 — as it was expensive for its day and production was terminated by the war. However, 1200 were bought by the British Purchasing Commission in 1939 and shipped to Britain, and one is inclined to wonder where they all ended up. The Super Match was a refined and carefully assembled version of the Super 38 model, with Stevens adjustable sights and with the top surface of the slide matted to prevent reflection.

The Colt Service Model Ace 22 LR rimfire pistol.

Service Model Ace (1937-45) The Ace had been visualized as a trainer for the 45 ACP M1911A1, but the minimal recoil of the 22 LR rimfire round gave a very pale imitation of full-bore shooting. The Service Ace was introduced to overcome this, and it adopted a unique floating-chamber system credited to David "Marsh" Williams. This was a loose component inside the barrel, which, when the cartridge was fired, was forced back against the breech face by a small proportion of the propellant gas to multiply the effect of the 22 cartridge. This gave the slide a heavy blow, moving it rapidly backward to give a recoil force that was very similar to that of the full-bore pistol. About 13,800 guns of this type were made, substantial quantities being acquired by the US Army. Pre-war guns were blued, though those made in 1942-5 were parkerized. They all had "SM" serial-number prefixes. A "New Service Model Ace" was made in small numbers in 1978-82 but was too expensive to sell in quantity.

Woodsman Match Target Model (1938) This was a special target version with a barrel milled from the solid rather than turned from steel bar stock. This made it easily recognizable by its flat sides, and the front of the frame was made deeper to accommodate the new barrel. The trigger action was hand finished, and the price was $41.50. Sales were not as good as had been hoped. It has been suggested that the heavier barrel spoiled the balance, but whatever the reason, the model was dropped in 1943 and never revived.

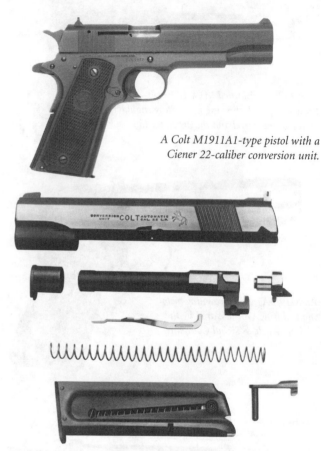

A Colt M1911A1-type pistol with a Ciener 22-caliber conversion unit.

The Colt 22-caliber conversion unit for the M1911A1.

Conversion Unit For those who were reluctant to buy a second pistol, Colt manufactured a "floating chamber" 22/45 conversion unit (1938-42, 1947-9?) that allowed the M1911 to be modified to fire 22 ammunition. Though seemingly expensive, it paid for itself after a few hundred rounds. The rather elaborate kit included replacement slide, barrel, barrel bushing, ejector, recoil spring, magazine and slide stop, and conversion was not something to be done in a few seconds. With all these parts in place, the M1911 virtually became the Ace. A curious 45/22 counter-conversion kit (1938-42) was also produced, allowing the owner of the 22 Ace to convert to 45 ACP. This was an even more involved business, and few of these kits were sold.

∼ AUTOMATIC PISTOLS, POST-WAR ∼

All-American Model 2000 (1991-4) This represented a major change of direction for Colt, abandoning John Browning's well-tried dropping barrel and adopting instead a design by C. Reed Knight and Eugene Stoner that used a rotating barrel to lock the breech. The frame of the pistol was of polymer material, while the barrel and slide were of steel. The barrel had lugs at the breech end, which locked into recesses in the slide. There was also a bottom lug on the barrel, which engaged with a helical cam track in a "cam block" in the frame. The rear end of the slide acted as the breechblock and carried a self-cocking firing

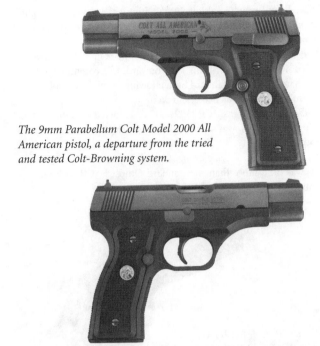

The 9mm Parabellum Colt Model 2000 All American pistol, a departure from the tried and tested Colt-Browning system.

mechanism. The trigger was connected to the sear, both being fitted with roller bearings to reduce friction, and a magazine carrying 15 rounds of 9mm Parabellum fit into the butt. There were no manual safety devices, and the only external lever was the slide stop. A notable feature was that this was entirely a self-cocking (or double-action-only) weapon.

Offered with polymer or aluminum-alloy frame, the pistol was loaded in the usual way. On pulling the trigger, the sear engaged with the striker and forced it back against a spring. Towards the end of the trigger movement, a cam and roller caused the end of the sear to drop and release the striker, which was driven forward by the spring to fire the cartridge in the chamber.

The recoil force drives the barrel and slide back, locked together by the barrel lugs engaging in the slide recesses. During this movement, the bottom lug on the barrel was drawn through the helical cam path in the frame, rotating the barrel through 30 degrees and so freeing the barrel lugs from the slide. The barrel stopped and the slide continued rearward, extracting the empty case and loading the recoil spring beneath the barrel. On the return stroke, a round was chambered and the barrel was then rotated back into the locked position. When the trigger was released, the sear automatically re-engaged with the striker, ready for the next shot.

The axial movement of the barrel produced very good accuracy. The roller bearings in the trigger mechanism produced a very smooth double-action pull comparable to the best type of revolver. But for all its apparent virtues, it proved to be one of the most embarrassing failures in the company's history. It met with very little enthusiasm, as there were stories of poor quality control and suggestions that the 9mm Parabellum would never be a popular caliber in the USA. The suggestions were rife, but none were substantiated. Nevertheless, sales were poor, and the company was losing money on the design; by 1994 production had ceased.

Cadet 22 This was introduced in 1994 as the "new Woodsman" and followed the same general lines, though with a rather more modern appearance. In stainless steel with polymer grips, the barrel is distinctly "bull" and topped by a ventilated rib. It has now been renamed "Colt 22 Auto". A 22 Target version appeared in 1995.

Combat Commander (pistol, 1971-99) Experience showed that the aluminum frame of the Commander wore more rapidly than some

people liked, so for the Combat Commander, Colt returned to the use of steel throughout the pistol, which, of course, put the weight up to 33 ounces. The guns were subsequently upgraded to 1992 Enhanced standards (see "Government Model, 45 ACP").

Combat Elite (1986) This was a variant of the standard Government Model or M1911A1 prepared for practical pistol contests. It had an enlarged grip safety, three-dot adjustable Accro combat sights, a beveled magazine aperture and an enlarged ejection port. The frame was of stainless steel, the slide was either blued carbon or stainless steel, and wraparound checkered rubber grips were standard. The chamberings were restricted to 38 Super Auto (nine-round magazine) and 45 ACP (eight rounds).

A Colt Combat Commander.

Colt's "Series 80" Combat Commander.

Commander (1949-98) This was produced in response to requests for a lighter pistol than the M1911A1, yet capable of firing the 45 ACP cartridge. The frame was made from high-strength aluminum alloy, though the slide remained steel. Slide and barrel were reduced in length, resulting in a handy pistol weighing only 26 ounces. As a natural consequence, the recoil was increased and the Commander required some skill to extract the best from it. It was also made in 9mm Parabellum, 38 Super and (for sale in Italy) 32 ACP Parabellum. The guns were subsequently upgraded to 1992 Enhanced, M1991A1, M1991 Model 0 and XS Model 0 standards (see "Government Model, 45 ACP"). The M1991A1 variant (1993-8) was offered from 1997 in stainless steel, the sights being changed to fixed three-dot "combat" patterns.

• *Commander Lightweight* A variant of the standard pistol with an aluminum-alloy frame, this was subsequently upgraded to M1991 Model 0 and XS Model 0 standards (see "Government Model, 45 ACP").

Compact (1994-8?) This was a variant of the M1991A1 45 ACP Government Model (q.v.), with a 3.25-inch barrel and a short butt designed to contain a six-round magazine. Guns made after 1997, constructed of stainless steel, had three-dot "combat" sights.

Concealed Carry Officer (1998-2001) Introduced as part of the 1992 "Enhanced" series, this was subsequently upgraded to M1991 Model 0 and XS Model 0 standards (see "Government Model, 45

ACP"). A stainless steel Commander-type slide, with a 4.25-inch barrel, was fitted on a lightweight aluminum-alloy frame with a short butt. A light trigger and a skeleton hammer were fitted; Hogue black rubber grips were standard; and the sights were three-dot combat style. The resulting pistol weighed about 26 oz empty; the magazine held 8 rounds.

Defender (1998 to date) This was a compact personal-defense version of the M1911A1, part of the 1992 "Enhanced" series. Chambered for the 40 S&W or 45 ACP, with a seven-round magazine, it had an aluminum-alloy frame and a stainless steel slide. The gun was about 6.8 inches long with a 3-inch barrel and weighed 23 oz empty. A lightweight trigger, a skeleton hammer and three-dot combat sights were among the features; grips were wraparound rubber. The original version was upgraded in 2000 to "Model 0" status (45 ACP only), gaining a brushed stainless finish, a skeleton trigger, a beveled magazine well, an extended safety catch and a "beavertail" grip safety lever.

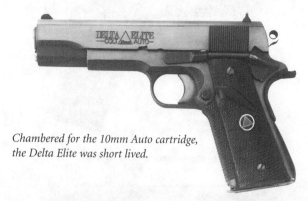

Chambered for the 10mm Auto cartridge, the Delta Elite was short lived.

Delta Elite (10mm, 1987) The Delta Elite was chambered to fire the then-new Norma 10mm Auto Pistol cartridge and was the first pistol in this caliber to be made by a major gunmaker. This was something of a gamble by Colt, since the 10mm cartridge had been trying to gain a foothold for about 10 years without much success, but their faith has been vindicated since then. It was basically an M1911A1 in a different caliber, with a slide mark that read "DELTA ELITE" over "—COLT AUTO—", the components being separated by a large triangle (for the Greek letter Δ, delta) containing "10mm". A motif of a red triangle inside a circle was molded into the wraparound Neoprene grips. The guns were offered in blued or stainless steel and had high-profile three-dot sights.

• *Delta Gold Cup* Dating from 1992, this was a version of the 10mm Delta Elite with a special trigger, adjustable Accro sights and the customary "Enhanced" features (see "Government Model, 45 ACP").

Double Eagle (pistol, 1989-2000) The Double Eagle was the first automatic pistol produced by the reorganized Colt Manufacturing Company, Inc., and it broke new ground: it was the first double-action pistol to be commercially offered by Colt. The basic M1911 action was allied with a double-action trigger mechanism with a de-cocking lever protruding from under the left grip above the magazine release. This allowed the hammer to be safely lowered with a round in the chamber and without touching the trigger. An automatic firing-pin lock disengages only during the last stages of trigger movement.

The Double Eagle shared the general appearance of the M1911A1 Government Model, but the trigger guard was shaped for a two-handed hold and the frontstrap was grooved. In addition, the trigger was a slender pivoting lever instead of the familiar sliding blade. The short-lived Mark I (designated retrospectively) was replaced in 1991 by the "Mk II/Series 90" version, which provided the basis for several variants. However, the Double Eagle was not particularly successful. Full-size guns, chambered for 10mm Auto or 45 ACP, were 8 inches long, had 5-

inch barrels and weighed about 39 oz without the detachable eight-round magazine. Made largely of stainless steel, they had fixed three-dot sights and black checkered Xenoy grips.

• *Double Eagle Combat Commander* (1991-7) Offered in 45 ACP, with a 40 S&W option from 1993 onward, this combined a 4.25-inch barrel with the standard butt, allowing the eight-round magazine to be used. It weighed about 36 oz.
• *Double Eagle Officer's ACP* (1991-7) Chambered only for the 45 ACP round, this was a short-barrel/short-grip version of the Double Eagle.
• *Double Eagle Officer's Lightweight* (1992-3) A short-lived pattern, this was little more than the standard Officer's ACP with an aluminum-alloy frame, reducing weight considerably.

The "Series 70" Colt M1911A1 Gold Cup National Match.

Gold Cup National Match Mark III (1957-70) These were carefully assembled and selected versions of M1911A1 pistols, usually chambered for the 45 ACP round. They had 1911-type mainspring housings, match-grade barrels and barrel bushings, skeletonized triggers with adjustable over-travel stops, adjustable target-type sights and an enlarged ejection port. Particular attention was paid to the fit of barrel and bushing. The lockwork was smoothed, and some of the sear surfaces were relieved to prevent undue friction. Minor changes were made to the extractor, recoil spring and slide-bearing surfaces. The guns were blued, with Colt medallions set into the checkered wooden grips. The slides were marked "GOLD CUP NATIONAL MATCH", and the serial numbers had an "NM" prefix. A few guns were made for the 38 Mid Range Wadcutter cartridge in 1961-74. A few guns were also made in Series 70 and Series 80 (see "Government Model, .45 ACP"), but the current design has now progressed to the M1991 Model 0 status.

Government Model (45 ACP) The original M1911A1-type "Mark III" commercial model was offered until 1971 but was then replaced by a modified design.

• *Government Model Mk IV Series 70* (1971-83) This had a heavier slide and a slotted barrel-bushing in pursuit of better accuracy. The transformation was also applied to the Gold Cup National Match pistols.

The "Series 80" Government Model Colt, the current version of the M1911A1.

The "Series 80" Gold Cup National Match pistol.

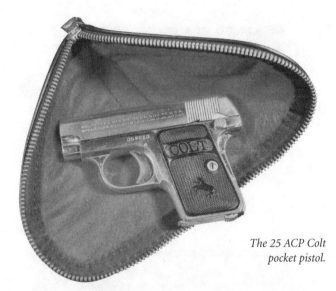

The 25 ACP Colt pocket pistol.

- *Government Model Mk IV Series 80* (1983-91) Also applied to the National Match pattern, this was an upgrade of Series 70 with a new passive firing-pin safety interlock and a revised half-cock notch. Stainless-steel construction was offered for the first time on a gun of this type.
- *Government Model Mk IV "Enhanced" Series 90* (1992-7?) The last of this particular group, applied to the Commander and the Combat Commander in addition to the standard guns, this incorporated a variety of changes: an extended or "beavertail" grip safety, a slotted Commando-style hammer, a relief-cut beneath the trigger guard, a beveled magazine well, a longer trigger, a flattop slide rib and diagonal retraction grooves. These were all needed to help Colt maintain its position in a marketplace that was fast becoming jammed with M1911/M1911A1 clones. See also "M1991".
- *Government Model M1991A1* (1992-8?) This was another improvement of the basic guns, though it remained a 45 ACP Colt-Browning with an overall length of 8 inches with a 5-inch barrel. The guns were parkerized and had black composition grips. A 9x23mm option was introduced in 1996.
- *Government Model M1991 Model 0* (1999 to date) Intended to replace all the previous versions of the M1911A1, but far less of a departure from the tried-and-tested Colt range as the Double Eagle, this incorporated another series of modifications. Matte or bright stainless finishes were standard. The upgrade was also applied to the Commander and Compact guns. Features include checkered rubber-composite grips and beveled magazine wells, but the manual safety catch and the grip-safety lever have reverted to the original designs. The trigger is a smooth-surface blade.
- *Government Model XS Model 0* (1999 to date) This is an "Enhanced" variant of the M1991 Series 0, applied to the Commander, Gold Cup, Concealed Carry Officers and Lightweight Commander patterns. The guns have checkered "double diamond" grips, usually made of rosewood, and (except for the Gold Cup version) diagonally-cut retraction grips that are duplicated at the muzzle. The safety catch is ambidextrous, a McCormick trigger is fitted, and the sights are 3-dot combat pattern. Chambered only for 45 ACP ammunition, the guns have stainless steel slides and aluminum-alloy frames.

Government Model (Series 70 and 80, 380 ACP, 1979-99) This was introduced for the benefit of those who liked the appearance of the M1911A1 but preferred something less powerful. It is a scaled-down Government model chambered for the 380 Auto (9mm Short) cartridge, but retains the locked breech of the larger weapon, though this is really not necessary in this caliber. There is no grip safety, and it is available in blued or nickeled finishes. Later production models incorporate an automatic firing pin lock — see 45 ACP version, above.

- *Government Model 380 Pocketlite* (1991-6?) This was similar to the Mustang, but had a 3.25-inch barrel and a magazine containing

seven 380 ACP rounds. The frame was aluminum-alloy, the slide was stainless steel and the grips were black checkered composition. The guns weighed about 15 oz empty.

Junior Colt (1957-70 and 1970-2) In the mid-1950s, the Colt company contracted with Unceta for the supply of an automatic pistol, the first 25 ACP (6.35mm Auto) examples being delivered in 1958 and the 22 LR rimfire version in 1959. These were sold as the "Colt Junior" to take advantage of the then-current demand for a pocket pistol without devoting time and money to development of a new design. The pistols were little more than the Astra 200 with appropriate markings, which included "MADE IN SPAIN FOR COLT'S" on the frame. The grips were inset with a medallion carrying the Colt trademark. About 67,000 guns had been made before the Gun Control Act of 1968 prohibited the importation of such a small weapon. Colt began manufacturing guns in the USA in 1970 but abandoned the project in 1972. A conversion unit for 22 Short RF ammunition was also made in small quantities.

The Colt "Series 80" 380 ACP Mustang.

Mustang (1987-99) Even smaller than the 380 Government and with a magazine holding only five 380 ACP rounds, this has achieved considerable popularity as a home defense weapon and as an off-duty police weapon. It was available in blue, nickel or matte stainless steel finish.

- *Mustang Plus II* (1988-99) This uses the barrel and slide of the Mustang allied to the frame of the 380 Government model, increasing the magazine capacity to 7 shots.
- *Mustang Pocketlite* (1987-2000) This is the 380 Mustang with a blued aluminum alloy frame, reducing the weight to only 12.5 oz. The price to be paid is, of course, more recoil.

Officer's ACP (1985-95) In the mid-1970s, Rock Island Arsenal developed the General Officer's Model pistol, a shortened M1911A1 for

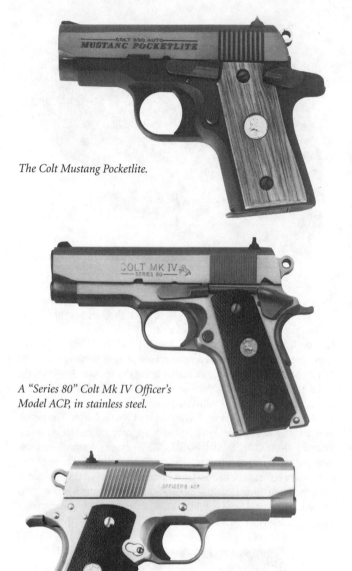

The Colt Mustang Pocketlite.

A "Series 80" Colt Mk IV Officer's Model ACP, in stainless steel.

The current Officer's ACP pistol, a compact 45-caliber Colt.

issue to general officers of the US Army and Air Force. Unavailable to the public, there was nevertheless a demand for it, and Colt responded by developing its own version. Like the Rock Island original, the barrel is shortened to 3.5 inches and the magazine holds only 6 rounds, making it a compact but powerful weapon. Finish may be blue, matte blue, satin-nickel (soon discontinued) or stainless steel, the grips being checkered walnut.

• *Officer's ACP Lightweight* Introduced in 1986, this relied on an aluminum-alloy frame to reduce the empty weight from the standard 37 oz to merely 24 oz.

Pocket Nine (1999-2001) This was a short-lived 9mm Parabellum personal-defense pistol with a double-action trigger and a bobbed hammer. Fitted with a stainless steel slide on an aluminum-alloy frame, it was 5.5 inches long, had a 2.75-inch barrel and weighed 17 oz without the 6-round magazine. The grips were wraparound rubber, the slide grooves were milled diagonally and the sights were three-dot combat patterns.

Pony (1997-2000) This was a tiny double-action gun, chambering the 380 ACP cartridge. It was about 5.5 inches long with a 2.75-inch barrel

and weighed 19 oz empty. The finish was Teflon or brushed stainless steel, the hammer was bobbed and the grips were black composition. The sights were fixed, the six-round magazine was released by a push-button behind the trigger and the slide-retraction grooves were vertical.

• *Pony Pocketlite* This was a lightweight version of the Pony, with an aluminum-alloy frame and stainless steel slide. It weighed about 13 oz.

Tac Nine (1999-2001) Chambered for the 9mm Parabellum cartridge, this was a minor variant of the Pocket Nine (q.v.) with a black oxidized finish on the stainless steel slide and a black anodized finish on the alloy frame. The sights had Tritium "night light" inserts.

Woodsman, post-war type Production of a greatly revised gun began again in 1947, now sometimes called "Second Series" to distinguish it from the original pre-war type. A slide-stop and a hold-open were added, and the magazine release became a push-button on the left side of the frame behind the trigger. The guns were finished in blue, the base of the butt was parallel to the bore-axis instead of cut at an angle and the grips were brown plastic. Changes were made in 1960, when a new or "Third Series" gun appeared, with the magazine catch on the heel of the butt; the grips were either black plastic or walnut.

• *Sport Model* (1947-55, 1960-77) This had a 4.5-inch round barrel and was made in both series. Production of Sport, Target and Match Target Woodsman pistols had amounted to 146,000 by 1955.

• *Match Target Model* (post-war type, 1948-75?) This was easily recognized by the slab-sided 4.5- or 6-inch barrel that had a deep flute running virtually the entire length beneath the bore in an attempt to shift the center of balance backwards. Colt Eliason rear sights were often fitted instead of the simpler adjustable pattern used on the Sport and Target models.

• *Target Model* This was little more than the Sport Model with a 6-inch barrel.

• *Challenger Model* (1950-5) The Challenger was a less expensive version of the Target and Sport models, lacking the hold-open and adjustable rear sight. The magazine catch lay on the butt heel and the barrels could be 4.5 or 6 inches long. Production amounted to about 77,000 guns.

• *Huntsman Model* (1955-77) A replacement for the Challenger, often promoted as a target-shooting beginner's gun, this was built on a standard "Third Series" frame but had fixed sights and barrels of 4.5 or 6 inches. Checkered black plastic grips were used until 1960, when walnut was substituted. Production amounted to about 100,000.

• *Targetsman Model* (1959-77) This was a variant of the 6-inch barreled Huntsman series with an adjustable rear sight and walnut thumb-rest style grips; the 6-inch barrel was standard. Production amounted to about 65,000 guns.

COLUMBIA ARMORY
Columbia, Tennessee, USA.

Although an address is confidently offered, there is some doubt as to whether this firm ever existed. It was found on a number of cheap revolvers under the names "Columbia" "Parker" and "Spencer", which were sold by Maltby, Henly & Co of New York in the 1888-1900 period. The patents marked on the pistols were those of John T. Smith, brother of Otis A. Smith, who operated a pistol factory at Rock Falls, Connecticut; and the balance of probability is that the two Smiths made the pistols and were happy to mark them "Columbia Armory" or any other fiction that their customers desired.

The pistols were all to the same design—a double-action, solid-frame "hammerless" 5-shot revolver. It was gate-loaded and had an unusual cylinder stop catch in the top of the standing breech, which could be pressed in with the thumb to allow the cylinder to be rotated for loading. This was the "Model 1892" and also appeared under the

Maltby, Henley name as the "Spencer Safety Hammerless" and the "Parker Safety Hammerless", being based on John T. Smith's patent covering a solid-frame revolver with a thumb-operated safety catch on the top surface of the hammer shroud and a "cocked" indicator above the cylinder. At first glance they appear to be hinged-frame revolvers, due to a prominent screw in front of the cylinder where the hinge normally falls, but this screw actually allows the trigger guard, lock and hammer unit to be swung down and out of the frame for cleaning, an ingenious idea that deserved greater success. The "Parker" was chambered for 32 caliber, the "Columbian" for 22 RF and 32 CF, and the "Spencer" for 32 Long CF cartridges.

After about 1898, the Smith firm submerges under a conflicting series of reports of amalgamation, liquidation and re-organization and the final fate of the company is not known.

COMPETITION ARMS

Tucson, Arizona, USA.

This company manufactures a single-shot pistol with interchangeable top-break barrels that can be supplied in a number of chamberings from 22 RF to 454 Casull. An adjustable rear sight is fitted, as is an optical sight mount. Production began in 1987.

COMPETITOR CORPORATION, INC.

New Ipswich, New Hampshire, and West Groton, Massachusetts, USA.

Promoters of the *Competitor* single-shot pistol, introduced in prototype in 1988 and offered in small quantities in 1991-7. The gun, which is distinguished by a unique rotating breechblock, had an adjustable trigger, adjustable sights and an exchangeable barrel (10.5-16 in). It was offered in more than 130 chamberings, ranging from 22 Short rimfire to 50 Action Express. The finish was usually a non-reflective blue, and the grip/forend could be wood, wood laminate or composite.

CONNECTICUT ARMS & MFG CO.

Naubuc, Connecticut, USA

The principal manufacturer of the single-shot Hammond Bulldog pistol.

COONAN ARMS

St Paul, Minnesota, USA.

The Coonan company set its heart on developing a 357 Magnum version of the Colt M1911A1, a difficult task given the physical problems of a long-rimmed cartridge. The *Model A* reached the market in 1985, offering the same method of a swinging link to drop the barrel out of engagement with the slide. The *Model B* (1987) adopted the solid lug and cam system of dropping the barrel. Both are generally similar to the M1911A1 but with straight-sided butts with walnut grips. Adjustable rear sights are fitted, and the slide release and safety catch are extended for easier operation. The *Cadet* (also known as the "Compact Cadet" and "Classic Compact Cadet") of 1993 is simply a smaller version of the basic model, still chambered for the 357 Magnum round but about 1.5 inches shorter. Trading ceased in 2002, and the current status of the project is uncertain.

COOPERATIVA OBRERA

Eibar, Spain.

The "Worker's Cooperative" of Eibar was a small workshop that produced only one pistol, the "Longines". This was a well-finished 32 ACP blowback that externally resembles the Browning 1910 but, as usual, reveals itself to be a standard "Eibar" when dismantled, using a recoil spring in the frame beneath the barrel. The appearance is also marred by the usual "Eibar"-type of hooked safety catch midway along the frame. The slide inscription reads "Cal 7,65 Automatic Pistol Longines".

FRANK COPELAND

Worcester and Sterling, Mass. USA.

A maker of which very little is known, Copeland produced two revolvers in the 1865-75 periods. The first was a 22 Short RF seven-shot, solid-frame, sheath-trigger weapon with a brass frame and octagonal barrel. Produced in the 1860s, this usually bears Copeland's name and "Worcester, Mass" on the barrel, though unmarked specimens are not uncommon. The second was in produced after 1870 and was in 32RF caliber but with a five-shot cylinder and an iron frame. This bears the "Sterling Mass" address on the barrel.

CRESCENT FIREARMS CO.

Also listed as the "Crescent Arms Co." or "Crescent Gun Co.", Norwich, Connecticut, USA.

Founded in 1892, this was one of the most prolific manufacturers of inexpensive shotguns — sidelock and boxlock, hammer or hammerless — to trade in the USA, making guns under a spectacular variety of brand names for dealerships that stretched nationwide. The business was purchased by H. & D. Folsom Arms Company, but continued to trade under its own name until amalgamated (in 1930) with the Davis-Warner Corporation to form "Crescent-Davis". It was then sold to the J. Stevens Arms & Tool Co. in 1932.

~ PISTOLS ~

Auto & Burglar Gun Made only in small numbers, this was a two-barreled version of the Certified Shotgun (below) in 410 or 20 bore.

Certified Shotgun Despite its name, this was a single-barreled 410 smoothbore with an automatic ejector and an exposed hammer made by the Crecsent-Davis Firearms Corp. until 1934 and thereafter by the J. Stevens Arms & Tool Co. until c. 1940. It will also be encountered under the name "Ever Ready". The barrel was usually 12.3 inches long, and the frame was sometimes color case-hardened. The walnut butt had a pronounced prawl or backward projection

Knickerbocker This is claimed to have been an adaptation of a Crescent double-barreled hammerless shotgun, with the barrels cut to 10 inches and a pistol-grip butt.

Victor Made sometime prior to 1930, this was a single-barreled break-open design with an exposed hammer and a top lever above the round-backed grip. The 12-inch barrel is chambered for 410 shotshells.

~ REVOLVERS ~

Columbian Another case of spurious labeling, these solid-frame double-action non-ejecting revolvers are marked "New York Arms Co", but this was, in fact, a trade name employed by Garnet Carter & Co of Chattanooga, Tennessee, and the revolvers were made in Norwich. They were usually chambered for 38-caliber centerfire ammunition, bore no patent or similar marks, and probably dated from 1892-1900.

Crescent Encountered under a variety of trade names, this was a 32 S&W break-open copy with a five-chambered cylinder and a double-action trigger system. Offered in blue or nickel-plate, it usually had molded rubber grips.

Faultless This was a solid-frame sheath-trigger "Suicide Special" made in the 1880s. Guns are usually encountered in 22 or 32 RF.

CROWN CITY ARMS, INC.

Cortland, New York, USA.

This company produced a copy of the Colt M1911A1 in 45 ACP, 9mm Parabellum and 38 Super calibers in the middle-to-late 1970s. They also produced a copy of the Colt Commander in the same calibers. Quality was adequate but no more, according to contemporary reports.

CRUCELEGUI BROTHERS

Crucelegui Hermanos, Eibar, Spain.

This gunmaking business specialized in "Velo-Dog" revolvers, which were produced in quantity between 1900 and 1925. The guns were all essentially similar. The most popular chambering was 6.35mm Auto, but 5mm, 7.65mm Auto, 8mm Lebel and others may be encountered.

Brong-Petit Yet another "hammerless" 6.35mm Velo-Dog type of solid-frame revolver, dating prior to 1914.

Bron-Sport This was a variation on the Brong-Petit, probably made from about 1912 to 1915. Basically a Velo-Dog type, it differed from the usual design in having a straight-sided butt resembling that of an automatic pistol and a conventional trigger in a large trigger guard. The upper section of the barrel was cut away at the sides to give some resemblance to an automatic pistol. The most common chambering is 6.35mm Auto, but 7.65mm Auto and 8mm Lebel have been reported.

C.H. Another of the Velo-Dog patterns, usually encountered in 6.35mm. The mark represents the manufacturer's initials.

Le Brong A name applied to an 8mm Lebel hammerless revolver in Velo-Dog style made in Eibar in the 1900s.

Puppy A name popular among Spanish makers of Velo-Dog and similar revolvers; see also Arizmendi, Gaztañaga, Ojanguren y Marcaido and Retolaza.

Velo-Mith Another of the many names that will be found not only on Crucelegui-made revolvers but also on the products of several other Spanish gunmakers.

CRVENA ZASTAVA

Zavodi Crvena Zastava ("Red Banner Factory"), Kragujevač, Yugoslavia (Serbia).

This was the old Serbian arsenal of Kragujevač working under the post-1948 Yugoslav government. In 1990, it changed its name to "Zastava Arms" (q.v.).

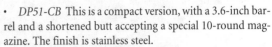

DAEWOO PRECISION INDUSTRIES LTD

Kumjung, Pusan, South Korea.

This is one of the several Daewoo subsidiaries and is, in fact, the old South Korean Arsenal at Pusan, which was taken over by Daewoo in 1983 and produces both military and commercial arms. However, the Daewoo industrial group ran into such severe financial problems at the end of the 20th century that the immediate future of its many manufacturing divisions remains unclear.

The K5 pistol, made by Daewoo, chambers the 9mm Parabellum round.

DP40 (or "DH40") This is a version of the standard DP51-B, chambering the 40 S&W cartridge. This restricts the magazine capacity to 11 rounds and raises the empty weight to 32 oz. The finish is usually matte gray and the grips are synthetic.

DP45 Comparatively short-lived, this was a 45 ACP version of the DP51. There is evidence to suggest that the delay system could not cope satisfactorily with the powerful cartridges, and the project was dropped after only a handful of prototypes had been made.

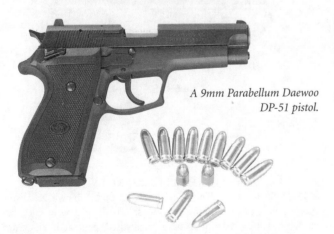

A 9mm Parabellum Daewoo DP-51 pistol.

DP51-B (or "Fastfire") This is the standard sidearm of the South Korean military forces and is a delayed blowback with a conventional double-action trigger system. The delay is obtained by using an annular grooved chamber into which the cartridge case extends under chamber pressure, thus resisting opening of the breech, but contracts after the bullet has left the barrel so as to permit the operating cycle to begin. Chambered for the 9mm Parabellum round, the pistol is about 7.5 inches long, has a 4.1-inch barrel and weighs about 28 oz. The magazine holds 13 rounds, restricted to 10 in the USA since 1994. The trigger guard is shaped to facilitate a two-hand grip, the safety catch is ambidextrous, the magazine catch is reversible and the hammer has a spur.

• *DP51-CB* This is a compact version, with a 3.6-inch barrel and a shortened butt accepting a special 10-round magazine. The finish is stainless steel.

• *DP51-SB* A combination of the full-size frame and the short slide/barrel assembly of the "CB" variant, finished in stainless steel, this can accept the standard 13-round magazine.

DP-52 (1994-8?) A 22 LR rimfire blowback, similar externally to the DP51, this had a 10-round magazine to comply with the post-1994 US legislation.

DP-40 is the same pistol in 40 S&W caliber.

DP-45 is the same in 45 ACP caliber. These are offered commercially.

DP-380 (or "DH-380") This is a copy of the Walther PP chambered for the 380 Auto (9mm Short) cartridge, with an eight-round single-column magazine. The guns are 6.7 inches long, have 3.8-inch barrels and weigh 23-24 oz empty.

CHARLES DALY

Harrisburg, Pennsylvania, USA.

An importer of a variety of Colt M1911A1 clones, apparently made in the Philippines by Armscor (q.v.). They have been sold under a variety of names since the 1990s. The *Field* is conventionally blued, the *Superior* has a blued slide and a stainless-steel frame, and the *Empire* is made entirely of stainless steel. Chambered for the 45 ACP round, the guns have barrels of 3.5, 4 or 5 inches. Magazine capacity is usually restricted to seven, though guns with "A2P" suffixes have staggered-column magazines holding 10 rounds. A "PC" suffix indicates a polymer frame, made under license from STI (q.v.) of Texas.

DANSK REKYLRIFFEL SYNDIKAT
("DRS", "DRS-MADSEN")

Later Dansk Industri Syndikat AS "Madsen" or "DISA-Madsen", Copenhagen, Denmark.

Schouboe Jens Tørring Schouboe, a Danish army officer, was also chief engineer of DRS and the inventor of the Madsen machinegun. In 1903, he patented a blowback pistol, and after trials had been completed, production began in 7.65mm Auto (32 ACP) chambering. Unfortunately, the strange-looking pistol failed to gain acceptance and work stopped after no more than 1000 had been made.

An early attempt to persuade military authorities to adopt large-caliber blowbacks, this 11.35mm Schouboe dates from 1907.

M1907 Undeterred by the failure of his small-caliber pistol, Schouboe enlarged the design to create an 11.35mm-caliber military pistol. However, believing firmly in the blowback system, he had to adopt some peculiar stratagems to achieve the desired performance. The solution relied on a very light bullet that was no more than a cupro-nickel jacket containing a wooden core and an aluminum base plug. This projectile developed a velocity of 1625 ft/sec but was so light that

*The Schouboe pistol in
its holster-stock.*

recoil was less than that created with conventional bullets. It moved so rapidly that it left the muzzle before the breech began to open.

The gun was a fixed-barrel blowback with a short slide/breechblock section at the rear but had few unusual features. It was tested by several governments — British and American among them — but was never adopted. Among the complaints were lack of stopping power, the absence of a breech-lock and poor accuracy arising from combining a light bullet with an inappropriate rifling twist.

Schouboe produced a variety of modified guns until he retired in 1917. It has been estimated that less than 500 pistols were made, many being given away as graduation prizes or marksmanship awards for Danish army cadets. Others were cased for presentation to a selection of dignitaries. Consequently, the M1907 is now extremely uncommon.

DARDICK CORP.

Hamden, Connecticut, USA.

David Dardick conceived this innovative pistol in 1949, though developmental questions prevented series production until 1954. The Dardick sold in small numbers but was unable to make much impact in a traditionally minded marketplace and production ended in 1962. The principle was subsequently licensed to another promoter but with a similar lack of success. It reappears periodically, particularly in relation to cannon and heavy machineguns, but has never been entirely successful.

The Dardick "Open Chamber" gun could be likened to a revolver in which the cylinder is formed with three triangular chambers in its periphery. This cylinder acts only as a transporter for the firing device, ammunition being carried in a box magazine inserted into the butt. Specially shaped cartridges, or "Trounds" as Dardick named them, were forced up the magazine by a spring to enter the open recess in the cylinder. The first movement of the trigger caused the cylinder to make a partial turn, presenting a fresh recess for the next round. The next trigger movement first positioned and then fired the first round behind the barrel, then moved on to simultaneously eject the case and present another recess so that it received a cartridge from the magazine. Subsequent trigger pressures fired and ejected cartridges until the magazine was emptied and the last round fired.

"Trounds" were held in the cylinder by the topstrap of the frame and the thin metal cylinder shroud, which had an opening to allow spent cases to be ejected at appropriate moments during the operating cycle. The cartridges were made by inserting standard commercial rounds into plastic outer cases made in the form of a trochoid (the section was triangular but with convex sides). Dardick envisaged that trochoidal brass cases would be made once demand had grown, but that particular stage was never reached.

Dardick pistols worked satisfactorily but were sufficiently different to engender sales resistance. Trounds were not readily available, and, by comparison with conventional rivals, the pistols were expensive; a M1500 cost $99.50 in 1960, at a time when the Colt Trooper could be had for $74.60. A combination of these factors caused the Dardick project to fail.

Model 1100 and Model 1500 The basic difference was size: the M1100 had a small grip and an 11-round magazine, while the M1500 had a larger grip to hold a 15-round magazine. Both were usually chambered for the 38 Dardick Special ammunition, which was simply 38 Special cartridges inserted in the plastic "Tround" casing, but by the use of adapters and interchangeable barrels, the guns could fire 38 S&W Long, 9mm Parabellum or 22 LR rimfire. The M1100 had a 3-inch barrel and the M1500 had a 6-inch barrel as standard, but other lengths were advertised. These included a special long barrel that, with the assistance of a shoulder stock, converted the Dardick pistol into a carbine.

DAVIS INDUSTRIES

Chino and Mira Loma, California, USA.

Founded by Jim Davis in 1982, this gunmaking business has specialized in small-caliber blowbacks and two-barrel Remington-type derringers.

~ TWO-SHOT PISTOLS ~

All Davis derringers have steel breechblocks and steel barrel-liners inserted in alloy frames. They also have a press-catch safety mechanism with an internal hammer block conforming with the Gun Control Act of 1968. Finish is either chrome plate or black Teflon.

Big Bore Series (1992 to date) Distinguished by a 2.75-inch barrel and black synthetic grips, guns of this type may accept 22 LR rimfire, 9 Parabellum or 38 Special ammunition.

"D" series (1986 to date) The original guns, offered with laminated wood or white pearl grips, have been made in 22 LR and 22 Magnum rimfire, 25 ACP or 32 ACP chamberings. Their barrels are 2.4 inches long.

Long Bore series (1995 to date) Available in the same chamberings as the "Bog Bore", these guns are easily identified by their 3.5-inch barrels.

The Davis P-32 pistol.

~ AUTOMATIC PISTOLS ~

P-32 (1986 to date) This is a simple 32-caliber blowback, distinguished more by good manufacturing standards and clean lines than mechanical novelty. The guns have striker-fired single-action lockwork and laminated wood grips; finish may be black Teflon or chrome. They are 5.4 inches long, with a 2.8-inch barrel, and weigh a substantial 22 oz. Magazines hold six rounds.

P-380 (1991 to date) An enlargement of the P-32, usually found in chrome finish with black synthetic grips, this chambers the 380 ACP (9mm Short) round and has a magazine capacity restricted to five cartridges.

DAVIS-WARNER

*Davis-Warner Arms Corporation, Assonet
and Norwich, Connecticut, USA.*

Formed in 1917 by the merging of shotgun-making N.R. Davis Company with the Warner Arms Company (q.v.), this gunmaking

The 32-caliber Davis-Warner "Infallible" pistol.

business operated from the Assonet factory of Davis until 1919 when they moved it to Norwich, Conn. Bought by H. & D. Folsom in 1930 and merged with Crescent Firearms Company, the business was finally sold to the J. Stevens Arms and Tool Co. in 1932 and lost its independent identity.

Davis-Warner continued to market the "Infallible" pistols that remained in the inventory alongside 32-caliber swing-cylinder revolvers and automatic pistols based on the 1906-type FN-Browning in 32 ACP and 380 ACP. The revolvers and the pistols were apparently made in Belgium.

D. DEBOUXTAY

Liege, Belgium

Bijou Sales name for a Velo-Dog pattern revolver in 6.35mm ACP caliber, manufactured in about 1908.

Lincoln A name that was very popular among Liége gunmakers and applied to a wide variety of revolvers produced from 1880 to 1914. Most were of the folding-trigger pocket variety, hammer and "hammerless" types, in chamberings ranging from 22 RF and 5.5mm Velo-Dog to 380. Other makers using this name included Ancion Marx, Bertrand, Dumoulin, Jannsen Fils et Cie, Le Page, Neumann Frères and Raick Frères, all of Liége, and Albrecht Kind of Germany. Most (or, indeed) all of the guns may have been made by Manufacture Liégeoise d'Armes à Feu.

WILHELM DECKER

Zella St Blasii (pre-1919) and Zella-Mehlis (post-1919), Germany.

In 1912, Decker patented a remarkable pocket revolver that might have had better success had war not begun in 1914. The hammerless solid-frame 6.35mm Auto (25 ACP) gun had a six-chamber cylinder, rotated

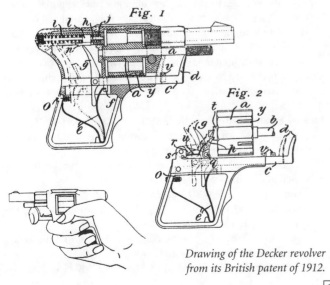

Drawing of the Decker revolver from its British patent of 1912.

and locked by a long bar that ran back beneath it. The bar also cocked and released the axial striker. The cylinder was loaded through a gate on the left side of the frame, spent cases being ejected backward through the same gate with the assistance of a pin carried in the cylinder arbor. A thin sheet-steel cover on the right side of the frame retained the cartridges and smoothed the contours to minimize snagging in the pocket.

Decker revolvers, made only in small numbers for a few years before World War I began, are rarely seen today. They were briefly promoted in Britain as the "Mueller Special Revolver" by R.H. Mueller of London.

F. DELU

Fabrique d'Armes F. Delu et Cie, Liége, Belgium.

A 6.35mm Auto blowback automatic broadly based on the Browning 1906, this dates from 1908-14. The only feature of note is the grip safety, which is not only very short but also protrudes sharply from the upper rear of the grip. Some guns lacked the grip safety, but it is not currently known which of the patterns is original. The slide is marked "FABRIQUE D'ARMES F.DELU & CO LIEGE – BELGIQUE" and the grips bear an "FD" monogram in a "circle" that is actually a letter "C" with a small "O" between its jaws.

DEMON

Manufactura de Armas "Demon", Eibar, Spain.

Whether this was a bona fide company or a sales name concealing some better-known manufacturer is something we have been unable to discover. The pistols, chambering either 6.35mm Auto or 7.65mm Auto ammunition, are run-of-the-mill "Eibar" types, though with some peculiarities of their own. The smaller gun has a large shield-shaped operating surface on the safety catch, which is at the left rear of the frame. The 7.65mm version comes in two forms; one is unremarkable, but the other has an extended butt frame to receive a 20-round magazine that makes the gun higher than it is long. The 6.35mm is marked with the company name and location on the left side of the slide — sometimes in French (the latter including "EIBAR – ESPAGNE") — the word "Demon" and a suitably diabolic face on the grips. The 7.65mm guns, which usually display "AUTOMATIC PISTOL "DEMON"…" on the left side of the slide above "32 CALIBER METAL COVERED BULLET", simply have the word "Demon" on the grips, without the devil-head motif.

DENEL

LIW Division of Denel, Pretoria, South Africa.

Vektor Z-88 This pistol was developed in 1986 against a demand from the South African Defense Force and went into production in 1989. It takes its title from the late T.D. Zeederberg, former general manager of LIW, and from its year of approval. The design is that of the Beretta 92, although the precise connection is not known, and it is unlikely that Beretta would have flouted the UN embargo on weapons technology that existed at that time. Nevertheless, the appearance, functioning and dimensions are exactly the same as the Beretta 92. Perhaps "imitation is the sincerest form of flattery".

Vektor SP There are two pistols in this group, the SP1, chambered for the 9mm Parabellum cartridge, and the SP2, chambered for the 40 Smith & Wesson cartridge. Both are to the same design, which is a development of the Z-88 insofar as it uses the same dropping wedge system of breech locking, though the open-topped Beretta style of slide has been abandoned for the more usual type. The slide is of steel and the frame of alloy. An automatic firing pin safety system is used in addition to a manual safety catch. The safety catch is duplicated on both sides of the pistol, and the magazine release can be fitted to either side as the user prefers. The SP2 has an accessory conversion kit consisting of a barrel, return spring and magazine, allowing it to be reconfigured

A Vektor SP1 Sport pistol, in 9mm Parabellum.

The South African Vektor SP2.

in 9mm Parabellum. The SP1 is in use by South African armed forces and is also manufactured under license by the Arms Corporation of the Philippines. There have been several variants, all dating from 1999.

- *SP1 and SP2 General's Model* These are 20mm shorter in overall length, with 103-mm barrels, and weigh 850g but are otherwise identical to the full-sized weapons.

DERINGER RIFLE & PISTOL WORKS

Philadelphia, Pennsylvania, USA.

Henry Deringer's name is immortalized (and usually misspelled) in the large-caliber single-shot pistols, which, apparently, occupied every gambler's vest pocket in the Old West. The majority of the genuine Deringer products appeared before 1870, but after his death, the name was continued by a company run by J.J. Clark. This made a range of fairly conventional rimfire revolvers based on patents by Charles Foehl. Trading ceased in 1879.

Centennial 1876 This name identified a series of revolvers made in the late 1870s. The basic weapon was the familiar 22 RF solid-frame sheath-trigger single-action type with a seven-chamber cylinder, though similar five-shot guns were made in 32 RF and 38 RF.

Model 1 A seven-shot 22 RF single-action break-open revolver, this was very similar to the then-current Smith & Wessons. It was made in 1873-5 but only in small numbers.

Model 2 This 22-caliber rimfire was similar to the Model 1, but the 3-inch barrel was cylindrical instead of octagonal and Foehl's patented cylinder-rotating pawl was replaced by a more conventional design. Five-shot 32 Short RF examples were also made.

ÉTABLISSEMENTS DERKENNE

Liége, Belgium.

Le Novo A five-chamber 6.35mm pocket revolver with a butt that folded up around the trigger and frame, this was invented by Dieudonné Oury and made for F. Dumoulin & Cie. Similar guns will also be found with the marks of Bertrand of Liége and Galand of Paris.

DESERT INDUSTRIES

Las Vegas, Nevada, USA.

Trading for a few years in the 1990s, this company acquired the assets of Steel City Arms (q.v.) and continued to market the *Double Deuce*, the *Two-Bit Special* and the *War Eagle*. Operations seem to have ceased in 1995.

DETONICS

Detonics Firearms Industries, Bellevue, Washington (to 1988); New Detonics Manufacturing Corp., Phoenix, Arizona, USA (1988-2000).

The Detonics company manufactures a range of pistols that are essentially based on the Colt M1911A1. The business has been reorganized on more than one occasion, with only the *Combatmaster* surviving from the earliest days.

Combatmaster This was a reduced-scale M1911A1, made almost entirely of stainless steel. Designed for serious use, the barrel was throated and had a polished feed ramp; the magazine aperture in the butt was beveled and polished; the trigger and sear were carefully tuned; the rear of the slide was angled to permit the hammer to be thumb-cocked rapidly; and the frame was redesigned to prevent the traditional "bite" of the hammer tang on the web of the thumb. Each barrel was carefully fitted, and the barrel was located by a "V"-block rather than a conventional muzzle bushing.

- *Mark I* (1977-81) This was offered only in matte-finish blue, in 45 ACP. See also "MC1" below.
- *Mark II* (1977-9) Another 45 ACP gun, this was distinguished from the Mark I solely by its satin-nickel finish.
- *Mark III* (1977-9) Chambered similarly to its predecessors, this was offered only in hard-chrome finish.
- *Mark IV* (1977-81) A variant of the Mark I, this 45 ACP pistol had a richly polished blue finish.
- *Mark V* (1979-85) Offered in 9mm Parabellum (seven rounds), 38 Super (seven) or 45 ACP (six), this was made entirely of matte-finished stainless steel.
- *Mark VI* (1979-89) Distinguished primarily by an adjustable rear sight, this was a minor variant of the Mk V. The sides of the slide usually had a high-polish finish.
- *Mark VII* Made only to special order, this was a Mark VI without sights. It could be chambered for the 9mm Parabellum or 38 Super rounds, both chamberings being discontinued in 1990, or for the 45 ACP. A handful was made in 1991-2 for the 451 Detonics round.
- *MC1* (1981-2000) Essentially the same as the "Mark I", a name it also carried for some time, this could be obtained in 9mm Parabellum, 38 Super or 45 ACP, though the two smaller caliber were discontinued in 1990. Except for a few guns with high-polish slides, made prior to 1983, construction was a combination of a non-glare blue slide and a matte-finish stainless steel frame. Rear sights were fixed. Barrels measured 3.5 inches, giving a weight of about 28 oz without the six-round box magazine.

Compmaster This was a 45 ACP Scoremaster (below) with a compensated barrel. It was made for a few years from 1988 but only in small quantities.

Ladies Escort Introduced in 1990, this was a compact 45 ACP pistol with 3.5 inch barrel and 6-shot magazine, reminiscent of the first Combatmaster. It was made in several forms:

- *Jade Escort* (1990) This had a stainless steel frame, but the slide and the grips were finished in jade green!
- *Midnight Escort* (1990-5?) Similar to the Jade Escort, this had a black frame and slide and grips finished in iridescent purple. The hammer and trigger were gold-plated.
- *Royal Escort* (1990-5?) This was distinguished by a satin-stainless frame, a black-stainless slide and black grips.

Military Combat (1979-84) Also known as "MC2", this gun —

available in the three regular chamberings — had a matted finish, fixed sights and non-slip Pachmayr grips.

O.S. Model (c. 1991-5) This was a short-lived variant of the Combatmaster, intended for use as a "back-up" or for off-duty personal defense. It was available only in 45 ACP, with fixed sights and satin-stainless or "black stainless" finish.

A 9mm Parabellum Detonics Pocket Nine pistol.

Pocket Nine (1985-6) A small double-action personal-defense pistol chambered for the 9mm Parabellum round, this incorporated a delayed blowback mechanism. Offered with a 3-inch barrel, a six-round magazine and a satin finish on the slide and frame, it weighed about 28 oz. However, the Pocket Nine was not particularly successful and was soon abandoned.

- *Pocket Nine LS* (1986) A "Long Slide" version of the basic design, this had a 4-inch barrel.
- *Pocket 380* (1986) A low-power version of the standard gun, with a 3-inch barrel and a six-round magazine, this chambered the 380 Auto (9mm Short) round.
- *Power Nine* (1986) This was little more than a 9mm Parabellum Pocket Nine with a high-polish finish on the sides of the slide. It was sold with two magazines, each numbered to the gun.

The Detonics 451 Scoremaster was a variant of the 1911-type Colt-Browning.

Scoremaster This was a full-size gun, offered in 45 ACP or 451 Detonics (the latter in 1991-2 only) with barrels of 5 or 6 inches. Micro-adjustable Millett sights and a grip-safety system were standard, the trigger was improved and the manual safety catch was extended.

Servicemaster This was a shortened version of the Scoremaster, with a 4.25-inch barrel and a coned barrel-locating system. The sights were exchangeable, matted "combat" finish was standard and an eight-round magazine was used.

DEUTSCHE WAFFEN- & MUNITIONSFABRIKEN ("DWM")

Charlottenburg and Berlin-Wittenau, Germany.

This large-scale gun-and-ammunition-making business is best known for the Mauser rifle, the Maxim machinegun and the Parabellum ("Luger") pistol.

The origins of this company go back to the foundation of Heinrich Ehrmann & Co in 1872 to manufacture brass cartridges. In 1878 this became the Deutsche Metallpatronenfabrik Loenz, and in 1889 it was sold to Ludwig Loewe of Berlin, a firearms and machine tool manufacturer. Loewe dropped the "Lorenz" part of the title and in subsequent years formed alliances with various other ammunition firms and generally prospered. In 1896, the company became Deutsche Waffen- und Munitionsfabrik and absorbed Loewe's arms manufactory.

The new company expanded steadily, prospering during 1914-18, but the post-war slump and the Versailles Treaty provisions hit the company hard. By 1922, it was no more than a holding company, calling itself the "Berlin-Karlsruhe Industriewerk" (BKIW). Rearmament in the 1930s pulled the firm up once more and in 1936 it reverted to the DWM title. War once more led to expansion, followed by the same sort of contraction, and in 1949 it became the "Industriewerke Karlsruhe" (IWK) and in the 1970s became "IWKA Industrieanlagen GmbH".

DWM manufactured a wide range of firearms during its life, but the only pistols amongst them were the Borchardt, the Parabellum and the DWM.

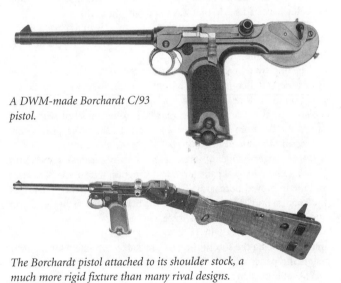

A DWM-made Borchardt C/93 pistol.

The Borchardt pistol attached to its shoulder stock, a much more rigid fixture than many rival designs.

Borchardt Over 1000 guns had been made by 1897, when Ludwig Loewe & Co. (q.v.) took over the Deutsche Metallpatronenfabrik Karlsruhe and re-named his new consortium "Deutsche Waffen und Munitionsfabrik" or DWM (qv). Pistols manufactured after January 1897 were marked "SYSTEM BORCHARDT PATENT." above "DEUTSCHE WAFFEN- UND MUNITIONSFABRIKEN." and "BERLIN." in three lines on the right side of the frame, retaining the patent mark on the toggle. Probably another 2000 were manufactured by DWM; the highest known serial number is 3013 and production ended in 1899.

The Borchardt only ever appeared in one form: a 152mm barrel, 8-shot magazine in 7.63mm Borchardt chambering. It is said that towards the end of the pistol's life a small number were made in 7.65mm Parabellum, but this has never been confirmed. A few, perhaps only one or two, were chambered for the 9mm Borchardt cartridge, an odd bottle-necked round that never went into quantity production.

Borchardt later made some attempts to improve his pistol, taking out patents in 1907, 1909 and 1911, but by this time, the superiority of the Parabellum was clear and the patents were never converted into actual weapons.

Parabellum ("Luger" prototypes and pre-production) The pistol was developed from the Borchardt pistol, patented in 1893, but it was

One of the prototype Borchardt-Luger pistols, tested in Switzerland in 1898.

soon evident that changes were needed. The Borchardt had several obvious weaknesses, including the delicacy of the return spring and the overhang of the spring housing behind the grip.

A solitary "Improved Borchardt" was sent to Switzerland in 1897 to substitute for the Borchardt-type C/93 in the army trials. On October 5, 1897, this Improved Borchardt was tried against a Bergmann and a Mannlicher. However, it was then replaced by the Borchardt-Luger and returned to DWM. It is believed to have had the return spring in the grip, would have been smaller than the original trials C/93, and would probably have had a grip that was raked backward.

The most obvious distinguishing features would have been a Borchardt-type toggle-breaking roller and the lengthy rearward overhang of the frame.

The Improved Borchardt was tested in Switzerland in October 1898 against several Bergmanns, a Mannlicher, the Mauser C/96 and a Krnka-Roth. Before the firing trials commenced, however, it was replaced by two Borchardt-Lugers, which were unlocked with cam-ramps on the frame instead of an internal roller. The pistols that arrived in Switzerland in November 1898, therefore, were the first of the true Lugers. One of these guns survives, called the "Third Experimental Model" by the Swiss to distinguish it from the Borchardt and the Improved Borchardt. They chambered a shortened version of the 7.65mm Borchardt cartridge that was better suited to the raked grip and magazine than the original type.

Changes were made in 1899 to satisfy the Swiss army, the most important being the substitution of a lockable grip safety for the fully automatic pattern of the Third Experimental Model. In May 1899, DWM submitted an improved Borchardt-Luger. Known as the "Fourth Experimental Model", this had a manually-operated safety lever recessed into the rear left side of the frame. It easily defeated a delayed blowback Mannlicher, but a revised prototype, weighing 835gm without its magazine, was supplied by DWM in early 1900. The name Parabellum, the telegraphic code-name of the manufacturer, was adopted at about this time.

Changes were soon made to the interface between the toggle links, and the head of the manual safety lever was progressively refined until it became a short raised flute that could be operated with the thumb of the firing hand. The standard Parabellum of this era, known as the "Old Model" after the introduction of the New Model in 1906, had a grip safety that could be locked by the upward movement of the manual safe lever and a rebound lock set into the right toggle grip. The toggle grips were distinctively cut away.

No sooner had the 7.65mm pistol reached service than doubts were being expressed about its "stopping power", forcing Luger to experiment with alternative cartridges until, by 1903, the neck of the existing 7.65mm case had been enlarged to accept a 9mm-diameter bullet.

The original 9mm-caliber Parabellums had combination grip-and-lever safety systems, toggle locks and dished toggle grips. The oldest guns were built around the existing receiver and frame design, until modified versions (about 2mm shorter) appeared c. 1904. The new short frame curves upward much more sharply ahead of the lock-ing-bolt spindle. However, though the two frames were used concurrently for some years and 9mm Old Model Parabellums may display either type, navy guns retained long frames until the middle of the First World War. A change from four- to six-groove rifling also dates from this period.

The "New Model" Parabellum, known during development as the "Model 1904", had a coil spring in the grip. A contract placed in December 1904 by the Dutch government is the earliest-known reference to construction of this type.

The first pistols to be purchased in quantity by the German authorities were issued to the navy from 1905 onward; though the earliest deliveries retained the leaf-type return spring and the lock let into the toggle grips. A short-barreled modification of the New Model was adopted for service with the German army in August 1908, and a long-barreled variant with a tangent-leaf rear sight (the lange Pistole 1908) followed in the summer of 1913.

Little was done to change the basic pistol design after the end of the First World War in 1918, and the post-war commercial market was saturated with war-surplus guns. The Dutch government ordered a few thousand guns for the Netherlands Indies Army (KNIL) in 1922, but these were "delivered" from Britain by Vickers Ltd (q.v.) in an attempt to hide the involvement of Berlin-Karlsruher Industrie-Werke, as DWM had become.

Pistols continued to be marketed by BKIW until 1930, many being marked with the well-known DWM monogram. A few thousand were exported, most notably to the Netherlands, and substantial numbers were sold commercially. However, the small-scale needs of the armed forces and the police were initially satisfied by Simson & Co. (q.v.), selected by the Allies as the only acceptable source of "official" handguns — though tens of thousands of guns were refurbished secretly and stockpiled away from prying Allied eyes. Mauser-Werke and Krieghoff became involved in Parabellum production in the 1930s, their exploits being described in the relevant entries.

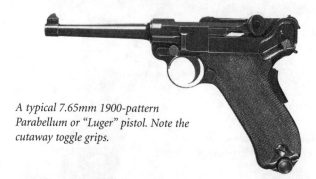

A typical 7.65mm 1900-pattern Parabellum or "Luger" pistol. Note the cutaway toggle grips.

Parabellum M 1900 (or "7.65mm Old Model") The first of the series to be adopted officially (in Switzerland in May 1900), these had 12cm barrels and the original long frames. A leaf spring lay in the grip behind the magazine, and a spring-latch was let into the right toggle grip to prevent the flat-topped breechblock bouncing back from the chamber face as the action closed. The toggle grips were knurled but were also cutaway at the rear in an attempt to improve grip. An automatic safety was let into the rear grip strap, and a manual safety, in the form of a small radial lever, lay in a recess in the rear left side of the frame. Guns were sold commercially, though never as effectively as the Mauser C/96. However, the Parabellum was the more successful militarily. Among the individual sales were:

- *Bulgaria* Acquired in small quantities for troop trials, these had the DWM monogram on the front toggle-link and a chamber mark consisting of a lion on a shield, supported by two lance-carrying lions within a pavilion. Possibly only a thousand were ever made. The safety-lever recess is marked in Bulgarian: "ОГЬНЪ".

An M1900 Parabellum attached to the US-made Ideal Holster Stock, which required special metal-backed wood grips on the gun.

An original 1900-type Parabellum carbine, with the action open. These guns had an auxiliary return spring in the fore-end.

- *Switzerland* Adopted officially in April 1900 as the "Ordonnanzpistole Modell 1900", these had the DWM monogram on the toggle and a cross-on-sunburst above the chamber. Several types of safety lever and triggers have been identified. Production amounted to 5000, plus a hundred converted from earlier trials guns.
- *USA* A thousand guns were delivered for trials in October 1901, but were unsuccessful. Survivors were sold to Bannerman in 1906, but surprisingly little is known about them. They had the DWM monogram on the toggle and a bald eagle clasping thunderbolts and arrows, surmounted by a cloud and stars, above the chamber. The serial numbers are customarily used to distinguish these from essentially similar guns sold commercially, but the exact range is still disputed.

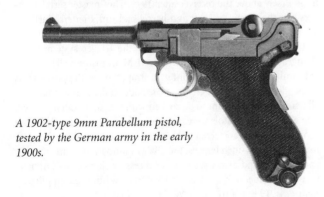

A 1902-type 9mm Parabellum pistol, tested by the German army in the early 1900s.

Parabellum M1902 (or "9mm Old Model") Another of the leaf-spring guns, this was essentially similar to the 7.65mm M1900 excepting for chambering. The barrel customarily measured 10cm (though longer examples are known), and apart from the earliest prototypes, the frames were reduced by 2mm.

- *German army trials guns* Small numbers of 7.65mm and 9mm-caliber pistols were purchased for trials. They could be distinguished only by a small military inspector's mark (usually a crowned "D")

on the left side of the receiver directly ahead of the trigger plate. They have short frames and grip safeties.

- *US Army "cartridge counter" guns* Fifty of these were acquired for trials in 1904, fitted with a cartridge indicating device developed by Groeger Powell and duly approved by the Cavalry School. An indicator attached to the magazine follower slid in a slot in the left side of the grip—covered with a protective celluloid plate and marked with a series of numbers—which allowed the state of loading to be seen at all times.

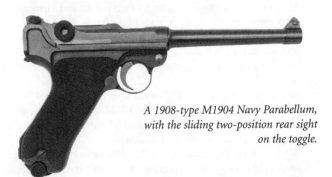

A 1908-type M1904 Navy Parabellum, with the sliding two-position rear sight on the toggle.

Parabellum M1904 ("Selbstladepistole 1904" or "Navy Model") Adopted by the German navy, these guns had 15cm (5.9in) barrels and two-position sights on the back toggle link. They were the first to incorporate the distinctive 1904-patent combination extractor/loaded-chamber indicator, set in the breechblock, but retained leaf-type return springs and had rebound locks in the toggle grips. The perfected version, delivered from 1906 onward, had coil springs and conventional flat-face toggle grips that lacked the locking latch. The grip safety was retained; though the direction of movement of the manual catch was changed c. 1912 to reduce accidents, as "old style" or "up-safe" catches could be disengaged when cocked-and-locked guns were holstered. Navy Parabellums made during the early part of World War I had short frames, and post-1916 deliveries had 1908-pattern actions that lacked grip safeties.

Navy guns could be identified by their markings, though a few "navy commercials" were also made. Proofmarks took the form of squared ("Imperial") crowns instead of the displayed-eagle markings associated with army issue, and navy inspectors' marks comprised simply a squared crown above "M", whereas army personnel were identified individually. Navy Parabellums could have an individual identifier — e.g., "W.W." for Wilhelmshaven dockyard (*Werft Wilhelmshaven*) — on the grip strap, but were dated only during World War I.

Parabellum M1906 (or "New Model") Developed in 1904, this was the first to combine the coil-type return spring and the 1904-patent extractor/loaded-chamber indicator. The 7.65mm guns had 12cm barrels and long frames; 9mm examples had 10cm barrels and short frames. The toggle grips were flat-faced, without the locking latch, and the mechanical hold-open of the Old Models was retained.

- *Brazil* About 5000 of these 7.65mm-caliber guns were purchased in 1911. They had 4.7-inch barrels, the DWM monogram on the toggle and an encircled "B" property mark. The extractor was marked "CARREGADA".
- *Bulgaria* Originally delivered in 1907-8 with 4.7-inch barrels, most of these 7.65-caliber guns were eventually converted to 9mm (4-inch barrels). They had the DWM monogram on the toggle and, like the earlier 1900-type delivery, had the Bulgarian lion-on-shield Arms over the chamber. The extractor was marked "ПЪЛЕНЪ", and "ОГЬНЪ" appeared in the safety-lever recess.
- *Germany, trials guns* Acquired for issue to machine-gunners in 1906-7 and numbered in their own sequence, these 9mm guns had 4-inch barrels. The DWM monogram appeared on the toggle, the

extractor was marked "GELADEN" and the safety-lever recess contained "GESICHERT". A small crowned gothic-letter inspector's mark will be found on the front right side of the receiver.

- *The Netherlands* Some sources credit the Dutch with suggesting the coil-spring improvement to the Parabellum, though the case is still largely circumstantial. Though a few guns were purchased for trials with the army, the only large-scale purchases prior to World War I were made on behalf of the colonial army, the *Nederlansch Indisch Leger* (given the prefix "Royal", *Koninklijke*, in 1911). Adopted in April 1910, these 9mm guns had 4-inch barrels and often gained brass marking plates on the left side of the frame. The extractor was marked "GELADEN" on both sides, but the safety-recess mark had become "RUST" beneath an arrow. The DWM monogram on the toggle distinguished the pre-1914 KNIL guns from post-1921 issues.
- *Portugal, army* These 7.65mm-caliber pistols, issued as the "M1909", had 4.7-inch barrels. The DWM monogram lay on the toggle, the "M2" cipher of King Manuel II lay over the chamber and the extractor was marked "CARREGADA".
- *Portugal, navy* The success of the 7.65mm army Parabellums persuaded the navy to follow, ordering 1000 9mm 4-inch barreled guns with a crowned foul anchor device over the chamber, complementing the DWM monogram on the toggle. However, before the order was complete, republicans overthrew the king; the last 200 pistols, therefore, were delivered with "R.P." (*Republica Portuguêsa*) instead of the crown above the anchor.
- *Russia* A few 9mm-caliber guns have been reported with crossed Mosin-Nagant rifles above the chamber and "ЭАРЯДЪ" on the extractor. It has been claimed that they were issued to army officers or the secret police, but it is also possible that they were made to the order of a wholesaler.
- *Switzerland* The components of more than 10,000 7.65mm Parabellums, with 4.7-inch barrels, were supplied prior to 1914 to permit assembly in the state firearms factory in Bern. All had the DWM monogram on the toggle-links, but pre-1909 guns had a cross-on-sunburst above the chamber and post-1909 examples had a cross-on-shield. Distinctive "Swiss cross" proofmarks and principal inspectors' marks (cartouches containing a small cross above an identifying letter) were also to be found.
- *USA* In 1907, DWM delivered a few guns chambering the 45 M1906 cartridge to the US Army. Trials favored the Colt-Browning, and nothing more was done. The 45-caliber Parabellums were much bulkier than normal and had a distinctively angular trigger instead of the standard curved design.

Parabellum M1908 (standard or short-barrel type, "Pistole 1908", "P. 1908", "P. 08") Adopted by the German army in 1908, this 9mm 10cm-barreled Parabellum included the coil-type return spring and the combined extractor/loaded-chamber indicator of the New Model, but the grip safety was omitted. A new manually applied safety lever raised a sliding plate vertically out of the left side of the frame, behind the cover plate, to block the lateral movement of the sear.

The earliest guns lacked a mechanical hold-open, allowing the action to close after the last spent round had been ejected. Field service soon showed this simplification to be a mistake, and the hold-open was reinstated early in 1913. A stock-lug was added to the heel of the standard Pistole1908 butt from August 1913.

Minor changes were made to the rear of the frame and the return-spring housing in 1915, but these had been present on all Parabellums made in Erfurt from 1911. The sear bar was changed in 1916 to allow the pistol to be cocked even if the safety catch was applied.

- *Bolivia* A few pistols bear marks of the national Arms or "EJERCITO DO BOLIVIA" above the chamber. It is still unclear whether these Parabellums, which seem to have been taken from pre-1914

commercial production, were acquired for trials or for the use of individual officers. Extractors were marked "CARGADO".

- *Bulgaria* Ten thousand pistols were purchased in 1910-11, numbered in two separate series. They had 9mm-caliber 4-inch barrels and a lanyard loop on the heel of the butt. The DWM monogram (uniquely) was above the chamber, allowing a simplified lion-on-crowned-shield mark to replace it on the toggle; the extractor was marked "ПЪЛЕНЪ", and "ОГЬНЪ" appeared in the safety-lever recess. A small rampant-lion proofmark appeared on the front right side of the receiver.
- *Finland (army)* Supplied in the 1920s by Berlin-Karlsruher Industrie-Werke ("BKIW"), as DWM had become, these were 7.65mm guns with 4-inch barrels. They can be identified by property marks (usually "SA" in a square) and also often by marking disks set into the grips. Many were converted to 9mm in the 1930s, when 4.7-inch Tikkakoski-made barrels were substituted.
- *Finland (prison service)* Purchased in the early 1920s from BKIW, these 7.65mm-caliber Parabellums had 4-inch barrels. They were distinguished by "VANKEINHOITOLAITOS" surrounding an encircled star-on-sunburst mark above the chamber and had DWM monograms on the toggle.

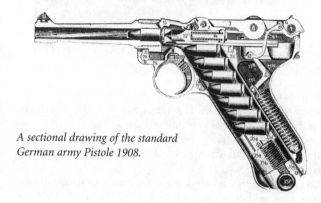

A sectional drawing of the standard German army Pistole 1908.

- *Germany* Service-issue pistols, excepting the type described below, all had 4-inch 9mm-caliber barrels. The first DWM-made guns lacked stock lugs and hold-opens, but these were reinstated in 1913. The earliest guns lacked chamber dates and had proof and inspectors' marks on the left side of the receiver ahead of the trigger plate. This had soon been changed to the right side, and a date was placed transversely above the receiver after 1910. The "master serial numbers" on the frame, receiver and barrel had suffix letters, partly to account for the large quantities involved and partly to ensure correct assembly; owing to the design of the trigger system, interchangeability could never be guaranteed. Many pistols will be found with unit markings on the front grip strap, though the process was suspended from 1916. A change was made to the sear at this time, allowing the Parabellum to be cocked with the safety catch applied.
- *The Netherlands* Pistols were purchased from BKIW shortly before production was transferred to Mauser (q.v.). Intended for the navy, they had 9mm 4-inch barrels, the DWM monogram on the toggles, and "RUST"-and-arrow safety-lever recess markings; "GELADEN" lay on both sides of the extractor. (Note: A few hundred supplied by Mauser in 1930-6 also bore DWM toggle marks.)

Parabellum M1908 (long-barrel type, "Lange Pistole 1908", "LP. 08") This was adopted in June 1913 to replace the revolvers and carbines serving the field artillerymen. Guns of this type had 20cm barrels, adjustable tangent-leaf rear sights and detachable stocks. The guns were marked similarly to the standard short-barrel equivalents.

DWM Introduced in the early 1920s, this was no more than a thinly-disguised copy of the Browning M1910, which DWM put on the market as their "Model 22". The original version had walnut grips, but in

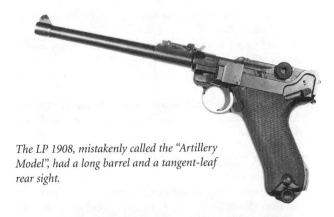

The LP 1908, mistakenly called the "Artillery Model", had a long barrel and a tangent-leaf rear sight.

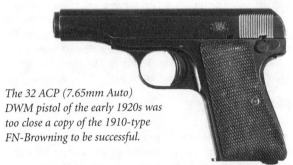

The 32 ACP (7.65mm Auto) DWM pistol of the early 1920s was too close a copy of the 1910-type FN-Browning to be successful.

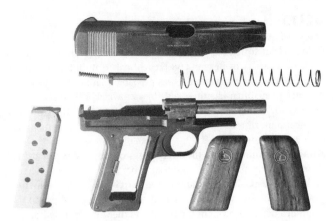

The Ortgies pistol dismantled into its principal components.

the following year, these were changed to black plastic and the pistol became the "Model 23", though this was purely a company reference and was never marked on the pistols. The only marking is the DWM monogram on the left side of the slide and on the black plastic grips. Production ceased in 1928; there is the suggestion that Fabrique Nationale brought legal action against the copying of their design, though this cannot be confirmed. Pistols remained on sale until 1931, and it is estimated that 40-50,000 may have been made.

DEUTSCHE-WERKE AG
Erfurt, Germany.
In 1921, Deutsche Werke AG, which had previously shown no interest in firearms, acquired the patents and machinery for production of the Ortgies (q.v.) pistol from its inventor. At that time, only a 7.65mm version was available, though designs for 6.35mm and 9mm Short (380 Auto) guns had been prepared. Deutsche Werke put all three calibers into production in 1922, beginning with the 6.35mm type. The 7.65mm pistol is identical with the 6.35mm design, except for size, but the 9mm variant exhibits minor variations.

Some 7.65mm and 9mm guns can be found with a manual safety catch on the left side of the frame at the top center of the butt; others rely on screws to hold the grip plates instead of the original "invisible" attachment.

A decorative Ortgies pistol, made by Deutsche Werke.

The markings may also vary. The earliest guns are marked "DEUTSCHE WERKE AKTIENGESELLSCHAFT WERK ERFURT" on the left side of the slide, and the original "HO" monogram medallion is let into the grips. Later examples display "DEUTSCHE WERKE" and "WERK ERFURT" on the slide, separated by a trademark consisting of a stylized cat formed from the letter "D". This motif is repeated on the grip medallions.

DICKINSON
E.L & J. Dickinson, Springfield, Massachusetts, USA.
Dickinson was one of the many small manufacturers who abounded in Massachusetts during and after the American Civil War. His original trade was in single-shot pistols, but in 1871, with patent restrictions removed, he produced a 32 RF revolver called the *Ranger No.2*. It was of good quality but much the same pattern as many competitors — a solid-frame, non-ejecting six-shot model with a cylindrical barrel and a bird's-head butt. Loading was through a groove in the right side of the frame, and unloading was done by pulling out the cylinder axis pin, removing the cylinder, and punching out the empty cases with the pin.

Having established this design, Dickinson then marketed it under a variety of other names, including "Earl Hood", "Earthquake", "Our Jake", "Sterling" and "Toledo" (a name also used by Hopkins & Allen). The company did not survive beyond the late 1880s.

D-MAX, INC.
Auburn, Washington, and Bagley, Minnesota, USA.
~ REVOLVER ~
Sidewinder (1992-8?) This was a large solid-frame Colt-like revolver, made entirely of stainless steel and fitted with adjustable sights. Hogue rubber grips were used to enhance control, the elongated six-chamber cylinder handling 45 Long Colt rounds or 410 shotshells interchangeably. The Sidewinder was about 14 inches long, with a 6.5-inch barrel and weighed about 57 oz empty. The muzzle accepted a detachable choke to concentrate the shot pattern.
~ AUTOMATIC PISTOL ~
D-Max (c. 1990-3) This was little more than a cut-down submachine gun modified to fire single shots from a closed-bolt blowback action. Chambered for the 9mm Parabellum, 10mm Auto, 40 S&W or 45 ACP rounds, the gun was 13.8 inches long, had a 6-inch barrel protected by a ventilated sleeve, and the detachable box magazine protruded from the left side. However, as the weight exceeded 5 lb, most shooters probably used a two-hand grip facilitated by a short walnut fore-end. Finished in "Max-Coat" polymer, with adjustable sights and a trigger-block safety catch, the D-Max was never made in quantity. The standard magazines held 30 rounds, and barrels of 8 or 10 inches were optional.

DOLNE

Louis Dolne, Liége, Belgium.

Dolne's claim to fame is a revolver developed in the 1860s that was made by a variety of Belgian and French makers until the end of the 19th century. The most prolific was probably Manufacture Liégeoise d'Armes à Feu, often identified only by a crowned "ML" mark (sometimes in the form of a monogram). Uncommon today, the guns may chamber pin-, rim- or centerfire ammunition, depending on manufacturer and their age.

Apache Acknowledging the street-gangs of Paris, who had named themselves after the Native American tribe, these revolvers offered a multi-threat capability. The guns lacked barrels, the bullets being fired straight out of the cylinder chamber through a hole in a topstrap that continued down the front of the cylinder to the wrought-iron frame. A folding knife blade, let into the lower part of the frame, could be extended in the manner of a flick-knife by pressing a catch. The brass butt was pierced and hinged to fold beneath the frame, which carried a folding trigger. By folding the weapon, it could then be grasped with the cylinder in the palm of the hand and the fingers through the holes in the butt … forming an efficient knuckleduster.

DORNHEIM

G.C.Dornheim AG, Suhl, Germany.

Dornheim — little more than a distributor — marketed pistols under the trade name Gecado for several decades.

Gecado The pre-1939 examples were 6.35mm and 7.65mm Auto "Eibar" automatics made in Spain by SEAM (q.v.), bearing "GECADO" in a diamond and offering only average quality.

Post-1945 guns, distributed by Gustav Genschow (q.v.) prior to 1959 and by Dynamit Nobel since then, usually prove to be minor variants of the 6.35mm Reck P-8 exposed-barrel blowback with the safety catch moved to the rear of the frame. The slides of these guns are usually marked "GECADO MOD 11 CAL 6,35 (.25)" above "MADE IN GERMANY".

DORNAUS & DIXON

Dornaus & Dixon Enterprises, Huntingdon Beach, California, USA.

This partnership was responsible for aCZ75 adapted by Jeff Cooper, the well-known US pistol shot and instructor, to chamber the 10mm Auto Pistol cartridge developed by Norma a few years earlier.

The weapons were otherwise unremarkable and due to their high price and the inability of the company to meet manufacturing schedules, failed to make the impact on the market that had been hoped. Manufacture ceased early in 1985 after possibly 1500 pistols had been made, but the 10mm cartridge was adopted by the FBI in 1989, and a resurgence of interest resulted in Peregrine Industries of Balboa, California, acquiring rights to the Bren Ten in 1990. The "Peregrine Falcon" was also to fail.

Bren Ten (1983-5) The basic construction and recoil-operated tipping-barrel mechanism remain those of the Czechoslovakian prototype (see "Česká Zbrojovka"), but the US-made derivative had much more angular lines.

The standard 10mm-caliber Bren Ten pistol, promoted by Dornaus & Dixon.

- *Dual-Master* This was offered with exchangeable 10mm and 45 ACP barrel/slide units.
- *Initial Issue Commemorative* Lightly engraved and detailed in gold, this deluxe gun was sold in a special presentation case.
- *Military & Police Model* This was the standard version, with an 11-round magazine.
- *Pocket Model* Distinguished by a shorter barrel/frame than normal, and a butt containing a nine-round magazine, this was made only in very small quantities.

DOWNSIZER CORPORATION

Santee, California, USA.

WSP (1997 to date) Distinguished by its squared contours and compact dimensions (3.3 inches overall, 11 oz empty), this is a single-shot break-open design with a double-action trigger mechanism. Originally chambered for the 9mm Parabellum, 357 Magnum, 40 S&W or 45 ACP rounds, the ultra-short synthetic grip makes the WSP difficult to fire accurately but allows a powerful punch to be delivered from a tiny package. Construction is largely stainless steel. The 9mm Parabellum and 40 S&W options were discontinued in 2001.

FRANZ VON DREYSE

Sömmerda, Germany.

Franz von Dreyse (1822-94) was the son of the inventor of the Prussian needle-gun, succeeding to the gunmaking business when his father died in 1867. The success of the Mauser rifles prevented Dreyse repeating his father's success, and profitability declined. Though a few needle-fire revolvers were made in the late 1860s in accordance with patents granted from 1852 onward to Georg Kufahl, production of handguns was restricted to the 1880s. Output was subsequently increasingly devoted to sporting guns until, in 1901, the near-bankrupt company was acquired by Rheinische Metallwaaren & Maschinenfabrik.

∼ REVOLVER ∼

Reichsrevolver The Dreyse facilities were put to making guns for the German army, just one of several contractors in the Thuringian Forest to participate (see "Spandau rifle factory") in a program that was intended to re-equip the armed forces as quickly as possible. The comparative scarcity of Dreyse "F. v. D." markings on the revolvers suggests that military-contract work was restricted to a single order, but so-called "Officers' Models", with non-standard features such as checkered rubber grips, double triggers and spurred trigger guards, have also been recorded.

∼ AUTOMATIC PISTOL ∼

Mannlicher Shortly before the 1901 transfer of business, Waffenfabrik von Dreyse is said to have made a small number of these pistols, essentially the prototypes of the M1901. The chronology is not clear, but it is possible that they included the experimental guns supplied to Swiss army trials as early as 1898.

DRULOV

Družstvo Lověna, Prague; later "Dilo" Svratouch (National Cooperative), Litomyšl, Czechoslovakia.

Formerly part of the state-controlled Czech firearms industry, this company specializes in inexpensive target pistols that are, nevertheless, well made and give good performance.

Model 70 Standard A bolt-action single-shot pistol, the bolt being operated by a knob protruding to the rear of the frame. Closing the bolt cocks the striker. The barrel is almost 10 inches long, carrying an adjustable front sight, and the rear sight is adjustable for elevation. The walnut wraparound grip has a prominent thumb-rest.

- *Model 70 Special* This is similar to the Standard model but is fitted with a set trigger. Inside the trigger guard is a horizontal setting lever and a button; pressing down the lever "sets" the trigger, and a slight pressure on the button fires the pistol.

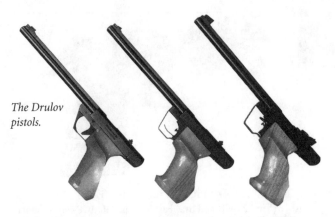

The Drulov pistols.

A 6.35mm (25 ACP) Duo, by Dušek of Opočno. This gun was made during the German occupation of Czechoslovakia — shown by the inclusion of "Opotschno" in the slide mark.

Model 75 A variant of the 70 Special with a somewhat different set trigger, different sights and a better grip. The set-trigger arrangement is similar to that of the 70 Special, but the setting lever springs back when released. That of the 70 Special remained down until the trigger button was pressed. The rear sight is also laterally adjustable.

Pav Designed by Pavliček, this was introduced in 1963. It is a cheap and simple drop-barrel single-shot weapon with a dovetailed front sight blade and a mere groove in the rear of the frame for a rear sight. The pistol is loaded by pressing a catch on the left side to open the barrel, placing a round in the chamber, cocking the firing pin by a knob on the striker and then closing the barrel. Cheap and cheerful, it was doubtless a good basic trainer for beginners.

DUMOULIN

F. Dumoulin et Cie, Liége, Belgium.

Le Novo A five-chamber 6.35mm pocket revolver with butt that folded up around the trigger and frame, invented by Dieudonné Oury and made for Dumoulin by Établissements Derkenne (q.v.).

Lincoln A name that was very popular among Liége gunmakers, it applied to a wide variety of revolvers produced from 1880 to 1914. Most were of the folding-trigger pocket variety, hammer and "hammerless" types, in calibers ranging from 22 RF and 5.5mm Velo-Dog to 380 CF. Among the other makers using this name were Ancion Marx, Bertrand, Debouxtay, Jannsen Fils et Cie, Le Page, Neumann Frères and Raick Frères, all of Liége, and Albrecht Kind of Germany. Most (or, indeed) all of the guns may have been made by Manufacture Liégeoise d'Armes à Feu.

DUŠEK

František Dušek, Opočno, Czechoslovakia.

Dušek set up as a pistol-maker in the late 1920s and made a number of 6.35mm blowback automatics under various names, most of which were based upon Browning originals (though lacking the grip safety

mechanism). He remained in business throughout World War II, and guns can be found with German markings. Dušek also accepted contracts to make and repair weapons for the occupying forces, his military output being identified by the code "aek". With the arrival of Communism in 1948, the business was nationalized and work was transferred to the Česká Zbrojovka plant.

Duo (1926-49) A 6.35mm blowback, this Browning derivative had a 2.25-inch barrel and a six-round box magazine. It was a good commercial success, selling widely throughout Europe and in the USA. It was also sold in Germany through an agent, Eblen of Stuttgart, whose name is sometimes stamped on specimens.

The guns are usually marked "AUTOMAT. PISTOLE "DUO" CAL. 6.35" on the left side of the slide, above "F. DUŠEK" and "OPOČNO"; the grips, which have distinctive squared checkering, display "DUO" in a circle. However, the slide inscription was rendered in German during the occupation of Czechoslovakia, when the location was given as "Opotchno". Production continued after 1949 as the Česká Zbrojovka Pistole "Z", with a modified slide incription and a "Z"-within-rifling motif on the grips. The guns that had been sold under other names prior to 1939 can often be identified only by their grips.

Ideal A variant of the Duo, marked "AUTOMATICKÁ PISTOLE RÁZE 6·35" over "IDEAL", though the grips, confusingly, are marked "Ydeal". It is probable that these guns, assuming they were handled by Dušek, were made in Spain immediately prior to World War I, as a typical example bears an Austro-Hungarian proofmark dated 1912.

Jaga Another camouflaged Duo, this is usually (but not invariably) marked "AUTOMAT. PISTOLE »JAGA« 6·35" on the slide; "Jaga" in a curved banner will be found on the grips beneath the retaining bolt.

Perla (1935-9) Based on the Walther Model 9, this had a fixed barrel and open-topped slide. There is no indication of the maker, as the slide displays nothing but "AUTOMAT. PISTOLE »PERLA« 6·35".

EAGLE ARMS CO.

New York, USA.

A little-known New York company that apparently made the 28-caliber Plant revolver under license between 1865 and 1870. It is, though, highly probable that the name was simply a sales device and was actually the company formally incorporated as Reynolds, Plant & Hotchkiss, which also operated as Plant's Manufacturing Co. See under "Plant" for further details.

EASTERN ARMS CO.

The "Eastern Arms Company" never existed, being merely a sales name employed by the Meriden Firearms Company (q.v.) for guns sold by F. Biffen & Co of Chicago. There were two revolvers that bore this particular name, in 32 and 38 centerfire chamberings. Both were hinged-frame double-action models with automatic extraction and were made between 1895 and 1915. They are readily identified by the peculiar form of front sight that characterized Meriden products.

JAVIER ECHANIZ

Eibar, Spain.

Defender This was a 7.65mm "Eibar" automatic of the usual type, made briefly in the 1920s.

ECHAVE Y ARIZMENDI ("ECHASA")

Echave, Arizmendi y Cia SA, Eibar, Spain.

This gunmaking partnership originated as Echave y Arizmendi in about 1911 and confined its attention exclusively to automatic pistols. Although the early models were of no particular merit, the partners improved the quality in the 1930s and after the Civil War were one of the four pistol makers permitted to return to the trade. Echave y Arizmendi enjoyed a good export business in the post-1945 years and also made the Model GZ pistol for the Manufacture d'Armes de Bayonne (see under "M"). Their export trade to the USA declined sharply after the 1968 Gun Control Act, however, and the business failed in 1979.

Basque This was the 32 ACP "Echasa" under a different name. The slide was marked "Basque Cal .32 Made in Spain" and the grips carried an oval with "Basque" inside.

Bronco (c. 1919-30) A routine copy of the 1906-type Browning, this was made in two forms: a 6.35mm Auto (25 ACP) and a 7.65mm Auto (32 ACP), identical but for size. The slide inscription read "[caliber] 1918 Model Automatic Pistol Bronco Patent No 66130". The patent referred to the "EA monogram" trademark molded into the grips.

Dickson Special Agent A name applied to 32-caliber Echasa pistols sold in the USA.

E.A. A 6.35mm Auto (25 ACP) "Eibar" blowback automatic based on the Browning 1906 model, this had a slide that was marked "6,35 1916 Model Automatic Pistol", with the maker's initials stamped into an oval on the frame. A predecessor of the Bronco, it lacked the grip safety.

Echasa "Echasa" became the company's trading name during the 1950s, a form of contraction common in Spain, and the Echasa pistol was a 7.65mm double-action blowback inspired by the Walther PP. The most significant difference lay in the method of dismantling. Instead of springing the trigger guard, as in the Walther, a sliding catch on the left rear of the frame allowed the slide to be removed. The safety catch was moved from the slide to the frame, the lockwork was considerably different and the hammer could not be lowered simply by pressing the safety catch. The Echasa leaves the impression that the harder parts of the copying job had simply been dodged. Several versions were made, differing largely in finish.

Fast This was simply the Echasa range under a different name, intended for sale in English-speaking countries in general and the USA in par-

An Echasa Model 761 "Fast" pistol.

ticular. The "Fast 221" was in 22 LR rimfire, the "Fast 631" in 25 ACP, the "Fast 761" in 32 ACP, and the "Fast 901" in 380 ACP (9mm Short). The standard "1"-suffix guns were made of blued steel and had black plastic grips. However, there were other options: the "633" was a chrome-plated 631 with white ivory grips, and the "902" was a blued 901 with walnut grips. The slides of "Fast" pistols all bore the Echasa trademark, "EA" divided by a "Y" that provides three spokes to the wheel-like design. "Fast" and "Echasa" were molded into the plastic grips, though "EyA" medallions were let into the wooden grips.

Lightning This was found on a gun that was little more than a Bronco marked "6,35 Automatic Pistol Lightning". Its grips bore the old "EA" monogram.

Lur Panzer A 22 LR rimfire blowback "Luger lookalike", this was little other than a copy of the Erma EP-22 (q.v.). The barrel extension was marked with "Lur Cal .22 LR Made in Spain" and the "EyA" mark and "Panzer" in a diamond motif was molded into the plastic grips.

Pathfinder Identical with the Bronco but for markings, this 6.35mm-caliber "Eibar" was renamed by Stoeger (q.v.) for sale in the USA.

Protector A name applied to 6.35mm "Eibar" pistols made by both Echave & Arizmendi and Santiago Salaberrin. The former was simply the "E.A." with minor changes in the design of the trigger guard and magazine catch.

Selecta Otherwise resembling the Protector, this had the top rear end of the slide relieved to form a thin central section doubling as a sight rib. There were four distinct models: *Double Safety*, in 6.35mm Auto (25 ACP) or 7.65mm Auto (32 ACP), with both applied and magazine safeties; and the *Triple Safety*, with an additional grip mechanism. The 6.35mm-caliber guns were marked "Model 1918", but the 7.65mm versions were the "Model 1919". The slide markings were all similar: the caliber accompanied by "1918 [or "1919"] Model Automatic Pistol Selecta Patent". The grips displayed the "EA" monogram.

BONIFACIO ECHEVERRIA

Eibar, Spain.

See also "Star"

Izarra Izarra is the Basque word for "Star" and this was the usual 7.65mm "Eibar" made after 1918. Notable for its quality, considerably better than most Spanish guns of this type, it also had an extended grip

The Echeverria 32 ACP Izarra blowback pistol, first in a long line of Stars.

that accepted a nine-round magazine. Some guns had long barrels protruding from the slide.

The 9mm Helwan was an Egyptian-made version of the Italian Beretta M951 Brigadier.

EGYPTIAN STATE FACTORY

Helwan A licensed copy of the Beretta M951 made in Egypt in the 1960s, this is identical to the Beretta except for Arabic markings on the slide.

EIG

USA.

The EIG Corporation was a distributorship in the USA in the 1950-70 era that sold European pistols marked with the "EIG" badge. The pistols were principally Röhm (q.v.) revolvers and Tanfoglio (q.v.) "Titan" automatic pistols. Japanese Miroku guns were also involved. It seems probable that the 1968 Gun Control Act ended this firm's activity by restricting importation.

ELY & WRAY

Springfield, Massachusetts, USA.

This was a partnership of Alfred B. Ely and F.W. Wray, formed in 1875. Ely was an experienced gunsmith and patentee; Wray may have been the financial backer. The firm produced a number of suicide special revolvers under such names as *American 38, Bang Up, Bloodhound* and *Tiger* before selling out to Harrington & Richardson, who continued to use the Ely & Wray brand names.

EMF CO.

Santa Ana, California, USA.

Founded in 1958, the EMF Company has handled a variety of Western-style revolvers made principally in Italy by Pietta (caplock) and Uberti (cartridge patterns).

Dakota (New Model Single Action Army Revolver) The original pattern was a Uberti (q.v.) Cattleman. This was not intended to be a replica of the original Colt and was offered in a variety of non-standard patterns with barrels ranging from 2 inches to 16 inches. Most had brass grip straps and high-profile adjustable sights that made them look a little like the Ruger Blackhawk. Though these guns sold in large numbers for more than 20 years, the rise of the "enthusiast" market persuaded EMF to substitute revolvers that were much more accurately based on the Colt SAA. These are now being sold as the "New Dakota" series.

Frontier Marshal This is an "economy" version of the New Dakota (below) and available only in 357 Magnum or 45 Long Colt. It has a color case-hardened frame, a blued barrel and a blued cylinder, but the grip straps and the trigger guard are made of polished brass.

Great Western II These "second generation" guns, closely modeled on the original 1873-type Colts, are offered in a variety of chamberings (357 Magnum/38 Special, 44-40 WCF, 45 Long Colt) and finishes. Barrel lengths are restricted to 4.75, 5.5 and 7.5 inches. The "Californian" has a blued barrel, case-hardened hammer and frame, and walnut grips. "Custom" examples may be finished in polished or satin nickel, overall blue, or blue with a case-hardened frame; the grips

are a high-quality simulated ivory. Engraved versions may have staghorn grips. Other guns have been made in stainless steel, or supplied "in the white" to allow purchasers to have them finished elsewhere.

Hartford The original series was made in several patterns, sharing the same basic Italian-made Single Action Army action. Guns can be obtained as "Old Models" (with a screw retaining the cylinder pin and a "bullseye" ejector-rod head) or a "New Model" (with a spring-latch retainer and a crescent-shape ejector-rod head that followed the contours of the barrel). Old Model revolvers are confined to traditional chamberings (32-20 WCF to 45 Long Colt), whereas the New Model will accept 357 Magnum/38 Special, 44 Special or 45 Long Colt.

- *Hartford Bisley* (or "Bisley 1894") Distinguished by the special high-grip frame and low-set flanged hammer spur, this could be chambered for 32-20 WCF, 357 Magnum, 38-40 WCF, 44-40 WCF or 45 Colt. Barrels could be 4.75, 5.5 or 7.5 inches long.
- *Hartford Buntline* This is simply a version of the basic 45 Long Colt Hartford revolver with a 12-inch barrel. A carbine has also been offered, with an 18-inch barrel, but has a shoulder stock permanently attached to the frame.
- *Hartford Combo* This name is sometimes applied to a set of two revolvers – Colt SAA and M1875 Remington – with exchangeable cylinders chambered for either the 45 Long Colt or 45 ACP rounds.
- *Hartford Deputy* This has a 3.5-inch barrel with an ejector-rod case and a standard straight-base butt. Chambering is restricted to 45 Long Colt.
- *Hartford Express* Offered in the same barrel-length options as the Bisley, this was chambered only for 45 Long Colt and had a Lightning-style grip (bird's-head style with a spur or "prawl" on a straight upper edge).
- *Hartford "Old West"* Made only in 45 Long Colt, in the three standard barrel lengths, these guns have an interesting "100 Year Old Antique Patina" finish, which creates a distinctive weathered gray.
- *Hartford Pinkerton* Sharing the Bisley chamberings, with the addition of 44 Special, this was restricted to a 4-inch barrel that retained the ejector case on the right side. The grip took traditional bird's-head form.
- *Hartford Premier* One of the finest of the EMF Colts, this usually offers a color case-hardened frame and hammer, high-polish blue on the barrel and simulated staghorn grips (though some guns have been bright or satin-nickeled). The action has also been honed to give a light and precise trigger pull. Restricted to 357 Magnum or 45 Long Colt, and with barrels measuring 4.75, 5.5 or 7.5 inches, the Premier may be encountered as a cased set.
- *Hartford Sheriff* A distinctively compact design, this matches a 3-inch barrel, lacking the ejector-rod case, with a standard butt. It is available only in 45 Long Colt.
- *Hartford US Army Model* Restricted to 45 Long Colt and the Old Model frame, these guns are made in two styles – "Cavalry" with the original 7.5-inch barrel and "Artillery" with a 5.5-inch barrel – to duplicate the guns acquired by the US Army in the 19th century. They have color case-hardened frames and hammers, blued barrels and straps, and plain walnut grips. A "U.S." mark lies on the left side of the frame beneath the patent acknowledgments, and a facsimile of an inspector's cartouche is pressed into the grip.

New Dakota These guns are essentially the same as the Great Western II series, with the same barrel-length options, but have brass straps with a black-nickel finish. The frame and hammer are color case-hardened, and the barrel remains a high-polish blue. Chamberings are restricted to 357 Magnum, 44-40 WCF and 45 Long Colt.

Remington These are re-creations of the principal rival to the Colt SAA. Very similar to the Colt externally, the 1875-type Remingtons can be distinguished by the prominent web beneath the barrel and the shape of the grip. The 1890 pattern was identical mechanically with its predecessor, but all the web was cut away except for a very short section immediately ahead of the frame. All EMF Remingtons may be obtained with engraving and special "custom" finishes.

- *Army Single Action* (or "Outlaw") Made only with a 7.5-inch barrel, this M1875 has been offered in 357 Magnum/38 Special, 44-40 WCF or 45 Long Colt. The standard guns are blued, with color case-hardened frames, and have plain walnut grips. The trigger guard is brass, though usually finished in black nickel.
- *Frontier Single Action* Identical with the Army Single Action in everything except barrel length (5.5 inches only).
- *Police Model* A replica of the 1890 gun, with most of the 1875-type under-barrel web removed, this is offered only in 45 Long Colt with a 5.5-inch barrel. The guns may be finished in blue or nickel and have a lanyard ring under the butt.

EMPIRE ARMS CO.

Also listed as "Empire State Arms Company".
This was a fictitious business name used by the Meriden Firearms Company (q.v.) in 1895-1905. The revolvers were the usual hinged-frame, ribbed-barrel "hammerless" pattern in 32 and 38 centerfire, recognizable by the Meriden front sight. The cylinders hold five or six rounds, depending on caliber.

ENFIELD (ROYAL SMALL ARMS FACTORY)

Enfield Lock, Middlesex, England.
In February 1879, the British Army found itself short of revolvers, and on March 11, the Superintendent of the Royal Small Arms Factory (RSAF) reported the purchase of 235 Tranter, 165 Colt and 100 Webley revolvers. He added that, as the Webley pistols were "slightly defective in their action, they have been returned for rectification".

The Director of Artillery, who was, at that time, the responsible authority for small arms, felt it to be unreasonable that, when 500 revolvers were needed, three different patterns had to be sought from the trade and 20 percent of those were found to be defective. Accordingly, on July 16, he called for a design of a revolver pistol to be produced by RSAF. In an astonishingly short time — 16 days — the Factory had produced drawings and had them approved. The prototypes went for trial to the Naval Gunnery Establishment, HMS *Excellent*, on January 14, 1880, and after some small changes, the design was sealed for issue on August 11, 1880, as the "Pistol Revolver, Breech Loading, Enfield, Mark 1".

After making small numbers of Webley revolvers in the years immediately after World War I had ended, the factory developed a 38-caliber adaptation that served the British Army until 1957, when the Browning GP35 automatic was adapted. The production of revolvers then ceased with no additional work being done on pistols before the Enfield factory closed down in 1988 and was subsequently demolished.

Enfield (1880 type) The 476 Enfield Mark I was a six-shot, hinged-frame, double-action revolver with an unusual extraction system; hinging down the barrel pulled the cylinder forward but retained the extractor plate in place, thus, in effect, drawing the cylinder off the empty cases. As the Captain of *Excellent* pointed out in his trial report, "the only fault being that in extracting the empty cartridges, the lower one hangs, the cylinder having to be revolved to clear it." Contrary to frequently expressed belief, the Enfield, with a 5.9-inch barrel, was not inaccurate. The trial report gives a 4.2-inch group at 25 yards off-hand, compared with 4.8 inches with the Tranter pistol.

However, there were two features on the original sealed pattern about which the Superintendent RSAF had second thoughts. The cylinder had the forward section of the chambers rifled, and the interior components of the lock were nickel-plated. Trials with some of the first production models showed that the rifled section of the chamber was

likely to choke with lead, and the nickel plating tended to flake off, particles falling into the lockwork and jamming the action. So on August 28 the approval was cancelled, and a fresh pattern was approved on September 13, 1880. It is of interest that a report of November 17 refers to an order for 5000 pistols for the Royal Navy, to be browned, and an unspecified number for the Indian army, which were to be nickel-plated externally.

- *Mark II* Use of the Mark I pistol during the first few months revealed some minor defects, and on April 12, 1881, the Superintendent of the RSAF submitted a Mark II design. The front sight was now rounded to prevent it catching in the holster; the cylinder had lie chambers taper-bored in order to reduce the chance of bullets loosening and to improve accuracy; the topstrap became part of the body forging instead of being a separate part; and a cylinder lock was added to prevent the cylinder revolving while the weapon was being carried in the holster. A minor detail of finish was that the butt grips were now to be plain instead of checkered. The cylinder lock was linked with the loading shield (similar to a gate), so that when the shield was opened, this lock was freed and the hammer locked, which in the words of the Superintendent, "so renders it impossible to fire the pistol, whilst loading, by accidentally pulling the trigger, which has been the source of frequent accidents". After some discussion, the pattern sealed on March 13, 1882.

In July 1887, a safety device was added to all Mark I and Mark II revolvers that prevented the hammer being jarred forward to fire a cartridge when in the rebound position. This was replaced by an improved design in 1889, and all pistols so fitted were stamped "S" on the left of the frame, below the barrel catch.

The pistol remained in service until the 1890s, but it was replaced for issue by the Webley Mark I on November 8, 1887, and this marked the end of pistol production for Enfield for several years.

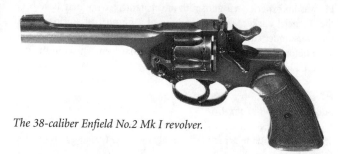

The 38-caliber Enfield No.2 Mk I revolver.

Enfield (1932 type) After World War I, the British Army turned away from the 455 caliber, since wartime experience had shown that such a powerful pistol demanded a high degree of training and constant practice. It was considered that a 38 firing a heavy bullet would be sufficiently lethal, and in 1932, the "Pistol, Revolver, No. 2 Mark I" — usually called the "Enfield 38" — was introduced. This was a modification of a Webley design, a six-shot hinged-frame double-action revolver with a 5-inch barrel.

The original cartridge for this was known as the 38 Webley Special, loaded with a 200-grain blunt-nosed bullet of lead. But there was some doubt about the ethical position, in view of the Geneva Convention's condemnation of soft-nosed "explosive" bullets, and in January 1938, the design was changed to a 178-grain jacketed bullet.

- *No. 2 Mark I** While the Enfield Mk I satisfied most customers, the Royal Tank Regiment objected that the hammer spur was prone to catch on the interior fittings of tanks as the crews were climbing in and out, and as a result of this complaint, the Mark I* was introduced in June 1938. This was the same weapon but had the hammer spur removed so that it could no longer be thumb-cocked to fire single action. The mainspring was lightened to reduce the trigger pull to 11-13 lb from the 13-15 lb of the Mk I, and the grips were formed with thumb recesses to give a better grip. Newly-made Mark I* revolvers were supplemented by conversions of the Mark I, altered as and when they were sent into workshops for overhaul and repair. Original Mark I examples are now rarely seen.

In addition to the Enfield production, Pistols No. 2 Mk I * were made by Albion Motors Ltd., of Scotstoun, Glasgow, from June 1941 to late 1943; about 24,000 were produced. These pistols are marked "Albion" on the right side of the frame. Components were also made by the Singer Sewing Machine Company of Clydebank and sent to Enfield for assembly. There are no pistols marked "Singer", but Enfield-made guns may be found with "SM" or "SSM" stamped on various components.

- *No. 2 Mark I*** This was introduced In July 1942 to accelerate production. The hammer safety stop was omitted, but this proved to be a false economy — dropping the pistol on to the hammer could fire it. These revolvers were all recalled after the war so that the stop could be reinstated, converting them back to the Mark I* pattern.

Webley A few 455-caliber Mk VI revolvers were made from 1921 onward. These were identical with the Webley (q.v.) pattern except for a more slender grip but can be distinguished from the original by the "Enfield" stamp on the right side of the frame below the hammer.

ENTERPRISE GUN WORKS
Pittsburgh, Pennsylvania, USA.
Eclipse This single-shot derringer, dating from the early 1870s, has a barrel that opens laterally. Chambered for 22, 32 and — very rarely — 25 Short rimfire ammunition, it has a nickel-plated wrought-iron frame and a walnut bird's-head grip.

ENTRÉPRISE ARMS
Entréprise Arms, Inc, Irwindale, California, USA.
This business specializes in pistols based on the Colt-Browning, the earliest dating from 1998. They are sold under designations such as "Boxer P500", "Elite P500", "Medalist P500" (discontinued by 2002), and the "Tactical Series" — P500 and Plus. There was also a "Tournament Shooter Model I", which had also been abandoned by 2002.

ENVALL
This unusual revolver was patented in 1885 by a Major Envall of the Norwegian army. The "trigger" actually cocked the hammer, and firing was performed by pressing a thumb-button in the top of the frame behind the hammer. The revolver was otherwise a reasonably conventional solid-frame, gate-loaded weapon, though with a curiously raked butt, which was probably necessary to ensure that the thumb fell naturally upon the firing button. A shoulder-stock could be fitted to convert the pistol into a species of carbine. The pistol was never given formal military approval, though small numbers appear to have been made for trials.

ERFURT RIFLE FACTORY
Koniglich preussisch Gewehrfabrik, Erfurt, Germany.
~ REVOLVER ~
Reichsrevolver Designed by the Prussian military Gewehr-Prüfungs-Kommission (see "Spandau arms factory"), these guns were made by a variety of contractors. Only a few Reichsrevolvers have been reported with Erfurt markings, almost exclusively the short-barreled M1883. They bear a "crown/ERFURT" mark on the left side of the frame beneath the cylinder, accompanied by the date.
~ AUTOMATIC PISTOL ~
Parabellum When the German army adopted the Pistole 1908 (Parabellum), the licensing agreement concluded with Deutsche

This view of an 1883-type Reichsrevolver shows the method of loading.

Waffen- und Munitionsfabriken (q.v.) allowing the government to install a duplicate set of production machinery. Purchased from Ludwig Loewe & Co., owners of DWM, this was installed in Erfurt in 1909-10. The first pistols were delivered in 1911, distinguished from the DWM-made examples by the "crown/ERFURT" mark on the front toggle link and the date of production over the chamber. The first batches were standard 4-inch barreled Parabellums, lacking the stock lug and manual hold-open mechanism. Both of these features were reinstated in 1913, and work continued until the end of World War I.

The Erfurt factory was also responsible for large numbers of long-barreled "Artillery Lugers" (LP. 08) delivered in 1915-18. These can be recognized by their toggle marks, the style of the "eagle" proofmarks on the receiver-side and the inspectors' marks. These can identify the source of components even though the original toggle-link may be missing.

ERMA
"Erma"–Erfurter Maschinenfabrik B. Geipel GmbH, Erfurt, Germany.
This gunmaking business is best known for the range of submachine guns, based on Vollmer's patents, that culminated in the immortal MP. 40 (widely, but mistakenly, known as the "Schmeisser").

In the 1920s, however, Erfurter Maschinenfabrik had developed a single-shot sub-caliber trainer for the Parabellum pistol, which was sold as the "Modell 20" (for 4mm primer-propelled ammunition) or "Modell 25" (22 LR rimfire). A version developed for use in the Mauser service rifle, known as the Einstecklauf 24 ("EL. 24"), was officially adopted by the German army in June 1927. It was followed by a magazine-feed version, (EL. 24 m. M.), accepted in January 1932, but the interest being generated in training persuaded Erfurter Maschinenfabrik to develop a semi-automatic mechanism that would fit the Parabellum. Patented in January 1927 by Richard Kulisch, a Berlin gunsmith, the "Selbstlade-Einstecklauf für Pistole 08" ("S.EL. für P. 08") was adopted in July 1932 and revived in post-war years (see below).

~ AUTOMATIC PISTOLS ~
Erma-Scheibe-Pistole ("Erma Target Pistol", 1936-8) The success of the Parabellum conversion kit persuaded Erma to develop a pistol for rapid-fire target shooting, introducing a blowback 22 LR rimfire semi-automatic in the mid-1930s. Subsequently known as the *Old Model*, this was a fixed-barrel blowback with an open-topped slide, a die-cast zinc-alloy frame and an external hammer. The slide had a stripping catch on the left side and the barrel, which was screwed into place, was easy to exchange. The standard lengths were 2.9, 4.9 and 7.9 inches, and there were many different sights and balance weights.

In 1937, an improved version, the *New Model*, appeared. The grip was at a sharper angle, the magazine was based on that of the Parabellum and the stripping catch was on the frame. The barrel was still interchangeable and there were differences in the barrel contour between the different styles available. The "Master" was supplied with a 300mm barrel as standard, the "Sport" with a 210mm barrel and the "Hunter" with a 100mm barrel. Production of all these stopped in 1940.
S.EL. für P. 08 ("Selbstlade-Einstecklauf für Pistole 08") This conversion unit allowed a 7.65mm or 9mm Parabellum to fire 5.6mm (22

LR) ammunition. It consisted of a barrel insert, a new toggle and breechblock, and a replacement magazine. The blowback breech mechanism contained its own return spring, as the normal spring — which remained in the butt after conversion — was far too strong to function with the 22 cartridge.

The S.EL. für P. 08 was marketed commercially as the "Modell 30", usually with a 5.9-inch barrel (though other lengths are known). The detachable box magazines held 5, 7 or 10 rounds. Sleeves were sold to fill the gap between the muzzle-nut of the barrel-insert and the muzzle of the gun, allowing the insert to fit virtually any Parabellum, from the 3.9-inch barreled guns introduced in the 1920s to the 5.9-inch "navy" pattern.

Virtually all were chambered for the 22 LR round, though a few hundred supplied to Switzerland in the 1930s were adapted for the 22 Long No. 7. Most of these inserts were apparently sold through Waffen-Glaser of Zürich.

ERMA (-WERKE)

Erma-Werke GmbH, Munich-Dachau, Germany (post-1945).
In 1945, Erfurt was enveloped in the eastern zone of occupied Germany, under Russian domination, and the original Erma company ceased trading. However, it is assumed that some members of the Geipel family, well aware of the consequences of staying in Thuringia, had moved westward. Work began again in 1946 in Dachau, refurbishing machine-tools and roller bearings in a factory that had been owned by Präzifix-Werke, and the Erma name was apparently readopted in 1948. In 1954, Interarms (q.v.) asked Erma-Werke to make new "Modell 30" sub-caliber inserts for the Parabellum. Production of these continued into the 1980s, alongside a variety of pistols — especially the blowback "Erma-Lugers" — and Smith & Wesson-style revolvers.

Erma handguns were successfully distributed in the USA for many years by Excam of Hialeah, Florida; Beeman Precision Guns of Santa Rosa, California; Mandall Shooting Supplies of Scottsdale, Arizona; and Precision Sales International of Westfield, Masschusetts. However, an ill-fated relationship with Harrington & Richardson increased competition, and increasing financial problems eventually forced Erma into liquidation in October 1997. A plan to move the manufacturing operations back to Suhl was never implemented.

~ REVOLVERS ~

These were based broadly on Smith & Wesson principles and were all solid-frame side-opening models with transfer-bar firing systems. A range of blank-firing and gas-cartridge guns was also made, which are difficult to distinguish from the firearms unless the distinctive markings (which will include an encircled "PTB") can be seen.

ER-422 Chambered for the 22 Long Rifle rimfire cartridge, with a six-chamber cylinder, this was offered with barrels of 2 or 3 inches. The longer option gave an overall length of 7.3 inches and an empty weight of 21 oz; sights were fixed. The guns were blued and had ERMA medallions let into their wood grips.

ER-423 Otherwise identical to the preceding gun, this was chambered for the 22 Magnum rimfire cartridge. The six-chamber cylinder was retained.

ER-432 Offered with 2- or 3-inch-barrels and a six-chamber cylinder, this was simply an ER-422 chambered for the 32 S&W Long cartridge.

ER-438 The most powerful of the range begun with the 422, this was a five-shot gun handling the 38 Special ammunition. The same barrel-length options were available, though, largely because of extra metal in the cylinder, the 3-inch-barreled ER-438 weighed 22-23 oz.

ER-440 This was a variant of the ER-438 made of stainless steel. The wood grips were usually retained.

ER-772 (1988-97) Offered in two basic patterns, this had a full-length ejector-rod shroud. The chamber held six 22 LR rounds, finish was usually blue and the sights were adjustable. The "Sport" revolver had

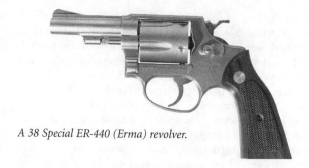

A 38 Special ER-440 (Erma) revolver.

standard grips, with stippling instead of checkering, and the "Match" pattern had an anatomical target-type grip with an adjustable palm shelf. The barrel was 6 inches long.

ER-773 (1988-97) This was a variation of the 772 chambered for the 32 S&W Long cartridge. It was also made in Sport and Match versions.

ER-777 (1993-7) Intended for sporting use, this was the 357 Magnum revolver in the "770" series. However, though it shared the general swing-cylinder construction of the others, it was strengthened to handle the power of the magnum cartridge and was substantially heavier than the other guns. Barrels could be 4, 5 or 6 inches long, and the grips were restricted to the conventional "Sport" type.

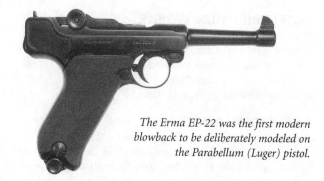

The Erma EP-22 was the first modern blowback to be deliberately modeled on the Parabellum (Luger) pistol.

~ AUTOMATIC PISTOLS ~

EP-22 (also known as "LA-22" or "La-22", 1964-71) This incorporated a blowback toggle system similar to the 1927-patent conversion kit, though the recoil spring was moved to the rear of the frame and the trigger system was more conventional than the P. 08 type. The guns were about 8.9 inches long, had 4.5-inch barrels and weighed about 35 oz. They had eight-round box magazines. As well as being of a size comparable with the standard 9mm Pistole '08, the EP-22 was also available as a 5.9-inch barreled "Navy" model and as a carbine with an 11.8-inch barrel, a wooden fore-end, a tangent-leaf rear sight and a detachable stock. Neither the "Navy" nor the carbine was ever made in quantity. The EP-22 was superseded by the KGP-69.

EP-452 Introduced in 1984, this had double-action lockwork, a radial safety catch mounted on the left rear of the slide and an external ring hammer. The external design was deliberately modeled on the Colt M1911A1, though the Erma was much smaller and chambered the innocuous 22 LR rimfire cartridge instead of the mighty 45 ACP. It was made of blacked alloy and had fixed sights; the grips were usually wood, with ERMA medallions let into the surface. The guns were typically 6.3 inches long, had 3.3-inch barrels and weighed 21-1/2 oz empty; magazines held eight rounds.

EP-457 This was simply a slightly enlarged EP-452 chambered for 32 ACP (7.65mm Auto) ammunition. Overall length was 6.5 inches, the barrel was 3.5 inches and empty weight was about 24-1/2 oz. The magazine held seven rounds, and the finish was "stainless" instead of blue.

EP-459 A version of the EP-457 chambering the 380 Auto (9mm Short) cartridge, this shared the general dimensions of the 32-caliber gun.

EP-552 Resembling the Walther PPK, though markedly different in detail, this had a blacked alloy slide and frame and molded plastic grips. The double-action trigger system and slide-mounted radial safety lever were retained. Overall length was merely 5.4 inches, with a 2.9-inch barrel, and empty weight was 14-1/2 oz. The detachable box magazine held seven 22 LR rimfire rounds.

The 25 ACP Erma EP-555 was clearly based on the Walther PPK.

EP-555 This was similar to the EP-552, but chambered the 25 ACP cartridge. Dimensions, weight and magazine capacity were also approximately the same.

EP-652 Little more than a modernized EP 552, this amalgamated the well-tried double-action trigger and slide-mounted radial safety lever with squared contours. These are particularly evident at the muzzle, as the 650-series guns lack the rounded contours of the 550 type. Though this suggests extra metal in the slide, and extra weight, the EP-652 weighs only about 13-3/4 oz empty. The guns were blacked, their sights were fixed and magazines held seven 22 LR rimfire cartridges. Grips were molded plastic.

Similar to the "555" model, the EP-655 has much squarer contours.

Chambered for the 22 LR round, the EP-752S is a rimfire version of the Erma PPK look-alikes.

EP-655 A 25-caliber version of the EP-652 that is quite similar to its 22 companion.

ESP 85 (1988-97) Destined for rapid-fire target shooting, this was a sophisticated blowback with an adjustable trigger and competition-grade sights. Offered with a variety of barrel weights and sight options,

the ESP-85 was blued and had stipple-finished anatomical grips with an adjustable palm-shelf. The barrels could be exchanged, allowing the shooter to fire 22 LR rimfire or 32 S&W Long Wadcutter ammunition. The guns were 10 inches long, had 6-inch barrels and weighed about 40 oz without weights. Magazines held either five or eight rounds, the latter being restricted to 22 caliber. A few guns were chrome plated, a few were made with left-hand ejection ports and grips (discontinued in 1994), and a "Junior" version had simpler grips. The designation is sometimes listed as "85A", but it is not clear what (if any) alterations were made to justify the suffix letter.

A 7.65mm (32 ACP) Erma KGP-68.

KGP-68 (or "KGP-32", 1968-71) This was an improved 32- or 38-caliber version of the EP-22, with a shorter action, a simpler trigger system and the return spring placed at an angle beneath the rear of the toggle/breech-block unit. A loaded-chamber indicator was also fitted. The guns were about 7.4 inches long, had 3.9-inch barrels, weighed about 22-1/2 oz empty and had fixed sights. The grips were generally wood, checkered with reeded (early) or plain (later) borders. The detachable box magazines held six 32 ACP/7.65mm Auto or five 380 ACP/9mm Short rounds.

KGP-68A (or "KGP-38", 1970-97) The US Gun Control Act of 1968 raised some safety problems, which were met by adding a spring-loaded intercepting bar in the rear of the frame to prevent the gun being fired if the magazine was not fully engaged. The designation acquired an "A" suffix and molded plastic "thumb-rest" grips, and production continued in the standard 32 and 38 calibers. Beeman sold this pistol as the "MP-08".

KGP-69 (or "KGP-22", 1970-97) An updated version of the EP-22, incorporating the magazine safety introduced in the KGP-68A, this was chambered for the 22 LR rimfire round and had an eight-round magazine. The grips were injection-molded plastic with an integral thumb-rest. A typical example was 7.8 inches long, with a 3.9-inch barrel, and weighed 29-1/2 oz.

SE 08/2 ("Selbstlade-Einstecklauf 08/2", c. 1956-85) The post-war version of the Parabellum ("Luger") conversion unit was originally made for Interarms, totaling about 3500 in 1956-62. These will bear Interarms' sunburst trademark as well as the Erma name. The unit was then sold commercially and remained in small-scale production for many years, total production being estimated at 10,000-15,000. Most were made with 5.9-inch barrels, weighed about 14 oz and had detachable eight-round magazines; chambering is invariably 22 LR rimfire. A few short-barrel inserts were made, with a conical muzzle shroud, but most rely on the sleeve and locknut attachment pioneered by the original S.EL. f. P. 08.

ERQUIAGA

Erquiaga, Muguruzu y Cia, Eibar, Spain.

The trading style was apparently "Erquiaga y Cia" until 1917 or 1918, when it changed to "Erquiaga y Muguruzu" and an "EM" monogram was adopted. The next change occurred in about 1921 when "Erquiaga Muguruzu y Cia" and "EMC" appeared.

Aguro (c. 1918-19) A 7.65mm "Eibar" automatic, this was simply a re-named post-war continuation of the wartime "Ruby" contract. The name was soon dropped in favor of "Fiel", below.

A 6.5mm (25-caliber) Erquiaga & Muguruzu "Diane".

Diana (1921?) This was the second-pattern 6.35mm "Fiel" automatic pistol (below), produced under a different name.

Fiel [No. 1] (6.35mm, c. 1919-25) With a slide marked "AUTOMATIC PISTOL 6,35 FIEL NO 1" above a depiction of the 6.35mm (25 ACP) cartridge, this was based on the 1906-type Browning. The grips may be plain, or have an "EM" or "EMC" monogram.

Fiel (6.35mm, second type, c. 1920-3?) The "No 1" on the 6.35mm model was probably put there to distinguish it from this gun, which was an entirely original design. A solid-frame assembly, forming a shroud over the top of the pistol, contained the removable barrel and the bolt. The 1.5-inch barrel was made with three bearing rings at muzzle, center and breech, and the center one was notched to engage with the safety catch that doubled as a barrel-locking pin. The bolt was tubular, containing the firing pin and spring; the reduced diameter of the rear two-thirds was intended to pass inside the return spring. This rear section of the bolt passed through the frame shroud and had a cocking knob screwed to it. Pulling this rearward would retract the bolt, compressing the return spring against the rear of the frame. A five-round magazine fit into the butt, and a removable side-plate gave access to the lockwork. However, despite such an ingenious design, this version of the Fiel does not appear to have had much success. It may be encountered with marks that include "AUTOMATIC PISTOL CAL. 6,35 FIEL" on the left side of the barrel shroud and an "EM" monogram on the grips.

Fiel (7.65mm, 1919-25?) This was originally a derivative of the 7.65mm-caliber "Ruby" pistols that had been made under sub-contract from Gabilondo during World War I and offered for commercial sale in 1918. The earliest guns had a long frame holding a nine-round magazine, checkered wooden grips, retraction grooves that had been cut radially and a lanyard ring on the left rear corner of the butt. Their slides were usually marked "ERQUIAGA Y Cⁱᵃ EIBAR "FIEL" CAL 7 ⁶⁵". The later guns had short frames with seven-round magazines, retraction grooves that had been milled vertically and slide marks that read "AUTOMATIC PISTOL CAL 7⁶⁵" above a representation of the 7.65mm Auto or 32 ACP cartridge. The safety catch was moved to the rear left side of the frame, and the grips had "EMC" monograms.

Marte (1920-5?) This was a simple 6.35mm "Eibar"-type blowback, based on the Browning of 1906 and essentially similar to the first small-caliber Fiel. The slide marks usually read "AUTOMATIC PISTOL CAL 6 ³⁵" over "MARTE", and the grips will display either "MARTE" or the "EMC" monogram.

ANTONIO ERRASTI
Eibar, Spain.
Errasti has an impressive list of trade names, most of them are sales names for the others and he only produced a few models. He began as a producer of cheap "Velo-Dog" revolvers in the early 1900s and during World War I obtained a contract to make the Italian 10.4mm "Bodeo" M1889 revolver. These offered surprisingly good quality and can only be distinguished from the Italian product by the inscription "ERRASTI EIBAR" on the right of the frame. More wartime sub-contracting brought Errasti into the automatic pistol business, and both revolvers and automatics were made throughout the 1920s and continued until the Civil War.

∼ REVOLVERS ∼
Dreadnought (1905-20?) These guns were offered in 22, 32, 38 and 44 calibers and were all hinge-frame pocket revolvers with ribbed barrels, prominent hinge bolts, small rounded butts and a removable cover plate over the lockwork. They were very similar to the revolvers being made by such firms as Iver Johnson and Harrington & Richardson 10 years earlier, but quality was generally mediocre and few have survived.

Errasti The revolvers of this name appeared in the 1920s and were based on the usual S&W Military & Police design — six-shot solid-frame swing-cylinder guns. Also called "Errasti Oscillante", they were available in 32, 38 and 44 caliber, though only the 38 is common.

Goliat Another name for the Dreadnought, above. It was usually found in 32 or 38 centerfire chamberings.

Oicet This 38-caliber revolver, copied from the Colt Police Positive, is believed to have been made in the 1920s.

Smit Americano Another name for the Dreadnought, above.

∼ AUTOMATIC PISTOLS ∼
Broncho Said to be sales name for the Errasti automatics, this may have been confused with "Bronco" (used by Echave y Arizmendi).

Errasti There were two models of these guns, one in 6.35mm and another in 7.65mm, but there were several minor variations. The finger grip cuts in the slide may be straight or curved, or the number of grooves may differ on otherwise identical pistols. The pistols are standard "Eibar" blowback Browning copies, and the differences are probably attributable to the out-worker system in which parts were made by independent machinists. The usual slide marking is "6 ³⁵ MODEL AUTOMATIC PISTOL – ERRASTI" on the left side of the slide, often above "CAL 25", with "ERRASTI" molded into the top of the grip and an encircled "AE" monogram within the checker panel. Some guns have been seen with unmarked slides (with retraction grooves cut vertically instead of radially), and the grip monogram set within a crowned scroll-like cartouche.

A "Model 31" revolver made by Manuel Escodin in 32-20 WCF.

MANUEL ESCODIN
Eibar, Spain.
Details of this company's history are obscure; the only known facts are that from 1924 to 1931 it produced a revolver, in 32 S&W and 38 Special chamberings, that was a copy of the S&W Military & Police model. A trademark comprising an ornate coat of arms is stamped (usually very badly) on the left side of the frame.

ESPERANZA Y CIA ("ECIA")
Guernica, Spain.
Founded in November 1925 by Juan Esperanza Salvador (see "Esperanza y Unceta", below), this arms-making business is best known for trench mortars. However, it also made blowback pistols and a series

of automatic-rifle prototypes of the same name. Reorganized after the end of the Second World War, ECIA SA traded until 1994.

Ecia Made only in 1929-33, this 7.65mm pistol, basically a simple "Eibar", had a hammerless self-cocking mechanism that relied upon a long trigger pull to cock and release the striker for each shot. Specimens are rare, and it is doubtful if many were made.

ESPERANZA & UNCETA

Esperanza y Unceta, also known as "Unceta y Esperanza"; Eibar and Guernica, Spain.

The company was the brainchild of Juan Esperanza Salvador (1860-1951), regarded as an expert in repeating weapons, who settled in Eibar in 1902. In 1908, Esperanza entered a partnership with gunsmith Juan Pedro Unceta, trading as "Unceta y Esperanza", and then began another with Isidro Gaztañaga. (c. 1911).

However, Esperanza withdrew from Gaztañaga y Esperanza in June 1913 and moved "Unceta y Esperanza" to Guernica. Production of the "Victoria" pistol began, the design being credited to a little-known inventor, Pedro Careaga, who has come to be regarded as the most famous inventor of small arms in Spain. The well-known "Astra" trademark was registered in Spain in this era.

Esperanza y Unceta, as the company was generally known after the move to Guernica, made the Campo-Giro pistol for the Spanish government prior to 1916, developing it into the Astra 400 or "Modelo 1921". Juan Esperanza had retained considerable independence, acquiring the defunct Alkartasuna (q.v.) in 1922, and left the partnership early in 1925, leaving his erstwhile partner to reorganize the business as "Unceta y Cia" (q.v.). Esperanza went on to found Construcciones Mecánicas SA (March 1925) and then Esperanza y Cia, listed previously.

Astra 100 This designation was applied to Victoria pistols up to 1915, when the name changed to "Astra 1911". There was also a "100 Special" manufactured after 1915 that had a nine-round magazine and which appears to be a commercial version of the 7.65mm Victoria.

An engraved 6.35mm Astra 200 blowback pistol.

Astra 200 (also called the "Firecat" in the USA) This was introduced in 1920 and remained in production until 1966. It was a 6.35mm blowback based on the Browning 1906 design, complete with grip and magazine safeties but with the safety catch midway along the frame in "Eibar" style. With a 2.2-inch barrel and a six-round magazine, it was offered in a vast range of finishes that gave rise to subsidiary numbering in the company catalogs — e.g., 200/1, 200/2.

Astra 202 (or "Firecat CE") This was a variant of the Model 200 with engraving, nickel plating and pearl grips.

Astra 207 An engraved and blued derivative of the Model 200.

Astra 300 Offered in 7.65mm Auto or 9mm Short (380 ACP), this was essentially a smaller version of the "400". It was first introduced in 1922 in 9mm and was adopted by the Spanish Prison Service. It was then offered commercially in both calibers, and in 1928, the 9mm version was adopted by the Spanish navy. During World War II, 85,390 of these pistols, in both calibers, were purchased by the German authorities for issue to the German army and Luftwaffe. Manufacture ceased in 1947 after a total of 171,300 had been made.

This is a 7.65mm (32-caliber) commercial version of the Astra 300 pistol.

The 9mm Spanish Astra 400, or M1921, could chamber and fire a variety of 9mm ammunition.

Astra 400 This was the first of the "tubular" Astra pistols derived from the Campo Giro design. The slide is tubular and the barrel seats into the frame by three lugs beneath the breech, much as in the Browning 1903 design. A coaxial recoil spring surrounds the barrel and is retained by a muzzle bush. The rear portion of the slide acts as a breechblock; there is an internal hammer and a grip safety.

The "400" is remarkable for two things. In the first place, this is a blowback automatic chambered for the 9mm Largo cartridge, probably the most powerful cartridge ever used in a blowback design. It succeeds by using a heavy slide and strong recoil and hammer springs, facts that become apparent when pulling back the slide in order to chamber a round.

The second unusual feature is that although chambered for the 9mm Largo cartridge, it will also chamber and fire the 9mm Parabellum, Steyr and Browning Long and the 38 Super Auto cartridges. This point is frequently a source of dispute, since shooters often try to fire all these rounds in order to prove or disprove the point and run into trouble, notably with the 9mm Parabellum. In this connection, certain points must be made clear. First, the pistols in question are often elderly and somewhat worn, which upsets the critical dimensions of the chamber; and secondly, it must be remembered that not only do different manufacturers adopt slightly different dimensional tolerances for their cartridges, but also that these dimensions can drift "within tolerance" from batch to batch. Anyone contemplating firing 9mm Parabellum ammunition (in particular) in an Astra would be well advised to test a variety of brands.

Such a wide acceptance of ammunition was intended solely as an emergency procedure, so that a soldier might not be immobilized for want of 9mm Largo when other ammunition was available; it is not recommended that other ammunition be fired from this pistol as a regular practice. Using 38 Super Auto should be particularly discouraged, as high pressure invariably blows out the caps and deforms the cases.

The Model 400 was introduced in 1921 and became the standard pistol of the Spanish army in that year. It was widely exported, and a few were purchased by the French army in the middle 1920s. Production ended in 1946, some 106,175 having been made. Experimental models in other calibers were made from time to time; at least one in 7.63mm Mauser is known.

Astra 1911 This was the first pistol to bear the Astra name, although the name was not actually registered as a trademark until November 1914. The Astra 1911 is no more than the contemporary Victoria pistol

The 7.65mm (32-caliber) Astra M1916 by Esperanza & Unceta.

re-named and was a standard "Eibar" copy of the Browning 1903 in 6.35mm or 7.65mm Auto chamberings. A grip safety was added in 1916 and work continued until 1918 at which time about 300,000 of the Victoria/Astra pattern had been made in the two calibers. The 7.65mm version was supplied to the French and Italian armies on military contracts in 1915/16, and the basic design was also produced commercially under various other names — Brunswig, Fortuna, Leston, Museum and Salso.

Astra 1924 A 6.35mm blowback automatic of "Eibar" type, based on the Browning 1906 design, this lacks not only a grip safety but also the customary "Eibar" safety catch. It offers rather better quality than most of its contemporaries. The left side of a typical export-style slide is marked "Esperanza y Unceta GUERNICA [Spain] 1924" over "ASTRA Cal 6.35 & 25". The grips bear a badge consisting of "ASTRA", with "E" above and "U" beneath to form part of a stylized sunburst.

Brunswig (1916-20?) This was a 7.65mm "Eibar", broadly the wartime Astra pistol made for commercial sale. The barrel, like most Esperanza products of the period, had "HOPE" engraved on it so as to be visible through the ejector port. Most slides are marked simply "7 ⁶⁵ 1916 MODEL AUTOMATIC PISTOL" over "BRUNSWIG" and between stylized arrowheads, each formed by three small wedge-like punch strikes. The identity of the manufacturer is betrayed only by "EU" in a cartouche on the left rear of the frame.

Campo-Giro Development of this pistol was undertaken in the Spanish ordnance factory in Oviedo (q.v.), but the lack of large-scale production facilities persuaded the government to contract with Esperanza y Unceta once the perfected "M1913" had been approved for issue to the army on January 5, 1914.

- *Model 1913* Removal of the breech lock, converting the Campo-Giro into a blowback, required an exceptionally strong barrel-return spring, and a shock absorber was added in the frame to reduce the hammering effect during recoil and run-out. About 1000 were then made in Guernica. They were 9.3 inches long, had 6.5-inch barrels and weighed 33.5 oz with an empty seven-round magazine.

- *Model 1913/1916* Adopted in September 1916, this slightly modified version of the M1913 could be recognized by the removal of the magazine catch from behind the trigger guard to the base of the

The perfected 9mm Campo-Giro, made by Esperanza & Unceta.

butt. Internally, a change was made so that the safety catch could be applied with the hammer down or cocked, in addition to the half-cock safety feature of the earlier pistols. Externally, the M1913-16 had two grip-retaining bolts compared with only one on the M1913. The Spanish army acquired 13,000 pistols in 1916-19, and an additional 500 were sold privately.

Fortuna (1916-20?) This name applies to 6.35mm and 7.65mm "Eibar"-pattern blowbacks made by Esperanza y Unceta concurrently with the Victoria models. The slide of a typical 6.35mm gun is marked "AUTOMATIC PISTOL CAL 6,35" above "FORTUNA" and "PATENT" between stylized arrowheads (see "Brunswig"). Most grips are marked "FORTUNA", though some have nothing but floral decoration.

Leston This was the Victoria pistol sold through Belgian dealers. Guns are said to be marked "THE AUTOMATIC LESTON 7 ⁶⁵ MM SPAIN" on the slide.

Museum The 6.35mm "Victoria" sold under this name in Belgium in the 1920s, probably through the Thieme & Edeler agency.

Salso This was another name for the Brunswig or Fortuna pistols, reputedly for sale in Belgium.

Union This was a line of cheap 6.35mm and 7.65mm "Eibar"-style automatics reputedly made for Esperanza y Unceta and Unceta y Cia between 1924 and 1931 by a sub-contractor. Four models, each marked "Automatic Pistol Union I", "Union II" etc., were produced—Models I and II in 6.35mm, and the Models III and IV in 7.65mm. They differed only in dimensions and magazine capacity. Examination of specimens suggests that more than one maker was involved; one "Model I" is identical with the 6.35mm pistol made by SEAM (q.v.), whilst another shows sufficient differences in machining to suggest an alternative source.

Victoria This was the brand name adopted by Esperanza y Unceta when they opened for business in 1908 and applied to 6.35mm and 7.65mm "Eibar"-type pistols based on the 1906-type Browning. The Victoria name was supplemented, or perhaps superseded, in 1914 by "Astra", and a grip-safety mechanism was added in 1916. Many 7.65mm pistols were supplied to France and Italy in 1915-16.

The earliest Victoria pattern was made in Eibar and is said to have had an external hammer. However, apart from the serial number 1, now owned by Unceta, no other guns of this type are known; production must have been small. After about 50,000 more conventional examples had been made, the factory moved to Guernica. Work continued until, by 1918, 300,000 guns had been made.

A 6.35mm Astra Victoria pistol.

Slides are marked typically "6 ³⁵ 1911 MODEL AUTOMATIC PISTOL" above "VICTORIA" and "PATENT" on the left side, each line being bracketed by stylized arrowheads made of three small wedge-like punch strikes. The grips display "VICTORIA" curved above a small encircled "EU" monogram, a mark that is sometimes duplicated on the slide behind and below the inscription. The slide-retraction grooves are milled radially.

ESPRIN BROTHERS

Esprin Hermanos, Eibar, Spain.

This partnership manufactured revolvers from 1906 until possibly 1917, when it ceased trading. The guns were of poor quality, using cast or soft metal, and the fact that they went out of business in the middle of a war must say something about their products.

Euska, Euskaro This was the name applied to all Esprin revolvers, hinged-frame models based on American designs of the 1890s such as the Iver Johnson and Meriden products. They were usually double action, though there are reports of a hammerless model copied from the S&W "New Departure". Calibers ranged from 32 to 44, and this brand is notable for the use of misleading inscriptions, such as "Use SMITH AND WESSON cartridges" stamped into the barrel.

EUROPEAN-AMERICAN ARMORY ("EAA")

Sharpes, Florida, USA.

EAA was once best known as an importer of Italian-made "Western" cartridge revolvers, usually purchased from Uberti, together with Tanfoglio and Astra pistols. However, some of the revolvers prove to have been acquired from Weihrauch, and Russian target pistols, made in Izhevsk, have also been distributed as "Baikals".

The products have included the *Standard Grade*, dating from 1991, and the *Bounty Hunter* and the *Big-Bore Bounty Hunter* (introduced in 1992), which are all Western-style Weihrauch revolvers. The *Bul* pistols are made in Israel by Transmark (q.v.), and the *European Model*, *Witness DA* (1991), *Witness Gold Team* (1992) and *Witness Silver Team* (1992) are all either made by Tanfoglio (q.v.) or are adaptations of Tanfoglio designs.

EXCEL INDUSTRIES

Chino, California, USA.

A maker of pistols based on the Colt-Browning action, including the *CP-45* and *XC-45* introduced in 2001. Offered only in 45 ACP, they measure 6.4 inches overall and have 3.25-inch barrels; weight ranges from 25 to 31 oz, depending on whether the standard six-round or "over-size" 10-round magazine is used. Construction is stainless steel, and the grips are checkered black nylon. The single-action trigger system relies on an external hammer, but there is an automatic firing-pin block and a manual safety catch.

EXTEGARRA

Extegarra y Abitua, Eibar, Spain.

See "Fabrique d'Armes [de Guerre] de Grande Précision."

FABBRICA ARMI SPORTIVE ("FAS")

Fabbrica Armi Sportive Srl, Settimo Milanese, Italy (formerly Italguns International).

The FAS target pistols were extremely popular in the 1970-90 period and were imported into the USA by companies such as Beeman Precision Arms of Santa Rosa, California; Mandall Shooting Supplies of Scottsdale, Arizona; and Nygord Precision Products of Prescott, Arizona. However, their chronology remains unclear. The first prototypes appeared in the early 1970s, and guns (specifically the CF 603 and SP 607) were still being distributed in 2000. Some sources suggest that the OP 601, SP 602 and CF 603 were all discontinued in 1987-8, but new guns were still being offered in catalogs such as *Guns Digest* a decade later.

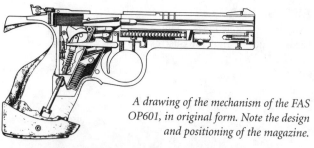

A drawing of the mechanism of the FAS OP601, in original form. Note the design and positioning of the magazine.

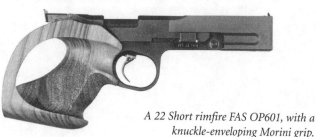

A 22 Short rimfire FAS OP601, with a knuckle-enveloping Morini grip.

OP 601 (originally known as the "Domino" or "IGI-Domino") Introduced in 22 Short rimfire in 1973, specifically for rapid-fire competition shooting, this was a slab-sided weapon with anatomical grips. The bolt moved in the receiver and was cocked by grips mounted on two arms that ran forward from the bolt, alongside the barrel section. The barrel was set low, almost an extension of the shooter's hand, and the sights were merely 0.6 inches above the bore. The trigger and lockwork, adjustable for let-off and over-travel, were contained in a detachable module. The five-round magazine was removed upward, allowing the grip to be adapted to suit virtually any individual marksman. Most guns had ported barrels to allow escaping gas to reduce the tendency of the muzzle to climb in rapid fire. The *Standard* barrel had six ports, the *High Speed* version had four, and the *Pentathlon* gun was restricted to two. Barrel weights can also be fitted. The Domino proved to be an excellent design and won a gold medal at the 1980 Olympics. It also provided the basis for a series of similar guns.

SP 602 This was a "Sports Pistol" version of the Domino, intended for slow-fire and similar competition shooting. It chambered the 22 LR rimfire round, lacked the barrel ports and had a trigger that could be adjusted from 3.5 oz to 36.5 oz. The front sight was a prominent blade instead of a small stud, and the retraction grips were greatly enlarged. Barrel weights could be fitted when required.

CF 603 This was essentially the same as the SP 602 but was destined for centerfire competitions and chambered 32 S&W Wadcutter ammunition. The trigger pull was restricted to about 48 oz to comply with ISU rules, and the grips were usually adjustable palm-shelf patterns.

The FAS SP607, chambered for the 32 S&W Wadcutter centerfire cartridge.

SP 607 A modernized version of the 22 LR rimfire SP 602, dating from 1994, this had improvements in the trigger mechanism and the takedown system. The sights were not only fully adjustable but set merely 0.35 inches above the barrel, and the five-round magazine was removed upward. The standard grips came in four sizes, from small to large. An adjustable version was also made with a palm shelf, and blanks could be obtained to allow "custom grips" to be made to suit an individual hand. The SP 607 was about 11 inches long, with a 5.6-inch barrel, and weighed about 37 oz.

FABRICA DE ARMAS GARANTIZADA ("FAG")

Eibar, Spain.

Apache A 38-caliber revolver, modeled generally on the Colt Police Positive, made by FAG but marketed by Ojanguren y Vidosa. The frame is marked "Apache" below the hammer on the left side, and there is a silvered medallion at the top of the grips (in Smith & Wesson style) with the Ojanguren "OV" monogram.

FABRICATION FRANÇAISE

This bland inscription can be found on the "Policeman" series of automatic pistols produced by Manufrance (q.v.) when, doubtless for sales reasons, the manufacturer chose to omit its name. The phrase is also associated with a variety of "Eibar"-type Spanish automatic pistols that were doubtless intended for sale in France or Francophone countries.

FABRIQUE FRANÇAISE D'ARMES DE GUERRE

Louhans, France.

This name appears on a small 6.35mm blowback automatic, a copy of the 1906-type Browning that offers better quality than the average "Eibar" pistol — even though the roughly shaped safety catch suggests Spanish origin.

The slide mark may read "FABRIQUE FRANÇAISE D'ARMES S^TE" over "BREVETÉ FRANCE". A similar gun, with a grip safety lever, is marked "SOCIÉTÉ D'ARMES PARIS" over "AUTOMATIQUE CAL. 6,35" and "BREVETE FRANCE", making three lines. Both guns have grips with an "SA" — or possibly "AS" — monogram, which has been claimed as "the registered mark of the Société d'Armes of Paris, an organization connected with the Société Française des Munitions SA". Confirmation is lacking.

The under-edges of the left side of the slides have two notches for the safety/stripping catch, a feature that is commonly associated with guns sold by Manufacture d'Armes des Pyrénées Françaises of Hendaye (see "Unique"). Many of these guns were actually made in Eibar, particularly prior to 1925.

FABRIQUE NATIONALE D'ARMES DE GUERRE ("FN")

Fabrique Nationale d'Armes de Guerre, Herstal, Belgium (1895-1990); FN Herstal SA, Herstal, Belgium (1990 to date).

See also under "Browning". Fabrique Nationale (FN) was set up in 1888 by a consortium of Belgian gunmakers with the sole intention of manufacturing Mauser rifles under license for the Belgian army, after which it would be closed down. But, like Frankenstein's monster, it took on a life of its own, eventually swallowing up its founders and competitors to become one of the world's major gunmakers, with interests that gradually extended to motorcycles, military trucks, armored cars, aircraft engines and ammunition as well as small arms. Eventually, like so many of these multi-faceted giants, it over-reached itself, got into financial trouble, and in 1990 was swallowed up by GIAT, the French armaments consortium. GIAT, in its turn, collapsed under its own weight, and in 1995 FN returned to Belgian ownership.

So far as pistols go, the greater part of FN's production has been bound up with John Browning's designs. But in the 1970s, the company began developing designs of its own, as well as a cooperative venture with Beretta, the results of which are listed herewith.

The FN Barracuda revolver, in 357 Magnum or 9mm Parabellum.

∼ REVOLVERS ∼

Barracuda The Barracuda was FN's one and only venture into the revolver business, and it was designed to supply those police forces that preferred revolvers to automatics. A conventional double-action, solid-frame, swing-out-cylinder, 6-shot weapon, it was chambered for the 357 Magnum cartridge and, oddly for a revolver, had the trigger guard shaped for a two-handed grip. A replacement cylinder allowed the firing of 9mm Parabellum cartridges, though these had to be fitted into a rosette-shaped clip so as to give the extractor something to work against. The hammer was propelled by a coil spring that could be adjusted to any of four different degrees of tension. However, although the Barracuda was a high-quality weapon, sales were disappointing since it appeared at a time (the late 1970s) when police forces were at last overcoming their distrust of automatic pistols. Production was stopped in 1987.

Manurhin In 1989, FN bought the revolver production portion of Manurhin (see "Manufacture de Machines du Haut Rhin") and set up a new company (FN France) with the intention of making the Manurhin revolvers under the FN name. The subsequent purchase of FN by GIAT in 1990 left this project in the air, and no clear statement of intent was forthcoming. In the event, GIAT had over-reached itself and in 1995 sold FN back to the Belgians while keeping Manurhin.

∼ AUTOMATIC PISTOLS ∼

In 1890, John Moses Browning had a disagreement with Winchester, with whom he had worked for several years, and went to Europe to find a company who would build an automatic shotgun the way he wanted it built. Fabrique Nationale was interested, and in addition to the shotgun, Browning eventually interested them in an automatic pistol that had been rejected in the USA. FN purchased the rights to the patents and set to work to develop them.

Later, Browning returned to the USA and interested Colt in his pistol designs with the result that FN and Colt came to an agreement in 1901 to divide the market: Colt took the western hemisphere and FN

the eastern, more or less. Britain was neutral territory in which both firms competed. Since that time, FN has produced Browning automatic pistols by the millions, to the extent that the word "Browning" is accepted in many European languages as being synonymous with "automatic pistol".

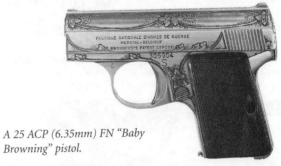

A 25 ACP (6.35mm) FN "Baby Browning" pistol.

Baby Browning Introduced in 1932, this was a 6.35mm blowback that differed from the Model 1906 in having no grip safety and in having the frame extend the full length of the slide, so giving a "square" shape to the front end of the pistol. The safety catch was a long lever beneath the left grip, the operating portion protruding just behind the trigger guard. Early models have the word "Baby" molded into the bottom of the grip plates, in addition to the "FN" monogram in the upper part. After 1945, the word "Baby" was omitted, and those made for the US market have the word "Browning" in place of the monogram. Work continued until the 1980s, but the influence of the design can still be seen in many ultra-compact personal-defense pistols (e.g., Bauer, Wilkinson).

BDA-9 Work began on these pistols in the late 1970s, and they were first announced in 1983. Basically, they were the 1935 brought up to date by adding a double-action lock, extending and shaping the trigger guard for a two-handed grip, fitting an ambidextrous safety catch that also acted as a hammer de-cocking lever, arranging the magazine release for right- or left-handed use, and mounting the sights into dovetails on the slide.

There is no safety catch; once the chamber has been loaded, the de-cocking lever is pushed up. This causes a safety block to interpose between the hammer and the firing pin, releases the hammer, and applies a brake to slow the hammer's descent. The automatic firing pin safety system of the Mark 3S is fitted, so that the BDA is quite safe against accidental discharge. When ready to fire, all that is needed is to pull the trigger to fire the first shot in double-action mode.

The idea was good, but there were a number of problems in converting the prototypes into production models, and no serious production was ever undertaken. The "family" was taken off the market in the mid-1990s.

- *BDA-9C* Announced in 1985, this was the "Compact" model, with a shorter (96mm) barrel and a shortened butt that held a 7-round magazine, saving about 5 oz. The de-cocking lever is ambidextrous.
- *BDA-9M* This was the 1985-vintage "Medium" model, with a 96mm barrel in a shortened frame.

The FN BDA-9M pistol, combining the action of the High Power with a double-action trigger system.

- *BDA-9S* was the standard pattern, originally dating from 1983, with a 118mm barrel and a 14-round magazine in a full-sized frame.

BDAO This is the same as the BDA-9 except that it is double-action-only, and for that reason, there is no cocking spur on the hammer. As the slide goes forward after cocking, and after each shot, so the hammer follows it, but the hammer is arrested before it can strike the firing pin. An automatic firing pin safety system ensures that the pistol cannot fire unless the trigger is pulled completely through to the full-cock position so that accidental discharges are practically impossible.

- *BDAOc* Introduced in 1998, this was simply a short-lived compact version of the BDAO.

The FN Target or "Challenger" sport pistol.

Challenger A name applied to the long-barreled "Standard Model" (q.v.) by the Browning Arms Company, for sale in the USA.

Fast Action This was a variant of the High-Power with the trigger system changed to embody a "hesitation cocking" feature. Retracting the slide cocked the hammer and loaded the chamber in the normal way, but when the slide had been returned, the hammer could be pushed forward manually. This set the mechanism so that a simple pull on the trigger would fire the gun. One of the goals of this system was a comparatively light trigger pull for the first "double-action" shot, instead of the long drag that often accompanied conventional designs of this type, and there was comparatively little difference between the first and subsequent shots in the Fast Action system. Unfortunately, the US JSSAP handgun trials of the 1970s, which led eventually to the standardization of the M9 (Beretta 92F) by the US Army, revealed that the Fast Action was far too weakly constructed to withstand the rigors of service. It had soon been abandoned in favor of the BDA described above.

Light but surprisingly large, the FN Five-seveN challenges our conception of a military pistol.

Five-seveN In the late 1980s, FN developed a highly innovative P-90 "Personal Defense Weapon" — a submachine gun to you and me — which, whilst being extremely compact and simple to use, was built around an entirely new cartridge that had formidable penetrative ability against body armor. After some initial misgivings, the weapon and cartridge gained acceptance in military circles, and in the early 1990s, FN set about developing an automatic pistol to fire the same cartridge.

The Five-seveN is a self-cocking semi-automatic introduced in 1995. The trigger action is rather unusual in that pressure on the trig-

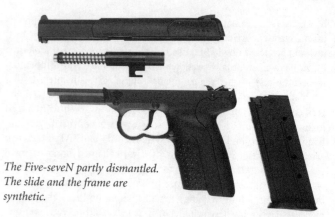

The Five-seveN partly dismantled. The slide and the frame are synthetic.

ger first loads the firing pin spring and then releases the firing pin. Unless the trigger is pressed, the firing pin is never under any sort of pressure, and thus there is no safety catch of the normal type.

Surprisingly, for a weapon of such power, the Five-seveN operates on the delayed blowback principle. The slide carries two notches on its under-surface. Set into the frame is a cross-shaft carrying two connected lugs. The barrel is a loose fit in the slide, and when the barrel and slide are assembled to the frame, a slotted lug beneath the chamber is so placed that the slot lines up with the cross-shaft. On firing, the pressure in the chamber forces the bullet up the barrel, and the friction and torque of the bullet's movement tends to take the barrel forward. At the same time, the gas pressure forces the cartridge case back and puts pressure on the slide to move to the rear. Barrel and slide move rearward together about 3 mm, at which point the slide notches engage the upstanding lugs on the cross-shaft and the slide is halted. As the bullet leaves the barrel, the friction and torque cease, and the barrel is free to move backwards. This causes the slotted lug to move over the cross-shaft and rotate it so that the twin lugs disengage from the notches in the slide, allowing the slide to continue moving rearwards to perform the usual extraction and reloading cycle while the barrel remains stationary. It all sounds very complicated but works with perfect efficiency.

The cartridge is considerably longer than the average pistol round, and 20 rounds are carried in the magazine, but the grip nevertheless fits the hand well and the recoil impulse is less than that from a 9mm Parabellum cartridge, so that the weapon is easily controlled. Synthetic materials have been used extensively in the design, so that the loaded pistol weighs some 30 percent less than a conventional 9mm Parabellum pistol of comparable size.

An accessory rail is formed in the front end of the frame, and a laser spot attachment is available. A sound suppressor has also been developed, capable of reducing the sound of discharge by some 30 dB using subsonic SB 193 ammunition. It is also possible to use the suppressor with standard ammunition, in which case, of course, the bullet noise will not be affected.

Forty-Nine This pistol got its name from being originally designed to fire the 40 S&W cartridge, after which the weapon was modified so as to fire the 9mm Parabellum cartridge. The mechanism includes what FN calls the "Repeatable Secure Striker" (RSS) System.

High Power (or "Hi-Power") Known variously as the "Model 1935", "HP" (for "High Power") or "GP" (for "Grand Puissance"), this originated in the aftermath of World War I, when John Browning decided to redesign the M1911 to incorporate lessons learned from trench warfare. It is also renowned as "Browning's last design" though this is something of an exaggeration and overlooks the part played in development by Dieudonné Saive and the FN Bureau des Études.

A desire to include a large-capacity magazine forced Browning to adopt a smaller cartridge than the 45 ACP (9mm Parabellum being selected as an ideal combination of power and size), and extensive

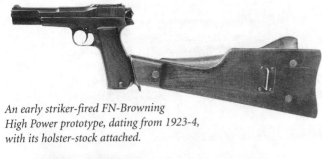

*An early striker-fired FN-Browning
High Power prototype, dating from 1923-4,
with its holster-stock attached.*

An FN-Browning High Power or GP-35 (a British No. 2 Mk I),
attached to its holster-stock.*

A hammer-fired High Power prototype, 1925.

changes were made in the firing mechanism. The prototypes incorporated single-column magazines. Strikers replaced hammers in the trigger system, to prevent dust and mud entering the action, and several types of stock were tried before the patent applications were filed in 1923.

The involvement of Fabrique Nationale, meanwhile, soon meant changes. Saive is said to have argued for a double-row magazine and a return to an external hammer that could be cocked manually in the case of a misfire. Improved prototypes had been made by the time Browning died unexpectedly in Liege in 1926.

*The perfected FN-Browning High Power
prototype, 1928.*

By 1929, the design had been refined to a point where production could be considered. Unfortunately, this coincided with the Wall Street Crash and the ensuing economic depression, and work was postponed. Not until 1934 did the FN management judge the market conditions to be right. The Belgian army accepted the pistol for service in 1935, and this success was rapidly followed by orders from Lithuania, Latvia, Romania, Estonia, China and Peru. In fact, none of these were completed; the Belgian army had priority, and World War II began before any of the foreign orders could be fulfilled.

The Model 1935 is an improvement on Browning's original "swinging-link" design of breech locking. Instead of the link, there is a fixed lump beneath the chamber into which a shaped path is cut. This path bears against a hardened transom in the frame so that as the barrel moves back, the shaped path pulls it down, disengaging the lugs from the slide. The only dubious feature is the trigger linkage; instead of

Browning's stirrup, used in the Colt and which passes around both sides of the magazine well, the 1935 uses a transfer bar in the slide, which also doubles as a disconnector. While undoubtedly efficient, it does mean that the trigger pull is neither so sensitive nor so amenable to refinement as that of the Colt. But since such "tuning" is only demanded by target shooters, and since the 1935 was designed as a combat pistol, this is of little consequence.

Originally, two versions were produced, the "Ordinary", with a normal fixed-notch rear sight, and the "Adjustable Sight Model", which had a tangent-leaf rear sight graduated to 500 meters and a slot in the backstrap of the butt to accept a wooden butt-stock. There was also a minor variant of this model that had a larger rear sight graduated to 1000 meters, a splendid piece of optimism. There was also said to be a selective-fire version of the "Adjustable Sight Model" that, when set to the automatic mode and fitted with the stock, could function as a submachine gun.

Other aberrant variations included an "Ordinary" model with a 9-round magazine, chambered for 7.65mm Parabellum or 7.65mm Longue, for trials by the Swiss and French respectively; neither were ever offered commercially. The French preferred the SACM-Petter M1935A on grounds of cost and complexity, and the Swiss eventually adopted the SIG-Petter to replace their Parabellums.

The original pre-war Belgian GP-35 customarily had the manufacturer's name over "HERSTAL BELGIQUE" on the left side of the slide, above "BROWNING'S PATENT DEPOSE". Liége proofmarks will also be present, and Belgian government inspectors' marks in the form of crowned letters within a cartouche will also be found on many individual components.

The FN factory was seized after Belgium had been overrun in 1940 and placed under German ownership as "DWM Lüttich" ("Lüttich" being the German name for Liége). The Model 1935 continued to be made as the "Pistole 640 (b)" with over 319,000 being made for the German forces. The paratroops, particularly, appreciated the large-capacity magazine. The slide marking on guns made under German supervision is usually identical with the pre-war FN legend, but the inspectors' marks prove to be small Waffenamt eagles over the individual inspector's number. Serial numbers usually lie on the right side of the slide and frame, and will usually also be visible on the barrel through the ejection port.

Several key FN personnel managed to escape to Britain in 1940-1 and were recruited by the Ministry of Supply. Among their baggage were drawings of the Model 1935, and although evidence is slender, it seems that a few pistols were made in Britain in 1941-2 (perhaps in the Enfield factory tool room); the approval of a "Pistol, Browning 9mm (FN), Automatic Mk 1 (UK)" was cancelled in April 1945 as part of a general stock-taking of obsolete designs, which suggests a formal introduction had been made. However, no progress was made and responsibility for the project was given to the John Inglis (q.v.) company of Toronto.

Shortly after World War II ended, Fabrique Nationale resumed manufacture, renaming the pistol the Model 1946 (for military sale) or the "High Power" (for commercial sale) — though the former designation never stuck, and the gun has always remained the "Model 35" to the rest of the world. The 13-round magazine remained standard, but an extended 20-round version could be supplied to order.

The High Power has been exceptionally successful and has sold in large quantities. FN sales literature was claiming sales to military, paramilitary and police forces in 50 countries in 1971 and 65 countries by the mid-1980s, and many different national markings will be found. In addition to licensed production in Britain, Indonesia and elsewhere, High Power copies have been made in China, in Hungary and by the Cao Dai rebels in Cambodia.

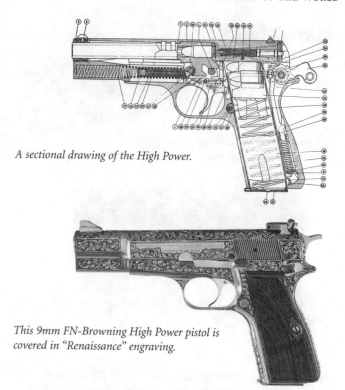

A sectional drawing of the High Power.

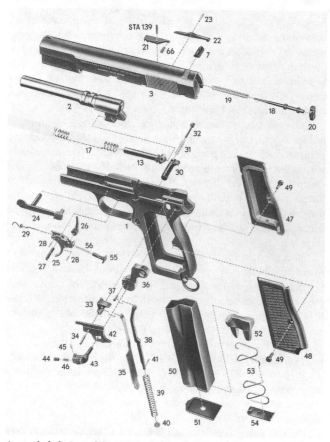

An exploded view of the FN-Browning GP 35.

Many guns have been sold commercially in a variety of guises. However, identification can be complicated by their designations. The pistol has always been known as the "Model 35" or colloquially as the "High Power", but FN Herstal SA, successor to Fabrique Nationale d'Armes de Guerre in the 1970s, also used a "Number 74" factory-designation prefix (for the Vigilante series) and catalog numbers that have been used so widely that they are now regarded as a legitimate form of identification.

A 9mm FN-Browning "Vigilant", a version of the High Power with fixed sights.

This 9mm FN-Browning High Power pistol is covered in "Renaissance" engraving.

- *Vigilante/Vigilant Model* This was the basic fixed-sight gun, with checkered polyamide grips. The 9mm Parabellum version could be obtained with a parkerized finish (Model 1001 with a lanyard ring, 1002 without it), or in black (1003 with lanyard ring, 1004 without it). Small quantities were also made in 7.65mm Parabellum, the code numbers being 1101, 1102, 1103 and 1104 respectively, but these were soon abandoned. By the early 1980s, only the 9mm guns survived. Vigilant-style guns have also been made for the commercial market (Model 1033) and with the Renaissance or Louis XVI-style decoration described below (see "Sport Model), the factory designations being Models 1122 and 1246, respectively.

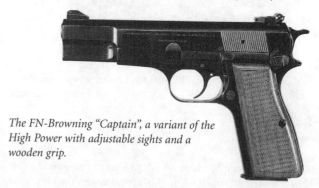

The FN-Browning "Captain", a variant of the High Power with adjustable sights and a wooden grip.

- *Capitaine/Captain Model* This had a 500-meter tangent-leaf rear sight, a replaceable front sight dovetailed into the slide and a stock-attachment groove milled into the backstrap. The options included 9mm Parabellum guns with parkerized or black finish (2001, 2002, 2003, 2004 depending on lanyard rings), and a similar 7.65mm Parabellum series (2101-2104). The basic 9mm guns, reintroduced in 1993 after production had stopped for several years, were still being offered as late as 1999.
- *Sport Model* Designated "Model 3001" in 9mm and "Model 3101" in 7.65mm Parabellum, this had a small adjustable rear sight and a high ramped-blade front sight. The grips were checkered walnut and the finish was usually polished black. A deluxe version — Models 3003 or 3103 in 9mm and 7.65mm Parabellum, respectively

— was offered with special high-gloss finish and checkered select walnut grips with a diamond-shape panel around the grip bolt. By 1980, the designation had advanced to Model 3033, owing to minor changes in the trigger mechanism. A decorative version (Models 3002 and 3102, depending on caliber) had Renaissance leaf-and-tendril "engraving" covering the slide and frame. This designation was subsequently advanced to Model 3142 by the addition of a gilded trigger lever and "old silver" finish. A later "Louis XVI" version (Model 3246) had photo-etched leaf, flower and ribbon decoration, nickel-plating and a gilded trigger.

The BN-Browning High Power "Competition", with a long barrel, an adjustable rear sight and wraparound Pachmayr grips.

- *Competition Model* Also known as the Model 5051, this was intended for target shooting. It was readily identified by its 5.9-inch barrel and adjustable counterweight/slide extension. A micro-adjustable rear sight was standardized, and the slide had a matted non-reflecting finish. The trigger was specially honed to give a pull of 4-4.5 pounds.

The FN-Browning High Power Mk 2 with an extended safety catch and molded grips.

High-Power Mk 2 By the 1970s, the Model 1935 was in use around the world, but other, newer designs were beginning to erode its position. For once, FN designers and engineers failed to analyze the markets correctly; instead of setting about a completely new design, they simply added a three-dot luminescent sighting system, an ambidextrous safety catch, a non-reflective finish (including the barrel) and anatomical grips. The Mark 2 pistol appeared commercially in 1985, but met with little success; it was not up to the usual high FN standards and there were complaints of unreliable performance. Production was stopped in 1987 in favor of the Mark 3.

High-Power Mark 3 Announced in January 1989, this was simply an improved Mark 2. New computer-controlled machinery improved the standard of manufacture, and the frame and slide were slightly re-dimensioned to make them stronger. The ejection port was enlarged and re-contoured, the grips were redesigned, and the sights were dovetailed into the slide so that they could be replaced with target sights when required. Offered in 9mm Parabellum and 40 S&W (the "HP-40" was rarely requested), the Mark 3 was intended for military use. Several

This High Power is a Mark 3, with an ambidextrous safety catch.

armies reportedly purchased it in small numbers, but the basic design was soon eclipsed by rivals such as the Glock and the Beretta.

- *Mark 3S* This was the standard Mk 3 with an additional automatic firing pin safety system that prevented the firing pin from moving except during the final movement of the trigger as the hammer was released. The pistol was intended for police use and commercial sale, the additional safety system being omitted from the standard military pattern owing to the higher state of training among soldiers. The Mark 3S was immediately adopted by the Belgian Gendarmerie.

International A derivative of the PA-22 and the Standard Model, this 22 LR rimfire target pistol was introduced in 1978 to conform with ISU rules. It had a stippled walnut grip with an adjustable palm rest, a heavy slab-sided barrel shroud, an adjustable weight beneath the muzzle and a matte-black non-reflective finish. The single-action trigger could be adjusted down to the 2.2-lb ISU minimum pressure setting, and an adjustable rear sight was standard. The guns were 298mm long, weighed about 1325gm and had 10-round detachable box magazines. An auxiliary safety system prevented the gun being fired if the magazine had been removed.

- *International II* Apparently dating from 1982, this was an improved form of the basic design, with changes in the sights and trigger mechanism to comply with changes in the ISU rules. The most obvious change concerned the rear sight, which was a solid-leaf "box" pattern instead of a crude-looking stamped-strip type. The finish is usually listed as blue, but it seems that at least some guns had a matte non-reflective coating.
- *International Medalist* The Browning Arms Company name for the Match 150 Model (q.v.) 22 rimfire target pistol.

An FN International II pistol, in 22 LR rimfire.

The FN Match 150 or "International Medalist".

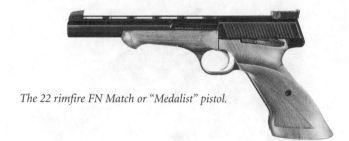

The 22 rimfire FN Match or "Medalist" pistol.

Match Model ("Medalist" or PA-22) Introduced in 1962, the "Pistolet Automatique Browning caliber .22" was the work of Bruce Browning, great-grandson of John. A fixed-barrel blowback, the gun had a sharply raked anatomical walnut grip, a schnabel-tip walnut fore-end and a large-diameter "bull" barrel with a ventilated rib. The rear sight was adjustable, and a mechanical hold-open held the slide back after the last round had been fired and ejected. The guns were also fitted with dry-firing devices and cartridge-case deflector pins. They had 6.75-inch barrels and provision for counterweights of 1-3 oz. Grips were 2.25 inches broad. The sighting radius and weight (with an empty magazine) were 9.75 inches and 46 oz., respectively.

This pistol was made for many years, often in highly decorative forms, laying the foundation not only for other 22 rimfire FN-Brownings but also the Buck Mark series that is still being made in the USA by the Browning Arms Company (q.v.).

• *Match 150 Model* A version of the "Match Model" complying with European ISU rules, this had a 5.9-inch barrel, no provision for fore-end or counterweights and a grip just 2 inches broad. The sighting radius was 8.6 inches and the gun weighed 42 oz with an empty magazine. Known in the USA as the "International Medalist", work stopped in the late 1970s when the "International" pattern appeared.

Model 125 Said to have been developed at the request of the Browning Arms Company, this was a 1970s modernization of the M10/22, with a distinctive squared one-piece slide (lacking the separate extension of its predecessor). It shared its adjustable sights with the High-Power Sport Model. The guns were 7 inches long, had 4.5-inch barrels and weighed 25-26 oz; grips were black polyamide, though walnut could be obtained to order. Comparatively few of these single-action striker-fired guns were made before production ended in favor of the Beretta-type M140DA (below) in the early 1980s. The M125 was chambered for the 32 ACP cartridge, had a nine-round single-column magazine, and boasted manual grip and magazine safety systems. A cocking indicator and a loaded-chamber indicator were also fitted.

The FN M140 DA pistol was a modification of the 80-series Beretta design.

Model 140DA Resemblance between this and the Beretta 81/84 types is no coincidence; the FN pistol is a slightly modified Beretta 81 with a spur hammer rather than a ring hammer and an all-enveloping slide with ejection port rather than the usual Beretta open-topped slide. Another difference is the placing of the safety catch on the slide, where it can be operated from either side, so that the pistol can be used

by right- or left-handed shooters. The Beretta Model 84 (in 9mm Short/380 ACP) is also modified in this way and is sold in the USA as the "Browning BDA Pistol". For relevant data, see Beretta Models 81 and 84.

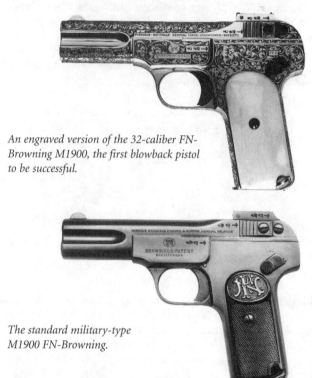

An engraved version of the 32-caliber FN-Browning M1900, the first blowback pistol to be successful.

The standard military-type M1900 FN-Browning.

Model 1900 (or Old Model) This blowback design, the first of its type to be commercially successful, was patented by John Browning in 1897. Browning offered his design to Colt's Patent Fire Arms Mfg Co. but was rebuffed. However, a chance meeting resulted in the grant of a license to Fabrique Nationale d'Armes de Guerre.

Work proceeded cautiously, until FN made about 4000 M1899 pistols to test public opinion. These were larger than the perfected 1900 pattern and had plain frames with unusually small grips.

The Model 1900, the first to use the 7.65mm ACP cartridge, had a 4-inch barrel and a 7-round detachable box magazine in the butt. The recoil spring lay in a tunnel in the slide above the barrel and was connected by a rod to a link pendant from the top of the slide and with its lower end engaged in the striker. In this way, the spring was used to power the striker, thus giving more than enough energy to ignite the most reluctant cap. The trigger mechanism was simple and robust, and the barrel was fixed to the frame.

After competing successfully against the Borchardt-Luger and a Mannlicher, the FN-Browning was adopted for arm officers and some sword-carrying NCOs of the Belgian army. Issues were subsequently extended to the gendarmerie, mounted artillerymen and cavalry NCOs, until, in 1910, all issue Nagant revolvers had been exchanged for Brownings. Guns were also offered commercially, to be purchased by many European police and paramilitary forces.

The earliest guns bore the manufacturer's mark on the left side of the slide, above a cartouche containing a pistol and the FN monogram; the monogram and S.G.D.G. (*Sans Garantie du Gouvernement*, "without government guarantee") could be found on the left side of the frame.

A lanyard ring was added to the left rear of the frame soon after production began, and the machining of the frame was altered to correct a weakness. The earliest grips were embossed with a representation of the pistol and a small "FN" logo, but these were soon replaced by more robust patterns displaying the "FN" monogram. Guns of this type bear the maker's mark on the slide above the pistol/monogram cartouche, which is repeated on the left side of the frame above "BROWNING'S-PATENT" and "BREVETE S.G.D.G."

A small radial-lever safety catch on the left rear of the frame was accompanied by "FEU" ("fire") and "SÛR" ("safe"). Inspectors' marks will be found on guns issued to the Belgian forces, occasionally accompanied by unit marks indicating that the pistols were used by "Other Ranks" as well as officers.

The design was unique and, so far as can be ascertained, was never pirated by any European gunmaker in the way that later designs were copied. Strangely, though, it seems to have had a considerable following in China, where innumerable poor copies have been made.

Production continued until some time in 1912. The "Old Model" is now often linked with the murder by Gavrilo Priničip of the Austrian Archduke Franz Ferdinand and his wife, thereby precipitating World War I. Photographs taken by the police in Sarajevo after the assassination, however, include only 1910-type FN-Brownings.

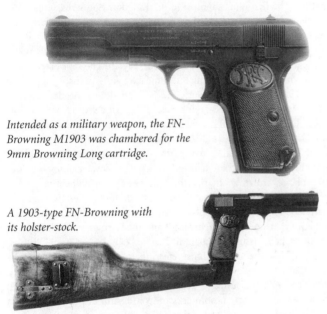

Intended as a military weapon, the FN-Browning M1903 was chambered for the 9mm Browning Long cartridge.

A 1903-type FN-Browning with its holster-stock.

Model 1903 A considerable change from its predecessor, this represented a considerable simplification and became the model for countless millions of Spanish and other imitations.

It was a blowback in which the return spring lay beneath the barrel. There was a concealed hammer inside the frame that struck the firing pin. There was a grip safety in the butt, and the five-inch barrel locked into the frame by means of lugs beneath the chamber that engaged in grooves in the frame. The pistol could thus be dismantled very easily by pulling back the slide and locking it there by means of a catch, then grasping the muzzle and rotating the barrel through 90 degrees to unlock it from the frame. The catch was then released, and the slide, complete with barrel and return spring, could be slipped forward off the frame.

The M1903 had a plain round-backed slide and a grip that was set square to the axis of the bore. It was chambered for the 9mm Browning Long cartridge, a round developed by FN to provide a useful chambering that could still be used in a blowback pistol. In fact, the cartridge fell between two stools, being unnecessarily large for a pocket pistol but too weak for military use. However, the manufacturer offered an optional 1000-meter tangent-leaf sight (particularly popular in the Far East) that could be attached to the top of the slide and a special wooden holster-stock. An extended 10-round magazine could also be purchased.

These accessories converted the M1903 into a pistol carbine, but it was not powerful enough to compete with its Mannlicher, Mauser and Parabellum rivals. The absence of a breech lock antagonized military authorities in Britain, Germany and the USA, but the 1903-type FN-Brownings sold well elsewhere. Buyers included the armies of Belgium, the Netherlands, Sweden and possibly Peru, and paramilitary or gendarmerie units in Russia, Turkey and Paraguay.

About 5000 "Russian" guns were purchased directly from Fabrique Nationale in 1904, distinguished by a mark of two crossed Mosin-Nagant rifles on top of the slide. This may point to military or police usage, but, equally, could be simply a gimmick to encourage commercial sales.

The M1903 was tested by the Swedish authorities at the infantry marksmanship school in 1903-4 as the *försöksmodell 03* (fm/03, "experimental model 03"), winning trials against Parabellum, Mannlicher, Colt-Browning and others largely because of its simplicity. The first "M/1907" guns were purchased from Fabrique Nationale, but later examples were made by Husqvarna (q.v.). Swedish FN-Brownings survived for many years, being brought out of store in 1986 when the Swedish Lahti pistol was withdrawn, pending the acquisition of new guns.

M1903 FN-Brownings guns were purchased for the Turkish gendarmerie in 1906-7. The guns display the encircled *Toughra* (a calligraphic cipher) of Abdülhamid II on the top of the slide, together with a property mark and an issue number in Arabic on the right side of the slide halfway between the trigger and the muzzle.

The M1903 was still being offered by Fabrique Nationale in the early 1920s, though it is unlikely that anything other than the assembly of pre-1914 components was being undertaken. It has also been claimed that a few pistols chambering the 9mm Short (380 ACP) cartridge were made under German supervision during World War I, but this has not been confirmed.

The 25 ACP (6.35mm) FN-Browning pocket pistol, introduced in 1906, was the inspiration for countless adaptations made in Spain prior to 1936.

Model 1906 This was more or less a scaled-down version of the Model 1903, designed around the 6.35mm ACP cartridge that, in turn, was designed for this pistol. The two appeared on the market together, and once again, FN had produced a design that was to be copied far and wide. The 1906 used the same form of construction as the 1903 except that it used a striker instead of an internal hammer, and there was no applied safety catch on the early production. After about 100,000 guns had been made, however, a safety catch was fitted to the left rear of the frame, largely because it made stripping easier. With this added, it became known as the "Triple Safety Model" since it now had applied, grip and magazine safeties. In the early days it was popularly called the "Baby Browning", but this name was later officially given to another model (below) and early references to the "Baby" should be carefully checked in order to be sure which model is being discussed. Production ceased when the Germans invaded Belgium in 1914, though it is suspected that a few guns were assembled from pre-war parts during hostilities and perhaps even in the immediate post-Armistice period.

The FN-Browning M1910 was the first of the streamlined designs.

Model 1910 This is a considerable change from its predecessors; instead of a slab-sided slide with the return spring under the barrel, the 1910 has a near-tubular slide with the return spring wrapped around the barrel and retained by a bayonet-joint collar around the muzzle, locking into the slide.

It was produced in 7.65mm ACP and 9mm Short calibers, had an 87mm barrel and a 7-shot magazine, was striker fired and had the Triple Safety features. It was widely adopted by police forces and had a considerable commercial sale worldwide. Production was suspended by the German invasion of Belgium in 1914 but began again after the Armistice. Sales were good enough to persuade Fabrique Nationale to continue work through the depression of the 1930s, but no new components seem to have been made after the Germans once again invaded in 1940. M1910 pistols from the 1940-4 period were most probably assembled from parts that had been in store.

The pistol was put back into production in 1946, with practically no changes to construction or markings and lasted until overtaken by newer double-action rivals in the early 1970s.

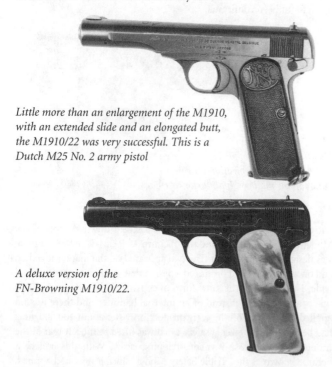

Little more than an enlargement of the M1910, with an extended slide and an elongated butt, the M1910/22 was very successful. This is a Dutch M25 No. 2 army pistol

A deluxe version of the FN-Browning M1910/22.

Model 1910/22 This was designed in response to a request from the Kingdom of Serbs, Croats and Slovenes (renamed "Yugoslavia" in 1929), which ordered 60,000 9mm pistols in February 1923. The specification included an eight-round magazine and a barrel measuring 12cm.

The quickest way to meet this was to modify the 1910 model, and this was done by lengthening the frame to accept a larger magazine and

by attaching a shroud to the muzzle (with a bayonet joint) to cover the extended barrel. This enabled the slide-making machinery of the 1910-type gun to be retained.

The M10/22 looked much the same as its immediate predecessor, except that the barrel and slide were longer and the grip portion of the frame was deeper. Some of the first guns made for the 9mm Short (380 ACP) cartridge had original 1910-type frames and six-round magazines, but this expedient soon gave way to the perfected large-frame model in 7.65mm ACP or 9mm Short. Small-frame guns are very rarely seen.

The action was conventional, with a single-action trigger and a striker running through the breechblock. The main spring was concentric with the barrel, permitting a slender rounded slide to be fitted, though the vertical joint with the shroud and the shroud-release catch on the left side of the muzzle ensure that the M10/22 is distinguished from similar-looking copies made in Spain.

Most M10/22 pistols bore the maker's mark on the left side of the slide, above "BROWNING'S PATENT DEPOSE" and the caliber designation. The first guns supplied to the Kingdoms of Serbs, Croats and Slovenes had standard FN slide markings and Liége proofmarks, but many subsequently gained Cyrillic markings on the slide that customarily translate as "Officers" or "State Troops". Others may signify police units in cities such as Belgrade, Split or Zagreb. The first batches had grips with the FN monogram, but some later guns, perhaps supplied to special order, have grips with the Serbian double-headed eagle, a crown, and a wild man carrying a club. The last deliveries were simply taken from commercial production.

The Dutch M25 No. 2 (10/22 type) FN-Browning pistols, purchased by the Royal Netherlands Army from 1926 onward, had standard FN commercial markings on their slides and grips. However, they were also given large "crown W" marks (the cipher of Queen Wilhelmina).

Fabrique Nationale was still making the M10/22 when the Germans invaded Belgium in 1940. Subsequently, more than 360,000 guns of this type were made for the Wehrmacht and the German paramilitary formations, being issued as 7.65mm "Pistolen 626 (b)" or 9mm "Pistolen 641 (b)" — the designations referring to a list of foreign-service weapons or *Fremdengeräte* drawn up by German military intelligence prior to 1939. The suffix "b" represented *belgisch*, "Belgian". These will bear German military proofmarks and Waffenamt inspectors' marks in the form of small displayed eagles. Quality deteriorated as the occupation approached its end in the late summer of 1944, but the basic design remained unchanged.

Work resumed in 1946 with hardly a change in construction or markings. It has been claimed that the last 10/22 was made in 1959, but assembly continued until the advent of the Model 125 in the 1970s. Post-war guns retained the two-part slide.

Model 1935 See "High Power", above.

Nomad A name applied by the Browning Arms Company to the short-barreled "Standard Model".

Practice 150 Model This was a version of the International (q.v.) with simple thumbrest-style walnut grips and a matte non-reflective finish.

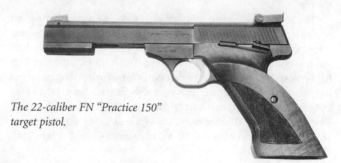

The 22-caliber FN "Practice 150" target pistol.

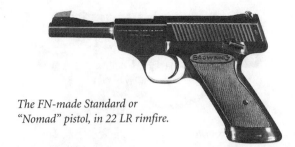

The FN-made Standard or "Nomad" pistol, in 22 LR rimfire.

Standard Model This was a 22 LR rimfire target pistol, offered with a barrel measuring 4.5 or 6.75 inches. It resembled the Colt Woodsman (q.v.) externally, with a well-raked grip and a slender unsupported barrel. The rear sight and the single-action trigger were adjustable. It offered an alloy frame, a blacked adjustable trigger, and black checkered Novadur grips.

Target Model This was an adaptation of the Standard Model (q.v.), with a steel frame that gave a weight of 34.5 oz (4.5-inch barrel) compared with 26 oz. The trigger lever was broad, with a grooved face, and gilded; the rear sight was adjustable. The guns were usually finished in blue, but chrome-plating and extensive Renaissance-style engraving could be specified. Production stopped c. 1978.

- *Target 150 Model* This was a minor variant conforming with the ISU competition rules and had a 5.9-inch barrel. The trigger was regulated for a pressure of no less than 1000gm (35.6 oz).

FAGNUS
A. Fagnus & Cie, Liége, Belgium.
Fagnus produced a small quantity of pinfire revolvers in the 1860s. Their only notable feature was the adoption of a vertical arm on the front end of the cylinder arbor, pointing downward, which could be used for punching empty cases out of the removed cylinder.

Fagnus-Spirlet The original Spirlet revolver, patented by a Belgian gunsmith in 1870, was a break-open design that pivoted around the top rear of the frame. The star-plate extractor was operated by striking a knob beneath the barrel on a solid object. Guns of this type were made in Liége in 1872-5 by F. Martin & Cie, sometimes in a simplified form that required the cylinder to be removed before spent cases could be expelled.

Fagnus made an improvement on the basic Spirlet design in the form of an uncommon 450-caliber military-style revolver that retained the basic design. The action was locked by an arm that extended from the butt to form the rear portion of the trigger-guard and then curved around the forward section of the guard. Springing this arm down and swinging it to the left released the front section of the guard, allowing it to be pulled downward to release a catch. The barrel and cylinder could then be swung upward, and additional pressure on the forward section forced the ejector star from the cylinder. The trigger was usually a double-action design.

FALCON FIREARMS MFG CO.
Granada Hills and Northridge, California, USA.
This company manufactures the "Portsider", an unusual left-handed version of the Colt M1911A1. Made from stainless steel, it has the ejection port on the left side of the slide, a special trigger, ring hammer, and the safety and slide stop catches on the right side of the frame.

FABRICACIONES MILTARES DEL EJERCITO ("FAMAE")
Santiago, Chile.
This military arsenal has manufactured two revolvers. The first, made in the late 1940s, was a virtual copy of the Colt Police Positive in 32 caliber. It has "Cart 32 Largo" on the barrel and a shield bearing the letters

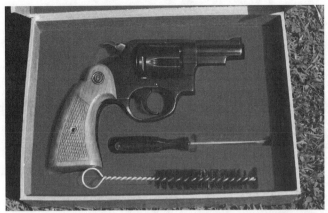

A typical 38 Special FAMAE revolver. Note the strange fluting on the cylinder.

"FAMAE" on the left of the frame. The second, manufacture of which began in the late 1970s, is a five-shot 38 Special, also based on the Colt system, with a FAMAE monogram in silver on the grips.

FEATHER INDUSTRIES
Boulder and Trinidad, Colorado, USA.
Best known for a series of 22-caliber auto-loading rifles, this company also promoted the AT-22 (1985-8) — a "handgun version" of the rifle with a 5.5-inch barrel and a 20-round magazine — and the *Guardian Angel* (1988-93?), a two-shot over/under derringer introduced in 1988. The derringer was initially offered only in 22 LR and 22 WM rimfire but was subsequently enlarged to accept 9mm Parabellum or 38 Super Auto rounds. Loaded with a pre-packaged "drop-in" magazine, it had a partly enclosed trigger, an internal hammer and fixed sight. It was made almost entirely of matte-finish stainless steel; grips were black composition.

FEDERAL ARMS COMPANY
This was a sales name adopted by the Meriden Firearms Company (q.v.), applied in 1895-1910 to conventional hinged-frame round-butt pocket revolvers with ribbed barrels. One was a 32-caliber five-shot, and the other was a similar 38; they may both be found in blue or nickel-plated finish.

FEDERAL ORDNANCE, INC
South El Monte, California, USA.
Best known as a creator of customized guns from a selection of military components, Federal has also offered the *Ranger* (1988-92). Sometimes advertised as the "Ranger G.I." or simply "G.I.", this was an all-steel version of the M1911A1 Colt-Browning. It was made largely with new parts and had checkered walnut grips. The sights were fixed.

FEGYVER ÉS GÁZKESZUELEKGYÁRA ("FEG")
Budapest, Hungary.
The "Arms & Gas Appliances Factory" is the post-1958 form of Fémáru és Szersámgepgyár (q.v.).

AKP-63 This is said to have been a short-barreled version of the AP-63, sharing the same depth of frame and the eight-round magazine.

AP-63 (or "Model AP") Chambered for the 9mm Makarov round, the PA-63 was the official Hungarian army sidearm; the AP was a commercial derivative in 7.65mm Auto. The basis of the Hungarian design is the Walam, which was little more than a copy of the Walther PP. The PA-63 had a bright-finish aluminum-alloy frame and a blued steel slide. The frame of the AP — also known as the "Attila-Pistol" — is usually anodized black. Checkered-plastic thumbrest-style grips were standard.

Attila This was simply an alternative name for the commercial version of the PA-63, applied for sale through agencies in West Germany and the USA.

FEG FP9 pistols were modified copies of the FN-Browning High Power, with a ventilated rib above the slide.

Another view of the FEG FP9.

FP9 This is a copy of the Browning GP35 High-Power; so close, in fact, that most of the parts will interchange quite easily, though the FP9 has a ventilated sight-rib above the slide. It was not adopted by any official body in Hungary but has sold widely in Western Europe and some have been used by small police forces. The markings on the slide can take several forms, often depending on the demands of a particular export market. A typical example reads "PARABELLUM" over "*Cal. 9mm*" on the left side, ahead of "*MADE IN HUNGARY FÉG–BUDAPEST*" in a single line. The FP9 was also marketed by Mauser-Jagdwaffen GmbH (q.v.) as the "Model 80SA".

P9R This is a variant of the FP9 with double-action lockwork and a slide-mounted safety catch that can drop the hammer when it is applied, locking the firing pin and placing a positive block between the hammer and the firing pin. The frame is blued steel. Left-handed models of these pistols were made in the mid-1980s, with the safety catch, slide stop and magazine catch on the right-hand side of the pistol. The P9R was also promoted by Mauser-Jagdwaffen GmbH (q.v.) as the "Mauser Model 90DA".

P9RA This was a minor variant of the P9R with an aluminum-alloy frame.

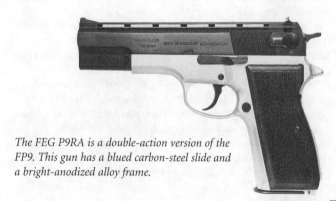

The FEG P9RA is a double-action version of the FP9. This gun has a blued carbon-steel slide and a bright-anodized alloy frame.

The 32 ACP FEG Model R pistol.

R (also known as "R-320") The "Model R" is a 7.65mm blowback of original design, though there are still some traces of Walther PP influence to be seen. It is a double-action weapon with a slide-mounted safety catch that drops the hammer when applied. There is a stripping catch on the left side of the frame, forward of the trigger, which allows the slide and barrel to be easily removed. The frame is of aluminum, the slide of steel, and the barrel is chromium-plated internally. A typical gun is marked "*Cal. 7.65mm Browning*" above "MADE IN HUNGARY FÉG–BUDAPEST" on the left side of the slide. Modified copies of this pistol have been made in Switzerland by ITM (q.v.).

R61 This was a shortened form of the 48M or "Walam", approximating more to the Walther PPK than the original Polizei-Pistole. It is chambered for the 9mm Makarov round, has checkered plastic grips without the Hungarian emblem, and also lacks the slide-mounted loaded-chamber indicator. Magazines hold six rounds. The left side of the slide is marked "R61" over "Cal 9mmM", separated from "FÉG" over "Budapest" by an enwreathed Hungarian police emblem.

RK69 This is said to be a reduced-scale version of the AP-63, approximating to the R61, chambered for the 7.65mm Auto or 9mm Short rounds. Comparable with the PPK, it has an aluminum-alloy frame.

The Tokagypt pistol was made by FEG for Egypt but was unsuccessful. It was little more than the Soviet Tokarev in 9mm Parabellum.

Tokagypt An adaptation of the Soviet Tokarev TT33 to fire the 9mm Parabellum cartridge, this also had a new manual safety catch and a one-piece wraparound plastic grip. It was designed and manufactured to satisfy a contract placed by the Egyptian government in 1958, but the army rejected the guns and the first batches were given to the police. It is said that the police were also unimpressed, and the contract was terminated long before completion. There is a possibility that the Tokagypt, which was otherwise sound, did not work satisfactorily in sand. But it is also possible that the cancellation may have owed more to politics than performance shortcomings. The balance of the contract was eventually released to the commercial market, many being sold in West Germany under the name "Firebird" (see "Hebsacker"). About 15,000 guns are thought to have been made.

The Tokagypt dismantled into its major component groups.

FELK, INC.

Midlothian, Virginia, USA.

A subsidiary of Felk Industries Pty, based in Australia, this promoter of a series of similar guns made in Spain began operating in 1998. Built on polymer frames, with steel slides, they were restricted to double-action only. The lockwork had a striker with an automatic safety, and the trigger had a pivoting-blade safety system inspired by the Glock. The trigger was adjustable, and the slide/barrel assembly could be exchanged when desired. The finish was usually grey-green, though some guns have been seen in black. The *MTS 919* chambered the 9mm Parabellum (9x19) round and had a 10-round magazine. The *MTS 400*, for the 40 S&W round, had a magazine capacity of eight, and the *MTS 450*, in 45 ACP, had a nine-round magazine. A typical MTS 919 is about 6.4 inches long, with a 3.5-inch barrel, and weighs about 20 oz empty.

FÉMÁRU FEGYVER ÉS GÉPGYÃR ("FFG", "FGGY")

Also listed simply as "Fegyergyár"; Budapest, Hungary.

The Hungarian state firearms factory is best known for Mannlicher rifles and the Roth-Steyr pistol, the service weapons of the empire of Austria-Hungary prior to 1918, but also made Frommer pistols in quantity. The trading style was changed to Fémáru és Szerszámgepgyár NV in 1958.

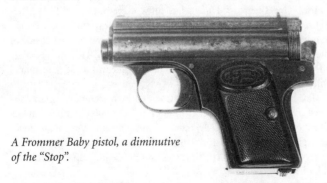

A Frommer Baby pistol, a diminutive of the "Stop".

Baby (c. 1912-25) Little more than a smaller edition of the Stop (below), this was intended as a 7.65mm pocket pistol. Some post-1919 examples were chambered for the 9mm Short cartridge, but none have been found in 6.35mm.

Frommer Rudolf Frommer was born in 1868 and, after qualifying as an engineer, joined FGGY in 1896. Appointed factory superintendent in 1900, he retained the position until he retired in 1935. Frommer died in the following year. He was a first-class engineer, with an original mind, and the pistols bearing his name were surprisingly successful — despite unnecessary complexity. Many of them served long and hard in military and police forces throughout Hungary and adjoining Central European states.

- *Model 1901* Frommer undoubtedly collaborated with Georg Roth and Karel Krnka during his working career. Though precise details are difficult to locate, the fondness of both Frommer and Krnka for long-recoil operation argues for cooperative effort. The first Frommer handgun was entered in a variety of military trials and even offered commercially from 1903 onward, but it never achieved success. Operated by long recoil, with a rotating bolt and an external hammer, the guns had a long slender barrel protruding from a combined frame/receiver and a long barrel jacket that not only formed part of the receiver but also supported the barrel during the recoil stroke. Only about an inch of the true muzzle projected from the shroud. Several chamberings were used, though most survivors accept the 8mm Roth cartridge that became the 8mm Roth-Steyr. The 10-round magazine, formed integrally with the butt, accepted cartridges that could be stripped from a charger through the top of the open action.

- *Model 1906* A transitional form of the 1901 design, this was simpler and more reliable. The operating principles were much the same, but the chambering was 7.65mm Roth (also known as "Roth-Frommer" or "Roth-Sauer"). The first guns retained the integral magazine, but later guns accepted conventional box entering beneath the butt. The modified magazine bore a resemblance to the Parabellum pattern, with large wooden finger grips at the bottom and a flute in the side to improve rigidity.

A 1910-type Frommer pistol, chambering the 7.65mm Roth-Sauer round.

- *Model 1910* The ultimate expression of the original design, this had a grip safety in the rear of the butt. Work continued until 1914. Some pistols have been reported with serial numbers in the 21000 range and output may have been larger than is generally believed.

Liliput (1921-9) This simple blowback was the first Frommer handgun design to break away from long-recoil operation, which was extremely expensive to make, and acknowledged that a locked breech

The Frommer "Liliput" was a 6.35mm blowback, lacking the complexity of the Baby.

The 32-caliber Frommer M1912 or "Stop" pistol, used by the Hungarian home-defense force during World War I.

A simplified form of the M1929, the M1937 was extensively used by the Germans in 32 ACP (7.65mm Auto). This is a 1941-vintage German gun, identified by the "jhv" code on the slide.

The Hungarian M1937 pistol dismantled into its principal components.

was unneccesary in small-caliber pistols. Fitted with an external hammer and grip safety, the "Liliput" laid the foundation for the pistols that replaced the Stop.

Stop (1912-30) This pistol was adopted by the *Honvéd*, the Hungarian element of the Austro-Hungarian army reserve, and then by the Hungarian army formed when the Austro-Hungarian empire disintegrated after World War I. Survivors remained in service until 1945.

The Stop was a fresh approach to long-recoil operation, relying on a double-spring assembly in a cylinder above the barrel. One spring controls the movement of the bolt while the other absorbs the recoil of the barrel and then returns the barrel to the firing position. This two-spring system is implicit in any long-recoil mechanism in which the barrel and bolt must move independently. The springs surrounded the barrel and bolt in the 1901 pattern, but placing them together in a cylinder provides a much more compact design — though complicating stripping and assembly.

At the instant of firing, the Stop is locked by a rotating head on the two-piece bolt. An inertia firing pin is struck by an external hammer, and the only safety device is a lever in the back of the grip. The barrel and bolt recoil for about an inch, allowing the bolt to be unlocked and held while the barrel returns to its forward position. The spent case is extracted and ejected during this phase. The bolt is then released to run forward, chamber the fresh round and rotate its head to lock the breech.

The original service pistols, chambered for the 7.65mm ACP cartridge, always bore a "Bp" mark (for "Budapest") followed by the Austro-Hungarian arms and the last two figures of the year of manufacture on the left side of the front web of the trigger-guard. Stop pistols were also made in 9mm Short after 1919, but these were intended for commercial sale and lacked the official markings. The "Stop" remained in production for some years and is still relatively common in Central Europe. A modified variant marked "M1939" has been reported, but authentication is lacking.

Model 1929 (1929-35) Initially offered only in 9mm Short (380 ACP), this was promptly adopted by the Hungarian army, and at least 50,000 had been made by time work ceased. It is little more than an enlarged Liliput, an external-hammer blowback with the barrel held in the frame by four lugs in Browning fashion. The M1929 was robust and simple and a more practical service weapon than the Stop. A 22 rimfire

The Hungarian M1929 pistol, in 9mm Short (380 ACP), was a blowback adaption of the Frommer Stop.

trainer was developed in 1933 but failed to gain military acceptance. The centerfire guns are marked typically "FEGYVERGYÁR – BUDAPEST" ahead of "29 M" on the left side of the slide and have wood grips that are finely grooved vertically.

Model 1937 (1937-45) Appearing the year after Frommer died, this was a simplification of the Model 1929. Adopted by the Hungarian army as the Model 37, accepting the 9mm Short round, it abandoned the separate pinned-in charging grips that lay at the rear of the 1929-type slide in favor of conventional grooves. The size of the hammer was reduced, and a finger-rest was added to the bottom of the grip. A grip lever was the only manual safety feature.

In 1941, the German government contracted with FGGY to make 50,000 1937-type pistols chambered for the 7.65mm Auto cartridge. Shortly after production had begun, the Luftwaffe demanded a manual safety catch, which was immediately fitted to the left rear side of the frame. The slides of Hungarian guns were marked "FEMARU-FEGYVER ÉS GÉPGYÁR RT. 37M" on the left side of the slide; German guns display "P. Mod. 37, Kal. 7,65." towards the front of the left side of the slide, with "jhv" over a two-digit date (e.g., "41") immediately ahead of the retraction grooves. German Waffenamt inspectors' marks will also be present.

Production of this pistol was extended by a second German contract and came to an end in 1944 after about 85,000 had been made. The 7.65mm gun was sturdy, accurate and pleasant to shoot, as it was heavier than most guns in this particular chambering. Many survived to serve the Hungarian armed forces and police long after World War II had ended.

Roth-Steyr Substantial quantities of the M1907 service pistol were made for the Austro-Hungarian army prior to World War I, distinguished by markings that included "FG" over "GY". Additional details will be found in the section devoted to Oesterreichische Waffenfabriks-Gesellschaft ("Steyr").

FÉMÁRU ÉS SZERSZÁMGEPGYÁR NV

Budapest, Hungary.

This style was used briefly in the 1950s by FGGY, until replaced by FÉG in 1958. The Frommers and their blowback derivatives were abandoned in favor of guns derived from the Walther PP, and Tokarev "48M" pistols were also made for the armed forces and police.

The FÉG Walam, "48. M" or M48 pistol was a minor variant of the Walther PP.

Another view of the FÉG Walam.

48M (or "Walam") Dating from the mid-1950s and apparently developed for police service, this was a straightforward copy of the Walther PP chambered for the 9mm Short/380 ACP cartridge, though the loaded-chamber indicator lies on the top left of the slide instead of protruding above the hammer. The designation causes confusion with the regulation Hungarian army 48M, a standard 7.62mm Soviet Tokarev. However, the guns are clearly marked "FÉMÁRU ÉS SZERSÁMGEP-GYÁR N.V. BUDAPEST" above "48.M. KAL. 9 mm". The checkered plastic grips usually bear the Hungarian state emblem.

FIALA ARMS & EQUIPMENT CO.

New Haven, Connecticut, USA.

The Fiala company marketed the *Fiala Magazine Pistol* from 1920 to 1923. Although it resembled the contemporary Colt Woodsman with its long exposed barrel, short slide and well-raked butt, it was a single-shot weapon. The 10-round magazine went into the butt, and the pistol was loaded by pulling back the slide and then pushing it home and locking it. After firing the shot, the slide was unlocked, pulled back to extract and eject the case, and pushed forward to load the next round. The object was to provide a simple pistol for beginners, a pistol that was claimed to be safer than an automatic and one that was also claimed to inflict less damage on the lead 22LR bullet during loading. Whatever the object, the public failed to take to it, and just over 4000 pistols were made in the 3 years, some of which were unsold as late as 1928.

The standard barrel, 7.5 inches long, could be removed by operating a turnscrew on the right side of the frame and replaced with a 2.75-inch barrel, turning the weapon into a pocket pistol. Alternatively, a 20.5-inch barrel and a shoulder stock turned the pistol into a carbine. The pistol was originally sold cased, complete with the three barrels,

the stock that could be clamped to the butt and cleaning apparatus.

Guns may be found not only with the Fiala name but also with Botwinck Brothers, Hartford Arms, Schall or Columbia names. However, the manufacture was actually done by the Blakeslee Forging Company of New Haven, and there are grounds for the belief that it was a Blakeslee design that the company sold guns to anyone who was interested and marked them accordingly.

GUILIO FIOCCHI SPA

Lecco-Belfedo, Italy.

∾ SINGLE-SHOT PISTOLS ∾

PGP 75 (Pardini) This is a single-shot bolt-action 22 rimfire Free Pistol with a very low-set barrel and a trigger that is "set" by a lever protruding from the wooden fore-end. Various styles of grips are available, including fully adjustable ones, and different barrel weights can be fitted.

∾ AUTOMATIC PISTOLS ∾

Pardini These pistols are designed for various levels of competition and are of two types, semi-automatic or single shot. The semi-automatics are of the currently fashionable pattern with the magazine ahead of the trigger-guard and slab-sided with a recoiling bolt inside the receiver. The "Gros Calibre" model is chambered for 32 S&W Long Wadcutter ammunition, the "Standard" for 22LR rimfire and the "Vitesse Olympique" for 22 Short. All are available with various grips, micrometer sights and different balance weights.

FIREARMS IMPORT & EXPORT CO. ("FIE")

Hialeah, Florida, USA.

As the name implied, this was a distributing business, originally handling a variety of European-made pistols in the USA under the FIE name. In the wake of the 1968 Gun Control Act, FIE began assembling some of the smaller pistols in Florida to avoid the new import restrictions. The FIE Titan series, near-facsimiles of the Tanfoglio Titan pistols, was among them. The Tanfoglio TA-90 pistol and the Tanarmi revolvers were also popular, the latter being sold under names that included "Buffalo Scout" and "Yellow Rose". Trading ceased in 1990.

F.M.E./F.M.G.

Fabrica de Materiel de Ejercito; Fabrica de Material de Guerra, Santiago, Chile.

This was the fore-runner of the present-day "FAMAE" (see entry above) and the name and initials will be found on a 6.35mm blowback automatic, a copy of the Browning 1906 complete with grip safety and safety catch at the left rear of the frame. It is of quite good quality and carries the company name on the slide, together with "FME" or sometimes "FMG" on the butt grips. Date of manufacture is unknown but was probably the early 1930s.

FOEHL & WEEKS FIREARMS MFG CO.

Philadelphia, Pennsylvania, USA.

This company was started in 1890 to exploit the patents of Charles Foehl and Charles A. Weeks, most of which related to details such as rebounding hammers and cylinder stops. The products were all five-shot revolvers in 32 or 38 caliber.

It is doubtful if production of these revolvers reached any great quantity since the company went out of business in the latter part of 1894. Weeks vanished from the scene, leaving Foehl to engage in other business before returning to firearms in partnership with Henry Kolb (q.v.).

Columbian A solid-frame 32- or 38-caliber revolver with removable five-shot cylinder, this dated from 1891-4. It was a fairly conventional weapon, the only patented feature being a rebounding hammer and a cylinder latch mechanism. The barrel bore the patent date of 20 January 1891.

Columbian Automatic This was a hinged-frame 38-caliber successor to the Columbian but was "automatic" only in the sense that a conventional cam-actuated ejector was fitted in the cylinder. It is doubtful if many were made before the company folded.

Perfect Also made 32 or 38, this was a "hammerless" self-cocking solid-frame revolver — though, like all such guns, a conventional hammer was concealed in the rise of the frame behind the cylinder.

FOREHAND & WADSWORTH

Forehand & Wadsworth, Worcester, Massachusetts, USA (1871-1890); Forehand Arms Co., Worcester, Massachusetts, USA (1890-1902).

Sullivan Forehand worked in the office of Allen & Wheelock and married one of Ethan Allen's daughters. Henry Wadsworth, an officer in the Union Army, joined Allen & Wheelock after the Civil War and he, too, married one of the Allen girls. When Thomas Wheelock died in 1864, Allen & Wheelock was reorganized as "Ethan Allen & Co.", allowing Forehand and Wadsworth to enter partnership with Allen. The business became "Forehand & Wadsworth" after Allen's death in 1871, initially continuing the existing range of guns but then gradually improving the basic designs.

The earliest Forehand & Wadsworth products were 22-caliber single-shot pistols of a type that had been made by Allen since 1865, but the first solid-frame revolvers soon appeared. Hinged-frame guns were introduced in the late 1880s, but Wadsworth lost interest in day-to-day operations and retired in 1890. Forehand continued trading as the "Forehand Arms Company" until he died in 1898.

Operations continued under the control of Sullivan Forehand's heirs but were soon sold to Hopkins and Allen. Guns bearing the Forehand name continued to be advertised until 1902, though there is no evidence that they were being made under the new regime and were probably old stock.

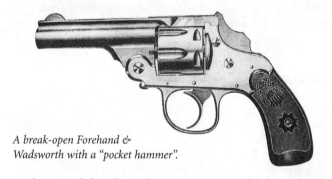

A break-open Forehand & Wadsworth with a "pocket hammer".

Pocket Models The earliest patterns were solid-frame double-action revolvers, in 32 and 38 caliber, with round barrels and five-chamber cylinders. Most display a patent date of July 24, 1875, somewhere on the left side of the frame, which also has a large detachable plate to give access to the lockwork. Guns of this type were still being made in the Forehand Arms period, though the barrel had become hexagonal and the company name was rolled into the topstrap above the cylinder.

Hinged-frame 32- and 38-caliber pocket revolvers were introduced in 1888, with the customary ribbed barrel, prominent hinge screw and spring catch above the standing breech. They were very similar to many other guns of this particular type and can be difficult to distinguish from the products of Harrington & Richardson or Hopkins & Allen.

Hammerless Models Promoted by the Forehand Arms Co. in 32 and 38 calibers, these were little more than the standard hinged-frame pocket models with light sheet-steel shrouds concealing the spurless hammers.

Bulldog One of the earliest revolvers made by Forehand & Wadsworth, this was initially offered only as a five-shot 38-caliber gun with a solid frame, a sheathed trigger and a hexagonal barrel. It was

then adapted to 44 caliber, retaining the solid frame, but acquired a larger butt, a trigger guard and double-action lockwork.

British Bulldog This name was applied to a series of revolvers made by Forehand & Wadsworth from c. 1875 until the 1890s. There were three models: a seven-shot 32, a six-shot 38 and a five-shot 44. All were double-action solid-frame designs, with a loading gate pivoted on the rear right side of the frame behind the cylinder, and had short bird's-head grips. The name "BRITISH BULLDOG" was rolled into the top-strap above the cylinder.

Russian Model This owed some of its design to Allen patents and was undoubtedly promoted to take advantage of the success of the Smith & Wesson "Russian" model. The 44 Forehand & Wadsworth gun bore a superficial resemblance to the S&W version, with a long ribbed barrel, but it was a solid-frame gate loader with hand ejection. The 32-caliber variant, conversely, did not resemble the S&W at all; it was little more than the sheath-trigger Bulldog with a rounded butt."

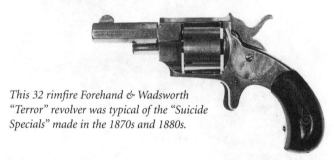

This 32 rimfire Forehand & Wadsworth "Terror" revolver was typical of the "Suicide Specials" made in the 1870s and 1880s.

Terror Another 32-caliber solid-frame revolver with a sheathed trigger, a round barrel and a bird's-head butt, this was otherwise comparable with the 32 Russian Model.

FORT WORTH FIREARMS

Fort Worth, Texas, USA.

This gunmaking business marketed target pistols that were effectively re-creations of the High Standards (q.v.), reflected in the inclusion of "HS" in many of designations. The *HSC, HSO, HST* and *HSV*, all introduced in 1995, were based on the Competition, Olympic, Tournament and Victor patterns, respectively. The *Matchmaster* (1997) shared the same frame/grip unit but had a massive slab-sided barrel shroud and a rear sight that was mounted on the half-length slide. A supplementary catch was added to allow the magazine to be released with the trigger finger, the magazine well was beveled, the frame was flattened ("Lo-Profile") and double extractors were fitted. The *Matchmaster Deluxe* had a full-length Weaver-type top-rib supporting the adjustable rear sight. Work ceased in 2001, allowing the High Standard (q.v.) name to reappear.

LUIGI FRANCHI

Luigi Franchi SpA, Fornaci, Italy.

This long-established gunmaking business is best known for its shotguns but has also developed rifles, submachine guns and an occasional handgun.

LF83 (1983-8) This was a conventional solid-frame double-action revolver, offered in 38 Special or 357 Magnum, with a six-chamber cylinder mounted on a side-swinging yoke. The barrel had a full-length rib and a full-length ejector-rod shroud. Several variants were offered — Compact, Standard, Service and Target — but the differences were confined largely to dimensions, and in the case of the Target Model, the addition of a ventilated rib and special sights.

AUGUSTE FRANCOTTE

Liége, Belgium.

Francotte was among the foremost Belgian revolver manufacturers

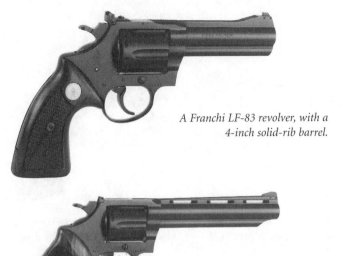

A Franchi LF-83 revolver, with a 4-inch solid-rib barrel.

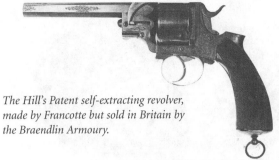

The Hill's Patent self-extracting revolver, made by Francotte but sold in Britain by the Braendlin Armoury.

This Franchi LF-83 has a six-inch barrel with a ventilated rib.

during the latter half of the 19th century, and a complete list of his products would be impossible; in the 1890s, he advertised no less than 150 different types of revolver. We can only remark here on his general range and mention some weapons of particular interest.

From 1860 to 1880, he produced, under license, numerous Adams and Tranter revolver designs, almost identical to the British-made models, and he also turned out good copies of Smith & Wesson designs. After making many Lefaucheaux pinfire revolvers, he made some modifications to produce the "Lefaucheaux-Francotte" revolvers, open-frame models, originally pinfire but later in various centerfire calibers. Principal among these was the 11mm Swedish M1871 Trooper's, the 10mm Danish M1882 Trooper's and the 9mm Danish M1886 Officer's revolvers.

With the arrival of the hinged-frame revolver, Francotte adopted the locking system frequently called the "Pryse", in which two transverse pins in the top of the standing breech are operated by two spring arms mounted vertically. He also adopted the Pryse cylinder catch, a milled knob in front of the cylinder that rotated half a turn, released the arbor pin and allowed the cylinder to be removed.

By the mid-1880s, Francotte's principal trade seems to have been that of wholesaling revolvers to gunsmiths who then put their own name on them. Francotte's name rarely appears with the only identification being a small "AF" stamped on the frame in an inconspicuous spot. For this reason, revolvers bearing the names of British and Continental gunsmiths should be examined closely for this mark.

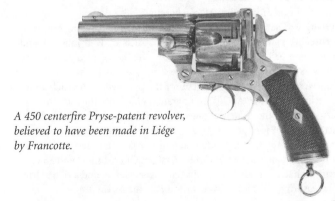

A 450 centerfire Pryse-patent revolver, believed to have been made in Liége by Francotte.

In the 1890s, he began to look further afield and produced an 8mm repeating pistol, one which was rather better thought-out than most of this class. With a magazine in the butt, it used the usual type of reciprocating bolt operated by a ring trigger. Models were certainly made, and some may have been sold, but surviving examples are rare. Equally rare is a four-barreled repeating pistol patented in 1885. No specimens attributable to Francotte are known, but the second model produced by the Braendlin Armoury (q.v.) appears to have been based on this patent and may have been licensed from Francotte.

In about 1912, he produced his only automatic pistol, a 6.35mm blowback of unusual design. The frame is formed at the rear so as to resemble the rear end of the usual slide, but it is actually a fixed housing into which a separate bolt recoils on firing. Attached to the bolt, at its forward end, is a hollow section that fulfills the purpose of a slide, containing the barrel and carrying a lug pressing against the recoil spring, which lies in the frame beneath the barrel. The finger grips, to permit cocking, are cut at the front end of the "slide" and there is a distinct gap between what look like two parts of the slide, in which lies the bolt. A five-shot magazine fits into the butt, and a safety catch on the left side also functions as a barrel-retaining pin. It was a well-made and ingenious design, but few were sold before the German occupation of 1914 put Francotte out of business. The company was revived after the war but has, since that time, concentrated on rifles and shotguns.

ADOLPH FRANK ("ALFA")
Hamburg, Germany.

∼ REPEATING PISTOL ∼

Alfa A German-made 230 four-barreled superposed repeating pistol marketed c. 1912 by Frank, and presumably named for him, since "Alfa" was his trademark. Usually highly ornamented and with mother-of-pearl grips, it has sufficient points of similarity to make it reasonably certain that it was a modification of the "Regnum" design made by August Menz.

∼ REVOLVER ∼

Alfa Frank also used the Alfa trademark on a number of cheap Belgian revolvers imported into Germany prior to 1914.

FREEDOM ARMS CO.
Freedom, Wyoming, USA.

In the late 1970s, this company took up the manufacture of a series of "mini-revolvers" that had previously been made by Rocky Mountain Arms and by North American Arms and then progressed to a Colt Peacemaker lookalike chambered for the awesome 454 Casull cartridge.

Mini-Revolvers They are, in essence, modern versions of the 1880s solid-frame, stud-triggered, bird's-head butt revolvers but of incomparably better quality. Modern features include a floating firing pin in the standing breech, an improved cylinder lock, improved trigger mechanism and a better-shaped butt giving a better grip. These guns were usually chambered for the 22 LR rimfire cartridge, but some "Magnum" models are made for the 22 magnum rimfire round.

A Freedom Arms FA-S-22LR "Mini-Revolver" housed in a belt buckle.

A Freedom Arms 454 Casull revolver, based on the Colt Single Action Army Model

The FA-S-22M mini-revolver.

- *Bostonian* Essentially the FA-L renamed, this retained the 3-inch barrel.
- *Celebrity* A variant of the Patriot or Ironsides, described below, in 22 LR or 22 WMR rimfire, this was sold in a belt-buckle mount.
- *FA-S* Eventually renamed "Patriot", this was the original compact 22 LR version, in stainless steel, with a 1.75-inch barrel.
- *FA-L* Distinguished by a 3-inch barrel, this was the first standard full-length pattern. It was subsequently renamed "Bostonian".
- *FA-BG* This was the "boot gun" with the longer barrel and a squared-heel butt. It became the "Minuteman".
- *Ironsides* Chambered for the 22 Magnum rimfire round, this was offered with barrels of 1 or 1.75 inches.
- *Minuteman* A standard 3-inch-barreled gun, this appears to have had squared grips instead of the bird's-head pattern. It was discontinued in 1988.
- *Patriot* This was the basic 22 LR version, with a 1.75-inch barrel.

Medium Frame Series This was derived from the original large-frame Model 83 in 1997, chambered for smaller cartridges than the Casull types. Most guns are available in Field and Premier Grades.

- *Model 97* (1997-2001) Confined to Premier Grade, this has a six-chamber cylinder accepting 357 Magnum, 41 Remington Magnum or 45 Long Colt. Barrel-length options are restricted to 4.25, 5.5 and 7.5 inches. Cylinders accepting 45 ACP or 38 Special rounds were once offered as optional extras; grips are now either impregnated hardwood or black synthetic micarta.

Large Frame Series The 454 Casull (or Magnum Revolver) cartridge was developed in the late 1950s by Jack Fullmer and Dick Casull of Salt Lake City, and revolvers were developed in the early 1960s. The cartridge is based upon the 45 Colt case, but the loadings are far more powerful and revolvers must be properly designed and built to withstand the high pressure and velocity developed. A few revolvers were made by Colt and Ruger in the late 1960s, but by the 1980s, only the Freedom Arms design remained in production. Most Freedom Arms guns are available in Field Grade, with a matte finish, Pachmayr rubber grips and a rear sight adjustable only for elevation; or in Premier Grade, with bright finish, laminated hardwood grips and a screw-

adjusted rear sight. By 2003, many of the large-frame guns were being advertised as "Model 83 353" or "Model 83-475" instead of the designations given below.

- *Model 83* (1985 to date) Made of high-grade steel, this offers traditional Peacemaker appearance, but can be recognized by its large dimensions and plain-surfaced cylinder. Barrel lengths range from 4.75 to 10 inches, and the chamberings (in addition to 454 Casull) have included the 357, 41 and 44 Magnums, 44 Remington Magnum, 45 Winchester Magnum, 475 Linebaugh and 50 Action Express. The five-shot M83 is available in both grades of finish.
- *Model 252* (1991 to date) This is a 22 LR rimfire derivative of the M83. A 22 Magnum rimfire cylinder can be obtained as an optional extra. Finish is satin stainless, and the barrel lengths range from 5.5 to 10 inches. "Silhouette Class" guns (now discontinued) had a large adjustable rear sight on top of the frame ahead of the hammer, and "Varmint Class" guns, currently fitted with black/green laminate hardwood grips, accept either Freedom Arms iron or optical-sight mounts.
- *Model 353* (1992 to date) An adjustable-sight version of the M97, available in either finish-grade, this chambers the 357 Magnum round. The barrels vary from 4.75 to 10 inches long. Two thousand guns were made in the cased deluxe "Signature Edition", with rosewood grips and high-polish finish. Their numbers are prefixed "DC", for Dick Casull. The "353 Silhouette" had a special 9-inch (357 Magnum) or 10-inch (44 Magnum) barrel and a special Iron Sight Gun Works rear sight.
- *Model 555* (1994 to date) Chambered for the 50 Action Express cartridge, this was offered in either Field or Premium Grade with barrel lengths of 4.75, 6, 7.5 or 10 inches.
- *Model 654* (1999 to date) Confined to 41 Magnum, this five-shot revolver has adjustable sights.
- *Model 757* (1999 to date) Chambered only for the 475 Linebaugh cartridge and available in both Field and Premier Grades, this has a five-chambered cylinder and barrels measuring 4.75-7.5 inches.

ANDREW FYRBERG

Worcester and Hopkinton, Massachusetts, USA.

Fyrberg was active for many years but was usually content simply to license his patents to other gunmakers such as Iver Johnson and Harrington & Richardson. In 1903, however, he decided to promote revolvers under his own name. However, it seems probable that the guns were made elsewhere. Except for the patented frame latch above the cylinder and the "AFCo." monogram molded into the butt, they are very similar to the contemporaneous Iver Johnson designs.

Automatic Ejector (1903-12?) Made in accordance with a patent granted in 1903, this double-action break-open design had an improved frame latch and cylinder retainer. Offered in 32 and 38 centerfire, it had a rounded butt, a five-chamber cylinder and a ribbed barrel measuring 3 inches (32 version) or 3.25 inches (in 38).

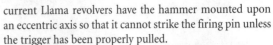

GABILONDO

*Gabilondos y Urresti, Guernica; later Gabilondo y Cia
and Llama–Gabilondo y Cia SA, Vitoria, Spain.*

This company began in 1904 as "Gabilondos y Urresti", manufacturing a variety of cheap Velo-Dog revolvers. When one Gabilondo brother left in 1909, the name became "Gabilondo y Urresti", and work on the Radium pistol began. In 1914, the partners began making an "Eibar"-type automatic under the name "Ruby" and, early in 1915, received an open-ended contract from the French government for 10,000 Ruby pistols every month — a request that was soon increased to a staggering 30,000 monthly.

Unable to meet the unprecedented demand, Gabilondo y Urresti sub-contracted work to five other gunmakers: SA Alkartasuna, Beistegui Hermanos, Eceolaza y Vicinai, Hijos de Angel Echeverria and Bruno Salaverria y Cia. The output of these six businesses was still too small, and it has been estimated that no more than 200,000 guns had been supplied to France by the end of World War I. The Italian army had also placed orders in Eibar, and though the program was supposed to be controlled by Gabilondo y Urresti and all the pistols were to be named "Ruby", it is suspected that anyone who could make pistols (or components) was recruited to help. One result was a glut of cheap blowback pistols after 1918; another was that many new gunmaking businesses were created.

Soon after the end of World War I, Gabilondo y Urresti moved to Elgoeibar and became Gabilondo y Cia. Manufacture of "Eibar"-type pistols was greatly reduced in favor of guns based on the FN-Browning M1910. The first of a new "Llama" series appeared in 1931, derived from the 1911-pattern Colt-Browning. These were well made and reliable and, particularly after the end of World War II, were sold in quantity throughout the world.

Shortly after the conclusion of the Spanish Civil War in 1939, Gabilondo y Cia moved to Vitoria. The first of a new range of Llama pistols appeared in the 1980s, beginning with the Omni. In 1992, unfortunately, at the mercy of a recession that gripped the Spanish gunmaking industry, the business failed. However (unlike Astra and Star), Llama-Gabilondo survived what had become a long-term crisis. A consortium of 60 shareholders and ex-employees formed Fabrinor SAL in January 2000, and the manufacture of handguns continues at a rate of about 20,000 annually; most are exported to the USA, though small quantities are supplied to the Spanish army and police.

∼ REVOLVERS ∼

These revolvers are all based on Smith & Wesson practice, with the yoke-mounted side-swinging cylinders released by a catch on the rear left side of the frame. Most of the guns in the Llama series were discontinued in the 1990s, the Model XXVI lasting longest. In 2000, only the Comanche and Super Comanche were still available.

Comanche A replacement for the Martial (below), this was a sturdy high-quality medium-frame revolver designed to fire Magnum ammunition. See also "Super Comanche".

- *Comanche I* (1977-82) Chambered for the 22 LR rimfire round.
- *Comanche II* (1977-82, 1986-7) Offered in 38 Special and, in the 1980s, in 22 LR rimfire.
- *Comanche III* (1975-2000) Originally chambered for the 357 Magnum cartridge, though a few were made in the 1980s in 22 LR rimfire, this had barrels of 4, 6 or 8.5 inches. A typical gun was about 11 inches long, with the 6-inch barrel, and weighed about 30 oz empty. The finish was either blue or satin-chrome and the grips were checkered walnut.

Llama series Note that all revolvers have the usual "Llama" inscription on the barrel, together with caliber and the Vitoria address. All current Llama revolvers have the hammer mounted upon an eccentric axis so that it cannot strike the firing pin unless the trigger has been properly pulled.

- *Model XXII* Olimpico This was designed as a 38 Special target revolver and has some unusual features including an adjustable anatomic grip, micro-adjustable rear sight, ventilated rib and a web joining the underside of the barrel to the ejector shroud.
- *Model XXVI* This is a less expensive version of the Model XXIX (below) with conventional grips and shrouded ejector rod.
- *Model XXVII* Similar to XXVI but chambered for 32 S&W Long and with a 2-inch barrel.
- *Model XXVIII* Offered only in 22 LR rimfire, with a 6-inch barrel, this has a ramped front sight and a micrometer rear sight.

A Llama-Gabilondo Match Model XXIX target revolver.

The Llama Model XXXII personal-defense revolver.

- *Model XXIX* Olimpico This is the Model XXII chambered for 22 LR rimfire ammunition.
- *Model XXXII* Olimpico This 32 S&W Long target revolver has an unusual cylinder that is about half the length of the frame aperture, allowing the barrel to be extended back into the frame space to meet it. The arbor is also visible. The ejector rod housing is the full length of the barrel and is squared off under the muzzle

Martial (1969-76) A robust 22 LR rimfire or 38 Special revolver, this was offered with ventilated-rib barrels measuring 4 or 6 inches. The front sight was mounted on a ramp and the rear sight was adjustable. The standard finish was blue, and the grips were checkered walnut.

The Llama Piccolo revolver.

Piccolo Called a "personal-defense" revolver and chambered only for 38 Special ammunition, this had smooth walnut grips and projections on the trigger guard suited to two-handed use. The cylinder held six rounds and the barrel was usually 2 inches long; empty weight was about 23 oz.

Scorpio Similar to the Piccolo, this had a conventionally rounded trigger guard and checkered walnut grips. Weight averaged 28 oz.

The Llama Super Commanche revolver.

Super Comanche This was an enlarged Comanche, built on a large frame, with a heavier barrel, a wide-face trigger, a broader hammer spur and "oversize" target-style grips.

- *Super Comanche IV* (1977-2000) Chambered for the 44 Magnum round, this was available with ventilated-rib barrels measuring 6 or 8.5 inches. The finish was blued steel.
- *Super Comanche V* (1977-88) Offered only in 357 Magnum, with barrels of 4-8.5 inches, this was also available only in blued carbon steel. The grips were walnut.

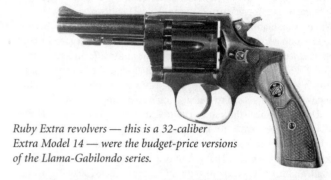

Ruby Extra revolvers — this is a 32-caliber Extra Model 14 — were the budget-price versions of the Llama-Gabilondo series.

Ruby Extra The "Ruby" name was revived in the 1950s to cover a range of revolvers that absorbed the model-numbers XII, XIII and XIV of the Llama series. They are all of Smith & Wesson pattern and are marked "Ruby Extra" in an oval on the left frame, together with a medallion "Ruby" at the top of the grips. Note also that the barrel inscription read "Gabilondo y Cia Elgoeibar Espana", the revolvers being made in Elgoeibar, the automatic pistols in Vitoria. Generally, it can be said that the "Ruby Extra" revolvers were Gabilondo's cheaper line.

- *Model XII* was a 38 S&W Long model with 5-inch barrel and square butt.
- *Model XIII* was in 38 Special with rounded butt and may be found with a 4-inch barrel with ventilated rib or with a 6-inch barrel, ventilated rib, micrometer rear sights and target grips.
- *Model XIV* came in either 22 LR rimfire or 32 S&W Long centerfire chamberings, with a variety of barrel lengths and sight options.

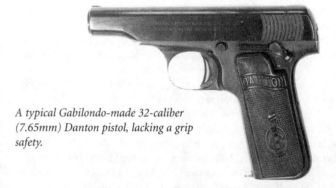

A typical Gabilondo-made 32-caliber (7.65mm) Danton pistol, lacking a grip safety.

∽ AUTOMATIC PISTOLS ∽

Danton (1925-33) This was made in two forms, both with a grip safety mechanism. It has been suggested that this is a Beristain design (see Gregorio Bolumburu, "Bufalo"), but authentication is lacking.

- *6.35mm type* Based on the Browning 1906, this had an unusual manual safety catch mounted at the top rear corner of the left grip, where it was controlled by a spring mounted in a slender horizontal tube. A grip-safety mechanism was subsequently added, possibly after the Beristain patents had expired. The slides were marked "AUTOMATIC PISTOL CAL 6 ^{35} (25) / "DANTON" PATENT 70724 TESTED" in two lines, with "DANTON" and the "GC" monogram on the grips.
- *7.65mm and 9mm Short type* These were based on the 1910-pattern FN-Browning, though there were many minor variants: 7-, 9- or

12-round magazines with grip lengths to suit. The first guns had the manual safety catch on the left side of the frame above the trigger, lanyard rings on the left side of the butt heel and vertical slide-retraction grooves. Their slide markings were similar to the 6.35mm type, except for the caliber notation and the inclusion of "DAN-TON" in the upper line. The grips usually bore the brandname and a cursive "GC" monogram. The later guns, which usually included "WAR MODEL" in the slide marking, had the spring-loaded safety catch on the rear left of the frame, a grip-safety mechanism and a press-button stripping catch (magazine release?) above the trigger.

Llama series (Colt-Browning type) These are all based, externally at least, on the M1911 Colt-Browning. But there are differences internally. The larger guns retain the swinging-link barrel depressor and a muzzle bush, but most of the small-caliber variants are simple blowbacks. It has proved difficult to classify all these guns, owing to confusion in most accessible sources. It is clear that only reference to the manufacturer's catalogs can authenticate the links between model-number and chambering.

The markings are subject to considerable variety, but can be classed in three groups. Those used prior to 1936 include "GABILONDO Y Cᴵᴬ – ELGOEIBAR (ESPAÑA)" over "CAL. 7,65 ᵐ/ₘ (32) "LLAMA"…" in two lines on the left side of the slide. Post-1936 slide markings are generally "LLAMA" ahead of "GABILONDO Y CIA – ELGOEIBAR (ESPAÑA)", above "CAL. 9 ᵐ/ₘ – 38 SUPER". Most recently, the marks have been reduced to simply "LLAMA" in distinctive outline lettering, ahead of (or above) the caliber designation on the left side of the slide, with "GABILONDO Y CIA. VITORIA (ESPAÑA)" on the right. A trademark of an encircled torch-and-hand within "LLAMA TRADE MARK" will be found on the grips.

Many guns will also be found with the names of the principal US importers, Stoeger Industries of South Hackensack, New Jersey, prior to 1993, and now Import Sports, Inc., of Wanamassa, New Jersey. These guns are customarily marked "MADE IN SPAIN" to comply with trade legislation.

* *Model I* (1933-54) This was a blowback design, chambered for the 7.65mm Auto round. The barrel was held in the frame by the locking pin that, in the locked-breech versions, anchored the bottom end of the swinging link. A lump beneath the breech acted as the locating piece and engaged the pin.
* *Model I-A* (1954-76) Another of the 7.65mm blowback pistols, this was little more than a Model I with a grip safety.
* *Model II* (1933-7) Similar to the Model I, this comparatively unsuccessful blowback design was offered only in 9mm Short (380 ACP).
* *Model III* (1936-54) A replacement for the Model II, chambered for the same cartridge, this embodied a few minor mechanical improvements.
* *Model III-A* (1955-98?) This superseded the Model III, the principal change being the addition of a Colt-style grip safety. It lasted in a slightly improved form — with a ventilated slide-rib and check-

A Llama-Gabilondo Model IIIA pistol.

ered polymer thumbrest grips — until the late 1990s. Chambered only for the 9mm Short (380 ACP) round, it was about 6.5 inches long, with a 3.6-inch barrel, and weighed 23 oz empty.

* *Model IV* (1931-54) Offered in 9mm Largo, this recoil-operated gun incorporated the swinging-link barrel-dropping system. The first of the Llama series to reach the commercial market, it lacked the grip safety of its Colt-Browning prototype.
* *Model V* (1931-54) This was simply a Model IV made for export to the USA, marked in English, and chambered for the 7.65mm Parabellum or "30 Luger" cartridge. An additional "Made in Spain" appeared on the slide to comply with US trade laws.

One of the blowback guns in the Llama series, this is a 380 ACP (9mm Short) Model VI.

* *Model VI* (1931-54) Chambered for the comparatively feeble 9mm Short cartridge, this nevertheless retained the breech lock.
* *Model VII* (1932-54) A variant of the locked-breech Model IV chambered for the 38 Super Auto round instead of 9mm Parabellum, this also lacked the grip safety.

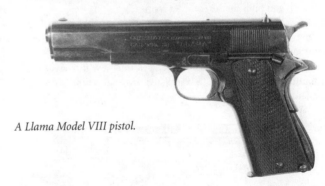

A Llama Model VIII pistol.

* *Model VIII* (1935-?) Offered only in 38 Super, this was similar to the Model VII.
* *Model VIII-A* (1954-76) This was a modernized version of the Model VIII, with a Colt-type grip safety in the backstrap
* *Model VIII-C* (1976-92?) A modern compact version in 38 Super, made to look much more like the original M1911 Colt-Browning.
* *Model IX* (1936-54) Originally offered only in 45 ACP, this retained the locked breech but lacked the grip safety.

A typical Llama Model IX, copied from the Colt-Browning M1911AI.

- *Model IX-A* (1954-76) Little more than a Model IX with a grip safety, it replaced the earlier gun.
- *Model IX-B* (1976-92?) This was a modernized version of the Model IX-A. The size was somewhat reduced and a spur hammer was fitted.
- *Model IX-C* (1977-98?) This was a large-frame gun, offered only in 45 ACP with a 10-round magazine and a ventilated slide-rib. It was about 8.5 inches long, with a 5.1-inch barrel, and weighed 41 oz empty. The finish was generally a matte blue-gray, the grips were black rubber and the sights were a three-dot combination.
- *Model IX-D* A compact version of the IX-C that retained the full-depth frame and 10-round magazine, this was 7.7 inches long and had a 4.25-inch barrel.
- *Model X* (1935-54) Despite being chambered for the ineffectual 7.65mm Auto (32 ACP) cartridge, this retained the swinging-barrel breech lock.
- *Model X-A* (1954-76) An improved version of the Model X, this had a Colt-type grip safety in the backstrap.
- *Model XI* (1936-54) Originally called the "Llama Especial", this differs from all other models. The grip frame projects forward at the toe to form a finger rest and was extended to accept a nine-round magazine. The barrel was 5 inches long, a ring hammer replaced the spur type and the grips were vertically-grooved walnut. Chambered only for the 9mm Parabellum round, it is among the best 9mm combat pistols ever made. It was widely used in the Spanish Civil War.
- *Model XI-A* (1954-76) A variant of the XI, above, with a Colt-type grip safety set into the backstrap of the grip.
- *Model XII-B* (1990-2?) Offered only in 40 S&W, this was a locked-breech gun built on the compact frame.
- *Model XV* (1955-?) This was a 22 LR rimfire blowback with grip safety. Also marked "Especial", it can be found in a wide variety of options with different grips, finishes and sights.
- *Model XVI* A deluxe version of the Model XV, this was usually found with engraving, a ventilated rib, adjustable sights and anatomical grips.

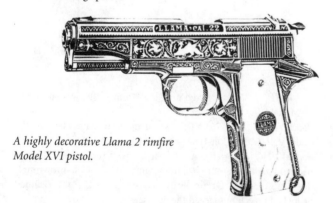

A highly decorative Llama 2 rimfire Model XVI pistol.

- *Model XVII* Chambered for the 22 Short rimfire round, this was a diminutive version of the Model XV, with the grip shaped for the fingers and streamlined external contours.
- *Model XVIII* This was a variant of the XV chambered for the 6.35mm Auto (25 ACP) round.

Max-I (1995 to date) Chambered for the 45 ACP round, this shares the Colt-Browning operating system of the locked-breech Llamas. However, the external appearance was altered to approximate more to the original straight-gripped M1911 than the Llama adaptations. A skeleton hammer was fitted, the manual and grip safety levers were extended and the retraction grooves were cut diagonally. The rear sight was adjustable, the front sight was a small fixed blade and the grips were black rubber. The standard long-frame ("L/F") guns had 5.1-inch

barrels, but an otherwise similar compact-frame version ("C/F", 1995-2001 only) had a 4.25-inch barrel. Magazines contained seven 45 ACP rounds. Construction could be blued carbon or bright-finish stainless steel, though a few duo-tone guns were made with blued slides and stainless fames.

- *Max-1 Compensator* (1996 to date) This is little more than a Max-I L/F with a triple-port compensator extending from the muzzle. The rear sight is usually a micro-adjustable type.

Micro-Max (1997 to date) Available in a variety of finishes, this is the current representative of the old blowback Llama guns, offered in 7.65mm Auto (32 ACP, eight rounds) or 9mm Short (380 ACP, seven rounds). The trigger is a single-action design, a "combat-style" ring hammer is fitted, the manual and grip safety levers have been extended and three-dot sights are fitted. Construction may be blued or satin-chromed steel, and the grips are black polymer thumbrest-style. The guns are about 6.5 inches long, with a 3.6-inch barrel, and weigh 23 oz empty.

Mini-Max (1996 to date) Chambered for the 9mm Parabellum (discontinued in 1997), 40 S&W or 45 ACP cartridges, this is a shortened version of the Max-I with a 3.5-inch barrel. Magazines contain eight 9mm, seven 40 S&W or six 45 ACP cartridges. The grips are checkered rubber, the front of the trigger guard has been squared to permit a two-hand grasp and the finish may be blue, satin-chrome or stainless steel. A few duo-tone guns have also been made.

- *Mini-Max Sub Compact* (1999 to date) This is a reduced-scale version of the Mini-Max, with the barrel reduced to 3.1 inches and a short butt holding a 10-round staggered-column magazine with a finger spur. The front of the trigger guard is rounded, but supplementary retraction grooves are milled vertically in the slide beneath the front sight.

Model 82 (1985-92?) Derived, to some degree, from the Omni, this did away with the roller-bearing slide feature and adopted a dropping-wedge breech-lock inspired by the Walther P. 38 and the Beretta 92. The goals included more reliable feeding and better accuracy from a barrel that was fixed in the frame. An ambidextrous slide-mounted safety conceals and locks the firing pin and disconnects the trigger bar. The hammer drops in a safe condition during the charging stroke, and so the first round is fired in double-action mode. The gun was adopted by the Spanish army in 1985, but did not appear on the commercial market until 1988.

Model 87 Competition (1989-92?) This was an enlarged and improved version of the M82. The barrel is longer and the slide extended by a combination balance weight/compensator with three gas-escape ports in the top surface. The frame and the magazine had a chemically treated nickel finish, the magazine catch was enlarged and the magazine opening was beveled. The trigger could be adjusted for length and sensitivity of pull.

- *Model 87 ISU Match* A few of these guns were made for competition shooting, with micro-adjustable rear sights. The compensator/muzzle brake attachment was absent.

Mugica These were "Llama" automatic pistols produced for sale by Jose Mugica, a gun dealer of Eibar. All were marked on the slide "Mugica-Eibar-Spain". They do not carry model numbers nor is there any indication of their Gabilondo origin. The equivalent Mugica catalog numbers were:

- *Model 101* was the Llama Model X.
- *Model 101G* was the Llama X-A.
- *Model 105* was the Llama III.
- *Model 105G* was the Llama III-A.
- *Model 110* was the Llama VII.
- *Model 110G* was the Llama VIII.
- *Model 120* was the Llama XI.

Omni (1982-5?) This had several novel features. It was in 45 ACP caliber and had a roller-bearing mounted slide and a double-action lock.

The breech lock was still the Browning link. It was originally produced as the "Omni I" in 45, "Omni II" in 9mm Parabellum with 9-round magazine and "Omni III" in 9mm Parabellum with a 13-round magazine, but only the Omni I was made in quantity.

Perfect This was a standard "Eibar" pistol that appeared in both 6.35mm and 7.65mm calibers. It was of relatively cheap quality and was marketed through Mugica to cover the lower end of the market. They can be identified by the word "PERFECT" on the grips, framing a floral design; some may have "MUGICA – EIBAR" on the slide, others "MUGICA – MADE IN SPAIN", and some have no mention of maker or vendor.

Plus Ultra (c. 1925-33) This was an aberrant model to satisfy those non-technical customers to whom "big" equated with "good". It was an ordinary 7.65mm "Eibar" automatic but with the grip frame lengthened to take a 20-round magazine. It looks deeper than it is long—an optical illusion, but one that may have helped sales. Suggestions have been made that the gun was developed in 1929 for the Japanese Government, but this seems highly unlikely. Yet, the Plus Ultra was popular during the Spanish Civil War (1936-9) with the flamboyant amateurs of the International Brigades.

Radium (c. 1912-15) This was an unusual little 6.35mm blowback pistol based on the FN-Browning of 1906 but without grip safety. The magazine, integral with the butt, is loaded by sliding the right-hand grip downward (carrying the elevator and spring) to expose the interior of the casing. Cartridges are simply dropped in until the magazine is full (six rounds), the grip can be replaced, and the magazine spring places the cartridges under pressure. The "Radium" seems to have been dropped in early 1915 due to pressure of war-work and was never revived. [Note: the only specimen traced for examination bore no maker's marks, and the attribution to Gabilondo should be treated as unconfirmed.]

Ruby This 7.65mm "Eibar"-pattern blowback was introduced commercially in 1914. Gabilondo y Urresti submitted specimens to the French army in the first weeks of World War I and received the substantial contract explained previously. However, the original army-type Ruby was abandoned, and the name was transferred to a copy of the 1910-type FN-Browning that was subsequently rechristened "Danton".

Ruby Arms Co. (6.35mm type) These guns, all based on the 1906 FN-Browning, will be found in a variety of forms. The original pattern was made with the safety catch on the left side of the frame above the trigger but was superseded by an improved design with the patented (no. 70724) spring-loaded catch on the rear left side of the frame behind the grip. A grip-safety mechanism was then added, and work continued. Most of the guns are marked "MANUFACTURED IN SPAIN BY "RUBY" ARMS CO" above the patent mark and the caliber notation. Most, but not all, of the grips also display "RUBY".

Ruby Arms Co. (7.65mm and 9mm types; c. 1925-32) These were adaptations of the Danton (q.v.), with a full-length grip-safety lever set in the backstrap and a conventional manual safety catch on the left side of the frame above the trigger (even though the slide markings retain a reference to "Patent 70724"). The magazines usually hold seven rounds. They guns are usually marked "MANUFACTURED IN SPAIN BY "RUBY" ARMS CO", and often lack Gabilondo marks.

Tauler (1933-5) This mark camouflaged Llama pistols (Models I–VIII) sold by Tauler, a gun dealer in Madrid in the early 1930s who could obtain contracts to supply the Guardia Civil, municipal police, the customs service and other official bodies. The markings may vary, but they are invariably in English and always include "TAULER".

GALAND
Charles François Galand, Liége, Belgium and Paris, France.
This Liége-based gunmaker made many contributions to revolver design. In 1872, he patented a double-action lock that was widely

adopted, notably by Webley in England and Colt in the USA, and his unique auto-extracting mechanism was also used under license elsewhere. Galand invented the "Velo-Dog" revolver, one of the most-copied revolver designs in history. Prior to 1870, he was working in Liége, but by 1872, his patent applications gave his address as "Paris", and his Velo-Dog revolvers, first made in quantity in 1894, were invariably marked "GALAND PARIS". Operations ceased in Belgium when the Germans invaded the country in 1914.

Auto-ejector The Galand revolver design can be listed as "Galand & Sommerville", "Galand-Perrin" and similar combinations arising from the participation of licensees or co-designers. The original pattern was basically an open-frame double-action revolver, usually with a six-chamber cylinder, with a lever, beneath the barrel and frame. The lever often doubled as a trigger guard and controlled a novel ejection system. As the lever was swung forward and down, the barrel and cylinder slid forward on the frame until a star-shaped extractor plate in the center of the cylinder was halted. However, as the cylinder continued to run forward, spent cases were held back on the extractor and simply fell clear of the breech. New cartridges were then loaded while the extractor plate was still out of the cylinder, relying upon the length of the bulleted cartridge to reach as far as the chambers. The lever was swung back to its original position, returning the cylinder to the breech face.

The design of the lever varied. Many of the original examples had levers that reached down the frontstrap of the grip, forming the entire trigger guard. Others were two-part designs that required the shooter to unlatch the rear section before the action could be opened. Levers of this type were replaced by a shorter design that formed the front section of the trigger guard and sprung (or was latched) into a post that formed the rear of the guard. The ultimate "New Model" Galand had a short lever beneath the barrel, which was locked in the frame beneath the front of the cylinder by a push-button or a small sprung bar.

Galand produced these revolvers in his own name, in a variety of calibers, from 1868 into the 1880s. Small numbers of 12mm-caliber guns were acquired for the Imperial Russian in the mid-1870s, and others went to the Romanian army in 1874.

- *Galand-Perrin* This term is frequently applied to guns that chambered 7mm, 9mm or 12mm Perrin "French Rim", "Thick Rim" or "Welt Rim" cartridges.

A 9mm Galand & Somerville revolver, with the action closed.

The Galand & Somerville revolver with the action open, showing how the cylinder slides forward to extract spent cases.

• *Galand & Sommerville* More common in England than Continental Europe, this gun has a shorter actuating lever that latched to the fore-end of the frame instead of running back around the trigger-guard. This was made in 380 and 450 calibers by Braendlin & Sommerville Ltd of Birmingham, which later, after various changes, became the Braendlin Armoury Company. Sommerville was Galand's co-patentee for the extracting system.

Le Novo This was a novel folding revolver, designed in Belgium by Dieudonné Oury (see "Derkenne"). The open-framed Galand version had a shrouded hammer, a folding trigger and a hollow metal butt that pivoted up beneath the frame to enclose the trigger. A lever on the frame extracts the cylinder arbor by means of a rack, allowing the cylinder to be lifted out for reloading. The knurled tip of the hammer protrudes through a slot in the shroud to allow thumb-cocking. Chambering generally proves to be 6.35mm Auto, suggesting that the guns date from 1907-14.

Tue Tue This was another remarkable little design, indicative of the wide market for small pocket revolvers in the days before the blowback automatic ousted them. One of the best pocket designs, dating from c. 1894, it has a concealed hammer, a solid frame and a cylinder that swings open to the right. A central extractor is operated by a rod, and the cylinder is locked by a latch on the right of the frame. The guns were originally made in 22 Short rimfire, 6mm Type Française and 5.5mm Velo-Dog chamberings, and it was subsequently adapted for the 6.35mm Auto cartridge.

Type démontable This was a greatly simplified design, made in two assemblies. The barrel was locked into the frame by a large "L"-shape lever on the lower right side of the frame, under and ahead of the cylinder. When this was pressed, the barrel and cylinder could be detached. Extraction was simply a matter of pushing the spent cases out of the individual chambers with the help of the projecting cylinder axis pin. Production of these revolvers does not seem to have been large, though a variety of styles and chamberings have been reported. They range from small pocket revolvers chambering 22 rimfire, 5.5mm Velo-Dog or 6.35mm Auto ammunition up to large military-style examples accepting 320 CF or 8mm Lebel cartridges. The simplicity of construction commended the design to imitators, and some "Galands" of this general type are suspected to have been made in the Far East.

A typical 5.5mm-caliber Galand "Velo-Dog" revolver.

Velo-Dog This, the original of its type, was an open-frame pattern similar to Le Novo without the folding butt. The trigger was a solid lever with a conventional guard, though later models adopted the slender hammerless folding-trigger appearance that characterized many later Velo-Dog designs.

The name "Velo-Dog" came from a combination of *velocipède* (bicycle) and "dog", the guns selling widely in the 1890s to allow cyclists to defend themselves from dogs that could attack them as they ventured into the depths of the countryside. The peculiar 5.5mm Velo-Dog cartridge had an unusually long and slender cartridge case loaded with a 45-grain jacketed bullet that made it less efficient than 22 LR rimfire.

Many of the guns made in 1900-14, indeed, accepted 22 LR or 6.35mm Auto cartridges, which were much more widespread than the 5.5mm type. Some rounds were even loaded with cayenne pepper or dust shot to satisfy cyclists with scruples, but the bullets had a more permanent effect.

GALEF

J.I.Galef & Co., New York City, USA.

The name of this import agency can be found on a number of Beretta automatic pistols and Italian-made "Western style" revolvers imported into the USA in the 1965-75 period.

GALESI

Industria Armi Galesi Figli, Collebeato, Brescia.

This company began making pistols in 1914, and although well known within Italy, they did not achieve widespread recognition until after World War II had ended, when Galesi products began to be exported more widely. See also "Rigarmi".

M1914 (1914-15, 1918-25) Introduced shortly before World War I began, this 6.35mm blowback was based on the 1906-type Browning but lacked the grip safety. Production was curtailed by the outbreak of World War I.

M1923 (1923-31) This resembled a diminutive M1910 FN-Browning with the return spring concentric with the barrel and was offered in 6.35mm or 7.65mm. The slides displayed "BREV. 1923. GALESI BRESCIA" on the left side, and the grips bore a crowned shield charged with a lion.

M1930 (1935-50?) Derived from the 1923 Galesi pistol and the FN-Browning of 1910, this was another striker-fired gun. Initially chambered for the 6.35mm Auto or 7.65mm Auto cartridges, it lacked a grip safety and the "sights" consisted of a groove in the slide top. The pre-war guns were usually marked "Industria Armi Galesi – Brescia – Brev. Mod. 1930" on the left side of the slide, but post-war examples often had "Industria Armi Galesi" on the slide above "Brev. Mod. 1930" on a banner that was clearly designed to resemble the Walther trademark. The grips, either wood or plastic, bore enwreathed "IAG" medallions.

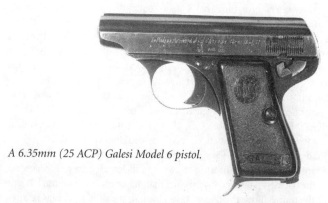

A 6.35mm (25 ACP) Galesi Model 6 pistol.

Model 6 (1936-50?) This was introduced in 6.35mm, 7.65mm and 9mm Short variant, the latter being developed for sale commercially but purchased for the Italian army during World War II. The Model 6 was the first of the Galesi pistols to include a spring-out locking piece, inserted in the rear of the frame to simplify the dismantling procedure.

Model 9 (1939-50?) The gun advertised under this designation (shared with the 1920s Walther design it greatly resembled) was made in 22 LR rimfire and 6.35mm Auto. It also came in a bewildering variety of finishes, grip materials and decoration.

Model 50, and the "500 series" (1950-85?) This was a cosmetic adaptation of the Model 6, with neater slide-retracting grooves and black synthetic grips with horizontal grooves molded into the base. Slide markings typically read *Armi Galesi – Brescia – Brevetto – Cal. 7,65*".

Most early grips were marked simply "AG" ("Armi Galesi") within a wreath, though later examples display "GALESI" on a ribbon across a stylized globe. The chronology and identification of the variants have proved difficult to establish.

- *Models 503-505* These were offered in 22 Short rimfire, 22 LR rimfire or 6.35mm Auto, the differing model numbers and a variety of suffixes indicating finish and decoration. The guns were 4.5 inches long and weighed about 12 oz.
- *Models 506-508* Identical mechanically with the preceding group, these guns were restricted to 22 LR. They were 5.2 inches long and weighed about 15.5 oz.
- *Models 512-514* Larger than their predecessors at 6.1 inches long and weighing about 20 oz, these were chambered for the 7.65mm Auto round.
- *Models 515-517* Also chambered exclusively for 7.65mm Auto ammunition, these guns, the largest and heaviest of the group, were 7.1 inches long and weighed 22 oz.

Rubi This name was applied to 6.35mm pistols made by Galesi for Establecimientos Venturini of Buenos Aires, Argentina, in the 1950s.

GAMBA

Armi Renato Gamba, Gardone Val Trompia, Brescia; SAB–Societa Armi Bresciane, Gardone Val Trompia.

Armi Renato Gamba was primarily a shotgun and rifle manufacturer, but began to make handguns on the basis of the Mauser HSc in the 1970s. Financial difficulties in 1984 led to a collapse, but the formation of Società Armi Bresciane ("SAB") revived the Gamba fortunes.

The Gamba 38 Special Trident revolver, with a 4-inch ventilated-rib barrel.

∼ REVOLVERS ∼

Trident This was a six-shot 38 Special revolver of a conventional solid-frame swing-cylinder design with barrels measuring 2 or 2.5 inches. Based generally on Colt practice, with a pull-catch to release the cylinder, it had a full-length ejector rod shroud and a front sight mounted on a full-length ramp. The similar post-1988 SAB version had barrels of 2.5 or 3 inches. Some guns will also be found with the marks of Mauser-Jagdwaffen, resulting from a marketing agreement dating from 1979.

- *Trident Golden Black* This was finished in highly polished black with gold-inlay decoration.
- *Trident Vigilante* Essentially a basic Trident mechanically, this had a 4-inch flat-sided barrel, a ramp-mounted front sight and a micro-adjustable rear sight. It became the "Trident Super 4" in SAB days.
- *Trident Match 900* Intended for target shooting, this amalgamated the basic Trident frame and a 6-inch slab-sided barrel. The barrel had a full-length ejector-rod shroud, the front sight was a blade, and the micro-adjustable rear sight was mounted on an extension of the frame that ran back above the hammer. The anatomical grip had a large prawl to fit the thumb web. The gun was available in either 32 S&W Long or 38 Special chamberings.

∼ AUTOMATIC PISTOLS ∼

Guardian A 7.65mm blowback pistol, this was virtually an enlarged "Personal" with double-action lock. It bore considerable resemblance to Tanfoglio designs, which may explain the source of the components. The "Guardian B/79" had a 12-round double-column magazine.

The 380 ACP Gamba RGP-81 was based on the Mauser HSc but had a larger magazine capacity and an extended grip.

HSc 80 As the name implies, this was a modification of the Mauser HSc made under license. The earliest Gamba-Mausers were virtually identical with the post-1945 HSc, except for their markings, but changes made in 1979 altered the outline by allowing a two-hand grip. A 15-round double-column magazine and a new magazine-release catch were fitted, and production continued as the "Model 80" ("HSc Super G-15" after 1988).

Personal This was a small 6.35mm blowback pistol with an exposed barrel and an open-top slide bearing a strong resemblance to the Tanfoglio Targa.

Based on the CZ 75, the SAB-Gamba G90 Combat was a 9mm double-action design.

SAB G90 In 1989, SAB introduced a completely new range of locked-breech military-style automatic pistols. Based on Tanfoglio components, they are virtual copies of the CZ 75 double-action pistol, using the Browning dropping-barrel method of locking the breech. The chambering was usually 9x21 IMI cartridge, the use of 9mm Parabellum being restricted in Italy to the armed forces and the police.

SAB G91 Compact The SAB military-pistol range was extended in 1990 by adding this gun, a diminutive of the G90 with a short barrel, a short slide and short butt containing a 12-round magazine. Finish may be black or chrome-plating.

SAB G2001 This was an updated version of the HSc 80, in 7.65mm Auto or 9mm Short.

GARANTAZADA

Fabrica d'Armas Garantazada, Eibar, Spain.

This name appears on a cheap 38-caliber revolver, a copy of the Colt Police Positive but with an unusual cylinder latch incorporated in the crane arm in front of the cylinder. The weapon was probably made in the late 1920s, and the cylinder latch is almost identical to that used on the Crucero revolver made by Ojanguren y Vidosa of Eibar in the same period. The inference is that "Garantazada" was simply a brand name.

GARATE BROTHERS

Garate Hermanos, Ermua, Spain.

Little is known about this gunmaking company, active from c. 1910 into the early 1920s.

The 25 ACP (6.35mm Auto) Cantabria revolver, made by Garate & Anitua, was typical of the guns that were made to resemble automatic pistols.

∾ REVOLVERS ∾

Cantabria (1900-30) This name was applied to Velo-Dog and Velo-Mith revolvers in 6mm, 6.35mm, 7.65mm and 8mm calibers, with 5-, 6- or 8-chamber cylinders. They had a tipping barrel retained in the frame by a catch above the standing breech, a concealed hammer with a cocking spur protruding through the shroud and a barrel unit — deliberately slab-sided and grooved — that resembled the muzzle of an automatic pistol. Folding triggers were fitted, and the butts were either angular like an automatic pistol or curved in revolver style.

Velo-Stark Apparently the brothers' first product, this was a solid-frame Velo-Dog type. It offered gate-loading, rod ejection, a folding trigger and a concealed hammer.

∾ AUTOMATIC PISTOL ∾

Cantabria (1918-22?) This name distinguished a poor-quality 6.35mm "Eibar"-style blowback pistol sold by Garate Hermanos, but probably manufactured elsewhere. Though the slide is marked "6 ^{35} 1918 Model AUTOMATIC PISTOL" over "PATENT "CANTABRIA"…" on the left side, the grips display a monogram that seems to consist of "L" and "G" in addition to "CANTABRIA" on a scroll.

GARATE & ANITUA

Garate, Anitua y Cia, Eibar, Spain.

This business made a wide range of handguns, varying the quality according to the demands of the prospective market; some were poor, but others were extremely well made. Garate & Anitua were one of the only two Spanish gunmakers to receive contracts from the British army during World War I, which was testimony to the quality that could be achieved. However, like many rivals, the company failed during the Spanish Civil War (1936-9) and was never revived.

∾ REVOLVERS ∾

Cosmopolite Oscillatory (1927-35) This 38-caliber six-shot gun was based on the Colt Police Positive, though the cylinder was locked by a sleeve on the ejector rod without the benefit of the customary thumb-operated latch.

El Lunar Also based on Colt lines, with a thumb-catch to release the cylinder, this was made in 1915-16 for the French army and chambered the 8mm Lebel cartridge. To resemble the Mle 1892 service revolver, the barrel was reinforced at the muzzle and close to the frame. El Lunar became known to French troops as the "92 Espagnole".

Lebel Rapide (or "El Lunar Lebel Rapide", 1918-25?) This combined features of the Smith & Wesson Military & Police model and the French Mle 1892. The frame, trigger-guard, cylinder-release catch and leftward-opening cylinder were based on Smith & Wesson practice, but the barrel, reinforced at the frame end and muzzle, drew its inspiration from the French design. The chambering was 8mm Lebel.

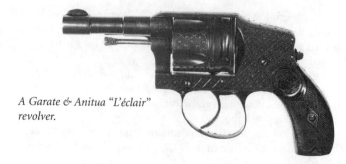

A Garate & Anitua "L'éclair" revolver.

L'éclair A solid-frame hammerless 6-shot revolver with a cylinder that swung to the right, this was chambered for the 5.5mm Velo-Dog cartridge. It dates prior to 1914 and was probably intended for sale in France.

GAC (or "GAC Firearms Mfg Co.", 1930-6) This mark is found on only one type of revolver, a 32-20 WCF or 38 S&W copy of the S&W Military & Police model, where it was stamped into the barrel. A surprising number arrived in Britain in 1940 and were issued to the Home Guard.

Made for the British during World War I, the Garate & Anitua "Pistol, Ordnance, Mk. 1 No. 1" chambered the 455 service cartridge.

Garate, Anitua This interesting six-shot tip-barrel double-action gun became an official British army service revolver during World War I, under the title "Pistol, O.P., [Old Pattern] No. 1 Mark I". It was approved on November 8, 1915, in the regulation 455 chambering and was declared obsolete in 1921. Few if any were sold commercially. The other "Garate, Anitua" pistol was a commonplace 7.65mm "Eibar" automatic of the usual type.

∾ AUTOMATIC PISTOLS ∾

Express (1920-5?) The first "Express" was a fixed-barrel model with open-topped slide reminiscent of the Mauser 1910 in its design. It was offered in 6.35mm initially, with a 2-inch top-ribbed barrel and a slide that formed the breechblock at the rear. The rear of the slide was marked "THE BEST AUTOMATIC PISTOL EXPRESS" on the left and "For the 6,35mm cartridge" on the right. The safety catch, on the left rear of the frame, often displayed the French markings "SÛR" and "FEU". The 7.65mm pattern was similar, but had a 4-inch barrel without the top rib. The grips of both pistols bore a representation of the pistol within an oval cartouche, unless they had the dragon motif of the distributor Tómas de Urizar.

The second model, also made in 6.35mm and 7.65mm, was a standard "Eibar"-type blowback. Minor variations have been encountered in the machining of the slide and frame and some guns had grip safeties. A typical example is marked "VERITABLE "EXPRESS" FOR THE 6 ^{35} CARTRIDGE" over "THE BEST AUTOMATIQUE PISTOL "EXPRESS"…" on the left side of the slide and may have a "GAC" monogram or a fox motif on the grips. Others were marked "F.A.M. GARATE Y ANITUA & Co EIBAR" over "THE BEST AUT. PISTOL "EXPRESS" FOR 25 CAL" ahead of a smaller "– MADE IN SPAIN –" (which may suggest export to the USA).

The third 6.35mm variant, apparently introduced in 1921, had an external hammer. The slide was marked "6 $\frac{35}{}$ AUTOMATIC PISTOL "EXPRESS"…" with "EXPRESS" on the grips, but there was no indication of the manufacturer. Unusually, the front-sight blade doubled as a loaded-chamber indicator, actuated by a lever in the slide that rested on the cartridge rim. The sight blade intruded into the line of sight only when the pistol was loaded.

Garate, Anitua (1916-18?) This was a large military-style "Ruby-type" 7.65mm blowback pistol, derived from the 1906 FN-Browning, with a nine-round magazine and a lanyard ring on the left side of the butt-heel. It is marked "PISTOLA AUTOMATICA CALIBRE 7$\frac{65}{}$ "over "GARATE ANITUA & CIA EIBAR (España)" on the left side of the slide. The safety catch is marked in French, suggesting supply to the French army during World War I.

La Lira (c. 1910-14) This unusual pistol would have been a faithful copy of the 1901-pattern Mannlicher but for two significant changes: the chambering was 7.65mm Auto, and a detachable box magazine replaced the original charger-loaded design. To conform to the shape of the butt, the magazine was distinctly curved and carries its own retaining catch. The result was praiseworthy, curing two defects of the Mannlicher that had restricted sales, yet La Lira does not seem to have prospered and survivors are rare. Wartime contracts may have persuaded Garate, Anitua to abandon it, but the Browning-type guns were undoubtedly easier to make. The breechblock is marked "SYSTEMA LA LIRA" on the left and "PARA CARTUCHES BROWNING" in two lines on the right. Some, but not all of the grips will bear "GAC" monograms.

Sprinter This is a 6.35mm blowback patterned on the Browning 1906 model and another of the firm's pre-1914 products. It is remarkable only for the polyglot two-line marking "THE BEST AUTOMATIQUE PISTOL "SPRINTER" / PATENT FOR THE CAL 6$\frac{35}{}$ CARTRIDGE" on the left side of the slide. The name was repeated on the grip, curved around an encircled "GAC-and-scroll" monogram. The destination was probably an entrepreneur in Liége. The safety markings are in French, and many of the guns have Belgian proofmarks.

Triumph All but identical with La Lira (q.v.), a Mannlicher copy in 7.65mm Auto, this carries no maker's name. The inscription on the breechblock reads "TRIUMPH AUTOMATIC PISTOL" on the left and "FOR THE 7$\frac{65}{}$ MM CARTRIDGE" in two lines on the right; the use of English suggesting export to the USA. The usual "GAC" monogram lies on the grips, and the only important difference from La Lira lies in the incorporation of the magazine catch in the backstrap of the butt.

Vesta This was a typical Eibar-type 6.35mm or 7.65mm Browning copy, probably made for a distributor. Considerable variety exists among the guns of this name, but very few display makers' marks. A 6.35mm exception is clearly marked "G.A. EIBAR 1924" ("Garate, Anitua") on the left side of the frame ahead of the trigger guard. A 7.65mm gun, however, is marked by Hijos de A. Echeveria.

GARBI, MORETTI Y CIA ("GMC")

Mar Del Plata, Argentine.

A 22 LR blowback automatic pistol, this weapon was of simple construction using an external hammer, a manually cocked bolt and an exposed trigger with no guard. It appears to have been made in small numbers in the mid-1940s.

GASSER

Leopold Gasser, Vienna and St Polten, Austria.

Gasser reputedly turned out some 100,000 pistols a year in the 1880s and 1890s. These were adopted by the Austro-Hungarian army and were widely distributed throughout Central Europe and the Balkans, the most common form being the "Montenegrin Gasser". His patents were also used in the "Rast & Gasser" Austrian service revolver of later design, though Leopold had died in 1871 and his brother Johann continued the business for many years. The company was wound up in 1903 and reformed as the Rast & Gasser (q.v.) partnership, under which the firearms business was run down and the firm converted to general engineering.

Gasser The original revolver was an open-frame model, with the barrel unit attached to the frame by a screw beneath the cylinder arbor. This arbor pin was screwed into the barrel unit and fitted into a recess in the standing breech. The cylinder was gate-loaded from the right side, and a rod ejector was carried beneath the barrel. A unique feature is the invariable presence of a safety bar on the right of the frame, below the cylinder. This bar carries pins that pass through holes in the frame to engage with the lock mechanism. Drawing back the hammer slightly allows one of these pins to move inward and prevent the hammer moving forward again when released, so allowing the pistol to be carried safely when loaded. Pressure on the trigger causes the pin to be withdrawn so that it does not interfere with the fall of the hammer on firing.

The M1870 Gasser became the Austro-Hungarian cavalry revolver. It used an 11.3mm centerfire cartridge usually called the "11mm Montenegrin", a long cartridge that had earlier been used in the Werndl single-shot pistol. It was later replaced by the Model 1870/74, which differed in having the frame of steel instead of wrought iron. A similar weapon was issued to the Austrian navy.

Gasser-Kropatschek The third Austro-Hungarian pistol of the time was the Gasser-Kropatschek M1876, designed as an officer's model and thus smaller than the standard revolvers. It was a re-design of the 1870 model instigated by Field-Marshal-Lieutenant Kropatschek, the changes being principally a matter of reducing weight by reducing the caliber to 9mm.

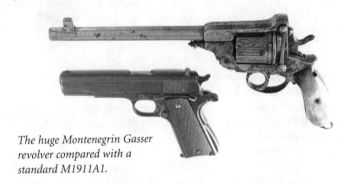

The huge Montenegrin Gasser revolver compared with a standard M1911A1.

Montenegrin Gasser This title covers a variety of weapons, all six-shot heavy-caliber revolvers. They originally appeared as open-frame models, similar to the M1870 and usually in the same 11.3mm caliber. Single- and double-action locks were used, grips were often in ivory or bone, engraving and gold inlay work was common and the predominant impression was one of weight and bulk. It is often said — though little hard evidence is available — that King Nicholas of Montenegro made the ownership of such revolvers mandatory on his male population … and also that His Majesty had a financial stake in the manufacturers. The story is weakened by the manufacture of "Montenegrin Gasser"-style revolvers by numerous small Belgian and Austrian firms in addition to Gasser himself. Later models were of hinged frame construction, using Galand's cylinder lock, and had a self-extracting mechanism. Most are marked "Guss Stahl", "Kaiser's Patent" and similar phrases. Genuine Gasser products are marked "GASSER PATENT" or "L.GASSER OTTAKRING PATENT" and often display a heart pierced by an arrow above "SCHUTZ MARKE".

A short-barreled 11mm Gasser break-open revolver.

Commercial patterns Gasser also produced a number of civil and police revolvers. The Gasser-Kropatschek, for example, appeared in commercial form, differing from the military issue in having an externally fluted cylinder instead of a smooth one. He also produced the "Post & Police" revolver, a solid-frame, non-ejecting, double-action model in 9mm caliber with a hexagonal barrel; a commercial version, generally of better finish; a commercial version of the M1874 in 9mm, open-framed; and a 9mm hinged-frame self-extracting model with the Galand double-action lock.

GATLING ARMS & AMMUNITION CO. LTD
Holford Mills, Perry Barr, Warwickshire, England.

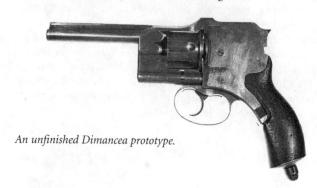

An unfinished Dimancea prototype.

Dimancea (1888-90) This revolver was patented by Captain Haralamb Dimancea of the Romanian army in 1885. It was a six-shot hammerless weapon in 380 or 450 caliber and employed a unique mechanism. It was a genuine hammerless design, rather than the usual concealed-hammer "hammerless", the trigger operating a star wheel inside the frame that revolved to strike a firing pin. There is no method of cocking, and the revolver can only be fired in the self-cocking mode, giving the effect of a double-action design without the excessive trigger pressure that is usually required. What looks like a hammer spur on the rear of the frame is the latch that allows the cylinder and barrel to be pushed to the left, pivoting about a bolt in the lower front of the frame. The barrel can then be pulled forward to operate a self-ejecting mechanism.

The guns bore the maker's marks and location on top of the barrel rib; some are also marked "DIMANCEA'S PATENT". Only a few revolvers were ever made; work ended when the Gatling business collapsed in 1890, to be taken over by Grenfell & Accles. The new proprietors continued to sell the remaining guns until they, too, failed in 1900. Dimancea returned to Romania in the late 1880s, was promoted Major, and became Sub-Director of Army Pyrotechnics, a post he held until his death in 1890.

GAUCHER ARMES
Saint-Étienne, France.
This gunmaking business has been making high-quality sporting weapons since 1834, and their current range includes rifles, shotguns

and two very specialized target pistols. The *Pallas P-1* is a substantial bolt-action single-shot chambered for the 22 Long Rifle cartridge and provided with micrometer sights. *The Phantom GP* is derived from the Pallas but has some distinctly different contours, a swept-back bolt and an integral barrel-silencer that reduced the noise of a subsonic 22 cartridge to about 53/55dB.

Variations of the Pallas have been sold in North America as the *GN-1 Silhouette* and *GP Silhouette* (introduced in 1990 and 1991, respectively). They have been distributed by several agencies, including Mandall Shooting Supplies of Scottsdale, Arizona.

The 7.65mm (32-caliber) Gavage pistol.

GAVAGE
Fabrique d'Armes de Guerre de Haute Précision Armand Gavage, Liége, Belgium.
This small gunmaking business began making an automatic pistol of similar pattern to the Clément in the 1930s. It had a fixed barrel and a barrel extension, with a rectangular bolt moving beneath the extension. Hammer fired, it chambered the 7.65mm Auto cartridge and had a Parabellum-like dismantling catch above the trigger. A safety catch lay at the rear of the frame. There were no maker's marks other than an "AG" monogram in the grip.

Guns that remained in stock were seized by the Germans in 1940, sometimes acquiring inspectors' marks, though the pistol does not appear in the official vocabulary. In addition to the manufacturing business, Armand Gavage was an arms dealer involved in supplying arms to the Republicans in the Spanish Civil War and was also a British MI5 agent.

GAZTAÑAGA
Isidro Gaztañaga, Eibar, Spain.
Gaztañaga entered the pistol business in the early 1890s with a cheap pocket revolver called the "Puppy". Shortly before World War I, this was dropped in favor of the usual "Eibar" copy of the Browning 1906, and 7.65mm pistols were subsequently made in quantity for the French army (apparently independently, not as a sub-contractor to Gabilondo). After the war had ended, the business continued to make "Eibar" automatics and Colt-copy revolvers.

～ REVOLVERS ～
Brown This was a "hammerless" Velo-Dog pattern with a solid frame, a five-chamber cylinder and a folding trigger. It was offered in 6.35mm Auto, 7.65mm Auto and 8mm Lebel chamberings.

Destroyer Introduced c. 1929, this was a Colt Police Positive copy chambering the 38 Special round. Contemporaneous reports suggest that it offered reasonable quality.

Horse Destroyer Apparently a variant of the "Destroyer", no specimen could be traced for examination. However, records in Eibar show that Gaztañaga registered this trade name.

Puppy Gaztañaga's first revolver was a solid-frame "hammerless" 5-shot weapon with a bird's-head butt, chambering the 22 LR rimfire and possibly also the 5mm Velo-Dog rounds. An ejector rod on the Abadie principle was fitted, a loading gate lay on the right side of the frame behind the cylinder and the trigger could fold. Similar revolvers were made by Arizmendi, Crucelegui,, Ojanguren y Marcaido and Retolaza (q.v.).

∼ AUTOMATIC PISTOLS ∼

Destroyer This name was applied to several differing "Eibar"-style pistols, dating from 1913 to 1935. Virtually all of the guns, excepting the 1919 type, had retraction grooves that were milled radially.

- *Model 1913* This was a 6.35mm FN-Browning 1906 copy, without the grip safety; the only odd feature was the use of the usual over-sized "Eibar" safety catch at the rear of the frame rather than above the trigger. Markings included "6 ³⁵ 1913 AUTOMATIC PISTOL / "DESTROYER" PATENT" in two lines on the left side of the slide, sometimes over "MADE IN SPAIN". The plastic grips bore an encircled "IG" above "DESTROYER".
- *Model 1914* This was the original 7.65mm version of the basic design, with a seven-round magazine and the safety catch on the left rear side of the frame. Apart from the caliber and the date, the slide marking was similar to the 1913 type. The grips were generally plain checkered wood.
- *Model 1916* Based on the 7.65mm Ruby, this was made for the French army. The magazine held nine rounds, the safety catch was moved to the left side of the fame above the trigger and a lanyard ring was attached to the left side of the butt heel. The slides of wartime guns were marked "CAL 7 ⁶⁵ PISTOLET AUTOMATIQUE "DESTROYER"…" above "I. GAZTAÑAGA – EIBAR" on the left side above the trigger aperture. A small "IG" in an oval usually lies on the left rear of the frame behind the checkered wooden grip. A variant, apparently marked "1916 MODEL", was made for the post-war commercial market with a shorter butt and a seven-round magazine.
- *Model 1918* When World War I finished, the opportunity was taken to revise the original 6.35mm gun by improving quality, moving the safety catch to the mid-frame position, changing the slide inscription to "CAL 6 ³⁵…" and omitting the quotation marks around the brand name.
- *Model 1919* The 7.65mm version reappeared as a copy of the 1910 FN-Browning but with a prominent stripping catch in the frame above the trigger and the safety catch at the rear of the frame. The advent of the stripping catch, which resembles the slide-stop of the Colt M1911, suggests some interior changes. However, it merely holds the slide to the rear while dismantling the barrel in the same way as a 1903-type FN-Browning. The guns usually bear "1919 MODEL" on the slide and have black plastic grips decorated with an "IG" monogram in an oval above "DESTROYER".

Indian A 7.65mm nine-shot "Eibar" automatic manufactured in the 1920s, this was identical with the "Army Model Destroyer".

Sûreté This is a modified version of the 1919-type Destroyer, without the auxiliary stripping catch. Doubtlessly intended to promote sales in France, the name appears in the slide marking; the only indication of manufacturer is an inconspicuous "IG" monogram stamped on the frame.

A 32-caliber Gaztañaga Sûrete pistol, lacking its lanyard ring.

GAZTAÑAGA, TROCAOLA & IBARZABAL
Eibar, Spain.
The gunmaking business operated by Isidro Gaztañaga (above) became "Gaztañaga, Trocaola y Ibarzabal" in 1933.

Super Destroyer This appeared to be a copy of the Walther PP but was really little more than a 1910-type FN-Browning with a muzzle bush retaining the return spring around the barrel. The lockwork is single action, and the slide-mounted safety catch, which merely locks the firing pin, has no effect on the external hammer. The slide was marked "PISTOLA AUTOMATICA CAL. 7.65 / "SUPER DESTROYER"…" in two lines, the name was molded into the black plastic grip and the finish was surprisingly good. The guns were apparently sold by José Mugica, a dealer in Eibar, but the beginning of the Spanish Civil War in 1936 brought production to an end after only two years.

GENERAL MOTORS
Guide Lamp Division of General Motors, Detroit, Michigan, USA.
Guide Lamp was a company skilled at pressing metal into peculiar shapes, and in 1942 they were given a government contract to produce the ".45 Flare Projector", which was designed to be assembled from stamped components. The company made a million in three months — one every 7.5 seconds, the only case on record of a pistol being made faster than it could be reloaded.

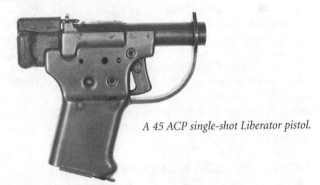

A 45 ACP single-shot Liberator pistol.

Liberator The "Flare Projector" was, in fact, a single-shot 45-caliber pistol to be dropped to resistance groups and other clandestine forces operating behind enemy lines. It was packed complete with ten 45 ACP rounds and a comic-strip set of instructions that even an illiterate could understand, all in a waterproof bag at a total cost of $2.10 "F.O.B. Detroit". It was a smoothbore with a 4-inch barrel and a manually operated breechblock. A sliding trap in the butt allowed five cartridges to be carried.

The striker was pulled back and rotated 90 degrees, allowing the breechblock to be lifted to reveal the chamber. A cartridge was inserted, the block was closed and the striker could be rotated back to the cocked position to lock the breech. Pressure on the trigger then released the striker. After firing, the breech was opened, the case was pushed out with a pencil or twig, and the weapon re-loaded.

The guns were christened "Liberator" when the secrecy that surrounded them was relaxed. About half were shipped to Britain, the remainder going to China and the Pacific. However, the value of the single-shot pistols was openly questioned; they were difficult to load, inaccurate and of far less value than the Sten Guns that were being made in Britain in huge numbers. Most of the pistols sent to Britain were dumped in the Irish Sea or melted-down to recover valuable raw material. The fate of those in the Far East, however, is less certain.

GENSCHOW
Gustav Genschow AG, Hamburg, Germany.
This business has been involved in the production of primers and ammunition since the 19th century, its various headstamps (including

"G", "GD", "GECO", "G G & Co" and "cxm") being well known. As one of Germany's leading distributors of sporting guns and ammunition prior to 1914, Genschow also marketed a variety of handguns.

∼ REVOLVERS ∼

Geco   A variety of hammerless solid-frame revolvers made by Francisco Arizmendi (q.v.) were offered. The 6.35mm versions, with folding triggers, could almost be classified as Velo-Dog types; the larger examples, though retaining the same general specification, could accept 7.65mm Auto, 32 S&W Long or 8mm French Ordnance cartridges.

German Bulldog   These were heavy solid-frame double-action guns, with pivoting loading gates and ejector rods beneath the barrel. Chambered for a variety of cartridges, including 32 S&W Long, 380 CF and 45 Long Colt, they were probably supplied by gunmakers in Belgium — Manufacture Liégeoise d'Armes à Feu, perhaps, or Henrion, Dassy & Heuschen (Manufacture d'Armes "HDH").

∼ AUTOMATIC PISTOLS ∼

Geco   These 6.35mm "Eibar"-type blowbacks were also acquired in Spain, perhaps from several differing sources. No other details are available.

GERING

H.M. Gering & Co., Arnstadt, Germany.
A gunmaking business active shortly after the end of World War I.
Leonhardt   This is exactly the same as the "Beholla" (q.v.) made by Becker & Hollander but differs from the others in this group (the Menta and Stenda) in not carrying military acceptance marks. Positive evidence is lacking, but what is known tends to suggest that in the early 1920s Gering bought up the stock of unfinished and unassembled components from Becker & Hollander and Stendawerke and assembled them into finished pistols bearing the Leonhardt name. Once this stock had been exhausted, Gering left the pistol business as abruptly as he had entered it.

GERSTENBERGER & EBERWEIN ("EM-GE")

Em-Ge Sportgerat GmbH & Co. KG, Gerstenberger & Eberwein, Gerstetten-Gussenstadt, Germany.
A successor to Moritz & Gerstenberger, trading prior to 1945 in Zella-Mehlis, this precision-engineering business recommenced the manufacture of revolvers and starting pistols in the 1950s.

Under the names "Em-Ge", "G & E", "Omega" and "PIC", and a bewildering collection of model numbers, the company has marketed a series of inexpensive solid-frame double-action revolvers chambered for 22 rimfire or 32 centerfire ammunition. The barrel lengths range from 2.25 to 6 inches, and the cylinders almost always have six chambers. One pattern is gate-loaded, with ejection performed by removing a pin carried in the cylinder arbor and punching out the cases; the other has a spring-loaded ejector rod on the bottom right side of the barrel, aligned with the loading gate.

The Em-Ge Model 22G rimfire revolver.

An Em-Ge M324 (4-inch barrel), in S&W Long chambering.

This M326T Em-Ge revolver has a 6-inch ventilated-rib barrel and an adjustable rear sight. It chambers the 32 S&W centerfire round.

Gerstenberger & Eberwein products sold widely in the USA until the 1968 Gun Control Act became effective in 1970; since then they have been confined largely to Europe.

GIACOSA

Luciano Giacosa & Co., Brescia, Italy.
This small Italian gunmaker manufactured inexpensive solid-frame non-ejecting double-action 32- and 38-caliber revolvers in the 1960s that were sold in the USA by the EIG Corporation and marked "EIG Italy" on the topstrap.

GLISENTI

Soc. Siderurgica Glisenti, Turin, Italy.
Glisenti entered the pistol business by manufacturing the 1889-type Italian army revolvers in such large numbers that the design is sometimes listed as a Glisenti. A reorganization at the beginning of the 20th century formed Società Siderurgica Glisenti, and the development of an automatic pistol began.

The gun was credited to Revelli, an army officer, but was undoubtedly influenced by the Mauser C/96 (which had been purchased by the Italian navy in 1899). Claims have been made that Revelli took some of the features from the Swiss Haussler & Roch pistol, but it is probable that this gun was also inspired by the Mauser. Trials to find a new Italian service pistol began in 1903, and, in 1906, the Glisenti company obtained machine tools from Britain to allow series production to begin.

In 1907, however, Glisenti sold manufacturing rights to Metallurgica Bresciana gia Tempini (q.v.). MBT had been making parts for the pistol for some time and now took over the entire project, buying more tools from Germany, but by late 1908, they were in production with a version of what had become known as the Glisenti pistol, chambering an odd 7.65x22 necked cartridge.

M1906   This 7.65mm gun failed to satisfy the Italian army and was redesigned to accept a 9mm cartridge copied from the German Parabellum. This developed a lower velocity than its German prototype in an attempt to reduce the recoil.

M1910   Formally adopted in 1910, this became the standard Italian service pistol. It is assumed that the contract allowed MBT to exploit the design commercially but that a duplicate production line installed in the Brescia small-arms factory was to satisfy military needs.

An Italian 9mm M1910 Glisenti pistol.

The need for reduced-charge ammunition was also dictated by the construction of the pistol. The breech was locked by a wedge, pivoted in the frame, that engaged in a recess beneath the bolt. When the gun was fired, the barrel, the barrel extension and the bolt moved back about 7mm, allowing the wedge to turn far enough to release the bolt. The barrel assembly stopped, retained by the depressed locking wedge, and the bolt continued to recoil. When the bolt returned to strip a new round out of the magazine, the wedge rose to free the barrel and re-engaged the bolt. The barrel-return spring then pushed the mechanism back into the firing position. But the operating cycle was so rapid that the effect was more of a delayed blowback than a locked breech.

The construction of the frame was also too weak to withstand the battering of a powerful cartridge. Removing a screw in the front of the frame, held by a spring catch, allowed the entire left side of the frame to be removed. This emphasizes that the main part of the frame lacks stiffness and does not give sufficient support to the left side of the barrel extension. Prolonged firing also loosened the side-plate.

Unlike most pistol designs, the closing stroke of the breech did not cock the striker. Pulling the trigger pushed the striker back against its spring before releasing it to strike the primer of the chambered round, resulting in an unnecessarily long and unpleasant trigger pull. Safety was provided only by a lever set in the front edge of the grip.

MBT made small quantities of the Brixia pistol, essentially an improved Glisenti intended for commercial sale, but the M1910 remained in production into the early 1920s. It had been supplemented from 1916 onward by large quantities of Spanish-made "Ruby"-type guns and by ever-increasing deliveries of the 1915-type Beretta. Finally, in 1934, the Beretta was adopted as the standard military and police handgun. Yet substantial quantities of old Glisenti pistols remained in service until the end of World War II.

GLOCK AG

Deutsch-Wagram, Austria.

Founded by Gaston Glock in 1963, this precision-engineering business — supplier of machine-gun belts, grenades, combat knives and entrenching tools — surprised the world in 1983 by winning a competitive trial to provide 25,000 pistols for the Austrian army. Glock had never made pistols before and unexpected success (in 1984 Norway became the first NATO army to adopt the Glock) forced the company to recruit sub-contractors until the Deutsch-Wagram facilities could be suitably enlarged. Since that time, however, the guns have acquired such a sound reputation for reliability and simplicity that subsidiaries have been opened in the USA (Smyrna, Georgia, 1985), Hong Kong (1988) and Uruguay (Montevideo, 1990). A new factory was opened in 1988 in Ferlach, the traditional home of the Austrian gunmaking industry, to handle ever-increasing demand. The 2,000,000th Glock pistol was exhibited at the SHOT Show in the USA at the beginning of 1999, and, by the end of 2000, more than 2.5 million guns had been sold to military and police forces in a hundred countries.

At the time of its introduction, there were a number of "scare stories" in the popular press, based on the use of plastic in the weapon and suggesting that it was an ideal terrorist gun that would evade detection at airports and other security checks. There was no substance at all in these stories, as it has been conclusively shown that there is more than sufficient steel in the construction to show up on even the most primitive X-ray or similar search device.

~ AUTOMATIC PISTOLS ~

The identification of Glock pistols is usually facilitated by the markings on the left side of the slide, which include the Glock trademark, the designation (e.g., "17", "23"), "AUSTRIA", and the chambering. The serial number and the proofmarks will be found on the right side of the slide and the right side of the barrel alongside the chamber, visible through the ejection port. The number also appears — on most guns, at least — on a metal plate set into the underside of the frame beneath the muzzle. Guns may also be found with marks of ownership, customarily on the slide, and a few special "commemorative editions" have been made.

These have included a thousand *Desert Storm* commemoratives, marked "OPERATION DESERT STORM" on the right side of the slide, above "January 16 – February 27, 1991" on the right side of the slide; two thousand guns presented to law-enforcement personnel responsible for security during the Atlanta Olympic Games, which bear "ATLANTA" over "GA. 1996" ahead of "USA" above the interlocking-ring Olympic symbol; and a group made for the National Rifle Association, which bear the individual gun number ahead of "…of 725" and an "NRA" logo on the right side of the slide near the muzzle. The Metropolitan Police of Washington DC and the Missouri State Highway Patrol are among the police organizations known to have had their marks placed on the slide.

All Glocks incorporate the "Safe Action Trigger" system, but the frames, in particular, have been the subject of variety. The original guns had plain-surface frames with the grip areas roughened to improve grip, but these were replaced in January 1986 by the so-called "pebble frame". This gave way in March 1989 to a version with checkering on the straps and then successively to a frame with finger-grips on the frontstrap (1995); to a frame with finger grooves and a rail beneath the muzzle that accepted light and laser projectors (1998); and finally to the current version that amalgamates finger grips, the rail, and a key-operated immobilizer in the rear of the grip behind the magazine well.

An extensive range of accessories includes a variety of front sights (polymer, steel, or Meprolight and Trijicon night patterns), different-height rear sights to correct aim, extended trigger releases and hold-open levers, and laser or light-projector holders. There are even two alternative trigger-spring units, developed at the request of the New York Police Department, to increase the pull to approximate that of a service revolver.

Magazine capacities given for each individual gun are those that Glock considers to be standard in all markets other than the USA, where magazine capacities have been restricted to 10 since 1994. It must be remembered, however, that each gun can accept virtually any magazine used within the same group as long as it is the same size or smaller than the gun for which the magazine was designed. Consequently, a "Compact" Glock will take the standard magazine, but not the sub-compact pattern; a sub-compact gun, conversely, having the shortest frame, will accept any of the magazines, which, in the case of 9mm Parabellum, could include the 33-round magazines associated with the Glock 18.

Magazine options associated with the 9mm Parabellum Glocks include 10, 12, 15, 17, 19, and 33 rounds; 357 SIG magazines hold 9, 13, 15 or 17 rounds; 380 ACP magazines hold 10, 12, 15, 17 or 19 rounds; 10mm Auto magazines are restricted to 10 or 15 rounds only; 40 S&W magazines may contain 9, 10, 11, 13, 15 or 17 rounds; and 45 ACP examples (with the exception of the special Glock 36 type) will hold 9, 10 or 13 rounds.

The 9mm Glock 17 in its case.

Glock 17 (1983 to date) Adopted in Austria in 1983 and approved by NATO a year later, this was the gun on which all the others have been based. Chambered for the 9mm Parabellum cartridge, using an adaptation of the familiar dropping-barrel breech lock, the Glock contains merely 34 parts (including two pins) and has a 17-shot double-column magazine. The frame is a composite construction of alloy and synthetic material, which helps in keeping the weight down. The self-cocking firing mechanism relies on pressure on the trigger to disengage a trigger-safety device before the striker can be cocked and then released to fire. At all other times, the striker is in the safe, half-cocked position. No manual safety devices are provided, as the Glock has a trigger safety, an automatic firing-pin lock, and an automatic trigger-bar safety device to prevent firing unless the trigger is correctly pulled. The guns are about 7.3 inches long, have 4.5-inch barrels with polygonal rifling and weigh 22 oz without their magazines. Ten-round magazines are currently standard in the USA, owing to the restrictions of the 1994 law, but a 19-round version can be obtained for use elsewhere. All Glock pistols have exceptionally durable Tenifer finish on their slides, giving a surface that is claimed to be harder than diamond.

- *Glock 17C and 17CC* These are variants with gas-escape ports in the barrel and a single slot cut in the slide on each side of the front sight. The "C" suffix signifies "Compensated"; "CC" is "Compensated Competition", showing that the guns have extended magazine and slide-release catches, specially honed triggers and adjustable rear sights. The "CC" suffix, however, is not usually recognized in Europe as a legitimate distinction.
- *Glock 17L Competition* (1988 to date) Little more than a Glock 17 with a 6-inch barrel, this competition-shooting "Longslide" derivative is 8.9 inches long and weighs about 24 oz without its magazine. The first 800-1000 Glock 17L pistols had compensators consisting of three gas-escape slots cut laterally across the barrel, but these were subsequently abandoned.

The long-barreled/long-slide version of the Glock 17, known as the "17L".

Glock 18 (1985 to date) This was developed by adding a fire selector and developing 19- and 33-round magazines to turn the gun into a machine pistol. The Glock 18 is about 1.3 inches longer than the Glock 17 and has a cyclic rate of fire of 1200 rds/min. It is not available commercially, being restricted to military and police customers, and has been made only in very small numbers.

A Glock Model 19 Compact pistol.

Glock 19 (1988 to date) A "compact" version of the Glock 17, this is 6.9 inches long, has a 4-inch barrel and weighs about 21 oz without its 15-round magazine. The earliest guns were made from cut-down Glock 17 frames, and the first commercial production had checkering on the grip straps.

- *Glock 19C and 19CC* Compensated versions of the Glock 19. See "Glock 17C and 17CC", above.

Glock 20 (1989 to date) Similar to the Glock 17, this is chambered for the 10mm Auto cartridge. It is 7.6 inches long, has a 4.6-inch barrel and weighs 27 oz without its 15-round magazine. Guns sold in the USA are currently restricted to 10 rounds.

- *Glock 20C and 20CC* Compensated versions of the Glock 20. See "Glock 17C and 17CC", above.

Glock 21 (1989 to date) Chambered for the 45 ACP cartridge, with magazines restricted to 10 (US market) or 13 rounds, this is otherwise similar to the Glock 20. It is 7.6 inches long and weighs about 26 oz without its magazine.

- *Glock 21C and 21CC* These are merely compensated versions of the Glock 21. See "Glock 17C and 17CC", above.

The 40 S&W Glock Model 22.

Glock 22 (1990 to date) A slight enlargement of the Glock 17, this is chambered for the 40 S&W cartridge. Dimensions are similar, but the gun weighs 23 oz without its standard 15-round magazine.

- *Glock 22C and 22CC* Compensated versions of the Glock 22. See "Glock 17C and 17CC", above.

Glock 23 (1990 to date) This is similar to the Glock 19, but chambers the 40 S&W cartridge. A 13-round magazine is standard.

- *Glock 23C and 23CC* Compensated versions of the Glock 23. See "Glock 17C and 17CC", above.

Glock 24 (1994-2001) Intended for competition shooting, this is a long-barreled version of the Glock 22, chambering the same 40 S&W

cartridge. Fitted with a 6-inch barrel, the Glock 24 is 8.9 inches long and weighs 27 oz without its 15-round magazine.

• *Glock 24C and 24CC* These are simply compensated versions of the Glock 24. See "Glock 17C and 17CC", above.

Glock 25 (1995 to date) Though externally similar to the locked-breech Glock 17, this is actually a simple blowback derivation chambered for the 380 Auto (9mm Short) cartridge. Offered with 15-round magazines, the Glock 25 is about 6.9 inches long, has a 4-inch barrel and weighs 20 oz.

Two sub-compact Glock pistols: 40 S&W Model 27 (top) and 9mm Parabellum Model 26 (bottom).

Glock 26 (1996 to date) The first of the "sub-compact" designs and mechanically identical with the Glock 17, this can be recognized by its short barrel and short grip. Chambered for the 9mm Parabellum round, it is 6.3 inches long, has a 3.5-inch barrel and weighs 20 oz. The standard magazines hold 12 rounds, but a 10-round version is made for sale in the USA.

Glock 27 (1996 to date) This is a sub-compact pattern in 40 S&W, with magazines holding nine rounds.

Glock 28 (1997 to date) A variant of the Glock 26 blowback in 380 ACP/9mm Short, this shares the short barrel/short grip "sub-compact" construction of the Glocks 26 and 27. It weighs about 19 oz and has a 10-round magazine.

Glock 29 (1997 to date) Another of the sub-compact series, this is chambered for the 10mm Auto round. It is 6.8 inches long, has a 3.8-inch barrel and weighs 25 oz. Magazines hold 10 rounds.

Glock 30 (1997 to date) Similar to the Glock 29 except for chambering 45 ACP, this has a magazine holding 10 rounds.

Glock 31 (1998 to date) Chambered for the 357 SIG cartridge, this is basically a Glock 17 in a different guise. It is 7.3 inches long and weighs about 23 oz without its 15-round two-column magazine.

• *Glock 31C and 31CC* Compensated versions of the Glock 31, these can be identified by the slots cut in the top of the slide alongside the front sight. See also "Glock 17C and 17CC", above.

Glock 32 (1998 to date) This is the compact version of the Glock 31, with a 4-inch barrel that reduces overall length to 6.9 inches. The magazines hold 13 rounds.

• *Glock 32C and 32CC* These are simply the compensated versions of the Glock 32. See "Glock 17C and 17CC", above.

Glock 33 (1998 to date) The sub-compact variant of the Glock 31, instantly identifiable by its short slide and short grip, this is 6.3 inches long, has a 3.5-inch barrel and weighs 20 oz. Magazines hold nine rounds.

Glock 34 (1997 to date) Chambered for the 9mm Parabellum round, this long-slide gun is 8.2 inches overall, has a 5.3-inch barrel and weighs about 23 oz. Magazines hold 17 rounds, but the most distinctive features are the ported barrel and the cut-out panel in the slide immediately behind the front sight.

Glock 35 (1997 to date) This is a 40-caliber version of the Glock 34, with identical porting arrangements. Magazines hold 15 rounds.

Glock 36 (1999 to date) The most powerful of the sub-compact Glock pistols, this chambers the 45 ACP cartridge and has a magazine restricted to six rounds in a single column. The guns are 6.8 inches long and weigh only 20 oz.

Glock 37 (2000 to date) This is a full-size gun, similar to the Glock 17, but chambering the new 45 Glock cartridge. The guns are 7.4 inches long and weigh 32 oz with a full 10-round magazine.

Training pistols The Glock 17T (introduced in 1997) can fire 9mm FX ammunition, loaded with color-marking or rubber bullets. Alternatively, 7.8 x 21AC practice cartridges can be used, each containing a charge of compressed air. Guns of this type are distinguished by their bright blue frames. There are also a variety of red-framed guns in the "P" and "R" series. "P" guns (currently confined to models 17P, 19P, 22P, 23P and 26P) are basically dummies, intended to familiarize potential Glock users before they get to the firing range. "R" guns (Glock 17R, 19R) are capable of projecting a "pulse" of laser light as the trigger is pulled, enabling training and instruction to take place in conjunction with video or film projection.

GRÄBNER

Georg Gräbner, Rehberg, Krems/Donau, Austria.

Kolibri (1914-25) Gräbner gave us the smallest-caliber automatic pistol and centerfire cartridge ever made. Placed on the market shortly before World War I began, the gun was based on the Pfannl (q.v.) Erika. This was small enough, but Gräbner decided to make an even smaller version intended to give women a self-defense weapon.

What effect a 3-grain bullet might have had on an aggressor is questionable; its velocity was perhaps 500 ft/sec — Wilson was unable to get it to register on a chronograph — so that the muzzle energy was about 2 ft/lb, less effective than all but the smallest air pistol.

The Kolibri was a smoothbore, with a fixed barrel and a reciprocating breechblock reminiscent of the Clément. The 3mm version, with a shorter barrel, is rarer than the 2.7mm version. A detachable 5-round box magazine was contained in the butt, and a safety catch lay on the left side of the frame.

FABRIQUE D'ARMES [DE GUERRE] DE GRANDE PRÉCISION

Eibar, Spain.

This "company" was actually a trading name registered by Extezagarra y Abitua of Eibar, a resounding title adopted in order to promote sales in Europe by suggesting French or Belgian origin. The title was often shortened by omitting "de Guerre", and the guns seem to have been acquired from a variety of sources. Consequently, it is now difficult to determine the chronology or attribution of many individual brand names — or to determine whether any of the many variations on the Grande Precision trading style were used deliberately by rival companies! These included "Fabrique d'Armes de Precision" (applied by José Aldazabal), and "Fabrique d'Armes de Guerre", used by gunmakers identified only by an "LE" monogram — Larranaga y Elartza — or the initials "L C."

Attributable guns The defining qualities of these, and the unattributable examples, are the presence on the slide of the Fabrique d'Armes [de guerre] de Grande Précision name, which may appear in a variety of lettering styles. They may also display "EC" monograms, often encircled, which is suspected to represent "Extegarra y Cia" — a successor to Extegarra y Abitua, if it can be realistically assumed that the original partnership was short-lived.

A Grande Précision 7.65mm-caliber Colonial pistol.

- *Bulwark* See "Beistegui Hermanos".
- *Colonial* See "Domingo Acha".
- *Helvece* See "Domingo Acha".
- *Libia* See "Beistegui Hermanos".
- *Looking Glass* See "Domingo Acha".
- *Titánic* See "Francisco Arizmendi".

Unattributable guns There are several of these:

- *Ca-Si* This is a 7.65mm six-shot "Eibar"-type gun with the safety catch in the mid-frame position and radial slide-retracting grooves. A sunburst surmounted by "CA-SI" appears on the grips. The attribution to Grande Précision is still uncertain, as no guns have been examined with appropriate markings.
- *Continental* Lacking a maker's mark, this 7.65mm gun has a drag-on motif on the grip, associated with Tómas de Urizar. The slide inscription includes a reference to Patent 16137.
- *Jupiter* A 6.35mm "Eibar" automatic of the usual Browning 1906 type, with an "EC" monogram but no manufacturer's mark. One gun, with the safety catch on the left side of the frame above the trigger and vertically milled grooves in the slide, includes "PATENT DEPOSE 43915" in its markings. The 7.65mm pattern, with the safety catch in the mid-frame position and retraction grooves that are milled radially, is marked similarly.
- *Liberty* A 6.35mm "Eibar"-type blowback with magazines of six, 10 or 11 rounds, this may be marked "MODEL 1913" or include "1924" in the inscription. None of the guns that could be traced bore any clue to their manufacturers.

The Grande Précision Minerve, a typical "Eibar-type" blowback pistol.

- *Minerve* (or "Minerva") Made by a gunmaker using an "LS" (or "SL") monogram. These are practically the same as the 6.35mm "Colonial" and the 7.65mm "Jupiter", both standard "Eibar" types. The grips on the 6.35mm version have a florid "LS" monogram in the top section, and both patterns have "LS"-monogram grip medallions. Other examples are unmarked.
- *Precision* A six-shot 7.65mm "Eibar" blowback identified only by a slide inscription that includes "PRECISION", but with a Ca-Si grip.

- *Princeps* Made by a gunmaker using the monogram "ET" or "TE", this 7.65mm "Eibar" was also sold by Tómas de Urizar (q.v.). One of the guns examined had no markings, a mid-frame safety catch and radial slide grooves; another, with the monograms, had the safety catch at the rear, vertically-milled grooves, and a full-length grip-safety lever set in the backstrap.
- *Principe* A six-shot 6.35mm, this lacked makers' marks.
- *Puma* A conventional 7.65mm gun — with a nine-round magazine and a suitably extended butt — this had the safety catch at the rear of the frame, vertical retraction grooves and a lanyard ring on the left side of the butt-heel. An unidentifiable shield of arms (probably a registered trademark of some type) was molded into the grips.
- *Trust* This 6.35mm "Eibar"-type gun, with a six-round magazine, is marked with nothing but its name in the slide inscription; the nine-shot 7.65mm version, conversely, has an ornate "TRUST" trademark ahead of the slide legend. Neither bears any indications of the manufacturer. The safety catch lies on the left side of the frame above the trigger, and the retraction grooves are usually vertical.
- *Trust-Supra* This six-shot 6.35mm or 7.65mm pistol is an almost exact copy of the Browning 1906, down to the grip safety and rear-mounted safety catch, though of obviously poorer quality. The slide carries the full Grande Précision name, but the grips display the dragon associated with Tómas de Urizar.

GREAT WESTERN ARMS CO.
Los Angeles, California, USA.
This company, operating only in 1953-61 from various California locations, sold a series of Colt SAA replicas in 22, 38 and 45 caliber under the names "Frontier", "Deputy" and "Buntline". They were of Italian origin.

GREEN
Edwinson C. Green, Cheltenham Spa, Gloucestershire, England.
Green was a "country gunmaker" of considerable repute, patenting numerous improvements relating to shotgun mechanisms, and it has been claimed that he invented the "over-and-under" shotgun. He also obtained British Patent 29321 of 1889, laying claim to various details of

A 450 centerfire revolver by E.C. Green.

Another Green break-open revolver, this time in 476 chambering.

revolver construction, including a stirrup-type barrel latch for hinged-frame revolvers with a cut-out on the rear face that prevented the barrel being unlatched if the hammer was down. As a result of this, he became involved in a long-drawn-out lawsuit with Webley, who claimed prior rights to the stirrup lock. Green showed that he had been making revolvers with this lock since 1883, and a beneficial agreement was reached with Webley. (Mr. Green's late grandson, who was still running the family business in Cheltenham in the mid-1970s, gave access to original documents relating to this lawsuit.)

Revolvers were made in a workshop in Cheltenham and can be frequently encountered. They were 450- or 455-caliber hinged-frame self-extracting "military-style" patterns with the Green Patent stirrup lock. Quality was good, and the revolvers were popular with British army officers. Manufacture ceased some time in the late 1920s.

GRENDEL

Grendel, Inc., Rockledge, Florida, USA.
This company made a limited range of double-action semi-automatic pistols characterized by frames and magazines made of high-strength polymers.

The Grendel P-10, showing the charger-loading feature.

P-10 (1989-95) Chambered for the 380 ACP round, this had a 10-round magazine loaded through the top of the action. The finish on the composite metal/polycarbonate frame/grip unit was usually matte black, but green Teflon and electroless nickel plating were available as options. The guns were about 5.3 inches long, with a 3-inch barrel, and weighed 15 oz empty. The sights were fixed.

P-12 (1992-4) A minor variant of the P-10, with the magazine capacity increased to 12 rounds to comply with the 1994 Gun-Control Act, this had a blued slide.

P-30 (1990-4) Easily distinguished from the other Grendels by its size — the barrel measured 5 inches — this 22 WMR pistol had a full-length grip that accommodated a 30-round magazine. The sights were fixed, the chamber was fluted, the safety catch was reversible and the frame/grip unit was made of Xytel. The guns were about 8.5 inches long and weighed 21 oz.

• *P-30L* (1990-4) A variant of the basic P-30 with an 8-inch barrel.
• *P-30M* (1992 only?) This was a P-30 with a detachable muzzle brake/compensator.

P-31 (1991-5?) Distinguished by an 11-inch barrel, fitted with a muzzle brake/compensator, this was a cut-down carbine chambering the 22 WMR round. Finished in matte black, it was 17.5 inches long and weighed 48 oz.

GRUSONWERKE AG

Magdeburg, Germany.
This company, which was renowned for armor plate before being swallowed by Krupp in 1893, made a brief foray into handgun design in the early 1890s. DWM produced a 7.4mm cartridge (No. 501) for a Grusonwerk gas-seal revolver, but it is doubtful if anything other than prototypes were ever made; no specimen is known to exist. The gun resembled rival gas-seal designs (see "Nagant"), but the barrel was pulled back into engagement with the cylinder instead of the cylinder moving forward to abut the barrel.

GUISASOLA

Fábrica de Armas Benito Guisasola, Eibar, Spain.
The only pistol attributed to this firm is a 38 revolver, a copy of the S&W Military & Police, produced in the late 1920s. The cylinder is released not by a catch on the frame but by a latch on the cylinder crane arm that is similar to the Ojanguren y Vidosa (q.v.) design. The Guisasola revolver can be identified by a prominent hammer axis pin passing through the frame, absent from the Ojanguren designs. It also carries a unique exhortation on the barrel: "USE U.S. STANDARD AMMUNITION".

GUISASOLA BROTHERS

Guisasola Hermanos, Eibar, Spain.
Undoubtedly connected in some way with Benito Gusiasola (above), perhaps a predecessor, this partnership made only a handful of guns.

∼ REVOLVER ∼

G.H. This was a 6-shot, double-action copy of the S&W Military & Police, dating from the late 1920s, with an S&W-type cylinder latch. It was chambered for the 38 S&W Long cartridge.

∼ AUTOMATIC PISTOLS ∼

G.H. Guns of this type were "Eibar" automatics in 6.35mm and 7.65mm, made by Gabilondo y Urresti — which casts doubt on the parentage of the Guisasola revolvers.

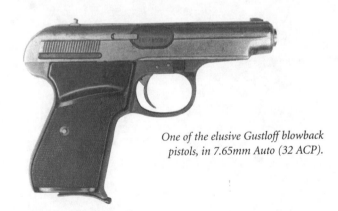

One of the elusive Gustloff blowback pistols, in 7.65mm Auto (32 ACP).

GUSTLOFF-WERKE

Suhl, Germany.
This engineering business made a variety of small arms during the Third Reich in factories in Suhl (code "dfb"), Weimar ("bcd") and Meiningen ("nyw").

Gustloff-Selbstlade-Pistole Work began on a 7.65mm blowback pistol in 1938, in the hope of attracting a military contract. The gun had a return spring around the barrel, an internal hammer and a unique hammer-spring tensioning lever protruding from the top of the left grip. This worked in conjunction with a double-action lock, reminiscent of the mechanism of the Sauer 38H. If the hammer was cocked, tension could be removed from its spring by using the lever; if the hammer was down, the pistol could be fired double-action by pulling the trigger.

A specimen pistol was presented to Hitler in January 1940, together with the suggestion that it might be a suitable police pistol. Arrangements were made for guns to be made in the Weimar factory, using, it has been alleged, inmates of the nearby Buchenwald concentration camp as the labor force, and Gauleiter Sauckel of Weimar made several applications for a prototype order. But no order ever appeared, and the project was abandoned.

Apart from details from correspondence by Sauckel, in the German State Records, few records or drawings of the project remain though a few guns survive (with both steel and die-cast zinc frames). Those that are marked usually display "G" in the form of a shield above "GUSTLOFF WERKE" over "WAFFENWERK SUHL" on the left side of the slide and a similar encircled "G" motif on the grips

Volkspistole A program was instituted by the German government in 1944-5 to develop a variety of emergency weapons (e.g., the "Volksgewehr" or "People's Rifle") for the Volkssturm and other home-defense organizations. This envisaged the mass-production of cheap and easily made weapons, though few of the plans made the transition from ideas to reality.

Several handgun prototypes have been identified, produced by Mauser and Walther, but the identification of the Gustloff participants is still uncertain. Common features included the standardization of the P. 38 magazine, the extensive use of stampings in construction and the use of the 9mm Parabellum cartridge. This hindered the development of blowback pistols, which would have been the simplest solution.

It is assumed that the Gustloff pistols incorporated a delay system inspired by the Volks-Gerät 1-5, a light semi-automatic carbine designed by Barnitszke, though the surviving guns of this type are now attributed to Mauser-Werke (q.v.).

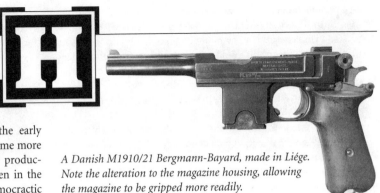

HAENEL

C.G.Haenel, Waffen und Fahrradfabrik, Suhl, Germany.
The Haenel firm dates back to 1840 and for much of its
early life was a general engineering company. The first
involvement with pistols appears to have been as a contractor, making the Commission-designed Reichsrevolver in the early
1880s. In the 1930s, Haenel moved away from pistols to become more
involved with submachine-gun design and military weapon production. Hugo Schmeisser died in 1946, and the factory, by then in the
Soviet zone of occupation (subsequently the German Democratic
Republic), had soon been absorbed into the state-controlled Ernst
Thälmann Werke. Airguns and sporting guns were made until trading
ceased in 1993.

∼ REVOLVER ∼

Reichsrevolver Haenel made these guns (see "Erfurt Rifle
Factory"), often in partnership with Spangenberger & Sauer and V.C.
Schilling. These guns bear cartouches containing "S. & S. – V.C.S." or "S.
& S. – V.C.S. – C.G.H." respectively.

∼ AUTOMATIC PISTOLS ∼

Haenel-Schmeisser This designation covers two essentially similar
6.35mm-caliber blowback pistols. In 1921, Hugo Schmeisser, who had
been working for Th. Bergmann, came to Haenel as chief engineer, and
he brought with him a pocket-pistol design that he had patented in 1920.

- *Model 1* This had one or two unusual features. The barrel was held
  in place by the recoil spring guide rod passing through a lump
  beneath the breech and into a recess in the frame, the safety catch
  was linked to the magazine catch so that the magazine could not be
  removed unless the pistol was set safe, and the catch could not be
  set to fire until the magazine was replaced. It was a well-made pistol and went into production in 1922, continuing until 1930. The
  slide was marked "C.G. Haenel Suhl, Schmeisser's Patent" and the
  grips carry an "HS" monogram.
- *Model 2* A new gun appeared in about 1927, whereupon the original version was retrospectively renamed "Model 1". The new pistol
  was mechanically the same as its predecessor but was shorter and
  more "squared-off" externally, lighter and looking as if it had been
  inspired by the Mauser WTP. The gun was marked "*C. G. HAENEL
  SUHL, SCHMEISSER'S PATENT*" above "*MODELL II*" on the left
  side of the slide with "SCHMEISSER" across the top of the grip.
  Production of the Model 2 does not appear to have continued for
  long, since they are less common than the Model 1.

HÆRENS TØJHUS

Copenhagen, Denmark.
The Danish government small-arms factory was responsible for a variety of handguns, including refurbishment of revolvers and production
of a version of the Bergmann-Bayard pistol.
M1910/21 In 1922, deprived of supplies for the Bergman-Bayard
from Belgium and faced with mounting losses of handguns through
wear and tear, the Danish government elected to copy the basic design.
The new version had large hard-plastic grips, and the cover-plate let
into the side of the frame was held by a screw instead of a spring catch.

Danish-made guns are marked "HÆRENS TØJHUS" (prior to
1923) or "HÆRENS RUSTKAMMER" (1923-32). Existing Belgian-
made M1910 pistols were modified as they fell due for repair, acquiring
large grip plates and sometimes also a "M1910/21" designation. The
guns remained in service throughout World War II. A decision had
been taken to replace them with the FN-Browning GP 35 in 1940, but
few (if any) of the latter had been delivered before the Germans over-
ran Denmark and Belgium.

*A Danish M1910/21 Bergmann-Bayard, made in Liége.
Note the alteration to the magazine housing, allowing
the magazine to be gripped more readily.*

HAMAL

Victor Hamal, Liége, Belgium.
Hamal patented a locked-breech automatic pistol of unknown (but
large) caliber in 1902. Inquiry of the patent agent elicited the fact that
the fees in respect to the patent had been paid by Webley & Scott, so
presumably the prototype model was made in Birmingham. It used a
cam-locked bolt moving in a barrel extension and had a removable
magazine ahead of the trigger guard in Mauser fashion. Photographs of
the pistol exist, but no example is known to survive.

HÄMMERLI

Lenzburg, Switzerland.
Founded as a gun-barrel manufactory in 1863, by Johann Ulrich
Hämmerli (1824-91), this became "Hämmerli & Hausch" in 1876 and
then "Rudolf Hämmerli & Co." in 1921. The business remained in the
family until Rudolf Hämmerli died in 1946, when the firm became
Hämmerli & Co. AG. It was acquired by SIG in 1971 and is now sometimes known as "SIG-Hämmerli", though only the P-240 pistol carries
this name.

The first Martini-action Free Pistols were made in 1933, though
many target rifles had been made (often on Vetterli or Schmidt-Rubin
actions) prior to this date. In 1951, however, the company acquired a
license to make the Walther Olympia-Pistole, which subsequently
inspired the "International" series. Limited quantities of high-quality
"Frontier" revolvers (Colt Peacemaker clones) were made in the 1960s
and 1970s, many being distributed in the USA by Interarms.

∼ SINGLE-SHOT PISTOLS ∼

Martini-action guns These Free Pistols, which owed something to
the success of German designs such as the Tell and Luna, made by Ernst
Büchel (q.v.) were intended for a specialized form of target-shooting.
Consequently, they showed great sophistication —especially in the
design of the trigger, the grips and the sights.

- *Model 33 Matchpistole* ("Modell 33 MP") The MP33 had an octagonal barrel chambered either for 22 LR rimfire or 22 Extra Long No.
  7. The action was opened by a lever set in the butt, and the three-
  lever set trigger was cocked by pressing a lever on the left side of the
  breech. The rear sight was mounted on an extension of the frame
  above the anatomical palm-rest grip. Only a hundred guns had been
  made by 1947, when similar numbers of slightly modified guns
  were made. Assembly ceased in 1949.
- *Model 100* This was a simplified form of the MP33, chambering the
  same two rimfire cartridges and retaining an octagonal barrel.
  However, the action was improved, the rear sight was modernized
  and a new five-lever trigger mechanism was developed (easily recognizable by the setting button protruding from the trigger blade).
  The trigger-pull could be adjusted to less than a third of an ounce.
  The rifling had six grooves instead of four, and the trigger-guard
  bow was enlarged. The first gun was tested in the summer of 1950,

series production began a year later and work stopped in 1956.

- *Model 101* (1956-60) This was a variant of the M100 with a tapered-cylinder barrel, a few minor changes to the action and an improved walnut grip. It could be distinguished from the otherwise-identical M102 by its non-reflective browned finish. Chambering was restricted to 22 LR rimfire.
- *Model 102* Introduced in 1956, this was identical with the M101 except for its high-polish finish.
- *Model 103* Made from 1956 until 1960, this was a variant of the M102, with similar attention paid to finish. It had an octagonal barrel and was habitually taken as the basis for the highly decorative guns made to individual order.
- *Model 104* Introduced in 1962, this was a modified M101 with a lightweight tapered-cylinder barrel. The most obvious identification features were the enlarged slab-side grip, the squared trigger-guard bow and a plain fore-end that lacked the schnabel tip of its predecessors. Production ceased in favor of the M106 in 1965.
- *Model 105* (1962-5) This was simply a variant of the M104 with an octagonal barrel.

The 22-caliber M106 Hämmerli-Martini Free Pistol.

- *Model 106* An improved 1965-vintage form of the M104 with a cylindrical barrel, this also had an improved five-lever set trigger with an adjustable let-off pressure from 0.5 to 3.5 ounces. The trigger blade lacked the setting button of the earlier designs. Assembly ceased in 1972.
- *Model 107* Made from 1965 to 1971, this was a version of the M106 with an octagonal barrel; consequently, many "deluxe" examples were made.

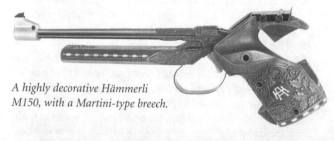

A highly decorative Hämmerli M150, with a Martini-type breech.

- *Model 150* The result of extensive development undertaken in 1968-9, this 22 LR rimfire Free Pistol was introduced in 1972 to replace the Models 106 and 107. It retained a Martini-type pivoting-block action, but this was opened by pulling upward on a lever on the left side of the breech, directly above the downward-moving lever that cocked the striker and set the five-lever trigger. The barrel floated freely above a wooden fore-end — bored to receive counterweights — and a newly designed anatomical grip lowered the line of the bore in relation to the shooter's hand. The M150 was replaced by the M160, below.

- *Model 151* This was a 1990-vintage replacement for the Model 150, differing principally in the design of the grips. It was itself superseded by the Model 160 (below).

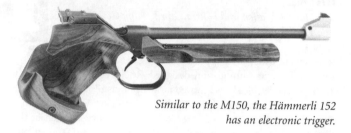

Similar to the M150, the Hämmerli 152 has an electronic trigger.

- *Model 152 Electronic* A variant of the M150 with an electro-magnetic trigger system powered by a battery in the fore-end, this appeared in c. 1974. The trigger gave a very short lock time and had an exceptionally light and precise pull, adjustable from a fifth of an ounce to 2.8 ounces. Indeed, it was so sensitive that it was said that a sharp puff of wind could fire the gun. Consequently, it was recommended that the power be switched off during loading.

The 22-caliber Hämmerli M160 target pistol.

- *Model 160* Dating from 1993, this was an improved version of the M150. Changes were made in the trigger system (adjustable from 0.35 to 3.5 ounces); the fore-end was synthetic; the trigger blade was adjustable for reach, cant and angle; and the walnut anatomical grip could be adjusted for rake. A variety of inserts for the front and rear sights were also available. Among the most obvious characteristics were the matt-finish barrel and the thumb-screw adjuster on the base of the grip.
- *Model 162 Electronic* Announced contemporaneously with the M160, this had an electronic trigger adjustable from one fifth of an ounce to 2.8 ounces. Identification was helped by red/green LEDs and associated toggle switches on the left upper face of the fore-end.

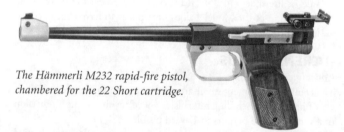

The Hämmerli M232 rapid-fire pistol, chambered for the 22 Short cartridge.

Model 120 A simplified single-shot 22-caliber "Sport Pistol" introduced in 1969, this abandoned the Martini breech in favor of a bolt sliding within the frame. Pulling outward on a lever on the left side of the breech retracted the bolt and exposed the chamber. Most guns had a 10-inch barrel, an alloy frame and a micro-adjustable rear sight. A ramp on the receiver accepted a telescope sight, which could be used in conjunction with a skeleton butt that attached to the back of the frame and the base of the butt. The standard M120 was 14.8 inches long and weighed about 44 ounces.

- *Model 120 HB* (or "Bull Barrel") Made only in small numbers, this had a 5.7-inch heavy barrel. It was mechanically identical with the standard pattern.

∽ REVOLVERS ∽

Based on the Colt Peacemaker, these "Frontier-style" guns were commissioned by Interarms. They were made only in small numbers.

Virginian Dragoon Made only in 357 Magnum or 45 Colt calibers, this offered the same barrel-length and fixed/adjustable sight options as its predecessor. However, the trigger guard and backstrap were chromed, the barrel and cylinder were blued and the frame was case-hardened. The guns were fitted with the Hämmerli "Swissafe" system, which relied on the cylinder arbor pin being pushed back until it locked. This prevented the hammer falling far enough to fire the cartridge. Virginian Dragoon revolvers could be identified by a narrow flute in the frame above the cylinder and by markings that included "PAT. Nº 3,803,741" over "DATE APR. 16, 1974" on the left side of the frame above the front of the trigger guard. Production was moved to the Interarms (q.v.) factory in 1976-7.

∽ AUTOMATIC PISTOLS ∽

Hämmerli-Walther series The pre-war Olympia-Pistole was also much too good a design to remain dormant, and production began in Switzerland in the small Hämmerli factory in Lenzburg. This company had a long and honorable association with target guns, including Martini-type Free Pistols, but had had no previous experience with auto-loaders.

Walther had offered Hämmerli the chance of entering a market with a proven design needing very little development, a license being concluded in March 1950. Hämmerli was granted worldwide sales rights, excepting South Africa, and royalties were paid to Walther until the early 1960s.

- *Model 200* Swiss-made guns differed from their German predecessors largely in the style and position of markings. The first slides to be made in Lenzburg had only 20 retraction grooves, milled diagonally, but shared the design of the Walther sights and barrel weights. The guns were 11.6 inches long and had 7.5-inch barrels. Many styles of decoration were offered at extra cost, and auxiliary weights, in three separate pieces, could be used in five differing combinations.

The pistols were mechanically identical with the pre-1945 German guns, with an internal hammer that struck an inertia-type firing pin, a radial-lever safety and a cross-bolt magazine release on the left side of the frame ahead of the grip.

Hämmerli slides were originally marked "Lenzburg Hämmerli-Walther Switzerland" on the left side, ahead of "Olympia-Pistole". "Hämmerli" took the form of the company trademark, "Walther" was cursive, and "Olympia-Pistole" was in italic. The serial numbers of 22 Short rimfire rapid-fire competition pistols began at 0-100; the 22 LR rimfire version commenced at 0-5000. The caliber marks appeared on the right side of the slide above the trigger aperture.

A new three-slot muzzle brake and compensator was introduced in 1954, when the design of the grips was changed. An adjustable trigger was fitted from 1956 onward, and a new two-slot compensator appeared in 1957 by a shorter two-slot design, when the supplementary weights were revised.

- *Model 201* (1955-7) Fitted with a three-slot compensator and an adjustable trigger, this was offered in 22 Short or 22 Long Rifle with alloy or steel slides, respectively. Owing to its 9.4-inch barrel, the Model 201 was soon banned under ISU rules.
- *Model 202* (1955-7) Offered in 22 Short and 22 Long Rifle, this was simply a version of the Model 201 with a special adjustable French-walnut palm-rest grip — intended for Free Pistol shooting — instead of the standard thumb-rest type.
- *Model 203* (1956-9) Introduced soon after the sensational appearance in the Melbourne Olympic Games of the long and unorthodox inverted-action Soviet MTsZ-1 target pistol, this short-barreled 202 conformed with then-current competition rules. The earliest guns had the wide palm-rest grip, but those made after another change of rules in 1957 had a narrower design. The M203 was 12.4 inches long, with a 7.5-inch barrel, and weighed 28.9 ounces (22 Short, six-round magazine, alloy slide) or 34.2 ounces (22 Long Rifle, eight-round magazine, steel slide).
- *Model 204* "Amerika-Modell" (1956-63) Introduced to satisfy US National competition rules instead of the European ISU legislation, this 22 LR rimfire gun had a multi-directional micro-adjustable rear sight mounted on the slide, a trigger pull of not less than 2lb and a sighting radius no greater than 9.5in. The guns also had a hold-open that held the slide back after the last round had been fired and ejected. The slide catch had to be pressed to allow the slide to close and chamber a new round once a fresh magazine had been inserted in the feed-way. The Model 204 had fixed French-walnut thumb-rest grips.
- *Model 205* "Amerika-Modell" (1956-63) Also available only in 22 LR, this was a variant of the 204 with an adjustable palm-rest grip. This gave an overall length of 12.5 inches.

Hämmerli-International series The Models 204 and 205 were the last of the true Hämmerli-Walther Olympia-Pistoles, being replaced in 1962 by the first "Hämmerli Internationals" (Models 206, 207). Only 4223 Hämmerli-Walthers had been made. Fewer, indeed, than Walther had made prior to the Second World War.

- *Model 206* Introduced in 1962, this was similar internally to the Hämmerli-Walthers even though few of the parts would interchange. Externally, however, the simplified contours of the frame and the slide were distinctly "squared" and the rear sight was placed on top of a rigid housing through which the slide recoiled. Versions were offered in 22 Short for rapid-fire shooting and 22 Long Rifle for other pistol competitions, magazine capacities being six and eight rounds, respectively. The 7.1-inch barrel was fitted with a standard three-slot muzzle-brake/compensator. There were 27 slide-retracting grooves, milled slightly diagonally; the French walnut grips followed the customary thumb-rest design, and a new adjustable trigger had been developed.

The guns were marked "Hämmerli International" on the left side of the slide ahead of "Lenzburg" over "Switzerland". "Hämmerli" took the form of the company trademark, and "International" was cursive. The caliber marks and "Olympia" were rolled into the right side of the slide. The M206 was distinguished from the otherwise similar 207 (q.v.) by the grips, which are the fixed thumb-rest type.

- *Model 207* (1962-8) This was little more than the Model 206 with a one-piece palm-rest grip adjustable for height and rake. The gun was 12.5 inches long, with a depth of about 5.9 inches and a width approaching 2 inches at the greatest point. It was offered in 22 Short (alloy slide) and 22 LR (steel slide), with magazine capacities of six and eight rounds, respectively. Auxiliary weights added 5-13 ounces, depending on configuration. Sufficient parts were stored to allow sales of new guns to continue into the 1970s.
- *Model 208* (1966-88) Chambered exclusively for the 22 Long Rifle round, this was introduced for the German "Gebrauchspistole" events — basically the ISU Standard Centerfire Pistol course shot with rimfire guns. The gun was little more than a shortened M207, without the muzzle brake. A trigger stop and a slide-lock were standard fittings, with a standard Walther-type radial safety lever and a cross-bolt magazine catch on the left side of the frame. The magazine release was moved in October 1967 to the base of the butt, and the manual safety was discarded when changes were made in the trigger a few months later.

The Model 208 was 10 inches long and had a 5.9-inch barrel. Shortening the barrel forced a change in the pitch of the rifling, which changed from a turn in 17.7 inches to one in 15.7 inches. The adjustable palm-rest grip gave an overall depth and maximum width conforming with the then-current ISU and most national-association rules

- *Model 208s* (1986 to date) An improved model of the 208, this was immediately recognizable owing to the deeply squared trigger guard. This allowed the trigger lever a 0.7-inch longitudinal adjustment, in addition to regulation for first stage or "take-up" length, take-up weight, second-stage or "let-off" length, and let-off weight. The sights were improved by the addition of an interchangeable rear-sight element.

- *Jubiläumspistole* Early in 1988, Hämmerli introduced the special commemorative variant of the Model 208 to celebrate the company's 125th anniversary. Supplied in a specially fitted case of walnut veneer, only 1000 guns were made.

- *Model 209* (1966-70) Introduced concurrently with the Model 208 and chambered only for the 22 Short rimfire cartridge, this rapid-fire pistol offered some unusual features. The trigger pull could be adjusted between 12.3 and 26.5 ounces, and a large adjustable muzzle-brake/compensator appeared at the muzzle. The slot in this brake was cut diagonally to deflect part of the propellant gases upward in an effort to counteract muzzle jump in concert with six holes bored into the top surface of the barrel. The three barrel ports nearest the muzzle were threaded to receive short plug-screws, enabling the gun to be adjusted to fire ammunition of differing powers. This feature is believed to have originated in France but had been copied in the Soviet Union by the time it was adopted by Hämmerli.

  Model 209 pistols made in 1968-70 had three additional longitudinal slots cut in the barrel behind the front sight to counteract the natural tendency of the shooter to pull the muzzle leftward. The magazine catch was moved to the butt heel, and the safety lever disappeared towards the end of 1967.

- *Model 210* (1966-70) This was a variant of the Model 209 with an adjustable palm-rest grip, which increased the maximum depth to 5.9 inches and the overall width to about 2 inches.

- *Model 211* (1966-88) This was simply a variant of the Model 208, chambering the 22 LR rimfire cartridge, with fixed thumb-rest grips. From the mid-1980s onward, these guns were fitted with the plain flat-sided grips of the Model 212 (q.v.).

- *Model 211s* Introduced in 1986, this was an improved form of the basic 211, incorporating the features described above for the Model 208s.

- *Model 212* This simplified form of the basic International design, dating from 1978, was designed for sporting use. Alternatively, when fitted with the optional safety catch, it satisfied the competition requirements of the German hunting association (DJV). The gun shared the action of the Model 208 but had a fixed-notch rear sight mounted on the slide. The retracting grooves were duplicated at the front of the slide, but the gun otherwise bore a remarkable resemblance to the pre-war Olympia-Pistole.

- *Model 215* Though the exemplary quaiity of the Model 208 cannot be argued, high price discouraged many prospective buyers. The M215, therefore, was introduced in an attempt to keep costs to a minimum. More than 30 machining and finishing stages were eliminated, though the pistol was still impeccably made and functioned flawlessly. The most obvious recognition feature was the humped base for the front sight.

- *Trailpistole PL-22*, or "Trailside PL-22"(1999 to date) This is the current representative of the Walther Olympia-Pistole derivatives, essentially a modernized Model 212. It has a one-piece-frame barrel shroud, often with a contrasting half-slide and muzzle weight. The grips may be colored synthetic moldings or walnut, often

including an adjustable palm rest. The rear sight is adjustable, but the top of the frame is grooved to accept optical-sight mounts. The trigger is an adjustable two-stage pattern. A typical example is 7.8 inches long, with the 4.5-inch barrel, and weighs about 28 oz empty; the optional 6-inch barrel increases weight by about 3 oz.

Model 230 Introduced commercially in 1970 after trials lasting two years (a prototype was exhibited at the Swiss industrial-design exhibition in 1969), this replaced the Hammerli-Internationals, which had been overtaken in rapid-fire competitions by more modern designs. The M230 was a 22 Short rimfire blowback with a separate breechbolt reciprocating within a frame that extended back above the shooter's hand, a trigger-release pressure regulated at 15.6-19.4 ounces and a

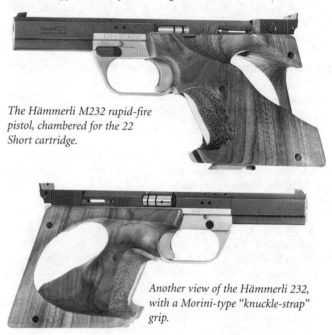

The Hämmerli M232 rapid-fire pistol, chambered for the 22 Short cartridge.

Another view of the Hämmerli 232, with a Morini-type "knuckle-strap" grip.

five-cartridge magazine in the butt. Dismantling could be undertaken without tools. The guns were about 11.6 inches long, had 6.3-inch barrels and weighed about 43.7 ounces. They could be recognized by their angular appearance and by the wedge-like extension beneath the rear of the frame. The *230-1* had a conventional grip, with a thumb-rest, whereas the *230-2* had an enlarged grip with a palm-rest. Production ceased in 1983.

The SIG-Hämmerli M240 pistol in 32 S&W Long Wadcutter.

Model 232 This short-barreled version of the M230 appeared in 1977, overall length being merely 10.4 inches. Six stabilizer holes were drilled directly into the upper surface of the 5.1-inch barrel to prevent the muzzle climbing during rapid fire, and the trigger was fully adjustable. The *232-1* (or "232A") had a conventional palm-rest grip;

the *232-2* ("Model B") had a hand-enveloping Morini grip, with a band of wood to restrain the back of the firing hand.

Model 240 (or "SIG-Sauer P-240") The rise in full-caliber target shooting led Hämmerli to combine with SIG to produce this pistol, which is essentially a target version of the SIG P-210 military pistol. It uses the same dropping-barrel breech lock, relying on engagement between a massive one-piece lug over the breech and the ejection opening. The P-240 was made to a very high standard of fit and finish. The barrel, for example, was swelled at the muzzle to form a lapped fit into the forward end of the slide (the fit was too precise to allow interchangeability).

The pistol was originally made specifically for 32 S&W Long and 38 Special Wadcutter ammunition, but persistent feed problems forced the latter to be abandoned in the early 1980s and work stopped altogether in 1986. A 22 LR fixed-barrel blowback version was made for practice or small-caliber competition shooting; and conversion units were developed to adapt centerfire guns to rimfire.

Model 280 Released in "pre-production form" in 1987 but not made in quantity until 1989, this exceptionally successful rapid-fire competition pistol marked another change in design, placing the magazine ahead of the trigger and adopting an alloy slide and a weight-saving carbon-fiber frame to allow precise adjustments of balance to be made with a variety of steel and carbon-fiber weights that attached to a rail beneath the frame ahead of the magazine. Chambered either for 22 LR rimfire or 32 S&W Long Wadcutter ammunition, the gun had a modular trigger unit (35.3 or 48 ounces). The trigger blade could be adjusted for reach, let-off point and over-travel, and the adjustable anatomical walnut grip had a palm-rest.

• *Model 280 Exclusive* Made in small numbers in 1996-7 to celebrate the first decade of competition successes, this was distinguished by a streamlined stabilizer weight that fit beneath the fore-end and extended back around the magazine housing. Marked "Exclusive", in an imitation of handwriting, the weights were available in blue, black, red, green or gold, the colors being repeated on the bolt, the retraction grips and the magazine-release button.

• *Model 280 Special* The standard 280 was extremely successful, but undeniably expensive. This 1996 introduction attempted to reduce costs without compromising efficiency, the most obvious changes being the "Hi-Grip" — molded synthetic instead of high-quality walnut — and fewer accessories.

SP-20 (1998-2001?) This was a target pistol, seen as a replacement for the Model 280. Offered in 22 LR rimfire or 32 S&W Long centerfire, it was about 11.8 inches long (with a 5.6-inch barrel) and weighed 35 oz without auxiliary weights. The anatomical "Hi-Grip" butt was available in five sizes, and the receiver could be anodized black, blue, gold, red or violet. The rear sight was micro-adjustable, the front sight could be set to three widths and a "JPS" buffer system was incorporated to alter the recoil characteristics so that (for example) a 22 gun could serve as a trainer for the 32 version. The detachable box magazine lay ahead of the trigger and the gun was designed to lie as low in the hand as possible.

HAMMOND

Grant Hammond Mfg. Co., New Haven, Connecticut, USA.
Hammond, an American, patented a gas-operated automatic pistol in 1914, but there is doubt as to whether it was ever made. He later became associated with Harrington & Richardson (q.v.), who made guns in the hope of gaining interest from the US Army.

HARRINGTON & RICHARDSON, INC.

Worcester (1874-1973) and Gardner (1973-87), Massachusetts, USA.
This company was formed in 1874 by Gilbert H. Harrington and William A. Richardson for the manufacture of revolvers. It was incorporated in 1888; both founders died in 1897. The company was reorganized in 1905, contracted and moved in 1973 and finally closed in 1987. It had made three million revolvers by 1907 and for many years maintained a reputation for reliability combined with low price.

The range of handguns was extensively revised after World War II and identified by new model numbers, which, for simplicity, are listed in numerical order. Unfortunately, H&R products were not sufficiently attractive to compete with foreign imports or the cutthroat firearms market of the 1970s and 1980s, and operations eventually failed. The New England Firearms Company has continued to make a few of the basic shotguns and revolvers, but the assets of the original company were acquired by Marlin in November 2000. See also "H&R 1871, Inc."

∼ REVOLVERS ∼

Aetna The first products of the firm were the inevitable cheap, single-action, stud-trigger, solid-frame revolvers under the name *Aetna No. 2* or *Aetna No. 2-1/2*. These were both five-shot 32-rimfire weapons, the No. 2 with a 2.5-inch octagonal barrel and bird's-head butt, and the No. 2-1/2 with a 2.44-inch barrel and square butt. The pistol was of better quality than most of its competitors, and its sales gave the company a good start in life. In 1876, an improved version, the *Model 1876*, appeared in 22, 32 and 38 rimfire chamberings, and in 1887, the company patented a double-action lock with "safety hammer" that led to a better revolver design.

American Associated with a "Suicide Special" made c. 1885-90 and also found on a solid-frame 32-, 38- or 44-caliber revolver dating from much the same era.

American Double Action Introduced in about 1888, this was a 32-caliber solid-frame gun, loaded through a gate on the right side of the frame behind the six-chamber cylinder. The cylinder could be removed simply by extracting the arbor pin. Revolvers of this type can

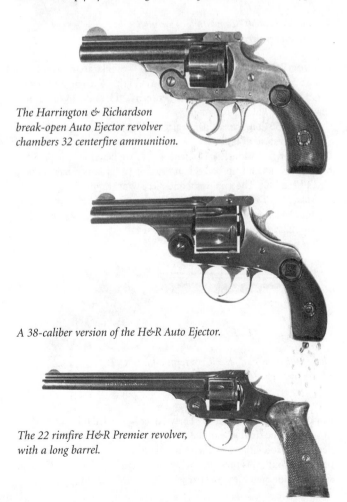

The Harrington & Richardson break-open Auto Ejector revolver chambers 32 centerfire ammunition.

A 38-caliber version of the H&R Auto Ejector.

The 22 rimfire H&R Premier revolver, with a long barrel.

be found with 2-, 4- or 6-inch octagonal barrels and usually have hard rubber grips with an ornate geometric design.

Automatic Ejecting Model The first of this series of tip-barrel revolvers appeared in 1897, developed from patents granted to H&R, Andrew Fyrberg and others. The guns had ribbed barrels, a spring-latch holding frame and barrel unit together, and a cylinder-retaining catch in the topstrap. They also introduced the later-familiar H&R pierced-target trademark, molded into the grips. Most of the guns were made in 32 or 38 centerfire, with barrels measuring 3.75, 4 or 5 inches.

• *Premier* A variant of the basic Automatic Ejecting design in 22 rimfire or 32 centerfire.

• *Bicycle* This was distinguished from the standard guns by the chambering, which was confined to 22 rimfire, and the 2-inch barrel.

• *Police* A variant of the Premier, in the same chamberings, this was fitted with a Safety Hammer.

• *Knife Model* Offered in 32 or 38 centerfire, this had a 4-inch barrel with a 2.5-inch knife blade that pivoted beneath the muzzle. Production was apparently small, with the 38-caliber version predominating.

Bicycle A top-break 22-rimfire double-action, 5-shot revolver chambered for the 32 S&W round, dating from the mid-1890s.

The nickeled M650 "Convertible" Harrington & Richardson revolver, in 22 LR and 22 Magnum rimfire.

Convertible (or "Model 649 Convertible") Similar to the M622, this had a 5.5- or 7.5-inch barrel and hardwood grips. Exchangeable cylinders allowed the shooter to choose between 22 LR and 22 WM rimfire chamberings.

• *Model 650 Convertible* Identical with the M649, this was finished in nickel instead of blue.

Defender (or "Model 925 Defender") Chambered for the 38 S&W round, this six-shot tip-barrel hand ejector had a 2-inch barrel and a bird's-head butt. The grip was a one-piece wraparound design.

• *Model 926 Defender* This designation was applied to two differing double-action tip-barrel guns: a five-shot 38 centerfire or a nine-shot 22 rimfire, both with 4-inch barrels.

One of the nine-shot "H&R Westerns", this is a 22 LR rimfire Model 949 with a 5.5-inch barrel.

Forty-Niner (or "Model 949 Forty-Niner") Loaded through a pivoting gate on the right side of the frame behind the nine-chamber cylinder, with a rod ejector on the right side of the barrel and a well-proportioned butt, this presented a "Western-style" appearance. The rear sight was adjustable and the trigger was a double-action type.

• *Model 950 Forty-Niner* Distinguished by nickel finish instead of blue, this was a minor variant of the M949.

Guardsman (or "Model 732 Guardsman") Finished only in blue, this was a 32-caliber solid-frame gun with double-action lockwork, a six-chambered cylinder, barrels of 2.5 or 4 inches, and a side-swinging cylinder. Ejection was undertaken manually.

• *Model 733 Guardsman* This was simply the M732 finished in nickel instead of blue and was usually restricted to the 2.5-inch barrel option.

The Harrington & Richardson M732 was a swing-cylinder revolver, in 32 S&W Long.

A convertible 22 LR/22 WM rimfire H&R Model 686 revolver, with a 5.5-inch barrel.

Gunfighter (or "Model 660 Gunfighter") A six-shot solid-frame "Frontier-Style" revolver chambering the 22 LR rimfire round, this had a spring-loaded ejector rod and a double-action lock. The barrel was 5.5 inches long, and the grips were walnut.

• *Model 686* Little more than an elongated version of the Gunfighter (M660), this was offered with barrel-lengths of 4.5–12 inches.

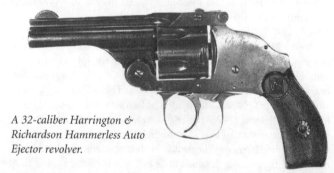

A 32-caliber Harrington & Richardson Hammerless Auto Ejector revolver.

Hammerless Model Introduced c. 1899, this was little more than the Automatic Ejecting Model with the rear of the frame raised to con-

A Harrington & Richardson M622, with a 4-inch barrel.

ceal the hammer in the usual manner. It was made in many guises, in 22, 32 or 38 caliber, with barrels of 2–6 inches.

Solid-frame designs, "numbered series":

• *Model 603* A six-shot solid-frame double-action revolver in 22 WMR with swing-out cylinder and single-stroke ejection. The 6-inch barrel had flat sides, and the grips were smooth walnut.

• *Model 604* This was a M603 with target-style bull barrel and a raised barrel rib.

• *Model 622* A six-shot 22 LR solid-frame double-action gun, this had a 2.5 or 4-inch barrel, a round butt with black Cycolac grips and was finished in blue.

• *Model 623* A nickel-plated version of the M622.

• *Model 632* A variant of the M622 chambering the 32 S&W Long cartridge.

• *Model 642* Another version of the M622, accepting the 22 WMR round.

• *Model 826* This introduced the "800 series Personal Defense" revolvers and was simply the M603 with a 3-inch heavy or "bull" barrel and a smooth cylinder chambered for 22 Magnum rimfire ammunition.

• *Model 829* A 22 LR rimfire variant of the M826, with a nine-chamber cylinder.

• *Model 830* A variant of the M829, this was finished in nickel instead of blue.

• *Model 832* Similar mechanically to the rimfire M826, this was chambered for the 32 S&W Long round. The cylinder had six chambers.

• *Model 833* A nickel-plated version of the M832, which it otherwise resembled.

• *Model 900* This was a double-action non-ejecting 22 LR rimfire gun with a nine-chamber cylinder. The barrel measured 2.5 or 4 inches.

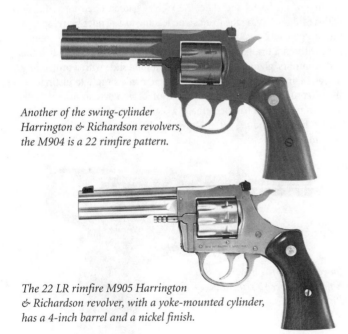

Another of the swing-cylinder Harrington & Richardson revolvers, the M904 is a 22 rimfire pattern.

The 22 LR rimfire M905 Harrington & Richardson revolver, with a yoke-mounted cylinder, has a 4-inch barrel and a nickel finish.

• *Model 903* Similar to the simpler M603, this nine-shot solid-frame double-action 22 LR rimfire revolver had a side-swinging cylinder and single-stroke ejection. The barrel was a flat-sided 6-inch pattern, and the grips were smooth walnut.

• *Model 904* A variant of the M903, this had a "bull" barrel with a raised rib.

• *Model 905* This was a nickel-plated version of the M904.

• *Model 922* A 9-shot 22-rimfire non-ejector with a solid frame and a double-action trigger system, this could be obtained with barrels of 2.5, 4 or 6 inches. The short-barreled version, known as the Bantamweight, had a round butt; the others had square butts.

• *Model 923* Distinguished by its nickel-plated finish, this was otherwise the same as the M922.

Models 1904, 1905 and 1906 Though the tip-barrel guns were very popular, H&R continued to make the cheaper and simpler solid-frame designs. A new design was introduced early in the 20th century. The 32- or 38-caliber Model 1904 had a 4-inch octagonal barrel and a good-sized butt. The 32-caliber *Model 1905* and 22 rimfire *Model 1906* were virtually indistinguishable.

New Defender A variant of the Sportsman with a 2-inch barrel as standard.

Safety Hammer Double Action This augmented the American Double Action, which used the same basic configuration. The rear face of the patented spurless "safety hammer" was concave and knurled, allowing the shooter to move the hammer back by pressing the trigger and then complete the cocking stroke with the thumb. The "safety" claim arose simply because the absence of a spur made the hammer less likely to catch in the pocket. The earliest guns were made for 32 centerfire ammunition but were soon so popular that they were supplemented by *Vest Pocket* models: a 7-shot 22 rimfire and a five-shot 32 rimfire, each with 1.1-inch barrels.

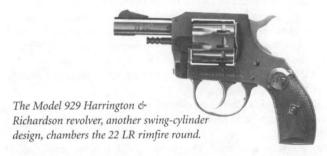

The Model 929 Harrington & Richardson revolver, another swing-cylinder design, chambers the 22 LR rimfire round.

Sidekick (or "Model 929 Sidekick") A nine-shot 22 rimfire with 2.5-, 4- or 6-inch barrels and double-action lockwork, this gun had a solid frame with a side-swinging cylinder. Rod-type ejection was used. The 4- and 6-inch barrel versions had adjustable rear sights.

• *Model 930 Sidekick* A variant of the M929, this was finished in nickel instead of blue and offered only with 2.5- or 4-inch barrels.

Special Another of the derivatives of Model 1906, this was a nine-shot 22 rimfire gun with a 6-inch ribbed barrel and target grips.

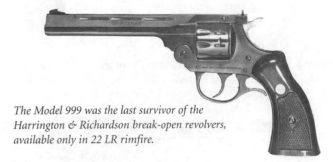

The Model 999 was the last survivor of the Harrington & Richardson break-open revolvers, available only in 22 LR rimfire.

Sportsman This tip-barrel revolver appeared in 1927, in single-action or double-action form. The design was based on the grip, size and balance of the USRA target pistol to produce a revolver capable of holding its own in competitions. Five interchangeable grip styles were offered, and the trigger guard had a spur that filled the gap between guard and grip to give a solid rest for the shooter's second finger. The chambers of the nine-shot cylinder were recessed, leaving a solid ring of steel around the outside of the cartridge rims to prevent metal splash from a case-head failure. The standard barrel length was 6 inches, though a 3-inch option could make an acceptable pocket pistol.

- *Model 999 Sportsman* (or "Deluxe Sportsman") Successor to the original 1927-type gun of the same name, this was a nine-shot tip-barrel auto-ejector with a 6-inch ventilated-rib barrel. The sights were adjustable, and the grips were generally checkered (though plastic versions have been seen). Chambering was restricted to 22 LR rimfire.

Trapper Introduced in 1907, this was based on the 22-caliber solid-frame M1906 but had a 6-inch octagonal barrel.

A 22 LR Model 939 H&R revolver.

Ultra Sidekick (or "Model 939 Ultra Sidekick") A 9-shot 22 LR rimfire gun with a 6-inch ventilated-rib barrel, this had a solid frame and a side-swinging cylinder. The rear sight was adjustable, the plastic grips had a thumb-rest and the barrel was distinctively flat-sided. A safety system prevented firing until unlocked with a special key, which appealed to those who bought the gun for domestic purposes.

- *Model 940 Ultra Sidekick* A variant of the M939, this had a round barrel.

USRA Model (1923-41) Introduced in 1923, this was a simple top-break revolver with an adjustable rear sight. A 10-inch barrel was standardized, though 7- and 8-inch alternatives were optional; the grips were also subject to variety. The popular USRA achieved considerable success in competitive shooting.

A typical 22-caliber Harrington & Richardson Young America revolver.

Young America This was similar to the original Safety Hammer model, in 22 rimfire or 32 centerfire. The *Young America Bulldog* was identical, except that it had a spur-type hammer.

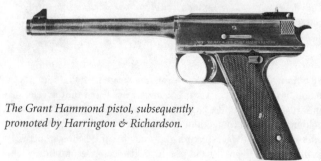

The Grant Hammond pistol, subsequently promoted by Harrington & Richardson.

∼ AUTOMATIC PISTOLS ∼

Grant Hammond (1915-17) This was a large, bulky 45 ACP pistol submitted to the US Army in 1917. It was recoil-operated, locked by a vertical plunger carried in the bolt that moved back inside the barrel extension. As barrel and bolt recoiled, the plunger was driven up by a cam to release the bolt to run back alone as the barrel extension was brought to a halt. The magazine was ejected automatically after the last shot had been fired, allowing a new magazine to be inserted with the minimum of delay. In general, the design was archaic — even for its time — and the guns were fragile and unreliable. The army rejected the Grant Hammond, which vanished into history after only a handful had been made.

The Harrington & Richardson 25 ACP pistol.

H&R Self-Loader (25 ACP version, 1913-16) Made under license from Webley & Scott, this was the Webley "Hammerless Model" of 1909. Like its prototype, the Harrington & Richardson pistol was hammerless in name only, the hammer being concealed internally, but the lockwork differed in detail. More obvious changes could be seen in the shaping of the barrel and slide; the Webley had an open-topped slide with a bridge carrying the front sight, leading to a slender barrel so that the bridge could pass across it in recoil. H&R used an open-topped slide without a bridge and built up the rear of the barrel to match the slide contours, giving the appearance of a solid slide with a protruding barrel. Many of these minor changes were made simply to distinguish the two products, and others avoided conflict with patents held by Colt. Though prototypes had been made as early as 1911, series production started in 1913 and ceased in December 1916 after 16,630 pistols had been made.

Based on the British Webley, this is the 32-caliber Harrington & Richardson pistol.

- *32 ACP version* (1916-24) Though this followed the original Whiting-patent Webley design in many respects, this had no direct Webley & Scott equivalent. It retained the internal hammer, the open-topped slide (with bridge), the slender barrel and the short grip-safety lever in the backstrap of the butt. A coil-type return spring replaced the Webley "V"-spring, and other changes were made in machining. The Harrington & Richardson pistol was introduced commercially in April 1916, superseding the 25 ACP design, and continued in production until June 1924. About 34,500 had been made when work finished, but sales were slow and new guns were still available from "factory stock" in the early 1940s.

HARRIS GUNWORKS, INC.
Phoenix, Arizona, USA
Best known for sporting and long-range sniping rifles, Harris has also made the *Signature, Jr.* long-range pistol. Introduced in 1992, this is built on a left- or right-hand bench-rest rifle action in titanium alloy or stainless steel. The guns can be supplied to order in virtually any chambering, usually with a barrel of about 12 inches and a weight of 5 lb. Some are single-shot, others may be fitted with a magazine; the combination grip/fore-end is almost always fiberglass.

HARTFORD ARMS & EQUIPMENT COMPANY
Hartford, Connecticut, USA.
This company is generally said to have come into existence in 1929, manufacturing the semi-automatic pistol, but studying the record of the Fiala Arms & Equipment Company (q.v.) reveals that the Blakeslee Forging Company, maker of the pistols sold as "Fiala", made the same pistol for a "Hartford Arms Co" to sell as "Columbia". Manufacture of these guns ceased in late 1923, but the external similarity of the semi-automatic pistol made by Hartford in 1929 and the manually-operated Columbia pistol made by Blakeslee in 1920-3 are too great to be entirely coincidental. Sales of the Fiala and its cousins were comparatively small, and it seems possible that the Hartford company re-designed the Fiala pistol into a proper semi-automatic.

Four differing patterns were made: a single-shot pistol, a repeater (virtually the Fiala/Schall/Columbia without the interchangeable barrel) and two blowback automatics. These guns looked very similar, with fixed barrels, half-slides and well-raked grips. Although several thousand good-quality pistols were made, the promoter failed in 1932. The Hartford assets including tools, stock and pistols were bought by High Standard (q.v.).
 ∼ SINGLE-SHOT AND REPEATING PISTOLS ∼
The slide of these guns remained closed when the pistol fired, to be unlocked, retracted manually, and returned to load a new round. A prominent safety catch lay behind the grip on the left side of the frame. The guns all had round barrels.
 ∼ AUTOMATIC PISTOLS ∼
These retained the safety catch behind the grip but had a second catch on the frame to double as a slide release and stripping catch. One of the guns had a round barrel, extending about 5 inches in front of the frame, but the other had a heavy slab-sided barrel that appears to be a continuation of the frame. All were marked with the company name on the left side.

HAWES FIREARMS
Los Angeles, California, USA.
This company was an importer rather than a manufacturer and distributed revolvers and automatic pistols under its own brand names.
 ∼ SINGLE-SHOT PISTOL ∼
Stevens Favorite A copy of a gun made in the 19th century by the J. Stevens Arms & Tool Co. (q.v.), this 22 rimfire had a tip-up barrel, plastic or rosewood grips, and fixed or adjustable sights.
 ∼ REVOLVERS ∼
Marshal series These were "Frontier" or "Western" types based on the 1873-model Colt Single Action Army revolver made in Germany by J.P. Sauer & Sohn (q.v.) and possibly also in Italy by Uberti or Armi San Marco. The guns all had six-chamber cylinders, regardless of caliber,

but the individual distinguishing characteristics are often difficult to determine.
- *Chief City Marshal* Available only in 45 Long Colt, this had a brass frame and adjustable sights.
- *Chief Marshal* This was chambered only for the two most common Magnum cartridges, 357 and 44, and had a 6.5-inch barrel. The guns were finished in blue, the trigger guard and the grip straps were brass and the rear sight was adjustable.
- *Denver Marshal* A variant of the Deputy Marshal, with adjustable sights and a brass frame.
- *Deputy Marshal* Advertised only in 22 LR and 22 Magnum rimfire, this had a 5.5-inch barrel.
- *Federal Marshal* Discontinued by 1992 and chambered for the 357 Magnum, 44 Magnum or 45 Long Colt rounds, this had a 6-inch barrel.
- *Montana Marshal* This was simply a Western Marshal with the trigger guard and backstraps of brass.
- *Silver City Marshal* Chambered for the 22 LR or 22 WM rimfire rounds, this had a 5.5-inch barrel. The sights were fixed and the finish was blue.
- *Texas Marshal* Little more than a "Western Marshal", this was finished in nickel instead of blue.
- *Western Marshal* Offered only in blue and in 22 LR rimfire, 22 WM rimfire, 9mm Parabellum, 357 Magnum, 44 Magnum, 44-40 WCF, 45 ACP or 45 Long Colt, this had barrels measuring 5.5 (22 only) or 6 inches. The sights were fixed.
Trophy A revolver of more modern type, based on the Sauer TR-6, this was a solid-frame double-action gun with a swing-out cylinder and hand ejection. It came in 22LR or 38 Special, with a six-inch barrel and adjustable rear sight.
- *Trophy Medallion* (or "Medallion") This was a simpler variant of the Trophy pattern, in the same chamberings, with a 3-, 4- or 6-inch barrel and fixed sights.
 ∼ AUTOMATIC PISTOLS ∼
Courier This was a 25 ACP pistol purchased from Rino Galesi (see "Rigarmi").
Diplomat A 380 ACP blowback automatic with an external hammer, dating from 1955-65, this is believed to have been either a Rigarmi or Bernardelli product.

HEBSACKER GESELLSCHAFT ("HEGE-WAFFEN")
Schwäbisch Hall, Germany.
Hege, more of a distributor than a manufacturer, has sold large quantities of handguns in Western Europe. These have included the "Hege AP-66", a Hungarian copy of the Walther PP made by FÉG, and the Spanish Astra Constable pistol. The FÉG Tokagypt was sold as the Firebird in 1967-75. After 1980, however, the company turned to the manufacture and distribution of blackpowder replica weapons.

HECKLER & KOCH GMBH
Oberndorf/Neckar, Württemberg, Germany.
The French army occupied the Mauser factory in Oberndorf in 1945. Though operations were continued into 1946, supplying standard German weapons to the French, protests from the other Allied nations forced work to cease. The factories were stripped of tools and equipment and effectively ceased to exist. In 1949, however, Edmund Heckler and Theodor Koch — ex-Mauser engineers — were allowed to reoccupy part of the old site to make machine tools, but they were eventually drawn into the Spanish CETME rifle project (initially as suppliers of machine tools). The result was the G3 rifle, which Heckler & Koch began to make for the Bundeswehr in 1959. This rifle laid the basis for an outstandingly successful range of small arms and associated equipment.

In 1990, however, a major contract for the revolutionary G-11 caseless-cartridge rifle failed to materialize, and H&K encountered financial difficulties. An announcement made in December 1990 suggested that the French state consortium (GIAT) was to purchase the business, but the agreement was cancelled in January 1991 and Heckler & Koch was acquired by Royal Ordnance (British Aerospace) of Great Britain.

The Heckler & Koch HK4 pistol can be seen as an improved version of the Mauser HSc.

The four interchangeable barrel/return-spring assemblies of the HK4.

The HK4 dismantled into its sub-assemblies.

other barrels and components, allowing the owner to change to any caliber at will.

The HK4 was sold in the USA in the 1960s in all calibers. From about 1968 to 1973, it was sold as the "Harrington & Richardson HK4" in 22 LR rimfire or 9mm Short, complete with conversion kit to another caliber.

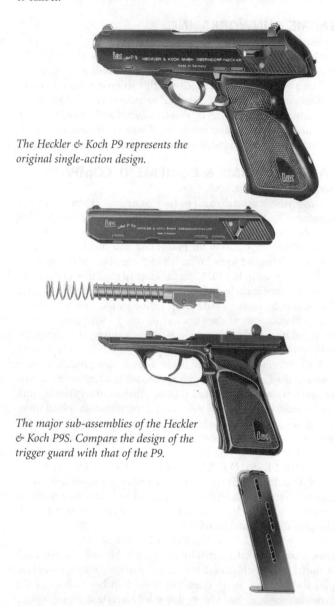

The Heckler & Koch P9 represents the original single-action design.

The major sub-assemblies of the Heckler & Koch P9S. Compare the design of the trigger guard with that of the P9.

HK4 (1964-83) The first of the H&K handguns, this was based on the Mauser HSc. The profile was different—the grips were plastic moldings with thumb-rests—but the dismantling, assembly and double-action lockwork were obviously derived from the earlier model.

The blowback pistol was offered in 22 LR rimfire, 6.35mm Auto, 7.65mm Auto or 9mm Short chamberings, though conversion from one to another was simply a matter of interchanging the barrels, return springs and magazines. The change from rim to centerfire also required a change to the strike of the firing pin, but this was also straightforward. The 9mm Short version could be purchased with a kit of the

P9 (1977-84) A delayed blowback, offered originally in 7.65mm and 9mm Parabellum, this incorporated a breech system derived from the G3. The front part of the two-part breechblock, mounted in the slide, carried two rollers that engaged recesses in the barrel extension. During the charging stroke, the heavy rear section of the bolt forced the rollers out into the recesses as the slide was closed. When the gun fired, the chamber pressure, acting on the bolt face through the base of the cartridge case, tried to force the rollers back. Careful shaping of the recesses in the slide tended to force the rollers inward, but movement was impossible until they had pressed on an angled tongue to force the heavy section of the breechblock backward. Once the inertia of the block (and the slide) was overcome, the rollers moved into the slide-body and the slide/breech-block assembly ran back to begin the reloading cycle.

The single-action P9 had a thumb-operated lever on the left side of the slide that allowed a cocked internal hammer to be lowered under

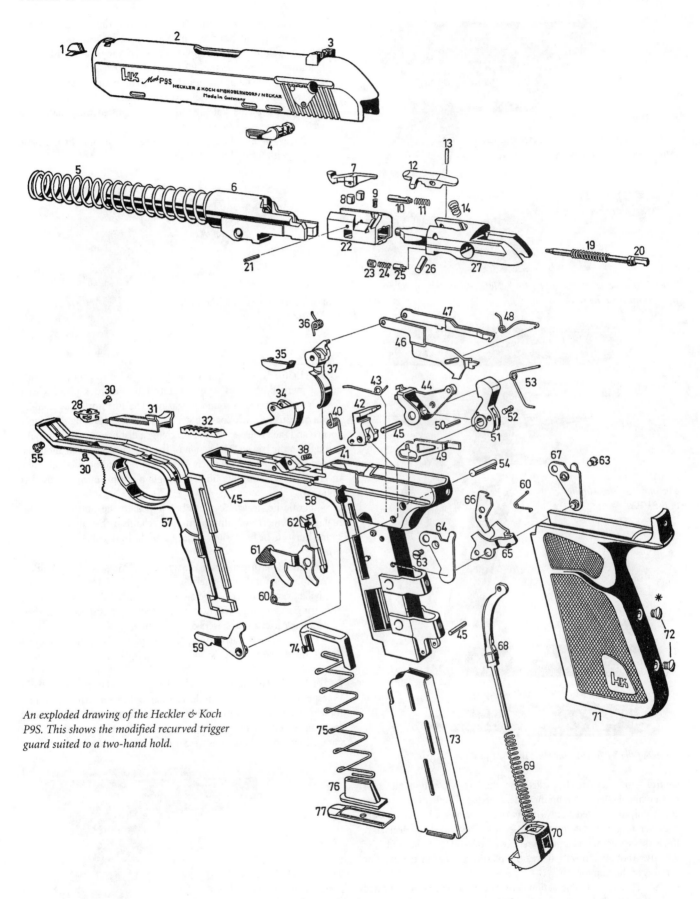

An exploded drawing of the Heckler & Koch P9S. This shows the modified recurved trigger guard suited to a two-hand hold.

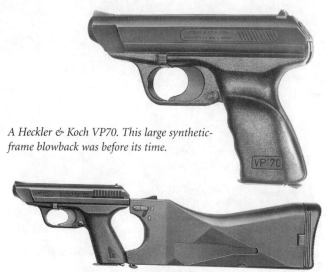

A Heckler & Koch VP70. This large synthetic-frame blowback was before its time.

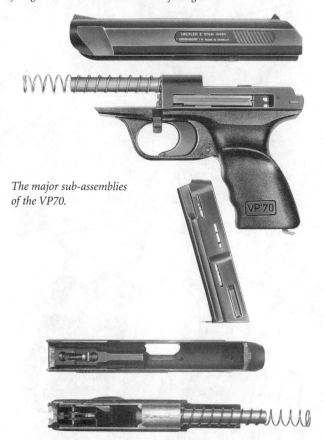

The VP70 attached to a shoulder stock. Note the position of the burst-firing control on the stock instead of the gun.

The major sub-assemblies of the VP70.

A view of the VP70 with the slide inverted to show the firing pin.

control — or, alternatively, cocked from the "down" position. The guns had a manual safety catch on the slide, a loaded-chamber indicator pin and a polygonal rifled bore with grooves that merged into the bore diameter to give a flattened-circle section. Developed by Heckler & Koch, this system was claimed to reduce friction on the bullet and raise velocity. Another innovation was the plastic coating on the exterior surfaces of the frame.

* *P9S* This was a double-action derivative of the P9, easily identified by the extended trigger guard and the position of the trigger lever. The trigger guard was altered in the mid-1970s to suit it to the fashionable two-handed grip, acquiring a reverse curve in the front

edge. The guns were initially chambered only for the 9mm Parabellum round, but a few in 45 ACP were made in 1977-80.

* *P9S Competition* A name applied in the USA to what is customarily known in Europe as the "P9 Sport" (below).
* *P9 Sport* As the name implies, this was a competition version of the P9S, with an extended barrel carrying a muzzle weight matched to the contours of the slide. It was also often fitted with anatomical walnut grips.
* *P9 Target* (or P9S Target) Names given to variants of the basic designs with fully adjustable sights.

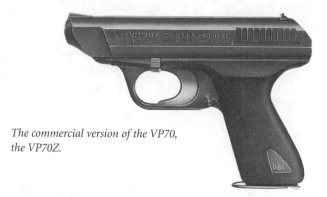

The commercial version of the VP70, the VP70Z.

VP70 (1970-83) An innovative design that failed to gain the acceptance it merited, this was a 9mm Parabellum blowback pistol with a fixed barrel and an 18-round magazine. The lockwork was double-action only, using a self-cocking striker mechanism. Pulling the trigger cocked and then released the striker, giving a distinctive two-stage pull-through on the trigger. The design of the trigger mechanism allowed a loaded VP70 to be carried safely even if loaded, and no manual safety mechanism was usually fitted (though a push-button catch was optional).

A plastic holster/stock could be clipped to the butt/frame unit, making a connection with the firing mechanism that allowed three-round bursts to be fired when a selector on the butt had been set appropriately.

* *VP70M* The original gun was given an "M" suffix (for Militär-Ausführung, "military pattern") soon after the introduction of the civilian version described below. A few cosmetic changes were made during a comparatively short production life, but sales, other than to a few African states, were disappointing.
* *VP70Z* (for Zivil-Ausführung, "civilian pattern") This abandoned the burst-firing holster/stock, selling simply as a semi-automatic pistol

P7 (or "PSP") This originated as the Polizei-Selbstladepistole ("PSP") in response to a demand from the German police authorities for a pistol with adequate performance but the minimum of handling required to bring it into action quickly. The VP70 had shown that 9mm Parabellum blowback designs were still regarded with some distrust, so

The 9mm Heckler & Koch PSP was subsequently known as the P7 and then as the P7M8.

the PSP reverted to delayed blowback. In the frame, beneath the barrel, lay a cylinder with a port to the barrel. Attached to the inner front of the slide was a piston rod, surrounded by a return spring, which entered the cylinder. As the pistol fired, gas under high pressure entered the cylinder. As the chamber pressure attempted to blow back the empty case and the slide, the piston rod was driven into the cylinder, where its movement was resisted by the high-pressure gas. This delayed the movement of the slide until the bullet was clear of the barrel and the gas pressure in the barrel fell, allowing the slide to move back. As the breech opened, the piston forced the gas out of the cylinder and into the barrel to escape from the muzzle and breech during the reloading cycle.

There was a small-but-perceptible opening of the breech at the beginning of the slide, before the cylinder pressure could rise far enough to check the movement of the slide. This could have caused case-head separations, but fluting the chamber surrounded the case with gas to prevent it bulging under internal forces.

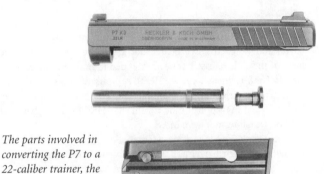

The parts involved in converting the P7 to a 22-caliber trainer, the P7K3.

The unique firing mechanism allowed the PSP to be brought into action exceptionally quickly. A pivoting lever in the front of the butt, resembling a grip safety, was squeezed instinctively by the firing hand to cock the striker ready for the first shot, made by simply squeezing the trigger. The striker remained cocked automatically, ready for the next shot, as long as the grip was maintained. If the pressure was released,

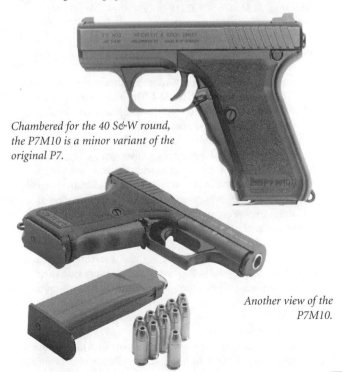

Chambered for the 40 S&W round, the P7M10 is a minor variant of the original P7.

Another view of the P7M10.

A nickel-plated P7M13, with a high-capacity double-column magazine.

the striker reverted to its rest position and the gun could be dropped in a safe condition. If the gun misfired, releasing and re-squeezing the grip allowed a second attempt to be made to fire a chambered round. The PSP, subsequently known as the "P7" in German police service, could also be silently de-cocked simply by pulling the slide back a short distance and releasing the cocking grip.

The PSP/P7 was very distinctive-looking, with a comparatively small and slender slide and a bulky grip that, because of the position of the striker-cocking lever, had a noticeable reverse taper — it was far broader at the top than the bottom. The grips were generally checkered plastic, and the finish, blue on most guns, could be nickel plate. The sights were fixed.

- *P7K3* (1988-95?) Although this outwardly resembled the P7, it lacked the gas-delay system. Blowback action was adequate for the low-pressure 7.65mm Auto or 9mm Short cartridges, neither of which demands a locked breech. A kit to convert the centerfire chamberings to 22 LR rimfire was also made.
- *P7M8* A finalized designation for the original PSP/P7, this was applied to guns with eight-round single-column magazines. They were still available in 2003.
- *P7M10* Introduced in 1993, this was chambered for the 40 S&W round. The magazine held 10 rounds.
- *P7M13* This was a variant of the P7M8 with a stagger-column magazine holding 13 rounds.
- *P7M45* (1987-9) Developed for sale in the USA, this was a modified P7M8 chambering the 45 ACP round. Tests showed that the gas-cylinder delay was inappropriate, failing to stop the breech from opening too quickly, and an oil-damped recoil suppressor was used. Inspired by the hydraulic buffers commonly embodied in the design of field guns and howitzers, this relied on a cylinder with a port in the piston-head. As the slide moved back, the piston head was forced through the oil, and the incompressible fluid passed through the port from one side of the piston to the other. This not only delayed the slide opening but also damped the recoil blow, making the P7M45 an exceptionally comfortable pistol to fire. However the complexity of the valve, which needed oil to pass back freely as the slide closed, presented the designers with problems that could not be overcome. After a small number of prototypes had been made, the project was abandoned.

USP (1993 to date) The "Universal Self-loading Pistol" was designed to incorporate the many features that the military and law enforcement agencies deemed to be vital. It uses the Browning cam-breech-locking system, allied with a patented recoil-reduction system that forms part of the recoil-spring/buffer assembly. The frame is a polymer molding, and the metal components are given an anti-corrosion finish. The USP was originally designed and made for the 40 S&W cartridge, but 9mm Parabellum and 45 ACP versions soon followed. Individual guns, considered as part of a modular series, can vary greatly in detail.

- *USP9 and USP40* The standard USP is now available only in 9mm Parabellum and 40 S&W, with (for the USA at least) 10-round magazines. The so-called "Law Enforcement" versions, which are regarded as standard in Europe, have magazine capacities of 13 40

Heckler & Koch's USP is based on the SOCOM pattern.

The Heckler & Koch "Mk 23 Mod. 0" or "SOCOM" pistol.

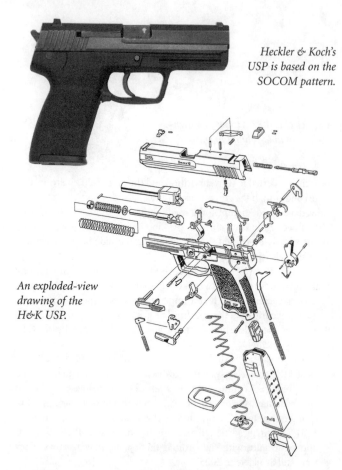

An exploded-view drawing of the H&K USP.

The H&K SOCOM pistol with its silencer attached.

S&W or 16 9mm cartridges. Offered in double-action or double-action-only versions, with the ejection port on the right or left side of the slide, the guns are made of carbon or stainless steel with what H&K calls "hostile-environment finish"; the grips are black polymer. The rear sight can be driven laterally in its dovetail to adjust the point of the impact, and an accessory rail is formed in the frame beneath the muzzle. Guns are typically 6.9 inches long, with 4.25-inch barrels, and weigh 28-29 oz empty. Post-1999 examples, particularly those sold in the USA, will be found with a key-operated lock in the butt.

- *USP9, USP40 and USP357 Compact* (1996 to date) This is little more than a shortened version of the standard gun, with a 3.6-inch barrel that gives an overall length of about 6.2 inches and an empty weight of 24 oz. Recognizable by size and by the vertical front surface of the trigger guard (to improve a two-handed grip), the USP Compact can be obtained in 357 SIG in addition to 9mm Parabellum and 40 S&W.

- *USP45 Expert* (1999 to date) Suitable for IPSC competition-shooting, this combines elements of the Heckler & Koch USP45 Tactical and Mark 23 pistols. It has a micro-adjustable rear sight, a specially developed trigger (single- or double-action to order) with an adjustable stop, a full-length slide and an "O"-ring seal on the barrel. The controls are ambidextrous. Expert pistols are about 8.75 inches long, have 5.2-inch barrels and weigh about 30 oz empty.

- *USP 45* (1995 to date) Essentially the same as the standard version, this chambers the 45 ACP round. Consequently, particularly as a 10-round magazine is retained, it is larger and heavier than its cousin: 7.9 inches long with a 4.1-inch barrel and an empty weight of 30.5 oz. Available in right- or left-hand versions, in carbon or stainless steel, with the standard black polymer frame, it is fitted with three-dot combat sights.

- *USP45 Compact* (1998 to date) A smaller version of the USP45, with an eight-round magazine, this exhibits changes in the contours

of the slide and frame. It is about 7.1 inches long with a 3.8-inch barrel and weighed 28 oz. Three-dot sights are retained, but the head of the slide release has been extended to make release easier.

- *USP45 H&K Commemorative* (1999) A thousand guns of this type were made to celebrate the manufacturer's 50th anniversary. They had a special high-polish blue finish, the "HK" logo in silver and gold on the slide, and were cased.

- *USP 45 Match* This is basically a target-shooting version of the USP 45, with a 6-inch barrel and a distinctive weight attached to the frame that protrudes ahead of the muzzle. Match-quality sights are fitted, the trigger is adjustable and the finish may be blue or stainless.

- *USP45 Tactical* A derivative of the USP-45, this has a barrel that projects from the slide, the muzzle being threaded to receive a silencer. The barrel is fitted with a bushing in the form of a neoprene "O"-ring; the trigger and the trigger-stop are adjustable; the frame is polymer; the magazine has an extended floor-plate; and the rear sight is fully adjustable. The Tactical version is a large gun, 8.65 inches long with a 4.9-inch barrel, and weighs about 36 oz empty. A 10-round magazine is standard.

- *USP Mark 23 Mod 0* (SOCOM) In 1990, the US Special Operations Command (SOCOM) requested proposals for a 45-caliber pistol that gave better accuracy than the M1911A1 and could be fitted with a silencer and a laser aiming projector. Colt and H&K both produced designs, the latter being selected for development in 1991. Prototypes were tested in 1992/3 and a production contract was awarded to Heckler & Koch in 1994. The initial purchases amounted to 1380 pistols, for $1186 apiece, accompanied by a similar number of silencers purchased from Knight's Armament Company and 650 laser aiming projectors.

The SOCOM pistol is generally similar to the USP (q.v.): a double-action design, hammer fired, with the breech locked by the Browning dropping-barrel system. An additional buffer is incorporated in the buffer-spring assembly to reduce the sensation of recoil and thus improve accuracy. The muzzle protrudes from the slide to accept a silencer (or "sound suppressor"), which is said to reduce noise by 25 dB. A slide lock allows the pistol to be fired without the slide recoiling when the silencer is fitted, preventing mechanical noise from the moving slide or an ejected cartridge case from compromising the silence of a shot. The front of the frame is grooved to accept the aiming projector, which can project either visible or infrared light, and the fixed sights have Tritium dots to improve performance in poor light.

- *Mark 23 Special Operations Pistol* (1996 to date) This is a commercial version of the SOCOM pistol, about 9.7 inches long with a 5.9-

inch barrel and weighing 43 oz. The black polymer grips are integral with the frame, three-dot combat sights are fitted, the magazines are restricted to 10 rounds (12 in European/"Law Enforcement" versions) and the trigger is a conventional double-action pattern.

P-11 The existence of this pistol had been known since the early 1980s, but it was not until 1997 that it was formally acknowledged and some details made public. It is a special weapon for underwater use by frogmen and similar operators, and it is reputed to be used by, among others, the German GSG9, British SBS and US SEALs. There is a strong suspicion that the similar Soviet weapon was actually based upon this German design, development of which began in the mid-1970s.

The pistol is actually little more than a butt, trigger and socket-like frame. A pre-loaded five-barrel module is slipped into the socket to complete the weapon. The five barrels are loaded with a special cartridge that uses an electric primer activated by a battery in the grip and that is loaded with a slender dart-like finned projectile. Pulling the trigger fires the barrels in sequence, launching the darts. When the last of the five barrels has been fired, the empty module is simply replaced.

HEINZELMANN
C.E. Heinzelmann, Plochingen, Germany.
Heinzelmann made the *Heim* pistol, a 6.35mm blowback automatic that externally resembles the Mauser WTP, but internally, is closer to the Browning 1910 with a fixed barrel and a coaxial return spring secured by a muzzle bushing. It carries the company's name on the slide and appears to have been made for a short time in the early 1930s.

HELLENIC ARMS
Heraklion, Greece
The EP7 is a variant of the Heckler & Koch P7M8, made under license. The company also makes H&K-type rifles for the Greek armed forces.

HELLFRITZSCH
Louis Hellfritzsch, Berlin, Germany.
This German inventor patented a locked-breech pistol, the subject of British Patent 19,448/1899 and an improvement protected by British Patent 9963/1902. Springs force the barrel backward and the bolt forward, the bolt spring being the stronger. When the gun fires, the barrel and bolt begin to move back. The bolt is rotated half a turn, but the barrel is rotated a half-turn in the opposite direction before being brought to a halt. This frees the bolt to run back to the limit of its travel before returning to strip a new round from a Mauser-style box magazine ahead of the trigger guard. The spring that is holding the barrel in its rear position is overcome by the force of the returning bolt, and the parts revolve to re-lock and then move back into battery. It is probable that prototypes were made, perhaps by Hellfritzsch himself (described in the patents as a "gunsmith" or "Gun Maker"), but no surviving guns have yet been found.

HEMBRUG ARMS FACTORY
Hembrug Geweerfabriek, Hembrug, the Netherlands.
The Nederlandsch Indisch Leger, or "Dutch Indies Army" was established in the 1880s to garrison the Dutch colonies in the Far East. Although customarily issued with guns that were similar to those of the Royal Netherlands army, the NIL was separately constituted and occasionally capable of procuring equipment independently. As far as handguns were concerned, the process included a special revolver and a variant of the Parabellum (q.v.). The guns did not bear property markings, other than the monarch's cipher, but could have distinctive unit markings either on the frame or applied to brass plates soldered to the frame. Granted the prefix *Koninklijke* ("royal") in 1905, the colonial army was disbanded in 1949 when Indonesia gained independence.

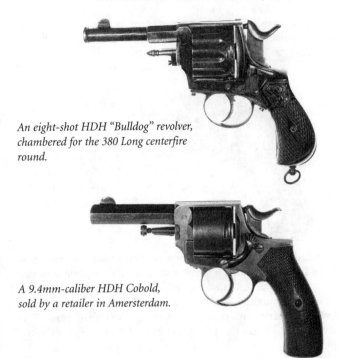

An eight-shot HDH "Bulldog" revolver, chambered for the 380 Long centerfire round.

A 9.4mm-caliber HDH Cobold, sold by a retailer in Amersterdam.

Model 1891 (NIL) This was a 9.4mm six-shot solid-frame revolver with gate loading and rod ejection, based on Galand (q.v.) lockwork. Although for service in the colonies, it was a far better design than the Beaumont revolvers issued to the home troops.

HENRION, DASSY & HEUSCHEN ("HDH")
Also known as "Manufacture d'Armes H.D.H.", Liége, Belgium.
This was among the larger Belgian gunmaking businesses, producing cheap revolvers at the turn of the century. Henrion, Dassy & Heuschen were the originators of the "Puppy" name, widely copied by others, and made their first automatic pistol shortly before World War I began. Work ceased when the Germans invaded Belgium and does not seem to have recommenced after the Armistice.

～ REVOLVERS ～
Cobold A military-style revolver dating from the 1880s, this was a five-shot solid-frame pattern with a hexagonal barrel and a bird's-head butt. It was loaded through a pivoting gate on the right side of the frame behind the cylinder and had an Abadie-style rod ejector in the center of the cylinder arbor. Guns were offered in chamberings ranging from 9.4mm Dutch service, 10.6mm German service and 450 CF. They also had a "safety catch" in the form of a pivoted lever that, when the decorated rear end was pressed down, lifted a hooked front end into the mouth of a chamber. This prevented the rotation of the cylinder, and, therefore, any movement of the hammer.

HDH These initials can be found on revolvers ranging from tiny 5.5mm "Velo-Dog" types to the bizarre 20-shot monsters so loved by Belgian and French makers.

- *Constabulary* Usually offered in 32 centerfire chambering, this was a solid-framed single-action revolver with a short barrel. A lanyard ring was often fixed to the base of the butt.
- *New Model* This was a five-shot hammerless open-frame 22 rimfire with folding trigger and a pocket butt, a real "pocket model".
- *Spirlet* Representing the lunatic fringe of revolver design were the guns made on this pattern, tip-barrel designs with oversized cylinder holding 20 5.5mm Velo-Dog or 6.35mm Auto rounds, or, alternatively, 16 7.65mm Auto cartridges. While all these were sold by HDH and so marked, they were also sold to the trade and may be found with gunsmiths' names, though the initials "HDH" will usually be found tucked away somewhere.

• *Type Ordnance* This was a tip-barrel revolver with automatic ejection, usually chambered for 8mm Lebel, 380 CF, 38 S&W or 450 CF cartridges. The barrel had a prominent rib.

Chambered for a 5.5mm cartridge, this Velo-Dog revolver was the work of HDH of Liége.

• *Velo-Dog* The HDH version was often more ornate than other guns of this genre. It had a tipping barrel with central ejection, a folding trigger and a six-chamber cylinder. The chambering was usually either 5.5mm Velo-Dog or 6mm "Type Française" rimfire.

Left Wheeler This oddly-named model, probably the last HDH revolver to be made, was a 32-caliber copy of the Colt Police Positive (q.v.).

Lincoln This was a 22-rimfire solid-frame vest-pocket revolver with a folding trigger, generally with ornate engraving and imitation pearl or ivory grips.

• *Lincoln-Bossu* Less ornate, this was a hammerless folding-trigger Velo-Dog in 5.5mm or 6.35mm caliber.

This 22-caliber folding-trigger Puppy, one of the smallest types of revolver to be found in Europe, was made by Henrion, Dassy & Heuschen ("HDH").

Puppy These small-caliber folding-trigger guns — 22, 5.5mm, 6.35mm and 7.65mm — were generally of Velo-Dog type. There were innumerable variations: hammerless, small hammer or large hammer, solid frame or tip-barrel. Many of them were extensively engraved and had ivory or mother-of-pearl grips.

∼ AUTOMATIC PISTOL ∼

H & D This was the company's patented blowback design, in 6.35mm caliber, with a rounded slide and a serrated breechblock section containing a striker. Beneath the barrel was a housing for the return spring. The frame was flat-sided, with a safety catch behind the grip, and was marked "H & D AUTOMATIC PISTOL PATENT". Guns of this type are now extremely rare, and it is unlikely that many were made before World War I stopped production.

HERITAGE MFG. INC

Opa Locka, Florida, USA.

∼ REVOLVERS ∼

Rough Rider (1993 to date) This was a 22 LR rimfire "Western-style" gun, loosely based on the Colt Single Action Army Model. Available in blue or nickel finish with squared-heel grips (bird's-head

style was optional), it had a hammer-block safety, a six-chamber cylinder and barrel lengths of 2.75, 3.5, 4.75, 6.5 or 9 inches. Empty weight was about 34 oz with the 6-inch barrel. An exchangeable cylinder chambering the 22 Magnum rimfire could be supplied to order. The grip material could be wood, wood-laminate or mother-of-pearl. The sights are fixed except for the 6.5-inch-barreled option, which has an adjustable rear sight.

Sentry (1993-9?) This was a simple double-action personal defense revolver with a six-chamber cylinder that could be removed (by withdrawing the cylinder axis pin) to reload. Chambered only for the 38 Special round, with a 2-inch barrel, the gun weighed about 23 oz empty. Finish could be blued or nickel-plated steel, the grips were checkered plastic and the sights were fixed.

∼ AUTOMATIC PISTOLS ∼

H25S (1993-2001) This was a small 25 ACP blowback, very similar to those that were made in quantity in Europe (cf., Astra Cub, Unique Mikros). Offered in blue or nickel, the gun was about 4.6 inches long (with a 2.25-inch barrel) and weighed 14 oz empty. The detachable box magazine held six rounds, the trigger was a single-action design, and a radial safety lever lay on the left side of the frame above the trigger.

Stealth (1995-2001) Chambered for the 9mm Parabellum or 40 S&W cartridges, this had a polymer frame and a stainless steel slide. Finish could be black, black chrome, or a "two-tone" version with the side panels of a black-chrome slide left bright. It was about 6.3 inches long with a 3.9-inch barrel and weighed only 20 oz without the ten-round box magazine. The action incorporated a gas-impingement delay system; the trigger was a conventional double-action design; an ambidextrous safety catch ran through the frame; and a magazine safety was fitted. The left side of the slide was marked "Heritage Manufacturing, Inc., Opa Locka, FL.", with "HMI" in an oval in the base of the grip checkering.

HERMAN

F. Herman, Liége, Belgium (?)

A 6.35mm blowback automatic of original design and marked "F HERMAN BREVETE", this was probably Belgian. The construction was unusual, as the frame extended upward to form just over half of what appeared to be the slide. The only part that moved is the top section that carried the breechblock, attached by screws and suspended behind the fixed barrel. Pulling the finger grips backward moved the upper section of the slide and the breechblock. The return spring was placed around the barrel, and a striker lay inside the breechblock. The upper section of the slide curved around the front of the gun to surround the barrel and retain the recoil spring.

HERTER'S, INC.

Waseca, Minnesota, USA.

Herter's, which ceased trading in 1978, sold a variety of Western-style revolvers made in Germany. These were sold under the names "Guide", "Single Six", "Power-Mag" and "Western" in 22 LR, 357 Magnum, 401 Herter Magnum (a wildcat cartridge) and 44 Magnum. The brand name "Guide" was also applied to a 22 LR rimfire solid-frame side-opening cylinder model of unknown make, probably also German.

HEYM

Fried. Wilh. Heym, Munnerstadt, Germany.

The Heym business was established in Suhl in 1865, patenting the first *Drilling* (three-barrel sporting gun) in 1891, but ceased trading at the end of World War II. Operations began again in Bavaria in 1949, but moved back to Gleichamburg in Thüringen in 1996. Renowned as a maker of high-quality shotguns and sporting rifles, Heym has also made airguns and a short-barreled 22 LR rimfire solid-frame double-action revolver. Sold in the USA as the Detective, by Hy Hunter (q.v.), this offered surprisingly good quality. Production was confined to the late 1950s.

HIGGINS

This brand name, correctly "J.C. Higgins", has been used by the Sears Roebuck mail-order company on a variety of sporting firearms, including several handguns.

∼ REVOLVERS ∼

These were purchased from High Standard in 1959-65.

- *Model 88* This was the Sentinel with a bird's-head butt.
- *Model 90* A variant of the Double Nine, this lacked the interchangeable cylinder of the High Standard prototype.
- *Natchez* A variant of the Double Nine with a bird's-head grip.
- *Posse* A short-barreled version of the Double Nine.
- *Ranger* This was also a Double Nine, under another name.

∼ AUTOMATIC PISTOLS ∼

- *Model 80* This was a slightly modified version of the 22 LR rimfire High Standard Dura-Matic.
- *Model 85* Made by Manufacture d'Armes des Pyrénées Françaises, this was little more than a Unique E-2 with different markings.

HIGH STANDARD

High Standard Mfg Co., Hamden, Connecticut; High Standard, Inc., East Hartford, Connecticut, USA.

This engineering business was formed in 1926 to make gun-barrel drills. The assets of the defunct Hartford Arms & Equipment Co. (q.v.) were purchased cheaply in 1932, allowing High Standard to enter the handgun business simply by putting the Hartford design into production under a new name. Improvements had soon been made, and an enviable reputation for accuracy was acquired. Handgun production stopped in favor of war work in 1942 but began again in 1943 to allow a training pistol to be supplied to the US armed forces. Fitted with a silencer, guns of this type were also issued to clandestine forces.

Commercial production resumed after World War II ended, and the first of a series of revolvers appeared in the 1950s. In the 1980s, however, increasing competition and cheap imports forced High Standard to close in January 1985. The distinctive pistols subsequently reappeared from Fort Worth, Mitchell and even Stoeger (q.v.), but litigation eventually resolved the questions that surrounded ownership of the brand names. The pistols are now being made only by the High Standard Mfg Co. Inc. (below).

∼ DERRINGERS ∼

DM 100 and DM 101 (1962-93) These two-shot over/under derringers were essentially updated versions of the Remington Double Derringer, with streamlined contours and a "half-guard" protecting the lever-like trigger. The barrel-block tipped down at the muzzle once a stirrup-like latch on the top rear of the frame had been released. Chamberings were restricted to 22 LR rimfire (DM-100) and 22 Magnum rimfire (DM-101). Finish was usually blue or nickel (electroless on guns made in 1982-3); grips could be walnut, or white or black plastic. Presentation guns were made with silver or gold plating, often to be sold in pairs in specially made presentation cases.

The guns bore a variety of markings, including the High Standard name and motifs of an eagle (prior to 1967) or a trigger (1967-9). Most of those made in 1969-83, however, lacked manufacturer's marks and simply bore "DERRINGER". Serial numbers were interspersed with other High Standard handguns from 1962, beginning in the 1,263,000 range, until new "D"-prefix numbers were adopted in 1975 (at D01001). After the move from Hamden to East Hartford, production began again in April 1977 at D13000 and continued until work stopped in the summer of 1983.

∼ REVOLVERS ∼

High Standard revolvers fell into two groups: solid-frame with swing-out cylinder and what might be termed "Western" models, based on the traditional Colt Frontier style. Some guns were sold under the J.C. Higgins name by Sears Roebuck (q.v.).

Camp Gun (1976-83) This was a steel-framed Kit Gun (below), chambered for the 22 LR or Magnum rimfire rounds, the cylinders being exchangeable. The rear sight was adjustable.

Crusader (1978-83) This was a large swing-cylinder double-action pistol, made only in 44 Magnum and 45 Long Colt (though 357 was also advertised). Only 500 guns were made, the first 50, with 8.4-inch barrels, commemorating High Standard's 50th anniversary; the remainder, with 6.5-inch barrels, were much plainer. The guns were blued with walnut grips and had adjustable sights. The most interesting feature, however, was the "geared" or rack-and-pinion mechanism that gave the yoke a uniquely smooth action.

Double Nine (aluminum-alloy frame type, 1958-70) The first of the "Western" models, this resembled the Colt Frontier model, though the ejector-rod sheath beneath the barrel was ornamental and the cylinder swung out to the left on a yoke. The "Double Nine" name originally came from the nine-chamber 22 LR rimfire cylinder and the double-action lockwork, though the origins were blurred when the optional 22 WMR cylinder was introduced (see below). The barrel was 5.5 inches long. Finish was nickel or blue, sometimes with gold-plated trigger guards and grip straps (blued guns only); grips could be black, ivory-colored plastic or simulated staghorn.

- *Steel-frame version* (1971-83) This was introduced to allow a 22 Magnum rimfire chambering to be offered. Most guns sold as a "Combo", accompanied by both cylinders. They were finished in blue or nickel, with wooden grips, and had adjustable rear sights.

Durango (1970-4) Made initially with an alloy frame and then with steel (1974 only), this was another of the nine-shot 22 LR High Standards. The barrels measured 4.5 or 5.5 inches, the sights were fixed or (5.5-inch barrel only) adjustable and the finish could be blue or nickel. Some of the blued guns had brass-color trigger guards and grip straps. The Durango was seen as an economy model of the contemporaneous Double Nine, lacking the interchangeable cylinder.

High Sierra (1974-83) Essentially a Double Nine with a 7-inch octagonal barrel, blued-steel frame, a gold-plated trigger guard and backstrap, this usually had fixed sights. Production of the original 22 LR version was confined to 1974, but the adjustable-sight "Combo", sold with exchangeable 22 LR and 22 WMR cylinders, lasted until High Standard ceased trading.

Hombre (1970-2) Made with a blue or nickel-finished aluminum-alloy frame, this was a nine-shot 22 LR rimfire revolver derived from the Double Nine. The barrel was restricted to a length of 4 inches, the sights were fixed and the squared-heel butt had walnut grips.

Kit Gun (1971-3) This was a solid-frame 9-shot 22 LR rimfire swing-cylinder gun, built on a good-sized alloy frame with an adjustable rear sight and double-action lockwork. The finish was confined to blue, the round-heel butt had walnut grips, the cylinder was locked by a catch on the yoke and the ejector rod lay unsupported beneath the barrel.

Longhorn (alloy frame type, 1961-70) This was a variant of the Double Nine, initially offered with barrels of 4.5, 5.5 or 9.5 inches, square-heel butts and fixed sights. The finish was confined to blue, though the grips could be walnut, plastic, simulated mother-of-pearl or simulated staghorn. Some guns also had gold trim on the trigger guard and the grip straps.

- *Steel-frame version* (1971-83) Introduced to allow a 22 Magnum rimfire option to be offered, these were blued, had walnut grips and had 9.5-inch barrels.

Marshall (1971-3) This was a special-promotion version of the 22 LR Double Nine, with a 5.5-inch barrel, a blue-finish aluminium-alloy frame, simulated staghorn grips and fixed sights. It came with a special trigger lock and a holster.

Natchez (1961-5) Made for Sears Roebuck, this was a 22 LR rimfire aluminium-alloy-framed Double Nine with a 4.5-inch barrel and a bird's-head butt with simulated ivory grip. The sights were fixed.

Posse (1961-5) Made exclusively for Sears Roebuck (see J.C. Higgins), this derived from the Double Nine. It had a 3.5-inch barrel, fixed sights and a blued aluminum-alloy frame with brass-color trigger guard and straps. The grips were walnut.

Power Plus (1983) A few of these five-shot double-action guns — based on the centerfire Sentinel — were made in 38 Special with blued steel frames and walnut grips. The cylinder was mounted on a yoke and swung out to the left to load.

Sentinel (first series, 1955-66) These nine-shot double-action revolvers had solid frames and yoke-mounted cylinders that swung to the left. They were made with barrels ranging from 2.4 to 6 inches and could be finished in blue or nickel. The grips were usually one-piece checkered brown plastic. However, the shortest barrel option was offered in 1957-62 with ivory-color grips; nickel plating on the cylinder, trigger and hammer; and frames that were anodized gold, pink or turquoise!

* *Sentinel Deluxe* (1965-73) This was simply the basic aluminum-alloy frame gun with two-piece walnut grips. The barrels were restricted to 4 or 6 inches, but the sights remained fixed.
* *Sentinel Imperial* (1962-4) This was a version of the basic gun, restricted to blue finish and barrels of 4 or 6 inches. It had two-piece walnut grips and an adjustable rear sight.
* *Sentinel Snub* (1967-73) Restricted to the 2.4-inch barrel option, this combined the aluminum-alloy frame with a round-heel butt. The grips were either walnut or brown plastic; finish could be blue or nickel.

Sentinel (second series, 1974-6) This was an improved version of the original gun, with changes in the action and a steel frame.

* *Mark 1* Offered in 22 LR rimfire, in nickel or blue, this was a 9-shot double-action design. Barrel lengths were 2, 3 or 4 inches, the ejector rod was shrouded and one-piece "oversize" wraparound walnut grips were fitted. The rear sight was fixed or adjustable, the latter being confined to the 3- and 4-inch options.
* *Mark 2* Made for High Standard by Dan Wesson (q.v.), this was chambered for the 357 Magnum round. Cylinder capacity was reduced to six rounds, the sights were fixed and the finish was restricted to blue. Barrels measured 2.5, 4 or 6 inches.
* *Mark 3* This was a minor adaptation of the Mark 2 with an adjustable rear sight.
* *Mark 4* A variant of the Mark 1, available in the same barrel-length/rear-sight combinations, this was chambered for 22 Magnum rimfire ammunition.
* *Sentinel Steel Frame* (1987-83) This nine-shot 22 rimfire gun was built on the basis of old Sentinel Mark 1 frames and could be obtained only with a 2-inch barrel (fixed sights) or 4-inch barrel (adjustable sights) — presumably as a way of ridding High Standard of old parts.

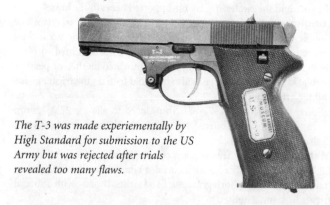

The T-3 was made experimentally by High Standard for submission to the US Army but was rejected after trials revealed too many flaws.

～ AUTOMATIC PISTOLS ～

Note: The introduction of guns with names instead of the letter-designations created an entirely new group. Unfortunately for the cata-

loger, High Standard made a variety of manufacturing changes that were applied only to certain guns in the "named series". Consequently, there may be several recognizably different patterns within each name. These are usually identified with series numbers, and there can be, for example, a "Series 104" Supermatic Citation as well as a "Series 107" Supermatic Citation. To prevent needless repetition, the principal characteristics of each series are summarized below. In addition, High Standard offered a variety of conversion kits that can blur identification still further. A good source of information is the contribution by John J. Stimpson, Jr. to *The Standard Catalog of Firearms* (2002 edition). Most of the guns made since the early 1950s have had their names on the slide or barrel-block, which makes identification easier.

* *Series 100* (1954-64) This introduced a small push-button barrel-release catch, protruding from the front of the frame ahead of the trigger guard, but the slide no longer shrouded the breech-face as preceding guns had done. Some of the guns retained the rib let into the top of the barrel and a slot in the underside of the barrel to receive balance weights.
* *Series 101* (1954-70) A minor variation of the preceding group, only applied to the higher-grade target pistols, this was identified by the omission of the barrel rib.
* *Series 102* (1957-60) This was distinguished by a modification to the takedown system, which was activated by pressing a large button on the right side of the frame. The rear sight (sometimes mounted on the barrel block) was improved, and the slide-retracting grooves were cut diagonally instead of vertically.
* *Series 103* (1960-3) Improvements were largely confined to machining and dimensions, making these guns difficult to distinguish from the their immediate predecessors (apart from markings).
* *Series 104* (1964-77) These guns were a minor revision of the preceding patterns, with changes to the barrels, and the trigger-stop screw moved from the frame to the trigger lever itself.
* *Series 105* Not used.
* *Series 106* (1964-8) This marked a wholesale design change. The original frame, with its slanting grip, gave way to a new pattern modeled on the M1911A1. Consequently, the 106-type guns are noticeably more "upright" than their predecessors. Rear sights were mounted on a bridge over the rear of the slide, maintaining the fixed relationship between the sights as the gun was fired, and the retraction grooves were moved to the front of the slide immediately behind the chamber.
* *Series 107* (1968-82) A minor improvement on Series 106, this was characterized by changes to the frame to eliminate the old spring hole in the back grip-strap that had previously required plugging. During the life of this group, production was moved (in 1976) from Hamden to East Hartford, Connecticut, and the slide markings changed accordingly.
* *SH Series* (1982-3) The last of the changes, this saw the replacement of the push-button takedown release with a hex-head cap screw.

Citation II (1982-3) Made in Series SH only, this had a slab-sided 5.25- or 7.25-inch barrel and a frame with smooth grip straps. The rear sight, mounted directly on the half-slide, was adjustable. The grips were checkered thumb-rest-style walnut and the finish was usually blue, though a few electroless nickel examples were made.

Custom 10-X (1980-3?, Series 107 and SH) This was a custom-made and hand-fitted target model in 22 LR rimfire. It had a 5.5-inch heavyweight "bull" barrel, a frame-mounted adjustable rear sight and a fully adjustable trigger.

Dura-Matic M-100 Made only in 1954, the original variant was a low-priced "fun gun" using a simplified construction system. The frame was held to the butt by a long bolt through the butt, the barrel unit was locked to the frame by a simple knurled nut above the stamped-strip trigger guard and the firing mechanism included a striker instead of a hammer. The sights were fixed, the plastic grips were made in a single piece and the slender tapering barrels measured 4.5 or 6.75 inches.

- *M-101* (1954-70) Externally similar to its predecessor, this had an improved barrel-lock nut. However, despite low price and surprisingly robust construction, the Dura-Matic failed to achieve popularity. Many of the guns made in the late 1960s were sold under the name "Plinker".

Field King (1950-67) The first guns of this type had heavy cylindrical barrels (4.5 or 6.75 inches), adjustable sights, blue finish and thumb-rest-style brown plastic grips. They were similar to the Supermatic (q.v.) but could not accept the auxiliary weights. The FK-100 (1954 only) was similar but had the new takedown system described in the Notes. The FK-101 was a minor modification, difficult to distinguish externally.

Flite King (1954-63) The first of this "lightweight" series, LW-100 (1954-7), had the frame and slide made of black-anodized alloy. The barrels were usually blued steel, sights were fixed and the brown plastic grips had a thumb-rest. This was replaced by the Models 102 and 103, which embodied the series changes listed above, but had steel frames.

Model A (1938-42) A deluxe version of the Model B, this had a distinctive frame with the base of the grip parallel to the axis of the bore instead of cut obliquely. The rear sight was adjustable, the grips were checkered walnut and the barrel measured 4.5 or 6.75 inches. About 7250 guns of this type were made, those dating later than August 1939 displaying the dismantling catch on the right side of the frame instead of the left.

- *Model H-A* (1940-2) Another of the "hammer versions" of the basic design, this was the rarest — with production amounting to merely 1040.

Model B (1932-42) Almost identical with the Hartford pistol, this was a fixed-barrel 22 rimfire with a half-length slide and an internal hammer. Barrels measured 4.5 or 6.75 inches, dimensions that were standardized throughout the entire pre-1942 range. The box magazine held 10 rounds and the rear sight was a fixed open notch. The guns were blued with checkered rubber grips, and the earliest examples incorporated some original Hartford-made parts. Guns made after August 1939 had the dismantling catch on the right side of the frame instead of the left, and production continued until about 66,000 guns had been made.

- *Model B-US* (1942-3) About 14,000 of these guns, High Standard's first "military model", were purchased by the US Army. Minor changes were made to the frame of the standard enclosed hammer Model B, the grips were checkered rubber and the barrel was restricted to 4.5 inches.
- *Model H-B* (1940-2) An external-hammer derivative of the Model B, this was made only in small numbers. Total production is estimated at 2100.

Model C (1936-42) Chambered for the 22 Short rimfire cartridge, this was not popular: less than 5000 were made, originally in a separate numbering sequence and then amalgamated with the Model B. Guns made after August 1939 had the dismantling catch on the right side of the frame instead of the left.

Model D (1938-42) A derivative of the Model A, this had large-diameter or "heavyweight" 4.5-inch or 6.75-inch barrels. Production was restricted to about 2500 guns, those made after August 1939 having the dismantling catch on the right side of the frame instead of the left.

- *Model H-D* (1940-5) This was little more than the "D" pattern with an external hammer. Production by the end of World War II had amounted to 6900, though assembly had slowed to a crawl in 1942.
- *Model H-D USA* (or "USA H-D", 1943-5) Purchased by the US Army, replacing the Model B-US (above), this was a slightly modified variant of the H-D with a manual safety catch on the left rear

of the frame behind the grip. The guns had fixed open-notch rear sights and checkered black rubber grips, the finish being blue (early) or parkerized (late). Purchases amounted to about 44,000.

- *H-D M* ("H-D Military", 1946-51) This was a commercial version of the H-D USA, introduced soon after World War II had finished, retaining the safety catch but with a better finish and brown plastic or walnut grips. Guns of this type were popular; total production is believed to have reached 150,000.
- *H-D MS* (1944-5) About 2000 silenced H-D type pistols were made for the OSS during World War II. They had specially perforated 6.75-inch barrels within large-diameter shrouds. The rear sight was a fixed open-notch.

Model E (1938-42) The heaviest version of the basic design, this could be obtained with 4.5-inch or 6.75-inch large-diameter barrels and thumb-rest-style walnut grips. Only about 2600 were made before the commencement of war work stopped production. Post-August 1939 examples had the dismantling catch on the right side of the frame instead of the left.

- *Model H-E* (1940-2) This was little more than a Model E with an external hammer; 2100 were made.

The High Standard Model G-380 pistol, chambered for the 380 ACP (9mm Short) round.

The right side of the High Standard G-380.

Model G-380 (1947-50) Immediately after World War II had ended, High Standard carried out a fundamental overhaul of its designs. The Hartford-type stripping catch that allowed the slide to be removed to the rear, while the barrel remained on the frame, was replaced by a system that allowed both the slide and the barrel to be detachable. A latch in the front of the trigger guard released the barrel (which was readily exchangeable), and the slide followed it forward and off the frame. Backward movement was prevented by an abutment that anchored the recoil spring. The gun was also chambered for the 380 ACP cartridge, unlike any other High Standard pistol design before or since, and had a six-round magazine. The safety catch was retained on the rear left side of the frame behind the checkered-plastic grip, the sights were fixed and the barrel was restricted to 5 inches. Finish was customarily blue. About 7500 guns were made.

Model G-B (1949-50) The first of the rimfire derivatives of the G-380, this was chambered for the 22 LR cartridge and had a 10-round magazine. The last of the short-frame guns to be made, readily identifiable by the obliquely cut grip base, the guns had fixed sights and readily exchangeable barrels of 4.5 or 6.75 inches. Finish was blue; grips were usually brown plastic. Production did not exceed 5000.

Model G-D (1949-50) Similar to the G-B pattern, this could be identified by larger-diameter barrels and an adjustable rear sight. The grips were checkered walnut, with a thumb-rest style available as an option; finish was invariably blue. About 3300 guns were made.

Model G-E (1949-50) Mechanically identical with the G-B pattern, this was the heaviest of the series. It could be distinguished by the large-diameter cylindrical barrels and adjustable sights, but only about 2900 were ever made.

Model G-O (or "Olympic", 1949-50) The first of the High Standard guns to be given a name, though also known by a "G"-series designation, this was chambered for the 22 Short rimfire cartridge and was specifically intended for rapid-fire shooting under NRA rules. Offered with barrels of 4.5 or 6.75 inches, which could be exchanged at will, the guns had grooves on the grip-straps to facilitate a good grasp and an adjustable rear sight on the slide. Most guns also accepted magazines with a slight curve, developed to increase the certainty of feed with rimmed cartridges, but a few took the standard straight-side design. Production is believed to have amounted to about 3000 guns.

Model S This designation has been applied to a small quantity of Model B and Model C pistols fitted with 6.75-inch smoothbore barrels. Only about 15 survive.

Olympic Originally known as "G-O" (see above). The first modifications led to a gun, still in 22 Short, with a heavy cylindrical 4.5- or 6.75-inch barrel, an adjustable rear sight on the slide, grooved straps and brown plastic thumb-rest grips. Weights could be added beneath the barrel, and a fill-strip was provided to plug the attachment groove when necessary. Magazines still held 10 rounds. The "O-100" version (1954 only) was identical, except for the new 100-series takedown system. The "O-101" was similar, but lacked the barrel rib, and the 6.75-inch barrel had a single compensating slot on each side of the front-sight ramp. The Models 102 and 103, difficult to distinguish externally, were basically 22 Short versions of the 22 LR Supermatic Citation, with grooved grip straps and barrels measuring 6.75, 8 or 10 inches. The rear sights were generally on the slide, and a 5.5-inch heavy "bull" barrel was offered with the "103"-type Olympic from 1962 onward. Series 104 guns were much like their "103" predecessors, but the barrel options were restricted to a 5.5-inch heavyweight "bull" pattern and an 8-inch flute.

Olympic ISU These guns of Series 102 and 103, difficult to distinguish, were little more than Olympics restricted to a 6.75-inch barrel with an integral muzzle weight. Their straps were usually grooved to improve grip. The Series 104 guns were much like their immediate predecessors but had detachable auxiliary weights. The rear sight lay on the slide. Series 106 introduced the military-style frame and stippled grip straps, though the sight remained on the slide. The guns in Series 107 had the rear sight on a bridge at the rear of the slide.

Olympic ISU Military Series 102 only. This was a variant of the Olympic ISU with the military-style grip and yoke-mounted sight. It dates from 1965.

Olympic Trophy ISU Made only in 103-series guise, this was an Olympic ISU with the same high-gloss blue finish that could be found on the Supermatic Trophy. However, very few guns of this type were ever made.

Sharpshooter Series 103, 107 and SH. For the less dedicated target shooter there was this gun, a lower-grade "Citation" in 22 LR rimfire with 5.5-inch bull barrel, thumb-rest grips and an adjustable rear sight on the slide.

Sport King The top-of-the-line High Standards were expensive: the "Trophy", for example, sold for $112 in 1960. For shooters with lesser ambitions and shorter pockets, a more utilitarian line was needed. The Field King and the Sport King were the first of this series to be introduced. "Sport Kings", in 22 LR rimfire with 10-round magazines, had lightweight round 4.5-inch or 6.75-inch barrels. They also had fixed open-notch rear sights, brown plastic thumb-rest grips and were usually blued. A mechanical hold-open was added two-thirds of the way

through the production run. The SK-100 (1954-7) was similar but had the new 100-series takedown system. Guns made in series 102 and 103 (1957-70, 1974-7) had tapering 4.5-inch or 6.75-inch barrels and the characteristics of their particular groups. Many of those made in 1974-7 were nickeled instead of blued. The guns in Series 107 had military-style frames and fixed rear sights; barrel-length options were restricted to 4.75 and 6.75 inches. "SH" pistols had a new dismantling system and optional electroless nickel finish.

• *Sport King Lightweight* (1956-64) This was a version of the standard Sport King with an aluminum-alloy frame. Most guns were black-anodized, but some sold in 1957-60 were nickeled.

Supermatic (1951-84) Chambered only for the 22 LR rimfire round, the earliest guns of this type had heavyweight cylindrical barrels, 4.5 or 6.75 inches long, and adjustable rear sights on the slide. They were usually blued, had grooved straps, and brown plastic thumb-rest style grips. The front sight was mounted on a rib dovetailed into the top of the barrel, and a groove beneath the barrel accepted either auxiliary weights or a filler-strip. Magazines held 10 rounds. The "S-100" (1954 only) was similar but had the 100-series takedown system. Series 101 had the group changes listed above, and the 6.75-inch-barrel option had a single compensator slot on each side of the front sight.

Supermatic Citation (1959-83) Made to the same general specification as the Trophy variant, this offered a lower quality of finish. Series 102 and 103 pistols were finished in ordinary blue, had checkered plastic grips and barrels that lacked the muzzle brake. The rear sight was mounted on the slide. A 5.5-inch heavy "bull" barrel was available from 1962 onward. Guns made in Series 104 had the rear sight on the slide, auxiliary barrel weights, grooved straps and checkered walnut thumb-rest grips. The barrels could be 5.5-inch "bull" or the 6.75-, 8- or 10-inch tapered patterns that were discontinued in 1964-5. Series 106 introduced the military-style frame, stippled grips and a rear sight that was mounted on a bridge at the rear of the slide. The barrels were either 5.5-inch "bull" or 7.25-inch fluted. Series 107 and "SH" representatives were similar to the 106 type but had alterations to the frame and, in the "SH" guns, a different dismantling system. Barrel options remained the same.

Supermatic Tournament (1959-81) Introduced in Series 102, this was a simplified form of the Trophy and Citation patterns, with tapering 4.5- or 6.75-inch barrel (with neither stabilizer nor weights), checkered plastic grips and a rear sight mounted on the slide. The 4.5-inch-barrel option was replaced by a 5.5-inch "bull" pattern in 1962. Series 104 guns, discontinued in 1965, had 5.5- or 6.75-inch barrels. Those in Series 106 had military-style frames, "bridged" rear sights and stippled grip straps; the "107" group had changes in the frame and smooth straps.

Supermatic Trophy (1959-83) Another of the Series 102 pistols, this was in 22 LR rimfire with a choice of 6.75-, 8- or 10-inch barrels that were fluted to hold the adjustable weights. The rear sight was mounted on the barrel block, above the chamber, to ensure that the relationship between the sights remained constant even if wear affected the movement of the slide, and the barrels had an enlarged collar at the muzzle to accept a detachable brake. The straps were grooves, the grips were walnut, the trigger was often gold-plated and a special high-polish blue finish was used. Series 103 guns were distinguished largely by their markings. However, a plain-sided 5.5-inch "bull" barrel was available from 1962, and a fluted 7.25-inch type appeared in 1963. Guns of this type were also made in Series 104, 106, 107 and SH. The "104" examples, discontinued in 1965, had 5.5-inch "bull" or 6.75-inch tapered barrels with detachable muzzle brakes, checkered straps, thumb-rest style walnut grips and an adjustable rear sight dovetailed into the top of the slide. The remainder all had military-style frames, the barrel options becoming 5.5-inch "bull" and 7.25-inch flute.

• *Olympic Commemorative Model* Made for the 1972 Munich games, this was a deluxe version of the Supermatic Trophy, with extensive scroll engraving on the frame and barrel, and the five-ring Olympic motif on the right side of the slide. Though High Standard had announced that a thousand "T"-prefix guns would be made, the deaths of Israeli team members in a terrorist attack cast a shadow over the project. Only 107 guns were completed.

Victor (1973-83) Made in Series 104, 107 and SH, this gun, while retaining the basic construction system begun with the "G" series, adopted a slab-sided barrel that continued the profile of the frame and slide. The 104-type guns — made only in 1973-4 — had 4.5- or 5.5-inch barrels with solid or ventilated straps, checkered walnut thumb-rest grips and adjustable sights that were integral with the rib. A few were made with 6.75-inch barrels with steel or aluminum-alloy ventilated ribs. Series 107 introduced the military-style frame, which was allied with the two short slab-sided barrel options and solid or ventilated ribs (initially steel, later aluminum-alloy). After 1977, a short groove was cut in the right side of the slide, immediately behind the chamber, to improve ejection. "SH"-type guns had an improved dismantling system.

HIGH-STANDARD MFG CO., INC.

Houston, Texas, USA.

A new business was formed in 1993 to perpetuate the name of the original High Standard business, which had collapsed some years earlier. Work on a few of the original target pistols continues. Current production includes the *Olympic Military* (introduced in 1994); the *Olympic Rapid Fire* (1996); the *Supermatic Citation* (1994; "MS" version, 1996); the *Supermatic Tournament* and *Supermatic Trophy* (1994); the *Trophy Target*; the *Victor* (1994); and the *10-X Model Target* (1994).

HI-POINT

Dayton, Ohio, USA.

These guns have been marketed under a variety of names. They were originally known as the "Stallard JS-9", after the designer, but have been offered as "Haskell" (the actual manufacturer) or even "Iberia" (sometimes listed as "Iberica") until the name settled on "Hi-Point" in the mid-1990s. The guns are currently being distributed by MKS Supply, Inc. Basically blow-backs, they have internal drop-safe trigger/hammer systems.

Model C This, the standard gun, is chambered for the 9mm Parabellum cartridge. It is about 6.7 inches long with a 3.5-inch barrel and weighs about 32 oz without its 8-round magazine. The stainless steel slide and the alloy frame have a black or chrome finish, and the grips are checkered acetyl resin. Sights, originally fixed, became an adjustable three-dot system in 2002.

- *Model C-P* (or "C-Polymer") This has a polymer frame, reducing empty weight to about 28 oz.
- *Model C-P Lightweight* This combines the polymer frame with an aluminum-alloy slide, reducing weight still further.
- *Model C-Comp* (1998 to date) An enlargement of the basic Model C, this has a 4-inch barrel with a compensator, slotted to receive a laser designator or a flashlight. The rear sight is adjustable, the trigger is restricted to single action and a 10-round magazine is standard.

Model CF (or "Model 380") This handles the 380 ACP round and has a magazine capacity of eight. The frame is polymer, giving an empty weight of about 29 oz with the 3.5-inch barrel. Three-dot combat sights have been fitted since 2002.

- *Model CF Comp* (or "380 Comp") This is a variant of the CF with a 4-inch barrel and a compensator/muzzle brake unit. It is supplied with a trigger lock, an alternative 10-round magazine and an action that is held open after the last shot has been fired.

Model JH (or "Model 45", 1991 to date) Derived from the JS (q.v.), this is a variant of the 9mm gun chambering the 45 ACP round. It is about 8 inches long, with a 4.5-inch barrel, and weighs about 39 oz

empty. The magazine holds seven cartridges. Made prior to 2002 with fixed sights, an alloy frame and black or chrome/black finish, the guns are now being provided with adjustable three-dot combat sights and a polymer frame.

Model JS (or "JS-9", 1991-8?) This was the original 9mm Parabellum gun, which provided the basis for the first 40 S&W and 45 ACP derivatives. It was 7.7 inches long, had a 4-inch barrel and weighed 39 oz without its eight-round magazine. The full-length 9mm pistol has now been replaced with the Model CP (above), and the alternative chamberings are now usually classified separately.

Model 40 (1991 to date) Chambered for the 40 S&W cartridge, this derives from the JS pattern (q.v.), weighing 39 oz empty. Magazine capacity is eight. Originally made with an alloy frame and black or black/chrome finish, the M40 is now being provided with a polymer frame. The sights are currently three-dot combat patterns.

HISPANO-ARGENTINA FABRICAS DE AUTOMOVILES SA ("HAFDASA")

Buenos Aires, Argentina.

HAFDASA entered the pistol business in the 1930s with the production—for the Argentine government—of a near-copy of the Colt M1911A1. It then made a 22-caliber rimfire automatic of unusual appearance, before abandoning the field as abruptly as it had entered.

A typical HAFDASA Ballester Molina pistol. Note the pattern of the slide-retraction system.

Ballester-Molina (1938-44) This was the original HAFDASA product, a close copy of the Colt M1911A1. The Argentine gun lacks the grip safety of its American prototype. It also has a somewhat longer slide and a smaller butt suited better for a small hand than the Colt. Externally, the quickest identifying mark is the irregular spacing of the finger grips on the slide, and the markings: "PISTOLA AUTOMATICA CAL .45 FABRICADO POR "HAFDASA" / "PATENTES INTERNA-CIONALES POR "BALLESTER-MOLINA" / "INDUSTRIA ARGENTI-NA" in three lines.

Substantial quantities served the Argentine army and police, and several hundred were bought by the British Purchasing Agency in 1939-40. These were eventually supplied to the Special Operations Executive ("SOE") and other clandestine organizations and are found in Europe more frequently than expected.

A 22 LR rimfire version, presumably a training pistol, was also manufactured in small numbers. It is externally identical to the 45 ACP pattern but is a simple blowback.

Criolla This was a copy of the 22-caliber Colt Ace (q.v.) pistol, sold commercially in the late 1930s. The slide is marked "La Criolla".

Hafdasa Because of the side marking, the Ballester-Molina is often called the "Hafdasa", though this name was rightfully carried only by an unusual 22-caliber blowback. The tubular receiver, carried on the frame, not only contains the barrel but also has a long ejection port cut in both sides. The rear section of the receiver encloses the bolt, with striker and recoil spring, which is retained by a screw-on end cap. The butt is wide and well-raked, and the whole pistol is well made and efficient, except for an awkward turn-button safety catch on the left grip. The pistol is cocked by grasping the serrated portion of the bolt through the ejection ports and pulling it back. The only marking is an "HA" monogram molded into the grips.

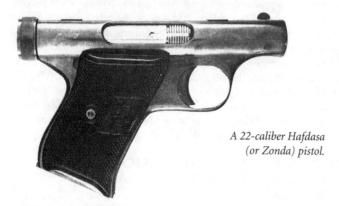

A 22-caliber Hafdasa (or Zonda) pistol.

Zonda Another name for the Hafdasa, found on the receiver.

HJS ARMS, INC.

Brownsville, Texas, USA.

Maker of a variety of ultra-lightweight derringers.

Antique Derringer (1994-8) Also mistakenly listed as "Antigua" or "Antiqua", this was a variant of the 22-caliber Frontier Four with a blued barrel cluster, a brass frame and brown plastic grips.

Frontier Four Derringer (1993-8) Derived from the Sharps & Hankins (q.v.) "cluster derringer", introduced commercially in 1859, this had a block of four barrels chambering the 22 LR rimfire cartridge. These were fired sequentially by a rotating firing pin in the standing breech. The sheathed-trigger pistols were made of stainless steel and had brown plastic grips; they were about 4 inches long with 2-inch barrels and weighed barely 6 oz.

Lone Star Derringer (1993-8) A single-shot tip-barrel cartridge derringer, based on the Southerner, this was made of stainless steel and had a beryllium firing-pin. Measuring a fraction under 4 inches long with a 2-inch barrel chambered for the 380 ACP round, it weighed about 6 oz.

HOLLY MANUFACTURING CO.

A spurious "company" brand name found on suicide special revolvers made by Reid (q.v.).

HOOD FIRE ARMS CO.

Norwich, Connecticut, USA.

Freeman W. Hood operated independently in Norwich from about 1873 to 1882, making and advertising guns on his own account, but then retired to concentrate on licensing his patents to other gunmakers.

The Hood pistols were almost all of the familiar solid-frame sheathed-trigger non-ejecting "Suicide Special" class, offered in 22 or 32 rimfire. They varied in barrel length, cylinder grooving and butt-shape, but otherwise followed a basic pattern. The names were used probably to differentiate between pistols sold through various distributors; the "Scout", for example, was sold by the Frankfurth Hardware Company of Milwaukee.

An almost infallible indication of a Hood revolver, whatever other names it may bear, lies in the rifling. To save time and expense, the revolver barrels were smooth-bored, but, to deceive prospective purchasers, the half-inch nearest the muzzle had five grooves in the bore. This gave the impression of rifling, though there was no effect upon the bullet apart from allowing gas to escape.

A.A.Co. An unidentified brand name, perhaps "American Arms Co.".

Alaska Made c. 1876-82, this was a seven-shot gun chambered for the 22 Short rimfire round. It had a sheathed trigger and a bird's-head grip.

Alert (or "Alert 1874") Chambering the 22 Short rimfire round, this had a solid frame, a 7-chamber cylinder, a sheathed trigger, a 2.25-inch round barrel and bird's-head grips. The barrel was rifled with five grooves, twisting to the left.

Alexia, Alexis Names applied to typical Hood "Suicide Special" revolvers that were essentially similar to the Alert listed previously.

Boy's Choice This was a solid-frame 7-shot 22 Short rimfire revolver with a sheath trigger made by Hood in the mid-1870s.

Brutus Another 22 Short rimfire solid-frame sheathed-trigger design, this seven-shot revolver dates from 1875-7. It was similar to the "Alaska" pattern.

Continental Conventional solid-frame Hood revolvers, dating from the late 1870s, these have the five false "rifling grooves" cut into the barrel at the muzzle.

Czar A seven-shot 22 Short rimfire revolver, this had a solid frame and a sheathed trigger. The butt was either saw-handle or squared-heel, and the barrels varied in length from 2 to 7.5 inches. Made in the 1875-1882 period, it had, rather unusually for a Hood product, three-groove rifling that extended for the full length of the barrel.

Hard Pan (c. 1875-85) These guns offered the usual solid-frame sheathed-trigger construction. Usually found with a 2.5-inch barrel, they are chambered either for 22 Short rimfire (seven chambers) or 32 Short rimfire (five chambers). False rifling is customary. Individual examples may be marked "HARD PAN" or "HARD PAN No 1".

International A cheap solid-frame, sheath-trigger revolver in 22 and 32 rimfire chamberings, this probably dates from 1875-82. It has false rifling at the muzzle.

Jewel No. 1 This was a brand name encountered on 22 rimfire solid-frame sheathed-trigger "Suicide Special" revolvers made by Hood in the 1870s.

Liberty This name was applied to a series of 22 and 32 rimfire revolvers made in 1875-1900 by Hood and other gunmakers, suggesting that it was owned by a distributor. The guns are typical solid-frame sheathed-trigger non-ejectors in 22 rimfire (seven shots) or 32 rimfire (five shots). Although they are simply marked "LIBERTY" on the barrel and are said to have been sold by Sears Roebuck as late as 1902, the Hood products — dating prior to 1882 — can be identified by their false rifling. The newer guns are either smoothbores or have full five-groove rifling.

Little John A sheath-trigger solid-framed "Suicide Special" made by Hood in the late 1870s with false rifling. It will usually be chambered for 22 or 32 rimfire cartridges, the cylinders having seven and five chambers, respectively.

Marquis of Lorne A 32-caliber sheathed-trigger solid-frame non-ejecting revolver made in the late 1870s.

Mohegan Another of the five-shot 32 rimfire non-ejecting "Suicide Specials" with a solid frame and a sheathed trigger, dating from 1875-82. One of Hood's better products, it usually has scroll engraving on the frame and grips of bone.

"New York Pistol Co." A name found on seven-shot 22 rimfire revolvers of the usual solid-frame non-ejecting type made by Hood prior to c. 1882.

Robin Hood A non-ejecting 22 rimfire revolver with a solid frame and a sheathed trigger, dating from about 1880.

Scout This was another of the many solid-frame revolvers made by Hood prior to 1882, with a solid frame and a sheathed trigger.

Tramp's Terror Dating from 1875-82 and generally found in 32 rimfire chambering (with a five-chamber cylinder), this combined a solid frame with a sheathed trigger. The mechanism was non-ejecting. Guns with this mark were also made by Johnson & Bye and Iver Johnson, suggesting that it was owned by a distributor.

Union Jack A typical Hood "Suicide Special", probably dating from the late 1870s, this offered the usual combination of a solid frame and a sheathed trigger. Like many of these guns, it was "false rifled" at the muzzle.

Wide Awake A non-ejecting solid-frame rimfire "Suicide Special" revolver, this sheathed-trigger pattern was probably made about 1880. The name is also found on revolvers made by Forehand & Wadsworth.

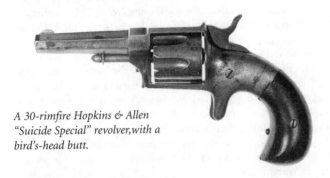

A 30-rimfire Hopkins & Allen "Suicide Special" revolver, with a bird's-head butt.

HOPKINS & ALLEN

Norwich, Connecticut, USA.

This once-powerful gunmaking business was founded in 1868 by two Hopkins brothers and C.H. Allen. They later allowed others to buy shares in the firm, and as a result, lost control of it in later years. The company made a huge variety of inexpensive revolvers under a variety of names but got into financial difficulties and in 1898 was re-organized as the "Hopkins & Allen Arms Co.". A disastrous fire in 1900 impeded progress, but the Forehand Arms Company was purchased in 1901 and trading improved. A contract to make Belgian rifles was secured shortly after World War I began in Europe, but before it could be completed, Hopkins & Allen were enveloped in the Marlin-Rockwell Corporation in 1917. The Norwich factory was put to making parts for the Browning automatic rifle, and with that, the Hopkins & Allen name finally vanished into gunmaking history.

Acme This revolver, made in 1893 for the Hulbert Brothers (successors to Merwin, Hulbert & Co.), was the same as the hammerless "Forehand 1891" model listed below. Chambered for 32 or 38 centerfire ammunition, it was a five-shot solid-framed non-ejector with a safety catch on the backstrap that prevented the hammer reaching full cock.

Aristocrat A pocket revolver manufactured for sale by the Supplee-Biddle Hardware Company of Philadelphia in 1870-1900, this solid-frame non-ejecting design was available in 22 Short rimfire (seven shots) or 32 Short rimfire (five shots). It had a sheathed trigger and single-action lockwork.

American Eagle This solid-frame sheathed-trigger revolver was made in 1870-1898 in 22 or 32 rimfire, with seven- and five-chambered cylinders, respectively. Identical guns were offered with other names such as "Monarch" and "Mountain Eagle".

Americus Another of the many names for the standard Hopkins and Allen 22 rimfire solid-frame sheathed-trigger seven-shot revolver, this presumably hid the identity of a distributor. It was manufactured between 1870 and 1900.

Automatic (1885-1910) The obsolescence of solid-frame guns, evident by the mid-1880s, persuaded Hopkins & Allen to introduce the first of their tipping-barrel patterns. An ejector automatically expelled spent cases when the barrel was opened. The barrel/cylinder assembly was latched to the frame by a neatly designed spring-loaded double latch, and a "hammerless" version, with the frame extended upward at the rear, could also be obtained. The chamberings were usually 22 rimfire or 32 centerfire types.

Bloodhound This was a seven-shot solid-frame revolver, accepting 22 Short cartridges, made about 1880. It had the usual single-action sheathed trigger.

Blue Jacket Made in the late 1870s, this was another solid-frame non-ejecting revolver with a sheathed trigger. It seems to have been offered only in a variety of rimfire chamberings: 22 Short (No. 1, seven shots), 32 Short (No. 2, five shots), 38 Short (No. 3, five shots) or 41 Short (No. 4, five shots).

Blue Whistler Virtually the same as Blue Jacket No. 2, this was a five-shot 32-caliber revolver with a solid frame and a sheathed trigger. The name has also been reported on shotguns made by the Crescent Arms Company but has yet to be linked with an individual distributor.

Captain Jack A solid-frame sheathed-trigger non-ejecting rimfire revolver made in the 1870s in 22 and 32 calibers.

Chichester A solid-frame sheath-trigger 38 Short rimfire revolver made by Hopkins & Allen in the 1880s, this had a five-chamber cylinder and a 10-inch barrel.

Czar These revolvers probably date from 1882-90. The most popular pattern was in 22 rimfire, with a solid frame, a sheathed trigger, a seven-chamber cylinder, a 3.5-inch octagonal barrel and a saw-handle butt. Most examples had scroll engraving on the frame, and many will also bear a dealer's name. A similar 32 rimfire version was also made, but not in such great quantities. The name has also been found on guns made by Hood (q.v.), which are assumed to date from an earlier era.

Defender This was a solid-frame non-ejector with a sheath trigger and a cylinder holding seven 22 rimfire or five 32 rimfire rounds. It dates from the late 1870s or early 1880s.

Dictator A 32 Short rimfire revolver made in the 1880s, this followed the customary solid-frame sheathed-trigger non-ejecting design of the period, with single-action lockwork and a saw-handle or bird's-head butt. The 2.9-inch barrel was round, and the five-chamber cylinder could be removed once the arbor had been released by its spring-clip.

Double Action No. 6 This was a simple solid-frame revolver, with a loading gate on the right side of the frame behind the six-chamber cylinder and double-action lockwork. Chambering was largely restricted to 32 centerfire, though a few rimfire examples may also have been made.

Faultless A typical Hopkins & Allen "Suicide Special", this was a solid-frame gun with a sheathed trigger. It was offered in 22 and 32 caliber, capable of seven and five shots, respectively.

A five-shot 38-caliber Hopkins & Allen Automatic Model, marked by the Warner Arms Co.

The Hopkins & Allen 32-caliber "Forehand Model 1891" revolver.

Forehand Model 1891 Made for Forehand & Wadsworth, this marked a reversion to cheap solid-frame non-ejectors. Distinguished by a pivoting loading gate on the right side of the frame behind the five-chamber cylinder, the 32-caliber gun accepted centerfire ammunition. A "hammerless" version was also available. The way in which the guns are constructed suggests that they were made on machinery that had previously been used to make the Double Action No. 6 (above).

Hopkins & Allen The first revolvers with the company's name were "Suicide Specials", similar to many of those described above, and the first steps forward were taken with the "Solid Frame Single Action" of 1875 — which could be charitably described as the original sheathed-trigger design with a conventional trigger and guard.

Imperial Arms Co. A name applied to the 32- and 38-caliber "hammerless" Automatic Revolver for sale through an unidentified distributor.

Joker This was a solid-frame non-ejector with a sheathed trigger. It is believed to have been confined to 32 rimfire, with a five-chamber cylinder and a bird's-head butt. The name was also used by Marlin (q.v.).

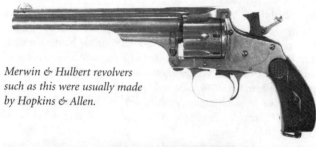

Merwin & Hulbert revolvers such as this were usually made by Hopkins & Allen.

A Hopkins & Allen 22 LR rimfire Safety Police revolver.

Another H&A Safety Police revolver, this time chambered for 38 centerfire ammunition.

Merwin & Hulbert This name graced a range of revolvers incorporating an ejection system patented in 1874-7 by Williams, Moore & Hulbert. Most of these guns will bear the Merwin & Hulbert name, but they were all made by Hopkins & Allen and will sometimes be marked accordingly. Additional details will be found in the "Merwin, Hulbert & Co." entry.

Monarch Another of the many names applied to solid-frame sheathed-trigger non-ejecting revolvers of the type common in the 1880s. The Hopkins & Allen version can be found in 22 and 32 rimfire chamberings, capable of firing seven and five shots, respectively.

Mountain Eagle A solid-frame non-ejecting revolver of the 1870s; see "American Eagle", above.

Ranger A 22 rimfire "Suicide Special", dating from the early 1880s. It

is a typical solid-frame design, with a seven-chamber cylinder and a sheathed trigger.

Red Jacket Another Hopkins and Allen solid-frame sheathed-trigger non-ejecting revolver of the 1880s, this was made in two patterns: "No. 1" was a seven-shot in 22 Short rimfire, and "No. 2" was a similar five-shot weapon in 32 Short rimfire. See also "Blue Jacket".

Safety Police Model (1907-15) After the re-organization of 1898 and the dreadful fire of 1900, Hopkins & Allen attempted to regain their former eminence by producing this revolver in 22 LR rimfire and 32 or 38 centerfire. This was a very good design; the tipping-barrel and ejection system came from the Automatic, but the lockwork was altered to prevent accidental discharge. This "Triple Action Safety" relied on a hammer mounted on an eccentric axis pin. The hammer could strike the firing pin only when the trigger was pressed to revolve the axis pin (and the nose of the hammer) downward; if the hammer was simply caught, pulled back and released, it struck an abutment on the frame before it could touch the pin. However, good as it was, the Safety Police Model came too late to save the company. Production struggled on until lucrative contracts from the belligerents in Europe were secured early in World War I.

Toledo Firearms Company This name appears on "Suicide Specials" made by Hopkins & Allen and E.L. Dickinson (q.v.).

Tower's Police Safety A mark found on solid-frame sheathed-trigger non-ejecting rimfire revolvers of the 1870s, usually attributed to Hopkins & Allen.

Universal These were conventional non-ejecting revolvers, with solid frames and sheathed triggers, made in the 1870s and 1880s in 22 Short and 32 Short rimfire chamberings.

XL series This brand name appeared in 1871, attached to the inevitable solid-frame sheath-trigger "Suicide Specials", and remained in production into the 1880s. There were several different patterns:

- *XL No 1* This was a seven-shot gun, chambering the 22 Short rimfire round.
- *XL No. 2* A variant of the No. 1 in 30 Short rimfire with a five-chamber cylinder.
- *XL No 2-1/2* Virtually identical with the XL No. 2, this differed principally in its chambering for the 32 Short rimfire.
- *XL No. 3* More powerful than the preceding No. 2 and No. 2-1/2, this was a five-shot gun chambering the 32 Long rimfire cartridge.
- *XL No. 3 DA* Introduced in 1885, this 32 Short centerfire revolver, with a 2.5-inch round barrel, adopted a conventional trigger guard, a double-action trigger system, a hammer with folding spur (to avoid catching in the pocket) and a square butt.
- *XL No 4* A survivor of the sheath-trigger period, this was still a single-action solid-frame non-ejector. The cylinder had five chambers, accepting the 38 rimfire cartridge.
- *XL No 5* A successor to the No. 4, essentially to the same pattern, this five-shot gun was intended to fire 38 centerfire cartridges. A rimfire version was also made in small quantities.
- *XL No 6 DA* This was a 38-caliber version of the No 3 DA, chambering centerfire ammunition.
- *XL No 7* The largest and most powerful of the original solid-frame sheath-trigger non-ejectors, this was chambered for the 41 rimfire cartridge.
- *XL Bulldog* This was similar to the No. 6 DA, with a double-action trigger and a conventional trigger guard, but was chambered for 32 or 38 Merwin & Hulbert centerfire ammunition.

HOURAT & VIE

Manufacture d'Armes Hourat et Vie, Pau, France.

Very little is known about this firm, which appears to have operated briefly during the 1930s in the south of France. With Pau being close to the Spanish border, it is hardly surprising that the "H.V." pistols are simply the 6.35mm "Eibar" type, albeit of an excellent standard of finish. It is possible that the major casting and machining was done in Eibar, allowing the parts to be exported to France for finishing and assembly. The slide is marked "FABRICATION FRANÇAISE" and "SYST. BREVETE HOURAT ET VIE", separated by an encircled "HV" monogram. A similar, but more ornate, monogram lies in a cartouche on the grips.

A typical H&R 1871, Inc., revolver.

H&R 1871, INC.
Gardner, Massachusetts, USA.
A lineal successor to Harrington & Richardson (q.v.), formed after the parent company collapsed, H&R offers a few of the original revolvers: *Model 929 Sidekick* (reintroduced in 1996), *Model 939 Premier* (1995), *Model 949 Western* (1994) and *Model 999 Sportsman* (1992). The company also marketed the *American*, developed in collaboration with Erma (q.v.) and briefly made in the USA by Amtec 2000.

HUNTER
Hy Hunter Firearms Co., Inc., Hollywood
and Burbank, California, USA.
Hunter was a distributor who dealt in a wide variety of firearms. The name will be found on the "Frontier Six Shooter", a Western-style single-action 22 LR rimfire revolver made in Germany by Röhm (q.v.); on the "Detective" and "Chicago Cub", both cheap 22-caliber pocket revolvers from Germany; and automatic pistols in 22, 25, 32 and 380 calibers under the names "Maxim", "Military", "Panzer", "Stingray", and "Stuka". The pistols are suspected to have been made in Italy, possibly by Galesi Figli or Rigarmi, but are sometimes mistakenly credited to Rhöner.

HUSQVARNA ARMS FACTORY
Husqvarna Våpenfabriks AB, Huskvarna, Sweden.
∼ REVOLVER ∼
Nagant M1887 This 7.5mm six-shot solid-frame rod-ejecting revolver was originally made for the Swedish army by the Nagant brothers in Liége. In 1897, however, Husqvarna obtained a production license and work continued until 1905. Small quantities were also made

The 9mm Swedish M40 Lahti service pistol, made by Husqvarna.

A right-side view of the Swedish M40 Lahti. This is the second-pattern gun, with the front of the trigger guard made flush with the frame.

for sale commercially, in 7.5mm and 38 S&W Long. There have also been reports of 22 rimfire versions, but it is suspected that these were later conversions — perhaps for training — and were not "factory original". Revolvers of this type were held in reserve for many years, and military-surplus guns were still being offered for sale in the USA as late as 1958.

∼ AUTOMATIC PISTOLS ∼
M07 Browning The decision to make FN-Brownings in Sweden was due to the German invasion of Belgium in 1914, which had cut supplies from Fabrique Nationale d'Armes de Guerre (q.v.). Production in the Husqvarna factory, begun in 1917, continued until 1941. The greatest annual output had occurred in 1918, owing to the need to re-equip, and in 1940 when war threatened.

The M07 was essentially similar to the FN-Browning M1903, but the slide was marked "HUSQVARNA VAPENFABRIKS AKTIEBOLAG" and "SYSTEM BROWNING". There were also a few minor dimensional changes, and the molded plastic grips have "crown h" marks instead of the FN monogram. Swedish pistols also display distinctive inspectors' marks and may have unit marks (e.g., "I 12 No. 245") on the left side of the frame above the grip.

M40 Lahti As World War II gripped the rest of Europe, the Swedish army realized that there would be a shortage of handguns in the event of universal mobilization. The Walther Heeres-Pistole had been adopted in 1939, but the outbreak of war had stopped supplies. As the FN-Browning GP-35 was also unavailable, the Swedes chose the Lahti. However, the Finnish small-arms factory was unable to supply standard 1935-type guns, owing to disputes with the USSR, and so production was licensed to the Svenska Automatvåpen AB. This company failed almost as soon as work had started, and the contract was passed over to Husqvarna. The first Husqvarna-Lahti pistols reached the Swedish army in 1942.

There were some differences between the Finnish L-35 and the Swedish M40. The Husqvarna gun has a slightly longer barrel, hexagonal at the breech reinforce, and the trigger guard is heavier. It lacks both the loaded-chamber indicator and lock-retaining spring of its Finnish prototype. The front sight is higher, with a vertical rear edge, and the grips carry the Husqvarna "crown h" motif. The first 5000 pistols had a reinforcing fillet on the receiver, above the guide rails, but this was then abandoned.

When work stopped in 1946, about 83,950 Lahti pistols had been made in Sweden — including about 1000 for commercial sale.

Unfortunately, modifications to the design, which included changes in the specification of the steels, were not particularly successful. The Lahti gave trouble in Swedish service, aggravated by the adoption of a high-powered 9mm Parabellum cartridge developed for use in submachine guns. A spate of cracked frames forced the withdrawal of the guns in 1980, and the ageing M07 FN-Brownings were issued from store while a new handgun was selected. This ultimately proved to be the Glock.

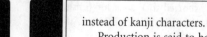

IAI

IAI-American Legends, Inc., Houston, Texas, USA.

Best known for military rifles, including "re-manufactured" Garands, IAI has also handled 1911A1-type Colt-Brownings.

M999 This was a comparatively short-lived variant of the M2000, offered either entirely in stainless steel or with a stainless-steel slide and a blued carbon-steel frame. Fixed sights and rubber combat-style grips were standard. The controls — slide-stop, safety catch and magazine catch — were all enlarged.

M2000 This is a variant of the M1911A1, supplied in standard or compact forms (5-inch or 4.25-inch barrels, respectively), with fixed sights, a 1911-straight-butt frame and a beveled feed ramp. It is parkerized, with checkered plastic or wood grips. The magazine holds eight 45 ACP rounds.

IAR, INC.

San Juan Capistrano, California, USA.

Importer of Uberti-made "Western" revolvers from 1996 onward, including the *1873 Six-Shooter*, *1873 Frontier* (introduced in 1997) and *1873 Frontier Marshal* (1998). The *Model 1872 Derringer* (1996) and *Model 1888 Double Derringer* (1999) are currently being made in the USA, the former on the machinery that was once used by Colt (q.v.).

TEODORO IBARZABAL

Eibar, Spain.

Little is known of Ibarzabal, except that he made a 45-caliber open-frame revolver, loosely based on the "Montenegrin" style, in the 1880s. One gun of this type survives in the museum in Eibar.

ILLINOIS ARMS COMPANY

A sales name applied to pre-1939 revolvers made by Friedrich Pickert (q.v.) of Zella Mehlis, Germany, for sale in the USA.

IMPERIAL ARMS COMPANY

A sales name adopted by Hopkins & Allen (q.v.) for 32- and 38-caliber "Automatic Hammerless" revolvers sold by an as yet unidentified distributor.

INAGAKI

Inagaki Gun Factory, Suginami, Tokyo, Japan.

Iwakichi Inagaki retired in 1924 from the artillery arsenal in Koishikawa, Tokyo, and opened a gun shop that made a variety of shotguns, sporting rifles and even airguns. When the Japanese became embroiled in war with China in 1937, the gunsmith designed a pistol. This was not submitted to the army until 1941, but there is a suggestion that production had not only begun some time earlier but also that a few hundred had been acquired for Japanese navy pilots.

Inagaki shiki ("Inagaki type") This was a simple 7.65mm blowback of conventional appearance except for a short length of exposed barrel in front of the slide. Its unusual features included the dismantling method, which relied on a peg extending upward from the front web of the trigger guard, and twin return springs held beneath the barrel by a screw and a transverse plate in the front of the slide. A leaf spring with a heavy head served as a hammer. The gun was about 6.5 inches long, with a 2.8-inch barrel, and weighed 23 oz without its eight-round magazine. The bluing was excellent, the grips were diagonally-grooved acacia, and an "IS" monogram lay on the rear right side of the frame. The probability that the gun was designed for the commercial market is shown by the safety-catch markings: "S" ("safe") and "F" ("fire")

instead of kanji characters.

Production is said to have stopped in 1943, after about 500 guns had been made, to allow a variant to be developed for the more powerful Japanese 8mm pistol cartridge. The enlarged Inagaki was not successful and only a few prototypes were made.

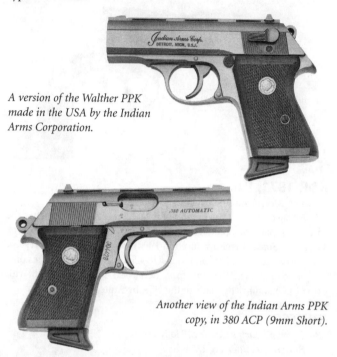

A version of the Walther PPK made in the USA by the Indian Arms Corporation.

Another view of the Indian Arms PPK copy, in 380 ACP (9mm Short).

INDIAN ARMS CORPORATION

Detroit, Michigan, USA.

This gunmaking business promoted a slightly modified copy of the Walther Model PP in 1975-7, chambered for the 380 ACP (9mm Short) cartridge. The guns were made of stainless steel and had a ventilated rib above the slide, but it has been estimated that only about 1000 were made.

INDIAN SALES COMPANY

Cheyenne, Wyoming, USA.

This distributorship sold the Herbert Schmidt (q.v.) KS21 revolver and HS4 automatic pistol under their name in the 1970s.

INDUSTRIA ARGENTINA

This mark has been reported on a 22 LR rimfire single-shot pistol, emanating from Argentina. It is also found on the frames of "Firestorm" guns acquired in Argentina by SGS Importers International. The "Compact Firestorm" (10-shot 22 LR and seven-shot 380 ACP) and the "Mini-Firestorm" (9mm Parabellum or 40 S&W, 10 shots) are made by Bersa as the Thunder 380 and Thunder 9, respectively. The "Firestorm Government Model", a 45 ACP M1911 clone, does not come from the same source.

INDUSTRIA ARMERA

R.S. Industria Armera, Eibar, Spain.

Omega This name has been reported on a 7.65mm "Eibar" blowback automatic made shortly after World War I. However, it is also associated with the guns made by Armero Especialistas, and its status is questionable.

An IMBEL-made M/973 Brazilian army pistol, copied from the 1911-type Colt-Browning. Note the designation and the property mark.

INDUSTRIÁ DO MATERIEL BELICÓ DE BRASIL ("IMBEL")

Fábrica Itajubá, Brazil.

M973 This is the current Brazilian service weapon, a close copy of the Colt-Browning M1911A1 in 9mm Parabellum instead of 45 ACP. Apart from a magazine capacity of nine rounds instead of seven, the principal differences can be seen in the markings and in the greater rearward overhang of the spur above the thumb web. The guns have 5-inch barrels and weigh about 35.5 oz empty.

M911A1 This is a straightforward copy of the traditional Colt-Browning, differing only in minor details and markings applied to the slide. Chambered for the 45 ACP round, it is accompanied by a seven-round single-column magazine, has a 5-inch barrel and weighs about 36.5 oz empty.

* *TP* Intended for competitive shooting, this is a M1911A1 with a heavy barrel and a variety of refinements. It weighs 37.5 oz.
* *TP Plus* Easily distinguished by a long 5.7-inch barrel protruding from the slide, drilled with six ports acting as a compensator, this also has an eight-round magazine.

A 45 ACP IMBEL Colt-Browning copy. Note the angle of the slide-retraction grooves, which differ from the original Colt-made guns.

GC Series A variant of the M973, these are distinguished by high-capacity ("Grande Capacidade") magazines, holding as many as 19 rounds in a double column, and an extended grip-safety lever.

* *MD1* The basic version, with a 5-inch barrel, had a frame and slide made of blued carbon steel, giving an empty weight of about 38.5 oz. It is offered in 9mm Parabellum (17-round magazine), 380 ACP (19 rounds) and 45 ACP (11 rounds).
* *MD1A1* Similar to the MD1, in the same chamberings, this had a matte-finish stainless steel frame.
* *MD1A2* Another variant of the MD1, this had a frame and slide of stainless steel, bright or matte finished.
* *MD1A3* Though a full-size gun, with the standard high-capacity magazine, this had an aluminum-alloy frame that reduces empty weight considerably. It is offered in 9mm Parabellum, 380 ACP and 40 S&W only.

* *MD2* These are essentially improved versions of the comparable MD1-series designs, with an additional automatic firing-pin safety. Heavy barrels with ramped feed are standard. Offered only in 40 S&W and 45 ACP, with magazine capacities of 14 and 11 rounds, respectively. The 5-inch barrel is standard.
* *MD2A2* This is a minor variant of the MD2, with the slide and frame of stainless steel. This reduces weight fractionally, but not enough to notice without weighing the gun. It comes in 40 S&W and 45 ACP only.
* *MD3A2* Distinguished by 12 ports cut in the barrel and two slots in the slide, acting as a compensator, this is otherwise comparable with the MD2 series. Chambered for the 40 S&W or 45 ACP round, the guns weigh about 39 oz empty; the slides and frames are made of stainless steel.
* *MD4* Offered only in 40 S&W, this is a double-action-only gun with a bobbed hammer. It can be recognized by the design and position of the trigger, which is a slender lever protruding from the frame at the mid-point of the guard instead of the customary sliding blade. The MD4 has a 5-inch barrel, a 16-round magazine and weighs about 38 oz empty. The slide is blued steel, and the frame is heavyweight aluminum-alloy.

SC series The "Super Compactas" guns are short-barrel, short-grip versions of the full-size patterns. Chambered for the 45 ACP round, they have 3.5-inch barrels and weigh about 31 oz with an empty 11-round double-column magazine.

* *MD1* The standard guns have carbon-steel slides and frames and are usually blued.
* *MD1A1* This differs from the MD1 only in the frame, which is made of stainless steel.
* *MD1A2* This gun offers frame and slide in stainless steel, matte or bright finish.

UC Series The "Ultra Compactas" guns , chambered for the 45 ACP round, are also offered in MD1, MD1A1 and MD1A2 versions (see "SC series", above). They retain the 3.5-inch barrel and short grip, but the single-column magazine is restricted to six rounds in an attempt to keep the grip as slender as possible.

INDUSTRIA NACIONAL DE ARMAS ("INA")

Saõ Paulo, Brazil

Now known as "IMBEL" (above), the state-owned ordnance factory made a small quantity of well-finished 32-caliber double-action solid-frame revolvers in the 1960s. Issued to the Brazilian air force and police, the guns were based on Smith & Wesson practice and had 2-inch barrels. An "INA" medallion was let into the grips and a trademark of a pouncing jaguar was engraved in the left of the frame of the guns that were destined to be sold commercially.

JOHN INGLIS & CO.

Toronto, Canada.

Inglis was a general engineering company with no particular interest in firearms until 1938, when the company contracted to make 5000 Bren light machineguns, the first of which was proofed in March 1940. Between then and 1945, some 163,000 guns were made for the British, Canadian and Chinese Nationalist Army.

In 1942, the company received a further contract to manufacture the FN-Browning Model 1935 automatic pistol for supply to the Chinese army. Drawings were not available, and six FN-made pistols retrieved from China were "reverse engineered" to produce working drawings. The need to convert all the metric dimensions to Imperial measure slowed progress, but production commenced in February 1944. When work ended in September 1945, 152,000 pistols had been made for China, Britain, Canada and Greece. On completion of the contract, Inglis closed the production line and left the firearms business.

Pistol No. 1 (GP-35) Two patterns were produced; the "Pistol No. 1", intended for China, had a 500-meter tangent sight and a butt that was slotted to take a shoulder stock. The "Pistol No. 2", for the British and Canadian armies, had a conventional fixed rear sight and no shoulder stock, though some early production guns had the butt appropriately slotted. A few experimental lightweight guns were also made with flutes cut in the sides of the slide.

- *Pistol, Browning, FN 9mm No 1 Mk 1* This had the adjustable rear sight and could accept a shoulder stock.
- *Pistol, Browning, FN 9mm No 1 Mk 1** Little more than a modified Mk 1, this had an improved ejector.
- *Pistol, Browning, FN 9mm No 2 Mk 1* Distinguished by its fixed "V"-notch rear sight, which could be adjusted only by driving it laterally along its doevatil, this also lacked the stock-attachment grooves on the butt heel.
- *Pistol, Browning, FN 9mm No 2 Mk 2* A variant of the No. 2 Mk 1, this incorporated the improved ejector. It did not accept a stock.

INTERARMS
Alexandria, Virginia, USA.

Although once considered primarily as distributors, Interarms made pistols and revolvers in the USA. Operations ceased in 2001.

∼ REVOLVERS ∼

Virginian The basic model was a Western-style six-shot weapon that incorporated lockwork and a transfer-bar safety system that had been patented by Interarms.

- *Virginian Dragoon* This had an adjustable rear sight and came in barrel lengths from 5 to 12 inches and in 357 Magnum, 41 Magnum, 44 Magnum or 45 Long Colt chamberings.
- *Virginian Deputy* Similar to the Dragoon, this was chambered for the 357, 44 Magnum or for 45 Long Colt. It had fixed sights.
- *Virginian 22* A reduced-size version of the Dragoon, made by Hämmerli in Switzerland, this was chambered only for the 22 LR rimfire round.
- *Virginian Dragoon Silhouette* Offered only in stainless steel with a 10.5-inch barrel, this 44 Magnum revolver had special adjustable long-range sights.

∼ PISTOLS ∼

Walther copies To avoid being penalized by the 1968 Gun Control Act, which prohibited the importation of many compact personal-defense pistols, Interarms has also made licensed copies of the Walther PPK/S "American" (introduced in 1980), PPK (1986) and TPH (1987).

INTERDYNAMICS OF AMERICA
Miami, Florida, USA.

This business operated in the early 1980s producing semi-automatic pistols modeled upon submachine guns, the designs of which originated with Interdynamics Forsknings AB of Sweden.

KG-99 (1981-3) Chambered for the 9mm Parabellum round, firing from a closed bolt, this had a 5-inch barrel (threaded at the muzzle for a silencer) within a sheet-steel shroud pierced with ventilation holes. The cocking handle projected upward from the left side of the receiver, and the grip/frame unit was a one-piece synthetic molding. The magazine, protruding vertically ahead of the trigger, usually held 36 rounds though small-capacity alternatives were available to restrict depth. The sights were fixed.

- *KG-99M* (1981-4) This was a compact version of the basic design, with a 3-inch barrel. The shroud was absent, but the muzzle was still threaded to accept a silencer. A 20-round magazine was standard but could be exchanged with the 36-round version.
- *KG-99 Stainless* (1984 only) This was a matte-finish stainless steel version of the KG-99 but was otherwise identical.

INTRATEC
Intratec USA, Inc., Miami, Florida, USA.

Formed to perpetuate the business of Interdynamics (above), this continued to promote the diminutive handguns derived from submachine guns.

∼ TWO-SHOT PISTOL ∼

TEC-38 (1986-8) This was a two-barreled derringer in 38 Special chambering. Based on the Remington double derringer (q.v.), it had a 3-inch tipping-barrel cluster. Unlike most guns of this type, however, the trigger system was double action.

∼ AUTOMATIC PISTOLS ∼

TEC-9 (1985-8) Based on the Interdynamics KG-99, this chambered the 9mm Parabellum round. The 5-inch barrel, threaded at the muzzle to accept a silencer, was contained in a ventilated sheet-steel shroud. The sights were fixed and the grip/frame unit was synthetic. The 36-round magazine was standard. A stainless steel version was also made.

- *TEC-9C* (1987) This was a carbine-length variant of the TEC-9, with a 16-inch barrel and an optional folding butt. It was too large to classify satisfactorily as a pistol.
- *TEC-9M* (1985-8) Also offered in stainless steel, this was a compact version of the basic design with a 3-inch barrel and a 20-round magazine.

TEC-22 (Scorpion, 1986-8) A derivative of the basic design, chambered for the 22 LR rimfire round, this had a 4-inch barrel and a 30-round magazine.

TEC-25 (1986) Similar to the 22 LR version (above), this chambered the 25 ACP round. It was made only in small quantities, as the rimfire ammunition — no less effective — was substantially cheaper.

IRAOLA Y SALAVERRIA
Eibar, Spain.

This was a small company that produced a 7.65mm "Eibar" blowback automatic in the early 1920s. There is nothing remarkable about the pistol, which is marked with the company name and "Automatic Pistol Cal 7 ⁶⁵".

WILLIAM IRVING
New York City, USA.

This gunsmith made 22 and 32 rimfire single-shot derringer pistols and solid-frame revolvers in 1862-3, during the American Civil War. The revolvers had a button set into the top of the tang to release the recoil shield on the right side of the frame. The shield could then be swung upward to expose a chamber; ejection was undertaken manually with the aid of a separate rod. Irving's name is also found on convertible 31 caplock/30 rimfire solid-frame sheathed-trigger revolvers made in accordance with a patent granted to James Reid (q.v.) in April 1863. It has been suggested that Irving's business was subsequently destroyed during the New York Draft Riots of 1864, but the confirmation is lacking.

ISRAEL MILITARY INDUSTRIES ("IMI")
Ramat Ha-Sharon, Israel.

Formed secretly in 1933, during the British Mandate in Palestine, this trading company now markets the products of Israeli government munitions manufacturers — ranging from small arms to electronic equipment and optical sights. These are often sold into the civilian market under the trade name "Samson". The Uzi submachine gun, the Galil rifle, the Negev light machinegun and the Desert Eagle and Jericho pistols are all manufactured by IMI. The company also promoted the 9x21mm pistol cartridge so strongly that it has become known as "9mm IMI". After a reorganization in 1993, IMI was renamed "Ta'as Israel Industries Company", but this change was ignored by the rest of the world and the original name was readopted in 1996.

Uzi Pistol (1984 to date) IMI's first venture in the handgun field, this

The 9mm Uzi pistol is little more than a cut-down submachine gun adapted for one-hand use.

Another view of the Israeli Uzi pistol.

is simply the current "Micro-Uzi" miniature submachine gun converted to semi-automatic form and divested of its folding butt. The result is cumbersome by comparison with conventional pistols but has an exceptional magazine capacity (20 rounds of 9mm Parabellum) and its weight and size allow for a very firm two-handed grip and controllable recoil. Like the submachine gun, it has adjustable sights, a cocking handle projecting from a slot in the top of the receiver, a grip safety and a manual safety catch above the left grip. The Uzi pistol is about 9.5 inches long, with a 4.5-inch barrel, and weighs about 58 oz empty. A loaded magazine adds another 14 oz.

Desert Eagle The origins of this large-caliber pistol have often been disputed. However, a 1984-vintage IMI leaflet states that the Desert Eagle was "Designed, developed and manufactured in Israel … based on a concept originally proposed by M.R.I. Ltd. [Magnum Research Industries] of Minneapolis, Minnesota, USA …" The gun was originally developed for metal silhouette and similar long-range competitive shooting, as well as hunting, and was to chamber the 357 Magnum cartridge. This had been developed for revolvers, and, though providing

The 41/44 Magnum Desert Eagle, available with exchangeable barrels.

very good performance, had a prominent rim. This caused problems not so much in firing and extraction/ejection, but during the feed stroke. The problem was solved by developing a magazine that allowed the rims to stagger laterally, and the Desert Eagle has a good reputation for reliability.

Eventually offered in 41 Magnum, 44 Magnum and 50 Action Express in addition to 357 Magnum, the gas-operated locked-breech pistol relies on a rotating bolt to lock the breech. Gas tapped from the barrel immediately ahead of the cartridge case is piped forward to just below the muzzle, where it enters a gas cylinder. A short-stroke piston inside the cylinder then drives the slide to the rear. A cam track in the slide engages with a lug to rotate and unlock the bolt, allowing the slide and bolt to run back to the limit of the opening stroke and cock the hammer. The parts are then returned by the spring in the frame beneath the barrel, stripping a new round into the chamber, and the gun can be fired again.

An ambidextrous safety catch on the slide can lock the firing pin and disconnect the trigger from the hammer. The standard lockwork can be replaced with an optional assembly allowing full adjustment of trigger pull. Various sight options are available and the slide top is grooved to accept a telescope-sight mount.

The guns were originally offered with a 6-inch barrel, though 8-, 10- and 14-inch options (some with MagnaPorting) were soon introduced. The standard finish on the carbon-steel slide and frame was black oxide, but stainless steel and aluminum-alloy frames have also been made. Special finishes have ranged from gold to "camouflage" and matte chrome with gold highlights!

In 1996, manufacture was switched to the USA, where Magnum Research (q.v.), after initially assembling Israeli-made parts, still makes the "Mark XIX" Desert Eagle in quantity.

Jericho 941 (1990 to date) Widely known in the USA as the "Baby Eagle", this bears a superficial resemblance to the Desert Eagle. Internally, however, it has more in common with the ČZ 75. The

A 357 Desert Eagle pistol, one of the few gas-operated designs that have been made in quantity.

A Desert Eagle with the long-barrel option and an optical sight, a combination that is suitable for metallic-silhouette shooting.

A short-barreled M941 Jericho (or "Baby Eagle").

An IMI M941 Jericho pistol dismantled into major sub-assemblies.

Jericho is a conventional double-action locked-breech pistol, with the slide moving on rails that are cut inside the frame. The breech lock is a variation of the Browning cam, and a slide-mounted safety catch retracts and locks the firing pin before dropping the hammer. The chambering was originally restricted to 9mm Parabellum, but a short-lived 41 Action Express version was also offered. Changing from one caliber to the other was simply a matter of changing barrels and magazines; the cartridges shared base dimensions. The interchangeability explains the designation.

- *941* The standard version is currently available in 9mm Parabellum and 40 S&W, with double-column magazines holding 16 and 12 rounds, respectively (both currently limited to 10 rounds in the USA). It is about 8.1 inches long, with a 4.4-inch barrel, and weighs about 35 oz without the magazine; three-dot combat sights are standard, with Tritium-type night sights as an option.
- *941F* This is a stainless steel version of the standard 941.
- *941FB* Made in 9mm Parabellum or 40 S&W (with magazines holding 13 and nine rounds, respectively), this is a short-barrel short-butt variant of the Jericho design. It is 7.25 inches long, with a 3.5-inch barrel, and weighs about 30.5 oz without a magazine.
- *941FBL* This is a minor variant of the 941FB with an aluminum-alloy frame, reducing weight to 22 oz without magazine.
- *941FS* Offered in 45 ACP (10-round magazine) in addition to 9mm Parabellum and 40 S&W, this combines a full-size frame with a 3.8-inch barrel, reducing overall length to 7.6 inches and empty weight to about 32.5 oz.

- *941PS* Designed for competitive shooting, this version of the 941 has a single-action trigger mechanism (with the trigger lever placed noticeably farther back in the trigger guard), and a 4.1-inch barrel with a compensator. This gives an overall length of about 8.3 inches. The slide is noticeably slimmer at the muzzle than the standard guns, and the front sight is set back to give space for the compensator.

ITALGUNS INTERNATIONAL ("IGI")

Zingone di Tressano, Italy.

IGI appeared in 1973, marketing a 22-caliber target pistol known as the "IGI Domino" or "Domino 601". However, IGI was merely a marketing organization; the pistols were made by Fabbrica Armi Sportive SrL (q.v.) of Settimo Milanese.

ITHACA GUN COMPANY

Ithaca, New York, USA.

In addition to a wide variety of sporting guns and rifles, Ithaca made M1911A1 pistols for the US armed forces during World War II, distinguished by their markings. The company also made and marketed the *X-Caliber* ("Excalibur") single-shot pistol in 1988-91. This tipping-barrel design, with a press-button release on the left side of the frame above the trigger, was apparently developed by Sterling Arms Company (q.v.) in the early 1980s. When Sterling encountered financial problems, manufacture passed to Ithaca. The X-Caliber was offered in chamberings ranging from 22 LR rimfire to 44 Magnum, with barrels measuring 10 or 15 inches. A dual-purpose firing pin allowed changes from rim- to centerfire ammunition to be made simply by exchanging the barrel unit. The "Model 20" was blued, and the "Model 30" had a protective coating of Teflon.

INDUSTRIAL TECHNOLOGY & MACHINES AG ("ITM")

Solothurn, Switzerland.

In 1984, this company began manufacturing a locked-breech pistol based upon the ČZ 75; indeed, the first pistols were identical copies made under license, but improvements and minor changes were soon made. However, ITM experienced problems with sub-contractors in Italy and Britain, and in 1990 became part of Sphinx AG (q.v.). The nomenclature of the pistols remained the same, but the Sphinx name replaced "ITM" on the slides.

The ITM PP, available in 32 ACP and 380 ACP (7.65mm Auto and 9mm Short), was a Swiss-made version of the Hungarian FÉG Model R.

The 9mm ITM AT84S was based on the Czeck ČZ 75.

An ITM AT84P-AA pistol chambered for the 41 Action Express round.

AT-84 This was the first pistol, a well-made 9mm Parabellum copy of the ČZ 75. Usually chambered for the 9mm Parabellum round, guns can be converted to 41 Action Express or 9mm Action Express. A universal magazine will accept ammunition of all three types, so that only the barrel and recoil spring need to be changed.

- *AT-84H* The "Hideaway" variant, this had a 10-round magazine.
- *AT-84P* A compact version of the full-size AT-84, this was 22mm shorter and 90g lighter.

AT-88 An improved AT-84, this featured greatly improved tolerances and finish. A slight dimensional change was made in the barrel, losing interchangeability with the earlier design. The barrels, made by Peters Stahl of Germany, had exceptional wearing properties and accuracy could be maintained for many tens of thousands of rounds. The safety catch could be applied whether the pistol was cocked or uncocked, and an automatic firing-pin safety system was added in 1987. An ambidextrous safety catch was standard, and an ambidextrous slide-stop catch was optional. Chamberings were restricted to 9mm Parabellum or 41 Action Express, conversion being possible simply by changing barrel and magazine.

- *AT-88H* An ultra-compact or "Hideaway" version of the basic pistols.
- *AT-88P* This was the compact version of the AT-88, shorter and lighter than its prototype.

Sphinx .3AT The first use of the Sphinx name was made in 1989, before the merger of the two companies. The gun was a fixed-barrel blowback chambered for the 9mm Short (380 ACP) round, with an automatic firing-pin safety, a self-cocking action, automatic de-cocking and ambidextrous controls.

IZHEVSK ENGINEERING FACTORY ("IMZ")

Izhevsky Mekhanichesky Za'vod, Izhevsk, Russia.

This engineering factory, created by the Soviet State from what had been the Izhevsk ordnance factory (founded in 1807 to make ammunition), has made a variety of small arms and sporting guns. These have included a surprisingly wide range of handguns. Since 1963, many IMZ products — including air rifles and gas-guns — have been marked "Baikal".

∼ SINGLE-SHOT PISTOLS ∼

IZh-1 A typical Olympic Free Pistol, this used a Martini-type pivoting breechblock operated by a side lever. Chambered for the 22 LR rimfire round, it was introduced in 1962. The sights and grips are adjustable.

IZh-3 An improved variant of the IZh-1, this had different sights and refined grips.

The Stechkin pistol (APS) with its holster-stock.

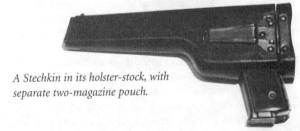

A Stechkin in its holster-stock, with separate two-magazine pouch.

Two members of the ITM AT88 series, the AT88S (top) and the compact AT88P (bottom).

∼ AUTOMATIC PISTOLS ∼

APS (or "Stechkin") This Soviet military pistol was unknown in the West until the early 1960s. It was clearly based on the Walther PP, but the double-action lock of the German design was replaced by a simple single-action type, and the slide-mounted safety catch has three positions — safe, single shots and automatic. With the catch in the rearmost position and a wooden holster-stock clipped to the butt, the APS can be used as a pseudo-submachine gun. The magazine is a 20-round box and the cyclic rate of fire is about 750 rounds/minute.

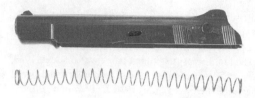

The Stechkin field-stripped.

Like all such compromises, however, the Stechkin was found wanting. It was far too big for the cartridge it fires, judged purely as a handgun, and as a submachine gun it was far too light to be readily controllable; even the official Soviet army manual recommended firing from the prone position and using a rest when possible. Apparently the military authorities reached the same conclusion, and the Stechkin was withdrawn in the mid-1970s. A few found their way to sympathetic countries, but most were scrapped.

IZh-HR30 This is a modern-looking target pistol, with the fashionable slab-sided appearance common to many rival designs. Chambered for the 22 LR rimfire round, it has micro-adjustable sights and anatomical grips. Unusual for a target gun, it also has a grip safety fitted in the butt.

• *IZh-HR31* A variant of the HR30, intended for rapid-fire contests, this chambers the 22 Short rimfire cartridge and has a compensator/muzzle-brake unit at the muzzle.

• *IZh-34M* An improved version of the HR-31, also intended for rapid-fire shooting, this chambered the 22 Short rimfire round. The gun has a special hammer, pivoted near the top to allow the bore to lie as low as possible in the hand, and adjustable trigger; the sights are micrometrically adjustable, and the anatomical grip has an adjustable palm-rest. The five-round magazine lies in the grip. With the assistance of grips on the tip of arms that extends forward on the frame-side, the IZh-34M is usually blued. About 11.8 inches long, it weighs about 42 oz.

• *IZh-35M* Intended for Standard Pistol (slow-fire) competitions, this is essentially the "34M" chambered for the 22 LR rimfire round. Constructional features duplicate those of the rapid-fire gun, though matte-finish stainless steel is used and the maximum permissible weight is 49 oz.

MP-443 ("Grach") The winner of a series of trials to find a new handgun for the Russian army (a process that also led to the approval of the PMM as an interim solution), this is a conventional double-action design — credited to Vladimir Yarygin — with a tipping-barrel locking system comparable with a wide variety of other guns. A similarity with the ITM/Sphinx AT-88 has been noted. Originally intended as part of a modular system that would enable the army to use old 7.62mm Tokarev ammunition that is still being stored in large quantities, the Yarygin pistol was standardized for a high-power variant of the 9x19mm (Parabellum) round designated "7N21", but it will be some years before it replaces the Makarov in service.

The production version is 7.8 inches overall, with a 4.4-inch barrel, and weighs about 34 oz empty. The double-row magazine holds 17 9mm rounds. The lockwork is a conventional double-action design, with an exposed hammer, and a safety catch in the rear part of the steel

frame locks the trigger, sear and hammer. The extractor doubles as a loaded-chamber indicator. Externally, the MP-443 has a squared-front trigger guard, a rear sight protected by sturdy "wings" and a one-piece wraparound grip that is fluted vertically in addition to horizontal grooves front and back. The magazine-release button is reversible.

• *MP-446* "Viking" This is a derivative of the MP-443 with a polymer frame, which reduces the weight to about 29 oz empty.

MP-451 This is a derringer with a tipping two-barrel block, chambered for the 9mm Short (380 ACP) round. The safety catch is combined with the barrel-lock, and the trigger protrudes from the frame only when the mechanism has been cocked by thumbing back the hammer — even though there is a conventional trigger guard. The gun fires sequentially, but is re-set when the barrels are opened. It is 5.3 inches long, with a 2.3-inch barrel, and weighs about 12.5 oz empty.

MTsM (sometimes listed as "MCM") This is the current Izhevsk-made version of the Margolin (q.v.) target pistol.

The 9mm Makarov pistol (PM) was undoubtedly inspired by the Walther PP. This example was made in the German Democratic Republic.

Below: Loading the Makarov.

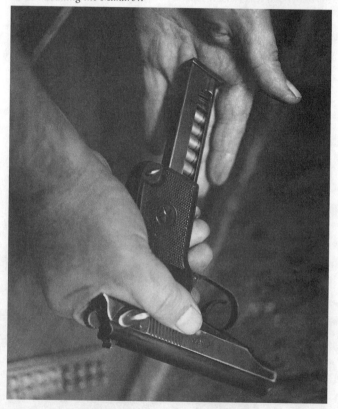

PM (or "Makarov", 1957 to date) The standard Soviet/Russian military pistol for more than 40 years, this is a modified copy of the Walther PP chambered for the Soviet 9x18mm cartridge, a design that is believed to have originated with the pre-war German "Ultra" round (see

"Walther"). It was probably developed in order to gain as much power as possible in a comparatively small blowback pistol, and there was probably also elements of standardizing a cartridge that none but the Soviet bloc used.

Credited to Nikolay Elizarov, the Makarov appeared in 1952 but underwent lengthy testing before replacing the TT (Tokarev) in Soviet service. Series production began in the mid-1950s. The pistol has been very successful and has been copied in other countries — notably as the "Pistole M" in East Germany and the "Type 59" in China. The Soviet model has a five-pointed star on the grip and a lanyard loop; the East German model has plain grips with no lanyard loop; and the Chinese equivalent usually has molded plastic grips with a shield displaying one large five-point star above four smaller ones. The guns all chamber the 9x18mm cartridge, are about 6.3 inches long with a 3.7-inch barrel, and weigh 25.7 oz with an empty eight-round magazine.

In 2001, it was announced that the Makarov was to be replaced by an entirely new 9x21mm design called the Gyurza (see "Tzitnochmash"), but it will be some years before the change is fully implemented.

- *PMM* (1994 to date) This was an adaptation of the PM by designers Pletsky and Shigapov. The most obvious change concerns the butt, which has been re-shaped to improve handling characteristics and thickened to allow a 12-round two-column magazine to be used instead of the original single-column type. Alterations have also been made to the chambering to allow upgraded Soviet/Russian high-pressure ammunition to be used.
- *IZh-70* This is the commercial version of the standard military-style PM, with fixed rear sight and plastic grips. It is chambered for the 9x18mm Makarov round and has an eight-round single-column magazine. The finish is better than military-grade examples and may be matte-nickel instead of blue. The grips may be black synthetic instead of regulation molded plastic, and an adjustable sight can be fitted to order.
- *IZh-70H* (sometimes identified as IZh-70N) Mechanically identical with the standard 9x18mm PM, this has a double-row magazine holding 12 rounds.
- *IZh-71* Identical with the IZh-70, this is chambered for the 9mm Short (380 ACP or 9x17mm) round. Magazine capacity remains eight rounds.
- *IZh-71H* (sometimes identified as IZh-70N) Mechanically identical with the standard PM, but chambered for 9mm Short (9x17mm) instead of 9mm Makarov (9x18mm), this has a double-column magazine holding 12 rounds. Guns distributed in the USA are restricted to 10 rounds.
- *MP-442* ("Baikal") Developed for the commercial market, this is an adaptation of the PM with an ergonomically-shaped wraparound grip and the front of the trigger guard squared to facilitate a two-hand grip. Supplied to order with a laser designator beneath the frame, the MP-442 retains the steel frame of the standard guns. Chambering is currently restricted to 9mm Makarov (9x18mm), but it seems likely that this will be extended to include 9mm Short (380 ACP). Three variants are offered: one with a standard eight-round magazine, another with a 10-round staggered-column magazine and a third with a 12-round double-column magazine. The 10- and 12-round guns are fractionally longer than standard (6.5 inches) and, in the case of the double-row magazine, substantially thicker (1.4 compared with 1.2 inches).

- *MP-448* ("Skyph", also listed as "PM-448", 2001 to date) This is essentially a PM or Makarov with a polymer frame, a reversible magazine-release button and fixed sights. Much the same size as a standard Makarov pistol, the MP-448 weighs merely 21 oz empty.
- *MP-448* ("Mini-Skyph") Chambered for the 9mm Short round (9x17mm) instead of 9mm Makarov, this is little more than a MP-448 with the barrel cut to 2.9 inches and the slide shortened accordingly. Overall length is about 5.7 inches, and the use of a polymer frame reduces empty weight to about 18.7 oz.

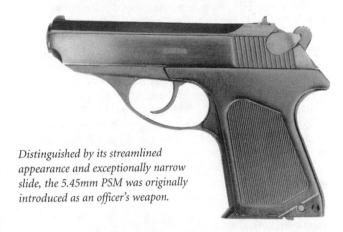

Distinguished by its streamlined appearance and exceptionally narrow slide, the 5.45mm PSM was originally introduced as an officer's weapon.

A right-side view of the Soviet PSM.

PSM ("Pistolet Samozaryadniy Malogabaritniy") Though unknown in the West for some years, this was originally developed as an ultra-compact officers' weapon, relying on comparatively high velocity and a special bullet to offset the small diameter of 5.45mm. The 5.45x18mm cartridge is effectively a necked 9mm Makarov. However, small size (only about 0.9 inches thick) soon commended the gun to internal-security units and police. The PSM resembles the Walther PP, a fixed-barrel blowback with a double-action lock, but there are differences in the lock mechanism and the safety catch has been moved from the side of the slide to a position alongside the hammer in an attempt to make the pistol as thin as possible. It is 6.1 inches long, with a 3.3-inch barrel, and weighs about 18 oz empty. The detachable box magazine holds eight rounds.

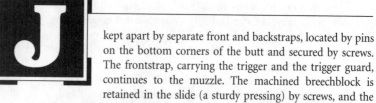

JACQUEMART

Jules Jacquemart, Liége, Belgium.

Jacquemart appears to have begun production of a pistol in about 1912. According to some reports, he died shortly after introducing it and his widow continued the business until work ended when the Germans invaded Belgium in 1914.

Le Monobloc (also known as "Monoblock") The pistol was a 6.35mm of original design. The frame, receiver and barrel were a single unit — explaining the name — and the external form of the barrel section was grooved similarly to the contemporaneous Pieper design. Inside the receiver lay a bolt with grooved finger grips, which protruded through slots in the receiver sides. The upper portion of the bolt was formed into a tube, through which the return spring and its guide rod passed; the forward end of the guide rod screwed into the front of the barrel unit, allowing the spring to be compressed as the bolt recoiled. The magazine held six rounds and the barrel was 2 inches long. The receiver was marked "LE MONOBLOC" over "PISTOLET AUTOMATIQUE" and "BREVETÉ" and the grips display an encircled cursive "JJ" monogram.

JAEGER

Franz Jaeger, Suhl, Germany.

Little is known of this maker of a distinctive pistol during World War I, except that "F. Jaeger & Co. GmbH" traded until 1945.

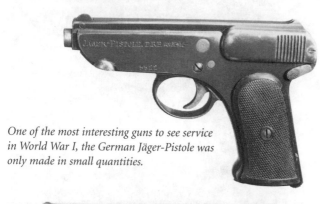

One of the most interesting guns to see service in World War I, the German Jäger-Pistole was only made in small quantities.

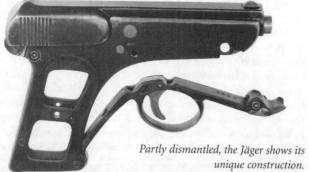

Partly dismantled, the Jäger shows its unique construction.

Jäger-Pistole (1915-17) This is a remarkable gun, designed with simplicity of manufacture in mind. Today's enthusiasts are familiar with the "sheet-metal and wire-spring wonders" developed since the 1940s to facilitate the mass-production of military weapons, but it is a shock to encounter a pre-1918 weapon that shows the same techniques.

With the exception of the slide, barrel, breechblock, butt-straps, return spring and striker, the parts are all sheet-steel stampings. The two plates forming the sides of the butt and frame contain a boss that secures the barrel by means of a block at the breech end. The plates are kept apart by separate front and backstraps, located by pins on the bottom corners of the butt and secured by screws. The frontstrap, carrying the trigger and the trigger guard, continues to the muzzle. The machined breechblock is retained in the slide (a sturdy pressing) by screws, and the front end of the slide forms a loop around the muzzle to constrain a return spring around the barrel. The breechblock carries the striker and striker spring, a simple trigger bar is set in a groove in the frame, and a 7-round box magazine fits into the butt. The slide is marked "Jäger-Pistole D.R.P. ANGEM.", sometimes with "– D.R.G.M." added, suggesting that many of the guns had been made before the patent was finally granted.

For all its simplicity, the Jäger cannot be called flimsy; it shoots well and is reliable. Yet the German army, not usually averse to designs that promised rapid production, never approved it as a *Behelfspistole* ("substitute pistol"), and it is doubtful that more than 10,000 were made.

JAMES

Alexander James Ordnance, Inc., Covina, California, USA.

Thomas Approximately 600 of these 45 ACP delayed-blowback pistols are said to have been made in 1975-8. They were relatively small, with a 3.5-inch barrel, and the necessary delay was obtained by a stirrup pressing against notches in the lower edge of the slide. The action was controlled by the pressure of the shooter's grip on the backstrap of the butt; the tighter the grip, the better the delay — but performance must have been marginal. The trigger mechanism was double action, and there was no mechanical safety other than a disconnector that prevented the gun being fired after the magazine had been removed.

JANSSEN SONS

Janssen Fils et Cie, Liége, Belgium.

The history of this gunmaking business, perhaps little more than a large-scale distributor, remains uncertain. Trading seems to have ceased when the Germans invaded Belgium in 1914 and resumed only briefly after the end of the war.

～ REVOLVERS ～

Lincoln This name, very popular with the Belgian gunmakers, was applied to a variety of revolvers made in 1880-1914. Most were of the folding-trigger pocket variety, hammer and "hammerless" types, in calibers ranging from 22 rimfire and 5.5mm Velo-Dog to 380 centerfire. Other makers using this name included Ancion Marx, Bertrand, Debouxtay, Dumoulin, Le Page, Neumann Frères and Raick Frères, all of Liége, and Albrecht Kind in Germany. Many, or indeed all, of the guns were made by Manufacture Liégeoise d'Armes à Feu.

Milady A name given to pocket revolvers by Ancion Marx in addition to Janssen, these were either of hammerless 5.5mm-caliber Velo-Dog revolvers or folding-trigger exposed-hammer revolvers in 6.35mm or 7.65mm Auto chamberings. Manufacture extended from c. 1895 to the German invasion in the summer of 1914.

～ AUTOMATIC PISTOLS ～

Jieffeco (1) Designed c. 1907 by Henri Rosier, this gun was originally marketed by Jannsen, though the guns may have been made by Manufacture Liégeoise d'Armes à Feu (see "Robar"). The name was derived from the phonetic version of "J" ("jie"), "F" ("effe") and the first two letters of "Companie".

The gun was a conventional 7.65mm-caliber blowback influenced by the 1900-type FN-Browning. What appears to be a slide is largely a fixed shroud around the fixed barrel; only the rear portion reciprocates, attached to a rod and return spring above the barrel. An ejection port is cut into the right side of the frame. A similar 6.35mm gun appeared

The 7.65mm (32-caliber) Jieffeco pistol was made by Robar prior to 1914.

in 1912, both being marked "PISTOLET AUTOMATIQUE JIEFFECO DEPOSE", often accompanied by "BREVETE S.G.D.G. PATENT 24875.08" on the left side of the frame. Strangely, this is actually the British patent number, which is perhaps why it was qualified with "S.G.D.G" — *sans garantie du Gouvernement*, "without government guarantee".

Jieffeco (2) This was the Robar-made New Model Melior, sold for a short period under the Jieffeco name in the early 1920s. The slide of this model is marked "AUTOMATIC PISTOL JIEFFECO", accompanied by "MADE IN LIEGE BELGIUM BREVETS 259178-265491" and sometimes also "Davis-Warner Arms Corporation New York". This suggests that it was named to take advantage of the goodwill created by pre-war sales in the USA.

JAPAN GUN CO. LTD

Nippon Jyuki KK, Tokyo and Notobe, Japan.
Founded in the early 1900s, this company specialized in sporting guns, until ordered to concentrate on war production. Bunji Hamada, owner of the business, decided to develop a 7.65mm automatic pistol for military use.

A typical Hamada pistol.

Hamada shiki The first pistol was a copy of the FN-Browning of 1910, but Hamada patented a variety of alterations in the barrel attachment, dismantling process and striker construction. The perfected design was successfully tested by the Japanese army in 1941 as the *Hamada shiki* ("Hamada type"), chambering the 7.65mm Auto round. Production immediately began in Tokyo and continued until February 1944, output amounting to 4500-5000 guns. They were 6.3 inches long, with a 3.5-inch barrel, and weighed 24 oz without the detachable nine-round box magazine.

Hake shiki Requests from the army for an 8mm handgun that would be easier to make than the regulation Type 94 led to an 8mm Hamada, tested in prototype form in 1942 but extensively altered by Major Kenji Yato of the 1st Army Technical Research Institute. Known as the *Hake shiki*, the new gun lost some of the simplicity of the original design and was much more difficult to make in quantity. Tested in March 1943 and officially approved for service as the "Type 2" (*ni-shiki*), the modified

Hamada was made only in small numbers in an old textile factory in Notobe. Five hundred were sent to be finished in the Toriimatsu factory of Nagoya arsenal in 1944, followed by another 1000 in 1945, and about 4000 sets of parts were surrendered at the end of World War II. The guns were 6.3 inches long, with a 3.8-inch barrel, and weighed about 28 oz empty. The magazines held six 8mm rounds. One of the most obvious recognition features was an oval depression in the slide immediately behind the chamber.

JENNINGS

Jennings Firearms, Inc, Stateline and Carson City, Nevada, USA.
Beginning in 1981, this company distributed the "J-22" (22 LR rimfire) and "J-25" (25 ACP) blowback automatics in a number of variants, largely matters of finish and grip material. See also "Bryco".

IVER JOHNSON

Iver Johnson's Arms & Cycle Co., Worcester and Fitchburg, Massachusetts (1883-1975); Iver Johnson's Arms, Inc., Middlesex, New Jersey (1975-82); Iver Johnson's Arms, Inc., Jacksonville, Arkansas (1982-86).
As noted under the entry "Johnson, Bye & Co" (below), Iver Johnson bought out his associate Martin Bye in 1883 and continued trading in Worcester under his own name. He moved to Fitchburg in 1891 and died in 1895, the business being carried on by his widow until her death, then by his sons and a grandson. Work continued on a range of revolvers, as well as bicycles, shotguns, rifles and machine tools, until the family connection ceased on the grandson's death in 1973. The company was sold in 1975, the new "Iver Johnson's Arms, Inc." moving first to Middlesex and then to Jacksonville. Operations failed again in 1986, but the surviving assets were sold back to the previous owners and absorbed into American Arms, Inc.; the Iver Johnson identity finally vanished.

Iver Johnson began simply by continuing some of the existing Johnson & Bye guns — American Bull Dog, Defender, Eagle, Encore, Favorite, Old Hickory — but moved away from this simplicity in 1883 to produce an aberrant design that was due to Andrew Hyde. Most of the old guns had been discontinued by 1887. Pre-1890 guns were generally built down to a price rather than up to a standard, but quality improved until a reputation for sound, inexpensive, if somewhat dated designs, was acquired. By 1910, Iver Johnson was claiming to be the largest producer of revolvers in the world.

∾ REVOLVERS ∾

American Bulldog (1974-6) Made only in small quantities, this was a double-action non-ejector in 22 rimfire, 32 S&W or 38 S&W centerfire with an adjustable rear sight. The barrels were 2.5 or 4 inches long, the cylinder held five rounds and the finish could be blue or nickel. The plastic grips bore "I J" in a circle.

Bengal No. 1 This was a five-shot solid-frame sheathed-trigger 22 rimfire gun. It had a tapered barrel and a bird's-head butt and was unusual in this class in not having the cylinder axis pin protruding beneath the barrel.

Cattleman Series These were single-action "Frontier"-style guns based on the Colt Single Action Army Revolver and made by Uberti (q.v.) for sale through Iver Johnson distributors in the USA.

• *Buckhorn* A Cattleman with adjustable sights.
• *Cattleman* Offered in 357 Magnum, 44 Magnum or 45 Long Colt, with 4.75-, 5.5-, 6- or 7.25-inch barrels, this had fixed sights.
• *Cattleman Buntline* Offered only with an 18-inch barrel, this had fixed sights and a walnut shoulder stock that could be attached to the butt.
• *Trailblazer* Restricted to 22 LR or 22 Magnum chamberings, with a 5.5- or 6.5-inch barrel and adjustable sights, this was the rimfire version of the basic Cattleman design.

Defender 89 An improved model of the Johnson, Bye & Co. gun of the same name, this was made from 1889 to 1895. The changes were relatively minor, and the general form remained the same: a solid-frame sheathed-trigger single-action non-ejector in 22 or 32 rimfire. The guns were usually marked "IMPROVED DEFENDER" on top of the frame.

Hijo Quick-Break A name used by Iver Johnson on "Safety Hammer Automatic Double Action" revolvers distributed by the Walzer Arms Company of New York c. 1955-65. They were offered as an eight-shot in 22 LR rimfire or a five-shot in 38 S&W.

Hyde Model Also known as the "Model 1879", though introduced commercially in 1883, this was the first US-made revolver to incorporate a side-swinging cylinder. The cylinder was carried on an arbor pin, pivoted at the front, and could rotate sideways out of the frame to the right and expose the chambers for loading. Iver Johnson initially made only five-shot 38 centerfire solid-frame double-action guns, but 32 centerfire and other chamberings were subsequently offered in small quantities. The same basic design was also produced by C.S. Shatuck (q.v.) in rimfire chamberings, but neither manufacturer had much success. Johnson abandoned it in 1887 with Shattuck following a year later.

Improved Model Target Dating from 1929, this 22 rimfire double-action gun was built on an extra-heavy frame and had a reinforced cylinder. Barrel lengths were usually restricted to 6 or 10 inches, the grips were walnut, the rear sight could be adjusted and the finish was blue.

Invincible, J.S.T. & Co. These marks have been found on cheap solid-frame revolvers made by Iver Johnson in the 1880s.

Knife Model Also dating from the 1880s, this combined the basic solid-frame design with a folding knife blade beneath the barrel.

Model 1900 (1900-47) This was a solid-frame double-action non-ejector in 22 rimfire, 32 Short rimfire or 32 Short centerfire chamberings, fitted with an octagonal barrel measuring 4.5 or 6 inches.

Petite Smaller than even the Safety Cycle Automatic Model (q.v.), this was a seven-shot solid-frame "hammerless" design, chambered only for the 22 Short rimfire round, with a one-inch barrel and a folding hammer. It could be considered as the American answer to the "Velo-Dog" but was too small to be taken seriously and did not remain in production for long. Only about 600 guns were made in 1908-9.

Post-World War II "numbered" guns Several new models appeared once the fighting had ceased; one innovation being the "Flash Control Cylinder" with the front face recessed to leave a solid rim enclosing the chamber mouths and the end of the barrel. This was intended to deflect any gas that leaked from the chamber/barrel junction.

* *Model 50 Sidewinder* (1961-75) A solid-frame eight-shot with 4.75- or 6-inch barrel, this was available with cylinders for 22 LR or 22 WMR. Gate-loaded, it was fitted with a rod ejector and a "Western-style" butt. Normally supplied with fixed sights, an adjustable-sight deluxe version was also made.
* *Model 55A Sportsman Target* (1955-75) Another eight-shot 22 LR rimfire non-ejecting revolver, this had a 4.75- or 6-inch barrel, a solid frame, fixed sights, blue finish and walnut grips. It was virtually the old "Target Sealed Eight" in modern form.
* *Model 55S-A Cadet* (1955-75) A small solid-frame non-ejector with a 2.5-inch barrel, fixed sights and a round butt, this was offered as an eight-shot (22 LR or 22 WMR) or five-shot (32 or 38 centerfire). It was blued, with plastic thumb-rest grips.
* *Model 57A Target* (1955-75) This was a variant of the Model 55A with a 4.5- or 6-inch barrel, adjustable sights and thumb-rest-style molded plastic grips.
* *Model 66 Trailsman* (1958-75) A break-open design with a heavy ribbed 6-inch barrel, adjustable sights and plastic thumb-rest grips (plain walnut was optional), this lacked the safety hammer feature. The cylinder had eight chambers accepting 22 LR rimfire rounds.

* *Model 66A Trailsman Snub* A minor variant of the Model 66, this had a 2.5-inch barrel and a rounded butt. It was offered as a 32- or 38-caliber five-shot in addition to the standard eight-shot 22 LR rimfire pattern.
* *Model 67 Viking* This was little more than a Model 66 with the safety hammer mechanism restored.
* *Model 844* Made in the 1950s, this was a 22-caliber double-action non-ejecting gun with a solid frame. The barrel measured 4.5 or 6 inches, the cylinder held eight rounds and the rear sight was adjustable.
* *Model 855* Introduced at the same time as the M844, this had a single-action trigger system. It was essentially a modernized form of the Trigger Cocker Single Action.

Rookie (1974-5) This was a double-action solid-frame non-ejector with a 4-inch barrel, blue or nickel finish and plastic grips. It was available only in 38 S&W Long centerfire, with a five-chamber cylinder.

A 38-caliber Iver Johnson Safety Automatic Double Action revolver.

Safety Automatic Double Action (1892-1950) By the mid-1890s, Iver Johnson had designed a new revolver, which appeared first in standard hammer form in 1892 and as a "hammerless" derivative in 1894. The guns were offered in 32 or 38 centerfire, but a 22 rimfire variant appeared in 1895. So many were sold that revolvers of this type remained the mainstay of the product line until after World War II had ended. The unique Safety Hammer became the most publicized feature of the company's advertising, the slogan "Hammer the Hammer" being a succinct description of its great merit. A transfer bar was attached to the trigger, the firing pin was mounted in the frame and the hammer was shaped so that it struck the frame without touching the pin. Only if the trigger was correctly pulled through did the transfer bar rise to a position where it could transfer the blow of the falling hammer to the firing pin. But if the pistol was dropped or the hammer was accidentally released during cocking, no discharge could occur, as the transfer bar was in its rest position and the hammer could only strike the frame. The "Automatic" designation referred to the ejection of spent cases as the barrel was tipped down.

A "new pattern" appeared in 1908 in hammer and hammerless form, chambered initially only for 32 or 38 Short centerfire ammunition (though 22 rimfire was introduced in 1910). Coil springs replaced the original leaf type, the tension of the mainspring could be adjusted and the connection between the mainspring plunger and the hammer became a ball-and-socket design. Barrel lengths of 4, 5 or 6 inches were regarded as standard.

* *Safety Automatic Double Action Hammerless* Introduced in 1894, this was a variant of the preceding gun, a break-open auto-ejector. It was offered as a seven-shot in 22 LR rimfire and as a five-shot in 32 S&W or 38 S&W centerfire. The earliest "hammerless" revolvers concealed the hammer beneath a clip-on shroud, but later examples had the contours of the frame altered to achieve the same purpose.
* *Safety Automatic Cycle Model* Made in hammer and hammerless forms, this was initially offered only in 32 centerfire with a 2-inch barrel. However, 22 LR rimfire and 38 centerfire options had been introduced within a few years of its first appearance in 1901.

Secret Service Special (or "SSS") A name used by the Fred Biffard Company, a gun dealer operating in Chicago in 1890-1910. The revolvers were supplied by Iver Johnson and the Meriden Firearms Company.

Sealed Eight Introduced after the end of World War I, this 22 rimfire break-open auto-ejecting revolver incorporated a cylinder with each of the eight chambers counter-bored at the rear to surround the cartridge rims.

- *Protector Sealed Eight* Offered only with a 2.5-inch barrel, for home defense and personal protection, this break-open auto-ejector retained the safety-hammer mechanism.

- *Supershot Sealed Eight* (1931-41, 1945-57) This eight-shot 22 LR rimfire solid-frame non-ejecting "sport revolver" had a 6-inch barrel and adjustable sights.

- *Target Sealed Eight* Another of the 1931 introductions, based on the solid-frame non-ejecting pattern, this could be seen as a continuation of the Model 1900. The principal feature was the counter-bored cylinders. It lasted until 1948, with a break in production for World War II.

Supershot (or "Super Shot", introduced in 1926) Made until the advent of the Sealed Eight version (see above), this was a 22 rimfire gun incorporating the safety-hammer system. It was built on an extra-heavy frame and had a 6-inch barrel. The cylinder capacity was initially six rounds, but a nine-round version, substituted in 1929, was still being sold in 1949.

Swift (c. 1890-1900) This gun was made exclusively for the John P. Lovell Arms Company of Boston, agents for Iver Johnson until the proprietor died in 1895. Most guns embodied an ejector mechanism patented in 1885 by Freeman W. Hood. The brand-name is said to honor "Captain Swift of the 5th US Cavalry", who supposedly designed the revolver in collaboration with Lovell, but there seems little substance to the story. The "Swift" was a break-open five-shot double-action 38-caliber revolver made in both hammer and "hammerless" forms. The only significant departure from contemporaneous Iver Johnson guns lay in the design of the frame latch (pulled down to unlock instead of lifted) and in the detail of the ejector.

Target (1925-32) This was a small-frame double-action 22-caliber revolver with a 9.5-inch octagonal barrel, walnut grips and blue finish. The rear sight was adjustable. See also "Improved Model Target".

Trigger-Cocker Single Action (1940-1, 1945-7) Made only in small quantities, with a 6-inch barrel and an eight-chamber counter-bored cylinder, this apparently used a variant of the 19th-century Tranter "hesitation cocking" system. This allowed the action to be cocked by pulling back on the trigger lever, but then fired — effectively in single-action mode — by using a small blade let into the rear of the trigger guard to release the hammer. Offered in blued steel, with walnut grips, the 22 rimfire guns also had an adjustable finger-rest on the front grip-strap.

U.S. Revolver Co. Marks of this type were applied to cheaper versions of the solid-frame Model 1900, and break-open Safety Automatic patterns, though they lacked the safety-hammer feature, had some consequent small changes in the lockwork and displayed less attention to finish. The revolvers were made in 22LR (hammer patterns only), 32 and 38 chamberings, and were sold alongside the "Iver Johnson" guns until the 1940s. They were marked "U.S. REVOLVER Co" on the barrel and had "US" molded into the grips.

~ AUTOMATIC PISTOLS ~

TP22 Added to the range when the company moved to Jacksonville, this was essentially a copy of the Walther PPK chambered for the 22 LR rimfire round. Offered in blued or nickel-steel, it had a 2.8-inch barrel and a seven-round magazine.

- *TP-25* This was a variant of the TP-22 chambered for the 25 ACP centerfire round.

The 22 rimfire Iver Johnson TP-22 pistol, based on the Walther TPH.

Iver Johnson's 380 ACP Pony was a version of a Spanish Star.

Trailsman Introduced in 1984, this was based on the discontinued Colt Woodsman, a fixed-barrel 22 LR rimfire "sport pistol". The guns were made with 4.5- or 6-inch barrels, blued finish, walnut or plastic grips and 10-round box magazines.

X-300 Pony A locked-breech automatic chambering the 380 ACP (9mm Short) round, this was a version of the Star–Echeverria (q.v.) Starfire marketed from 1975 onward. It was apparently assembled in the USA from parts made in Spain.

J.H. JOHNSON

J.H. Johnson, Great Western Gun Works, Pittsburgh, Pennsylvania, USA.

Continental Revolvers produced by the Great Western Gun Works in 1875-85. A 22RF seven-shot and a 32RF five-shot, both were solid-frame, non-ejecting sheath-trigger models with bird's-head butts of the common pattern. Guns of this type were also sold as *Great Western*.

JOHNSON, BYE & COMPANY

Worcester, Massachusetts, USA.

This gunmaking business was formed in 1871 in Worcester by Iver Johnson and Martin Bye in order to manufacture cheap revolvers. Manufacture of a number of models took place until 1883, when Bye left the business, leaving his one-time partner to continue trading as the Iver Johnson Arms Co. (q.v.). The revolvers produced by the firm went under a number of names. All except the "American Bulldog" and "Eclipse" models were of the same pattern: a solid-frame, sheath-trigger, non-ejecting revolver of low quality in 22RF, 32CF, 38CF and 44CF calibers. The barrel was frequently octagonal.

~ SINGLE-SHOT PISTOL ~

Eclipse Distributed by the John P. Lovell Arms Company of Boston, the attribution of this pistol to Johnson & Bye remains uncertain. It was a tiny 22 rimfire pattern with the barrel held on a vertical pivot so that the breech swung sideways to load. The bird's-head grip and sheathed trigger were similar to those used on the revolvers of the same name.

∼ REVOLVERS ∼

Most of the guns made prior to 1879 bore no marks, other than the brand names.

American Bull Dog A name associated with a range of revolvers manufactured from 1881 onward, with short octagonal barrels, solid frames, double-action lockwork and nickel plating. The grips were marked with a dog's-head motif. They were offered in 32 and 38, rim- or centerfire, and had five-chamber cylinders.

Boston Bulldog This name was applied to a variant of the American Bull Dog sold by John P. Lovell & Sons of Boston. The basic design was a solid-frame double-action revolver in 22 Short rimfire, 32 Short rimfire, 32 S&W or 38 S&W centerfire, usually with a 2.5-inch barrel though other lengths were available. The 22 Short version was a seven-shot, but the others all had five-chamber cylinders.

British Bulldog A series of revolvers made in 1881-82 and sold through Lovell of Boston. There were three five-shot patterns, in 32, 38 and 44. All were solid-frame single-action sheathed-trigger non-ejectors.

Defender Introduced in 1875, this was a solid-frame non-ejector with a sheathed trigger, "saw handle" and an octagonal barrel. Chamberings were restricted to 22 Short rimfire, 32 Short rimfire, 38 Short rimfire and 38 Short centerfire. Most had half-flute cylinders, though the 38 CF guns usually had long flutes.

Eagle A sales name for a series of double-action revolvers made from 1879 onward. They were the first double-action guns to be made by Johnson & Bye but retained the general appearance of their contemporaneous solid-frame sheath-trigger cousins. The butt was usually a bird's head. The chambering was usually 38 centerfire (five shots), accompanied by a 3-inch barrel, but guns in 22 rimfire (7-shot), 32 centerfire and 44 centerfire have been reported.

Eclipse One of many sheathed-trigger solid-frame single-action revolvers made by Johnson & Bye, this is believed to have been sold by the John P. Lovell Arms Company of Boston.

Encore Applied to a range of seven-shot 22 rimfire and five-shot 32 RF and 38 RF solid-frame sheathed-trigger revolvers, this name was used by Johnson & Bye in 1874-83. The guns resembled the Favorite model but had round or part-round barrels.

Favorite Made from 1873 onward, this was similar to the Defender described previously, with a solid frame, an octagonal barrel, a sheathed trigger and a bird's-head butt. Chambered almost exclusively for rimfire ammunition, the "Favorite" and "Favorite No 1" were seven-shot guns in 22-caliber; "Favorite No 2" was a five-shot in 32-caliber; "Favorite No 3" was a five-shot in 38-caliber; and "Favorite No. 4" was a five-shot in 41-caliber.

• *Favorite Navy* A name applied to a Favorite with a round (instead of octagonal) barrel. The Encore was very similar.

Lion A name given to solid-frame, sheath-trigger non-ejecting revolvers offered in 22, 38, 41 and 44 rimfire chamberings.

Old Hickory (1) A name applied to solid-frame single-action revolvers with a sheathed trigger, offered in 1873-8 in 22 rimfire (seven shots) with a round barrel and a fluted cylinder, or as a five-shot 32 Long rimfire with a round or octagonal barrel. The grips could be hard rubber, ivory or pearl.

• *Old Hickory* (2) Introduced in 1877, this was a double-action solid-frame gun with a conventional trigger guard, an octagonal barrel, nickel-plated finish and rubber grips. Chamberings included 22, 32, 38 and 44 rimfire. The 22-caliber version had a seven-chamber cylinder and a 2.5-inch barrel; the others were six-shot, with barrels measuring 2.5 or 4.5 inches.

Smoker Introduced in 1875 in chamberings that ultimately ranged from 22 rimfire to 41 rimfire, this was a sheathed-trigger design with a fluted cylinder and a "Russian Handle" (prawled grip).

Star Vest Pocket A name applied to 22 and 32 rimfire revolvers made by Johnson & Bye in the late 1870s, but nothing more than the solid-frame non-ejectors of the period.

Tycoon Introduced in 1873, this was simply the Favorite under another name.

JYVÄSKYLÄ ARMS FACTORY ("VKT")

Valtions Kivääritehdas, Jyväskylä, Finland.

The Finnish state small-arms factory was best known for a variety of small arms, including Mosin-Nagant rifles, Lahti-Saloranta light machineguns and the Lahti pistol.

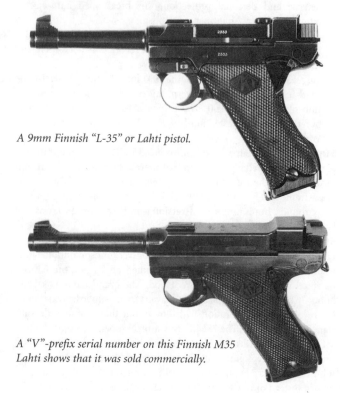

A 9mm Finnish "L-35" or Lahti pistol.

A "V"-prefix serial number on this Finnish M35 Lahti shows that it was sold commercially.

M1935 Lahti This was designed in the late 1920s by Aimo Lahti, prototypes chambered for the 7.65mm Parabellum round being tested by the Finnish army from 1929 onward. A patent was granted in Finland in February 1934. The intention was to make pistols in 7.65mm and 9mm Parabellum, to use stockpiled ammunition, but the final "Pistooli L-35" was restricted to 9mm.

Although the shape invites comparison with the Parabellum, there is no other similarity, the mechanism being more akin to the Bergmann, using a bolt moving in a barrel extension and locked by a vertically-moving yoke. The most unusual feature is the incorporation of a bolt accelerator in the form of a bell-crank lever pivoted on the left side of the barrel. As the barrel and bolt come to the end of the recoil stroke, the lower arm of this crank strikes a lug on the frame, causing the longer upper end to swing back and strike the bolt as it unlocks. This thrusts the bolt back mechanically, instead of relying simply on momentum to carry the bolt back to the limit of its travel. One theory suggests that this was due to the longer-than-average recoil stroke, which might have diminished the momentum by the time the bolt unlocked; another takes the view that the accelerator was needed to ensure reliability in the sub-zero temperatures to be expected in Finland.

The value of the additional complication has been doubted, and even the manufacturer completed one batch of guns without accelerators. The rapid recall of these guns for alteration suggests that the accelerator was useful, if not truly essential.

Production was slow, preventing widespread issue of Lahti pistols until 1939. The first few had beechwood grips and front sights that had been forged integrally with the barrel, but the grips were changed to molded plastic and the separate front-sight blade was dovetailed into the barrel. The guns all had lugs on the butt to take a Mauser-type wooden holster-stock, though only 200 stocks were made. All but the last batches had loaded-chamber indicators on top of the barrel extension.

About 500 had been made by the time of the 1939/40 Winter War, which temporarily halted production. Changes were made to the production methods, accompanied by changes in the guns, and work resumed. The yoke-retaining spring had been removed and the machining of the barrel extension was simpler. Deliveries recommenced in 1941, and about 4500 guns had been made before the "Continuation War" of 1944 interrupted progress. Work re-started in 1946, continuing until about 9000 pistols had been made by c. 1951.

The Finnish Lahti performs reliably, but production relied greatly on hand-fitting and the use of high-quality steels persuaded the Finns to experiment with a simple "m/44" Colt-Browning clone. Supplies of Lahti pistols, which had never been large, dwindled to a point where

VKT made about 1250 replacement Swedish-style slides in 1958-61. These were fitted to surviving pistols, which were then known as Vammakoski ("repaired"). Eventually, the surviving M/23 Parabellums were brought out of store while the Finnish army sought a new service pistol.

If the Lahti has a weakness, it is its complicated dismantling process — a task that is almost impossible without proper tools. This was generally regarded as a price worth paying to ensure reliability in some of the worst climatic conditions in the world. Markings are usually restricted to a "VKT" monogram, set in a diamond, which appears on the top of the receiver above "L-35" and the Finnish army property mark of "SA" within a square. The monogram also appears on the grips.

The serial number lies on the left of the frame and the barrel extension. Numbers without prefix are Finnish army weapons, but about 1000 pistols that failed inspection were sold commercially with "V"-prefix numbers.

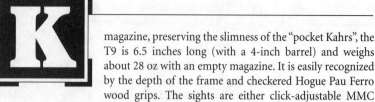

KAHR ARMS

Blauvelt, New York State, USA.

This gunmaking business made its name with a series of ultra-compact pistols that offered an ideal combination of size and power. They have also attained a good reputation for quality. In addition to the standard Kahr-type pistols, the assets of Auto-Ordnance (q.v.) were acquired in 2001, and Kahr now also makes a series of surprisingly traditional M1911A1 clones.

Kahr pistols are locked-breech designs, relying on a modification of the Browning dropping-barrel system with a lug above the chamber locking into the roof of the slide. The guns also embody a special patented cam-operated double-action trigger system, which not only releases the firing-pin lock but also completes cocking during the final stage of the trigger pull — not only a safety feature, but also giving a remarkably smooth trigger movement.

K9 (1994 to date) Chambered for the 9mm Parabellum round, this is the standard version made of matte-finish stainless steel with a wrap-around polymer grip and fixed bar/dot combat sights. Tritium "night light" dots are optional. The guns are about 6 inches long, with 3.5-inch polygon-rifled barrels, and weigh about 23 oz without the seven-round box magazine. The "K9 Elite 98" is a deluxe version distinguished by the high-polish finish instead of matte and a laser-etched logo.

- *MK9* Introduced in 1998 with a special short trigger stroke, this is a short-barrel, short-butt version of the K9. It is only 5.3 inches long, with a 3.1-inch barrel, and weighs 24 oz empty. Magazine capacity is restricted to six rounds (seven if the standard magazine is substituted). The slide and barrel are matte-finish stainless steel, though the "MK9 Elite 98" version has a high-polish finish. Grips are usually textured nylon.
- *P9* (2000 to date) Similar externally to the K9, this has a textured black polymer frame/grip unit that reduces weight to 18 oz with an empty magazine. The slide is matte-finish stainless steel.
- *P9 Covert* Intended for use where concealment is important, this combines the full-length barrel/slide unit with a short-butt frame that reduces depth by about a half-inch. Magazine capacity is restricted to six rounds, though the standard full-length magazine (which will protrude beneath the butt) can be substituted when necessary.
- *PM9* Distinguished by a black polymer frame with a short butt, a short barrel and stainless-steel slide, this is 5.3 inches long and weighs only 16 oz empty. Magazine capacity is six rounds. The slide may be finished in bright matte or given a protective "Black Diamond" coating.

K40 (1994 to date) A 40 S&W version of the K9, this has a six-round magazine. About 6.1 inches overall, it weighs 24 oz without the magazine. The "K40 Elite 98" has high-polish finish and an additional laser-etched logo on the slide.

- *MK40* (1998 to date) Fitted with a 3.1-inch barrel, reducing length to 5.4 inches and weight to about 26 oz empty, this has a specially shortened trigger stroke and a short butt that restricts the capacity of the standard magazine to five rounds. The grips are black textured nylon and construction is either matte (standard) or high-polish ("Elite 98") stainless steel.
- *P40* A polymer-frame version of the K40, introduced in 2000, this weighs about 19 oz with an empty magazine.
- *P40 Covert* A short-butt version of the P40, retaining the polymer frame, this accepts a five-round magazine. It weighs about 18 oz empty.

T9 Introduced in 2002, this is an enlargement of the 9mm Parabellum K9 designed for general use. Fitted with an eight-round single-column magazine, preserving the slimness of the "pocket Kahrs", the T9 is 6.5 inches long (with a 4-inch barrel) and weighs about 28 oz with an empty magazine. It is easily recognized by the depth of the frame and checkered Hogue Pau Ferro wood grips. The sights are either click-adjustable MMC three-dot ("T9 Target 9") or fixed Novak low-profile three-dot sights with Tritium inserts ("P9 Tactical 9"). The guns are made largely of matte-finish stainless steel.

Colt–Browning clones (2001 to date) Formerly marketed by Auto-Ordnance, these stay much more faithful to the original design than many of the modern "re-creations".

- *1911A1 Parkerized* The basic matte-black "Mil-Spec" version, offered with a 5-inch barrel and fixed sights, is about 8.5 inches long and weighs 39 oz empty. Virtually indistinguishable from military-service issue, it has controls that duplicate the original designs, retains the lanyard loop on the butt heel and is marked "MODEL 1911A1 U.S. ARMY" on the left side of the slide. Only the slide-retraction grooves (angled forward to extend the line of the grip) betray modern Auto-Ordnance origins.
- *1911 Deluxe* This has a polished blue finish, one-piece wraparound rubber grips and high-profile three-dot combat sights. It lacks the lanyard loop and is marked "AUTO-ORDNANCE CORP." over ".45 CALIBER AUTOMATIC" on the left side of the slide behind the "Thompson signature" logo.
- *T1911A1* Finished in blue, this version has brown plastic grips with a "Thompson signature" medallion. It lacks the lanyard loop.

K.B.I. INC

Harrisburg, Pennsylvania, USA.

This company was associated with the distribution of the US-made PSP-25 pistol (see "Palmer Security Products") and "Charles Daly M1911A1P" pistols made in the Philippines by Armscor (q.v.).

KEL-TEC CNC INDUSTRIES, INC.

Cocoa, Florida, USA.

P-11 (1995 to date) This is a compact double-action-only 9mm Parabellum pistol with a blued, stainless-steel or parkerized slide and a black polymer grip/frame unit. The sights are adjustable and the detachable box magazine holds 10 rounds. The P-11 is 5.6 inches long, has a 3.1-inch barrel and weighs about 14 oz without its magazine.

- *P-40* (1998-9?) A variant of the P-11 chambered for the 40 S&W cartridge, it is about 5.8 inches long, with a 3.3-inch barrel, and weighs 16 oz empty. Magazines hold nine rounds.

P-32 (1999 to date) Chambered for the 32 ACP round, this is a blow-back personal-defense pistol with a blued steel slide and frame. It is merely 5 inches long, with a 2.7-inch barrel, and weighs about 6-1/2 oz without its seven-round box magazine. An optional 10-round magazine extends beneath the butt.

F.W. KESSLER

Also listed as "Keszler"; Suhl, Germany.

Kessler began trading in 1869, entering into a partnership with his son by 1914. The trading style had become "B. Kessler & Erben" by 1930 and "F.W. Kessler KG" by 1939. Best-known for shotguns and Martini-action sporting rifles, Kessler also developed a pistol.

Kessler-Pistole (c. 1909) The shape is reminiscent of the FN-Browning of 1900, with a hump on the rear of the frame. However, what appears to be a slide is actually the hinged upper part of the frame, and a separate breechblock, retracted by grooved spurs projecting externally, reciprocates independently. The grips display the Arminius-head

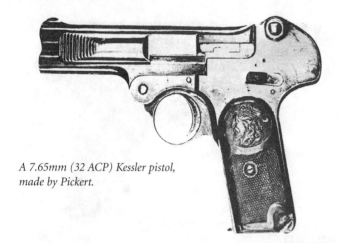

A 7.65mm (32 ACP) Kessler pistol, made by Pickert.

trademark associated with Friedrich Pickert (q.v.), and there is little doubt that Kessler sub-contracted the work. It is assumed that production was meager; no survivor could be traced for examination.

KIMBALL ARMS COMPANY
Wayne, Michigan, USA.

This gunmaking business was responsible for the Kimball pistol, a delayed-blowback design developed in the 1950s by John W. Kimball. Delay was achieved by allowing the barrel to recoil a short distance with the block, after which the barrel was held and the block allowed to continue. In addition, the inner surface of the chamber was grooved so that the expanded cartridge case would be more resistant to extraction and thus hold the breech closed for a little longer until the pressure fell.

It has been said that Kimball's purpose was to produce a military weapon and to produce a pistol that would allow hunters to carry only one type of cartridge. It was doomed on either score; the military would not countenance a pistol without a breech-lock, and no self-respecting hunter carried M1 carbines. Moreover the 30 M1 Carbine cartridge was designed to be fired in an 18-inch barrel; the propellant did not burn properly in the 5-inch barrel of the Kimball, and the expulsion of unburned grains from the muzzle led to ballistic irregularity.

The Kimball pistol was an unsuccessful attempt to chamber a handgun for the 30 M1 Carbine cartridge.

Kimball pistol (1955-8) The design was much like a 22-caliber target automatic, with an exposed barrel, a short slide at the rear and molded plastic grips. The construction was largely of blued carbon steel. Experience soon showed that the 30-caliber cartridge was too powerful for the design, leading to broken frame lugs and the chance of the slide flying off backwards. Although Kimball planned to produce the weapon in chamberings such as 22 Hornet, 357 Magnum and 38 Special, all suitable for handguns, only 238 pistols were ever made. Virtually all were chambered for the 30 M1 round, though there were a few in 22 Hornet and, perhaps, a prototype or two in 357 Magnum.

• *Aircrew Model* (1955-6) A variant of the basic 30-caliber Kimball automatic, this was fitted with a 3.5-inch barrel. Sometimes listed as

the "Combat Model", it was manufactured in very small numbers. The problems with unburned propellant were more marked in the short barrel than in the standard 5-inch type.

KIMBER MFG, INC.
Yonkers, New York, USA.

This gunmaking business, originally better known as a maker of rim- and centerfire rifles, was founded as "Kimber of Oregon" in 1979, but failed in 1991. Reorganized as "Kimber of America" in Clackamas, Oregon, in 1993, the company began to make handguns in 1995 and then consolidated operations in New York in 1997. The current trading name was adopted at the same time.

Browning-type pistols (metal frame, 1995 to date) Designed for Kimber by gunsmith Chip McCormick, these are essentially improved versions of the M1911 Colt-Browning. Most guns have duplicated retraction grips, skeletonized hammers and triggers, deepened ejection ports, 1911-type straight-side butts and extended or "beavertail" grip safety levers. A new firing-pin safety system was introduced in 2001, the guns that are so fitted including "II" in their designations.

• *Compact* [II] This is distinguished by a direct-fitting 4-inch barrel (lacking the traditional muzzle bushing) and a butt that is about 0.4 inches shorter than standard. Made only in 45 ACP, the Custom pistol lacks the duplicate slide-retraction grips at the muzzle. The "Compact Stainless" was made largely of stainless steel, and the "Compact Stainless Aluminum" — somewhat lighter than the standard 34-oz empty weight of the steel-frame guns — had a stainless steel slide and a stainless-finish aluminum-alloy frame.

• *Custom* [II] Originally introduced in 1996 and upgraded in 2001, this has a full-length (5-inch) barrel, an eight-round magazine and a variety of special features, including match-grade stainless-steel barrel and bushing and Wolff springs. The finish is usually bead-blasted black oxide, though the grips may be checkered black rubber, rosewood or walnut. Chamberings may be 38 Super, 40 S&W or 45 ACP. The sights may be fixed Kimber or three-dot Meprolight type. The "Custom Walnut" has double-diamond checkering; the Custom Stainless is made largely of stainless steel; and the "Custom Target Stainless" (38 Super and 45 ACP only) has adjustable sights. The "Custom Heritage Edition" (2000-1) had a classical seven-round magazine, hand-checkered rosewood grips and an inscription on the slide. The "Custom Royal" was a variant of the standard gun with a high-polish blue finish and checkered double-diamond grips of select walnut.

• *Eclipse Custom II* (introduced in 2002) Similar to the Custom II, this has a black anodized stainless-steel slide and frame with the flats polished to give a two-tone appearance. Gray/black wood laminate grips and Meprolight night sights are standard. The series includes the "Eclipse Pro II", with a 4-inch "bull" barrel and a standard grip; the "Eclipse Pro Target II", with a 4-inch barrel, the full-length grip and an adjustable rear sight; the "Eclipse Target II", with an adjustable bar-dot rear sight and a 5-inch barrel; and the "Eclipse Ultra II", with a 3-inch barrel and short grip.

• *Gold Match* [II] Similar to the Custom pattern, this 45 ACP gun has a stainless-steel barrel with match-grade chamber and a hand-fitted barrel bushing. The rear sight is adjustable, the double-diamond checkered grips are rosewood and the trigger is aluminum. A stainless-steel version, the "Gold Match Stainless", is currently being offered in 40 S&W and 45 ACP.

• *Pro Carry* [II] (1998 to date) This is similar to the Compact version, with a direct-fitting 4-inch heavyweight "bull" barrel. The standard 45 ACP guns have an aluminum-alloy frame, but the "HD" ("Heavy Duty") version, offered in 38 Super and 45 ACP, has a stainless-steel frame that raises empty weight from about 30 to 38 oz. The "Pro Carry Stainless" was the original stainless-steel version.

- *Super Match* [II] (1999 to date) This is a version of the Gold Match intended for high-level competition shooting. It has a stainless-steel barrel and chamber, a stainless-steel frame and an adjustable Kimber rear sight. A test target is supplied with each pistol.
- *Ultra Carry* [II] (1999 to date) This is a short-barrel version of the Compact (q.v.), with a 3-inch barrel engaging directly with the slide. The grip is the short pattern, 0.4 inches less than standard, and a special slide-stop is fitted. Empty weight is about 25 oz, owing to an aluminum-alloy frame. The "Ultra Carry Stainless" is similar but heavier, being made entirely of stainless steel.

Browning-type pistols (polymer frame, 1999 to date) These guns are easily distinguished by their weight, which is customarily less than that of comparable steel or aluminum-alloy framed equivalents, and by the amorphous shape of a trigger guard that has been adapted for a two-hand grip. A major improvement to the frame was made in 2002, when the polymer frame was molded over a stainless-steel or aluminum-alloy skeleton.

- *Custom Polymer* [II] The standard gun, made only in 45 ACP, had a 5-inch barrel and fixed sights. The "Pro Carry Polymer [II]" was similar but had a direct-locking 4-inch heavyweight barrel. "Stainless Polymer [II]" was little more than the standard gun with a slide of stainless instead of blued carbon steel, and the "Ultra Polymer [II]" had a 3-inch barrel and a short butt.
- *Ten II Polymer series* The original guns were replaced by the "High Capacity Ten II" group, with flush-fitting double-column magazines holding 10 rounds for sale in the USA or 14 for use elsewhere. They also exhibit a variety of detail improvements. The "Gold Match Ten II Polymer" has an adjustable rear sight and polished flats on the stainless-steel slide; the "Pro Carry Ten II Polymer" has a 10-round magazine, fixed sights and a 4-inch barrel; the "Stainless Ten II Polymer" is a minor variant of the standard gun, with a stainless-steel slide and fixed sights; and the "Polymer Ultra Ten II" is a 3-inch barreled version of the standard gun, with a short butt, that weighs only about 24 oz empty.

Custom guns In addition to the standard patterns, Kimber makes a variety of "Custom Shop" and CDP ("Custom Defense Program") guns. These incorporate a variety of special features and are exceptionally difficult to classify. Some details will be found in the *Standard Catalog of Firearms*.

ALBRECHT KIND ("AKAH")

Suhl, Thüringen, Germany.
Founded in 1853, this distributor of sporting guns, clothing and hunting equipment maintained extensive gunsmithing facilities prior to 1945 and even made leatherware (including holsters) in a factory in Alstadt-Hachenburg/Westerwald. The Kind name, a trademark of an oak leaf and acorns, or brand names such as "Eichel", "Schutzmann" and "Tanne", will be found on a variety of revolvers such as the Kolb "Baby Hammerless" and Belgian-made "Constabulary", "Lincoln" or "Kobold" types (often made by Manufacture Liégeoise des Armes à Feu, q.v.) sold in Germany prior to 1939. Trading is currently centered on Hunstig bei Dieringshausen.

A. KLESESEWSKI

Berlin, Germany.
Suspected to signify nothing other than a distributor, this name appears on a 6.35mm "Eibar" pistol, with a slide marked "AMERICAN AUTOMATIC PISTOL CAL. 6.35" and a vulture-like motif (possibly a condor) on the butt. The same motif appears on an identical pistol, marked "CAL. 6.35 MODEL AUTOMATIC PISTOL" over "ORIGINAL MODEL – VICTORIA ARMS CO", that probably dates from the early 1920s. These guns bear no resemblance to any of the "Victoria" designs produced by Esperanza y Unceta (q.v.), and their origins are unresolved.

The 7.65mm Kohout Mars pistol, made in Czechoslovakia.

KOHOUT

Kohout & Společnost, Kdyně, Czechoslovakia
This engineering business began making handguns in about 1927 and continued work until shortly before the Germans seized Czechoslovakia in 1939. It also made two small pistols for sale by Pošumavska Zbrojovka (q.v.), its successor.

Mars The first gun of this name — chambered for the 7.65mm Auto round — was based on the 1910-type FN-Browning but lacked the grip safety and relied on a striker instead of a hammer. The second type was 6.35mm-caliber, based on the FN-Browning 1906, again without grip safety. These guns were usually marked "MARS 7.65" (or "6.35") on the left side of the slide, above "KOHOUT & SPOL KDYNE", and had "Mars" molded into the grips beneath the head of the god of war.

KOISHIKAWA ARMS FACTORY

Koishikawa arsenal, later Tokyo artillery arsenal, Tokyo, Japan.
Prior to the early 1890s, the service pistol of the Japanese armed forces had been the Smith & Wesson New Model No. 3 revolver, but a decision was taken to end the reliance on foreign suppliers and concentrate the manufacture of service weapons in military arsenals. Except for small quantities of contract work, this policy was followed until 1945.

The 9mm Japanese 26th Year Type revolver.

～ REVOLVER ～

Meiji 26th Year Type (1893-1925) This handgun was introduced in the 26th year of the reign of the Emperor Meiji. The design was little more than a mixture of features taken from other guns: the lockwork appears to be based on a Galand design, the hinged frame and frame latch are Smith & Wesson, a hinged side-plate covering the lockwork comes from then-experimental French 1892-type Modèle d'Ordonnance and the general shape may be due to Nagant or Rast and Gasser — opinions differ. The absence of a cocking spur, intended to avoid snagging clothing and firing accidentally, forces reliance on double-action mode.

Chambered for a uniquely rimmed low-power 9mm cartridge of Japanese origin, the 26th Year Type revolvers were made in the

Koishikawa factory in Tokyo. When much of the factory was destroyed in the great earthquake of 1923, production stopped. Assembly continued until stockpiled parts had been exhausted, but the revolver had been superseded by the 14th Year Type pistol.

Survivors were still being encountered in 1945, which was a testimony to the quality of the original workmanship. The bluing, indeed, was often superb, and though the steel could be soft by Western standards, the revolver made a much better combat weapon than the idiosyncratic Japanese pistols.

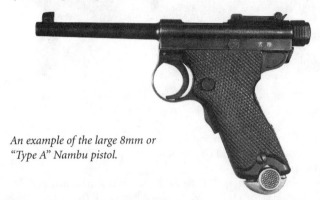

An example of the large 8mm or "Type A" Nambu pistol.

∼ AUTOMATIC PISTOLS ∼

Nambu Type "A" (large) (1902-6) This was designed by a Japanese army officer, Kijiro Nambu, but its status has always been contested, and many attempts have been made to discredit its designer. Though Nambu claimed that his experimentation dated back to the "30th Year Automatic Pistol Plan" of 1897, begun after a commission led by Nariake Arisaka had returned with news of the latest European developments, the inspiration for the Nambu pistol has been claimed variously as the Mauser C/96, the Swiss Häussler-Roch pistol (patented in 1903) or the Italian Glisenti of 1906-7. The probability is that the Mauser C/96, which had been patented in Germany at the end of 1895, influenced all these guns independently.

An 8mm "Nambu-type self-acting pistol", later known as "Type A", had been perfected by 1902. Small numbers were subsequently made in the Koishikawa factory of Tokyo artillery arsenal for trials with the Japanese army, but the budget was too restricted to allow adoption. However, Nambu pistols were made for the commercial market, and some were subsequently sold to China and Siam. Though the Nambu was never sanctioned by the army, the Russo-Japanese War (1904-5) found the troops so short of weapons that officers were given permission to buy the pistols privately.

The first batches made in Tokyo (c. 1903-6) had exceptionally cramped trigger-guard bows, rounded triggers, lanyard loops that were welded in position and wood-bottom magazines. They also had butt heels cut to receive a large wood-bodied holster/stock unit.

• *"Improved Type A"* (1906-23) This was developed in response to complaints voiced by buyers. The most obvious changes were the enlargement of the trigger guard to admit a gloved finger and an aluminum-alloy magazine base. The cocking-piece grooves were altered, and the lanyard loops were retained in rings.

Work continued on a small-scale basis, until the Japanese navy adopted the "Army Model" Nambu for the Special Naval Landing Force (marines) in September 1909. The Tokyo artillery arsenal was unwilling to accept the order, subcontracting it to the Tokyo Gasu Denki KK ("Tokyo Gas & Electric Company", q.v.). Both contractors ceased work on the Type A in 1923. Most pistols have ideographs reading *nambu shiki* ("Nambu type") on the right side of the frame, and many also bear three ideographs (*riku-gun shiki*, "army type") on the left. This suggests commercial sale, as the precise designation marks found on other small arms are lacking.

Although resembling the Parabellum outwardly, the mechanism of the Nambu is closer to that of the Mauser C/96. The Nambu has a slender barrel, forged integrally with the receiver, and a one-piece frame carrying a tangent-leaf rear sight. The barrel and barrel extension recoil on the frame; a hinged arm, with an upper lug, is attached to the barrel extension and is forced up by a ramp in the frame, so that the lug enters a recess in the bolt. On recoil, the hinged arm holds the bolt closed until it passes off the ramp, whereupon the arm drops and the bolt is freed to move away from the barrel. A single recoil spring is fitted at the left side of the bolt, and the bolt carries an internal striker and a grooved external cocking grip at the rear end. There was a grip safety in the front edge of the butt, and an eight-shot magazine went into the butt. The pistol was chambered for an 8mm bottle-necked cartridge, also designed by Nambu.

The Nambu balances well, despite the main spring chamber protruding from the left side, and has a light and precise trigger. Material and finish is usually excellent, though the quality of the striker spring was notoriously bad; pockets for spare springs were even provided in the holster!

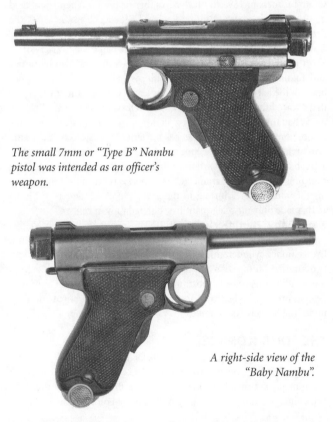

The small 7mm or "Type B" Nambu pistol was intended as an officer's weapon.

A right-side view of the "Baby Nambu".

Nambu Type "B" (small, 1909-23) Commonly called the "Baby Nambu", this was developed to equip officers who felt that the standard gun was too large to carry conveniently. Made to the same design as the "Type A", the "B" was chambered for the 7mm bottle-necked cartridge and had a fixed open-notch rear sight instead of the tangent-leaf pattern. It was only 6.8 inches long and weighed 21 oz without its seven-round magazine.

The earliest guns had a wooden magazine bottom and a pinched-in cocking knob, together with a single-diameter firing pin. After about 450 had been made, however, the magazine base became aluminum, the cocking knob became rounded and the firing pin was changed to multiple-diameter form.

The Koishikawa factory ceased work in 1923, owing to internal reorganization after the great earthquake, but TGE continued assembly until c. 1929. Virtually all these guns were purchased privately by officers, but the Baby Nambu never achieved popularity. It was almost twice the price of comparable imported pistols.

Taisho 14th Year Type The Tokyo artillery arsenal made these 8mm-caliber service pistols in the refurbished Koishikawa factory from 1928 until the machinery was moved to Kokura in 1931. See "Nagoya Arsenal" for constructional details.

KOKURA ARMS FACTORY

Kokura army arsenal, Kokura, Japan.

Taisho 14th Year Type This small-arms factory made 8mm service pistols from 1933 until 1936, when all production was concentrated in the Nambu-Seisakusho (q.v.) factory in the Kokabunji district of Tokyo. The Kokura production machinery had come from the Tokyo artillery arsenal (see "Koishikawa", above) in 1931. See "Nagoya Arsenal" for details of construction.

HENRY M. KOLB

Philadelphia, Pennsylvania, USA.

Trading in association with Charles Foehl (late of Foehl & Weeks), Kolb set up business in 1892 to make 22-caliber revolvers. When Foehl died in 1912, his place was taken by Reginald F. Sedgely, and in 1930, the firm ultimately became R.F. Sedgely & Company.

Baby Hammerless (1892-1930) A generic name for a variety of 22 Short rimfire five-shot solid-frame revolvers with concealed hammers and folding triggers. The earliest patterns had a knurled arbor pin beneath the barrel and a vertical spring-catch on the right of the frame that allowed the pin to be withdrawn to release the cylinder. The *1910 model* had three bands of knurling on the pin, and the catch was mounted horizontally. The *1918 model* has the letter "S" instead of "K" in the grip moldings, marking the appearance of Sedgely. The *1921 model* had a much thinner and plain arbor pin and a spring-loaded retaining sleeve engaging in a slot in the frame. A *1924 model* was much the same except for the addition of knurling to the arbor pin. A 32 centerfire Model 1910, made only in small quantities, differed only in caliber.

New Baby Hammerless (1911-30) Henry Kolb patented this break-open design in 1910. Offered only in 22 Short rimfire, with a five-chamber cylinder, this had a ribbed barrel and a frame-latch with two knurled buttons. An improved 1911-patent latch, passing behind the standing breech, was substituted for the original version almost as soon as production began. Work continued until Kolb retired and then under the Sedgely (q.v.) name.

THEODOR KOMMER

Th. Kommer Waffenfabrik, Zella Mehlis, Germany.

Shortly after the end of World War I, this gunmaker introduced a 6.35mm pocket pistol. Though little more than a copy of the 1906 Browning, the muzzle was enlarged and knurled on the Models 3 and 4

A typical 6.35mm Kommer pistol.

A partial view of a dismantled Kommer pistol, showing the barrel-attachment system and the open magazine well.

to provide a grip for dismantling — much easier than the usual struggle with a tight and oily barrel. Production ceased in favor of war work in the early 1940s.

- *Model 1* (c. 1921-8) The standard 6.35mm blowback had an eight-round magazine and a slightly curved backstrap. The maker's name and address may lie on the top of the slide, with "… "KOMMER" SELBSTLADE-PISTOLE CAL. 6,35" on the left side of the slide and, on the earliest guns at least, "Kommer" in script on the frame ahead of "D.R.G.M." These guns also have a "TK" monogram in an oval panel on the checkered plastic grips.

- *Model 2* (1925-40) This was virtually the same as the Model 1 but had a straight-sided grip and a six-round magazine. The markings duplicated those of the Model 1 in content, if not exactly in style, but the frame is usually marked "D.R.P.a." ("German patent sought [but not granted]") and the butt is marked "Th. K" in a round-edged panel.

- *Model 3* (1927-40) Recognizable by the knurled collar at the muzzle and the length of the butt, extended to accept an eight-round magazine, this was marked similarly to the Model 2 — though the frame mark was often "D.R.P." over "ANG." The grips were marked "Th. K."

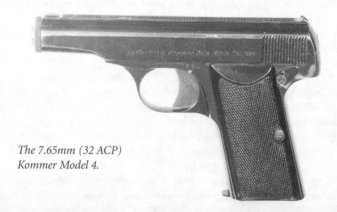

The 7.65mm (32 ACP) Kommer Model 4.

- *Model 4* (1936-40) The last Kommer pistol, this short-lived 7.65mm pattern was based on the 1910-type FN-Browning, though it lacked the grip safety and was fired by a striker instead of a hammer. The quality was much better than the 6.35mm guns. A knurled collar appeared at the muzzle, the butt held a seven-round magazine and the left side of the slide bore "Waffenfabrik Kommer Zella Mehlis Cal. 7,65" in slanted lettering. A cocking-indicator pin was added in the back of the slide after serial numbers had reached the 12000 group.

KOMURO ARMS FACTORY

Tokyo, Japan.

This gunmaking business is best known for an aberrant pistol, introduced in 1904, that is one of the rare class of "blow-forward" weapons. Instead of the breechblock being driven backward, the block remains still and the barrel moves forward to extract and reload.

Hino-Komuro (1908-12) Designed by Kumazo Hino, a Japanese army officer, the gun was submitted to the Japanese army as a potential military weapon but was rapidly rejected on the grounds that the safety features were not good enough. Hino then went to the Komuro brothers, who financed the project and equipped a factory in the hope of profiting from sales to the Chinese revolutionaries led by Sun Yat Sen. Work began in 1908, but the Chinese were not interested. Nor were many other people; production was meager and ended when serial numbers had reached only into the 1100 group.

The magazine fit into the butt, and the barrel was pulled forward until engaged by a latch. The movement of the barrel also operated a cartridge lifter to position the first round in the feed way. Pressing the trigger then released the latch, and the barrel ran back far enough to allow the bullet and the head of the cartridge to enter the chamber. When the grip safety was squeezed, the barrel could run back to chamber the round, driving the base of the cartridge against a fixed firing pin in the standing breech. A combination of bullet friction and gas pressure drove the barrel forward, stripping the empty case from the chamber, and a mechanical ejector threw it clear before the lifter brought up the next round.

The pistol was invariably chambered for the 7.65mm Auto cartridge (32 ACP), although one specimen in 8mm Nambu chambering is known to exist.

A comparison between the Norwegian M1912 and M1914 Colt Brownings.

KONGSBERG ARMS FACTORY

Kongsberg Vapenfabrik, Norway.

The Norwegian army took delivery of 300 45-caliber M1911 Colt-Browning pistols in 1913, issuing them for field trials as the "M/1912". These were successful enough to allow the "M/1914" to be adopted in April 1915. Production of this Norwegian copy of the M/1912 began in Kongsberg in 1915, the first 500 — made largely by hand — being delivered in 1917-19. The only real difference between the original Colt-made guns and the copies concerns the Norwegian slide-stop lever, which was enlarged to make operation easier. About 22,440 guns had been made by 1940. The left side of the slides was marked "11.35ᵐ/ₘ AUT. PISTOL M/1914". Another 10,000 were made during the German occupation (1940-5) for issue to the German armed forces as "Pistolen 657 (n)", and several hundred were assembled from parts in 1945-6. These went to the Norwegian army, ending with gun number 32854.

In early 1987, to explore the possibilities of returning to pistol manufacture, the Kongsberg management decided to make a special test-batch of M1914 pistols. These bore the same markings as the original pre-1946 guns and were numbered from 32855 to 32874. They proved that handguns could be made if required and were then sold commercially in the USA for $1500 apiece; an additional distributor's mark, "BENET ARMS AFTON VA." had been added on the right side of the slide.

KORTH

Korth-Vertreibs GmbH, now Korth Germany GmbH, Ratzeburg/Holstein, Germany.

Founded in 1954 by Willi Korth, a railway engineer, this gunmaking business made alarm revolvers (using steel salvaged from scrapped MG. 34) until the first cartridge revolver appeared in 1964. A pistol was developed shortly before Korth's death in 1982 but did not reach the market for some years afterwards. At one time associated with the Dynamit Nobel Group, the Korth business was purchased in 2000 by Freylinger & Company of Levange, Luxembourg, but work continues in Ratzeburg.

∾ REVOLVERS ∾

Made from 1964 to date, these guns are renowned for their exceptional quality and are priced appropriately. They are conventional solid-frame swing-cylinder double-action guns with full-length ejector shrouds, ventilated barrel ribs, automatic ejection, adjustable firing-pin strike and adjustable triggers. The cylinder-release catch, uniquely, lies alongside the hammer on the right side of the frame.

The 357 Magnum Korth Sportrevolver, with a ventilated-rib barrel.

Offering excellent quality, the Korth Target revolver has micro-adjustable sights and an anatomical grip.

- *Combat* This is the standard version, with barrels measuring 3 or 4 inches and conventional checkered walnut grips. Chamberings are restricted to 22 LR and 22 Magnum rimfire, 38 Special or 357 Magnum. The earliest guns (1966-8) had five-chamber cylinders, but those made since 1968 have been six-shot.
- *Sport* Distinguished by a 5.25- or 6-inch barrel, with a ventilated rib and an adjustable rear sight, this is distinguished by its conventional checkered-walnut grip. Chambering is currently restricted to 357 Magnum.
- *Target* Similar to the Sport pattern and with the same barrel-length options, this has a micro-adjustable target-type rear sight and an anatomical grip with an adjustable palm shelf. It is available in the four regular chamberings: 22 LR rimfire, 22 WM rimfire, 357 Magnum or 38 Special. It weighs 43 oz with a 6-inch barrel.

∾ AUTOMATIC PISTOLS ∾

Made only to order, in very small quantities, this is a large high-quality design locked by a wedge system that allows the barrel to move axially in pursuit of exemplary accuracy. The Korth has been chambered for a variety of cartridges, though the options are currently restricted to including 9mm Parabellum, 9x21 IMI, 357 SIG and 40 S&W.

- *Standard version* (1985 to date) Announced in 1982, but not available commercially for some time, this has a double-action trigger system and adjustable sights. It weighs about 40 oz, with a 5-inch barrel, and has a double-column magazine holding 13 9mm Parabellum rounds. Minor changes were made to the lockwork in 1987 that did not affect the operating system, and "production" — these are really semi-custom handguns — is still underway.
- *Single-action version* Introduced in the spring of 2001, this is identical with the preceding gun except that the trigger mechanism is simplified. The trigger lever lies noticeably farther back in the trigger guard than on the double-action alternative.

KORRIPHILA

Korriphila-Präzisionsmechanik GmbH, Ulm/Donau, Germany.
This precision-engineering business is best known in gunmaking circles for handguns designed by Edgar Budischowsky. These were originally distributed exclusively by Waffen-Frankonia of Würzburg, but the current products are promoted by Intertex-Korriphila of Eislingen.
TP-70 Apart from double-action lockwork and exemplary quality, this was a conventional blowback design with a slide-mounted safety catch. It was sold in the USA in the 1970s as the "Budischowsky", honoring its designer.
HSP-701 (1982 to date) An interesting delayed-blowback pattern, this relies on a separate breechblock within the slide and a transverse roller. When the gun fires, the roller has dropped into a recess in the frame and prevents the breechblock from moving back until an operating finger on the slide raises the roller out of its seat. Only about 30 guns are being made annually, confined to 9mm Parabellum (nine-round magazine) and 45 ACP (seven rounds), although 7.65mm Parabellum, 9mm Police, 9mm Steyr, 38 Special and 10mm Norma options have all been offered in the past. The guns have 4- or 5-inch barrels and weigh about 39-42 oz depending on their features. A few single-action examples have also been made.
- *Odin's Eye* This is a fascinating deluxe version of the basic HSP-701, differing from the standard pattern in the material of the frame and slide. It is the only automatic pistol ever to have been made in hand-forged damascus steel. The guns are fantastically expensive, but truly "one-of-a-kind", as the patterning on the metalwork is unique to each particular component.

ALFRED KRAUSER

Zella-Mehlis, Germany.
This gunsmith made blowback pistols in accordance with patents granted to Hugo Helfricht in 1920-1.
Helfricht (c. 1921-9) The construction of this pocket pistol is unusual. The slide is shallow while the frame is deep, and the ejection port is split between the two, the lower half being cut out of the frame and the upper half out of the slide. When the pistol is at rest, the two halves are not aligned, with the upper portion lying alongside the barrel and the lower portion revealing the side of the breechblock. When the pistol is fired, the slide moves back and the two halves align just as the cartridge case is ejected.

The method of assembly is also unique. The front end of the frame has two hook-like projections on the left inner side, engaged by two hooks that form part of a rod passing along the inner top of the slide (through the top of the breechblock) to end in a slotted boss at the rear end of the slide. The return spring is concentric with this rod. When the

slide recoils, the hooks engage and hold the front end of the rod, allowing the slide to move backwards and compress the return spring.

To dismantle the pistol, all that is needed is to press the slotted boss inward with a coin, against the pressure of the return spring, and give it one-third of a turn to disengage the hooks; the slide can now be withdrawn backwards off the frame.

There were four patterns of this 6.35mm blowback pistol. Models 1–3 have the slide and frame ending above the front of the trigger guard, exposing the barrel for about half of its 2-inch length. Model 4 is more conventional, with the slide and frame enveloping the barrel. However, the guns are not marked with model numbers, and the differences between them are not easily seen.
- *Model 1* has a cylindrical seating at the top front end of the slide that acts as a bearing for the dismantling shaft, with the slotted boss protruding about a quarter of an inch behind the slide. It also has an unusual safety catch, a long lever passing beneath the left grip with a knurled operating stud just behind the trigger, and a large hook, which locks into the slide, at the other end. Moving this lever locks the slide and also locks the trigger. The guns are usually marked "PATENT" ahead of "HELFRICHT" in a round-cornered cartouche on the left side of the frame, with "KH" on the grip.
- *Model 2* has the front end of the slide flat, with the boss protruding at the rear. The safety catch and markings are the same as the Model 1.
- *Model 3* has the front end flat and the boss flush with the rear of the slide. The Model 3 also shares the safety-catch design of the Model 1. The markings are also similar.

A first-type 6.35mm (25 ACP) Helfricht Model 4, showing the unusual split ejection port.

The left side of a Helfricht Model 4.

- *Model 4* does not have the protruding barrel and is marked "Helfricht's – Patent Mod. 4" on the frame, with "KH" on the grip. The safety catch is also much more conventional.

Helkra Although there is documentary evidence suggesting that the "Helkra" pistol was the same as the 6.35mm and/or 7.65mm Helfricht, no gun could be traced for examination and the style of marking remains unknown.

HEINRICH KRIEGHOFF

Heinrich Krieghoff Waffenfabrik, Suhl, Germany.

A well-established maker of sporting guns and rifles, Krieghoff developed a semi-automatic rifle during the 1930s and became keen to acquire a military contract —particularly from the Luftwaffe, which was seeking to order machineguns. As a form of bait, Krieghoff acquired tooling for the Parabellum pistol from the liquidators of Simson & Co. (q.v.). It was once fashionable to claim that Krieghoff held an exclusive contract to supply the air force, but publication of handgun inventories has now undermined the claim.

Parabellum The army had first call on P. 08s being made by Mauser-Werke, and this, combined with a very low price quoted by Krieghoff, persuaded the Luftwaffe to order 10,000 pistols in 1935. It seems that parts for 15,000 were made, to ensure sufficient allowance for wastage. Consequently, about 1300 guns that failed the rigorous inspection process were marketed commercially; they were distinguished by "P"-prefix serial numbers and must not be confused with the DWM and Mauser-made guns that had been sold by Krieghoff prior to 1935. These often had the Krieghoff name on the left side of the frame and usually had suffixed serial numbers. They also bore the distinctive sword-and-anchor trademark, sought in December in 1928.

The air force contract was completed in 1938. The guns had the trademark, flanked by "H" and "K", on the toggle link above "KRIEGHOFF" and "SUHL". The coded date "G" (1935) and "S" (1936) above the chamber were superseded first by "36" and then "1936", a style that continued until "1945". During the early part of the war, another 1000 pistols were assembled, and about 100 "P"-prefix guns were sold commercially. A last batch of 150-200 was put together in 1944, and finally, in the brief twilight between the American occupation of Suhl and its takeover by the Soviets, about 250 were assembled from surviving parts. Most of these were probably bartered with US Army personnel.

KAREL KRNKA

Weipert and Vienna, Austria-Hungary.

Karel Krnka (often confusingly named in patent applications as "Charles" or "Carl") was a gifted and prolific designer best known as the author of *Die principiellen der automatische Handfeuerwaffen*, published in 1902 under the pseudonym "Kaisertreu". The son of the renowned gunsmith/inventor Sylvestr Krnka, Karel was born in 1858 and served in the Austro-Hungarian infantry for several years. The first of many improvements to infantry rifles were patented in this period.

He then left the service and went to England to become the chief engineer of the short-lived Gatling Arms & Ammunition Company (q.v.), but this business collapsed in 1890 and Krnka returned to Prague. After working as a patent agent, he became manager of the Roth cartridge factory in 1898, patenting a number of automatic-pistol designs in collusion with his employer. Krnka moved to the Hirtenberg Cartridge Company after Roth died in 1909, remaining there until returning to what had become Czechoslovakia in 1922. There he worked for Československá Zbrojovka until his death in 1926.

Krnka's earliest handguns were notable more for their mechanical ingenuity than practicality, and few were made. It was not until his association with Roth — and possibly with Frommer — that his designs became more practical, though even then his predilection for the long recoil system of operation made them too complicated to succeed. Yet the part played by Krnka in the development of guns such as the Roth-Sauer, Roth-Steyr and Steyr-Hahn has been largely overlooked.

∾ REPEATING PISTOLS ∾

The first patent in this group, granted to Krnka in 1888, protected a mechanically operated pistol incorporating a bolt action driven by a ring trigger. Only a prototype had been made prior to his return to

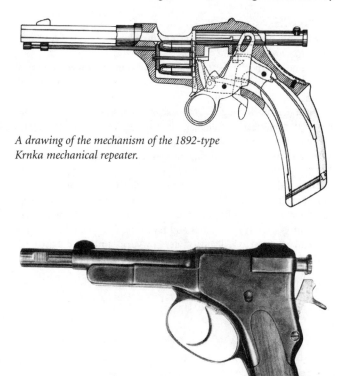

A drawing of the mechanism of the 1892-type Krnka mechanical repeater.

This prototype Krnka pistol, probably made in the Roth factory, is said to date from 1895.

Prague, where an improved "Model 1892" was announced. This was only made in tiny quantities, owing to the emergence of the semi-automatic pistol that made mechanical repeaters obsolete.

∾ AUTOMATIC PISTOLS ∾

By the middle of the 1890s, Krnka had begun working on automatic pistols and in 1895 patented a design with two characteristic features: an integral magazine in the butt, charger-loaded through the open action, and long recoil operation. The barrel and bolt recoiled together across the top of the magazine; the bolt was then rotated to open and held back while the barrel ran forward alone. As the barrel stopped moving, it released the bolt to run forward, chamber a new round and rotate back into engagement. An external hammer provided the firing impulse.

Krnka pistols were made in considerable numbers, but survivors rarely give a clue to their origins. Some were clearly the work of Roth, whose name is customarily attached to them — probably more by virtue of his ownership of the company than participation in the design process — but little else is known.

KRONBORG ARMS FACTORY

Kronborg Geværfabrik, Kronborg, Denmark.

This long-established Danish government arms factory occasionally made or modified handguns until production began in the 1880s in the Copenhagen site ("Geværfabriken Kjobenhavn", best-known as "Hærens Tøjhus").

M1865 Designed by Georg Christensen, this solid-frame revolver had a folding trigger and a safety catch between the hammer and the frame. Issued to cavalrymen and artillerymen, it originally chambered an 11mm pinfire cartridge. Survivors were altered in the Copenhagen factory in the 1890s to chamber an 11.4mm centerfire round, which were re-issued as the "M1865/97".

KYNOCH

The Kynoch Gun Factory, Aston Cros, Birmingham, Warwickshire, England.

The name of Kynoch is better known in the ammunition world than in the handgun trade, though the two businesses involved were both founded by the same man.

George Kynoch bought out Pursall & Phillips, percussion cap makers of Witton, near Birmingham, and set up business in 1862. This became "Geo. Kynoch & Co Ltd", but Kynoch left for South Africa in 1889 to set up a gun importing business and died in Bloemfontein in 1890. The "Kynoch Gun Factory" was a separate entity, created by Kynoch and partners to make small arms for the government of the Transvaal. These included Gras-type rifles assembled from Chassepot components that had been in store in Birmingham since the Franco-Prussian War of 1870-1. Rifles and revolvers were made in a factory that had belonged to William Tranter (q.v.) prior to 1885, but the business was soon in financial trouble and was liquidated in 1889.

Kynoch revolver Patented by an engineer named Henry Schlund, this had an unusual firing system based on the mechanism of the caplock Tranter revolver. Pulling the lower of two triggers cocked a concealed hammer, and pressure on the upper trigger fired the gun. The Kynoch pattern was a six-shot break-open design in 380, 450 or 476 CF chamberings, with a hammer that was concealed in a rise at the rear of the frame. Pressing a knurled catch, placed where the hammer would normally be found, allowed the barrel to drop and forced a star ejector from the center of the cylinder.

- *1885 type* Guns made in accordance with the original patent have the cocking trigger below the trigger guard. Comparatively few of these revolvers were made, possibly less than 100.
- *1886 type* A patent of improvement protected a modification of the 1885-type gun with both triggers inside the guard. It is reckoned that only about 600 guns of this type were made prior to 1889.

CHARLES LANCASTER

London, England.

Charles William Lancaster, best known for the invention of oval-bore rifling, worked in partnership with his brother Alfred until 1867 and then continued alone until his death in 1878. The business was acquired by Henry Thorn, its manager, but retained the Lancaster name.

Lancaster pistol Popular in the 1880s and 1890s, this was customarily a break-open four-barreled repeater. The barrels were in a solid block, two above two, that tipped down to load. Most were chambered for the large British-type centerfire cartridges — e.g., 450, 455 or 476 — that were popular with army officers who distrusted the revolver. A few were even offered in 320 CF or 380 CF, and many were rifled on Lancaster's oval-bore system to let them fire ball or shot charges interchangeably.

- *First type* Four firing pins were carried in the breech face, together with a tubular striker with zig-zag grooves on its circumference. Pulling the trigger pushed the striker back against a spring, and a pin, riding in the grooves, turned the striker through 90 degrees to align the striker-lug with one of the firing pins. Further trigger pressure released the striker to fly forward and hit the pin. The next pull on the trigger rotated the striker through another 90 degrees, to hit the next firing pin, and the process continued until all four cartridges had been fired.

- *Second type* A simplification of the design, this abandoned the separate firing pins and firing-pin springs in favor of a revolving striker that struck the primers of the cartridges directly. Production seems to have been short-lived, though two-barreled guns of this type were also made.

LANDSTAD

Halvard Landstad, Christiania (now Oslo), Norway.

This mechanical engineer patented an automatic revolver in 1899, with a flattened two-chambered feed-block or "cylinder". The upper chamber was aligned with the barrel but lay ahead of a reciprocating bolt carrying a striker and an extractor. In addition, the top cartridge in a detachable magazine in the butt lay directly behind the lower chamber.

After a loaded magazine had been inserted in the butt, a rod beneath the barrel was pulled back to retract the bolt. When the rod was released, the bolt ran forward to cock the striker and strip the top cartridge from the magazine into the lower chamber. When the trigger was pressed, a pawl rotated the feed-block through 180 degrees to position the cartridge behind the barrel; the block was locked in place and the striker was released to fire the cartridge. The bolt was blown back, extracting and ejecting the spent case, and returned to re-cock the striker and push a new round into the lower chamber.

The principal goal of this complexity was to allow a loaded handgun to be safely carried by preventing the cartridge arriving in front of the striker unless the trigger had been pressed. Landstad certainly achieved his aim, but at the expense of considerable complication. Only one gun of this type is currently known to survive, chambered for the 7.5mm Norwegian service cartridge and marked "SYSTEM / "Landstad" / MODEL No 1. 1900" in three lines on the right side of the frame. It is doubtful if more than a handful of prototypes were ever made.

LANGENHAN

Fredr. Langenhan Gewehr- und Fahrradfabrik, Zella St Blasii (to 1919) and Zella Mehlis (1919-45), Germany.

Valentin Friedrich Langenhan began trading as a gunsmith in Mehlis in 1842 and moved to Zella St Blasii in 1855. By the end of the century, his successors were making revolvers, sporting guns and rifles, air guns and bicycles. During World War I, the firm, by then owned by Fritz and Ernst Langenhan, produced an automatic pistol. Bicycle production was abandoned, and sporting guns and small-arms components were made until 1945. The Langenhan pistol design was granted protection in 1915 and supplied in quantity to the German army as a *Behelfspistole*. About 50,000 were made, but few if any were ever sold commercially.

The 7.65mm (32 ACP) Langenhan FL-Selbstlader, showing the locking yoke and the retaining screw above the rear of the frame.

F.L. Selbstlader This was a 7.65mm blowback of conventional form in all respects other than the breechblock, which was a separate unit. The barrel was screwed into the frame and the return spring, in the upper part of the slide, bore against a fixed block above the breech. The breechblock ran on slides on the left side of the frame, but much of the right side of the frame was cut away to form an ejection port.

A yoke, hinged to the slide, engaged lugs on the breechblock and was locked in place with a large screw. This was the main claim to originality in the design but was a dubious advantage; experience has shown that as the gun wears, so the yoke loosens and the locking screw unscrews slightly with each shot. Unless the screw is re-tightened from time to time, the yoke will jump out of engagement and the block will be blasted off the slide into the shooter's face.

After about 3500-4000 guns had been made, the right side of the frame was modified. The ejection port was cut back so that the right side of the breechblock, no longer supported by a rail, simply ran along the top of the frame. The side of the block was milled to fit flush with the frame and slide, and the exterior surface was blued so that no ejection port was visible. At about the same time, the trigger bar and disconnector, originally hidden inside the frame on the right, were let into the left so that both were visible. The final change was to adopt black hard rubber grips instead of the original wooden ones.

The markings reflect these changes; the earliest guns (comparatively rare) were marked "D.R.P. ANGEM" over "F.L. SELBTSLADER 7,65" on the left of the slide. With the adoption of the flush breechblock, the description was changed to "F.L. SELBSTLADER" over "D.R.G.M. 625263" on the right of the slide. Finally, with the addition of the new trigger bar, "– 633251" was added to the inscription. The F.L. was about 6.5 inches long, had a 4.1-inch barrel and weighed 23 oz empty.

Model I This was a smaller version of the F.L. pattern, chambered for the same 7.65mm cartridge but with the magazine restricted to six rounds. The gun was 5.4 inches long and had a 2.9-inch barrel. The markings were the same as the perfected F.L.

Model II After the war, Langenhan offered this 6.35mm pistol on the commercial market. It was a reduced-scale version of the 7.65mm pattern, but the yoke was replaced by a cross bolt that passed through the slide and the breechblock. The magazine held eight rounds. New guns

A 6.35mm Langenhan field-stripped. Note that the connection between the slide and the breechblock is now a sturdy pin.

were still being offered in 1936, but it seems unlikely that any production had taken place since the late 1920s. They were usually marked "Langenhan 6,35" on the right side of the slide, sometimes accompanied by the model designation. About 5.7 inches overall, with 3.1-inch barrels, they weighed about 18 oz and had seven-round magazines.

Model III Introduced shortly after the preceding pattern, this shared the same basic construction but was only 4.8 inches long and weighed about 15.5 oz. The short butt contained a six-round magazine.

LAR MANUFACTURING, INC.

West Jordan, Utah, USA.

Thus gunmaking business made a variety of pistols based on the 1911-type Colt-Browning but recognizable by their squared lines and barrels that often extended from the slide.

Grizzly series (1983-2001) The original *Mark I* version was cham-

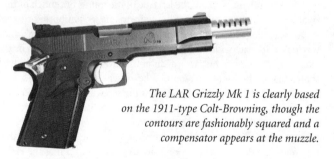

The LAR Grizzly Mk 1 is clearly based on the 1911-type Colt-Browning, though the contours are fashionably squared and a compensator appears at the muzzle.

bered for cartridges that included the 357 Magnum, 38 Special, 10mm Auto, 45 ACP and 45 Winchester Magnum ("WinMag"). Magazines usually held seven rounds. Barrels could be 5.4-10 inches long, often with compensators built into the muzzle of the longest options. Adjustable Millett sights and an ambidextrous safety catch was fitted, and the finish on the carbon-steel slide and frame could be parkerized, blue or chrome; grips were usually black rubber.

• *Mark II* Made for a few years from 1986 onward, this was restricted to short barrels, fixed sights and a standard safety catch.
• *Mark IV* Chambered only for the 44 Magnum round, this was otherwise similar to the Mark I. The barrel-length options were restricted to 5.4 and 6.5 inches, and the finish was either blued or parkerized steel.
• *Mark V* This was little more than a variant of the Mark IV chambered for the 50 Action Express round. Production was comparatively small.

LARRANAGA Y ELARTZA

Eibar, Spain.

Jubala A 6.35mm "Eibar" automatic of no outstanding merit, this is said to have been made for sale by Fabrique d'Armes de Grande

Précision (q.v.). The safety catch lies on the left side of the frame above the trigger, and the slide-retraction grooves are usually milled radially. A typical slide mark reads "FABRIQUE D'ARMES DE GUERRE / "JUBALA" MARQUE DEPOSÉ" in two lines on the left side of the slide, with a "LE" monogram on a shield and "JUBALA" above a warrior's head on the rubber grips. It has been dated to 1914 but more probably originates in the early 1920s.

LASAGABASTER HERMANOS

Eibar, Spain.

Douglas A 6.35mm "Eibar"-type blowback pistol, with the safety catch on the frame above the trigger and radially-milled retraction grips, this is marked "6 ^{35} 1914 MODEL AUTOMATIC PISTOL / "DOUGLAS" PATENT" on the slide. However, it seems more likely that it dated from the early 1920s. The grips are marked "Douglas" beneath the initials "LH".

LASERAIM TECHNOLOGIES, INC.

Little Rock, Arkansas, USA.

Laseraim made handguns modeled on the 1911-type Colt-Browning. However, they had modernized contours, extended squared trigger guards and rails beneath the front of the frame to allow a designator to be fitted. Series I was offered only in 10mm Auto or 45 ACP, with eight- or seven-round magazines, respectively. The 6-inch ported barrel had a slotted compensator attached to the front of the slide and was made of stainless steel with a protective black Teflon finish. Series II was similar, but the barrel was only five inches long and lacked the compensator. A compact form was offered with a 3.4-inch barrel. Series III shared the 5-inch barrel, but this was ported and compensating slots were cut across the slide behind the front sight.

JOSEF LAUMANN

Vienna, Austria-Hungary.

The Laumann pistol was a bolt-action clip-fed mechanically-operated repeater very similar to others of the same period (e.g., Schulhof, Bittner), but it has a special place in pistol history since it was transformed into one of the earliest self-loading pistols — the Schönberger (see "Oesterreichische Waffenfabriks-Gesellschaft").

LEE ARMS COMPANY

Wilkes Barre, Pennsylvania, USA.

A maker of cheap solid-frame sheathed-trigger non-ejecting "Suicide Special" revolvers in 1880-9, succeeding the Pittston Arms Company (q.v.). The guns were marked *Imperial*, *Red Jacket*, *Royal* or *Wm. Tell*, and could be chambered for 22, 30 or 32 rimfire ammunition. Some will be marked with an 1881 patent date, referring to improvements made by Roland Brewer, the factory superintendent. The company name was provided by its president, J. Frank Lee; there was no connection with the gun's designer, James Paris Lee.

EUGÈNE LEFAUCHEUX

Paris, France.

The French gunsmith Casimir Lefaucheux perfected the pinfire cartridge, and in 1851, introduced a "pepperbox" revolver. His son Eugène (1820-71) is credited with the development of the eponymous open-frame pinfire revolver, often with a double-action trigger system patented in 1853 by Chaineux. Lefaucheux revolvers were made in huge quantities, and beginning with the French navy M1858, served a variety of military forces throughout the world in the 1860s and 1870s. They were also made in huge quantities for commercial sale. Though the output of genuine Lefaucheux guns ceased shortly after the Franco-Prussian War (1870-1), work continued elsewhere in France and Belgium until 1914.

The guns ranged from tiny 5mm-caliber pocket revolvers — with folding triggers and spurless hammers — to enormous 30-shot monsters, remarkable principally for their clumsiness, and 12mm-caliber guns that offered acceptable man-stopping performance. One of the best-known makers of pinfire guns was Francotte (q.v.) of Liége, who adopted the descriptive title "Lefaucheux-Francotte".

Most "Lefaucheux" patterns had a characteristic two-piece open-top construction, with the barrel held in the frame by the cylinder axis-pin and a screw running either up through the frame ahead of the hammer or horizontally into the frame from the front lower part of the cylinder web. However, some enterprising manufacturers offered solid straps above the cylinder, dovetailed into the standing breech, and a few even used frames forged in a single piece to provide additional strength.

LEPAGE, LE PAGE

Manufacture d'Armes Le Page SA, Liége, Belgium.

This business began as "Le Page et Chauvot" late in the 18th century and by 1860 was making a range of pinfire revolvers. After World War I, the business was reorganized as a "Société Anonyme", and in 1925 began making automatic pistols. However, despite a sound design and good workmanship, the pistols failed to prosper and are uncommon today.

This "Bull Dog" is typical of the revolvers made by Le Page in the late 19th century.

∼ REVOLVERS ∼

The first Le Page revolvers were Lefaucheux-pattern pinfires, in a variety of calibers. An *Infanterie Monténégrin* pattern was a close copy of the Gasser (q.v.), though with a proprietary cylinder lock. With the arrival of self-extracting revolvers, Le Page produced a *Type Brasilien* with a tip-up hinged frame and lever extractor on broadly Spirlet principles but then reverted to solid-frame gate-loaded types. Most common was the *Constabulary* pattern, the usual short-barrel large-caliber double-action revolver with bird's-head butt. The *Type Mexicain* was similar, excepting for a ring trigger that was rarely seen as late as the 1890s. More effective was the *Type Militaire*, chambering the French 8mm revolver cartridge.

The name *Lincoln* was applied to a wide variety of revolvers made in 1880-1914, from folding-trigger hammer and "hammerless" types in 22 rimfire and 5.5mm Velo-Dog to study solid-frame patterns in 380 centerfire. Many of these guns, whatever their markings suggest, prove to have been made by Manufacture Liégeoise d'Armes à Feu (q.v.).

∼ AUTOMATIC PISTOLS ∼

Le Page (1) The patented Le Page design is a fixed-barrel blowback automatic with an open-topped slide and an external hammer. The slide contains the return spring, beneath the barrel, and the breechblock section stands proud of the barrel line. The only interesting feature is the packaging of the lockwork and the hammer in a removable unit forming the backstrap of the butt, which can be easily removed once the safety catch has been detached. The guns were offered in

A 7.65mm Le Page blowback pistol.

7.65mm Auto, 9mm Short and 9mm Browning Long chamberings, the largest version having a large butt containing a 12-shot magazine and distinctive finger grooves on the frontstrap. A wooden clip-on holster-stock was also provided. Typical markings read "MANUFACTURE D'ARMES LEPAGE – LIEGE – BELGIQUE" in a single line on the left side of the slide, above "CAL. 7,65 BREVET No 305326"; "LEPAGE" was also molded into the plastic grips.

Le Page (2) This was a 6.35mm gun introduced to satisfy the pocket-pistol market, though it was nothing but an unremarkable copy of the 1906-type FN-Browning without the grip safety.

LERCKER

Bologna, Italy.

The Lercker pistol was a selective-fire machine pistol in 25 ACP caliber designed in 1950. Of fairly conventional pistol shape, it was cocked by pulling back the bolt, which was then held back by the sear, so that when cocked, the pistol was somewhat awkward, with a large rear overhang. On pulling the trigger, the bolt closed, loading and firing the round in one movement. A selector lever permitted firing either single shots or automatic at a cyclic rate of about 1200 rounds per minute. Whilst the Lercker was a workable weapon, the small size of the cartridge prevented it from being taken seriously as a police or military weapon, and it is understood that no more than 150 were made.

LES, INC.

Also known as "LES Importers"; Skokie, Illinois, USA.

This distributing business sold the *Rogak P-18* in the USA in the 1970s. This was actually the Steyr (q.v.) MPi 18. Guns were made, or at least assembled under license, in the USA, but the quality control was poor and work soon ended. The guns chambered the 9mm Parabellum round and had 5.5-inch barrels. Magazine capacity was 18.

LIGNOSE

Actiengesellschaft Lignose, Suhl, Germany.

Lignose bought the Bergmann (q.v.) company in 1921, taking over the factory in Suhl. Among the acquisitions was the Chylewski (q.v.) one-hand pistol, which became the *Einhand*. Another was the Bergmann Taschenpistole, which also had its name changed to Lignose. Both were

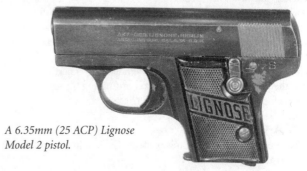

A 6.35mm (25 ACP) Lignose Model 2 pistol.

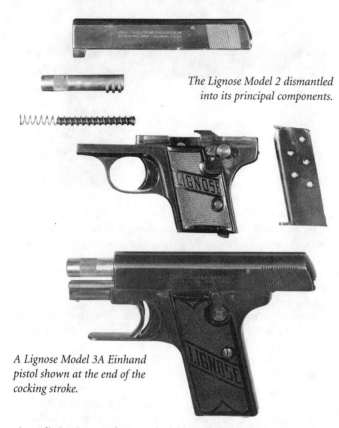

The Lignose Model 2 dismantled into its principal components.

A Lignose Model 3A Einhand pistol shown at the end of the cocking stroke.

given distinctive numbers, as had been the Bergmann practice; the Taschenmodelle became "2" and "3", while the Einhand versions became "2A" and "3A". The number "1" had been reserved for a prospective Einhand in 7.65mm, which, together with a 9mm Short version, was never made. Excepting the changes in markings and designation, there were few significant differences between Lignose and Bergmann products. Later in the 1920s, a variant of the "2A" was made with the magazine extended to give a nine-round capacity on the normal frame.

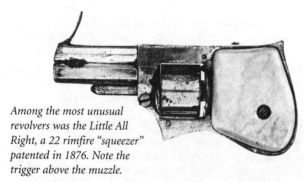

Among the most unusual revolvers was the Little All Right, a 22 rimfire "squeezer" patented in 1876. Note the trigger above the muzzle.

LITTLE ALL RIGHT FIREARMS COMPANY

Lawrence, Massachusetts, USA.
This was formed to make the *Little All Right*, an unusual solid-frame 22 Short rimfire five-shot revolver patented in 1876 by Edward Boardman & Andrew Peavey. A folding trigger, above the muzzle, worked a rod that revolved the cylinder and tripped a concealed hammer. The butt was wedge-shaped, lying behind the cylinder; the objective was to "palm" the gun, with the 1.75-inch barrel protruding through the fingers. One finger was used to operate the trigger.

LLAMA-GABILONDO

The name of a long line of pistols made by Gabilondo (q.v.) of Eibar from 1931 to the present day.

LUDWIG LOEWE

Ludwig Loewe & Co., Berlin and Charlottenburg, Germany.
Loewe began as a small engineering company before it began making sewing machines. During the Franco-Prussian War, it took on several military contracts to manufacture weapons and components and realized that, given the state of Europe, there was probably more to be made from munitions than sewing machines. In the early 1880s, Loewe acquired sizable holdings in Waffenfabrik Mauser, then purchased Deutsche Metallpatronenfabrik Lorenz, and finally amalgamated everything to form Deutsche Waffen- & Munitionsfabriken ("DWM", q.v.).

Ludwig Loewe made a large number of good quality S&W Russian Model copies in the late 1870s.

Smith & Wesson-type revolvers Copied directly from the "Russian Model" pattern, about 70,000 guns of this type were made in 1878-80 for the Russian government at a time when the American manufacturer was unable to honor a new contract. They are similar to the short-barreled cavalry pattern but clearly display Loewe's name in Cyrillic on the barrel rib instead of Smith & Wesson markings.

Borchardt Hugo Borchardt (1845-1924), born in Magdeburg, migrated to the USA at the age of 16 and subsequently became an American citizen. He became a skilled engineer and worked with various US gunmakers, being responsible for the Sharps-Borchardt rifle and assisting in the development of revolvers for Winchester. In 1883, he went to Hungary to become works director of Fegyvar és Gépgyár of Budapest, returned briefly to the USA in 1890-2, then returned to Europe to seek handgun patents in Germany. Borchardt is reputed to have approached Fabrique Nationale d'Armes de Guerre, unsuccessfully, before reaching agreement with Loewe.

The Borchardt pistol used the toggle lock, subsequently adapted by Georg Luger, but it is probable that the idea was provided by the Maxim machineguns that had been demonstrated in Austria and Hungary at a time when Borchardt was in Budapest. The toggle breaks upward and is linked to a clock-type return spring in a large housing at the rear of the frame. The idea of placing the magazine inside the butt may have derived from Borchardt's association with James Paris Lee in the USA.

The construction of the pistol looks awkward—the butt being almost at right-angles to the frame and the frame overhanging much too greatly at the rear—but at least the grip is at the center of balance, and the reports of the day testify to good balance, exceptional accuracy and low recoil. A shoulder-stock could be attached to the spring housing to make a passable light automatic carbine, accurate out to 200 yards or more.

Also known as the "C/93", after the year in which the patent had been granted, the Borchardt pistol was marketed commercially in the mid-1890s. They are marked "WAFFENFABRIK / LOEWE / BERLIN." in three lines above the chamber, with "D.R.P." over "75837" on the toggle, and "SYSTEM BORCHARDT. PATENT." on the right side of the frame. Though work passed to DWM at the beginning of 1897, the pistol was regarded with considerable respect by the gunsmiths of the day. Commercial success was denied by high price and excessive size.

LORCIN ENGINEERING

Mira Loma, California, USA.

Lorcin was best known for a variety of blowback pistols, made from 1989 until 2001.

∽ TWO-SHOT PISTOL ∽

Derringer This had a barrel cluster that tipped down once the latch had been released. It was chambered for the 357 Magnum, 38 Special or 45 ACP rounds and packed a considerable punch in a package that measured merely 6.5 inches long (with a 3.5-inch barrel).

∽ AUTOMATIC PISTOLS ∽

L-9 This was a 9mm Parabellum version of the basic design, with a 4.5-inch barrel and a 10-round magazine. The gun weighed 36 oz empty but was only made in small quantities.

L-22 Chambered for the 22 LR rimfire cartridge, this was 5 inches long, with a 2.5-inch barrel, and had a 10-round box magazine. Empty weight was 16oz. The guns generally had black plastic grips with horizontal flutes and squared trigger guards shaped to allow a two-hand hold.

L-25 Measuring merely 4.8 inches overall, with an empty weight of 13 oz, this had a magazine containing seven 25 ACP cartridges. The "LT-25" was identical but had an aluminum-alloy frame that reduced weight by about 3 oz. The trigger guard was rounded, the finish was usually bright stainless steel and the grips could be white plastic simulating ivory or mother-of-pearl.

L-32 Little more than an enlargement of the L-22, this chambered the 32 ACP round. Magazine capacity was seven.

L-380 An enlargement of the L-32, this had a 3.5-inch barrel and a seven-round magazine. Chambering was restricted to 380 ACP. The "LH-380" had a 4.5-inch barrel and a 10-round magazine and was available in black, satin or bright chrome.

LOWELL ARMS COMPANY

Lowell, Massachusetts, USA.

This was a successor to the business of Rollin White, active 1865-8. White had made weapons covered by his own patent, approved by Smith & Wesson, but the reorganization of the company was not so successful and a lawsuit was threatened. Smith & Wesson seized nearly 2000 Lowell revolvers and work ceased.

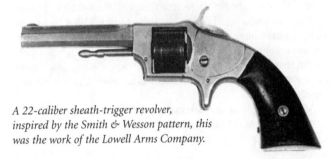

A 22-caliber sheath-trigger revolver, inspired by the Smith & Wesson pattern, this was the work of the Lowell Arms Company.

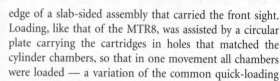

MACCHINE TERMO BALLISTICHE ("MATEBA")

Pavia, Italy.

The Mateba revolver was designed by Emilio Ghisoni with a view to producing a weapon suitable for ISU rapid fire contests. The novelty of the design lay in the positioning of the cylinder, low down and in front of the trigger guard, so that the barrel was as low as could be achieved within the restrictions of the ISU rules. The rear end of the weapon resembled an automatic pistol but concealed a conventional double-action hammer mechanism, striking a long firing pin. An outside cocking lever, above the left grip, allowed the hammer to be cocked for single-action firing.

MTR series Two models were developed, the "Sport and Defense" and the "Combat", the only difference being that the former had a large rib above the barrel carrying the front sight, while the latter had a plain barrel with the foresight mounted on the receiver. All had a cylinder that was mounted on a crane to open to the left and down, retained by a sliding latch in front of the cylinder. There was also a carbine design, which was little more than the revolver mechanism with a suitably long barrel and a shoulder stock.

- *MTR8* was the basic weapon, an eight-shot chambering the 38 Special cartridge; the MTR8M was similar but for the 357 Magnum.
- *MTR12* was a 12-shot in 38 Special, and the MTR12M was the 357 Magnum version.
- *MTR14* was a 14-shot chambering 22 LR rimfire ammunition.
- *MTR20* was a 20-shot in 22 LR.

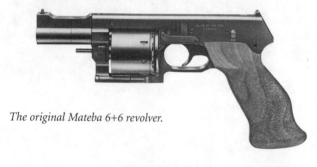

The original Mateba 6+6 revolver.

The Mateba compared with a conventional 357 Magnum Smith & Wesson.

MTR6+6 The MTR8 and its variants were given a great deal of publicity in 1983-4, when there were stories that the project would be backed by Franchi. However, nothing came of these, and a new Mateba design appeared in 1985. This had the cylinder placed more-or-less conventionally above the trigger, but the barrel was placed ahead of the bottom chamber so the turning moment as the gun fired was reduced to a minimum. The side-opening cylinder hinged upward, perhaps the only one of its type to do so, and the barrel was formed in the lower edge of a slab-sided assembly that carried the front sight. Loading, like that of the MTR8, was assisted by a circular plate carrying the cartridges in holes that matched the cylinder chambers, so that in one movement all chambers were loaded — a variation of the common quick-loading device. The designation of the 357 Magnum MTR6+6 arose because the six-chamber cylinder was supplemented by another six rounds in a loading plate in the base of the butt. The MTR6+6 was more successful than the MTR, but was never made in quantity.

- *2006M* A six-shot gun with a 2-, 3- or 4-inch barrel, this was chambered for 357 Magnum or 38 Special ammunition. It also had an interchangeable barrel. The supplementary loading plate in the butt was abandoned, and the cylinder was loaded like that of any other revolver.
- *2007S* This was a seven-shot 38 Special derivative, with barrels measuring 3, 4 or 6 inches.

MAGNUM RESEARCH, INC.

Minneapolis, Minnesota, USA.

Best known as the inspiration behind — and distributor of — the Israeli-made Desert Eagle, Magnum Research has also handled a variety of other handguns and even manufactured them in the USA.

∼ SINGLE-SHOT PISTOLS ∼

Lone Eagle (1991 to date) Intended for target shooting (including silhouette competitions), this is a large gun with a rotating-block breech system. It is usually supplied with a 14-inch barrel, though the chambering can range between 22 Hornet and 22-250 to 444 Marlin. The barrel is usually drilled and tapped to accept optical-sight mounts, but fixed or adjustable open sights can be fitted to order. A *New Model*, introduced in 1996, offers an interchangeable barrel in 15 chamberings and an optional muzzle brake. The finish is black or chrome, and the one-piece grip/frame unit is made of a synthetic compound called Lexan.

∼ REVOLVERS ∼

BFR Little Max (1998 to date) A single-action solid-frame design, this is chambered for the 22 Hornet, 454 Casull, 45 Long Colt or 50 AE rounds. Barrels are usually 7.5 inches long, but a 6.5-inch option is available in 45 Colt and 454 Casull, and a 10-inch version in 454 Casull only. Construction is largely stainless steel, and the rear sight is adjustable.

BFR Maxine (1998 to date) A long-cylinder version of the Little Max, this can be chambered for 45 Long Colt/410 shotshell (7.5-inch barrel) or 45-70 Government (7.5 or 10-inch barrels). Sights are adjustable.

∼ AUTOMATIC PISTOLS ∼

The *Desert Eagle* and what Magnum Research habitually sells as the *Baby Eagle* (the Jericho 941) are included in the Israeli Military Industries section.

Mountain Eagle This is a large 22 LR rimfire blowback gun with a synthetic grip/frame unit and a cylindrical aluminum-alloy receiver containing a reciprocating bolt. The composite barrel has a distinctively blind slotted under-rib replicating the shape of the Desert Eagle. Overall length is about 10.6 inches, with the standard 6.5-inch barrel, and weight averages 21 oz without the 15-round box magazine (a 20-round version is optional). The rear sight is adjustable and the front-sight insert can be changed.

- *Compact Edition* Mechanically identical with the full-length gun, this has a 4.5-inch barrel and a shortened grip.
- *Target Edition* This is a minor variant of the standard pattern, with an 8-inch "accurized" barrel, a jeweled bolt and a two-stage trigger.

MAKÍNA VE KIMYA ENDÜSTRÍSÍ ("MKE")

Tandogan-Ankara, Turkey.
This company, set up in the late 1940s, made a copy of the Walther PP in 7.65mm and 9mm Short calibers.

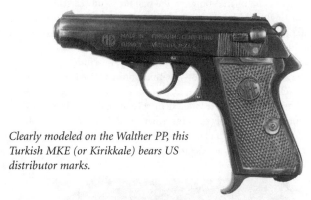

Clearly modeled on the Walther PP, this Turkish MKE (or Kirikkale) bears US distributor marks.

MKE (also known as "Kirikkale") This was a copy of the Walther PP, made in Turkey without the benefit of license from the 1950s onward. There are few obvious differences, although the magazine release lies on the heel of the butt instead of running through the frame behind the trigger and the magazine extension has a spurred finger rest. The guns were originally made by Kirikkale company and were marked "Kirrikale Tüfek Fb Cap 7.65mm" (or "9mm") on the left side of the slide; the grips often bore "F.j.M" on the left side and a star-and-crescent emblem on the right. The later MKE-made guns, sometimes also advertised as the "PK" or "TPK", had the encircled "MKE" trademark on the left side of the slide, ahead of "Kirikkale Cap 9mm". Manufacture ceased in 1973 but resumed in the 1990s. Guns may be encountered with the marks of US distributors, including the Firearms Center of Victoria, Texas, and Mandall Shooting Supplies of Scottsdale, Arizona.

MALTBY, CURTIS & COMPANY

Later Maltby, Henley & Co, New York City, USA.
Maltby, Curtis and Turner formed Maltby Curtis & Co. in c. 1875. An interest in the assets of the bankrupt Norwich Pistol Company was purchased in 1881, the gunmaking business re-emerging a few weeks later as the Norwich Falls Pistol Company. Many of the revolvers made by the new Norwich Falls operation bore Maltby, Curtis & Co. marks until work ceased in 1887. Maltby, Curtis & Co. became Maltby, Henley & Co. in 1889.

It seems that much of the stock of the Norwich Falls Pistol Company had been purchased immediately after the 1887 foreclosure, and guns of this type continued to be sold for many years. It has also been suggested that Maltby, Henley & Co. "acted as sales agents for [revolvers of] the Columbian Arms Company", but this was a trading style of the Crescent Arms Company and was more commonly applied to shotguns. The revolvers were usually cheap solid-frame double-action patterns, some "hammerless". Trading finally ceased c. 1896.

MANN

Fritz Mann Werkzeugfabrik, Suhl, Germany.
Mann began trading in 1919 by marketing a most unusual 6.36mm blowback automatic pistol, but it subsequently proceeded to more conventional designs.
New Model In 1930, Mann advertised that the Taschen-Pistole would be available to special order chambered for an entirely new necked 6.35mm cartridge developing 1050 ft/sec with a 62-grain bullet, a considerable improvement on the performance of the standard 6.35mm (25 ACP) cartridge. However, the only illustration of the cartridge in existence is the drawing provided in the Mann advertise-

ments, and no specimen of the cartridge or the pistol has ever been found. There seems no good reason why Mann should have developed the special cartridge when he had been unable to succeed with a perfectly serviceable gun in a standard chambering, and it seems likely that he was "flying a kite" to see whether interest could be raised. The economic depression of the early 1930s ensured that it was not …

The 6.35mm (25 ACP) Mann pocket pistol.

Old Model (or "M1920", c. 1921-4) This was a solid-frame design with a removable 1.65-inch barrel and a separate bolt. The return spring lay in a tunnel above the barrel, constrained by an operating rod that screwed onto the end of the bolt. Finger grips at the muzzle allowed the barrel to be removed from the frame by rotating it through 90 degrees and pulling forward. The whole pistol weighed only 9 oz, without its five-round magazine, and was one of the smallest ever made in this caliber. Serial numbers suggest that about 18,000 were made.

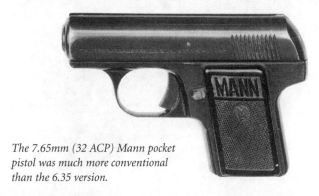

The 7.65mm (32 ACP) Mann pocket pistol was much more conventional than the 6.35 version.

Taschen-Pistole (c. 1924-9) It has been said that Mann intended to produce his 1920-patent pistol in 7.65mm caliber but decided instead on a more conventional design. The new gun resembled the 1906-type FN-Browning externally, but the return spring was concentric with the barrel, and the barrel was anchored in a lump on the frame by a helical thread instead of lugs. The Mann pistol was offered in both 7.65mm Auto and 9mm Short, and about 45,000 had been made before their manufacturer became just one of many victims of the economic depression.

MANUFACTURE D'ARMES À FEU

Liége, Belgium (sic).
This imaginary company was a sales ploy used by Gregorio Bolumburu (q.v.) of Eibar. Its name is usually found on the Rex pistol, a good-quality copy of the FN-Browning of 1910, but has also been noted on a simple 7.65m "Eibar" model apparently based on the Regina.

MANUFACTURE D'ARMES DE BAYONNE ("MAB")

Bayonne, Département Basses-Pyrénées, France.
Founded in 1921, MAB made a wide range of sound and simple pistols for many years. In 1940-4, when the factory was under German supervision, the pistols were being produced for Wehrmacht and police use

and marked with the German acceptance marks. Commercial production resumed in 1945, and in the 1960s, MAB obtained a contract to provide the French military forces with a 9mm Parabellum pistol. In the middle 1980s, however, the factory was closed after the company had gotten into difficulties; a rescue attempt failed and work never recommenced. This left the French forces without an indigenous handgun supplier, and they eventually settled on a variant of the ubiquitous Beretta 92.

The slide-marks of Bayonne-made pistols originally took the form "PISTOLET AUTOMATIQUE CAL 7,65" over (for example) "MAB BREVETE MODELE C" on the left side; later guns were marked in the form "PISTOLET AUTOMATIQUE MAB BREVETE [– S.G.D.G.]" over "MODELE D".

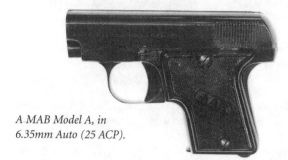

A MAB Model A, in 6.35mm Auto (25 ACP).

Model A (1921-85) This was a 6.35mm blowback automatic based on the Browning 1906 with grip, magazine and applied safety devices. The magazine held six rounds.

Model B (1932-49) A 6.35mm pistol with obvious Beretta overtones, this had a barrel that was formed as part of the frame and a slide that was open-topped for most of its length.

A typical 7.65mm-caliber MAB Model C.

Model C (1933-85) The first MAB design to have the return spring concentric with the barrel, this also had a butt that was unusually deep from front to rear — giving the pistol an ungainly appearance, but offering a good grip. The gun was originally produced in 7.65mm Auto chambering, but this was soon followed by 9mm Short. The slide marking took the usual MAB form, but the 9mm model may be marked ".38" if destined for export to Britain or the USA.

Model D (1933-85) Little more than a lengthened Model C, this had the same general layout but a 4-inch barrel, a nine-round magazine and a butt with a lanyard loop on the heel. Introduced in 7.65mm but soon

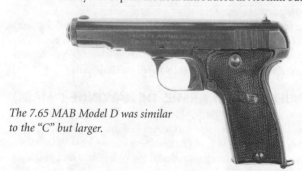

The 7.65 MAB Model D was similar to the "C" but larger.

offered in 9mm Short chambering as well, it remained in production until the company's demise. Alterations were made to the appearance in the early 1950s, giving noticeably more streamlined contours.

Model E (1949-85) A post-war design, this was an enlargement of the Model D chambered only for the 6.35mm Auto cartridge. It was easily distinguished by its squared slab-sided appearance and a ring hammer that protruded from the back of the slide. The magazine held 10 rounds.

Model F (1950-85) This was an unusual 22 LR rimfire pistol, basically the same as the Model B — with an open-topped slide — fitted with barrels varying from 2.65 to 7.25 inches and a 10-round magazine. The adjustable sights were offered in several patterns. The grip was raked much more sharply than the other MAB designs, but the Model F pointed well and, particularly when fitted with one of the longer barrels, made a useful beginner's target pistol.

The MAB Model G, in 22 LR rimfire.

Model G Introduced in 1950, this external-hammer gun was offered in 22 LR rimfire or 7.65mm Auto, with magazines holding 10 and eight cartridges, respectively. Aluminum-alloy frames were sometimes used.

The MAB Model GZ was made in Spain by Echasa. Note the design of the hammer and the retraction grooves in the slide.

Model GZ (c. 1955-65) Virtually identical externally with the Model G, this was made for MAB by Echave y Arizmendi of Eibar. The return spring remained concentric with the barrel, but the dismantling catch lay on the left rear of the frame. The slide was marked in the standard MAB fashion, with "MODELE GZ"; however, guns of the same type were also sold in Spain and were marked "ECHASA – EIBAR (ESPAÑA) CAL .32 (7.65ᵐ/ₘ)" over "MODELO GZ-MAB ESPAÑOLA". They were also made in 22 LR rimfire, 6.35mm Auto and 9mm Short.

Model R (1951-85) Similar to the Model D in appearance, this had an external hammer instead of an internal striker.

- *R Court* A variant of the R Longue introduced in the mid-1950s, this chambered the 7.65mm Auto round known in France as "7,65mm Court" ("short") to distinguish it from the Longue version.
- *R Longue* This, the original version, was chambered for the French 7.65mm Longue cartridge, which was still then in widespread use in the armed forces and the police.
- *R Para* Chambered for the 9mm Parabellum round, this was redesigned internally so that a rotating barrel locked the breech. Gas

pressure initially attempts to drive back the slide, but a lug on the barrel, engaged in a spiral track in the slide, ensures that the barrel is revolved as the slide moves back. Rotation is resisted by the torque of the bullet as it follows the rifling, though, like the Savage pistol (q.v.), the "breech lock" is more in the nature of a delayed blowback. The R Para was efficient enough to sell in small quantities, but it was never as popular as the 7.65mm blowback versions.

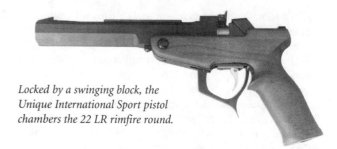

Locked by a swinging block, the Unique International Sport pistol chambers the 22 LR rimfire round.

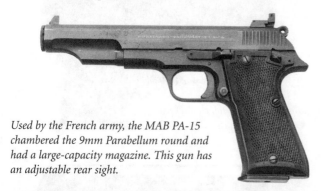

Used by the French army, the MAB PA-15 chambered the 9mm Parabellum round and had a large-capacity magazine. This gun has an adjustable rear sight.

Model P (c. 1966-85) This was a militarized version of the "R Para", strengthened to military standards and with the butt extended to take either an 8-round or a 15-round magazine, the guns being known as P-8 and P-15 (or PA-8 and PA-15, for "Pistolet automatique"). The rotating-barrel lock was retained, but the pistols were sturdier than their predecessors and often had matte finishes. The French army purchased the PA-15 in the early 1970s to supplement the dwindling stocks of MAC Model 50 pistols and used them until replaced by the Beretta 92G in the 1990s.
- *PA-PF1* A target-shooting version of the PA-15, this has a lengthened barrel and slide and is fitted with target sights. It was still being used by French armed forces competition-shooting teams in the late 1990s.

Winfield This name identifies MAB pistols sold in the USA by the Winfield Arms Corporation of Los Angeles. Early models were marked "Made by MAB in France for WAC" on the slide, often behind the brand names.
- *Le Cavalier* This was the MAB Model C under another name.
- *Le Chasseur* This was a modification of the 22 LR rimfire Model F with an external hammer. It had a nine-round magazine, an adjustable rear sight and thumb-rest-style plastic grips.
- *Le Gendarme* Winfield's name for the MAB Model D.
- *Le Militaire* A name applied to the 9mm Parabellum Model R Para, owing to its large size and "military" chambering.

MANUFACTURE D'ARMES DES PYRÉNÉES
("MAPF", "UNIQUE")
Manufacture d'Armes Pyrénées Françaises ("MAPF" 1923-88); Manufacture d'Armes "Unique", Hendaye, France (1988 to date).
This company was set up in 1923 and has confined its manufacture to automatic pistols. In pre-1939 days it was notable for the vast number of sales names and pseudonyms under which its "Unique" range was sold, names often applicable to one particular outlet or dealer. Prior to 1939, its products were aimed at the domestic defense, police and military market, but since 1945, activity has gradually turned to the production of target pistols. Present-day products enjoy such a high reputation in the competition world that the company changed its name to "Unique" in the late 1980s — the brand name had become better known than the trading name.

The "Unique" pistols can be broadly divided into two phases, pre-1939 and post-1945. The former were generally Browning copies, but the latter show more originality. In addition to carrying the "Unique" name, guns have been sold under names ranging from Audax and Burgham Superior to Vindex and Western Field. Virtually all the sur-viving brand names were abandoned after the German invasion in 1940 and the subsequent partition of France.

Browning-type pistols (1906 type) A variety of guns of this type, all derived from the 6.35mm FN-Browning pocket pistol (or at least from the Spanish "Eibar"-type simplification), have been linked with this particular manufacturer. However, not all are appropriately marked and the attributions are often conjectural.

The proliferation of these pistols is comparable with the exploits of the Spanish Basque gunmakers in Eibar, just across the border from the French Basques in Hendaye. It seems possible that at least some of the parts of the "French" guns were purchased in Spain, which may explain the differences between individual patterns. Most of the guns, however, have the safety catch on the left side of the frame above the trigger (with "S" and "F" on the frame), vertical slide-retracting grooves and magazine-release catches on the heel of the butt. The slide marks often include the manufacturer's name, the location ("HENDAYE") and "LE VERITABLE PISTOLET FRANÇAIS "UNIQUE"…" in their markings, and a trademark of a lion is often molded into the grips.
- *Audax* This was a 6.35mm gun, with a grip safety and a radial safety lever projecting from the top of the left grip. Apart from the inclusion of "FABRICATION FRANÇAISE" beneath the slide inscription, there is no indication of origin.
- *Duc* See "[Le] Tout Acier", below.
- *EBAC* Said to have been made for "Piot–Lepage" of Paris, this has a slide marked "MARQUE DEPOSEE CAL 6.35 m/m" and grips with "EBAC" within a diamond. It is assumed that the initials refer to a distributorship.
- *Furor* This was a 7.65mm gun, with an extended grip holding a nine-round magazine and a lanyard ring on the left side of the butt heel. It bore "MANUFACTURE d'ARMES des PYRÉNÉES HENDAYE" on the slide, with the brand name and an encircled-head mark (with "PARIS" and "L.D.& C.") on the checkered plastic grips. The abbreviation is said to represent "Louis Dumoulin & Cie".
- *Lepco* This was a 6.35mm gun made for the "Lepco Firearms Company" (L. Le Personne & Co.), a distributor working in London. The slide marks usually include "MADE IN FRANCE".
- *[Le] Majestic* The slides of these guns are usually marked "PISTOLET AUTOMATIQUE A DOUBLE SURETE / "LE MAJESTIC" CAL 6.35" in two lines. The "Double Sûreté" term referred to the presence of manual and magazine safety devices. Their grips have similar detailing to the "Lepco".
- *[Le] Sans Pareil* Another of the 6.35mm guns with a six-round magazine, this was marked "FABRICATION FRANÇAISE" over "LE SANS PAREIL" on the left side of the slide. Also said to have been made for "Piot–Lepage".
- *[Le] Tout Acier "Duc"* The slide of this 6.35mm gun was marked "PISTOLET AUTOMATIQUE CAL 6,35 / LE TOUT ACIER – "DUC" / FABRICATION FRANÇAISE" and the grips displayed "DUC" in a floral motif.
- *Triomphe Français* The slide of this 6.35mm pistol, in addition to the brand name, displayed "CAL 635 m/m S.F.M. ACIER CANON SPECIAL". This has been taken to indicate distribution by the well-known ammunition manufacturer, Société Française des Munitions

("SFM") but may simply be a recommendation to use French-made ammunition. The grip often has a plain diagonal band across the checkering.

- *Others* Among the questionable attributions are "Burgham Superior"; "Capitan"; "Cesar", which is probably the "J. Cesar" of Tómas de Urizar; "Chantecler"; "Chimère Renoire" (sic); "Colonial", usually associated with Fabrique d'Armes de Grande Précision (q.v.); "Demon" or "Demon Marine"; "Elite"; "Gallia", which is usually marked "FABRIQUE A ST ETIENNE" and shows differences in construction; "Ixor"; "Mars"; "Perfect"; "Rapid-Maxima"; "Reina"; "St Hubert"; "Selecta"; "Sympathique"; "Touriste"; "Unis", which appears on the frames of several different guns and may be a distributor's mark; and "Vindex". In addition, several guns — including those with Audax or Unique markings — bear "UNIS" over "FRANCE" within a cartouche on the left side of the frame behind the grips. The significance of this is also unknown, unless it is a clue to a distributor.

Browning-type pistols (1910 type)

- *Audax* A sales name for two automatic pistols made for sale by the Cartoucherie Française of Paris in 1931-9. One was the 6.35mm copy of the 1906-type Browning described above, but the 7.65mm version was based on the 1910 FN-Browning design, with the return spring concentric with the barrel, a grip safety, a similar manual catch to the small-caliber pattern and an odd bulge on the heel of the butt to improve grip. The guns were marked "PISTOLET AUTOMATIQUE CAL 7,65mm / "AUDAX" MARQUE DÉPOSÉE / FABRICATION FRANÇAISE" in three lines on the slide, with "Audax" on the grip.

The 6.35mm Unique Mikros.

Mikros This name covers two pistols, made from 1934 to 1939, and obviously inspired by the Walther Model 9. The first was a 6.35mm, identical to the Walther in every respect, even down to the peculiar screws that held the grips. The second was a 7.65mm model and simply an enlarged version of the 6.35mm, something that Walther never attempted.

- *Mikros-58* This was a post-war revival of the Mikros name that appeared in the 1950s; it was a much different pistol, resembling the larger "Unique" models. It had a fixed barrel and open-topped slide, with an external hammer, which could have a ring or spur head. It was made in 22RF and 6.35mm versions, both the same size, though the 22 could be obtained with a 4-inch barrel as a target pistol. Now known simply as the "Mikros", it is currently available in 6.35mm caliber only.

Unique series

- *Kriegsmodell* All the above models were in production in 1940 when the factory was taken into German control. Production was continued to German orders, the Model 17 being selected for manufacture as the "Kriegsmodell". The earliest examples bore the full commercial markings on the slide, but this was soon changed to "7,65 COURT 9 COUPS "UNIQUE"…" with "7,65m/m" and "9 SCHUSS" in a roundel on the grip. The contours of the butt were

changed, gaining a rounded backstrap, and — finally — an external hammer appeared to conform to German preferences. Many Kriegsmodells will be found with military inspection marks, but others may have been sold commercially during World War II.

A Unique Model 10 pistol, chambered for the 6.35mm Auto (25 ACP) round.

The Unique Model 12, with a grip safety. Note the "UNIS" mark on the rear of the frame.

- *Models 10–14* Introduced in 1923 and the first of the series, the "Model 10" was a striker-fired 6.35mm blowback in FN-Browning 1906 style, lacking only the original grip safety. A distinctively "Eibar"-type safety catch lay on the left side of the frame above the trigger. Like most pre-war Uniques, the Model 10 had an oval "lion" badge on the grips.

  The "Model 11" was identical with the Model 10 in all respects but had a grip safety and a loaded-chamber indicator that protruded from the top of the slide. The "Model 12" was a minor variant of the Model 11, retaining the grip safety, but omitting the loaded-chamber indicator. The "Model 13" was little more than a Model 12 with a longer butt and a seven-round magazine instead of the original six-round type. The "Model 14" was a Model 12 with an even larger butt and a nine-round magazine.

- *Models 15–17* The "Model 15" was the first 7.65mm model, also introduced in 1923, and was simply an enlarged Model 10. It retained the six-round magazine. The "Model 16" had a seven-round magazine, and the "Model 17" had a nine-round magazine.

This Unique Model 17 was made under German supervision during World War II.

- *Models 18–21* Another of the 7.65mm-caliber guns, the "Model 18" was based on the 1910-type FN-Browning, with a concentric return spring and a muzzle bush. No grip safety was fitted, but it had a lanyard ring at the bottom of the butt. The magazine held six rounds. The "Model 19" and "Model 20" were similar, with seven and nine-round magazines, respectively, and the "Model 21" was simply a Model 19 in 9mm Short.
- *Model 52* This moved closer to the design finally adopted for the Models D and E. The slide was extensively cut away and the barrel was fixed, leading to a new system of dismantling controlled by a lever on the right of the frame. Chambered for 22 LR rimfire ammunition, it had a 3.1-inch barrel. Comparatively few were made, as it was superseded by the D and E models.

The DES/32U was a centerfire version of the better-known DES/69U, firing the 32 S&W Long Wadcutter cartridge.

A Unique Bcf-66.

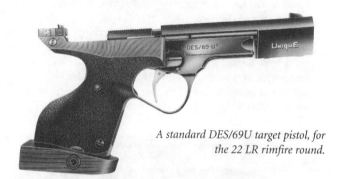

A standard DES/69U target pistol, for the 22 LR rimfire round.

- *Model Bcf 66* The first post-war design, offered only in 9mm Short, this introduced a new system of nomenclature. It had a fixed 3.5-inch barrel, an open-topped slide and an external hammer. Finish was usually blued steel, with molded thumb-rest-style plastic grips.
- *Model C* This 7.65mm pistol was virtually the wartime Kriegsmodell in civilian guise. The slide inscription changed to "7.65 COURT 9 COUPS "UNIQUE"…" above the company name, and the grips displayed an encircled "PF" monogram. "7.65mm Court" is the French term for the 7.65mm Auto (32 ACP) cartridge, a distinction made necessary by the existence of the French 7.65mm Longue round.

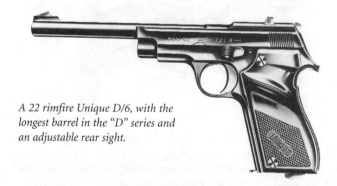

A 22 rimfire Unique D/6, with the longest barrel in the "D" series and an adjustable rear sight.

- *Model D* This was a 22 LR rimfire design, offered in D/1, D/2, D/3, D/4, D/5 and D/6 versions, differing in the length of the barrel, the design of the sights, the shape of the grips and the availability of auxiliary weights. The longest barrels could be fitted with compensators if required. All used the fixed-barrel open-topped-slide construction adopted for almost all postwar "Unique" pistols and had detachable 10-round box magazines.
- *Model DES/32U* This was a centerfire version of the DES/69U and was very similar externally except for the more prominent slide-retracting grips on the arms that extend forward along the frame

above the trigger guard. Micro-adjustable sights and a walnut anatomical grip were standard. It chambered the 32 S&W Long Wadcutter.
- *Model DES/69U* Offered only in 22 LR rimfire, with a 10-round magazine, this is essentially a Model D with a 5.9-inch barrel, a special wide trigger, the rear sight on a bridge at the rear of the frame and the anatomical grips carried up to shroud the lower part of the frame and slide so that the retraction grooves lie at the muzzle. The guns also have exposed hammers and a notable gap between the end of the slide and the rear-sight bridge. They are extremely accurate, winning the French national pistol championship for 12 successive years in the 1970s and 1980s.
- *Model DES/823U* A specialized rapid-fire target pistol in 22 Short rimfire chambering with an enclosed hammer, this had a special alloy frame and a shock-absorbing system to reduce the recoil sensation. Compensating vents in the muzzle could be plugged to "tune" the pistol to particular brands of ammunition.
- *Model DES/2000U* A modernized version of the 22 LR rimfire DES/69U, this has anatomical walnut grips carried higher on the frame so that the characteristic gap between the slide and the sight-bridge is not as obvious. The slab-sided barrel block and the enlarged trigger guard also contribute to a more modern-looking appearance.

The DES/2000U is a modernized form of the 22-caliber DES/69U.

- *Model DES/VO* A modified DES/69U for rapid-fire competitions and chambered for the 22 Short rimfire round, this has a squared-off barrel block with vents drilled into the bore to act as a compensator.
- *Model E* Exactly the same as the "D", with the same options and variations, this was chambered for the 22 Short rimfire cartridge.
- *Model F* This is essentially the Model C in 9mm Short, with an eight-round magazine.
- *Model Fr-51* A variant of the Model C, this is heavier and more robust. Consequently, it found favor with French police units in the 1950s and 1960s.
- *Model "International Sport"* This is a single-shot 22 LR rimfire target pistol, locked by a swinging-block breech operated by an under-lever formed as the trigger guard. The trigger and the sights are adjustable, a rail above the barrel accepts optical-sight mounts, and the grip and the fore-end are formed in a single piece of walnut.
- *Model K* The factory designation for the "Mikros" model; the "Kn" variant was nickel-plated.
- *Model L* This has been made in three patterns: "Lc" in 7.65mm Auto, "Ld" in 22 LR rimfire and "Lf" in 9mm Short. Offering the usual open-topped slide and external hammer, the guns can be found with steel or alloy frames. The 22-caliber guns have a 3.1-inch barrel, but the barrels of the 7.65mm and 9mm versions measure 3.3 inches.

A Unique Model L.

The 7.65mm-caliber Unique Model Rr-51 Police derived from the "Kriegsmodell" made under German supervision during World War II.

- *Model Rr-51* This, like the Fr-51, has served police units. The principal difference is the chambering — 7.65mm Auto — but the gun is otherwise a sturdier Model C. One specimen examined was marked "MODEL Rr POLICE CAL 7,65mm (.32) 9 COUPS" on the left side of the slide.

US-market guns These were sold under a variety of names, including:

- *Corsair* (or "Unique Corsair") This was the Unique Model D-1 22-caliber target pistol sold in late 1950s.
- *Escort* (or "Unique Escort") A name for the Model E-1, sold in the USA in 1955-65.

- *J.C. Higgins* Used by Sears Roebuck, the internationally renowned mail-order distributors, the "J.C. Higgins Model 85" was the 22-caliber Model E-2 with a 4-inch barrel.
- *Ranger* (or "Unique Ranger") A 22 LR rimfire pistol introduced in the early 1950s, this was based on the Model C. It could be obtained with 3.5-, 5.3- or 7.3-inch barrels.
- *Western Field* Another 22-caliber target pistol, comparable to the Colt Woodsman, this was sold by Montgomery Ward. It had a fixed 6-inch barrel and a 10-round magazine. An identical pistol was also sold by Manufrance as the "Auto-Stand".

MANUFACTURE DE MACHINES DU HAUT RHIN ("MANURHIN")
Mulhouse, France.

This company has largely been concerned with the making of machine tools and has made a particular specialty of ammunition-making machinery. In the years just after World War II, the company acquired a license to manufacture Walthers.

In 1989, the ammunition machinery and pistol side of the Manurhin business was sold to FN Herstal SA (q.v.). A new company, "Browning France SA", was created to market the MR73 revolver under the Browning name, but before this venture had properly begun, FN was taken over by GIAT (see under "Browning" for details). In the mid-1990s, GIAT disposed of FN but retained Manurhin, amalgamating it with another of its subsidiaries to form Matra-Manurhin Defense. Manurhin is now concerned solely with the manufacture of ammunition-making machinery, and the handgun business was sold in the late 1990s to Chapuis Armes.

～ REVOLVERS ～

MR32 (c. 1976-83) A match-shooting version of the MR73 chambered for the 32 S&W Wadcutter cartridge. The hammer spur and trigger blade are broader than normal, barrel weights can be attached and the frame is extended backward to provide a thumb-web.

MR38 (c. 1976-83) An alternative designation for the 38 Special version of the MR32 and sharing the same features — except that the thumb-web was formed by an extension of the anatomical walnut grip instead of the frame.

A 357 Magnum MR-73 "Defense & Police".

MR73 (1973 to date) In the early 1970s, Manurhin developed a solid-frame double-action revolver with side-swinging cylinder very similar to the contemporary Smith & Wesson models. The MR 73 had some unique features, including a combined roller-bearing and leaf-spring trigger system, giving a very smooth pull.

- *Defense et Police* ("Defense and Police", also known as "M73V") These guns had 2.5-, 3- or 4-inch barrels and fixed sights. They could be chambered in 357 Magnum/38 Special or 9mm Parabellum, the latter being done by providing an exchangeable cylinder.
- *Gendarmerie* Used in quantity by the French Gendarmerie National, GIGN and other specialist police units, this has a 3-inch barrel with a prominently ramped front sight and an adjustable "no snag" rear sight with rounded edges.

- *Match* Intended for specialist target-shooting, this has a heavy 5.75-(38 Special) or 6-inch (32 S&W Wadcutter) barrel with a full-length ejector-rod shroud and an adjustable sight that is carried back above the hammer. The finish is usually a matte blue, and the anatomical grips may be walnut or composition. Guns of this type are about 10.8 inches long and weigh 38 oz. A few revolvers of this type, intended for metallic-silhouette shooting ("MR73 Silhouette" or "MR73 Long Range"), have been fitted with barrels of 9.1 or 10.8 inches, and a special 7.9-inch barrel version, fitted with a bipod, was issued to GIGN personnel in the 1980s.
- *Sport et Competition* (or "Model 73S") Usually distinguished by adjustable target-pattern sights, these had 4-, 5.25-, 6- or 8-inch barrels chambering 32 S&W Long, 357 Magnum or 38 Special ammunition. The 357/38 versions could accept the optional 9mm Parabellum cylinder.

MR88 (1990 to date) This was an adaptation of the F1 Special Police revolver (a product of cooperation between Manurhin and Ruger), which once equipped the Gendarmerie National. Developed using the latest computer-assisted design programs and made of the best material available, the MR88 is available in two patterns. The biggest change, though not obvious externally, concerns the inclusion of a transfer bar in the trigger system.

- *Models D and DX* Made of blued or stainless steel, respectively, with 3-inch or 4-inch barrels, these are service/defense guns with fixed "combat" sights. Chambering is restricted to 357 Magnum/38 Special, though an exchangeable 9mm Parabellum cylinder can be obtained.
- *Model SX* The sports pattern, available only in stainless steel, has a ramped front sight and a fully adjustable rear sight on top of the frame ahead of the hammer. Barrels measure 4, 5.25 or 6 inches, all with full-length ejector-rod shrouds. Grips may be composition or walnut, often with thumb-rests.

MR96 (2000 to date) This is a modernized form of the MR88, with special attention paid to ergonomics. Consequently, the grip flows more smoothly into the frame than its predecessor (in a search for greater control), and the angle of the grip to the bore has been altered. The guns have ventilated barrel ribs, full-length ejector-rod shrouds and the front of their trigger guards is shaped to facilitate a two-hand grip. The MR96 is intended for sporting use. It can be obtained only in polished blue and has composition grips. Barrels may be 3, 4, 5.25 or 6 inches, giving overall lengths of 8.9-11.9 inches and weights of 38-65 oz. Chamberings are currently restricted to 357 Magnum/38 Special.

RMR ("Ruger-Manurhin-Revolver", 1981-4) This arose from an attempt by Manurhin to produce a cheaper weapon than the MR73, which was proving to be too expensive for many cost-conscious police agencies in France. The result combined a frame supplied by Ruger with an MR73 barrel/cylinder assembly. However, production was comparatively small, and the RMR was replaced by the SP F-1.

SP F-1 ("Special Police F-1", 1984-8) Problems arose with the use of Ruger frames, and Manurhin decided to withdraw from the agreement. Work on the RMR stopped, and the F-1 was substituted. Though similar externally, it had a Manurhin-type detachable side-plate instead of the Ruger design. Sales were comparatively small, and as the F-1 lacked the quality of the standard MR73, work stopped altogether in the late 1980s.

∼ AUTOMATIC PISTOLS ∼

Manurhin-Walthers The PP and PPK were identical with the original Walther products excepting for the words "Manufacture de Machines du Haut-Rhin" on the left front of the slide and "Lic. Excl. Walther", with model and caliber, at the left rear. The grips had the word "Manurhin" mounded into the upper part and "Lic Excl Walther" in the lower.

Pistols with these markings were imported into the USA by the Thalson Import Co of San Francisco in the early 1950s. They were later

A short-barreled Walther P1K with Manurhin marks. Guns of this type were supplied to the West Berlin police prior to the reunification of Germany, avoiding treaty restrictions.

imported by Interarms of Alexandria, Virginia, but these were differently marked; the Manurhin name did not appear, the Walther trademark was on the slide with the words "Mark II" underneath and "Made in France" was on the left rear of the slide. Both PP and PPK models were imported as the "Mark II", though they did not differ from the other version.

The license agreement lapsed when Walther returned to pistol making, but Manurhin continued to make them under contract to Walther until the mid-1960s. These were marked in Walther fashion and cannot be distinguished from the Ulm product.

PP (c. 1955-64) This was a facsimile of the pre-war gun with a few minor changes in the safety system and alterations in manufacturing tolerances. The guns were about 6.75 inches long, had 3.9-inch barrels and weighed 23-24 oz depending on chambering. Magazine capacities were seven rounds in 9mm, eight in 7.65mm and ten in 22 rimfire. They all had ring hammers, safety catches with 60-degree radial movement and fixed sights. They were blued with checkered black plastic grips, and the left side of their slides was generally marked "MANUFACTURE DE MACHINES" over "DU HAUT-RHIN" and "LIC. EXCL. WALTHER" over "Mod. PP. Cal. 7,65mm" (or "9mm"), the two groups being separated by the Manurhin-and-cogwheel trademark. The Manurhin trademark in a diamond-shaped frame and "LIC. WALTHER. PP." were molded into the grips. Chamberings were 22 LR rimfire, 7.65m Auto (32 ACP) and 9mm Short (380 ACP).

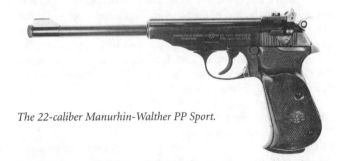

The 22-caliber Manurhin-Walther PP Sport.

PPK (c. 1955-64) A smaller version of the PPK, with a one-piece grip that wrapped around the rear of the frame, this was also offered in three chamberings. The smaller dimensions are its most obvious characteristics, though "PPK" will be found in the slide and grip markings. The Manurhin-PPK was about 6.1 inches long and had a 3.25-inch barrel. Weight varied from 16 oz for the alloy-framed 22 rimfire variant to 20.5 oz for the steel-framed centerfire guns. The 9mm pattern was available only in steel. Magazines held one fewer cartridge than the PP equivalents.

PP Sport (Sporter, Sportmodell or "Model S", c. 1955-64) The origins of this have been disputed, and the date of introduction is sometimes claimed to have been as late as 1962. However, a Manurhin instruction manual marked "E55" (English language, 19<u>55</u>?) may hold the key. The guns were offered only in 22 Short and 22 LR rimfire, with barrels of 6 (rare) or 8.4 inches. The latter gave an overall length of 11.1 inches and a weight of 26 oz. The most obvious features included a barrel protruding from a standard-length slide, a ramped front sight on a collar around the muzzle, an adjustable rear sight on the slide ahead of the spurred ring-hammer and the design of the thumbrest-style grips, which had a distinctive rounded base. The slides were marked "Mod. Sport. Cal. .22 LR".

- *PP Sport-C* (or "Model SC") This was identical with the standard gun, except that the trigger was a special single-action "competition" pattern (with a pull regulated to about 44 oz) instead of the standard double-action type.

MANUFACTURE FRANÇAISE DES ARMES ET CYCLES ("MANUFRANCE")

Saint-Étienne, France.

The history of this company goes a long way back, and its first activities within our period appear to have been the production of pinfire revolvers of the cheaper type. Some of these were bizarre specimens, such as the 16-shot 32 "Le Terrible", the 10-shot 8mm "African" and the "Rédoubtable", a 6mm gun relying on two barrels and a cylinder with two rows of chambers to provide a 20-shot capacity. Other, more conventional designs followed, including the inevitable Velo-Dog types. Shortly before World War I began, the company began to make the idiosyncratic Le Français automatic and continued production into the 1960s.

SINGLE-SHOT PISTOLS

Buffalo Stand (c. 1912-70) Offered in 22 Long or 6mm "Type Française" rimfire chamberings, this single-shot pistol embodied the patented Manufrance action that consisted of a shot rotating bolt set in a sliding carrier block. The receiver was a steel monoblock, the bolt handle was a turned-down spatulate pattern, the trigger guard had a finger-spur and the rear sight was a quadrant design prior to 1939. Most post-war guns, however, had tangent-leaf sights. A typical Buffalo Stand pistol was 16.5 inches long and weighed about 49 oz. The 1928 catalog offered the No. 31 (plain), No. 32 (lightly engraved) and No. 33 (deluxe) patterns.

Populaire (c. 1900-40) Chambered for the 6mm "Type Française" rimfire cartridge, this was a simple bolt-action rifle with a handle that locked down ahead of the split receiver bridge. An automatic extractor was fitted in the bottom of the bolt way, and the half-stock had extensive checkering on the fore-end and pistol-grip. The sights were adjustable but comparatively primitive. Length was usually about 17.3 inches, and weight averaged 32 oz. The 1928 Manufrance catalog lists three patterns: No. 5 was plain, No. 6 was lightly engraved and the deluxe No. 7 had a barrel of "Hercules Steel".

REPEATING PISTOLS

Gaulois An alternative, and more common, name for the "Mitrailleuse" repeating pistol.

Mitrailleuse This was a repeating "palm-squeezer" pistol introduced in 1893, firing the same cartridge as the contemporary Turbiaux "Le Protector" palm-squeezer. The Mitrailleuse was a rectangular box

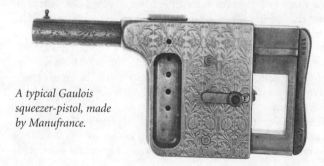

A typical Gaulois squeezer-pistol, made by Manufrance.

with a barrel protruding from one corner, the rear of the box being a moving grip unit. When grasped in the hand, with the fingers around the front and beneath the barrel, the heel of the palm bore on the rear section, and closing the hand squeezed the rear section into the box. A single-column magazine was contained in the front edge of the box, and as the grip was pushed in, a round was pushed from the magazine into the chamber. Further compression then released the firing pin, which was cocked during the first movement of the grip.

The Mitrailleuse was marketed as a home and personal-defense weapon, its principal attraction being the absence of bulk compared with a revolver. But the arrival of the small automatic pistol rapidly drove all these types of pistol from the market, and it ceased manufacture in about 1910. Shortly after its introduction — about 1897 — it was re-named the "Gaulois", and it is this version that is most commonly encountered. A similar mark has also been reported on a 6.35mm "Eibar" automatic of unknown provenance.

REVOLVERS

African A pinfire revolver manufactured from about 1860, it was an open-frame pattern with a 10-shot cylinder and was in 9mm caliber. The name probably derives from the popularity of these large-capacity revolvers in the French colonies.

L'Agent A 5-shot "Constabulary"-style double-action solid-frame revolver with rod ejection chambered for the 8mm French Ordnance cartridge. It was adopted as a police revolver in some Départements of France in the 1890s.

Le Colonial Resembling an overgrown Velo-Dog, this was a solid-frame "hammerless" non-ejecting revolver chambered for the 8mm cartridge made in the 1890s. The butt is straight and the frame rises behind the cylinder to conceal the hammer. A loading gate is fitted on the right side.

Le Petit Formidable Dating from the early 1900s, this was a 6.35mm five-shot solid-frame non-ejecting revolver with double-action lock. It almost qualifies as hammerless, as only the tip of the hammer protrudes through a slot in the raised frame.

Manufrance Under this style the company produced a number of revolvers prior to World War I. They were all solid-frame double-action designs, chambering either the 7.65mm ACP or the 8mm French Ordnance cartridge.

AUTOMATIC PISTOLS

Autostand This was a 22-caliber target pistol marketed by Manufrance but made by Manufacture d'Armes des Pyrénées. It was little more than the standard Unique Model E-1 fitted with a special 5.9-inch barrel.

Franco This was the 6.35mm Le Français "Policeman" model with a fresh name for sales purposes.

Le Français This range of pistols began with a 6.35mm model designed by Étienne Mimard (1862-1944). A patent was sought in August 1913 and granted in 1914. A small number of guns were made prior to World War I, but successful exploitation was delayed until hostilities had ended.

Le Français pistols were all made to the same basic design: a blowback automatic with hinged drop-down barrel and a self-cocking striker. The principal novelty is the hinged barrel, which can be released by a lever to allow the breech to rise clear of the slide for cleaning and loading — in much the same manner as the Pieper design. The barrel catch is linked to the magazine to ensure that the barrel flies open as the magazine is withdrawn, a certain method of preventing inadvertent firing of the round left in the chamber. The slide is conventional in appearance, but the recoil spring lies vertically in the front edge of the grip and an "L"-shaped lever beneath the left grip plate links the slide to the spring. This lever pivots close to the lower edge of the grip, and the lone vertical limb engages with the slide while a short toe presses up against the coil spring.

The slide carries a striker and its spring, together with a separate retraction spring to keep the tip of the striker inside the breech face. When the trigger is pulled, the trigger bar forces the striker back against the mainspring and is then cammed free, allowing the striker to fly forward to fire the cartridge. There is no extractor, the empty case being blown from the chamber by residual gas pressure as the slide opens.

The magazine is often found with a spring clip on its bottom plate, allowing the carriage of an extra cartridge. After the magazine is inserted, this spare round is taken and loaded into the chamber and the barrel closed. This feature meant that the pre-1945 guns lacked retraction grips, as there was no need to retract the slide to cock or chamber a round. The magazine of the 9mm army model can be partly withdrawn and locked clear of the slide, allowing single rounds to be fired by inserting them directly into the chamber while a full magazine was kept in reserve.

The design was ingenious, but the army model was doomed from the start by being designed around the 9mm Browning Long cartridge, a round that never attained the popularity sought by its inventors. It was too weak to be effective in combat, and the pistol could not be easily redesigned to take a more powerful cartridge. The 6.35mm models, on the other hand, were reliable and serviceable enough to see considerable commercial success. The design was obsolete by the 1960s, and as private ownership of pistols was increasingly restricted, Manufrance finally abandoned the Le Français pistol.

- *Modèle 1950* (1951-69) An updated form of the pocket model, chambered for the more powerful 7.65mm Auto (32 ACP) round, this was the only Le Français pistol to have conventional retraction grips on the slide. Its modernized appearance was at least partly due to the trigger guard, which was forged as part of the frame instead of being a simple sprung strip. M1950 pistols, also known as "No. 8466", are usually marked with "MANUFRANCE" instead of the full company name that had characterized other guns in the series. They were not particularly successful, and only about 10,000 were ever made.

This pocket-model 6.35mm (25 ACP) Le Français pistol shows how the barrel could be tipped for loading.

- *Modèle de Poche* ("Pocket Model", 1914-66) Chambered for the 6.35mm Auto (25 ACP) cartridge, this was the first of the series to be made. The grips — which usually bore the company's enwreathed "MF" monogram trademark — were originally held by two screws, but by 1928, were being held by one. A change had also been made to the way in which the sear spring operated. The original magazine was held in the butt by a catch that had to be pushed forward towards the butt-toe. This catch was actually part of the magazine base, but the system was replaced by a conventional bolt running laterally through the slide in 1935. Manufrance catalogs of the 1920s listed four patterns (No. 1 to No. 4), depending on the degree of decoration, but these designations had been changed by 1939 to the 800 series. Unlike the other patterns, which were steel, No. 812 had an alloy-frame that reduced unloaded weight to 8.5 oz.

Pre-war guns may be found with several different safety devices. Production continued until the mid-1960s, the magazine being changed to a skeletal pattern, with a large central void, in 1964.

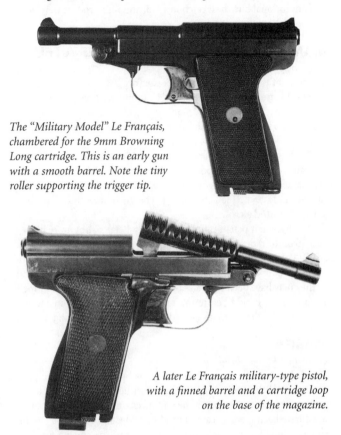

The "Military Model" Le Français, chambered for the 9mm Browning Long cartridge. This is an early gun with a smooth barrel. Note the tiny roller supporting the trigger tip.

A later Le Français military-type pistol, with a finned barrel and a cartridge loop on the base of the magazine.

- *Type "Armee"* (1928-45?) Chambered for the ineffectual 9mm Browning Long cartridge, this was 8 inches long, had a 5-inch barrel and had a plain barrel/slide construction that gave it a weight of 37 oz. Circumferential grooves were added to the breech in 1931, when longitudinal flutes were also milled in the barrel beneath the chamber. This reduced weight to about 32 oz and gave an unmistakable appearance. The wooden grips acquired a plain brass disc at this time, replacing the original composition pattern that had borne the enwreathed "MF" monogram. Post-1931 magazines also had a loop on the base for a single cartridge, which was used to load the chamber once the barrel had been tipped open. Le Français pistols were extensively tested by the French army in 1928-33 but were rejected owing to the lack of an extractor and the design of the double-action trigger system. However, many guns were used during World War II, when the slide was reinforced and a gas-escape hole was cut through the face of the breechblock into the striker channel. Production does not seem to have resumed in earnest after 1945, though some guns were undoubtedly assembled from pre-war parts. Catalogs published at the end of the 1920s allocate the model numbers 12 (plain), 14 (lightly engraved) and 16 (deluxe engraving) to the army pistols, the designations changing to models 850, 856 and 862 by 1938.

- *Type "Champion"* (1926-33?) Intended as a target pistol, this had a 5.9-inch barrel and a special magazine extension (*rallonge*) with sprung straps that could be slipped over the grip. The gun was sold in the 1920s as the "No. 10"; alternatively, the "No. 15" could be obtained, which was a cased version of the standard 6.35mm gun with an exchangeable 22-caliber barrel.

- *Type "Policeman"* (1922-68) This was little more than the 6.35mm pocket model with a 3.3-inch barrel. Catalogs from the 1920s revealed the customary four degrees of decoration (No. 5 to No. 8), the designations being altered to the 800 series prior to 1938. The original magazine-retaining arrangements were replaced with a conventional butt-heal catch in 1935, and four grooves were added above the chamber in 1965.

MANUFACTURE LIÉGEOISE D'ARMES À FEU

Liége, Belgium.
A version of the full title of Robar & Co. (q.v.).
Liége, Liégeoise This name will be found on three pistols, including the Robar "New Model Melior", an elegant and well-made 6.35mm blowback. The slide is marked with the title given above and "BREVETS – 259178 – 265491 – LIEGE – BELGIUM".

The other two pistols are different, 6.35mm or 7.65mm "Eibar"-type guns offering much poorer quality than the Melior pattern. They are marked similarly but with "SOC. AN." added to the name and "LIEGE (BELGIQUE) PATENT 51350" beneath it. The grips have an oval with the letters "ML" and a crown.

The five-digit patent number is scarcely Belgian, but more likely to be a Spanish trademark registry (marks of this type are usually included in "Patents"). Consequently, the guns are either outright forgeries made in Spain in 1915-17 at a time when Liége was in German hands, or they may have been commissioned by Robar for sale in the immediate post-1918 period before the manufacturing facilities in Liége — dismantled by the Germans — had been restored to working order.

MARGA

Uldarique Marga, Belgium.
This Belgian army officer developed a gas-operated automatic pistol, patented in Belgium in 1905-7. A gas port beneath the barrel led gas back to a piston that actuated the bolt mechanism. A prototype or two must have been made because DWM cartridge no. 458 was a 7.65mm rimless round for this particular weapon, but no specimen is known to survive.

MARGOLIN

Mikhail Margolin, Tula and Izhevsk, USSR.
In 1923, at age 19, Margolin was blinded in a military accident. After leaving the hospital, he began to design target pistols by making clay or wax models that provided the basis for draftsmen to produce working drawings. Many of the guns achieved great distinction in international shooting contests in the 1950s and 1960s, in particular, and are still being made in the Izhevsk (q.v.) engineering factory. They have often been sold commercially as "Baikal" or "Vostok", particularly in English-speaking countries.

∼ SINGLE-SHOT PISTOLS ∼

MTs-2-3 Developed c. 1950, this was a single-shot 22 rimfire pistol with a bolt-type breech mechanism and a button trigger that can be "set" by pulling the trigger-guard downward.
MTs-55-1 An improved version of the MTs-2-3, this reverted to a Martini-type pivoting block mechanism. Though the trigger is a conventional blade instead of a button, it is still set by pulling down on the guard.

∼ AUTOMATIC PISTOLS ∼

MTs Intended for competitive shooting and chambered for the 22 LR rimfire round, this is a comparatively simple blowback design distinguished by a micro-adjustable rear sight. Early versions were plain-barreled; later versions have a muzzle brake/compensator on the muzzle.
MTsU This was a minor variant of the MTs, chambered for the 22 Short cartridge. It was somewhat smaller than its near-relation.
MTsZ-1 Designed specifically for the 1956 Olympic Games, held in Melbourne, this was essentially a standard MTs turned upside-down. The barrel lay below the line of the hand and the breech mechanism

A Margolin 22 LR rimfire MTs target pistol.

was inverted, though the magazine was in the proper place. The design was advantageous, as the position of the barrel reduced the turning couple that tended to raise the muzzle during rapid fire to virtually nothing. After its first Olympic campaign, therefore, the rules were rapidly rewritten to exclude the MTsZ-1 from competitions simply by deciding that its overall length was too great.

MARLIN

John M. Marlin and the Marlin Firearms Company,
New Haven, Connecticut, USA.
John Marlin is best known for his lever-action rifles, though inexpensive pistols were made from 1872 onward. The business was reorganized as the "Marlin Firearms Company" in 1881, and in 1887, it introduced a double-action revolver. Contemporary reports suggest that these guns were inferior and the Marlin handgun business closed down in 1900 to allow work to concentrate on longarms.

∼ SINGLE-SHOT PISTOL ∼

Never Miss (1872-5) This appears to have been Marlin's first handgun, offered in 22 Short, 30 Short, 32 Short and 41rimfire. The barrel pivoted on a vertical post to allow the breech to move sideways for loading, and a sheathed trigger was used. The grip was a bird's-head pattern, and the finish could be blue or nickel. The automatic ejector was patented by Marlin in April 1870.

The 22-caliber Marlin Little Joker was a typical sheathed-trigger "Suicide Special" of the 1870s.

∼ REVOLVERS ∼

Joker (or "Little Joker", 1872-5) This was a seven-shot 22 Short rimfire revolver with a solid frame, a sheathed trigger, and a bird's-head butt.
Marlin (1) The first of this name was a break-open gun based on Smith & Wesson patterns, first appearing in 1873. It was offered in 22, 30 and 32 rimfire chamberings, supplemented by 38 centerfire in 1878. An improved design appeared in 1887, sharing the same basic construction and chambered for 32 and 38 centerfire ammunition.
Marlin (2) Dating from the 1890s, this was a solid-frame 44-caliber revolver with a cylinder that swung out of the right side of the frame. However, these double-action weapons were never successful and do not appear to have been made in any quantity.

MARS

Mars Automatic Pistol Syndicate, Birmingham, Warwickshire, England.
This promotional agency was formed in January 1904 to further the cause of the "Mars" pistol, designed by Hugh Gabbett Fairfax. The inventor had been forced into bankruptcy only 16 months previously, and even though the British army had lost interest, the backers clearly felt that the gun had development potential. There is no evidence that Gabbett Fairfax had anything to do with the syndicate, and as a bankrupt, he would have been confined to advisory positions.

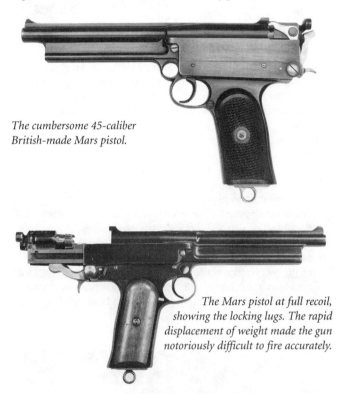

The cumbersome 45-caliber British-made Mars pistol.

The Mars pistol at full recoil, showing the locking lugs. The rapid displacement of weight made the gun notoriously difficult to fire accurately.

Webley & Scott, makers of the pre-1902 guns, were developing pistols of their own; any Mars pistols made after 1904, therefore, would have been made elsewhere. Several plausible candidates have been put forward, including Westley Richards of Birmingham, but little else is known. It has even been claimed that the guns were imported from Belgium, but none that could be traced for examination had anything other than British proofmarks.

British Patent 25,565/1905 was accepted in September 1906 in the name of the Syndicate and a mechanical engineer named Clement Brown, but the improvements were too late to salvage the reputation of the Mars pistol and the promotional agency was dissolved in 1907.

MARSTON

William W. Marston, The Phoenix Armory, New York City, USA.
Marston succeeded the business of Marston & Knox in 1854 and traded until his business was destroyed in the Draft Riots of 1863. He made single-shot pistols and 1857-patent break-open derringers, in 22 or 32 rimfire, with a three-barrel monoblock and a striker that fired each barrel in succession from the bottom upward. Marston made caplock revolvers, but he has also been linked with solid-frame single-action "Suicide Special" revolvers marked "Washington Arms Company", dating from the early 1870s. Evidence for this is lacking.

T. MARTIN

This gunmaker patented a 6.35mm automatic pistol in France in 1905. It was a fixed-barrel blowback, fired by a striker and had a grip safety. A later patent, granted in 1909, introduced a method attaching the bar-rel by sliding it backwards into a dovetail in the frame and securing it with a flat plate pivoting on the frame. Very few guns of this type seem to have been made, and it is possible that the inventor later became associated with the Bernardon-Martin pistol (q.v.).

MARTZ

John V. Martz, Lincoln, California, USA.
This gunsmith is best known for the "Martz Lugers", incorporating one of the very few worthwhile mechanical improvements in the Luger or Parabellum pistol to appear since the 1930s. The Martz Safe Toggle Release or "MSTR", conceived in 1968 and patented in the USA in 1976, allows the breechblock (normally held back after the last shot has been fired and ejected) to close on an empty chamber when the safety lever is pressed. Alternatively, the system can be used to strip a new round into the chamber when a new magazine has been inserted. In addition to converting hundreds of standard P. 08s, Martz has made a variety of modified guns.

Martz Lugers These guns may be identified by the presence of "MSTR" on the left frame rail and "JVM" in an oval beneath the trigger plate. Finish is usually blued, with walnut grips, but plated versions are known. In addition to the variants listed individually below, Martz has made a few guns for the 38 Super round and about eight for 45 ACP. Arising from an attempt to make a gun resembling (though not actually duplicating) the legendary "big bore" pistols submitted to the US Army trials of 1907, the latter are made by cutting apart two original P. 08 frames and widening the frames to accept the broader magazine required to accept the 45 ACP cartridge. This also necessitates new toggle-train components, but the guns have been surprisingly popular. Barrel lengths range from 2.5 to 7.9 inches.

- *Luger Rimfire Magnum* Chambered for 22 WM rimfire ammunition, this has been made only in small quantities. Barrels usually measure 4 or 4.7 inches.

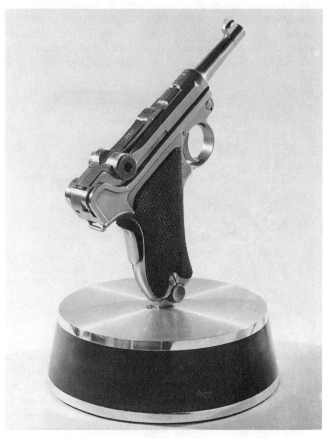

This Martz Baby Custom Luger was originally a 7.65mm M1908 Portuguese army pistol with a 4.7-inch barrel.

- *Baby Luger* An otherwise standard pistol fitted with MSTR, these guns usually have barrels of 2 or 3 inches. Most of them have been chambered for the 9mm Parabellum round, but a handful has been made in 7.65mm Parabellum and 380 ACP. Total production has amounted to a few hundred.
- *Luger Carbine* Offered in 22 WM rimfire, 7.65mm Parabellum or 9mm Parabellum, these will be found with 11.8- or 15.8-inch barrels, wood fore-ends and special rear sights. The long barrel has always been the more popular of the options.

MAUSER

Gebruder Mauser (1872-84); Waffenfabrik Mauser (1884-1922); Mauser-Werke AG (1922-45); Mauser-Werke Oberndorf GmbH (1953 to date).

The origins of this great gunmaking business lay in the development of a single-shot bolt-action rifle by the Mauser brothers in 1867-9 and the adoption of the 1871-model Mauser rifle by the Prussian government. Paul and Wilhelm Mauser began trading in December 1872, intending to make parts for the new rifles, and "Gebrüder Mauser & Co." was formed when the Württemberg government firearms factory in Oberndorf was acquired in 1874. The rifle was the foundation of the company's fortunes, not only because of its financial significance but also because its reliability and consistent high quality ensured that the name Mauser on a firearm was a guarantee of fitness that even those with only a passing knowledge of weapons could appreciate. Wilhelm Mauser died in 1882, robbing the business of its guiding hand, and a reorganization of the business led to Waffenfabrik Mauser AG in 1884. In the late 1880s, Ludwig Loewe & Co. (q.v.) purchased a large stake in Mauser, and at the beginning of 1897, a cartel consisting of Mauser, Fabrique Nationale d'Armes de Guerre, Deutsche Waffen- & Munitionsfabriken and Österreichische Waffenfabriks-Gesellschaft was formed to split increasingly lucrative contracts between the participants. Mauser continued to make rifles until the end of World War II, alongside a variety of handguns. However, many of the pistols (especially the earliest designs) were much too complicated to succeed. The same could also be said of the company's semi-automatic rifles.

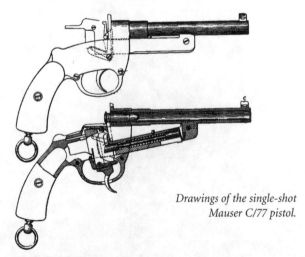

Drawings of the single-shot Mauser C/77 pistol.

～ SINGLE-SHOT PISTOLS ～

C/77 A fixed-barrel gun chambering a 9mm rimmed cartridge, this had a falling-block breech operated by a thumb latch in the place normally occupied by a hammer. When the latch was pressed down, the breechblock dropped into the frame, carrying the internal hammer, lockwork and trigger with it (the trigger passed down through a slot in the trigger guard). The hammer was cocked during this opening movement, and the spent case was automatically ejected as the breech opened.

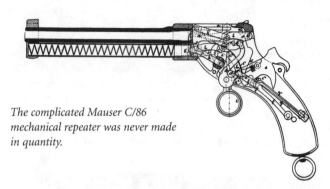

The complicated Mauser C/86 mechanical repeater was never made in quantity.

～ REPEATING PISTOLS ～

C/86 Mauser next turned to the mechanical repeating pistol, producing a design that might have been influenced by the 1884-type Mauser infantry rifle. The pistol also had a tube magazine beneath the barrel but was operated by a complicated system of levers. This lowered the breechblock, collected a cartridge, lifted the block, rammed the cartridge home, and finally closed the breech and released the hammer to fire. It was not a success.

～ REVOLVERS ～

C/78 The single-shot pistol found few takers, and so it was superseded by a revolver. This was built in several patterns and was protected by the same series of patents. The oldest type was a solid-frame 9mm-caliber double-action gun with a cylinder that was revolved by a stud, carried on a rod in the frame, working in "zig-zag" slots cut in the periphery. As the hammer was cocked, the stud moved forward and, by following the groove, turned the cylinder to align the next chamber with the barrel. As the hammer fell, the stud returned down a straight groove in the cylinder, ready for the next shot, and thus acted as a cylinder stop.

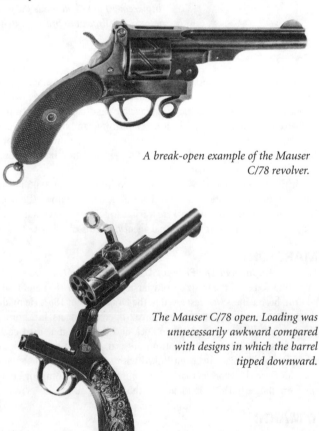

A break-open example of the Mauser C/78 revolver.

The Mauser C/78 open. Loading was unnecessarily awkward compared with designs in which the barrel tipped downward.

The solid-frame model was soon replaced by a tip-up design in which the barrel/cylinder unit pivoted about the top of the standing breech. A ring catch in front of the trigger locked the parts together. When the breech was opened, the barrel unit swung free and then farther travel, against a spring, forced out a central ejector to expel the empty cases. Six-shot revolvers of this type were offered in 7.6mm, 9mm and 10.6mm caliber. The largest was offered to the Gewehr-Prüfungs-Kommission ("rifle-testing commission"), but apprehensive about the mechanical complication of the Mauser, the testers preferred the solid-frame, non-ejecting "Reichsrevolver" (see "Spandau"). As a result, the 10.6mm Mauser revolver is rarely encountered, the smaller commercial calibers being more common.

A rarely-encountered "third pattern" M1878, known as the "Improved Model", had a neater method of locking the frame and tipping-barrel unit together with a sliding catch.

～ AUTOMATIC PISTOLS ～

C/96 or M1896 Not until 1894 did Mauser accept the merits of automatic pistols. At that time, he had in his employment three brothers named Feederle, one of whom was the Superintendent of the Oberndorf factory. The brothers had been designing an automatic pistol in their spare time, and Mauser, sufficiently impressed with progress, ordered them to turn the plans into reality. The first prototype was completed in March 1895 and patents were taken out in Mauser's name in 1895-6, a common commercial practice of the day, as designs developed by employees were regarded as company property.

The Mauser C/96, as this design was known, differed but slightly from later models, a testimony to the essential correctness of the original concept, but it went through several minor changes during its first few months of production as improvements suggested themselves. The cartridge selected was the 7.65mm Borchardt, which made Borchardt somewhat aggrieved when, in later years, he saw the success of the Mauser pistol in comparison to his own design. Mauser had the cartridge loaded to give a slightly higher velocity, creating the "7.63mm Mauser" round; the caliber had not changed at all, but the new name not only identified with the pistol but also suggested that the pistol and cartridge had been created by Germany's foremost gun-designer.

The mechanism used a locked breech, a rectangular bolt moving in a square-section barrel extension. Beneath the bolt, attached to the extension, is the locking piece, a steel block with a lug in its upper surface that engaged with a slot in the underside of the bolt. The bottom of the locking piece rode on a ramp in the frame so that when the barrel and extension were forward and the bolt closed, the locking piece was forced upwards to secure the bolt. The bolt carried a long firing pin, and there was an external hammer. The magazine, which was loaded by means of a charger, was in front of the trigger-guard.

On firing, the barrel, extension and bolt all moved backwards for about 2.5mm, after which the locking piece slid down the ramp and released the bolt. The barrel stopped, the bolt ran back and cocked the hammer, then returned, driven by the recoil spring which was inside

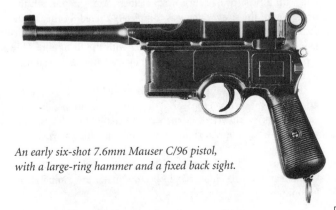

An early six-shot 7.6mm Mauser C/96 pistol, with a large-ring hammer and a fixed back sight.

A typical C/96 with its holster-stock.

the bolt, and drove a fresh cartridge out of the magazine and into the chamber. Barrel and bolt moved forward, the locking piece rode up the ramp, and all was ready for the next shot.

The C/96 was strictly a handgun; it had a fixed sight and was not fitted for a shoulder stock. The hammer had a large spur head, which, when the hammer was forward, obscured the sights as a reminder that the pistol was uncocked. Alongside the hammer was the safety catch, a rocking bar that locked the hammer when down.

A Mauser C/96 carbine.

- *Carbines* A few of these were made prior to 1914, often by enterprising gunmakers who simply adapted a Mauser pistol that had been purchased either directly from the factory or through a distributor. Attempts were to develop machine-pistol variants of the C/96 during World War I, but the Bergmann submachine-gun proved to be preferable.

- *Copies* Thousands of C/96-type guns were made in China by the Taku Naval Dockyard and Shansei Arsenal, and near-copies were made in quantity in Spain by gunmakers such as Unceta y Cia ("Astra") and Zulaica ("Royal"). The Chinese-made guns were essentially similar to the Mausers, but the material was inferior, the finish was far poorer and the ideographs that appear on the frame are easy to recognize. The Spanish-made guns offer far better quality and also a variety of design differences — including a rate-reducing mechanism in the grip of some Astra machine pistols. These guns are all considered in the relevant sections.

- *Early commercial guns* The first C/96 pistols were semi-experimental, and survivors exhibit many differences in detail before the design began to stabilize. The first guns were apparently made with six-round magazines and distinctive barrels that had a "step" immediately ahead of the receiver. Guns were also made with 10- and 20-round magazines. These also had adjustable tangent-leaf rear sights, instead of the fixed open-notch rear sight of the guns with 6-round magazines. Barrels were usually 5.5 inches long, though a few 4.7-inch examples are known.

Ultimately, the 10-round magazine, loaded through the top of the action with a charger or "stripper clip", was standardized. Another important early change was to use two lugs on the locking piece and two recesses in the bolt, spreading the load more evenly and allowing the bolt recesses to be shallower. This in turn strengthened the bolt.

For the first two years of production, the hammer had a cone-shaped head, but in 1899, this was replaced by a large ring that lasted until the introduction of a small-ring pattern that did not obscure the sights. Panels that had once been milled surprisingly deep into the frame became shallower, and the horizontal grooves in the walnut grips were increased from 23 to 34 (which looked better but gave a poorer grip in adverse conditions). The standard pre-1912 commercial C/96 had a 5.5-inch barrel with an adjustable rear sight and either grooved walnut or checkered rubber grips, the latter being relatively rare. Rubber grips made prior to 1909 custom-

A commercial "Bolo" C/96, with a short barrel and decorative grips, dating from 1905-6.

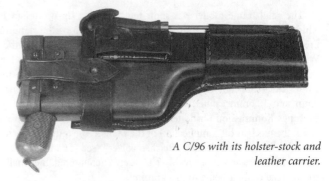

A C/96 with its holster-stock and leather carrier.

arily bore a distinctive "WM" ("Waffenfabrik Mauser") monogram. The Mauser banner trademark was added to the frame after this date.

The heel of the butt of most pistols was grooved to take a wooden holster-stock, the rear sight was an adjustable tangent-leaf type graduated to 500 or 1000 meters, and the pitch of rifling was changed from the original one turn in 26 calibers to one in 18 calibers to give better long-range stability to the bullet. Producing a gun that combined the characteristics of a pistol and a light carbine was intended to attract military interest, but the military proved exceptionally resistant to the idea and the Mauser C/96 was not purchased in quantity by the German army until 1915.

Early in the production of the C/96, a change in frame construction changed the appearance of the pistol. Until this time all production had the sides of the frame recessed over the trigger and above the grips, in a distinctive rectangular pattern, but now the frame was made flush-sided, without recessing or ornamentation. This, in some subtle way, seems to detract from the pistol's appearance; Mauser must have thought so too and soon reverted to the recessed pattern. Further minor improvements were made to the design; the disconnector was improved along with the trigger pull, and the firing pin was made more easily removable.

The first of what came to be called the "Bolo" model (a slang term for "Bolshevik") appeared in the early 1900s with a 3.9-inch barrel and fixed sights. A few guns apparently had six-round magazines, but 10 rounds were standard.

• *Export-Modell* In about 1907, a number of C/96 pistols were chambered for the 9mm Export cartridge. These appear to have been intended as hunting weapons (used with the shoulder stock) for the South American market and were not generally available in Europe. They were mechanically the same as the 7.63mm model and had a 140mm barrel with six grooves.

• *German trials guns* (1898-1903) The authorities ordered 145 guns in 1896, but delivery was not made until the summer of 1898 — an interesting commentary on the state of production at this time.

Mauser C/96 pistols were made for the German army during World War I in 9mm Parabellum, the caliber being marked on the grip.

These were followed by others in 1899 and then by "improved" guns in 1901-2. Trials showed that the action of the C/96 was prone to jam, and, even though improvements were constantly being made to the magazine and the feed ramp, the Parabellum (Luger) was ultimately preferred.

• *German army model* (1915-18) With the outbreak of war in 1914, the German army ordered 150,000 C/96 pistols in 9mm Parabellum. Except for the caliber, these were the same as the 7.63mm model, were identified by a figure "9" carved into the wooden butt grips and were colored red (or occasionally black). The grips usually have 24 horizontal grooves and the genuine military-issue guns will bear inspectors' marks in the form of small crowned Fraktur ("gothic") letters. However, standard commercial-type 7.63mm guns impressed into service may also bear these marks.

Dating from 1899-1900, this C/96 has a plain-side frame and a tangent-leaf rear sight. Guns of this type were purchased by the Italian navy.

• *Italian navy purchase* (1899) The Italian navy bought 5000 guns in 1899, the first major military purchase of an automatic pistol. They had tangent-leaf sights, distinctive flat-sided frames and large ring hammers. They are also usually marked "DV" on the left side of the receiver alongside the chamber.

• *New Safety Model* (1912) The next major change in the "Military Model" (as the C/96 and its successors are always known) came in 1912. The 140mm barrel was rifled with six grooves instead of four and with a twist of one turn in 25 calibers. More important, the operation of the safety catch was completely altered. In this "Neue Sicherung C/12", the safety catch could only be set to safe if the hammer was pulled back out of contact with the firing pin. This type of safety can be quickly identified by the letters "NS" stamped into the hammer.

Production of "NS" guns, usually identified by their 30-groove grips and "NS" mark on the rear of the hammer, continued into the early part of World War I. Many were purchased by officers, large numbers were impressed to serve rank-and-file (particularly artillerymen to compensate for a lack of long-barreled Parabellums) and some seem to have gone to Turkey in 1917-18. German and Austro-Hungarian inspectors' marks are comparatively common.

- *Officer's Model* (1902) This was a reversion to the original "hand pistol" concept, with a 3.9-inch barrel, a six-round magazine, a fixed open-notch rear sight, a large ring hammer and a short curved butt without a stock groove. It is believed that this is the six-shot "light-weight" pattern acquired for trials with the German army in 1902. Possibly 30 were made.
- *Persian contract* A few guns of this type were acquired during the early 1900s, perhaps as late as 1911-12. They may be distinguished by markings in Arabic and by an enwreathed lion-and-sunburst motif on the frame panel. Acquisitions have been estimated as 500-1000.

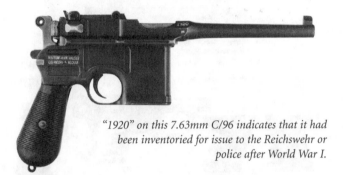

"1920" on this 7.63mm C/96 indicates that it had been inventoried for issue to the Reichswehr or police after World War I.

- *Post-war models* (1920-30) After the war, the Treaty of Versailles forbade the production of 9mm-caliber pistols, other than those that were issued to the army and police, and restricted barrel-length to no more than 100mm (3.93 inches). Mauser therefore reverted to 7.63mm caliber and a 99mm barrel, selling large numbers to the Russians during the civil war that followed the 1917 revolution. These short-barreled guns became known as the "Bolo", after the then-current slang term for "Bolshevik". Most of them had tangent-leaf sights graduated to 1000 meters and a slot for the holster-stock. However, the confused political state of Germany immediately after World War I allowed the creation of hybrid guns of all types. The Mauser was no exception to this rule and will be found with almost every conceivable combination of barrel, sight and grips. Most genuine post-1920 guns will have the banner trademark on the panel set into the left rear of the frame. Police markings are also often to be found.
- *Turkish army purchase* (c. 1897/8) Small numbers of these 7.63mm-caliber "cone-hammer" guns were purchased at a time when Mauser was supplying the Turkish army with large quantities of bolt-action rifles. It is not clear whether they were destined for officers or (perhaps) the Sultan's bodyguard, but they have sights marked in Arabic numerals, the date "1314" on the right side panel and the Toughra (a calligraphic cipher) of Sultan Abdul Hamid I on the left. Estimates of quantity range from 100 to 1000.

C/06-08 The failure of the C/96 to challenge the Parabellum (Luger) in the German army trials forced Mauser to develop a new design based on patents granted in 1900-6 to protect a variety of automatic rifles. It has been said that the C/06-08 was a speculative venture in response to a request from the Brazilian army, but it is much more likely that it was created in response to the German army's preference for the Parabellum (Luger) pistol at the expense of the C/96.

A military observer recorded in October 1906 that trials of a "completely redesigned" Mauser pistol would begin as soon as it had been submitted, but the Parabellum was adopted for the infantry machine-gun detachments in March 1907 and it is believed that the Mauser had been rejected (if indeed it had appeared at all). It has been claimed that the first version, the C/06, had a raked grip with the magazine in the butt, but the perfected C/06-08 reverted to the C/96 layout, though the

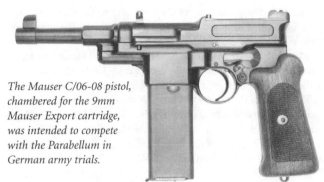

The Mauser C/06-08 pistol, chambered for the 9mm Mauser Export cartridge, was intended to compete with the Parabellum in German army trials.

butt was enlarged to give a better grip and a detachable box magazine was fitted ahead of the trigger guard.

The principal changes lay in the firing system, which relied on a striker, and the use of struts to lock the breech. Two levers were hinged to the barrel extension in such a way that they lay within the extension sides and allowed the bolt to move between them. As the bolt closed and the barrel moved forward, the front ends of these levers were cammed inward behind the bolt to lock it in position. When the gun was fired, and after a short recoil movement, the levers were cammed out to release the bolt.

Very few C/06-08 pistols were made, all chambering the 9mm "Mauser Export" cartridge that had been created from the 7.63mm simply by opening up the case mouth and inserting a larger bullet. The guns shared many of the vices of the automatic rifles, as they were complicated, expensive and prone to failure.

M1909 Work began about 1907 to develop a range of pistols that could challenge the Brownings being sold exceptionally successfully by Fabrique Nationale d'Armes de Guerre. The striker-fired M1909, an ambitious design chambering the 9mm Parabellum cartridge, formed the basis of most of the blowbacks that followed. It had a fixed barrel with an open-topped slide. Lugs on the barrel beneath the breech and the muzzle were both bored axially, allowing them to be dropped into holes in the frame to receive a long locking pin (pushed into a hole running the length of the frame) that passed through both lugs and held the barrel securely. The pin itself was secured by a bayonet joint and spring catch. Unfortunately, the M1909 was unsuccessful — even though special cartridges with light bullets and low-pressure charges were developed. Only a few guns were made.

M1910 Problems with the M1909 showed that the basic design was better suited to lighter loads, and a 6.35mm (25 ACP) version was developed. Known as the "Mauser-Selbstladepistole Kal. 6,35mm" (and not by a year date), it was extremely successful commercially, selling about 60,000 between 1910 and 1913. The earliest guns had a barrel-locking pin that was retained solely by friction and a bayonet joint into the front of the frame. The plate on the left side of the frame, covering the lockwork, not only had an obliquely-cut front edge but was also retained by a pivoting latch above the trigger. This was eventually

A typical 6.35mm (25 ACP) Mauser M1910.

changed to a spring-catch under the front edge of the frame (the so-called "M1910/14"), and production continued into the period of World War I.

M1912 The M1909 appears to have been designed around a special 9mm round that had a lighter bullet and a weaker charge than the usual Parabellum round, but even the reduced-charge round was too powerful. The action of the M1909 was too violent to be acceptable, and so a recoil brake was added to transform it into a delayed blowback. This became the M1912, tested in Brazil, Russia and elsewhere. The cartridge was now a variant of the 9mm Mauser Export, using a 125-grain streamlined bullet and identified as DWM No 487C. Only about 200-250 M1912 guns were made, mostly with fixed open-notch rear sights and plain-heel butts, though a few examples with adjustable sights have been reported. A few guns were sold commercially, but most were destined for military trials.

The Mauser WTP1, a 6.35mm (25-caliber) vest-pocket pistol.

The Mauser WTP1 field-stripped.

The Mauser M12/14 pistol, chambered for the 9mm Parabellum round, was a delayed blowback.

- M12/14 This designation was applied to a variant of the M1912 with a stock-lug on the butt. Ironically, about 800 guns of this type — probably the bulk of production — were used by the British Royal Navy during World War I. Official records credit the original purchaser as Brazil, but it seems that Chile, anticipating the delivery of two battleships and four large destroyers, was a more likely source. Mauser had delivered the pistols directly to the shipyards in Britain shortly before hostilities began. Consequently, they will occasionally be found with signs of British ownership. The M12/14 was about 7.3 inches long, had a 4-inch barrel and weighed 34 oz without its eight-round detachable-box magazine.

M1914 (1914-18, c. 1921-34) The "Mauser Selbstladepistole Kal. 7,65mm" was an enlargement of the 6.35mm 1910-pattern blowback chambered for the 7.65mm Auto round. A small spring catch was added beneath the front edge of the frame to positively retain the locking pin, and the cover plate was changed to a rectangular form sliding in dovetails in the frame; it could be removed only when the slide had been taken off. The first 2750 guns had a curiously hump-backed slide, but this was then changed for a straight-top design. Military inspectors' marks and signs of police issue will often be found on these guns, and it is assumed that production continued until the end of World War I, even though the 6.35mm version may have been discontinued before beginning again in the early 1920s. Barrels may be 3.5 inches (common) or 4.5 inches (rare) long.

WTP (subsequently known as "WTP1", 1921-39) The *Westentaschenpistole* ("WTP", "vest-pocket pistol") was designed shortly after the end of World War I. Chambered for the 6.35mm Auto cartridge and fitted with a six-round detachable magazine, it had an all-enveloping slide and a one-piece plastic grip that had to be removed before the pistol could be dismantled. The tail of the striker protruded from the rear face of the slide when the mechanism was cocked.

M1930 (1931-7) The perfected version of the C/96, this had a 5.2-inch barrel, grips with only 12 grooves and the new three-position "Universal Safety". The safety catch could be pulled down to lie along-side the hammer, allowing the pistol to be fired; it could be pushed fully upward to block the hammer; or, in an intermediate position, everything —hammer, trigger and bolt — was locked. This was the last variant of the Military Model and remained in production until the C/96 family was finally abandoned. The guns generally had fixed magazines, but a few were made with 10-, 20- or 40-round detachable boxes to compete in the Far East and South American markets, where competition had been intensified by Spanish imitations such as the Royal and Azul pistols. Among these were some that allowed selective automatic fire, and, to remain competitive, Mauser was forced to produce something similar. No selective-fire capability was included, and though the M1930 was a much more sensible proposition, the large-capacity adaptation (sometimes labeled "M711") failed to compete in a market that saw full-automatic weapons as status symbols.

Parabellum ("Luger", 1930-45) The DWM production line for the manufacture of the P.08 was moved to the Mauser factory and thereafter Mauserwerke was the principal contractor. Some of the pistols still carried the DWM badge until 1934, but the familiar "Mauser Banner" appeared on most of them, which were in both 7.65mm and 9mm caliber. Guns may still be found with the Schiwy sear and Walther magazine safeties, patented in the early 1930s, or showing signs of having once had them. These features were intended to prevent accidents occurring in police service, but neither was an unqualified success.

Manufacture of Pistolen 08 continued throughout the Third Reich, though the nationalization of Simson & Company (which eventually became Gustloff Werke) initially meant that work was concentrated in the Oberndorf factory. Mauser made modest quantities in the 1930s, exporting Lugers to countries as diverse as the Netherlands, Persia and Siam, but the orders were never large.

In 1934, however, series production began again for the *Wehrmacht* — the German armed forces — and had reached six-figure sums by the end of the decade. This era saw the gradual supersession of wooden grips by molded bakelite patterns.

Large-scale production continued until 1942, when Mauser, then the last major supplier of Parabellums, began to make the P.38 in quantity. The last few batches of P.08s, despite acceptance by Waffenamt inspectors, were exported to Portugal and Bulgaria in 1943. Yet small quantities of 7.65mm Parabellums were made until the end of World

War II for the forestry service and, apparently, commercial sale, and the French continued to use the parts that had been found in the Oberndorf factory until the Spring of 1946. Others were assembled in post-war years, the bulk of which went to supply the souvenir market among occupying troops. In addition to the patterns listed below, Mauser also supplied pistols to Latvia and Sweden. Used for trials in the late 1930s, in 7.65mm and 9mm Parabellum, most of these guns had 118mm (4.65in) barrels instead of the standard 120mm (4.72in). They do not appear to have distinctive marks of any kind and can be recognized only by their serial numbers.

- *German military guns* Mauser-made military pistols may display the code "S/42" on the toggle, together with a code letter indicating the year, "K" for 1934 and "G" for 1935. In the following year, the system was revised; the Mauser code became "S/42", the chambers were dated in full ("1936"-"1939"), and work continued until another change was made. The toggle mark was shortened to "42", confined to 1939-40, and the date was then shortened to "41" (for 1941). This combination of simplified numerical code and date was also short-lived, as the "42" code was then changed to "byf", a style that continued in use until the end of the war. [See also "Krieghoff".]

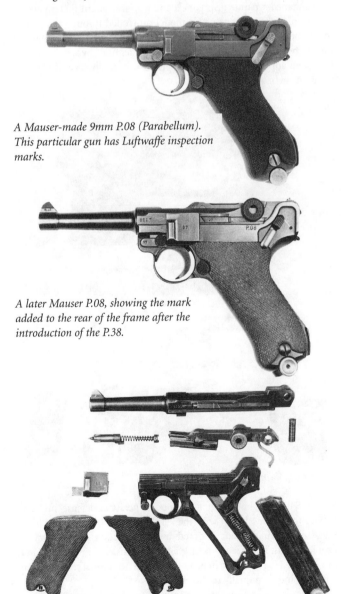

A Mauser-made 9mm P.08 (Parabellum). This particular gun has Luftwaffe inspection marks.

A later Mauser P.08, showing the mark added to the rear of the frame after the introduction of the P.38.

A "42"-code Mauser P.08 field-stripped.

Most post-1940 guns, issued after the introduction of the Walther P.38, will also display "P.08" on the left rear side of the frame. The style of the inspectors' marks — small linear eagles over a number, sometimes prefaced by "WaA" — will usually distinguish army from Luftwaffe issues, at least until the air force inspectorate was subordinated to the army weapons office (Heereswaffenamt) in 1943.

- *German commercial guns* These can be found in a wide variety of styles. The earliest retained the Mauser banner trademark on the toggle (and were sometimes also dated), but many of the guns made in the period immediately prior to World War II had "S/42" on the toggle and a date such as "1938" above the chamber. The most obvious distinguishing characteristics are the commercial proofmarks, "crown/N" prior to February 1, 1940, and "eagle/N" afterwards. The finish is usually a high-gloss blue, and the grips are finely checkered walnut.

- *German police guns* These were supplied by Mauser, apparently only in 1938-41. They had the banner mark on the toggle, chambers dated in full and inspectors' marks in the form of large linear eagles accompanied by the letters "C", "F" or "L"; serial numbers have "v", "w", "x" or "y" suffixes. A few of the earliest guns may have been fitted with the Schiwy sear safety, but most were subsequently converted to standard operation. However, the safety mechanism will usually have left traces of its existence.

- *German Democratic Republic* (East Germany) An extensive refurbishment/assembly program ended in the GDR in the 1950s. Usually intended for the People's Police or Volkspolizei, these P.08s can be identified by markings, plastic grips with a concentric-circle mark and magazines coded "2/1001". Many have been retrieved in recent times from trouble-spots such as the Middle East and Vietnam.

- *The Netherlands* A few hundred "Pistols No. 1" were supplied to the Dutch navy in the 1930s, running on from deliveries that had been made by DWM/BKIW. Standard 4-inch-barrelled 1908-type guns, they had short frames, retained the DWM monogram trademark on the toggle and had "crown/crown/U" proofmarks instead of "crown/N". They also have "RUST" in the safety-lever recess on the left rear of the frame, accompanied by an arrow, and the extractor has "GELADEN" on both sides.

- *Persia* The army received about 3000 "short" and 1000 "long" pistols in 1936-7, which were issued as the "Model 1314". The short guns were standard 4-inch-barrelled P.08s, but the "long" pattern had the 7.9-inch barrel and tangent-leaf rear sight assembly of the LP.08 drawn from components that had been stored since the end of World War I. Distinguishing features included the Mauser name in Arabic on the toggle, a lion within a crowned wreath above the chamber, the designation in Arabic on the front right side of the receiver and Arabic marks on the extractor and in the safety-lever recess. The serial numbers and the graduations on the LP.08-type rear sights were also in Arabic.

- *Portugal* The Portuguese purchased two types of Parabellum from Mauser. The Guardia Nacional Republicana purchased a few hundred 1906-type guns (with grip-safety mechanism) in the 1930s, distinguished by 4.7-inch barrels and "v"-suffix serial numbers, and the army bought substantial numbers of P.08. The police guns bore the Mauser banner on the toggle and had a distinctive "GNR" monogram above the chamber; the army "Model 943" examples had "byf" on the toggle, "42" above the chamber and German military proof and inspectors' marks. Army guns were supplied from the last batches of Parabellums made for the Wehrmacht, which, owing to the advent of the P.38, were deemed to be superfluous to requirements. Only their numbers (in the "m"-block) distinguished them.

- *Siam* A few hundred P.08 and about a hundred LP.08 were acquired in the 1930s for the police. They had a Mauser banner on the toggle, chambers dated "1936" or "1937", and commercial proofmarks. The safety-lever recess and the extractor were unmarked. An inventory number (in Siamese) and a stylized lion-head property mark will be found on the rear of the frame.
- *Turkey* Several types of Parabellum were acquired prior to World War II. The most common is the security-police or "EIUM" model, which has the Mauser banner on the toggle, a "TC" monogram above the chamber and "Emniyet Işleri" over "Umum Müdürlüğü" on the right side of the receiver. The extractor and the safety-lever recess are marked "ates" and "emniyet" respectively; proofmarks are German commercial, but all the Turkish guns also bear Waffenamt inspectors' marks. A few P.08s were acquired by the air force and the army, the receivers being marked "Hava Ordusuna Mahsustur" and "Subaylara Mahsustur", respectively. The air force guns also have a "TC-and-crescent" chamber mark.

Schnellfeuerpistolen (1933-41) The failure of the M1930 to challenge its fully-automatic Spanish imitations persuaded Mauser to develop a "quick-firing pistol" designed by Josef Nickl. Sometimes listed as the "M1933", this had a plain rectangular bar-switch on the right side of the frame. When pushed forward to "N", the pistol functioned in the usual way; when pulled back to "R", however, a secondary sear came into operation and the weapon could fire automatically at about 850 rounds per minute.

A second version was soon introduced, using a different fire-selector mechanism developed by Karl Westinger. The differences were largely internal, simplifying the automatic mechanism, and the only external change could be seen in the form of a new "pointed-oval" selector plate. This gun was sometimes known as the "M1936" or "Model 712" (the latter apparently being a Genschow catalog designation).

The perfected Schellfeuerpistolen sold well enough to keep the Spanish imitations at bay. Many thousands were sold to China and about 100 went to the Yugoslav army in 1933. In 1938-9, the remaining stock was taken by the German army as the "Reihenfeuerpistole Mauser, Kal. 7,63mm" and issued to the Waffen-SS.

A 1934-type Mauser pistol with navy markings.

M1934 (1933-41) This was a modernized version of the 1914-type pocket pistol, offered in 6.35mm and 7.65mm Auto. The small-caliber guns are much rarer than the 7.65mm version and may date only from 1933-5. The design had undergone a facelift; the wooden grip was much more rounded than its predecessor, and the elegant spring-loaded catch that had held the locking pin was replaced by a simpler and cheaper catch made from bent steel strip. The finish was a high-polish blue, though nickel-plating could be obtained to order. Yet the M1934 was still fundamentally the 7.65mm model that had been introduced in 1914 and that had been eclipsed by the Walther PP and PPK. Though substantial quantities were acquired by the police, the para-military and the armed forces (recognizable by their inspectors' marks), the M1934 was clearly a developmental dead-end. Mauser's designers immediately set to work to develop something more modern.

The 7.65mm M34 Mauser pistol dismantled into its major components.

WTP2 (1938-42, 1945-6) This 6.35mm (25 ACP) blowback was an improved version of the original WTP. It was slightly smaller but with better-shaped separate grip panels and a trigger guard that allowed a better hold. The striker on this model protruded through the rear of the frame to signal a cocked condition. A few hundred guns assembled under French supervision in 1945-6 can be identified by serial numbers that were applied with an electric pencil and an absence of German commercial proofmarks.

The 6.35mm-caliber (25) Mauser WTP2.

The principal components of the Mauser WTP2.

HSc (1940-6) The search for a pocket/personal-defense pistol to replace the M1934 began with the "HS" (Hahn Selbstspanner, "hammer, self-cocking") that adopted a double-action trigger system. Problems with infringements of Walther patents slowed progress, but, in 1937, the HSa appeared in prototype form. Additional changes led to the HSb, and then finally to the HSc.

Made almost exclusively in 7.65mm Auto (though a few 22 LR rimfire and 9mm Short examples are known), the HSc was a fixed-barrel

The Mauser HSc was introduced to compete with the Walther PP.

A field-stripped Mauser HSc pistol.

design with an all-enveloping slide that encloses all but the spur of the hammer. The first 2000 guns had the retaining screws placed very low on the grips, but this was soon changed. Most of the guns were issued to the armed forces, particularly the Luftwaffe, but some will be seen with police acceptance marks, and others were undoubtedly sold commercially. The HSc differed greatly from previous Mauser personal-defense pistols, as it was elegantly streamlined with a shapely well-raked grip that gave a good hold. About 252,500 were made before World War II ended, and, after a pause, production was resumed under French supervision. About 17,500 were made for the French armed forces in 1945-6.

HSV (1937-8?) This was a locked-breech design, relying on a pivoting block beneath the barrel to engage the frame as the gun fired. Made only in small numbers during the period in which the Walther Armee-Pistole was being transformed into the Heeres-Pistole (and thus into the perfected P.38), the HSV was clearly intended as a rival. It had a slender Parabellum-like barrel protruding from a half-length slide, a double-action trigger system with the spur of the hammer protruding from a slot in the rear of the slide and an elegant well-raked grip.

The most interesting feature, however, was the design of the return springs, which lay in the frame on either side of the magazine, acting on the slide by way of rocking arms. The subject of a patent granted to Ernst Altenburger and Alexander Seidel in 1938, this system may have been inspired by the Webley & Scott (q.v.) pistol used briefly by the British in World War I. It permitted the slide to be made much narrower than the competing Walther design. Unfortunately for Mauser, the HSV — assumed to represent "Hahn, Selbstspanner, Verriegelt" ("hammer, self-cocking, locked[-breech]") — was a failure. It may have inherited too many of the drawbacks of the Parabellum and the HSc: a comparatively weak breech-closing stroke, unsatisfactory feed from a magazine that was set at too great an angle to the bore and lockwork that was too delicate for military service.

P. 38 (1942-6) Towards the end of 1941, in response to a request received some months previously, the Mauser factory in Oberndorf tooled for the Walther P.38 (q.v.) and production of the P.08 gradually

ceased. The first Mauser-made P.38s were delivered in October 1942 with distinctive matte-finish slides and the code "byf" above a two-digit date on the left side.

The guns were numbered in blocks of 10,000, but unlike Walther examples, were not reduced to "01" at the beginning of each year. When 9999z was reached, the series began again at "01a", but the style of the suffix letters changed from cursive to upright. The last guns were coded "svw" over "45", which may suggest a re-location of final assembly to another location. It has even been suggested that this was in Czechoslovakia, but it is much more likely to have been close to the Oberndorf factory.

About 308,000 Mauser-Pistolen 38s were made for the German authorities during World War II, the last batches combining a weakly blued barrel and phosphated slide and frame. The French occupation forces, realizing that they were short of handguns, then continued work. About 5000 P.38s were assembled from existing parts, usually with the duotone finish, and then a quantity in excess of 37,000 new guns were made. Retaining the "svw" code, but dated "45" or "46", these had a distinctive dark-gray finish. Work finally stopped at the end of April 1946, and the facilities were dismantled.

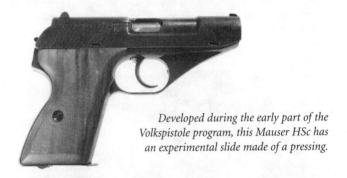

Developed during the early part of the Volkspistole program, this Mauser HSc has an experimental slide made of a pressing.

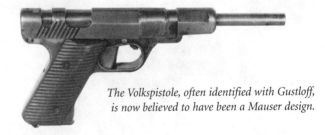

The Volkspistole, often identified with Gustloff, is now believed to have been a Mauser design.

Volkspistolen (1944-5) These guns arose from programs instituted by the German government to develop emergency weapons for the Volkssturm and other home-defense organizations. Work began in 1943, when the first attempts were made to simplify a variety of service weapons in the hope of making better use of machine time and conserving the most vital raw materials.

Mauser submitted an HSc with a simplified stamped-sheet slide, and Walther may have contributed a similar adaptation of the P.38. More ambitious were a Walther prototype with a rotating barrel-lock, adapted from the Steyr-Hahn, and Mauser project M.7057, which relied on a transverse groove in the barrel (above the chamber) rising to engage a shoulder crimped in the slide. The Mauser had a double-action trigger system, a radial safety lever high on the left side of the slide and an exposed hammer. The return springs were simplifications of the 1938 Alternburger/Seidel system, one being placed on each side of the magazine.

The first true Mauser Volkspistole, however, was double-action blowback V.7082. Made largely of sturdy pressings crudely welded together, this had a striker-fired ignition system. It was tried against a similar Walther design in the summer of 1944, but the testers demanded the reinstatement of a hold-open and the addition of a lanyard ring. When the guns reappeared, they had single-action lockwork.

The absence of breech-locks remained a weak point in the designs, and the authorities requested that some form of delay should be incorporated. It is not known if Walther made any progress with this, but Mauser adapted the V.7082 to include a gas-bleed system that was once attributed to Gustloff-Werke (q.v.). Propellant gas was allowed to leak through ports in the barrel, pointing forward and upward, to impinge on the inside of the slide. This tended to hold the parts together until chamber pressure had dropped to a safe level but was susceptible to fouling. One gun of this type was duly tested in January 1945 against a double-action blowback, but the war ended before any conclusions could be drawn. Two common features were the extensive use of stamped sheet-metal in the construction and the standardization of the Walther P-38 magazine.

MAUSER-JAGDWAFFEN GMBH

Oberndorf/Neckar, Germany.

After 1945, there was a gap of some years before the German gunmakers returned to business, after which, apart from producing the HSc, Mauser concentrated upon rebuilding their rifle trade. They were tempted back by the lure of the Parabellum, which retained an interest for collectors. The Mauser firearms business was acquired by SIG in 1999.

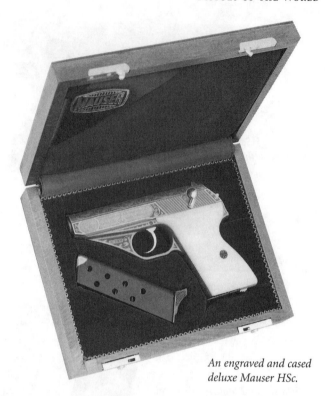

*An engraved and cased
deluxe Mauser HSc.*

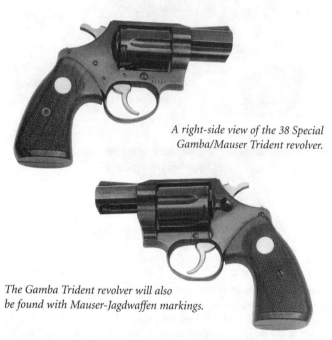

*A right-side view of the 38 Special
Gamba/Mauser Trident revolver.*

∼ AUTOMATIC PISTOLS ∼

HSc (1968-81) The rise in interest in pre-war German handguns, inspired by the Parabellum (Luger) and the Walther PP/PPK series, persuaded Mauser Jagdwaffen to recreate the HSc in 7.65mm Auto and 9mm Short (32 and 380 ACP). The guns were essentially the same as those made prior to 1946, excepting markings. A few thousand "American Eagle" guns were made for Interarms in the 1970s, but interest in the project waned until, in 1982, rights were sold to Renato Gamba (q.v.) and production recommenced in Italy.

Mauser-Parabellum 29/70 (1970-2) The Parabellum pistol will always carry an air of glamour, and Mauser created a new production line in 1970 at the behest of Interarms. The guns were similar external-

*The Gamba Trident revolver will also
be found with Mauser-Jagdwaffen markings.*

∼ REVOLVERS ∼

Trident Mauser licensed the manufacture of the HSc to Renato Gamba of Italy, receiving in return the right to market the Gamba Trident revolver in Germany.

*The original 7.65mm Mauser-Parabellum 29/70
was very similar to the Swiss 06/29 W+F type.*

The post-war version of the Mauser HSc.

*A "factory cutaway" 9mm 29/70 Parabellum
with Interarms markings.*

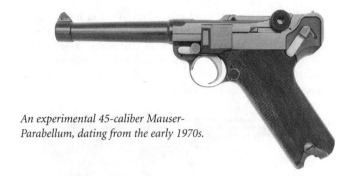

An experimental 45-caliber Mauser-Parabellum, dating from the early 1970s.

ly to the Swiss 06/29 W+F patterns, with straight front grips and safety levers with circular heads. They were offered in 7.65mm and 9mm Parabellum, usually with 4.7-inch and 4-inch barrels (a few 5.9-inch barrels were made) and serial numbers prefixed "10" and "11" respectively. An "Original Mauser" banner trademark lay on the toggle. Those made for the European market had "GELADEN" on the left side of the extractor, but those sold in the USA by Interarms were usually marked "LOADED". The Interarms name and sunburst trademark appeared on the front right side of the receiver. Most were finished in blue, with checkered walnut grips, but plated and engraved deluxe examples were made to special order.

Mauser-Parabellum 06/73 (1971-88) Introduced commercially towards the end of 1971, this was mechanically similar to the 29/70 pattern. However, the shape of the grip and the design of controls such as the safety lever and takedown catch were altered to more closely resemble the P.08 than the Swiss 06/29 W+F. The basic 7.65mm and 9mm guns were very similar to their predecessors and continued the same serial-number sequences. They were extremely well finished in blue (a satin-chrome finish was introduced in 1973), many being engraved and inscribed to order, and were expensive products aimed squarely at the collector market. Once that appeared to have been satisfied, in the mid-1980s, Mauser closed down the line and it is unlikely that the Parabellum will ever re-appear. But there have been several special commemorative issues, almost always with a descriptive inscription (in German) on the left side of the frame above the grip.

The Mauser-Parabellum 06/73, though it retained the grip safety, was much more like the German P. 08 than the Swiss 06/29 W+F.

A deluxe version of the 7.65mm Mauser-Parabellum 06/73.

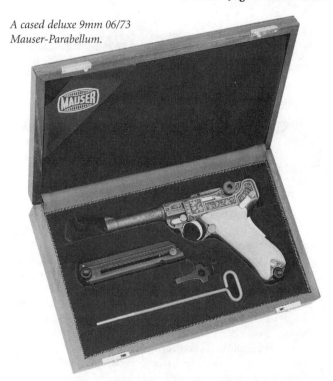

A cased deluxe 9mm 06/73 Mauser-Parabellum.

- *American Eagle Model* (1984) Marked "9mm Parabellum" (not "9mm Luger") on the barrel and with "GELADEN" on the extractor instead of "LOADED", these were made for sale in Germany and Switzerland. They had 4-inch barrels and an "American Eagle" marking over the chamber. Only about 80 were made, with five-digit "AE"-prefixed numbers. The left side of the frame was marked "Mod. 1902" over "American Eagle".
- *Artillery Model* (1985-6) Distinguished by a tangent-leaf sight on a 7.9-inch barrel, this 9mm-caliber gun was an 06/73 altered to approximate with the LP.08. It lacks the grip safety, has "A"-prefix serial numbers and was issued with a board-type shoulder stock. The left side of the frame was marked "Erinnerungsmodell" over "Lange Pistole 08".
- *Bulgarian Model* (1975) Made to commemorate the adoption of the Parabellum by the Bulgarian army, this was a 7.65mm 06/73 with a 4.7-inch barrel and the toggle grips cut away or "dished" to resemble the 1900 or "Old Model". It had the Arms of Bulgaria over the chamber, the "Original Mauser" banner on the toggle and Cyrillic lettering on the extractor and the safety-lever recess. The left side of the frame was marked "70 Jahre / Parabellum–Pistole / Königreich Bulgarien" in three lines.
- *Gamba Model* (1973) Made for the well-known Italian gunmaker (q.v.), these 9mm Parabellum guns — with 4-inch barrels — had the Mauser banner mark on the toggle and a chamber mark consisting of a displayed eagle over "RG". They also have a mark containing "SERIE SPECIALE RENATO GAMBA" on the right frame rail. Only a few hundred were made with distinctive "RG"-prefix numbers, but a substantial number were never delivered. These were deactivated for a Stuttgart dealer in 1976 and sold lacking both "RG" numbers and nitro proofs. However, they do have the special Gamba chamber and frame-rail markings.
- *German Army Model* (1983-4) Made to celebrate the 75th anniversary of the adoption of the P.08, this lacks the 06/73-type grip-safety mechanism and can be identified by the mark on the frame. It is also marked "1908" above "1983" over the chamber. The serial numbers had a "C" prefix, and the "9mm Luger" barrel marking signaled an intention to sell the guns in North America. The left side of the frame was marked "75 Jahre / Parabellum–Pistole / Mod. 08".

A 9mm Mauser "Navy commemorative" pistol, with 15c barrel and two-position rear sight. Note the "KM"-prefix serial number.

- *Navy Model* (1979) Issued to mark the 75th anniversary of the adoption of the Pistole 1904 by the Imperial German Navy, this was an 06/73 with a 5.9-inch barrel, the sliding two-position rear sight on the rear toggle link, a stock lug on the butt heel and "GELADEN" on the left side of the receiver. Unlike the Artillery or German Army commemorative models, the Navy pattern retains the grip-safety mechanism. It also had "KM"-prefixed numbers. The mark "70 Jahre / Parabellum–Pistole / Kaiserliche Marine" appeared on the left side of the frame.
- *Russian Model* (1975) These 9mm Parabellum guns, with 4-inch barrels, were made to acknowledge the distribution of Parabellums in Russia prior to World War I, though the status of the "adoption" has since been questioned. They had crossed Mosin-Nagant rifles above the chamber and Cyrillic markings on the extractor and in the safety-lever recess. The left side of the frame was marked "70 Jahre / Parabellum–Pistole / Kaiserreich Rußland" in three lines.

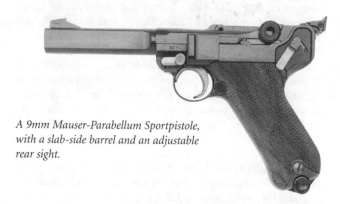

A 9mm Mauser-Parabellum Sportpistole, with a slab-side barrel and an adjustable rear sight.

- *Sportmodell* (or "Sport Model") Usually offered in 9mm Parabellum (a very few 7.65mm guns were made) with a 4.7-inch heavy barrel, this was only made in small quantities. The heavy barrel was either fluted or slab-sided, and the rear sight was fully adjustable. A few guns will bear the name of Interarms and a sunburst trademark on the front right side of the receiver.
- *Swiss Model* (1975-6) Made to celebrate the 75th anniversary of the adoption of the Parabellum by the Swiss army, this was a 7.65mm-

The 7.65mm-caliber Swiss commemorative Mauser-Parabellum 06/73.

caliber gun with a 4.7-inch barrel. The guns had the "Original Mauser" banner trademark on the toggle and a cross-on-sunburst mark above the chamber. The extractor was marked "GELADEN", but the safety-lever recess was left blank. The left side of the frame was marked "75 Jahre / Parabellum-Pistole / 1900–1975" in three lines of an angular-looking lettering.

The 9mm "Cartridge Counter" commemorative Mauser-Parabellum, celebrating the US Army purchase in the early 1900s.

- *US Army Cartridge Counter* (1982) These were 9mm guns with 4-inch barrels and "LOADED" on the left side of the extractor and an American Eagle motif above the chamber. They also had the left side of the grip cut away to reveal a cartridge-counting scale inspired by the Powell Indicating Device fitted to the 1902-pattern US Army test guns. The "Original Mauser" mark appears on the toggle, and the marks of the Ulm proof house will be found. The left side of the frame displays "Mod. 1902" over "Cartridge Counter".

The Mauser HSP was developed for German police trials in the mid-1970s but was only made in small numbers.

HsP Designed by Walter Ludwig, this gun was developed in the 1970s to answer a demand from the Federal German Police for an automatic pistol that could be carried loaded and cocked in perfect safety but brought into action without the need for manipulating safety devices or pulling back slides or hammers. Several manufacturers put up ideas, and Mauser's design was the HsP (apparently for "Hahnsicherung, Polizei").

A recoil-operated double-action design, the HsP had a breech that was locked by a swinging wedge beneath the barrel, controlled by a cam track in the frame. A combined safety catch and de-cocking lever was built into the left-side grip, and a stripping catch similar to that of the Parabellum lay on the left side of the frame. However, the police expressed a preference for the Heckler and Koch design (which became the P7 series) and Mauser abandoned the HsP project. It is doubtful if more than a couple of hundred were made.

M2 This is a modern-looking double-action-only pistol, offered in 357 SIG (10-round magazine) or 40 S&W (eight rounds). The squared contours of the slide hide a striker and a rotating barrel lock. An automatic firing-pin safety system is fitted, a pin projects from the top of the slide when the chamber is loaded, a magazine safety is present and the trigger holds the striker at half cock during the firing cycle; additional pressure on the trigger completes the retraction of the striker and fires the gun. A manual safety lever projects from the back of the frame, moving laterally to the left to the firing position. The slide is Nitron-finish chrome-nickel steel, the frame is alloy, the grips are polyamide and the retraction grips are widely spaced. Empty weight is 29 oz with the standard 3.5-inch barrel; overall length is 6.9 inches. The sights are usually dot-and-square combat patterns.

Made in Hungary, the 9mm Mauser Model 80SA was a variant if the FÉG FP9.

Another of the Hungarian guns, the Mauser M90DA was the FÉG P9R.

Model 80 (also known as "Model 80SA") Announced in 1992, this was a clone of the FN-Browning GP-35 ("High Power") made by FÉG of Budapest as the "FP-9". It had a 4.7-inch barrel and weighed 35 oz without its 14-round magazine. It was supplied to Mauser "in the white" to be marked and finished to the customary high standards expected by German purchasers.

• *Model 90DA* This was a double-action variant of the Model 80, equivalent to the FÉG P9R but lacking the ventilated rib above the barrel and with a slender trigger lever placed well forward within the guard.

• *Model 90DAC* A "Compact" version of the Model 90DA (or FÉG P9RK), this was only sold in small quantities. It can be identified by its 4.1-inch barrel and trigger guard that has been squared to facilitate a two-hand hold.

MAXIM GUN & AMMUNITION COMPANY

Crayford, Kent, England.
Hiram Maxim patented this pistol in 1896 in collusion with his principal assistant, Louis Silverman. Perhaps as many as 10 were made, but none were ever sold commercially. The Maxim-Silverman was a striker-fired blowback of admirable simplicity, with a hollow lightweight bolt sliding inside a tubular receiver. There were only four parts in the bolt, in addition to the sear: the trigger and its spring, the magazine and the barrel. The receiver, trigger guard and frame were made in a single piece. The pistols would have handled well, owing to the grip-rake angle of 45 degrees, and chamberings are said to have included 8mm Schönberger, 7.65mm Borchardt and 455 Webley.

Why Maxim chose to discontinue work is something of a mystery, but it is suspected that the sharply raked grip may have contributed to feeding problems and the British army authorities would certainly not have countenanced any semi-automatic pistol firing from an unlocked breech.

MAYOR

Ernest & François Mayor, Lausanne, Switzerland.
This pistol was designed and patented in 1919 by Ernst Rochat of Nyon. Having no manufacturing facilities, Rochat entered into an agreement with the Mayor brothers, gunsmiths trading nearby, to make the pistol. The Mayor establishment was small, however, and less than 1000 guns were made. Work ceased prior to 1930, owing to competition from bigger gunmaking businesses, but new guns were still being sold in 1933. The Mayor pistol is uncommon today but worth saving because workmanship and finish were excellent.

The original version of the 6.35mm (25-caliber) Swiss Mayor Arquebusier pistol.

Arquebusier This was a 6.35mm blowback with the fixed barrel protruding from the slide and an unusually long overhang behind the grip. The earliest examples had a one-piece slide with a cutout over the barrel serving as an ejection port. Later guns had a two-piece slide, with only the rear or breechblock section moving on recoil. This allowed ejection to take place through the gap created as the two parts of the "slide" moved apart. The pistol frame was made in halves, the right-hand part carrying the trigger and lockwork and the left part not only carrying the safety catch but also retaining the internal components when the two sides were put together. The first guns had external extractors, a lever-type safety catch and sights that stood above the slide. Later examples had internal extractors, a groove in the slide to acts as a sight and a sliding safety button.

The left side of the slide was marked with "MAYOR" over "ARQUE-BUSIER", behind a trademark comprising "R" above "N", separated by a fish. The motif, in a diamond, was also impressed into the wooden grips.

MB ASSOCIATES

San Ramon, California, USA.
This business was formed in 1960 by Robert Mainhardt and Art Biehl, entrepreneurs looking for suitable ideas to back. In the event, few good ideas appeared and the two men became interested in weapons technology, deciding that "since the existing technology was over 50 years old and nothing really new had happened in that time" (Mainhardt's words), there was room for improvement. Eventually they hit on the idea of small spin-stabilized rockets and, having developed the rockets, produced a hand-held launcher known as the "Gyrojet" — little more than a large pistol firing 13mm rockets instead of conventional ammunition.

Whether MBA knew it or not, the Germans (as usual) had introduced a 20mm spin-stabilized rocket launcher in 1944. Nevertheless, the Gyrojet rockets were a considerable technical feat; at 13mm-caliber and about 1.5 inches long, they had a solid head and a tubular body containing a solid propellant. The base was closed by a venturi plate with four jets, angled to give spin as well as forward thrust, and had a percussion primer placed centrally.

The launcher resembled an automatic pistol in general outline and carried six rockets in the butt. The hammer was above the trigger and struck backwards to hit the nose of the rocket and thus drive it back so that the percussion cap was impaled on a fixed firing pin in the standing breech. This ignited the rocket, and as it accelerated, so the hammer was thrust down and re-cocked.

The MBA Gyrojet Mark I Model B was really a hand-held rocket launcher.

Gyrojet pistol This, along with shoulder-fired "carbines" in a variety of experimental calibers, appeared on the commercial market in 1965. The handgun sold on its novelty value (even at the high price of $2500), but the sought-after military contract did not appear. The accuracy was far below that of a conventional pistol — one report spoke of 11-inch groups at 10 yards — and the rapid decline in velocity so soon after launching did nothing for penetration or accuracy. The ammunition was also very expensive.

After the restrictions on weapons over 50-caliber (12.7mm) had been imposed by the 1968 Gun Control Act, a few Gyrojet pistols were made in 12mm caliber until the project failed and work ceased in 1970. The Trebor Corporation of Dublin, California, announced the availability of the "Gyrojet Rocket Handgun" in a "limited collector's edition" in 1984, together with a quantity of inert rocket projectiles, but this project also failed to prosper.

MENDOZA

Productos Mendoza SA, Mexico City, Mexico.
Better-known for machineguns and submachine guns, this gunmaking business was also responsible for a 22 LR rimfire sport pistol in the 1960s. The *K-62* resembled a Western-style revolver, with a well-flared grip and a prominent hammer, but was actually a single-shot pistol with a drop-down barrel held by a simple stirrup catch. A three-round "quick loader" was attached to each side of the frame where the cylinder would have been.

MENZ

August Menz, Waffenfabrik August Menz, Suhl, Germany.
August Menz came into the automatic pistol business by way of a contract to manufacture the Beholla pistol (see "Becker & Hollander") for the German army in 1916-18, producing it as the "Menta". From this beginning, he went on to produce a number of pistols of his own design. Menz was bought out by AG Lignose in 1937.

∼ REPEATING PISTOL ∼

Regnum This was a brutally simple repeating pistol, consisting of a rectangular butt supporting a frame with trigger and guard. A hammer was concealed in the rear of the frame. A block of four 6.35mm-caliber barrels pivoted in the frame, released by a push-button, tipped forward for loading. Once the block was returned and locked, pressure on the trigger fired the four barrels in succession. Dating from c. 1905-14, the guns rarely bear Menz's name but do have "AM" monograms on the grips; they also bear "D.R.G.M. U. AUSLANDS-PATENT" on the frame.

∼ AUTOMATIC PISTOLS ∼

Bijou An alternative name for the 6.35mm Liliput.
Kaba, Kaba Spezial These were sales name for the Liliput pistol sold through dealers.

A 6.35mm (25 ACP) Menz Liliput "Model 1925" pocket pistol.

Liliput Similar in concept to the Walther Model 9, this compact "vest-pocket" automatic went on sale in 1920. The first version was a tiny blowback automatic in 4.25mm caliber, chambering a cartridge that had originated with the "Erika" pistol made by Pfannl prior to 1914. Menz adopted the 4.25mm round to keep his pistol as small as possible. Though the cartridge was far from common, the Liliput appears to have enjoyed some success, as examples engraved "MODELL 1927" are common. Nevertheless, Menz was sensible enough to see that it would be more popular in a more popular caliber and offered a 6.35mm version in 1925. A handful was eventually made in 7.65mm.

Menta After the First World War had ended, Menz retained the machinery used to make this Beholla copy and continued to offer guns for commercial sale, including a scaled-down version in 6.35mm Auto.

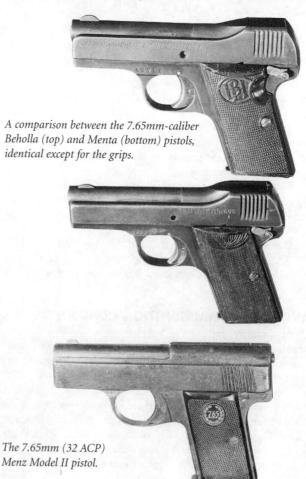

A comparison between the 7.65mm-caliber Beholla (top) and Menta (bottom) pistols, identical except for the grips.

The 7.65mm (32 ACP) Menz Model II pistol.

Model II Instead of pursuing the 7.65mm Liliput, Menz chose to market a separate pattern under his own name. The front of the slide was originally cut square but was tapered beneath the muzzle after about 500 guns had been made.

Modell III This 7.65mm pistol was a radical re-design. Menz abandoned the open slide of the Liliput — and the shoddy Liliput standard of manufacture — for a better quality pistol with a fixed barrel, a concentric return spring and a full-length slide similar to that of the 1910-type FN-Browning. The gun had an external hammer and a slide-removal catch above the trigger. It was advertised as the "Polizei und Behörden Modell" and the slide was duly marked ""*MENZ*" *P&B PIST. CAL. 7,65*" over "*MOD. III*", but whether he had any success in getting it adopted by police forces is questionable; the guns are extremely uncommon and serial numbers suggest that only a few hundred were ever made. The grips bore an enwreathed "AM" monogram. A "Model IV" — a double-action version of the Model III — is said to have been made in small numbers but probably only in prototype form.

- *Modell IIIA* This was a "double-action-only" variant of the standard gun with the hammer cut back until it was virtually flush with the slide.

Okzet Another of the names associated with the 6.35mm Liliput pistol.

P&B Special Menz's last design, this was similar to the Model III but had an enlarged trigger guard to give the range of movement needed in a double-action trigger. The external hammer was retained, but the safety catch, placed on the end of the slide, became a vertically moving latch rather than the usual rocking arm. It is assumed that this was a way of avoiding infringements of patents granted to Walther and others to protect slide-mounted safety systems. The left side of the slide was marked "*AUGUST MENZ WAFFENFABRIK SUHL*" over "*PB "SPECIAL"*…" and the grips carried the word "Special". This pistol appeared in 1935/6 but did not sell well, was never adopted by any official body and is now quite rare. The Menz business was acquired by Lignose in c. 1937, and the remaining stocks of Menz pistols were sold by the new owners under the "Bergmann-Erben" name.

Westentaschen ("Vestpocket") This 6.35mm model was made only in small numbers. It appears to have been based on the Menta but embodies a few obvious improvements. The firing pin acts as a cocking indicator, protruding through the rear of the slide. The barrel is retained by a pin passing through the frame below the slide. And the barrel has a secondary anchor in the return-spring guide rod that not only protrudes from the front of the frame but also has a groove around the end to allow it to be pulled out to free the barrel.

MERIDEN

Meriden Firearms Company, Meriden, Connecticut. USA.

This shadowy gunmaking business had its origins in the last decade of the 19th century, and traded until c. 1915. The mystery lies in who owned it and just how much actual manufacturing was done. Various suggestions have been put forward: that the business was owned by the mail-order house of Sears, Roebuck; that it was part of Andrew Fyrberg's operations; or that it was an offshoot of the Stevens Arms & Tool Company. Stevens was well known for shoulder arms and single-shot pistols but also owned some useful revolver patents. Consequently, it has been suggested that Stevens-made revolver components were assembled in Meriden.

Aubrey Correctly "A.J. Aubrey", this was used as a brand name on revolvers sold by Sears, Roebuck & Co. in 1900-30. Aubrey, patentee of several gun-related accessories, was the manager of Sears' manufacturing division. Offered in 32 Long and 38 Long centerfire chamberings, the five-shot guns were standard Meriden top-break double-action products.

Chicago Arms Co. A sales name applied to revolvers made for the Fred Biffar Company of Chicago, c. 1870-90. The revolvers were of 32- and 38-caliber top-break five-shot double-action patterns with ribbed barrels.

Eastern Arms Co. See "Meriden".

Empire Automatic This brand name distinguished a five-shot hinged-frame double-action revolver distributed by the H.D. Folsom Company of Chicago in 1895-1915. The revolvers were made in 32 and 38 caliber and were "automatic" only in the sense that the empty cases were automatically ejected when the revolver was opened. The guns were usually provided with 3-inch barrels, though 4- and 5-inch barrels can also be found.

Empire State See "Meriden". Possibly marketed by Sears, Roebuck & Co.

Federal See "Meriden".

Howard Arms Another of the brand names used by the Fred Biffar Company of Chicago, this graced 32 and 38 hinged-frame double-action revolvers dating from 1895-1915.

Meriden Whatever the provenance, the Meriden factory made a variety of essentially similar revolvers. There were two basic groups: conventional hammer and "hammerless" (concealed hammer) patterns, with ribbed barrels, hinged frames, automatic extractors and five-chamber cylinders. Calibers were restricted to 32 and 38, usually with 3-inch barrels though other lengths will be found. Quality might be charitably described as "average" and, by and large, it would be hard to tell a Meriden product from many contemporaneous rivals were it not for the design of the front-sight blade — with two short ornamental curves that sweep up from the barrel surface at each end.

Secret Service Special This was a sales name used c. 1890-1910 by the Fred Biffar Company of Chicago on two differing revolvers. One was made by Iver Johnson and the other by Meriden.

MERRILL

The Merrill Company, Rockwell City, Iowa (to 1979),
then Fullerton, California, USA.

Merrill manufactured a single-shot drop-barrel pistol in 1977-85. The gun was a conventional design with an octagonal barrel (9 or 12 inches long), tapped and drilled for optical sight mounts, and a striker that protruded from the standing breech to show that the action was cocked. An interchangeable barrel allowed chamberings from 22 LR rimfire to 44 Magnum centerfire to be used. However, reports suggested that the design, satisfactory in 22 caliber, lacked robustness and accuracy in the larger sizes.

MERRIMAC

Merrimac Arms & Mfg Co., Newburyport, Massachusetts, USA.

This was a trading name used by the Brown Manufacturing Company (q.v.) on single-shot derringer pistols made in 1869-73.

MERWIN

Merwin, Hulbert & Company, New York City, USA.

The company originated as Merwin & Bray in 1863, becoming "Merwin & Simpkins" in 1868, "Merwin, Taylor & Simpkins" in 1869 and, finally, "Merwin, Hulbert & Co." in 1871. The business acted as an agent for Plant caplock revolvers made by various companies during the American Civil War, and then promoted guns made by Hopkins & Allen (q.v.). Merwin & Hulbert controlled several patents used by Hopkins & Allen and eventually, in 1874, purchased a controlling interest in the manufacturing company. Consequently, many Hopkins & Allen-type revolvers will be encountered with nothing but Merwin & Hulbert markings. Though Joseph Merwin died in 1879, the two Hulbert brothers continued trading under the existing name until reorganizing the business as "Hulbert Bros. & Co., Inc." in 1892. This company failed in 1896, contributing greatly to the collapse of Hopkins & Allen two years afterwards.

Merwin & Hulbert also promoted their own designs of ammunition, in 32, 38 and 44 centerfire, differing in dimensions from other cartridges of the same nominal caliber. The Merwin & Hulbert revolvers were chambered for these cartridges, though the dimensional differences were so small that they could usually be persuaded to chamber and fire better known cartridges as well. Consequently, Merwin & Hulbert were never able to make their fortunes from the sales of ammunition.

M&H revolvers These were made in several styles by Hopkins & Allen (q.v.) in 1875-92. The design was unusual. The barrel and barrel extension were attached to the remainder of the revolver by a combination of the cylinder arbor pin and an interlock at the front of the frame. Pressing a spring catch allowed the barrel unit to be rotated laterally around the arbor pin and then pulled forward, taking the cylinder with it. A star-plate extractor attached to the standing breech then withdrew the fired cases from the cylinder. The barrel could then be returned and re-locked, and the cylinder could be loaded through a gate on the right side of the frame.

The open-frame design proved to be weaker than solid-frame competitors such as the Colt Peacemaker and had soon been strengthened by adding a strap that ran back above the cylinder to engage the standing breech. This was undoubtedly a wise move, as many of the Merwin & Hulbert revolvers were 44 caliber. Many were chambered for the 44-40 WCF cartridge and will be marked appropriately on the frame; others, unmarked, accepted the 44 Merwin & Hulbert cartridge, which is difficult to distinguish from the better known 44 S&W Special.

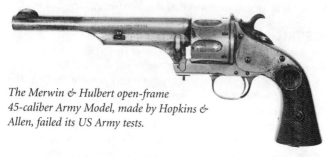

The Merwin & Hulbert open-frame 45-caliber Army Model, made by Hopkins & Allen, failed its US Army tests.

- *Frontier or Army Model* This was a large 44-caliber gun, usually encountered with a 7-inch barrel and a square butt (though 3.5- and 5.5-inch barrels are known). Some examples may be marked "WINCHESTER 1873", a reference to the ubiquitous 44-40 WCF cartridge. The earliest guns were open-framed and had oval "flutes" in the cylinder surface that had soon been replaced with a more conventional design. Later changes included the addition of a strap above the cylinder and the development of double-action lockwork, presumably to compete with the Colt Lightning. Revolvers of this type were tested by the US Ordnance Board in 1877 but had soon been rejected for military use.
- *Pocket Army Model* Also chambering the 44 M&H or 44-40 rounds, this was a derivative of the Frontier pattern with a 3.5-inch barrel

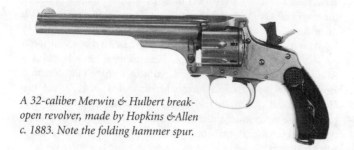

A 32-caliber Merwin & Hulbert break-open revolver, made by Hopkins & Allen c. 1883. Note the folding hammer spur.

and a beaked "skull-crusher" butt drilled to accept a lanyard. The guns were originally open-frame, but the supplementary topstrap and the optional double-action lockwork had both appeared by the early 1880s.
- *Pocket Model* (single action) This was a diminutive of the Army patterns, built on smaller frames but still offering the unique "twist and pull" extraction system. The earliest examples, with five-chamber cylinders, were not only open-framed but also had sheathed triggers. The cylinder arbor pin protruded from the frame, and the cylinder was loaded through an aperture cut in the recoil shield. Guns of this type had soon acquired sliding loading gates and a shroud around the arbor pin and eventually acquired conventional trigger guards. They were almost always in 38 caliber with five-chamber cylinders.
- *Pocket Model* (double action) These either had seven or five 32-caliber chambers and were built on a medium-size frame; there was also a small-frame 32-caliber five-shot pattern. All double-action Merwin & Hulbert revolvers had conventional trigger guards and will sometimes also be found with folding hammer spurs.

METALLURGICA BRESCIANA GIA TEMPINI ("MBT")
Brescia, Italy.

MBT made the Glisenti (q.v.) pistol for the Italian army but subsequently embarked on a program of improvement. The revised design had a stronger frame and abandoned the grip safety, but the other changes were largely cosmetic.

The 9mm Brixia or "M1912" pistol was an improved form of the Italian Glisenti army pistol.

Brixia M1912 The modified Glisenti was submitted to the Italian army and tested experimentally prior to World War I. However, there was deemed to be too little improvement to justify rejecting the current 1910-type service pistol. MBT then offered the Brixia for sale commercially, but hostilities began before it could make an impression. The project was never revived. The Brixia resembles the Glisenti, but the left side of the frame is flat instead of paneled and the grips are marked "MBT".

MEXICO CITY ARMS FACTORY
Fabrica Nacional de Armas de Mexico, Mexico City.

Obregon Patented by Alejandro Obregon in 1934 and made in 1934-8, this pistol resembles the Colt M1911A1 at first glance. It shares the same general outline, hammer and grip safety, but an unusually long slide latch/safety catch lies on the left side of the frame. In addition, the Obregon slide becomes tubular towards the muzzle instead of the slab-side construction of the Colt. The magazine is slightly different, and some individual guns have an additional safety mechanism to lock the hammer when the magazine is removed.

The major difference concerns the locking system, a turning barrel reminiscent of the Savage or Steyr-Hahn (instead of the tipping barrel of the Colt-Brownings) that explains the shape of the slide. The barrel is held in the frame by lugs that ride in helical cam-ways, and a third

The Mexican Obregon pistol looks like the 1911-type Colt-Browning externally but has a rotating-barrel lock.

The Japanese Miroku Liberty Chief revolver, in 38 special.

barrel-lug engages an angular slot in the slide. When the gun fires, the barrel and slide recoil, securely locked together, until the third lug rides in its cam-way to revolve the barrel about 20 degrees. This allows the locking cam to align with a straight slot and the slide can run back alone once the barrel has been brought to a halt. An additional delay is created by the torque created by the bullet in the rifling, which opposes the rotation of the barrel.

It is generally accepted that less than 1000 Obregon pistols were made. Manufacturing the pistol proved to be difficult and expensive; purchasing standard 45-caliber Colt-Brownings commercially proved to be more cost-effective. No Obregon pistols were ever sold commercially, owing to contemporaneous restrictions placed on civilian use of 45 ACP ammunition.

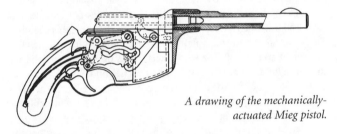

A drawing of the mechanically-actuated Mieg pistol.

MIEG

Armand Mieg, Heidelberg, Germany.

In 1890, Mieg patented a complicated mechanical repeater that relied on a system of levers to operate a turn-bolt mechanism. The chambering was a special 6.65mm necked cartridge, DWM design no. 396, but the pistols never progressed beyond the prototype stage. A patent granted in 1893 then transformed the repeating pistol into a semi-automatic, relying upon an improved system of levers to delay the opening of the turning bolt. The new gun chambered an 8mm necked cartridge, DWM no. 372, but only a few handmade examples existed. None are known to survive.

MIKKENGER

Mikkenger Arms Company, Dallas, Texas, USA.

This company produced a number of single-action Western-style revolvers in the 1970s, chambering 44 Magnum or 45 Long Colt ammunition. Gate-loaded solid-frame guns based on the Colt Peacemaker, they had an Allen screw under the loading gate to secure the cylinder arbor pin. The revolvers being marketed in 1978 were numbered as high as 5000, but it seems unlikely that these reflect *actual* production figures. Work ceased in the early 1980s.

MIROKU

Miroku Firearms Mfg Co., Kochi, Japan.

This company, founded in 1965, has made a number of 38 S&W Special revolvers copied from the solid-frame double-action swing-cylinder construction pioneered in the USA by Colt. The *Model VI* was a six-

shot pattern with a 2-inch barrel, sold in the USA as the "Liberty Chief", and there was also a smaller five-shot *Special Police Model*. Manufacture ceased in the mid-1980s.

MITCHELL

Mitchell Arms, Inc., Santa Ana, California, USA.

Mitchell originally attained success by distributing a wide variety of guns imported from abroad, including a range of handguns originating in Yugoslavia (now Serbia, see "ZCZ"). Production of a variety of designs was then undertaken in the USA, though it seems likely that at least some of the parts were either imported from Europe or made elsewhere in North America. Operations failed in 1997, and, though some components were sold to Brolin Arms (which itself ceased trading in 1999), the Mitchell guns are no longer common.

∼ REVOLVERS ∼

Single Action Army This was a Western-style revolver based on the Colt Peacemaker and offered in chamberings ranging from 22 Long Rifle RF to 45 Long Colt — though ultimately concentrated on 357 Magnum, 44 Magnum and 45 Long Colt. Barrel lengths ranged from 5 to 12 inches, with an 18-inch "Buntline" pattern to be used with an optional shoulder stock.

∼ AUTOMATIC PISTOLS ∼

Parabellum ("Luger") Announced in 1992, the *American Eagle 08*, an homage to the German P.08 (albeit made of stainless steel), enjoyed a brief success before the project was sold by Stoeger. The Stoeger-Luger is still in series production.

High Standard Mitchell also made a series of target pistols based on the High Standard (q.v.) range, largely because Alexander Mitchell had once worked for this particular manufacturer. However, a lengthy dispute over rights to the designs was resolved in favor of the High Standard Mfg Co. (q.v.) and Mitchell decided to concentrate instead on a range of good-quality Colt-Brownings. Individual target-pistol patterns included the "Citation II", "Olympic ISU", "Sharpshooter II", "Trophy II" and "Victor II", which were all generally comparable with the original patterns of the same name (see "High Standard"). The "Sportster" was a sports pistol inspired by the old Sport King, with a long slender barrel and the front sight mounted on a muzzle collar.

Colt-Browning clones These featured refinements that included long barrels and slides, extended controls, duplicated slide-retraction grooves, special sights, wraparound grips and skeleton hammers. They have included the "Baron", "Monarch" and "Sovereign", all dating from 1992-4, and the Gold Series ("Gold Standard", "Gold Wide Body", "Gold Tactical") introduced in 1994. Ambidextrous Gold Series guns were announced in 1996, but only a few were made before trading ceased. Among the most interesting of the Mitchell Colt-Brownings was the "Alpha" (1995), which featured interchangeable single-action/double-action trigger modules. The Mitchells generally chambered the 45 ACP round, though an enlarged 44 Magnum version, with a 5.5-inch barrel and a six-round magazine, was announced in 1996.

MKS

MKS Supply, Inc., Dayton, Ohio, USA.

The distributor of Hi Point (q.v.) firearms, sometimes listed as the manufacturer.

MOLGORA ("MMM-MONDIAL")

Modesto Molgora, Milan, Italy.

This firm, essentially a toymaker, has made an enormous range of blank, cap and starting pistols. There has also been a cheap six-shot "personal-defense revolver", a double-action solid-framed non-ejector chambered for 22 Short RF or equally ineffective 6mm Flobert cartridges.

An MOA Maximum single-shot lever-action pistol.

MOA CORPORATION

Dayton, Ohio, USA.

This company ("Minute-Of-Angle") makes the *Maximum* pistol, a single-shot design introduced in 1983 specifically for long-range competitive shooting. A dropping-block breech mechanism is operated with a looped lever that follows the contours of the front strap of the butt. Chamberings currently range from 22 Long Rifle rimfire to 454 Casull centerfire, by way of a selection of pistol and rifles cartridge that includes 22 Hornet, 223 Remington, 243 Winchester, 250-3000 Savage, 30 M1 Carbine, 30-30 WCF, 357 Magnum and 375 H&H. With a hand-fitted barrel, guns of this type are often capable of achieving half-inch groups at 100 yards.

The Douglas barrel (8.75, 10.5 or 14 inches long) carries adjustable sights but is also tapped and drilled to accept optical-sight mounts. A typical gun is 18.5 inches long, with the 14-inch barrel option, and weighs a substantial 78 oz. Metalwork may be blued carbon or stainless steel, often with contrasting parts; the butt and the fore-end are usually walnut.

MOHAWK ARMS COMPANY

Or simply "Mohawk", this appeared on revolvers and shotguns made prior to 1915 by the Crescent Arms Company.

MOORE

Moore's Patent Firearms Company, Brooklyn, New York, USA.

Daniel Moore opened his factory in Brooklyn in 1861, making pistols and revolvers until the end of the American Civil War. Operations were reconstituted in 1866 as the "National Arms Company" (q.v.).

⁓ SINGLE-SHOT PISOLS ⁓

Derringer A 41-caliber rimfire gun with a barrel that swung out to the right for loading, combined with an all-metal "knuckles" butt, this was patented in the USA in February 1861 and made in large numbers until the business was eventually purchased by Colt. The Moore (or "National") No. 1 and No. 2 Knuckle Dusters duly laid the basis for the Colt No. l and No. 2 patterns.

⁓ REVOLVERS ⁓

Early rimfire guns Seven-shot revolvers in 32, 38 and 44 rimfire made in accordance with a patent granted in September 1860, these guns had barrel-cylinder groups that rotated laterally to load. Predictably, they fell foul of the Rollin White patent owned by Smith &

Wesson. Moore lost the resulting lawsuit, and the guns made in 1863 were marked "MADE FOR SMITH & WESSON".

Teat-fire guns The failure of the rimfire revolvers persuaded Moore to circumvent the White patent with a revolver that had "blind" chambers in the cylinder. These could be loaded from the front with 32-caliber metallic cartridges ignited by a protruding "teat" on the base. The teat, which contained a fulminate igniter, projected through a small hole bored in the rear face of the chamber, where it could be struck by the falling hammer. Six-shot revolvers of this type were first made in 1863 but were soon improved by the addition of a combined extractor/cartridge retainer developed by David Williamson. Work continued even after the advent of the National Arms Company. Most guns had open frames, sheathed triggers, plain-surface cylinders and bird's-head butts.

MORAIN

Paris, France.

The name of the Parisian gunsmith Georges Morain can be found on an 8mm "Velo-Dog" "hammerless" folding-trigger revolver of better-than-usual quality. The barrel marking of "G. MORAIN BREVETE" suggests that he may have been making the guns in accordance with a patent that has yet to be traced. Production was probably confined to 1895-1910.

MORINI

Morini Competition Arms SA, Lamone, Switzerland.

This company, originally best known for grips and shooting accessories, graduated in the 1980s to making guns of its own. In addition to a small range of good-quality target pistols, it also makes gas-powered designs.

CM22M Intended for rapid-fire competition shooting, this chambers the 22 rimfire round and is about 11.8 inches long with a 5.1-inch barrel; weight averages 42.7 oz with a steel frame, or 33.5 oz with the aluminum-alloy alternative ("CM22M Alu"). The gun is a typical modern target pistol with the axis of the bore set as low as possible in the hand, an anatomical grip with an adjustable palm shelf and a detachable box magazine ahead of the open-base trigger aperture. Construction is modular — including a red-colored polymer trigger/hammer housing and cocking grips extending under the front part of the barrel housing. The mechanical trigger can be adjusted for length of pull, rake, let-off point, over-travel and release pressure (first stage 14-28 oz, second stage 3.5-35 oz). The guns are usually marked "Morini™ CM 22M" on the left side of the barrel housing, ahead of "MADE IN SWITZERLAND" in three lines. A "MC" monogram lies on the front of the barrel housing and on the left grip.

CM32M Similar to the CM22M, but intended for use in full-bore competitions, this chambers the 32 S&W Wadcutter round. It weighs about 44.5 oz without its detachable magazine. The trigger housing is usually blue instead of red.

CM84E Derived from an earlier mechanical-trigger gun designated "CM80", this is a single-shot dropping-block Free Pistol chambering the 22 LR rimfire round. It is built to an advanced specification that includes an adjustable grip angle, an adjustable bore axis, an adjustable sight radius (13-15 inches), various sight options and a range of muzzle counterweights. About 19.5 inches long, with an 11.4-inch barrel and an empty weight of 43.7 oz, the CM84E has an adjustable electronic trigger system with a safety beam. The gun is easily identified by the trigger guard, which is an open-ended bow, and by the shape of the top of the breech.

MORITZ

Heinrich Moritz, Zella St.Blasii (to 1919) and Zella-Mehlis (1919 onward), Germany.

Hei-Mo A brand name registered by Heinrich Moritz in 1917, this was applied to a 7.65mm-caliber blowback pistol dating from the early

1920s. It is basically an "Eibar", with the familiar Eibar safety catch halfway along the frame, but the barrel is octagonal and protrudes about half an inch from the slide — which facilitates stripping, as the construction duplicates that of the 1903-type FN-Browning. The only markings are "Kal 7,65" on the slide and "D.R.G.M." on the frame, but these could easily have been stamped on in Spain.

He-Mo A 7.65mm blowback pistol similar to the Hei-Mo, this had an open-top slide (similar to that of the 1934-type Beretta) and a cylindrical barrel. It was marked "HE-MO GES. GESCH." on the left side of the slide, above the vertically ribbed wooden grip, and probably dates prior to 1930.

MOSSBERG

O.F. Mossberg & Sons, New Haven, Connecticut, USA.
This gunmaking business is best known for rifles and shotguns, but Oscar F. Mossberg also obtained a variety of handgun patents. Most of these were assigned to manufacturers such as Iver Johnson, but, in 1906, he patented a novel four-barrel repeating pistol.

∼ REPEATING PISTOLS ∼

Novelty The 1906 design had the barrels two-over-two in a dropdown block, and the revolving firing pin was operated by squeezing the grip. It was designed for use as a "palm-squeezer", held in the hand with the barrels protruding between the fingers, and was usually in 22 Short, though guns in 32 Short RF are sometimes found. Mossberg assigned the patent to the Shattuck Company (q.v.) of Hatfield, Massachusetts, and it was made for some years as the "Unique" for several years. However, Shattuck failed during World War I and the patent reverted to Mossberg, who began making essentially similar guns as the "Novelty".

Brownie In 1920, Mossberg decided that there was a market for an improved Novelty, which he patented in July 1920. The design was very much the same as its predecessor, a four-barreled repeater with a dropdown barrel-block/trigger unit retained by a sliding catch on top of the breech. As the trigger is pulled, the hammer is cocked and a separate link moves the rotating firing pin (attached to the hammer face) to the next notch, aligning it with appropriate barrel. The sear slips off the hammer at the end of the trigger stroke, and the pistol fires. The 2.5-inch barrels could fire 22 Short, 22 Long or 22 Long Rifle rimfire cartridges interchangeably and a simple manual extractor emptied all four barrels simultaneously.

The first 2500 pistols, made before the patent was granted, are marked "PAT APPLIED FOR" on the right side of the receiver. Once the patent had been granted, this changed to "PAT JULY 27 1920", although at least one has been noted erroneously marked "JAN." instead of "JULY". It has been estimated that some 37,000 were made before production ended in 1933.

MUGICA

José C. Mugica, Eibar, Spain.
The name of this distributor soon became synonymous with a group of Llama pistols sold in the 1930s. See "Gabilondo".

MÜLLER

Bernhard Müller, Winterthur, Switzerland.
Müller patented his automatic pistol in Switzerland in September 1902, submitting a 7.65mm version to Swiss army trials in 1904 and details of a projected 45-caliber version to the US Army trials in 1905. A cumbersome design, with a Parabellum-like butt containing a detachable box magazine projecting beneath a massive slab-sided receiver, it was locked by a rotating bolt. The bolt was opened by a cam track during a short recoil stroke and an internal hammer could be re-cocked by an external lever in the event of a misfire. Unfortunately, small-but-vital defects were found during the Swiss trials, and the pistol faded into obscurity after perhaps only 10 had been made.

MUSGRAVE

Musgrave (Pty) Ltd, Bloemfontein, South Africa.
Ben Musgrave was a keen hunter who began developing his own ideas of a sporting rifle in his garage and then founded a gunmaking business in 1950. He continued making sporting rifles until such severe financial problems were encountered in the early 1970s that the firm was rescued in 1975 by Armscor, the national munitions consortium. The business was still known as "Musgrave", but in 1995, in a massive re-organization of the South African arms industry, a consortium called Denel replaced Armscor and absorbed Musgrave completely. The factory became a manufacturing unit of Denel Pty, though work on sporting guns continued.

Musgrave pistol During the early 1990s, the General Manager, A.J. Koch, set his designers to the task of producing an automatic pistol with the minimum number of parts and the simplest form of construction. The result was a large 9mm blowback that — despite good features — failed to find widespread acceptance. Consequently, the project was abandoned after only a few guns had been made.

The 9mm Parabellum Musgrave pistol was a simple design with a synthetic grip/frame unit and a bolt reciprocating inside the tubular receiver.

NAGANT

E. & L. Nagant Frères, later Fabrique d'Armes Léon Nagant (to 1910), then Fabrique d'Armes et Automobiles Nagant Frères (post-1910); Liége, Belgium.

Émile Nagant, a Liége gunsmith, obtained several revolver patents in the late 1870s protecting an assortment of minor improvements dealing with dismantling systems and ejection. He developed a series of revolvers that gained considerable popularity in military circles, allowing the Nagant brothers' gunmaking business to flourish, but by 1900, Léon had died and Émile had become blind. Léon's sons preferred to make automobiles, and although even this activity came to a stop when the Germans occupied Liége in 1914, trading continued until 1931.

～ TWO-SHOT PISTOL ～

Constabulary Model ("Modèle de Gendamerie") Introduced in 1874 to replace a caplock, this was essentially a double-barreled version of the Remington rolling-block pistol chambering a 9.4mm centerfire cartridge. A thousand guns were made in 1874 and another thousand, with an improved frame, in 1877. They served the Belgian gendarmerie until replaced by revolvers in the 1890s.

～ REVOLVERS ～

Standard patterns All these were basically similar: solid-frame, six-shot, double-action with gate loading and rod ejection, with no extraordinary features about them.

The Belgian 9mm M1878 Nagant revolver.

The Belgian M1883 Nagant revolver, issued to officers and senior NCOs.

- *M1878*, Belgium Originally adopted by the Belgian army for its officers (though issue was subsequently extended), this six-shot 9.4mm double-action weapon was retained until World War I. The M1878/86 (or "M1886") was a simplified version, recognized by small oval depressions in the cylinder instead of the flutes that had characterized the original M1887. Guns used by the customs service will be marked "DOUANE BELGE".
- *M1883*, Belgium Based on the 1878 design, but with the lockwork restricted to single action, this 9.4mm-caliber gun also had a distinctive plain-surface cylinder. It was originally issued to NCOs and others — including field artillerymen and wagon drivers — who lacked carbines.
- *M1884*, Luxembourg Adopted for officers in 1887, and sometimes listed as "M84/87", this was a variant of the 1878-pattern Belgian

gun chambered for the 7.5mm Swiss service cartridge. Small quantities of 1882 Schmidt-type revolvers had previously been acquired from Switzerland, explaining what would otherwise have seemed an odd choice of cartridge.

A variant of the 7.5mm M1884 was also made with a safety catch in the form of a lever, pivoted on the left side of the frame, with a hooked nose that could lock into a chamber to prevent the cylinder rotating. Perversely, guns of this pattern were also issued to the Belgian prison service in the 1890s in the same 7.5mm chambering.

The M1884 gendarmerie revolver, made only in tiny quantities, had a long barrel with a sleeve that could accept a detachable 4-inch bayonet blade. It chambered the 9.4mm Belgian cartridge instead of the 7.5mm Swiss type.

- *M1887*, Sweden The victor of tests that had begun in 1885, this was a 7.5mm variant of the M1884. Most of the guns made prior to 1897 emanated from Liége, but later examples were made by Husqvarna. Swedish guns had a distinctively squared front sight.
- *M1891*, Serbia The designation of these guns has never been confirmed. They were essentially similar to the Belgian M1878/86 but had an Abadie-type gate on the right side of the frame that disconnected the hammer when the gun was being loaded.
- *M1893*, Norway The Norwegian authorities had bought a few 1883-type single-action 9.4mm-caliber Nagants in the mid-1880s but ultimately adopted a minor variant of the 7.5mm M1887 Swedish gun with a semi-circular front sight. About 12,000 were supplied from Liége, supplemented by a few hundred acquired from Husqvarna in 1900 (to replace guns that had been lost in service) and a handful made — largely by hand — in the Kongsberg ordnance factory.
- *Brazilian navy model* This was an enlargement of the M1878/86, a double-action six-shot gun chambered for a 44-caliber rimmed cartridge (11.2x20R). It was marked "MARINHA DOS E.U. DO BRASIL" and had a plain-surface cylinder.
- *Others* Nagant-type revolvers were sold commercially and extensively copied not only in Liége but also in Spain. The Belgian-made guns included a modified "Nagant-type" revolver made by Ancion-Marx (marked "JAM" in a triangle) with simplified lockwork that dropped out of the bottom of the frame. Nagant-type revolvers were also made in Germany, by Simson & Co., and 44-caliber Belgian-type guns ("11.2x22R") are said to have served with the armed forces in Argentina.

Gas-seal patterns Léon Nagant patented a gas-sealing revolver in 1892-5, the only design of its type ever to succeed commercially. The cylinder was moved forward during the cocking movement of the hammer so that the coned rear end of the barrel entered the mouth of the chamber in the cylinder. It was then locked in place by an "abutment" behind the cartridge to be fired, so that not only was the cylinder held but the base of the cartridge was supported. However, construction of this type required an abnormally long firing pin to reach across the gap and through the abutment to strike the cartridge cap.

The cartridge case was extended to enclose the bullet, and, as the cylinder and barrel came together, the slightly tapered case-mouth entered the rear of the barrel. When the gun was fired, gas pressure and the movement of the bullet expanded the case-mouth to bridge any gap between chamber and barrel, preventing the loss of propellant gas.

Arguments have always raged about the value of this complication; there is no doubt that the gas is sealed, but the improvement in performance is generally considered not to be worth the effort. Comparison between otherwise-identical gas-sealing systems and conventional revolvers is clearly impossible, but it has been calculated that the difference in velocity might be in the order of 70 ft/sec. The muzzle velocity of the 7.62mm Soviet revolver cartridge is 1000 ft/sec with a 108-grain bullet, giving a muzzle energy of 240 ft/lb. Reducing the velocity by 70 ft/sec reduces the energy to 208 ft/lb, but, as 60 ft/lb is widely accepted as a minimum "knock-down" figure, the difference in performance does not seem to justify the additional mechanical complication. However, TOZ-36 target revolvers have been made on the basic Nagant action, which may give better accuracy as a result of consistent ballistics.

An 8mm-caliber Taisho 14th Year Type pistol, with the enlarged trigger guard adopted in 1940.

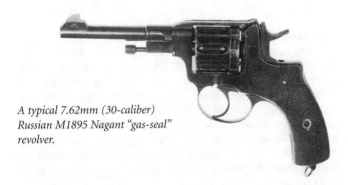

A typical 7.62mm (30-caliber) Russian M1895 Nagant "gas-seal" revolver.

- **M1895** The Nagant brothers had cooperated in the development of the Mosin-Nagant infantry rifle, and, doubtless owing to this connection, the Russians were persuaded to adopt the gas-seal revolver. The first 20,000 guns were made in Liége, but production was subsequently undertaken in Tula (q.v.). Gas-seal revolvers are also said to have seen military service in Greece and Romania, but details are lacking. Guns were also made for commercial sale in 7.62mm and 7.5mm chamberings, the latter being used with standard short-case ammunition that invalidated the gas-seal feature. The 1895-type revolver-manufacturing machinery was sold to the Polish arsenal at Radom in 1929, where the "Ng30" was made until production of the Radom automatic pistol commenced.
- **M1910** This was an improved version of the original gas-seal design developed by the sons of Léon Nagant (who had died in 1900). The lockwork was simplified, and the cylinder, mounted on a yoke, swung out of the right side of the frame. This feature — shared with the French M1892 Modèle d'Ordonnance — was intended to allow a horseman to reload while holding the reins with his left hand.

   The M1910 is said to have been developed for trials in Greece, but the advent of the Second Balkan War in 1912 stopped progress and the genuine Nagant-made guns are rarely encountered. The German invasion of Belgium in 1914 stopped work altogether, though not before copies had been made by a Liége-based gunmaker named Grah. These have cylinders that swing to the left.

NAGOYA ARMS FACTORY

Nagoya Army Arsenal, Atsuta and Toriimatsu (Kasugai) Factories, Japan.

Handguns were made in two different factories in the Nagoya area from individual components supplied from several others. The production history is difficult to summarize, but additional information can be found in Harry Derby's book, *The Hand Cannons of Imperial Japan*.

Taisho 14th Year Type Though the Nambu pistol (see "Koishikawa") had achieved official recognition, it had proved to be too expensive to be purchased in quantity and was not being bought by officers in sufficient numbers. Kijiro Nambu began re-designing the pistol in 1916, seeking to simplify construction and reduce costs. By 1924, however, he was superintendent of the army arsenal in Tokyo and carried the rank of lieutenant general. At this point, Nambu retired

from the army to pursue commercial interests, and it is assumed that the final design of the new pistol was entrusted to the arsenal staff.

The changes included providing dual recoil springs, one on each side of the bolt; replacing the grip safety with a manual catch; fitting a magazine safety; simplifying the sights and creating a slimmer butt with horizontally-grooved wooden grips. These and a variety of minor changes reduced the production cost and the army duly approved the design for issue to NCOs and purchase by officers. The modified Nambu was officially adopted in 1925, the 14th year of the Taisho Era.

Experience was to show that the 14th Year Type had some very poor features. The safety lever was awkwardly placed, but far worse was the absence of a mechanical hold-open — an empty magazine was exceptionally difficult to withdraw from the butt — and an inherent weakness in the firing pin, which was solved initially by simply issuing spare strikers to be carried in the holster.

The changes that were made to the guns were too little and too late. The trigger guard was enlarged in 1940 to allow use with a gloved hand, a change that had been suggested by experience in Manchuria, and an additional magazine-retaining spring was inserted in the lower front grip-strap in 1940. The firing pin and its guide were redesigned late in 1941.

Production began in the Atsuta factory of Nagoya arsenal in November 1926 and in the rebuilt Tokyo (Koishikawa) arsenal in May 1928. The Tokyo machinery was moved to Kokura Arsenal (q.v.) in 1931 but moved again in 1936 to the Kokubunji factory of the Nambu Rifle Manufacturing Company. Tokyo continued to make parts until 1935, but these were sent to Kokura to be assembled.

Only a few thousand pistols were assembled in Nagoya-Atsuta, but in late 1941, a new production line was created in the Toriimatsu factory of Nagoya Arsenal. Work continued there until August 1945 with output amounting to 125,000-130,000 guns.

The 14th Year Type pistols displayed the designation on the rear left side of the frame, in ideographs that read "Ku-yon nen shiki", and had a serial number prefixed by the manufacturer's mark in a panel in the frame behind the right-side grip. The 100,000-gun number blocks were prefixed with a kana character and accompanied by an acceptance date taking the form of "15.10" — the 10th month of the 15th year of the Showa reign-period, October 1940.

NAMBU

Nambu-Seisakusho Kabushiki Kaisha/Chuo Kogyo Kabushiki Kaisha, Tokyo.

The Nambu Rifle Mfg. Co., created by Kijiro Nambu after his retirement from the Japanese army in December 1924, eventually managed to become the sole source of 14th Year Type pistols after the machinery from Kokura arsenal had been installed in the Kokubunji district of Tokyo in the autumn of 1935. On December 1, 1936, however, Nambu was amalgamated with two other engineering businesses to create Chuo Kogyo KK, though the Nambu trademark used on firearms remained unchanged. Operations were re-established in 1949 as "Shin Chuo Kogyo" (q.v.).

Taisho 14th Year Type The first guns were apparently accepted in December 1935 with work continuing—increasingly restricted after 1942 by work on the Type 94—until August 1944. Total production has been estimated at 110,000-115,000.

The 8mm Type 94 pistol, among the poorest designs ever to be adopted for military service.

Type 94 pistol This was developed by Nambu and his associates in 1929, but the design was subsequently changed and re-changed so many times in response to requests from the army ordnance office that comparatively few of the original ideas remained by the mid-1930s. The goal had been to develop a cheaper alternative to the 14th Year Type pistol, but the result proved to be difficult and far more expensive to make.

The designation reflected a change in Japanese nomenclature, which, instead of the traditional reign-period (*neng?*) basis, reverted in 1930 to a simpler system reckoned from the mythical foundation of Japan in 660 BC; 1934, therefore, was "Year 2594".

The Type 94 chambered the standard 8mm Nambu cartridge and was locked by a vertically moving block that held the slide and barrel together until cammed out of engagement during a short recoil stroke. A sturdy hammer firing mechanism replaced the objectionable striker of the 14th year Type, but the sear was exposed on the left side of the frame and could be jarred out of engagement if a cocked pistol was carelessly handled. Moreover, faulty design allowed the possibility of Type 94 pistols firing before the breech was properly locked. Good-quality constructional materials were used in the earliest guns, and the finish was also satisfactory. As the war ran its course, however, manufacturing standards rapidly deteriorated even though the basic design remained constant.

Type 94 pistols were made exclusively in the Chuo Kogyo factory until the end of World War II. It has been estimated that about 70,000 were made. They had distinctive slab-sided receivers and a slender grip for use with a gloved hand, which also restricted the capacity of the magazine to six rounds. Popular with Japanese tank, vehicle and aircraft crews, owing to their compact dimensions, the guns bore the designation on the left side of the frame above the trigger and had the serial number, date and acceptance marks on the rear right side.

NATIONAL ARMS COMPANY
Brooklyn, New York, USA.
A successor to the Moore Patent Firearms Company (q.v.), this gunmaking business continued to make Moore teat-fire revolvers and Moore derringers until purchased by Colt (q.v.) in 1870. Colt continued production of the derringers for some time, but closed the Brooklyn factory and moved work to the Colt Armory in Hartford, Connecticut. It has been claimed that the National operations were purchased simply because Moore and his successors had represented the only serious competition to Smith & Wesson during the life of the White patent, producing something over 30,000 revolvers, and Colt wanted a clear field when the patent expired.

NAVY ARMS CO.
Ridgefield, New Jersey, USA.
This gunmaking business was best known as an importer of firearms made in Italy, particularly from Pietta and Uberti, but now maintains manufacturing facilities (known as "Replica Arms") in the USA. The founder of Navy Arms, the late Val Forgett, has been credited with almost single-handedly revitalizing the revolver-making business in and around Gardone Val Trompia, driven by the demand that has been created in the USA. Navy Arms continues to publish fascinating catalogs of Western firearms and accessories and has marketed a variety of handguns.

∼ REVOLVERS ∼

Colt type These have included a range based on the Peacemaker, including metallic-cartridge conversions of the *1851 Navy*, *1860 Army* and *1861 Navy* caplock revolvers, all introduced in 1999, and the 1873-pattern *Single Action Army*, *Cavalry* and *Artillery* patterns dating from 1991. The P*inched Frame* model, dating from 1997, replicates the original Colt revolvers that had rear sights created by pinching the metal of the topstrap upward to form a "U" notch. The *Flat Top Model* (1997) has an adjustable rear sight, and the *Bisley* patterns — standard and Flat Top (1997-8) — re-create the characteristically humped frame and high-set grip. The *Shootist Model* of 1999 is another version of the Peacemaker.

Smith & Wesson type A modern version of the 45-caliber *Model 1875*, or "S&W Schofield" announced in 1994, has been offered in "Hide-Out", "Wells Fargo", "US Cavalry" and "Deluxe" guise. These were joined in 1999 by a *New Model Russian* revolver, rarely seen amongst modern replicas.

The Mamba pistol, designed and produced in South Africa, was to be distributed in the USA by Navy Arms.

∼ AUTOMATIC PISTOLS ∼

Mamba The Mamba was a double-action stainless steel 9mm Parabellum pistol developed in South Africa in the early 1970s, incorporating a variant of the Colt-Browning mechanism embodying a cam to drop the rear end of the barrel. A handful was made (probably by the Sandcock-Austral Company) for submission to the South African Defence Force, but the guns were too unreliable to be acceptable. Plans to make them commercially in South Africa, with the expectation of sales to the USA through Navy Arms also miscarried. Navy Arms then acquired the rights, intending to make blued carbon or stainless steel Mamba pistols in the USA. Unfortunately, teething troubles with the design were so serious that the entire project was abandoned in 1983.

NEUMANN
Neumann Frères, Liége, Belgium.
Lincoln This name was very popular among Belgian gunmakers in 1880-1914. Most of the guns were folding-trigger pocket revolvers, hammer and "hammerless" alike, chambering cartridges ranging from 22 Short RF and 5.5mm Velo-Dog to 380 CF. Ancion Marx, Bertrand, Debouxtay, Dumoulin, Jannsen Fils et Cie, Le Page and Raick Frères, all of Liége, and Albrecht Kind of Germany have all been identified with "Lincoln" markings. Most of the guns seem to have emanated from Manufacture Liégeoise d'Armes à Feu.

NEW ENGLAND FIREARMS CO.

Gardner, Massachusetts, USA.

This was formed from the remnants of Harrington & Richardson (q.v.) and is best known for sporting rifles and shotguns built on the proven break-open action. The company has also offered simple solid-frame revolvers under the names *Standard* (1988), *Ultra* (1989) and *Lady Ultra* (1992).

The 7.65mm German Nordheim pistol.

NORDHEIM

Gotthilf von Nordheim, Zella Mehlis, Germany.

Nordheim made a 7.65mm blowback automatic in the late 1920s, though new guns were probably still being sold as late as 1933. The design was inspired by the 1910-model FN-Browning, with a return spring that was concentric with the barrel and a screwed-in bush at the muzzle to restrain the spring. The bush is much larger than the Belgian prototype, has prominent ribs and projects some distance from the slide. The barrel protrudes nearly half an inch from the bush. The slide is marked "*DEUTSCHE SELBSTLADE PISTOLE*" over "*CAL 7,65 ZUM PATENT ANGEM.*" and the grips may bear a "GvN" monogram.

NORTH AMERICAN ARMS CO. LTD

Quebec, Canada.

This company, occupying the factory of the moribund Ross Rifle Company, obtained a contract to manufacture the 45-caliber Colt M1911 for the US Army in 1918. The production line was created, but no guns had been made when World War I ended. After the Armistice, about a hundred pistols were assembled from a variety of parts. However, the project was abruptly terminated and the Canadian-made M1911 is among the most desirable of Colt-Brownings. The slide is marked with the company name on the left side.

NORTH AMERICA ARMS CORPORATION ("NAACo")

Toronto, Canada.

This had no connection with the 1918 predecessor and operated for a short period between 1957 and 1962, making a few bolt-action rifles and some single-barrel shotguns.

Brigadier Designed by Robert Herman, this was simply a somewhat enlarged version of the Browning GP35 designed around a new and

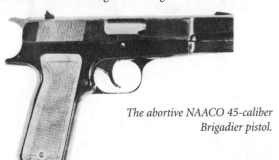

The abortive NAACO 45-caliber Brigadier pistol.

powerful 45-caliber cartridge also developed by the company. This, the 45 NAACO, was based on a cut-down 30-06 rifle cartridge case carrying a standard 45 ACP bullet; it developed a muzzle velocity of 1600 ft/sec and a muzzle energy of 1307 ft/lb. The pistol used an alloy frame and had the trigger and its mechanism in a removable module that also carried the hardened-steel grooves in which the slide could run back. In spite of the alloy frame, the pistol weighed 4.25 lb; it had a 5-inch barrel and an eight-round magazine and must have been a handful to shoot.

Only a single prototype was made, initially without a number though "195901" (a combination of its number, "1", and the date) was subsequently added to the barrel and slide. It was intended that the trigger module could be replaced by another unit that incorporated a selective-fire mechanism. A 20-shot magazine and butt-stock could be fitted, the stock also carrying a perforated barrel guard, which fit over the slide of the pistol when the whole thing was assembled. This produced a species of submachine gun known as the Borealis. However, this combination was never actually made, existing only as an artist's impression. NAACo hoped that the Brigadier and the Borealis would be adopted by the Canadian army, but the project died in 1960.

NORTH AMERICAN ARMS COMPANY

Spanish Fork and Provo, Utah, USA.

This company makes a "Mini-Revolver" that could be considered the modern equivalent of the solid-frame sheathed-trigger non-ejectors of the 1880s, though quality is exemplary and the material is flawless.

A typical North American Arms Mini-Revolver, in 22 Magnum rimfire.

The North American Arms Black Widow (22 LR) and Mini-Master (22 Magnum rimfire) are "mini-revolvers" with oversize grips, ventilated barrel ribs and prominent sights.

The Mini-Revolver can be fired without removing it from its leather holster.

Mini-Revolver This single-action non-ejector is made from stainless steel and beautifully finished. It carries an inertial firing pin, and the cylinders have intermediate safety notches between the chambers, allowing it to be carried with all five chambers full but none aligned with the hammer. Manufacture began in 1974 with a 22 Short RF version, followed in 1976 with a 22 LR model. Later, a 22 WMRF version was added.

- *Black Widow* Similar to the Mini-Master, this has a heavy 2-inch barrel, a plain cylinder and rubber grips. Fixed or adjustable Millett low-profile sights are standard.
- *Mini* Currently offered in 22 Short, 22 LR and 22 Magnum rimfire, this five-shot gun has a 1.1- or 1.6-inch barrel. Weight is only about 4 oz with the short barrel, overall length being a mere 3.65 inches. The guns are made entirely of stainless steel (polished or matte finish) and have laminated wooden grips.
- *Mini-Master* Introduced in 1989, this has a 4-inch ventilated-rib barrel, giving a length of 7.8 inches and an empty weight of about 10-11 oz. The five-chamber cylinders accept 22 LR or 22 WMR rimfire ammunition. The grips are "oversize" black rubber, the cylinder has a plain surface and the rear sight may be adjustable.

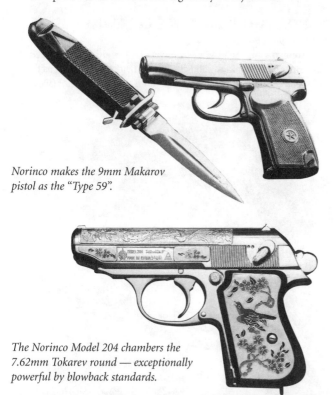

Norinco makes the 9mm Makarov pistol as the "Type 59".

The Norinco Model 204 chambers the 7.62mm Tokarev round — exceptionally powerful by blowback standards.

NORTH CHINA INDUSTRIES CORP. ("NORINCO")

Beijing, People's Republic of China.

Created in the late 1960s, this engineering combine still makes some of the guns described under "Chinese State Factories".

Type 77 This blowback is a remarkable copy of the 1930s Lignose "Einhand" pistol. The reverse-curved front of the trigger guard is linked to the slide so that curling the forefinger around the guard and pulling backward draws the slide back to cock the pistol. Releasing the finger allows the slide to close, chambering a round, and the finger can then be placed inside the trigger-guard ready to fire. (On firing, of course, the front end of the trigger guard remains static.) The fluted chamber reduces the gas pressure acting on the base of the case by leaking a proportion of gas past the case wall, easing extraction. The cartridge fired is the same rimless 7.62mm Type 64 as used by the Chinese State Factories silenced pistols.

The Chinese Type 77 pistol, chambered for the 9mm Makarov round, has a one-hand cocking system.

Cocking the Type 77.

The Type 77S is a larger and more powerful version of the Type 77, but it retains the one-hand cocking feature.

Type 80 Another oddity, this is a reincarnation of the Mauser Schnellfeuerpistole of the 1930s, though with some modernization. It remains basically Mauser in outline, with the magazine ahead of the trigger and the same lug-locked Mauser bolt acting in the barrel extension. But the detachable box magazine is canted forward, perhaps to improve the reliability of the feed, and the squared-off butt is much more modern than the original Mauser design. A clip-on telescoping stock and even a bayonet can be provided to order. The cartridge is the standard 7.62mm Type 51 and the manufacturers claim accuracy to 150 yards with the stock fitted.

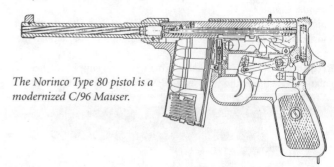

The Norinco Type 80 pistol is a modernized C/96 Mauser.

M1911A1 series These are straightforward copies of the Colt-Browning of the same designation, differing only in a few very minor details, and have formed the basis for many customizations. They can usually be identified by the slide marks, which read, for example, "MODEL OF THE 1911 [logo] 45 AUTOMATIC" on the left side of the slide, or, on the "Compact" patterns, "1911A1 C 45 ACP"; "MADE IN CHINA BY NORINCO" may appear in a single line on the left side of the frame.

NORTH KOREAN ARMS FACTORIES

The North Korean People's Army carries two pistols made in the state-owned arsenal.

Type 64 This is none other than the FN-Browning "Old Model" of 1900 resurrected for production in North Korea. Making of spurious Brownings has long been a cottage industry in China and Manchuria, and the NKPA has probably done little more than to organize this tradition. The guns are stamped "7,62" but are chambered for the 7.65mm Auto (32 ACP) cartridge. A variant with a short slide and an elongated barrel has its muzzle threaded to receive a silencer.

Type 68 A locally-made version of the Soviet 7.62mm Tokarev TT-33, this has a shortened slide and barrel that, together with the deeper slide, gives the gun a stocky appearance. The swinging link has become a fixed cam, and the magazine catch has been moved to the heel of the butt. The finger grooves are diagonal instead of vertical and the chamber accepts standard Soviet-block pistol cartridges.

NORTON

Norton Armament Company, Mount Clemens, Michigan, USA.

Mini-Revolver A name applied to a very small 22 Short pocket revolver with a sheathed trigger and a solid frame.

Budischowsky This was a small double-action automatic pistol offered in 22 LR rimfire or 25 ACP. It was made of stainless steel. Marketed in the USA in 1973-7, it was little other than the Korriphila (q.v.) TP-70 pistol of German origin.

NORWICH FALLS PISTOL COMPANY

Norwich, Connecticut, USA.

Formed by Maltby, Curtis & Co. in 1883, this gunmaking business succeeded the Norwich Pistol Co. (q.v.). Production finally ended in 1887 with the failing fortunes of the promoter, but the creation in 1889 of Maltby, Henley & Co. suggests that stocks of parts, pistols and machinery may have been used by this new company to continue production for a short period. Unfortunately, records no longer exist to show just what the various organizations made and sold, or what names were used on pistols at what times. The whole question of the inter-relationship of the companies and the pistols produced is involved, debatable and one which offers considerable scope for research. Many of the revolvers made by the original Norwich Pistol Company were perpetuated by its successor, complicating accurate dating.

America This was a 32 Long RF revolver manufactured about 1883-5. It had a solid frame, a seven-chamber cylinder, double-action lockwork and a 3-inch barrel. The design was patented by William Bliss in 1878.

Chieftain A solid-frame 32 rimfire revolver with a sheathed trigger, this also had a five-chamber cylinder and a 2.3- or 2.7-inch octagonal barrel. The grip may be a saw-handle type or conventionally squared. It was made for sale by Maltby, Curtis & Co. in the mid-1880s.

Challenge A 32 rimfire five-shot single-action design with a solid frame and a sheathed trigger, this was another of the guns manufactured to the 1878 Bliss patent.

Crescent See "Norwich Pistol Co."

Defiance Another of the usual 22-caliber rimfire solid-frame guns with a sheathed trigger and a bird's-head grip, this dated from 1878-88.

Gypsy This was a 22 rimfire solid-frame sheath-trigger revolver, typical of the 1870s. The general details, particularly the cover-plate over the lockwork, suggests that it was made by the Norwich Falls company.

Hartford, Hartford Arms Co. Revolvers marked with this name were made in the 1878-90 period. They represented the usual type of

32 rimfire solid-frame non-ejector with a sheathed trigger, a five-chamber cylinder and a saw-handle butt.

Maltby & Henley 32 rimfire revolvers made for sale by the parent of the Norwich gunmaking business, probably assembled elsewhere after business had collapsed.

NORWICH PISTOL COMPANY

Norwich, Connecticut, USA.

The company that produced such a fearful roster of inexpensive revolvers, and, moreover, did it in a matter of a few years, was set up in 1875 in Norwich, Connecticut, by the New York sporting-goods company Maltby, Curtis & Co., to make firearms, roller-skates, tools and other artifacts to be sold by Maltby, Curtis and their associated dealers across the USA. It appears to have operated entirely separately from its parent, so much so that in 1881 it went bankrupt. Maltby, anxious not to lose the source of supply, bought the remains of the company and re-christened it the "Norwich Falls Pistol Co." (q.v.). Several of the guns being made by the original business were perpetuated by the Norwich Falls Pistol Co.

∼ REVOLVERS ∼

Basic or "Norwich" pattern This was made under a variety of names, disguising the usual solid-frame non-ejecting design with a sheathed trigger. One common feature is that they are almost always marked "April 23 1878", referring to a patent granted to William H. Bliss, superintendent of the manufactory. Chamberings ranged from 22 to 44, almost always rimfire prior to 1881. Some of the guns were subsequently perpetuated by the Norwich Falls Pistol Company (see preceding entry).

- *Challenge* A 32 rimfire five-shot single-action design.
- *Crescent* Assumed to have been made for the Crescent Arms Company, best known for inexpensive shotguns, these had five- or six-chamber cylinders (plain or fluted) and a 2.5-inch octagonal barrel. The butt was rounded with walnut or ivory grips.
- *Defiance* A 22-caliber rimfire gun. Identity of brand name owner unknown.
- *Excelsior* A 32 rimfire five-shot gun.
- *Hartford Arms* These were made for either the Simmons Hardware or the Shapleigh Hardware Company (or perhaps both) of St Louis, Missouri.
- *Metropolitan Police* This was a 32 rimfire gun, sometimes marked by Maltby, Curtis & Co. It is believed to have been supplied to distributors Siegel & Cooper of New York.
- *Nonpareil* Presumably made for a distributor, as yet unidentified.
- *Parole* A distributor's brand name. See "Nonpareil".
- *Patriot* A distributor's brand name. See "Nonpareil".
- *Penetrator* A distributor's brand name. See "Nonpareil".
- *Pinafore* A distributor's brand name. See "Nonpareil".
- *Prairie King* A distributor's brand name. See "Nonpareil".
- *Protector* A distributor's brand name. See "Nonpareil".
- *Spy* A distributor's brand name. See "Nonpareil".
- *True Blue* A distributor's brand name. See "Nonpareil".
- *U.M.C.* Whether this gun exists has been debated, as the suggestion has been made that the "Model name" has been confused with the identity of the ammunition maker, the Union Metallic Cartridge Company. Alternatively, UMC may have bought revolvers to help advertise their products.
- *Winfield Arms* A brand name applied to guns distributed by H. & D. Folsom of New York City.

Bull Dozer Sold by J. McBride & Co. in 1875-83, this was a 22, 38, 41 or 44 rimfire revolver with a solid frame and a sheathed trigger. The cylinders held seven 22 rounds or five of the others. Unlike most Norwich Pistol Company products, the Bull Dozer does not acknowledge the 1878 Bliss patent.

OESTERREICHISCHE WAFFENFABRIKS-GESELLSCHAFT ("OEWG")

Steyr, Austria. Subsequently Steyr-Werke AG; Steyr-Daimler-Puch AG; and Steyr-Mannlicher GmbH.

This company was created in 1863 by Josef Werndl to convert muzzle-loading military rifles into breech-loaders. In 1869, it was established as a joint-stock company; after World War I it became Steyr-Werke AG and diversified into automobile and general engineering. In 1934, it absorbed the Austro-Daimler and Puch companies to become Steyr-Daimler-Puch, and during the 1930s, it became part of the Rheinmetall-Solothurn axis, acting as the production facility for weapons designed by Rheinmetall and engineered by Solothurn. A sales organization, Steyr-Solothurn AG, was set up in Zurich to market military arms produced by this consortium. At one stage, it is reported, Rheinmetall owned a substantial part of Steyr, and when Austria was occupied in 1938, Steyr consequently became part of the Reichwerke Hermann Goering. After World War II, the company produced farm machinery and motorcycles, and firearms manufacture was resumed in the 1950s.

Steyr's involvement with pistols appears to have begun while making various experimental weapons for Krnka, Roth and other Austro-Hungarian inventors in 1885-95 before progressing to better things.

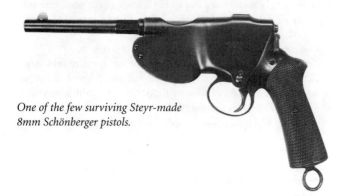

One of the few surviving Steyr-made 8mm Schönberger pistols.

Schönberger This is generally accepted as being the first practical automatic pistol to be offered commercially, though only a handful was ever made. The basic design originated with Josef Laumann, a Viennese gunmaker, who, in 1890, patented a repeating pistol with a reciprocating bolt operated by a finger-ring. Pushing the ring forward opened the bolt; pulling it back drove the bolt forward, stripping a 7.7mm cartridge into the chamber from the Mannlicher-type clip magazine. As the ring reached the end of its stroke, it enveloped a trigger protruding from the butt until the trigger was tripped and the gun fired. A duplicated cocking lever on the frame-side allowed the breech to be opened for loading.

A few of these manually-operated Laumann pistols were made, but in November 1891, the inventor submitted a new patent claiming automatic operation. Shortly afterward, guns of the new pattern appeared with the Steyr name and "Schönberger". Study of Laumann's US patents reveals that he had assigned his second repeater and automatic-pistol patents to the "Gebruder Schönberger" of Vienna. Thereafter, Laumann appears to have taken no part in the production of his design.

For several years, it was believed that the Schonberger was a locked breech design operated by primer set-back, an opinion that originated with R.K. Wilson in *A Textbook of Automatic Pistols* (1943). However, this claim appears to have been based on a misleading description in the official British *Abridgements of Patents ...*, which, in turn, was derived from Laumann's Provisional Specification. But the Final Specification reveals that the pistol was nothing other than a delayed blowback.

The bolt carried a swivel link that was pressed into a recess in the receiver by the forward movement of the firing pin. When the gun fired and the bolt tried to move backward, the link was forced from its recess to engage a spring-loaded forked arm that pivoted in the receiver. This restrained the movement of the bolt until the link lifted free of its recess and the resistance offered by the forked arm and its spring had been overcome. Careful design of the arm ensured that resistance was at its greatest during the initial opening of the bolt, and, conversely, the closing pressure was greatest as the new round was entering the chamber from the clip-loaded magazine ahead of the trigger guard. A single cocking lever, on the right side of the frame, allowed the action to be opened for loading.

The cartridge was a rimmed and necked 8mm round, customarily identified as the "8mm Kromar", which was no surprise, as both guns were made by Oesterreichische Waffenfabriks-Gesellschaft. However, specimens of this cartridge have also been cycled through a Schönberger pistol action without difficulty.

A handful of Schönberger pistols were made in the Steyr factory, clearly marked "WAFFENFABRIK" over "STEYR" on the left side of the frame, but the date is disputed. Customarily listed as "1892-3", which would number the guns among the earliest practicable self-loaders, it seems more likely that they were made for military trials, c. 1895.

Mannlicher The original 1894 blow-forward model made by Schweizerische Industrie-Gesellschaft (q.v.), though an interesting design, was far from perfect. Trials soon revealed the undesirability of the operating system, and Mannlicher moved to other things. The success of his rifles ensured that the Steyr factory was keen to be involved.

This Mannlicher pistol, a forerunner of the so-called M1901, was tested in Switzerland in 1898-9.

Drawings of the 1900-type Mannlicher.

- *M1896* This was a fixed-barrel blowback, with a bolt that reciprocated within the receiver. A charger-loaded six-round box magazine was placed above the front of the trigger guard, and the lockwork was designed to be thumb-cocked by a hammer extension that protruded at the rear of the frame. The gun was thus a true "autoloader", but not an "auto-cocker". The hammer itself lay within the receiver, rising into a slot towards the front of the under-surface of the striker to fire the gun. The pistol originally chambered the same 7.6mm rimmed cartridge as the Model 1894, but very few were made. A blowback firing a 115-grain bullet at merely 800 ft/sec was too feeble to arouse military interest, and the gun was far too large to be promoted as a pocket pistol.

- *M1901* A refinement of the 1896 blowback design, this is often considered to be the most elegant automatic pistol ever made. It was patented in 1898 and had appeared in prototype form in the trials that began in Switzerland in May 1899. These may have been made by "Waffenfabrik Neuhausen" (SIG), but others were made by Waffenfabrik von Dreyse (q.v.). Most of the early guns chambered an otherwise unknown rimless straight-taper 8mm cartridge, but this was soon altered to a caliber of 7.63mm. Mannlicher chose not to adopt the existing 7.63mm Mauser round, which was too powerful, and designed a new rimless straight-sided cartridge that fired an 85-grain bullet at about 1025 ft/sec. This created the Model 1901, and series production began in Steyr.

The gun was successful enough to be purchased privately by officers of the Austro-Hungarian army, though the military authorities rejected it officially in 1904-5 largely owing to the lack of a breech-lock. However, the manufacturer had established a sizable export market in South America and the Mannlicher pistol was more common there than in Europe due largely to official adoption in Argentina in 1905.

These Mannlichers had a fixed barrel that screwed into the frame and introduced the "open-topped slide". The slide — a one-piece forging — consisted of a short breechblock behind the barrel, carrying the extractor and the firing pin, with two arms that extended forward to join beneath the barrel. The return spring was located at the rear in a hole beneath the breech and extended forward to anchor on a stud formed inside the front junction of the slide arms. Consequently, any rearward movement of the slide immediately began to compress the spring.

A large hammer in the rear of the frame engaged the trigger by way of a simple linkage on top of the right side of the frame, protected by a removable plate. The "V"-type mainspring lay on the other side of the frame with the lower arm pressing on the hammer and the upper arm resting on a small lever. The tip of the small lever engages in a notch in the underside of the slide. This mechanism is covered by a protective plate that is joined to the left-hand sideplate by a forward-sweeping arm locked beneath the return spring by a spring catch.

When the gun was fired, the slide recoiled and forced the lever in the slot beneath the right side of the slide out of engagement. However, the movement of the lever was resisted by pressure from the mainspring that had to be overcome in addition to the pressure required to compress the return spring beneath the barrel. The slide rotated the hammer back to the cocked position, pressing up the lower limb of the mainspring to give more resistance to the retarding lever. The design of the parts increased the frictional forces opposing the travel of the slide, helping to slow the opening movement of the breech and absorbing some of the energy. The recoil of the Mannlicher was much softer than might be expected from such a lightweight slide.

The slide was returned from the limit of the backward stroke, chambering a fresh round and leaving the hammer cocked for the next shot. The safety catch was a small hinged block at the rear of the slide, which, when pressed down, prevented the hammer reaching the firing pin. The magazine — integral with the butt — was loaded from a charger through the open action. A small catch on the right side of the frame above the grip could be pressed once the slide had been drawn back, allowing the force of the magazine spring to forcibly eject the contents of the magazine.

The semi-experimental nature of the earliest Mannlicher pistols created many minor variations. The first guns had a different safety catch, a large thumb-lever on the left side of the frame that locked the hammer internally, and the leading edge of the front sight was rounded instead of vertical. Guns made in 1900-1 had a rear sight that was little more than a groove on a post forged as part of the standing breech, where it was surrounded by the front edges of the breechblock when the breech was closed. Some time in 1902, the post was superseded by a notch in the rear end of the slide that not only maximized the sight radius but also lowered the sight line. Consequently, the height of the front-sight blade was reduced and its upper surface was sloped much more sharply.

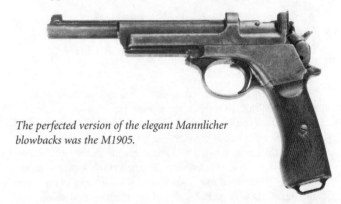

The perfected version of the elegant Mannlicher blowbacks was the M1905.

The normal barrel length was 5.5 inches (140mm), but guns were made with short barrels and short grips. The "pre-production guns" made in 1900-1, perhaps totaling 300, bore "PATENT MANNLICHER" on the left front side slide arm. The marking "WAFFENFABRIK" over "STEYR" appeared on the lock-cover plate on the left side of the frame for the remainder of 1901, but the mark changed in 1902 to become "SYSTEM / MANNLICHER" on the right side of the frame and "Md. 1902 / WAFFENFABRIK / STEYR" in three lines on the left. The year in this designation was altered annually until 1905. The "M1905" was acquired in small numbers by Argentina. These guns have the Argentine Arms in an oval cartouche on the right side of the frame above the grip, and all the markings in five lines on the left.

The 1900-type guns were numbered separately, though all of those made from 1901 onward were numbered in a single cumulative series. It has been estimated that about 12,000 were made.

- *M1903* Patented in 1896 and made in small quantities for trials in Switzerland in October 1898, this was the last Mannlicher pistol to appear commercially. It was a locked-breech design chambered for a special 7.63mm necked rimless cartridge, which shared the dimensions of the Mauser 7.63mm round but was loaded to give merely 1250 ft/sec instead of 1450 ft/sec. This was a short-sighted policy, however, as the Mannlicher action was not strong enough to withstand firing Mauser ammunition regularly, and it would have been better to have chosen either a different cartridge or strengthen the pistol. There is some evidence that a pistol-carbine chambering a long-case cartridge loaded with a 116-grain bullet and possibly capable of developing 2000 ft/sec was produced experimentally. The locking system of the M1903 was robust enough in theory, even though the original gun was found to be lacking in practice.

An experimental 1896/1903-type Mannlicher pistol, submitted to the Swiss trials of 1898.

The 8mm-caliber M1907 or Roth-Steyr pistol, with its holster and an empty charger.

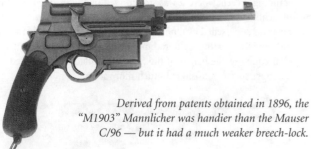

Derived from patents obtained in 1896, the "M1903" Mannlicher was handier than the Mauser C/96 — but it had a much weaker breech-lock.

A Roth-Steyr at full recoil.

The bolt moved in a rectangular barrel extension doubling as the receiver, riding on top of the frame, and a steel-strut bolt lock was attached to the rear of the extension. When the action was closed, the front end of the strut was forced up behind the bolt by a ramp in the frame. When the gun fired, the barrel, the barrel extension and the bolt ran back about 0.2 inch, securely locked together, until the locking strut moved down a supporting ramp in the frame and out of the bolt path. The barrel and the barrel extension were then brought to a halt, allowing the bolt to continue moving backward to compress the return spring.

When the spring reversed the motion, the bolt returned to strip a new round from the box magazine (ahead of the trigger) into the chamber. As the bolt closed, a separate barrel-return spring in front of the magazine pushed the barrel, extension and bolt forward until the ramp raised the head of the locking strut behind the bolt. Pressing the trigger allowed the internal hammer to strike a firing pin contained in the lower section of the bolt. A lever on the right side of the frame could be used to re-cock the mechanism in the event of a misfire, and a safety catch beneath the end of the barrel extension acted directly on the hammer.

The strut-type lock was theoretically strong enough to handle the 7.63mm Mauser cartridge, but the remainder of the pistol was not. The Mannlicher was handier than the C/96 but was much less robust, less reliable and never attained such great popularity. A fully stocked carbine was offered with an 11.8-inch barrel, and the M1903 pistol could be obtained with a holster-stock. These guns were extensively, but unsuccessfully, tested by the Austro-Hungarian army in 1903-5. The carbines were briefly popular as hunting weapons but their low power was a handicap.

It is unlikely that more than 3000 guns were made prior to 1914, and the death of Ferdinand von Mannlicher in 1904 had brought development to an end.

Roth-Steyr Cooperation between Georg Roth (q.v.) and the Steyr factory began in the early 1900s, but the prototype of this particular pistol is said to have been an unsuccessful Theodorovič design of the 1890s that had failed to impress the Austro-Hungarian Militär-Technische-Komité. Success awaited the substitution of a barrel-locking system developed by Karel Krnka (q.v.).

A few Krnka-Roth pistols of the so-called "Modell II" or "M1904" were tested extensively by the Austro-Hungarian authorities throughout 1905, against 7.65mm and other Mannlichers, and performed well enough to encourage field trials to be undertaken in the spring of 1907. An improved pistol chambering a unique 8mm rimless cartridge was adopted on December 5, 1907, to replace the revolvers in the hands of the cavalry and mounted artillery. The original trials guns had an additional lever on the left side of the frame above the grip and were more angular than the perfected version.

The unique operating mechanism was one of the few Krnka-Roth designs to use anything other than long recoil. The most remarkable feature of the M1909 was the bolt, extending for the full length of the receiver. The front part of the bolt was hollowed to surround the barrel, the rear part being solid except for the striker chamber. The bolt fit inside a tubular receiver that was machined as part of the pistol-frame forging.

Cam-grooves inside the hollow section of the bolt received two lugs on the breech-end of the barrel, while two lugs at the barrel muzzle fit into grooves in the muzzle bush. When the pistol fired, the bolt and barrel ran back for about half an inch, securely locked together. As the parts moved backwards, the lugs on the muzzle rotated in the helical grooves cut in the muzzle bush; simultaneously, the helical grooves in the bolt rotated the lugs on the rear of the barrel through 90 degrees. When the initial movement had been completed, the lugs at the muzzle of the barrel stopped against the groove-ends in the muzzle bush and the lugs on the rear of the barrel were aligned with the straight rearward extension of the grooves cut inside the bolt. The barrel was stopped, allowing the bolt to continue backward alone.

The bolt was stopped at the end of its travel by a spring inside the tubular receiver ahead of the magazine, returning to strip a cartridge from the integral magazine in the butt and then lift the cartridge through a slot in the underside of the bolt before ramming it into the chamber. The combination of lugs and the cam-grooves then rotates the barrel back to the locked position and returns it to battery.

The striker mechanism was also unusual. As the bolt ran forward from the limit of its recoil stroke, the striker was held back by the sear; but the striker spring remained under comparatively little compression. Pulling the trigger then forced back the striker to compress the spring before the sear could release the striker to fire the gun. A similar system was embodied in the Roth-Sauer pistol (q.v.). It is said to have been developed as a safety feature for cavalrymen; the conscious effort required to fire the Roth-Steyr would reduce the amount of accidents that occurred if horses became skittish while pistols were being used.

The walnut grips were grooved diagonally, a lanyard loop lay on the base of the butt, the rear sight was formed in the rear edge of the charger guides and the heads of the hold-open catch and cartridge-retaining latch on the left side of the frame were checkered. Service experience revealed the guns would accidentally "double" (fire more than one shot for a single press of the trigger), and a separate disconnector was added in the sear train in 1909 after about 7000 had been made. New-pattern guns had an additional axis pin, visible on the right side of the frame above the grip.

The Roth-Steyr was never marketed commercially. After its official adoption, it was made in Steyr for some years and then additionally at the Fegyvergyar factory in Budapest during World War I. Pistols were marked "WAFFENFABRIK STEYR" or "FEGYVERGYÁR BUDAPEST" on the top surface of the barrel casing and also displayed acceptance marks such as "W-n [eagle] 11" on the back of the frames. Many had a brass disc let into the right grip to receive unit markings. About 90,000 were made and some were still being used by the Italian army (which had obtained them in 1919 as war reparations) as late as 1941.

The 7.65mm Pieper pistol was made in the Steyr factory as the M1909.

M1909 This was purely a commercial pistol and was built to the patents of Nicolas Pieper (q.v.) of Liége. They were tip-down barrel blowback automatics in both 6.35mm and 7.65mm caliber, and the differences between the Steyr weapons and those of Pieper are very minor. Manufacture of these pistols was suspended in 1914, resumed in 1921 and continued until 1939.

M1911 ("Repetierpistole M12") This pistol, which can be seen as an improved form of the Krnka-Roth and Roth-Steyr, was developed in the Steyr factory as a commercial venture. The venture is usually credited to Karl Murgthaler, assisted by Helmut Bachner and Adolf Jungmayr. Patents were sought in 1911-12, but work is believed to have started in 1910.

The gun had a conventional full-length slide protecting the barrel. Two lugs on the top of the barrel engaged recesses in the slide, and a helical lug beneath the barrel engaged a groove in the frame. When the gun was fired, the slide and the barrel moved backward, securely locked together, until the helical lug had been drawn back far enough to rotate the barrel about 20 degrees to disengage the locking lugs from the slide recesses. As this happened, the barrel was brought to a stop when its fourth lug struck a transom in the frame. The slide continued back alone, extracting the empty case, cocking the external hammer and returning to strip a new cartridge from the magazine. The barrel and the slide then moved forward until the helical lug had rotated the lock-

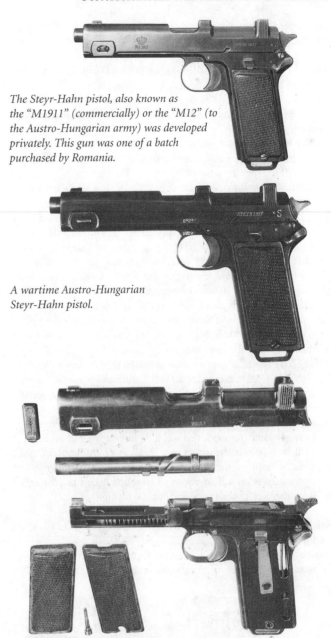

The Steyr-Hahn pistol, also known as the "M1911" (commercially) or the "M12" (to the Austro-Hungarian army) was developed privately. This gun was one of a batch purchased by Romania.

A wartime Austro-Hungarian Steyr-Hahn pistol.

The Steyr-Hahn pistol dismantled into its principal components. Note the cams and locking lugs on the barrel.

ing lugs back into engagement with the slide, and the moving parts had returned to battery.

The magazine, integral with the butt, was loaded by pulling back the slide to open the action, inserting a charger and forcing the cartridges downward with the thumb. A quick-release catch allowed the contents of the magazine to be ejected through the open action.

The pistols were chambered for the powerful 9mm Steyr round, which fired a 115-grain bullet with a muzzle velocity of 1115 ft/sec. The cartridge was similar dimensionally to the Bergmann-Bayard, but the bullet was usually steel-jacketed and had more of a point than other 9mm designs.

The original semi-experimental M1910 is rarely seen, but it can be identified by the prominent "flats" surrounding the transverse wedge through the slide beneath the muzzle. The 1911-pattern guns have much smaller flats with rounded corners, and the so-called "M1912" has a differently shaped wedge and a front sight that is formed as a separate component instead of integral with the slide forging. The M1911 was adopted by the Chilean army as the "M1911" and the M1912 by the Romanian army in 1913. Chilean guns have "EJÉRCITO DE CHILE" on the right side of the slide and the national Arms on the left; Romanian guns have a large crown above "Md. 1912" on the left side of the slide. Both types can be found with additional Austro-Hungarian marks, indicating that they were seized before delivery. Guns used in Poland after the end of World War I may be found with additional single-headed eagle markings.

The 1911-type pistol was also offered commercially prior to World War I, though sales were presumably restricted and comparatively few guns of this type are now to be found. They are usually marked "*OESTERR. WAFFENFABRIK STEYR. M. 1911. 9 ᵐ/ₘ 12.*", in a single line on the left side of the slide and have commercial proofmarks. When the fighting began, the Austro-Hungarian authorities pressed the "Repetierpistole M 12" into emergency service on a grand scale. Service pistols were usually marked "STEYR", the date, and a large "S" on the rear left side of the slide, with acceptance marks — e.g., "W-n [eagle] 15" — on the left side of the trigger-guard bow. Serial numbers took the form of blocks of 10,000, distinguished by suffix letters.

The Bavarian army also purchased M12 pistols to alleviate temporary shortages of Parabellums. Ten thousand were acquired in April 1916 and another 6000 in March 1918, but small-scale deliveries were still being made at the end of the war.

The M12 was reliable and robust and, after the German annexation of Austria in 1938, continued to serve the army and police. Many were rebarreled for the 9mm Parabellum cartridge and bear a large "08" mark on the left side of the frame.

- *Repetierpistole M12/16* Issued during the First World War in surprisingly large numbers, this was little more than a standard M12 with alterations in the trigger system to allow continuous fire and a radial selector on the right side of the frame above the grip. The perfected version had an elongated 16-round magazine protruding from the butt. Cyclic rate was about 800 rds/min.

OESTERREICHISCHE WERKE ANSTALT ("ÖWA")

Vienna, Austria.

The demilitarized rump of the Austro-Hungarian arsenal in Wiener-Neustadt, this engineering business made handguns in the early 1920s.

The 6.35mm (25 ACP) ÖWA pistol.

ÖWA Patented in 1920 in the name of the "Staatliche Industriewerke", this 6.35mm pistol bears an external resemblance to the Pieper/Steyr drop-barrel design, although the barrel is fixed and the constructional details are different. The slide is pivoted at the front of the frame and can be released by a large catch at the rear end. The part of the slide behind the barrel is cut away to receive a separate reciprocating breechblock that is slotted to pass around an abutment at the end of the frame (to which the slide catch locks). The return spring lies above the breechblock. A hammer in the frame comes up through the slotted portion of the block to strike the firing pin, and a sliding safety catch on the left side can be applied to lock the hammer.

The original version of the ÖWA had stepped breechblock grips and a straight frame shoulder above the trigger guard; later guns had squared grips and a noticeable curve in the frame above the guard. A typical gun was marked "CAL 6.³⁵ ARSENAL VIENNA AUSTRIA" on the upper left side of the slide above "PAT. I.A. KULTURSTAATEN" ("Patented in all civilized nations"), though the earliest examples were marked "PATENT ANGEMELDET" ("Patent being sought"). The grips display "ÖWA", though the later guns have the umlaut (the two dots above "O") *inside* the letter instead of above it. "Made in Austria" will be found on guns that were intended for export, particularly to the USA.

OJANGUREN Y MARCAIDO

Eibar, Spain.

Records of this company are few, but it appears to have been formed in the 1890s for the manufacture of "Velo-Dog" revolvers. This continued to the World War I period when manufacture changed to more modern styles of revolvers based on Smith & Wesson designs. The company continued to operate through the 1920s but disappeared in the early 1930s, a victim of the economic depression.

Brow This was a "hammerless" solid-frame five-shot Velo-Dog revolver, usually with a folding trigger though sometimes found with a conventional trigger and trigger guard. Fitted with a loading gate and a rod ejector, it was introduced between 1905 and 1910 in 6.35mm Auto, 7.65mm Auto and 9mm Short chamberings. It can be identified by the word "Brow" on the barrel and an "OM" monogram in a circle on the frame.

Cilindro Ladeable A 32-caliber revolver dating from the 1930s, this was a copy of the Smith & Wesson Military & Police model. It can be identified by "CAL 32 LARGO" on the barrel and the "OM" monogram on the grips. It also carries a near-copy of the Smith & Wesson monogram on the left side of the frame, surrounded by the words "TRADE" and "MARK".

El Blanco Dating from the 1920s and based on the Colt Police Positive, this was a 22 rimfire six-shot revolver with a solid frame and a yoke-mounted cylinder. "El Blanco Model de Tiro" was similar but larger, in 38-caliber. Both guns offered good quality and were fitted with adjustable sights.

Militar y Policia A 38-caliber copy of the S&W Military & Police model, dating from 1925-35, this can be identified by the "OM" monogram on frame and butt.

OM Revolvers of this type were made during and after World War I. They were copied from the S&W Military & Police model, differing only in chamberings that ran from 22 LR rimfire to 38 Special. All are marked with the "OM" monogram on the frame.

Puppy Popular among makers of Velo-Dog and similar revolvers in Spain, this name was also used by Arizmendi, Crucelegui, Gaztañaga and Retolaza. The Ojanguren & Marcaido version is the same as the "Brow", but has a six-chamber cylinder chambered for the 22 Short rimfire round.

Velo-Mith The name "Velo-Mith" was used generically to identify a six-shot hinged-frame advance on the Velo-Dog design. The general appearance — "hammerless", with a folding trigger—resembles a typical Velo-Dog, but the barrel is usually flattened and reinforced to resemble the slide of an automatic pistol. The hinged frame has a top latch locked by a thumb-piece above the hammer shroud, and ejection is automatic. Chamberings included 6mm Type Française rimfire and 6.35mm Auto, 7.65mm Auto or 9mm Short centerfire.

OJANGUREN Y VIDOSA

Eibar, Spain.

The relationship between this partnership and Ojanguren & Marcaido has yet to be resolved, though it is suspected that O&V began as a separate entity, producing automatic pistols, and then absorbed the remains of O&M in the early 1930s. It is noticeable that O&V revolvers are virtually identical with O&M models, similarities in detail being beyond coincidence and arguing production on the same machinery. Ojanguren & Vidosa ceased trading, along with many other Spanish gunmakers, during the Civil War of 1936-9. It is also worth considering if Ojanguren & Vidosa was simply a distributor of guns made elsewhere in Eibar.

∼ REVOLVERS ∼

Crucero This was applied to "Apache" revolvers, made by Fabrica de Armas Garantizada (q.v.), which were being sold by Ojanguren y Vidosa.

Ojanguren These guns were based on Smith & Wesson practice and were all but identical with those made by Ojanguren y Marcaido. They can only be distinguished by the trademark of "OV" on a circle, very much like the "OM" trademark, and the names on the barrels of some of them.

- *Model de Expulsion a Mano* ("hand ejector") Two types of 32-caliber patterns were made, one with a 6-inch barrel and square butt and another with a 3-inch barrel and round butt. The designation may be found on the barrel.
- *Militar y Policia* In 38 Long Colt chambering, this had a 6-inch barrel and a squared butt.
- *Legitimo Tanque* Another 6-inch-barreled gun, this time in 38 S&W Special and fitted with adjustable sights. The butt was squared.

∼ AUTOMATIC PISTOLS ∼

Apache Eibar-type blowback pistols bearing this name were offered by several gunmaking businesses in the 1920s, almost always in 6.35mm Auto (25 ACP) chambering. One pattern has a slide cutaway similar to the Retolaza "Gallus", with vertical slide-retracting grips, but others have plain slides and grips that are cut radially. The left side of the slide is typically marked "Pistola Automatica Browning / "APACHE"...", sometimes accompanied by the caliber designation. Some guns have grips embossed with "APACHE" and a motif of a sinister-looking head wearing a beret, showing that the name denoted Parisian gangsters instead of Native Americans, and an "OV" monogram in a diamond. Others display nothing but the monogram.

A typical 7.65mm-caliber (32) Crucero pistol, made by Ojanguren & Vidosa.

Crucero This 7.65mm pistol, an enlarged version of the Salvaje pattern described below, is nothing but a standard "Eibar" type. The left side of the slide is marked "Pistola Automatica" / "CRUCERO" – Eibar (Guipuzcoa) España", in two lines, and sometimes also "Marca Registrada Junio 1917"; the grips display a warship motif and an "OV" monogram.

Furia This is a better-than-average "Eibar" 7.65mm blowback pistol bearing the two-line slide marking "Pistolet Automatique Francaise / Fabrique a St Etienne (acier garanti)" and the name "FURIA" embossed in the top of the grips. Though these guns are often attributed to Manufacture d'Armes des Pyrénées Françaises (see "Unique"), the presence of the Indian-head trademark of Ojanguren y Vidosa on the grips suggests that at least some of the guns were made (or perhaps simply sold) in Spain in the early 1930s. The Furia butt has an unusual curved backstrap, swelling at the base to fit the hand.

Salvaje Apart from the contours of the slide, which are more rounded, this 6.35mm pistol is almost the same as the Apache described above. The grip shows the head of a Red Indian, with feathered headdress, beneath "SALVAJE" on a curved band. The left side of the slide is marked "Pistola Automatica Browning / "SALVAJE" Patentada" in two lines, sometimes with an additional caliber mark.

Tanque The design of this 6.35mm pistol showed some originality. A solid block beneath the barrel, running for most of its length, fit into the frame to be secured by a screw at the front end. The slide had an odd shape, tapering away from the breech to leave a rib over the rounded forward portion that ended just in front of the trigger. This gave the pistol its top-heavy appearance. The barrel was only 1.5 inches long, the magazine held six rounds and the slide was marked "6.35 "TANQUE" Patent". A motif of a Renault two-man tankette beneath "TANQUE", in a circle, was molded into the grips together with an "OV" monogram in a diamond.

ORBEA

Orbea Hermanos and "Orbea y Cia", Eibar, Spain.
The Orbea brothers were amongst the earliest of Spanish pistol manufacturers and the most inventive. The arms museum in Eibar owns a gas-operated Orbea automatic revolver, made in 1863, that uses a piston beneath the barrel and a system of levers to cock the hammer, rotate the cylinder and eject an empty case. The gun was never made in quantity and was doubtless highly temperamental with the crude ammunition of the day, but it reflects great credit on its designers and establishes Eibar as the likely birthplace of the automatic pistol.

Unfortunately, the Orbea family subsequently concentrated on a run of unimaginative copies, producing a 44 S&W Russian-type gun for the Spanish army in 1884, and continued to make swing-cylinder examples adapted from S&W or Colt patterns. The business is believed to have been reorganized as "Orbea y Cia" in the early 1930s but was then terminated during the Spanish Civil War of 1936-9. This would account for the rarity of the solitary pistol of the name.

∼ REVOLVERS ∼

Colon A 32-caliber six-shot solid-frame double-action revolver with swing-out cylinder, this was copied from the Colt Police Positive. Production was confined to 1924-34, as the "Colon Model 1925". The guns are identifiable by "OH" monograms on rounded-heel butt and frame.

Iris Another Colt copy, available in 32-20 WCF, 32 Long or 38 Special, this was little more than a Colon with a 6-inch barrel and a square butt.

M1916 This was a six-shot 10.35mm revolver based on the ribbed-barrel Smith and Wesson top-break revolver made for the Italian army in 1914-18. The grips on the bird's-head butt stopped short of a prominent beak at the toe, allowing a hole to be drilled for a lanyard. Many revolvers of this type were sold commercially after the end of World War I and may be found with Italian gun dealers' names stamped into the frame.

O.H. This name was applied to a range of revolvers bearing nothing but the "OH" trademark on the frame or grips. They were all copied

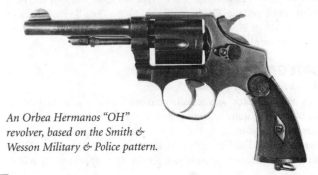

An Orbea Hermanos "OH" revolver, based on the Smith & Wesson Military & Police pattern.

from the S&W Hand Ejector or Military & Police patterns, with 4-inch or 6-inch barrels and round or square butts. Chamberings included 22 LR rimfire, 32 S&W Long, 32-20 WCF, 8mm French or 38 S&W Special, and a few guns even accepted the 5.5mm Velo-Dog cartridge — perhaps the only instance of a modern swing-cylinder revolver using this particular round. The guns usually date from 1918 or later and may be marked "Model 1925"; some will also bear marks such as "38 S & W SPECIAL / U.S. SERVICE CTGS" on the side of the barrel. Most of the guns made after the approval of laws governing proofing procedures (in December 1929) will bear Eibar proofmarks.

∽ AUTOMATIC PISTOL ∽

Orbea This 6.35mm gun is distinguished by unusual construction. The barrel terminated in a strangely-shaped block that not only carried the front sight but was also held in the frame by a screw passing up in front of the trigger-guard. The external shape of the muzzle block matched the slide, which, therefore, was noticeably shorter than normal. The return spring was carried in the top of the slide, a striker was contained in the breechblock and a grip safety was fitted in the backstrap. There was no other safety system. The slide was usually marked "ORBEA y CIA – EIBAR ESPANA" over "PISTOLA AUTOMATICA CAL 6 35".

ORBEA

La Industrial Orbea, Eibar, Spain.

∽ REVOLVERS ∽

La Industrial A six-shot solid-frame revolver resembling the S&W Military & Police model with a 4-inch barrel marked "LA INDUSTRIAL ORBEA – EIBAR", this was manufactured from 1915 to 1935. The standard guns were 32 caliber, but examples in 8mm Lebel chambering have also been reported.

∽ AUTOMATIC PISTOL ∽

La Industrial This was a 6.35mm-caliber "Eibar" blowback, marked "LA INDUSTRIAL – ORBEA" on the left side of the slide, above "CAL 6 ³⁵", with "ORBEA" in a cartouche on the grips. A decorative monogram also appears on the grips; this reads "OH", which suggests that "La Industria Orbea" was simply a trading style of Orbea Hermanos (above).

FERNANDO ORMACHEA

Eibar, Spain.

∽ REVOLVER ∽

Bron-Grand A Velo-Dog-patterned "hammerless" revolver, this was probably made between 1906 and 1915. It was the usual solid-frame folding-trigger type with the frame raised behind the cylinder to conceal the hammer. It was available in 6.35mm or 7.65mm Auto chamberings.

∽ AUTOMATIC PISTOLS ∽

Duan A 6.35mm "Eibar" blowback dating from the 1920s, this offered no better than average quality and could be distinguished from many competitors only by the inscription "AUTOMATIC PISTOL CAL 6 ³⁵ DUAN", sometimes accompanied by "FABRIQUE EN ESPAGNE" on the slide and an ornate dragon molded into the grips.

Merke This was another "Eibar"-type 6.35mm pistol of the early 1920s based on the FN-Browning of 1906. The slide was usually marked "MODEL AUTOMATIC PISTOL" over "MERKE", with "MK" in a circle on the slide and the grips.

ORTEGA

D.F. Ortega de Seija, Madrid, Spain

This "manufacturer" was actually no more than a large-scale distributor of sporting guns (including pistols and revolvers) that had been purchased in Eibar.

Benemerita Used in 1920-35, this name could be found on 6.35mm and 7.65mm Eibar-type blowback pistols. They appear to have been

"A.A.A." guns made by Antonio Aldazabal (q.v.) of Eibar. The smaller gun is usually marked "1918 MODEL AUTOMATIC PISTOL / "BENEMERITA" PATENT CAL 6 ³⁵" in two lines on the left side of the slide and has a lion's-head motif on the grips, beneath "BENEMERITA" and above "MARCA REGISTRADA". The 7.65mm model is marked similarly, except for the change in caliber. (Other dates — e.g., 1916, 1919 — have been found in the slide inscriptions, suggesting that they give a clue to the year of manufacture.)

HEINRICH ORTGIES & CO.

Heinrich Ortgies (& Co.), Erfurt, Germany.

Although born in Germany, Ortgies lived in Liége for several years. There he designed an automatic pistol that was patented in 1918. The inventor then returned to Germany, where the first 7.65mm-caliber guns were marketed. The terms of the agreement remain unknown, but it is assumed that Ortgies originally contracted with Deutsche-Werke (formerly the local Prussian small-arms factory) to make the components that were then assembled, marked and sold under the Ortgies name. Subsequently, however, Deutsche-Werke acquired the rights and began promoting the pistol under its own name. Ortgies himself appears to have taken no further interest in firearms.

The 7.65mm Ortgies pistol. Though marked by Deutsche Werke, this gun has the Ortgies monogram on the grips.

Ortgies This was an extremely well-made and well-finished striker-fired blowback, with a 3.4-inch barrel and a detachable eight-round magazine in the butt. The method of attaching the barrel, the design of the disconnector and the way in which the grips were retained were all patented separately.

The barrel was formed with a flanged lump beneath the chamber that engaged in a claw-like seating in the frame; the barrel could be turned sideways through 90 degrees to disengage the claw and could be lifted out of the frame. The disconnector was a spring-loaded stud protruding from the frame, which was held down by the slide until the breech was properly closed. A recess in the slide then allowed the stud to rise, reconnecting the trigger and sear for the next shot. The wooden grips were held by spring-steel clips inside the butt frame, reached by removing the magazine.

The grip safety would remain locked in the backstrap of the butt until pressing a button at the top of the left grip allowed it to spring out again. The grip-safety spring also drove the striker, so that squeezing the grip safety placed additional pressure on the spring to ensure a firm strike on the primer of a chambered round.

Guns sold by Ortgies were marked "ORTGIES & Co – ERFURT" over "ORTGIES PATENT" in two lines on the left side of the slide and have bronze medallions with "HO" monograms let into the grips. See also "Deutsche Werke".

ORUETA

Orueta Brothers (Orueta Hermanos), Eibar, Spain.

Alfa These guns were sold by Armero Especialistas Reunidas (q.v.) of Eibar, c. 1920-33. The oldest patterns were based on the early top-break Smith & Wesson double-action revolvers, with a prominent rib above the barrel and automatic ejectors. They differed principally from their

US-made prototypes in quality of construction (which was much poorer) and the design of the butt, which was squared. They were made in 32, 38 and 44 centerfire chamberings. They were superseded by copies of the S&W Military & Police design. However, the first type lacked the lug that supported the tip of the ejector rod and had a Colt-type "pull-back" cylinder release. The second type reverted to the S&W design, with a barrel lug and a push-type cylinder release. Both chambered the 38 Long Colt cartridge.

Oculto This name was applied to 32- and 38-caliber copies of the Smith & Wesson "New Departure" double-action hinged-frame revolvers dating from the 1920s.

OSGOOD

Osgood Gun Works, Norwich, Connecticut, USA.
This 1880-vintage gunmaking business made a double-barreled revolver designed by Freeman W. Hood, but sales did not meet expectations and trading ceased in 1882/3.

Duplex A modernized version of the better-known Le Mat revolver of the US Civil War era with a shotgun charge in a separate barrel, this was an eight-shot 22 Short rimfire revolver with a hinged frame, a single-action trigger, a sheathed trigger, a decoratively molded gutta-percha grip and an auxiliary barrel (chambered for 32 Short rimfire ammunition) that not only served as the cylinder arbor pin but also extended back through the frame. The hammer had a movable two-position firing pin, which could fire either the 22 cartridges in the cylinder chambers in the usual manner (upper position) or the 32 cartridge in the lower barrel (lower position). The Duplex was handicapped by the lack of automatic extractors, and the frame latch — a strap hinged to the barrel in front of the cylinder that snapped over the standing breech — was also a poor design. The latch was effectual when the gun was new but loosened with wear until it could be dangerous.

The original guns, now rarely seen, were marked "DUPLEX", "PAT. DEC 7 1880", and "OSGOOD GUN WORKS – NORWICH CONN." After the failure of the business, the guns appear to have been sold under the brand name "Monarch". This is usually associated with Hopkins & Allen (q.v.), which may hold a clue either to the actual manufacturer or to the eventual distributor.

OVIEDO ARMS FACTORY

Oviedo, Spain.
The government-owned arms factory was best known prior to World War I for Mauser-action rifles, but they also made a few handguns.

Campo-Giro Lieutenant-Colonel Don Venancio López de Ceballos y Aguirre, Count of Campo-Giro, was an officer of the Spanish army who began work on an automatic pistol in about 1900. The first prototypes were made and tested in 1903/4 and are generally known as the "1904 Model". A variety of modified patterns subsequently appeared, but towards the end of the production run in 1918, complaints began to be made about frame failures. Aguirre had been killed in a riding accident in 1915, and so the problem was passed to Esperanza y Unceta (q.v.). The gun was redesigned, becoming the "Astra 400", and taken into Spanish service in 1921.

- *Model 1904* This was a locked-breech pistol, the lock being a laterally-sliding wedge beneath the barrel, controlled by a cam track in the frame. The magazine was in the butt and an external hammer fired the pistol. The caliber of these early models is in some doubt; one survivor is said to have been chambered for a 7.65mm cartridge, perhaps the 7.65mm Parabellum or 7.8mm Bergmann No.5 (which, despite its designation, shared the same projectile diameter). Another has been reported in 9mm. Though Aguirre referred to the cartridge as the "9mm Campo-Giro", it is assumed to be the same as the 9mm Bergmann[-Bayard], renamed "9mm Largo" with the advent of the Model 1921 (Astra 400) pistol.

- *Model 1910* An improved version of the pistol was then developed around the 9mm Largo round. Some changes were made to the frame, making it more comfortable to hold, and 25 examples of the "Model 1910" were made in Oviedo in 1911. Extensive testing revealed a need for modification, and an improved pistol was adopted in September 1912.

- *Model 1912* Five hundred were ordered in November 1912, but teething troubles led to the substitution of a simplified blowback design that abandoned the locking wedge of pre-1912 guns.

- *Model 1913* Manufacture of the perfected gun was entrusted to Esperanza y Unceta (listed under "E").

OYEZ ARMS COMPANY

Liége, Belgium.
This small firm manufactured a 6.35mm automatic pistol prior to 1914 based on the contemporaneous Pieper tip-barrel design. It is possible that the Pieper design, which only appeared commercially in 1912, was licensed to Oyez; this would date the project to 1913-14, which would account for the scarcity of the pistol.

PACIFIC INTERNATIONAL

Pacific International Marketing Company, Inc., Sacramento, California, USA.

Vega This was a stainless steel copy of the Colt M1911A1, marketed with fixed or adjustable sights in the late 1970s. It was available either as a complete converted pistol ($329 with fixed sights, $370 with adjustable sights) or as a kit of stainless frame and slide components for home conversion of an existing M1911A1.

PAGÈS

V.-F.-E. Pagès, Paris, France.

In 1880, Pagès patented a unique multi-shot pistol consisting of an open-frame butt with two tangs running forward, top and bottom to support a block carrying six short superimposed barrels. A bank of firing pins lay behind the barrels, with a vertical shaft carrying six cams. Space for the fingers of the firing hand was provided between the two barrel-support tangs, with a trigger in the top of the aperture.

The block of barrels could be swung open to load, probably using one of the 6mm "palm-squeezer" rounds, and latched back into position. Pressing the trigger then rotated the vertical shaft through a part-turn, allowing a cam to retract and then release the first firing pin. This sequence continued until all six barrels had been fired.

The firing mechanism undoubtedly worked efficiently, but the pistol was cumbersome and expensive compared with contemporaneous pinfire pocket revolvers. The Pagès pistol was never made in quantity and remains practically unknown today.

PARA ORDNANCE

Para Ordnance Mfg Co., Scarborough, Ontario, Canada (also sometimes marked "Fort Lauderdale, Florida").

This gunmaking business, founded in 1985 to make a "Dye Marking Tactical Machine Pistol", has been making specialized adaptations of Colt-Browning type pistols since 1988. These have always been distinguished by an attention to detail that has been recognized by a variety of awards, including *Guns & Ammo's* "Innovation of the Year, 2001". Among the major changes to Browning's original design have been to the frame, which has been adapted to high-capacity magazines; to the trigger system, culminating in the introduction of the LDA double-action; and to the way in which the barrel locks into the slide at the muzzle, solved by great attention to detail and adherence to manufacturing tolerances judged in ten-thousandths of an inch. All Para-Ordnance guns have internal firing-pin-blocking safety mechanisms in addition to the classical grip and manual patterns; plunger tubes and grip bushings that are made integrally with the frame instead of separate components; lowered and flared ejection ports; beveled magazine wells and extended or "beavertail" grip safety levers. The barrels also have feed-ramps to guide ammunition of virtually any type into the chamber.

∼ AUTOMATIC PISTOLS ∼

These are all built to essentially the same design, relying on the single-link barrel depressor patented by John Browning in 1911. Many of the guns offer high-capacity magazines that, owing to the provisions of the Assault Weapons Bill of 1994, are restricted in North America to police or military use. Found on the right side of the slide, the designations give a clue to magazine capacity and caliber; for example, the "P14-45" chambers the 45 ACP round and has a 14-round magazine. The left side of the slide is usually marked "Para-Ordnance" in outline semi-script lettering.

Single-action ("Performance Plus" guns) These come in a variety of sizes, usually with the option of an alloy frame. Except for stainless-steel guns, which are bright, the finish is usually black. Grips are usually black synthetic, with the Para-Ordnance "P and concentric circles" logo.

- *P10 series* Models 10-9 (in 9mm Parabellum), 10-40 (40 S&W) and 10-45 in (45 ACP) all have 10-round magazines suited to the US domestic market. These are contained in an ultra-short "sub-compact" grip that gives an overall length of 6.5 inches (with a 3.5-inch barrel) and a depth of merely 4.5 inches. The guns weigh 24 or 31 oz, depending on the material of the frame.
- *P12-45* Only available in 45 ACP, this compact-frame handgun measures 7.1 inches overall with a 3.5-inch barrel and has a depth of 5 inches. It weighs 26 oz (alloy frame) or 34 oz (steel frame).
- *P13-45* Chambered only for the 45 ACP round, this is 7.8 inches long, has a 4.25-inch barrel and weighs 28 or 36 oz depending on the material of the frame. The gun is about 5.3 inches deep.
- *P14-45* Another of the 45 ACP guns, this is 8.5 inches overall, has a 5-inch barrel and a full-size frame, giving an overall depth of 5.75 inches. Weight is 31 or 40 oz., depending on frame metal.
- *P16-40* Offered in 40 S&W, with a full-size frame, this conforms with the same specification as the 14-45 except for chambering and a 16-round magazine. It is available only in blacked carbon or bright stainless steel.
- *P18-9* Another variant of the 14-45, made only in stainless steel, this chambers the 9mm Parabellum round and has an 18-round magazine.

Single-action "Limited" guns (1998 to date) Based on the standard P10-45, P12-45, P13-45, P14-45 and P16-40, these offer a variety of features that are usually associated with "semi-custom" guns. These include micro-adjustable competition-style rear sights (standard sights are retained on the P10-45 and P12-45), ambidextrous safety levers, a trigger over-travel stop and a lightweight competition skeleton hammer. The larger guns (P13 upwards) have a second set of slide-retraction grooves behind the muzzle. The designation marks on the slide are accompanied by "Limited" in formal script.

Double-action (LDA) guns (1999 to date) These guns incorporate one of the most innovative changes ever to have been made to Browning's original design, an efficient double-action trigger system credited to Ted Szabo, President of Para-Ordnance. The guns are immediately recognizable by shape and position of the trigger, a slender elegantly curved lever instead of the sliding 1911-type blade. The first guns to be offered in this configuration were Models 12-45 LDA, 14-40 LDA, 14-45 LDA, 16-40 LDA and 18-9 LDA, variants of the single-action guns described previously.

- *Model 7-45* (2000 to date) This is a 45 ACP handgun with a seven-round single-column magazine patterned on the original (but with Para-Ordnance improvements). It has checkered "double-diamond"-style cocobolo grips and a rounded backstrap that is reminiscent of the M1911A1.
- *C7-45 LDA Para Companion* (2001 to date) A "Compact" version of the 7-45 with a short barrel, an abbreviated frame and cocobolo grips; magazine capacity remains seven rounds, owing to the innovative design of the magazine follower. The designation "Para Companion" appears on the left side of the slide.
- *C6-45 LDA Para Carry* (2001 to date) This "sub-compact" is currently the smallest 45-caliber double-action-only personal-defense gun available commercially. It is 6.5 inches long with a 3-inch barrel and only 4.75 inches deep. The magazine holds six rounds. The stainless-steel slide and frame give the gun a weight of 30 oz, much greater than most representatives of this class — but a useful way of soaking up the recoil of such a powerful cartridge!

- *P7-45 LDA LE* and *P16-40 LDA LE* (2002 to date) These are "Law Enforcement" derivatives of the standard guns, with spurless hammers.
- *Para Companion-Carry Option* (2003) This is essentially a Para Companion with some of the features of the smaller Para Carry, including a spurless hammer, a bobbed grip safety and night sights.
- *Para CCW* (2003) Similar to the Companion-Carry Option, this has a 4.25-inch barrel instead of the 3.5-inch type. Both the 2003 introductions are made only in stainless steel and have checkered cocobolo grips.
- *Tac-Four* and *Tac-Four LE* (2003) Offering a combination of a 13-round magazine and a 4.25-inch barrel, this also has a spurless hammer and a bobbed grip-safety lever. Available only in stainless steel, it is 7.7 inches long and weighs about 36 oz. "LE" signifies "Law Enforcement", and black synthetic grips are found instead of the standard double-diamond checkered cocobolo pattern.

Double-action (LDA) "Limited" guns (1999 to date) This is currently restricted to variations of the Models 7.45 LDA, 14-45 LDA, 16-40 LDA and 18-9 LDA. They include the refinements associated with the single-action Limited pistols described previously, including the duplication of the retraction grips behind the muzzle. The designations (e.g., "14.45 LDA") on the right side of the slide are accompanied by "Ltd." in formal script.

PARDINI

Pardini SpA, Lido di Camaiore, Italy.

This gunmaking business offers a range of semi-automatic pistols, usually destined for specialized competition shooting.

∼ SINGLE-SHOT PISTOLS ∼

K-22 Intended for Free Pistol competitions, this is a 22 LR rimfire pistol with a bolt-action breech that is claimed to give better support to the base of the cartridge than rival tipping-block designs. It has a fixed grip, intended to be sculpted to the requirements of an individual owner, an adjustable sight radius and auxiliary weights attached to a rod carried back over the muzzle from the front-sight cradle. It is 18.1 inches long with an 11.8-inch barrel and weighs 38.8 oz without its weights.

∼ AUTOMATIC PISTOLS ∼

Blowbacks These are intended for Standard Pistol and Full-Bore Pistol shooting, chambered for the 22 LR rimfire or 32 Smith & Wesson Wadcutter centerfire rounds. They are similar designs, with the barrel set as low as possible, a separate breechblock reciprocating within a closed slab-sided receiver, the rear sight at the extreme rear of the frame and an anatomical grip. Some of the guns bear the manufacturer's mark on the frame above the trigger, but the bright-finished horizontal ribs on the trigger housing provide a more obvious recognition feature.

- *Models GP* and *GPE* (also known as the "Schumann" patterns) These guns are virtually identical externally, chambered for the 22 Short round and destined for rapid-fire competitions. They differ in the design of the trigger: the GP is mechanical; the GPE is electronic. They also have grips that envelop the hand but lack the adjustable palm-rest of the other Pardini pistols and are designed to be adapted to an individual shooter's hand. To conform to restrictions on overall length, the extended grip has forced a reduction in barrel length to 3.9 inches.
- *Model HP* The centerfire version of the HP can be identified by the strengthened frame (lacking the bolt aperture of the rimfire version) and the magazine, which protrudes beneath its housing.
- *Model SP* The basic 22 rimfire gun is 11.6 inches long with a 4.7-inch barrel and weighs about 39 oz.

Browning type Intended for practical-pistol competition shooting, these guns embody a cam-finger variant of the tilting-barrel lock. The grip is raked to give better instinctive "pointability", the trigger guard is squared to facilitate a two-hand grip and the slide-retraction grips have

been duplicated at the muzzle. The magazine release is ambidextrous, and the trigger and sights are adjustable. Grips are walnut, the steel slide is blacked and the alloy frame is anodized black.

- *PC-9* Chambered for the 9x21 IMI round, this has a 17-round double-column magazine. The standard version is 8.9 inches long with a 5.3-inch barrel and weighs 39.5 oz empty.
- *PC-9S* This is basically a variant of the PC-9 with a special single-action trigger mechanism and a three-slot compensator attached to the muzzle. The slide is hard-chromed, the frame is bright anodized, the grips are selected walnut and a special Pardini optical-sight mount can be attached when required. The barrel measures 5.3 inches, giving an overall length of 10.4 inches and an empty weight of about 44 oz.
- *PC-40* A variant of the PC-9 in 40 S&W, this has a magazine holding 13 rounds.
- *PC-40S* A compensated version of the PC-40, comparable with the PC-9S except for the chambering.
- *PC-45* This 45 ACP version has a 13-round magazine (currently limited to 10 in the USA).
- *PC-45S* This is basically a long-barreled compensated version of the PC-45, otherwise comparable with the PC-9S described above.

PARKER-HALE

Parker-Hale Ltd, Birmingham, Warwickshire, England.

This gunsmithing business, best known for sights and target rifles, also made adapters that allowed Webley, Smith & Wesson and other revolvers to fire 22 rimfire ammunition for practice purposes. The changes usually involved the insertion of 22-caliber sleeves in the barrels and chambers, and alterations to the firing pins.

PASSLER & SEIDL

Weipert, Bohemia, Austria-Hungary.

Designed by Ferdinand Passler and Josef Seidl and patented in Austria-Hungary in 1887, this 7.7mm-caliber repeating pistol was made in limited numbers — probably in the gunmaking center of Weipert in Bohemia. The reciprocating bolt, operated by a finger-operated ring trigger, fed cartridges into the chamber from a clip-loaded six-round magazine in the frame ahead of the trigger. The Passler & Seidl pistol can be distinguished from others of this class by a long spring-loaded cartridge follower, pivoting the barrel, that runs through a slot in the frame into the magazine.

PATRO

Patro di Roberto Palama, Borgovercelli, Italy.

A small, but highly respected gunmaker, Patro has specialized in target pistols. These have "packaged" trigger systems, low-set barrels and magazines ahead of the trigger guard. The *Olimpionico* chambers the 22 Short rimfire round, for use in rapid-fire competitions, and the *M2 Standard* is offered in 22 LR rimfire. The guns feature all-steel construction and the customary trigger, sight, grip and balance-weight options.

PAVLIČEK

Frantiček Pavliček, Litomyšl, Czechoslovakia.

This gunmaker created the single-shot 22 rimfire *Pav* target pistol in the early 1930s, a simple but well-made gun that proved to be popular in central Europe prior to World War II. Pavliček briefly resurrected his operations after 1945, but the business (like all other gunmakers in the country) was nationalized in 1948. The pistol subsequently became the "Model P" and was still being made in the 1980s (see "Drulov").

PETERS STAHL

PSW-Vertriebsgesellschaft mbH, Aachen, Germany.

Originally primarily a barrel maker, supplying target-grade barrels to a

A Peters-Stahl 22 rimfire conversion unit for the FN-Browning High Power.

variety of gunmakers, this business diversified in the 1970s. It has made 22 RF adapters for pistols such as the Browning High-Power and SIG P-210, and the *PSP Multi-Caliber* conversion. The PSP was a modified Colt M1911A1 adaptable to 38 S&W Special, 9mm Parabellum, 38 Super or 45 ACP chamberings simply by changing the barrel, springs and magazine.

The product range currently includes the *PSP 07 Sport* and the *PSP 2000*, the latter being offered in *High Capacity*, *Millennium Model* and *Trophy Master* guise. These guns are "squared" Colt-Browning clones with skeletonized hammers, speed triggers, extended controls, duplicated slide-retraction grips and grips that may be walnut or walnut/rubber composites. Barrels measure 5 or 6 inches, each with full-length slides, and the sights are generally adjustable. The *Trophy Master* has a rounded trigger guard and magazine capacities of seven 45 or eight 9mm rounds. The *High Capacity* version has a squared "two-hand" trigger guard bow and a magazine holding 10 (US market) or 15 9mm rounds. The *Millennium Model* has a frame and slide coated in titanium.

PFANNL

Franz Pfannl, Krems an der Donau, Austria.

Erika (or "Pfannl-Miniature-Selbstladepistole") Developed in 1910-12 and introduced commercially shortly before World War I began, this odd-looking pistol introduced an equally idiosyncratic 4.25mm centerfire cartridge made exclusively by the Hirtenberg Cartridge Company. The cumbersome design belied the tiny caliber, with a raked butt placed far enough from the chamber to allow the magazine to enter the frame in the space between the rear of the trigger aperture and the frontstrap. The barrel unit, hinged at the rear of the frame and pinned to the front, was allied with a bolt that moved beneath the overhanging section of the barrel extension. A rod running through the center of the return spring, which was placed in a tube above the barrel, hooked over a lug in the bolt-top. Both sides of the bolt were grooved to assist the charging stroke.

The Erika seems to have been made until c. 1926, though the total output was probably less than 3500-3750. Minor changes had been made during the production life. The length of the butt changed, and guns may be found with barrels measuring 1.5 or 2.25 inches. Pfannl may have licensed the basic design to George Gräbner (q.v.) of Rehberg, who developed the ultra-small-caliber Kolibri. It is suspected that Pfannl also may have made the Kolibri, as his "FP" monogram will be encountered on the grips of both Erika and Kolibri pistols.

PHELPS

E.F. Phelps Mfg Co., Evansville, Indiana, USA.

This company has made the *Eagle 1* and *Heritage 1* revolvers, heavy-weight enlargements of the Colt Single Action Army pattern chambering 444 Marlin or 45-70 Government cartridges. The barrels may be 8 or 12 inches long, empty weight being about 70 oz (8-inch barrel).

PHILLIPS & RODGERS, INC.

Conroe, Texas, USA.

Medusa 47 Introduced in 1996, this is a double-action "multi-caliber" revolver capable of chambering, firing and extracting more than 25 different 357, 38 and 9mm-caliber cartridges. Fitted with a slab-sided barrel, 2.5-6 inches long, the Medusa usually displays blue finish and rubber "Gripper" grips. It can be identified by the narrow horizontal flutes in the barrel block. The front sight is interchangeable.

PHOENIX ARMS

Ontario, Canada.

This gunmaking business made the Raven Arms (q.v.) *P-25*, which is now being offered under the Phoenix name in bright chrome, polished blue or satin nickel with grips of synthetic ivory, "pink pearl" or gloss black. Phoenix has also been responsible for the *HP-22* (22 LR rimfire) and *HP-25* (25 ACP), which are similar bright-chrome or polished-blue blowbacks with black checkered grips. Introduced in 1993, these guns have magazines that contain 11 and 10 rounds, respectively, the former currently being restricted to eight or 10 in the USA. They also have distinctive ventilated-rib slides and optional interchangeable target-shooting long-slide/long-barrel units. The HP-22 is 5.1 inches long, has a 3-inch barrel and weighs about 20 oz empty.

PICKERT

Friedrich Pickert, Arminius Waffenfabrik, Zella St Blasii (pre-1919) and Zella-Mehlis (post-1919), Germany.

The demand for cheap pocket revolvers appeared to be insatiable in the early 1900s, prompting at least one German gunmaking business to challenge the domination of the Belgians. Founded in 1865 to make sporting guns, the business of Friedrich Pickert made inexpensive revolvers from the beginning of the 20th century until World War II.

Arminius This name, that of a tribal leader who had defeated the Romans, was applied to an entire range of handguns, and a motif depicting the head of a warrior was embossed in the grips of all the revolvers. Although the basis of the revolvers was an obsolescent design, the guns were well-made, reliable and offered good value. Their features usually included a solid frame, a swinging loading gate on the right side of the frame behind the cylinder and a rod ejector beneath the barrel (though some of the simplest examples had cylinders that had to be removed for loading). The double-action firing system sometimes took the form of a "hammerless" self-cocking variant, with a concealed hammer that struck a floating firing pin in the standing breech. Virtually all hammerless guns had radial safety catches on the rear left side of the frame, but some triggers folded upward against the frame and others had conventional guards. Several of the individual patterns had a folding trap in the bottom of the butt, allowing five or six spare cartridges to be concealed.

Most Pickert revolvers chambered standard commercial cartridges, though some of those made in prior to 1914 accepted the 5mm Pickert round, also known as "5.2x16.5R", that had been developed from the 5mm Bergmann pistol pattern c. 1900.

∼ SINGLE-SHOT PISTOLS ∼

- *TP1* A 22-caliber target pistol with a 7.9-inch drop-down barrel and a firing mechanism with an exposed hammer.
- *TP2* Similar to TP1, this had a double set trigger and concealed hammer.

∼ REVOLVERS ∼

Arminius revolvers are often extremely difficult to classify: it seems that length, cylinder capacity and caliber could be combined and permuted indefinitely. The list that follows covers the standard models on sale between the wars, but it is far from exhaustive.

- *Model 1* A typical "hammerless" revolver, with the hammer concealed in the frame, this chambered 22 Short or LR rimfire ammunition. It had a seven-chamber cylinder and a barrel measuring about 1.9 inches.

- *Model 2* This 22-caliber gun had an external hammer and a 4.7-inch barrel.
- *Model 3* Another of the pseudo-hammerless patterns, this had a folding trigger beneath the frame. Chambered for the 6.35mm Auto (25 ACP) round, it had a five-chamber cylinder and a 1.9-inch barrel.
- *Model 4* Otherwise similar to the Model 3, this accepted the 5.5mm Velo-Dog round.
- *Model 5/1* One of the exposed-hammer guns, this had a five-chamber cylinder, a 2.6-inch barrel and accepted the 7.5mm Swiss ordnance-revolver cartridge.
- *Model 5/2* Similar to the Model 5/1, this had a larger cylinder capable of accepting either eight Swiss 7.5mm or five 7.62mm Nagant "non-gas-seal" rounds. The barrel was 2.6 inches long.
- *Model 7* Fitted with an external hammer, this 320 centerfire gun had a five-chamber cylinder and a 2.6-inch barrel.
- *Model 8* This has been listed as a pseudo-hammerless pattern, chambered for the 320 centerfire or 7.65mm Auto (32 ACP) rounds, with barrels that were 1.9 or 5.5 inches long. The trigger folded up against the underside of the frame.
- *Model 9* Chambered similarly to the Model 8, this had an external hammer and a conventionally guarded trigger. It had a five-chamber cylinder and a 2.4-inch barrel.
- *Model 9A* This was little more than a Model 9 with 3.1-inch barrel.
- *Model 10* One of the pseudo-hammerless patterns in 320 centerfire or 7.65mm Auto (32 ACP), this had a folding trigger, a five-chamber cylinder and a 1.9-inch barrel.

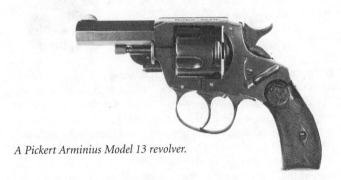

A Pickert Arminius Model 13 revolver.

- *Model 13* A conventional external-hammer five-shot gun in 380 centerfire, this had a 2.6-inch barrel.
- *Model 13A* Chambered for the 22 Long rimfire round, this had an external hammer, a conventional trigger guard, an eight-chamber cylinder and a 5.3-inch barrel.
- *Model 14* Another of the pseudo-hammerless Arminius patterns, this 380 centerfire gun had a five-chamber cylinder and the near-customary 2.6-inch barrel.

HENRI PIEPER

Henri Pieper & Cie, then Henri & Nicolas Pieper and eventually Anciens Établissements Pieper, Herstal-lèz-Liége, Belgium.

After training as an engineer in Germany, Heinrich "Henri" Pieper began mass-producing rifle barrels in 1866 and after opening a second factory, specialized in this particular art. Towards the end of his life, he designed a gas-seal revolver, but he allowed the patent to lapse after only four years, which allowed Nagant (q.v.) to prosper from it. Pieper died in 1898 and the company was taken over by his son Nicolas, to be renamed "Anciens Établissements Pieper" (AÉP) in 1905. A new factory was built in Herstal in 1907-8 to satisfy large-scale orders for rifle and shotgun barrels, but Nicolas Pieper, having patented a novel automatic pistol, had left AÉP by this time to pursue his own ideals. Gun

barrel making and work on the Bayard pistols kept the production lines going until the Germans invaded Belgium in 1914. However, unlike the other Liége gunmaking businesses (and doubtless owing to German origins), Pieper then supplied parts for the Parabellum pistol to the Erfurt small-arms factory. Trading survived World War I, the Great Depression of the early 1930s and World War II, though Pieper was owned by Krieghoff (q.v.) in 1933-45. Business is currently confined to sporting shotguns and rifles. The name "Bayard", registered by Henri Pieper, was customarily used in conjunction with the figure of a mounted knight. This represented the French soldier Pierre Terrail, seigneur de Bayard (1473-1524), the "knight without fear and beyond reproach".

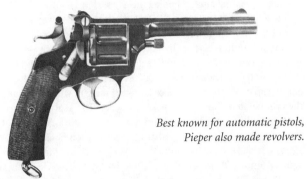

*Best known for automatic pistols,
Pieper also made revolvers.*

~ REVOLVERS ~

Bayard (swing-cylinder type) The original gun of this type appeared c. 1887. It had a solid frame, a yoke-mounted cylinder that swung out to the left after a latch on the rear left side of the frame had been pulled back and a double-action trigger mechanism. The contours were squared, giving the impression of solidity. Chamberings included 7.5 Swiss and 8mm Lebel, but production seems to have been restricted by the absence of military orders and the development of the gas-seal design.

Pieper subsequently copied the Smith & Wesson Hand Ejector in 32 and 38 centerfire, with a variety of barrel lengths from 4 or 6 inches. The long-barreled guns generally had squared butts; the others were generally rounded. The presence of the Bayard name or trademark, or "AÉP" within a circle, will usually identify them.

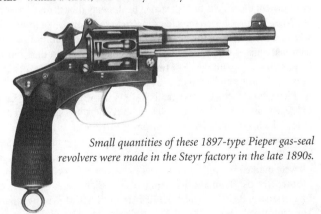

*Small quantities of these 1897-type Pieper gas-seal
revolvers were made in the Steyr factory in the late 1890s.*

Bayard (gas-seal type) The first of these, derived from the standard swing-cylinder design, dated from the late 1880s. However, Pieper allowed the original 1886 patent to lapse after just four years, and the gun was never particularly successful, even though some were made in the Steyr factory of Oesterreichische Waffenfabriks-Gesellschaft to take part in the trials that led to the adoption of the Rast & Gasser pattern.

The cylinder was cammed forward during the trigger stroke, relying on the case mouth of an elongated 7.62mm cartridge to seal the joint between the barrel and the chamber at the instant of firing. Ironically, this system proved to be very successful for Léon Nagant (q.v.) after Pieper allowed patent-protection to lapse. However, the Nagant revolver lacked the yoke-mounted cylinder of the Pieper and was reckoned to be more durable.

Pieper-Reynoso These guns embodied an auto-ejecting system patented by García Reynoso of Buenos Aires, an officer of the Argentine Army. Each time the gun was fired, the fall of the hammer was used to drive an ejector that expelled the preceding spent case through a gate in the shield behind the cylinder. However, diverting some of the power generated by the falling hammer weakened the blow on the primer of a chambered round, risking unreliability. The Reynoso ejector was incorporated on some of Pieper's revolvers, particularly those that also embodied the gas-seal mechanism.

Pieper also made Reynoso-patent revolvers with a feed case in the rear of the frame that could accept a loaded five-round clip. After firing the five rounds in the chamber of the cylinder, spent cases being ejected automatically, five additional pulls on the trigger could be used to transfer the cartridges in the feed-case to the cylinder chambers. The empty clip could then be replaced, leaving the gun with five rounds in the cylinder and another five held in reserve. The goal was to prevent the shooter from ever holding an empty gun, but it was achieved at the cost of such great complexity that the project soon failed. The DWM 1904 cartridge catalog listed the "Reynoso Pistol" cartridge in two calibres—7.8mm (DWM 423) and 5mm (DWM 420)—which suggests that Pieper intended to promote full-size military and reduced-scale pocket revolvers.

∼ AUTOMATIC PISTOLS ∼

Bayard These blowbacks were based upon patents granted in 1907 by Bernard Clarus. The shallow front portion of the slide covers the barrel, while the full-depth rear section contains the breechblock and the firing pin. The rear section also contains the hammer, suspended upside-down from a cross pin in the slide. An inverted sear lies behind the hammer, hung in such a way that it intercepts the trigger bar only when the slide is forward and the breech has been closed. Rollers on the sides of the hammer align with ramps formed in the rear of the frame. The return spring lies above the barrel, contained at the rear in a tube screwed into a frame transom and enclosed at the front in an anchor that forms the base for the front sight. Pressing the sight back, and letting it rise from the slide, allows the return spring and its guide rod to be removed; the slide is then detached by drawing it back and upward.

When the pistol fires, the slide runs back, carrying the hammer and sear, and the rollers on the hammer ride up the frame-ramps until the hammer engages with the sear. The slide comes to a halt, then moves forward under the influence of the return spring to strip a new round into the chamber and leave the sear held by the trigger bar.

Pieper bought the Clarus patents in 1908, allowing the first 7.65mm (32 ACP) pistols to be sold in 1909. A 9mm Short version followed in 1911, which was followed by a 6.35mm version in 1912. The guns incorporated a standardized series of components, the only differences being the barrels, magazine platforms, breech faces and return springs. All were marked in similar manner, with the caliber (e.g., "CAL 380 9MM MODELE DEPOSE") on the left front of the slide above " ANCIENS ETABLISSMENTS PIEPER " and "• HERSTAL – BELGIUM •" in two lines. The grips usually bore "BAYARD" on a diagonal band, and the mounted-knight trademark can also be found on the frame.

• *Model 1923* Clarus-patent pistols remained in production until 1914, resuming after the German occupation of Belgium had been ended in 1918, but changes were introduced in 1923 to make the guns more attractive. Superficially, the new range resembled the 1910-type FN-Browning though the suspended hammer and sear system was retained inside the slide. The Piepers were offered in 6.35mm and 7.65mm, the former being notably smaller than the latter. Typically, they were marked "ANCIENS ETABLISSEMENTS

A 6.35mm Pieper "New Model" pistol.

PIEPER HERSTAL – BELGIUM" on the left side of the slide, over "CAL 7.65 MODELE DEPOSE" ahead of the mounted-knight trademark and "BAYARD". The Bayard name also appeared on the grip band.

• *Model 1930* Improvements to the magazine catch and internal details allowed Pieper to add "MODELE 1930" to the slide marking. Most pistols also have an encircled cursive "AEP" mark on the grips instead of the Bayard name. Production continued until the Germans invaded Belgium again in 1940.

The 9mm Bergman-Bayard pistol, with the original type of magazine.

Bergmann-Bayard The failure of arrangements made in Germany to make Bergmann-"Mars" pistols for the Spanish army forced Theodor Bergmann to license production to Anciens Établissements Pieper. Though a few German-style guns seem to have been sold under the Pieper name, changes were soon made; the barrel was lengthened, the frame was broadened, an integral barrel extension was adopted and the rifling was changed to six-groove left-hand twist. The new gun became the "Pistolet Bayard Modèle 1908", although commonly called the "Bergmann-Bayard".

Pieper subsequently delivered guns to the Spanish, Greek and Danish armies. The earliest guns (1908-10) had hard rubber grips carrying the Bayard trademark, and the walls of the magazine housing were smooth. Markings included the mounted-knight trademark and "BAYARD" on the magazine housing, with "BREVETE" over "S.G.D.G." and "ANCIENS ETABLISSEMENTS PIEPER" over "HERSTAL – LIEGE" and "BERGMANN'S – PATENT" on the left side of the receiver. In 1911, however, the Bayard mark was removed to allow finger-tabs to be formed in the magazine housing. The Danish guns delivered in 1911-14 took this form. However, the German occupation of Belgium during World War I brought production to an end. Deprived of their supplies, the Danes ultimately decided to make copies of the Bergmann-Bayard in the government small-arms factory in Copenhagen (See "Hærens Tøjhus").

Legia This was a 6.35mm pocket blowback made in a factory established by Pieper in Paris during the 1920s. It was based on the Baby Browning and differs only in the method of retaining the barrel, which is screwed into the frame rather than using lugs. The same pistol was sold in Belgium as the "New Pieper". The standard magazine was a six-shot type, but an extended 10-shot model with additional sideplates to extend the pistol butt grips was also available.

NICOLAS PIEPER

Herstal-lez-Liege, Belgium.

This business was operated by the son of Henri Pieper, who left Anciens Établissements Pieper c. 1905 to exploit his pistol design. Trading continued until the Germans invaded Belgium in 1914, and then recommenced on a small scale in 1919 and continued until terminated by the economic depression that began in 1929.

Arico This 6.35mm-caliber pistol was presumably given this name for sale through a dealer. A typical example is marked simply "PISTOLET AUTOMATIQUE N. PIEPER" over "ARICO" on the left side of the slide.

Pieper These guns, made in accordance with patents granted from 1905 onward, existed in two forms: fixed barrel ("Demontant") and tip-barrel ("Baaculant"), each being offered in a choice of size or chambering. All Pieper pistols have checkered grips bearing an "NP" monogram in an oval cartouche, though the content of the slide markings can vary from the simple "Nicolas Pieper Brevete" to "PISTOLET AUTOMATIQUE N. PIEPER BTE S.G.D.G.", sometimes accompanied by "DEPOSE". A few guns have even been seen with markings that acknowledged four British patents granted in 1905-8 and a single Swiss patent, no. 403358.

- *Basculant* Pieper's original tip-barrel guns were offered in several types. These included the Model N, with a seven-round magazine and an overall length of about 6.1 inches and an empty weight of 21 oz; the "Model O", also in 7.65mm, with a shorter barrel and a six-round magazine; and the 6.35mm pocket model, or "Model P", which was similar in size and weight to the Model C Demontant.
- *Demontant* The fixed-barrel version of the Pieper blowback pistol, these were marketed in at least three patterns. "Model A", in

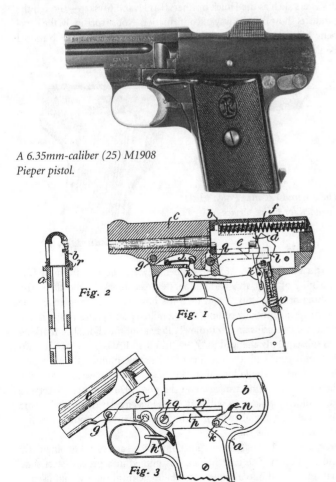

A 6.35mm-caliber (25) M1908 Pieper pistol.

Fig. 2

Fig. 1

Fig. 3

Drawing of the tip-barrel Pieper, from a British Patent granted in 1908.

7.65mm, was the largest and had a seven-round magazine; "Model B" was a similar 7.65mm gun but had a shorter barrel and a short butt holding a six-round magazine; and the 6.35mm "Model C", a compact pocket pistol, had a short barrel/short butt construction that gave an overall length of 4.9 inches and an empty weight of only 11 oz.

- *Model 1909* This was a simplified form of the original 1905-patent design offered in both tip-barrel "Basculant" and fixed-barrel "Demontant" form. They had straight-topped slides and small projecting cocking grips that doubled as the rear sight.
- *Model 1920* Offered in small numbers immediately after the end of World War I, these were essentially similar to the Pieper-type tip-barrel pocket pistols made in Austria-Hungary by Oesterreichische Waffenfabriks-Gesellschaft. Markings distinguish them from Steyr-made examples.

Oyez A variant of the 1909-type 7.65mm gun, probably made for a specific distributor. The only specimen traced for examination bore nothing other than Belgian proofmarks and the trade name.

PIETTA

Fabbrica d'Armi F.lli Pietta di Giuseppe & C. snc, Gussago, Brescia, Italy.

Best known as a maker of caplock revolvers, including Colt, Remington and Starr look-alikes, Pietta has also made copies of the Colt Single Action Army Revolver ("Peacemaker").

Single Action A close copy of the Colt, this usually has a color case-hardened frame, a blued barrel, a blued cylinder and blacked-alloy or brass trigger-guard and grip straps. The grips are customarily plain walnut. Chamberings are restricted to 22 LR rimfire, 32-20 WCF, 357 Magnum, 9mm Flobert (restricted to Europe), 38-40 WCF, 44 Special, 44-40 WCF and 45 Long Colt. Barrels range from 3.5 to 24.6 inches, though the guns are most commonly encountered with the 4.75-, 5.5- or 7.5-inch options. "Target" patterns have adjustable rear sights.

- *1894 Bisley Model* This is a duplicate of the high-grip Colts, available in either standard or Target patterns with fixed and adjustable rear sights, respectively. Chamberings are restricted to 22 LR rimfire, 32-20 WCF, 357 Magnum, 38-40 WCF, 44-40 WCF and 45 Long Colt, with the barrel-length options restricted to 4.75, 5.5, 7.5 and 10 inches.

PINDAD ARMS FACTORY

Pabrik Sendjata Ringan Pindada, Pindad, Indonesia.

This government-operated arsenal made a licensed copy of the 9mm Browning High-Power (or GP-35) pistol in 1955-65. It is to exactly the same dimensions and can only be distinguished by the marking of the factory name on the slide, followed by "P1A 9mm" together with the enwreathed Indonesian five-pointed star.

PIRLOT

Pirlot Frères, formerly Pirlot & Frésart; Liége, Belgium.

Chamelot-Delvigne Pirlot Freres were the patentees of a double-action revolver lock, which is always referred to as the Chamelot-Delvigne lock for reasons lost in history. It became an extremely popular mechanism due to its robustness and reliability, and it was adopted by several countries for their service revolvers in the 1870-1900 period. Irrespective of who designed or made the pistols, they all came to be known as Chamelot-Delvigne. So far as we are able to ascertain, those revolvers correctly known by this name are as follows:

- *Model 1871* A solid-frame revolver in 11mm centerfire caliber, adopted by the Belgian army in 1878 as a trooper's revolver.
- *Model 1872* The Swiss had adopted possibly the earliest Chamelot & Delvigne pistol in the late 1860s; this was in two versions, a 12mm for Guides and a 9mm for artillery NCOs. In 1872, this was over-

hauled by Stabsmajor Schmidt, who made some minor changes to the lock and changed the caliber to 10.4mm rimfire, making it the *M1872*. A variant model in 10.4mm centerfire was then adopted by Italy. It was a solid-frame, gate-loaded six-shot weapon, with rod ejector and folding trigger.

- *Model 1874* This was the Italian M1872 in 9.4mm centerfire, adopted by the Netherlands as an officer's revolver and in 11mm centerfire by the French for both officers and men.
- *Model 1872/78* In 1878, the Swiss changed to 10.4mm centerfire caliber and adopted a new Schmidt revolver. In order to standardize ammunition supply, they recalled the 1872 rimfire weapons and converted them to centerfire, whereupon they became the "Chamelot, Delvigne and Schmidt M1872/78".
- *Model 1879* Adopted by the Italian army as an officer's revolver, this was an improved M1872.

PITTSTON ARMS COMPANY
Exeter, Pennsylvania, USA.

Founded in 1877 to make cheap single-action "Suicide Special" revolvers with solid frames and sheathed triggers, this gunsmithing business was rapidly succeeded by the Lee Arms Company (q.v.). It is not known which of the Lee-type guns were made in Exeter, nor how the Pittston products were marked.

PLANT
Ebenezer Plant and Plant's Mfg Co., Southington, New Haven, and then Plantsville, Connecticut, USA.

Founded by Ebenezer Plant in 1860, this made 42-caliber "cup primer" revolvers to the patents of Willard Ellis and John White. The guns loaded from the front of the cylinder, evading the Rollin White patent controlled by Smith & Wesson. The earliest were break-open patterns, but these were superseded by a solid-frame design with an ejector designed by Henry Reynolds (patented in 1864). Convertible caplock/cartridge revolvers were also made in small numbers. Plant's factory burned down in 1866, but guns were then made by Marlin until business failed in 1867. Plant-type revolvers may be found with a variety of marks, including those of Merwin & Bray, the Eagle Arms Company, Marlin, and Reynolds, Plant & Hotchkiss.

PLZEŇ
Zbrojovka Plzeň, Pilsen, Czechoslovakia.

This company was formed in the 1920s by the famous Škoda arms-making business — renowned for artillery and heavy weapons but not for small-arms other than the Škoda machinegun and the Salvator-Dormus pistol of the 1890s.

Plzeň Credited to Alois Tomiška, this 7.65mm-caliber "squared-off" version of the FN-Browning blowback pistol of 1910 lacked the original grip safety. The left side of the slide was marked "AKCIOVA SPOLEČNOST DŘIVE ŠKODOVY ZÁVODY" over "ZBROJOVKA PLZEŇ" ("Limited-liability company formerly Skoda …, Pilsen factory"). The pistol was intended as a commercial venture but was not as successful as the promoters had hoped; the project had soon been transferred to Zbrojovka Praga (see below).

POND
Lucius W. Pond, Worcester, Massachusetts, USA.

Pond built six-shot 32- and 44-caliber rimfire revolvers in accordance with a patent obtained in July 1860 by Abram Gibson, but work on these Smith & Wesson-type guns, locked by a distinctive lever, soon stopped in favor of an "evasion" (of the patents controlled by Smith & Wesson) patented in 1862 by John Vickers. This fired rimfire cartridges inserted in individual thimbles that were loaded into the front of the cylinder. Guns of this type were offered in 22 or 32 caliber and may

have an 1864-patent ejector designed by Freeman Hood. Dating from c. 1870, the *Dead Shot* was a 22 rimfire revolver with a sheathed trigger, a solid frame and a squared butt.

POWERS
J. Powers, Holly, Michigan, USA.

Magmatic A prototype automatic pistol made in the late 1970s. It was in 44 Auto-Mag caliber and used a rotating bolt to lock the breech. The bolt was unlocked by a gas piston, after which residual chamber pressure blew the bolt open. The barrel could be removed and replaced by one in 45 ACP caliber with no changes being necessary to the breech face or other mechanism. Four guns were made, but there was no commercial production.

POŠUMAVSKÁ ZBROJOVKA KDYNĚ ("PZK")
Kdyne, Czechoslovakia.

Sometimes considered to be a trading name employed by Kohout Společnost (q.v.) of Kdyně, this business was responsible for the *PZK* and *Niva* pistols, 6.35mm blowbacks based on the FN-Browning 1906. Simply the Kohout "Mars" under different names, they were made only in small numbers. The German invasion of Czechoslovakia ended production. A typical example is marked "AUTOMAT. PISTOLE" over "P Z K" on the left side of the slide, with a "PZK" logo on the grips. A small caliber mark, "6 ³⁵" may also be found.

PRAGA
Zbrojovka Praga, Prague, Czechoslovakia.

This small-arms manufacturing company was founded in 1918 by Antonín Novotný, a gunmaker who is said to have employed talented designers such as the Holek brothers, Krnka and Myška — though the products show little by way of confirmation. Not surprisingly, the company failed to prosper and, in 1926, was foreclosed by the National Bank.

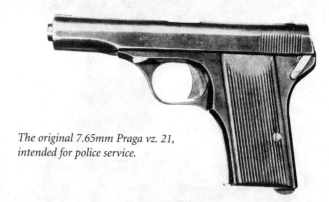

The original 7.65mm Praga vz. 21, intended for police service.

Praga vz. 21 (1) A 7.65mm-caliber blowback derived from the FN-Browning of 1910, this had a separate breechblock, lacked the barrel bushing of its prototype and used the nose of the slide to retain the return spring. Initially promoted as a military and police pistol, it had plain wooden grips and "Zbrojovka Praga" on the slide. The marking was subsequently changed to "ZBROJOVKA PRAGA / PRAHA" in two lines, and guns with the insignia of the Prague municipal police have been reported. The failure of the Praga as a military weapon forced a change of marketing strategy, and the post-1923 commercial version had molded plastic grips with "PRAGA" in a circular cartouche. Some guns had long barrels with muzzles that protruded about 1.2 inches from the tip of the slide.

Praga vz. 21 (2) This was a 6.35mm blowback pistol of singularly unusual design. The breechblock was pinned in a pressed-steel slide that was shaped into a finger grip where the front sight would usually be found, and a folding trigger lay beneath the frame. However, the

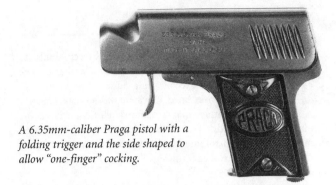

A 6.35mm-caliber Praga pistol with a folding trigger and the side shaped to allow "one-finger" cocking.

The 25-caliber (6.35mm) PAF Junior pistol, made in South Africa.

Praga is not a "one-hand" pistol. The chamber could be loaded normally, but the slide could then be eased back until the trigger locked up under a lip on the slide beneath the muzzle. This allowed the gun to be pocketed safely without requiring the additional complication of a safety catch. When the gun was drawn, the forefinger was placed in the finger grip to pull the slide back far enough to release the trigger. The trigger then sprang down to allow the forefinger to fire the gun.

The slide was marked "ZBROJOVKA PRAGA / PRAHA / PATENT CAL. 6,35" in three lines, with "PRAGA" on the grips. Quality could charitably be described only as adequate.

PRECISE IMPORTS CORPORATION ("PIC")

Or "P.I.C., Inc.", Decatur, Illinois, USA.
This dealership distributed guns and ammunition in 1955-65. The "PIC" mark could be found on a variety of handguns, including German-made Gecado automatic pistols and Model 22K Em-Ge revolvers.

PRESCOTT

Prescott Pistol Company, Worcester, Massachusetts, and Hatfield, Connecticut, USA.
Formed in the early 1850s by gunmaker Edwin Prescott, this manufacturing business made Smith & Wesson-type rimfire revolvers for Merwin & Bray from 1860 until prevented from continuing in 1863 by successful S&W litigation. The 22- and 32-caliber sheathed-trigger guns were accompanied by a few 38-caliber "Navy Models" with conventional trigger guards. Most of the revolvers incorporated a cylinder latch patented by Prescott in October 1860. Trading continued until 1870 or later, but few handguns seem to have been among the post-Civil War products.

PRETORIA ARMS FACTORY ("PAF")

Pretoria, South Africa.
This company operated for a short time in the 1950s, making the *Junior*, a 6.35mm automatic based on the Baby Browning, though without the grip safety. It was well made with the early models having raised sights and the later models having merely an aiming groove in the slide top. The slide carried a badge of two crossed cartridges in a wreath, repeated in the grip moldings, ahead of ""JUNIOR" / VERVAARDIG IN AUID-AFRIKA / MADE IN SOUTH AFRICA" in three lines. Ten thousand guns are said to have been made, but they are rarely seen outside South Africa.

Pryse's "Army Model" break-open revolver was widely used by British officers, in chamberings such as 450 and 476.

PRYSE

Charles Pryse the Younger, Birmingham, Warwickshire, England.
This gunmaker succeeded his father, the elder Charles, in 1873 and traded until 1888. He received a British Patent in 1876 to protect an "improved trigger mechanism for revolvers", but he lacked the facilities to make guns on anything other than a limited scale and was content to license his design to companies such as Francotte (q.v.) in Liége and Webley (q.v.) in Birmingham. The principal claim to novelty lay in a cylinder-locking pawl that engaged secondary notches on the cylinder when the trigger was at rest, unlocking only as the trigger was pulled. After the cylinder had revolved, a lump on the trigger then engaged in the primary notches and held the cylinder secure during the fall of the hammer.

PYRÉNÉES ("MAPF", "UNIQUE")

See "Manufacture d'Armes des Pyrénées Françaises".

RADOM ARMS FACTORY

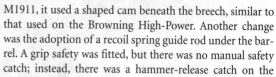

Fabryka Bronie w Radomiu, Radom, Poland; now Zaklady Metalowe Lucznik, Radom.

The Radom Arsenal has been the principal Polish small arms facility since 1920. Prior to 1939, it manufactured two military pistols, the Nagant revolver and the Radom automatic. Since 1945 its production has not been revealed, but it is assumed that copies of Soviet Makarov pistols, as well as other Warsaw Pact weapons, have been made there. In the 1990s, it succumbed to the European disease and became "privatized" as the Zaklady Metalowe Lucnik.

~ REVOLVER ~

Ng 30 This was simply the 1895-pattern Russian Nagant (q.v.) revolver, made in Radom from 1930 onwards. It was chambered for the Russian 7.62mm cartridge, lacked the gas-seal feature of the original and had a rounded-blade foresight instead of the sharper Russian pattern. Serial numbers suggest that as many as 20,000 may have been made. They were marked "F.B." over "RADOM" over "Ng30" on the rear left side of the frame beneath the hammer.

~ AUTOMATIC PISTOLS ~

Vis-35 The development of this pistol presents an unusual story. Desperate to prevent the adoption of the Czechoslovakian vz. 24 (q.v.), Pyotr Wilniewczyc, an engineer employed by the National Armament Factory (PWU), raised such vocal objections that he was allowed to develop a pistol that was little more than an idea. He completed the basic design with the assistance of Jan Skryzpinski and, after successful test-firing, obtained a patent in February 1932. The Polish government duly purchased manufacturing rights in 1933, a de-cocking mechanism was added, and the first deliveries of what had become the Pistolet Vis wz. 35 (but is now more commonly known as the "Radom") were made to the Polish army in 1936.

The Vis was a modified Browning design, using the usual locking lugs on the barrel, but instead of the swinging link used in the Colt M1911, it used a shaped cam beneath the breech, similar to that used on the Browning High-Power. Another change was the adoption of a recoil spring guide rod under the barrel. A grip safety was fitted, but there was no manual safety catch; instead, there was a hammer-release catch on the slide, which, when pressed, retracted the firing pin and then allowed the hammer to fall. The pistol could then be carried safely with a round in the chamber and was readied for firing by simply thumbing back the hammer.

At the rear of the frame was a stripping catch that resembled the safety catch on a Colt M1911, but it did nothing except lock the slide back when dismantling the pistol. It is a bulky and rather heavy weapon for its caliber and, because of its weight, very comfortable to shoot.

Radom pistols bore the Polish eagle on the left side of the frame, separating the place and date of manufacture (e.g., "RADOM" over "1939r") from the designation and an acknowledgment of the patent ("VIS-WZ. 35" over "PAT.NR.15567"). The checkered plastic grips displayed "FB" within an inverted triangle (*Fabryka Broni*, "arms factory"). Approximately 18,000 guns had been made when the Germans invaded Poland in 1940. Managerial staff was imported from Steyr-Daimler-Puch, and handgun output was diverted to the Wehrmacht. These pistols customarily bear German proof and inspectors' markings. Slides are marked "F.B.RADOM VIS MODEL 35. PAT. NR. 15567" in a single line, usually above the German designation "P.35 (p.)". Designation marks will also be found on reissued ex-Polish weapons. Interestingly, the Radom factory was one of the very few munitions makers that was never allocated a production code by the Germans; it operated under its own name throughout the war.

The construction and finish of wz. 35 pistols made prior to the beginning of 1944 were eminently acceptable, but a progressive deterioration led to the omission of the stock-slot on the heel of the butt, the deletion of the stripping catch on the left rear of the frame and the substitution of radially-grooved wooden grips for finely checkered plastic. When the Germans evacuated Radom in the face of the Russian advance in the autumn of 1944, large numbers of components were evacuated to the Steyr factory (or to one of its subsidiaries) and work continued into 1945. The quality of these, which bear the code "bnz", was exceptionally poor. Production under German control has been estimated at 310,000 guns.

• *Modern version* In 1992, Zaklady Metalowe Lucznik put the Radom pistol back into production, principally for collectors but also as a service pistol for anyone so inclined. The original engineering drawings of 1937 were used as the basis, and the pistol is virtually identical though with very slight differences in weight and overall

A Polish 9mm VIS-35 or Radom pistol. This example bears German inspection marks and "P. 35 (p)" on the slide.

The Radom pistol field-stripped, showing it to be a variant of the 1911-type Colt-Browning.

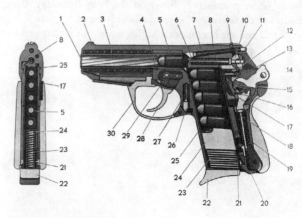

A drawing of the Polish P-64 pistol, derived from the Walther PPK.

length. It is, of course, to an exceptionally high quality of manufacture and finish.

P-64 This replaced the obsolete Pistolet TT (the Soviet Tokarev) in the Polish army. It bears a strong resemblance to the Soviet Makarov, fires the same ammunition and is simply another copy of the Walther PP, albeit with some cosmetic changes largely in the interest of simplifying manufacture and keeping down the cost. A blowback weapon using a double-action trigger mechanism, it has the safety catch on the slide where it doubles as a de-cocking lever and also moves the firing pin into a safe position before it lowers the hammer. The pistol appears to have been reliable and was in service for just over 20 years before being replaced by an even cheaper version.

The Polish 9mm P-83 pistol was an updated P-64 suited to modern manufacturing techniques.

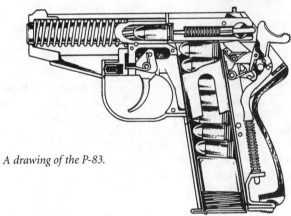

A drawing of the P-83.

P-83 This was developed in the late 1970s as a cheaper and easier-to-manufacture replacement for the P-64. Its general appearance and operation are similar to the P-64, a fixed-barrel blowback, but there is more use of pressings and precision castings in the design and less machining work required. The lockwork is double action, and a slide-mounted lever drops the hammer safely onto the loaded chamber, lowering the end of the firing pin out of the hammer path as it does so. It also has a loaded-chamber indicator.

In its original form, the P-83 was chambered for the 9mm Makarov round, but in later years, it was chambered for the 9mm Short (380 ACP) cartridge in the hopes of finding an export market. A minor point of interest is that the dismantling method was changed from the hinged trigger guard of the Walther to a pull-down catch inside the trigger guard copied from the pre-1945 Sauer 38H.

P-93 This is a further development of the P-83, which it generally resembles. The principal difference is the placement of the de-cocking lever on the frame, above the left-side grip instead of on the slide. The hammer is a ring type, rather than a spur, and the rear sight is

The 9mm Polish P-93 is an improvement on the P-83.

adjustable. The original caliber was 9mm Makarov, but the manufacturer says that "it can be adapted for" the 9mm Short/380 ACP cartridge. Just how this adaptation is done is still unresolved.

MAG-95 A conventional double-action locked-breech military pistol with overtones of Browning and SIG, this has obviously been designed with export sale in mind, being chambered for the 9mm Parabellum cartridge. The tapering frame resembles the Browning GP35, but the barrel locks into the central ejection port in a similar manner to the SIG 220 series. There is a frame-mounted de-cocking lever, a slide-stop lever and also a stripping catch on the left side; an automatic firing pin safety system is incorporated. The barrel is chromed internally, and a laser target indicator can be fitted to the front of the frame. An elongated 20-round magazine is optional.

- *MAG-98* A variant of the MAG-95 with an alloy slide and a recoil buffer, reducing the weight to 875g.

RAICK

Raick Frères, Liége, Belgium.

Kobold Sales name for a series of revolvers of the "Constabulary" type, short-barreled solid-frame double-action guns with rod ejectors and bird's-head butts. Some had folding triggers; others had fixed triggers with guards. Most had a manual safety catch on the left of the frame that locked the hammer. They were customarily chambered for 320 CF, 380 CF, 44 Russian and 450 CF cartridges and were frequently distributed by gunmakers and retailers (e.g. J.B. Rongé in Belgium and Albrecht Kind of Germany).

Lincoln A name that was very popular among Liége gunmakers, this was applied to a wide variety of revolvers produced in 1880-1914. Most were of the folding-trigger pocket variety — including hammer and "hammerless" types — in chamberings ranging from 22 rimfire to 5.5mm Velo-Dog and 380 centerfire. Other makers using this name included Ancion Marx, Bertrand, Debouxtay, Dumoulin, Jannsen Fils et Cie, Le Page and Neumann Frères, all of Liége, and Albrecht Kind in Germany. Most (or, indeed) all of the guns may have been made by Manufacture Liégeoise d'Armes à Feu.

RANDALL

Randall Firearms Company, Sun Valley, California, USA.

This short-lived gunmaking business, active only in 1983-5, made a bewildering variety of Colt-Browning clones — 24 different models in just two years. Most of the products were designated with a letter prefix and a three digit-number. The letters codes were "A" for right-hand ejection, "B" for left-hand ejection, and "C" for a featherweight frame with right-hand ejection; the numbers identified the frame type, slide configuration and caliber. For example, Model A121 ejected to the right, had a "Service Model" frame and a flattop slide with fixed sights. Chambering was 45 ACP. The complicated history of Randall is difficult to summarize in a few sentences, but more information can be found in the *Standard Catalog of Firearms*.

An 8mm Rast & Gasser M1898 revolver.

The Reck R-12 revolver, with the marks of the US distributor Spesco.

A Reck R14 revolver.

RAST & GASSER

Vienna, Austria-Hungary.
Probably the last pistol to carry the name of Gasser (q.v.) was the Rast & Gasser *Model 1898* Austro-Hungarian service revolver in 8mm caliber. This was an 8-shot solid-frame model, gate-loaded with rod ejection. The right-side loading gate was on the Abadie system, disconnecting the hammer from the trigger when opened for loading. The Rast & Gasser looks somewhat angular today, and the grip angle is poor from the instinctive shooting viewpoint, but the guns were extremely well-made and reliable.

The Raven Arms P-25 pistol.

RAVEN ARMS

Industry, California, USA.
This company, which failed in 1984, made a good-quality 25 ACP blowback automatic called the "P25". This had an all-enveloping slide and generally resembles the Baby Browning, though lacking a grip safety. It also had an unusual safety catch that, when applied, also locked the slide. The *MP25* had a diecast frame and walnut or ivory grips. See also "Phoenix Arms".

RECK

Karl Arndt Reck Sportwaffenfabrik KG, Lauf/Pegnitz, Germany.
In the 1950s and 1960s, Reck manufactured a 6.35mm blowback automatic known as the "P-8", which was widely sold in Europe and also extensively exported to the USA, where it sold under such names as "La Fury" and "Chicago Cub". It was striker-fired, made largely of alloy, could be obtained in a variety of finishes and sold cheaply. Reck also made a derringer-like 22-caliber single-shot pistol and a solid-frame non-extracting six-shot 22-rimfire folding-trigger revolver called the "Recky".

The Gun Control Act of 1968 ended the importation of small pistols into the USA, and increasing competition, together with growing restrictions on ownership of pistols, forced Reck to turn increasingly towards starting and alarm pistols. The business was absorbed by a sporting-goods conglomerate in the 1980s and now operates as the Reck Division of Umarex-Sportwaffen of Arnsberg, making only starting and similar pistols.

～ REVOLVERS ～

Baby Introduced in the late 1950s, this, like most of the Reck pistols of that time, was a simple five-shot 22 rimfire revolver with a folding trigger and the front sight mounted on a distinctive collar around the muzzle.

Chicago Cub This was another of the cheap 22 rimfire solid-frame revolvers manufactured in the 1950s. It was sold in Europe as the "Recky" and in the USA as the "Chicago Cub". The Gun Control Act of 1968 ended the importation.

～ AUTOMATIC PISTOL ～

LA Fury, La Fury A 6.35mm blowback automatic, more or less based on the Baby Browning, made in the 1970s.

REID

James Reid, New York City and Catskill, New York State, USA.
Best known as the patentee of a combination revolver/knuckleduster, Reid began his gunmaking career in 1862. Many of the wartime guns will be found with the names of Fitch or Irving of New York City, who were presumably acting as distributors.

～ REVOLVERS ～

Civil War type These were made in a variety of shapes and sizes but usually had plain-surface cylinders and sheathed triggers. The design was clearly inspired by the contemporaneous Smith & Wesson, with a barrel that pivoted up and back once a catch on the lower front of the frame had been released.

- *Number 1* Chambered for the 22 rimfire cartridge, this had a seven-chamber cylinder and a 3.5-inch octagonal barrel. The frame was usually blued iron, and the grips were walnut.
- *Number 2* This was an enlargement of the No. 1, chambered for 32 Short rimfire ammunition. The cylinder held five rounds.
- *Number 3* A modification of the No. 2, a five-shot 32, this had a grip that curved noticeably more sharply than its predecessor. Plugs in the rear of the chambers allowed percussion-cap nipples to be substituted.

- *Number 4* Apparently also known as the "Navy Model", this was another convertible rimfire/caplock. The rammer was solid and a multi-part rammer was attached beneath the barrel. Chambering is believed to have been 32 or 38 rimfire, which equated to 31- and 35-caliber cap-and-ball.

Derringer This was a conventional revolver based on the Knuckle Duster but lacking the finger-hole butt. Introduced in 1879, the guns had 3-inch octagonal barrels, 5-chamber fluted cylinders and conventional squared-heel butts with walnut grips. The *No. 3* had a silver-plated brass frame, a blued barrel and a blued cylinder; the essentially similar *No. 4* had a polished brass frame. Production ceased in 1884.

Knuckle Duster The "My Friend" pattern was revised in the mid-1870s when two new designs appeared. The *No. 1* had a 3-inch barrel and the *No. 2* had a 1.8-inch barrel, the changes being made, presumably, to prevent accidents occurring when the fingers of the firing hand strayed across the firing chamber of the barreless pattern. Offered in 38 or 41 rimfire, the Knuckle Dusters could be identified by the finger-hole in the butt. They had brass frames, usually silver-plated, and plain-surface cylinders. The barrel and cylinder were usually blued. The trigger was set in the front of the butt, but the cylinder-release catch projected from the lower front of the frame beneath the barrel. Production stopped in the early 1880s.

My Friend Patented in 1865, this distinctive "barreless" revolver was offered as a seven-shot 22 or a five-shot 41 rimfire. The frame, made of blued iron or brass (often silver plated), had a large finger hole cast into the slab-sided butt to enable the gun to be used as a knuckleduster. The sheathed trigger is set into the front of the butt, and a small sliding cylinder-release catch lies under the frame.

New Model My Friend Only a handful of these guns were made in 1884, apparently in 32 centerfire. They had five-chamber cylinders, 2-inch barrels and a conventionally shaped grip cast integrally with the frame. A slender loop stretching forward from the toe of the butt to the rear of the trigger sheath provided the "knuckles".

The Reiger mechanically-operated repeating pistol with the feed-spool detached.

REIGER

Erwin Reiger, Vienna, Austria.

Reiger was one of many inventors, mostly Austro-Hungarian, who developed a mechanical repeating pistol in the late 1880s. His version is similar to most others, relying upon a rotating bolt driven by the action of a ring trigger. Pushing forward on the trigger retracts the bolt; pulling back closes the bolt, driving a cartridge from the magazine (ahead of the trigger guard) into the chamber and cocking the striker. Continued pressure trips the striker and fires the round. The Reiger was unusual in employing a rotary magazine instead of a clip-fed box and appears to be chambered for the 7.7mm Bittner cartridge. Like all mechanical repeaters, specimens of the Reiger are extremely uncommon partly because they worked efficiently only when meticulously

cleaned and oiled and partly because of the advent of the automatic pistol in the same era.

REISING

Reising Arms Co., Hartford, Connecticut;
Reising Mfg Corp., New York, USA.

Patented by Eugene Reising in 1916-21, this 22-caliber target pistol had a long barrel pivoting around the front of the frame. Releasing a locking catch allowed the barrel to tip down for cleaning. The slide resembled that of the Mannlicher, with a solid rear and arms at the sides that were linked at the front to compress a return spring in the frame beneath the rear end of the barrel. A 10-shot magazine fitted into the butt.

After making about 3500 pistols in Hartford in 1921, Reising moved his business to New York in 1922. Another 1000 guns were made, but sales were not encouraging and production stopped in 1924. The pistols carry the company name and address on the left side of the slide, with a bear's-head motif and the slogan "It's a Bear" molded into the bakelite grips. Minor differences can be detected between the Hartford and New York-made pistols, doubtless reflecting improvements that were suggested during production.

REMINGTON

E. Remington & Sons, Ilion, New York State; Remington Arms Company, Ilion, New York State; Remington-Arms–Union Metallic Cartridge Co., Ilion, New York State, and Bridgeport, Connecticut, USA.

This company was founded by Eliphalet Remington in 1816 and from the 1850s onwards produced a variety of pistols of varying quality. The original business collapsed in 1886, unable to compete with Colt and Winchester, but was revived in 1888 as the "Remington Arms Company". Interest in handguns had declined only to revive in the 1920s with an outstanding automatic pistol that, however, failed to achieve the success it deserved. Remington thereafter concentrated on shoulder arms until returning to the handgun field with the unusual bolt-action Fireball.

∼ SINGLE-SHOT PISTOLS ∼

Vest-pocket Model (1865-88) About 25,000 of these tiny 22 rimfire tip-barrel pistols were made. They had 3.25-inch barrels, sheathed triggers, exposed hammers, slab-sided iron frames that were either blued or silver plated, and walnut grips with a distinctively serpentine base.

Navy Model (1865-70) These 50-caliber guns, chambered for rimfire ammunition, were made only in comparatively small numbers. They can be identified by the rolling-block breech, shared with the outstandingly successful rifle. A pivoted breechblock, which carries the firing pin, can be swung back and down — in a similar arc to that of the hammer — to expose the chamber for loading. After closing the breech, the hammer is released, but as it begins to fall, the hammer breast moves behind the breechblock to give positive support as the firing pin is struck.

- *M1865* This had an 8.5-inch round barrel, a blued case-hardened frame, and a butt and fore-end of walnut. The most distinctive features, however, were the round-back grip and the sheath trigger. Total production is estimated to have been about 6500.
- *M1867* Similar mechanically to the M1865, this had a conventional trigger guard and a 7-inch barrel. Production amounted only to a couple of thousand.

Army Model (1872-88) An improved version of the Navy Model, chambered for 50-caliber ammunition, the M1871 had an 8-inch round barrel, a prawled backstrap and a squared butt. About 6000 were made, including substantial quantities for commercial sale.

Target Models The rolling-block pistol proved to be accurate and dependable and was ideally suited to target shooting. The guns were essentially lighter and more elegant versions of the 1871-pattern Army pistol, offered in a variety of chamberings and finishes.

- *M1891* Only about 100 guns of this type were made in 1891-8, usually with 10-inch half-octagon barrels and adjustable sights. The rear sight lay on the barrel. Chamberings were restricted to 22 short and long rimfire, 25 Stevens, 32-20 WCF and 32 S&W centerfire; the frame was case-hardened, and the woodwork was select walnut.
- *M1901* Little more than the 1891 pattern with the rolling-block thumb-piece moved to the left, out of the sight line, and the rear sight on the frame instead of the barrel, this was also made only in small quantities. Chamberings were similar to the earlier guns, with the probable addition of 44 Russian.

XP-100 Fireball More than 30 years after the demise of the Model 51, Remington returned to the handgun business with this pistol, which combined the bolt action of the Model 700 rifle with a 14.5-inch ventilated-rib barrel. The stock was originally nylon-based plastic, with a fore-end tip separated by a thin white-line spacer and a diamond motif on the fore-end. The grip was ambidextrous, and a hollow in the fore-end allowed up to five 130-grain 38-caliber bullets to be inserted to adjust the balance. The rear sight was adjustable, and the receiver was drilled and tapped for optical-sight mounts.

The XP-100 was designed to chamber the 221 Remington Fireball cartridge but from 1980 was also offered in 7mm BR ("Bench Rest") — a proprietary Remington cartridge made by cutting down the 308 Winchester case.

- *XP-100 Custom* Introduced in 1986, this is essentially a Silhouette with a nylon or walnut stock. Chamberings have included 223 Remington, 250-3000 Savage, 6mm BR, 7mm BR, 7mm-08 and 35 Remington.
- *XP-100 Hunter* Characterized by a 14.5-inch barrel, tapped and drilled for optical-sight mounts, this lacks open sights. It also has a laminated wooden stock and has been offered in similar chamberings to the Custom version (excepting 250-300 Savage and 6mm BR)
- *XP-100R* (1998 to date) Available in 22-250, 223 Remington, 260 Remington and 35 Remington, this has a 14.5-inch barrel drilled and tapped for optical sights. The most obvious feature is the fiberglass stock, which has a conventional pistol-grip butt at the rear of the action instead of the more familiar design with the pistol grip set forward at the point of balance.
- *XP-100 Silhouette* Chambered for the 7mm BR or 35 Remington rounds, this offers a 15-inch barrel, drilled and tapped for optical-sight mounts, and a plain synthetic stock.

~ REPEATING PISTOLS ~

Zig-Zag derringer (1861-2) Only about 1000 of these interesting 22 short rimfire guns, patented in 1858-60 by William Elliot, were ever made. They have a revolving six-barrel cluster, 3.3 inches long, operated by a ring trigger and a series of zig-zag grooves in the barrel-cluster surface. The barrels tip upward at the breech to load and are fired by an internal hammer.

Remington-Elliot derringer (1863-88) The failure of the "Zig-Zag" pattern (above) inspired this tip-barrel cluster-barrel gun, which was essentially a fixed-barrel pepperbox chambering either 22 rimfire or 32 rimfire ammunition (five and four shots, respectively). Finished in blue or nickel with rubber grips, the guns had revolving firing pins. Production is estimated to have totaled 25,000, but it is likely that manufacture had ceased by the mid-1870s and that the guns being sold in the late 1880s had been in store for many years.

Double Derringer (1866-1935) Designed and patented in 1865 by Joseph Rider, this 41-caliber over-and-under design was extraordinarily successful as a hideaway or "back-up" defense. Remington made about 150,000 of them, and derringers of this type — sturdy, simple and reliable — are still being made by gunmaking businesses through-

out the world. The barrels pivot upward to load, once the catch on the right side of the frame has been released, automatically re-setting the auto-sequencing firing pin. The iron frame was generally blued or nickeled, and the grips could be walnut, rosewood, rubber, ivory or mother-of-pearl. The earliest guns lacked extractors, but a manual system was fitted after only a few hundred had been made, and then replaced in turn by a mechanically-operated extractor. Markings may give a clue to age: pre-1888 examples bear the marks of E. Remington & Sons, those made between 1888 and 1911 are marked "Remington Arms Company", and 1912-35 output bore the mark of the Remington Arms–Union Metallic Cartridge Company. Double Derringers are about 4.8 inches long with a 3-inch barrel and weigh about 11 oz empty.

Magazine Repeating Pistol (or "Rider derringer", 1871-88) Patented in August 1871 by Joseph Rider, this was an extremely simple design with a tubular magazine beneath the barrel, an oddly-shaped grip and a stud trigger. The breechblock was hidden in the frame, with a cocking spur protruding ahead of a smaller spur on the hammer. Pulling the breechblock spur backward drew back and cocked the hammer, operated the extractor and raised a cartridge from the magazine. Releasing the cocking-spur allowed the breechblock to run forward under spring pressure, stripping a cartridge into the chamber and lowering the cartridge-lifter to pick up the next round. The 32 Extra Short rimfire cartridge was apparently developed specially for this pistol, to allow five rounds to be loaded into the restricted magazine space and keep the breech as short as possible. Overall length was about 5.9 inches with a 3-inch barrel. Only about 10,000 guns of this type were made.

~ REVOLVERS ~

In addition to the purpose-built guns listed below, Remington also offered rimfire adaptations of the well-known 36- and 44-caliber caplocks. These included the first batch of military-style revolvers ever to be converted, the work being undertaken by Smith & Wesson in 1866.

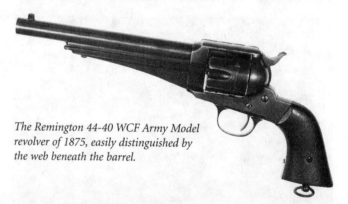

The Remington 44-40 WCF Army Model revolver of 1875, easily distinguished by the web beneath the barrel.

Army Model 1875 Developed to compete with the Colt Peacemaker, this could be recognized by the prominent stiffening web beneath the barrel. Loaded through a pivoting gate on the rear right side of the frame behind the cylinder, with an ejector-rod case offset to the lower right side of the barrel, the standard single-action M1875 had a 7.5-inch barrel. Chamberings were restricted to 44 Remington, 44-40 WCF and 45 Long Colt. The finish could be blue (with color case-hardening on the frame) or nickel-plate, and the grips were usually walnut. Lanyard rings were usually fitted to the base of the butt. Production continued until the late 1880s, but only about 25,000 were ever made.

- *Model 1890* (1891-4) A lightened version of the M1875, lacking all but the vestiges of the stiffening web beneath the barrel, this was made only in 44-40 WCF. The barrels measured 5.5 or 7.5 inches, finish could be blue or nickel and the grips were customarily black rubber with an "RA" monogram. Production ran to little more than 2000 guns.

Iroquois (1878-88) A 22 rimfire revolver with a solid frame and a sheathed trigger, this offered better quality than the usual "suicide special". It had a bird's-head butt, a 2.25-inch barrel and a seven-chamber cylinder. The popularity of the Iroquois is difficult to assess, owing to estimates of production that range from as low as 10,000 to as high as 50,000 or more. Most bear the company name on the barrel, and many guns are nickel-plated.

New Line These were based on a design by William Smoot, an employee, but conformed with the same formula as many rivals — solid frames, sheathed triggers, single-action lockwork, and bird's-head or round butts — but the quality was far better than average.

- *Number 1* (1874-88) This was a five-shot gun in 30 rimfire with a spring-loaded ejector rod offset to the right of the barrel so that it aligned with the chamber directly ahead of the loading gate. It had a 2.75-inch octagonal barrel and, originally at least, a rotating recoil shield. Made of iron, blued or nickel-plated, the No. 1 had grips of walnut or rubber.
- *Nunber 2* Similar to No. 1, this chambered 32 rimfire ammunition. Production in 1878-88 is said to have totaled about 20,000 guns.
- *Number 3* Similar to No. 1 and chambered only for 38 rim- or centerfire ammunition, this was made in two versions. The original had a round butt and lacked the barrel rib; the later pattern had squared butt contours and a prominent barrel rib. It has been estimated that 25,000 were made.

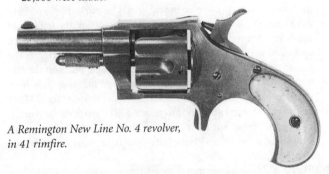

A Remington New Line No. 4 revolver, in 41 rimfire.

- *Number 4* (1877-88) Chambered for 38 Short or 41 Short rim- or centerfire cartridges, with a 2.5-inch barrel, this differed from the others in the series. It had a tapered round barrel and lacked an ejector, a prominent knurled arbor pin being removed to release the cylinder from the frame. Only about 10,000 No. 4 revolvers were made.

A Remington-made M1911 pistol, dating from World War I.

∽ AUTOMATIC PISTOLS ∽

Colt M1911 A contract to make 150,000 45 M1911 Colt-Browning pistols was placed with Remington–UMC in December 1917, but the end of World War I stopped work in December 1918 after only 13,152 had been produced. They were identical mechanically with the guns made by Colt (q.v.), but the left side of the slides displayed Remington–UMC marks.

Model 53 Shortly before the USA entered World War I, Remington had begun to develop a pistol designed by John Pedersen. An experimental 45 ACP version was offered to the armed forces, interesting the US Navy in particular, but the war ended before adoption could be formalized and the pistol re-emerged as the Model 51 (below).

The M53 was about 8.3 inches long, with a 5-inch barrel, and weighed 35 oz without its seven-round box magazine. The barrel was fixed with a concentric return spring, and a separate lightweight breechblock unit was carried in the slide. When the gun fired, the block and the slide recoiled together for about 2mm until the bottom rear section of the breechblock was temporarily stopped against a transom in the frame and the slide moved back alone. Once the slide had moved far enough, a ramp disengaged the breechblock from the transom and the slide and breechblock once more ran backward together.

The system is generally described as a "delayed blowback", but the breech actually opens immediately as the gun is fired — like any other blowback. The only departure from standard practice is the momentary halting of the breechblock, with the case protruding slightly from the chamber (and doubtless with gas leaking all around it), until the opening movement is resumed.

The hammer was cocked at the end of the opening stroke of the slide/breechblock unit, which was then returned by the spring to strip a fresh cartridge into the chamber. As the action came to the end of the forward stroke, the interaction of sloping faces in the slide and on the breechblock once more forced the block downward.

The Pedersen-designed Remington M51 pistol, in 380 ACP.

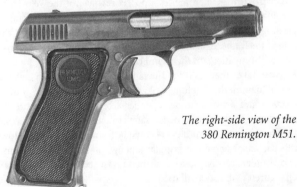

The right-side view of the 380 Remington M51.

- *Model 51* Placed on the market in September 1919 in 380 ACP (seven-round magazine) and followed in 1921 by a 32 ACP version (eight rounds), this remained in production until 1927 — though new guns were still being sold from stock in 1934. The first guns were marked "PATENT PENDING"; later examples acknowledged patents granted in 1920 and 1921, and 16 grooves replaced the original nine. Virtually all were blued, with black plastic or rubber grips marked "REMINGTON" over "UMC" within a circle. Total production has been estimated at about 54,000 guns in 380 ACP and 11,500 in 32 ACP.

The M51 was essentially a small-caliber version of the M53, though the hammer was mounted internally. It was about 6.6 inches long, with a 3.5-inch barrel, and weighed 21.2 oz empty. The grip safety, which normally lay flush with the butt, protruded from the backstrap if the action was cocked; and the manual lever could be set to safe only when the hammer was cocked.

The Remington was exceptionally well made and has always been praised for its handling qualities. However, the only justification for the use of the Pedersen breech system with low-powered ammunition lay in the alleged reduction in recoil. Additional complication called for precise machining and the need to fit intricate components with care. Consequently, the M51 was expensive enough to deter prospective purchasers.

REPUBLIC ARMS, INC.

Chino, California, USA.

This gunmaking business promoted the *Patriot* pistol, introduced in 1997. This was a double-action-only 45 ACP gun with a 3-inch barrel and fixed sights. It also had a black polymer frame with integral checkered grips and a stainless-steel slide. The magazine held six rounds, giving a loaded weight of about 24 oz; overall length was about 6 inches.

REPUBLIC ARMS PTY

Johannesburg, South Africa.

This made a double-action *Republic* revolver in 38 Special, a five-shot solid-frame design with a side-opening cylinder on Smith & Wesson lines. It was to be produced with a 2- or 3-inch barrel and was extensively advertised in South Africa in 1979, but little was heard of it thereafter and it is probable that production never began and that only prototypes were made.

RETOLAZA

Retolaza Hermanos ("Retolaza Brothers"), Eibar, Spain.

Retolaza began working in the 1890s, making the inevitable Velo-Dog pocket revolver, and circumstantial evidence suggests that they were among the pioneers of automatic pistol manufacture in Eibar. They joined the 1915 "gold rush" and continued producing cheap automatics until the Spanish Civil War (1936-9) ended their activities.

～ REVOLVERS ～

Brompetier A "hammerless" pocket revolver of the Velo-Dog type manufactured between 1905 and 1915. Of the usual solid-frame non-ejecting pattern, it had a folding trigger and a safety catch on the left side of the frame. Available in 6.35mm and 7.65mm Auto, it carried the name "Brompetier" on the round barrel.

Puppy Like other pistols of the same name from Spanish makers, this was a "hammerless" folding-trigger revolver with a solid frame, rod ejection and a five-chamber cylinder accepting the 22 Short rimfire round. The butt was rounded, a safety catch lay on the rear left side of the frame and the word "PUPPY" could be found on the barrel. However, this particular name was popular among Spanish makers of Velo-Dog and similar revolvers, as Arizmendi, Crucelegui, Gaztañaga and Ojanguren y Marcaido all used it.

Velo-Brom Otherwise identical to the "Brompetier", this had an octagonal barrel and chambered either 5.5mm Velo-Dog or 8mm Lebel cartridges. The length of these cartridges ensured that the Velo-Brom cylinder was longer than usual, each division between the chambers being marked by one and a half flutes.

Velo-Mith Like many other guns of this name, the Retolaza version was a hammerless hinged-frame folding-trigger revolver with the front part of the barrel shaped to resemble the 1900-type FN-Browning automatic pistol. It can be found in 6.35mm and 7.65mm calibers.

～ AUTOMATIC PISTOLS ～

Like the products of many other Spanish gunmakers, the Retolaza output is often difficult to identify. It is probable that some of the pistols, such as the Liberty, were also made elsewhere — possibly in different periods or perhaps for a particular distributor.

Gallus A 6.35mm-caliber "Eibar"-type blowback automatic, this probably dates from the early 1920s. However, few of the guns bear anything other than "PISTOLET AUTOMATIQUE 6 35 GALLUS" on the slide and have "CAL 6,35" encircled on the grips. Attribution to Retolaza, therefore, requires authentication.

Liberty Several different guns of this name have been reported.

• *6.35mm type* The oldest of these is believed to be a copy of the FN-Browning of 1906, with a grip safety in the backstrap and the manual safety catch on the left rear side of the frame. The slide grips are milled vertically. Most of the guns that could be traced were marked by Fabrique d'Armes de Grande Précision (q.v.) and had "LIBERTY" on a band running across the grips diagonally. Later guns, lacking the Grande Précision name, are usually much larger with extended butts containing eight-round magazines and have the "LIBERTY" band horizontally in addition to an encircled panther's (lion's?) head trademark on the grips; some are marked "AUTOMATIC PISTOL CAL 6³⁵" in a single line, while others display "CAL .25 – 1924 AUTOMATIC PISTOL – EIBAR" above "LIBERTY" in two lines. The safety catch has been moved forward above the trigger, the grip safety is absent and many of the guns were proofed in Italy.

• *7.65mm type* Also associated with Bolumburu, this is little more than the wartime Ruby pistol, even though it may be marked " ‹7 65 1914 Automatic Pistol ›" over "…"LIBERTY" Patent" on the left side of the slide. It has vertical slide grips, prominent sights and a safety catch on the mid-point of the left side of the frame above the trigger. The magazine holds eight rounds and a lanyard ring appears on the rear bottom left side of the butt. Guns of this type that may have been made for sale to the French and Italian forces during World War I may have had wood grips and an encircled "RH" mark on the rear left side of the frame, but most of them, distinguished by plastic grips with a wheat-ear design on the horizontal band, were probably sold commercially after 1918.

Military This was a long-butt 6.35mm Liberty, with "MILITARY" on the slide and grips.

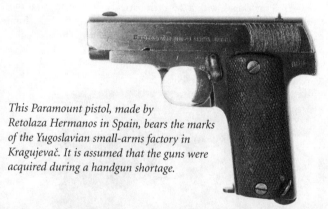

This Paramount pistol, made by Retolaza Hermanos in Spain, bears the marks of the Yugoslavian small-arms factory in Kragujevač. It is assumed that the guns were acquired during a handgun shortage.

Paramount This name, popular in Spain, has often been associated with Retolaza. However, most 6.35mm and 7.65mm guns are usually attributed to Apaolozo Hermanos (q.v.) and there seems no reason for doubt.

Retolaza This was a standard "Ruby"-type gun, possibly made during World War I. It has radially milled slide grips, a safety catch above the trigger on the left side of the frame (often marked in English), prominent sights, plain checkered grips and a lanyard ring on the lower left side of the butt. The mark on the left side of the slide usually reads "7 ⁶⁵ 1914 MODEL AUTOMATIC PISTOL" over " – RETOLAZA – ", with "RH" in an oval on the left rear of the frame.

Stosel It has been suggested that this was Retolaza's first automatic, a belief based on a name that was probably bestowed in honor of the commander of the Russian Port Arthur garrison during the Russo-Japanese War of 1904-5. Even though Anatoly Stessel (usually "Stossel" in English-language literature) had soon been court-martialed and disgraced, newspaper accounts had ensured that he enjoyed a hero's reputation outside Russia. However, it seems likely that the guns were made while the name was still well known, which suggests 1908-10.

- *6.35mm type* It is difficult to decide which of the sub-variants came first, but the honor probably belongs to those that are marked simply "≺ 'STOSEL' Patent ≻", with a crown in an oval cartouche in the top of the grips; these guns also have finely-milled vertical retraction grips in the slide. Next came essentially similar guns with coarse retraction grooves in the slide, plain checkered grips and markings that included "PISTOLA AUTOMATICA CAL 6 ³⁵" over "…'STOSEL' No 1" on the left side. A change was then made to radially milled retraction grooves and grips displaying not only the crown but also "STOSEL" on a diagonal band. These guns are usually marked "6³⁵ MODEL AUTOMATIC PISTOL" over "1912 'STOSEL' PATENT".

- *7.65mm type* The earlier of the two known patterns is identical mechanically to the striker-fired 6.35mm version, but it is larger, has prominent sights and a lanyard ring lies on the lower left side of the butt. It is marked "7⁶⁵ — MODEL AUTOMATIC PISTOL" over "1912 'STOSEL' PATENT", with a general-on-horseback motif in the grip cartouche and "STOSEL" on the grip-band. The later gun, with a magazine holding nine rounds instead of seven, has slide grooves that are milled vertically, plain-bordered checkered grips and a hammer-type firing system. Its slide is usually marked "≺ 7⁶⁵ 1914 AUTOMATIC PISTOL ≻" over "≺ 'STOSEL' No 1 PATENT ≻".

Titan Often identified with Retolaza, this seems to have been made by Suinaga y Aramperri (q.v.). It is similar to but not identical with the 6.35mm "Gallus".

The Retolaza Hermanos 7.65mm Auto (32 ACP) "Titanic" pistol.

Titanic Another example of the Spanish talent for topical names, this appeared in 1913, the year after the sinking of the famous steamship. The presence of the mark on a variety of different guns suggests that it was a brand name applied by an unidentified distributor.

- *6.35mm type* One of these was the usual Browning 1906 derivation, similar to the "Gallus", with a recessed rib on top of the rear portion of the slide. Others bear "FA" within a crowned heart, the mark of Francisco Arizmendi (q.v.), and some are marked by Fabrique d'Armes de Grande Précision.

- *7.65mm type* A conventional "Eibar"-type pistol, with a six-round magazine, this was certainly a Retolaza product. Marked "7⁶⁵ 1914 MODEL AUTOMATIC PISTOL" over "…'TITANIC' EIBAR", it also has an oval containing "RH" (for "Retolaza Hermanos") on the frame and shares the slide-cut with the 6.35mm Gallus-type gun. The grips display "TITANIC" arched around a "RHyC" monogram, flanked by the caliber designation. A second pattern is similar but lacks the slide-cut. It has plain checkered grips, prominent sights and a lan-

yard ring on the butt. The slide mark omits "Model" and substitutes "PATENT" for "Eibar".

RÉUNIES

Fabrique d'Armes Réunies (1909-14), Belgium.

This company was set up in 1909 to produce the "Dictator" pistol, which was patented in the company's name. The inventor is unknown. Work ceased when the Germans invaded Belgium, and although guns have been seen with the marks of "Fabrique d'Armes Unies" (q.v., in the "U" section), these are believed to have been made in Spain in 1918-31.

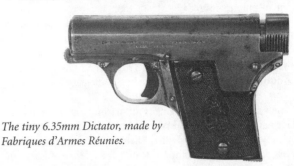

The tiny 6.35mm Dictator, made by Fabriques d'Armes Réunies.

Dictator (also sold as "Centaure") Patented in 1909, this was manufactured only until the Germans invaded Belgium in 1914. The design was most unusual, with the frame and the tubular receiver forged in one piece. The barrel is attached to the front of the receiver by a screwed block, and the rear end of the barrel fits into a circular bushing that runs on the inside of a tubular bolt. This bolt, the unique feature of the design, is solid at the rear — forming the breechblock, carrying the striker and terminating in a ribbed cocking piece — but the remainder is hollow, completely enclosing the barrel when forward.

The bolt reaches to the rear of the muzzle bushing in the receiver and is held in alignment by a screwed collar that surrounds the barrel and retains the co-axial return spring. A small catch beneath the muzzle locks the receiver bushing in place, preventing it from unscrewing due to bullet torque. The rear of the spring is retained by the breech-end bushing, and, oddly, the safety catch lies on the right side of the frame.

A five-shot magazine goes into the butt in the usual manner. A feed slot and an ejection port are cut in the hollow section of the bolt. Another ejection port is cut through the wall of the receiver, but the ports align only when the bolt has recoiled.

The configuration of the Dictator is interesting, qualifying, without doubt, as the first telescoping, wrap-around or overhung bolt — a feature that was hailed as a great leap forward when it appeared in submachine guns in 1944-5 to combine a bolt of sufficient mass with a short reloading stroke. The purpose of the Dictator design is unclear, but it was probably due simply to a desire to avoid infringing existing patents.

The receiver bears the manufacturer's name, with a motif of an equestrian statue on top of a column, accompanied by "DICTATOR", in an oval cartouche on each of the grips.

RH-ALAN

Zagreb, Croatia.

HS-95 This pistol was briefly seen in 1991, marketed as the "CZ 99" by Zastava Arms (q.v.) of Kraguyevač. The subsequent political upheaval and the fragmentation of Yugoslavia closed down communications, and nothing more was heard until the design reappeared in 1995 under new ownership. The HS-95 incorporates a few cosmetic changes compared with the CZ 99 but is basically an adaptation of the SIG-Sauer 220 series—locked by raising the squared barrel-block into the ejection port, fitted with a similar double-action-firing/de-cocking system and including an automatic firing-pin safety. The contours of the HS-95 butt are noticeably more rounded than the SIG-Sauers, but the general appearance is similar. Pistols are apparently issued to Croatian army personnel and are also offered for export.

RHEINISCHE METALLWAAREN- & MASCHINEN-FABRIK ("RM&M", "RHEINMETALL")
Düsseldorf, Sömmerda and elsewhere; Germany.
Founded in Düsseldorf in 1889 as an engineering business and anxious to capitalize on the industrial boom that had followed the creation of the German empire in 1871, RM&M soon became involved with artillery, building guns to the designs of Heinrich Ehrhardt. Though initially struggling to overcome the supremacy of Krupp, RM&M (often known simply as "Rheinmetall" after 1914) found a sizable export market for field artillery and, in 1901, gained a foothold in the small-arms market by purchasing the ailing Waffenfabrik von Dreyse (q.v.).

A variety of small-arms, ranging from machineguns to handguns, was made until the end of World War I. Restricted to the production of light guns by the Treaty of Versailles, Rheinmetall continued clandestine development throughout the 1920s, managing design offices in the Netherlands and Russia before becoming involved with Solothurn AG in Switzerland and Steyr in Austria. The Third Reich led to a wholesale expansion with Rheinmetall amalgamating in 1936 with Borsig of Berlin to become "Rheinmetall-Borsig", specializing in heavy engineering that encompassed artillery and railway locomotives. Dismantled in 1945 and reorganized once again, Rheinmetall GmbH is still a major source of weaponry.

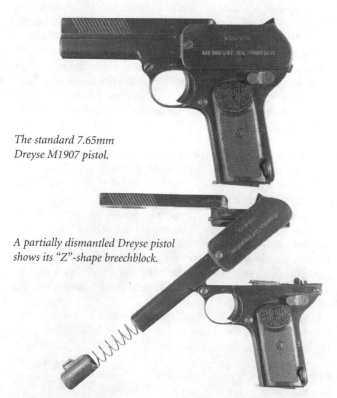

The standard 7.65mm Dreyse M1907 pistol.

A partially dismantled Dreyse pistol shows its "Z"-shape breechblock.

Dreyse (7.65mm type) The guns bearing this name, the work of Louis Schmeisser, were patented in Germany in 1905. The essence of the design was a cranked slide, with an extension along the top of the barrel and a short breechblock section behind the chamber. The breechblock was confined by a flat-sided frame, bridged by a transom formed as the rear sight, which blocked the backward movement of the front part of the slide once the limit of recoil had been reached. The breechblock protruded from the rear of the frame at this point.

The return spring, concentric with the barrel and enclosed by the frame, was held by a sprung latch on a collar that engaged the front end of the slide. Consequently, the finger grips lay towards the front of the slide. A striker-type firing system was used, allowing the tail of the firing pin to protrude from the back of the breechblock when the gun was cocked.

A latch on the rear of the gun released the entire top section of the frame/slide unit to pivot around a transverse pin through the lower part of the frame ahead of the trigger guard. This allowed the "cranked" slide to be removed.

The Dreyse pistol presented an obsolescent appearance, with the deep slab-sided frame and small-looking grips, but was sturdy, reliable and pleasant to shoot. The earliest batches seem to have been made exclusively for the Saxon state police, displaying "K. S. Gend." ("Royal Saxon gendarmerie") and an issue number on the left side of the frame, over "Rheinische Metallwaaren- & Maschinenfabrik" in a single line above "Abt. Sömmerda". Guns that were sold commercially had "DREYSE 1907" instead of the police markings, though even these may be found with the marks of other police units (e.g., Bremen, Dresden, Leipzig) on the frame. Guns made from c. 1914 were marked simply "RHEINMETALL ABT. SÖMMERDA" on the frame, but virtually all Dreyse pistols — regardless of age — had decorative "RMF" monograms on the grips.

Minor changes were made during a production life that extended into the immediate post-war period. The most important concerned an alteration in the firing mechanism, which dates from 1913-14. Instead of simply being held back on the sear until released by the trigger, the firing pin was pushed back as the trigger was pressed to complete compression before release. This appears to have been adapted from the original 9mm Dreyse described below, perhaps as a safety feature but possibly also to allow a second pull of the trigger in the event of a misfire. A recess was cut in the top front of the slide during World War I to facilitate removing the recoil-spring retaining bushing.

The 6.35mm (25-caliber) Dreyse pocket pistol.

This partially dismantled 6.35mm Dreyse shows that it is quite unlike the 7.65mm version internally.

Dreyse (6.35mm type) Introduced shortly after the 7.65mm gun, sharing some similarity externally, this was a conventional blowback inspired by the 1906-type FN-Browning. The Dresye lacked the grip safety of the Browning and retained the unique patented method of assembly. The barrel was located by a cylindrical lump under the chamber, held in a recess in the frame by a metal rib dovetailed into the top surface of the barrel and the breechblock sections of the slide. The rib, which reciprocated with the slide, carried the sights, sprung snugly in its groove. Pulling the rear sight upward allowed the entire rib to be lifted, pulled back and removed from the slide. The pistol could then be dismantled. Spent cases were ejected to the right. The earliest guns seem to have borne nothing other than "DREYSE" on the left side of the slide, but later examples added "Rheinische Metallwaaren- & Maschinenfabrik Abt. Sömmerda" in a single line. An "RMF" monogram was always found on the grips.

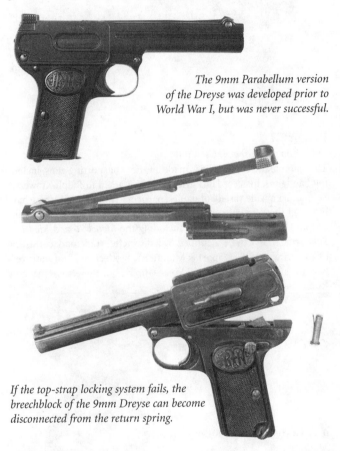

The 9mm Parabellum version of the Dreyse was developed prior to World War I, but was never successful.

If the top-strap locking system fails, the breechblock of the 9mm Dreyse can become disconnected from the return spring.

Dreyse (9mm type) Chambered for the powerful 9mm Parabellum cartridge, this was the last of the Dreyse pistols to appear. An enlargement of the 7.65mm blowback pattern, it demanded a very strong recoil spring and a patented cocking system in the form of a long arm pivoting on a transverse pin above the muzzle. The arm carried the front sight, a rear sight doubling as a finger-grip, and two lugs that projected downward. The recoil-spring bushing extended about 2 inches back from the muzzle, becoming a sleeve that enveloped the front of the return spring and ended in a vertical lug to engage one of the lugs beneath the arm. The second (rear) lug on the arm locked into a recess on the top of the slide.

To cock the pistol, the finger-grip was raised to disconnect the cocking arm from the return-spring sleeve; the arm was then retracted, taking the slide back without encountering any pressure from the spring. Pushing the parts back to their rest position closed the breech, chambering a new cartridge, and the cocking arm was then snapped back into engagement with the return-spring sleeve. When the gun fired,

therefore, movement of the slide, cocking lever and return-spring sleeve — all securely locked together — duly compressed the return spring.

The cocking system undoubtedly worked satisfactorily when the guns were new, but excessive wear in the lugs allowed the arm to leap from its engagement at the instant of firing. The slide, no longer connected with the return spring, would then slam back violently and jam the gun. Fortunately, the solid transom in the top of the frame was strong enough to prevent the slide from being blown off the frame towards the shooter.

The perfected 9mm Dreyse has a self-cocking striker mechanism (see 7.65mm version, above), and the upper part of the frame was held by a sturdy bolt instead of a spring catch. However, the production history of the basic design is uncertain. It is possible that the first 9mm guns pre-dated the adoption of the Parabellum pistol by the German army (1908) and that they were intended for trials. Certainly, some guns were made with the single-action striker system and the plain slab-sided frame adapted from the 7.65mm pattern; they also had lanyard loops that were placed low on the left side of the butt parallel to the backstrap. Markings paralleled those of the perfected commercial-type 7.65mm Dreyse. Later guns, possibly introduced in 1911, had the modified trigger and a prominent radial lever above a panel milled out of the left side of the frame above the grip. The markings, with "DREYSE" transferred to the right side of the frame, lay above the lever in two lines. The grips retained the decorative "RMF" monogram, but the lanyard loop was placed diagonally and the lower rear corner of the left grip was cut away appropriately.

Guns of this type were still available in 1915, though production was never large, and were still being sold in the 1920s from old stock. Although never formally approved by the German army, a few undoubtedly saw service during World War I. A simplified version developed experimentally in this period abandoned the separate cocking system in favor of a conventional slide with retraction grips milled vertically behind the front sight. The strength of the return spring would have made the "improved Dreyse" hard to cock, and it is assumed that this and the lack of a breech-lock failed to impress the German military authorities; the Walther Model 6, another 9mm-caliber blowback, was treated similarly.

The post-1920 Rheinmetall pistol was far simpler than the Dreyse.

Rheinmetall A new 7.65mm pistol developed soon after the end of World War I, this was introduced commercially in 1922. Though based on the FN-Browning of 1910, the dismantling system was unusual; the slide was pulled back and locked, after which the rear section, with the finger grips, could be unscrewed from the rest of the slide. This allowed the front portion of the slide to be slid forward off the frame and made a threaded muzzle bushing unnecessary. Held in a ring seating in the frame, the barrel could be removed by turning it until a tab below the chamber came clear of a recess, then pulling backward. The grips were wood, and the tail of the striker protruded from the rear of the slide as a cocked indicator.

Catalog illustrations dating from the start of the 1920s show a prominent rear sight and a matted rib on top of the slide, but these features (if they were ever used) were soon abandoned in favor of a simple sighting groove in the slide. The slide marking originally read "Rheinmetall Abt. Sömmerda" on the left side, flanked by tiny encircled-diamond trademarks. Later examples displayed simply "Rheinmetall 7,65". Work continued until 1927, when, with sales declining in the face of a deteriorating economic situation, Rheinmetall elected to concentrate on heavier weapons. A few unsuccessful 9mm Parabellum guns are said to have been made for military trials sometime in 1925-32.

RHEINISCHE WAFFEN- & MUNITIONSFABRIK ("RWM")

Cologne, Germany.

The affairs of this company remain mysterious. It has sometimes claimed, on the basis of a misunderstanding of German orthography, that RWM was a trading style invented by Francisco Arizmendi and Arizmendi y Goenaga (qq.v.) of Eibar. However, it is more likely that the business simply imported Spanish-made handguns such as the Waldman/Walman series for sale in Germany in the 1920s. Virtually all the guns have German proofmarks.

There has been much debate concerning the origins of the 6.35mm Continental pistol, which was probably made in Spain for sale in Germany. The transparent grips are not original.

The Continental field-stripped. No German proofmarks are visible.

Continental (1) This model is a cheap Spanish-made 6.35mm "Eibar" blowback, made of soft metal, poorly finished, but notable for an unusually efficient safety catch that locks the trigger and the internal hammer securely together. The slide is marked "…"CONTINENTAL" KAL 6,35" over "RHEINISCHE WAFFEN & MUNITIONSFABRIK – CÖLN", though the use of "C" instead of "K" in "Cöln" is not in itself significant — but merely typical of pre-1920 German usage.

Continental (2) Apparently based on the Webley & Scott Police Model automatic of 1906, chambered for the 7.65mm Auto cartridge, this seems to date from the 1920s. The left side of the slide is marked "• CONTINENTAL •" over "AUTOMATISCHE PISTOLE CAL. 7,65 ᵐ/ₘ" and "SYSTEM CASTENHOLZ".

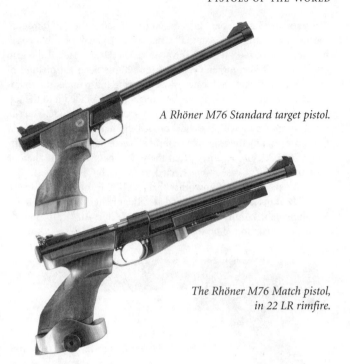

A Rhöner M76 Standard target pistol.

The Rhöner M76 Match pistol, in 22 LR rimfire.

RHÖNER

Obereisbach-Weisbach, Germany.

This gunmaking company has made a variety of sporting guns, including handguns, in accordance with patents granted to Ralph Krawczyc. Sold under a wide variety of names, particularly in the USA, these have included the Western-style *Frontier Six-Shooter* and a variety of bolt-action 22 rimfire target pistols including the *Model 76* and *Model 76 Silhouette*. Most can be identified by a distinctive trademark consisting of an encircled "SM" ("Sport & Munition") between fields of short vertical lines. Rhöner has also sold blank-firers, but these were made by Röhm and possibly also Reck.

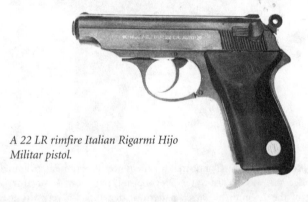

A 22 LR rimfire Italian Rigarmi Hijo Militar pistol.

RIGARMI

Rigarmi di Rino Galesi, Brescia (post -1951).

Founded by a son of the Galesi (q.v.) brothers, this gunmaking business has also made caplock revolvers based on Colt designs. Many of the pistols were sold in the USA prior to 1970, distinguished by names such as "Hijo" or "Hijo Militar" (sold by Sloan of New York City) and "Maxim" (by Hy Hunter). They may be found in a variety of finishes—black, chromed, engraved — and with grips of wood, plastic, mother-of-pearl or simulated ivory. The slides are usually marked "RINO GALESI – RIGARMI – BRESCIA – BREV. CAL. 6,35" in a single line, with an encircled "RG" on the grips.

Rigarmi series Inspired by the Galesi pocket pistols, these are simple blowbacks chambered for the 22 LR rimfire or 6.35mm Auto (25 ACP) rounds.

- *Model 53* The standard 6.35mm version, with the ejection port on the right side of the slide and a radial safety catch on the rear left side of the frame.
- *Model 54* An adaptation of the basic design chambered for the 22 LR rimfire cartridge, this had the slide cut away so that the open-top ejection aperture appeared on both sides of the breech. The safety catch was moved forward ahead of the trigger to allow a dismantling catch to take its place at the rear of the frame.
- *Model 55* This was a 6.35mm version of the Model 54, with the same safety and dismantling catches, but reverted to the 1953-type slide with the ejection port on the right side.
- *Model 57* A heavier version of the Model 55, 5.3 inches long and weighing about 15 oz empty.

Italia Militar Introduced in the early 1960s and resembling the Walther PP externally, this simple blowback chambered the 22 LR rimfire or 7.65mm Auto (32 ACP) centerfire rounds. The double-action trigger mechanism and slide-mounted safety catch/de-cocking lever typify many of the guns of this type, though the angular backstrap helps identification.

- *Italia 69* (or "Model 69") A version of the Italia Militar intended for target shooting, this had a long barrel that protruded from the slide to carry the front sight on a muzzle collar.

ROBAR

SA Manufacture Liégeoise d'Armes à Feu
Robar et Cie, Liége, Belgium.

This firm began as "Robar & de Kerkhove" and went through numerous minor changes of name before La Société Anonyme Robar et Cie was liquidated in 1958. Robar & de Kerkhove began producing inexpensive pocket revolvers in the 1890s, turning to automatic pistols shortly before World War I began. Work was resumed in 1920 and continued, interrupted by World War II, until the early 1950s. The guns were widely exported and are still commonly encountered.

∼ REVOLVERS ∼

Lincoln Robar produced a number of revolvers in 1895-1914 that were mostly solid-frame rod-ejecting double-action "Bulldog" types in 320, 380 and 450 centerfire chamberings. A 320 folding-trigger "hammerless" pocket model was also produced under this name.

∼ AUTOMATIC PISTOLS ∼

Liege, Liegeoise These names were sometimes applied to the New Model Melior, but identification may be complicated by the existence of Spanish pistols of the same name. See "Manufacture Liégeoise d'Armes à Feu".

A typical 6.35mm (25-caliber) Melior pistol, made by Robar & Co.

Melior (old model) The Rosier-designed Jieffeco pistol, marketed by Jannsen Fils (q.v.), was probably made by Robar. The terms of agreement — if agreement there was — remain unclear, but Robar was able to market an essentially similar gun under the name "Melior". Similarly externally to the 1900-type FN-Browning, the gun was marked "Brevete S.G.D.G. Patent 24875.08" on the frame, with a cursive

"Melior" on the grips. Some guns have additional vertical grooves milled in the sides of the barrel housing behind the muzzle, which, owing to the use of a separate reciprocating breechblock, are assumed to have been intended to assist dismantling.

Also made by Robar, this is a 7.65mm New Model Melior pistol dating from the 1920s.

Melior (new model) In 1920, Robar introduced a totally new design in 6.35mm and 7.65mm calibers, eventually joined by versions in 22 LR rimfire and 9mm Short. The guns resembled the FN-Browning of 1910 externally, but the breechblock was a separate unit that had been inserted in the slide from the rear. A dovetailed locking plate, passing across the top of the slide, engaged in a groove in the breechblock. Releasing a spring latch and driving the locking plate outward allowed the slide to be removed forward over the barrel, leaving the breechblock behind.

The grip safety originally ran the full depth of the backstrap, but this was changed to a half-length pattern after about 50,000 7.65mm and about 100,000 6.35mm-caliber guns had been made. However, after only about 10,000 additional small-caliber pistols had been made, the grip safety was abandoned.

The Melior appears to have sold steadily from its inception until the 1950s, excepting World War II. The normal marking was "MELIOR" over "BREVETS – 259178 – 265491 – LIEGE – BELGIUM", but some guns reportedly bear "MFR LIEGEOISE D'ARMES A FEU". A caliber mark will often be found on the frame, "6,35 B^R" or "7,65 B^R" on the earliest and simply "6,35MM" or "7,65MM" thereafter. The grips were originally marked "MELIOR" in a curved cartouche with an "RT" or "R-and-hammer" motif; later examples had "MELIOR" and "LIEGE" in an annulus containing an "RCo" monogram.

The guns made after the end of World War II were modernized, lacking the grip safety and fitted with plastic grips. The large 7.65mm type retained the distinctive breechblock construction but had a streamlined web beneath the muzzle. Some guns bear the name "MERCURY", for sale by Tradewinds of Tacoms in the USA, but others have slides displaying "SA MANUFACTURE LIEGEOISE D'ARMES A FEU ROBAR & CO" in a single line.

Melior (vest-pocket model) This was a tiny 6.35mm blowback with an open-top slide, retaining the removable breechblock feature. A few guns were made in the late 1920s or early 1930s, but economic depression forced the project to be abandoned. The guns were only about 4.1 inches long and weighed 8.3 oz empty.

Phoenix Robar apparently applied this name to a 6.35mm Melior made for "Phoenix Arms" of Lowell, Massachusetts — presumably an otherwise-unidentified US distributor. A gun of the same name was made in Spain: see "Unattributed Spanish".

ROCK RIVER ARMS

Cleveland, Illinois, USA.

This source of semi-custom M1911 clones, generally restricted to 45 ACP, began work in the late 1990s.

Colt-Brownings Most guns have skeleton hammers, extended or "beavertail" grip-safety levers, duplicated slide-retraction grips behind the muzzle and other special features.

- *Basic Limited Match* Otherwise similar to the Bullseye Wadcutter pattern, this has adjustable Bo-Mar open sights. The "Basic Limited Hi-Cap" is similar but is distinguished by a double-column magazine contained in wide-grip frames acquired from Entréprise Arms, Para-Ordnance and other manufacturers.
- *Bullseye Wadcutter* Fitted with a Rock River optical-sight mounting rib on the slide, this is intended for long-range competition shooting.
- *Elite Commando* This offers a 4-inch barrel/slide on a National Match frame with duplicated retraction grips and an enlarged ejection port. An aluminum-alloy trigger, tritium-illuminated night sights and checkered "double-diamond" cocobolo grips are standard.
- *Limited Match* Fitted with a host of internal refinements and extended cocobolo grips, this is guaranteed to shoot 1.5-inch groups at 50 yards.
- *Match Master Steel* Another of the 38 Super ACP guns, this is similar to the Ultimate Match Achiever but has a lightweight skeletonized slide.
- *National Match Hardball* Offered in blue with a conventional hammer and grip-safety spur, this has a Bo-Mar rear sight and an undercut front sight dovetailed into the slide. It also lacks duplicated slide grips.
- *Standard Match* This is similar to the Elite Commando but has a 5-inch barrel and a conventional adjustable rear sight without "nightlight" inserts.
- *Ultimate Match Achiever* Chambered for the 38 Super ACP cartridge, this is intended for IPSC competitions. It has a three-slot compensator at the muzzle, a slide that is cut down at the rear and a mount for an optical sight attached to the right side of the frame above the trigger-guard web.

ROCKY MOUNTAIN ARMS CORP.

Salt Lake City, Utah, USA.

This firm was the original manufacturer of the "Mini-Revolver" from 1972 to 1974, after which the design was taken over by the North American Arms Co (q.v.).

RÖHM

Röhm GmbH, Sontheim/Brenz, Germany.

This gunmaking business has produced a bewildering range of handguns, sold not only under its own designations but also under dozens of other brand names. Most of the latter were intended for the US market in the days before the 1968 Gun Control Act severely curtailed the import of minuscule pistols.

∼ REVOLVERS ∼

Röhm revolvers may bear identifiable medallions in the grip carrying the letters "RG" and the model number. This medallion sometimes carries the sales name — e.g., "Hy-Score", "EIG" — and additional markings may lie on the barrel. Construction falls into three broad groups: the cheap solid-frame gate-loading patterns; the cheap solid-frame models with swing-out cylinders; and the better-quality solid-frame models with swing-out cylinders. There is also a substantial range of starting, gas and alarm pistols, numbered in the same sequence as the bullet-firing guns.

Burgo Found on RG-10 revolvers sold in Germany by Burgsmüller of Kreiensen.

EIG This mark was applied to revolvers — usually RG-10 or RG-12 — that were sold in the USA by the Eig Corporation.

Hy-Score The "Hy-Score Model 108" was actually a variant of the RG-10 with an additional safety catch and distributed in the USA by the Hy-Score Arms Company of Brooklyn.

Liberty (or Liberty 12) An unidentified brand name encountered on RG-12 revolvers distributed in the USA.

RG-7 Chambered for the 22 Short rimfire round, this non-ejector had a 1.25-inch barrel, a solid frame and a loading gate.

RG-10 Among the most common guns of the type, this six-shot solid-frame non-ejector was offered only in 22 LR rimfire with a 2.25-inch barrel. However, many minor variations in finish, butt shape, grip material and hammer-spur design will be encountered, depending largely on the whims of the purchasers.

The 22-caliber Röhm RG10 has been sold under a variety of names, including the "Valor" shown on the grips of this example.

- *RG-10s* A variant of the RG-10 with a rounded trigger guard, instead of the usual square shape, and a large "oversize" butt.

RG-11 Chambered for the 22 LR rimfire round, this solid-frame non-ejector had a 3.6-inch barrel and finger grips formed into the frontstrap of the butt.

RG-12 Similar to the RG-11, this had a loading gate on the rear right side of the frame behind the cylinder and an ejector rod beneath the barrel.

A Röhm RG14, in 22 LR rimfire.

RG-14 Offered only in 22 LR rimfire, with a 1.75-inch barrel, this had a six-chamber swinging cylinder that was held in the frame by a spring catch on the yoke.

RG-20 Similar to the RG-14 but in 22 Short rimfire, this had a 3-inch barrel.

Another of the simple swing-cylinder Röhm designs, this is an RG23.

RG-23 Another of the swing-cylinder guns, this had a 1.5-inch barrel. Chambering was restricted to 22 LR rimfire.

RG-24 A variant of the RG-23 with a 3.5-inch barrel.

RG-31 Chambered for the 38 Special round, this was a more substantial product than the rimfires. The five-chamber swing-out cylinder was retained by a crane catch, and the barrel was merely 2 inches long.

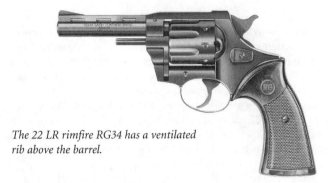

The 22 LR rimfire RG34 has a ventilated rib above the barrel.

RG-34 Chambered for the 22 Short rimfire round, this had a good quality solid frame, a swing-out cylinder locked by a thumb-catch behind the cylinder and a ribbed barrel.

*   *RG-34A* A minor variant of the RG-34, this had an adjustable rear sight and a broadened hammer spur.
*   RG-34T Fitted with an adjustable rear sight, a ramp-mounted front sight, a heavy barrel, a broad trigger, a hammer spur and wooden anatomical grips, this provided a good beginner's target revolver.

RG-35 Identical mechanically with the RG-34, this chambered the 22 LR rimfire round.

RG-36 Another of the guns derived from the RG-34, this chambered the 32 S&W Long cartridge.

*   RG-36T This was a derivative of the RG-36 built on the same frame, intended for target shooting. The sights were adjustable, a broad trigger and hammer were fitted, and the anatomical grips were usually walnut. (Note: The RG-36T is sometimes claimed to have been chambered for the 22 Magum rimfire round, which may have once been an option.)

One of the more powerful Röhm revolvers, the RG38S chambers the 38 Special round.

RG-38 Adapted to accept the 38 S&W Special cartridge, this is otherwise an RG-34 with an adjustable rear sight and a broad hammer spur.

*   *RG-38T* An RG-38 with a ventilated barrel rib and adjustable competition-style sights.

RG-40 Chambered for 38 Special ammunition, this had a six-chamber swing-out cylinder held by a thumb-catch; barrel length was merely 2 inches.

RG-57 A strengthened version of the best-quality design with a steel frame, this has been offered in 38 Special, 357 Magnum, 41 Magnum,

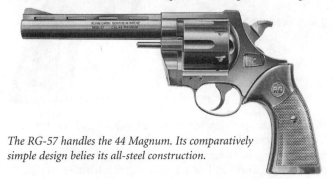

The RG-57 handles the 44 Magnum. Its comparatively simple design belies its all-steel construction.

44 Special, 44 Magnum or 45 Colt. The cylinders have six chambers, and the barrels measure 4 or 6 inches.

*   *RG-57T* An RG-57 with adjustable sights, a broad trigger, a wide hammer spur and better-quality grips.

RG-63 This was a "Western-style" single-action solid-frame revolver based loosely on the Colt Single Action Army, offered in 22 LR or Magnum rimfire, and 32 S&W Long or 38 S&W Special centerfire chamberings.

RG-66 Similar to the RG-63, this had an adjustable rear sight and interchangeable cylinders, offered in 22 LR and 22 Magnum rimfire combinations. The barrels measured 4.75 or 6 inches.

The Röhm RG66T is a "Western Style" 22-rimfire gun inspired by the Colt Peacemaker. It has an adjustable rear sight.

*   *RG-66T* A target version of the RG-66 with adjustable sights and an adjustable trigger stop.

RG-86 A strengthened but otherwise similar version of the RG-66, this retained the same interchangeability of cylinders.

RG-88 A very good quality 38 Special or 357 Magnum six-shot revolver with a ventilated barrel rib and fixed sights, this had a steel frame. A 6-inch barrel was standard on both versions, though shorter barrels have been supplied to order.

*   *RG-88T* An RG-88 with adjustable sights.

Romo The RG-10 sold by an unknown US dealer.

Thalco The RG-10 sold in the USA as the "Thalco Plinker" by the Thalson Import Company.

Valor An RG-10 with an additional safety catch (see "Hy-Score"), sold in the USA through an unidentified dealership.

Vestpocket The RG-10 Sold by the "Rosco Arms Company", location unknown.

Western Style A brand name for a modified RG-10 with a rod ejector beneath the barrel, bearing no resemblance to the true western-style RG-63.

Zephyr Yet another name for the RG-10 of unknown provenance.

～ AUTOMATIC PISTOLS ～

Röhm began producing blowback pistols in the 1970s, deriving the design from the well-established range of starting pistols.

RG-26 This is a simple striker-fired 6.35mm automatic with an alloy frame and a steel slide. The magazine holds six rounds.

RG-27 A much better design than the RG-26, this shows an affinity with the Walther TPH, with a double-action lock, an exposed hammer and a safety catch on the slide.

RÖMERWERKE

Suhl, Germany.

This gunmaking business offered 22 rimfire pistols c. 1925-33 that were distinguished by exchangeable 2.5- and 6.5-inch barrel units suited to personal defense and target shooting, respectively. The guns had a slab-sided half-slide and barrel-block unit, transforming into a near-cylindrical barrel with a narrow top rib. They were striker fired and had detachable eight-round box magazines in the butt. Markings included "RÖMERWERKE" over "A.G. SUHL" on the left side of the slide ahead of the retraction grips and had either an "RWS" ("Romerwerke, Suhl") monogram or a motif of "R" pierced by a sword on the grips.

A short-barreled Römerwerke pistol. A caliber mark — "22 Long Rifle" — in English suggests that an export market was being sought.

The Römerwerke pistol field-stripped, showing the two-part barrel/slide construction.

RONGÉ

J.B. Rongé et fils, Liége, Belgium.

Rongé was a revolver maker active in 1880-1900. His principal product was the usual type of cheap "Bulldog" revolver in 320, 380 and 450 calibers, but he also made two substantial military-style weapons. The first of these was the 41centerfire *Frontier*, a solid-frame six-shot double-action revolver with a swinging loading gate, a rod ejector beneath the barrel and a finger-spur beneath the trigger guard. This was accompanied by a 44-40 WCF *Frontier Army Model* of otherwise similar pattern.

A short-barrel short-butt 45 "Bulldog" revolver attributed to Rongé fils.

Rongé also appears to have acted as a "trade house", supplying revolvers to gunsmiths throughout Europe who then applied their own names. Consequently, many oddly named weapons may prove to come from this particular source. On examination, his revolvers will be found to have "JBR" or "RF" stamped on the frame in some inconspicuous place, or on the grips.

ROSSI

Amadeo Rossi & Co., Sao Leopoldo, Brazil.

This company was founded in 1881 by an immigrant Italian gunsmith, growing to become the largest independent gunmaker in South America. Rossi has made rifles, shotguns, revolvers and even a few automatic pistols. The revolvers are generally based upon Smith & Wesson practice, solid-frame guns with swing-out cylinders retained by a thumb-catch behind the cylinder and a lug under the barrel.

～ REVOLVERS ～

The first guns to be made in the early 1950s were 38 Special personal-defense patterns with 1.5-inch barrels and a 22 LR rimfire sporter with a 5-inch barrel. The cylinder and crane were locked in the frame by a spring sleeve concentric with the ejector rod. Later guns, often distributed in the USA by the Garcia Corporation of Teaneck, New Jersey, concentrated on 3- and 6-inch barrels. The 3-inch option could be supplied in 22 LR, 22 Magnum rimfire, 32 S&W Long (all six-shot) or 38 Special (five shots), in blued or nickel finish. The guns all had adjustable rear sights. The 6-inch barrel was initially restricted to a 22 LR rimfire target revolver with fully adjustable sights.

From these beginnings, the range expanded considerably. Most of the revolvers are marked "Amadeo Rossi & Cia Sao Leopoldo RB" on the barrel, with the company monogram on the right side of the frame and "ROSSI" on the molded grips.

Lady Rossi (introduced in 1995) Chambered for the 38 Special round, this has been offered with 2- or 3-inch barrels with shrouded ejectors. Overall length with a 3-inch barrel is about 7.5 inches, weight is about 21 oz, the construction is stainless steel and the grips are rosewood. A "Lady Rossi" mark will be found on the frame.

Model 13 (Princess) This is the current version of the early model in which the cylinder locking is done by a sleeve on the ejector rod. A 22 LR six-shot with 3-inch barrel, it has an alloy frame and is usually nickeled.

· *Model 25 Princess* Dating from 1965, this is a 1.5-inch-barreled version of the Model 13.

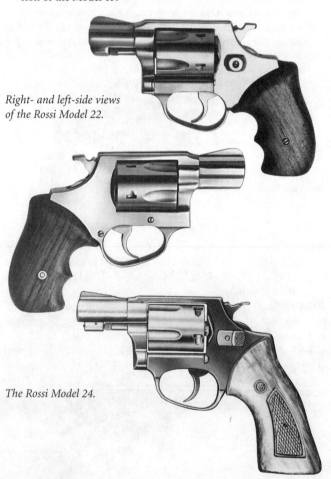

Right- and left-side views of the Rossi Model 22.

The Rossi Model 24.

Model 20 (Ranger) Introduced in 1964, this is chambered for the 32 S&W Long cartridge and has a six-chamber cylinder locked in the frame by a thumb-catch and a barrel lug. Made only with a 3-inch barrel, the Model 20 also had an improved trigger mechanism.

* *Model 28 Ranger* A smaller version of the Model 27, with six-shot cylinder.

Model 27 (Pioneer) A 38-caliber derivation of the Model 20, this appeared in 1966. It had a five-chamber cylinder and a 4-inch barrel.

* *Model 31 Pioneer* Introduced in 1967, this was a 32-caliber version of the Model 27 retaining the standard 4-inch barrel but with an additional chamber in the cylinder.
* *Model 32 Pioneer* A 38-caliber Model 27 with 6-inch barrel.
* *Model 33 Pioneer* A Model 27 with 3-inch barrel.
* *Model 87 Pioneer* Introduced in 1981 and chambered for 38 Special ammunition, this was derived from the Model 27. Made from stainless steel, it also had a one-piece hammer instead of having a separate pinned-in firing pin.

A Rossi Model 38 revolver.

Model 38 (Champion) A development of the 38-caliber Model 27, this had a 4-inch barrel and an adjustable rear sight.

* *Model 39 Champion* This was the 32 version of the Model 38, with six chambers instead of five.
* *Model 40 Champion* Introduced in 1969, this was a variant of the Model 38 with a heavy 6-inch barrel and a better grip.
* *Model 41 Champion* A 32-caliber Model 39 with a 6-inch barrel and better-shaped grips.

Model 42 (Senator) Introduced in 1970, this was a six-shot 22 LR rimfire gun with a 1.9-inch barrel and fixed sights.

The Rossi M43.

* *Model 43 Senator* A version of the Model 42 with a 3-inch barrel.

Model 47 (Sportsman) A variant of the Model 42 with a 1.9-inch barrel and an adjustable rear sight.

* *Model 48 Sportsman* Mechanically identical with the Model 47, this had a 3-inch barrel.
* *Model 49 Sportsman* Similar to the Model 47, this had a 4-inch barrel and generally heavier build.
* *Model 50 Sportsman* This was simply a Model 49 with a 5-inch barrel.
* *Model 51 Sportsman* A Model 49 with 6-inch barrel.

Model 68 (Champion II, 1978-85) The first of a new series, the "Champion II" was based on the "Pioneer" series but with an adjustable rear sight and ramp front sight. The Model 68 was a five-shot weapon in 38 Special with a 75mm barrel.

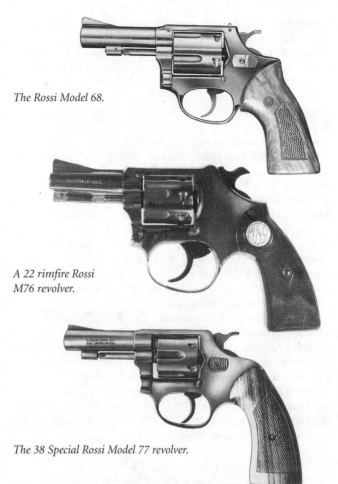

The Rossi Model 68.

A 22 rimfire Rossi M76 revolver.

The 38 Special Rossi Model 77 revolver.

* *Model 68S* (1993-?) A modernized version of the M68, this had a 2- or 3-inch barrel with a shrouded ejector-rod. The sights were fixed, finish was blue or nickel and the grips were customarily walnut. Empty weight was about 23 oz with the 3-inch barrel.
* *Model 69 Champion II* (1978-85) Little more than a 32-caliber version of the Model 68, this had a six-chamber cylinder.
* *Model 70 Champion II* (1978-85) A further derivative of the Model 68, this version is a 22 LR model with a 3-inch barrel.

Model 84 (1985-7?) Chambered for the 38 Special round, this had a six-chamber cylinder. The solid-rib barrels measured 3 or 4 inches, the finish was generally blue and the grips were walnut. The sights were fixed.

Model 85 (1985-7?) This is believed to have been a variant of the M84 with an adjustable rear sight.

Model 88 Discontinued in 1985, this was a Model 87 with 6-inch barrel and adjustable rear sight, made of stainless steel and with the one-piece hammer.

* *Model 88S* (or "88 Stainless") Introduced in 1983 and another of the guns chambering 38 Special ammunition, this had a barrel measuring 2 or 3 inches and a five-chamber cylinder. The grips were wood or later rubber, and the empty weight was about 22 oz.

Model 89 This was originally little more than a variant of the M88 chambered for the 32 S&W Long centerfire round. It was abandoned in 1985.

* *Model 89S* (1983-?) This was simply a variant of the short-barreled M88S in 32 S&W Long. It was made of stainless steel.

Model 93 Introduced in 1985 in 38 Special, this had a 3-inch barrel. The gun was made of blued carbon steel and usually had wood grips.

Model 94 A variant of the M93, this had a 4-inch barrel with a solid rib.

Model 96 Fitted with adjustable sights, this was a long-barreled version of the M93 and M94. The barrel measured 6 inches.

Model 351 (introduced in 2001) Chambered for the 38 Special round and strengthened to fire "+P" loads, this had a five-chamber cylinder and a 2-inch barrel. Constructed of blued steel, it had rubber grips.

Model 352 A variant of the M351 made of stainless steel. It also dates from 2001.

Model 461 Announced in 2001 and fitted with a six-chamber cylinder, this 357 Magnum personal-defense revolver had a 2-inch barrel and walnut (later rubber) grips. It weighed about 26 oz empty.

Model 462 (2001 to date) This was a stainless-steel version of the M461, invariably found with rubber grips.

Model 511 (Sportsman, 1986-90?) A modernized Model 51 (q.v.), this had a 4-inch barrel with a full-length ejector-rod shroud. Construction was stainless steel and the grips were usually walnut.

Model 515 Dating from 1992, this handles the 22 Magnum rimfire round. It has a six-chamber cylinder, a 4-inch barrel with a solid rib and a small frame made of stainless steel. The grips may be wood or rubber, and the sights are adjustable.

Model 518 This is a 22 LR rimfire version of the M515, sharing similar characteristics other than chambering.

Model 677 (1997 to date) Chambered for the 357 Magnum round, this six-shot gun was offered only with a 2-inch barrel, matte blue finish and black rubber grips. It weighed about 26 oz empty.

Model 720 (1992 to date) Made with a five-chamber cylinder and a 3-inch solid-rib barrel with a full-length ejector-rod shroud, this 44 Special revolver was made of stainless steel and weighed 28 oz. The grips were invariably black rubber.

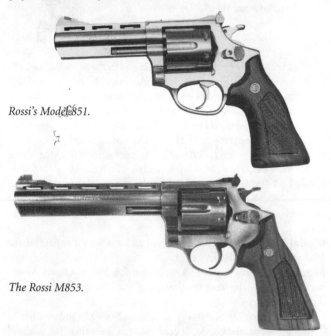

Rossi's Model 851.

The Rossi M853.

Model 851 (1991 to date) Chambering the 38 Special round, this six-shot gun had a 3- or 4-inch barrel with a ventilated rib, adjustable sights and walnut grips. Construction was stainless steel. An upgraded version, "851 +P", was introduced in 2001. This is restricted to a 4-inch barrel and blue finish.

Model 877 (1996 to date) A six-shot design in 357 Magnum, this had a 2-inch heavy barrel and weighed about 26 oz empty. It was made of stainless steel and had black rubber grips.

Model 951 (1985 to date) This six-shot 38 Special revolver offered ventilated-rib barrels (3 or 4 inches long) and adjustable sights. Made of blued steel, the M951 had walnut grips.

A typical Rossi Model 881 revolver.

The Rossi M941.

A Rossi M971 revolver.

Model 971 (1988 to date) The basic pattern, chambering the 357 Magnum round, had a 4-inch barrel with a solid rib and a full-length ejector-rod shroud. Made of blued steel, it had walnut grips. A "+P" version with a forged-steel frame was introduced in 2001.

- *Model 971 Comp* (1993 to date) Readily identifiable by the short two-slot compensator protruding from the muzzle of the 3.25-inch barrel, this was about 9 inches long and weighed 32 oz empty. Construction was stainless steel; grips were black rubber.

- *Model 971S* (or "971 Stainless", 1989 to date?) This was simply a version of the standard gun made of a different material. It had black rubber grips instead of walnut.

- *Model 971 VRC* (1996) The "Ventilated Rib Compensated" version of the M971 was offered with 2-, 4- or 6-inch barrels. These had integral gas-escape ports and ejector-rod shrouds. Made of stainless steel with black rubber grips, a typical long-barreled gun weighed about 39 oz.

Model 972 Chambered for the 357 Magnum round, this was introduced in 2001 in "+P" configuration with a forged stainless-steel frame. It is essentially an M971 with a 6-inch barrel.

Model 988 (Cyclops, 1997 to date) Chambered for the 357 Magnum round, this six-shot gun had a 6- or 8-inch barrel with a solid rib and a deep full-length ejector-rod shroud doubling as an underlug. Four gas-escape ports were cut into the barrel on each side of the front sight. The guns were made of stainless steel and had black rubber grips. They weighed 44 oz or 51 oz, depending on barrel length.

A Roth-type pistol (or "Krnka-Roth") submitted to trials in Switzerland in 1898.

This large Roth-type pistol, probably a prototype, dates from c. 1900-1. Note the detachable box magazine in the butt.

ROTH

Georg Roth, Budapest, Austria-Hungary/Hungary.

Roth was primarily an ammunition engineer, eventually operating two factories in Vienna and Pressburg (now Bratislava), but he also seems to have had some facility for weapons design. In 1898, he employed Karel Krnka (q.v.) to manage one of his factories. Since Krnka was a gun designer, the two men soon began to collaborate on designs, though it seems reasonably certain that the major part of the gun work was done by Krnka and that Roth merely contributed ideas and, most importantly, developed suitable ammunition.

Roth's name attaches to several pistol designs. Invariably the design was due to Roth & Krnka (and possibly Rudolf Frommer), but since Roth had no manufacturing capability, they were farmed out to other companies for production; as a result, the name of the manufacturer was added to that of Roth. Details of the Roth-Sauer will be found in the entry devoted to J.P. Sauer & Sohn; details of the Roth-Steyr will be found under "Oesterreichische Waffenfabriks-Gesellschaft".

RPM

Twin Lakes, Arizona, USA.

This gunmaking business is responsible for the *RPM XL*, a single-shot target pistol once marketed by R&R Sporting Arms, Inc., of Brea, California. Developed specifically for long-range silhouette shooting, the RPM can be identified by its squared contours (particularly the trigger guard) and the considerable rake of its grip. A sophisticated hammer-fired design, it has a tipping barrel controlled by a sprung lock and a hammer-block safety mechanism. A cocking indicator is also present. The trigger can be adjusted for pull-weight and over-travel. The front sight is a hooded replaceable post, or sometimes a Patridge-type blade, and the rear sight is fully adjustable. However, most guns are used with optical sights and the barrel-top is appropriately drilled and tapped to

receive the mounts. Chambered for cartridges ranging from 22 LR rimfire to 45-70 Government, the barrels measure 8, 10.75, 12 and 14 inches. Construction may be blued or stainless steel, or a combination of a blued barrel and a stainless frame. Grips are currently Goncalo Alves wood, with thumb-rest and palm-shelf. A left-hand action is available on request, and some guns are fitted with muzzle brakes. The *RPM XL Hunter* is a barreled action, lacking grips and sights.

RUPERTUS

Jacob Rupertus and the Rupertus Pistol Mfg Co., Philadelphia, Pennsylvania, USA.

Active from 1858 until the end of the 19th century, Rupertus was a prolific patentee of revolving firearms, pellet feeders and breech-loading rifles. Beginning with simple single-shot caplock pistols, he progressed to eight-shot pepperboxes and a variety of "Army Model", "Navy Model" and "Pocket Model" caplock revolvers.

∼ SINGLE-SHOT PISTOLS ∼

Offered in 22, 32, 38 and 41 rimfire, these had half-octagonal barrels measuring 3-5 inches, usually marked "RUPERTUS PAT'D. PISTOL MFG. CO. PHILADELPHIA" in a single line. A few thousand guns were made c. 1870-85.

∼ MULTI-SHOT PISTOLS ∼

These had double 3-inch barrels that swung to the left for loading. Chambered only for the 22 Short rimfire round, they had sheathed triggers and sliding firing pins. Finish was generally blue, with walnut or rosewood grips. Production is assumed to have been small.

∼ REVOLVERS ∼

In November 1871, Rupertus received a patent protecting the design of the *Empire*, a revolver with a solid frame, a sheath trigger and a bird's-head butt. Guns of this type were made in 22 rimfire (seven shots), 32 rimfire (five shots) or 41 rimfire (five shots). The 22 version had a plain-surface cylinder, but the others were fluted; barrels were usually 2.9 inches long. Finish could be blue or nickel-plate, with walnut or occasionally molded rubber grips. Some guns were marked "EMPIRE PAT. NOV. 21 71" on the topstrap and others displayed "Empire No 1"; the presence of the patent date is usually conclusive identification of a Rupertus "Suicide Special".

Guns of this pattern were also made under names such as "Hero", "Protector" (for sale by the "Protector Arms Company" of Philadelphia) and "Ranger" (a name used by many other manufacturers).

RYAN MFG CO.

New Haven, Connecticut, USA.

Edward Ryan was a pistol manufacturer of some substance, having a factory in New Haven with about 45 employees, and a sales outlet, the "Ryan Pistol Mfg Co", in New York. From the late 1870s until his death in 1891, Ryan produced the usual Suicide Special solid-frame sheathed-trigger non-ejectors in the form of a seven-shot 22 rimfire and a five-shot 32.

THOMAS J. RYAN

Norwich, Connecticut, USA.

This small gunsmithing business was active from 1874 until c. 1878. It is possible that Thomas Ryan was Edward Ryan's father. See above.

Napoleon These revolvers were of the usual solid-frame non-ejecting type with sheathed triggers and bird's-head or square butts. Chamberings were confined to 22 and 32 rimfire.

SABATTI & TANFOGLIO

Magno Val Trompia, Brescia, Italy.

This engineering business was formed in 1947 and made its first 6.35mm-caliber pocket pistols in 1953. Production continued until 1961, when Sabatti retired and Tanfoglio continued alone (see "Giuseppe Tanfoglio").

Sata One of the original designs, this appeared in 22 and 6.35mm versions, both of similar appearance but different construction. Both were fixed-barrel striker-fired models with coaxial recoil springs. The 22 model was chambered for the Short cartridge, and the slide was retained by an abutment at the rear that slid into recesses in both slide and frame. In the slide, it acted as an anchor for the striker spring, and in the frame, it was held by a clip.

The 6.35mm model used a similar system, but the abutting piece formed the upper end of an arm pivoted to the butt frame and forming the top of the backstrap. It could be released by rotating the safety catch through 180 degrees from the "fire" position.

SAFARI ARMS COMPANY/SCHUETZEN PISTOL WORKS

Tempe, Arizona, USA.

The affairs of these interlinked businesses have proved difficult to unravel. Since the Enforcer, a compact version of the Colt M1911A1 with ornate grips and various sight options, was announced in 1979, a range of similar guns has appeared—some under the Safari banner and others under the Schuetzen name!

In 1997, for example, the Schuetzen range of guns comprised the "Big Deuce", "Big Deuce II", "Griffon", "Reliable", "4 Star" and "Renegade"; the Safari brand was being carried by the "Cohort" (introduced in 1996), the "Enforcer" and "Enforcer CarryComp II", "GI Safari" (1996), "Matchmaster" and "Matchmaster CarryComp" (1993). By 2003, no Schuetzen-brand guns were being listed in *Gun Digest*. The "Enforcer", "GI Safari", "Carrier" (1999), "Cohort", "Match Master" and "CarryComp" were still listed, but the last two were apparently being made by Olympic Arms.

SAINT-ÉTIENNE ARMS FACTORY

Manufacture Nationale d'Armes de Saint-Étienne ("MAS").

Until the 1870s, the French armed forces relied upon contract supplies from commercial makers for their revolvers, but after the Franco-Prussian War (1870-1) had shown the folly of these arrangements, a regulation handgun was developed for production in the state-owned factories.

~ REVOLVERS ~

Model 1873 This was a sturdy double-action solid-frame gun, with Chamelot-Delvigne lockwork and a plain six-chamber cylinder accepting 11mm centerfire cartridges. A loading gate on the right side of the frame behind the cylinder could be opened to allow spent cases to be

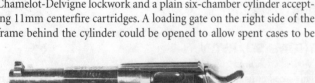

A French 11mm-caliber M1873 revolver.

expelled individually with the aid of a rod sliding in a tubular case offset beneath the barrel (though, alternatively, a button on the frame could be pressed to detach the cylinder). The barrel was partly octagonal and a lanyard ring lay on the base of the butt. Markings were confined to "Mre d'Armes" over "de St-Etienne" on the right side of the frame beneath the front of the cylinder and "MLE 1873" on top of the barrel. The maker's prefix letter ("S" for Saint-Étienne) and the date of acceptance could be found on the right side of the barrel. Guns of this type were about 9.5 inches long, with 4.5-inch barrels, and weighed about 42 oz. Survivors were still being encountered in 1940.

- *Model 1874* The officer's pattern was identical mechanically with the M1873 but had a shorter barrel, a fluted cylinder and metal removed from the frame inside the butt to reduce weight. It was about 9 inches long and weighed 35 oz empty. Commercial-type guns were also made by Manufacture Française des Armes et Cycles de Saint-Étienne and a variety of Belgian gunmakers prior to 1900.

Model 1887 The first attempts to develop an improved revolver in 1885 led to an experimental 11mm solid-frame six-shot design with a loading gate on the right side of the frame behind the cylinder and an ejector rod beneath the barrel. By 1888 — and the advent of smokeless propellant — the design had been changed to fire an 8mm bullet, and about 1000 were made. However, dissatisfaction with the design forced the factory design staff to produce a better weapon.

The French 8mm M1892 "Lebel" revolver.

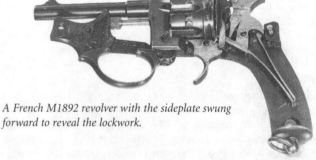

A French M1892 revolver with the sideplate swung forward to reveal the lockwork.

M1892 ("Modèle d'Ordonnance" or "Lebel") The perfected French revolver was a solid-frame design chambering six 8mm rounds (8x27R). The lockwork was based on the 1873 design, but a rebounding hammer and a hinged sideplate were added, and the cylinder, mounted on a yoke, could be swung out to the right. This allowed mounted men to reload while holding both the gun and the reins in the left hand. A hand lever ensured that the spent cases were ejected collectively.

What appears to be a loading gate on the right side of the frame actually releases the cylinder lock and immobilizes the hammer, but a variant, the rarely encountered *Modèle à Pompe*, relies on a thick sleeve surrounding the ejector rod beneath the barrel to lock the cylinder. Pressing a latch and pulling the sleeve forward released the cylinder from the frame; pushing the sleeve back then ejects the spent cases.

The M1892 was a sound design, well made and reliable, that remained in military service until World War II and in police hands into the late 1950s. Similar guns were made commercially in France, Belgium and Spain. The only real weakness lay in the ammunition, as an 8mm-diameter 120-grain bullet moving at merely 720 ft/sec was a poor choice for a combat pistol.

∼ AUTOMATIC PISTOLS ∼

SE-MAS The prototype "SE-MAS Type A No 4" was the culmination of a series of experimental pistols submitted to the French army, but it was not successful. An odd-looking blowback chambering the idiosyncratic French 7.65mm Longue cartridge, it had the return spring around the barrel and a suspended hammer mechanism in the rear of the slide. The SACM (Petter) design was preferred.

The French MAS M1935S, a simplified form of the Petter, was a sturdy gun chambered for the ineffectual 7.65mm Longue cartridge.

M1935S In 1938, with war looming closer, Saint Étienne engineers redesigned the 1935-type SACM (q.v.) pistol to make it easier to mass-produce. The basic mechanical features remained the same, but the contours became more angular and a matte finish was developed. The locking system changed from the original Browning-derived barrel ribs, locking in grooves inside the slide, to a simple lug on the barrel locking into a single recess in the slide. Some of the lockwork components were also simplified, though their functions remained unaltered.

The original SACM design became the "Mle 1935A", while the "utility" model made by the three principal French small-arms factories — Châtellerault, Saint-Étienne and Tulle — became the "Mle 1935S". However, only a few guns had been made when the Germans invaded France in 1940, and only the Mle 1935A remained in production prior to 1945.

MAS 1950 Combat experience in Europe and Indo-China had showed the M1935S to be efficient but also that the 7.65mm cartridge was too weak to be effective. The obvious answer to the problem was to redesign the 1935-type gun to fire 9mm Parabellum ammunition, lengthening the grip to take a nine-round magazine. The Mle 1950 was also made in Châtellerault ("MAC 50"), the source being betrayed by the third letter of the mark on the right side of the slide: "C" for Châtellerault, "S" for Saint-Étienne.

PA-MAS 9mm G-1 Manufacture of the M1950 ended by 1960, by which time the army had a sufficient stock for the foreseeable future. Subsequent demands were met by purchasing the PA-15 made by Manufacture d'Armes de Bayonne (q.v.), but by 1988, when the armed forces decided that more pistols were needed, no facilities remained to make them. A competitive trial then led to the selection of the Beretta 92F, and guns were purchased directly from Beretta to satisfy the needs of the Gendarmerie Nationale. Licensed production began in Saint-Étienne for the French navy in 1990, and the army adopted the Beretta in 1992.

The PA-MAS G-1 is similar to the Beretta 92F but only has a de-cocking lever instead of the safety-catch/de-cocking combination.

When the de-cocking lever has been pressed and the hammer has been lowered, releasing the lever allows it to spring back to the normal position. The pistol can be fired by simply pulling through on the trigger. Beretta has since offered the variation commercially as the Model 92G.

SAKO

Oy Sako Ab, Riihimaki, Finland.
Founded in 1919, Sako adopted its name (an acronym of Suojeluskuntain Ase- ja Konepaja Osakeyhito, "Arms & Engineering Workshop of the Civil Guard") when a move to Riihikami was completed in 1927. Sold to the Red Cross in 1944, to prevent the facilities being seized by the Soviet Union, Sako survived to become part of Sako-Valmet Oy in April 1987. Best known for rifles, sporting and military, Sako has also marketed handguns.

The Sako 22-32 target pistol.

22/32 Developed in the late 1970s, this competition pistol, as the name suggests, could be converted to fire any of the three main competition cartridges: 22 Short rimfire, 22 Long rimfire, and 32 S&W Long centerfire. The pistol was supplied as a package containing a butt/frame unit and three slide/barrel units, one in each chambering. The resulting pistol was a simple blowback with a separate bolt moving inside the slide. Various sight and grip options were available.

The Sako Triace pistol with its exchangeable barrel/breechblock units and magazines.

Triace This gun superseded the 22/32 pattern in 1978, an improved version with cast frame, fully adjustable grips, better sights and an improved adjustable trigger mechanism.

SALABERRIN

Santiago Salaberrin, Eibar, Spain.
The name of this gunmaker, or perhaps retailer, has been associated with a variety of "Eibar"-type pistols sold under the names *Etna*, *Invicta* and *Protector*. However, none of the guns that could be traced for examination showed any evidence that Salaberrin had made them. The Etna was marked "MODELE DEPOSE / "ETNA" CAL 6 35" on the slide and had a "JA" or "AJ" monogram on the grips. No 7.65mm

Invicta-type gun could be traced, and the Protector bore nothing but "AUTOMATIC PISTOL CAL. 6^{35}/ "PROTECTOR" / SPAIN" on the slide.

SALAVERRIA

Iraola Salaverria y Cia, Eibar, Spain.

Salaverria's workshop made 7.65mm Ruby pistols under contract to Gabilondo (q.v.) during World War I, continuing work until the early 1920s.

Destructor Two guns of this "Eibar" type were made, one in 6.35mm and another in 7.65mm. A typical small-caliber example is marked "AUTO MODEL" on the slide, but the grips display an encircled "IS" monogram in a circular cartouche over "DESTRUCTOR" on a scroll.

SAN PAOLO

Armi San Paolo, Gardone Val Trompia, Brescia, Italy.

This company took over the production of the S&W-style revolvers developed by J.P. Sauer & Sohn when the latter company became heavily involved with the manufacture of SIG automatic pistols in the late 1970s. It also makes a variety of "Western-style" revolvers based on the Colt Peacemaker and Remington New Army models.

CASIMIR SANTOS

Eibar, Spain.

El Cid Named after a legendary medieval hero who saved Spain from the Moors, this was a typical "Eibar" blowback based on the FN-Browning of 1906. It is usually marked "6^{35} 1915 Model Automatic Pistol" on the left side of the slide, above "EL CID". The grips have a crown in a circle, and the slide-retraction grips have been milled radially.

MODESTO SANTOS

Eibar, Spain.

Another of the small Eibar companies formed in 1915 to take advantage of the French army contracts, Santos began by producing the usual "Eibar" 7.65mm blowback automatics that were supplied to the French army through an intermediary called "Les Ouvriers Réunies". A series of 6.35mm and 7.65mm pistols of the usual simplified Browning pattern were sold throughout the 1920s under a variety of names.

A 7.65mm (32-caliber) Modesto Santos Action No. 2 pistol.

Action This name was first applied to the original 7.65mm guns made for the French army in 1915-18, which may be marked "LES OUVRIERS REUNIES ACTION NO 2 MLE 15". In addition, the name is associated with a 6.35mm pistol dating from c. 1919-25. This may also have been exported to France, as it is usually marked "PISTOLET AUTOMATIQUE MODELE 1920 CAL. 6^{35}/ "ACTION" …" on the left side of the slide and has a "MS" monogram molded into the grips.

Corrientes This was an alternative name for the 6.35mm-caliber "Action" (above), dating from the early 1920s.

M.S. Similar to the other guns in this particular series, this could be distinguished by the maker's name on the slide and standard "MS" monograms on the grips.

SAUER

J.P. Sauer & Sohn, Suhl (to 1945); J.P. Sauer & Sohn, Eckernforde/Holstein, Germany (1949 to date).

By the end of the 19th century, this old company (a descendant of Spangenberg & Sauer) had attained a reputation for first-quality rifles and sporting guns and had been involved in manufacturing the Reichsrevolver until the early 1890s. Their first commercial pistol was the "Bär", followed by the Roth-Sauer. This seems to have stirred up some interest, and in 1913, Sauer produced a pistol design of its own. Further designs followed, culminating in the Model 38 H, one of the best designs of the 1930s.

After 1945, the company "voted with its feet" and was re-established in West Germany, returning to pistol manufacture in the early 1950s. Sauer pistols had always been made to the highest standard, of first-class material, and it is strange that production of the Model 38 H did not resume after World War II. Guns were also made for other firms, in particular for Sterling Armaments (q.v.). In the late 1970s, the company entered into an agreement with SIG of Switzerland to produce SIG designs in Germany under the name "SIG-Sauer". This allowed SIG a greater market than could be reached from perennially neutral Switzerland, owing to restrictions placed on the export of firearms, and the revolver-making machinery was sold to Armi San Paolo in Italy.

Made by Sauer, the two-barrel 6.35mm (25-caliber) Bär pistol was very compact.

～ MULTI-SHOT PISTOL ～

Bär (c. 1900-10) Patented by Burkhard Behr of Zürich in 1898, this was made in Suhl prior to World War I. It resembled a revolver in layout, but the barrel was a flat, fluted unit with two superposed barrels. Behind it, in the place of a cylinder, was a flat block with four chambers, the upper two being aligned behind the two barrels. Behind this was a hammer concealed within a high frame and carrying a rotating firing pin unit. On pulling the folding trigger, the hammer was raised and dropped to fire the upper chamber; the next pull caused the firing pin to rotate so that it fired the next lower chamber. A catch in the top of the frame was then pressed, allowing the chamber block to be rotated so as to bring the two lower loaded chambers to the top, whereupon they could be fired by pulling the trigger as for the upper two chambers. By releasing the catch and giving the block a half-turn, all the chambers were exposed at the sides of the weapon and could be emptied by using a pin carried in the butt, then reloaded. It was originally produced in a special 7mm rimmed caliber, but after c. 1907, the 6.35mm Auto (25 ACP) cartridge was preferred.

～ REVOLVERS ～

Western Six Shooter A single-action revolver broadly based on the Colt M1873, it was followed by a number of other similar designs largely intended for export to the USA at the time of the "fast draw" craze in the middle 1950s. Most of these were sold through the Hawes company and are detailed under that entry.

TR6 This Smith & Wesson-styled solid-frame revolver was a six-shot personal-defense weapon.

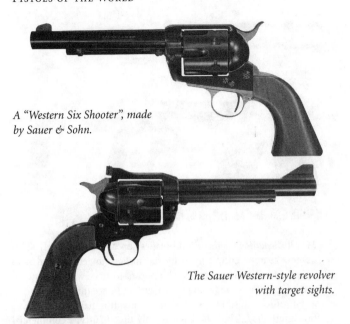

A "Western Six Shooter", made by Sauer & Sohn.

The Sauer Western-style revolver with target sights.

SR3 A heavy S&W-style target revolver with ventilated rib, adjustable sights and an adjustable trigger.

~ AUTOMATIC PISTOLS ~

Roth-Sauer (c. 1905-9) Patented by Roth and Krnka in 1900 and manufactured by Sauer, this, like so many of Krnka's designs, was unnecessarily complicated and used the long recoil system of operation. The barrel and bolt recoiled locked together by a lug on the bolt engaging in a recess on the breech. At the end of the recoil stroke, the bolt struck a cam that rotated it 20 degrees to unlock and was then held while the barrel went forward again. During this movement, the case was extracted and ejected, and as the barrel stopped, it tripped the bolt, which then came forward to chamber a fresh round. As the bolt entered the breech, it rotated to lock, and as the locking was completed, the locked assembly ran forward a further short distance to the firing position.

The 7.65mm Roth-Sauer pistol.

Firing was by a partially self-cocking striker mechanism; as the bolt closed, the striker was held by a sear, with its spring in partial compression. Pulling the trigger further compressed this spring and then released the striker. It was not fully self-cocking; once the striker had been released, it could only be re-cocked by manually re-cycling the bolt.

All this complication tends to look out of place when one considers that the cartridge was a special 7.65mm round designed by Roth and somewhat weaker than the normal 7.65mm ACP round. Other mechanical features of interest on the Roth-Sauer include use of the cocking knob as a safety that locked the action when rotated and an integral magazine in the butt that was charger-loaded through the open bolt-way. The pistols are marked "Patent Roth" on top of the frame, and

the grips carry an oval frame with Sauer's *Wildmann* ("wild man", "savage") trademark.

The Roth-Sauer was made only in small numbers. However, these were sufficient to allow a substantial quantity — perhaps 250 — to be purchased for service with Landesaustellung Windhoek, the colonial gendarmerie in German South-West Africa, c. 1911. It is assumed that these guns had remained in stock and were available at a competitive price in an era when the army had first call on supplies of the regulation Pistole 1908 (Parabellum).

An "Old Model" 7.65mm (32-caliber) Sauer pistol, introduced shortly before World War I began.

Sauer-Pistole (7.65mm version, c. 1913-31) Designed by Heinz Zehner and patented in Germany in 1912, this 7.65mm blowback appeared commercially in 1913. Its novel construction features included a fixed barrel with a concentric spring, a light tubular slide and a separate breechblock held in the slide by a screwed end-cap that was locked by a spring catch. A seven-shot magazine went into the butt, and the pistol was striker-fired. A safety catch on the left side locked the sear and disengaged the trigger when applied. Most of these guns bore the maker's mark in German ("& Sohn"), but a few, undoubtedly intended for export, were marked in English ("Prussia", "& Son"). Guns of the latter group also bear "PAT'D MAY 20 1912" on the left side of the slide, which suggests that they were destined for the USA, as pre-1914 British patent legislation did not require the patent date to be specified, whereas it was obligatory in the USA. The first few thousand guns had additional safety bolts through the lower part of the frame behind the trigger-guard web. They also lacked a rear sight, a rudimentary groove in the end-cap sufficing, but a small standing-notch sight doubling as the end-cap lock soon appeared instead. Grips that had been checkered bakelite, with a plain lozenge around the retaining bolt, became a plainer design with "S & S" in a panel.

Changes were made to the basic design in the mid-1920s when the contours of the frame were altered (the underside of the trigger guard, for example, became horizontal), the retraction grips were extended to cover the rear of the tubular slide in addition to the end-cap and the safety lever was altered to double as a hold-open. The grips of these pistols, which are sometimes now called "M1926", were usually black bakelite with "Sauer" and "Cal. 7,65" in separate panels. Total production has been estimated at 175,000 guns. Many guns were purchased by German officers during World War I, though few of these would have borne inspectors' or comparable military marks. Others undoubtedly served the police during the Weimar Republic, and a few were distributed as reparations immediately after World War II. Some reportedly bear "POLITI" ("police") marks together with a crowned axe-wielding lion of Norway.

- *6.35mm version* (c. 1914-29) It has been claimed that these guns were introduced commercially in 1914, but that the outbreak of war restricted sales. Work undoubtedly recommenced in the early 1920s, but the simpler "WTM" was preferred. The original guns were small-scale duplicates of the perfected rear sight/end-cap lock 7.65mm type. The second pattern was similar but had an auxiliary safety catch or Zusatzsicherung that locked the trigger bar. Guns of this type can be identified by the small pivoting catch beneath the safety-lever shank on the left side of the frame. It is suspected that these were developed in the hope of satisfying the demands of the police. The third-pattern 6.35mm Sauer, probably dating from 1926-8, had the safety system altered to double as a hold-open. Usually finished in blue (though nickel-plated examples are known), the guns had bakelite grips with a decorative "S&S" monogram in an oval panel.

The tiny Sauer vest-pocket pistol, chambering the 6.35mm Auto (25 ACP) round.

WTM (c. 1922-8) The first of these 6.35mm Auto (25 ACP) pocket pistols is said to have been designed as early as 1920, though it is suspected that production did not begin for several years. The Westentaschen-Modell ("WTM", "vest-pocket model") was a compact blowback distinguished by an enlarged ejection port in the slide. A separate breechblock was held in the slide by a spring catch, the striker protruded from the rear of the slide when the pistol was cocked and vertical retraction grips were milled at both ends of the slide.

- *1928 pattern* An improved version of the original design, this had simpler contours and a breechblock that was forged integrally with the slide. The retraction grips, confined to the rear of the slide, were milled obliquely.
- *1933 pattern* The contours of the slide were revised once again in an attempt to modernize, and the ejection port was moved to the right side. Work continued until war began in 1939.

M1930 This was a refinement of the last, or 1926-type, 7.65mm general-purpose pistol. The essence of the original 1912-patent Zehner design was retained, but the grip was changed and a sleeve was added at the rear of the return spring. Most guns were blued, with checkered bakelite grips displaying a simple "SuS" monogram. However, nickel-plated and specially engraved examples could be obtained to order, and some have been seen with stainless-steel barrels (marked "NIROSTA"). Others had duraluminum frames. Chamberings were restricted to 22 Lang (22 Long rimfire, very rare) and 7.65mm Auto (32 ACP). Many guns of this type were sold to the Netherlands in the early 1930s by way of distributor Joh. Munts of Amsterdam. These are said to have been used by the Dutch armed forces, police and government departments such as the finance ministry. Some were fitted with lanyard rings and others had loaded-chamber indicators.

The 7.65mm Sauer Behörden-Modell, introduced in the early 1930s, had a distinctive blade-type safety-catch set into the trigger.

A Sauer Behörden-Modell pistol field-stripped.

- *M1930 Behörden Modell* ("Authorities" or "Official" model) This name was apparently coined by the makers to recommend it to police and military users, which appears to have worked, since it was adopted in some numbers by German police forces and also as a staff officers' pistol by the German army. It remained in production until 1937. The gun was basically the 1930-type commercial model with a loaded-chamber indicator and a small catch inserted in the trigger to act as a security lock. Unless the catch had been pressed inward by the finger, the trigger was locked to prevent inadvertent discharge if, for example, the loaded weapon was dropped. It is assumed that this feature was demanded by the police. Many of these guns, which were known to the police as "Pistolen S&S BM", will be found with appropriate marks. Some were also purchased on behalf of the paramilitary groups.

Model 38 This was a completely new design and, but for the war, would certainly have left its mark on the commercial market. The demands of World War II, however, ensured that virtually all of the guns went to the military, the paramilitary and police forces. Army-issue guns usually display linear-eagle marks, usually applied by inspector no. 37, whereas the police issue have inspection markings in the form of single letters (e.g., "C", "F", "L") alongside a simplified eagle and

The Sauer 38H was one of the most advanced designs of its type. This is a 7.65mm (32-caliber) version.

The Sauer 38H, showing the de-cocking lever on the left side of the frame across the magazine well.

may also have a unit marks on the grip straps. Paramilitary acquisitions may bear the mark of the purchasing group — e.g., "SA DER NSDAP" — or a regional abbreviation. The dating of the earliest commercial guns may be helped by a change in the proofmark, from "crown/N" to "eagle/N", which took effect on April 1, 1940.

- *Model 38* (1939) This was a fixed-barrel blowback with the recoil spring around the barrel and a separate breechblock unit pinned into the slide. The lockwork was double action, and an internal hammer was connected to a de-cocking lever on the left side of the frame (partially concealed by the grip). This allowed the cocked hammer to be lowered under control, or an uncocked hammer could be brought to full-cock by thumb action.

- *Model 38 H* (1939-45) The perfected version of the Model 38, this was distinguished by the addition of a safety lever on the left side of the slide above the grip. This Hahnsicherung, or "hammer safety", locked the hammer to prevent it reaching the inertia-type firing pin. The guns were still fitted with the magazine-safety system and a loaded-chamber indicator pin. The finish was customarily blue with checkered bakelite grips, but nickel or chrome-plating could be applied to order. A few pistols were engraved, often for presentation to high-ranking military officers or government officials, and a few were chambered for the 22 LfB (22 LR rimfire) cartridge. A few long-barreled *Jägermodelle* are also said to have been made in 1939. Duraluminum frames were made in small quantities, the resulting *Leichtmodell* (lightweight model) weighing about 5 oz less than normal. Manufacturing standards, particularly finish, declined as the war progressed. Noticeable changes included the omission of the Sauer & Sohn name from the left side of the slide (only the caliber mark remained) and the deletion of the safety catch and loaded-chamber indicator pin. The guns made immediately prior to the fall of Suhl to men of the US Army, in April 1945, were very poor indeed.

SAVAGE ARMS COMPANY
Utica, New York, USA.
The Savage Arms Company was founded in 1894 by Jamaican-born Arthur W. Savage, who had become a jackaroo in Australia, managed a coffee plantation in Jamaica, designed a torpedo adopted by the Brazilian navy and superintended the Utica Belt Railroad before sitting down to design a lever-action sporting rifle.

The rifle was extremely successful, allowing Savage to sell his interests in the company in 1904 to continue his previous footloose ways — founding a tire company here, growing citrus fruit there, oil drilling somewhere else and even prospecting for gold before he died in 1941 at age 84.

The Savage Arms Company was purchased by the Driggs-Seabury Ordnance Company in 1915 and reorganized in 1919 as the "Savage Arms Corporation". In later years, Savage absorbed the J. Stevens Arms and Tool Company, the Davis-Warner Company and sundry other firearms manufacturers, rising to become one of the leading manufacturers in the United States prior to a final collapse in the 1990s.

Though renowned for bolt- and lever-action rifles, Savage also made substantial quantities of handguns in 1907-28. Some have claimed that the guns were designed by William Condit or Arthur Savage himself, but the first relevant British patent was granted to Major Elbert H. Searle in 1905. Later patents of 1909-10 name both Searle and Condit. Condit also appeared as a co-patentee in another 1905-vintage British patent protecting an abortive recoil-operated pistol with vertical locking system and an internal hammer.

∼ SINGLE-SHOT PISTOL ∼
Model 101 After an absence from the pistol business of nearly 40 years, Savage returned in 1960 with a single-shot pistol chambered for the 22 LR rimfire cartridge. The pistol had the appearance of a Frontier-style revolver, but the barrel and "cylinder" were an integral unit that swung out of the frame for ejection and reloading. It was withdrawn from sale in 1968.

∼ AUTOMATIC PISTOLS ∼
Excepting the abortive 25-caliber blowbacks, all Savage pistols were made in accordance with the Searle patent. The barrel, concentric with the return spring and the slide, had lugs above and below the chamber. The bottom lug was a square lump that anchored the barrel in the frame, allowing it to move radially but not linearly. The upper lug was a curved cam that fitted a track in the slide. A removable breechblock in the rear of the slide carried a striker and spring.

When the gun fired, the reaction on the base of the cartridge case attempted to blow the slide to the rear in the usual blowback fashion. Owing to the engagement of the slide track and the lug on the top of the barrel, however, rearward movement was resisted and the interaction of track and cam rotated the barrel 5 degrees counterclockwise. The slide recoiled once the cam track straightened.

Searle claimed that sufficient resistance to the rotation of the barrel was provided by the bullet engaging the rifling, which twisted in the opposite direction to keep the breech closed until the bullet had left the muzzle. The merits of the system have been disputed ever since. Searle's contention that the breech was locked at the instant of ignition cannot be disputed, but how long does it stay locked? The theory of bullet reaction in the barrel is open to arguments. The inventor maintained that the rotation of the bullet as it passed through the right-handed rifling tended to turn the barrel clockwise and resist opening. But there is an equally valid argument that maintains that the bullet will resist the turning moment placed upon it by the rifling and place a counterclockwise torque on the barrel — a phenomenon encountered in light artillery on more than one occasion. Spark-gap photographs made in Germany in the late 1920s apparently showed that the breech of the 7.65mm Savage opened faster than that of a 6.35mm Browning, a pure blowback (although, given the relative powers of the two cartridges, this is perhaps not so surprising.)

It seems likely that the Savage breech does not remain locked until the bullet leaves the muzzle and should rightly be classed as a sophisticated delayed blowback — in effect if not intention — efficient enough to handle the 45 Colt M1906 cartridge.

One of the 45-caliber Savage pistols tested by the US Army in 1907-9.

M1907 (or "Model H", US Army trials) Savage was preparing a 32-caliber pistol when, in 1906, the army announced that trials would be held to find a new service pistol. Work began to create a gun to fire the experimental 45 M1906 round. It performed encouragingly enough to persuade the General Staff to decide that 200 Colt-Browning and 200 Savage pistols should be issued for field trials. A total of 230 Savage pistols were tested in 1909-10, but the rival Colt design was preferred and the Savages that survived the trials were sold at auction in 1912. It is said that 20-30 additional 45-caliber pistols were made experimentally, with a variety of features, but the project was then abandoned.

The 32 ACP M1907 Savage pistol.

M1907 Introduced commercially in August 1907 in 32 ACP and in 1913 in 380 ACP (9mm Short), this had a serrated "hammer" at the rear of the slide that was actually the top surface of the cocking piece. The cocking piece was pivoted on the lower part of the bolt unit, which formed the rear part of the slide, and the firing pin was pinned in its upper arm; lower arms extended into the frame. When the slide ran back, the lower arms were pulled across the frame, forced up and forward, and (owing to the pivot) drew back the upper arm to cock the striker. An extension of the upper arm formed a spur that allowed the striker to be thumb-cocked.

The 1907-type Savage had a circular tip on the safety catch, lacked any indication of the safety-catch positions, and the unusual sheet-steel grips snapped into place on the frame. The company name, caliber and patent date could be found on top of the slide, with a circular motif of an American Indian head and the words "SAVAGE QUALITY" on the grips. The pistols were certainly extremely well made.

The Savage was adopted only by the Portuguese army, which took small quantities of the 1907-type guns with rounded cocking-piece extensions as the "M/908" and some late 1907 models with spur-type extensions as the "M/915". The purchases were made during World War I, when supplies of Parabellums were interrupted. The Savage pistols were replaced in military service in the 1920s and relegated to the Guardia Nacional Republicana. They were finally sold commercially and are not as uncommon in Portugal as elsewhere in the world.

M1915 A major redesign led to the replacement of the exposed cocking piece by a concealed version, the addition of a grip safety and a hold-open catch in the trigger guard to lock the slide open after the last spent case had been ejected. Another innovation was the engraving of "SAVAGE" in large letters on the frame above the left grip. The 1907 model remained in production until 1916, the only change concerning the replacement of the original nine broad retraction grooves with 28 narrow grooves.

M1917 The "hammerless" 1915 pattern was not particularly well received and had soon been withdrawn in favor of a gun that discarded the grip safety and restored the visible cocking piece, using a narrow spur that had been tested on M1907 guns made in 1915-16. The butt became noticeably wedge-shaped, which looked ugly yet improved the

An M1917 Savage. Note the spur-type hammer.

handgrip, and the grips themselves were held by screws. The gun remained in production until 1926 (32 ACP version) and 1928 (380 ACP version), but it seems that the Savage, expensive to make, could simply no longer compete in the market.

25-caliber guns Savage also developed a blowback pocket pistol, but events conspired against it. The first attempt was made in 1915, when the pressure of war contracts led to the idea being shelved. The idea was apparently revived in 1916, but the entry of the United States into the war brought even more contracts. Another revival occurred in 1919, but Savage finally decided against the project in the depressed post-war economic climate. A small run of pre-production pistols was made but never offered for sale commercially. Some guns had long barrels, the design of the sights can vary and the magazine capacity may be six or seven rounds.

SAVAGE ARMS, INC.

Westfield, Massachusetts, USA.

An outgrowth of the original Savage business, which failed in the 1990s, this still concentrates on bolt-action rifles.

Centerfire series These guns are built on the left-hand "M110" action, a well-proven front-locking design originating in the early 1950s. The pistols all eject to the right and, unless stated otherwise, have internal box magazines, composite stocks and 14-inch barrels.

* *M510F Striker* Weighing about 5lb, this is chambered for the 22-250 Remington, 243 Winchester or 308 Winchester rounds, magazine capacity being three rounds.
* *M516BSAK* This is a variant of the 516BSS with a muzzle brake, available in 22-250 and 223 Remington chamberings only.
* *M516BSS* A stainless-steel version of the basic 510 and introduced in 1999, this has a laminated thumb-hole butt. Chamberings have included 223 Remington, 243 Winchester, 7mm-08, 260 Remington and 308 Winchester; magazines hold merely two rounds.
* *M516FSAK* A minor variant of the 516FSS, this has an additional muzzle brake.
* *M516FSS* Derived from the 510F, this is made entirely of stainless steel and usually has a black stock.

Rimfire series These are built on a lighter right-hand bolt action with detachable box magazines ahead of the trigger.

* *M501F Sport Striker* Offered with a 10-inch barrel, this gun feeds from a detachable 10-round box magazine. Chambering is restricted to 22 LR rimfire. Introduced in 2000, these are also drilled and tapped for optical sight mounts.
* *M502F Sport Striker* A variant of the M510F in 22 Magnum rimfire with a five-round magazine.

SCHALL

Schall & Co., New Haven, Connecticut, USA.

This business provided spare parts and servicing facilities for Fiala (q.v.) pistols after the failure of their original promoter. It also assembled a few 22-caliber repeating pistols from a combination of the parts that had been in store and some new fabrications. The rear sight is simpler than the Fiala design, and the wooden grips are ribbed.

SCHILLING

V. Chr. Schilling, Suhl, Germany.

Schilling, a long-established gunmaker, first came to prominence by making the M79 and M83 Reichsrevolvers in partnership with Spangenberg & Sauer and C.G. Haenel. These guns bear cartouches containing "S. & S. – V.C.S." or "S. & S. – V.C.S. – C.G.H.", respectively. Work ceased in the 1890s when Schilling returned to the manufacture of military rifles (Gew. 88), sporting rifles and shotguns. Pistols were made for Theodor Bergmann (q.v.) until 1904 when Schilling was purchased by Sempert & Krieghoff. The Bergmann contracts were immediately rescinded, though rifles were still being made under the Schilling name in 1918.

SCHMIDT

Herbert Schmidt, Ostheim an der Rhön, Germany.

Schmidt has made revolvers that have been sold under a variety of names including "AMCO", "Bison", "Buffalo Scout", "Burgo Mod 21", sold by Karl Burgsmüller of Kreiensen; "Cheyenne Scout", "Deputy Adjuster", "Deputy Magnum" and "Deputy Marshal", possibly sold by Hawes Firearms of San Francisco; "EIG E8", sold by the EIG Corporation of Los Angeles; "Eusta" and "Gecado Model 21", sold by Albrecht Kind; "Geroco", "Indian Scout", "LAs Deputy", "Liberty", "Liberty Scout", "Madison", "NATO", "Omega", "PIC Model 11", "PIC Model 21" and PIC Model 121", sold by the Precise Import Corporation; "Spesco", sold by the Spesco Corporation of Atlanta; "Texas Scout", "Valor", "VOL" and "Western", probably sold by the Western Arms Corporation of Los Angeles.

The "PIC Model 11" was a six-shot double-action gun with a solid frame, a swing-out cylinder and a 2.5-inch barrel; the "Liberty 11" and "EIG E8" were similar. A target-shooting version of the basic revolver, with a 5.5-inch barrel, has also been produced. Schmidt's "Western-style" 22 rimfire revolvers had either an ejector rod beneath the barrel or a detachable cylinder arbor and attracted the "Deputy" and "Scout" names. The guns may betray their origins with small encircled "HS" marks on the frame or the maker's name stamped into the lower edge of the butt frame that becomes visible only when the grips are removed. They will also have German proofmarks that distinguish them from essentially similar revolvers made by Uberti and others in Italy.

A four-barrel Schüler "Reform" pistol.

SCHÜLER

August Schüler, Suhl, Germany.

Reform This was a repeating pistol of unusual pattern. The butt, frame, trigger and guard, and hammer all resemble revolver practice, but in front of the frame lies a four-barrel block with the barrels arranged vertically. The block was removed, loaded with four 6.35mm cartridges and replaced; pulling the trigger dropped the hammer on the round in the top barrel and fired it. The next pull lifted the block and brought the second barrel into alignment with the hammer; the next brought the third barrel, and so on. As the second barrel fired, a small hole blew some of the powder gas into the first barrel and blew out the empty cartridge case. After the fourth shot, the block was removed and the fourth case had to be punched out before reloading.

The pistol was made between about 1907 and the time World War I began; the genre was popular, as the guns were thin, light, easily carried in the pocket and cheaper than contemporaneous automatic pistols.

SCHULHOF

Josef Schulhof, Vienna, Austria-Hungary.

Best known for rifles, Schulhof was another of the many Austro-Hungarian inventors of mechanically operated repeating pistols. His

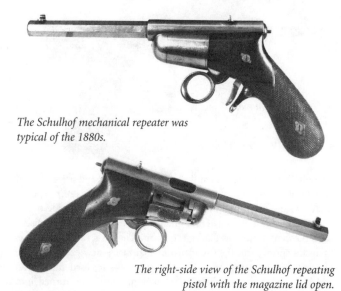

The Schulhof mechanical repeater was typical of the 1880s.

The right-side view of the Schulhof repeating pistol with the magazine lid open.

design, patented in 1884, relied on a reciprocating bolt driven by a ring trigger. It was made in small numbers, in 8mm and 10.6mm calibers, though some reports also speak of a version using the 320 centerfire revolver cartridge. He also made a variety of single-shot dropping-block target pistols.

SCHUTZ & LARSEN

Otterup, Denmark

This company is principally known as a maker of barrels and target rifles but produced the *Model 51*, a distinctive bolt-action 22-caliber Free Pistol with the usual options of grips and sights. Production, never large, was confined to 1952-7.

SCHWARZLOSE

A.W. Schwarzlose GmbH, Berlin, Germany.

Andreas Wilhelm Schwarzlose, though born in Germany, served for some years as an armorer in the Austro-Hungarian army. After gaining additional gunmaking experience in Suhl, he began designing automatic pistols and later developed a delayed blowback machinegun that was adopted by Austro-Hungary, the Netherlands and Bulgaria prior to 1918. A factory was opened in Berlin to make small-arms but was closed by the Allied Disarmament Commission in 1919. Schwarzlose then acted as a consultant until his death in 1936.

Early designs The first pistol, perfected in 1892, was a remarkable design that has been likened to an automated form of the Remington rolling-block breech. The hammer and a breechblock pivoted on the same axis-pin in a frame that supported a magazine, beneath the barrel, containing seven rimmed cartridges carried nose-down. When the gun fired, the barrel was allowed to recoil just far enough to drive the hammer and breechblock backward. As the block pivoted downward, a feed-arm lifted a cartridge from the magazine and aligned it with the chamber. Spring pressure then returned the block to chamber the cartridge and return the feed-arm to its original position. The hammer stayed back until the trigger was pressed. A gun of this type is said to have survived in the Musée d'Armes in Liège until stolen in 1970, but series production was never undertaken.

His next design was a long recoil weapon of considerable ingenuity, using a rotating bolt. Although mechanically simple, it too never saw production. But by 1897, Schwarzlose had perfected a design that he thought worth producing, and in 1898, the first model appeared of what became known in Britain as the "Standard Model".

M1898 (or "Standard Model") This was a locked-breech pistol firing the 7.63mm Mauser cartridge, the locking being performed by a rotat-

A 7.65mm Schwarzlose M1898 pistol.

ing bolt with four lugs. When the gun fired, the bolt and barrel moved back until the barrel was stopped by compression of the return spring. A stud in the frame, working in a cam track in the underside of the bolt, had meanwhile rotated lugs on the bolt head far enough to disengage the bolt from the barrel extension. The bolt ran back alone, against a spring, and then returned to chamber a new cartridge. The lugs entered the barrel extension, the barrel was released, and barrel and bolt ran forward to battery, the locking lugs being turned into engagement during the closing stroke. The striker had been cocked and was held back on the sear until the trigger was pressed.

The "Standard" was a simple design that should have prospered, but it had been pre-empted by the Mauser and is said to have been unreliable. Sales were slow, until the remaining guns were apparently sold to the Russian revolutionaries in 1905.

M1900 This delayed blowback had a toggle-lock that unfolded as the bolt recoiled, a precursor of the system used in the Schwarzlose machinegun. The pistol was less fortunate, existing only in prototype form.

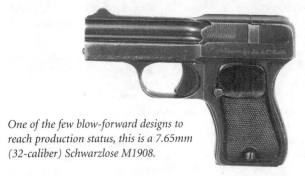

One of the few blow-forward designs to reach production status, this is a 7.65mm (32-caliber) Schwarzlose M1908.

M1908 Schwarzlose abandoned all previous ideas and produced something new: the only blow-forward pistol ever to attain commercial success. The breech formed part of the frame, and the barrel was free to slide forward against a return spring. To load, the barrel was pulled forward and allowed to fly back, collecting a cartridge from the butt magazine, forcing it against the breech face and cocking an internal hammer at the same time. When the gun fired, the barrel ran forward and stripped itself of the empty case (which was knocked clear by a mechanical ejector) before returning to reload and re-cock for the next shot. A grip safety in the frontstrap of the butt could be locked in the "fire" position by a pushbutton.

Blow-forward pistols were made in Berlin from 1908 to 1911, many being distributed in North America by the Warner Arms Company of Brooklyn; these have the Warner name on the barrel beneath the Schwarzlose marks. When work ceased in Berlin, Warner purchased the rights, tools and dies, and made a small quantity of pistols in the USA.

SCHWEIZERISCHE INDUSTRIE GESELLSCHAFT ("SIG")

Neuhausen am Rheinfalls, Switzerland.

Also known in the early days as "Waffenfabrik Neuhausen" or "Fabrique d'Armes Neuhausen", SIG was established in 1853 to make

railway rolling stock but has since attained an enviable record for excellence in the design and manufacture of firearms. The company has specialized in military weapons, primarily for the Swiss army, and since 1945 has been making pistols that rank among the world's best. A link was forged in the 1970s with J.P. Sauer & Sohn (q.v.), allowing SIG designs to be made in Germany. SIG now also owns Hämmerli (q.v.).

~ AUTOMATIC PISTOLS ~

Note: From 2002 onwards, SIG handguns made of stainless steel have been offered with a synthetic Nitron coating on the metalwork. This gives them a matte-black finish. Others have been offered in "Two-Tone", which normally combines a bright-finish stainless-steel slide with a blacked aluminum-alloy frame.

An 1894-type 7.65mm Mannlicher pistol, made by "Fab. d'Armes Neuhausen" — SIG.

Mannlicher Ferdinand Ritter von Mannlicher was born in 1848 and spent much of his life working for the North Austrian Railway. In 1876, during a visit to the Centennial Exhibition in Philadelphia, he was impressed by the exhibits of Winchester and other gunmakers and returned to Austria to design a repeating rifle of his own. This was successful enough to attract the attention of the Austro-Hungarian army, which adopted the perfected "straight-pull" Mannlicher rifle in 1886. He was also responsible for a variety of self-loading rifles and automatic pistols.

The first Mannlicher pistol appeared in 1894. When it was fired, the barrel moved forward from the breech against a spring, an extractor on the standing breech retaining the spent case until it could be ejected by the pressure of the next cartridge (or the magazine platform) rising below it. The barrel was held at the end of the forward stroke until the shooter released the trigger and a catch was tripped to allow the barrel to return. A new round entered the chamber as the breech closed.

A firing pin attached to the hammer passed through a hole in the standing breech, as in contemporary revolver practice. The self-loading action did not affect the trigger system, as the hammer had to be cocked by the thumb or raised and dropped by pulling through on the trigger in double-action style. The hammer rebounded after firing to withdraw the firing pin from the breech face — otherwise, of course, the pistol would have fired as soon as it re-loaded.

In prototype form, the Mannlicher apparently chambered an 8mm rimmed cartridge shared with the Salvator-Dormus pistol (see "Škoda"), but the series-made large-caliber guns chambered a rimmed round that has become known as the "7.6mm Mannlicher M94".

A 6.5mm pattern was then produced, chambering another rimmed straight-sided cartridge, though some of the original drawings for the 6.5mm pistol show a rimless necked cartridge. It is doubtful if more than 60 of these were made.

The 1894-type pistol was made in 1894 and 1895, introducing a characteristic system of marking that has been the source of innumerable arguments; guns may be marked "Model 1894" or "Model 1895" according to the year in which they were made. Minor changes were made during their short production life, and variants may be found without the automatic barrel-retaining catch, with a single-action trigger mechanism or experimental safety devices.

The production history of the original Mannlicher pistol is unclear. It is assumed that the prototypes were made in Austria-Hungary, perhaps in Steyr or the North Austrian Railway workshops, by Gasser or even by Škoda. The only large-scale contribution was made by SIG, where a handful of 7.6mm guns tested in 1894 was succeeded by about 60 6.5mm guns made in 1895. These had "FAB. D'ARMES" curved over "NEUHAUSEN" on the left side of the frame above the rear web of the trigger guard.

Petter The Swiss army began seeking a replacement for the 06/29 W+F Parabellum pistol in the 1930s, persuading SIG to acquire rights to the patents of Charles Petter. The original Petter pistol, developed by Société Alsacienne de Constructions Mecaniques (q.v.), had been adopted by the French army as the "M1935". SIG made prototypes in 1937-40, but these were little more than near-copies of the M1935. By 1944, however, a small number of *Neuhausen 44/16* (so-called from the year and the 16-shot magazine capacity) and *Neuhausen 44/8* pistols were submitted for trials against the government-sponsored Pistole 43 W+F Browning (see "Bern Arms Factory"). The results favored the SIG design, which was refined to become the SP 47/8.

SP 47/8, or P-210 This was a locked-breech design using the familiar shaped-cam beneath the breech to pull the barrel out of engagement with the slide. The hammer, sear and other lock components were carried in a removable module, and the slide ran on rails formed inside the frame instead of externally. The design of the rails complicated the manufacturing process but supported the slide better than normal and contributed to both accuracy and the longevity of the pistol.

A deluxe form of the SIG SP 47/8 or P210.

The SP 47/8 was marketed commercially from 1948 in 9mm Parabellum and adopted by the Swiss army as the *Ordonnanzpistole SIG Modell 49* ("OP 49"). It was subsequently approved by the West German Border Police and the Danish army but was too expensive to encourage large-scale sales. Conversion kits allowed 22 LR rimfire or 7.65mm Parabellum centerfire ammunition to be used when required.

In 1957, the designation of the SP 47/8 was changed to "P-210" to conform to company nomenclature policy. Production finally ceased in 2002, but new guns will probably be available from stock for several years. In addition, Danish and Swiss military-issue pistols, displaced by more modern equipment, are now being refurbished for commercial sale.

- *P-210-1* This was the original military-pattern pistol, with fixed sights, polished blued finish, wood grips and a lanyard loop on the butt.
- *P-210-2* Another of the military-style guns, this had a matte sand-blasted finish, wood or black plastic grips and fixed sights.
- *P-210-4* A special model for the West German Border Police, this was essentially similar to the 210-1.
- *P-210-5* Made specially for target shooting, this had a 6-inch barrel, adjustable sights and a specially adjusted trigger. Guns made during the late 1990s also had a compensator attached to the muzzle and a rail for sights and accessories beneath the frame ahead of the trigger guard. Undoubtedly the finest automatic pistol of its day, the P-210-5 retailed at $2100 in the USA in 2000.

The SIG P-210-6, with wooden match-style grips and an adjustable rear sight.

- *P-210-6* The standard target pistol in the 210 series, this retained the standard 4.7-inch barrel but had adjustable sights and a specially adjusted trigger mechanism. Empty weight was about 32 oz.
- *JP-210* (or Jubiläumspistole 210) Five hundred of these were made in 1977 to celebrate the 125th anniversary of SIG, with special high-polish blue finish, gold plating on the hammer, trigger, dismantling catch and safety lever, and walnut grips carved with an oakleaf design. The guns were numbered from JP001 and had the SIG logo ahead of "1853-1978" on the slide.
- *P-210-8* Introduced in 1998 and derived from the P-210-6, this shared the 4.7-inch barrel and adjustable sights. It also had a special heavy frame, an adjustable trigger stop, select walnut grips and a blued sandblast finish. Empty weight was about 37 oz.

P220 In the 1960s, SIG began developing a simpler version of the P-210, introduced commercially in 1974 as the "P220" and immediately adopted by the Swiss army as their *Pistole 75*. This weapon was the first of the SIG-Sauer designs, combining a de-cocking lever and lock mechanism inspired by the pre-war Sauer Model 38 H with a locking system adapted from the P-210.

The P220 is a double-action pistol that uses the same cam system of lowering the barrel, but the chamber area is squared to rise into the ejection port — a simplified locking system that has been widely copied. Guns have been offered in 7.65mm Parabellum (discontinued

A typical SIG-Sauer P220 pistol, with non-typical target-style sights.

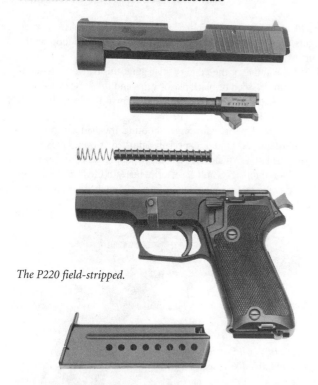

The P220 field-stripped.

The SIG-Sauer P226, in 9mm Parabellum.

M1911A1 Colt-Browning. The SIG is 7.7 inches long with a 4.4-inch barrel and weighs 27 oz empty. The magazine catch could be reversed, and the magazine capacity was increased from 8 to 15 rounds. The P226 was beaten only on the basis of "best and final price" by Beretta, but a small quantity was purchased for the British Special Air Service in 1991. Guns are currently being offered in 357 SIG, 9mm Parabellum or 45 ACP, with optional extended magazines holding 15 or 20 rounds. The latest versions also have traditional double-action or double-action-only lockwork.

- *P226 Sport* Introduced in 2001, this 9mm Parabellum gun is made of stainless steel. It has adjustable target sights and a large slab-sided muzzle weight. The grips are generally black-rubber Hogue designs.

in 1992), 9mm Parabellum (discontinued in 2001), 38 Super and 45 ACP, the only significant difference being that the 45-caliber version has a push-button magazine release behind the trigger instead of a sprung latch on the heel of the butt. This merely reflects the preferences of the US market. Magazine capacity is nine 7.65mm, 9mm or 38 rounds, or seven rounds in 45 ACP. The latest guns are available with either traditional double-action or double-action-only lockwork.

- *P220 ST* A designation applied to a variant of the basic gun with a stainless-steel slide and an alloy frame. It has Hogue grips and an accessory rail beneath the front of the frame.
- *P220 Sport* Introduced in 1999 in 45 ACP only, this offers a 5.5-inch barrel with a compensator/muzzle weight. The guns are made of stainless steel, have black rubber grips and weigh about 44 oz empty. Magazine capacity is seven rounds.

A deluxe 226 celebrating 125 years of SIG weapons production.

- *JP226* (or Jubiläumspistole 226) Five hundred of these guns were made in 1977, to mark the 125th anniversary of SIG. They have gold-line inlays on the slide and gold plating on the trigger, hammer, de-cocking lever and magazine catch. Finish is high-polish blue and the slide inscription includes "1853-1978".

P228 This appeared in the late 1980s, though it is little more than a refinement of the P225 with a 13-round magazine. Most of the components of the P225, P226 and P228 are interchangeable, as are most of the accessories. The first US government contract was placed in 1992 as

A SIG-Sauer P225.

P225 Similar to the P220, this military-style pistol is smaller, lighter and carried one round fewer in the magazine. An automatic firing-pin safety compensates for the lack of manual safety features. The P225 is about 7.1 inches long with a 3.9-inch barrel and weighs about 26 oz without its eight-round single-column magazine. Finish may be matte blue, K-Kote polymer or electroless nickel. The grips are usually black plastic.

P226 This was developed from the P225 in the 1980s to satisfy the demands of a US Army that was searching for a pistol to replace the

The compact SIG-Sauer P228.

The SIG-Sauer P228 with accessories, including an oversize magazine and sight-adjusting tools.

A recent example of the SIG-Sauer P230 personal-defense pistol. This particular gun is chambered for the 9mm Short (380 ACP) round.

a result of trials held in January 1990 in the US Army Military Police School, Fort McClellan, Alabama. The SIG submission proved to be the best "off-the-shelf" acquisition. The P228 has since been adopted by the US Navy as the "M11 Pistol", for issue to aircrew and investigators. The M11 has a special non-corrosive finish and "U.S. M11" on the right side of the frame. Guns are being assembled in the Sigarms factory in the USA, though many of the parts are apparently supplied from the Sauer factory in Germany.

P229 (1991 to date) Excepting slight changes in the contours of the slide, this was simply a P228 chambered for the 40 Smith & Wesson cartridge (though a 9mm Parabellum option was introduced in 1996). The standard model — originally an option known as "P229SL" — has a blacked stainless-steel slide and an anodized-alloy frame. It is about 7.1 inches long, with a 3.8-inch barrel, and weighs 28 oz without its 12-round magazine (currently restricted to 10 rounds in the USA). The 357 SIG round was developed specifically for this gun in 1994, the work being entrusted to the Federal Cartridge Company. In an attempt to duplicate the performance of the 357 Magnum cartridge in an automatic pistol, 40 Smith & Wesson cases were necked to take a 357 bullet, the result being known as the "357 SIG". Muzzle velocity averages about 1350 ft/sec with a 125-grain bullet, which is slightly slower than the average 357 Magnum revolver firing the same bullet but deemed to be acceptable enough.

The SIG-Sauer P229SL.

- *P229 Nickel* Featuring a stainless-steel slide and frame with a coating of nickel, this was introduced in 1998.
- *P229 Sport* (1998 to date) Currently available only in 357 SIG, this has a 4.8-inch barrel with a compensator, adjustable sights and a 10-round magazine. It is made of stainless steel and weighs about 41 oz.

P230 Introduced in 1976, this was a simple blowback personal-defense pistol available in 22 LR rimfire, 6.35mm (25 ACP), 7.65mm (32 ACP) and 9mm Short (380 ACP) chamberings. It introduced the

concept of an automatic firing-pin lock in SIG guns, allowing the manual safety catch to be discarded—unless the trigger was properly pulled through, in either double- or single-action mode, the firing pin could not be driven forward by the hammer. Many post-1996 guns have been sold in "Two-Tone", with a bright-finish slide and a blacked frame, but others are conventionally blued. The grips are customarily black plastic moldings. Magazine capacity ranges from 10 22 LR rimfire rounds to seven 9mm Short rounds, empty weight being 16–21 oz depending on caliber and the material of the frame.

P232 This was introduced in 1997 to replace the P230, but it is little more than a redesign taking advantage of modern manufacturing techniques. Slight changes have been made in the slide contours; and since 1998, Tritium-insert night sights, black-rubber Hogue grips and all-stainless-steel construction have been favored. Guns are also now being made in traditional double-action or double-action-only guise and have been advertised as the "Personal Size Weapon". Chambering is currently restricted to 9mm Short (380 ACP), though a few 7.65mm guns have been made.

The SIG-Sauer P239 ultra-compact design.

P239 Introduced commercially in 1996, this was simply the P229 altered to accept the new 357 SIG round (see P229, above). No changes were needed in the breech face or magazine, though the magazine capacity was reduced to seven rounds to allow a slim grip to be used. This was better suited to "concealed carry" than the wide-bodied P229. Optional 9mm Parabellum and 40 S&W P239 chamberings were announced in 1998, with magazines of eight and seven rounds, respectively, and a double-action-only trigger system was introduced at the same time. A typical 357-caliber pistol is 6.6 inches long with a 3.6-inch barrel and weighs 25 oz empty.

P245 Announced in 1999, this is a compact 45 ACP SIG-Sauer with a single-column magazine holding six rounds. Offered in blue, "Two-Tone" or K-Kote polymer finish, it has black plastic grips. Overall length is 7.2 inches with a 3.9-inch barrel, and empty weight averages 28 oz.

SIG-PRO series Introduced in 1998, these guns combine a blued-steel slide and a matte-finish polymer frame with improved grips (often with a rubber insert) and an accessory rail under the front of the frame ahead of the trigger guard. Currently available only in 9mm Parabellum (*M2009*) and 40 S&W (*M2340*), they have 10-round magazines and weigh 25-28 oz. Barrel length is 3.9 inches.

SCOTT
Walter Scott, Birmingham, Warwickshire, England.
Trading from Princip Street in Birmingham in 1871-80, Scott sold a variety of firearms, including Smith & Wesson revolvers. He was an inventor of note, receiving several patents for sporting guns and accessories.

Thornton's Patent This mark will be found on revolvers made in the 1870s, referring to a British Patent protecting a trigger mechanism for revolvers granted in 1876 to Amedee Thornton de Mouncie — who also styled himself "Baron Thornton" when it suited him. He described himself as an English citizen in the patent but appears to have had some connections in the gun trade in Britain and Belgium.

De Mouncie submitted six revolvers to the British War Office in 1877. Made by Scott, these were tested by the staff of the Royal Small Arms Factory. The design was regarded as interesting, but the workmanship was poor. De Mouncie then became involved with Michael Kaufmann, who later worked for Webley, and the two visited the Royal Small Arms Factory to discuss improvements in the "Thornton" revolvers.

The factory superintendent drew attention to an improvement that could be made in the firing mechanism, and de Mouncie attempted to patent the modification in May 1878. He then abandoned the project, selling rights in the 1876 patent to Kaufmann, and vanished into obscurity.

Michael Kaufmann submitted a revolver that incorporated the improvement suggested by Enfield, obtaining an appropriate patent in 1878. The lockwork was subsequently incorporated in the Enfield (q.v.) revolver, but, in a subsequent examination of patent claims, "Thornton's Patent" was found to cover a revolver lock that had been patented in Belgium in 1875 by Jean Warnant.

Warnant had appointed de Mouncie as his agent, hoping that the patent could be obtained in Britain, but de Mouncie had other ideas and filed the specifications in his own name. He then appears to have sold shares in the patent to a variety of people, prior to the final agreement with Kaufmann, and vanished with the proceeds.

SECURITY INDUSTRIES OF AMERICA
Little Ferry, New Jersey, USA.
This company appeared in 1976, offering a five-shot revolver in 38 Special or 357 Magnum, both made of stainless steel. They followed Smith & Wesson lines, and indeed the 357 Magnum model used a frame of exactly the same dimensions as the S&W Model 60. The venture did not survive for very long.

SEDGELY
R.F. Sedgely, Philadelphia, Pennsylvania, USA.
Known also as "Sidewalk Sedgely" from his habit of conducting most of his business whilst perambulating the streets of Philadelphia. His antecedents are obscure and he first came under notice as a partner of H.J. Kolb of Philadelphia after the death of Charles Foehl, Kolb's original partner in a small revolver manufactory. In 1930, Kolb retired, and Sedgely took over the business, operating it under his own name until 1938, when it went into liquidation. He reappeared shortly afterwards with a machinegun design of unknown parentage that he offered to the US Army in 1939-40 without success.

SEECAMP
L.W. Seecamp Co., Inc., New Haven, Connecticut, USA.
This company began making a small blowback automatic in 25 or 32

caliber in 1980. The two models are identical but for caliber and are of stainless steel. The action is rather unusual, as they are hammer-fired, but the hammer follows the slide home after each shot and the trigger action is self-cocking, raising and dropping the hammer at each trigger pull. These pistols have had particular attention paid to exterior smoothness and the 32-caliber model has found good sales as a concealed pistol for law officers. The *LWS-32 Stainless DA* pistol, introduced in 1985, was still being made in 2002.

The Semmerling LM-4, sometimes regarded as a semi-automatic, is actually a manually-operated repeater.

The Semmerling LM-4 with a grip and sideplate removed to expose the lockwork.

SEMMERLING CORPORATION
Newton, Massachusetts, USA.
This company began making the *LM-4* pistol in the mid-1970s, the most recent revival of a manual "pull-forward" principle. Chambered for the 45 ACP cartridge, it was extremely small and doubtless the system of operation helped to keep the recoil sensation within reasonable bounds. The pistol was prepared by inserting a magazine in the butt, then pulling the slide fully forward before releasing it. The firing mechanism was self-cocking, fired by a long pull-through of the trigger. The LM-4 achieved some popularity as a self-defense weapon and is now being made by the American Derringer Corporation (q.v.).

SEYTRES
M. Seytres, Saint-Éienne, France.
Little is known of this gunmaker, who in 1920-39 offered a number of blowback automatic pistols in both 6.35mm and 7.65mm under the trade name *Union*. However, as all these guns are very obviously "Eibar" types, even to the distinctive safety catch midway along the frame, it is likely that Seytres merely distributed Spanish-made guns in France. Some features of the pistols suggest that they were made by Esperanza y Unceta, but this is by no means certain. All are marked with "Union" on the grip. Some have a trademark of an American Indian head; most have slides marked "PISTOLET AUTOMATIQUE FRANCAISE / FABRIQUE A ST ETIENNE" in two lines, often accompanied by a caliber mark.

SHARPS

Christian Sharps and Sharps & Hankins, Philadelphia, Pennsylvania, USA.

Sharps is probably best known as the designer and maker of a unique four-barreled pistol in which the four barrels form a unit that can be slid forward on the frame for loading and in which the hammer carries a revolving firing pin that turns so as to fire the four rimfire barrels in succession. These pistols originated in a design patented in 1859 and were made in a variety of rimfire chamberings — 22 Short (Model 1), 30 Short (Model 2), 32 Short (Model 3) and 38 Long (Model 4) — from the creation of Sharps & Hankins in 1860 until Sharps' death in 1874. They were also made under license by Tipping & Lawden (q.v.).

Sharps patented a number of revolver features, but revolvers of his own make are extremely rare and fall before our period. However, "Un Officier Superieur", writing in 1894, referred to the army of Saxony being equipped with a "Sharps Model 1873" revolver. However, these were Suhl-made copies of the sheath-trigger Smith & Wesson No. 2, in 10.75mm rimfire (M1873) or 10.75mm centerfire (M1874), with additional safety catches that blocked the hammer and lanyard rings on the butts.

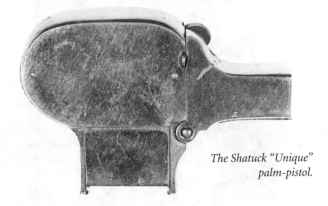

The Shatuck "Unique" palm-pistol.

SHATUCK

C.S. Shatuck Arms Company, Hatfield, Massachusetts, USA.

Charles S. Shatuck manufactured an aberrant revolver, designed by Andrew Hyde, in 1879-87. In appearance, it was the usual solid-frame, stud-trigger, bird's-head-butt pattern of the day, but the cylinder arbor pin was carried on a vertical axis in an extension to the frame, and thus the cylinder could be swung sideways out of the frame for extraction and re-loading. No extractor mechanism was used, the cases being poked or shaken out. Shatuck produced this gun in 32 and 38 rimfire, and the same design was also manufactured in 32 and 38 centerfire by Iver Johnson in the same era; neither firm had much success. See "Mossberg" for details of Shatuck's activities with the Mossberg-designed "Unique" pistol.

SHERIDAN

Sheridan Products, Inc., Racine, Wisconsin, USA.

Sheridan manufactured the "Knockabout" pistol in the 1953-62 period. This was a single-shot 22 LR rimfire design, hammer-fired, that resembled an automatic pistol. Apart from the barrel, the gun was made of steel pressings and plastic. The name was appropriate — it was good for "plinking", but not much else.

SHIN CHUO KOGYO KK

Tokyo, Japan.

This company is the post-1945 incarnation of the old Chuo Kogyo (q.v.) business that had made Taisho 14th Year Type and Type 94 pistols. The "New Nambu" pistols have no other connection with the original Nambu design.

The Model 57B New Nambu pistol was only made in prototype.

A New Nambu M60 revolver in 38 Special.

~ PISTOLS ~

Model 57A This was a 9mm automatic based on the Colt M1911A1 design but with a magazine safety and no grip safety. It was developed but never put into production.

Model 57B A 7.65mm blowback automatic modeled on the Browning 1910 pattern but with an external hammer and a loaded-chamber indicator. It was submitted for adoption by both military and police forces but was turned down and did not go into production.

~ REVOLVERS ~

Model 58 The company entered the pistol field again in the late 1950s with contracts to supply pistols to the Japan Self-Defense Force and police forces. The "Model 58" was a five-shot solid-frame revolver with swing-out cylinder, based on Smith & Wesson practice, which was adopted by the Japanese police in 1961 and later by the Maritime Safety Guard. It has also been sold commercially.

SIMSON

Simson & Co., Also known as "Waffenfabrik Simson", Suhl, Germany.

Simson specialized in sporting rifles and shotguns but in 1922 obtained a contract to supply the German services with Parabellum pistols, a contract that lasted until 1932. Both of the pocket pistols were of good quality, but in 1934, the company (which had Jewish antecedents) was sequestered by the State and became part of the Gustloff Werke. The Parabellum machinery was removed and sent to Krieghoff and the production of the Simson pistol ceased. The company was reconstituted after 1945 and now makes shotguns.

Parabellum When World War I ended, Simson, relatively untainted by involvement with the arms industry, was given the license to refurbish Parabellum pistols for the Reichswehr and the police services. Production machinery was obtained from the Erfurt small-arms factory, to allow new guns to be made if parts ran short, and about 10,000 guns were made in 1925-8. These were marked "SIMSON & Co" over "SUHL" on the toggle but were otherwise standard Pistolen 08.

M1922 Work on the Parabellum encouraged Simson to introduce a new 6.35mm blowback pocket-pistol in 1922. This offered good quality and had a slide that was distinctly rounded although the frame was

The 1927-type Simson 6.35mm (25-caliber) pocket pistol.

flattened above the grips. The barrel was held in the frame by a lug under the breech, into which the recoil spring guide rod fit, and the slide was held on the frame by a spring catch in the front edge of the trigger guard. Striker fired, the Model 1922 had a six-shot magazine and a 1.8-inch barrel. The pistols can be recognized by the markings on the slide and frame: "SELBSTLADE PISTOLE SIMSON D.R.P." above "WAFFENFABRIKEN SIMSON & Co SUHL". In addition, "Simson" was molded into the black plastic grips.

M1927 An improved version of the M1922, this had a frame that was flat throughout its length, though the slide was still rounded. The Simson intercutting-triangle trademark was added on the left of the frame above the rear of the trigger guard.

The Sirkis Industries SQR pistol, in 9mm Parabellum.

A compact 9mm Sirkis SD9.

SIRKIS
Sirkis Industries Ltd, Ranat-Gan, Israel

Also known as "Sardius", this mark will be found on a double-action personal-defense pistol, the *SQP*, chambering the 9mm Parabellum round. The guns are blued with prominent diagonal retraction grips filling much of the rear portion of the slide and have checkered plastic grips. They are 6.9 inches long with a 3.9-inch barrel and weigh about 31 oz without its detachable nine-round box magazine. The *SD-9* is similar but smaller, with a 3-inch barrel and a seven-round magazine.

ŠKODA
Pilsen, Czechoslovakia.

This company was founded in 1869 by Emil Škoda, an Austrian-born engineer who had trained in German shipyards. The business soon

became known for heavy guns but eventually offered services ranging from steel-making to the construction of railway locomotives. Its contributions to small-arms history, however, were uninspiring.

Salvator-Dormus Dating from 1894, this pistol was designed by Archduke Karl von Salvator and Lieutenant Georg Ritter von Dormus — two distinguished officers who were better known for the invention of the Škoda machinegun. Salvator had died in 1892, but von Dormus always insisted on recognizing his collaborator's name.

The pistol was a blowback, among the first of the type, chambered for a rimmed 8mm cartridge. The barrel was concentric with the return spring and the barrel jacket. An operating arm, provided with a cocking handle, lay beneath the barrel, the rear end of the arm passing into the receiver where it connected with the bolt. The gun had an external hammer and had an integral magazine in the butt that accepted a five-round clip through the open action. A follower forced the rounds from the clip into the bolt-way, and after the last round had been chambered, the empty clip fell through a slot in the bottom of the butt.

A few of these pistols were made, presumably in the Škoda factory in Pilsen, but the Salvator-Dormus could offer neither a locked breech nor performance that was good enough to satisfy the Austro-Hungarian army. Very few examples survive.

A 9mm JSL G2 LS Sterling Spitfire pistol, based on the ČZ 75.

SLOUGH
John Slough Ltd ("JSL"), Hereford, England.

Spitfire. Developed in 1987-90 and placed in limited production in 1991, this was a locked-breech design adapted from the Czech ČZ 75. The entire pistol was made from stainless steel and tolerances were generally tightened to 5 microns by the use of computer-controlled machines. The sights were fully adjustable. The action was designed to allow double action or single action to be chosen, and so the pistol could be "cocked and locked" in safety. Though designed as a combat pistol, the Spitfire was sufficiently accurate to be used for target work. Guns were made in 9mm Parabellum, 9x21 IMI and 9mm Major chamberings, in a variety of configurations, but the total ban on the ownership of pistols in the United Kingdom — and bureaucratic difficulties encountered exporting pistols to Europe — led John Slough to cease work in 1997.

SMITH
Otis A. Smith, Middlefield and Rock Fall, Connecticut, USA.

Smith designed an assortment of revolver mechanisms in the 1870s, under his own name or in conjunction with his brother John T. Smith, and then began to make "Suicide Specials" in quantity. The Smith brothers also seem to have been involved in the production of weapons for Maltby & Curtis before going out of business in the late 1890s.

Early guns These were all solid-frame non-ejecting guns with sheathed triggers offered in 22, 32, 38 and 41 rimfire chamberings. They can be distinguished by Smith's name and an 1873 patent date. What appears to be an oversized cylinder arbor pin is, in fact, a patented quick-release that allows the cylinder to be detached for reloading. Guns of this type may be marked "Mohawk Mfg Co." or "Parker Revolver Co.", which were probably figments of Smith's imagination.

New Model This was a ribbed-barrel five-shot 32 rimfire gun, with a sheathed trigger and a push-button cylinder release on the left of the frame.

Model 83 In 1881, Otis Smith patented and produced the "Model 83 Shell Ejector", a tip-barrel revolver with a cam-operated self-ejecting mechanism. The ribbed barrel, sheathed trigger and single-action lockwork were retained, and this 32 rim- or centerfire five-shot gun must have been among the last of its type to be developed. It was well made, but the ribbed barrel, the "saw-handle" grip and the absence of a trigger guard give it an odd muzzle-heavy appearance.

Model 92 This was a more conventional solid-frame gun with a "hammerless" double-action trigger system and an exposed cylinder stop that, when pressed, allowed the cylinder to rotate freely. A five-shot in 38 rim- or centerfire, the revolver had a conventional trigger guard and a rounded grip.

SMITH & WESSON
Smith & Wesson, Inc, Springfield, Massachusetts, USA.
The history of Smith & Wesson began in 1852 when Horace Smith and Daniel Wesson entered a gunmaking partnership in Norwich, Connecticut. The business started with the manufacture of an improved version of the Jennings repeater, firing hollow-based ammunition by using fulminate of mercury as the propellant, but was soon in financial difficulties. A consortium of New Haven businessmen, headed by Oliver Winchester, then bought-out the partners and formed the Volcanic Repeating Arms Company; Smith & Wesson temporarily parted company.

During this period, Daniel Wesson, who had moved to Springfield, Massachusetts, not only produced the first rimfire cartridge but had also built a revolver to fire it. To do this, he required possession of the Rollin White patent for bored-through cylinders, but this, once gained, meant that Smith & Wesson would shortly be in an unassailable position in the revolver trade. They had to wait because Colt held master patents on revolvers, but they were fully prepared and tooled up when the patents expired in 1857. They leapt into production of the first metallic cartridge breech-loading revolver.

These early "tip-up" revolvers gave the partners much useful background for their future designs. The caliber of these revolvers was only 22, the reason being that the firm could not produce and anneal a copper cartridge cast that would stand up to greater charges.

Other firms made cartridges under license from Smith & Wesson, and several cheerfully ignored the patent laws, thereby involving the partnership in endless lawsuits. In the course of some of these successful suits, Smith & Wesson took over their rivals' stock and weapons. Among them was the business of Lucius W. Pond, who had been making a cartridge in 44 caliber. When Smith & Wesson produced their own 44-caliber revolver 6 years later, in 1869, they may have used the Pond or Henry cartridges. The resulting "44 S&W" became one of the most famous of all revolver rounds, rivaling the popularity of the 45 Long Colt for decades. The S&W Model No. 3 was the first "big-bore" revolver to be specifically designed in the USA around self-contained metallic-case ammunition.

The acquisition of impressive contracts from the Russian government, though making Smith & Wesson a fortune, also virtually handed over the entire Wild Western market to Colt, which was quick to take advantage. When the Russian contract came to an end in the late 1870s, Smith & Wesson turned their attention to the home market only to find that sales were very difficult, despite the attractions of a revolver that simultaneously ejected all cases and could be quickly and easily loaded.

This was a distinct setback for Smith & Wesson, who needed the publicity of the home market to keep sales buoyant, and until World War I, there was a continual struggle with American rivals to keep the firm ahead.

The first double-action S&W revolver was introduced in 1880. The Safety Hammerless was the first mass-produced revolver to have an enclosed hammer and a double-action-only trigger mechanism; the 32/44 and 38/44 guns were the first revolvers ever to be fitted with adjustable rear sights; and the first S&W with a yoke-mounted cylinder was introduced commercially in 1896. However, this gun proved to be too fragile to withstand the rigors of military service, and not until the legendary 38-caliber Military & Police ("M&P") revolver appeared in 1899 could Smith & Wesson rival Colt. But the M&P is still in production after more than a century.

More than 75,000 455-caliber revolvers were supplied to the British army during World War I, and the introduction of the K-22 Outdoorsman and 357 Magnum saw the company through the worst of the Great Depression. A highlight of this period was the advent in 1935 of the 357 Magnum cartridge and a suitably strengthened revolver. The low point was the Model 40 Light Rifle, a 9mm carbine developed for the British government, which was such a disaster that S&W nearly collapsed. The situation was resolved by selling the British huge number of revolvers to offset the advances that had been made — including 568,000 38-caliber M&P-type guns.

The Chiefs Special of 1952 was the first revolver to feature not only an alloy frame but also an alloy cylinder, though the latter was soon replaced by steel. The Model 39 pistol, which was first made in 1954, was the first 9mm double-action design to reach series production in the USA. It was also the first double-action pistol to reach service with any state-government agency, being used by the Illinois State Police in 1968.

The Wesson family lost control immediately after World War II when Carl Hellstrom became President. When Hellstrom died unexpectedly in 1963, the company was purchased by the Bangor Punta Corporation and had soon diversified into a variety of law-enforcement products including holsters, night sights and riot-control gear. The first stainless-steel revolver (the Model 60 Chiefs Special) appeared in 1965, and the Model 59, the first double-action pistol to be made in the USA with a large-capacity magazine, appeared in the early 1970s alongside the Models 581, 586, 681 and 686 "L"-frame revolvers.

Smith & Wesson are still among the best-known large-scale revolver manufacturers, and their products are renowned all over the world … even though markets are being eroded by cheaper rivals — including, ironically, a variety of Smith & Wesson clones made in South America. Rationalization in the 1980s was followed by the purchase of Bangor Punta by the Lear-Siegler Group, which in turn sold out to Forstmann, Little & Company in 1986. The new owners wanted only the automotive and aerospace elements of Lear-Siegler, and eventually Smith & Wesson was sold to F.H. Tompkins plc of London. It was ironic that one of America's oldest and best-known gunmakers should be purchased by a company based in Britain — a country that has one of the most paranoiac views of firearms in the Western world.

Finally, in 2001, Tompkins sold its stake in S&W to the Saf-T-Hammer Corporation, formed by one-time Smith & Wesson employees, and the business reverted to US control. The parent group is now known as the Smith & Wesson Holding Corporation. A ruthless review of business has led to the disappearance of many well-established designs, especially among the pistols. However, the exploitation of titanium-alloy cylinders and scandium-alloy frames, the introduction of the mighty 500 Magnum cartridge (as powerful as many assault-rifle rounds!), the exploits of the Performance Center, and the distribution of Walther USA products — perhaps temporarily — will hopefully ensure that Smith & Wesson products will be seen for many years to come.

Smith & Wesson's first single-shot target pistol, in 38 S&W Long centerfire.

The Smith & Wesson No. 3 American Model, in 44-caliber.

～ SINGLE-SHOT PISTOLS ～

First Model (1893-1905) The origin of the first Single-Shot Model stemmed from someone in the Smith & Wesson factory who took a standard Third Model 38-caliber revolver and fitted a single-shot barrel to the hinged frame. This barrel was locked at the topstrap and had an ejector running through the solid lower part of the breech, where the cylinder would be on a revolver. This neat conversion produced a useful target pistol that was soon also being offered in 32 S&W Long. Over-sized rubber grips gave a good hand-grasp, and barrels of 6, 8 or 10 inches gave exemplary accuracy.

By 1893, target shooters were successfully demanding a 22 LR rimfire version. For a little extra money, the buyer could also have barrels in 32 or 38. Production of the First Model totaled only 1250, but a substantial quantity of conversion units were sold independently.

Second Model (1905-9) In 1905, the firm decided that the combination revolver was too good a bargain, and the single-shot target pistol was made as a separate item. The opportunity was taken to simplify the frame, and so the recoil shield was removed. A target rear sight was fitted as a standard. Chambering was restricted to 22 LR rimfire, the barrel was 10 inches long and the finish could be blue or nickel. When work ceased, about 4600 of these guns had been made.

Third or "Perfected" Model (1909-23) This looked as though it was little different from the Second Model. However, a double-action trigger mechanism was fitted — even though often restricted to single action — and the fall of the hammer was accelerated. Most of the lock components were shared with the Perfected Model 38-caliber revolver. The standard barrel was 10 inches long, but others could be supplied to meet specific requirements.

The Perfected Model, an immediate success, was adopted by the American national shooting teams in 1910, 1911 and 1912. This set the seal of approval in the highly specialized target-pistol field, and sales were good. A particular feature of the Olympic pistols was that the chamber was shorter than normal, so that the bullet had to be forced into the chamber in order to close the breech. This arrangement meant that the bullet did not have to jump a gap to reach the rifling, no gas pressure was lost, and accuracy and consistency were marginally improved. When work finished, about 6950 Perfected Model single-shot pistols had been made.

Straight Line Model (1925-36) Designed to replace the Perfected Model pistol, this was an unmitigated disaster and only 1870 were made. Unfortunately, reliance on a unique "straightline" action ensured that the hammer fall and trigger pull was never constant from shot to shot, and the pistol soon got a bad name that it never lost. The hammer and sear were little more than sliding plungers, and they not only jammed but also turned out of line. Excessive lubrication could also slow the hammer fall, owing to the precision of the tolerances maintained during the manufacturing process. Smith & Wesson eventually developed a conventional rebounding hammer, but this improvement was too late to restore the Straight Line pistol's reputation. Ironically, apart from its fundamental fault, the gun handled well and was exceptionally accurate. It was also among the first 22-caliber pistols to be consciously fitted with a recessed chamber head as protection against blown rims.

～ REVOLVERS INTRODUCED PRIOR TO 1945 ～
Listed in alphabetical order of model-name.

American Model (or "Model No. 3 American", 1870-9) This was the first revolver to take advantage of the patents of William Dodge and Charles King, and in so doing, kept the firm ahead of its rivals, who after 1869 were able to use the expired Rollin White patent. The Dodge and King patents involved opening the frame at the rear of the cylinder and pivoting the barrel assembly at the front of the lower strap while at the same time providing a system for the simultaneous ejection of the empty cases. The actual mechanism of the ejector was bulky and clumsy, but it was continuously refined over the years and is now common in any top-break revolver.

The whole success of the weapon lay in the cartridge. The case was of brass, with a centerfire primer and Berdan system of ignition. The bullet weighed 218 grains, the powder charge was 25 grains, the muzzle velocity was 650 ft/sec and the muzzle energy was 205 ft/lb. The bullet was of slightly less diameter than the case, in order to get it into the mouth, and as a result, it was a poor fit in the bore. However, it shot well enough at up to 50 yards and soon made a respectable name for itself.

The other reason for the popularity of the American was the fact that it ejected all the empty cases at once, rather than having the shooter punch them out one at a time. Although this feature, and the cartridge, did not impress the U.S. Army sufficiently to cause them to buy, it caught the eye of others.

- *First pattern* (1870-2) Introduced at a time when Colt was still converting caplocks to fire metal-case ammunition, the S&W American Model represented a huge advance in handgun technology. Its 8-inch barrel was perhaps a little too long, making the gun difficult to handle in situations requiring speed rather than precision; 6- and 7-inch barrels were made in small numbers, but are rarely encountered. A low rounded front sight was let into the top rib of the barrel, and the rear sight was a simple open notch in the barrel catch. The deep fluting between the six chambers in the cylinder added to the gun's handsome appearance. The finish was generally blue, but nickel-plated versions were also made; grips were usually walnut. Total production amounted to about 8000, including a few hundred chambered for the 44 Henry RF cartridge instead of the 44/100 Smith & Wesson centerfire type.

  A thousand guns were ordered for the US Army in 1871, 800 in blue and the remainder nickel-plated. They bore "U.S." on top of the barrel and had the "O.W.A." marks of inspector O.W. Ainsworth on the grips.

- *Second Model* (1872-4) This was an improved American Model, with an inter-connecting lock to prevent the barrel being opened unless the hammer was at half or full-cock. This had been an original feature of the first model, abandoned after complaints that it was inconvenient but reinstated to prevent accidents.

  Made in a period when the Russian contracts were underway, these guns showed some of the improvements made in the "Russian Model" of the day, including a larger trigger pin betrayed by a noticeable hump in the underside of the frame level with the rear web of the trigger guard. The front sight was steel, instead of weak nickel silver, and several small machining changes were made.

Production totaled 20,735, including about 3000 chambering the 44 Henry rimfire cartridge. A few guns had barrels measuring 5.5-7 inches, but the 8-inch pattern was standard.

It should be noted that hybrid guns combining the features of the first and second patterns can also be found, assembled during a period of transition to use parts that would otherwise have been left in store or scrapped.

Bekeart Model (or "22/32", 1911-53) This was one of the more unusual success stories in the lengthy history of Smith & Wesson, and the one most often quoted in defense of tinkering with factory designs. Philip Bekeart, a San Francisco arms dealer, had been urging S&W to make a heavy-frame 22-caliber revolver for target shooting. He suggested that the then-current 32-caliber frame would be ideal, but Smith & Wesson doubted there would be sufficient demand to justify tooling. Bekeart promptly ordered 1000 (though only 292 were delivered), and production began. Genuine "Bekeart" guns were built on 32 Hand Ejector frames numbered in the 138000 series and had additional "production numbers" on the butt ranging from 1 to about 3000. A 6-inch barrel, a heat-treated six-chamber cylinder for the 22 Long Rifle RF cartridge and special "oversize" grips on the standard butt were standardized. The sights were adjustable.

• *Hand Ejector, 22-caliber, Model 22/32* (1912-53) This was the lineal successor to the Bekeart, numbered in its own series and lacking the separate production numbers. Whatever doubts Smith & Wesson may have had were allayed by sales that exceeded a quarter of a million. The 22/32 proved to be an excellent compromise, benefiting greatly from the generally excellent lock design of the Ejector Models.

Double Action (32 caliber, First Model, 1880) The first double-action Smith & Wesson revolver was much the same as its Single Action counterpart, except for the addition of a trigger guard. Less obvious was the adoption of a rocking-bar cylinder stop, demanding two rows of notches on the cylinder, and a trigger mechanism arranged to give a longer pull with better leverage in the double-action mode. A five-chamber cylinder and a 3-inch round barrel were standard, and the round-heel butt had plain-surface rubber grips. Only 30 of these guns were made, mostly finished in blue though a few were nickel-plated. They were distinguished by the straight-sided detachable sideplate, which was soon found to weaken the left side of the frame too greatly.

A second-pattern 38-caliber S&W Double Action revolver.

• *Second Model* (1880-2) This was essentially the same as its predecessor, but the detachable sideplate had become oval. The rubber grips had an S&W monogram and either checkering or a floral design. About 22,000 guns were made.
• *Third Model* (1882-3) Most of the important changes in this pattern were made internally, where the rocking-bar cylinder stop had been replaced by a more conventional pawl. Consequently, the cylinder only had a single set of stop notches, and the "free groove" that had characterized the first and second models was abandoned.
• *Fourth Model* (1883-1909) Though a few insignificant internal changes had also been made, the most obvious feature of this gun

A fourth-model 38 DA Smith & Wesson revolver.

was the rounded contours of the rear of trigger guard, as the preceding 32 DA examples had been squared. Production amounted to 240,000, making the fourth model one of the most successful of the Smith & Wesson revolvers made prior to World War I.
• *Fifth Model* (1909-19) This was a minor adaptation of the fourth model, with a front sight that was formed integrally with the barrel instead of being a separate component pinned into the muzzle. About 44,600 were made.

Double Action (38 caliber, First Model, 1880) This was essentially similar to the 32-caliber gun, with the straight-edge sideplate and the same general characteristics. About 4000 were made in blue or nickel, with checkered rubber grips.
• *Second Model* (1880-4) Fitted with a new irregularly-shaped sideplate, strengthening the sidewall of the frame, this gun was most successful: 115,000 were manufactured during its short production life.
• *Third Model* (1884-95) This had changes made in the trigger mechanism to refine the single-action pull. It proved very popular, and 204,000 were sold in 5 years. Barrels measured 3.25-10 inches, though the 8- and 10-inch options were rarely specified.
• *Fourth Model* (1895-1909) Identified by a change to the sear and the elimination of the rocking-bar cylinder stop (and the second cylinder stop notch), this duplicated the design of the 32-caliber equivalent. Altogether, 216,600 of these revolvers were manufactured.
• *Fifth Model* (1909-11) This incorporated some small changes to the front sight (which had become an integral part of the barrel) and ejector mechanism, but only 15,000 were made. The basic design was gradually overtaken by the Perfected model, which had appeared in the same year.
• *Perfected Model* (1909-21) Differing markedly from the preceding models, this had a barrel latch and a cylinder lock. The latter was released by a sliding thumb-catch on the left of the frame, similar to the fitting on the swing-cylinder guns. The lockwork was also changed to include the improvements that had appeared in the 32-caliber models, and the trigger guard (formerly separate) was forged as part of the frame. About 59,400 guns were made in a separate numbering sequence.

Double Action (44 caliber, Old or First Model, also known as "DA Frontier" or "New Model Army", 1881-1913) Closely resembling the Russian Frame Models, this top-break auto-ejecting revolver attempted to encroach on the Colt market. A sturdy and dependable gun with a good reputation for reliability, it never achieved the popularity of the Single Action Army revolver and could make no impression in the Western states of America.

The internal mechanism was modeled on the successful 38-caliber DA, and the trigger pull was considered attractively light for such a large gun. The frame was slightly shorter from the top latch to the butt than the New Model No. 3 single-action 44, owing to the shorter hammer movement, but in most other respects, the guns were the same. Most double-action guns chambered the 44 S&W Russian round, though a few were supplied in 38-40 and 44-40 WCF. Barrels measured 3.5-6.5 inches, with the shortest available only to special order, and the six-chamber cylinder had distinctive double stops and a "free groove". Production amounted to about 54,000.

Sometimes considered as separate models, as they were numbered separately, about 15,300 44-40 guns were made in 1886-1916 and a few hundred in 38-40 in 1900-10. All guns chambered for Winchester ammunition had cylinders that were 1.56 inches long instead of the otherwise-standard 1.44 inches.

- *Favorite* (or "Western Favorite", 1882-3) About 1000 of this unsuccessful lightweight derivative of the 44-caliber Double Action Model were made with slender 5-inch barrels and rebated six-chamber cylinders. Finish could be blue or, more commonly, nickel plate; the grips were walnut or rubber. The rear sight was reduced to a groove along the top rib; and the manufacturer's name, address and the patent claims were rolled into the cylinder instead of the barrel.

Hand Ejector (22 caliber, K-22 First Model, "Outdoorsman", 1930-40) This revolver was a logical extension of the practice of fitting 22-caliber cylinders and barrels to heavy frames in order to produce a satisfactory target revolver without having to ask an outrageous price. A similar construction would produce a robust 22 revolver for hunters and campers who wanted a small-caliber gun not only suitable for vermin shooting but also one that would withstand the rigors of outdoor life. In the Outdoorsman, the only change from the Model 1905 Fourth Change 38—which was the basic frame—lay in the change of caliber, the use of a floating firing pin in the frame and a flat-faced hammer.

- *Second Model* ("Masterpiece", 1940-2) For the Second Model K-22, an anti-backlash trigger and speed-lock action were installed, with consequent improvements in the shooting. Only 1600 were made before war production stopped the line.

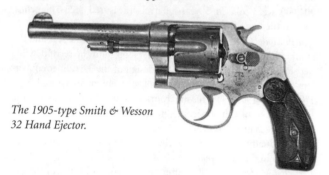

The 1905-type Smith & Wesson 32 Hand Ejector.

Hand Ejector (32 caliber, Model of 1896 or "First Model", 1896-1903) Developed to fire the 32 S&W Long centerfire cartridge, this was Smith & Wesson's first swing-out cylinder revolver, but it was an uninspired design. The frame was clean, simple and, in general principles, followed the style of preceding Smith & Wessons — apart from the crane pivot in the bottomstrap. The six-chambered cylinder was retained by a center pin that locked into a hole in the rear of the frame, and the action was opened simply by pulling the head of the cylinder axis-pin forward. There was no locking mechanism at the front of the frame. The cylinder stop was activated by the hammer, a method that S&W had dropped in 1881, and the stop notches were lined with hardened shims to reduce wear. The barrel (3.25, 4.25 or 6 inches long) had a front sight that was pinned into the top-rib. Although not a novel design, the M1896 Hand Ejector set the pattern for the future, gaining a firm place in the market by selling about 19,700 guns against concerted opposition from Colt and the other members of the American gun trade.

Hand Ejector (32-caliber, Model of 1903 or "Second Model", 1903-17) The faults of the First Model soon became apparent, and its replacement was a very different gun. The unsatisfactory cylinder stop was moved to the bottomstrap and the cylinder axis-pin was locked at both ends. The front of the pin was held in a solid lug, forged as part of the barrel, and a thumb piece on the rear left side of the frame (conveniently placed for the thumb) could be pressed forward to release the cylinder — a strong and sensible arrangement that held the cylinder positively in place. The top rib was abandoned in favor of a slightly tapering barrel measuring 3.25, 4.25 or 6 inches. The finish was blue or nickel, the heel and toe of the butt were rounded, and the grips were usually checkered rubber. The 32 Hand Ejector became one of Smith & Wesson's steady money-spinners, undergoing changes and improvement in minor details, and was offered with adjustable sights instead of the standard fixed patterns. Production amounted to about 19,400 when the first major changes were made.

- *First Change* (1904-6) This had a different cylinder stop and some alterations to the trigger. About 31,700 were made.
- *Second Change* (1906-9) More changes were made in the trigger mechanism, and a rebound slide was added; production totaled 44,400.
- *Third Change* (1909-10) This gun had additional improvements in the lockwork and a hammer that fell farther. Output was limited to merely 624 guns.
- *Fourth Change* (1910 only) This was essentially the "third change", with a few small detail changes to the mechanism. Production amounted to 6400.
- *Fifth Change* (1910-17) The most commonly encountered variant of the M1903 32-caliber Hand Ejector, this had some entirely redesigned components in the trigger system. More than 160,000 guns of this type were made, providing the basis for the so-called "Bekeart Model" (q.v.) 22-caliber target revolver; when the last "fifth change" example had been sold, the output of "Second Model" patterns had reached more than a quarter of a million.

Hand Ejector (32-caliber, Model of 1910 or "Third Model", 1911-42) Few customers could have been aware of the progressive alterations that were put into the many variants, but in 1911, further changes had been made, and the resulting revolver was announced as a completely new Third Model. This was no more than the 1903 Model with a much-improved mechanism. A hammer block was fitted, which positively prevented the hammer falling onto a cartridge unless the trigger was pulled. When work finished at the beginning of World War II, about 274,000 had been made.

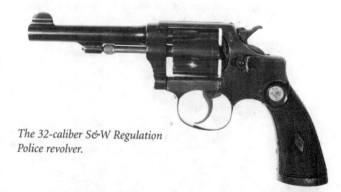

The 32-caliber S&W Regulation Police revolver.

- *Regulation Police Model* (1917 onward) This was a version of the standard 32 Hand Ejector with a squared butt. Production continued after the end of World War II, when it became the standard 32-caliber S&W revolver.
- *K-32 First Model* ("Masterpiece", 1938-41) Towards the end of the life of the 32-20 model, its target version was obviously well out of date, and it was decided to replace it with a more modern design. The K-32 used the 38 Military & Police frame and was chambered for the 32 S&W Long cartridge. It was very accurate, but production only lasted for a short time before war interrupted it. It was reintroduced in 1946 and continued until 1973 as the Model 16 (q.v.).

Hand Ejector (357 caliber, 1935-41) The original Magnum loads were developed by Smith & Wesson in collaboration with Winchester on the basis of suggestions made by the gun writer Philip Sharpe. Sharpe had asked for high-performance ammunition to be chambered in the 38/44 ("N" frame) revolver, and the 357 Magnum was the result. The cartridge was deliberately made longer than the 38 Special to prevent accidents. The first revolvers were made in 1935, little more than the 38-44 Outdoorsman in a stronger grade of steel and with chambers that were recessed to enclose the cartridge rims. The barrels measured 3.5-8.4 inches and had full-length ribs. The finish was restricted to bluing and the grips were checkered walnut.

Smith & Wesson had expected sales to be slow and had been happy not only to number each gun but also issue a certificate of registry. Demand soon proved to be greater than anticipated, and registry was abandoned in 1938 after about 5500 revolvers had been made. These are marked "REG." and the number on the cylinder yoke. Another 1150 357 Magnums were then made without registration numbers, until work stopped for the duration of the war at the end of 1941. The guns were eventually reintroduced, to become the Model 27 (q.v.). However, the "Magnum philosophy" also gathered speed in post-war years and several other calibers duly appeared.

Hand Ejector (Model of 1899 or "Military & Police, First Model" ("M&P"), 38 caliber, 1899-1902) Known first as the "Military & Police" and latterly as the "Model 10", this revolver has enjoyed an unbroken production run of more than a century. Though modifications have been made, the basic design has remained the same, and the present-day Model 10 can easily be seen to be the same pistol as the 1899 model.

The First Model closely resembled the 32 Hand Ejector First Model, except that it was stronger and introduced the thumb-catch cylinder release on the left rear side of the frame. However, the yoke was still locked only at the rear. The guns were chambered either for the 38 S&W or 32-20 WCF rounds (the latter being built on the "38" frame instead of the "32" as so often claimed) with barrels measuring 4, 5, 6 (38-caliber version only), 6.5 and 8 inches (38-caliber only). Finish was blue or more rarely nickel, the base of the butt was squared and the grips were checkered walnut or rubber. Production amounted to about 21,000 in 38 S&W and 5311 in 32-20. The US Navy purchased 1000 commercial-type guns in 1900, stipulating that they should be chambered for the 38 Long Colt cartridge and have a 6.5 inch barrel with left-hand twist. A "U.S.N." mark appeared on the butt. The US Army followed the navy lead in 1901, acquiring another 1000. These bore "U.S. ARMY" and "MODEL 1899" and had inspectors' marks on the grips. However, experience in the Philippine Insurrection showed that a 45-caliber weapon was necessary and the purchases were not repeated.

Hand Ejector (Model of 1902 or "Military & Police, Second Model" ("M&P"), 38 caliber, 1902-3) An improved version of the original design, this incorporated the additional frontal lock for the cylinder, a sturdier ejector rod and a refined trigger system. Offered in 38 S&W (total production: 12,900) or 32-20 WCF (4500), the guns had round-heel butts. The 8-inch barrel option was abandoned.

• *First Change* (1903-5) These reverted to the square-base butt and had alterations to the machining of the frame. Made in 38 S&W (28,645 guns) and 32-20 WCF (8313 guns), they had barrels measuring 4, 5 or 6.5 inches.

Hand Ejector (Model of 1905 or "Military & Police, Third Model" ("M&P"), 38 caliber, 1905-6) This gun went through several minor sets of changes, and when production finally stopped in 1942, more than a million had been made. The first pattern, made only for 2 years, was a refinement of the M1902, with a double-locking cylinder. Offered in 38 S&W or 32-20 WCF, in blue or nickel, the guns could have barrels measuring 4, 5, 6 or 6.5 inches. The butts were generally squared, though a rounded version was offered in 38 S&W only. The

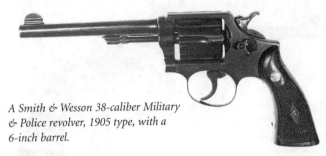

A Smith & Wesson 38-caliber Military & Police revolver, 1905 type, with a 6-inch barrel.

grips were checkered rubber, though walnut (and adjustable sights) could be fitted to guns destined for target shooting. Production totaled 15,100, including about 4300 in 32-20.

• *First Change* (1906-8) The alterations, largely internal, are difficult to recognize. About 46,700 38-caliber guns and a little over 11,000 in 32-20 were made.

• *Second Change* (1908-9) More changes were made internally in this version, which can be identified most easily by serial numbers. Production amounted to 26,900 in 38 S&W and 11,700 in 32-20 WCF.

• *Third Change* (1909-15) In addition to minor improvements in the lockwork, this gun had barrel options restricted to lengths of only 4 or 6 inches. Production totaled about 94,800 in 38 S&W and an unknown number in 32-20 WCF.

• *Fourth Change* (1915-42) The most common of the M1905 variants, this was offered with barrels of 2, 4, 5 and 6 inches. The 2-inch barrel, restricted to 38 S&W, was intended for close-range personal defense and appealed greatly to policemen. When work finally stopped at the beginning of World War II, more than 758,000 of these Hand Ejectors had been made in 38 S&W and about 81,000 in 32-20 WCF.

Made for Britain during World War II, this is a 38-200 Smith & Wesson.

• *British Service Model* (1940-5) Known to British servicemen as the "Pistol No 2, Smith & Wesson", this was simply the standard M&P chambered for the British 38-200 cartridge. About 1,125,000 were made for British and Commonwealth service, with a variety of finishes and grips. A new type of safety hammer block was introduced in 1944, but otherwise changes were few. It got a reputation for misfires because British caps were harder than American, but an adjusting screw in the butt could place more pressure on the mainspring and this fault was easily cured. It was far more popular than the Enfield revolver and remained in use well into the 1950s.

Hand Ejector (44 caliber, First Model, also known as "Triple Lock" or "New Century", 1908-15) Considered by many to be the high-water mark of revolver design, this was a standard hand-ejector revolver with side-swinging cylinder; but, in addition to the usual breech face and barrel lug latches, the cylinder lock incorporated a latch placed centrally in the front edge of the frame. The ejector rod was enclosed in a shroud beneath the barrel, the first time that this had been done. However, quality and strength came at a price. Machining and assembly needed to be exceptionally precise. Consequently, only 15,375 of the

This 455-caliber Smith & Wesson New Century revolver was sold for service in Britain during World War I.

The Smith & Wesson 45 ACP M1917 revolver needed half-moon clips to function properly.

beautifully-made New Century revolvers were made in 38-40 WCF, 44-40 WCF, 44 S&W Special (the most popular), 44 S&W Russian and 45 Long Colt. Offered in blue or nickel with checkered walnut grips, they had barrels measuring 5 or 6.5 inches (though a few were supplied to special order with 4-inch barrels). A special batch of about 5000 were made early in World War I. Chambered for the 455 British service cartridge, these had 6.4-inch barrels and blue finish. Some have been reported with the Broad Arrow property mark. About 100 guns of this type, possibly rejected by inspectors or remaining on hand after the war, were sold commercially in the USA.

- *Second Model* (1915-37) A wartime version of the New Century model, possibly prepared to satisfy the British purchasing agencies, this lacked the Triple Lock and the under-barrel ejector-rod shroud. The travel of the hammer was increased to ensure that even the least sensitive primer would be fired. About 69,800 455-caliber guns with 6.5-inch barrels were made in 1915-17—almost all going to Britain—but 17,500 were sold commercially in 1915-37 in 38-40 WCF, 44-40 WCF, 44 S&W Special and 45 Long Colt. Barrel-length options were restricted to 4, 5 and 6.5 inches. Target revolvers of this type had 6.5-inch barrels and adjustable sights.

- *Third Model* (1926-1949) Originally made to the order of a Texas firearms distributor, who took many of the first 3500 made, this reintroduced the barrel shroud (but not the Triple Lock feature). The three standard barrel lengths — 4, 5 and 6.5 inches — were available for standard pistols and a 6.5-inch version for the adjustable-sight target revolver. The chambering was usually 44 Special, though a few were made to special order in 44-40 WCF and 45 Long Colt. Production stopped in 1940 but resumed in 1946, though the 357 Magnum rivals were surpassing the 44 Hand Ejector in performance.

- *38/44 Model* (1930-41) Commonly called the "thirty-eight on a forty-four frame", this followed the design of the 44 Hand Ejector but was chambered for 38 Special and had a 5-inch barrel. A special cartridge known as the Hi-Speed was developed with a muzzle velocity of 1115 ft/sec (versus 870 for the standard one), and it was intended mainly for police use.

  It could be considered as a forerunner of the Magnum category, and it was revived in 1950 as the Model 20 but did not stay in production for long. The target version of the 38/44 was always listed separately as the "Outdoorsman" and had a 6.5-inch barrel with adjustable rear sight. It, too, was revived after 1945, but few were made.

Hand Ejector (45 caliber, Model of 1917, 1917-46) When World War I began in 1917, the US Army desperately needed handguns in the standard 45 ACP chambering. Colt and Smith & Wesson modified their standard contemporary heavy revolvers to take this cartridge, using a three-cartridge "half moon" clip that had been designed by Joseph Wesson. The S&W revolver was a variant of the second-type 44 Hand Ejector with the cylinder shortened at the rear to leave space for the clips and the base of the pistol cartridges. Unlike Colt, Smith & Wesson were wise enough to machine a slight step in each chamber. This allowed car-

tridges to be loaded and fired without the clip, as their mouths seated on the chamber-step. Ejection was another story entirely!

The M1917 had a 5.5-inch barrel and a lanyard ring on the base of the butt. Finish was exclusively blue, and the grips were smooth-surfaced walnut. Marks included "U.S. ARMY" and "MODEL 1917" on the butt together with a variety of inspectors' marks. Work continued until 1919, a total of 153,311 being supplied to the Army from the 163,500 that had been made. It is assumed that the others were sold commercially.

The M1917 was sold on the commercial market until 1949, distinguished by high-gloss finish and checkered walnut grips. In addition, 25,000 went to Brazil in 1938; these have the Brazilian Arms (a sword piercing a star) on the sideplate let into the right side of the frame. Production of 1917-type Smith & Wesson revolvers is believed to have totaled 210,320. A modified version, the Model 25 (q.v.) for target use, was introduced in 1955.

Jet Magnum (22 Remington Jet chambering, 1961-73) This pistol was designed to fire the Remington high-velocity cartridge, which used a long, bottle-necked case and developed 2200 ft/sec muzzle velocity. The revolver was conventional but specially strengthened to withstand the pressure, and chamber inserts could be used to allow firing the more usual 22 rimfire cartridges. Two floating firing pins were fitted, and the hammer could be set to fire either, one being for rimfire and the other for the centerfire Jet round. In the event, the cartridge was rather too much of a good thing, setting back and giving trouble with jammed cylinders, and the pistol was eventually discontinued.

Kit Gun (22/32, 1935-53) The Kit Gun got its name from being intended to be carried by campers and outdoorsmen as part of their camp kit. It used the standard 32 target frame and cylinder with a 4-inch barrel. The sights were fully adjustable.

Ladysmith (First Model, 1902-6) This small hand-ejecting revolver was another of Daniel Wesson's own designs and was meant as a personal-protection weapon to be carried by women, hence the name. (It was also topical in Europe, where the siege of Ladysmith in the South African War was still a fresh memory.) The guns had 2.25-, 3- or 3.5-inch barrels and butts that were too small to be held easily in the average male hand. Offered in blue or nickel with checkered rubber grips, the guns had seven-chamber cylinders and weighed only about 9.5 oz. Chambering was restricted to 22 Long Rifle rimfire. The first pattern had a lock only at the rear of the cylinder, operated by a small checkered-head catch on the rear left side of the frame. About 4600 guns of this type were made.

- *Second Model* (1906-10) This was similar in size and weight to the first pattern but had an additional locking point at the front of the cylinder yoke. The release catch was abandoned in favor of a simple pull on the cylinder axis-pin. Barrel-length options were restricted to 3 and 3.5 inches, and about 9400 guns were sold.

- *Third Model* (1910-21) Essentially similar to the second pattern, with the same axis-pin cylinder release, this also had a rebounding hammer (with which nobody could quarrel) and barrel lengths that ranged from 2.25 to 6 inches. The longest barrel was apparently intended to be for target work, a role that the Ladysmith could never adequately fulfill. The butt-base was squared, making it easier to hold, and the grips were smooth walnut with gold Smith & Wesson medallions let into their surface. Sales reached about 12,200 guns before work ceased. The name remained dormant until revived for an entirely new range in 1990 (see below).

Model No. 1 (first pattern, 1858-60) Introduced commercially in January 1858, this tiny 22-caliber rimfire sheath-trigger revolver was a landmark in firearms history — even though it was not appreciated for some time. The pistol weighed about 10 oz with the standard 3.25-inch octagonal barrel and had a seven-chamber cylinder. The grips were rosewood, the barrel and the cylinder were blued and the brass frame was usually silver-plated. Releasing a catch beneath the barrel allowed the barrel to tip upward around a transverse pivot in the frame above the front of the cylinder. This disengaged the spigot that held the cylinder, and the cylinder fell into the shooter's hand.

Several variations of this gun exist. The action of the first 1000 was locked by a bayonet catch, but this was then changed to a sprung side-latch on the lower left side of the frame ahead of the cylinder. Rifling changed from three to five groups after about 4200 revolvers had been made, and the revolving recoil shield was replaced by a more conventional pawl-and-ratchet in the region of gun number 5500.

A "second issue" 22-rimfire Smith & Wesson No. 1 revolver.

- *Second pattern* (1860-8) A modified design appeared in May 1860, by which time about 11,700 guns had been made. The frame was flat instead of rounded, the detachable sideplate was shaped irregularly instead of circular and the length of the barrel was marginally reduced. The guns bore three patent dates (the latest being December 18, 1860). Work continued until about 115,000 had been made, including substantial quantities that had been nickel- or silver-plated.
- *Third pattern* (1868-82) The No. 1 was substantially altered after the Civil War to appeal to the growing commercial market. The barrel was round, with a top-rib; the cylinder was fluted; and the butt became a rounded bird's-head type. Unlike the preceding guns, which had brass frames, the third pattern was made entirely of iron. About 131,000 had been made when work stopped, but it seems unlikely that any had been made for some time and that "new" guns were simply being taken out of store. Most had 3.25-inch barrels, though a 2.6-inch option — rarely ordered — was introduced in 1872.

Model No. 1-½ (first pattern or "Old Model", 1865-8) This was a lightweight version of the No. 2, chambering the 32 Short RF cartridge. It had a five-chamber cylinder, a squared butt and a 3.5-inch octagonal barrel. Most of the components were sub-contracted to King & Smith of Middletown, Connecticut, and then assembled in the Springfield factory. Consequently, particularly when the second pattern was introduced, a variety of guns were made combining old and new parts.

- *Second pattern* (or "New Model", 1868-75) About 101,000 of these were made, distinguished by their round rib-topped barrels measuring 2.5 or 3.5 inches, fluted cylinders and bird's-head butts. The cylinder stop was moved to the top of the frame.

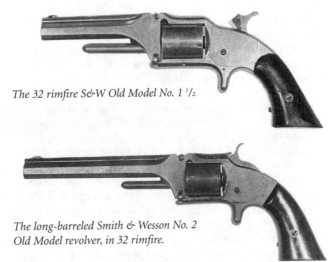

The 32 rimfire S&W Old Model No. 1 ½.

The long-barreled Smith & Wesson No. 2 Old Model revolver, in 32 rimfire.

Model No. 2 ("Army" or "Old Model", 1861-74) This was simply an enlargement of the No. 1, chambering a 32 Long rimfire cartridge that fired a 90-grain bullet. It had an iron frame, an octagonal barrel (4-6 inches long), a six-chamber cylinder and a squared butt. Finish could be blue or nickel; grips were usually rosewood. Though the 22-caliber No. 1 also sold in quantity, the No. 2 was the only metallic-cartridge handgun available at the beginning of the Civil War that offered enough hitting power to be considered as an acceptable "back-up" for personal defense. Demands were such that there was a perpetual back-log of orders, forcing Smith & Wesson to sub-contract the No. 1-1/2, and about 77,000 No. 2 revolvers had been made when work ceased. Alone in the "Civil War series", it had not been modernized to suit the post-war commercial market.

New Model Single Action (or "New Model No. 3", 1878-1912) For several years after the end of the Russian order, Smith & Wesson experimented with improvements to the basic "Russian Model" revolver design, and once production had begun, the New Model soon established itself as a precision shooting weapon. The profile of the original butt had been copied from English practice and had never been popular with American shooters. Wesson took the opportunity to abandon the prawl, which was reduced to merely a hint of a protrusion on the backstrap, and the grip was widened. The curve of the butt was reduced and the finger-spur on the trigger guard was removed. Finally, the extractor gear of the then-current 38-caliber single-action gun was fitted and the long lug under the barrel was appropriately shortened, improving the balance.

Offered in blue or nickel with checkered rubber or plain walnut grips, the New Model could be obtained in 15 chamberings ranging from 32 S&W to 455 British Service. The surface of the cylinder was fluted between each of the six chambers, and barrels measured 3.5-8 inches — though the 6.5-inch option (and the 44 S&W Russian cartridge) was standard. The cartridge was improved in 1887 by concealing the lubrication for the bullet in the neck of the case, which kept the outside of the bullet clean.

The reputation of the New Model was made by a professional marksman, Ira Paine, who defeated all comers in Europe and the USA with his Smith & Wesson. Many of the 35,800 guns that were made went abroad: the Japanese navy acquired 1500, the Japanese army took a few hundred (allegedly for artillerymen), a few hundred accompanied by shoulder stocks went to police units in Australia, and about 5500 altered to accept the 44 Henry rimfire cartridge went to Turkey in 1879-83. Turkish guns had a lanyard ring on the butt heel. And Schuyler, Hartley & Graham sold 2000 centerfire revolvers to Argentina, with "EJERCITO" above "ARGENTINO" on the trigger guard.

For some reason, the 38-40 WCF New Model No. 3 revolvers were numbered in a separate sequence and are often considered to be a separate pattern. Offered in blue or occasionally nickel, with checkered rubber or plain walnut grips, they were mechanically identical with the standard guns. Only 74 were made in 1900-7.

- *New Model Frontier* (1885-1908) Intended to compete directly with the Colt Single Action Army Revolver, this was an adaptation of the Russian model. Unfortunately for Smith & Wesson, the Colt was far too strongly entrenched and sales of the Frontier only reached 2072 pieces. The gun was little more than a standard New Model No. 3 (q.v.) accepting the 44-40 WCF round. Barrels measured 4, 5 or 6 inches, finish was blue or nickel and the grips were checkered rubber or smooth-surface walnut. The cylinder was 1.57 inches long instead of 1.43 inches for the 44 S&W Russian cartridge, the frame and the topstrap being lengthened commensurately. This completely upset the natural balance of the original design.

- *Target Revolver* (1887-1910) Designed by the renowned pistol-shot Ira Paine—originally for his own use—this was marketed commercially once S&W realized that it had sales potential. The gun amalgamated the frame of the 44-caliber New Model No. 3 with a 6.5-inch barrel/six-chamber fluted cylinder assembly chambering special cartridges. The bullets of the 32-44 and 38-44 S&W Gallery (or "Target") rounds were enclosed in elongated cartridge cases. The 32-44 Gallery and 32-44 Target versions gave muzzle velocities of 575 ft/sec and 740 ft/sec respectively, producing soft recoil in such a heavy gun and giving consistently good accuracy. However, though it shot well, the New Model Target Revolver never caught the public's imagination; sales totaled only about 4300. A few detachable shoulder stocks were made but are now exceptionally rare.

*A Smith & Wesson "Buggy Rifle",
in 44-40 WCF.*

Revolving Rifle (or "Pocket Rifle", 1879-87) This was designed as a small-caliber repeating rifle suitable for shooting small game. The basis was an improved Model 3 Russian frame, chambered for a new 320 round. A shoulder stock was slotted to the butt, and a screwed-on extension gave 16, 18, or 20 inches of barrel length. A molded hard rubber fore-end improved handgrip. Guns could be fitted with an adjustable peep sight, which fit onto the wrist of the stock, and an exchangeable post-and-bead front sight. The identity of the chambering has been debated, but may have been the 320 Long Center Fire, a round of European origin manufactured by Winchester at this time.

The Smith & Wesson shot well but suffered from the usual trouble of revolver rifles: flash from the front of the cylinder burned the left wrist, and many shooters disliked having a flash so close to the face. Output in 1879-80 totaled 960, and another 17 were assembled from parts prior to 1887. Guns of this type were no longer listed in Smith & Wesson catalogs after 1890.

Russian Model (44 S&W Russian, first pattern, 1871-4) In 1870, the Imperial Russian army decided to equip its cavalry and artillerymen with a modern revolver, eventually choosing a variant of the 44 American Model chambered for a new cartridge. The case was enlarged in diameter to accept a bullet of the same diameter as the bore and crimped to hold the bullet. The chamber was then bored out to take the larger case; the bullet weight increased to 246 grains and the charge reduced to 23 grains. These changes put the muzzle velocity up to 750 ft/sec and the energy to 308 ft/lb, while accuracy was improved by better bullet fit. It was a revelation to an industry in which, at that time, most ballisticians worked by guesswork and experience.

The first Russian contract, placed in 1871, asked for 20,000 six-shot

guns fitted with 8-inch barrels. Externally similar to the American Model (q.v.), they had minor changes in the ejector mechanism and a more robust trigger-axis pin, which required a swelling in the underside of the frame level with the rear trigger-guard web. The barrels were marked in Cyrillic, a proofmark in the form of a large double-headed eagle was applied and the inspectors' marks consisted of Cyrillic letters beneath tiny eagles.

An additional 4655 guns were sold commercially, with English-language barrel inscriptions (which included "RUSSIAN MODEL") and, occasionally, barrels of 6 or 7 inches instead of the standard 8. There were also about 500 guns, rejected by the Russian inspectorate, that were altered for the 44/100 S&W cartridge for sale on the domestic market. These could have Cyrillic or English markings, the latter often struck over Cyrillic marks that had been ground away.

- *Second or "Infantry" pattern* (1873-8) Experience soon persuaded the Russians to make changes. The barrel was shortened to 7 inches, a prawl (a slight extension) appeared on the rear of the backstrap to prevent the butt rolling down into the hand on firing and a finger spur was added to the trigger-guard. However, whether these minor changes improved the weapon is a matter of individual opinion; Daniel Wesson hated the re-shaping of the butt, and he was not alone.

Total production of this pattern has been estimated at 85,200, of which 70,000 were Cyrillic-marked guns going to Russia with lanyard rings on their butts. About 6700 were sold commercially with English-language markings, including about 500 chambered for the 44 Henry rimfire round. Some guns were nickel-plated instead of blued, and, except for presentation pieces, grips were almost always walnut. Turkey took about 2000 44 Henry RF revolvers in two batches, the first being built on special rimfire frames and the second converted from standard centerfire components. The Japanese navy took 5000, marked with two horizontal zigzag lines across an anchor on the butt and inspectors' ideographs on the barrel.

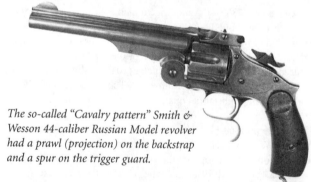

*The so-called "Cavalry pattern" Smith &
Wesson 44-caliber Russian Model revolver
had a prawl (projection) on the backstrap
and a spur on the trigger guard.*

- *Third or "Cavalry" pattern* (1874-8) Sometimes known as the "New Model Russian" or "M1874", this was an adaptation of the second pattern destined for cavalry and artillerymen. Consequently, the long-barreled guns, which were being produced concurrently, were retrospectively classed as the "Infantry Model". Cavalry-type guns had 6.5-inch barrels, short extractor housings and front sights made integrally with the barrel instead of separately. About 60,600 were made, slightly more than 40,000 going to Russia. About 13,500 were sold commercially in 44/100 S&W (common) or 44 Henry RF (very rare) with barrel marks in English, and the Turks took 5000 rimfire guns built on the basis of altered centerfire frames. The Japanese navy acquired 1000 with bars-and-anchor marks. Guns of this type were also made in Charlottenburg by Ludwig Loewe (q.v.) and, eventually, by the Russian small-arms factory in Tula.

Safety Hammerless Model (32 caliber, First Model, 1888-1902) Little more than a smaller version of the top-break auto-ejecting 38-

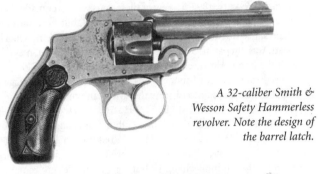

A 32-caliber Smith & Wesson Safety Hammerless revolver. Note the design of the barrel latch.

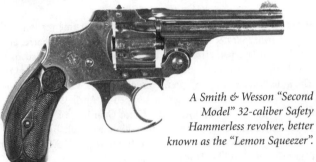

A Smith & Wesson "Second Model" 32-caliber Safety Hammerless revolver, better known as the "Lemon Squeezer".

caliber Safety Hammerless (below) chambered for the 32 S&W cartridge, this took the lead from modifications made to its big brother and enjoyed a steady popularity throughout a long life. It was an ideal pocket weapon, selling to those who took little heed of ballistic performance (the 32-caliber bullet was fired at such a low velocity that it was unlikely to inflict more than a minor wound on an assailant at anything other than close range). The guns had fluted five-chamber cylinders and round barrels of 2, 3 or 3.5 inches, each with a raised top rib. The butt had a rounded heel and toe, grips being walnut or checkered rubber with "S&W" monograms; finish was blue or nickel. The barrel was released by a pushbutton catch in the center of the topstrap. Production amounted to about 91,000 guns.

- *Second Model* (1902-9) This was a minor adaptation of the preceding pattern, with a "T"-bar latch instead of the pushbutton. The front sight, a separate component, was pinned into the barrel rib. About 78,600 guns of this type were made. The so-called "Bicycle Model", with a 2-inch barrel, is particularly scarce.
- *Third Model* (1909-37) Distinguished from the second pattern largely by the design of the front sight, which was forged integrally with the top-rib, this also had a few machining revisions internally. About 73,000 were sold, though it seems unlikely that much production had been undertaken after World War I.

Safety Hammerless Model (38 caliber, First Model, "New Departure" or "Lemon Squeezer", 1887) This gun was often known as "New Departure" to the factory and "Lemon Squeezer" to the general public. Although the "hammerless" (i.e., concealed hammer) system was not entirely new (it had been seen on a few percussion revolvers), this S&W version was the first successful one to be made commercially; and it also had an entirely novel safety device, the grip safety.

Daniel B. Wesson introduced the grip safety lever which projected through the back tang of the butt. It ran for most of the length of the tang and fit into the palm of the shooter's hand. The lever was directly linked to a safety latch, which prevented any cocking action by the hammer until the lever was squeezed. The latch then moved out of the way and the hammer could be cocked by pulling the trigger. The hammer was a small internal one, and it fired the cartridge by striking a small firing pin. An ingenious arrangement of the sear angles allowed a short hesitation just before the hammer fell, so that the hammer could be practically fully cocked by a strong pull on the trigger; and

when the dwell point was reached, the shooter could correct his aim and complete the pull. This last part of the motion required a markedly lower pull and allowed a reasonably accurate shot to be made. The barrel, cylinder and ejector were all but identical with the 38 DA model, and the same ammunition was used.

Only about 5250 examples of the first-pattern revolver were made. They had "Z"-bar latches set into the top rear of the frame and 6-inch barrels. Most were blued, but a few were nickel-plated; grips were checkered rubber.

- *Second Model* (1887-90) For the Second Model, the barrel catch was changed to a pushbutton protruding above the frame, and the safety lever spring was strengthened. About 37,200 were made in blue or nickel with checkered "S&W monogram" rubber grips.
- *Third Model* (1890-8) Another change was made to the barrel catch, which was milled flush with the frame to prevent accidental release, and an interlock between the catch and the hammer prevented the hammer falling unless the action was securely closed. By this time, the Safety Hammerless was selling well, and some 73,500 third-type guns were made. The US Army purchased 100 guns in 1890 for tests with the cavalry but concluded that they were too fragile and complicated for general service; the swing-cylinder Colt was taken instead. These Smith & Wessons were numbered at the end of the "second pattern" block but had third-model features and 6-inch barrels marked "U.S.".
- *Fourth Model* (1898-1907) Made only in 38 S&W centerfire, a fact that was acknowledged by the addition of a "caliber mark" on the barrel shortly after production had begun, this gun was distinguished by a "T"-bar barrel latch. This was similar to those fitted to other top-break S&W designs. Just why these constant barrel catch changes were thought necessary is no longer known, but the "T"-bar was successful enough to remain unchanged until the end of the Safety Hammerless series in 1940. Production of fourth-model guns totaled about 104,000.
- *Fifth Model* (1907-40) The last model of the New Departure was distinguished by the construction of the front sight, formed integrally with the barrel instead of a separate component pinned into the rib above the muzzle. The design had now stabilized so completely that very few alterations were made during the rest of its life. A 2-inch barrel was optional, recognizing that the main use of these revolvers was self-defense — size and speed of reaction counted more than precision marksmanship. About 41,500 of these guns were made, though only a few thousand buyers specified the short barrel.

Schofield Model (or "Model No. 3 Schofield", first pattern, 1875-6) This was practically the same as the 44-caliber American Model (q.v.), but it had a new barrel catch invented by Major (later Colonel) George W. Schofield. The extractor system was improved, and the length of the barrel was reduced to 7 inches. The cartridge was developed by Smith & Wesson specifically to impress the US Army, on the basis of experience gained with the 44 S&W Russian round, but velocity was well below that of the 45 Long Colt even though the Schofield revolver proved to be accurate and pleasant to fire. The US Army took 3000 guns, with "U.S." property and inspectors' marks, but only 35 were sold commercially.

- *Second pattern* (1876-7) Changes had been made to the extractor and some of the minor components, resulting in this gun. The US Army took 4000, distinguished by their "U.S." markings, and an additional 650 were sold commercially. However, the issue of two 45-caliber handgun cartridges for military service (45 Long Colt, 45 S&W Schofield) not only caused confusion but also led to some serious accidents. The Schofield revolver was soon withdrawn. Some were sold to National Guard units, but others went to the military-surplus wholesalers Francis Bannerman & Sons and Schuyler,

Hartley & Graham. Some of the Schuyler guns had their barrels shortened to 5 inches, were nickeled and then sold to Wells, Fargo & Company in the 1880s. These guns will bear "W.F. & CO." on the frame or barrel.

Single Action (or "Model No. 1-½ CF", 32 caliber, 1878-92) The idea for this revolver came from Colt, who introduced a 32-caliber gun in 1875 with immediate success even though the cartridge was no more refined than many Colt designs. Smith & Wesson delayed a reply until the introduction of this graceful version of the contemporary auto-ejecting S&W 38, with a sweeping bird's-head grip, a sheathed trigger and a fluted five-chamber cylinder. A half-cock position was omitted from the earliest guns, but the adoption of a rebounding hammer reduced the danger of carrying the gun with the hammer resting on an empty chamber. Prior to the introduction of 8- and 10-inch options in 1887, barrels were restricted to lengths of 3-6 inches. However, orders for the longest barrels remained few and far between. Most guns were blued, though nickel plating will also be encountered; their grips could be wood, rubber, celluloid or ivory.

The 32 S&W CF cartridge followed the company's design philosophy of reducing the powder charge and enlarging the case diameter to accommodate a bullet that fit tightly in the bore, giving exemplary accuracy. The standard barrel was 3.5 inches long, but a 6-inch barrel was also available. The revolver was a steady seller until discontinued, after 97,540 had been made.

Single Action (38 caliber, First Model, 1876-7) Colt had gained a head start over S&W with their introduction of the 38 Short CF cartridge while Smith & Wesson were too committed to the Russian orders to respond. When S&W moved to catch up, the result was a far better cartridge based on lessons learned with the 44 Russian — using an over-size bullet to engrave in the rifling and seal the bore. The result was more accurate than the Colt 38 and soon proved popular.

The "Baby Russian" revolver built to take the 38 S&W cartridge was virtually a scaled-down 44 Russian Model, retaining the same top-break auto-ejecting design and general outline (even though it had a sheathed trigger, which was then still popular commercially). The fluted cylinder had five chambers. The barrels were originally 3.25 or 4 inches long, though a 5-inch option was subsequently added. Finish was blue or nickel; and the butt had a rounded heel. The grips were rosewood, walnut or checkered rubber with S&W medallions. About 26,000 guns were made in 1876-7, two-thirds of this total being nickel-plated.

• *Second Model* (1877-91) The extractor gear on the original Baby Russian revolver, a replica of the 44-caliber Russian Model design, was heavy and complicated. Consequently, these modified 38-caliber guns had a simpler ejector, and the housing beneath the barrel was much shorter than its predecessor. The cylinder can be taken out with a straight pull, instead of a twist-and-pull, and an additional safety device on later examples released the cylinder at half cock to allow it to revolve freely. About 108,000 of these revolvers were made with barrel lengths of 3.25-10 inches, the longest options being comparatively rare.

• *Third Model* (1891-1911) Offered with barrel lengths of 3.25, 4 or 6 inches, in blue or nickel finish, this was introduced shortly after S&W had failed to get an army order for their New Departure (q.v.) revolver. Possibly influenced by the military tests, the third model had a conventional trigger guard, an enlarged hammer spur and a rebounding lock that allowed the gun to be carried fully loaded. Finish was customarily blue, though many individual guns were nickel-plated, and the grips were invariably checkered rubber with S&W medallions. With a 6-inch barrel, this revolver was delightful to use and soon became popular with the target-shooting clubs. About 28,000 had been made when work ceased and the Single Action, clearly outdated, was quietly dropped from Smith & Wesson's extensive range.

• *Mexican Model* (c. 1892-5) Few of these guns were ever made. They are essentially the same as the third-model 38, but have sheathed triggers, flat-side hammer spurs and lack the half-cock notch. The sheath was a separate component, instead of being made integrally with the frame. However, S&W also offered a "conversion kit" that allowed standard third-model guns to revert to sheathed triggers, and it can be difficult to identify the "Mexican" guns.

Terrier (or "38/32 Terrier", Model 32, 1936-70) This was a 2-inch-barrel version of the 38 Regulation Police, with minor changes. The frame was that of the 1903 Model 32 Hand Ejector but fitted with a 38-caliber barrel and a five-shot cylinder. Post-war production had a ramp foresight and other minor changes, but the basic design remained unchanged.

Victory Model (1942-5) This was simply a wartime version of the 38-caliber Military & Police revolver, with a 2- or 4-inch barrel and a sandblasted-and-parkerized finish. A lanyard ring was added to the base of the squared-base butt, which had smooth-surface walnut grips. The guns had "V" or "VS"-prefix serial numbers, which had reached VS811119 by the time production stopped in April 1945. They were issued to the US armed forces, the Coast Guard, the Department of Justice and many other agencies and will occasionally be found with identifying marks on the butt or the frame (e.g., "U.S.C.G." for the Coast Guard, "U.S.M.C." for the Marines).

∾ REVOLVERS, POST-1945 AND "NUMBERED SERIES" GUNS ∾

In 1957, faced with a product range of steadily increasing complexity, Smith & Wesson elected to adopt numerical designations. This relegated the names to a secondary role, though the tendency (increasing as the years have passed) has been to give guns both names and numbers — for example, "Model 586 Distinguished Combat Magnum". The basis for the listing below is straightforward numerical order.

Variants within each model are usually signified by a suffix. "Model 26-4", therefore, is the fourth change to be made to the basic design. The changes can be difficult to detect externally, but S&W is particularly good at stamping the designation into the barrel or frame, leaving little doubt over identification. The complexity of these sub-variants is best appreciated from one of the specialist books on the subject (S&W recommends *The Standard Catalog of Smith & Wesson*, 2nd edition, by Jim Supica and Richard Nahas and published by Krause Publications).

Among the most obvious are the changes in the number of screws on the right side of the frame that retain the sideplate, which reduced from four to three and now finally to two. The change from four to three occurred in 1955 on the small "J" and medium or "K"-frame designs and in 1956-8 on the large "N"-frame guns. The screw ahead of the trigger guard on the underside of the frame (retaining the cylinder-stop plunger and its spring) was deleted in 1961-2. The cylinder-release latch found behind the cylinder on the rear left side of the frame was altered from a flat to contoured pattern in the mid-1960s. Another easily detected change is the method of attaching the barrel to the frame, which had previously relied on a cross pin, which was altered in 1977. The recessed-head chambers were abandoned at the same time.

Smith & Wesson revolvers are built on only a handful of basic frames. The "I" frame was the smallest, accommodating 22-, 32- and a 38-caliber designs. This has now been replaced by the "J" frame, slightly larger. Most of the 38-caliber guns are built on the medium or "K" frame, and the "N" is reserved for the Magnums (357, 41, 44) and traditional large-body cartridges such as 44 S&W Special and 45 Long Colt.

K-32 (Combat Masterpiece) A few of these guns, basically little more than the K-32 (Model 16, q.v.) with 4-inch barrels, were made prior to the change of designation system in 1957.

Model 10 (38 Military & Police, 1957 to date) This 38 S&W Special Hand Ejector, originating prior to World War I, is still virtually the

A heavy-barreled version of the 38-caliber Smith & Wesson Model 10.

A 357 Magnum S&W Model 13.

same as the original version — at least externally. Built on the medium "K" frame, with barrels measuring 2-6 inches, the Model 10 has been offered in blue or nickel and with a rounded or square-base butt. The grips are invariably checkered walnut.

- *Model 10-1*, which had a heavy barrel, appeared in 1959.
- *Models 10-2* (standard barrel) and *10-3* (heavy barrel) were introduced in 1961, marking an increase in the width of the front-sight blade and a change in the extractor-rod thread to left-hand.
- *Models 10-4, 10-5* and *10-6* Dating from 1962, these designations referred to the elimination of the screw in front of the trigger guard but applied to different guns: the "10-4" was an alteration of the basic Model 10, "10-5" was an alteration of the Model 10-2 (standard-weight barrel) and "10-6" was an adaptation of the heavy-barreled Model 10-1.
- *Current guns* Modernized forms of Model 10-6, these are offered only with a 4-inch heavy barrel. The front sight is mounted on a serrated ramp and the rear sight is a fixed open notch. Made of blued carbon steel, with Uncle Mike's rubber grips, they weigh about 36 oz.

Model 11 This designation was given to the "British Service Model", a 38/200 variant of the 38 Military & Police revolver supplied to Britain during World War II. Many orders for this gun — usually originating from British colonial and ex-colonial police forces — were received in the 1950s and 1960s when the basic pattern was retained.

The Smith & Wesson Model 12.

Model 12 (38 Military & Police Airweight, 1952-86) This is a short-barreled lightweight version of the Model 10 Military & Police, originally made with an alloy frame and cylinder. However, the cylinder proved to be too weak to withstand prolonged use and a steel version was introduced in 1954. This increased weight by about 4 oz.

- *Model 12-1* had a left-hand extractor-rod thread and lacked the screw hole running up into the frame ahead of the trigger guard.
- *Model 12-2*, introduced "for the record" at the same time as 12-1, had the width of the front-sight blade increased from a tenth to an eighth of an inch.

Model 13 (Aircrewman, 1953-4) This designation was given by the USAF to a small number of Model 12 revolvers supplied by S&W for issue as survival weapons. They were all marked "M13" on the back-strap but were rapidly rejected owing to the weakness of the alloy cylinders. This is not an "official" Smith & Wesson designation, as it predates the adoption of the numerical system by several years.

Model 13 (38 Military & Police Heavy Barrel, 357-caliber, 1974 to date) A strengthened Model 10 with a different barrel, this was developed at the request of the New York State Police in 1974 and later placed on open sale.

A single-action target-shooting version of the Model 14, this S&W revolver also has an adjustable rear sight.

Model 14 (K-38 Masterpiece, 1946-81) Chambering the 38 S&W Special round, this was little more than a Model 10 with a 6-inch barrel and adjustable sights. In 1959, alternative barrel lengths were offered, and a special single-action version with a faster lock time was produced in small numbers in 1961-3.

- *Model 14 FL* (Full Lug, 1991-2?) Apparently made only in small numbers, this was simply a reintroduction of the Model 14 with a 4-inch barrel fitted with a full-length ejector-rod shroud.

The 4-inch-barreled Smith & Wesson M15, in 38 Special.

Model 15 (K-38 Combat Masterpiece, 1950-87) This was a variant of the Model 14 with a 2- or 4-inch barrel, for pocket use, though still with adjustable sights.

Model 16 (K-32 Masterpiece, 1947-73) This was a variant of the Model 14 built on the medium "K" frame but chambered for the 32 S&W Long cartridge. Comparatively unpopular, only 3630 were made in the production life that exceeded 25 years.

- *Model 16 Magnum* (or "Full Lug", 1990-3) An adaptation of the original Model 16, this had a full-length ejector-rod shroud and chambered the 32 H&R Magnum round. It also had Goncalo Alves grips instead of walnut.

Model 17 (K-22 Masterpiece, 1946-99) This differed from its predecessors in having adjustable sights, a ribbed barrel measuring 4, 6 or 8.4 inches, and special checkered walnut grips. Finish was invariably blue. The longest barrel was discontinued in 1993.

The Smith & Wesson Model 17, also known as the K-22 Masterpiece.

• *Model 17 Plus* (1996 to date) This is a new version of the basic M17 with a 10-chamber cylinder and 6-inch barrel with a full-length ejector rod shroud. The front sight is a Patridge design, the rear sight is adjustable, the grips are a black-rubber Hogue pattern and the finish is matte black.

A Smith & Wesson M18 revolver.

Model 18 (K-22 Combat Masterpiece, 1950-72) This was much the same as the Model 15, but in 22 LR chambering. It had a 4-inch barrel, a ramped front sight and an adjustable rear sight.

The S&W Model 19, or 357 Combat Magnum.

Model 19 (Combat Magnum, 1954-95?) Built on the medium "K" frame, yet chambering the powerful 357 Magnum round, this arose from a suggestion made by Bill Jordan of the US Border Patrol. The gun originally had a 4-inch barrel with a heavy extractor shroud, but a 6-inch version was introduced in 1963 and a 2.5-inch version (with a round-butt frame) followed in 1968. The bulky grips, made of walnut or Goncalo Alves, have a "Speed-loader" cutaway on the left side. The rear sight is click-adjustable; the design of the front sight varies with barrel length and date of production. The M19 has also provided the basis for specially cased commemorative issues, including the "Texas Ranger" and the "Oregon State Police", accompanied by a bowie knife and a special belt-buckle, respectively.

Model 20 (38/44 Heavy Duty, 1930-66) Introduced to provide a more powerful handgun than those that were then serving the US police forces, this also introduced the 38 Special cartridge. Made on the large "N" frame, with barrels of 3.5-8.4 inches (the 5-inch version was standard), the guns were either blued or nickel-plated and had check-

ered walnut grips. However, despite initial popularity, production amounted to only about 20,000.

Model 21 (44 Military M1950 or "44 Hand Ejector, 4th Model", 1950-66) Though carried in the Smith & Wesson catalogs for many years, this "N"-frame gun in 44 Special, was not successful; only about 1200 were ever made. They generally had 5-inch barrels, fixed sights, plain walnut grips and blue finish.

Model 22 (45 Military M1950, 1951-66) Chambered for the 45 ACP — requiring half-moon clips — or 45 Auto-Rim cartridges, this was the post-World War II version of the M1917. Blued, with a 5-inch barrel and plain walnut grips, the guns all had "S"-prefix numbers. Only about 4000 were made, owing to the ever-increasingly popularity of the Magnum patterns.

Model 23 (38/44 Outdoorsman, 1931-42, 1949-66) Another of the pre-World War II guns built on the large "N" frame to provide a sturdy sporting revolver, this was essentially a Model 20 with an adjustable rear sight. It also had a 6.5-inch barrel, blued finish and checkered walnut "Magna" grips. About 4760 were made prior to 1942, but a modified version with a ribbed barrel appeared after the war. Production of post-1949 guns totaled 8365; about 2300 were made largely from old components, and only the remaining 6000 had the new ribbed barrel.

Model 24 (44 Target M1950, 1950-66) Chambering 44 S&W Special, this "N"-frame design was basically a Model 21 with adjustable sights. Popular with long-range handgunners until the advent of the 44 Magnum, the M24 was discontinued after a little over 5000 had been made. It was reintroduced briefly in 1983-4 in a modernized form but has now been abandoned.

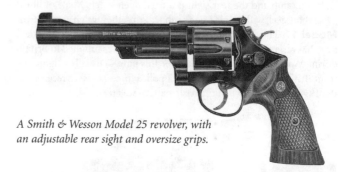

A Smith & Wesson Model 25 revolver, with an adjustable rear sight and oversize grips.

Model 25 (45 Target M1950, 1955 to date) A modified version of the M1917 45-caliber Hand Ejector (above), this offered heavy barrels measuring 4, 6.5 or 8 inches with ejector-rod shrouds. Finish was blue or nickel, the bulky grips were checkered walnut and the rear sight was adjustable. Chambered for the 45 ACP or 45 Auto-Rim cartridges, the guns lost popularity when the 44 Magnum appeared.

• *Model 25-1* This was made with a left-hand ejector rod thread.
• *Model 25-2* Fitted with a 6-inch barrel, this lacked the cylinder-stop plunger retaining screw under the frame ahead of the trigger guard.
• *Model 25-3* A cased deluxe gun produced in 1977 to celebrate the 125th anniversary of Smith & Wesson, this was made only in small numbers.
• *Model 25-5* This is the current production version. Newer guns are built on the revised "N" frame, standardized for the 44 Magnum. As the Magnum cartridge is longer than 45 ACP, a noticeable gap appears between the front of the 45-caliber cylinder and the inner face of the frame.

Model 26 (45 Target M1950, 1950-61) Made on the "N" frame in comparatively small numbers and in three sub-variants (M26, M26-1 with a left-hand ejector rod thread, and M26-2 without the cylinder-stop plunger screw in the frame), this had a slender tapering 6.5-inch barrel and adjustable sights. Complaints that the gun was too muzzle-light for effective target shooting were answered by introducing the M25. Production amounted to about 2800.

The Smith & Wesson Model 27 revolver chambers the 357 Magnum cartridge.

Model 27 (357 Magnum, 1948 to date) The post-war version of the 357 Hand Ejector (q.v.) has been subject to a variety of changes. Offered with barrels of 3.5-8.4 inches, it was offered in blue or nickel and had checkered walnut grips. A 3-screw sideplate was adopted in 1958.

* *Model 27-1* (introduced in 1961) This had a left-hand thread on the extractor rod.
* *Model 27-2* (1962) Owing to a change in the design of the cylinder stop, this variant lacked the hole drilled into the frame ahead of the trigger guard for the plunger and its spring. It also had a ramped front sight, adjustable rear sight, an ejector-rod shroud and oversize grips. A target-type hammer and Goncalo Alves grips were standardized in 1975.

Also known as the "Highway Patrolman", this is the Smith & Wesson 357 Magnum Model 28.

Model 28 (Highway Patrolman, 1954-86) This was a "budget" version of the 357 Magum Model 27 produced to interest law-enforcement agencies that wanted the power of the M27 but were not prepared to pay the price. The M28 had a matte-blue finish, a sandblasted barrel rib (instead of machined checkering or ribbing) and checkered walnut grips. The barrels originally measured either 4 or 6.5 inches, but the latter was eventually replaced by a 6-inch version. Most guns had an adjustable rear sight and a Baughman quick-draw front sight on a ramp.

Model 29 (44 Magnum, 1956-97?) This gun was developed in the mid-1950s to satisfy shooters who were demanding more powerful cartridges than the 44 S&W Special and guns that could withstand the battering of such loadings. Remington developed the 44 Magnum load in 1954, and Smith & Wesson produced the Model 29 to fire it. The new

The 44 Magnum S&W Model 29 revolver.

Magnum cartridge cases were deliberately made longer than 44 Special to prevent accidents. Offered in blue or nickel with contoured checkered walnut grips, the M29 was originally offered with a 6.5-inch barrel; 4-inch and 8.4-inch options were introduced in 1957 (the former lasting only until 1993), and a few hundred guns were made in 1958 with 5-inch barrels. The original four-screw sideplate was replaced by a three-screw pattern at about the same time. Magnum revolvers have proven to be extremely popular — greatly helped by the Dirty Harry films — and have inspired a variety of alterations. See also M629.

A Model 30 Smith & Wesson, also known as the "32 Hand Ejector", chambered for the 32 S&W Long round.

Model 30 (32 Hand Ejector, 1949-60) This was a modernized version of the original M1903 32 Hand Ejector (1903-42) built on the "I" frame. It was chambered for the 32 S&W Long cartridge and had a six-chamber cylinder. Barrels measured 2, 3, 4 or 6 inches, the sights were fixed and the round butt had checkered walnut grips. Finish could be blue or nickel. Guns made after 1960, known as Model 30-1, were built on the more robust "J" frame. They lasted in production until 1976.

A Smith & Wesson Model 31.

Model 31 (32 Regulation Police, 1950-60) This was little more than a M30 (above) with a squared-base butt.

* *Model 31-1* Originally built on the "I" frame, a change to "J" was made in 1960. The designation was amended and work continued until the mid-1970s.
* *Model 31 Target* (or "Regulation Police Target") Introduced in 1957, only about 200 of these were made. They could be distinguished from the standard M31 by the adjustable rear sight.

Model 32 (38/32 Terrier, 1936-42, 1948-60) This was a 38-caliber revolver built on the "I" frame that was customarily associated with the 32-caliber designs. The number of chambers was reduced from six to five to allow the larger cartridge to be used. The Model 32 had a 2-inch barrel, a round butt with checkered walnut grips and fixed sights.

* *Model 32-1* With upgraded standards that came in 1960 with the adoption of the "J"-type frame, this variant lasted until 1974. Finish was blue or nickel.

Model 33 (38 Regulation Police, 1936-42, 1948-60) This was a five-shot 38 S&W Long version of the 32-caliber Model 31, with a squared butt and a 4-inch barrel. Known as the "Model 38-32" to Smith & Wesson, the gun was offered in blue or, more rarely, nickel-plate finish.

* *Model 33-1* An improved version of the basic design, introduced in 1970, this was built on the "J" frame and lasted in production until 1974.

The Smith & Wesson M34 revolver,
or "1953 Model 22/32 Kit Gun".

Model 34 (22/32 Kit Gun, 1936-42, 1946-8, 1953 to date) Essentially a 22-caliber Hand Ejector built on a 32-caliber frame, this pre-war design, temporarily abandoned when World War II began, was made again in small numbers (probably from pre-1942 parts) after hostilities had ceased. A modernized version was introduced in 1953 with a coil-type main spring and a new micro-adjustable rear sight. Available in blue or nickel with checkered walnut grips, the Model 34 was revised in 1960.

• *Model 34-1* (1960 to date) When the "J" frame replaced the "I" type, the designation was advanced. See also "Model 51".

Model 35 (22/32 Target, 1953-60) This was the last of this particular series, the role having been taken over by the "Masterpiece" revolvers. The guns had a 6-inch barrel, squared walnut grips (often an "over-length" design) and adjustable sights. The finish was blue, or, less commonly, nickel plating.

• *Model 35-1* The "I" frame was replaced by the "J" pattern in 1960, creating this variant; work then continued until 1973.

The 38-caliber Chief's Special,
or Model 36 Smith & Wesson.

Model 36 (38 Chiefs Special, 1950 to date) This was the first snub-nosed gun to re-appear after 1945, built on the small "J" frame with a barrel of 2 or 3 inches and a rounded butt. The cylinder held five 38 Special rounds. A squared-base butt option was introduced in 1952, finish could be blue or nickel and the walnut grips were invariably checkered. A heavy 3-inch barrel appeared in 1967 and was standardized in 1975; the 2-inch-barrel option was abandoned in 1993.

• *Model 36 LS* (38 LadySmith, 1989 to date) The "Ladysmith" title was revived for a new range of pistols, including some semi-automatics. In keeping with the modern age, they are not as lady-like as the original 22 rimfire patterns. They have five-chamber cylinders, for 38 Special ammunition, and originally had rosewood grips. Guns being made in 2003 have 1.9-inch barrels, fixed sights and Dymondwood grips. Made of blued carbon steel, they weigh about 20 oz.

• *Model 36 Target* (38 Chiefs Special Target, 1955-65) Made only in limited quantities, this was little more than an M36 with an adjustable rear sight. Offered with barrels of 2 or 3 inches, in blue or nickel, the guns made in 1957-65 were marked "MODEL 36" on the cylinder yoke. However, this was then changed to "MODEL 50" (q.v.).

Model 37 (38 Chiefs Special Airweight, 1952 to date) The earliest batches of this five-shot 38 Special revolver were made with alloy frames and alloy cylinders, but the latter proved to be too weak and

A lightweight version of the Chief's Special,
the Model 37 had an alloy frame.

were replaced by steel after 1954. Offered with the same 2- and 3-inch barrel options associated with the Model 36, the M37 is still in production. Guns made after 1998 have been strengthened to fire "+P" ammunition and those being made in 2003 have matte-black finish and black-rubber Uncle Mike's "boot" grips. The barrel now measures 1.9 inches, and the sights consist of a blade on a serrated ramp and a fixed open notch.

The Model 38 S&W or "Bodyguard
Airweight", with an enclosed hammer.

Model 38 (38 Airweight Bodyguard, 1955 to date) Built on an alloy frame, with barrels measuring 2 inches (common) or 3 inches (exceptionally scarce), this had the back of the frame extended upward to enclose all but the tip of the hammer. Finish was blue or nickel, the grips were checkered walnut and the notably slender butt had a rounded backstrap. Guns made since 1998 are rated as suitable for "+P" ammunition.

The Smith & Wesson M40 Centennial,
in 38 Special.

Model 40 (38 Centennial, 1952-74) Introduced to commemorate the centenary of Smith & Wesson, this was a revival of the Safety Hammerless or "New Departure" design with a five-chamber cylinder mounted on a yoke instead of a break-open mechanism. The M40 was built on a modification of the "J" frame, adapted to accept an enclosed hammer and a grip safety set in the backstrap, and had a steel frame. Sights were fixed, finish was blue or nickel and the grips were checkered walnut. See also "Model 42" and "Model 640".

Model 42 (38 Centennial Airweight, 1953-74) This was simply a lightweight model of the Model 40, with a frame made of aluminum alloy instead of carbon steel. The first 40 guns had an alloy cylinder but proved to be too weak to withstand the strains imposed by even moderately loaded 38 Special ammunition. A steel cylinder was substituted.

Model 43 (22/32 Kit Gun Airweight, 1954-74) Built on a "J" frame, this was virtually the same as the standard Model 34 but had a light alloy frame and a 3.5-inch barrel. The butt could be rounded or squared, the finish was blue or nickel, grips were invariably checkered walnut and the rear sight was adjustable. A few guns were made with 2-inch barrels, and a handful was chambered for 22 WMRF instead of the standard 22 LR rimfire pattern. See also "Model 51".

Model 45 (1948-57, 1963) Made for the US Postal Service, this was a standard 38-caliber M&P adapted to become a 22 LR rimfire trainer. Guns of this type are rarely seen in collections, as production was severely restricted.

The S&W Model 48 revolver.

Model 48 (K-22 Masterpiece Magnum, 1959-86) This is identical mechanically with the Model 17 but chambers the 22 WMRF round instead of 22 LR (though the cylinders are exchangeable!). It is usually blued and has a barrel measuring 4, 6 or 8.4 inches.

The Model 49 Smith & Wesson was an all-steel version of the M38.

Model 49 (38 Bodyguard, 1959 to date?) The Bodyguard is a postwar revival of the "hammerless" design, though in this case there is a vestigial spur showing above the frame sides. A five-shot gun with a 2-inch barrel (the 3-inch option was rarely requested), the M49 was made entirely in carbon steel — unlike the alloy-frame M38, which was externally identical. See also "Model 649".

Model 50 (38 Chiefs Special Target, 1965-75) Clearly marked "MODEL 50" on the cylinder yoke, this was essentially the Model 36 Chiefs Target (q.v.) under a new designation. Only about 2300 guns were made in 1955-75, in several recognizable different sub-variants, but perhaps only 1000 bore the revised designation.

Model 51 (22/32 Kit Gun Magnum, 1960-74) This was a variant of the Model 34 (q.v.). Made in blue or nickel with walnut grips, the M51 was chambered for the 22 Winchester Magnum rimfire cartridge instead of 22 LR. Squared-base butts were standardized, though about 600 round-butt guns were made in the early 1960s.

Model 53 (Magnum Jet, 1961-74) Chambered for the 22 Remington Jet centerfire round, this was offered with barrels of 4, 6 or 8.4 inches. The guns were usually blued and had oversize checkered walnut grips.

The frame-mounted firing pin was duplicated so that the Model 53 could also fire 22 LR rimfire ammunition, as long as suitable liners had been inserted in the chambers. About 15,000 guns of this type were made, including a substantial number marked "53-1" and "53-2".

Model 56 (1962-4) Fifteen thousand of these 38 Special five-shot guns with 2-inch heavy barrels on a medium "K"-type frame were made for the US Air Force and had a "U.S." mark on the backstrap. Most were destroyed at the end of their service lives, but a few were sold commercially; these lack official markings, other than a few that escaped destruction.

Chambered for the 41 Magnum round, the S&W M57 did not sell in large quantities.

Model 57 (Magnum, 1964-82) This is virtually an enlarged Model 10 M&P chambered for the 41 Magnum cartridge and developed principally for police use and for those who felt that 44 Magnum was too much of a good thing for everyday use. Built on the "N" frame, the guns have barrels measuring 4, 6 or 8.4 inches. The ejector-rod shroud is a half-length type. They are blued with checkered "over-size" walnut or Goncalo Alves grips and have adjustable rear sights. Individual variants have included the Models 57-1 (1982-8), 57-2 (1988-90), 57-3 (1990-3) and 57-4 (1993 to date).

The Smith & Wesson M58, "41 Military & Police" revolver.

Model 58 (Military & Police Magnum, 1964 to date) This was an economy version of the Model 57 developed principally for police use and adapted from the 44 Hand Ejector design to chamber the 41 Magnum round. Made only with fixed sights and a 4-inch barrel, it could be finished in blue or nickel and had checkered walnut grips.

Model 60 (1965 to date) This was a stainless-steel version of the Model 36 (q.v.), originally chambered for the 38 Special cartridge. It was offered with a 2-inch barrel (usually with fixed sights) or a 3-inch "full lug" barrel and an adjustable rear sight. The trigger was serrated; the grips were usually walnut.

An updated design appeared in 1996, with a 2.1-inch barrel and Hogue black-rubber combat grips. It is chambered for the 357 Magnum and 38 Special interchangeably, thanks to a cylinder that has been lengthened. A short-cylinder version of the new gun, accepting 38 Special only, reappeared in 1998.

The guns being made in 2003 have 2.1- or 3-inch barrels, cylinders that will chamber 357 or 38 Special cartridges interchangeably and a weight of 22.5 or 24 oz empty. The front sight is pinned into a ramp at

A Smith & Wesson Model 60 "Chief's Special Stainless", in 38 Special.

the muzzle, and the rear sight is a simple fixed notch. Finish is satin stainless steel; grips are usually black-rubber Uncle Mike's.

- *Model 60 LS* (LadySmith, 1989 to date) This was originally a version of the M60 with a 2-inch barrel, rosewood grips on the slender butt and a laser-engraved design on the frame. A long-cylinder variant chambering 357 Magnum and 38 Special interchangeably was introduced in 1996 and is still being made in 2003. It now has a 2.1-inch barrel, Dymondwood grips and a glass-beaded finish. The sights are the same as the current M60.

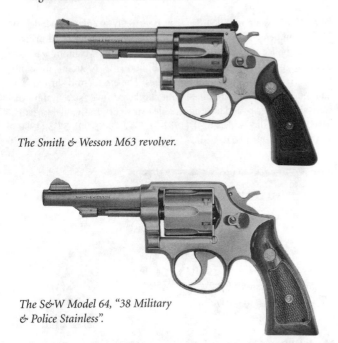

The Smith & Wesson M63 revolver.

The S&W Model 64, "38 Military & Police Stainless".

Model 63 (Kit Gun, 1977 to date?) This is a stainless-steel version of the Model 34 (q.v.).

Model 64 (38 Military & Police Stainless, 1974-7) As the name suggests, this is little more than the Model 10 M&P in stainless steel. Chambered for the 38 Special round with a six-chamber cylinder, the M64 was superseded in about 1977.

- *Model 64-1* This was an improved M64 with a 4-inch heavy barrel. Options available in 2003 include heavy barrels of 2, 3 and 4 inches, all with a combination of serrated ramp and fixed-notch sights. Grips are black-rubber Uncle Mike's; finish is satin stainless.

Model 65 (357 Military & Police Heavy Barrel Stainless, 1974 to date) A stainless version of the Model 13 developed at the request of the Oklahoma Highway Patrol and then placed on open sale. It is currently restricted to a 4-inch heavy barrel.

- *Model 65 LS* (LadySmith, 1992 to date) A lightweight version of the Model 65, originally with a 2-inch barrel, this also had rosewood grips on a slender butt with a rounded backstrap. The current ver-

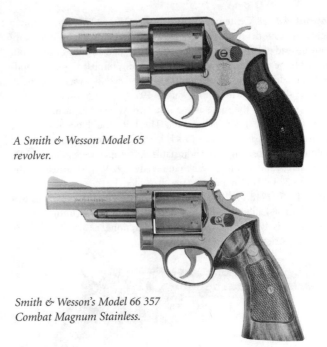

A Smith & Wesson Model 65 revolver.

Smith & Wesson's Model 66 357 Combat Magnum Stainless.

sion has a 3-inch heavy barrel, fixed sights and a Dymondwood grip. The finish is glass-bead.

Model 66 (38 Combat Magnum Stainless, first type, 1970-83) Made with adjustable sights, a squared-base butt and checkered walnut grips, this gun was originally offered only with a 4-inch barrel. However, a 2.5-inch barrel appeared in 1974 and was sometimes combined with a round-butt frame. A 6-inch barrel and target sights were introduced in the 1980s. The 2003 options include a barrel of 2.5 or 4 inches, black-rubber Uncle Mike's grips and a combination of ramped red-insert front sight and an adjustable rear sight set in the top rear of the frame. The finish is satin.

The Model 67 S&W Combat Masterpiece Stainless.

Model 67 (38 Combat Masterpiece Stainless, first type, 1972-7) Little more than a stainless-steel version of the Model 15 (q.v.), this had a 4-inch barrel and a six-chamber cylinder accepting 38 Special cartridges. It was superseded by the Models 67-1 (1977-88), 67-2 (1988-93) and 67-3 (1993 to date). The guns being sold in 2003 have ramp-mounted front sights with red inserts, an adjustable rear sight and Uncle Mike's rubber grips.

Model 73 Built in the early 1970s on a special "C" frame with a 2.5-inch barrel, this six-shot 38 Special revolver is now rarely seen; most of the 5000 that were made were subsequently destroyed, and it is claimed that only 20 examples survive.

Model 242 (AirLite, 1999-2001) Built on the medium "L" frame, this fired 38 S&W Special "+P" ammunition. Provided with a 2.5-inch barrel, a seven-chamber cylinder and a "semi-concealed" hammer, the M242 had a matte-finish alloy frame and a titanium cylinder. The blacked front sight was pinned into the barrel rib, and the rear sight was a fixed open notch. Black rubber "boot" grips were standard.

Model 296 (AirLite, 1999 to date) Otherwise similar to the M242, with the same combination of frame and cylinder, this five-shot revolver was chambered for the 44 S&W Special round. It had a 2.5-inch barrel, a concealed hammer and weighed about 19 oz empty.

Model 317 (AirLite Ti, 1997 to date) Featuring a stainless-steel barrel, a titanium cylinder and an aluminum-alloy frame, this 22 LR rimfire gun has an eight-chamber cylinder. The gun is about 6.2 inches long, has a 1.9-inch barrel and weighs about 10.5 oz. The ramped front and open-notch rear sights are fixed, and the grips are a "boot" of synthetic Dymondwood or rubber Uncle Mike's Combat. Built on a "J" frame, the M317 has an "AirLite" logo on the sideplate on the right side of the frame.

* *Model 317 Kit Gun* (AirLite Ti, 1998 to date) A variant of the standard M317, this has a 3-inch barrel and an adjustable rear sight. Guns made after 2001 have HiViz green-dot front sights. Grips may be Dymondwood or Uncle Mike's Combat patterns. Empty weight is about 12 oz.
* *Model 317 LadySmith* (AirLite Ti, 1998 to date) This gun has a 2-inch barrel, slender Dymondwood grips and an empty weight of about 10 oz. It also has a cursive "Lady Smith" legend on the right side of the frame above the trigger.

Model 329 (PD Sc, 2003) Chambering 44 Magnum, this is built on a scandium-alloy "N" frame and has a six-chamber titanium-alloy cylinder. The barrel is 4 inches long with a HiViz green dot sight, and the gun is finished in dark gray (cylinder) and matte black (barrel and frame). Wooden Ahrends finger-groove and rubber Hogue wraparound grips are supplied with each gun, which is about 9.5 inches long and weighs 26 oz empty. The electron-orbital and AirLite logos appear on the right side of the frame.

Model 331 (AirLite Ti, 1999 to date) Built on the "J" frame, this six-shot revolver chambers the 32 H&R Magnum round. Fitted with a 1.9-inch barrel, it has a gray titanium cylinder and an aluminum-alloy frame, cylinder yoke and barrel shroud. This gives a two-tone matte finish. The barrel is a stainless-steel liner within the alloy shroud. Wood or rubber Uncle Mike's "boot" grips are standard, and the guns weigh about 12 oz empty.

Model 332 (AirLite Ti, 1999 to date) This is a double-action-only variant of the M331 (above), with the hammer concealed within a high-back frame.

Model 337 (AirLite Ti, 1999-2002) Chambering 38 Special "+P" ammunition in a five-chamber cylinder, this gun matched an aluminum-alloy frame with a titanium cylinder and wood or rubber grips. The barrel was 1.9 inches long, with a blacked front sight pinned in the rib above the muzzle. The guns also had a distinctive logo consisting of an S&W monogram placed within eight electron orbitals on the sideplate. The "AirLite" logo was transferred to the right side of the frame above the trigger.

* *Model 337 Kit Gun* (AirLite Ti, 2000-2) This was a 337 with a 3-inch barrel and an adjustable rear sight. Guns made after 2001 also had HiViz green-dot front sights. Empty weight was about 13.5 oz.
* *Model 337 PD* (AirLite Ti, 2000 to date) Allegedly developed for "Police Department" use (hence the "PD" suffix in the designation), this matches a distinctive gray titanium cylinder with matte-black finish on the frame and barrel. Hogue Bantam grips are standard.

Model 340 (AirLite Sc, 2001 to date) A five-shot double-action-only design with the hammer enclosed within a high-back scandium alloy frame, this chambers the 357 Magnum round and has a 1.9-inch barrel. The front sight is pinned into the barrel rib, the rear sight is fixed, Hogue Bantam grips are used and the finish is a combination of a gray titanium cylinder and matte "stainless" barrel/frame. The guns weigh about 12 oz empty.

* *Model 340 PD* (2001 to date) This was simply a variant of the standard M340 AirLite Sc with a gray cylinder, blacked frame and

blacked barrel. The front sight is either a ramped blade with a red insert or an orange HiViz fitting.

Model 342 (AirLite Ti, 1999 to date) This is another double-action-only design, similar to the M340 with a 1.9-inch barrel, an alloy frame and a titanium cylinder, but it chambers 38 Special "+P". The grips can be wood or a rubber Uncle Mike's "boot" design.

* *Model 342 PD* (AirLite Ti, 2000 to date) A variant of the standard gun described previously, with a dark gray finish and Hogue Bantam grips.

Model 360 (AirLite Sc, 2001 to date) Built on the small "J" frame with a 1.9-inch barrel, this is chambered for 357 Magnum/38 Special "+P" ammunition. The front sight is a blade pinned into a serrated ramp and the rear sight is a fixed open notch. The M360 weighs about 12 oz empty and has Hogue Bantam grips.

* *Model 360 Kit Gun* (AirLite Sc, 2001 to date) Essentially the same as the standard M360, this has a 3.1-inch barrel, an orange-dot HiViz front sight and an adjustable rear sight set in the top rear of the frame. The black rubber grips are usually Uncle Mike's Combat pattern.
* *Model 360 PD* (AirLite Sc, 2001 to date) This version of the M360 has a grayed titanium-alloy cylinder matched with a matte stainless barrel and frame. The front sight is either a red insert on a ramp or an orange-dot HiViz; the rear sight is fixed, and the grips are usually Hogue Bantams.

Model 386 (Mountain Lite Sc, 2001 to date) Built on a scandium-alloy "L" frame, now with a seven-chamber titanium "Plus" cylinder, this 357 Magnum gun has a 3.5-inch barrel and a HiViz green dot front sight. The rear sight is adjustable. The finish is a dark matte gray, and the grips are Hogue Bantam patterns. The designation appears in outline lettering on the right side of the barrel.

* *Model 386 PD* (AirLite Sc, 2001 to date) A variant of the standard M386, this has a matte black/dark gray finish, a 2.5-inch barrel and a ramped red-insert or orange-dot HiViz front sight. Empty weight averages 17.5 oz.

Model 396 (2000 to date) Chambered for the 44 S&W Special and weighing about 18 oz empty, this "L"-frame gun has a five-chamber titanium cylinder and an aluminum-alloy frame. The barrel measures 3.1 inches, the front sight is a green-dot HiViz type and the rear sight is adjustable.

Model 442 (Centennial Airweight, 1993 to date) Originally offered with a 2-inch barrel, an alloy frame and a steel cylinder, this 38 Special five-shot revolver also has an enclosed hammer. It has been made in blue or satin-nickel finish and usually has rubber "combat" grips. The front sight is mounted on a serrated ramp and the rear sight is a fixed open square notch. Guns being made in 2003 were blacked and had Uncle Mike's "boot" grips. Empty weight averages 16 oz.

Model 500 (2003) Chambered for the awesome 500 S&W Magnum, the world's most powerful handgun cartridge (developing a muzzle energy of 2600 ft-lb), this five-shot stainless-steel revolver is built on the unique "X" frame. It has an 8.4-inch "ported" barrel, a ramped front sight and an adjustable rear sight let into the top of the frame. Hogue rubber grips are standard. The M500 is about 15 inches long and weighs 73 oz.

Model 520 (1980-90?) Built on the large "N" frame, this was chambered for the 357 Magnum round. It had a 4-inch barrel, fixed sights, blue finish and checkered walnut grips.

Model 547 (9mm Military & Police, 1980-85) This short-lived experiment was a variant of the Model 10 M&P chambered for the 9mm Parabellum cartridge, offered with a 3-inch or 4-inch heavy barrel. At that time, many police and military forces were adopting 9mm in automatic pistols and submachine guns, and the Model 547 was intended to satisfy those who wished to standardize caliber but retain some revolvers. The curve of the grip was tightened to resist the heavier recoil, but the gun was otherwise conventional. Finish was usually blue, and the grips could be checkered plastic, checkered walnut or contoured Goncalo Alves. The M547 did not prove to be popular.

The S&W Model 547 revolver, for the 9mm Parabellum round, had the butt curved more sharply than usual.

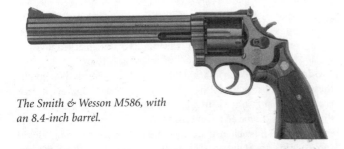

A Smith & Wesson M581.

Model 581 (Distinguished Service Magnum, first type, 1980-6) Built on the medium "L" frame and chambered for the 357 Magnum cartridge, this had a 4-inch "full-lug" barrel and fixed sights. Finish was blue or nickel, and the grips were usually checkered walnut. The original manufacturing pattern was replaced by the Models 581-1 (1986-7), 581-2 (1987-8) and 581-3 (1988-99).

Model 586 (Distinguished Combat Magnum, first type, 1980-6) Another of the "L"-framed 357 Magnums, this was similar to the M581 but had adjustable sights, extended "target" grips and a specially-regulated trigger system. Barrels could be 4, 6 or 8 inches long. The basic M586 was superseded in 1986 by the Model 586-1; then came the 586-2 (1987-8), 586-3 (1988-93) and 586-4 (1993-9). The "Model 585-6" was a special version made for Brazil in 1993-5, in 38 Special instead of 357 Magnum.

The Smith & Wesson M586, with an 8.4-inch barrel.

Model 610 (1998-9) Sometimes known as the "Classic Hunter", this stainless-steel gun was built on the "N" frame and chambered the 10mm Auto round in a plain-surface cylinder. The barrel was a 6.5-inch "full-lug" design with an ejector-rod shroud running its entire length. The front sight was an exchangeable design, the rear sight was adjustable and the grips were a black rubber Hogue wraparound type. The gun weighed about 52 oz empty. It was "reintroduced" in 2001 with a 4-inch barrel, reducing weight by about 2 oz.

Model 617 (1996 to date) This is simply a stainless-steel version of the Model 17 Plus (q.v.), currently offered with barrels measuring 4 or 6 inches and black rubber Hogue finger-groove grips. The short-barrel gun is offered with a 10-chamber cylinder, but the 6-inch-barreled gun

A stainless-steel M624 Smith & Wesson revolver.

may be six- or 10-shot. It is assumed that the six-chamber cylinder will be abandoned in due course.

Model 624 (Magnum Target Stainless, 44-caliber, 1985-2000) The Model 624 is simply a stainless steel version of the Model 27 with a change of caliber.

Model 625 (or "Model 625-2", 1989 to date) This is a stainless-steel version of the Model 25-2, with a 5-inch barrel and Pachmayr SK/GR grips. It is intended for "bowling pin" target shooting. The guns being offered in 2003 have Patridge front and adjustable rear sights, Hogue grips and "full-lug" barrels of 4 or 5 inches. These give an overall length of 9.4 or 10.4 inches and weights of 43 and 45 oz, respectively. A glass-bead finish is standard.

- *M625 Mountain Gun* (1996-2002) Chambered for the 45 Long Colt round, this has a tapered 4-inch barrel with a ramped front sight. The adjustable rear sight is set in the top rear of the frame, which is drilled and tapped for optical-sight mounts. A 45 ACP version was announced in 2000, but the Mountain Gun was considered a limited edition and only about 2500 were made.

Model 627 (1989) A minor variant of the 357 Magnum Model 27, made entirely of stainless steel, this has a 5.5-inch barrel with a full-length ejector-rod shroud. The contoured wooden grips were made of Goncalo Alves. Production totaled merely 4500.

Model 629 (44 Magnum Stainless) A stainless-steel version of the "N"-frame Model 29, this has a full-length ejector-rod shroud and contoured walnut or Goncalo Alves grips. The current version is offered with a 4- or 6-inch barrel, a red-insert ramped front sight, an adjustable white-outline rear sight on the top rear of the frame, and black rubber Hogue grips. The short-barrel option is 9.6 inches long and weighs about 41.5 oz empty.

- *Model 629 Backpacker* (1994-2001) This was a variant of the M629 with a round-butt frame, a 3-inch barrel and an adjustable rear sight. Made in stainless steel, it had Hogue rubber grips and weighed about 40 oz empty.
- *Model 629 Classic* (1990 to date) A minor variant of the M629, this has a full-length ejector-rod shroud, a chamfered cylinder and rubber Hogue "combat" grips. The front sight is exchangeable, the rear sight is adjustable and the top of the barrel is drilled and tapped for optical-sight mounts. The guns being made in 2003 — with 5-, 6.25- or 8.4-inch barrels — usually have Patridge front and adjustable white-outline rear sights, though a green-dot HiViz/adjustable "V"-notch combination is optional with the 6.25 inch barrel. A typical example is 12 inches long, with a 6.5-inch barrel, and weighs about 49 oz empty.
- *Model 629 Classic DX* (1991 to date) A variant of the M629 Classic, this has been sold with two sets of grips and five exchangeable front-sight inserts. The standard barrel-length options are 6.5 and 8.4 inches, with full-length ejector-rod shrouds, but a 5-inch pattern was offered in 1992-3.
- *Model 629 PowerPort* (1996 to date) Easily identified by a compensator made integrally with the barrel, requiring the front sight to be set back from the muzzle, this has a 6.5-inch "full-lug" barrel, a Patridge front sight, an adjustable rear sight and Hogue "combat"

The S&W Model 629 44 Magnum revolver, made of stainless steel.

grips. The top of the barrel rib is drilled and tapped for optical-sight mounts. Guns of this type weigh about 54.5 oz empty and are about 12 inches long.

- *Model 629 Mountain Gun* (1993-4, 1999-2001) Originally introduced as a limited edition of about 2500 guns, this featured a 4-inch barrel and drilled-and-tapped holes in the frame that accept optical-sight mounts. The blacked front sight was pinned into the barrel rib, and the rear sight was adjustable. Finish was satin stainless, and the rubber grip was a Hogue round-butt design.

Model 631 (1990 to date) Chambered for the 32 H&R Magnum round, this has been offered with either a 2-inch barrel (fixed sights) or a 4-inch barrel (adjustable rear sight). It offers a stainless-steel finish, though the frame is aluminum alloy, and weighs about 22 oz empty.

- *Model 631 LadySmith* (1990 to date) A variant of the M631 with a 2-inch barrel, rosewood grips and a laser-engraved frame.

Model 632 (Centennial, 1990-93?) Made only in small numbers, this was a variant of the enclosed-hammer series chambered for the 32 H&R Magnum cartridge. It had a 2-inch barrel and an alloy frame. The finish was "matte stainless".

Model 637 (Airweight, 1996 to date) Essentially similar to the M37 Chiefs Special Airweight (q.v.), this has an alloy frame and stainless-steel finish instead of blue. Guns made since 1998 all have a "+P" rating. The guns currently being offered have 1.9-inch barrels, Uncle Mike's "boot" grips, serrated ramp front sights and fixed-notch rear sights. They have a glass-bead satin-stainless finish and display "Airweight" on the right side of the frame. Empty weight is about 15 oz.

Model 638 (Bodyguard Airweight, 1996 to date) This is little more than the M38, retaining the alloy frame and shrouded hammer, with a glass-bead stainless-steel finish instead of blue. Post-1998 guns (with the same features as the M637 described previously) are strengthened to fire "+P" 38 Special ammunition.

Model 640 (Centennial, 1985-95) A stainless-steel version of the M40 (q.v.), this was chambered for the 38 Special cartridge. Offered with barrels measuring 2 or 3 inches (the latter being abandoned in 1993), it lacked the grip safety of its prototype. A modified 357 Magnum/38 Special gun was introduced in 1995 with a longer five-chamber cylinder, a 2.1-inch barrel and rubber "combat" grips. The front sight is pinned into a ramp at the muzzle, and the rear sight is a fixed square notch. Finally, a new 38 Special derivative, with the original short cylinder but otherwise like the 357, reappeared in 1998. The guns being sold in 2003, with 1.9-inch barrels and "Airweight" on the right side of the frame, are identical with the M637 except for the grips, which are Uncle Mike's Combat instead of the shorter "boot" design.

Model 642 (Centennial Airweight, 1985-92, 1996 to date) This is a variant of the M640 Centennial, with an aluminum-alloy frame and a 2-inch barrel. Work stopped on the original version in the early 1990s, but the M642 was subsequently reintroduced in an improved form distinguished by rubber "combat" grips. Guns made since 1998 have been strengthened to handle "+P" ammunition safely. Those being sold in 2003 had 1.9-inch barrels, fixed sights and Uncle Mike's "boot" grips. The finish is satin stainless.

- *Model 642 LS* (LadySmith) Introduced in 1996, this had a 2.1-inch

barrel, rosewood grips on the original slender rounded butt and laser engraving on the frame. The current version has a 1.9-inch barrel, Dymondwood grips, fixed sights and a glass bead finish.

Model 647 (2003) This is chambered for the 17 Hornady Magnum rimfire round. Built on a stainless-steel "K" frame with an 8.4-inch "full-lug" barrel, the gun is about 13.5 inches long and weighs 53 oz empty. The front sight is pinned into the muzzle ramp, the rear sight is adjustable and black rubber Hogue finger-groove grips are fitted.

Model 648 (1996-2001, 2003) Derived from the Model 17, this six-shot revolver is made entirely of satin-finish stainless steel. Chambering the 22 WMRF round, the current version has a 6-inch barrel — with a full-length ejector-rod shroud — and black rubber Hogue finger-groove grips. The front sight is pinned in the ramp; the rear sight is adjustable. Satin-finish stainless steel is used throughout. The 2003 version of the M648 is about 11.1 inches long and weighs 45 oz empty.

Model 649 (Bodyguard Stainless, 1985 to date) A version of the M49

The Smith & Wesson M649 was a stainless-steel variant of the M49.

(q.v.) made of stainless steel, this can handle 357 Magnum and 38 Special ammunition interchangeably — though a short-cylinder version, restricted to 38 Special (and "+P"), was introduced in 1998. The standard grips were originally walnut. Guns being advertised in 2003 have 2.1-inch barrels, a blade-type front sight pinned into a muzzle ramp, an open fixed-notch rear sight and Uncle Mike's Combat grips. The finish is currently satin stainless.

Model 650 (1983-8) Built on a stainless-steel "J" frame, this gun had a 3-inch heavy barrel and a six-chamber cylinder accepting the 22 WM rimfire round. The butt was rounded and the sights were fixed.

Model 651 (1983-8) This was a comparatively short-lived stainless-steel version of the 22 WMRF Model 51, with a 4-inch barrel and a "J" frame. Made only with a squared butt, it also had adjustable sights. The original pattern was superseded by the Models 651-1 (1988-9) and 651-2 (1989-90).

Model 657 (Magnum Stainless, 357-caliber, 1980-99, 2001-2) The 41 Magnum had a resurgence in popularity in the early 1980s and this "N"-frame model was introduced to take advantage of it. It was originally made with 4-, 6- or 8.4-inch barrels, but the 4-inch option was dropped from the line in 1993. The Model 657 reappeared in 2001 with a 7.5-inch barrel, a front sight pinned into the muzzle ramp and an adjustable rear sight. The grips are now black-rubber Hogue combat instead of checkered walnut, and the empty weight has risen to about 52 oz.

- *Model 657 Classic Hunter* (2003) A minor variant of the M657 with a plain-surface cylinder, this has a 7.5-inch full-lug barrel with a "Power Port" compensator ahead of the front sight, which is set noticeably back from the muzzle. The sights consist of a pinned blade at the front and an adjustable open notch at the rear; black rubber Hogue grips are standard, and the metal parts have a satin finish. The guns are 11.9 inches long and weigh about 52 oz empty.

Model 681 (Distinguished Service Magnum Stainless, 1981-92) This

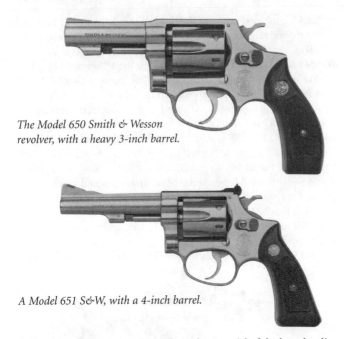

The Model 650 Smith & Wesson revolver, with a heavy 3-inch barrel.

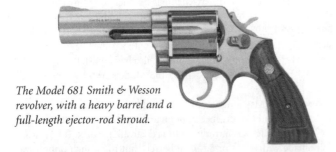

A Model 651 S&W, with a 4-inch barrel.

differed from the M581 principally in the material of the barrel, cylinder and frame.

Model 686 (Distinguished Combat Magnum Stainless, 1980 to date) Offered in the same variants as the carbon-steel M586 (except for the "-5" type), this was made entirely of stainless steel. The guns being sold in 2003 chamber 357 Magnum/38 Special "+P" interchangeably, have barrel lengths of 2.5, 4 or 6 inches, and a combination of ramped red-insert front and adjustable white-outline rear sights. The 6-inch-barreled option is usually accompanied by Hogue rubber grips instead of the Uncle Mike's pattern associated with the shorter guns. A typical gun is 9 inches long, with a 4-inch barrel, and weighs about 41 oz empty.

• *Model 686 Magnum Plus* (1996 to date) Though similar to the standard M686, this has a seven-chamber 357 Magnum cylinder (one more than normal) and full-lug barrels measuring 2.5, 4 or 6 inches. The front sight is a red blade mounted on a ramp, the rear sight is adjustable, and the barrel rib is drilled-and-tapped for optical-

The Smith & Wesson Model 686.

barrel with a full-length ejector-rod shroud. The cylinder had five chambers, the rear sight was adjustable and the grips were black rubber Hogue designs. The guns weighed about 48 oz empty.

Model 940 (1985-99?) A derivative of the Centennial series chambered for the 9mm Parabellum cartridge, this retained an enclosed hammer but lacked the original grip-safety mechanism. The barrel options have been restricted to 2 inches (abandoned in 1993) and 3 inches. Construction was stainless steel, and the grips were usually black rubber Hogue "combat" type. Sights were fixed.

∼ AUTOMATIC PISTOLS ∼

In the latter part of the 19th century, Smith & Wesson did well by developing special cartridges and building revolvers around them, the cartridges gaining international acceptance. When they tried the same thing with an automatic pistol, it was a near disaster, and this appears to have played a big part in them deciding to concentrate on revolvers for many years afterwards. It was not until the 1950s that they dipped their toe back into the water and the 1970s before they really began to make serious moves into the automatic pistol business. By 1990, they had a range of automatics every bit as good as their revolvers.

Automatic Pistol (35-caliber, 1913-21) Smith & Wesson were not keen on the automatic pistol, but as this new device began eroding their pocket-revolver market, they produced one of their own in 1913. Instead of attempting to develop something entirely new, the patents of Clément (q.v.) were bought; this was a simple blowback pistol albeit of unusual design. The principal feature was a separate bolt working in the receiver and exposed at both sides, running in slots. The barrel and a "topstrap" were a single unit and hinged up about a pin in the upper rear of the frame, above the bolt. The recoil spring was above the barrel, and there was a grip safety beneath the trigger guard.

A defect of the early automatics was that lead bullets jammed in the feed ramp, but jacketed bullets wore the barrel badly. Smith & Wesson produced a 35-caliber bullet with a jacketed nose and a lead skirt, thus getting the best of both worlds.

Unfortunately, it was more expensive than the usual types, and the owners quickly found that 32 ACP would almost fit, at a lower price. The 32 ACP was a little more powerful than the 35 S&W, and jams were frequent, which did nothing for sales, and by 1921, when production sensibly ceased, only 8350 had been sold. There were many minor variants on the original design.

The original 1913-type Smith & Wesson 35-caliber pistol.

dard M686, this has a seven-chamber 357 Magnum cylinder (one more than normal) and full-lug barrels measuring 2.5, 4 or 6 inches. The front sight is a red blade mounted on a ramp, the rear sight is adjustable, and the barrel rib is drilled-and-tapped for optical-

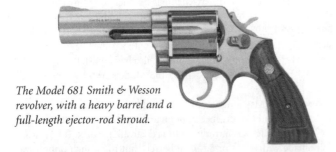

The Model 681 Smith & Wesson revolver, with a heavy barrel and a full-length ejector-rod shroud.

sight mounts. The guns are satin-finish stainless steel and have black rubber Hogue grips.

• *Model 686 Plus Mountain Gun* A variant of the M686 Plus, retaining a seven-chamber cylinder, this has a tapering 4-inch barrel with a half-length ejector-rod shroud. The sights are adjustable and black rubber Hogue grips are standard. Empty weight is about 44 oz.

• *Model 686 PowerPort* (1995 to date) This has a 6-inch barrel with a full-length ejector-rod shroud and an integral compensator. Consequently, the pinned blacked Patridge sight is set back from the muzzle. The barrel is also tapped and drilled to accept optical-sight mounts. The rear sight is adjustable, the grips are sculpted black-rubber Hogue patterns and the finish is satin stainless.

Model 696 (1997-2001) Built of stainless steel on the "L" frame and chambered for the 44 S&W Special round, this gun had a 3-inch heavy

Automatic Pistol (32-caliber, 1924-36) Undismayed by the poor reception of the 35 model, S&W tried again, changing the caliber to the standard 32 ACP and simplifying the design. But it was still expensive to make, with a sale price some 30 percent above that of the competition, and this, together with the US firearms laws of 1926 and the Depression, was enough to ruin its chances. Less than 1000 were sold.

Chiefs Special series (1999 to date) These are small "ultra-compact" derivatives of the basic Smith & Wesson double-action pistol design. They are easily identified by "Chiefs" and "Special" on the left side of the slide, separated by the S&W monogram logo.

· *CS9* Chambered for the 9mm Parabellum cartridge, this has a 3-inch barrel and a 7-round magazine. An alloy frame and a steel slide give a weight of about 21 oz. The current guns have wraparound back-rubber Hogue grips and three-dot sights; the rear sight is a Novak Lo-Mount Carry pattern. Finish is currently glass-beaded stainless steel.

· *CS40* Identical with the CS9 but chambered for the 40 S&W round, this has a 3.25-inch barrel and weighs about 24 oz without its 7-round magazine. A "Two Tone" limited edition was introduced in 2001, with a blacked alloy frame and a satin-finish stainless-steel slide. Only a few guns of this type have been made.

· *CS45* The largest of the Chiefs Special series, this is offered only in 45 ACP. The barrel measures 3.25 inches, giving an overall length of 6.5 inches and an empty weight of about 24 oz. Magazines hold six rounds. The grips, sights and finish duplicate the current CS9 (above).

∼ ENHANCED SIGMA SERIES ∼

See "Sigma series", below.

Model 22A (1997 to date) A new blowback design intended to supplement the 422 series, this is easily recognized by its well-raked grip and a separate rail for optical sights above the steel slide. Guns are currently being offered with barrels of 4, 5.5 and 7 inches, giving an overall length of 8-11 inches and weights of 28-42 oz without their 10-round magazines. A fixed Patridge front sight and an adjustable target-type rear sight are standard on all but the post-2001 5.5-inch heavyweight or "bull-barrel" option, which can also have a green-dot HiViz front sight. Guns with 4-inch barrels have black polymer grips, while those with standard 5.5- and 7-inch barrels have Soft Touch grips. The bull-barrel guns have thumbrest-type wood grips (with Patridge front sights) or Soft Touch grips (with HiViz front sights). All Model 22 pistols have alloy frames and stainless-steel slides, finished in black.

· *Model 22A Target* A designation sometimes applied to the target-shooting version of the basic 22A, with the 5.5-inch heavy "bull" barrel, adjustable sights and laminated thumbrest-style grips.

· *Model 22S* (1997 to date) This differs from the 22A solely in the material of the slide and frame, which are entirely gray-finish stainless steel. This raises weight to about 41 oz with the standard 5.5-inch barrel. The options are currently the same as those of the 22A, except that the 4-inch barrel is not available. HiViz sights are usually orange-dot types.

· *Model 22S Target* (1997 to date) An alternative designation for the original stainless-steel version of the Model 22A Target listed previously, this can be easily distinguished by its finish. In addition, it weighs about 48 oz with an empty magazine.

Model 39 (1957-82) Credited to Joe Norman, S&W's chief designer, this was the first large-caliber double-action design to be manufactured in the USA. Work began soon after World War II had ended, and the prototype, known as "X-46", was finished in October 1948. Work continued slowly until the US Army requested pistols for trials in 1953. The first double-action guns were assembled in December 1954, followed by a pair of single-action alternatives. When the numerical designation system was adopted, these became the Model 39 and Model 44 (q.v.), respectively.

The well-tried Browning locking mechanism was retained, relying on a shaped cam beneath the chamber pulling the barrel down far enough to disengage a single lug above the chamber from the inside of the slide. Applying the Walther-style safety catch/de-cocking lever on the rear left side of the slide locked the firing pin and lowered the hammer. The M39 was accurate and reliable enough to attract the attention of the US armed forces, but only the US Navy and the Special Forces purchased guns of this type in quantity. Chambered for the 9mm

The 9mm Parabellum S&W Model 39 was the first double-action pistol to be made in the USA.

Parabellum round, with an 8-round single-column magazine, the M39 had a 4-inch barrel and blue or nickel finish. Grips were checkered walnut. Most of the guns had steel slides and alloy frames, but about 930 steel-frame examples were assembled in 1966 from parts that had been in-store for some time.

The thumb piece of the de-cocking/safety lever was lengthened in 1957 after about 2000 had been made, but this did not affect the designation. However, replacing the original spring-claw extractor with a narrow bar powered by a coil spring produced the "Model 39-2" in 1971. The "Model 39-1" was the 1961-vintage 38 AMU, subsequently designated "Model 52-A" (q.v.).

Model 41 (or "Model 41 Target", 1957 to date) This, S&W's first 22-caliber target automatic, was a carefully made and very accurate blowback design. The steel slide and frame made the gun comparatively heavy (41-44 oz depending on barrel), but the additional weight reduced the effect of body tremors and the guns soon attained a reputation for shooting exceptionally accurately "out of the box". Barrel options were restricted to a 5-inch lightweight pattern, a slab-sided 5.5-inch heavy type (guns so fitted were sometimes known as "M41 HB"), and a 7.4-inch version that could accept auxiliary weights on a rail beneath the muzzle. The 5.5-inch barrel could be ordered with a front sight that extended beyond the muzzle, and the 7.4-inch variety would accept a compensator/muzzle weight. Finish was almost always blue, and the thumb-rest style grips were invariably checkered walnut.

The basic design was revised in 1994 when hardwood grips replaced walnut. The original S&W-type micro-adjustable rear sight gave way to a Millet design, and the top of the frame was drilled and tapped to receive optical-sight mounts.

Guns being made in 2003 were restricted to 5.5- and 7-inch barrels, with Patridge front and adjustable target-type rear sights. They have hardwood thumb-rest grips and are finished in blue. The long-barreled gun, 12 inches overall, weighs about 42 oz without its 10-round magazine.

· *Model 41-1* (1960-2) Intended for rapid-fire competitions, this was chambered for the 22 Short rimfire round. The frame and slide were alloy, and the 7.4-inch barrel, compensator and auxiliary weights were standard. However, the gun was not particularly successful and only about 1000 were made.

· *Model 46* (1960-8) Developed in 1959 for the US Air Force, this lacked some of the detailed equipment of the Model 41. The guns were fitted with 7-inch barrels and finished in a dull blue. However,

A heavy-barrel Smith & Wesson M41 22 rimfire target pistol.

the standard 5-inch light or 5.5-inch heavy barrels were also used during the time that small-scale commercial production was undertaken (c. 1964-8). Only about 4000 guns were ever made, more than half of them with the 7-inch barrel.

Model 44 (1954-6) This designation was reserved for the single-action derivative of the Model 39 (q.v.). However, production had ceased some months before the numerical designations were adopted — after only about 800 had been made — and none of the "Model 44" guns were ever marked in this way. The single-action pistols were carried in S&W catalogs until the summer of 1959 in the hope that interest would be stimulated, but nothing more came of the project.

Model 52 (first type, 1961-3) Although resembling a combat weapon, this was designed specifically as a target pistol. It is little more than a Model 39 chambered specifically for 38 S&W Special Mid-Range Wadcutter ammunition, with micro-adjustable target sights and an adjustable trigger stop. The design of the barrel bushing was adjusted to minimize wear, and extra care was taken during assembly. The barrel was 5 inches long, the grips were checkered walnut and the magazine capacity was usually restricted to five rounds. Production totaled about 3500.

- *Model 52A* This was a version of the Model 39 (q.v.), developed in 1960-1 in response to a request from the US Army Marksmanship Unit, that chambered a cartridge known as the "38 AMU". Smith & Wesson initially designated the AMU guns "Model 39-1" but then had a change of heart and switched to "Model 52". However, the Army rejected the Smith & Wesson submission, and all 87 guns were sold commercially in 1964. They originally had barrels marked "38 A.M.U. CTG.", visible through the ejection port, and could be identified by "A"-suffix designations on the left side of the frame above the trigger guard. The suffix was intended to distinguish them from the true Model 52 described previously.
- *Model 52-1* (1963-71) This was a refinement of the original Model 52, with a purpose-built single-action trigger mechanism instead of the conventional double-action pattern restricted to single action by a set screw.
- *Model 52-2* (1971-93) The last variation of the basic design could

Smith & Wesson's Model 59 pistol, based on the M39, introduced a double-column magazine.

be identified by the design of the extractor, which was a narrow bar driven by a coil spring instead of the original broad sprung claw. Guns of this type are still being assembled on an irregular basis by the S&W Performance Center and advertised as the "most accurate 9mm target pistol available".

Model 59 (1971-82) First made experimentally in the summer of 1964, this project was not accorded priority until the US Navy ordered some for trials in 1969. The gun was an enlarged Model 39, chambering the 9mm Parabellum cartridge, with a 14-round double-column magazine. The butt had a straight backstrap, instead of the curved one of the earlier pistol, and the grips were checkered plastic. The grip straps were serrated (on all but the earliest guns) to facilitate grasp.

Model 61 (or "Escort", 1970-4) Development of this gun, the only true "pocket pistol" ever to be made by Smith & Wesson, began in 1963. The M61 was chambered for the 22 LR rimfire round and had a 2.5-inch barrel. Offered in blue or nickel finish with checkered black plastic grips, it had rudimentary fixed sights and a 5-round single-column magazine in the butt. The designation advanced to "61-1" in May 1970, when a magazine safety system was fitted; to "61-2" in September 1970, when a barrel-nut was added; and finally to "61-3" in July 1971, when a forged aluminum-alloy frame was adopted.

The Model 61 Escort, a 25 ACP pocket Smith & Wesson, was not particularly successful.

Model 410 (1996 to date) This is an economy version of the 4000 series, originally with fixed sights, a one-piece plastic grip and a matte-blue finish on the alloy frame and carbon-steel slide. Chambered for the 40 S&W cartridge, it has a 4-inch barrel and a traditional double-action trigger system. The de-cocking lever/safety catch lies on the slide. The "Value Series" M410 being made in 2003 has a straight backstrap, black polymer grips and either white-dot sights or a combination of a green-dot HiViz front sight and a fixed open "V"-notch. The alloy frame and carbon-steel slide have a matte-black finish.

- *Model 410S* (2001 to date) A minor variant of the M410 and available only with white-dot combat sights, this offers a bead-blasted matte alloy frame and a satin-finish stainless-steel slide.
- *Model 410 Two-Tone* (1998 only) This limited edition had a bright finish alloy frame and a black slide.

Model 411 (1993-4) The predecessor of the M410 (above), this was the original budget-price version of the 40-caliber 4000 series (q.v.), with a 4-inch barrel, an alloy frame, a steel slide, fixed sights and a wraparound rubber grip. Overall length was about 7.5 inches, weight averaging 29 oz without the 11-round magazine. The finish is matte blue. The restriction in magazine capacity introduced in the USA in 1994 led to the designation "M410" being substituted for "M411".

Model 422 (1987-2001) The Model 41 relied on the breechblock unit moving in a slotted slide and attached to the return spring by arms reaching forward below the barrel, somewhat similar to the 1901-type Mannlicher. The design of the Model 422, however, was different. The barrel lies at the bottom of the barrel-unit so that the thrust lies low in the shooter's hand, and there is a half-slide with an integral breechblock behind the barrel unit. The grip is slender and more upright, with a trigger guard that is recurved to allow a two-hand grip.

- *M422 Field* Offered with barrels of 4.5 or 6 inches, with an alloy frame and a matte-blue steel slide, this had a 10-round magazine. The sights were fixed and the grips were checkered plastic.
- *M422 Target* A minor variant of the Field model, this had adjustable sights and checkered walnut grips.

Model 439 (1979-88) This was an improved form of the Model 39 chambered for the 9mm Parabellum cartridge and with the 8-round single-column magazine. It had a new adjustable rear sight protected by prominent lateral wings, an ambidextrous safety catch/de-cocking lever, a new trigger-actuated firing pin lock and an improved extractor.

The S&W Model 439 was a modernized M39, with a single-column magazine.

Model 457 (1996 to date) Chambering 45 ACP ammunition, this member of the "Value Series" incorporates a traditional double-action trigger system with a de-cocking lever/safety catch on the left side of the frame ahead of the hammer. The gun is about 7.25 inches long with a 3.75-inch barrel and weighs 29 oz without its 7-round magazine. The alloy frame and carbon-steel slide are finished in matte black; the one-piece wraparound grip is black polymer, with a straight backstrap. Three-dot combat sights are standard.

- *Model 457S* (2001 to date) This is a minor variation of the M457. It has a bead-blasted finish on the alloy frame and a satin finish on the stainless-steel slide.

Model 459 (1979-87) This was an improved form of the Model 59, chambering the 9mm Parabellum cartridge. The magazine remained a 14-round double-column type. A new adjustable rear sight was protected by prominent lateral wings, the safety catch/de-cocking lever became ambidextrous, a trigger-actuated firing pin lock was developed and the extractor was improved.

Model 469 (1983-8) This was a specially shortened version of the Model 459, developed to meet a US Air Force specification. It had a shortened M459 frame with a curved backstrap, a fashionably recurved trigger guard and a "bobbed" or spurless hammer. The lightweight alloy frame and the steel slide had a matte sand-blasted blue finish. The butt had textured black plastic grips, and a spur on the magazine base acted as a finger rest. Barrels measured 3.5 inches, and the magazines held 12 9mm Parabellum rounds in double columns.

The Smith & Wesson M459 was a variant of the 439 with a double-column magazine.

Model 559 (1980-3) This was a steel-frame version of the Model 459, made only in small numbers. The magazine held 14 9mm Parabellum rounds.

Model 622 (1987-2001) This was little more than a stainless-steel version of the M422 (q.v.) made in the same "Field" and "Target" patterns.

- *Model 622 VR* (1996-2001) Distinguished by a ventilated rib above the barrel, this also had a blacked trigger and a rounded trigger guard that lacked the recurve of its predecessors. The sights were adjustable and the grips were black polymer.

Identified by its small size and bobbed hammer, the compact S&W Model 469 chambered the 9mm Parabellum round.

Model 639 (1984-8) This was little more than a variant of the Model 439 made entirely of stainless steel.

Model 645 (1985-8) This was an enlarged 45 ACP derivative of the 9mm Model 439. The muzzle was carried in a fixed-barrel bushing, giving better accuracy and simpler field stripping. The magazine well was beveled to facilitate quick loading, and the magazine body had numbers to indicate the ammunition remaining. There were three safety systems: a slide-mounted safety catch locked the firing pin and dropped the hammer; an automatic firing-pin safety locked the firing pin except when the trigger was about to release the hammer; and a magazine safety locked both trigger and hammer when the magazine was removed. Made of stainless steel, the guns had 5-inch barrels, fixed or adjustable sights, and ambidextrous controls. Their magazines held eight rounds in a single row.

The 9mm S&W Model 559.

Model 659 (1982-8) This was a stainless-steel version of the 9mm Parabellum Model 459, with ambidextrous controls and a 14-round magazine.

Model 669 (1986-8) A short-lived stainless-steel variant of the Model 469, this was made only in small quantities.

Model 745 (IPSC, 1986-90) Chambered for the 45 ACP cartridge, with an eight-round single-column magazine, this was a special single-action version of the M645 described above. It had a stainless-steel slide, a carbon-steel frame, adjustable sights and checkered walnut grips.

Model 908 (1995 to date) This is an "economy" version of the stan-

Smith & Wesson's Model 639 was a stainless-steel version of the M439.

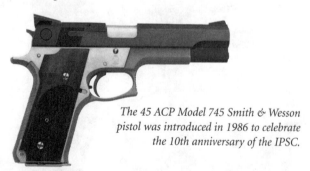

Chambered for the 45 ACP round, the S&W Model 645 was an enlargement of the basic M39 design.

dard 9mm Parabellum compact guns, with fixed sights, an alloy frame, a carbon-steel slide and a traditional double-action trigger. The decocking lever/safety catch on the slide is ambidextrous. The finish is matte blue and the grips are one-piece plastic with a straight backstrap. It is 6.9 inches long with a 3.5-inch barrel and an empty weight of about 26 oz without its 8-round magazine. The guns being made in 2003 had three-dot combat sights and matte-black finish.

- *Model 908S* (1999 to date) Essentially the same as the M908, this has a bead-blasted aluminum alloy frame and a satin-finish stainless-steel slide.

Model 909 (1995-7) This was a full-size gun, with a 4-inch barrel and a backstrap that curved to fit the shooter's palm. It also had a single-column magazine.

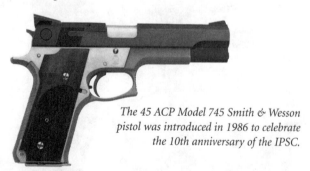

The 45 ACP Model 745 Smith & Wesson pistol was introduced in 1986 to celebrate the 10th anniversary of the IPSC.

Model 910 (1995 to date) Another of the full-size 9mm Parabellum versions, this has a straight backstrap and a double-column magazine that, for the US market at least, is currently restricted to 10 rounds. The gun is about 7.4 inches long and weighs 28 oz empty. The sights are usually three-dot combat patterns, but orange-dot HiViz front and open "V"-notch rear sights are optional. The alloy frame and carbon-steel slide are blacked.

- *Model 910S* (1999 to date) This is a minor variant of the M910 with a stainless-steel slide. The alloy frame has a matte bead-blasted finish.

Model 915 (1993-7?) This 9mm Parabellum pistol had a 4-inch barrel, giving an overall length of about 7.5 inches and a weight of 28 oz

without the magazine. Finished in matte blue with a wraparound rubber grip, it also had fixed sights.

Model 1000 series (1990-2001) Chambered for the 10mm Auto cartridge, these guns were otherwise similar to the 5900 series. However, they were somewhat larger and usually had reduced-capacity magazines.

- *Model 1006* Made entirely of stainless steel, this has a 5-inch barrel and a 9-round magazine. The sights may be fixed or adjustable.
- *Model 1066* Essentially similar to the M1006, this is a compact variant with a 4.25-inch barrel. It was discontinued in 1993.

A Model 1076 "FBI" Smith & Wesson, chambered for the 40 S&W round.

- *Model 1076* This is a special design, originally intended for the FBI, with the de-cocking lever on the left side of the frame instead of the slide.
- *Model 1086* Discontinued in 1993, this was a variant of the compact M1066 with a double-action-only trigger mechanism. It was readily identified by its short, plain-sided slide.

Model 2206 (1990-2001) A blowback design chambered for the 22 LR rimfire round, this has an adjustable rear sight and a barrel measuring 4.5 or 6 inches. The detachable box magazine held 12 rounds until 1994 and 10 thereafter. The frame and slide are stainless steel.

- *M2206 TGT* (1995-2001) The target-shooting adaptation of the basic pistol with a selected 6-inch barrel, this also had a matted top-rib to minimize reflections. The front sight is a Patridge design, and the rear sight is a micro-adjustable Millet pattern. The trigger has a serrated blade and an adjustable stop.

Model 2214 (1990-2001) Also known as "The Sportsman", this 22 LR rimfire plinker had a 3-inch barrel and an eight-round magazine. The frame was blacked alloy, the slide was blued carbon steel and the grips were plastic.

Model 3900 series (1989-2002, except some TSW patterns) This consists of a variety of 9mm Parabellum guns derived from the Model 39 and 439, the so-called "First Generation" and "Second Generation" patterns. They all have single-column magazines (cf., Model 5900).

- *Model 3904* This had a 4-inch fixed barrel, an eight-round magazine, a steel slide and an alloy frame with a recurved trigger guard. The wraparound one-piece grips were Delrin and three-dot "combat" sights were standard.
- *Model 3906* This was a stainless-steel version of the M3904.

The 22-rimfire Model 2206, in stainless steel.

A 9mm Model 3904 Smith & Wesson, with a one-piece grip and fixed sights.

- *Model 3913* A shortened "Mini" or "Compact" version of the M3904 with a 3.5-inch barrel (though retaining the full-capacity magazine), this had a steel slide and an alloy frame. The trigger guard was usually rounded.
- *Model 3913 LS* This "LadySmith" pistol is mechanically identical with the original M3913, but the design was altered to eliminate the step in the underside of the frame immediately ahead of the trigger guard. The guns being made in 2003, with 8-round magazines, have white-dot front and two-dot Novak Lo-Mount Carry rear sights; gray straight-back polymer grips; and a glass-bead finish to the alloy frames and stainless-steel slides.
- *Model 3913 TSW* (1997 to date) The first of the "Tactical Smith & Wesson" (TSW) series to be listed, this is really little more than the M3913 — 9mm Parabellum, 8-round magazine — with a "stainless" finish on the alloy frame and stainless-steel slide. The front sight is a single white-dot type, the rear sight is a two-dot Novak Lo-Mount Carry and a rail for designators or light sources has been added beneath the front of the frame. The guns also have fixed barrel bushings, ambidextrous de-cocking levers and checkering on the front butt-straps. The TSW series is easily identified by markings that include "TACTICAL", preceded by the caliber ("9", "40", "45"), on the left side of the slide ahead of the manufacturer's address and the S&W monogram logo.

  The current M3913 TSW is 6.75 inches long, has a 3.5-inch barrel and weighs about 25 oz without its magazine. The black one-piece polymer grips have a straight back, and the sights are combinations of a white dot and two-dot Novak Lo-Mount Carry patterns. The alloy frame has a matte finish, achieved by bead-blasting, and the slide is satin-finish stainless steel
- *Model 3914* A stainless-steel version of the M3913.
- *Model 3914 LS* The stainless-steel equivalent of the M3913 LS, this also shared the straight-line frame contours.
- *Model 3953* (1990-3, 1998-2002) This was the double-action-only version of the M3913.
- *Model 3953 TSW* A "Tactical Smith & Wesson" version of the double-action-only 9mm Parabellum M3953, with an accessory rail beneath the frame. See "M3913 TSW" for additional details.
- *Model 3954* (1990-3) A double-action-only version of the M3904, this can be recognized by its smooth-sided slide. The safety catch/de-cocking lever has been eliminated.

Model 4000 series (1990-2002, except TSW patterns) These guns are generally similar to the 5900 series but chamber the 40 S&W cartridge that was evolved to compete with the 10mm Auto round. The S&W design is shorter than 10mm Auto, requiring no modification to magazine wells that were originally designed for the 9mm Parabellum round.
- *Model 4003* Chambered for 40 S&W instead of 9mm Parabellum, this looks like a heavier version of the M5903. It has a 4-inch barrel, an 11-round staggered-column magazine (10 rounds on guns sold in the USA after 1994) and a serrated hammer. The frame is alloy,

and the slide is stainless steel with empty weight being about 29 oz.
- *Model 4003 TSW* (1997 to date) A "Tactical Smith & Wesson" version of the traditional double-action M4003, with an accessory rail beneath the frame. The guns being made in 2003 had a white dot front sight, a two-dot Novak Lo-Mount Carry rear sight and black polymer grips with a straight backstrap. Their frames and slides had a satin finish. See "M3913 TSW" for additional details.
- *Model 4004* Discontinued in 1993, this had an alloy frame and a blued carbon-steel slide.
- *Model 4006* Apart from the change in caliber, this was virtually identical to the M5906. It was made of stainless steel and had an 11-shot magazine. Guns of this type weighed about 8 oz more than those with alloy frames.

The 40-caliber S&W M4006 pistol, with an adjustable rear sight.

- *Model 4006 TSW* (1997 to date) A "Tactical Smith & Wesson" version of the traditional double-action stainless-steel M4006, with an accessory rail beneath the frame. Examples from 2003 had white dot sights, the rear sight being adjustable for elevation, and weighed about 38 oz compared with 29 oz for the alloy-frame M4003 TSW. See "M3913 TSW" for additional details.
- *Model 4013* A compact version of the M4003, this had a 3.5-inch barrel and an 8-round magazine. The slide was stainless steel; the frame was alloy.
- *Model 4013 TSW* (1997 to date) A "Tactical Smith & Wesson" version of the traditional double-action M4013 compact, with an accessory rail beneath the frame. The guns being made in 2003 had 9-round magazines, black polymer grips with a curved backstrap and a combination of bead-blasted alloy frame and satin-stainless slide. The front sight was a white dot and the rear sight was a two-dot Novak Lo-Mount Carry design. See "M3913 TSW" for additional details.
- *Model 4014* This was a short-barreled variant of the M4004, with a blued steel slide and an alloy frame.
- *Model 4026* An adaptation of the M4006 and made entirely of stainless steel, this had the de-cocking lever on the frame instead of the slide.
- *Model 4040 PD Sc* (2003) The first of the "compact" S&W pistols to feature a scandium-alloy frame, this 40 S&W gun has a seven-round single-column magazine, a 3.5-inch barrel and Hogue combat grips. The three-dot sights include a Novak Lo-Mount Carry rear sight. Finish is matte black, with the "electron orbital" logo on the left side of the frame above the trigger and "AirLite PD" on the left side of the slide. The pistol weighs 26 oz without its magazine.
- *Model 4043* Introduced in 1991, this was a full-size double-action-only gun with a 4-inch barrel, a carbon-steel slide and an alloy frame.
- *Model 4043 TSW* (1997-2002) A "Tactical Smith & Wesson" version of the traditional double-action M4043, with an accessory rail beneath the frame. See "M3913 TSW" for additional details.

- *Model 4046* A double-action-only version of the M4006 dating from 1991, this had a plain-sided slide and a semi-bobbed hammer. It is made entirely of stainless steel.
- *Model 4046 TSW* (1997-2002) A "Tactical Smith & Wesson" version of the double-action-only stainless-steel M4046, with an accessory rail beneath the frame. See "M3913 TSW" for additional details.
- *Model 4053* This was a double-action-only version of the M4013. It had a 3.25-inch barrel, an 8-round magazine, an alloy frame and a plain-sided stainless steel slide.
- *Model 4053 TSW* (1997-2002) A "Tactical Smith & Wesson" version of the double-action-only M4053, with an accessory rail beneath the frame and a nine-round magazine. See "M3913 TSW" for additional details.
- *Model 4054* Abandoned in 1993, this was a double-action-only version of the compact 40-caliber M4014 with a blued steel slide.
- *Model 4056 TSW* (1997-2002) Incorporating a traditional double-action trigger system, this 40-caliber gun had a 3.5-inch barrel and a 90-round magazine. It also had white three-dot "combat" sights, a curved backstrap and wraparound grips. Finish was matte stainless, though the frame was alloy. Weight with an empty magazine was about 36 oz.

Model 4500 series (1989-2002, except TSW patterns) The largest of the "Third Generation" Smith & Wessons, these double-action pistols all chamber the 45 ACP cartridge.

- *Model 4503* Offered with a 5-inch barrel and an 8-round single-column magazine, this has a blued steel slide and frame.
- *Model 4506* A version of the M4005 made entirely of stainless steel, this may be found with fixed or adjustable sights.
- *Model 4513 TSW* (1997 to date) A "Tactical Smith & Wesson" version of the compact traditional double-action guns, with an accessory rail beneath the frame. The slide is blued steel, the barrel measures 3.75 inches and the single-column magazine holds seven rounds. The guns are 7.75 inches long and weigh about 29 oz. They have a combination of white-dot front and two-dot Novak Lo-Mount Carry rear sights. The black polymer grips have straight backstraps, the alloy frame is bead-blasted and the stainless-steel slide has a satin finish. See "M3913 TSW" for additional details.
- *Model 4516* (1990-1, 1994 to date?) This is the compact version of the M4506, with a 3.75-inch barrel and a 7-round magazine. The slide and the frame are both made of stainless steel.
- *Model 4536* A "compact" stainless-steel gun with a 3.75-inch barrel and a 7-round magazine, this has the de-cocking lever on the frame instead of the slide.
- *Model 4546* Easily identified by its plain-sided slide, this is a 5-inch-barreled gun with a double-action-only trigger system and a "semi-bob" hammer. It is made entirely of stainless steel.
- *Model 4553 TSW* (1997-2002) A "Tactical Smith & Wesson" version of the compact double-action-only design, with an accessory rail beneath the frame. The slide was blued steel, the barrel measured 3.75 inches and the single-column magazine held seven rounds. See "M3913 TSW" for additional details.
- *Model 4563 TSW* (1997 to date) A "Tactical Smith & Wesson" version of the traditional double-action M4505, with an accessory rail beneath the frame. The slide is blued steel, the barrel measures 4.25 inches, the gun weighs about 31 oz and the single-column magazine holds eight rounds. The front sight is a white dot, and the rear sight is a two-dot Novak Lo-Mount Carry. The black polymer wraparound grips have a straight backstrap; finish is a combination of a bead-blasted alloy frame and a satin-finish stainless steel slide. See "M3913 TSW" for additional details.
- *Model 4566 TSW* (1997 to date) This is a stainless-steel version of the M4563 TSW (above), weighing about 39 oz. See "M3913 TSW" for additional details.

- *Model 4583 TSW* (1997-2002) A double-action-only version of the M4563, with a plain-sided slide and an accessory rail beneath the frame. See "M3913 TSW" for additional details.
- *Model 4586 TSW* (1997-2002) This was a stainless-steel variant of the M4583, retaining the double-action-only trigger system and the accessory rail beneath the frame. It was made of stainless steel. See "M3913 TSW" for additional details.

Model 5900 series (1989-2002, except TSW patterns) In 1989, Smith & Wesson announced their "Third Generation" series of pistols, replacing all previous heavy-caliber models except the Model 52. Features incorporated in these pistols included a fixed barrel bushing, greatly improved trigger pull, three-dot sights, improved wraparound grips, beveled magazine aperture and the triple safety system described above. Sights may be fixed or adjustable. The guns all chamber the 9mm Parabellum round and have double-column high-capacity magazines.

- *Model 5903* This conventional de-cocking gun has an alloy frame and a stainless-steel slide. The magazine holds 15 rounds and the front of the trigger guard is recurved to allow a comfortable two-hand grip.
- *Model 5903 TSW* (1997 to date) A "Tactical Smith & Wesson" version of the traditional double-action M5903, with an accessory rail beneath the frame. The slide was originally blued steel, the barrel is 4 inches long and the double-column magazine is restricted (in the US market at least) to 10 rounds. The guns being made in 2003 are 7.5 inches long and weigh 29 oz empty. They have white-dot front sights, two-dot Novak Lo-Mount Carry rear sights and black polymer grips with a curved backstrap. Finish is a combination of a bead-blasted alloy frame and a satin-stainless slide. See "M3913 TSW" for additional details.

The Model 5904 Smith & Wesson, a 9mm pistol with a high-capacity magazine.

- *Model 5904* A variant of the M5903, this has an alloy frame, a carbon-steel slide and stainless-steel barrel. Magazine capacity is 15, and the trigger guard is usually rounded.
- *Model 5906* This is an M5904 made entirely of stainless steel.
- *Model 5906 Special Edition* Introduced in 1993, this offered a special machined finish on the frame and slide, and one-piece wraparound Xenoy grips. A Novak LoMount Carry rear sight was fitted.
- *Model 5906 TSW* (1997 to date) A "Tactical Smith & Wesson" version of the traditional double-action M5906, with an accessory rail beneath the frame. The sights were originally fixed, though an adjustable rear sight and Tritium-insert night sights could be obtained to order. Guns being made in 2003 had white-dot front sights and either fixed two-dot Novak Lo-Mount Carry rear sights or two-dot sights that are adjustable for elevation. Construction is satin-finish stainless steel throughout. See "M3913 TSW" for additional details.
- *Model 5926* This was a variant of the M5906, stainless steel throughout, with the de-cocking lever on the frame instead of the slide. It was abandoned in 1993 after only a few had been made.

- *Model 5943 TSW* (1997-2002) A "Tactical Smith & Wesson" version of the double-action-only design, with an accessory rail beneath the frame. The slide was blued steel, the barrel was 4 inches long and the double-column magazine was restricted (in the US market at least) to 10 rounds. See "M3913 TSW" for additional details.
- *Model 5946* A 9mm double-action-only design, this can be identified by the lack of a de-cocking lever or safety catch — and also by a distinctive "semi-bob" hammer.
- *Model 5946 TSW* (1997-2002) A "Tactical Smith & Wesson" version of the M5946, retaining the double-action-only trigger system. It had an accessory rail beneath the frame, a blued-steel slide, and double-column magazines that are restricted (in the US market at least) to 10 rounds. See "M3913 TSW" for additional details.

Model 6900 series (1989-2001) These are compact versions of the 5900 pattern with 3.5-inch barrels and 12-round double-column magazines.

A compact design with a fixed sight, the Smith & Wesson M6904 chambers the 9mm Parabellum cartridge.

- *Model 6904* This version has an alloy frame, a steel slide and a stainless-steel barrel. The sights are fixed, the front of the guard is shaped to facilitate a two-hand grip and the hammer is generally bobbed.
- *Model 6906* A stainless-steel version of the M6904, this is identical mechanically.
- *Model 6946* Readily identifiable by the plain slide, this is a double-action-only version of the stainless-steel M6906.

Sigma series (1994 to date) This represents a considerable departure from the traditional Smith & Wesson pistols and an attempt to compete with guns such as the Glock (q.v.) that incorporated a variety of synthetic components. The Sigma pistol has a stainless-steel barrel, a carbon-steel slide and a polymer frame/grip unit. It is locked by a variation of the Colt-Browning rising barrel, using a cam-bar in the frame to raise the squared chamber-top into the ejection port, and is fired by a striker instead of a hammer. Safety is ensured by the design of the two-piece trigger lever, which rocks back until a small blade no longer aligns with the frame; the trigger can then be pulled back to fire the gun. Immediately before the striker is released, the trigger disengages the firing-pin lock that otherwise prevents the gun from firing if it is dropped on a hard surface. There is also an interlock to prevent the trigger releasing the striker if the magazine has been removed.

An "Enhanced Sigma" series was introduced in 1999, initially distinguished by "E"-suffix designations, though, with the introduction of other patterns, the distinction is no longer being used. Enhancements included a shorter trigger pull, improvements to the extractor and ejector, an enlarged ejection port, a guard-lip on the frame beneath the hold-open latch and checkering on the sides of the grip. A rail for designators or light-projectors was added to the frame ahead of the trigger guard.

- *SW9C* (1994 –2001) The "Compact" 9mm Parabellum version of the Sigma had a 3.5-inch barrel.
- *SW9E* (1999-2002) The "enhanced" version of the full-size gun, with the improvements listed in the introductory text above. The slide is black Melonite-finished stainless steel, and the sights have Tritium "night light" inserts.
- *SW9F* (1994-2001) This was the "Full-size" version in 9mm Parabellum, originally designed with a 4-inch barrel and a 17-round magazine though now supplied with capacity restricted to 10 rounds to satisfy the current US gun laws.
- *SW9G* (2001 to date) A variant of the SW9F, this has a stainless-steel slide finished in black Melonite and a polymer frame in NATO green. The sights are currently three-dot combat patterns.
- *SW9M* (1995-2001) An "ultra-compact" version of the basic design, this has a 3.25-inch barrel and a magazine restricted to seven rounds. It weighs about 18 oz empty.
- *SW9P* (2001 to date) This "Ported" variant is distinguished by a slot on either side of the front sight that allows propellant gas to bleed through ports in the barrel to act as a rudimentary compensator. The current guns have three-dot combat sights and Melonite finish on the slide. The polymer frame is black.
- *SW9V* (1998-2002) These are 9mm Parabellum guns with white-dot "combat" sights, satin-finish stainless-steel slides and gray or black polymer frames.
- *SW9VE* (2001 to date) An "Enhanced" version of the SW9V (see introductory text for details), with a stainless-steel slide. The guns being made in 2003 are about 7.25 inches long, have 4-inch barrels and weigh 25 oz without their 10-round magazines. The sights are three-dot combat patterns, the frame is black polymer and the slide is satin-finish stainless steel.
- *SW40C* (1994-2001) The "Compact" variant of the 40 S&W Sigma had a 3.5-inch barrel.
- *SW40E* (1999-2002) An "Enhanced" version of the SW40F, with an assortment of detail improvements (see introductory text), black Melonite finish on the stainless-steel slide and Tritium "night sight" inserts.
- *SW40F* (1994 –2001) The "Full-size" 40 S&W version, this has a 4-inch barrel. The magazine was designed to hold 15 rounds, but is now restricted to 10 rounds to comply with current US gun laws.
- *SW40G* (2001 to date) A variant of the SW40F, this has a stainless-steel slide finished in black Melonite and a polymer frame in NATO green.
- *SW40M* (1995-2001) Distinguished by its 3.25-inch barrel and shortened grip, restricting magazine capacity to seven rounds, this is the ultra-compact representative of the 40-caliber Sigma series.
- *SW40P* (2001 to date) Distinguished by slots on either side of the front sight to allow propellant gas to bleed through ports in the barrel, this 40 S&W pistol is otherwise the same as the SW9M.
- *SW40V* (1998-2002) These are 40-caliber guns with white-dot "combat" sights, satin-finish stainless-steel slides and gray or black polymer frames.
- *SW40VE* (2001 to date) An "Enhanced" version of the SW40V, with the detail improvements described above (see introductory text). The slide is stainless steel.

SW99 series (2000 to date) Developed with an eye on military contracts, this is an intriguing combination of a polymer frame supplied by Walther (essentially similar to that of the Walther P99, q.v.) and a slide manufactured by Smith & Wesson. The features include a special safety trigger system ("Saf-T-Trigger"), a de-cocking button flush with the slide, a magazine-release button integrated with the trigger guard and a rail for designators and light projectors beneath the muzzle. The Melonite-finish slide has two sets of retraction grips (front and rear) and adjustable white-dot or Tritium night sights. Like the Walther, the Smith & Wesson is a striker-fired adaptation of the Colt-Browning barrel-dropping system, relying on a cam-finger instead of a link and on the squared chamber-top rising into the enlarged ejection port instead of two barrel-ribs engaging recesses in the underside of the slide. The tip of the striker projects from the back of the slide when the mechanism is cocked. A pivoting extractor bar doubles as a loading indicator, exposing a red mark on the lower rear of its recess when a cartridge is in the chamber. The shape of the butt can be altered by exchanging the backstrap.

- *SW99* (9mm types) The full-size gun is 7.1 inches long, has a 4-inch barrel and weighs about 25 oz without its 10-round magazine. It has white-dot or Tritium sights and is finished in black (self-colored polymer frame/grip unit, Melonite on the stainless-steel slide). A compact version introduced in 2003 is 6.6 inches long, has a 3.5-inch barrel and weighs about 23 oz. It is immediately recognizable by its short butt, though use of a staggered-column magazine allows 10 rounds to be carried.
- *SW99* (40 S&W types) Identical mechanically with the 9mm Parabellum guns, these are also made in full-length and compact versions. Magazine capacities are 8 rounds for the compact and 10 rounds for the standard gun, which is 7.25 inches long and has a barrel measuring 4.1 inches.
- *SW99* (45 ACP type) Introduced in 2003, this is 7.4 inches long, has a 4.25-inch barrel and weighs about 26 oz. The magazine holds nine rounds in a staggered column. Sights, construction and finish are the same as the 9mm and 40-caliber guns.

SW380 (1995-9?) Though customarily included in the Sigma series, this is a compact blowback design chambering the 380 ACP cartridge. It has a simplified short-butt frame, and the sights are nothing but a groove along the top of the slide. The gun is about 5.8 inches long, with a 3-inch barrel, and weighs 14 oz without its six-round magazine.

SW1911 (2003) This is a modernized version of the M1911A1 Colt-Browning, incorporating a firing-pin safety release and a variety of special components, including Wolff springs, a Texas Armament match trigger, a McCormick skeleton hammer and manual safety, a Briley barrel bushing, and a Wilson extended "beavertail" grip safety. Chambered for 45 ACP, with an 8-round single-column magazine, the SW1911 is about 8.7 inches long with a 5-inch barrel and weighs 39 oz without its magazine. A two-dot Novak Lo-Mount Carry rear sight and a single-dot front sight are standard, together with black rubber Hogue grips and satin-stainless finish. The S&W monogram logo and "SW1911" lie on the left side of the slide.

∼ PERFORMANCE CENTER GUNS ∼

Originally intended as a "custom gunshop" responsible for the special features and decoration specified by individual clients, the role of the Smith & Wesson Performance Center has changed radically in recent years. In addition to traditional gunsmithing services, guns are now made in quantity either for sale through Smith & Wesson distributorships or for specialist agencies such as Lew Horton or Banger Distribution. Many different guns have been made in quantities ranging from handfuls to hundreds.

Special guns The current Smith & Wesson catalog reflects that the Performance Center "pistols feature hand-fit titanium coated bushings and slide stops for superior accuracy, and hand-lapped frames and rails for a smooth and tight fit that yields improved durability and accuracy. Revolvers feature chamfered cylinder charge holes for easy loading and extraction, adjustable-weight full under-lug barrels and porting to reduce felt recoil as well as integral scope mount slots and interchangeable front sights …" Information concerning many of these special designs will be found in the current edition of the *Standard Catalog of Firearms*. However, the guns supplied to S&W distributorships can be considered as semi-production "company items". The following are typical of the range:

- *Model 66 F Comp* Distinguished by a 3-inch ported barrel with a full-length under lug, this also has chamfered chambers in the cylinder to facilitate reloading; a matte glass-bead finish on its stainless-steel barrel, frame and cylinder; and a trigger stop. The

grips may be walnut "combat" or Hogue Bantam patterns. Guns of this type are about 8 inches long and weigh 35 oz empty.

- *Model 500 S&W Magnum Hunter* Designed to make the best of the powerful 500 S&W Magnum round, this is effectively a 21st-century version of the old Smith & Wesson Pocket Rifle (q.v.). It has a 10.5-inch barrel with a tapering full-length barrel shroud, an integral compensator and an integral Weaver-type sight rail. The grip is a special dual-density Hogue Sorbathane wraparound rubber design. The revolver also has a ball-detent yoke latch, a micro-adjustable rear sight, an exchangeable-blade front sight and a key-operated safety lock. Special features include a precision-crowned muzzle, a flash-chromed forged hammer and trigger, and an embossed mainspring. Finish is glass-bead over stainless steel. The guns, which come with a sling, are about 18 inches long and weigh a substantial 5 lb 2 oz.
- *Model 629 Comped Hunter* Something of a shock for the traditionalist, this 44 Magnum six-shot revolver is distinguished by a tapering under lug running the length of its 7.5-inch barrel to an integral two-slot compensator. A secure yoke lock-up is assisted by a sprung ball detent. The guns are stainless steel, with a glass-bead finish, and have laminated rosewood finger-groove grips. The front sight has an orange insert, the rear sight is adjustable vertically and a removable stainless-steel scope-mount rail can be attached to the barrel rib. The Comped Hunter is 12.6 inches long and weighs 52 oz.
- *Model 647 Varminter* Chambered for the new 17 Hornady Magnum rimfire round, this is another of the pistol-carbines. Made of stainless steel, with a glass-bead finish, it has a 12-inch fluted barrel with a half-length shroud carrying an integral sight rail. The front sight, mounted on a collar, can be removed when not needed. A bipod adapter is fitted, the yoke is retained by a ball detent and the hammer and trigger are flash-chromed forgings. The key-operated safety lock is also a standard feature. Overall length is about 17 inches with weight averaging 54 oz.
- *Model 945* This is a modern stainless-steel variant of the 45 ACP M1911A1 Colt-Browning, with a 5-inch barrel and an 8-round single-column magazine. The grips are a black-and-silver checkered laminate, a Wilson adjustable rear sight is standard, the safety lever is ambidextrous and the spherical barrel bushing has a titanium coating. A firing-pin plunger safety system is fitted, and the retraction grips, duplicated at the muzzle, are a fish-scale pattern. The M945 is about 8.75 inches long, weighs 42 oz and has a glass-bead finish.

Commemorative guns Smith & Wesson has also produced a variety of commemoratives, though the factory records are said to be incomplete. Information will be found in specialist sources such as the *Standard Catalog of Smith & Wesson*. A few of the most important items are listed below:

- *Model 25* (125th Anniversary Commemorative, 1977) This was a variant of the Model 25 produced in 45 Long Colt to celebrate the founding of the company in 1852. Ten thousand were made with a special gold-line version of the S&W monogram logo on the sideplate, but only 52 were finished in "Class A"—engraved, with ivory grips and accompanied by a rosewood-finish wooden case. The serial numbers had an "S&W" prefix.
- *Model 27* (Limited Edition 357 Magnum Commemorative, 1985) This was produced to celebrate the half-centenary of the commercial introduction of the legendary Magnum round in 1935. The guns had special Goncalo Alves grips, target hammers and triggers, a checkered topstrap and a ribbed 5-inch barrel. The sideplate bore "The First Magnum" over "April 8, 1935", filled in gold, within floral scrolls. The right side of the barrel was marked "50th Anniversary" over "S&W .357 Magnum" separating the dates "1935" and "1985". Production totaled 2500 guns, with "REG" serial-number prefixes.

SOCIEDAD ESPAÑOL DE ARMAS Y MUNICIONES ("SEAM")

Fabrica de Armas de Sociedad Español de Armas y Municiones, Eibar, Spain.

This was a sales organization rather than a manufactory. Most of its products appear to have come from Tomas de Urizar (q.v.) while others are identical to the products of the Fabrique d'Armes de Grande Précision (q.v.), another puzzling organization. SEAM has also been linked with the Sivispacem and Waco pistols, but these are believed to have been marketed by Thieme & Edeler (q.v.).

Praga This was a 7.65mm "Eibar"-type blowback, marked simply "CAL 7 ^{65} "PRAGA"…" on the left side of the slide; it is identifiable as a SEAM product only by the grip design, a floral band with a crown in the center. The name was probably adopted to profit from the reputation of the contemporaneous Czechoslovakian pistol and may even indicate the market into which the guns were to be sold.

SEAM (Browning type) The 6.35mm pistols bearing this name exist in several patterns, with 10, 11 or 13 finger grooves on the slide. The 11-groove version has been found with grips displaying "FL" and crossed swords, and the 10-groove pattern offers a superior finish. However, they are difficult to place chronologically. Some guns have been found with the full company name on the left side of the slide, often accompanied by "EIBAR ESPAÑA", but others display "FABRICA DE ARMAS S.E.A.M" above "PATENTE No 11627 CAL 6 ^{35}" on the slide and two different "SEAM" motifs on the grips. The presence of Spanish proofmarks indicates (depending on content) a date no earlier than 1923.

A 7.65mm "Eibar" pistol has also been identified with similar markings on the grips but only "AUTOMATIC PISTOL CAL. 7.65" over "FABRICA DE ARMAS S.E.A.M." on the slide.

The 6.35mm (25 ACP) SEAM pistol.

SEAM (Walther type) Básed on the 6.35mm Walther Model 9, though with a few manufacturing shortcuts, this had a smooth open-top slide, broad retraction grooves and a safety catch at the rear of the frame. The slide was marked "SEAM PATENT No 11.627" over "Pocket Model Cal. 6,^{35}"; the grips bore a SEAM medallion. The Spanish proofmarks suggest a date later than 1929.

Silesia This was a 7.65mm "Eibar" of below-average quality with "Automatic Pistol Cal 7^{65} "Silesia"…" on the slide and the SEAM medallion in the grips.

SOCIÉTÉ ALSACIENNE DES CONSTRUCTIONS MECANIQUES ("SACM")

Cholet, France.

After World War I had ended, the French army decided to adopt an automatic pistol. Designers attached to the small-arms factories, particularly in Saint-Étienne, began work at a leisurely pace and the opinions of commercial manufacturers were canvassed. Eventually, after a competition that had included the SE-MAS blowback and a 7.65mm version of the prototype FN-Browning High Power, a design forwarded by SACM gained approval for service as the "Modèle 1935".

This gun had been developed on the basis of patents granted in

1934 to Charles Petter, a Swiss national employed by SACM, though the design was little more than a variation on the Browning swinging-link system with the firing mechanism incorporated in a separate removable unit. The M1935 was well made, comfortable to hold and extremely reliable — though the safety catch came under criticism, being nothing but a simple half-round shaft at the end of the slide that could be rotated to prevent the hammer striking the firing pin. But, like the 1892-type revolver before it, the M1935 was handicapped by a useless cartridge. The 7.65mm Longue propelled an 87-grain bullet at 1100 ft/sec, an improvement on the M1892 revolver but still poor by military standards.

The 7.65mm Longue French SACM (Petter) M1935A pistol.

SOCIÉTÉ FRANÇAISE D'ARMES AUTOMATIQUES

Saint-Étienne, France.

Nothing is known of this company, which failed to survive World War I.

Automatique Française This unusual 6.35mm pistol was manufactured prior to 1914, based generally on the Mannlicher design with a fixed barrel and a slide that had arms passing alongside the barrel. The arms joined transversely to restrain the return spring. The barrel was exposed for most of its length. The butt was broad, with an oddly shaped grip safety in the frontstrap. The magazine-release button lay under the heel of the butt, and the grips were ornately decorated moldings. The right side of the slide was marked "AUTOMATIQUE FRANCAISE" and the company name appeared on the left side of the frame.

SOCIÉTÉ FRANÇAISE DES MUNITIONS ("SFM")

Paris, France.

Autogarde This five-shot Velo-Dog pattern revolver, chambered for the 7.65mm Auto (32 ACP) cartridge, was sold by Société Française des Munitions in 1900-14. SFM was primarily an ammunition manufacturer, and so it is probable that the gun was made in Belgium. It has a folding trigger and a shrouded hammer with only the spur visible above the raised frame sides. An "SFM" monogram lies on the butt.

SOKOLOVSKY CORPORATION

Sunnyvale, California, USA.

This is a "prestige" weapon for those who simply had to have the biggest and best. Advertised as the "Rolls-Royce of automatic pistols", the *Automaster* is a large 45 ACP using the usual Browning method of locking. There is an odd overhang at the rear, but there are no external excrescence — no pins, screws, slide stop or safety catch protruding from the sides. A finger-operated "safety blade" lies to the right of the trigger, together with a slide decelerator and a ready-to-fire indicator. Its price is in excess of $4500, by far the most expensive pistol in the world, and only about 50 guns have been made since work began in 1984.

SPANDAU ARMS FACTORY
Spandau, Germany.

∼ REPEATING PISTOL ∼

Schlegelmilch Louis Schlegelmilch was the Chief Engineer at the Spandau Arsenal in Berlin, and in 1890-1, he developed a mechanical repeating pistol. According to contemporary reports, this pistol fired a "high-powered, bottle-necked, smokeless powder rifle cartridge" carried in a magazine ahead of the trigger-guard. The mechanism was the usual type of bolt, but the pistol used an external hammer that, when thumb-cocked, drew back the bolt and then released it to go forward and chamber a cartridge. So far as can be determined, only a handful of prototypes were ever made.

∼ REVOLVER ∼

Reichsrevolver Designed by the Gewehr-Prüfungs-Kommission based in the Spandau factory, these guns were made by Gebr. Mauser & Cie for the Württemberg army and by Schilling, Haenel and Spangenberg & Sauer for the armies of Prussia and Saxony. Guns have also been reported with the marks of J.P. Sauer & Sohn, the Erfurt rifle factory and Waffenfabrik Franz von Dreyse. The marks applied by each of these contractors are described in the appropriate entries.

- *M1879* ("Infantry" or "Trooper's Model") Adopted in March 1879, revolvers of this type were issued to dragoons (from 1881), cuirassiers (1885), NCOs, standard-bearers and musicians of the infantry regiments (date unknown), and field artillerymen (1887).

  The guns had a lanyard ring attached to the butt cap and a prominent rib around the muzzle. The trigger was a single-action pattern, and a large radial safety lever was fitted on the left side of the frame. The chambers are recessed into the cylinder so that the entire head of the cartridge is enclosed; a stranger feature is the numbering of each individual chamber on the outside of the cylinder. Extraction was primitive: shooters were required to punch spent cases out of the loading gate individually using a rod that was carried on top of the ammunition pouch. A half-cock notch on the hammer allowed the cylinder to rotate freely by disengaging the cylinder-locking bolt.

- *M1883* ("Cavalry" or "Officer's Model") This was a short-barrel derivative of the 1879-type Reichsrevolver, though the date of its adoption is still uncertain. It is mechanically similar to its predecessor but has a short barrel and the cylinder axis pin is retained by a vertical leaf spring with a small press-catch. The butt of service weapons was rounded, and a lanyard ring was generally present — though essentially similar guns were offered commercially with better finish, diced rubber or checkered walnut grips, spring-loaded ejector rods and double-action triggers. These, however, do not display military inspectors' marks.

  Though replaced by the Pistole M1908 prior to World War I, many remained in store when the fighting began. These were immediately re-issued, which accounts for the markings applied by ammunition-column and similar second-line formations on backstraps or butt caps. Some survived to show up in the hands of Volkssturm units in World War II.

  The 10.6mm ammunition was commercially available until 1939. Reichsrevolvers will chamber the 44 S&W Russian cartridge, but full smokeless powder loads are not recommended.

∼ AUTOMATIC PISTOL ∼

Parabellum Regulation 1908-type Parabellum ("Luger") pistols are occasionally reported with "SPANDAU" on their toggles instead of the more common "ERFURT". They have been subjected to great controversy, but the explanation is simple: they were cannibalized, probably in 1918, from guns that had failed proof. Their receivers often bear marks applied by inspectors working in the Deutsche Waffen- & Munitionsfabriken factory in the Wittenau district of Berlin in addition to those applied in Spandau. Guns will also usually display the "crown over RC" mark of the Revisions-Commission.

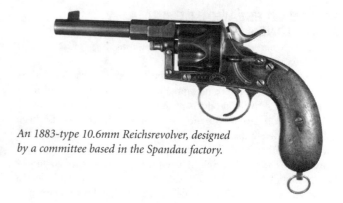

An 1883-type 10.6mm Reichsrevolver, designed by a committee based in the Spandau factory.

SPANGENBERG & SAUER
Suhl, Germany.

This gunmaking business was noted for its part in a consortium (with C.G. Haenel and V.C. Schilling) known as the Handfeuerwaffenfabrik Genossenschaft Suhl, making Reichsrevolver M79 and M83 from 1879 to 1885. At that point, Spangenberg died and Sauer left the combine to become J.P. Sauer & Sohn (q.v.). The guns customarily bear cartouches containing "S. & S. – V.C.S." or "S. & S. – V.C.S. – C.G.H.", depending on the constitution of the cooperative.

SPESCO CORPORATION
Atlanta, Georgia, USA.

Falcon Distributed in the early 1960s, this was a 6.35mm blowback automatic pistol made in Germany by Karl Arndt Reck (q.v.) as the "Reck Model 8".

SPHINX AG
Porrentrury, Switzerland.

This machine-tool and engineering business acquired ITM (q.v.) in 1989, along with rights to the handguns being made in Solothurn. The nomenclature of the pistols remained the same, but the Sphinx name replaced "ITM" on the slides. In 2001, Sphinx was purchased by Oerlikon and renamed "ASAI – Advanced Small Arms Industries". The guns are now being distributed in the USA by Magnum Research of Minneapolis.

Sphinx .3AT The first use of the Sphinx name was made in 1989, before the merger of the two companies. The gun was a fixed-barrel blowback chambered for the 9mm Short (380 ACP) round, with an automatic firing-pin safety, a self-cocking action, automatic de-cocking and ambidextrous controls.

AT 2000 S The Sphinx version of the AT-88 series is available in the same three variants as the AT-88. The slide is marked "ITM Solothurn AT 2000 P", while the frame is marked "Sphinx Made in Switzerland". The standard "S" model has fixed rear sights and wooden or rubber grips. An adjustable rear sight with Tritium inserts, a 25-shot magazine and barrels for 9mm Parabellum or 41 AE are available as options.

- *AT 2000 H* The "Hideaway" version of the AT 2000 series, this is dis-

The ASAI (Sphinx) One-Pro 45-caliber pistol.

tinguished by a short barrel and a short butt.

- *AT 2000 HDA* This is a double-action-only derivative of the PDA gun, with a short butt in addition to a short barrel.
- *AT 2000 P* The compact version of the basic design.
- *AT 2000 PDA* A double-action-only version of the basic compact variant.
- *AT 2000 SDA* An adaptation of the AT 2000, the SDA is self-cocking (SDA, "Standard Double Action [only]"). It retains an external hammer, without a spur.

AT .380 This is an improved version of the .3AT described above. Fixed sights are standard, but adjustable sights, luminous sights and wooden grips are optional. A special version chambered for the 9x18mm Police cartridge, with a 15-round magazine, can be supplied to order.

A 9mm-caliber Sphinx AT 2000 HDA.

A Sphinx AT 2000 PDA.

The Sphinx (ITM) AT .380 pistol.

A sectional drawing of the Sphinx AT .380.

SPREEWERKE GMBH

Berlin, Germany.

Best known as a manufacturer of heavy artillery, this company was recruited to make handguns during World War II. The guns were assembled in a factory in the village of Grottau-Zittau in occupied Czechoslovakia (Reichsprotektorat Böhmen-Mahren).

P. 38 The first Spreewerke-made Walther (q.v.) pistols were delivered in May 1942. They bore a "cyq" code, the date on the slide and were numbered in a single sequence of 10,000-gun blocks. When the "z"-block was reached towards the end of the war, the tail of the "y" in the code broke away and a few thousand guns were made with what appears to be a "cvq" mark. Spreewerke guns make the greatest use of sub-contracted parts and have the poorest surface finish. About 275,000 had been made when the war ended, but the post-war Czechoslovakian authorities subsequently assembled small quantities (3,000-5,000?) from parts found in the Grottau factory.

SPRINGFIELD, INC.

Geneseo, Illinois, USA.

The original Springfield Armory, a government-operated small arms arsenal, closed in 1975, but a private company of the same name was established shortly afterwards. This traded as "Springfield Armory, Inc.", offering a variety of rifles and pistols until reorganized as "Springfield, Inc." in 1993.

∼ SINGLE-SHOT PISTOL ∼

M1911A2 SASS ("Springfield Armory Single Shot") This was an interesting single-shot pistol, essentially an M1911A1-frame fitted with a receiver and an exchangeable 10.75- or 15-inch barrel carrying adjustable target-type sights. The barrel can be pivoted downward to expose the chamber. Chamberings were restricted to 223 Remington, 243 Winchester, 7mm BR, 7mm-08, 308 Winchester (long barrel only), 357 Magnum (short barrel only), 358 Winchester (long barrel only) and 44 Magnum (short barrel only). Springfield supplied complete guns, which generally had a matte-blue finish and checkered black-rubber Pachmayr grips. The magazine was replaced by an extended aluminum-alloy finger rest.

∼ MULTI-SHOT PISTOL ∼

M6 Scout This is a shortened version of the two-barrel over/under M6 Survival Rifle, originally designed for the USAF, with a conventional trigger lever instead of the elongated "gloved-hand" design associated with the original gun. A simple break-open design, locked by a catch that protrudes above the breech, the Scout can be dismantled exceptionally rapidly to allow a 16-inch "carbine" barrel assembly to be substituted for the 10-inch "pistol" unit. A detachable side-folding butt can also be obtained. Chamberings are restricted to 22 LR rimfire or 22 Hornet centerfire (upper barrel) and 45 Long Colt/410 3-inch shot-shells (lower barrel). Finish is either parkerized or bright stainless steel.

∼ AUTOMATIC PISTOLS ∼

Most of the Springfield handguns are based on the proven Colt-Browning system, upgraded with a variety of special features suited to

The M1911-A2 SASS pistol by Springfield Armory, Inc.

21st-century requirements. These include improved adjustable sights, ambidextrous safety levers, the proprietary "High Hand" extended or "beavertail" grip safety, lightweight triggers, beveling on the slide and ejection port to reduce the chances of snagging clothing, slender cocobolo grips and captive dual-spring recoil spring assemblies. Many of the guns also have what Springfield calls the "ILS" (Integral Locking System) set into the backstrap, which allows the action to be locked with a key.

Springfield Armory also operates a Custom Shop, where a variety of limited-production and even "one-off" guns have been made. These are not always easy to classify, and it can be difficult to determine the status of individual models.

Springfield Armory's M1911A1 Champion pistol.

Champion Little more than a compact version of the Service Model, this 45-caliber handgun has a 4-inch barrel and a full-length grip accepting eight-round magazines. The original version (blued or "Mil-Spec" parkerized) had fixed three-dot sights and walnut grips, but the revised version, introduced in 1996, was offered only in stainless steel with cocobolo grips and Novak low-profile Tritium sights.

• *Champion Comp* This was a version of the original ring-hammer gun with a single-port compensator and an extended return-spring guide. Restricted to blue finish and usually found with walnut grips, it weighed 38 oz without its eight-round magazine (seven rounds in the latest examples).

• *Champion MD-1* This was a 380 blowback, approximating to the standard locked-breech Champion externally. It had a matte gray-black finish and checkered black plastic grips. The most obvious feature was the extractor, which was exposed on the right side of the slide behind the ejection port. Made with a steel frame, guns of this type weighed about 31 oz without their magazines.

Combat Commander (1988 to date) Based on the "Mil-Spec" 45-caliber M1911A1, this had a bobbed spur-type hammer and a 4.25-inch barrel instead of the standard 5-inch pattern. It was available in blue or parkerized steel and had walnut grips.

Made in blued or stainless steel, the Springfield Armory M1911A1 Compact is restricted to 45 ACP.

Compact This was a smaller version of the Standard Model, similar to the Champion, with a 4-inch barrel and a shortened grip containing

a six-round magazine. The guns are 7.75 inches long and weigh 32 oz empty. The original examples had fixed three-dot sights, ring hammers and checkered black plastic grips. Later examples have Novak night sights, skeletal hammers and cocobolo grips. Finish can be parkerization (Mil-Spec) or polished blue.

Distinguished by a short, broad butt, the Springfield Armory High Capacity Compact version of the M1911A1 has a double-column magazine.

• *Compact High Capacity* A variant of the basic design only available in stainless steel. It accepted a two-column magazine containing 10 or 11 45 ACP cartridges for the post-1996 North American commercial and law-enforcement markets, respectively.

• *Compact Lightweight* This had a steel slide and alloy frame with a matte-blue finish, reducing weight to about 27 oz.

• *Compact Lightweight Comp* A version of the standard alloy-frame lightweight gun, this could be distinguished by a single-port compensator at the muzzle and an extended return-spring guide. Most guns had ring hammers, were about 8 inches long and weighed 30.5 oz.

Custom Pistols The products of Springfield Armory's own customizing operations, these are usually made to order and, according to the requirements of individual buyers (and a vast selection of accessories), can vary greatly in detail. However, most guns have had specially honed triggers, extended safety levers, chamfered magazine wells, enlarged ejection ports, heavy "throated" barrels with polished feed ramps and special return springs. The M1911A1-style guns have included:

• *Basic Competition* This was a refinement of the Standard Model with the same spur hammer but with an adjustable Bo-Mar rear sight and a refined skeletal match-grade trigger. Finish was customary blue, the grips were walnut and chamberings were usually restricted to 45 ACP (though others have been supplied to individual request).

• *Bullseye Wadcutter* This was a target pistol with a skeleton hammer, a Videcki speed trigger adjusted to a pull of about 3.5 pounds and a Bo-Mar Bullseye sight rib on top of the slide. The beavertail grip safety was standardized, together with blue finish and walnut grips. Checkering appeared on the front grip strap and the flat mainspring housing. Most guns were in 45 ACP, but other chamberings have been supplied on request.

• *Bureau Model* (1998-2000?) This was made with a 5-inch match barrel, a speed trigger, Novak sights, checkered grip straps and Black-T (Teflon) finish. The guns were marked "BUREAU MODEL" on the left side of the slide and had FBI-prefix numbers.

• *Competition Grade Combat Pistol* Available in 9mm Parabellum, 38 Super or 45 ACP, this had low-profile combat sights, a Videcki match trigger and Pachmayr wraparound rubber grips. Finish could be blue or Metaloy.

• *Custom Carry Gun* A variant of the M1911A1 available in 9mm Parabellum, 38 Super or 45 ACP, this had low-profile combat sights. Grips were usually walnut; finish could be blue or Metaloy. The magazine was the standard seven-round inline pattern.

• *Distinguished "Limited Class"* Specifically intended to comply with

USPSA Limited Class competition rules, these guns had refinements such as Bo-Mar BMCS combat sights, ambidextrous controls, extended magazine releases, beavertail grip safeties and a recoil buffer system. Particular attention was paid to the fit of the parts, and checkering was applied to the frontstrap, the mainspring housing and the underside of the trigger guard. Usually supplied in 45 ACP, with other chamberings on request, the stainless-steel pistols had walnut grips.

- *Expert* Similar to the Trophy Master Distinguished design described below and available in the same chamberings, this had a Bi-tone finish (blued slide, bright stainless-steel frame) and black rubber Pachmayr wraparound grips.

- *Expert "Limited Class"* Destined for USPSA competition-shooting, this was a Distinguished "Limited Class" (q.v.) pistol with a Bi-tone finish — blue on the slide, bright stainless-steel frame — and black rubber Pachmayr wraparound grips. The flat mainspring housing and Bo-Mar BMCS combat sights were retained.

- *High Capacity Full-House Race Gun* A competition pistol chambered for a variety of cartridges, including 9x25 Dillon and 45 ACP, this was distinguished by a three-port compensator and a hard-chrome finish. The rear sight could be a micro-adjustable Bo-Mar, a proprietary Springfield Armory design or a C-More optical sight could be substituted. The guns had titanium triggers, ambidextrous controls and checkering on the grip strap and mainspring housing; grips were normally synthetic. Magazine capacities were 15 45 ACP, 17 9x25 Dillon or 19 38 Super rounds.

- *Master Grade Competition Pistol* (1998 to date) Made in two patterns, "A" and "B" (the latter with a compact one-port compensator at the muzzle), these had adjustable Millett or Bo-Mar combat sights, National Match barrels, ambidextrous manual safety levers, extended or "beavertail" grip safeties and a ring-type hammer. The grips were usually wraparound Pachmayr rubber designs, with a rubberized mainspring housing at the rear of the grip, but checkering, jeweling and special grips were available on order.

- *National Match Hardball* Fitted with a honed match-trigger system, a recoil buffer and an adjustable Bo-Mar rear sight, this was also designed to comply with HRA rules. Unlike other Springfield Armory target pistols, the NMH sight extended back over the spur-type hammer. The guns were available only in 45 ACP, were blued steel and had walnut grips.

- *National Match Pistol* Offered in blue or parkerized finish in 9mm Parabellum, 38 Super or 45 ACP, this target pistol was essentially a standard M1911A1 with a heavy barrel, a specially adjusted barrel bushing and a heavy-duty return spring. The rear sight was a high-profile micro-adjustable type, the front sight being a substantial blade.

- *NRA PPC Model* Intended to comply with US National Rifle Association practical-pistol competition rules, this 45 ACP gun had fully adjustable low-profile match sights, with the rear-sight base extending forward to the ejection port. Finish was blue; grips were walnut.

- *Squirtgun* Made in two patterns, "Springfield Formula" and "CMC Formula", this was little more than a Trophy Master with a modular frame and an extended 20-round magazine. Chamberings included 9mm Parabellum, 9x21, 9x23, 38 Super and 45 ACP; finish was hard-chrome.

- *Super-Tuned Series* Comprising variants of the Champion, Standard and Standard V-10, this was introduced in 1997. The guns had 4-inch or 5-inch barrels, depending on pattern, and were chambered exclusively for the 45 ACP cartridge. Great attention was paid to the fit of individual parts. The extractors and the ejectors were specially polished, together with the feed ramps and barrel-throats. The triggers were a special speed pattern, with extensive skeletonization, and the grip safeties took an extended beavertail form. The guns were polished blue or parkerized and had walnut

(later cocobolo) grips.

- *Trophy Master Distinguished* Offered in 9x21 IMI, 38 Super, 10mm Auto, 40 S&W, 45 ACP and in a variety of custom chamberings, this was a variant of the High Capacity Full-House Race Gun (q.v.) with a skeletal speed trigger and single-column magazine holding seven 45 ACP or nine 38 Super cartridges. Finish was usually hard-chrome; grips were walnut.

Defender This was a version of the Springfield M1911A1 "Mil-Spec" with adjustable three-dot "combat" sights, an extended manual safety lever, serrations on the front grip strap, a bobbed spur-type hammer, an enlarged ejection port, a skeletal Videcki speed trigger and a beveled magazine well. Available in blue or parkerized steel, it chambered the 45 ACP round.

Factory Comp This was a variant of the Standard Model (q.v.) with a three-port compensator, giving an overall length of 10 inches and a weight of about 40 oz. The guns were usually blued with checkered walnut grips. An adjustable rear sight was fitted. Guns were available in 38 Super and 45 ACP, with nine- and eight-round magazines, respectively.

High Capacity Another name for the Service Model High Capacity (q.v.) pistol, made in Standard and Compact forms.

- *High Capacity Factory Comp* This was a variant of the Factory Comp (q.v.) pistol, with a frame that had been adapted to accept magazines holding 13 45 ACP or 17 38 Super rounds (altered to 10 rounds for the post-1996 domestic market). The compensator had two (38-caliber) or three (45-caliber) ports. Skeleton hammers were fitted, together with matte-blue finish and black plastic grips.

Lightweight An alloy-frame version of the Standard Model (q.v.), these guns had three-dot sights, ring hammers and walnut grips. Chambered for 9mm Parabellum, 38 Super and 45 ACP — with magazines holding 9, 9, and 7 rounds, respectively — the guns weighed about 29 oz.

Long Slide (1997 to date) Characterized by the 6-inch barrel and a slide that is an inch longer than normal, this is basically a stainless-steel Service Model. It has adjustable target sights but lacks the additional attention given to the Trophy Match Long Slide (which is otherwise identical).

- *Long Slide V-16* A variant of the standard gun with 16 small gas-venting ports in the barrel and an aperture cut in the slide-top directly behind the front sight. This helps to reduce muzzle jump and aids recovery time in rapid-fire.

A standard or "Mil-Spec" version of the Springfield Armory, Inc., M1911A1 pistol.

M1911A1 (1985 to date) This is simply a re-creation of the standard 45 ACP Colt-Browning, with a 5-inch barrel and a single-column magazine containing seven rounds. Offered in stainless steel or with a parkerized finish, the gun has three-dot combat sights and black rubber grips. Mil-Spec guns have spur hammers, short grip-safety levers, the original type of safety lever on the left side of the frame and narrow retraction grooves. The slides are marked "SPRINGFIELD ARMORY" on the right side, together with a trademark that resembles the escutcheon of the US Ordnance Department. This escutcheon originally lay immediately behind the ejection port but has now been removed to the muzzle. The designation "MODEL 1911-A1" appears above the caliber on the left side of the slide, with the company address on the right side of the frame above the trigger. See also "Standard Model".

Micro-Compact (Lightweight, 2002 to date) The smallest of the Springfield Armory Colt-Browning derivatives, this is essentially an Ultra-Compact (q.v.) with a 3-inch barrel and an alloy frame (apparently excepting the "black stainless" option introduced in 2003). The standard finishes are bright or black stainless steel, OD Green, Armory Kote and Bi-tone — bright stainless slide, blacked alloy frame. Chamberings were restricted to 45 ACP until 2003, when a 40 S&W option appeared. Magazines all hold six rounds.

Night and Night Light (1996-8) These were made exclusively for Lew Horton Distributors, featuring Millett night sights and black-rubber Hogue wraparound grips. The chamberings seems to have been confined to 45 ACP. The Night model, with a steel frame, was essentially a Springfield Compact; the Night Light patterns, with alloy frames, were based on the Standard and Compact forms.

Omega (1987-91) An attempt to break away from the Browning link system, this pistol adopted the cam-finger method of elevating the squared barrel-block into an ejection port that ran completely across the slide. Developed around the then-new 10mm Auto cartridge, options had soon been extended to include 38 Super and 45 ACP. The barrels measured 5 inches (standard) or 6 inches (optional) and had polygonal rifling. Compensating ports could be cut into the muzzle, except for the 38 Super chambering, and the dual extractors allowed caliber to be altered merely by exchanging the barrel and return spring. A conversion kit allowed any M1911A1 pistol to be upgraded to Omega standards. Unfortunately, interest in the 10mm Auto round soon waned in favor of 40 S&W, and the Omega project was soon abandoned. A typical 6-inch-barreled gun was 9.5 inches long and weighed about 45 oz with an empty seven-round magazine.

The Omega Match pistol, in 10mm Auto chambering.

- *Omega Match* A minor variation of the standard gun, this had a long barrel and more sophisticated sights.

Operator This is a variant of the Service Model (q.v.) with a Picatinny Rail sight-mount forged integrally with the frame ahead of the trigger guard. The standard gun is parkerized, with cocobolo grips, low-mount Novak Tritium sights and a heavy 5-inch "bull" barrel, but a variant is offered with "Armory Kote" finish, black synthetic grips and Bo-Mar sights. A stainless-steel *Micro Operator* (2003) with a 3-inch barrel and Novak sights can also be obtained for use with an XML light projector.

P-9 (1990-3) A modified copy of the Czech ČZ75, this incorporated improvements such as a sear-safety mechanism, a strengthened hold-open and low-profile sights. The slide top was ribbed to reduce glare. Chamberings were 9mm Parabellum, 40 S&W and 45 ACP, magazines capacities being 16, 12 and 10 rounds, respectively.

- *P-9 C* (Compact) (1991) This was a short-barreled version, made only in small numbers.

- *P9 Factory Comp* (1991-3) This could be identified by the triple-port compensator attached to the muzzle, an extended magazine release, ambidextrous controls and an adjustable rear sight. The rear of the frame was extended back above the thumb-web, and ultra-slim walnut grips were fitted. The finish was Bi-tone, a combination of a blued frame and a bright stainless-steel slide.

- *P-9 SC* (Sub-Compact, 1991) A smaller version of the Compact, this had a short butt that reduced magazine capacity by several rounds.

- *P-9 Ultra IPSC* (1992-3) Made in small numbers for competition-shooting under IPSC rules, this had a 5-inch barrel/slide assembly and target sights. Pachmayr rubber wraparound grips were standard. An IPSC logo appeared on the right side of the slide.

The Springfield P-9 is derived from the ČZ 75 series.

PDP Series ("Personal Defense Pistols") This designation was applied to a range of guns — Champion Comp, Defender, Factory Comp, High Capacity Factory Comp, Lightweight Compact Comp — fitted with compensators. The guns are listed here individually.

Service Model The standard 45 ACP Colt-Browning adaptation in the Springfield range, this has ambidextrous controls, the extended grip safety, a lightweight trigger, retraction grips duplicated immediately behind the muzzle and many other refinements. Finish may be blued steel, "OD [Ordnance Department] Green", parkerized, and black or bright stainless steel. Grips are usually cocobolo, but can be black synthetic. Magazines hold seven rounds and most guns have Novak low-mount sights. Ring-type hammers are standard.

- *Service Model High Capacity* (1998 to date) Sharing the general characteristics of the standard pattern, this has a special forged-steel frame adapted to accept a 10-round staggered-row magazine. Finish is restricted to parkerizing.

- *Service Model Lightweight* (introduced in 2003) This matches a stainless-steel slide with a blacked alloy frame, reducing weight considerably.

- *Service Model Target V-12* This is distinguished by fully-adjustable Bo-Mar sights and 12 small gas-venting ports bored in the top of the barrel to reduce muzzle-jump.

Standard Model These guns had fixed three-dot sights, ring hammers, walnut or black plastic grips and were offered in blue or stainless steel. Chamberings were restricted to 9mm Parabellum, 38 Super and 45 ACP, magazine capacities being eight (45 ACP) or nine (9mm, 38 Super). Weight was about 36 oz (blued steel) or 39 oz (stainless steel) with overall length being 8.6 inches; 5-inch barrels were standard. The Service Model (q.v.) replaced the Standard Model in 1998.

- *Standard High Capacity* Available in 9mm Parabellum and 45 ACP in a parkerized finish with black plastic grips, this was adapted to accept magazines containing 17 9mm or 13 45-caliber rounds (10 rounds for the US domestic market after 1996). Three-dot combat sights were standard. A polished-blue finish was introduced in 1997.

Tactical Response Pistol (TRP, 1998 to date) This is a commercial equivalent of the TRP-Professional Model built by Springfield under contract to the FBI. Its features include checkering on the front grip strap and the mainspring housing, a match-grade barrel and a specially regulated barrel bushing. Finish may be stainless steel or Armory Kote (a form of Teflon), Novak Tritium night sights are standard and the grips are usually cocobolo. The seven-round magazines have a buffered or "pad" base. The Operator (q.v.) is similar to the TRP but has an integral rail for light projectors.

TGO (or Leatham Legend Series) Endorsed by Rob Leatham, one of the world's best pistol-shots, these 45 ACP Colt-Browning derivatives have special barrels and sighting arrangements.

- *TGO-1* has a National Match barrel, a low-mount Bo-Mar rear sight and a Dawson fiber-optic front sight.
- *TGO-2* is similar to TGO-1, with a stainless-steel throated match barrel and bushing.
- *TGO-3* has the same barrel/bushing assembly as TGO-2, but the rear sight is a Springfield Armory design. It usually has a bright stainless steel slide and a blacked steel frame, whereas the others have blacked slides and bright frames.

Trophy Match (1994 to date) Designed for practical pistol shooting, especially bullseye competitions, this matches the frame of the Service Model with a 5-inch barrel. The rear sight is a micro-adjustable target pattern, the frontstrap is checkered and the match-grade barrel is accompanied by a specially adjusted bushing. Restricted to 45 ACP and 9mm Parabellum (introduced in 1997), the Trophy Match has a trigger pull some 20 percent lighter than the Service Model. Once offered additionally in blue or Bi-tone, it is now available only in stainless steel. The original guns had the Springfield escutcheon at the rear of the slide, immediately behind the ejection port, and a trophy motif at the front.

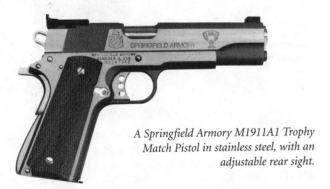

A Springfield Armory M1911A1 Trophy Match Pistol in stainless steel, with an adjustable rear sight.

- *Trophy Match Long Slide* A variant of the Trophy Match with a 6-inch match-grade barrel and match sights, these guns are tuned individually to ensure consistent performance.

Ultra Compact (1996 to date) Readily distinguished by its 3.5-inch barrel and short-grip frame, this 45 ACP handgun has fixed three-dot combat or Novak Tritium sights. The manual safety catch lies on the left side of the frame, and the grip safety, initially a beavertail, is now a bobbed design. The overall length of the guns, initially 7.13 inches, declined to 7 inches as a result. The standard finishes are parkerization (combat sights) and bright stainless steel (Novak sights), the grips being black plastic and cocobolo, respectively. The earliest guns used a Compact frame, which accepted a special seven-round magazine, but this was subsequently replaced by an ultra-short frame taking six-round magazines.

- *Ultra Compact V-10* Otherwise identical with the standard pattern, this has 10 small gas-venting ports in the barrel and an aperture in the top of the slide behind the front sight.
- *Ultra Compact High Capacity* This is simply a standard gun with the frame altered to accept magazines holding 10 or 11 rounds (commercial and law-enforcement markets, respectively).

- *Ultra Compact Lightweight* A variant of the standard gun with a blacked alloy frame and a bright stainless-steel slide.
- *Ultra Compact Lightweight MD-1* This was a 380 blowback, approximating to the locked-breech Ultra Compact Lightweight externally. It had a matte gray-black finish and checkered black plastic grips. The most obvious feature was the extractor, which was exposed on the right side of the slide behind the ejection port. Weight was about 24 oz.

XD series Abandoning the P-9 left Springfield Armory without a modern double-action personal-defense handgun. The XD fills this void. Matching a steel slide with a polymer frame, it has a striker that doubles as a cocking indicator, a loaded-chamber indicator let into the top surface of the slide, a dual-spring recoil system and a light-rail molded integrally with the frame beneath the muzzle. A grip safety is fitted in the thumb-web area and a pivoting blade inserted in the trigger ensures that the gun will not fire unless the trigger-lever is deliberately retracted. Markings include the Springfield Armory name on the right side of the slide and frame, the latter as "SPRINGFIELD INC. GE. ILL.", and the designation "SA-XP" molded into the lower right side of the grip. "XP" also appears on the right side of the slide between the forward retraction grips and the ejection port. The standard guns have 4-inch barrels and can be supplied in black, Bi-tone (with a stainless-steel slide) or OD Green. Chamberings are currently restricted to 357 SIG, 9mm Parabellum and 40 S&W. Sights may be Trijicon or Heinie Tritium Slant-Pro types.

- *XD Sub-Compact* This is a variant of the standard pistol with a 3.1-inch barrel. Offered in black or OD Green, optionally with Heinie Tritium sights, it accepts an XML designator beneath the frame.
- *XD Tactical* Identifiable by its 5-inch barrel and suitably lengthened slide, this is available in black or OD Green. Three-dot combat sights are standard.
- *XD Tactical Pro* This is a variant of the standard XD Tactical pistol with a Dawson fiber-optic front sight. Chamberings are restricted to 9mm Parabellum and 40 S&W.
- *XD V-10* A version of the standard pistol with 10 small gas-venting ports in the barrel and slots in the frame immediately behind the front sight. Finish is usually black.

SPRINGFIELD ARMORY

National Armory, Springfield, Massachusetts, USA.

Founded in 1782, though no guns were made for the first 12 years of its existence, this arms-making establishment is best known for the production of rifles. However, handguns have been made in small quantities. Disregarding "one-off" and developmental models, such as the Phillips gas-operated design tried at a time when the adoption of the Colt-Browning was by no means certain, the only series production to have been undertaken in the last 100 years concerned the 45-caliber M1911 pistol. A license negotiated with Colt allowed the creation of a duplicate production line in the Springfield factory and the manufacture of 50,000 guns. The factory was greatly enlarged during the two world wars but declined in importance after 1945 and had been reduced to the status of

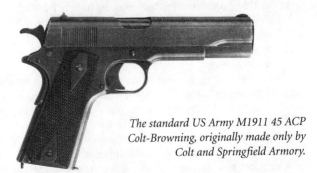

The standard US Army M1911 45 ACP Colt-Browning, originally made only by Colt and Springfield Armory.

Made by the National Armory in Springfield, this experimental pressed-steel version of the M1911A1 dated from World War II.

a large-scale repair shop by 1980. It was then closed, allowing Springfield Armory, Inc., of Geneseo, Illinois, to purchase many "USGI" (US Government issue) components that had remained in store.

M1911 A description of the gun will be found in the Colt section. The first Springfield-made pistols were delivered in 1914, work continuing only until the end of 1915. Output totaled about 31,000, with serial numbers ranging from 72571 to 133186 (in four comparatively small blocks interspersed with Colt deliveries). They were identical with Colt-made guns, with the designation on the slide and property marks on the frame, but they had different manufacturer's marks.

SQUIRES, BINGHAM MFG. CO. ("SQUIBMAN")

Luzon, Philippines; now known as Armscor (q.v.).

This company began in the 1930s as importers, but in the 1950s began manufacturing sporting rifles and later revolvers. Their products are well-made but are rarely seen in Europe. The company changed its name to "Armscor, the Arms Corporation of the Philippines" in the late 1980s, and its present products will be found under that name.

Model 100DA A 38 Special six-shot general-purpose double-action revolver based generally on Colt practice, this had a side-opening cylinder operated by a pull-back thumb catch. The barrel had a ventilated rib and there was an adjustable rear sight. *The Model 100 was a* cheaper version with a plain tapered barrel, and the *Model 100DC was* a middle grade version with ramp front sight on a cylindrical barrel.

Thunderchief This was a development from the Model 100DA with a heavier barrel but still with ventilated rib, full-length ejector shroud and fully adjustable sights. It was normally found in 38 Special caliber, but 22 LR and 22 WM rimfire versions were also made.

STAR–BONIFACIO ECHEVERRIA SA

Eibar, Spain.

This company began in 1905 with an automatic pistol design attributed to Juan Echeverria; unfortunately, like so many Spanish firearms makers, their records suffered during the Spanish Civil War and thus there is much that is not known about the company's history. The original models under the trade name "Star" were, to some extent, modeled upon the 1901 Mannlicher, but they were far from being Mannlicher copies, as some writers have suggested. Although the name "Star" was used from the first, it was not registered as a trademark until 1919, at which time Bonifacio Echeverria had become the company director and principal designer.

In the early 1920s, the original pattern of Star pistol, with open-topped slide, was augmented by a new model with a full slide, based on the Colt M1911. This appeared in various patterns, including some with selective-fire capability. During the Civil War, the factory was extensively damaged, and the company records were destroyed by fire. After the war, Star was one of the four companies permitted to continue with pistol manufacture; and at the present time, their products

have a high reputation, and they are currently providing the Spanish army with their latest pistol.

The list of models produced under the "Star" name is long and confusing. Early models were given year designations, but in the 1920s, a letter designation was adopted, which was then complicated by adding letter suffixes to indicate variations. At the same time, there were also models with distinctive names. A new series of numbered models appeared in the 1980s, but the business collapsed in July 1997 during a severe recession in the gunmaking business that also claimed Astra-Unceta (q.v.). The stock was acquired by Mecanizado, Tratamiento y Montaje de Armas SAL, but, though existing components were assembled, practically no new manufacturing has been undertaken. The remaining guns were soon dispersed in the USA.

M1908 This, the first "Star", was introduced late in 1907 but was not advertised until 1908. It was a fixed-barrel blowback with an open-topped slide. The breechblock section of the slide consisted of two raised portions with a reduced center section carrying a top-mounted extractor. The rearmost section of the block was ribbed to form a finger grip, the safety catch was a hinged block attached to the back of the slide and the external hammer completed the resemblance to the 1901-type Mannlicher. Below the slide, though, the Mannlicher's graceful butt, delicate trigger-guard and integral magazine had given way to a thick rectangular butt, a squared-off trigger guard and a detachable box magazine.

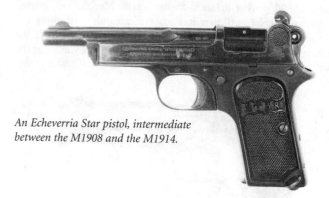

An Echeverria Star pistol, intermediate between the M1908 and the M1914.

This model appeared in 8-shot 6.35mm form with a 3-inch barrel and was simply marked "Automatic Pistol Star Patent" on the slide, with plain checkered hard rubber grips.

M1914 Found in both 6.35mm and 7.65mm calibers, this was an improvement of the M1908. The top of the breechblock was flat instead

The 7.65mm (32-caliber) Star Model 1 (or M1919).

of stepped, and two prominent round bosses were formed as finger grips. A few guns have been seen with round grips and a stepped-top block and are assumed to have been transitional. The Star trademark, a six-pointed star surrounded by rays of light, first appeared in the 1914 Model.

M1919 (or "Model 1") The principal improvement in this pattern concerned the dismantling procedure. The earlier guns had a serrated stud behind the trigger that allowed the slide to be removed, but the 1919 system relied on a catch in the frame ahead of the trigger guard. Guns were made in 6.35mm Auto, 7.65mm Auto and 9mm Short chamberings and in a variety of barrel lengths. They usually carried the maker's name "BONIFACIO ECHEVERRIA – EIBAR – ESPAÑA" and the Star trademark.

Model 28 This appeared in the early 1980s and was Star's first double-action automatic, incorporating several modern features. The slide runs on internal frame rails, and the safety catch on the slide is ambidextrous, withdrawing and locking the firing pin when applied. The trigger and hammer are not affected by the safety catch, and it is possible to pull the trigger and drop the hammer after the safety has been applied and also to pull the trigger and drop the hammer for "dry firing" practice. There is also a magazine safety, but this can easily be removed by the owner.

A line drawing of the Star Model 30M, sharing features with the Colt-Browning and the Smith & Wesson.

The Model 28 DA Star pistol, the first of the double-action designs.

The 9mm Star Model 31P.

The *28DA* was submitted for adoption by the Spanish army but turned down, after which it was placed on commercial sale. There are two variant models: the *Model 28P DA* is about 12mm shorter than the Model 28DA but is otherwise the same; the *Model 28PK DA* is the same as the 28P DA but has a light alloy frame.

This version of the Firestar, the Model 40, chambered the 40 S&W round.

The 9mm Star Model 30M.

The Firestar M45 was a 45 ACP version of the Star double-action design.

Model 30 This is an improved version of the M28 with an ambidextrous safety that locks the firing pin, though the "free trigger" feature has been retained. The *Model 30M* is entirely of steel, while the *Model 30PK* has a light alloy frame. Both use a 15-shot magazine, loaded-chamber indicator and adjustable rear sights. The Model 30M was adopted by the Spanish army in 1989.

Model 31 An improved version of the M30, this embodies a de-cocking system. It chambers the 9mm Parabellum or 40 S&W cartridges with a double-column magazine holding 15 or 11 rounds, respectively (still restricted to 10 in the USA). The *Model 31P* has a steel frame and weighs about 39 oz. The *Model 31 PK* is similar but is restricted to 9mm and has an alloy frame that reduces empty weight to 30 oz.

Firestar Introduced in 1990, this is a compact pistol with a steel frame and slide, a cam-dropped breech and three lugs on the barrel. The muzzle-end of the barrel is coned and shaped to lock securely with

the slide for each shot, rendering the muzzle bushing redundant. This direct interaction of muzzle and slide also enhances accuracy. The lockwork is single action, but the safety catch is ambidextrous and an automatic firing-pin safety is present. The magazine is a single-column type, often with a spurred base-plate, and the grips are generally rubber; finish may be blue or brushed chrome.

· *Firestar M40* Chambered for the 40 S&W cartridge, this has a 3.4-inch barrel and weighs about 30 oz without its magazine.

· *Firestar M43* The standard 9mm Parabellum version, sharing the dimensions of the M40.

- *Firestar M43 Plus* Dating from 1993, this offers a lightweight aluminum-alloy frame with a noticeably humped backstrap and a staggered-row magazine holding 10 rounds. Empty weight is merely 24 oz.
- *Firestar M45* Slightly larger and heavier than the other guns in the series, this chambers the 45 ACP round. Empty weight is about 35 oz, and the barrel is 3.6 inches long.

Lancer This was the Model CU chambered for 22LR and re-named for the American market.

An example of the Megastar pistol.

Megastar Introduced in 1992, this is a double-action locked-breech pistol chambered for either the 10mm Auto or 45 ACP rounds. It has a de-cocking/safety lever on the slide, a ring hammer, a squared trigger guard and "Combat" sights. Finish may be blue or brushed chrome; grips are usually black rubber. A typical 10mm gun has a 4.6-inch barrel and weighs a substantial 48 oz without its 12-round magazine.

Military Model (or "Modelo Militar") Introduced in 1921, this uncommonly-seen pistol represents a transitional stage between the designs derived from the Mannlicher and those that were based on the Colt-Browning. Broadly, the "Military Model" is a version of the Colt M1911, using the same swinging-link lock, but the grip safety is absent and the rear of the slide is raised to form a flat-topped section (but with the extractor on the right side). The safety catch fit into the boss on the

A 9mm Short (380 ACP) Star Model A with mother-of-pearl grips.

left side and rotated a bar that prevented the hammer reaching the firing pin. The pistol was chambered for the 9mm Largo (Bergmann-Bayard) cartridge and was probably intended to compete for a Spanish army contract, but the army chose the Astra. Echeverria then offered the "Military Model" commercially, adding 38 Super and 45 ACP chambering options.

Model A This, dating from 1924, had a slide that was based much more closely on the Colt M1911 than the Modelo Militar and a safety catch on the left rear of the frame. The retraction grips were milled vertically and the rear sight, mounted in a rounded slot in the slide, doubled as a firing-pin retainer. The hammer had a small hole as well as a spur. The Model A was available in 7.63mm Mauser, 9mm Largo or 45 ACP chamberings. The butt could be slotted to take a shoulder stock, and later examples had a full-length grip safety let into the backstrap.

Model B This was much the same as the "A" but had the backstrap humped in the manner of the Colt M1911A1, a change that indicates introduction after 1926, and it chambered the 9mm Parabellum round. The hammer had a good-sized spur and the vestigial hole was eliminated. The Model B remained in production for many years, as work resumed after the end of the Spanish Civil War in 1939 and over 35,000 were purchased by the German army in 1941-44. Manufacture did not end until 1984.

The 9mm Star "Super B".

- *Model Super B* This appeared in 1946 when it was also adopted by the Spanish army. It featured an improved dismantling system — with a take-down lever on the right side of the frame — and abandoned the swinging-link lock in favor of a solid cam. A loaded-chamber indicator was fitted and white dots were added to the sights. Production ended in 1983.

Model BS This was introduced in the early 1970s, chambered for 9mm Parabellum. Its principal feature was its size, probably the smallest major-caliber locked-breech pistol at that time. It retained the Colt configuration but lacked the grip safety and weighed only 25 oz without the 8-round magazine. The frame was steel.

- *Model BKS* Also known as the "Starlight", this was a lightweight version of the BK, with an aluminum-alloy frame. It weighed merely 20 oz without the magazine. The earliest guns had vertical slide-retracting grooves, but these subsequently became diagonal.

Model BM Little more than a smaller version of the Model BS, this had a 4-inch barrel and a steel frame. Chambered for the 9mm Parabellum round, with an eight-round magazine, it could be obtained in blue or chrome finishes.

- *Model BKM* This was simply the BM with an alloy frame, saving a considerable amount of weight.

Model C Introduced c. 1928, this was the Model B chambered for the 9mm Browning Long cartridge.

Model CO (1930-7) This 6.35mm-caliber blowback reverted back to the open-topped slide configuration but showed changes that obviously came from experience with the "A", "B" and "C" models. The rear of the slide was straight and had vertical finger grooves, the forward stripping catch vanished and the slide became a one-piece assembly riding on top of the frame. Dismantling was merely a matter of pulling the slide back and lifting it. The safety catch was under the left butt plate and the hammer was spurred.

Model CU Introduced in 1937 to replace the "CO", this had an aluminum-alloy frame and the safety catch moved to the rear.

Model D Dating from 1930, this 9mm Short (380 ACP) pistol followed the general Colt-Browning shape but had the combination rear sight/firing-pin retainer of the Military Model and a "CO"-type safety lever protruding from the left-hand grip. Guns of this type were adopted by Spanish police forces, the Model D becoming known as the "Police & Pocket Model". Work ceased in 1941.

Model DKL This appeared in 1958, a modified "D" with a light alloy frame. The butt was shaped to fit the hand, the safety catch lay behind the butt on the left rear of the frame and the rear sight no longer retained the firing pin.

Model E Introduced in the early 1930s and made until 1941, this was a 6.35mm vest-pocket gun comparable with the Walther Model 9. It had a fixed barrel and an open-topped slide but also a prominent comb and an external hammer. The safety catch lay behind the trigger.

Model F This was the first of a range of 22-caliber Star pistols. The line began with the "F" or "FTB" pattern, with an open-topped slide and an external hammer allied with a 7.5-inch barrel. This appeared in the 1930s and was discontinued in 1941, only to be revived after World War II, still as the "Model F", with a 4.3-inch barrel and fixed sights. The Model F laid the basis for a series of guns, virtually all chambering the 22 LR rimfire cartridge and provided with 10-round magazines.

• *FM* The last of the line, produced in 1973, this was an "F" with a new frame that had a solid metal web in front of the trigger guard.

• *F Olympic* This had a 7.1-inch barrel with an adjustable rear sight, a muzzle brake and optional barrel weights. The "F Olympic Rapid Fire" was similar but chambered the 22 Short rimfire round.

• *FR* Made in 1967-72, a modified form of the Model F, this had a new slide stop and hold-open catch on the left of the frame, let into the top of the grip. The barrel introduced the modernized slab-side design.

• *FRS* A target-shooting version of the "FR", this had a 6-inch barrel and adjustable sights.

• *F Sport* Similar mechanically to the Model F, this had a 6-inch barrel and fixed sights.

• *F Target* This was a variant of the Model F with a 7.1-inch barrel and adjustable sights.

Model H Another of the guns introduced in the mid-1930s and shortly before the Spanish Civil War began, this was an enlargement of the Model CO in 7.65mm Auto (32 ACP). It was made only until 1941.

• *Model HF* This is virtually a "CO" in 22 LR rimfire, a diminutive "H" and more-or-less comparable with an "F" with a 2.5-inch barrel. Very few appear to have been made.

• *Model HK* A variant of the "HF" pattern, this was chambered for the 22 Short cartridge instead of the Long Rifle type. Production was meager.

• *Model HN* The "H" in 9mm Short (380 Auto), this co-existed with the "H" and was abandoned at the same time.

Model I This was an "H" with a 4.7-inch barrel and a better-shaped grip. It was introduced in 7.65mm Auto as a police pistol, but apparently the barrel was too long for comfort and it was augmented in service by the "HN" with a 3.9-inch barrel. Production stopped in 1941 but was resumed after the war. Some time in the 1950s, it was replaced by the Model IR, with a thumb-rest grip and slab-sided barrel.

Model M This was essentially the Model B chambered for 9mm Short (380 Auto) ammunition.

• *Model Super M* An improved form of the Model M, comparable with the "Model Super B" (q.v.).

Model MD This was a fearsome device, a "Model B" with a selective-fire switch that allowed fully automatic operation. Introduced c. 1930, it was available in 7.63mm Mauser, 9mm Largo, 38 Auto and 45 ACP. The 7.63mm, 9mm and 38-caliber versions could be supplied with extended magazines holding 16 or 32 rounds, while the 45-caliber magazines held 13 or 25 rounds. A 40-round 9mm magazine has also been seen but may not have been a "factory" item. These extended magazines came with a shoulder stock that allowed a modicum of control when using the pistol as a submachine gun. Guns of this type were officially adopted by the Nicaraguan government but otherwise found little favor.

Model P A post-war replacement for the Model B in 45 ACP, this had a 5-inch barrel. Finish was customarily blue, with checkered walnut grips.

Model PD Announced in 1975, this was a surprisingly small 45 ACP pattern. Only 7.5 inches long with a 3.75-inch barrel, it nevertheless accepted an eight-round magazine, plus a round in the chamber, and

was one of the first truly concealable and compact pistols in this caliber. The reduction in size meant some mechanical changes; thus the barrel only had one locking lug on top, the recoil spring and guide were in an assembled unit, there was no grip safety and the frame was alloy. The rear sights were adjustable.

Model S Adopted by the Spanish air force in 1941, this was a Model B chambered for the 9mm Short (380 ACP) round.

Model SI This was similar to the Model S but chambered the 7.65mm Parabellum cartridge. Never popular, it was discontinued c. 1956.

Model SM Chambered for the 9mm Short cartridge, this had the butt extended to hold a 10-round single-column magazine. The finish was generally blue and the grips were checkered walnut.

• *Model Super SM* This was a modernized version of the Model SM, embodying the "Super" modifications described under "Model B". The thumbrest-style molded plastic grips were distinctive.

Starlight An American sales name for the Model BKS and later the Model BKM.

Starfire An American sales name for the Model DK.

Starlet The North American sales name for the Model CU.

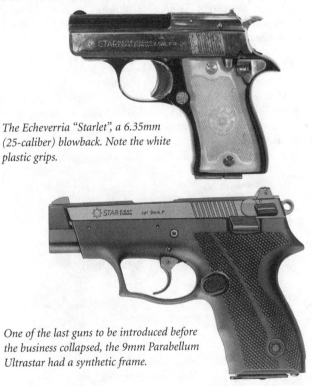

The Echeverria "Starlet", a 6.35mm (25-caliber) blowback. Note the white plastic grips.

One of the last guns to be introduced before the business collapsed, the 9mm Parabellum Ultrastar had a synthetic frame.

Ultrastar Dating from 1994, this is a compact 9mm Parabellum or 40 S&W personal-defense pistol with a steel slide and a polymer frame. The lockwork is double-action, the safety catch is ambidextrous and the rear sight is adjustable. The guns are 7 inches long with a 3.6-inch barrel and weigh about 26 oz empty. Magazine capacity is nine 9mm or seven 40-caliber rounds.

STEEL CITY ARMS

Pittsburgh, Pennsylvania, USA.

This company made small blowback automatic pistols for some years, variously as the *Double Deuce* in 22 LR rimfire and the *Two-Bit Special* in 25 ACP (though both types were marketed under the "Double Deuce" name towards the end of production). They were essentially modified copies of the Walther TPH made of stainless steel and fitted with grips of exotic hardwoods.

The 9mm Parabellum *War Eagle* pistol was announced in 1986, though production did not begin until 1990. This was a double-action, exposed-hammer pistol with an unusual near-cylindrical slide, an ambidextrous safety on the rear of the slide, adjustable sights and 4- or 6-inch barrel.

STENDAWERKE GMBH
Suhl, Germany.
Stendawerke took over production of the "Beholla" (q.v.) pistol in early 1919. Many of these were assembled from parts made by Becker and Hollander, so that they may have conflicting markings — Stendawerke on the slide but Becker & Hollander on the grips. Mechanically, the worst feature of the Beholla design was the method of attaching the barrel by a pin, which required holes in the slide and tools to dismantle the pistol. Stenda patented a modification in which a dovetailed lump on the barrel beneath the chamber slid into a slot in the frame from the left side. A sliding catch locked the barrel and the slide, so that the slide could be removed first and then the barrel … the opposite of Beholla practice. A genuine Stenda pistol can be identified by the lack of holes in the slide and by the presence of the catch above the trigger. Work continued into the mid-1920s but then ceased after about 25,000 pistols had been made.

STERLING ARMAMENT CO. LTD
Dagenham, England.
Sterling was best known for submachine guns, which equipped the British and many other armies. In 1983, the company management decided to produce a pistol for police use and announced that the range of Smith & Wesson-style revolvers previously made by J.P. Sauer & Sohn (q.v.) would be made in Britain. Unfortunately, "teething trou-

The British Sterling 357 Magnum revolver.

bles" were so severe that Sterling ran into financial difficulties and was acquired by an Anglo-Canadian consortium. This sold the operations to Royal Ordnance plc in 1988, and the entire product range was abandoned.

Three revolvers had been proposed, all in 38 Special: the *Compact* had a short barrel, fixed sights and a small round butt; the *Target* had a 6-inch barrel, square butt and adjustable sights; and the *Service* had a 4-inch barrel, square butt and fixed sights.

STERLING ARMS CORPORATION
Gasport, later Lockport, New York, USA.
Sterling began in the late 1950s, producing a series of inexpensive blowback automatics. The line began with two 22 LR "sport" pistols and progressed to a variety of personal-defense designs. Trading ceased in 1986, but the X-Caliber has since reappeared elsewhere.

∼ SINGLE-SHOT PISTOL ∼
X-Caliber This was a single-shot hinged-barrel sporter, offered in 22 LR and 22 WM rimfire, 357 Magnum or 44 Magnum. The caliber could

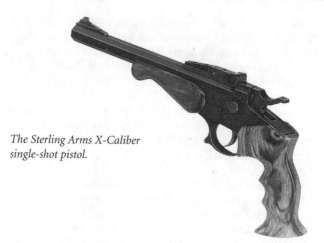

The Sterling Arms X-Caliber single-shot pistol.

be changed simply by changing the barrel. It had an adjustable rear sight and was tapped and drilled for optical-sight mounts. There were two standard barrel lengths, 8 and 10 inches, and various grip options.

∼ AUTOMATIC PISTOLS ∼
280 series (target pistols) This contained a variety of 22-caliber external-hammer guns, similar in appearance to the Colt Woodsman or the High Standards, with half-slides and detachable 10-round magazines accepting the 22 LR rimfire round.
- *Model 283 Target* This was offered with a heavy barrel measuring 4, 4.5 or 8 inches. It had adjustable sights and black plastic grips.
- *Model 284 Target* Similar to the 283, this had a tapering 4.5- or 6-inch barrel with the front sight on a muzzle collar.
- *Model 285 Husky* Derived from the 283, this was restricted to a 4.5-inch heavy barrel and a fixed rear sight.
- *Model 286 Trapper* A variant of the Model 284 with a 4.5-inch tapering barrel and fixed sights.
- *Model 287 PPL 380* Chambered for the 380 ACP (9mm Short) cartridge, this was 5.1 inches long, with a 1-inch barrel, and weighed 22 oz without its six-round magazine. It was effectively a cut-down target pistol and was soon replaced by the purpose-built 300 series.
- *Model 288 PPL 22* Another of the short-barreled guns, this was chambered for the 22 LR rimfire round and had a 10-round magazine.

300 series These guns, intended for personal defense, were conventional blowbacks that resemble an amalgam of Browning and Walther features. The 25 ACP M300 was 5 inches long with its 2.5-inch barrel and weighed 14 oz without its six-round magazine. Finish may be blue or nickel plate, the grips generally being black plastic.
- *Model 300S* This was a stainless-steel version of the M300.
- *Model 302* Similar to the Model 300, this chambered the 22LR rimfire round.
- *Model 302S* A stainless-steel version of the M302.

400 series Introduced in 1973, the Model 400 was a double-action, external-hammer model in 380 ACP (9mm Short) chambering.

The 25 ACP Sterling pocket pistol.

- *Model 400 Mark 2* Introduced in 1979, this was characterized by a more slender appearance.
- *Model 400S Mark 2* A stainless-steel variant of the preceding gun.
- *Model 402* Essentially a M400 in 22 LR rimfire.
- *Model 402 Mk 2* This gun accepted the 32 ACP (7.65mm Auto) cartridge, making it more useful as a self-defense weapon than the original M402.
- *Model 402S Mark 2* Similar to the 32-caliber M402 Mk 2 but in stainless steel.

A 32-caliber Sterling Arms "Mark II" pistol.

Model 450 (or "45 DA") Sterling began work on this double-action 45 ACP police and military pistol in 1979, but business floundered before much progress could be made and the project was abandoned after only a handful of prototypes had been made. They had double-action lockwork, a tipping-barrel lock and a small hole drilled through a lug on the two-hand trigger guard. Made of blued carbon steel with walnut grips, a typical example was 7.7 inches long with a 4-inch barrel and weighed about 36 oz without its eight-round detachable box magazine.

J. STEVENS ARMS & TOOL COMPANY

Chicopee Falls, Massachusetts, USA.

This firm began as J. Stevens & Co. in 1864, and in 1888 was incorporated, taking on the new title given above. The business was acquired by the owners of the Savage Arms Corporation in 1920, becoming a semi-autonomous division of Savage.

The first pistols Work began in 1864 with the "Vestpocket Model" and the "Pocket Pistol", both of which continued in production into the 1890s.

- *Vestpocket* This was a 22 or 30 Short rimfire gun, with a blued or nickel-plated iron frame, a sheathed trigger and a 2.75-inch octagonal barrel that hinged down to load.
- *Pocket model* Also offered in 22 or 30 Short rimfire, this was slightly larger than the Vestpocket. It had a silver- or nickel-plated brass frame, a blued barrel, a sheathed trigger and a spring to open the barrel when a button was pressed. After about 15,000 guns had been made, in 1886, the barrel-tipping spring was discarded in favor of manual operation; experience had shown that the spring tended to wear out. Another 10,000 guns were made before work finally ceased in 1896.
- *Gem* Introduced in 1872, also in 22 or 30 Short rimfire, the 3-inch half-octagonal barrel of this gun turned around a vertical pivot so that the breech opened sideways for loading. The only Stevens design to eschew the tip-down system, the Gem was made until 1890. Production totaled only a few thousand, made with nickel-plated brass frames and blued or nickeled-iron barrels.
- *No. 41* A replacement for the Pocket Model, chambered for the 22 or 30 Short rimfire rounds, this had an external hammer, a sheathed trigger and a separate firing pin in the standing breech. Offered in blued or nickeled finish, it had a square-bottom butt with walnut grips. About 90,000 guns had been made when assembly stopped in 1916.

Gallery Models Stevens made 22 rimfire rifles that sold extremely well and, in 1887, took a momentous step in small-arms history with the introduction of the 22 Long Rifle rimfire cartridge. This was accomplished simply by combining the established 22 Long case and a 40-grain bullet. A series of target pistols chambered for the 22 Long had appeared in 1880, and these were now adapted for the Long Rifle round to produce guns that were marvels of accuracy in their day.

The "Gallery Pistols" all used tip-down barrels and were fitted with Paine-type front sights (a bead on a post) and a rear sight that could be adjusted for elevation with a sliding wedge. The hammer had to be half-cocked to permit the barrel to be opened. The guns were surprisingly large for 22 rimfires and had hand-filling grips that endeared them to target shooters. Chamberings included 22, 25 or 32 rimfire, and 32, 32-44, 38 or 38-44 centerfire.

- *Diamond or No. 43 Model* Lighter even than the Gould pattern, this was the lightest and smallest of the group. Chambered only for the 22 LR rimfire cartridge, with 6- or 10-inch half-octagonal barrels, nearly 100,000 guns were made from 1886 to 1916.
- *Conlin or No. 38 Model* Supplied with a finger rest on the trigger guard, this was made in two versions. The original (1880-4) had a sheathed trigger inside the guard, but the later pattern, made until 1903, had a conventional trigger. Total production scarcely exceeded 6500 guns.
- *Gould or No. 37 Model* This was a lighter version of the Lord, but only about 1000 were made between 1889 and 1903.
- *Lord or No. 36 Model* Introduced in 1880, this had a heavy 10-inch barrel. Only a little more than 3000 had been made when work finally ceased in 1911.
- *Off-Hand or No. 35 Model* (1907-42) This was the last Stevens pistol, almost a reversion to the Gallery models of the 1880s, with an external hammer and a half-octagonal tip-down barrel 6, 8, 10 or 12.25 inches long. The firing pin lacked a separate bushing and the butt, which had walnut grips, had a weighted base. The original No. 35 Target pattern, discontinued in 1916, had sophisticated adjustable sights. It could be obtained in 22 LR rimfire, 22 Stevens-Pope or 25 Stevens centerfire

The post-1923 version was essentially similar, but the chambering was usually limited to 22 LR rimfire, and the sights were simplified. Production totaled about 43,000 when stopped by the entry of the USA into World War II. Guns of this type were also made between 1929 and 1934 as the Autoshot 35, with an 8-inch or 12.5-inch smoothbore barrel chambered for the 410 shotgun cartridge.

The 22 rimfire Stevens Model 10.

A Stevens Model 10 with its shoulder stock.

Target Model No. 10 (1919-33) The Gallery pistols remained in production until their popularity waned in the early 1900s, and many of the smaller guns were still available until 1916. When Stevens returned to commercial production after the end of World War I, the No. 10 was announced. Though still a single-shot tip-barrel design, it resembled an automatic pistol with an exposed barrel ahead of a rectangular receiver. A catch on the left side, designed on a cam principle, drew the barrel back towards the standing breech as it was locked. Consequently, any wear in the hinge bolt was taken up. The No. 10 had an internal hammer, with a cocking plunger that protruded from the rear of the receiver. About 7000 guns were made.

STEYR-MANNLICHER GMBH

Steyr, Austria.

After World War II, the Steyr manufactory confined its attention to motorcycles and other engineering and did not return to firearms until the mid-1950s.

SP Developed in the 1950s, this personal-defense pistol was a 7.65mm blowback of modern appearance with a self-cocking lock. The barrel was fixed to the frame and carried its recoil spring around it, secured into the slide by a knurled collar around the muzzle. There was no safety catch. It appears not to have sold very well and manufacture ceased in 1965.

Pi-18 Announced in 1974, this was a delayed-blowback design using a gas delay system. The barrel was fixed to the frame but was externally shaped to form a sort of piston. The slide was internally shaped to fit closely around this piston so as to leave an annular cylinder around the barrel. Gas was directed into this space from just ahead of the chamber, and the high pressure, forcing itself against the front of the slide, was sufficient to delay the opening of the breech until the bullet had left the bore and the pressure began to drop. There was an external hammer and a slide-mounted safety catch. The magazine held 18 shots in a double column, so that the butt was not exceptionally thick. It was also produced in selective-fire form, in which a third position on the safety catch gave automatic fire, and in this form, a 36-shot magazine and a shoulder stock were provided.

Prototypes were made in Steyr, but it is believed that the automatic feature raised problems over export due to the restrictive Austrian peace treaty then in force. Steyr licensed production to an American company, L.E.S. of Morton Grove, Illinois, who produced the standard semi-automatic version as the P-18. Quality control was poor, the pistol gathered a poor reputation for reliability and eventually Steyr terminated the agreement and took another look at the design.

The 9mm Steyr GB.

GB This was the improved version of the Pi-18. The delayed blowback system works exactly the same way, but the detail design was improved and the selective-fire option was abandoned, thus making it possible to manufacture in and export from Austria. The GB proved to be an excellent pistol, the gas-delay feature soaking up some of the recoil, so that it was very quickly brought back into the aim. In spite of the large mag-

azine capacity, it was comfortable to hold and it proved to be most reliable in use. Nevertheless, it was expensive and military adoption eluded it; the final straw came with the Austrian army's rejection in favor of the Glock in 1985, and production ceased in 1988.

SPP (Special Purpose Pistol) This is a semi-automatic version of the Tactical Machine Pistol or "TMP", a submachine gun. It uses the same synthetic frame and receiver and operates in the same delayed-blowback mode by means of a rotating barrel. The principal difference is that the pistol has no forward handgrip and a slightly greater length of exposed barrel and jacket in front of the receiver.

M Series In the late 1990s, Ingenieur Aichner, the company's designer, set about developing an entirely new range of pistols. This drew upon the company's exceptional knowledge of synthetic materials and their employment in gun design to produce a conventional dropping-barrel recoil-operated pistol with synthetic frame and steel slide. It was designed from the start to be produced in 40 S&W and 9mm Parabellum chamberings. To produce a smooth recoil action with the heavy 40-caliber bullet, the barrel and breech recoil some 3.5mm together before unlocking, which also gives the pistol very good accuracy. The firing mechanism is entirely self-cocking (or double-action only) and there are a variety of safety systems: a trigger safety similar to that of the Glock, a manual safety and an "Integrated Limited Access Lock" with key — the first such safety lock to be actually incorporated into the design of a pistol.

Introduced in 2000, the *M-9* and *M-40* were followed by the *S-9* and *S-40*, these being compact versions using 91mm barrels instead of the 102mm of the M types. They were followed in 2001 by the *M-357*, chambered for the 357 SIG cartridge, and the *M-9** and *S-9**, which were chambered for the 9 x 21mm IMI cartridge and sold only in Italy.

A German-made 7.65mm (32-caliber) Stock pistol.

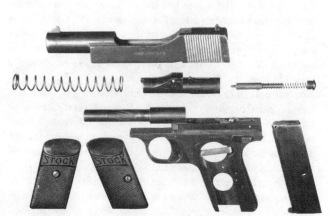

The principal components of the Stock pistol.

STOCK

Franz Stock Maschinen- und Werkbau-Fabrik, Berlin, Germany.
Designed by Walter Decker and patented in 1915-18, the Stock pistols were made from 1923 until the mid-1930s. They were well-made pistols in 22 LR rimfire, 6.35mm and 7.65mm Auto chamberings, and the patented features covered the assembly of the breechblock and the magazine safety.

The Stock was a fixed-barrel pistol with enveloping slide and coaxial recoil spring. The center of the slide was open-topped, and the breechblock was a separate unit held in the rear of the slide by a hook at the rear end of the extractor engaging in a lip on the underside of the slide. A screwed cap in the end of the block, protruding through the rear of the slide, retained the firing pin and spring. Stripping the pistol for cleaning was simply a matter of lifting the front of the extractor and pressing in the screwed cap; the breechblock came loose and could be lifted through the top of the slide.

A.F. STOEGER & COMPANY/STOEGER ARMS

Later the Stoeger Arms Corporation, and then the Stoeger Arms Division of Stoeger Industries, New York and South Hackensack, New Jersey, USA.
Adolf Stoeger founded his sporting goods distributorship in New York soon after World War I, importing Parabellum pistols (among other things) into the USA. Stoeger astutely noticed that although the name was "Parabellum", everybody called them the "Luger" and, in 1923, registered the word Luger as a trademark. He then made arrangements with Berlin-Karlsruher Industrie-Werke (as DWM had become) for all his purchases to be marked "A.F.Stoeger Inc. New York Luger Registered US Patent Office" on the right side of the frame. This continued until World War II began in Europe in 1939.

In more recent times, the Stoeger Arms Company has revived the name. In 1976, it introduced a totally new pistol that looked like a Luger but had a fixed barrel and embodied a simplified blowback-type toggle system. These 22 LR rimfire pistols were made for Stoeger by Replica Arms, a subsidiary of Navy Arms (and after Stoeger dropped it in 1986, the gun was revived and was marketed as the "Navy Arms Luger".) The frame was an aluminum forging with the barrel inserted from the front and pinned in place. Steel inserts supported the bolt movement that was controlled by an external toggle.

Two basic models were made, the standard *Stoeger-Luger* and the *Stoeger Target Luger*, the latter having an extension at the rear of the frame to support an adjustable sight. Both were available with 4.5-inch or 5.5-inch barrels. They were prominently marked "LUGER" in a floral decorative scroll on the right side of the frame.

Stoeger has also made a copy of the genuine 1908-type Parabellum, after apparently preventing the production of the Mitchell Arms version. The *American Eagle Lugers* have been made since 1994, distinguished by their markings. A "Navy" Model has a sliding two-position rear sight on the rear toggle link and a 6-inch barrel.

STURM, RUGER & COMPANY

Southport, Connecticut, USA.
William B. Ruger (1916-2002) began producing his 22-caliber blowback automatic in 1949, and it became an immediate success due to its simplicity, reliability, accuracy and reasonable price. Shortly after this, he realized there was a vast number of people who wanted a Single Action Colt but whose ambition was thwarted because Colt had discontinued the model. Ruger therefore began production of single-action revolvers; and to such good effect that Colt reconsidered their decision, and innumerable other makers began producing near-Colts. The Ruger designs, however, were far from being mere reproductions. They are well-engineered revolvers with evidence of original thought, and they have been periodically improved to incorporate all the latest innovations in safety and technology. In more recent years, the company introduced a line of double-action revolvers for police and home defense, as well as percussion revolvers, rifles and carbines.

∼ SINGLE-SHOT PISTOL ∼

Hawkeye (1963-4) In the early 1960s, there was considerable interest in the USA in the development of high-velocity small-caliber revolver loads, and in 1961, the 22 Remington Jet cartridge appeared, together with the Smith & Wesson M53 revolver. Shortly afterwards came the 256 Remington Magnum, another bottle-necked round claiming 2400 ft/sec velocity. High-power cartridges such as these had problems, particularly when the cases sat back far enough in the chamber to jam the cylinder action. Ruger solved this problem by producing the "Hawkeye", a single-shot pistol in the form of a "Blackhawk" revolver. What appeared to be the cylinder was a breechblock. When this block was open, a cartridge could be placed in a loading trough; the "cylinder" was then rotated to align the trough with the barrel, and the cartridge could be pushed forward into a chamber formed in the end of the barrel. Rotating the cylinder back again placed solid steel behind the cartridge. Pressing the trigger allowed the hammer to strike a firing

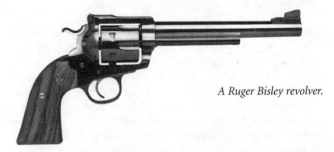

A Ruger Bisley revolver.

pin that ran through the breechblock, which could then be opened to allow a cam-like extractor to unseat the empty. Although an elegant engineering solution and capable of excellent accuracy (recognized by provision for optical-sight mounts), the "Hawkeye" never gained great popularity. It was discontinued after only about 3300 had been made. Blued, with walnut "Ruger medallion" grips, they had 8.5-inch barrels.

∼ REVOLVERS ∼

All of the revolvers made in 1976, regardless of type, were marked "MADE IN THE 200TH YEAR OF AMERICAN LIBERTY".
Bearcat (1958-70) This reduced-scale Single Action (q.v.), similar to but cheaper than the Single-Six, had fixed sights, a 4-inch barrel and was chambered only for the 22 LR rimfire cartridge. The most obvious feature was the cylinder, with an "engraving" rolled into its plain surface. The frame was alloy, anodized black, with separate straps that could be finished in black or imitation brass; the barrel was blued steel. The grips were plastic impregnated wood until 1963, and the "medallion" walnut type thereafter.

The New Bisley revolver, in 22 LR rimfire or 32 H&R Magnum centerfire.

Bisley Model (1986 to date) An adaptation of the Blackhawk with the distinctively cramped-looking high-grip Bisley frame and a low-swept hammer spur, this was originally offered with adjustable sights and in chamberings that included 22 LR rimfire, 32 H&R Magnum,

357 Magnum, 41 Magnum, 44 Magnum and 45 Long Colt. Barrels are restricted to 6.5 and 7.5 inches, but the cylinders may be fluted or roll-engraved. Finish is usually satin blue, and the grips, made of Goncalo Alves wood, have Ruger trademark medallions.

• *Bisley Vaquero* (1998 to date) Offered in 44 Magnum and 45 Long Colt, with a 5.5-inch barrel, this amalgamates the Bisley-type frame with fixed sights — a blade at the muzzle and an open notch ahead of the hammer. Finish is restricted to blue, with a simulated color case-hardened frame.

The 357 Magnum Ruger Blackhawk "Western Style" revolver.

Blackhawk (first pattern or "Flat-top type", 1955-62) This was introduced in answer to requests for a more powerful version of the Single Six. It was of the same pattern but chambered for the 357 Magnum cartridge, with a 4.6-, 6.5- or 10-inch barrel and a micro-adjustable rear sight. The guns were blued and had checkered rubber grips, replaced soon after production began by walnut. The advent of the 44 Magnum cartridge led to the introduction of a suitably chambered Blackhawk (1956-62), sometimes called the "Ruger 44 Magnum", with a heavier frame and a larger cylinder. Barrels were restricted to 6.5, 7.5 and 10 inches, but the gun proved to be a handful to shoot and was supersed-

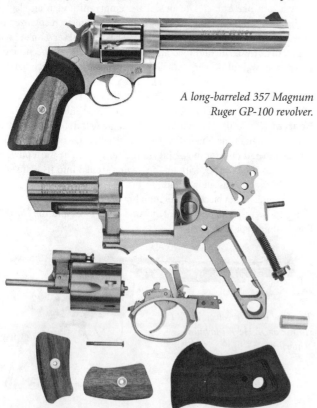

A long-barreled 357 Magnum Ruger GP-100 revolver.

The Ruger GP-100 partly dismantled.

ed by the Super Blackhawk (q.v.). Production of first-pattern Blackhawks totaled 72,000, with the 357 Magnum outnumbering the 44 version about three-to-two.

• *Convertible Pattern* A few of these exchangeable-cylinder guns were made, options being restricted to 357 Magnum/9mm Parabellum and 45 Long Colt/45 ACP.

• *Second Pattern* (1962-72) This was a comparatively minor variant, with a rear sight formed by "pinching" two fences in the top of the frame to form a short groove. Chamberings were restricted to 30 M1 Carbine (7.5-inch barrel only), 357 Magnum (4.6 or 6.5 inches) and 45 Long Colt (4.6 or 7.5 inches). A 41 Magnum option was introduced in 1964, barrel options duplicating 45 Long Colt, but the 30-caliber option was discontinued in the same period. Finish was blue, and grips were usually walnut with Ruger-trademark medallions.

Buckeye Special (1989-90) This was a short-lived variant of the New Model Single Six (q.v.), available in 32 H&R Magnum, 32-20 WCF, 38-40 WCF or 10mm Auto.

GP-100 (1986 to date) Intended to replace the Security Six, this offered a heavy frame designed to withstand the pounding of heavy loads, a "Cushioned Grip" (a combination of Goncalo Alves inserts in a rubber surround) and a completely new system for locking the cylinder during firing. It has been available in blue or stainless steel, with 3-, 4- and 6-inch barrels. The rear sight is outlined in white and the front sight has a colored insert to facilitate aim. All versions of the GP-100 are chambered for either 357 Magnum or 38 Special cartridges.

The 22 LR/22 WM rimfire New Bearcat.

New Bearcat (1993 to date) This was to the same design as the original but with an improved investment-cast steel frame, a transfer bar mechanism and two interchangeable cylinders, one for 22 Long Rifle, the other for 22WMRF. Two versions are offered, one in blued steel and the other in stainless steel; grips are walnut.

New Model Blackhawk (1973 to date) This is virtually the original Blackhawk modified by the addition of the transfer-bar in the lockwork. The chamberings and barrel-length options duplicate those of the pre-1972 guns. However, the stainless-steel New Model Blackhawk is only available in 357 Magnum, 44 Magnum and 45 Long Colt, and the convertible model (usually blued) is restricted to 357 Magnum/9mm Parabellum and, from 1998 onward, 45 Long Colt/45 ACP.

A New Model Blackhawk, with a 4.6-inch barrel chambering the 45 Long Colt cartridge.

- *SRM Model Blackhawk* (1981-4) This was a version of the basic revolver promoted for metallic-silhouette shooting and chambered for the powerful 357 Maximum cartridge, with 7.5- or 10.5-inch barrels. Even though the frame and barrel were made of stainless steel, the SRM Blackhawk proved to be too susceptible to gas erosion to be successful. It was abandoned after less than 10,000 had been made.

New Model Single-Six (1973 onward) The first few of these guns, distinguished by adjustable sights, were made for one year only. Chambering was confined to 22 LR rimfire, the finish could be blue or stainless steel, and the revolvers had a star prefix to their serial numbers. Barrels could be 4.6, 6.5 or 9.5 inches.

The Ruger New Model Super Single-Six revolver, convertible for 22 LR or 22 WM rimfire ammunition.

Two Ruger New Model Single-Six revolvers.

- *Colorado Centennial Single-Six* (1975) A total of 15,000 of these were made with stainless-steel frames and blued barrels and fittings. Barrels measured 6.5 inches, and the guns were sold in cases with centennial medallions let into the lid.
- *Fixed-Sight New Model Single-Six (1)* (1973-97) The adjustable-sight pattern was superseded by a fixed-sight variant. The first 1500 — 500 each with 4.6-, 5.5- or 6.5-inch barrels — had a drift-adjustable rear sight, but the production guns had the sight formed by pinching the topstrap. Offered in blue or glossy stainless steel, the perfected guns had barrel options restricted to 5.5 or 6.5 inches, weight being 35 and 38 oz, respectively.
- *Fixed-Sight New Model Single-Six (2)* (2000 to date) Essentially similar to the 22 rimfire version, this was reintroduced in 32 H&R Magnum. Offered only with a 4.6-inch barrel and a short-grip Vaquero-style frame with a fixed rear sight, the guns are made in blue or stainless steel and have simulated ivory grips.
- *SSM Single-Six* (1984-97) These chambered the 32 H&R Magnum cartridge and had adjustable sights. The first 800 had "SSM" on the frame, but the distinctive mark was then dropped.

New Model Super Blackhawk (1978 to date) This was a modernized version of the Super Blackhawk, with a transfer-bar safety system. Construction was blued or stainless steel. Changes made in 1998 led to the introduction of a "Hunter" frame (stainless steel only) and laminated wood grips; barrel options were restricted to 4.6 and 7.5 inches.

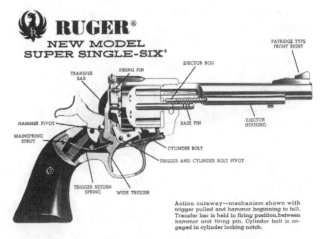

A cutaway view of the Ruger New Model Super Single-Six.

New Model Super Single-Six (1973 to date) This was little more than the original Single Six with a new transfer-bar trigger mechanism developed to satisfy the provisions of the Gun Control Act of 1968. No single-action revolver based upon the original Colt Single Action Army model could possibly pass the new tests, and most of the revolvers being made in the USA were either re-designed or removed from sale. The Ruger, thanks to the floating firing pin, was closer to the new safety standards than most. Its lockwork could be changed simply by making the hammer strike the standing breech unless a "transfer bar", fitted to and raised by the trigger, was interposed between the falling hammer and the firing pin to transfer the blow and fire the pistol. When the trigger was released, the transfer bar was withdrawn and no amount of blows on the hammer could possibly fire the cartridge that lay ahead of the firing pin.

At the same time, the traditional half- and quarter-cock notches were removed, leaving the hammer with only two possible positions — cocked or uncocked. Since the loading gate was originally linked with the half-cock notch, the mechanism had to be altered so that the transfer bar and cylinder lock were withdrawn when the loading gate was opened, allowing the cylinder to turn freely for loading.

The standard guns had 4.6-, 5.5-, 6.5- or 9.5-inch barrels that were usually chambered for 22 LR rimfire, though an exchangeable 22 WMRF cylinder could be supplied on request. They had adjustable sights and were usually blued, with walnut "medallion type" grips.

Police Service-Six (1973-88) The Security-Six, as noted below, was originally produced with either fixed or adjustable sights, but the two options were soon separated. Thereafter, the Security-Six came with an adjustable rear sight, while the fixed-sight model became the "Police Service-Six". The contours of the butt were slightly changed to make concealment easier, and the 6-inch barrel option was withdrawn after only a few had been made. The basic revolver, the blued Model 107

The Ruger New Model Super Blackhawk Hunter, with a barrel rib that accepts optical-sight mounts.

A 357 Magnum Ruger Police Service-Six revolver, in stainless steel.

("M707" in stainless steel), chambered the 357 Magnum round; the blued M108 (and stainless M708) accepted the 38 Special; and the M109, not made in stainless steel, took 9mm Parabellum ammunition. The Parabellum option was withdrawn in 1984, but the others lasted until the end of production.

The Ruger Redhawk.

Redhawk (1986 to date) This large-frame double-action revolver was introduced in 41 Magnum then offered additionally in 44 Magnum (1992 onward). The guns are blued, have smooth walnut grips and 5.5- or 7.5-inch barrels.

- *Stainless Redhawk* This was made in small numbers in 357 Magnum in 1985, before the blued 41-caliber version appeared, but was then offered in 41 Magnum until the 44 Magnum option was standardized in 1992. An additional 45 Long Colt option was available from 1998.

Security-Six (1970-85) Announced in late 1968 but not made in quantity for some months, this was Ruger's entry into the field of modern double-action revolvers. It is a solid-frame model with side-opening cylinder operated by a thumb-catch on the frame. The ejector rod is secured in a shroud, forged integrally with the ribbed barrel, and the

A cutaway drawing of the Ruger Security-Six.

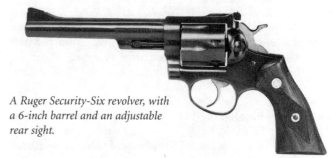

A Ruger Security-Six revolver, with a 6-inch barrel and an adjustable rear sight.

lockwork includes the patented transfer bar. In 357 Magnum chambering, the Security-Six was offered with barrels of 2.75, 4 or 6 inches and squared walnut-gripped butts. Finish could be blue (Model 117) or stainless (M717). The sights were adjustable. The earliest fixed-sight guns were also marked "SECURITY SIX", but this particular pattern was almost immediately renamed "Service Six" (q.v.).

Single-Six (1953-72) The first Ruger revolver, this was based loosely on the Colt M1873: a solid-frame, six-shot single-action pattern with a pivoting loading gate on the right side of the frame behind the cylinder and a sliding-rod ejector offset to the right and below the barrel. However, the leaf-type mainspring was replaced with a coil spring, making the action more robust, and a floating firing pin was let into the standing breech. The earliest guns were chambered only for 22 LR rimfire ammunition and had 5.5-inch barrels, though 4.6-, 6.5- and 9.5-inch options were added in 1959. The first 60,000 guns had angular loading gates, but these were replaced by contoured gates, which were more in keeping with the original Colt design. Most guns were blued, with checkered rubber grips (smooth walnut from 1962). The grip medallions had a black background until 1971 when they became silver.

- *Single-Six Convertible* This was simply a Single Six offered with two cylinders, one chambering 22 LR rimfire and the other chambering 22 WMRF.
- *Single-Six Lightweight* (1956-8) Made with an alloy frame and a 4.6-inch barrel, this was abandoned after only 12,000 had been made. The first guns had alloy cylinders with steel chamber liners, but these proved to be too weak and were replaced by all-steel cylinders. The guns had silver or black-anodized frames; alloy cylinders were finished similarly, but the steel examples were conventionally blued.
- *Single-Six Magnum* Only made for about 3 years, this 22 WMRF, suitably marked on the frame, was replaced by the Convertible. Barrel-length options were restricted to 6.5 inches.
- *Single-Six New Model* The post-1973 replacement for the original design. See "New Model Single-Six".

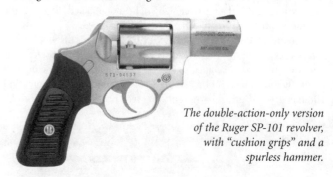

The double-action-only version of the Ruger SP-101 revolver, with "cushion grips" and a spurless hammer.

SP-101 (1989 to date) This was announced in 1988 as the "small-frame revolver" of the series, for police service or home defense. Chambered for 22 LR rimfire (six shots), 357 Magnum, 38 Special or 9mm Parabellum (five shots each), the SP-101 has a frame that is strengthened in particular areas to provide the greatest possible strength. Made only in stainless steel, the gun has 2-, 3- or 6-inch barrels (the longest in 22 only) and windage-adjustable sights. The grips are black synthetic. A double-action-only "Spurless Hammer" version was introduced in 1993 in 357 Magnum/38 Special, with fixed sights and a five-chamber cylinder.

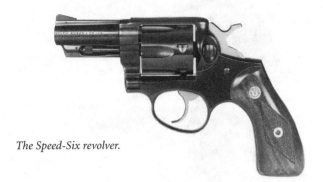

The Speed-Six revolver.

Speed-Six (1973-85?) This is the same pistol as the Security-Six but with fixed sights, a round butt and a 2.75- or 4-inch barrel. Finish was blue, and grips were checkered walnut. Chamberings were restricted to 357 Magnum (Model 207), 38 Special (M208) or 9mm Parabellum (M209); stainless-steel versions were designated Models 737, 738 and 739, respectively. A few guns also had spurless "bobbed" hammers to facilitate concealment.

Super Bearcat (1971-4) This was made entirely of blued steel, except for some of the earliest examples that retained the brass-anodized alloy trigger guard of the standard Bearcat to rid the stores of existing parts.

Super Blackhawk (1959-72) An enlargement of the basic Blackhawk design, this owed its introduction to the difficulties of controlling a standard gun chambered for the 44 Magnum cartridge. The "Super" was essentially similar mechanically but had a longer grip, a square-backed trigger guard and a cylinder that had been strengthened by omitting the usual flutes between the chambers. The barrel was 7.5 inches long, though, owing to an oversight, 600 6.5-inch-barreled guns were made in the mid-1960s. The guns were blued, with walnut "medallion" grips; a few had brass grip straps.

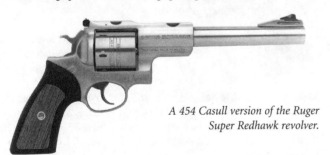

A 454 Casull version of the Ruger Super Redhawk revolver.

Super Redhawk Introduced in 1987, this was an enlarged and greatly strengthened Redhawk, the principal visible change being the extension of the frame around the barrel for some distance in front of the chamber. The wide topstrap and the barrel rib incorporate optical-sight mounts, construction is stainless steel and the grips incorporate the Ruger "Cushioned Grip" system in which the Goncalo Alves panels are set in a rubber shock-absorbing seat. The guns were originally chambered only for the 44 Magnum round with 7.5- or 9.5-inch barrels; but a 454 Casull option was introduced at the beginning of 1999, and the 480 Ruger cartridge followed in January 2001. Post-1999 guns are stronger than their 44-caliber predecessors and usually have 7.5- or 9.5-inch barrels.

Super Single-Six (1964-72) This was a variant of the Single-Six (q.v.) with adjustable instead of fixed sights. Barrels were restricted to

5.5 and 6.5 inches, though a few hundred were made with the 4.6-inch type. Finish was usually blued-steel cylinder/blacked-alloy frame, but 100 guns were nickel-plated.

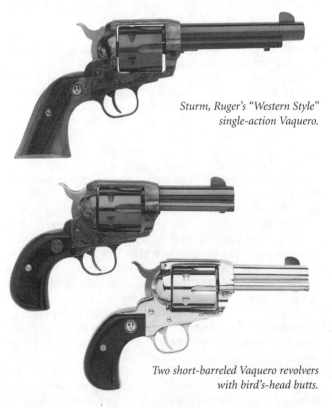

Sturm, Ruger's "Western Style" single-action Vaquero.

Two short-barreled Vaquero revolvers with bird's-head butts.

Vaquero (1993 to date) A fixed-sight version of the New Model Blackhawk, this was originally offered in 44 Magnum and 45 Long Colt. A 44-40 WCF option was added in 1994. Barrels measure 4.6, 5.5 and 7.5 inches, and the finish may be blued or stainless steel. Blued guns customarily have a simulated color case-hardened frame.

• *Vaquero Birdshead* (2001 to date) Currently being offered in 45 Long Colt with a 5.5-inch barrel, this has short round-heel grips. Finish may be blue or stainless steel.

∼ AUTOMATIC PISTOLS ∼

Note: Most of the Ruger pistols made after 1980 have been offered in stainless steel in addition to blue finish. Their designations are customarily given an additional "K" prefix. The KMK-6 is a stainless-steel version of the blued-steel MK-6, and sometimes excepting the material of the grips, the two guns are identical. Sturm, Ruger & Company has also made some special-issue guns for individual distributors but not in the quantities (or diversity) associated with Colt and Smith & Wesson. More than three million Ruger pistols had been made by 2003.

Standard Model (1949-82) The bedrock of the Ruger line, this 22 LR rimfire blowback was designed shortly after the end of World War

A cutaway view of the Ruger 22 rimfire "Standard" pistol.

II. It uses a fixed, exposed barrel with a tubular receiver in which a cylindrical bolt moves. The bolt can be retracted by two serrated wings that protrude at the rear of the receiver. There is an ejection port on the right side and a 9-shot magazine goes into the butt. The pistol was fired by an internal hammer, the mechanism being designed to give a short lock time. The rear sight was dovetail mounted to be laterally adjustable, and the tapering barrels measured 4.75 or 6 inches. Bill Ruger deliberately modeled his design on the Luger ("Parabellum"), capitalizing on the similarity of name, and it had a well-raked grip inspired by its German antecedent. The earliest guns had checkered composition grips, with the company's hawk-and-monogram trademark on a medallion with a red background. The death in 1951 of Alexander Sturm, one of the founding partners, was reflected in a change to a black background that was retained for the lifetime of the pistol (and has only recently been changed on the Mk II). A few hundred guns were assembled in Mexico and will bear "HECHO EN MEXICO" on the frame.

Mark I (1951-82) Within a short time of the introduction of the "Standard", a demand arose for a target model, and this appeared as the "Mark I" in 1951. It used the same frame and receiver but had fully adjustable sights. The first guns were made with a 6.9-inch barrel; but a tapered 5.25-inch barrel was offered in 1952-5, and a 5.5-inch cylindrical heavyweight or "bull" pattern appeared in 1963. A few guns will be found with muzzle brakes, and those that were purchased by the US Army for marksmanship training bore "U.S." on the frame. Ruger also made made 5000 "Red Eagle Commemoratives" in 1976, apparently to mark the 25th anniversary of the death of Alex Sturm; they were made of stainless steel.

Mark II Competition Model (or "MK-678GC") Introduced in 1991, this is an adaptation of the Mk II Target with a stainless-steel frame and barrel, a 6.9-inch bull barrel that is tapped and drilled for optical-sight mounts, an undercut Patridge-type front sight and checkered wooden thumbrest-style grips. A thousand guns were made in 1995 with 5.5-inch slab-sided barrels, but they lacked the "COMPETITION" marking on the frame. However, the flat-side barrel was subsequently introduced to regular production.

The 22 rimfire Ruger Mark II "Government Target Model" pistol, with a slab-side barrel.

Mark II Government Model (or "MK-678G") Based on the Mk II Target pistol, with a 6.9-inch heavy barrel, this is available in blue or stainless steel. Guns purchased by the US armed forces display "U.S." on the frame.

Mark II Standard Model (1982 to date) This replaced the original Standard Model. Improvements included a new magazine release, a better magazine, a hold-open catch, a modified high-speed trigger mechanism and a refined safety catch. Grips became checkered Delrin.

- *MK-4* This has a 4.75-inch barrel, fixed sights and weighs about 35 oz. It is made in blue or stainless steel.
- *MK-4B* A heavyweight version of the MK-4 with a 4-inch "bull" barrel and adjustable sights, this gun weighed about 38 oz. The grips were either checkered Delrin or wood laminate.

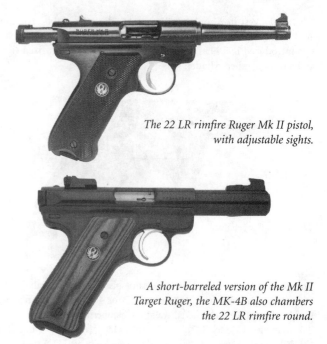

The 22 LR rimfire Ruger Mk II pistol, with adjustable sights.

A short-barreled version of the Mk II Target Ruger, the MK-4B also chambers the 22 LR rimfire round.

- *MK-6* A variation of the preceding gun, this offers a 6-inch barrel and adjustable sights. Finish may be blue or stainless steel. Weight is about 37 oz.
- *MK-6 NRA* (1997) Only 650 of these were made to help raise funds for the National Rifle Association. They had a high-polish blue finish, simulated ivory grips and an NRA inscription and serial number ("… of 650") inlaid in gold.
- *MK-10* Easily distinguished by its 10-inch barrel, this is mechanically identical to the standard Mk II. It has adjustable sights and may be obtained in blue or stainless steel.

A Mark II Target Model Ruger pistol, with adjustable sights.

Mark II Target Model (or "MK-678", 1982 to date) A replacement for the Mk I and available in blue or stainless steel, this was offered with a variety of barrels: 5.25-inch taper (1990-5 only), 5.5-inch heavy or "bull", 6.9-inch taper and 10-inch heavy. The guns all have adjustable target-type rear sights.

22/45 (1992 to date) Introduced in the early 1990s and sometimes known as the "Mk II Bull Barrel", this was the mechanism of the Mark

The Ruger 22/45 pistol.

II pistol placed on a frame that duplicated the dimensions and feel of the 45 ACP M1911. The Ruger magazine latch was also identical with its Colt-Browning prototype. The barrel and receiver are stainless steel, but the frame is made of a fiberglass-reinforced polymer called Xytel. Barrels may be 4-inch tapered, 5.25-inch tapered (1992-4 only) or a 5.5-inch heavyweight "bull" type. Except for guns with 4-inch barrels, which are fixed, the sights are target-type adjustable.

- *KP4* A derivative of the 22/45, this has a 4.75-inch tapered barrel, fixed sights and a weight of about 28 oz. Construction is stainless steel.
- *KP514* Made only in stainless steel in 1992-4, this had a 5.25-inch tapering barrel and adjustable sights. Weight was about 42 oz.
- *P4* Made in limited numbers in 1995, this entered series production in 1997. It has a 4-inch "bull" barrel and adjustable sights. The metalwork is blued.
- *P512* Essentially similar to the P4, this has a 5.5-inch barrel. The barrel/receiver unit is finished in blue or stainless steel (KP512).

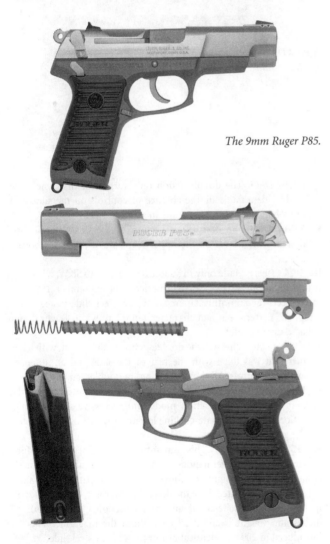

The 9mm Ruger P85.

A partly dismantled Ruger P85.

P-85 (1987-95) The first of the "P"-Series, this was Ruger's first heavy-caliber automatic pistol. It was a conventional double-action locked-breech automatic, using the familiar Browning swinging link method of locking. Instead of using lugs on top of the barrel to lock into recesses in the slide, the chamber area was squared off and this entire section locked into an enlarged ejection port that extended right across the top of the slide. The frame was of lightweight alloy, hardened to resist wear,

and the slide and barrel were of steel. There was an external hammer, and the safety catch was on the slide; it was ambidextrous and locked the firing pin, blocked the hammer and disconnected the trigger. Chambered for the 9mm Parabellum or 9x21 IMI rounds (the latter being comparatively rare), the P-85 was a sound, no-nonsense combat pistol with excellent accuracy.

P-89 (1991 to date) After the introduction of the P-85, slight modifications were made as a result of experience, and the model became known as the P-89. It was made to the same general design as the original P-85 but with small changes in manufacture and dimensioning. The safety catch is fitted on both sides of the slide and locks the firing pin, disconnects the trigger and blocks the fall of the hammer when applied. The magazine release is in the forward edge of the butt and can be operated by either hand. A stainless-steel version, introduced in 1992, is known as the "KP-89".

- *P-89DC* A de-cocking version of the basic design, with a radial lever on the rear left side of the slide above the grip. The standard gun is blued, but the KP-89DC is made of stainless steel.

RUGER 9mm P89DAO
Double Action Only Pistol

The new *RUGER* stainless *KP89DAO* (top) fires only in the double-action mode. There is no separate manual safety or decocking lever. Hammer spur has been bobbed and finger grooves added to rear of slide.

Magazine capacity of the new *RUGER* stainless *KP89DAO* is 15 rounds of 9mm Luger ammunition.   Catalog number KP89DAO

The KP-89 DAO.

- *KP-89 DAO* Made only in stainless steel, betrayed by the "K" prefix, this is a double-action-only version. It lacks the de-cocking and manual safety levers and has a hammer that lies flush with the rear of the slide.
- *KP-89X* (1993) Only about 6000 of these stainless-steel guns were made in 7.65mm and 9mm Parabellum (exchangeable barrels and springs) and with 15-round double-column magazines. The safety catch could be positioned for right- or left-handed shooters at will.

P-90 (blued) and KP-90 (stainless steel) (1991 to date) Fitted with a manual safety and a conventional double-action trigger mechanism that fired the second and successive shots from the single-action posi-

A 45 ACP Ruger KP-90 DC, in stainless steel.

tion, this chambered the 45 ACP round. A seven-round single-column magazine was standard.

KP-91 DAO (1992-5) Made only in stainless steel, in 40 S&W, this was a double-action-only design with a hammer that lay flush with the slide.

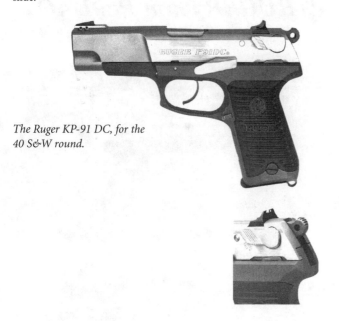

The Ruger KP-91 DC, for the 40 S&W round.

•   *KP-91 DC* (1992-5) A de-cocking variant of the KP-91 DAO, this could be identified by the de-cocking lever high on the left side of the slide above the grip. It fired the second and successive shots in single-action mode.

P-93 DAO (1993 to date) Chambered for the 9mm Parabellum cartridge and with a 15-round magazine (at least until 1994), this is a compact double-action-only design with a 3.9-inch barrel and a weight

The Ruger KP-93 DC is a "compact" with a 15-round magazine.

of about 24 oz without the magazine. There are no controls on the slide, and the hammer lies flush with the rear of the slide; all shots are fired in double-action mode. Post-1994 guns sold into the North American market have magazine capacities restricted to 10 rounds.

•   *P-93 DC* The de-cocking version of the P-93 DAO, this has a prominent de-cocking lever on the side of the slide above the grips. The controls are ambidextrous. Stainless-steel guns have an additional "K" prefix in the designations.

P-94 (1994 to date) A semi-compact gun with a 4.25-inch barrel, this has been made in 9mm Parabellum and 40 S&W, magazines holding 15 and 11 rounds, respectively (post-1994 North American-market guns are restricted to 10 rounds). A standard P-94, which fires the first shot double-action and successive shots in single-action mode, has a manual safety lever. It weighs about 33 oz. The "KP-94" is made of stainless steel.

A P-94 DAO Ruger, with a synthetic frame.

•   *KP-94 DAO* The double-action-only version of the basic design, readily identifiable by the absence of controls on the slide and a flush-lying hammer. Made only in stainless steel.
•   *KP-94 DC* The de-cocking version of the basic stainless-steel design, with a lever on the upper rear part of the slide above the grip.

KP-944 (1994) Made only in stainless steel and 40 S&W, with an 11-round magazine (10 in North America after September 1994), this introduced the smoothly tapered stainless-steel slide instead of the "stepped" pattern that had characterized the previous Ruger designs. It had a manual safety.

•   *KP-944 DAO* This was the double-action-only variant, with a hammer that was flush with the rear of the slide and an absence of external controls. All shots were fired in double-action mode.
•   *KP-944 DC* The de-cocking variant of the basic pistol, this fired the first shot in double-action mode and successive shots in single-action mode. It has a de-cocking lever on the side of the slide above the grip.

KP-95 (1996 to date) This gun introduced a fiberglass-reinforced polymer frame to Ruger handguns and is readily identifiable. The slide is stainless steel, the sights are three-dot "combat" patterns and a manual safety catch is fitted. Like the de-cocking variant, the gun fires once in double-action mode and then as a single action. Overall length is 7.3 inches and weight is about 29 oz without the magazine. The P-95, introduced in 2001, is identical except for a blued-steel slide.

•   *P-95 DAO* The double-action-only version, this has a hammer that lies flush with the rear of the slide.
•   *P-95 DC* The de-cocking version has a lever on the side of the slide above the grips. Unless this has been activated, the gun fires second and successive shots in single-action mode.

KP-97 DC (1999 to date) This de-cocking design chambers the 45 ACP round and has a seven-round single-column magazine. It also has a polymer frame, a stainless-steel slide, fixed sights and an empty weight of about 27 oz.

- *KP-97 DAO* Introduced in 2000, this is the double-action-only version of the KP-97 DC, easily identified by its spurless hammer. This lies flush with the slide.

SUINAGA Y ARAMPERRI

Eibar, Spain.

This partnership made 38-caliber revolvers in the 1920s, basing them on the Smith & Wesson Military & Police model. They could be identified by an "S&A" mark on the rear left side of the frame above the grip.

SUPER SIX LTD

Elkhorn, Wisconsin, USA.

This firm makes the *Golden Bison* revolver, based on the Colt 1873 Single Action Army but chambered for the 45-70 Government cartridge. This, being a rifle round, demands a sizeable revolver, and this weapon is 15 inches long with an 8-inch barrel, built on a manganese-bronze frame. It is a luxury product, sold in a fitted wooden case and with a lifetime guarantee. The *Golden Bison Bull* is the same basic weapon but with a 10.5-inch heavy barrel.

SWIFT RIFLE COMPANY

London, England.

This company was a manufacturer of training devices, but it manufactured an automatic pistol in 1944 in the hope of interesting the British army.

Tarn The pistol was designed by a Polish exile in England, named Bakanowski, and was a simple blowback in 9mm Parabellum. It was a conventional-looking fixed-barrel gun with a slide that resembled the 1910-type FN-Browning, the return spring concentric with the barrel. The breechblock was a separate component, held into the slide by a large wedge across the top.

Tested by the Ordnance Board in 1945, the Tarn was too poorly made to perform adequately. The strong spring and heavy construction needed to keep the breech closed until the chamber pressure had dropped made it awkward to handle. The action was violent and accuracy was poor. The Board rejected the pistol and nothing more was heard. Four guns were submitted for test, and it is unlikely that more than 10 were ever made.

T

TALLERES DE ARMAS LIVIANAS ARGENTINAS ("TALA")

Punta Alta, Argentina.

This small company manufactured two 22 LR automatic pistols in the post-1945 period. They generally resembled the Colt "Woodsman" in style, having short slides behind tubular fixed barrels and a well-raked butt. The standard model had a 3.3-inch barrel and fixed sights; the "Super E" Model had a 5.1-inch barrel and an adjustable rear sight. The company's name and address appear on the left side of the slide.

TANFOGLIO BROTHERS ("TANARMI")

"Tanarmi"–Fratelli Tanfoglio, Gardone Val Trompia, Brecia, Italy.

Fratelli Tanfoglio SNC was formed by the sons of Giuseppe Tanfoglio (below) in 1970 with the intention of enlarging production facilities that had become too restricted. After reaching agreement to share common components in 1974, work spent adapting the Czechoslovakian ČZ 75 led to the exceptionally successful TA90. This was extensively distributed in North America by Excam and others and laid the basis for a series of derivatives. A reorganization of the Tanfoglio businesses in 1982 created Fratelli Tanfoglio SPA. The products of this company are still distinguished by "Tanarmi" trademarks and "TA"-prefixed designations (cf, "Targa" and "GT" for Giuseppe Tanfoglio).

A 32-caliber Fratelli Tanfoglio Titan II pistol, distributed by FIE.

∼ REVOLVERS ∼

TA22 (or "Buffalo Scout") This, in several variations, was a 22 LR rimfire single-action revolver in "Western style" marketed in the USA during the 1965-75 period. Most of the variations were matters of finish—chrome, blue, brass backstrap and so forth—but some were available in 22WMRF chambering.

TA76M This is the current version of the "Buffalo Scout", a single-action six-shot revolver in 22LR or 22WMRF.

∼ AUTOMATIC PISTOLS ∼

TA18 A 9x18mm Police version of the TA90.

TA41 Ultra This, in effect, is the TA90 in 41 AE chambering with an alloy frame, a frame-mounted safety catch and a very high standard of finish. The slide is marked "I.P.S.C. Approved", and it is probably the most powerful pistol generally available to the commercial market in Italy.

TA90 This is a military-style pistol of high quality, generally resembling the ČZ 75, from which it has been copied. In 9mm Parabellum with a 15-round magazine, breech locking is by the usual Browning cam system. The trigger is double-action, and a manual safety on the slide locks firing pin, hammer, sear and trigger. Nine millimeter Short and 9mm Parabellum ammunition is classed as "military caliber" by

Two FIE-distruted "TA 90" 9mm Parabellum pistols, by Fratelli Tanfoglio.

the Italian authorities, and civilian ownership of weapons in these chamberings is prohibited; hence the popularity of the GT series in Italy (see "Giuseppe Tanfoglio").

• *TA90 Baby* This is the compact version of the TA90, 27 mm shorter and with a 12-round magazine.

• *TA90S* A target version of the TA90 with a 5.9-inch barrel (instead of the standard 4.7 inches), a muzzle weight, a muzzle compensator and an adjustable rear sight. For domestic consumption it is complemented by the *GT21S*, the same pistol but for the 9x21mm cartridge.

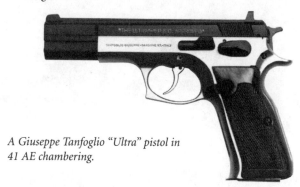

A Giuseppe Tanfoglio "Ultra" pistol in 41 AE chambering.

• *TA90K Pitbull* This is the "combat" version of the TA90, having the safety moved to the frame and the smaller slide stop lever. Normally in 9mm Parabellum, it is also available in 41 AE, and a spare barrel in the alternative caliber can be purchased to allow quick conversion. The domestic equivalent is the *GT41K* with the choice of 9x21mm or 41 AE.

TA380 This was the export designation of the GT32 (by Giuseppe Tanfglio, q.v.), with a seven-round single-row magazine.

TA382 A variant of the TA380 with a staggered-row magazine containing 11 rounds.

GIUSEPPE TANFOGLIO

Fabbrica d'Armi Giuseppe Tanfoglio, Magno Val Trompia, Brescia; Giuseppe Tanfoglio SRL, Gardone Val Trompia, Brescia, Italy.

This gunmaking business succeeded Sabatti & Tanfoglio (q.v.) in 1961, introducing the first of the "GT" series of pistols a year later. These were followed by the first Western-style revolvers and two-barrel Remington-type derringers. By the late 1960s, it had become obvious that business was rapidly outgrowing its facilities. Giuseppe Tanfoglio's sons then formed Fratelli Tanfoglio (see above) in nearby Gardone, principally to develop military-style pistols.

Giuseppe Tanfoglio retained the blowback pistols, but production of revolvers was continued by his sons. The two companies agreed to

A 25-caliber Tanfoglio
Titan pistol.

The 25-caliber (6.35mm)
Titan pocket pistol.

share a common range of components in 1974 and eventually, in 1982, a major reorganization saw the creation of Giuseppe Tanfoglio SRL. The products of this company are still distinguished by "Targa" trademarks and "GT"-prefixed designations (cf, "Tanarmi" and "TA" for Fratelli Tanfoglio).

It should be noted that Tanfoglio products have been distributed widely in the Americas and will be found with a variety of markings. These include the stamps of distributors such as the EIG Corporation, Excam and FIE. Among the brand names commonly applied to the guns was "Titan".

～ REVOLVERS ～

Buffalo Scout This was the original 22-caliber Western-style gun, introduced c. 1965 and made by Fratelli Tanfoglio (q.v.) after 1970.

～ AUTOMATIC PISTOLS ～

GT21 The GT21 is essentially the same as the TA90 but chambered for the 9 x 21mm IMI cartridge and with some minor changes in contour. The trigger guard has a deeper curve on the bottom surface and the butt contour is slightly changed for a better grip. The standard model is the same size as the TA90 and has a 15-shot magazine.

A 9x21 Giuseppe Tanfoglio
GT21 Baby pistol.

- *GT21 Baby* has the same construction as the GT21 but is smaller and has a 13-shot magazine.
- *GT21 Baby Combat* has the safety on the frame and the modified slide stop lever.
- *GT21 Combat* model is as for the Standard but with the safety mounted on the frame and a less protruding slide stop catch.

GT22 This is a 22LR blowback automatic with fixed barrel, open-top slide and external hammer. The magazine has a finger-rest to afford a better grip.

The long-barreled GT22T pistol,
in 22 LR rimfire.

- *GT22T* This was a target version with a 150mm barrel and adjustable rear sight.

GT27 A 6.35mm automatic that is similar to, but smaller than, the GT22 and without the finger-rest.

GT30 This is essentially a TA90 chambering the 7.65mm Parabellum round.

GT32 A 7.65mm model, again to the same general plan as the GT22 but larger. It is also available in 9mm Short as the "TA380", but only for export.

The Giuseppe Tanfoglio-marked
GT32 pistol.

- *GT32/2* This was a variant model with a 12-shot magazine, instead of the seven-shot of the standard model. Similarly, the "TA382" is the same design in 9mm Short with an 11-shot magazine.

TAURUS

Forjas Taurus SA, Porto Alegre, Rio Grande do Sul, Brazil.
This company was founded in 1939 to make Smith & Wesson-type revolvers and is now part of a group that makes products ranging from hand tools to sports equipment. By the early 1990s, the company was employing more than 3000 people in four factories in Brazil and, thanks to a subsidiary in Miami, had risen to become the second most important distributor of handguns in the USA after Smith & Wesson. Taurus International Firearms, Inc. (subsequently "Taurus Firearms, Inc.") makes the PT-22 and PT-25 pistols that could not otherwise be imported owing to the provisions of the 1968 Gun Control Act.

～ REVOLVERS ～

Unless specifically identified to the contrary, these are invariably solid-frame swing-cylinder double-action guns modeled on Smith & Wesson practice. The different models vary in barrel lengths, sights and grips, though they are built on only a handful of basic frames — small (22, 32 and some small 38-caliber patterns), medium (357 Magnum, 38 and 44 calibers) and the large "Raging Bull" type, chambering some of the most powerful mass-production handgun cartridges and incorporating an additional locking latch on the left side of the frame ahead of the cylinder.

"Plain" barrels usually lacked shrouds for the ejector rods. "Heavy" barrels customarily had shrouds and ribs, though the latter could be solid or ventilated depending on the individual pattern. Virtually all Taurus revolvers made since the mid-1970s have incorporated floating firing pins and transfer-bar safety systems that comply with the US Gun Control Act.

Many guns have been advertised with "S" suffixes to their designations, which simply indicated that they were made of stainless steel. This distinction tended to disappear after the mid-1990s and is now rarely drawn. The current tendency is to allocate designations that have been expanded to include the barrel length, finish and special features — e.g., "M85B2CH" would be a Model 85 revolver in blued steel with a 2-inch barrel and a concealed hammer.

Markings vary considerably, particularly after the formation of the US subsidiary. The barrels of the original Brazilian-made revolvers were marked "FORJAS TAURUS S.A." above "P. ALEGRE • RS • BRASIL". Guns sold into the US market usually had "TAURUS • BRASIL" on the left side of the barrel, with the caliber designation (e.g., "CAL. .357 MAGNUM") on the right. The encircled bull's-head trademark appeared on the left side of the frame beneath the hammer and on the medallions set into the grips. "TAURUS INT. MFG." above "MIAMI, FLA." is on the right side of the frame above the trigger, with the serial number above "MADE IN BRAZIL" on the front right side.

Model 17 Tracker (announced in 2002) Chambered for the 17 Hornady Magnum rimfire round and with a seven-chamber cylinder, this is offered with a 6-inch barrel, adjustable sights, rubber grips and matte stainless-steel finish. It weighs about 46 oz empty.

• *Model 17 Silhouette* (announced in 2002) This is easily identified by its 17 HMR chambering and 12-inch ventilated-rib barrel. The pressure of the main spring and the position of the trigger stop can both be adjusted. Empty weight is about 58 oz.

Model 22H (Raging Hornet, 1999 to date) Chambered for the 22 Hornet centerfire round, this offers a 10-inch ventilated-rib barrel and an eight-chambered cylinder. The sights are adjustable, the finish is matte stainless steel and the grips are black rubber. The gun weighs about 50 oz empty.

Model 30C (Raging Thirty, announced in 2002) Fitted with a 10-inch ventilated-rib barrel, this bulky eight-shot double-action revolver chambers the 30 [M1] Carbine cartridge and requires "full-moon" clips to extract the rimless cases satisfactorily. It weighs 72 oz empty.

Model 44 (1994-2001?) Made of blued or stainless steel, this six-shot gun chambered the 44 Magnum cartridge. The standard barrels measured 4, 6.5 and 8.4 inches, the two longer options (with ventilated ribs instead of solid) having integral compensators. Sights consisted of a ramp at the front and an adjustable open notch at the rear. Grips were usually hard rubber, though wooden patterns could be obtained on request.

Model 45 (Raging Bull, 1997-2001?) This was a variant of the Model 44 (above) chambered for the 45 Long Colt round. Barrel-length options were restricted to 6.5 and 8.4 inches.

Model 65 (1978 to date) Identified by its slender grips, this 1978-vintage six-shot design can accept 357 Magnum or 38 Special cartridges interchangeably and has fixed sights. The solid-rib barrels lacked ejector-rod shrouds and measured 2.5 inches (from 1992 only), 3 inches (discontinued in 1992) or 4 inches. Overall length was 9.4 inches with the 4-inch barrel, empty weight being about 37 oz. The guns were blued with hardwood grips, until a stainless-steel version appeared in 1993.

Model 66 (1978 to date) Little more than a Model 65 with adjustable sights, this could be fitted with 3-, 4- or 6-inch barrels. A 2.5-inch barrel replaced the 3-inch type in 1992. Offered in blued steel or (from 1993) stainless steel, the M66 weighs about 35 oz with a 4-inch barrel. In 1998, the basic pattern was changed to accommodate a seven-cham-

The Taurus Model 66 revolver.

ber cylinder; finish may be blue or stainless steel, and rubber grips are now standard.

• *Model 66 CP* (1993 to date) This offers 4- or 6-inch solid-rib barrels with integral compensator slots alongside the front sight. The ejector-rod heads are shrouded.

• *Model 66 Silhouette* (2001 to date) Fitted with a 12-inch barrel, this seven-shot gun also has adjustable sights. The grip is black rubber, and construction may be either blued carbon or matte stainless steel.

Model 70 A six-shot design in 32 S&W Long, this had a plain 4-inch barrel and small grips. Guns in this chambering were abandoned in the late 1980s in favor of 32 H&R Magnum derivatives.

Model 71 This was a variant of the Model 70, also in 32 S&W Long, with a heavy solid-rib barrel. The sights were fixed.

Model 73 Originally introduced for the 32 S&W Long cartridge, this was re-introduced in 1989 for the comparatively short-lived 32 H&R Magnum but has now reverted to the original chambering. It has a six-chamber cylinder, a 3-inch ribbed barrel with a half-length ejector-rod shroud, and fixed sights. The large grip is usually walnut.

Model 74 Another of the guns chambered for the 32 S&W Long round, this was apparently a Model 73 with adjustable sights. It was made only in small quantities.

Model 76 Also originally chambering the 32 S&W Long round but subsequently adapted for 32 H&R Magnum, this six-shot target revolver had a 6-inch barrel and adjustable sights. It was available only in blue.

Model 80 (1980-2001?) A six-shot in 38 Special, this had fixed sights, small hardwood grips and a heavyweight tapering 3- or 4-inch barrel. The ejector-rod head lacked a shroud and the gun weighed 30 oz empty. Finish was originally blue or (much more rarely) nickel-plating, but a stainless-steel option – sometimes designated "M80 SS" – was introduced in 1993.

A Taurus Model 82 revolver.

Model 82 (1980-2001?) Similar to the Model 80 in caliber, finish and barrel-length options, this also had fixed sights. However, it had a heavy barrel with a prominent top rib and weighed about 34 oz. A stainless-steel "M82 SS", latterly offered only with a 4-inch barrel, was introduced in 1993.

- *Model 82B* (1997-2001?) A strengthened version of the basic design, this could handle 38 Special "+P" ammunition. Restricted to a 4-inch barrel and blue finish but retaining a six-chamber cylinder, it weighed 37 oz.

Model 83 (1977-2001?) This 4-inch-barreled six-shot revolver, in 38 Special only, had a ribbed barrel with a half-length ejector-rod shroud and large wooden grips. The front sight was a Patridge design, and the rear sight was adjustable. The guns were originally finished in blue, or more rarely plated with nickel, until a stainless-steel option ("M83 SS") was introduced in 1993.

Model 85 (1980 to date) Distinguished by oversize grips and an ejector-rod shroud extending virtually to the muzzle, this 38 Special personal-defense revolver was offered with fixed sights and heavy solid-rib 2-, 3- or 4-inch barrels. The 4-inch option was discontinued in 1992. Guns have been made in blued, nickeled or (from 1993) stainless-steel finish. The original hardwood grips were replaced in 1996 by rubber Uncle Mike's Boot Grips.

The 38 Special Taurus Model 85.

This short-barreled Taurus M85CH revolver has a spurless hammer.

- *Model 85CH* Introduced in 1991, specifically for short-range personal defense, this had a 2-inch barrel and a spurless "Concealed Hammer". Removing the cocking notch on the hammer ensured that the gun could only be fired in double-action mode.
- *Model 85 Ti* (or "85 ULT", 1999 to date) The first of the "Titanium Series" to be listed here, this five-shot in 38 Special has a 2-inch barrel and fixed sights. It is distinguished by a titanium-alloy cylinder and frame/barrel sleeve, with a rifled stainless-steel liner. Most guns have ported barrels and, where appropriate, are rated for "+P" ammunition. The grips are invariably black rubber, but three finishes are offered: bright blue, matte blue and matte gold.
- *Model 85 UL* (1997-9) This "Ultra-Lite" variant was built on an aluminum-alloy frame, reducing empty weight to 17 oz. Made only with a 2-inch barrel, in blue or stainless steel, it had rubber grips.
- *Model 85 UL/Ti* (1999 to date) A replacement for the preceding gun, this is now designated "M85 UL". It is fitted with a 2-inch barrel that lacks gas-escape ports and combines a titanium-alloy cylinder with a conventional aluminum-alloy frame. The sights are fixed.

Model 86 Made only in small numbers, this was similar to the Model 83 but had a 6-inch barrel. It was originally chambered for 32 S&W Long (discontinued in 1991) or 38 Special ammunition and had a checkered Brazilian hardwood grip. The trigger was adjustable, the hammer had a broad "target" spur, and the finish was blue. Some guns were apparently made with barrels that had an elongated matte-finish sight rib with an adjustable weight, but most had a tapering lightweight barrel with an unshrouded ejector-rod head.

Model 87 A six-shot 38 Special gun, this was offered with 3-inch or 4-inch barrels.

Model 88 Similar to the Model 87, this had an additional 2.5-inch barrel option.

Model 90 This 22 LR rimfire revolver had a six-chamber cylinder. The 4-inch plain barrel lacked a rib and an ejector-rod shroud, and small grips were fitted.

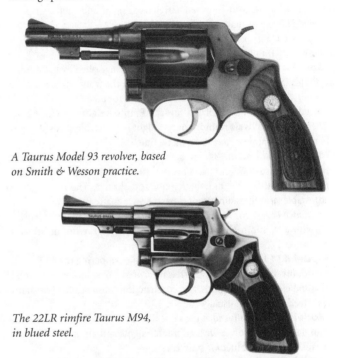

A Taurus Model 93 revolver, based on Smith & Wesson practice.

The 22LR rimfire Taurus M94, in blued steel.

Model 94 (1989 to date) Chambered for the 22 LR rimfire cartridge, this has a nine-chamber cylinder and adjustable sights. The ribbed barrels have half-length ejector-rod shrouds. They were originally restricted to 3 or 4 inches, but a 5-inch option was introduced in 1996. Large hardwood grips are standard. The guns were all blued until the introduction of a stainless steel in 1993.

- *Model 94 UL* (1997 to date) Offered only with a 2-inch barrel and an aluminum-alloy "Ultra-Lite" frame, this 22 LR rimfire gun has a rubber grip. It weighs 14 oz empty and may be obtained in blue or stainless finish.

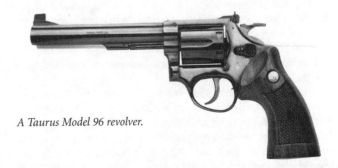

A Taurus Model 96 revolver.

Model 96 (1989-2001?) A six-shot 22 LR rimfire target revolver, this had adjustable sights, an adjustable trigger, a broad-spur "target" hammer and a heavy 6-inch barrel. It was available only in blue with hardwood grips.

Model 217 (Target Silhouette, announced in 2002) Another of the Taurus revolvers chambered for an unusual cartridge — in this case, 218 Bee — this offers an eight-chamber cylinder and a 12-inch ventilated-rib barrel with adjustable sights. The main spring and the trigger stop are also adjustable. Offered in matte-finish stainless steel, with black rubber grips, the M217 weighs about 52 oz empty.

Model 218 (Raging Bee, announced in 2002) Also chambered for the Bee cartridge, this seven-shot revolver has the double cylinder-yoke locking system and a heavy 10-inch ventilated-rib barrel. The grips are rubber, the main spring and trigger stop are adjustable, the construction is matte stainless steel and the empty weight is about 75 oz.

Model 415 (1999 to date) Another of the five-shot 41 Magnum guns, this has a 2.5-inch ported barrel, fixed sights and rubber grips. It is made largely of matte-finish stainless steel.
• *Model 415 Ti* (or "M415 ULT") This is a variant of the M415 with an alloy frame. See "M85 Ti" for additional details.

Model 416 (Raging Bull, 1999 to date) Distinguished by the double cylinder latches (one on the rear and one on the front left side of the frame), this is chambered for the 41 Magnum round and has a 6.5-inch ported barrel with a ventilated top-rib. Empty weight is about 62 oz. The cylinder holds six rounds, the rear sight is adjustable, grips are rubber and the stainless steel has a matte finish.

Model 425 (Tracker, 2000 to date) Chambered for the 41 Magnum round, this five-shot gun has a heavy ported 4-inch barrel with a solid rib and a full-length underlug/ejector-rod shroud. The rear sight is adjustable, and the stainless-steel parts have a matte finish.
• *Model 425 Ti* (or "M425 ULT") A five-shot 41 Magnum revolver with a titanium-alloy frame and a distinctive gray finish. See also "M 85 Ti".

Model 431 (1991-2001?) A five-shot gun chambering the 44 Special round, this had fixed sights. Barrels measured 3 or 4 inches, with solid ribs and ejector-rod shrouds, and construction could be blued or stainless steel. Grips were usually rubber.

Model 441 Announced at the same time as the M431, this was a five-shot 44 Special revolver with adjustable sights and an optional 6-inch barrel. It could be blued or stainless steel.

Model 444 (Raging Bull) This is little more than a fixed-sight version of the Model 44 (q.v.). Barrels may be 4, 6.5 or 8.4 inches long.

Model 445 Chambered for the 44 Special round, this has a five-chamber cylinder, fixed sights and black rubber grips. The barrel may be ported. Construction is blued or stainless steel.
• *Model 445 CH* (1997 to date) This is simply a concealed-hammer version of the standard gun, with the trigger system restricted to double-action-only.
• *Model 445 Ti* (or "M445 ULT", 1999 to date) A lightweight variant of the M445, this has a 2-inch barrel and a titanium-alloy frame. See also "M85 Ti".

Model 450 (1999 to date) This is similar to the Model 445, but chambered for the 45 Long Colt cartridge. Barrel-length options are restricted to 6.5 and 8.4 inches.
• *M450 Ti* (or "M450 ULT", 1999 to date) A variant of the M450 with a titanium-alloy frame, this has a 2-inch ported barrel and fixed sights. See also "M85 Ti".

Model 454 (Raging Bull, 1997 to date) Chambered for the powerful 454 Casull round, this five-shot revolver has a 5-, 6.5- or 8.4-inch compensated barrel. The sights are adjustable, construction may be blued or stainless steel and the grips are either rubber or walnut. A typical example weighs 56 oz with the longest of the barrels.

Model 455 (Stellar Tracker, announced in 2002) Adapted to fire 45 ACP ammunition and requiring a five-cartridge "full-moon clip", this may be obtained with 2-, 4- or 6-inch barrels. Empty weight is about 38 oz, with the longest barrel. The sights are adjustable, the grips are usually rubber and construction is matte-finish stainless steel.

Model 460 (Tracker, announced in 2002) This five-shot revolver, chambering the 45 Long Colt cartridge, may be obtained with 4- or 6-inch ventilated-rib barrels. Fitted with an adjustable rear sight, it is made of matte-finish stainless steel and has black rubber grips.

Model 480 (Raging Bull, 2001 to date) Chambered for the awesome 480 Ruger round, with a 5-chamber cylinder, this can have ported ventilated-rib barrels 5, 6.5 and 8.4 inches long. The front sight is a Patridge-type blade, the rear sight is an adjustable open square notch and the soft rubber grips help to soften the recoil forces. Construction may be blued or matte-finish stainless steel.

Model 605 (1995 to date) This personal-defense revolver chambered the 357 Magnum cartridge and had fixed sights. The last digit of the designation, "5", indicated the number of chambers in the cylinder. Offered in blue or stainless steel, the 605 had a 2.25- or 3-inch barrel with a solid rib and a full-length ejector-rod shroud. The grips, originally Brazilian hardwood, have been rubber since 1996.
• *Model 605C* ("Custom", 1999 to date) This has a 2.25-inch compensated barrel with a single gas-escape slot on each side of the front sight. It may be purchased blued or in stainless steel.
• *Model 605CH* This was simply a variant of the 605 with a 2.25-inch barrel, a spurless "Concealed Hammer" and the trigger mechanism restricted to double-action only. Available in blue or stainless-steel finish, the guns weigh about 24 oz.
• *Model 605CHC* A variant of the M605, combining the concealed hammer and the compensated 2.25-inch barrel, this can be obtained in blued or stainless steel. The designation sometimes includes the finish and barrel length (i.e., "Model 605CHSS2C").

Model 606 (1998-2001?) Chambered for the 357 Magnum round, this had a 2-inch barrel and fixed sights. Available in blued or stainless steel with rubber grips, the M606 had a trigger system that could be restricted to single-action, double-action, or double-action-only (the latter usually accompanied by a spurless hammer).

Model 607 (1995-2001?) Another of the 357 Magnum designs, available in blued or stainless steel, this had a seven-chamber cylinder. The 4- and 6.5-inch barrels had integral compensators; the longer barrel also had a ventilated rib. The grips were black rubber, and the rear sights were adjustable.

Model 608 (1995 to date) Fitted with rubber grips, a red ramp front sight and an adjustable rear sight, this was essentially an eight-shot version of the 607. The same barrel options were offered. Made of blued or stainless steel, the M608 weighs 52 oz with the longer of the two barrels.

Model 617 (1998 to date) Little more than a seven-shot version of the six-shot 357 Magnum Model 606 with a 2-inch barrel, fixed sights and rubber grips, this can be obtained in blued or stainless steel.
• *Model 617CH* A concealed-hammer version of the standard M617, this also has lockwork restricted to double-action-only.
• *Model 617CP* (1998 to date) A minor variant of the standard M617, this has three gas-escape ports cut into the barrel on each side of the front sight.
• *Model 617 Ti* (or "M617 ULT", 1999 to date) This has a seven-chamber cylinder, a 2-inch barrel and fixed sights. Its construction duplicates the M85 Ti (q.v.).

Model 627 (2000 to date) A seven-shot 357 Magnum, this revolver has a 4-inch ported barrel with a heavy full-length ejector-rod shroud. The finish is restricted to matte stainless steel, and the grips are generally black rubber.
• *Model 627 Ti* (or "M627 ULT") Fitted with a 4-inch ported barrel, a seven-chamber cylinder and adjustable sights, this is otherwise similar to the M85 Ti (q.v.). It is finished in gray.

Model 669 (1988-2001?) This 357 Magnum revolver had a 4- or 6-inch solid-rib barrel, a full-length ejector-rod shroud, an adjustable rear sight and a replaceable-insert front sight on a short ramp. Finish could be blued or stainless steel; the grips were Brazilian hardwood.

The 357 Taurus Model 669 Magnum revolver, in blue.

• *Model 669CP* (1992-2001?) This had a 6-inch barrel with integral compensating slots, one on each side of the front sight. A seven-chamber cylinder was standardized in 1998.

A 357-caliber Taurus M689, in stainless steel.

Model 689 (1990-2001?) Chambering the 357 Magnum round, this was a variant of the 669 with a ventilated rib above the barrel — and, therefore, lighter by about 2 ounces. Seven-chamber cylinders were standardized in 1998.

Model 731 Ti (or "M731 ULT", 1999 to date) Chambered for the 32 H&R Magnum round, with a six-chamber cylinder, a 2-inch barrel and fixed sights, this shares the constructional features of the M85 Ti (q.v.).

Model 741 (1991-2001) This six-shot gun, with 3-inch or 4-inch heavy solid-rib barrels, was little more than a Model 74 (in 32 H&R Magnum) with adjustable sights. Weight averaged 30 oz with the longer barrel. The original guns were blued, with hardwood grips, but a stainless-steel option was announced in 1993.

Model 761 (1992-2001) A variant of the M741 with a heavy 6-inch solid-rib barrel and adjustable sights, this weighed about 34 oz. Finish was restricted to blued steel.

Model 817 (1999 to date) Chambered for the 357 Magnum round, this is an "Ultra-Lite" pattern with an alloy frame. The cylinder has seven chambers, the solid-rib barrel (which may be ported) is restricted to 2 inches, the sights are fixed and the construction may be blued or stainless steel.

Model 827 (1998 to date) This is simply a variant of the M817 with a 4-inch heavy barrel and adjustable sights. Grips are usually rubber; construction may be blued or stainless steel.

Model 889 (1990-2001?) This was little more than a 689 (q.v.) chambered for the 38 Special round.

Model 939 Another of the nine-shot 22 rimfire revolvers and discontinued in the early 1990s, this was offered with barrels of 3 or 4 inches. It had adjustable sights.

Model 941 (1992 to date) Chambered for the 22 Magnum rimfire round, this is little more than the Model 94 (q.v.) with an eight-chamber cylinder and solid-rib barrels measuring 3 or 4 inches. The ejector-rod head is shrouded. A 5-inch barrel option was announced in 1996, when rubber grips replaced the original hardwood pattern. Sights are adjustable.

• *Model 941UL* (1997 to date) Distinguished by an "Ultra-Lite" aluminum-alloy frame, reducing weight to 10 oz (2-inch barrel), this may have a blue or stainless finish.

Model 970 (Tracker, 2001 to date) This seven-shot 22 LR rimfire gun has a 6-inch ventilated-rib barrel and adjustable sights. The grips are rubber, and the construction is matte-finish stainless steel. Empty weight averages 54 oz.

Model 971 (Tracker, 2001 to date) This is nothing more than an M970 chambered for the 22 WM rimfire cartridge.

Model 980 (Silhouette, 2001 to date) Chambering 22 LR rimfire ammunition, with a seven-chambered cylinder, this gun has a heavy-weight 12-inch ventilated-rib barrel with an integral rail for optical-sight mounts. Grips are rubber, construction is matte-finish stainless steel and empty weight is about 68 oz.

Model 981 (Silhouette, 2001 to date) A variant of the M980 (above) chambering 22 WM rimfire instead of 22 LR.

∼ AUTOMATIC PISTOLS ∼

Most of the Taurus pistols originated as license-built Berettas, though the ranges have since deviated in detail. The Brazilian-made guns have never offered the variety of trigger mechanisms that has characterized the Italian prototypes. The original Brazilian-made guns bore markings such as "TAURUS PT 92 AF 9mm para." on the left side of the slide ahead of the trademark, often with "TAURUS INT. MFG." above "MIAMI, FLA." on the right side of the slide above the trigger. "MADE IN BRAZIL" customarily appeared on the front right side of the slide on guns distributed in the USA. Medallions let into the grips also bore the trademark. By the early 1990s, however, the US guns were sporting a modernized legend: a linear form of the trademark ahead of "TAURUS® INT. MFG. INC" in a single line, above "MIAMI, FL."; the lettering took a much squarer form than previously, with "TAURUS" in bold outline.

The 22 LR rimfire Taurus PT22 pistol, derived from the tip-barrel Berettas.

PT22 (1992 to date) This 22 LR rimfire pistol has a 2.75-inch barrel and an eight-round magazine. Overall length is about 5.3 inches; empty weight is just 12 oz. The trigger is a double-action design, the sights are fixed, and the grips are usually Brazilian hardwood. Finish may be blue, blue with gold accents, nickel, or two-tone blue/nickel. To comply with restrictions imposed by the Gun Control Act of 1968, the guns are now being assembled in the USA.

PT25 (1992 to date) A 25 ACP version of the PT22, introduced at the same time and also assembled in the USA, this has a nine-round magazine.

PT51 Replaced by the PT25, this was a 25 ACP tip-barrel blowback, in blue or nickel, with a 2.4-inch barrel and an eight-round box magazine in the butt. The magazine release was set into the left grip.

PT55 Chambered for the 22 LR rimfire round, this was another tip-barrel Beretta adaptation. Finished in blue or nickel, it had a 2.75-inch barrel and a seven-round magazine. It was replaced by the US-made PT22.

A 7.65mm (32-caliber) Taurus PT57, based on the 92-series Beretta pistols.

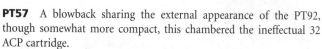

A Taurus AF-D with the marks of the US subsidiary.

PT57 A blowback sharing the external appearance of the PT92, though somewhat more compact, this chambered the ineffectual 32 ACP cartridge.

- *PT57C* A "Compact" version of the original pistol, this had a 4-inch barrel and a 12-round staggered-column magazine. Some post-1991 guns were made of stainless steel.
- *PT57S and PT57SC* These seem to have been improved variants of the original guns, with ambidextrous safety levers.

PT58S (1988-2000?) Chambered for the 380 ACP cartridge, with a 4-inch barrel and a 12-round staggered-row magazine, this variant of the PT57 had fixed sights and an ambidextrous safety catch; finish could be blue, nickel or (from 1991) stainless steel.

PT91 (1991-4) This was a short-lived derivative of the PT92 chambering the 41 Action Express round. It had a 10-round magazine, a two-position safety lever and weighed about 34 oz.

PT92 This was essentially a Brazilian version of the 9mm Parabellum Beretta Model 92 (q.v.), made under license in Porto Alegre. Made only with a double-action trigger system and a 15-round staggered-row magazine, the original guns had conventional "right-handed" controls. These were apparently improved in 1983, when the "AF" version appeared with ambidextrous safety and magazine-release features, and then on the introduction in 1990 of the "AF-D" guns with a proprietary three-position safety/de-cocking lever above the rear of the grip.

Pressing the lever fully downward dropped a cocked hammer safely on a loaded chamber; a spring on post-1992 guns automatically returned the lever to its intermediate position. Guns with an "S" in their designations (e.g., "PT92 AFS D") had frames and slides made of stainless steel. However, though the designations have often been incorporated in Brazilian slide designations, they now appear only in the serial numbers of the pistols distributed in the USA.

The standard PT92 was 8.5 inches long and weighed about 33.5 ounces. Finish was customarily blued steel, but nickel-plating and stainless-steel finishes may also be encountered. PT92 sights were always fixed.

- *PT92 AFC* Also known simply as the "PT92C", this "Compact" derivative of the 92 AF had a 4.25-inch barrel and a shortened butt accepting a 13-round magazine.
- *PT92B* The current version of the PT92 series – the only one to remain in production – has a double-action trigger mechanism, with a three-way safety/de-cocking lever and three-dot "combat" sights. Chambered for the 9mm Parabellum round, the guns have 10-round magazines (for the US market) and 5-inch barrels that give an overall length of about 8.5 inches; empty weight is 34 oz. Construction may be blued or stainless steel, often found with gold accents. Adjustable night sights can be supplied on request.

A 9mm Taurus PT92 AF-D.

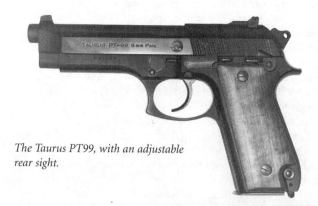

The Taurus PT99, with an adjustable rear sight.

A stainless-steel version of the Taurus 92, this AF-D chambers the 9mm Parabellum round.

PT99 Sometimes mistakenly identified as a "single-action" version of the PT92, this was really little more than the 9mm Parabellum PT92 with an adjustable rear sight. Finish could be blued, nickel or stainless steel.

- *PT99 AF* (1983-91) Made with ambidextrous safety levers and magazine-release catches.
- *PT99 AF D* (1992 to date) Still current, this offers a 5-inch barrel, a 15-round magazine (restricted to 10 in the USA) and the perfected de-cocking mechanism.

PT100 (1991-7, 2001 to date) A variant of the PT92, chambering the 40 S&W cartridge, this had a 5-inch barrel and an 11-round magazine (limited to 10 in the USA after 1994). Its sights were fixed, though the rear sight could be driven laterally in its dovetail, and the construction could be blued, nickeled or stainless steel. Empty weight was about 34 oz.

PT101 (1991-7, 2001 to date) This was a variant of the PT100, chambering the same 40-caliber ammunition but with a three-dot "combat" sighting system. Tritium-insert night sights are among the optional extras.

PT111 (Millennium, 1998 to date) Derived from the M911 (below), the guns in this series abandon the locking system of the Beretta – effectively that of the Walther P.38 – in favor of the simplified Colt-Browning dropping-barrel system. A squared block above the chamber rises into the ejection port. The PT111 chambers the 9mm Parabellum round, has a 3.25-inch barrel and 10-round magazine, and weighs about 16 oz empty. Overall length is 6 inches. The trigger is a double-action-only pattern. The closed-top slide may be blued carbon or matte-finish stainless steel, but the frame is a polymer molding.

* *PT111 Ti* (announced in 2002) Similar externally to the standard gun, this has a titanium-alloy slide and Tritium-insert night sights.

PT132 (Millennium, 2001 to date) Externally similar to the PT111, this is a simplified blowback version chambered for the 32 ACP (7.65mm Auto) round. The magazines hold 10 rounds.

PT138 (Millennium, 1999 to date) A blowback variant of the PT111 chambering the 380 ACP or 9mm Short cartridge. The barrel is 4 inches long and the magazines hold 10 rounds.

PT140 (Millennium, 1999 to date) A 40 S&W variant of the PT111, retaining the breech-lock. It has a 3.25-inch barrel, a 10-round magazine and weighs about 19 oz empty.

PT145 (Millennium, 2000 to date) Chambered for the 45 ACP round, this retains the locked breech of the PT111. Fitted with a 3.25-inch barrel and a 10-round magazine, it weighs about 23 oz empty. Teething troubles prevented the MP145 entering series production until 2002.

PT400 (1999-2001) Chambered for the 400 CorBon round, this was essentially the same as the PT908. A stainless-steel version was usually designated "PT400SS".

PT908 (1993-2001?) Chambered for the 9mm Parabellum cartridge and relying on the modified SIG-type Colt-Browning tipping-barrel locking system, this also had a perfected de-cocking trigger system, fixed three-dot "combat" sights and an eight-round single-row magazine that allowed the grip to be slimmer than normal. The grip had straight straps and the slide abandoned the familiar Beretta-type open top for a closed pattern. The standard barrel was 3.8 inches long. The first guns had wooden grips, but those delivered after 1996 used synthetic rubber. Slides could be blued, satin-nickeled or stainless steel; frames were forged aluminum-alloy, finished to duplicate the slide.

PT910 (1998-2001?) Chambered for the 10mm Auto cartridge, with a nine-round single-row magazine, this "908" derivative has now been abandoned.

PT911 (1997-2001) A variation of the PT908, this had a closed-top slide with squared contours (similar to the SIG-Sauers), adjustable sights and a 4-inch barrel. The magazine capacity was, in the USA at least, restricted to 10 9mm Parabellum rounds. Made of blued or stainless steel, the guns had black rubber grips.

PT922 (announced in 2002) This is a 22 LR rimfire blowback with a double-action trigger mechanism, adjustable sights and a 10-round magazine. Though bearing an external resemblance to the locked-breech PT92, the slender 6-inch barrel protrudes past the half-length slide; the result has been likened to the Walther P. 38, though the Taurus pistol is noticeably longer in relation to its height. Construction may be blued or stainless steel.

PT938 (1997 to date) This was a blowback version of the PT908, lacking the breech lock and chambering the 380 ACP (9mm Short) round. The guns are about 6.5 inches long, have 3.7-inch barrels and weigh about 27 oz; magazines hold 10 rounds.

PT940 (1996 to date) A variant of the PT908 chambering the 40 S&W cartridge, with a 4-inch barrel and an empty weight of about 28 oz, this now has three-dot "combat" sights. The single-column magazine held 10 rounds.

PT945 Announced in 1995, this PT908 derivative chambered the 45 ACP round and had an eight-round single-row magazine and a three-way safety/de-cocking lever. It was 7.5 inches long, had a 4.25-inch barrel and weighed about 29 oz empty. Construction could be blued or stainless steel closed-top slides (with optional gold accents), blued or bright-finish alloy frames, and grips could be of rubber, rosewood or mother of pearl.

* *PT945C* This was a "compensated" variant, with gas-escape ports in the slide alongside the front sight.
* *PT945S* (1998 to date) This chambers the 45 Super cartridge but is otherwise much the same as the standard "945".

PT957 (1999 to date) Another of the pistols based on the PT908, with the three-position de-cocking lever and an ambidextrous safety catch, this chambers the 357 SIG pistol cartridge. It is about 7 inches long with a 4-inch barrel and weighs about 28 oz empty; the magazines hold 10 rounds.

TEXAS LONGHORN

Texas Longhorn Arms Company (sometimes known as "Texas Armory"), Richmond, Texas, USA.

Most of the guns offered by this engineering business — obvious from the names — are "Western-style" single-action revolvers based on the Colt Peacemaker of 1873. An unusual detail is that (with the exception of the "Right Hand"), the loading gate and ejector rod are fitted to the left side of the gun, so that they can be reloaded without relinquishing the grip. All these weapons were hand-made, but work ceased in 1998.

∼ SINGLE-SHOT PISTOL ∼

Jezebel (or "The Jezebel") This was a hinged-barrel 22 LR or 22 Magnum rimfire single-shot target pistol announced in 1986 and offered commercially from 1988 onward. It was made entirely of stainless steel and had a 6-inch barrel.

∼ TWO-SHOT PISTOL ∼

Defender (1983) was a two-barrel derringer, offered in several chamberings.

∼ REVOLVERS ∼

Grover's Improved No. 5 Introduced in 1988, this had a flattop Bisley-like frame, target sights and special cylinder-pin latches. Only 1200 were made, with 5.5-inch barrels.

Mason Commemorative Offered only with a 4.75-inch barrel, this commemorative had mason's square-and-dividers insignia inlaid in gold on the frame. It dates from 1984.

Right Hand Introduced in 1984, this was basically a South Texas Army with the loading gate placed conventionally, on the right side of the fame behind the cylinder.

South Texas Army This was regarded as the standard model in the range, offered only in 357 Magnum, with a 4.75-inch barrel and conventional flare-heel grips.

Texas Border Special (1984) Offered in 44 S&W Special and 45 Long Colt, with a 3.5-inch barrel, this also had Pope-type rifling. It was blued, with a color case-hardened frame and bird's-head-type walnut grips.

Texas Sesquicentennial Announced in 1986, celebrating the 150th anniversary of the creation of the Texan state, this had ivory grips and was engraved in the style of Louis Nimschke.

West Texas Flat Top Target (1984) Based on the Colt Bisley target revolver, with a 7.5-inch barrel and target-style sights combined with a flat-topped frame. Chamberings were restricted to 32-20 WCF, 357 Magnum, 44 Special and 45 Long Colt.

THÄLMANN

VEB Fahrzeug und Jagdwaffenfabrik Ernst Thälmann, Suhl, Germany.

This was the East German State-controlled firearms consortium set up in about 1950 by amalgamating all the independent gunmakers of the Suhl district after the area came under communist control. Among the products were shotguns and sporting rifles sold under the "Simson" and "Merkel" names, the "Haenel" airguns and some Bühag (q.v.) pistols.

THAMES

Thames Arms Company, Norwich, Connecticut, USA.

One of the many small gunmaking businesses that flourished in the vicinity of Norwich in 1870-1900, Thames was responsible for conventional hinged-frame ribbed-barrel, double-action revolvers sold under the name "Automatic" — though this referred merely to their "automatic" self-ejecting action. Chamberings were customarily 22, 32 or 38 rimfire, the 22 having a seven-cartridge cylinder and the others being restricted to five.

These guns carry a variety of patent dates, principally 1886, and resemble some of the Hopkins & Allen products in detail. However, similarities with the Meriden revolvers can also be detected, and it is assumed that the various Norwich firms of the day used the same subcontractors.

THAYER, ROBERTSON & CAREY

Norwich, Connecticut, USA.

This name appears on a 38-caliber hinged-frame five-shot revolver identical to the Thames model and is assumed to be either a fictitious brand name or the mark of an otherwise obscure dealership.

THIEME & EDELER

Eibar, Spain.

Herr Thieme first appears in 1897 as a partner in the "Nimrod Gewehrfabrik Thieme & Schlegelmilch" of Berlin. Makers of shotguns, they disappeared in about 1910, but shortly thereafter, the DWM catalogue listed "Cartridge No. 547, 7.65mm Pistol, Thieme & Edeler, Eibar" suggesting that Thieme had taken a new partner and moved his operations to Spain. The listing of this cartridge is not sufficiently detailed to indicate whether it was a special design or merely the normal 7.65mm Auto round made under contract. Thieme & Edeler appear to have imported Spanish-made pistols for sale in Germany. Typically, they are 6.35mm or 7.65mm guns with Grande Précision (q.v.) "PRINCEPS" markings on the slides and a distinctive "TE" monogram on the butt.

THOMPSON/CENTER ARMS

Rochester, New Hampshire, USA.

This gunmaking business was founded in 1966 by Warren Center, who had designed a pistol and who owned the K.W. Thompson Tool Company.

Contender Introduced commercially in 1967, with a patented selectable rimfire/centerfire firing system, this is a single-shot tip-barrel

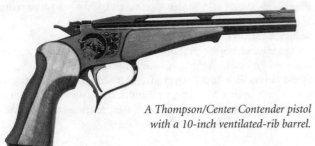

A Thompson/Center Contender pistol with a 10-inch ventilated-rib barrel.

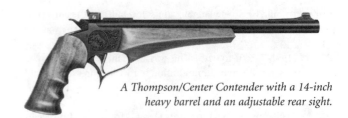

A Thompson/Center Contender with a 14-inch heavy barrel and an adjustable rear sight.

The Thompson/Center Contender Alloy II, with a 10-inch heavy "bull" barrel.

external hammer pistol of the highest quality. The standard barrel lengths are regarded as 10-inch octagon, 10-inch heavy (or "bull") and 10-inch vent-rib. A barrel can be easily removed and replaced by one of another caliber; in order to cater for changes between rimfire and centerfire, there is a dual firing pin that can be adjusted from one to the other ignition system. Since its inception, the Contender has been made available in chamberings ranging from 17 Bumblebee to 45/410, including 223 Remington, 30-30 WCF, 357 Magnum, 9mm Parabellum, 38 Special, 44 Magnum and 45 Long Colt.

• *Alloy II Contender* This is similar to the basic Contender but has an alloy frame.

Hunter This designation is usually reserved for a variant of the Contender gun with a 12- or 14-inch barrel with a compensator. Optical sights are regarded as standard.

Super Contender This is distinguished by the barrel, which may be a 14-inch "bull", a 14-inch ventilated-rib, a 16-inch tapered or a 16-inch ventilated-rib pattern.

Encore Introduced in 1996, this was designed expressly for use with high-pressure ammunition and has a stronger frame with higher side walls. The Encore barrels cannot be exchanged with the Contender fittings, though a special blackpowder version of the basic gun is also made.

THORSSIN

J. Thorssin & Son, Alingsås, Sweden.

This engineering business made the *Hamiltonpistol*, a semi-automatic design patented in Sweden in December 1900 by Count Gustav Hugo

The 6.5mm Swedish Hamilton pistol.

Röhss Hamilton of Gothenburg. The blowback gun had a clip-loaded magazine ahead of the trigger guard in Bergmann fashion but was distinguished by a curved bolt that moved radially down into the butt. The 1903-vintage Swedish trial reports reveal that it fired a specially under-loaded version of the 6.5mm Bergmann round, loaded with a 4.1-gram bullet, at 228 m/sec (748 ft/sec). The gun shot extremely badly and was withdrawn shortly after the accuracy trials began; it never reappeared. It is assumed that only a handful of prototypes were made, including a version that had a detachable box magazine pictured in Dr. J.H. Mathews' *Firearms Identification*.

TIPPING & LAWDEN

Caleb & Thomas Tipping-Lawden, Birmingham, Warwickshire, England.

Brothers Caleb and Thomas Tipping-Lawden opened their gunmaking business in 1837 but, although Thomas patented several sporting guns in 1861-2, preferred to make the designs of others under license. Revolvers were made during the caplock era for Deane, Lang and others, but the Tipping-Lawden brothers retired in 1877 and sold the business to P. Webley & Son. Production of Sharps pistols and Thomas revolvers ceased immediately, though guns were still being sold "from stock" in 1881. The trading style was invariably "Tipping <u>&</u> Lawden".

∼ REPEATING PISTOL ∼

Sharps Rights to this four-barreled pistol were apparently acquired from the executors of Christian Sharps in 1874. The guns fired the barrels sequentially; they were made in 22 and 30 rimfire for sale in Britain and also in 6mm, 7mm and 9mm rimfire for distribution in Europe.

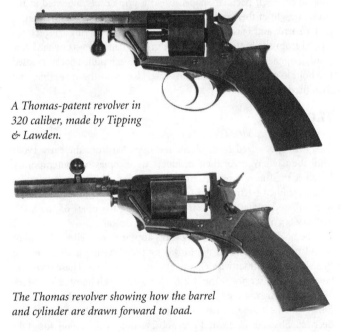

A Thomas-patent revolver in 320 caliber, made by Tipping & Lawden.

The Thomas revolver showing how the barrel and cylinder are drawn forward to load.

∼ REVOLVER ∼

Thomas Patented in 1869 by John Thomas of Birmingham, England, this was a solid-frame five-shot weapon using an unusual method of extraction in which the cylinder was carried in an over-long frame aperture. A knob beneath the barrel could be used to turn the barrel counter-clockwise, allowing a helical groove in the barrel to ride across a stud in the frame. This caused the barrel to move forward, pulling the cylinder away from the ejector plate to strip spent cases from the chambers. Loading was performed through a pivoting gate on the right side. The Thomas-patent revolver remained in production for about 7 years, about 1200 being made principally in 320, 380 and 450 centerfire though other chamberings have been reported.

TOKYO GAS & ELECTRIC COMPANY

Tokyo, Japan.

Nambu The manufacture of Type A and Type B pistols (see "Koishikawa") continued until the late 1920s. These guns were identical with their immediate Tokyo-made predecessors, excepting for flat-sided frames. The stock slot was then eliminated, further changes were made to the frame and work continued. Type "B" or "Baby Nambu" pistols were made until c. 1929. Guns of this type could be recognized by the manufacturer's mark, which consisted of "GTE" in a circle.

TOMIŠKA

Alois Tomiška, Pilsen, Bohemia, Austria-Hungary (later Czechoslovakia).

Born in Bohemia in 1876, Tomiška patented an automatic pistol with a double-action trigger system in 1908. A few guns were made by Wiener Waffenfabrik prior to World War I, and work resumed in the early 1920s. By this time, however, the designer was working for Jihočeská Zbrojovka (q.v.), where he reputedly designed the "Fox" automatic pistol. When the company was assimilated into Česká Zbrojovka, Tomiška continued design work until his death in 1946.

Little Tom Made in both 6.35mm and 7.65mm, this was a fixed-barrel blowback with the return spring around the barrel, an enveloping slide, an external hammer and a double-action lock. A sliding plate on the right side of the frame concealed the lockwork and could be removed once the slide was off. The safety catch lay in the frame, above the trigger. The slide ended in a pair of wings that enclosed most of the hammer and left only the serrated top exposed for cocking.

The production history of these guns is still very difficult to determine. The earliest were apparently marked "WIENER WAFFENFABRIK" above "PATENT" on the left side of the slide, with ribbon bearing "Little Tom" molded into the grips. The guns made after World War I display "WIENER WAFFENFABRIK. PATENT. LITTLE TOM. CAL. 7 $^{65}_{m}$/m" (or "6 35 m/m") in a single line on the left side of the slide. Those intended for export to English-speaking countries often had "(.25)" or "(.32)" appended to the mark. The grips usually display a "WWF" monogram on the grips, often on a small brass medallion. Many also have Austrian proofmarks dating from 1921-30.

Guns made, or perhaps simply sold, by Tomiška in Czechoslovakia were marked similarly to the post-1920 Austrian guns, excepting that the slide mark read "ALOIS TOMISKA – PLZEN – PATENT LITTLE TOM 6.35mm (.25)" and the medallion on the wooden grips displayed an "AT" monogram.

TRANSMARK

Tel Aviv, Israel.

Bul M5 This is basically a copy of the Colt M1911 using a synthetic frame and stainless slide. The trigger guard is shaped for the two-handed grip, and the hammer ends in a serrated ring rather than the usual spur. The M5 is available in either 45 ACP or 9mm Parabellum chambering, and the synthetic frame allows the use of a larger-capacity magazine than might be expected — 13 45 rounds or 18 9mm Parabellum (though magazines sold in the USA currently contain only 10 rounds to comply with the 1994 Act). The "Commander" version has fixed sights, but with the facility to add an optical sight, and has the barrel extended and slotted to act as a compensator. The "Standard" model has fixed and micro-adjustable sights and a normal length barrel.

TRANTER

William Tranter's Gun & Pistol Factory, Birmingham, Warwickshire, England.

Tranter (1816-90) was a Birmingham gunmaker of considerable repute and an active inventor in several disciplines. After succeeding a gunsmith named Dugard in 1841 and trading as a partner in Hollis,

Sheath & Tranter, he began trading on his own account in the early 1850s. Tranter is renowned as the patentee of a pepperbox (1849), for a series of revolvers (1853-68), and a variety of sporting guns. He was most active during the caplock era, often making guns for others. Many of the revolvers that were sold by English "country gunmakers" in the middle of the 19th century under their own names will be marked "Tranter's Patent" on the frame. However, Tranter also sub-contracted or licensed manufacture of his own designs elsewhere, and it is not impossible to find guns marked "Tranter's Patent" that were not made in Birmingham. The relevant patents protected trigger mechanisms, lockwork, extracting systems and methods of construction, and careful examination is often necessary to determine which particular patent was being acknowledged.

Army Model (or "M1878") The most important of all the Tranter revolvers made between 1870 and 1885 (when the inventor retired from business) was the British army's "Pistol, Revolver, Breech Loading, Tranter, Interchangeable" introduced in July 1878. The official approval gave the following details: "(1) the cylinder is short and has six flutes ... (2) the ejector rod has a direct action, and (3) the base of the cylinder is completely guarded. Length of barrel 6 inches, Caliber .433 ..." It was a solid-frame gate-loader with a rod ejector, based on earlier Tranter caplocks, and remained in British military service until superseded by the Webley in 1887.

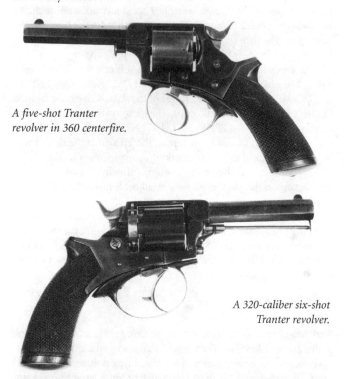

A five-shot Tranter revolver in 360 centerfire.

A 320-caliber six-shot Tranter revolver.

Others Revolvers offered commercially were more-or-less to the same specification as the Army pattern, though the cylinders were commonly smooth-surfaced (without the flutes of the military pattern) and could be supplied in a variety of rim- and centerfire chamberings. Particularly interesting was a 32 RF seven-shot pocket model, with a sheath trigger and a cylinder arbor pin that doubled as an ejection rod — a practice common with commercial Tranter designs. The single-action lockwork of the pocket revolver was also unusual, as most Tranters were double-action.

TREJO

Armas Trejo SA, Zacatlan, Mexico.

This company produced three interesting pistols in the 1955-65 period. The *Tipo Rafaga Model 1* and *Model 2* were both in 22 LR caliber and

their shape was based upon the Colt M1911 pattern, though they were simple fixed-barrel blowback designs. The unusual feature was the presence of a fire selector lever on the right side behind the trigger, which allowed either semi- or full-automatic fire. The Model 1 was quite plain, while the Model 2 had a ventilated rib above the slide and an adjustable rear sight.

The company also produced a *Model 3* in 9mm Short chambering, but this, sensibly, did away with the selective fire feature and was a straightforward semi-automatic.

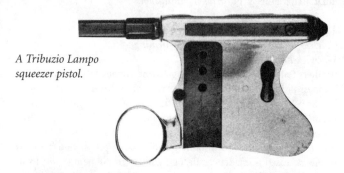

A Tribuzio Lampo squeezer pistol.

TRIBUZIO

Catello Tribuzio, Turin, Italy.

Tribuzio made the Lampo pistol, patented in 1890. This was one of the many mechanical repeaters developed around that time, but one that seems to have been moderately successful, since specimens appear from time to time. Of peculiar shape, it had a grip deeply indented at the back, straight at the front and containing a removable box magazine, and a barrel and barrel extension above the grip. A ring trigger protruded from the bottom front of the grip. When this was pushed forward, it opened the bolt by a direct linkage; when pulled back, it closed the bolt, loading an 8mm Gaulois cartridge from the magazine, and then fired the round.

TROCAOLA

Trocaola, Aranzabal v Cia, Eibar, Spain.

This firm specialized in revolvers and operated from the early 1900s until the Civil War. All their products were copies of contemporary Smith & Wesson or Colt designs, in 32, 38 and 44 calibers, beginning with the ribbed-barrel hinged-frame models, both hammer and "hammerless", and, after World War I, progressing to copies of the S&W Military & Police and the Colt Police Positive models.

The quality varies; pre-1914 pistols appear to be well made and of sound material, which is reinforced by their sharing a 1915-vintage British army contract with Garate, Anitua y Cia (q.v.). These revolvers entered British service as the "Pistol O.P. with 5 inch barrel, No 2 Mark 1". A specimen examined has the inscription "Fa de Trocaola, Aranzabal Eibar" on the frame and is, of course, in 455 British caliber. It was declared obsolete in 1921. (The abbreviation "O.P." stood for "Old Pattern".)

The weapons produced after 1921 varied widely in quality, though the *Modelo Militar* in 44 Special and using the Smith & Wesson "Triple Lock" (the only known example of this mechanism being copied) was of good material and workmanship.

Trocaola revolvers are identifiable by the company trademark, a monogram of "TAC" in a circle, placed on the left of the frame and resembling the S&W monogram.

TSINNTOCHMASH

TsINN–tochnogo mashinostroeniya, Klimovsk, Russia.

These guns are the work of the central research and development bureau of the Precision Engineering Company. The SPP, together with an accompanying rifle, was the first underwater weapon to be publicly revealed. Its general resemblance to the Heckler & Koch design may be coincidence; on the other hand, there may be a limited choice of design options in this restricted field of endeavor.

∼ REPEATING PISTOLS ∼

SPP-1M This underwater pistol was designed by Vladimir Simonov in 1969-71. It consists of a frame with four barrels in a square formation, with a large breechblock at the rear that contains the firing mechanism. This breech unit is unlocked and the barrel unit tipped down in shotgun fashion, allowing a clip containing four cartridges to be loaded into the barrels. The barrel unit is then moved back into place and locked and the weapon is ready to fire. Pressure on the trigger will drive a self-cocking mechanism to fire one barrel at a time. The muzzle velocity and range vary according to the depth of water and the consequent water pressure; the effective range varies from 55 feet at a depth of 15 feet to 20 feet at 130 feet deep.

The cartridge consists of a rimless necked case, designated 4.5x145, which has been based on the standard 7.62x39 assault-rifle round. This contains a drag-stabilized dart, 4.5 inches long, with a muzzle velocity in air of about 660 ft/sec. The gun is approximately 9.6 inches long and weighs about 33.5 oz empty.

∼ AUTOMATIC PISTOLS ∼

P-9 Gyurza Designed by Pyotr Serdyukov in the late 1980s, this pistol competed unsuccessfully against the Yarygin (see "Izhevsk") in the Russian army trials of the early 1990s, but it attracted the attention of the FSB (Federal security service, lineal successor to the KGB) in 1996 and was finally standardized for military and police service in 2003.

Based on the Walther P. 38, sharing a pin-actuated tilting locking block with the Beretta 92 series, the Gyurza is an interesting gun. It is chambered for a special 9x21 cartridge, firing a cored bullet that is said to penetrate 30 layers of Kevlar fabric and two .05-inch sheets of titanium at a distance of 110 yards or .15 inches of steel armor at 65 yards. It has also been claimed that groups with diameters of 12.6 inches can be achieved at 110 yards. The muzzle velocity is said to be 1360 ft/sec with a 103-grain bullet, giving a muzzle energy of 426 ft/lb.

The external appearance of the Gyurza suggests an enlarged Makarov, but the frame is made of polymer material and steel-rail inserts carry the steel slide. A partially exposed hammer permits single- or double-action firing, a Glock-type trigger safety is used and a tiny grip-safety blade protrudes from the backstrap (too small for effective use, this is usually immobilized with tape in service). The first guns lacked a slide-stop, but this was added after a few thousand had been made. The P-9 is 195mm long and weighs about 1180gm empty. The magazine holds 18 rounds in a double column.

Known in military circles as the SPS, or *Samoziariadniyi pistolet Serdyukova*, the Gyurza is usually listed in FSB inventories as the "Vektor".

PSS Designed by Viktor Levchenko, this is little more than a conventional blowback pistol with double-action lockwork, but it achieves silence by firing a special cartridge. The pistol has a very broad grip, owing to the unusual 7.62x41 silent cartridge, and the separate breechblock reciprocates instead of a conventional slide. The SP-4 cartridge has a necked case containing a piston above the propelling charge. When the gun is fired, the propelling charge ignites and generates gas. This drives the piston forward, transmitting sufficient energy to the base of the bullet, through a stem or "nose" on the piston, for the projectile to reach 50 meters or more. Muzzle velocity is about 200 m/sec.

When the piston reaches the neck of the cartridge, it jams in place and seals the propellant gases — and hence the noise, smoke and flash — inside the case. There is virtually no "firing signature"; the pistol then automatically ejects the spent case and strips a new round from the six-round box magazine.

TTIBAR
Ttibar Industrias SRL, Buenos Aires, Argentina.
A 22 LR rimfire automatic pistol probably made in the 1950s, the "Ttibar" was broadly based on the lines of the Colt Woodsman. However, instead of a half-slide behind the fixed barrel, the separate bolt reciprocated within a rectangular receiver, and the bolt and return spring were retained by a large knurled cap at the rear of the receiver. There is a cocking lever lying beneath the barrel, which, when drawn back, presses the bolt back to cock and load. An adjustable rear sight was fitted, and the general effect was of a beginner's target pistol.

TULA ARMS FACTORY
Tulskiy Oruzheinyi Za'vod, Tula, USSR/Russia.
This, the principal state-owned ordnance factory, was founded in 1648 to make gun barrels and was elevated to the status of a gun manufactory in 1712. In addition to handguns, Tula is best known for Mosin-Nagant and Tokarev rifles.

∼ REVOLVERS ∼

Smita i Vessona These were faithful copies of the revolvers made first by Smith & Wesson (q.v.) and then by Ludwig Loewe, who installed the machinery in the Tula factory on which they were built. Production is said to have begun in 1880 and lasted until the decision was taken to develop a modern small-caliber replacement. The Russian-made "4.2 Line" (10.6mm) guns could be distinguished by the mark on top of the barrel, in Cyrillic, which included the Tula name "ТУЛЬCKIN" and the date of manufacture.

An 1895-type Russian Nagant gas-seal revolver, made during World War II.

M1895 The adoption of the 7.62mm (30-caliber) Nagant (q.v.) "gas-seal" revolver was accompanied by the purchase of a license to make guns in Tula. However, the first 20,000 guns were supplied from Belgium and were marked "L. NAGANT" and "LIEGE" in lines that arched around "BREVETE" on the left side of the frame beneath the hammer; a date lay beneath the mark. They could also be distinguished from essentially similar guns sold commercially (and even a few Spanish copies) by their military proof- and inspectors' marks.

Production began in Tula in 1899 and stopped in mid-1942, though guns were still being assembled until 1944. The earliest guns bore a Cyrillic mark on the left side of the frame that read "Imperial ordnance factory, Tula" above the date; marks of this type can be identified by the central line, which reads "ТУЛЬCKIN". By the beginning of July in 1914, about 436,000 1895-type revolvers had been made.

Some guns will be found with the marking defaced (or, at least, the "Imperial" portion) during the post-Revolutionary Civil War, but the date is usually untouched. Work began again in Tula in 1919, but the markings were changed. Guns made prior to 1924 display "ПЕР.ТУЛ.ОР.ЗАВ" — "First Tula Ordnance Factory" — between "P.C.Ф.C.P." ("Russian Soviet Federal Socialist Republic") and the date; post-1924 guns are marked "C.C.C.P." ("Union of Soviet Socialist Republics") above the arsenal mark and the date; and those made after c. 1929 bear an arrow within a large five-point star above a date that can be as late as 1944. Production was stopped in favor of the Tula-Tokarev (TT) pistol in 1933 but began again in 1935 after the pistol had demonstrated serious operating problems.

The original Belgian-made guns, and most of those made after 1919, have double-action lockwork. The guns made in Tula prior to 1917, however, were invariably restricted to single action. In the words of an ex-Tsarist soldier, "If anything went wrong, you could mend it with a hammer". The Nagant was greatly favored by Soviet tank and armored-vehicle crews, as its fixed barrel was easier to use from a firing port than the reciprocating barrel of the TT. The standard gun was about 235mm long, with a 115mm barrel, an empty weight of 750gm and a seven-chamber cylinder.

- *Short version* Distinguished by a short barrel and a shortened butt, this was merely 207mm long with a 90mm barrel and an empty weight of about 675gm. It is said to have been developed for plainclothes agents of the GRU, to aid concealment, but is now often associated with the Okhrana (the Tsarist secret police), the Cheka (the Soviet version of the Okhrana) and the KGB. The date of introduction is still contested.
- *Training version* Chambered for the 22 LR rimfire round, without the cylinder-camming gas-seal mechanism, this was made in small numbers — apparently in the 1925-33 period.

TOZ-36 This was a gas-seal revolver chambered for the 7.62mm Nagant revolver cartridge and introduced in the 1960s to facilitate target shooting.

∼ AUTOMATIC PISTOLS ∼

TOZ (or "TK" ("Tula-Korovin")) This small general-purpose pistol was designed by Sergey Korovin and manufactured between 1926 and 1935. It was a 6.3mm fixed-barrel blowback that was loosely based on the Mauser Model 1910 pattern and which fired a peculiar Soviet cartridge that was dimensionally the same as the common 25 ACP/6.35mm Browning but which carried a somewhat heavier charge and delivered a higher velocity. Since the 25 ACP round can be loaded and fired in the TOZ, it came to be accepted in the West as a 25-caliber gun, but recent research into Soviet archives revealed the existence of the 6.3mm round.

The TOZ was originally intended to be a target and sport pistol, but it rapidly became popular with officers of the Red Army who preferred it over the regulation TT-33 Tokarev and was eventually accepted as the ex officio staff officers' pistol.

The barrel is anchored into the frame by the safety catch and can be easily removed for cleaning. The pistol was made under the TOZ name at first, these initials being molded into the grips, but in about 1930, the design was slightly changed to include some small alterations to the slide contours and the grips, now secured by internal locks (similar to the Ortgies) instead of the conventional screws; this became the TK model.

Tula-Tokarev ("TT") The standard pistol of the Soviet armed forces for many years, this was designed by Fedor Vassilyevich Tokarev in the late 1920s and was approved for service in 1930.

- *1930 pattern* Basically it was a Browning swinging-link locked-breech design with some changes to improve reliability and simplify manufacture and maintenance. The principal changes from, say, the Colt M1911 were the assembly of the hammer and lockwork in a removable module and the absence of any form of safety device other than a half-cock notch on the hammer. A smaller but innovative feature was the forming of the magazine lips into the frame, leaving the magazine with a simple constricted mouth; this ensured that the feed lips, the most vulnerable part of the average automatic pistol, were entirely protected against accidental damage. Production of the TT-30 began in 1930, and while precise figures are not available, it has been assumed that about 93,000 were made before the TT-33 replaced it.

A pre-war Soviet 7.62mm TT-33 pistol.

A 1953-vintage Soviet TT-33. Note the design of the slide-retraction grooves compared with the previous illustration.

A sectional drawing of the TT-33, showing how the locking lugs were milled entirely around the barrel.

- *1933 pattern* In 1933, the design was slightly changed. The 1930 model had the usual two locking ribs machined on top of the barrel, but the 1933 modification changed this into two collars machined completely around the barrel. These could be formed during the shaping of the barrel and thus cut out one machining operation — the milling of the lugs — which simplified manufacture. Another, minor, change was to make the butt backstrap part of the frame forging instead of a separate component. This became the "TT-33", which completely replaced the TT-30.

  Manufacture of the TT-33 began in 1934 and continued until the mid-1950s in the USSR. The total made is not known, but from the few known figures of pre-war and wartime production, it is possible to estimate that it may be in the region of 1.75 million.
- *TT-R-3 and TT-R-4* These were sub-caliber trainers, firing the 22 LR rimfire round. The basic "R-3" model was difficult to distinguish from the standard service pistol, but the "R-4" version had a long barrel protruding from the slide and adjustable sights.
- *Others* Tokarev pistols were made throughout the Soviet bloc and in satellite states. The Chinese version was designed *Type 51*, Yugoslavia used the *M-57* and others emanated from Radom (in Poland) for the Czech, Polish and East German forces.

TULLE ARMS FACTORY

Manufacture Nationale d'Armes de Tulle ("MAT"), Tulle, France.
This government-owned ordnance factory was involved in the manufacture of handguns, particularly the MAS 35 (see "Saint-Étienne") and

the MAC 50 (see "Châtellerault"). These can sometimes be identified by the presence of "MAT" marks.

TURBIAUX

Jacques Turbiaux, Paris, France.

Jacques Edmond Turbiaux invented what is probably the best-known and most common survivor of all the "palm squeezer" pistols: the *Protector*. This took the form of a disc, some 2 inches across and half an inch thick, from one edge of which protruded a barrel and from the other edge a lever arrangement. The disc contained a revolving block with seven 8mm or 10 6mm chambers for rimfire cartridges.

The Protector was held in the palm of the hand with the barrel lying between the first and second fingers, these resting against "horns" on the casing, and with the lever against the heel of the palm. Clenching the fist forced the lever inwards, which rotated the block to align a cartridge with the barrel, locked it, cocked the firing pin and released it. On relaxing the hand, a spring forced the lever out, thus preparing it for the next shot. To load, a cap on the left side of the casing was rotated, allowing the "cylinder" to be lifted out for emptying and re-loading. The cartridges used were the 6mm Protector or the 8mm Gaulois, both having extremely short cases and neither developing much power.

Turbiaux promoted this weapon with some success; he patented it in 1882 and "Le Protector" enjoyed a great deal of popularity, especially in France. Specimens made by him are marked "Le Protector Systeme

The Turbiaux Protector squeezer pistol.

E.Turbiaux" around the central cap. Sales appear to have lasted well into the 1890s, but by that time, he had licensed production in the USA to the Minneapolis Firearms Company (q.v.).

There the "Protector" was made in 32 Short RF by J. Duckworth of Springfield, Massachusetts; these bore the Minneapolis company name and the date of Turbiaux' US patent. The company then ran into trouble, apparently due to poor quality control, and the patents were bought by P.H. Finnegan late in 1892. See "Chicago Firearms Company".

UBERTI

Aldo Uberti e C SNC, Gardone Val Trompia, Italy.

This company was founded in 1959 and began by making reproduction cap-and-ball revolvers, such as the early Colts, Remingtons and Confederate types. It then began making "Western" cartridge revolvers and in more recent years has produced a more modern revolver design. The guns are currently marketed in the USA by a wide range of agencies, including American Frontier Firearms, Cimarron Arms, EAA, EMF, Navy Arms, the United States Patent Fire Arms Co. and Uberti USA.

Uberti regularly provides components to customers. These are "Phantom" long-range target revolvers marketed in Germany by Hege Waffen.

～ SINGLE-SHOT PISTOLS ～

Remington Rolling Block The 1871-pattern target pistol has been re-created with a 9.5-inch half-octagonal barrel, a color case-hardened frame and walnut woodwork. The butt takes a "saw handle" form. Chamberings have included 22 LR and 22 WM rimfire, 22 Hornet, 222 and 223 Remington, 357 Magnum and 45 Long Colt. The guns are typically about 14 inches long and weigh 42-44 oz.

～ REVOLVERS ～

Uberti's first single-action "Colt 1873" type was marketed in the USA as the *Cattleman* by LA Distributors of New York and was also sold by the Iver Johnson company. It was available initially only in 357 Magnum, 44 Magnum and 45 Long Colt.

Colt Peacemaker type

*   *Buckhorn* Similar to the Cattleman but somewhat larger and heavier, this was strengthened to take the 44 Magnum round. Current "Buckhorn Target" guns are convertible 44 Magnum/44-40 WCF, with adjustable sights set in flat-topped frames. A "Buntline" variant has been made with an 18-inch barrel.

A typical Uberti-made 45-caliber Cattleman "Western Style" revolver. This particular gun has an adjustable rear sight.

*   *Cattleman* These single-action revolvers are currently being offered in 22 LR and 22 WM rimfire, 357 Magnum, 38 Special, 44-40 WCF, 44 Special, 45 ACP and 45 Long Colt, with barrels of 3, 3.5, 4, 4.75, 5.5 or 7.5 inches, the three shortest options being restricted to 44-40 WCF and 45 Long Colt chamberings. The standard finish is blue, with color case-hardened frame and brass straps, but steel straps and nickel plating are optional. The grips are almost inevitably one-piece walnut. The "Cattleman Target" and "Cattleman Target Stainless" have improved sights and a square-shouldered frame, while the "Cattleman Buntline" has the usual ultra-long barrel.
*   *Bisley* Introduced in 1997, this duplicates the high-set grip of the original Colt version; the "Bisley Model Flat Top" (1998) has an adjustable rear sight set in a flattened high-sided frame.
*   *New Thunderer Model* Made exclusively for Cimarron Arms (q.v.), this is a single-action "re-creation" of the 1877-type Colt, offered in 357 Magnum, 44 Special, 44-40 WCF or 45 Long Colt. The barrel lengths have been restricted to 3.5 and 4.75 inches, and the finish could be blue or nickel. The grips are hard rubber.
*   *Phantom* This is a special variant of the Buckhorn, with a 10.5-inch barrel, an anatomical one-piece walnut grip, the trigger guard

altered to give a better two-hand grip and an adjustable rear sight.
*   *Regulator* A name applied to variants of the Cattleman distributed in the USA by Tristar Sporting Arms.
*   *Tornado* Chambered for the 454 Casull round and made only in sandblast nickel finish, this has been offered with a 4.75-, 5.5- or 7.5-inch barrel, the longest option having integral compensating ports drilled in the muzzle.
*   *Stallion* A 22-caliber (Long Rifle or Magnum rimfire chamberings) diminutive of the Cattleman series, this is generally fitted with one-piece walnut grips. The finish may be blue, with color case-hardening on the frame, or nickeled overall.
*   *Trailblazer* A predecessor of the Stallion and sharing similar characteristics. Barrel lengths varied from 4.75 to 7.5 inches, and many of the guns were nickel-plated.

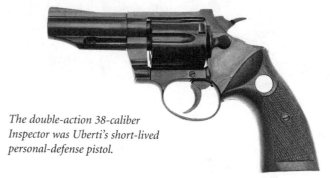

The double-action 38-caliber Inspector was Uberti's short-lived personal-defense pistol.

Inspector This was a modern solid-frame swing-cylinder design based generally on Colt practice. Offered customarily in 38 Special with a six-chamber cylinder, the guns were made with a variety of barrel lengths (2-6 inches with fixed sights, 4 inches and 6 inches with adjustable sights). A 32 S&W version was also made in small numbers. Finish could be blue or chrome, with walnut grips.

Remington type These are based on the 1875-type single-action revolver, originally produced to compete with the Colt Peacemaker. Lanyard rings on the butt provide an instant identification.

*   *Model 1875 SA Army Outlaw* Available in 357 Magnum, 44-40 WCF, 45 Long Colt and 45 ACP, with a 7.5-inch round barrel. The finish may be nickel-plating overall or blue with color case-hardening on the frame and a brass trigger guard; the grips are usually walnut.
*   *Model 1890 SA Police* Available in the same chamberings as the M1875, this has a 5.5-inch barrel and lacks the prominent under-barrel web of its predecessor. Finish may be blue or nickel, with walnut grips.

Smith & Wesson type

*   *Model 1874 Russian* (or "New Model Russian") Introduced in 1999, this six-shot break-open design is chambered exclusively for the 44 S&W Russian cartridge. Finish is polished blue, with walnut grips.

The gun is about 12 inches long, with the standard 6.5-inch barrel, and weighs 40 oz empty.

- *Model 1875 Schofield* Chambered for 44-40 WCF or 45 Long Colt ammunition, this top-break auto-ejector — introduced in 1994 — can be obtained with barrel lengths of 3.5, 5 or 7 inches. Finish is blue; grips are walnut.

ULTRA-LIGHT ARMS, INC.

Granville, West Virginia, USA.

This gunmaking business, best known for its bolt-action rifles, also offers a pistol bolt on a left-hand short rifle action. The *Model 20 Hunter's Pistol* appeared in 1987 with a 14-inch Douglas barrel, a graphite-reinforced Kevlar half-stock and a five-round magazine. Chamberings have included most of the best-known short-case rifle cartridges. A gray-stock variant, apparently known as the "Model 20 Reb Hunter", appeared in 1996.

UNATTRIBUTABLE DESIGNS

This section contains a variety of pistols and revolvers that cannot be satisfactorily linked with any particular gunmaker. This is usually due to the fact that they follow comparatively standard patterns (e.g., "Suicide Special" revolvers or "Eibar"-type FN-Browning copies) or bear nothing but the name of a distributor. Proofmarks may help to refine the search but will not be found on the American guns nor on many of the Spanish examples made prior to the 1920s.

American guns

- *Baby Bulldog* A 22 rimfire double-action hammerless folding-trigger revolver; also found in 32 caliber. Maker unknown, c. 1885.
- *Buffalo Bill* This revolver from the 1875-85 period was the usual 22 Short rimfire 7-shot solid-frame sheathed-trigger type. According to the markings, it was sold by the Homer Fisher Company, but the actual manufacturer is unknown.
- *Bulls Eye* Another of the many revolvers of the 1870-80 period, this was a 22 Short rimfire 7-shot with a sheathed trigger and a solid frame. Maker unknown.
- *Clipper* A seven-shot 22-caliber solid-frame-sheathed trigger revolver of the 1875-80 period.
- *Chicago Ledger* A five-shot sheathed-trigger solid-frame 22-caliber revolver dating from the 1880s. With a bird's-head butt, it resembles the usual "Suicide Special" but has a notably prominent hammer spur.

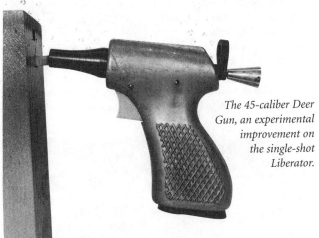

The 45-caliber Deer Gun, an experimental improvement on the single-shot Liberator.

- *Deer Gun* This was a modernized "Liberator" (see "General Motors"), a single-shot pistol intended to be dropped to guerrilla and resistance forces operating behind enemy lines. The Deer Gun was developed under the auspices of the CIA for use in Southeast Asia during the Vietnam War. The butt and frame of the pistol were an aluminum casting, with a steel barrel. The barrel was unscrewed and removed from the frame, and a 9mm Parabellum cartridge was inserted into the chamber. The barrel was then screwed back into the frame and the pistol was fired by simply squeezing the exposed trigger to cock and release the striker. A simple flap on the striker acted as a safety catch. Like the Liberator, the Deer Gun had a hollow butt that could hold four or five cartridges and a short wooden rod that acted as an ejector. There was the usual set of graphic comic-strip instructions showing illiterates how to use the weapon. Several thousand guns were made in 1964, each packed in a polystyrene foam box ready for air-dropping. A political decision prevented the Deer Gun from being used, and all but a handful were scrapped.

- *Imperial* Solid-frame sheathed-trigger revolvers of the 1875-85 period, these will be found in 22 or 32 Short rimfire. The 22-caliber version has a plain-surfaced seven-chamber cylinder; the 32 version is a five-shot with a fluted cylinder. Either type will be marked "IMPERIAL NO 1" or "IMPERIAL NO 2", with no obvious distinction between them.

- *Kittemaug* This was a 32 rimfire solid-frame sheathed-trigger non-ejecting revolver of the usual 1870s pattern, parentage unknown.

- *Leader* Applied to revolvers distributed by the Charles Williams hardware stores of New York, these were offered as seven-shot 22-caliber or five-shot 32-caliber solid-frame non-ejectors, with the type of bird's-head grip common in 1875-90. The only marking is the "LEADER" name on the barrel.

- *Liberty* See "Hood Firearms Company".

- *Scott Arms Company* This name has been reported on a five-shot 32 Short rimfire non-ejecting revolver with a solid frame and a sheathed trigger, probably dating from 1875-85. It was probably a figment of the imagination of a well-established gunmaker.

Belgian guns

- *British Bulldog* The Webley break-open revolver was extensively copied in Liége and sold with no markings other than the title; no manufacturers' names are to be seen, but small variations in pattern and finish suggest the involvement of several gunmakers in the 1885-1910 period. Many of the guns can be distinguished from Webley patterns only by the absence of Webley markings.

- *Bullfighter* Chambered for the rimmed 300 centerfire cartridge, this revolver is representative of the "Bulldog" class common in the 1890s — with a short barrel and a bird's-head grip. Most of the guns were exported and will frequently carry a dealer's name or trademark.

- *Le Martigny* A 6.35mm blowback automatic, similar externally to the FN-Browning of 1906, this had an unusual external hammer mounted in the rear of the frame. The hammer fell between two "wings" forming the rear of the slide but cannot be thumb-cocked and, indeed, is only visible when cocked. The only specimen traced for examination bore Liége proofmarks and, as it offered reasonable quality, is assumed to have been Belgian instead of Spanish.

French guns

- *Bicycle* A 22-caliber single-shot pistol styled like an automatic pistol, this probably dates from c.1910.

- *Merveilleux* A "palm-squeezer" pistol of uncertain provenance and probably made in Saint-Étienne between 1898 and 1910. It resembles the more common Gaulois, being little more than a square box with a barrel protruding from one corner and a grip at the rear, shaped so that the gun could be easily concealed in the hand. Instead of pressing the rear grip inwards to operate the mechanism, the Merveilleux had a grip at the front that could be squeezed back by the fingers to cock and release the striker and load the chamber from an internal box magazine. It fired a special 6mm Merveilleux cartridge, somewhat longer than the more common 6mm Gaulois equivalent, which suggests that sufficient guns were made to make the manufacture of ammunition worthwhile.

German gun

- *Kobra* Possibly dating from the 1920s, this unusual 6.35mm blow-back automatic has a fixed barrel carried in a block that appears to be the front of the slide but is actually stationary. The half-length slide has wings that run forward alongside and under the barrel block. The grip is in the usual place, but the trigger guard extends to the front of the frame. The Kobra has an external hammer and a safety catch on the left rear side of the frame. "KOBRA", framed by a snake, will be found on the left side of the slide ahead of "CAL. 6.35 D.R.P.".

Romanian gun

- *Buescu* "Captain Buescu's Model 1876" was a solid-frame gate-loading six-shot revolver of conventional pattern and unknown (probably Romanian) make. It was originally issued as the "Galant-Lebeau M1874" and modified to Buescu's ideas, though the improvements are difficult to detect from surviving guns and no relevant patent has yet been traced.

South African gun

- *Lynx* Developed in 1977-9, this was a five-shot solid-frame 357 Magnum revolver built on Smith & Wesson lines and with a 3-inch ventilated-rib barrel. It was advertised commercially early in 1979, but it is believed that few (if any) were sold and that the company failed within months. No specimen has been seen.

Spanish guns

In addition to countless anonymous 6.35mm and 7.65mm copies of the 1906-type FN-Browning pistol, there are numerous guns marked simply "FABRIQUE A ST. ETIENNE" or "FABRICATION FRANÇAISE". Even though these often have French safety-catch markings and French or Belgian proofmarks, they undoubtedly originated in Spain in the 1910-30 period.

- *Alamo Ranger* A 38-caliber six-shot double-action revolver, this is usually marked "ALAMO RANGER EIBAR 1929" "MADE IN SPAIN" and ".38 Ctg", and will also have Eibar proofmarks. The revolver has a solid frame, a loading gate on the right side behind the cylinder and relies on a detachable arbor pin to release the cylinder. The quality of material and the finish is generally poor.
- *Arva* This was a 6.35mm automatic pistol copied from the Clément (q.v.), with an additional grip safety. Opinions vary as to its manufacturer; some claim Belgian while others say Spanish. No specimen has yet been traced for examination and the provenance remains uncertain. Spanish origins seem most likely.
- *Asiatic* This 6.35mm pistol was identical with the Cobra (see below), apart from markings.
- *Aurora* A 6.35mm automatic pistol, based on the Browning 1906 pattern, this will usually display "SPAIN" or "MADE IN SPAIN" stamped into the frame. Safety catches marked "FEU" suggest sales in France.
- *Automatic Pistol* There are many cheap Spanish 6.35mm (25 ACP) and 7.65mm (32 ACP) guns with no markings on the slide other than the words "AUTOMATIC PISTOL". Among the many variants encountered have been:
1) A 6.35mm blowback marked "Automatic Pistol Cal. 6 35" on the slide, with "CAL. 6,35" and floral sprigs on an oval cartouche on the grips. This gun has coarsely milled vertical retraction grooves and Spanish proofmarks.
2) A similar gun with finer retraction grooves and a grip safety, marked simply "CAL 6,35 MODEL AUTOMATIC PISTOL" in a single line on the left side of the slide.
3) A 6.35mm pattern marked simply "1911 MODEL AUTOMATIC PISTOL", with narrow vertical retraction grips.
4) Another 6.35mm gun, similar to the preceding variant, but dated "1916" instead of "1911". The retraction grips are milled radially.

5) An extended-butt 6.35mm-caliber gun, with a nine-round magazine, marked "PISTOLA AUTOMATICA" on the left side of the slide.
- *Burgham Superior* A 6.35mm "Eibar"-type pistol, possibly destined for sale in France. See also "Manufacture d'Armes des Pyrénées Françaises" under "M".
- *Cobra* The "POCKET MODEL COBRA" has been reported in 6.35mm and 7.65mm calibers but is nothing other than a commonplace "Eibar"-type automatic. None of the guns available for examination bore proofmarks, suggesting origins in the early 1920s. Similar guns have been seen with nothing other than "CAL 6.35 MODEL AUTOMATIC PISTOL" on the left side of the slide and a striking-cobra motif on the butt. See also "Asiatic", above.
- *Coq* An exceptionally poor-quality 6.35mm "Eibar" blowback based on the FN-Browning of 1906 but lacking the grip safety. Marked merely "K-25" on the left side of the slide, it probably dates from the early 1920s.
- *Cowboy, Cow Boy* Another 6.35mm "Eibar"-type pistol, this may be marked "COW-BOY FABRICATION FRANCAISE / MARQUE DEPOSEE" or, alternatively, "COW-BOY" separated from "MODEL AUTOMATIC PISTOL" by an encircled gun-slinging cowboy motif. The grips may have a cowboy on a prancing horse, with "COW" above "BOY".
- *Defense* A 6.35mm 1906-type FN-Browning copy lacking the grip safety, this was marked "PISTOLET AUTOMATIQUE CAL. 6 35 / "DEFENSE"…" suggesting export to France — though the only specimens examined both had Belgian "proof of foreign arms" marks. The grips bore a motif of seven balls surrounded by six stars on a wreath.
- *Eles* Another of the many 6.35mm Spanish-made pistols that has been listed elsewhere but never seen in specimen, this was mentioned by H.B.C. Pollard in his book *Automatic Pistols* (published in 1920), which suggests that it originated during World War I and vanished shortly afterwards.
- *Eley* Another 6.35mm "Eibar" of unknown make, this certainly had nothing to do with the British cartridge-making business of the same name.
- *Favorit* A Browning-type 6.35mm "Eibar" blowback, this was marked "AUTOMATIC PISTOL FAVORIT" on the left side of the slide, with "FAVORIT" on the grip-band. Spanish proofmarks were usually present.
- *Joffre* A 7.65mm Browning copy pistol of unknown origin, this will also usually be marked "MODEL 1916" — a mark used by several Spanish gunmakers to suggest war-contract origins and an assurance of reliability to.
- *Joha* Found on 6.35mm and 7.65mm-caliber guns, this is believed to have been sold in Finland. Attempts have been made to link the pistols with "Kone- e Asepaja" of Türkü, but it seems much more likely that the distributor had the initials "J. H."— phonetically "Jo-Ha". The 6.35mm gun lacks a grip safety and is marked "AUTOMATIC

"Le Basque", a typical Eibar-type pistol distributed by Tómas de Urizar.

PISTOL "JOHA"…" on the slide, with a cursive "Joha" in the top of the molded plastic. The larger version, with radial retraction grips and a sighting groove along the slide, is marked "AUTOMATIC PISTOL JOHA". Spanish proofmarks are also sometimes present on the small-caliber guns.

- *Le Basque* A 7.65mm blowback, based on the 1906 FN-Browning, this was marked "CAL 7 65 "LE BASQUE" MARQUE DEPOSÉ" on the left side of the slide. It also had floral-band grips reminiscent of Bolumburu and Retolaza products.
- *Liberty* See remarks under "Retolaza Hermanos".
- *Lusitania* Another 7.65mm blowback automatic of the usual "Eibar" type, this is usually listed as marked with nothing other than the name and "Model 1915" — suggesting that the name commemorated the sinking of the RMS Lusitania in that year. However, one example is reportedly marked "<«LA ARMERA ELGOEIBARRESA» CAL. 7 65> " over "–"LUSITANIA"–", suggesting not only a possible manufacturer but also that the derivation of the name was actually the Roman province of Lusitania.
- *Mosser* A 6.35mm "Eibar" blowback based on the Browning 1906, dating prior to 1914. The slide is marked "THE VERITABLE MOSSER AUTOMATIC PISTOL SUPERIOR" and the grips carry the word "SUPERIOR".
- *Paramount* The guns of this name were usually made by Apaolozo Hermanos in Eibar, but there are also several unidentifiable "Paramounts" without distinguishing features.
- *Phoenix* One gun of this name was made in Belgium by Robar & Cie (q.v.), but there is also a Spanish-made "Eibar" 6.35mm pistol with an external hammer partly concealed within a slot in the rear of the slide, allowing only the serrated top to be seen when down. It also has an unusual dismantling catch in the form of a knurled button midway along the frame on both sides. Markings are restricted to "PHOENIX ARMS PATENT" on the slide and a crown above "PHOENIX" on the grips. Some sources attribute this pistol to the "Victoria Arms Co" of Eibar, but it may have been distributed by Tómas de Urizar.
- *Republic* A 7.65mm "Eibar" automatic of unknown origins, this is marked simply "AUTOMATIC PISTOL "REPUBLIC" PATENT" on the slide, above "CAL 7 65". Comparing it with other guns suggests manufacture by Arrizabalaga (q.v.) in the 1920s.
- *Vulcain* Marked simply "…"VULCAIN" AUTOMATIC PISTOL C. 6 35" on the slide, with "VULCAIN" on the grip-band, this "Eibar"-type pistol probably dates from the 1920s.
- *Zwylacka* A 6.35mm blowback pistol of unknown origin, this is an unusual design and of first-class quality. It rather resembles a Baby Browning though with the butt deepened behind the trigger area to give a better grip. The slide contains a separate cylindrical breech-block fitting into a boring in the rear of the slide and held in by a cross-screw with a knurled head showing at each end. It bears no marks other than "AUTOMATIC PISTOL" on the slide and Liége proofs, though the specimen examined had an undecipherable shield molded into the grips. It is much more likely to have been made in Spain in the early 1920s than Belgium.

UNCETA Y CIA

Esperanza y Unceta, later Unceta y Cia; Eibar and Guernica, Spain.
A partnership between Pedro Unceta and Juan Esperanza was founded in Eibar in 1908 to make an automatic pistol called the "Victoria". The business moved to Guernica in 1913, becoming Esperanza y Unceta, and undertook production of the Campo Giro pistol for the Spanish army. The "Astra" name (q.v.) was registered in 1914.

During World War I, Esperanza y Unceta became involved in contract work for the French and Italian armies. After the war, they produced their first "tubular" pistol, derived from the Campo Giro, and saw it adopted into Spanish service as the Model 1921 (known commercially as the "Astra 400"). Production of Astra pistols was continued alongside a line of cheaper Eibar automatics during the 1920s, until the trading style changed to Unceta y Cia in 1925.

∼ AUTOMATIC PISTOLS ∼

Guns made prior to 1925 are listed under "Esperanza"; those introduced between 1925 and 1955 are listed here; and the post-1955 designs are listed under "Astra".

Astra 500 According to various reports, this was a variant of the 400, slightly smaller (7.1 inches overall instead of 8.5 inches) and chambered for the 9mm Browning Long round. The Unceta company does not recognize this particular model designation, nor does it have production records, and it seems reasonable to conclude that the Astra 500 does not exist.

The Astra 600.

Astra 600 This was a smaller version of the 400 chambered for the 9mm Parabellum cartridge and manufactured in 1943 to meet an order from the German government. A few guns were also offered in 7.65mm Auto or 7.65mm Parabellum chambering — the evidence is conflicting. A total of 10,450 had been delivered to the Germans until, late in 1944, German occupation of the Franco-Spanish border ceased. Work then continued in 1946, another 49,000 being made for sale commercially (though some were apparently supplied to West German police forces after 1945).

Astra 700 This was a 7.65mm Auto version of the M400 made in 1927. Only 4000 were manufactured and all were sold commercially.

The Astra 700 Special was derived from the FN-Browning of 1910. This is a 7.65mm (32-caliber) example.

- *Astra 700 Special* This was a rationalization of the M700. The pistol was made smaller, as befitted the smaller cartridge, and was altered in shape, the slide having the sides flattened to resemble a 1910-type FN-Browning. Overall length was 6.3 inches and the magazine held 12 rounds. The M700 was the first pistol to carry the "Unceta y Cia" name, and the plastic grips had a new version of the trademark — a circle with the "ASTRA" between the letters "U" and "C" and surrounded by a sunburst.

Astra 900 series In the late 1920s, several Spanish gunmakers took advantage of economic troubles that had afflicted Mauser to introduce copies of the Mauser C/96 Military Model. The goal was to capture traditional Mauser markets in China and, particularly, Spanish-speaking Central and South America. Unceta y Cia developed the "900 Series".

The Astra lockwork, pinned to the right side of the frame, differs from the Mauser pattern in several respects. The bolt lock, pinned to the barrel extension, is forced up into engagement with the bolt by the spring-loaded trigger bar. When the parts recoil, the bolt and the barrel remain locked together until the end of the bolt lock is driven downward by striking a transom in the frame, freeing the bolt as the barrel stops. The downward movement of the bolt lock also presses on the trigger bar to act as a disconnector. The bolt runs back to cock the hammer before returning to chamber a new round. The barrel-return spring then forces the barrel forward, allowing the bolt lock to rise into engagement once more.

An Astra Model F machine-pistol, with its holster-stock.

The 9mm Astra Model F.

The Astra Model F with the grip removed to show the rate-reducing escapement built into the frame.

- *Model 900* Introduced in 1927, about 9000 of these had been sold to China within a year. The Astra resembles the Mauser C/96 externally, but a sliding cover plate on the left side gives access to the lockwork and a separate barrel-return spring lies in the frame beneath the chamber. The standard of manufacture is very high, and the finish is generally excellent.

  Chambered for the 7.63mm Mauser cartridge, the M900 is much the same size as the Mauser but somewhat heavier owing to heavier-gauge metal in the barrel and barrel extension. Guns were supplied to the Spanish security police and Guardia Civil in addition to the export successes.

- *Model 901* Developed in response to a demand from China, this 7.63mm-caliber gun added a selective-fire mechanism to the basic design. A selector on the right side of the frame, working in an arc, acted on the trigger bar to prevent it re-engaging with the hammer until the trigger was released. When the gun was firing automatically, a secondary sear held the hammer back until the barrel was forward and the bolt had been locked. The rate of fire was about 850 rds/min. Experience showed that the fixed 10-round magazine was too much of a restriction, and only about 1600 guns were ever made.

- *Model 902* Introduced late in 1928, this was simply the M901 with a fixed 20-round magazine and a 7.5-inch barrel. Virtually all of about 7000 guns went to China. A few are said to have been made without the selective-fire switch.

- *Model 903* Developed from the M902 and announced in 1932, this had detachable 10- or 20-round box magazines. Sales to China were being restricted by competition and the advent of the Spanish Civil War (1936-9); though 3450 were made, 2004 survived in store to be taken by the German government in 1940 and 1943.

- *Model 903E* This embodied insignificant internal changes in the design of the magazine release and magazine platform but was made only in small numbers. These are included in the M903 total given previously.

- *Model 904* A pre-production 7.63mm version of the 9mm Model F (below), this had a rate-reducer, some minor changes to the fire selector switch and hold-open device for the bolt. The 904F was produced to demonstrate changes demanded by the Guardia Civil, particularly the reduction in the rate of fire. Only 10 were made in 1933.

Astra Model F Designed specifically to meet the requirements of the Guardia Civil, this was similar to the Model 903 but chambered the 9mm Largo (Bergmann-Bayard) cartridge and had a retarder built into the butt to keep the automatic fire-rate down to 350 rds/min. Detachable 10- or 20-round box magazines were standardized. About 1100 Model F pistols were made in 1934-5, 950 being delivered to the Guardia Civil in June 1935. The remaining 150 were seized by the

Basque provisional government on the outbreak of the Civil War in 1936.

Astra 1000 After World War II had ended, Unceta y Cia began a new numbering series with this model, a 7.65mm Auto version of the Model 200 with a 12-round magazine and a 5.1-inch barrel. It was made in small numbers in the late 1940s.

Astra 2000 This was an external-hammer variant of the M200, made without the grip safety and available in 6.35mm Auto (25 ACP) or 22 Short rimfire chambering. The centerfire version could be converted to rimfire with a special kit. The Astra 2000 was promoted in the USA as the "Colt Junior", but when the Junior was withdrawn from sale in the USA in 1970, the Astra version was reintroduced as the "Cub".

Astra 3000 The old Model 300 was revived in 1948 and made until about 1956 under this designation. A loaded-chamber indicator pin was added in the back of the slide and the design of the grips was modernized, but the two patterns are otherwise identical. The Astra 3000 was offered in 7.65mm Auto (seven-round magazine) or 9mm Short/380 ACP (six-round magazine).

UNIES

Fabrique d'Armes Unies, Spain?
The identity of this trading company is difficult to establish, and it has sometimes been considered as a lineal successor to Fabrique d'Armes Réunies (q.v., under "R"). However, there is little doubt that the revolvers were made in Spain, and it is possible, despite the marks on the guns, that the "Unies" name was deliberately chosen for its similarity with a Belgian precursor. Proofmarks, if any, may prove to be the arbiter.

The principal product was a revolver known as the *Texas Ranger* (or "Cowboy Ranger"), a Colt Peacemaker copy in 38 S&W Special. The guns appeared in the early 1920s and are customarily marked "TEXAS RANGER FOR .38 S&W SPECIAL CTDGES" on the left, and "FAB D'ARMES UNIES LIEGE BELGIUM" on the right. Quality was no better than mediocre.

UNION ARMERA EIBARENSE ("U.A.E.")

Eibar, Spain.

Very little is known of this firm, which appears to have been a cooperative of small gunmakers in Eibar working prior to 1914. Their only positively identified product was a 6.35mm "Eibar" blowback based on the Browning 1906 and marked simply "U.A.E.".

UNION FIREARMS COMPANY

Toledo, Ohio, USA.

This company produced sporting rifles and shotguns in the early years of the century and then turned to the making of pistols with two unusual designs.

∼ AUTOMATIC PISTOL ∼

Riefgraber This was patented by J.J. Riefgraber in 1903-7 and manufactured some time prior to 1914. It was an unusual weapon, operating on a combination of short recoil and gas. The barrel and barrel extension, which carried the bolt, were inside a casing, and ports in the barrel directed gas into this casing so as to give a boost to the recoil. The bolt was locked by a rocking arm in the barrel extension, which was moved by a lug in the frame after a short recoil movement. The bolt then continued backwards, cocking the hammer; but instead of the normal return stroke, the hammer held the bolt open until a grip, resembling a grip safety in the rear of the butt, was pressed in. This released the bolt to chamber a fresh round and lock, and let the hammer fall until arrested by the sear. The pistol was produced in 32 or 38 caliber, chambering rimmed revolver cartridges, and it is believed that no more than 100 were made.

∼ REVOLVER ∼

Lefever This was patented by Charles Lefever in 1909 and which might well have been inspired by the Webley-Fosbery (q.v.). It consisted of a butt and frame supporting a cylinder and barrel unit free to recoil on the frame. The cylinder bore helical grooves that engaged with a pin on the frame so that when fired, the barrel and cylinder recoiled along the frame and the action of the groove and pin caused the cylinder to rotate and align the next cartridge. This system differed from Fosbery's in that the cylinder made the complete movement during the recoil stroke and did not rotate during the run-out stroke; the Fosbery cylinder turned half the distance on each stroke. The five-shot Union revolver chambered the 32 S&W cartridge but was no more successful than the Reifgraber pistol. Few were made, and when production ceased, probably about 1912, the Union Firearms Company left the handgun business.

MANUFACTURE D'ARMES "UNIQUE"

Hendaye, France.

This is the current trading style, adopted in 1988, of Manufacture d'Armes des Pyrénées Françaises (q.v., listed under "M").

UNITED STATES ARMS CORPORATION

Riverhead, New York, USA.

Abilene A trade name for a number of single-action revolvers based generally on the Colt M1873 pattern and marketed in 1978-82. Available in 357 Magnum, 44 Magnum and 45 Colt chamberings, it came with barrel lengths varying from 4.625 to 7.5 inches. See also "US Arms Co."

UNITED STATES PATENT FIRE-ARMS MFG. CO.

Hartford, Connecticut, USA.

Despite the name, this is a distributor of Italian-made "Western-style" revolvers under names such as the "Nettleton Cavalry Revolver" (and "Artillery" type), the "Bird Head Model", the "Flattop Target" and the "Bisley Model". The guns are apparently supplied by Uberti (q.v.).

TÓMAS DE URIZAR

Barcelonar, Spain.

Urizar was a major distributor of firearms and ammunition, buying his pistols largely from the Eibar district. These may be encountered in a variety of patterns, but only rarely do they bear the Urizar name. Most can be identified by a dragon motif on the grips, though Urizar also used a club-wielding savage and even a rabbit. Among the manufacturers involved were Garate Anitua y Cia and Fabrique d'Armes de Grande Précision (q.v.).

∼ REVOLVER ∼

Dek-Du A rather unusual revolver produced between 1905 and 1912 by Tomas de Urizar of Eibar. It was generally of the Velo-Dog pattern, "hammerless" and with a revolver-style butt; the barrel is part octagonal, mostly cylindrical, with a pronounced collar holding the front sight. The cylinder is large and contains 12 chambers in a single ring. It was available in either 5.5mm Velo-Dog or 25ACP chambering. A spring catch held the cylinder arbor, and the cylinder was removed for loading.

The 7.65mm Urizar Princeps pistol.

*A 7.65mm (32-caliber) Venus,
sold by Tómas de Urizar.*

∼ AUTOMATIC PISTOLS ∼

Celta A 6.35mm "Eibar" copy of the 1906 FN-Browning, this is identical with the "J. Cesar" excepting for its markings: "AUTOMATIC PISTOL / "Celta"…" in two lines on the left side of the slide and the dragon motif on the grips.

Continental A 6.35mm pistol made by Fabrique d'Armes de Grande Precision (marked appropriately on the slide) and sold by Urizar, with dragon-motif grips.

Express Sales name for a blowback automatic pistol produced by Tomas de Urizar of Eibar in three distinct versions, one sold under the Urizar name and the other two supplied to Garate Anitua y Cia and sold by them.

J. Cesar Also known simply as "Cesar", this is another Spanish-type 6.35mm blowback pistol. The slide is usually marked "AUTOMATIC PISTOL "J. CESAR"…" in a single line, with the dragon on the grips.

The origin of the gun is uncertain. Several have been seen with "CESAR" on the grip-band above a motif of the Roman general, but these lack Urizar markings — unless "J. Cesar" was itself an Urizar brand name.

Le Secours   This was a 7.65mm blowback in the "Eibar" style, marked "PISTOLET AUTOMATIQUE / "LE SECOURS" BREVETE" in two lines on the left side of the slide. It also has the Urizar dragon on the grips, but the identity of the manufacturer remains unclear.

Puma   A 6.35mm "Eibar" based on the 1906-type FN-Browning, this lacks maker's marks but bears the Tómas de Urizar dragon trademark on the right grip. It may have been made by Fabrique d'Armes de Grande Précision in the early 1920s.

URREJOLA Y CIA

Eibar, Spain.

One of the many small Eibar firms that sub-contracted some of the Ruby pistol work in 1915-18, Urrejola y Cia continued to make the same pistol in 7.65mm under their own name in the early 1920s. The quality was poor and the competition considerable, and they appear to have gone out of business before 1925.

US ARMS CO.

New York City, USA.

This small gunmaking business apparently made a series of the usual solid-frame sheathed-trigger non-ejecting revolvers in 1870-80. The guns were offered in 22 Short RF (seven-shot), 32 Short RF (six-shot), 38 Short and 41 Short rimfire (five shots apiece). Confusion arises from the fact that Iver Johnson subsequently also made revolvers — though not to the same patterns — using "U.S. Arms Co" as a sales name.

VALENCIA ARMS FACTORY

Valencia, Spain.

R.E. The initials stand for "Republica Espana" and the R.E. pistol is simply a copy of the Spanish army's Astra 400 pistol produced during the Spanish Civil War. The Republican forces were unable to obtain weapons from most of the established factories, since these were in Nationalist hands, and set up a factory in Valencia to make this pistol. Apart from the "RE" monogram on the butt and the absence of the usual Astra markings, the pistol is exactly the same as the Astra 400.

VALTRO

Valtro SPA, Brescia Italy.

This gunmaking business has offered sporting guns and a Colt-Browning pistol, marketed as the *M1998A1*. It is distinguished by a 5-inch barrel, checkered grip straps, an extended or "Beavertail" grip safety and duplicated slide-retraction grooves at the muzzle. Finish is usually blue, with select walnut grips.

VENUS-WAFFENWERK(E)

Zella-Mehlis, Thüringen, Germany.
See "Oscar Will".

MANUFACTURE D'ARMES VERNEY-CARRON

Saint-Etienne, France.

An old-established company, and still in business making shotguns, Verney-Carron's name appears on two pistols. The first was actually the 1912-model 6.35mm Star — the design that resembles a small Mannlicher — and the second was a typical 6.35mm "Eibar" based on the FN-Browning of 1906, though without the grip safety. Both will be found with slides marked "MANUFACTURE D'ARMES / VERNEY-CARRON" and the 6.35mm Eibar-type gun also has "VerCar" on the grips.

A short-lived British-made Victory MC5 pistol.

VICTORY ARMS COMPANY

Brixworth, England.

This company announced the *Victory MC5 Multi-Caliber Pistol* in 1988. It was a fixed-barrel locked-breech design with an open-top slide and an external hammer, usually chambered for the 9mm Parabellum round. The breech was locked by a pivoting block beneath the slide,

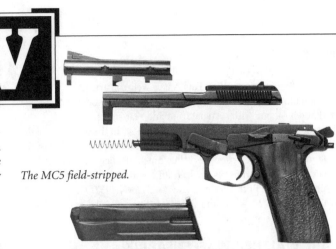

The MC5 field-stripped.

and the barrel could be easily exchanged. Optional chamberings included 38 Super Auto, 10mm Auto, 41 Action Express and 45 ACP. The magazine well was large enough to accommodate the differing magazines, and it was claimed that a single design of breech-face could cope with the various cartridges. The standard barrel was 4.4 inches long, and optional lengths of 5.9 and 7.5 inches were available. The lockwork was double-action and a de-cocking lever dropped the hammer on to a locked firing pin.

The left side of the frame was somewhat cluttered with a takedown latch, slide release latch and de-cocking lever, and the whole pistol was quite large — 8.5 inches overall with the smallest barrel. A 17-round magazine added to its bulk. However, despite extensive and generally favorable publicity, the design never attracted attention and trading ceased in 1989. The design migrated to the USA, but has never been successful.

VOERE GMBH

Vohrenbach, Austria.

In 1940, the Krieghoff company created a subsidiary in Kufstein, Austria. This began to make school and office furniture after the end of World War II, as "Tiroler Maschinenbau & Holzindustriegesellschaft m.b.H.", until the first air rifles appeared in 1951. This allowed the formation of Tiroler Sportwaffen und Apparatebau GmbH, but the business ran into financial difficulties in 1964 and was purchased by Voere of Vöhrenbach, Germany, a year later. The trading style changed to Tiroler Jagd- und Sportwaffenfabrik and then again in 1988 to "Voere-Kufsteiner Geratebau & Handelsgesellschaft mbH."

The company is best known for a variety of sporting guns but introduced the bolt-action VEC-91 rifle in 1991. This was chambered for the 6mm UCC, or "Unique Caseless Cartridge" (sometimes listed as 5.7x26), and embodied an electronic ignition system powered by batteries in the butt.

The system was extended in 1995 to two bolt-action pistols: the single-shot *VEC-95CG*, with the butt at the mid-point of the black synthetic half-stock, and the *VEC95-RG* with a detachable five-shot box magazine and the grip at the rear of the stock. The guns have 12- or 14-inch barrels, drilled and tapped for optical sight mounts, and a sliding safety catch on the tang behind the bolt handle.

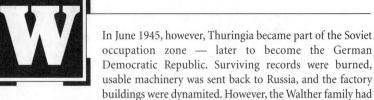

WAHL

Albin Wahl, Zella-Mehlis, Germany.

Stern ("Star", c. 1925-35) This was a well-constructed 6.35mm blowback pistol of conventional type. Two models are known — one with vestigial front and rear sights, and the other, perhaps newer, with an aiming groove in the top of the slide. The "sighted" model also has an unusual aperture in the left side of the slide, opposite the ejection port, but much smaller and set into the upper angle. Its purpose is unclear, unless it was simply a chamber-inspection port. Both models have "– *STERN-PISTOLE CAL. 6,35 WAHL'S D.R.G.M.* –" on the slide and "Stern Pistole" over "A.W.Z." molded into the grips.

CARL WALTHER WAFFENFABRIK

Zella St Blasii and Zella-Mehlis, Germany.

Carl Walther (1860-1915) was apprenticed to a gunsmith before founding his own business in Zella St Blasii in 1886, initially making target rifles. The success of the Browning-designed blowback pistols being made by Fabrique Nationale d'Armes de Guerre inspired Walther to create a rival, helped by his son Fritz (1889-1966) and a cousin, Friedrich Pickert. However, the first attempt failed, and not until German patent 256606 was granted on November 22, 1911, was real progress made. This protected what came to be known as the "Model 1". Introduction dates as early as 1908 have been misleadingly quoted, but these arose from a desire to pre-empt Mauser.

The Model 1 led to a variety of guns protected by a patent granted in January 1913 to protect the design of the combination rear sight/loaded-chamber indicator, but none of the revised designs had been made in quantity before Walther outgrew its facilities in 1915 and sold the factory to Oscar Will. When pistol production in Zella St Blasii stopped at the end of World War I, a workforce that had totaled 75 in 1915 had grown to nearly 500. Walther subsequently made optical-instrument components until production of the Models 4, 5 and 7 resumed in 1920/21. During the intervening period, the villages of Zella St Blasii and Mehlis had united, forming the town of Zella-Mehlis.

Work began again in the early 1920s, leading first to the conventional Models 8 and 9 and then, at the end of the decade, to the ground-breaking *Polizei-Pistole*. Said to have derived indirectly from the Tomiška "Little Tom" (q.v.), this was protected by a German patent granted in November 1930. The compact *Kriminalpolizei-Pistole* (PPK) was selected by the *Ehrenwaffe des Politischen Leiters* ("honor weapon of the political leaders") and the 22 rimfire Olympia-Pistole helped gain all the medals in the 1936 Olympic Standard Pistol competition.

The success of the PP/PPK series encouraged Walther to enter the military market with the *Militärische Pistole* of 1934, an enlarged PP chambering the 9mm Parabellum cartridge. This was soon replaced by a locked-breech design, most of the design being undertaken by Fritz Barthelmes. Patents were sought in the mid-1930s, enclosed-hammer *Armee-Pistolen* were made in small numbers, and a much-modified exposed-hammer Walther pistol was finally accepted by the Heereswaffenamt in February 1940.

Production of pistols and rifles continued throughout World War II, though external finish of the guns declined. The company developed simplified designs in this period, including a sophisticated rotary-barrel locked-breech pistol and a stamped-metal version of the Polizei-Pistole.

Zella-Mehlis and its environs were captured by the US Army in 1945, and before World War II had ended, the priceless collection of weapons in the Walther factory museum was looted by US servicemen.

In June 1945, however, Thuringia became part of the Soviet occupation zone — later to become the German Democratic Republic. Surviving records were burned, usable machinery was sent back to Russia, and the factory buildings were dynamited. However, the Walther family had fled westward. Business began again, with mechanical calculators made in a borrowed workshop in Heidenheim an der Brenz, and the beginnings of Carl Walther Sportwaffenfabrik (q.v.) were laid in Ulm in 1950.

A 6.35mm (25-caliber) Walther Model 1.

The Walther Model 1 field-stripped.

～ AUTOMATIC PISTOLS ～

Model 1 (1910-14) The design that began Walther's pistol business, this is sometimes claimed to have been introduced in 1908 (too optimistically) even though the relevant patent was not granted until 1911. Unlike many contemporaries, Fritz Walther did not simply copy the 1906-type Browning. His pistol was a 6.35mm (25 ACP) striker-fired blowback with a fixed barrel and an open-topped slide. There were two versions; the older has a stripping catch inside the front of the trigger-guard bow while the later, which dates from 1912, has a larger catch on the right side of the frame. The pistol also has a jacket around the barrel, an unusual feature that prevents dismantling until it is unscrewed and removed. The guns were 4.5 inches long, had 2-inch barrels and weighed about 13 oz. The detachable magazine held six rounds. Total production is believed to have been about 31,000.

Model 2 (1914-15) Developed in 1913 and marketed in very small numbers before World War I began, this 6.35mm blowback was a simplification of the Model l. It had a conventional full-length slide with an ejection port on the right side, and the recoil spring — concentric with the barrel — was retained by a screwed muzzle bush. The firing system had an internal hammer, and the rear sight-leaf doubled as a loaded-chamber indicator. This 1913-patent sight-leaf normally lay flush with the slide but rose when there was a round in the chamber. Superseded by the Model 5, the Model 2 was 4.3 inches long, had a 2.1-inch barrel and weighed about 10 oz. The detachable box magazine held six rounds. Only about 10,000 guns were made.

Model 3 (1913-15) This was little more than a Model 2 enlarged to suit the 7.65mm Auto (32 ACP) cartridge. The ejection port was moved to the upper left of the slide — an aberration that persisted for several years in Walther designs, causing the ejected case to sail disconcertingly across the shooter's line of sight. The screwed bush holding the recoil spring in the Model 2 slide was replaced by a bayonet-jointed pattern, locking into studs inside the slide. A small spring catch beneath the muzzle retained the bush. The Model 3 is among the scarcest of pre-1918 Walthers with production amounting to a mere 3500.

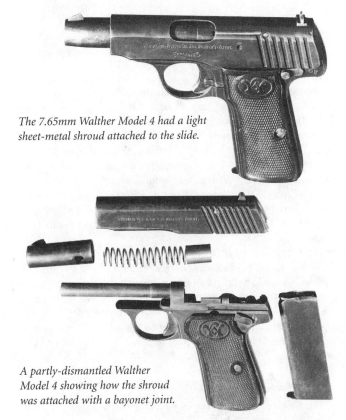

The 7.65mm Walther Model 4 had a light sheet-metal shroud attached to the slide.

A partly-dismantled Walther Model 4 showing how the shroud was attached with a bayonet joint.

Model 4 (1915-29) Despite an optimistic introduction date of 1910, which Walther has always itself perpetuated, this did not appear until World War I had started. One of the first guns to be made in the newly-extended Walther factory, the 7.65mm Model 4 — larger than its predecessors — seems to have been developed in answer to demands from the military. It was little more than a Model 3 extended to take an eight-round magazine, and the barrel was lengthened from 2.6 inches to 3.3 inches. The slide was based on the Model 3; indeed, the earliest Model 4 guns had leftover Model 3 slides complete with the pop-up rear sight/loaded-chamber indicator. The slide was lengthened by an extension piece, held by the same type of bayonet catch and stud-lock as the Model 3, though the spring lock under the muzzle was abandoned.

The Model 4 was purchased in large numbers by German army authorities during the war. Exactly how many guns were made is unknown, but the total may well have exceeded 100,000. They had a simplified slide with a fixed "V"-notch rear sight and a modified dismantling system.

Production of the Model 4 continued after the end of the war, with post-1919 guns being identified by slide marks that read "Zella-Mehlis" instead of "Zella St. Blasii". Work ceased in the mid-1920s, but new guns were being delivered from store until the end of the decade. They

A typical 6.35mm (25 ACP) Walther Model 5.

were 6 inches long and weighed about 19-1/2 oz. It has been estimated that about 300,000 were made.

Model 5 (1915-25) Introduced at the same time as the Model 4, this was an improved Model 2 made to somewhat better standards. Apart from the rifling, which changed from four grooves to six, it could be distinguished from the Model 2 by the substitution of a fixed-notch rear sight for the earlier rear sight/loaded-chamber indicator combination. The Model 2 slide inscription read "Selbstlade Pistole Cal 6,35 Walther's Patent", but the Model 5 simply bore "Walther's Patent Cal 6,35". The Model 5 was about 4.3 inches long, had a 2.1-inch barrel and weighed about 10 oz without its six-round magazine. Guns made prior to 1919 had nine wide retraction grooves, but post-war guns had 16 narrow grooves; production totaled about 60,000.

Model 6 (1916) Virtually an enlarged Model 4 chambering the 9mm Parabellum cartridge with the ejection port moved back to the right side of the slide, this gun attempted to satisfy military demands. However, the simple blowback action was stressed to its limit by the powerful cartridge and the authorities, unhappy with performance, acquired little more than a few hundred for trials. Total production seems to have exceeded 1000, but few examples survive. The guns were 8.3 inches long, had 4.7-inch barrels and weighed about 33 oz. Their magazines held eight rounds.

Model 7 (1916-20) A smaller 6.35mm-caliber version of the Model 4, this had a Model 5-type slide with an extension shroud, rightward ejection and a 3-inch barrel. Internally, a hammer replaced the striker of the preceding pocket pistols. Most of the guns were sold commercially, being favored by military officials and staff officers; tens of thousands were made before work ceased in November 1918. A few guns assembled after 1919 bear "Zella-Mehlis" on the slide instead of "Zella St. Blasii" and had 16 narrow retraction grooves milled into the slide instead of nine broad grooves.

Model 8 (c. 1922-42) Walther's first post-war pistol broke new ground. The slide extension was replaced by a full-length ribbed-top

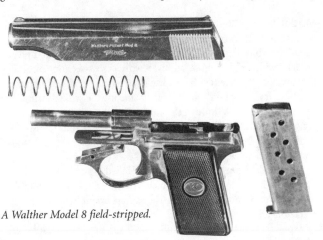

A Walther Model 8 field-stripped.

slide, tapering at the muzzle. Patented in 1920, the trigger guard doubled as a stripping catch. The guard pivoted on the butt and ran up through a slot in the frame to stop rearward movement of the slide. On all but the earliest guns, which had a thumb catch in the trigger-guard web, it was necessary only to pull the guard down and spring it aside. The slide could then be removed by pulling it back, up and off the frame.

The 6.35mm Model 8 was large enough to allow a good grip and was extremely well finished. It remained in production until the early 1940s, total output amounting to about 250,000 guns. No changes had been made in the basic design, apart from a simplification of the extractor and firing-pin assembly in the early 1930s. The guns were 5.1 inches long, with 2.8-inch barrels, and weighed 13 oz; eight-round magazines were provided. Finish was usually polished blue, but nickeled, gilded and even gold-plated guns have been seen. Some also display engraving, arabesque and oakleaf styles predominating. The composition grips had distinctive medallions, with the "CW" monogram on a field of sky-blue cloisonné enamel. Later grips also displayed the Walther banner trademark, which also lay on the left side of the slide.

A 6.35mm Walther Model 9 vest-pocket pistol.

A partly dismantled Model 9.

Model 9 (c. 1922-40) One of the smallest and neatest of all vest-pocket pistols, this 6.35mm-caliber Walther was patented in 1921. A fixed-barrel blowback with an open-top slide, it is virtually an updated Model 1 with a slide held by an insert with a cross-section resembling the number "8". Retained by a spring catch, this "8"-block is pushed into both frame and slide at the rear, anchoring the striker spring. The striker-tail runs back through the block when the action is cocked, acting as an indicator. The only inherent drawback is that the Model 9 striker spring, being somewhat small, loses its elasticity over a period of years and can deliver weak strikes.

The Model 9 was the last of the numbered Walther pistols. It was merely 3.9 inches long, with a 2-inch barrel, and weighed about 9 oz without the six-round magazine. The earliest examples had concealed extractors and retraction grips that were milled slightly diagonally, but an exposed extractor was soon substituted and the grips became verti-

cal. Though the standard finish was a rich blue, decorated and engraved options could be requested (see Model 8, above). The grips were initially the cloisonné-enamel medallion design, but this was replaced by a transverse retaining bolt that ran through a steel washer. A few guns were made in the 1930s with duralumin frames.

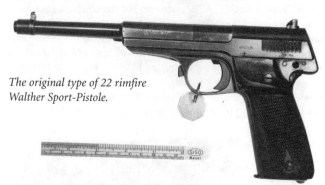

The original type of 22 rimfire Walther Sport-Pistole.

Automatische-Sport-Pistole (1926) This 22-caliber blowback was introduced in the mid-1920s, selling steadily but unspectacularly for some years. In 1932, a German marksman firing one of these guns unexpectedly took a silver medal at the Los Angeles Olympic Games, and pistols were soon being misleadingly sold in the USA as "Model 1932". The Walther was built on the frame of the abortive Model 6 (q.v.) but had an open-top slide around its fixed barrel. It had an internal hammer, the safety catch lay on the frame and the barrel originally measured either 5.9 inches or 9.1 inches. After the Olympic games, a 7.5-inch barrel was added to the options. A few guns were fitted with alloy slides and chambered the 22 Short cartridge for use in rapid-fire competitions.

PP (1930-45) This could be regarded as a logical development of the Model 8, enlarged to chamber the 7.65mm Auto (32 ACP) cartridge, with double-action lock and an external hammer, but the design was refined until it rendered every other pocket pistol obsolete overnight. A signal pin indicated a loaded chamber; the magazine catch lay in the grip frame behind the trigger, instead of on the butt-heel; and the safety catch on the slide could be applied to release the hammer and lock the firing pin.

A 7.65mm Walther PP. This was a wartime gun, with the "ac" manufacturer's code on the slide.

A partly dismantled Walther PP.

"PP" stood for *Polizei Pistole* ("police pistol"), revealing Walther's intention. In this role it was outstandingly successful, attracting several export orders in addition to serving throughout Germany by 1939. The PP sold extensively to the German paramilitary formations and was purchased in quantity for the armed forces during World War II. Its small size commended it particularly to army tank crewmen and Luftwaffe pilots.

A few small changes were made to the PP in the 1930s, beginning with the replacement of the original two-piece or "split" firing pin with a sturdier one-piece design, and strengthening the rear part of the frame forced a change to be made to the sear. The loaded-chamber indicating pin — once optional — was virtually standardized after 1933, and the 90-degree rotation of the safety lever was reduced to 60 degrees in 1938. Finish deteriorated as the war ran its course, and the frame was simplified in 1943 to save machine time. The signal pin was omitted altogether from 1944 onward. However, except for a group of "ac"-code guns made in 1944-5, Polizei-Pistolen all bear the Walther name and address, the banner trademark and the model designation.

Although the original Polizei-Pistole was originally offered only in 7.65mm Auto and 9mm Short, variants chambering the 6.35mm Auto and 22 LR rimfire cartridges appeared in 1933. Only a few hundred 6.35mm guns were ever made, and even the rimfire version, which lacked the signal pin, is comparatively scarce. A standard pre-1945 PP was 6.7 inches long, had a 3.9-inch barrel and weighed 24-1/2 oz. The magazine capacity varied according to caliber: seven 9mm Short, eight 7.65mm or 10 22 LR rounds.

Polizei-Pistolen will be found with a variety of marks applied by police and paramilitary units, though many fakes exist. Police guns will bear inspectors' marks in the form of displayed eagles accompanied by single letters ("C", "F"). Unit marks may also be found, "P.D.N." identifying the police department in Nuremberg. Marks applied by the Sturm-Abteilung (SA), the Nationalsozialistische Kraftfahrkorps (NSKK) and the Reichsfinanzverwaltung (RFV) have all been authenticated, together with "Rplt." for the Danish state police or *Rigspoliti*. A helpful guide to dating concerns the proofmarks, which changed from a crowned "N" to an eagle over "N" with effect from April 1, 1940.

Walther licensed production of the Polizei-Pistole to Manurhin (q.v.) in the early 1950s, but as the design was too attractive to be ignored, copies appeared in many countries. Despite the availability of cheaper versions, the PP was slow to lose popularity. Walther recommenced production in the mid-1960s and continued work until the mid-1990s, when the decision was taken to import American-made guns from Interarms (q.v.). Details of the post-war Ulm-made guns will be found in the next section.

PPK (1931-45) The success of the Polizei-Pistole as a holster pistol inspired the introduction of a compact model, allegedly developed for use in shoulder holsters at the request of the Prussian state police. This was the "PPK" or *Kriminalpolizei-Pistole*, named for its appeal to investigative plain-clothes policemen.

A pre-war Walther PPK.

The PPK was a smaller version of the PP, identical in every mechanical respect except for a significant change in the construction of the butt. Instead of being forged with a steel backstrap and separate grip plates, the PPK had a simple rectangular grip-frame without a backstrap and a molded one-piece plastic grip. An optional finger-rest on the magazine base — also available with the Polizei-Pistole — could improve grip if required. The changes made in the design of the PPK duplicated those of the PP, except that the PPK firing pin was always a one-piece design. The most obvious change concerned the rotation of the safety lever, which was reduced from 90 degrees to 60 degrees in 1938.

Production of the PPK began in 7.65mm Auto and 9mm Short and was then extended to 6.35mm Auto and 22 LR rimfire. The 6.35mm PPK, like the equivalent PP, was very rare; it was discontinued in 1935 after only a few hundred had been made. The 7.65mm PPK was 6.1 inches long, had a 3.3-inch barrel and weighed 20-1/2 oz empty. The detachable box magazine held seven rounds.

Guns will be found with the marks of the police and paramilitary units (see PP, above), but the most important variation was the *Ehrenwaffe des Politischen Leiters*. Destined for high-ranking party officials, this gun had special "Adlergriffe" or "eagle grips", with a swastika-clutching displayed eagle molded into the upper panel.

MP (1) (1934) An enlarged Polizei-Pistole chambering the 9mm Parabellum service cartridge, this was intended as a replacement for the P.08 — hence the designation *Militärische Pistole*. Though a logical design progression, it is doubtful if Walther ever expected it to be accepted and the gun may simply have kept the authorities busy while something better was developed. Mechanically the same as the Polizei-Pistole but much larger (8 inches overall with a 5-inch barrel), the MP was soon abandoned. Its designation was subsequently applied to locked-breech prototypes.

MP (2) (1934-5) This replaced the MP (1). It embodied an experimental recoil-operated mechanism with a locking block on each side of the breech. Consequently, the slide had two shallow protrusions on each side, running back as far as the rear of the trigger guard. The hammer was internal and the trigger was double-action. Trials presumably showed that this gun had promise but was too complicated. Consequently, it was abandoned in favor of the Armee Pistole described below.

Olympia-Modell (1934-5) Realizing that the demands of the 1936 Olympic Games, to be held in Berlin, would be an ideal way of showcasing German superiority, the national shooting association (Deutscher Schützen-Verband, "DSV") asked Walther to develop a special pistol that would give German marksman an edge over their rivals. The basic layout of the Automatische-Sport-Pistole was retained, but the streamlined contours of the new prototypes owed much to the Polizei-Pistolen. They had exposed hammers and a frame that was carried back over the hand to allow an auxiliary sight-block to be attached. Experience of competition soon showed that the guns were better than their predecessors, but not good enough, as separating the sights, with the front sight on the slide and the rear sight on the frame block, promoted inaccuracy; and the trigger system was insufficiently sensitive. The design was returned to Walther for revision.

Olympia-Pistole (1935-40) This matched the general layout of the Olympia Modell with a trigger system with an ultra-rapid hammer fall. The hammer was internal, allowing the sights to be mounted on the barrel and slide. Testing suggested that the new Walther had exceptional potential as a target pistol, and the development of a duraluminum slide allowed a 22 Short rimfire version to be created specifically for rapid-fire competitions. The steel slide was usually reserved for the sporting derivatives, which chambered the 22 Extra Long No. 7 or 22 LR rimfire rounds. Production began late in 1935, together with special match-grade ammunition developed by RWS, and the guns were soon

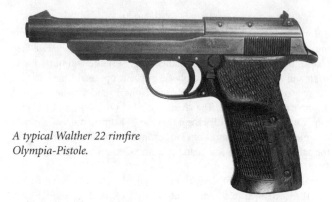

*A typical Walther 22 rimfire
Olympia-Pistole.*

*A 9mm enclosed-hammer Walther Armee-Pistole,
with its holster-stock.*

being offered commercially. They were spectacularly successful, though commercial sales prevented the Germans from making a clean sweep of the medals in rapid fire; Von Oyen and Hax took gold and silver, while the bronze went to a Swede firing an Olympia-Pistole. The basic design was licensed to Hämmerli (q. v.) in the 1950s.

Assembly seems to have stopped shortly after World War II began, and no gun has yet to be authenticated with the "eagle over N" proofmarks that would date it later than April 1, 1940. Though presentations were made in 1941 (and possibly later), these guns have "crown/N" proofs and were presumably taken from store. Olympia-Pistolen, which were appropriately marked on the left rear of the slide and had "O"-prefix serial numbers, were made in several guises:

• *Funfkampfmodell* Destined for use in modern pentathlon, a blend of horsemanship, shooting and fencing, this was chambered for the 22 LR rimfire cartridge and had a steel slide. Three supplementary weights could be fitted to the rail beneath the slab-sided barrel and the frame. The checkered walnut grip, with a flared heel after 1939, also had checkering on the thumb-rest — banned in rapid-fire competitions — and a wooden extension to the magazine base filled the space between the grips. Funfkampfmodelle usually had 9.6-inch barrels, giving an overall length of 13.1 inches, and weighed about 45 oz with all the auxiliary weights in place. The magazine held 10 rounds.

• *Jagdmodell* (or "Jäger Modell") Intended for casual target practice, this had a 4.7-inch barrel that reduced overall length to 7.9 inches and weight to about 27 oz with an empty magazine. The guns were usually supplied in 22 LR, with steel slides and 10-round magazines, but a variant in 22 Short (with an alloy slide and a six-round magazine) was also made in small numbers.

• *Schnellfeuermodell* Chambered for the 22 Short rimfire round, with an alloy slide and a steel frame, this was the basic rapid-fire version. The barrel was 7.5 inches long, the guns weighed about 40 oz with the solitary frame weight and the magazines held six rounds. The guns could be recognized by the heavy cylindrical barrel assembly, which was noticeably "stepped" in front of the frame-tip.

• *Sportmodell* This was a variant of the 4.7-inch barreled Jagdmodell (above) intended for sporting use. Its grips lack the sophisticated shaping of the target patterns.

• *Standardmodell* Essentially similar to the Funfkampfmodell, this was usually sold with a 7.5-inch cylindrical barrel and squared auxiliary weights. The barrel weights are used in a most peculiar manner. One has a collar around the muzzle and attaches directly to the under-frame weight at the rear, allowing the two small weights to be secured beneath it. Most standard guns are in 22 Short RF, with alloy slides, but a few steel-slide examples were made in 22 LR.

AP (1935-7) Derived from the recoil-operated Militärische Pistole (2), this had a simplified locking system that relied on a pin-like actuator and a "U"-shape block or "wedge". The barrel and slide rode on the frame, the top of the slide being cut away to expose the breech end of the barrel. The upper surface of a locking wedge in the frame, beneath

the barrel, was supported by a ramp and the sprung actuator to engage a recess under the barrel; simultaneously, side wings engaged recesses in the slide.

Barrel and slide moved back together as the gun fired. The barrel lug carrying the actuator pin struck a transom in the frame, forcing the tip of the pin to depress the locking wedge to disengage the slide. The slide was then freed to reciprocate and complete the loading cycle.

The Armee Pistole had an internal hammer, with the double-action lock and a slide-mounted PP-type safety catch limited to a rotation of 60 degrees. Return springs on each side of the frame bore against the lower edge of the slide, while a slide lock and a stripping catch lay on the left side of the frame. The slide had a single longitudinal projection instead of the two that had characterized the MP (2).

A few hundred guns were made for trials, but the army expressed a preference for an external hammer. Made in small batches, largely by hand, Armee-Pistolen often varied in detail. A typical 9mm specimen measured 8.5 inches overall, had a 4.7-inch barrel and weighed 28 oz without its eight-round detachable box magazine. A few guns chambered the 7.65mm Parabellum cartridge, but the existence of prototypes in 38 Super and 45 ACP (intended to impress the North American market) has yet to be authenticated.

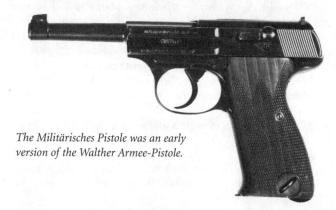

*The Militärisches Pistole was an early
version of the Walther Armee-Pistole.*

MP (3) (1937) This was the first of the series to have a flush-sided slide, though it retained the enclosed hammer of the Armee Pistole. Only a few were made (perhaps no more than 10), but they included at least one in 45 ACP instead of the standard 9mm Parabellum. Surviving guns also have extra-deep trigger guards, which may suggest that they were intended for trials in cold climates (Sweden, perhaps) where a gloved finger would be used.

MP (4) (1937-8) This was essentially an adaptation of the enclosed-hammer MP (3) with the back of the slide cutaway to reveal the hammer. Some guns had PP-type ring hammers, but most had the spurred design that was perpetuated on the P.38. Internally, the lock that prevented the gun from firing unless the trigger was pressed applied to the firing pin instead of the hammer. This is assumed to have been done to satisfy the military authorities. If the hammer-lock failed, the gun would not work; if the firing-pin lock failed, however, there was a good chance that the gun could still be fired. Most guns also had rectangular-head firing pins that retracted into the breechblock when the safety catch was applied.

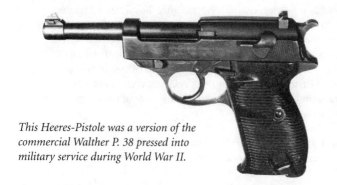

This Heeres-Pistole was a version of the commercial Walther P. 38 pressed into military service during World War II.

A wartime Walther-made P. 38 dismantled into its main component groups. Note the locking block above the trigger and the actuating pin protruding from the back of the rear barrel lug.

HP (1938-45) The "Heeres-Pistole" was little more than a refined MP (4). The earliest guns were essentially series-made prototypes, and several changes were made before the perfected HP could be accepted by the Wehrmacht. The lockwork was based on the Polizei-Pistole, a loaded-chamber signal pin was fitted, and the safety catch of the earliest pistols not only retracted the head of the firing pin into the breech-block section of the slide, but it also locked the pin in place and then dropped the cocked hammer. The hammer struck the slide body instead of the firing pin. However, the original rectangular-head firing pin was soon replaced by a simpler non-retracting cylindrical pattern.

Heeres-Pistolen were submitted to trials in Sweden, where the design was adopted as the "Automatiska pistol M/39" and also offered for sale commercially in 7.65mm or 9mm Parabellum, the former chambering being rarely seen. The 38 Super Auto and 45 ACP options were offered by Stoeger in the USA, but it is unlikely that anything other than a few prototypes had been made when World War II began. In addition, war terminated the Swedish contract after only about 1500 commercial-type 9mm pistols had been delivered. This forced the Swedes to accept the Lahti (q.v.), which had placed only third in the original trials.

A surprising number of detail changes were made in the design of the Heeres-Pistolen, which was not really stabilized until about 1000 had been made. They included a reduction in the depth of the slide, changes to the loaded-chamber indicating pin and a broadening of the decocking-lever thumb-piece. A more important change concerned the extractor, once concealed and easily jammed, which was soon exposed on the right side of the side behind the ejection port.

The army authorities regarded the Heeres Pistole as acceptable for service, requesting purely minor changes to facilitate mass-production; these were agreed by Walther and the modified gun became the 9mm Pistole 38 (or "P.38"). However, Heeres-Pistolen with commercial markings were made until the middle of 1944; these were mechanically identical with the military P.38 described in the next entry.

P. 38 (1940-5) The principal mechanical difference between the prototype Heeres-Pistolen and the perfected military-issue derivative lay in a slight simplification of the safety system: applying the safety catch simply locked the firing pin without withdrawing it from the path of the hammer. When the hammer was finally released by the safety, it struck the rear of the pin. Movement was prevented only by the engagement of the safety-catch shaft with the pin body — safe enough in guns made to peacetime standards, but not as secure in those made right at the end of the war when standards of metallurgy had declined.

The extractors of the first 1500 P.38 were concealed within the slide, and a simplified cylindrical-headed firing pin replaced the original rectangular pattern after about 4500 guns had been made. A duraluminum frame was developed experimentally, probably before series production began, but was not durable enough to replace the forged-steel pattern. The guns were 8.5 inches long, had 5-inch barrels and weighed about 34 oz empty. The detachable box magazines held eight rounds.

The first army order was given to Walther in April 1939 with the first deliveries being made in August. These early guns had "0"-prefix serial numbers, and the banner trademark lay on the left side of the slide. After about 13,000 0-prefix guns had been made, the authorities allotted Walther the numerical code "480" in September 1940 — applied in conjunction with the banner mark — but this was replaced by an "ac" code only two months later. The letter code was used until the end of the war, though the style changed in 1943 from a "stacked" or two-line code/date mark (e.g., "ac" over "42" for 1942) to a single-line or "monoblock" design ("ac 44"). The most important of the contractors numerically, though by no means the most rapid, Walther made about 480,000 P. 38 by 1945.

Comparatively few changes had been made once the design had been stabilized, though the standards of finish (and the metallurgical quality of some of the parts) declined as hostilities progressed. The grips, finely checkered plastic on the earliest guns, were changed in 1940 to a ribbed pattern that was easier to hold if the gun was wet or greasy. Simplified hold-open catches and coarsely serrated "cog" hammers were introduced in 1943, the frame was strengthened in the vicinity of the trigger axis pin and phosphated sheet-steel grips were accepted in 1945.

Pistols were also made in large quantities by Mauser and Spreewerke, with a few assembled in the ČZ factory in Strakonice; details will be found in the appropriate sections. The employment of three prime contractors and several major sub-contractors, often in German-occupied Czechoslovakia, means that Pistolen 38 will be found with a variety of markings.

KPK (1938-9?) This appears to have been an experimental adaptation of the PPK, possibly intended for a paramilitary organization. Few were made and fewer survive. The design was basically a 7.65mm PPK with a light alloy frame and the slide lengthened to almost completely conceal the hammer. The slide was marked "KPK" with the Walther banner trademark, the one-piece plastic grips bearing the swastika-clutching *Reichsadler*.

UP ("Ultra Pistole") This project was apparently begun by an ammunition manufacturer, Gustav Genschow & Co. of Durlach, in a bid to explore the limits of blowback operation. The goal was to replace the standard Browning-type pocket-pistol cartridges — 6.35mm Auto, 7.65mm Auto, 9mm Short — with ammunition that offered better performance, yet avoided the need for a breech-lock. Designs for 6.45mm, 8mm and 9mm Ultra rounds were finalized in 1938, and a few pistols were converted to fire them. Ultimately, however, no one was keen to gamble on new calibers when the likelihood of war held so little promise for commercial exploitation. The project was shelved, and the war effectively killed it.

It is said that 20,000 rounds were made in each chambering, most being used in test firing. The identity of the pistols involved remains something of a mystery, but, as the PP/PPK series was in full production, it seems much more likely that guns of this type served as test-beds rather than the Mauser HSc or Sauer 38. Neither of the latter was being made in quantity in this period. A special "Walther" prototype has also been linked with the Ultra project, though the origins of such a distinctive design — with a half-length slide and the return spring assembly in the grip — remain uncertain.

The special pistols were either tested virtually to destruction or returned to their original form once the trials had been completed. Any guns that survived were probably dispersed in 1945; ammunition is similarly scarce. The project was not entirely forgotten, as it is generally accepted that the 9x18mm Makarov and 9x18mm Police cartridges were both inspired by knowledge of the Ultra program.

Volkspistole (1944-5) Faced with ever-growing problems of providing enough small arms to equip the armed forces, especially the home-defense Volkssturm units, the German government instigated a variety of emergency programs at the end of World War II. These included the development of a "People's Rifle" (Volksgewehr) and a comparable pistol, a process described in greater detail in the Mauser section.

The demand was simply for a cheap mass-produced pistol capable of handling the regulation 9mm Parabellum cartridge, preferably with a breech-locking system. Prototypes were made by Gustloff, Mauser and Walther, but practically nothing is known about the Walther pistols — except that they varied from a P.38 with a simplified slide to crude stamped-metal constructions.

The official records reveal the submission of a locked-breech Walther prior to June 1944, but this was unsuccessful and two new "much simplified" guns had arrived by November.

One simplified Walther matched a rotating-barrel lock adapted from the Steyr-Hahn, then in German police service in some numbers, with a double-action trigger system. It had a forged-steel frame with a butt fabricated from stampings, a drop-forged slide, a barrel that could be made on a lathe and a proliferation of stamped parts. But if this can indeed be classified as a "Volkspistole", it was undoubtedly too complicated to impress the authorities.

A hybrid gun combining a P.38 frame with a full-length stamped-steel slide enveloping the barrel is also known, but this was also too wasteful in both time and material. It was probably superseded by the first of the large double-action blowbacks, one survivor displaying a Walther banner on the slide and a simplified lever-type safety protruding ahead of the checkered wooden grips. However, the authorities disliked the trigger mechanism (which was too complicated and too coarse) and asked for a modified single-action version that incorporated even more stampings. The result was the crudest of the Walthers, with a single-action trigger and a simple lathe-turned barrel pinned into the frame. Virtually every minor part was a stamping, and the magazine-release catch was reduced to a bent spring.

Still dissatisfied with the blowbacks, the development commission then insisted that a breech lock was essential. It is assumed that the Walther projects were abandoned at this point. Though claims have been made that guns were made with a Browning tipping-barrel system, the testers preferred the delayed-blowback Gustloff and Mauser designs. The war ended before anything other than trials could be undertaken, and Volkspistolen of any type are now very rarely seen.

CARL WALTHER SPORTWAFFENFABRIK

Ulm/Donau, Germany.
The US Army reached Zella-Mehlis on April 12, 1945, and work in the

Walther factory ceased. Shortly after hostilities had ceased, Fritz Walther and his family transferred to what was to become the American occupation zone. Work initially concentrated on mechanical calculators, made in a small workshop in Heidenheim an der Brenz, and purpose-built factories had soon been erected in Niederstötzingen and Gerstetten. Finally, in 1950, Walther purchased an old cavalry barracks in Ulm/Donau and (with a work force of just six men) began to make air rifles.

The Allies allowed work to recommence on the P.38 in 1954, and the first new series-made guns left the Ulm production line in 1957 (though Manurhin assembled a few thousand guns for export to Portugal in the same era). The firearms business grew rapidly throughout the 1960s, with the success of the PP series, the TPH and the new target pistols. However, difficulties encountered in mass-producing a pre-war design, together with the preference of German police for other designs, forced Walther to develop a Browning-style tipping barrel instead of the Barthelmes block. The P88 (announced in 1983) became just one of many similar designs competing in the military/police market, predictably failing to compete with long-established rivals such as the Beretta 92 and SIG-Sauers.

The once-large and powerful gunmaking business became a shadow of its former self, greatly hindered by the early death of Karl-Heinz Walther (1922-83). It was purchased in 1994 by Umarex Sportwaffen GmbH & Co. KG of Arnsberg, experienced a rise in fortunes with the successful development of the P99 and continues to work today on a reduced scale while diversification is sought. Walther pistols were handled in North America by a variety of agencies, including the Thalson Arms Company, until Interarms (q.v.) became involved first in the distribution and then in the manufacturer of the PP, PPK , PPK/S and TPH in the USA. On August 1, 1999, agreement was reached with Smith & Wesson to make a modified version of the P99 under license.

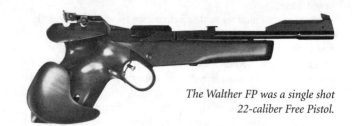

The Walther FP was a single shot 22-caliber Free Pistol.

~ SINGLE-SHOT PISTOL ~

FP (1979-89?) Entirely different from the other Walther target pistols, this single-shot Free Pistol has a Martini-type dropping block operated by a lever on the right side of the frame. The firing circuit is electronic; a solenoid firing pin is actuated by a trigger switch and a 9-volt battery. Opening the breech breaks the firing circuit; closing the breech restores the circuit and charges a capacitor to power the solenoid. A "ready light" indicates when the system is ready to fire.

~ REVOLVER ~

R-99 (1999-2000) Offered briefly in the "La Chasse" range, this was a Röhm design with Walther marks; both companies are owned by the Umarex Group. Chambered for the 357 Magnum round, the R-99 had a six-chamber cylinder and blue or stainless-steel finish. The grip was dark-gray synthetic.

~ AUTOMATIC PISTOLS ~

P-1A1 (1989-92) This was an improved P-5 (q.v.) with an additional cross-bolt safety catch in the slide. When applied, the catch forced the firing pin down to align with the recess in the hammer face. The basic operating system remained unchanged. The P-1A1 was 7.1 inches long, had a 3.5-inch barrel and weighed about 29 ounces empty. The P. 38/P-1-type magazine held the customary eight rounds.

A 9mm Walther P1A1.

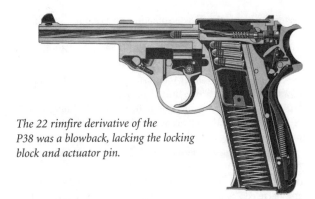

The 22 rimfire derivative of the P38 was a blowback, lacking the locking block and actuator pin.

P. 38 or P-1 (1957-95) When the German Federal Republic reconstituted its army in the 1950s, the Bundeswehr requested the P.38 as its standard handgun. A series of prototypes was begun in 1954, and the gun eventually re-entered production. The first delivery to the Bundeswehr was made in May 1957.

The new Ulm-made P.38 was very similar to its wartime predecessor, though so many minor changes had been made that only a few components will interchange. The greatest changes were the introduction of a duraluminum frame and the safety system. A supplementary automatic firing-pin safety device was unlocked only as the hammer was about to fall, removing one of the objections to the pre-1945 system in which the hammer-face rested on the head of the firing pin.

The P.38 was officially renamed "P-1" in 1963. Prolonged service experience showed that the slide was weak, ironically just where the manufacturer's mark had been rolled into its surface, and a strengthened design was adopted in July 1968. Guns of this type were initially identified by a star mark ("★") until all the older guns had been converted; the mark was then abandoned. The 100,000th pistol was delivered to the Bundeswehr in April 1960, but comparatively few export orders were obtained. A few guns went to Austria, some to Chile, and others to Norway and Portugal, but the P.38 was never able to challenge the domination of the FN-Browning GP-35 ("High Power"). Guns with Manurhin marks were assembled in Ulm but shipped to Mulhouse to be finished. These then went to the police forces in West Berlin and also to Austria, satisfying local regulations.

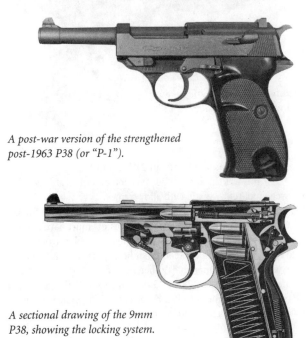

A post-war version of the strengthened post-1963 P38 (or "P-1").

A sectional drawing of the 9mm P38, showing the locking system.

Commercial production also recommenced, some of the guns being offered in 7.65mm Parabellum (1968-76 only) in addition to 9mm Parabellum. These guns have the deer's antler mark of the Ulm proof house on the left side of the frame, accompanied by a proof date (not necessarily the same as the date of manufacture). More than 250,000 P.38 had been sold commercially by 1975. A few changes were made to the safety system during the production life of the P.38/P-1 series, and the steel frame replaced the alloy version in 1987.

Though the P.38/P-1 sold in large numbers, particularly to the German military and police, exports were comparatively meager and commercial sales were hamstrung by price. In 1939, the A.F Stoeger Company of New York had sold the "Model HP" for $75. When the P.38 returned to the USA in 1960, the price was $96, but the standard alloy-frame 9mm gun cost $995 by 1990 … and the steel-frame version retailed for $1400. A variety of special-edition and commemorative guns were made, but production steadily declined until work stopped. The P-5 (below) was an attempt to modernize the basic Barthelmes/Walther design.

- *P.38* (rimfire version, 1965-90) Popular as a trainer and externally similar to the centerfire pistol, this was a simple blowback adaptation chambered for the 22 LR rimfire round. The magazine held 10 rounds.
- *P.38 IV* See "P-4".
- *P. 38 Jubiläumsmodell* (1988) This was produced to celebrate the 50th anniversary of the P.38, being marked appropriately "50 Jahre P 38 1938-1988" on the left side of the slide. The finish was high-polish blue, with gold plating on the extractor, the hammer and the trigger. There was oakleaf carving on the walnut grips. Purchasers were allowed to select their own serial number (as long as it was below 500), and to have their name added on the right side of the slide.
- *P.38k* (1974-9) Made only in very small numbers, from October 1974 onward, this was simply the standard pistol with the barrel reduced to 2.75 inches and the front sight mounted on the tip of the slide instead of the barrel. The basic P.38 was simply too large to be

A short-barreled P.38k.

concealed easily, and the P.38k is sometimes seen simply as an interim solution while the P-5 (q.v.) was being developed. The truth is probably that it was seen as an advertising gimmick, duplicating "the pistol of the secret police".

PP (1964-2001) Though Walther was permitted to begin making airguns in 1950, work on cartridge-firing handguns was prevented until the mid-1950s. In the intervening period, the pre-war Olympia-Pistole and the PP/PPK series had been licensed to Hämmerli and Manurhin, respectively. Working in Alsace, an area with a large German population even though returned to France in 1945, Manurhin was particularly sympathetic to Walther's requests.

Work began c. 1953 and, by 1955, the PP and PPK had been joined by a long-barreled "Sport" model. When Walther was allowed to resume handgun production, beginning with the P.38 for the German armed forces, Manurhin continued to make PP and PPK pistols, even though many bore Walther slide marks. Work in Mulhouse-Bourtzwiller continued until 1964, when manufacture switched to Ulm.

A post-war Ulm-made PP, in "9mm kurz" (9mm Short, 380 ACP).

German-made guns continued to appear until the late 1970s, when the basis of the project switched to the Interarms factory in the USA. Thereafter, Walther assembled US-made parts into guns that had German slide markings. Assembly ceased in 1999, the last 500 guns being offered in a commemorative series in 2001. German-made PPs were generally blued, with walnut grips, but stainless-steel (US-made) examples were seen in increasing numbers in the 1990s and were still being offered in 2001.

- *PP Fiftieth Anniversary* (1979) Offered only in 22 LR rimfire and 9mm Short (380 ACP), this gun was richly blued, with gold-filled inscription on the slide, and hard-carved grips displaying oakleaves, acorns and the Walther banner trademark. It was supplied in a matching walnut case.
- *PP Last Edition* (2001) Five hundred guns have been offered, in PP or PPK guise, with special high-polish finish and the legend "Last Edition" over "1929-1999" on the right side of the slide. They also come in a presentation box containing a video of Walther's history. There were only 50 Polizei Pistolen in 7.65mm Auto (32 ACP) and 100 in 9mm Short (380 ACP).
- *PP Super* (c. 1975-82) Development of this enlargement of the PP began in 1972 to suit the 9mm Police cartridge that was being promoted by Hirtenberg. Long-term trials were undertaken in 1974, but the police preferred locked-breech designs and ultimately took the P-5 (Walther), P-6 (SIG-Sauer) and P-7 (Heckler & Koch) instead. Walther then decided to market the PP Super commercially from 1975 onward. The guns incorporate the improved safety system of the P5, with the firing-pin head inside a recess in the hammer face except when the trigger is being deliberately fired. A squared trigger guard facilitated the fashionable two-handed grip but did little for appearance. The PP Super was 6.9 inches long,

A post-war PPK, in 22 LR rimfire.

with a 3.6-inch barrel and weighed 27 oz empty. The magazine held seven rounds. Sales were comparatively few.

PPK (1964-2001) The history of the post-war PPK duplicates that of the PP (q.v.). Licensed to Manurhin, it was made in France until 1964 — even though many guns bore German marks — before returning to Ulm, and then transferring to the USA in the 1970s. Walther subsequently assembled Interarms-made parts until 1999, when the entire project was stopped. A few high-polish blue guns were offered in 2001 as part of the "Last Edition" commemorative series, though stainless-steel examples were still being offered from regular commercial stock.

- *PPK/E* (2000 to date) This recent variant of the PPK series, despite its Walther marks, is believed to emanate in Hungary (see "FÉG") to offset shortages due to the termination of Interarms' "Walther American" production in the USA. Differences can be seen in the design of the retraction grips, which stand out of the slide instead of groove-milled into the surface, the shape of the grips (which have a shallow thumb-rest) and the contours of the frame and the slide. Guns of this type have a 3.75-inch barrel and are currently being chambered only for the 7.65mm Auto cartridge, though 22 LR rimfire and 9mm Short versions were offered prior to 2000. The magazines hold seven 9mm, eight 22LR or eight 7.65mm rounds.

A presentation pistol celebrating the 50th anniversary of the Walther PPK.

- *PPK Fiftieth Anniversary* (1979) In 22 LR rimfire and 9mm Short (380 ACP), this was similar to the PP version described above. A few guns were apparently made with alloy frames.
- *PPK/S* (1969-2001) Dimensional restrictions introduced by the US Gun Control Act of 1968 demanded that pistols must have a minimum depth of 4 inches; the PPK measured 3.9 inches from slide-top to magazine-bottom and could not be imported. As it had been selling well in North America, Walther, reluctant to lose such a valuable market, devised the PPK/S ("S" for "Special"). This was simply a PP frame carrying the barrel and slide of the PPK, increasing overall depth to 4.1 inches and allowing importation to continue. Ultimately, the problem was solved by licensing production of the PP and PPK to Interarms (q.v.), avoiding the problem altogether. PPK/S production stopped in Ulm when work began in North

Intended to circumvent the US Gun Control Act of 1968, the PPK/S combined the length of the PPK with the frame-depth of the PP.

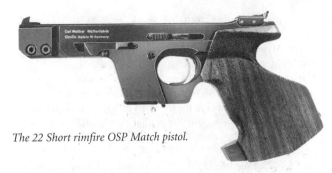

The 22 Short rimfire OSP Match pistol.

America. The stainless-steel and bi-color (blue slide, stainless frame) versions, unique to Interarms, were still being imported into Germany in 2001.

• *PPK Last Edition* (2001) A few guns of this type, interspersed with the PP pattern (above), were offered with special finish and an appropriate commemorative inscription on the slide.

TP (1961-4, 1968-71) Offered in 6.35mm Auto or 22 LR chamberings, this was a modernized version of the Model 9. Construction was similar, though the TP was about an inch longer than its predecessor, and its butt had a far better shape. Placing the safety catch on the slide provided the one major mechanical change; operating the catch disconnected the sear and locked the striker. The guns were 5.2 inches long, had 2.6-inch barrels and weighed about 12 oz without their six-round magazines. One of Walther's less successful designs, the TP lasted less than a decade before replaced by the TPH. Production amounted to about 12,000 in 6.35mm and only about 2,500 in 22 rimfire.

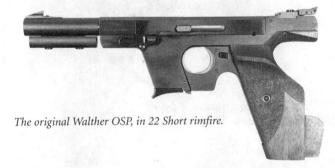

The original Walther OSP, in 22 Short rimfire.

OSP (1962 to date) The Olympia-Schnellfeuer-Pistole is a far cry from the pre-war Olympia Modell. Gone are the graceful curves, as the severely functional OSP is merely a machine for delivering bullets accurately. For all its graceless shape, it balances well and feels good in the hand; and accuracy is beyond reproach. The OSP is still a fixed-barrel blowback, but a bolt, cocked by wings on each side, reciprocates in the rectangular receiver. The grip is a massive anatomical pattern; the detachable box magazine fits into a housing in front of the trigger guard, and a stripping catch appears on the right side of the frame. The rear sight is fully adjustable, the trigger may be set to differing release pressures and the 4.5-inch barrel is chambered for the 22 Short cartridge. A change from eight- to six-groove rifling was made shortly after production began, and four vents were bored into the barrel-top of some guns from 1964 onward. Pistols made before 1971 had rounded barrel contours and a near-circular trigger aperture; later guns share the slab-sided barrel of the GSP.

• *OSP Match* (1985-93) This was a modification of the standard gun with five compensating ports in the barrel-block top and a sliding bar (supporting the front sight) that could be slid forward to cover one of the ports. This allowed the gun to fire special low-pressure 22 Short ammunition in a bid to improve control in rapid fire. The

grips were attached by a single central bolt, allowing them to be adjusted to suit individual hands. The OSP Match was only 11 inches long, compared with 11.5 inches for the standard OSP.

• *OSP 2000* (1992 to date) This was a variation of the OSP Match, with a longer and slightly lower sight line and a walnut Morini-style grip that extends over the back of the firing hand. The guns are 11.7 inches long and weigh about 41 oz. The detachable box magazine, in the frame ahead of the trigger guard, holds five 22 Short rounds.

A typical 22 LR rimfire Walther TPH.

TPH (1968-2001) This scaled-down PP — with a full slide, a double-action lock and an exposed hammer — replaced the uninspiring TP. Available in 22 LR rimfire or 6.35mm Auto (25 ACP) and introduced after the Gun Control Act of 1968 had been passed, the tiny TPH could not be imported into the USA; the depth from slide top to the base of the magazine failed to meet the Gun Control Act's "4-Inch Minimum" criterion by about 0.3 inch. Ultimately, however, the problem was solved by licensing manufacture to Interarms (q.v.). The guns are 5.3 inches long, have 2.8-inch barrels and weigh 11-1/2 oz empty; their frames are alloy and the magazines hold six 6.35mm rounds. A stainless-steel version, made in the USA, will also be seen with standard Walther markings.

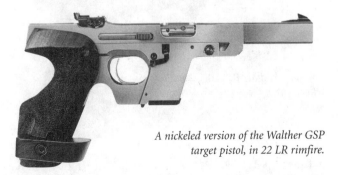

A nickeled version of the Walther GSP target pistol, in 22 LR rimfire.

GSP (1968-2000) The Gebrauchs-und Standard Pistole, the current Walther Standard Pistol, was a modification of the highly successful OSP. It introduced the modern slab-side barrel and has a very noticeable oval trigger aperture. It chambers 22 LR rimfire ammunition and has a shorter sight radius than its companion.

• *GSP-C* (subsequently known as "GSP 32", 1968-2000) This center-fire adaptation of the GSP chambers the 32 S&W Wadcutter cartridge. A conversion unit (comprising bolt, barrel and magazine) can transform it to 22 LR if required.

• *GSP Expert* (1999 to date) An improved version of the basic design, in 22 LR rimfire or 32 S&W Wadcutter, this has a new barrel system with a vibration damper in the form of a plastic sleeve. A detachable compensator/counterweight lies at the muzzle, and the grips are usually natural/blue-stained wood laminate. The Expert is about 11.6 inches overall.

• *GSP Jubiläumsmodell* (1993) Offered only in 22 LR rimfire, this had a nickeled frame and gray/black wood-laminate grips. A quarter-century of success was marked by a "25 Jahre" mark on the right side of the barrel.

The 22-caliber Walther GSP Junior.

• *GSP Junior* This was a lightened short-barreled version of the standard gun.

• *GSP MV* This was simply a version of the basic 22 rimfire pistol with a satin-nickel finish.

• *GSP MV32* Little more than a matte-nickel version of the standard centerfire gun, this was available only in 32 S&W chambering.

KSP2000 (1999 to date) This is a Russian Izhevsk ("IZh") target-pistol design, assembled and finished in Germany. The right side of the slide bears Walther markings in addition to "Cooperation with Baikal". Chambered only for the 22 LR rimfire cartridge, the KSP is intended as an inexpensive competition pistol that nonetheless offers features such as a barrel that lies low in the hand, a separate reciprocating-bolt blowback action, precisely adjustable sights and an adjustable trigger. The anatomical grips are usually a green/brown/blue-dyed laminate design.

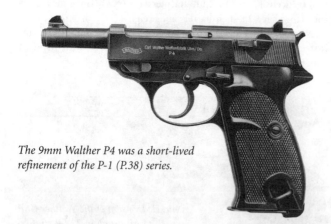

The 9mm Walther P4 was a short-lived refinement of the P-1 (P.38) series.

P-4 (or "P.38 IV", 1976-82) Announced in October 1974, but not offered commercially until 1976, this was a modified P.38 with a strengthened solid-top slide, a steel reinforce in the alloy frame, a shortened barrel and a recessed hammer face. When the hammer is in its rest position, the firing pin enters the recess; as the weight of the hammer is taken on the rear face of the slide, the firing pin cannot be struck. When the trigger is pressed, an auxiliary arm in the lockwork lifts the firing pin until it can be struck by the solid face of the hammer. Guns of this type were 7.5 inches long, had 4.3-inch barrels and weighed about 28 oz. The detachable box magazines held eight rounds.

P-5 (1977-95) A progression from the P.38, this was developed in 1975 in response to requests made by the West German police for a standard pistol, but it was not made in quantity until after the trials had been concluded. The P.38 lockwork was combined with a shortened barrel and an all-enveloping slide. The firing pin and recessed-hammer safety system of the P-4 were retained, but the slide-mounted safety catch was replaced by a de-cocking lever on the left side of the frame. The ejection port lies on top of the slide, spent cases traveling towards the left — an interesting reversion to early Walther designs. The goal of the redesign was to eliminate the manual safety device, often an encumbrance when the pistol is needed, but ensure perfect safety at all other times. The P-5 is 7.1 inches long, has a 3.6-inch barrel and weighs about 35 oz with an empty magazine. Interestingly, all three of the principal competitors in the police trials were adopted with the SIG-Sauer P225 and the Heckler & Koch PSP becoming the P-6 and P-7, respectively. Though the Walther was adopted by the state police in Baden-Württemberg and 45,000 were purchased for the Dutch national police, it proved to be the least popular of the three designs — perhaps because it was the most conventional and the most expensive to make. Production ceased after more than 150,000 had been made.

• *P-5 Compact* (1986-2002) A shorter and lighter P-5, intended for use where concealability is paramount, this has a light alloy frame, wooden grips and a round-tip hammer that is less likely to catch in clothing. The guns are 6.6 inches long and weigh 27-1/2 ounces without their eight-round magazines.

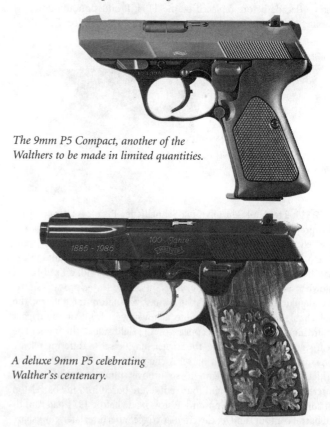

The 9mm P5 Compact, another of the Walthers to be made in limited quantities.

A deluxe 9mm P5 celebrating Walther'ss centenary.

• *P5 Jubiläumsmodell* (1986) Produced to celebrate the Walther centenary, this was marked "1886-1986" and "100 Jahre" over the Walther-banner trademark on the left side of the slide. It had a high-polish blue finish and carved oakleaf decoration on the walnut grips. The extractor, the trigger and the hammer were all gold-plated.

The 9mm P88 was the first locked-breech Walther to abandon the P38-type locking system in favor of a modification of the Browning tipping-barrel.

P88 (1983-92) This was the first locked-breech Walther to abandon the well-tried locking wedge in favor of the SIG variation of the Browning-cam system, in which the squared top of the barrel-block rises into an enlarged ejection port on the slide. The P88 retained the P-5 double-action trigger and safety system, suitably modified. The magazine release and de-cocking lever were duplicated on both sides of the frame. The P88 was 7.4 inches long, had a 4-inch barrel and weighed 32 oz empty. The magazine held 15 rounds. Finish was usually blue, with walnut grips, but matte "military" finish and plastic grips could be obtained on request. However, the P88 was unable to make much headway in a crowded marketplace, and with the increasingly evident trend towards reductions in size and weight, it was replaced with the P88 Compact (below) in the early 1990s. The basic full-length design has since been perpetuated in the specialized "88 series" target pistols.

- *P88 Compact* (1990 to date) Little more than a shortened P88, retaining the same de-cocking/safety system and the same automatic firing-pin safety, this has been offered only in 9mm Parabellum and 9x21 IMI chamberings. It soon proved to be much more pop-

The 9mm Walther P88 Compact.

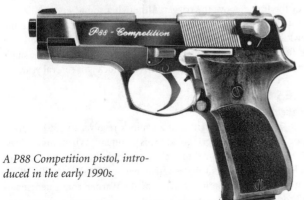

A P88 Competition pistol, introduced in the early 1990s.

ular than the full-length gun and is still being offered from stock. In 9mm Parabellum only (14-round magazine).

- *P88 Champion* (1993-7) A target-shooting version of the P88, this was characterized by barrels of 4, 5 or 6 inches and an adjustable target-type rear sight. The 5-inch barrel had a compensator/counterweight at the muzzle. The trigger mechanism was restricted to single-action-only, the de-cocking option being abandoned. Guns could be obtained in blue or bi-color, with a blued slide and a bright finish stainless-steel frame. The grips were checkered walnut.
- *P88 Competition* (1993-7) Essentially similar to the Champion, restricted to the 4-inch and 5-inch compensated barrel options, this had a fixed rear sight.

P99 (1997 to date) Developed to satisfy the demands of the technical commission of the German police academy, this pistol has many interesting features. The striker-type ignition system is claimed to be the first of its type to offer the advantages of a traditional SA/DA hammer mechanism with the simplicity of construction conferred by a linear striker. The elimination of a hammer prevents snagging, the tail of the striker doubles as a cocking indicator by protruding through the rear of the slide and the de-cocking lever is recessed into the top of the slide. The controls are ambidextrous, and the extractor pivots to reveal a red dot when a cartridge has been chambered. The standard P99, available only in 9mm Parabellum (16-round magazine) or 40 S&W (12 rounds), has a steel slide, a polymer frame and three exchangeable backstraps, allowing the profile of the grip to be adapted to suit individual preferences. The finish is usually black Tenifer — a Teflon-based coating — though military-style matte-gray/green can be supplied on request.

The 40-caliber gun, which is 7.25 inches long and weighs 23 oz without its magazine, is about a quarter-inch longer and 1 oz heavier than the 9mm version; this is due almost entirely to an elongated barrel. Individual guns can be fitted with flashlights and laser designators, and a silencer can be attached if the optional 4.6-inch barrel is substituted for the standard 4-inch type.

The trigger mechanism is among the most interesting features of the P99, as it can be set to give a long pull (0.6 inches) for the first shot in double-action mode and the second and subsequent shots in single-action mode. It also includes an "anti-stress" safety consideration that ensures the gun can only be fired by a very deliberate pull on the trigger instead of an accidental jerk. Alternatively, a "rapid-fire" position can be selected, ensuring a 0.2-inch trigger travel for all shots fired in single-action mode.

In addition to the standard cartridge-firing versions of the P99 and a version licensed for production in the USA (the Smith & Wesson P40), Walther also offers a "P99 Simunition" chambered for 9mm paint balls and FX rubber bullets and a 4.5mm-caliber "P99 CO2" carbon-dioxide-powered trainer. The former has a blue frame; the latter may be red, black or yellow.

- *P99 DAO* (sometimes called "P990", 1999 to date) The trigger mechanism of these guns is regulated to give a consistent pull of about 7-8 lb with a 0.6-inch travel. All shots are fired from a double-action cycle.
- *P99 Luxusmodell* (1999 to date) This is simply a variant of the basic P99 with oakleaf or arabesque decoration on the slide and frame, and walnut inserts in the backstrap. A variety of "La Chasse" series guns were made in the late 1990s, including a standard version with hand-cut engraving on a gray slide and a "DU" variant with laser-cut engraving on a blued slide. These guns have a distinctive logo consisting of a leaping hart, the Walther banner trademark and "La Chasse".
- *P99 Millennium* (2000) Offered in 9mm Parabellum and 40 S&W, this had a high-polish blue finish and "COMMEMORATIVE FOR THE YEAR 2000" on the slide. The frame remained black polymer, but the backstrap insert was walnut.

- *P99QA* (2000 to date) Intended for special-response units, this is a "Quick Action" variant relying on a partially "pre-cocked" striker to reduce the contrast between single- and double-action operation. The trigger has a consistent pull of about 6-7 lb and an equally consistent travel of about 0.3 inches. The de-cocking lever has been reduced to a button let into the top left surface of the slide ahead of the rear sight, preventing accidental release.
- *P99 QPQ* (2000 to date) This is a standard P99 with a silver Tenifer QPQ protective finish on the slide and a blacked frame, giving a distinctive bi-color appearance. The DAO version is sometimes listed as the "990 QPQ".

P22 (1998 to date) Externally similar to the P99, this is a 22-caliber blowback design with a ring-tipped hammer exposed at the rear of the slide and duplicated retraction grips behind the muzzle. Extensive use of synthetic components, including a lightweight polymer frame, keeps weight to merely 15.2 oz without the magazine. The standard guns are 6.3 inches long and have 3.4-inch barrels. Three exchangeable backstraps alter the shape of the grip to suit individual preferences, the controls are ambidextrous and a multiplicity of firing-pin, magazine and anti-drop safety systems meets the most demanding criteria.

- *P22 Target* A long version of the P22, this has a counterweight that resembles (but does not function as) a compensator. It is about 7.8 inches long, has a 5-inch barrel and weighs 18.5 oz. Conversion units can be obtained to adapt a standard P22 to P22T standards.

WAMO MFG CO.

San Gabriel, California, USA.

Powermaster (1956-66) This 22-caliber single-shot bolt-action pistol had a raked grip and long exposed barrel. It resembled the High Standard guns of the same period but had fixed instead of adjustable sights and was undoubtedly of poorer quality. The bolt operated within a fixed receiver and was controlled by a guide rod that ran through a hole in the rear of the receiver, protruding just over an inch when the bolt was opened. The Powermaster was also notable for the bolt handle, placed on the left side of the receiver where it was ideally suited to right-handed shooters.

WARNANT

L. & J. Warnant Frères, Hognée, Belgium.

The Warnant brothers established themselves as jobbing gunmakers in the mid-19th century, producing a variety of sporting guns. Jean Warnant then began working on revolver locks and eventually patented a double-action lock that was widely adopted by others. Warnant made hinged-frame revolvers in 1870-90, largely based on contemporary Smith & Wesson practice, with round barrels, folding triggers and automatic ejection by means of a pierced plate behind the cylinder. A large-caliber *Modèle Militaire*, with vertical arms on the standing breech to lock the topstrap to the frame and a similar ejector, was generally the most robust of a series that included commercial equivalents in 320, 380 and 450 centerfire chamberings.

In the early 1900s, the Warnant brothers took to the automatic pistol with a confusion of patents and designs. Their first attempt to break away from the revolver had come with the "Warnant-Créon" repeater, a mechanical pistol with a hinged Martini-type breechblock and a tubular magazine beneath the barrel, but this never got far beyond the prototype stage. Their next patent protected the hinged-barrel automatic pistol associated with Pieper (q.v.), but the Warnants had a secondary patent in which the fixed-barrel unit was pinned to the frame.

The brothers licensed one design to Pieper and decided to exploit the solid-frame version themselves. Once again, however, they were foiled by fate; before the 1912-type pistol — a sound design — could become established, World War I began and Hognée was overrun by the invading German army. The Warnant enterprise became an early casualty of the war.

~ AUTOMATIC PISTOLS ~

Durabel (c. 1912) This was the 6.35mm Auto (25 ACP) 1908-type Warnant pistol sold under another name. The slide merely displayed "Durabel Automatic Pistol Cal. 6,35", but the Warnant monogram was embossed in the center of the grips.

1908 type (1908-14) The barrel of this 6.35mm-caliber pistol was forged integrally with the frame, and the sheet-metal receiver contained a separate bolt that consisted of a tubular section passing over the barrel and a rectangular breech-block section that lay behind the barrel. The recoil spring was inside the tubular section of the bolt, and the mechanism could be operated by pulling back on two serrated wings exposed at the rear of the receiver. A five-shot magazine went into the butt. Less than 2000 guns of this type had been made when an improved version appeared. The receiver was made of milled steel and could be removed complete with bolt and recoil spring by drawing it back, lifting the rear end and sliding the whole assembly forward over the short barrel.

1912 type (1912-14) This was a 7.65mm (32 ACP) pistol of an entirely different design, similar to the familiar M1903 FN-Browning but with a separate breechblock. The slide had a wide slot in the rear end into which the block was inserted and held in place by a heavy cross bolt. This construction not only avoided patent infringement but also simplified stripping; by removing the retaining bolt, the breechblock could be removed from the rear and the slide taken forward over the fixed barrel.

WARNER ARMS COMPANY

Brooklyn, New York, and Norwich, Connecticut, USA.

The Warner Arms Co. of Brooklyn was constituted in about 1912, having bought the tools and remaining stock of the M1908 blow-forward pistol from A.W. Schwarzlose of Berlin (q.v.). This pistol was then marketed in the USA as the "Warner", being marked "Warner Arms Corporation" with or without the usual Schwarzlose markings. This venture, hardly surprisingly, failed, and in 1913 production stopped. Warner then purchased the rights to an automatic pistol credited to Andrew Fyrberg (q.v.). Guns of this type were sold as the "Infallible" with the firm moving to Norwich to begin manufacture. Warner also made a cheap hinged-frame double-action 32-caliber revolver in this period, indistinguishable from the contemporary products of the Meriden or Iver Johnson companies. In 1917, it merged with another company to become the Davis-Warner Arms Company, moving to Assonet before returning to Norwich in 1919. The business was subsequently acquired by H. & D. Folsom and merged with the Crescent Arms Company in 1930.

Infallible (1915-19) Protected by patents granted to Andrew Fyrberg in July 1914 and March 1915, this striker-fired 32 ACP blowback had a bolt that reciprocated in a fixed receiver, a barrel that tipped upward to facilitate cleaning and a fragile-looking radial safety lever on the left side of the frame above the trigger. Although a sound-enough design, it was delicate and not very reliable. It was also far from handsome and sat awkwardly in the hand. It failed to achieve popularity, and it is doubtful if more than about 1500 were made — probably in a single run in 1915—leaving guns to be sold "from stock" for several years.

JAMES WARNER

Springfield, Massachusetts, USA.

Born in 1811 and the patentee of a caplock revolver in 1851, Warner became involved in the Springfield Arms Company. When this business failed in 1860, he continued to make guns under his own name. They included a 30-caliber rimfire derivative that infringed the Rollin White patent controlled by Smith & Wesson, yet Warner continued small-scale production until his death in 1870.

WEATHERBY, INC.

South Gate and Atascadero, California, USA.

Roy Weatherby began operations in 1945, seeking to market high-velocity sporting rifles that offered a better performance that those that were available commercially. The first rifles incorporated FN-Mauser actions, but the introduction in 1959 of the "Mark V", made first in Germany and now Japan, was the key to success. This gun established not only the Weatherby name but also the powerful Weatherby Magnum cartridges.

Mark V CFP ("Center Fire Pistol", 1998 to date) This was an adaptation of the standard right-hand bolt action, offered only in 22-250, 243 Winchester, 7mm-08 and 308 Winchester. The barrel is a lightweight 15-inch tapering pattern, fluted to maximize rigidity, and the magazine holds three rounds. The pistol-grip half stock is a wood laminate.

- *Mark V Accumark CFP* (2000 to date) This is a minor variant of the standard CFP, offered in the same four chamberings, with a matte-black stock made of Kevlar reinforced with fiberglass.

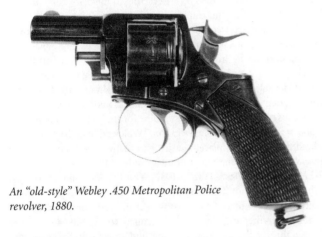

An "old-style" Webley .450 Metropolitan Police revolver, 1880.

WEBLEY (& SCOTT)

P. Webley & Son (1860-1879); Webley & Scott Revolver & Arms Co. Ltd. (1879-1906); Webley & Scott Ltd. (1906 to date).
Birmingham, Warwickshire, England.

This famous firm can trace its roots to James Webley, born in 1808 and the son of a button-maker, who became a "percussioner" and set up in business in the early 1830s. His brother Philip, born in 1812, was apprenticed to a gun-lock filer when he was 14 years old. After serving his apprenticeship for 7 years, Philip became a journeyman gun-lock filer and joined his brother in business in 1834.

In 1838, Philip married Caroline Davis, daughter of a deceased "bullet mold and gun implement manufacturer" whose business was being continued by his widow. Philip Webley eventually succeeded to the Davis business when his mother-in-law died. His first son, Thomas William ("T.W."), was born in 1838, and in 1859, the firm became "P. Webley & Son". Philip had four children, but only Henry, born in 1846, joined his brother and father. The business was then often known as "P. Webley & Sons".

James and Philip Webley had specialized in caplock revolvers, each developing a respectable business. However, James died suddenly in 1856 and his business was absorbed by his brother. Samuel Colt decided that there was insufficient market in Europe in this period to warrant a separate factory and closed his London operations, leaving the revolver market wide open. Philip Webley promptly expanded his business to meet the demand, obtaining several government contracts. For more than 40 years, beginning in 1887, Webley & Sons were the sole suppliers of revolvers to the British armed forces.

Philip Webley died in 1888, aged 76; his wife died 3 years later, leaving the company in charge of Thomas William and Henry. Finally, in 1897, the Webley business was amalgamated with those of W.C. Scott & Sons (shotgun makers) and Richard Ellis & Sons (rifle & shotgun maker) to form the Webley & Scott Revolver & Arms Co. Ltd. Henry Webley retired, though he subsequently returned to become a director, while Thomas William became Managing Director until his death in 1904.

A further reorganization took place in 1906, when the business became Webley & Scott Ltd. This continued to make revolvers until the 1970s, when repressive legislation and the widespread adoption of automatic pistols by military forces killed the revolver trade in Britain. Webley & Scott continued making shotguns, air rifles and pistols for some years but eventually gave up the struggle in 1980, when the shotgun-making operations separated to become "W. & C. Scott Ltd". Finally, in 1982, the designs, patent rights and tooling for the manufacture of Webley revolvers were sold to a company in Karachi, Pakistan, though the Webley name was retained by the remnants of a once-grand company that thereafter concentrated on airguns.

Webley was never afraid to try new ideas and always employed the best designers. However, after the merits of an idea had been demonstrated, the management of the company tended to do little other than introduce modifications (if experience suggested them) while maintaining the character of the basic pattern. This practice has had two major effects. First, it hindered survival when depression hit the British gun trade in the 1960s; and, secondly, it created innumerable minor variations in detail that still frustrates the enthusiast.

Moreover, though most manufacturers will drop obsolete models as soon as production of new designs is running smoothly, Webley continued making individual designs as long as anyone showed an interest in them. This not only hinders dating the introduction of individual guns but also results in a bewildering array of variations. Consequently, it is proposed to deal with the most significant changes within each group in turn, owing to the problems of maintaining developmental threads within strict chronological order. Many minor variants — presentation models, versions made for country gunsmiths, or pistols with special markings for police forces — have been omitted, but sources of additional information are listed in the Bibliography.

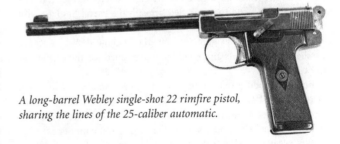

A long-barrel Webley single-shot 22 rimfire pistol, sharing the lines of the 25-caliber automatic.

∼ SINGLE-SHOT PISTOL ∼

Target Pistol (1911) Two 22-caliber target versions of the 32-caliber 1906-type automatic pistol were developed as potential training pistols. Although they resembled the automatic, they had no recoil spring and the slide had to be unlocked and cycled by hand for every shot. Two versions were offered, one with a 4.5-inch barrel and another with a 9-inch barrel. The shorter model was adopted by the Metropolitan Police as a trainer. An improved version — the "improvements" concerning grips and finish — was popular with target shooters and continued to be marketed until the 1950s.

∼ MULTI-SHOT PISTOL ∼

Under-and-Over Pistol (1890) This is an oddity in the Webley series, though the company had made a similar weapon in the 1870s in a variety of calibers. There seems to have been no record of success, and so a revival of the basic design after 20 years is interesting. The pistol was in 450 caliber with a pair of 3-inch barrels that rotated about a central pin. They were turned by hand and locked by a small spring-loaded lug. However, guns of this type are very rare and are unlikely to have seen much commercial success.

The original Webley 442-caliber RIC Model revolver.

A No. 2 Webley RIC revolver, chambering the 442 centerfire round.

∼ REVOLVERS ∼

RIC No. 1 Model (1867-1914) Destined to remain in production for over 50 years, this compact revolver was adopted by the newly-formed Royal Irish Constabulary ("RIC") in 1868 and was the subject of many presentations, among the recipients being Lt-Col George A. Custer of the 7th US Cavalry Regiment (1869). There were many variants in different calibers and barrel lengths, but all were of the solid-frame pattern and of great durability and reliability. The design was widely copied in Europe, where short-barreled solid-frame revolvers in large calibers were commonly known as "Constabulary" revolvers, irrespective of what their makers called them.

The original RIC model was a solid-frame double-action revolver with a 4.5-inch barrel screwed into the malleable cast-iron frame. The barrel had an odd shape, rounded on the bottom but merging into a thin flat surface at the top to give the suggestion of a ribbed barrel even though the "rib" could not be discerned. Viewed from the front, the shape of the barrel might even be called "tear-drop". The six-chamber cylinder was plain, with locking notches close to the forward end. The gun was loaded through a gate on the right side, and ejection was undertaken with a rod that swiveled beneath the barrel to align with the loading gate. Empty cases could then be punched out singly. The caliber was 442, an odd figure that apparently allowed Webley to use the bullet-casting molds and machinery developed for the earlier 54-gauge caplocks.

This basic model remained in production for several years, in which time the range of calibers was extended to cover 320, 380 and 450 centerfire cartridges. There were also different lengths of barrel, the 2.5-inch option proving popular with police forces, and commercial sales of the revolver gave rise to decoration and grips of selected wood or ivory.

The version with the plain cylinder (with stop-notches towards the front) is generally known as the *First Model No. 1*. The *Second Model No. 1* of c. 1880 was similar but had a fluted cylinder with the cylinder stops at the rear edge, a 4-inch barrel and an ejector rod mounted on the frame.

RIC No. 2 Model (1881-1914) This appeared early in the 1880s, though the No. 1 model remained in production. The No. 2 has a plain cylinder (suggesting appearance before the No .1 Second Model), with the cylinder ratchet stop catches at the rear end of the cylinder where they were engaged directly by the trigger. The barrel was cylindrical and the front sight was mounted on a slight ramp that tapered almost as far as the frame. The butt of guns in 442 and 450 caliber was solid walnut, retained by two screws, while the smaller 320 and 380 versions had a frame that required two separate butt-grips fitted conventionally. The five-chamber cylinder on these smaller-caliber guns was also originally

plain, though subsequently superseded by a fluted pattern. Though superseded by later designs, the No. 2 remained in production until World War I.

RIC No. 3 Model (c. 1883-95) Reverting to the tear-drop barrel of the No. 1 RIC pattern, this can be identified by the absence of the ejector rod. This was screwed into a hole in the solid butt, to be removed when necessary. The cylinder was plain; the earliest examples had rectangular stops at the front, but these had soon been removed to the rear. However, the design of the lockwork ensured that these stops only prevented rotation in one direction, and the weight of cartridges in the cylinder often caused the cylinder to turn backwards in a holster or if jolted. This placed a fired case next in line for the hammer, a potentially fatal weakness in the police weapon. Webley added a friction brake to hold the cylinder in place, but this eventually caused a bright band of wear to appear in the center of the cylinder.

RIC No. 1 New Model (1883-1932) This five-shot gun was the last of the Royal Irish Constablulary patterns to be made in large numbers, differing from the preceding versions in chambering options: 320, 380 or 450 centerfire and eventually extended to include 455 caliber (though this version had a larger frame and longer cylinder, as did the Metropolitan Police 450 model). Cylinders were fluted, with ratchet stops at the rear end. The New Model remained in production for many years and was still carried in the Webley catalog when World War II began, probably the last large-caliber solid-frame non-ejecting revolver in production anywhere in the world.

No. 2 Bull Dog (1878-1914) This was derived from the RIC model, becoming one of Webley's most successful designs. It remained in production in various forms until World War I began. It was intended purely as a commercial project, most being exported throughout the Empire, but at least one mounted infantry regiment carried guns of this type during the South African War of 1899-1902. The basic form was a short-barreled large-caliber solid-frame revolver with a distinctive bird's-head butt and a cylinder that, depending on the size of the cartridges, had five or six chambers. The Bull Dog was widely copied in several countries, particularly in Belgium, and offered in a variety of calibers.

A solid-frame Webley 450 No. 2 Bull Dog.

- *First Model* (1878) This, like the RIC No. 1, was given a plain cylinder and a tear-drop barrel that was also "swamped"— greater in diameter at the muzzle than the breech — and the cylinder held only five rounds. It was chambered for the 442 cartridge, the barrel length was 2.5 inches and the double-action lock was the normal Webley pattern. The range of calibers had been extended to 380 and 450 by 1881. These Webley revolvers were always marked "BULL DOG" or "BRITISH BULL DOG"—never "Bull-Dog", "Bulldog" or "Buldog", all of which will be found on Belgian copies. Nor were all small Webley revolvers "Bull Dogs", as only 442- and 450-caliber examples were so marked. Guns in 320 and 380 calibers were merely "Webley No. 2, R.I.C Pattern".

- *Second Model* (1883) This had a fluted cylinder, saving a little weight, and a longer butt that gave a better hold — a necessary feature in a caliber as large as 450.

No. 1 Pug (c. 1873-1900) This first appeared in 41 rimfire, probably in the early 1870s, and could be considered as the forerunner of the essentially similar Bull Dog series. It was also the first Webley revolver to feature the bird's-head butt, and the muzzle of the 2.4-inch barrel was rounded to reduce the chances of snagging the lining of a pocket. Later versions of the Pug were produced in 44 and 450 centerfire. The most obvious identification feature of a Webley Pug is the curved spring lever, providing a half-cock position, that lies on the left side of the frame alongside the hammer.

The 450 centerfire Tower Bull Dog, made by Webley in the 1870s.

Tower Bull Dog (450-caliber, 1885-90) This variant appears to have been made only in small numbers. It is little different from the general run of Bull Dogs, though the frame is more angular and has a prawl above the grip to give a better hold. The hammer spur is more flared upward than on other Bull Dogs. It carries the marking "London Tower" with a representation of the Tower of London, Britain's most famous fortress, stamped on the frame in front of the cylinder. It seems likely that it was produced to the order of a specific Birmingham gunsmith, Thomas Turner, though the words "London Tower" were a Webley registered trademark.

Ulster Bull Dog (450-caliber, c. 1885-90) The date of this model remains uncertain, though it is believed to have been made to a special order placed by the gunsmith Braddell of Belfast. It was generally as the Webley No. 2 model, a short-barreled six-shot "constabulary" type, but the bird's-head butt was longer than normal and made by brazing the butt of a British Bull Dog to the frame of a Webley No. 2. Only a limited number were made and they are among the rarer Webleys.

Silver & Fletcher's Patent (c. 1885-1900) Hugh Silver and Walter Fletcher patented a combined safety and ejection device for revolvers in Britain in December 1884. It was subsequently fitted to a few Webley RIC-type guns, all apparently in 450 caliber. Like most devices of its type, the mechanism relied too greatly on the falling hammer to drive a lever and flick a spent cartridge case out of the loading gate. It inevitably interfered with the free fall of the hammer and was a source of misfires if the cartridge caps were harder than normal. The ejector was an extra expense and was not a commercial success. Guns that were

An 1883-type Webley RIC revolver with Silver & Fletcher's self-extracting hammer.

fitted with it were usually marked "Silver & Fletcher's Patent" and "The Expert". Webley's name did not appear and the revolvers were numbered in a series of their own; they may also bear the marks of S.W. Silver & Co. of Cornhill, London, which traded until 1904. Silver's marks may be found on other revolvers, often imported from Belgium, but few will display the patented ejector.

A 455-caliber Webley No. 4 revolver.

A 455-caliber Webley No. 5 revolver, with the markings of the Orange Free State on the grip.

Chambered for the 360 centerfire round, this is a commercial version of the Webley No. 5 revolver.

No. 5 Army Express (1878-1914) It has been suggested that the introduction of this gun was due to a desire to compete with the Colt Double Action Army model; if so, Webley won hands down, because the DA Army was not one of Colt's better designs, while the Army Express attained considerable popularity.

The Army Express models were heavy and powerful weapons designed for service use. The first model was a six-shot 455 model that was an advance on anything Webley had hitherto produced. This is generally known as the "Army Express Revolver" and was not in production for long. It was a solid-frame weapon using the frame of the RIC but with a 6-inch barrel and a spring-loaded ejector rod on the right side, aligned with the loading gate. The gate locked the hammer at half-cock when opened, and when the hammer was cocked, it locked the gate shut. The butt was one piece of walnut and had a lanyard ring.

A special 476-caliber single-action version of the "Express" was produced to the order of the Cape Mounted Rifles in South Africa. This appears to have been the only single-action centerfire revolver ever made by Webley. It is recognizable by the octagonal 5.5-inch barrel, small trigger-guard and a more sharply curved butt that had hitherto been common on Webley designs.

While the first Army Express was still being sold, Webley's produced a new version and called it "Webley's New Model Army Express". It was almost the same as the earlier version but had a bird's-head butt, and the grips were in two separate pieces. The interlocked safety loading gate was abandoned, and a simple gate was fitted, with a small knob for opening and closing it. There were also small changes in the design of the cylinder arbor and retaining catch, largely to prevent fouling from creating friction. It was normally chambered for the regulation 455 Mark 2 cartridge or for the 476 Enfield, though specimens chambered for the 45 Long Colt and 44-40 WCF have been seen. Numbers were issued to units of the South African Republic in the 1880s, and some were fitted with Silver & Fletcher safety hammers and extractors.

The final model in the Army Express series appeared in 1886 and was a pocket model for the home-defense market, using a 3- or 4-inch barrel and chambered for the 360 Rook Rifle cartridge. It could also chamber and fire the 38 Smith & Wesson or 380 Webley cartridges. The principal mechanical difference was the arrangement of the ejector rod inside the cylinder arbor, from which it could be withdrawn and swung to align with the loading gate when needed. The same design (patented by John Adams) was widely used on the various RIC models. Production of the Army Express series ended in 1914.

A 476 Webley-Pryse.

No 4, or Webley-Pryse Webley began experimenting with self-extracting revolver designs in about 1870, building various experimental models on RIC frames. A side-opening design was considered and abandoned, and eventually a hinged-frame design attributed to Edward Wood was approved (though no relevant patent has ever been traced). This used a simple latch to lock over the end of the topstrap and had a star-shaped ejector in the center of the cylinder that was cammed out as the barrel moved down. Webley adopted this as a first approximation and then set about refining it.

In 1877, Webley began production of a new self-extracting hinged-frame revolver. Basically an improved Wood design with the 1876 patents of Charles Pryse incorporated, the two principal features of this gun were the rebounding hammer and the cylinder lock. The hammer was arranged so that the mainspring lifted the hammer up to half-cock when the trigger was released after firing. The hammer was then held in that position and could not be accidentally driven forward; very few

revolvers of any make, since that time, have failed to use the rebounding hammer, though not, usually, rebounding as far as half-cock.

The cylinder lock was a stud or arm actuated by the trigger, which locked into a special ring of slots in the cylinder so as to hold the cylinder firmly with a chamber lined up with the barrel and free it only when the trigger was pulled. As the trigger was pulled, the lock withdrew and the cylinder was revolved to the next chamber, and as the fresh chamber lined up, a second spring-loaded stud engaged in the slot and locked the cylinder once more.

Another Pryse feature was the frame-locking latch, a double bolt through the top of the standing breech and into the topstrap controlled by two arms that lay down the side of the standing breech. Both arms had to be pressed in, withdrawing both bolts, before the gun could be opened to extract and reload.

The Pryse patents were licensed to other makers as well as Webley, but the Webley-Pryse revolvers were probably the widest range available. They appeared in all the major calibers, from 320 to 577, and all were of the same basic design with barrels of 3 to 5.7 inches. After 1885, these revolvers incorporated a safety bolt beneath the barrel release to prevent the hammer from being cocked if the barrel was not properly closed and locked. The pistols are generally marked "Webley No. 4" on the left of the topstrap, together with the caliber, and they appear to have continued in production until 1900.

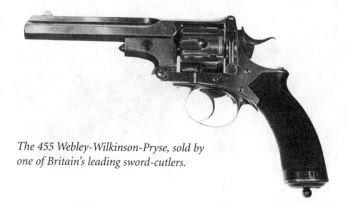

The 455 Webley-Wilkinson-Pryse, sold by one of Britain's leading sword-cutlers.

Webley-Wilkinson-Pryse At the time the Pryse models were being marketed, Webley also made a special series of Pryse revolvers for Henry Wilkinson & Son ("Wilkinson Sword Company" after 1885), the London sword-cutlers. Wilkinson supplied swords to officers, and he reasoned that when an officer bought a sword, it would be sensible to sell him a revolver also. (British officers of the period were not issued with swords or revolvers; they had to purchase their own, and the revolver make was immaterial provided that it accepted the service cartridge.)

Wilkinson commenced his plan in 1878 by having a pistol made in Belgium in 450 caliber. The two principal differences between this and the Webley guns were the cylinder stops, which are to the rear of the cylinder, and a slightly different cylinder release. The barrel was 6.5 inches long and had five rifling grooves. This model was introduced in 1878. A later model in 1880 was in 455/476 caliber and had a 5.4 inch barrel.

It would seem, though, that these Belgian-made revolvers did not meet Wilkinson's desire for quality, and so he approached Webley. All subsequent Wilkinson patterns were made by Webley, finished to a very high standard, and had the top barrel rib engraved "WILKINSON & SON PALL MALL LONDON". Wilkinson also added a six-pointed star, the "HW" trademark and a proprietary serial number either under the trigger guard or on the bottom of the butt. The sights were of German silver, a blade at the front and, at the rear, a silver triangle set into the steel notch.

The first Webley-Wilkinson appeared in 1884 and was quite clearly based upon the contemporary No. 4 Pryse revolver. However, the small-frame hinge bolt is distinctive.

In 1888, however, a completely new model appeared, which owed little to the No. 4 design and was unique to the Wilkinson series. The hexagonal barrel had the front sight set into a ramp, the cylinder was deeply fluted, the extraction system was changed, identifying this model by its larger hinge bolt, and a large coin-slotted screw in the frame retained the cylinder. The frame was basically that of the No. 4 revolver but much modified, with a new mainspring and a round-ended butt that curved more sharply than previous patterns. Standard finish was a lustrous blue with the trigger, hammer and barrel-locking levers left bright, but nickel finish was available and popular with officers serving in tropical countries owing to its superior resistance to corrosion.

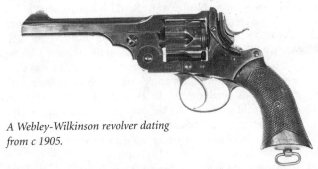

A Webley-Wilkinson revolver dating from c 1905.

Webley-Wilkinson In the 1892 Webley-Wilkinson model, Pryse influence declined and the revolver was virtually all the work of Webley, particularly the stirrup barrel latch and cylinder assembly. Another Wilkinson model was introduced in 1905, taking the standard six-shot 455 Mark IV service revolver as the pattern and only differing in respect to the usual refinements demanded by the Wilkinson range. In this particular model, a small fillet was screwed behind the trigger guard to prevent the middle finger of the firing hand from being caught by the recoil, but there are no significant changes to the Webley original version. Indeed, the name of Webley is stamped on the right side of the frame along with the Webley number.

The 1911 Wilkinson was little different from the 1905 type, and by this time, there was little pretense that they were anything other than selected production Webley revolvers even though they still carried the additional Wilkinson serial number. The only significant change lay in the rifling, which now became six-groove instead of seven.

Target versions of the Wilkinson revolvers were also made in small numbers with longer barrels, more carefully finished trigger pulls, heavily checkered butts, triggers and backstraps. The usual target barrel was 7.5 inches long.

Webley Improved Government Model ("Webley-Kaufman") Michael Kaufman was a talented designer who worked for Webley from 1878 to 1881 and developed some useful mechanical arrangements for revolvers, among them a new type of hinged frame latch and a new lock mechanism. The frame lock was a push-button on the standing breech that operated a three-part bolt that passed through the breech and the topstrap. When locked, the joints of the bolt fell within the body of the frame and topstrap and the gun was locked; when pushed, the three bolt sections lined up with the two parts of the breech and the central topstrap so that the gun could be opened. The lock mechanism contained only five parts and produced a light-but-crisp action. The revolvers that incorporated these and other refinements are generally known as Webley-Kaufman models, though the correct factory designation was the "Webley Improved Government Model". Indeed, the only Kaufman feature that survived throughout the series was the improved lock mechanism.

The first models were six-shot double-action revolvers with 5.25-inch barrels in 450 centerfire. These were soon followed by the second model, which saw some minor improvements, one of them being the abandonment of the push-button operation of the barrel lock for a design that, still using the three-part bolt, adopted the familiar hinged arm that could be pressed in by the thumb and was thus easier to use. The cylinder lock was modified, and some pistols were given a safety lock that prevented opening the cylinder while the hammer was cocked. This model was usually in 455 caliber, though some were made in 476. All Kaufman weapons were marked "MK" inside a triangle, with a number beneath; this relates to the Kaufman features and provided a separate record that facilitated royalty payments. The Webley serial number is stamped on the left side of the buttstrap.

W-G Model 1882 ("Webley-Green") This important line of revolvers was always known as the "W.G.", and they ran in a series from 1882 to 1896 with manufacture continuing beyond that date. The "Green" part of the name comes from Edwinson C. Green, who was the original inventor of the "stirrup" method of barrel locking (see under "Green" in the body of the book for further details of his work). Nevertheless, some degree of controversy still surrounds this question, largely due to attempts made by Webley enthusiasts to promote the alternative term "Webley Government".

W-G revolvers were a combination of all the best earlier Webley ideas, which formed a harmonious whole. The lockwork was provided by Kaufman, and the cylinder-release system came from Webley-Pryse with input from Wilkinson and the government-sponsored Enfield. The bird's-head butt was retained, and, instead of the usual round ends, the cylinder flutes took an angular form known in the trade as "church steeple". This first model was in 455/476 chambering and had a 6-inch barrel.

- *W-G Model 1885* The cylinder release was changed from the Pryse pattern to a larger slotted screw that could be turned by a coin. The extractor was changed in minor ways so that it became an original Webley design rather than an amalgam of other designs. The caliber and barrel were unchanged.

The 455 Webley "W-G" revolver, 1889.

- *W-G Model 1889* The significant change here was to abandon the bird's-head butt and adopt one with a widely flared bottom, with the usual flattened lanyard ring. This greatly improved the grip and shooters began to find the W-G a good target revolver, so much so that special 7.5-inch barrel models were made with improved sights. All the 1889 W-G models were stamped "W.G. Model 1889", whereas the previous models had been marked "Webley Patents". The year 1889 marked the first year that Webley revolvers indicated the date of production.
- *W-G Model 1892* The caliber was reduced to 455 and the barrel standardized at 7.5 inches; the flared butt was retained. Changes were made to the lockwork, the ejector and the cylinder release, the principles of which have been retained in Webley revolvers ever since. The cylinder release, patented in 1891, allowed for manual release of the cylinder once the action was open but automatically

locked it in place when the action was closed. The cam and lever for operating this system were screwed to the left side of the barrel lug and, with slight variations, have been a Webley recognition feature ever since.

- *W-G Army Model 1892* This rarely-seen model can be regarded as the first of the W.G. Army series. In many ways, it was the 1882 model brought up to date; it used the same 6-inch barrel (in 450, 455 or 476) and the bird's-head butt, together with fixed sights, but it incorporated the improved cylinder release and action of the standard Model 1892.

A Webley 476-caliber W-G Army Model, 1892.

A 455 Webley W-G Target Model revolver with a 7.5-inch barrel.

- *W-G Target Model 1893* This brought in only one change from the previous year's design: the adoption of a flat-faced hammer and a floating firing pin set in the standing breech. The reason for this change is not known, and it did not survive for long. Another minor change was the abandonment of the practice of stamping the year of issue on revolvers, an 1889 innovation that had only lasted four years. It has been suggested that its abandonment was due to objections from retailers that the age of their stock was thereby revealed to customers. A final feature was that this was the last Webley revolver with the angular fluting; subsequent models were standardized with round-end flutes on the cylinder.
- *W-G Target Model 1896* The target models (previously called the standard "W.G." models) were more or less fixed on the 1892/3 design, with very minor changes. The visible difference was the adoption of the rounded flutes on the cylinder and the return to a conventional hammer carrying its own firing pin.

Pocket Hammerless Model 1898 In 1898, Webley produced a small hinged-frame pocket revolver with a concealed hammer. A six-shot 320, it had a 3-inch barrel and sharply curved butt. Above the

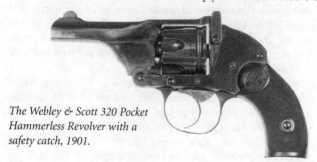

The Webley & Scott 320 Pocket Hammerless Revolver with a safety catch, 1901.

hammer shroud was a sliding safety catch, and the frame was locked by a simplified barrel latch that carried the rear-sight notch.

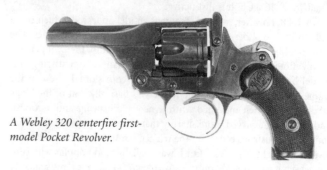

A Webley 320 centerfire first-model Pocket Revolver.

Pocket Hammer Model 1901 This reverted to an exposed hammer and had an even simpler barrel latch, which had no thumb lever but was serrated on top so that it could be drawn back with the thumb. Both this and the 1898 hammerless remained in production until 1934.

442 Mark I The company had always realized that the best basis for the business would be government contracts, and for this reason, it spent a great deal of effort in designing carefully-made weapons with completely interchangeable parts. In 1880, the British government adopted the Enfield revolver (q.v.), but this was not satisfactory and the search for a better one continued. By 1886, the choice was down to either the Smith & Wesson hinged-frame design or a new Webley, and after trials, the Webley was approved in July 1887.

The first gun was a six-shot hinged-frame design in 442 caliber, with a 4-inch barrel and bird's-head butt, not far removed from the contemporary commercial Bull Dog models. The lock mechanism was refined to only five components, and the mainspring operated the entire lock action, dispensing with at least five minor parts and thus improving reliability. The butt grips were a departure from tradition in being made from black Vulcanite instead of wood. Another innovation was the adoption of a separate recoil shield in the standing breech. This, the face of the breech and the half-round wings at each side, was made replaceable due to erosion of the firing-pin hole, and was dovetailed into place and secured by a screw. This was adopted after production of the Mark I pistol had got under way, and the change was considered sufficiently important to change the designation to Mark I*.

The British Army Webley Mk II revolver.

- *442 Mark II* By 1894, there had been a sufficient number of small modifications to the Mark I design to justify drawing up a fresh pattern and calling it Mark II. The separate recoil shield of the Mark I* was incorporated along with a new hammer with larger spur, a modified barrel latch and somewhat more graceful butt.

It is worth noting that production of the various marks of Webley revolver frequently overlapped, and it is difficult to say with certainty when production started and stopped. It is probable that existing contracts, say for the Mark I, were allowed to be completed even though the Mark II had been approved and a manufacturing contract issued. In the case of the Mark II, there are a number of specimens known that were made in 1900, four years after the Mark III had been introduced.

The Webley Mk III service revolver.

- *442 Mark III* Approved in October 1897, this was generally the same as the Mark II but with a new barrel unit and cylinder assembly, adapted from the W-G 1892 model. This gave a more satisfactory cylinder release and less friction when the cylinder rotated. There were also small changes to the recoil shield and extractor lever, though they remained interchangeable with those of earlier Marks. Production of the Mark III continued for some time after the Mark IV was introduced and certainly throughout the South African War.

455 Mark IV (1899) The Mark IV was the first service model to be produced solely in 455 caliber; the earlier marks were available in 442, 455 and 476 as required, but by 1899, the 455 round had been standardized and the earlier ammunition was obsolete. It is often called the "Boer War Model" because its introduction coincided with the start of that war and many volunteer units were armed with it. Apart from the standardization of caliber, there were few changes from the Mark III. The specification for the frame and barrel unit was changed to a higher grade of steel, and some components were now case-hardened to resist wear. The hammer spur was widened, as were the cylinder locking slots. Altogether, the changes were concerned with improving reliability without making any changes to the operating of the weapon.

- *455 Mark V* (1913) This was virtually the same as the Mark IV but with a slightly larger cylinder and with corresponding adjustments to the frame. The increased size was in order to give additional strength so as to have a good safety factor to cater for smokeless powder cartridges. The approved pattern was fitted with a 4-inch barrel, but in 1915, a "Land Service Only" pattern with 6-inch barrel was approved; and some were made with 7.5-inch barrels.

A 1918-vintage Webley & Scott Mk VI 455-caliber revolver opened, showing the operation of the stirrup latch and the star-plate extractor.

- *455 Mark VI* (1915) This might be considered the "perfected" or "definitive" Webley, since it was the last military model and remained in use until World War II, though officially replaced by a 38-caliber weapon some years previously. The change from the Mark V was not great; the barrel length was 6 inches, and the butt shape changed from the bird's head to a squared-off pattern.

The Mark VI was host to one or two eccentric inventions. The Pritchard-Greener Bayonet, for example, was a 7-inch bayonet that fit onto the Mark VI by locking on the barrel lug, holster guides and foresight block. It could be used without interfering with the operation of the revolver and may have been of some use in trench fighting. Another addition was a shoulder stock, but few of these appear to have been used.

The Mark VI continued in service after the war ended, and in 1921, its manufacture was transferred to the Royal Small Arms Factory at Enfield Lock, where production continued at a low rate. These Enfield products are identical with the Webley models except for being suitably marked by a crown stamp and the word "Enfield". Production ended in 1932 with the introduction of the Enfield 38 revolver.

22 RF Mark VI (1918) In order to provide for cheaper practice and to encourage shooting on indoor ranges, a 22-caliber version of the Mark VI was produced for training purposes. The cylinder and barrel were changed, but the rest was standard Mark VI, thus giving a realistic feel. The cylinder was much shorter than that of the 455 version, and the barrel was thus brought back in the frame to meet it, leaving a large gap in front of the cylinder. A round 22-caliber barrel was fitted and the foresight was raised to bring it into line with the rear sight.

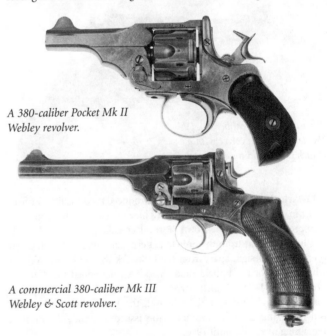

A 380-caliber Pocket Mk II Webley revolver.

A commercial 380-caliber Mk III Webley & Scott revolver.

Marks II and III (commercial models, 1896-97) Throughout the manufacture of the government revolver, there was a parallel production for police and commercial markets, though these were in 38 (and sometimes 32) caliber. They followed the same pattern as the army weapons.

The Marks II and III were short 38-caliber revolvers with 4-inch barrels and bird's-head butts, though with a prawl behind the hammer to protect the thumb. Some were produced with conventional hammers, others with flat-faced hammers and floating firing pins. The Mark III abandoned the curved butt and adopted a short square-ended butt, which probably gave a more secure grip. Some police models were fitted with a safety catch on the left side of the frame.

W.S. Army and Bisley Target Models In 1904, Webley & Scott introduced a target revolver that was marked on the topstrap either "W.S.Army Model" or "W.S.Target Model". Both were the same weapon and are usually known under the collective title of "Bisley Target Revolvers". They were in 455 caliber and foreshadowed the future Mark VI in appearance, though they were built from Mark IV components. Barrels were 4, 6 or 7.5 inches long, and the usual target sights were fitted.

22 Mark IV Target Model (1929-55) A successful 22 rimfire target version was produced that had the same sized cylinder and barrel as the 38-caliber weapon. This allowed realistic practice on cheaper ammunition and was popular with police forces.

32 Mark IV (1929-55) The standard Mark IV was also produced in 32 caliber, the dimensions being otherwise unaltered.

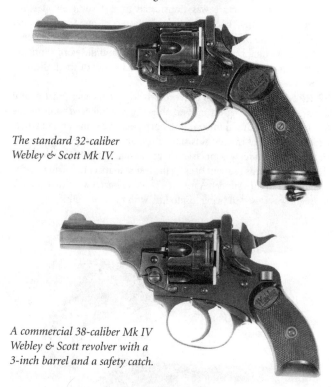

The standard 32-caliber Webley & Scott Mk IV.

A commercial 38-caliber Mk IV Webley & Scott revolver with a 3-inch barrel and a safety catch.

38 Mark IV (1929) When the army introduced the 38-caliber Enfield (q.v.) in 1927, the connection with Webley ended, and the firm went into production with their own 38 revolver, calling it the Mark IV. It was little different from the Enfield pattern, since that had been based on a Webley design, apart from the lockwork that was pure Webley; whereas that of the Enfield model had been developed there. It was produced in 4- and 5-inch barrel lengths and sold widely to police forces. When World War II broke out, the War Office placed large orders for this 38 Mark IV, and it was issued alongside the Enfield, remaining in service until 1956.

- *38 Mark IV Target Models* (1929-55) Target versions were made from the start of the series with the main differences being in the careful selection during manufacture and the fitting of suitable sights, all target models having a laterally-adjustable rear sight. Models made after 1945 had a 6-inch barrel.

Mark IV Pocket Models These were little different from the Mark III Pocket variety, except for the revised mechanism and a holster guide. All had 3-inch barrels and were chambered for either 32 or 38 cartridges. A small number were made in 22 LR rimfire.

～ AUTOMATIC REVOLVER ～

The arrival of the automatic pistol in the 1890s led to long arguments about the relative merits of revolvers and automatics, some of which

persist to this day. Colonel Vincent Fosbery, VC, invented a type of automatic revolver that he claimed combined the virtues of both types of weapon, and his idea was taken up by Webley.

Webley-Fosbery This was never an approved issue weapon but was permitted to officers as their service sidearm until 1918. However, despite its many virtues, it was never made in large numbers. It was more expensive to make, was vulnerable to dirt and grit, and once the slide jammed the weapon was useless. Manufacture ended in early 1915, crowded out by war contracts for conventional revolvers.

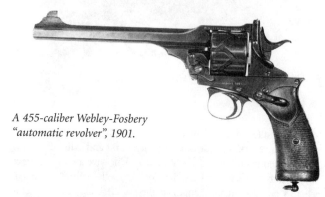

A 455-caliber Webley-Fosbery "automatic revolver", 1901.

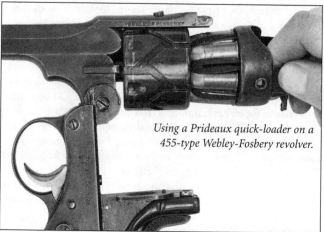

Using a Prideaux quick-loader on a 455-type Webley-Fosbery revolver.

- *455 Model 1901* The Webley-Fosbery revolver was in two units: the frame and the barrel/cylinder, the latter moving across the former. When fired, recoil caused the barrel unit to slide backwards, cocking the hammer; at the same time, a stud in the frame engaged with zigzag grooves in the cylinder and so turned the cylinder one-twelfth of a revolution. The barrel unit was then pushed forward again by a recoil spring, leaving the hammer cocked, and during this movement, the cylinder was given another one-twelfth turn so that as the barrel came to rest, the unfired chamber was aligned with the barrel.

Inevitably, the division into two parts increased the size of the weapon, and the Webley-Fosbery was no pocket revolver, being some 6 oz heavier than their equivalent conventional types. But they were very pleasant to shoot, due to the recoil-absorbing action of the moving parts, and they became very popular with target shooters. So much so, in fact, that after 1918, when it was no longer an official weapon, it was excluded from competition on the grounds that it gave shooters an unfair advantage.

This first production model used as many parts of the existing Mark IV army revolver as possible, including the 6-inch barrel, sights, hammer and cylinder arbor. A safety catch on the left side locked the two moving units and the hammer in whatever position it was in. A Target Model with 7.5-inch barrel was also made and fitted with target sights.

- *38 Model 1901* This was made at the same time as the 455-caliber version, and wherever possible, the same components were used. The cylinder, however, had to obviously be specially made, but by keeping it to the diameter of the 455 model, it was possible to have eight chambers. It is easily recognized because the pattern of the zigzag grooves had to be modified. It is also of interest to note that the chambering was not for any existing 38 revolver cartridge but rather for the 380 Auto pistol round (9mm Short), which, being semi-rimmed, was capable of being extracted by the normal mechanism. It also gave better ballistics than any available revolver rounds. These 38-caliber models were renowned for their accuracy, making many competition records, but relatively few — less than 300 — were made.

- *455 Model 1902* Some minor changes were soon made. Most notable was the moving of the cylinder flutes from the back of the cylinder to the front. Some were produced with the "Pryse" flat-topped barrel, and some target shooters preferred to remove the safety catch.

- *38 Model 1902* Similar changes were made to the 38-caliber model, changes aimed at simplifying manufacture and which made little or no difference to the operation.

- *455 Model 1914* The 1914 models were simply a refined version of the 1902 model, without significant changes. The *Target* version was made with a 7.5-inch barrel, and a very few were made with 4-inch barrels, though this may have been to special order.

∼ AUTOMATIC PISTOLS ∼

Mars Webley & Scott were the principal manufacturers of this, an early attempt to provide a high-velocity handgun powerful enough to convince the British army of its merits as a "man-stopper". The gun was the work of Hugh William Gabbett Fairfax (often wrongly spelled "Gabbet") of Leamington Spa, England, who was granted British Patent 14,777/1900 to protect his recoil-operated pistol.

The inventor had approached Webley & Scott as early as 1898, but the Board of Directors was unimpressed. However, within a year, Gabbett Fairfax had raised sufficient money for development work to begin. The pistols were offered in four chamberings, 8.5mm Mars, 360 Mars and 45 Mars (two lengths of case), and British army trials began in March 1901. The pistols were ultimately rejected in 1903, but Gabbett Fairfax had been declared bankrupt in September 1902 – a situation he ascribed to the absence of British army orders! – and work ultimately passed to the Mars Automatic Pistol Syndicate (q.v.). Webley's commitments had ceased well before this point. Probably no more than 50 had been made.

The Mars was a large gun with a detachable box magazine in the butt. When it fired, the barrel and breechblock ran back in the frame, and the uppermost cartridge in the magazine was withdrawn backward. Lugs on the bolt head were rotated out of engagement as the end of the backward stroke approached. The barrel then ran forward alone. A cartridge lifter raised the cartridge into the feed way, and the bolt was released to run forward, load the chamber, re-lock the mechanism and allow the bolt and barrel to return to battery. The external hammer, which had been rolled backward as the breech opened, was cocked and ready to fire.

Unfortunately, the pistol was notoriously difficult to handle. Trials suggested that it was reasonably reliable, but a typical 360-caliber example was 11.9 inches long, weighed 52 oz without its 10-round magazine and balanced badly. The power of the cartridge, the excessive weight of the reciprocating parts (the barrel, breechbolt and carrier assembly) and the length of the operating stroke usually ended with the muzzle pointing skyward after each shot. The Captain of HMS Excellent, the British Royal Navy gunnery school, reported in 1902 that "No one who once fired the pistol wished to shoot with it again …"

The 8.5mm cartridge fired a 140-grain bullet at 1750 ft/sec, and the long 45 propelled a 220-grain bullet at 1200 ft/sec. Not until the Auto-Mag (q.v.) was made 70 years later did anything eclipse the Mars.

The first, or 1904-type Webley & Scott 455-caliber pistol.

Webley-Whiting During their brief, unsuccessful and doubtless educational flirtation with the "Mars" pistol at the turn of the century, Webley & Scott set about developing their own design, and the first experimental model appeared in 1903. It was designed by W.J. "Bill" Whiting, the works manager, and it chambered the 38 Auto round. A second design for the 38 Auto and for a new 455 rimless cartridge appeared in 1904. Both these prototypes were made only in limited numbers.

The Webley automatics are immediately recognizable by their upright and square appearance, the graceful lines of the revolvers having been completely lost. They were never very popular even though they shoot quite well once the shooter is familiar with them.

A 32-caliber Webley & Scott 1906-type pistol, with a safety catch on the hammer.

32 Model (1906) This blowback pistol was the first automatic offered for sale and continued to be made until 1939. It was adopted by the Metropolitan Police in 1911. Throughout its existence, the 32-caliber pistols underwent various changes, some fundamental, but all intended to simplify manufacture or improve operation. The most obvious of these changes was in the safety catch that, in the first models, lay on the left side of the external hammer. By pressing this down when the hammer was at half-cock, the pistol could be locked and carried safely in a loaded condition. On later versions, the catch was placed on the frame above the left grip.

The barrel length was 3.5 inches, and the magazine held eight 32 ACP (7.65mm Auto) or 380 ACP (9mm Short) rounds.

25 External Hammer Model (1906) This is simply a scaled-down version of the 32-caliber blowback, with the mechanism simplified to the extreme. It was an ugly weapon and so small that it was difficult to hold, but it remained in production until 1939.

25 Hammerless Model (1909) A refinement of the 1906 hammer model and even lighter, this was the smallest Webley pistol ever made. Like most such weapons, it was not really hammerless, having the hammer concealed within the slide. It was this pistol that Harrington & Richardson (q.v.) chose to make in the USA.

9mm Model (1909) This was developed to satisfy enquiries from Europe that demanded a powerful chambering but not the heavy 455-caliber option offered in 1906. This, of course, was a locked-breech weapon and used a lug above the breech to lock into a recess in the

A 25 ACP Webley & Scott hammerless pocket pistol.

A 9mm (380 ACP) Webley & Scott pistol.

The Webley & Scott 455 Mark I pistol, 1913.

455 Pistol, Self-Loading, Mark I (1912) This is often called the "Navy Model" since it was adopted by the Royal Navy in 1913 and retained by them until 1945. It used the 455 Webley & Scott rimless cartridge, had an external hammer, a grip safety and a 7-shot magazine. The breech-locking system was identical with that of the 9mm model described above.

• *455 Pistol, Self-Loading, Mark I No. 2* (1915) This was approved in April 1915 for issue to the Royal Flying Corps, and it was also issued in small numbers to Royal Horse Artillery. It could be fitted with a shoulder stock and an additional safety that held the hammer at full cock. These adjuncts were considered of value because they allowed aviators to use the pistol single-handedly to fire at enemy aviators, and a special rear sight was fitted to aid in this use. Needless to say, its use in this role must have been minimal, and in mid-1916 they were withdrawn from flying use. Numbers of the pistols survived in the Royal Air Force for many years afterwards. Their use in the RHA was equally short-lived, since it was found that the mechanism was easily jammed by the mud and dirt of the battlefield.

9mm Jurek In the late 1940s, a Polish engineer named Marian Jurek obtained employment with Webley & Scott, bringing with him various proposals for automatic weapons. By that time, the British army had decided that its next sidearm would be an automatic pistol and was conducting a desultory series of trials to find if there was anything better to consider than the Browning 1935 High Power. Webley & Scott thought they saw an opportunity to regain their pre-eminence as pistol suppliers and began developing a Jurek design.

In its simplest terms, this was a Walther P-38 with the Colt-Browning dropping barrel replacing the Walther locking wedge. There were some minor refinements to the method of mounting the barrel, to give an air of originality to the whole thing, but the parentage is in no doubt. It worked well, firing the British standard 9mm Mark 2Z cartridge, but by the time Jurek perfected the design and built his second prototype, the army had made up its mind on the Browning. Webley prudently dropped the whole idea — particularly as there was no obvious commercial market in Britain. Jurek then left Webley and set up shop as a general gunsmith, specializing in custom-built target pistols.

～ SUB-CALIBER ADAPTERS ～

The "Morris Tube" was patented in 1881 and widely adopted by the British army as a sub-caliber training device. In its basic form, it was a barrel insert for the Lee-Metford and Lee-Enfield rifles that fired a special 297 cartridge. The Morris patents also covered a 22 rimfire adapter, and with the easier availability of rimfire ammunition, this eventually replaced the 297 versions. Webley adapted this system to their revolvers using a barrel insert that carried its own chamber; the cylinder was removed and the insert slipped into the barrel. Some were provided with an extractor that used the revolver's cam to force it out and so eject the spent case as the action was opened. Later types used a shorter insert barrel and a replacement cylinder with 22-caliber chambers, so that the revolver would work in the proper way and fire six shots.

front end of the short slide. Barrel and slide would recoil together until two sloping ribs on the sides of the breech caused the barrel to drop and the lug to come free from the slide recess. The recoiling slide re-cocked the hammer, and a fresh round was loaded on the return stroke. It was chambered for the 9mm Browning Long cartridge and was fitted with a grip safety in the butt backstrap.

9mm South African Model (1920) The 9mm model of 1909 was unsuccessful in obtaining any official orders, though it sold reasonably well commercially. In 1920, the South African Police adopted it with a manual safety catch mounted on the slide instead of the grip safety, and the modified guns were offered commercially until 1930. They are sometimes referred to as the "1909 Second Version".

Webley & Scott's 9mm High Velocity Hammerless Model, 1910.

38 High Velocity Hammerless Models (1910 and 1913) These two pistols were not a commercial success, but they represent a step in the progress of the Webley design. They were intended for military use and adopted the 38 Auto round. They were identical in shape and operation to the 455-caliber pistol of 1912 (below) but weighed much less. A concealed hammer mechanism was shared, with the principal difference between the two models being that the 1910 used only a grip safety and its successor had a manual safety catch on the frame.

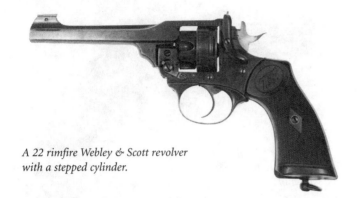

*A 22 rimfire Webley & Scott revolver
with a stepped cylinder.*

So many adapters and converters were marketed to fit Webley revolvers that it is difficult to list them all. Interested readers should refer to the Bibliography for sources of information.

WEIHRAUCH ("ARMINIUS")

Hermann Weihrauch, Zella St Blasii (prior to 1919), Zella-Mehlis (1919-45) and Mellrichstadt (1948 to date), Germany.

Founded in 1899, this gunmaking business was also renowned for the quality of its bicycles by the time World War II began. Machine-gun parts and optical-sight mounts were made during hostilities, marked "eea", but Thuringia fell under Soviet domination in 1945 and the business ceased to exist. However, the Weihrauch family, like the Walthers and many others, had been able to escape westward before the final partition. Work began again in Bavaria in 1948, and the first of a highly successful series of airguns was put into production in the 1950s. This was followed by the first cartridge revolvers c. 1961. These have usually borne "HWM" ("Hermann Weihrauch, Mellrichstadt") and an "Arminius" trademark associated prior to 1945 with Pickert (q.v.). Though guns distributed by Albrecht Kind were usually marked "Gecado", many other brand names – e.g., Dickson Special Agent, Omega – have been used in the USA.

∼ REVOLVERS ∼

The Weihrauch Arminius guns are very different from the old Pickert Arminius designs, being side-opening hand-ejector patterns inspired by the Smith & Wessons. They offer good quality and have the "Arminius" trademark – a bearded head with winged helmet – on the left side of the frame beneath the cylinder latch. The designation is usually engraved on the cylinder yoke with the caliber and chambering marked on the left side of the barrel; "Made in Germany" may appear on the frame of revolvers exported to the USA, together with "READ OWNER'S MANUAL BEFORE USE".

Many of the guns made prior to the early 1990s had ventilated barrel ribs. However, owing to a change in production methods (and doubtless also to a desire to minimize costs), the ribs now have little more than blind recesses.

HW 3 This is a compact double-action swing-cylinder design offered in 22 LR, 22 WM rimfire (eight shots apiece) or 32 S&W Long (seven shots). The guns are blued with fixed sights and currently have black

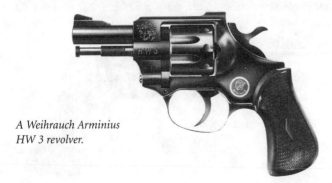

*A Weihrauch Arminius
HW 3 revolver.*

synthetic "combat" grips. They have been sold in Europe under the "Gecado" brand name and in the USA in the 1960s as the "Dickson Bulldog". The barrels are 2.8 inches long.

• *HW 3 Duo* This designation applies to guns supplied with interchangeable 22 LR/22 Magnum rimfire cylinders.

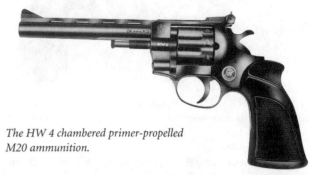

*The HW 4 chambered primer-propelled
M20 ammunition.*

HW 4 This designation was apparently originally applied to a 22-caliber revolver with barrels measuring 2.5-6 inches, a blue or chromed finish, and a square or flared butt. The current HW 4, however, has fixed sights, a 2.5-inch barrel and an eight-chamber cylinder accepting 4mm M20 primer-propelled ammunition. The guns are 6.7 inches long and weigh 25 oz with black synthetic "combat" grips.

• *HW 4 T* A variant of the 4mm HW 4, this gun has a rear sight that is adjustable for windage and elevation. The barrels may be 4 or 6 inches long, finish is blue and the grips may be black synthetic or checkered walnut (4-inch barreled option). The long-barreled version has special walnut "Sport" grips, giving an overall length of 11.1 inches and a weight of about 32.5 oz.

HW 5 Essentially an HW 3 with a 4-inch barrel, this can also be obtained in 22 LR rimfire, 22 Magnum rimfire and 32 S&W Long. Finish, sights and grips are identical with those of the short-barreled gun. The 32-caliber version was sold in the USA in the 1960s as the "Omega".

• *HW 5 Duo* An exchangeable-cylinder version of the HW 5 chambered for 22 LR rimfire and 22 Winchester Magnum rimfire.

The HW 5 T revolver.

• *HW 5 T* A variant of the HW 5 with an adjustable rear sight.

HW 7 Supplied with a 6-inch barrel, black synthetic "combat" or wood grips and fixed sights, this is simply a long-barreled version of the HW 3 and HW 5 listed previously.

• *HW 7 S* Chambered only for the 22 LR rimfire round and with an eight-chamber cylinder, this revolver has a laterally-adjustable front sight and wooden grips.

HW 9 This is a 22 LR revolver intended for competitive use. It has a recessed barrel rib, a micro-adjustable rear sight, an adjustable trigger with a trigger shoe, a broad-spur hammer and walnut thumb-rest grips. The standard model has a 6-inch barrel and an alloy frame and weighs about 35 oz.

The Arminius (Weihrauch) HW 7.

- *HW 9 Sport* This is a target-shooting version of the HW 9 ST, recognizable by its anatomical grip, with an adjustable palm rest and non-slip stippling. The 6-inch barrel is standard and the empty weight is about 48 oz.
- *HW 9 ST* Similar to the HW 9 and chambered for the 22 LR rimfire round, this "Sports-Target" revolver may be distinguished by the slab-side barrel that incorporates a full-length ejector-rod shroud. It has a checkered wooden grip. The steel frame and the heavyweight barrel increase weight to about 46 oz.

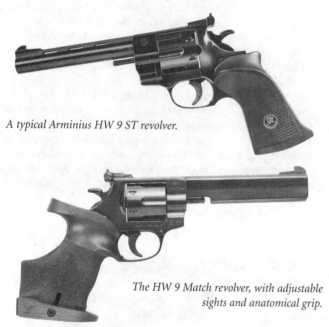

A typical Arminius HW 9 ST revolver.

The HW 9 Match revolver, with adjustable sights and anatomical grip.

- *HW 9 ST Silhouette* Introduced in 1994 in 22 LR rimfire and specifically for metallic target shooting, this has a six-chamber cylinder and an extraordinarily long barrel (10 or 10.75 inches) that raises weight to 58-60 oz. The rear sight and the trigger are adjustable, a trigger shoe and a broad-spur hammer are standard, and the grips are the checkered wooden "Sports" pattern with thumb rests. The front sight is hooded, the rear sight has a lightweight hood running the length of the frame and matted rails lie beneath and on the left side of the heavyweight "bull" barrel. An optical-sight rail can be fitted if required. Guns with 10.75-inch barrels – the longest that can be fitted to comply with the IMSSU 12.6-inch (320mm) sight-radius rule – have a matte-nickel finish, the others being blued. Those made after 1997 also have a Bo-Mar rear sight with a flip-up hood that extends back above the hammer and grip.

HW 38 Chambered for the 38 Special cartridge, this six-shot revolver may be obtained with 2.5- or 4- or 6-inch barrels. The guns are blued, have fixed sights and are generally fitted with synthetic "Combat" grips (often wood on the 6-inch-barreled examples). The barrels have ribs with "blind" recesses that give the appearance of being ventilated. A

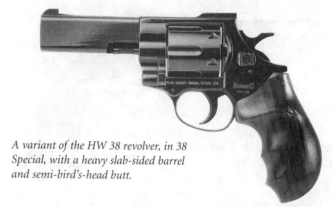

A variant of the HW 38 revolver, in 38 Special, with a heavy slab-sided barrel and semi-bird's-head butt.

typical 6-inch-barreled HW 38 is about 11 inches long and weighs about 31 oz.

- *HW 38 T* This is similar to the standard gun but has a micro-adjustable rear sight and a walnut thumb-rest "Sport" grip to facilitate target-shooting.

HW 68 Now discontinued, this was a lightweight HW 4 with a 2.5-inch barrel and a black-anodized alloy frame. The cylinders, which were readily exchangeable, were chambered for either 22 LR or 22 WM rimfire cartridges.

The Weihrauch HW 357 T, chambered for the 357 Magnum round.

HW 357 Identical with the HW 38 in all respects other than chambering, this was strengthened for the 357 Magnum round. Primarily a personal-defense weapon, it has fixed sights and a synthetic "Combat" grip.

- *HW 357 Match* This is a variant of the "T" pattern fitted with the same micro-adjustable rear sight and checkered wooden "Sport" grip, but it has the slab-side barrel of the HW 9 ST (above) with the full-length ejector-rod shroud.
- *HW 357 T* A variant of the standard HW 357 with a micro-adjustable rear sight suited to target shooting, this also has a walnut "Sport" grip.

Windicator A strengthened version of the standard Weihrauch swing-cylinder design, this accepts 357 Magnum and 38 Special ammunition interchangeably. It is blued, with fixed sights, synthetic "Combat" grips and a six-chamber cylinder. Empty weight is about 32 oz.

WSA ("Western Single Action") A single-action revolver based on the Colt Single Action Army Model, this is available in 22 LR rimfire, 22

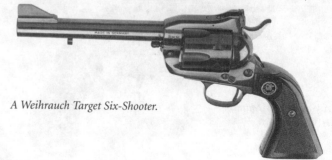

A Weihrauch Target Six-Shooter.

*Weihrauch Arminius
Western Six-Shooters.*

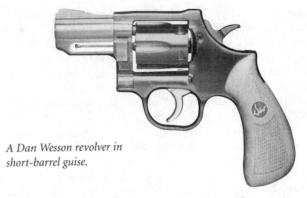

*A Dan Wesson revolver in
short-barrel guise.*

Magnum rimfire, 357 Magnum, 44 Magnum and 45 Long Colt. The most important difference from the original design concerns the floating firing pin and transfer bar, which connects the hammer and firing pin when the trigger is pulled, to comply with the US Gun Control Act of 1968. The centerfire guns, offered with 4.75- or 7-inch barrels, have color case-hardened frames and plain walnut grips. The rimfires (6/7.5-inch barrel only) are similar but finished entirely in high-polish blue. The grip straps and the trigger guard are polished brass.

• *WSA Target* This was a variant of the standard pattern with a micro-adjustable rear sight. It is no longer in production.

DAN WESSON FIREARMS

Monson and Palmer, Massachusetts, USA.

Founded in 1968 by the great-grandson of Daniel Wesson, this company developed an ingenious and practical design of revolver that allowed rapid interchange of barrels and grips. The guns were well received, and sales were promising. In January 1991, however, a restructuring to create Wesson Firearms, Inc., disguised the impact that cheaper rivals – especially imports – were having on the marketplace. Profitability rapidly declined and eventually, in 1995, Wesson was declared insolvent. However, the assets were purchased by the New York International Corporation, and trading recommenced in 1996 (see next entry).

～ REVOLVERS ～

The guns are all solid-frame double-action swing-cylinder types incorporating a yoke that is retained by a press-catch on the lower front left side of the frame and a patented interchangeable-barrel system.

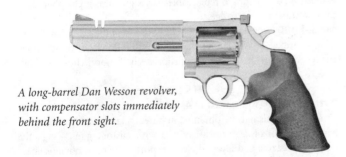

*A long-barrel Dan Wesson revolver,
with compensator slots immediately
behind the front sight.*

The barrel is screwed to the frame in the usual way and is then enclosed in a shroud that incorporates the ejector-rod housing and foresight. This shroud butts against the frame, and a barrel-retaining nut is then screwed into the muzzle so as to hold the shroud firmly in place and place the barrel under tension. The shroud is automatically aligned with the foresight precisely vertical and the sight adjustment is maintained when barrels are interchanged. The spare barrels are supplied with feeler gauges that ensure the correct cylinder-to-barrel clearance when the new barrel is being inserted.

The earliest guns (Models 8-12), dating from 1970-1, had external barrel-locking nuts. These had soon been superseded by a recessed-nut design that required a separate spanner. Dan Wesson revolvers also featured a wide variety of interchangeable sights. An attachment stud projecting downward from the rear of the frame allowed an almost limitless range of grips to be fitted.

Guns have often been sold in *Pistol-Pacs* (P22, P32, P45), providing additional barrel lengths (2-4, depending on caliber), additional grips and a variety of replacement sights. Some have even included a walnut blank to allow the owner to carve grips to suit a personal style or preference. *Hunter Pacs* (HP22, HP32, HP15, HP40, HP41, HP44 and HP445) were restricted to guns firing Magnum ammunition. They offered only two barrel-shroud options – 8-inch ventilated ribs, light and heavy – but included Burris 1.5-4x or 2x optical sights and appropriate mounts.

Often listed as "Series" instead of "Model", the Dan Wesson guns may include the caliber or chambering in their designations. The prefix "7" indicates stainless-steel construction.

Model 8 (and Model 708, 1971-5; 1977-95) Chambered for the 38 Special cartridge, the original guns had external barrel-locking nuts. Sights were fixed. The Model 8 was reintroduced in the late 1970s, effectively the "new" Model 14 in a different chambering. The Model 708 appeared at the same time.

Model 9 (and Model 709, 1971-5; 1977-95) A minor variant of the Model 8 with an adjustable rear sight, it was discontinued in its original form and then reintroduced within a few years as a 38-caliber version of the "new" Model 15.

Model 11 (1970-1) The original production variant of the Wesson revolver, fitted with the original external barrel-locking nut, this was chambered for the 357 Magnum cartridge. Barrels could be 2.5, 4 or 6 inches long, the sights were fixed and the grips were walnut.

Model 12 (1970-1) This was simply a version of the 357 Magnum Model 11 with adjustable "target" sights and a more sophisticated grip.

Model 14 (and Model 714, 1971-5; 1976-95) The first of the Wesson revolvers to feature the recessed barrel-locking nut, this chambered 357 Magnum ammunition. An improved version was substituted in 1976, which offered 2-, 4- or 6-inch barrels in "Service Shrouds". The sights were fixed and the walnut grips were the slim Service pattern.

• *Models 14 and 714 Fixed Barrel Service* These had 2.5- or 4-inch barrels and slender Service grips. They were intended for purchasers (e.g., policemen) who did not require the barrel-change feature.

Model 15 (and Model 715, 1971-5; 1976-95) Offered only in 357 Magnum, these guns had ramped front and adjustable rear sights. The improved version was offered with barrels measuring 2-10 inches, accompanied by the standard or Service shrouds; weight ranged from 32 to 50 oz, depending on barrel length. The grips were usually wooden target patterns.

• *Models 15 and 715 Fixed Barrel Target* Minor variants of the standard adjustable-sight 357 Magnum guns, these lacked the interchangeable barrels. Barrel lengths were restricted to 3 or 5 inches.

Model 22 (and Model 722, 1976-95) Chambered for 22 LR rimfire ammunition, these guns have been offered in a variety of options. Barrels measured 2-8 inches and were accompanied by standard, ventilated-rib or heavy ventilated-rib shrouds. The sights were adjustable and the grips were target patterns. Weights ranged from 36 to 49 oz, depending on the individual barrel/shroud combination.

- *Models 22M and 722M* A 22 Winchester Magnum rimfire version of the standard Model 22.
- *Model 22 Silhouette* Chambered for 22 LR rimfire ammunition, with a six-chamber cylinder and single-action lockwork, this was distinguished by a 10-inch barrel with a ventilated-rib shroud. The guns weighed 55 oz, or 62 oz with the heavyweight shroud.

Model 32 (and Model 732, c. 1985-95) Chambered for the 32 H&R Magnum centerfire round, this was offered with adjustable sights, a target grip and 2-, 4-, 6- or 8-inch barrels with a choice of shroud. Weight varied from 35 to 53 oz.

Model 38P (and Model 738P) Apparently made only in small quantities, this was a fixed-barrel gun chambering the 38 Special cartridge. It was specifically intended to appeal to police and similar authorities. Distinguished by a five-chamber cylinder and a 2.5-inch barrel, it had fixed sights, wood or rubber grips and weighed about 25 oz empty.

Model 40 (Supermag, 1988-95) Chambered for the 357 Maximum cartridge (subsequently rechristened 357 Supermag), this was sold with a variety of barrels (4-10 inches) and ventilated-rib shrouds, though a slotted ventilated-rib shroud was available with the 8-inch barrel. Adjustable sights and target-style grips were standard, and in 1993, a Compensated Barrel Assembly ("CBA") was added to the options.

Model 41 (and Model 741, 1983-95) Chambered for the 41 Magnum, this was offered with barrels ranging from 4 to 10 inches, giving weights of 40-70 oz. The shrouds were generally standard ventilated-rib patterns, sights were adjustable and the grips were wood or rubber target types.

Model 44 (and Model 744, 1983-95) This was a variation of the M41 chambered for the 44 Magnum round.

Model 45 (and Model 745, 1983-95) Chambered for the 45 Long Colt cartridge, this was otherwise identical with the Models 41 and 44.

- *Models 45 and 745 Pin Gun* These fixed-barrel revolvers built on the Model 44 frame chambered rimless 45 ACP ammunition (with or without half-moon clips). The 5-inch barrel had a two-slot compensator and was fitted with a standard or heavyweight ventilated-rib shroud. Sights were adjustable, and a target-type grip was standard.

Model 322 (and Model 7322, 1988-95). Chambered for the venerable 32-20 WCF round, this was otherwise comparable with the Model 32.

Model 375 Chambered for the 375 Supermag round.

Model 445 (and Model 7445, 1989-95) Chambered for the 445 Supermag round, this gun could be fitted with barrels measuring 4-10 inches. Most had ventilated-rib shrouds (standard or heavy), though slotted shrouds could be obtained with the 8- and 10-inch options. The sights were adjustable and the grip was a target pattern. An optional Compensated Barrel Assembly ("CBA") appeared in 1993.

- *Model 7445 Alaskan Guide Special* (1992-3?) Fewer than 500 of these guns were made, with 4-inch compensated barrels (5.5 inches overall) and heavy ventilated-rib shrouds. The sights were adjustable, the grips were synthetic and the finish was blacked titanium nitride. Empty weight was about 56 oz.

WESSON FIREARMS CORPORATION

Norwich, New York State, USA.

This is the outgrowth of the Wesson Firearms, Inc. (formerly Dan Wesson Firearms, above). Trading recommenced in 1996, when an opportunity was taken to rationalize the product range, and the first Colt-Browning M1911-type pistols appeared in 1997.

∼ REVOLVERS ∼

The highly successful Dan Wesson interchangeable-barrel system has been retained, but a few of the older guns have been abandoned. The organization of the "New Generation" product-range is now based more on categories than individual models, and several new revolvers have appeared.

New Generation guns (1997 to date) Basic details of the individual guns will be found in the preceding section, excepting the three listed below. Most of the current products have ventilated-rib shrouds, often the heavyweight pattern, and adjustable sights. Black rubber Hogue finger-groove grips are considered to be standard. Hunter Pacs and Pistols Pacs are still being offered with the Models 15, 22, 32, 40, 41, 44, 45, 414, 445, 460 and 3220, together with all the "7"-prefix stainless-steel equivalents. The Hunter Pacs may contain Burris or Weaver optical sights.

- *Compensated Series* Offered with 4-, 6- or 10-inch barrels with an integral two-slot compensator immediately ahead of the front sight, this group contains the Models 15, 41, 44, 45, 360 and 460, plus the "7"-series versions.
- *Large-frame Series* These six-shot guns – Models 41, 44, 45, 360 and 460, together with the stainless-steel versions – are offered with 4-, 6-, 8- or 10-inch barrels.
- *Small-frame Series* Available with 2.5-, 4-, 5.6-, 8- and 10-inch barrels, this includes the Models 22, 22M, 32, 3220 and 15, and their stainless-steel ("7"-prefix) derivatives.
- *Standard Silhouette Series* Introduced in 1999, this is currently confined to the Models 722, 740, 741, 744, 7360, 7414 and 7445. All but the Models 741 and 744, which can also be obtained with 10-inch barrels, have 8-inch barrels with ventilated-rib slotted shrouds. Patridge front sights and micro-adjustable rear sights are standard.
- *Supermag-frame Series* The Models 40, 414 and 445, with the stainless-steel equivalents, can be obtained with 4-, 6-, 8- and 10-inch barrels.
- *Super Ram Silhouette Series* ("SRS", 1999 to date) This is restricted to the same guns that constitute the Standard Silhouette Series (above). They have Bo-Mar sights (hooded front, adjustable rear) and plain or fluted cylinders.

Model 3220 This is the current designation for what was originally designated "Model 322" – chambered for the 32-20 WCF cartridge. The stainless-steel version is now the "M73220".

Model 360 (1999 to date) Built on a large frame, this gun chambers the 357 Magnum round.

Model 414 A standard replaceable-barrel gun, this is chambered for the 414 Supermag cartridge.

Model 460 (1999 to date) The M460 can accept the 45 ACP, 45 Auto-Rim, 45 Super, 45 Winchester Magnum or 460 Rowland rounds interchangeably, provided that the appropriate half-moon clips are available.

∼ PISTOLS ∼

Patriot (2002) Introduced in 45 ACP in two patterns, "Expert" and "Marksman", this may be obtained in blue or stainless steel. Though it has a selection of features associated with custom guns – e.g., the beveled magazine and lowered ejection port – the most obvious characteristic is the wedge-like "Combat/Carry" rear sight.

PointMan series (2000 to date) These 45 ACP pistols are locked by the familiar recoil-operated Colt-Browning tipping barrel system. They incorporate a variety of improvements, but the most obvious identification features are the duplicated slide-retracting grooves (front and rear) and the "DW" medallions set into the grips. The guns all have skeleton hammers and triggers, extended or "beavertail" grip safety levers and beveled ejection ports.

- *PointMan Dave Pruitt Signature* (2001 to date) Customized by an IDPA Grand Master, this features a variety of "custom" refinements, including chevron-type retraction grips, finely checkered "double-diamond" cocobolo grips, a beveled magazine well, a lowered and flared ejection port and a match trigger of the customer's choice.

- *PointMan Guardian* This is a compact version of the PointMan Major, with a 4.25-inch barrel. The slide and frame are made of blued carbon steel.
- *PointMan Guardian Deuce* A two-tone version of the Guardian, this offers a blued carbon-steel slide and a satin-finished stainless-steel frame.
- *Pointman Hi-Cap* This is little more than a PointMan Minor adapted to accept a 10-round double-row magazine.
- *PointMan Major* Made of stainless steel, this gun has a special match-quality barrel, an interchangeable front sight and an adjustable rear sight mounted on a raised rib. The grips are rosewood.
- *PointMan Major Aussie* (2002) This has a Bo-Mar rear sight and a special sighting rib along the top of the slide. A Southern Cross emblem (five stars and four bars) is laser-engraved on the front right side of the slide.
- *PointMan Major Tri-Ops* (2002) This is a set of three slides, barrels, return springs and magazines (9mm Parabellum, 10mmm Auto, 40 S&W) in a special case.
- *PointMan Minor* This is a lesser version of the Major, with a blued carbon-steel slide and a standard barrel.
- *PointMan Seven* The basic version of the range, this is made of blued carbon steel and lacks the sight rib. A stainless-steel version has also been made in small numbers.

FRANK WESSON
Worcester and Springfield, Massachusetts, USA.
Franklin "Frank" Wesson was the elder brother of Daniel Baird Wesson, co-founder of Smith & Wesson. Perhaps best known for a "two-trigger" break-open rifle produced during the American Civil War (1861-5), he was also responsible for a variety of handguns. These included the pistols described below and at least one revolver that was never produced in quantity. Operations ceased in the early 1880s.

∼ SINGLE-SHOT PISTOLS ∼
Tip-up pattern Introduced in 1858 in accordance with a patent eventually granted to Wesson & Harrington in 1859, this chambered the 22 Short rimfire Smith & Wesson cartridge. The guns originally had 4-inch octagonal barrels and slender brass frames. The sliding barrel-release catch projected ahead of the sheathed trigger.

The perfected 22-caliber small-frame guns, made from 1858 until 1865, had rounded frames and half-octagonal barrels measuring 3, 3.5 or 6 inches. Finish was blue, and the grips were customarily rosewood. A modified pattern, with a flat-sided frame and a detachable circular sideplate to give access to the lockwork, was made from 1865 until 1871. A medium-frame pattern (1859-70) made of iron instead of brass had a 4-inch half-octagon barrel chambered for the 30 or 32 rimfire rounds. The trigger and its sheath were lengthened in 1862, and the frame was strengthened at the hinge-point.

Rolling-barrel pattern Patented by Wesson in May 1870, this had a barrel that rotated laterally around a longitudinal pivot set in the breech face. Most of the guns, which had brass or iron frames, were sold as "Pocket Rifles". Chambered for rimfire cartridges ranging from 22 Short to 44 and with barrels as long as 24 inches, they were usually accompanied by skeleton stocks. However, a few short-barreled pistols were also made, and the shortest of the rifles, with 10-inch barrels, could still serve as handguns. Most guns have a half-cock notch on the hammer, and some – especially 32-caliber or larger – had a press-catch on the frame to lock the hammer at half-cock.

∼ REPEATING PISTOL ∼
In July 1869, Frank Wesson received a US Patent protecting a two-barrel "over and under" derringer, with a flat barrel block that rotated

around its longitudinal axis to bring a second cartridge under the hammer. The barrel block could be turned to an intermediate position to allow spent cases to be ejected and the chambers reloaded. The guns were made in three sizes in 1868-80. The smallest, chambering the 22 Short rimfire round, had a barrel measuring 2 or 2.5 inches. The 32 version had 2.5- or 3.5-inch barrels, and the largest, chambering the 41 rimfire cartridge, had 3-inch barrels. A sliding bayonet was sometimes housed between the barrels.

WESTINGER & ALTENBURGER ("FEINWERKBAU")
Oberndorf/Neckar, Germany.
Best known for air- and gas-guns, Feinwerkbau has also made a range of high-class 22 rimfire target rifles. The current AW93 rapid-fire target pistol combines a Russian Izhevsk design with German precision engineering. See also "Walther".

WHITE
Rollin White Arms Company, Lowell, Massachusetts, USA.
This gunmaking business was operated by the patentee of the bored-through revolver cylinder, a design exploited with such dazzling effect by Smith & Wesson (q.v.). It became the Lowell Arms Company in 1864. With the removal of White from control, the continued production of revolvers with bored-through cylinders invited Smith & Wesson to successfully sue for patent infringement.

WHITE-MERRILL
The White-Merrill Arms Company, Boston, Massachusetts, USA.
A White-Merrill design was among the pistols tested by the US Army in the 1907 trials that eventually resulted in the selection of the Colt M1911. The first design, of 1905, was a delayed blowback relying on the resistance of the hammer to provide, by means of differential leverage, the necessary delay in opening the breech. This proved unsuccessful, and the 1907 model tested by the US Army had a locking system remarkably like that of Browning: three ribs on top of the barrel locked into the front end of the half-length slide. The unusual feature of this pistol was the provision of a finger-operated lever beneath the trigger guard, which, when squeezed, drew back the slide to allow the weapon to be cocked by one hand. This feature is said to have been provided for the benefit of the US Cavalry, who could thus retain control of their horse while cocking the pistol. The test specimen, however, was "still in a primitive state of development" and promptly rejected by the US Army trials board. With that, the White-Merrill was abandoned.

WHITNEY ARMS COMPANY
Whitneyville, Connecticut, USA.
This firm was founded by the famous Eli Whitney at the beginning of the 19th century, and it became a pioneer in the field of machine-tool operation and mass-production. By the 1870s, though, their status had declined, having been overtaken by other firms, and their only products in our field of interest were a collection of cheap revolvers of the

A 38 rimfire Whitney "Whitneyville Armory House Pistol".

"suicide special" type. These were all the usual solid-frame, stud-trigger, non-ejecting pattern, appearing as 7-shot 22RF and 5-shot 32RF models with barrels of 1.5 to 3.5 inches. They may be found marked "Whitneyville Armory" or with the sales names of Defender and Eagle and Monitor.

WHITNEY FIREARMS, INC.

North Haven, Connecticut, USA.

This firm, which had no connection with the previous one, produced a novel 22-caliber blowback automatic that was among the most handsome pistols ever made. Indeed, we suspect this to have been its principal fault, as it may have looked too "space age" to be taken seriously.

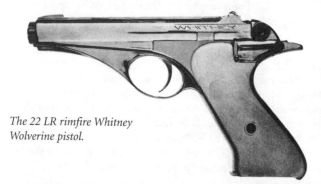

The 22 LR rimfire Whitney Wolverine pistol.

Lightning or Wolverine Designed by Robert Hillberg in 1954, while he was working for the Bellmore-Johnson Tool Company, the Whitney pistol was made in a small factory in State Street, North Haven. Only 10,000 were made in a single production run, distribution exclusively being in the hands of J.L. Galef of New York. The business was sold to Charles E. Lowe Company in 1956, and a few additional guns were made largely from components remaining from "Whitney" production. Guns remained in stock until the early 1960s.

The pistol was a rather complex design. The light alloy frame carried a well-raked butt and a tubular receiver. Into the receiver went a cylindrical "slide" into which the breechblock was pinned at the rear end, terminating in a cocking grip. The front portion of the slide was occupied by the barrel, which passed through the front end and was secured to the receiver by a screwed collar. The breech end of the barrel was of enlarged section, so as to ride inside the slide and centralize the barrel, and the recoil spring was held between this section and the front of the slide.

On firing, the breechblock recoiled, taking the slide with it and compressing the recoil spring. Cutouts in the slide allowed for ejection of the spent case and the feeding of a fresh cartridge from the butt magazine. The "full-floating" firing pin or striker, a flat stamping, was held in the breechblock without the assistance of a spring.

The pistol was initially called "Lightning", but early models were also marked "Whitney" on the left of the receiver and "Wolverine Whitney Firearms Inc" on the right. The name "Wolverine" was dropped at about serial number 24,000, after the Lyman Sight Company drew attention to its use on telescope sights. The left-side inscription then became "Caliber .22 Patent Pending The Whitney Firearms Co Hartford Conn USA". It was then sold simply as the "Whitney Auto-Loader" until distribution ended in 1963.

WICHITA

Wichita Arms Company. Wichita, Kansas, USA.

Originally called the "Wichita Engineering & Supply, Inc.", this company developed a single-shot bolt-action hunting pistol in 1978 on the basis of a left-hand version of its better-known rifles.

Classic (1978 to date) Chambered for virtually any cartridge up to 308 Winchester, this mates a standard left-hand action, with a ball-type

bolt handle, with a tapered 11.25-inch barrel. The walnut half-stock has a pistol grip with a thumb rest and a pronounced schnabel forend tip. Engraved versions have also been made in small numbers.

International (1989 to date) Though sometimes mistakenly listed as another of the bolt-action derivatives, this is actually a single-shot break-open design with a press-button latch on the left rear side of the frame. The grip portion of the frame is modeled on the Colt M1911A1, and the grip-plates and forend are walnut. Chamberings range from 22 LR rimfire to 357 Magnum, barrel-length options usually being restricted to 10.5 and 14 inches. Adjustable open sights are standard, though optical-sight mounts can be substituted to order (guns with telescope sights are sometimes designated "Hunter"). Construction may be blued carbon or satin-finish stainless steel.

MK 40 This is a variation of the Silhouette pistol (below), with a 13-inch barrel and "multi-range" sights. Supplied with a composition or walnut stock, it may be blued carbon or satin-finish stainless steel.

Silhouette (1979 to date) Distinguished by a heavyweight 15-inch barrel, squared contours and a spatulate ("butterknife") bolt handle, this pistol is currently being chambered only for 7mm HMSA or 308 Winchester ammunition. Target-type adjustable sights are standard, the front sight lying immediately above the squared forend tip.

A 32-caliber (7.65mm) "Little Tom" pistol made by Wiener Waffenfabrik.

WIENER WAFFENFABRIK

Vienna, Austria(-Hungary).

This gunmaking business was responsible for the Tomiška "Little Tom" pistol, production apparently beginning after the end of World War I. They made some small changes in the contour of the slide and replaced Tomiška's name and address on the slide with "WIENER WAFFENFABRIK", the right side carrying the serial number and "MADE IN AUSTRIA". The grips, plastic for the 6.35mm and wood for the 7.65mm, had the Wiener trademark: two "W" letters superimposed, with the right-hand stroke of the lower "W" formed into an "F". Total Vienna production, in both calibers, is believed not to have exceeded 10,000 when production ended in about 1925.

Although not a particularly important pistol, the Little Tom deserves credit for being the first production double-action automatic, a feat usually credited to the later Walther PP.

WILDEY

Wildey Firearms Co., Inc., later "Wildey. Inc.", Cold Spring and New Burg, New York; Cheshire and Brookfield, Connecticut, USA.

This firm began operation in the 1970s with the unique Wildey gas-operated automatic pistol. Designed by Robert Hillberg (see also "Whitney Wolverine"), the prototype was made by the Bellmore-Johnson Tool Company in Hamden, Connecticut, and chambered a Magnum cartridge developed by Bellmore-Johnson, Hillberg and David Findlay. Application for what became US Patent 4,291,481 was made in March 1979. W.J. "Wildey" Moore then created a manufacturing/distribution agency.

A Wildey 45-caliber pistol.

The gun is a fixed-barrel design in stainless steel and has a three-lug rotating bolt. Gas is tapped from six ports bored radially in front of the chamber. The gas passes into a chamber around a breech containing an annular piston. This is driven back by the gas and unlocks and then drives the bolt backwards against a recoil spring. This gas operation appears to soften the recoil somewhat, and although a heavy weapon firing powerful loads, the Wildey is not unpleasant to fire.

The history of the gun has been somewhat checkered. Chamberings have included 357 Peterbuilt, a variety of Winchester Magnum cartridges (30, 9mm, 10mm, 11mm, 45), and 475 Wildey Magnum, but are currently restricted to 357 Peterbuilt, 45 Winchester Magnum and 475 Wildey Magnum. The length of the interchangeable barrels can range from 5 to 10 inches, all with distinctive ventilated ribs.

WILKINSON

Wilkinson Arms Company. Parma, Indiana; Covina and El Monte, California, USA.

This gunmaking business has specialized in small-caliber automatic pistols, named after designer Ray Wilkinson's wife and daughters.

Diane (c. 1977 to date) This is a well-made, if conventional, 25 ACP blowback. It has been made in "Standard" and "Lightweight" forms, the latter featuring a light alloy frame.

Linda This is a pistol-carbine chambered for the 9mm Parabellum cartridge, with a walnut forend and a 30-round detachable box magazine in the grip. Measuring 12.3 inches overall, with an 8.4-inch barrel and an empty weight of 77 oz, it is only barely classifiable as a "handgun".

Sherry (1985 to date) Chambered for the 22 LR rimfire round, this diminutive gun is only 4.4 inches long and weighs merely 9.2 oz without its six-round magazine. A cross-bolt safety catch locks the hammer. The finish may be blue overall, or a combination of a blued slide and a gold-anodized alloy frame.

WILL

Venus Waffenwerke Oscar Will, Zella St Blasii (prior to 1919) and Zella-Mehlis (post-1919), Germany.

This gunmaking business, founded in Zella St Blasii in 1844, traded until Oscar Will sold his business to Wilhelm Foss in 1923. Foss continued trading as "Venuswaffenwerke, vorm. Oskar Will" until 1945 (see "V"). Will is best known for the shotguns and rifles that were made in the Zella factory, but his name will also be encountered on handguns, airguns and a variety of accessories.

∽ SINGLE-SHOT PISTOLS ∽

Will's marks have been found on guns ranging from tiny swinging-breech "personal defence" guns chambered for BB or CB Caps (known in Europe as "Type Flobert" or "Übungsmunition") to surprisingly sophisticated target pistols. However, it is difficult to decide which of these were truly Will designs, as most of the cheaper examples were undoubtedly made in Belgium.

Break-action types The simplest of these, probably emanating from Liége, had a press-catch on the left side of the frame, which allowed the breech to rise. Some guns had extractors, but few expelled the spent case entirely. The lockwork generally relied on an exposed spurred hammer, and the better guns had set-trigger mechanisms. The sights, though often adjustable, were rarely noteworthy.

The Will-made guns were much more sophisticated than the Belgian purchases. One pattern was built on sporting-rifle lines, with a double trigger that incorporated a "set" element. Characteristically, these guns had 15.7-inch barrels that were octagonal at the breech and cylindrical for much of their length but with a short octagonal section at the muzzle. They also had automatic ejectors and self-cocking strikers. Fixed sights were generally regulated for 75 meters, the trigger guard (which doubled as the operating lever) had a prominent finger spur and the checkered walnut grip had a pronounced prawl (or hump) on the backstrap. Chamberings were typically 6mm centerfire, 6.5x27R, 6.5x48.5R or 32-20 WCF.

- *Venus Präzisions-Scheiben-Pistole* This was an improved form of the break-open design with a squared high-back frame instead of a low rounded sporting-rifle pattern. The underlever was simplified and an adjustable single trigger was fitted. Guns of this type, which were supplied in quantity to A.L. Frank ("Alfa") prior to World War I, could be chambered for Flobert (primer-propelled), 6mm centerfire or 32-20 WCF ammunition.

Falling-block types These had a sturdy breechblock, containing the hammer and its spring, which dropped down through the frame when the operating-lever/trigger-guard unit was pulled downward. Ejection was customarily automatic, and the trigger system almost always incorporated a setting lever. The rear of the operating lever usually had a pivoting spring-loaded latch to engage a notched post on the trigger plate. Chamberings were restricted to rimfire ammunition – 22 Short, 22 Long, 22 Extra Long, 6mm and 9mm.

Swinging-block types These came in two basic forms: one with a breechblock that swung laterally to the right (the "Mariette System") and another that swung upward on two arms ("Warnant System") to expose the chamber. Though the quality of the fittings and decoration could be surprisingly good, swing-breech guns usually had fixed sights and simple triggers. Most, if not all, had come from Belgium.

∽ REVOLVERS ∽

Catalogs published prior to 1914 reveal a surprising variety of designs, ranging from tiny open-frame rimfire guns with folding triggers to substantial "Constabulary" and "Army Model" solid-frame patterns chambering the 320 or 380 centerfire rounds. The largest of all was the "Ordonnanz-Modell", chambered for the 10.6mm cartridge introduced for the Reichrevolvers, though among the most interesting were the break-open Smith & Wesson auto-ejector copies and the 12-shot folding-trigger "Detectiv-Revolver" that chambered minuscule 230 centerfire ammunition. But few if any of these guns were made in Germany. Most were undoubtedly made in Liége by companies such as Henrion, Dassy & Heuschen ("HDH") and will bear Belgian proofmarks in addition to the Will name or "Venus" trademark.

∽ AUTOMATIC PISTOL ∽

Venus-Pistole Made in small numbers prior to World War I, this was a fixed-barrel blowback on Browning lines. The top of the frame was rounded to support the lower portion of the slide and barrel, the return spring lay above the barrel, and the breech section of the slide was not only carried higher than the remainder but also had prominent retraction ribs. The gun had an internal hammer, and a radial safety lever lay on the left rear of the frame. The slide was marked "Original Venus Patent", with an "OW" monogram molded into the grips. The Venus-Pistole is said to have been offered in 6.35mm (25 ACP), 7.65mm (32 ACP) and 9mm Short (380 ACP) chamberings, but none could be traced for examination, and it is suspected that only the two smaller versions were ever offered commercially. They are said to have performed with better-than-average accuracy, but production had already ceased by 1914.

WILSON COMBAT

Berryville, Arkansas, USA.

This gunmaking business is responsible for a range of custom and semi-custom pistols based on the Colt M1911A1. The original parts were acquired from Springfield Armory, but, since 1997, Wilson has made its own slides and frames. Among the semi-custom guns are the Tactical Carry KZ-45 with a polymer frame and a range of "M1996A2 Service Grade" patterns – including "Classic", "Classic Rimfire", "Protector", "Protector Compact", "Sentinel Ultra Compact", "Tactical" and "Target".

The custom guns, made only to order, include the "Combat Classic", "Defensive Combat Pistol", "Stealth Defense System" and "Tactical Elite" patterns. They can include virtually any part that is available for the M1911A1, including triggers, extended safety levers, skeleton hammers and muzzle bushings. Details of the range can be found in the *Standard Catalog of Firearms* (2002 edition), pp. 1232-5. There is also a "Custom Carry Revolver" based on the Smith & Wesson Model 66.

WINCHESTER

Winchester Repeating Arms Company,
New Haven, Connecticut, USA.

The history of this long-established gunmaking company is tortuous and best appreciated from specialist studies such as *Winchester. The Gun that Won the West* by Harold Williamson (1962) and *Winchester Repeating Arms Company* by Herbert Houze (1996).

Best known for its rifles prior to 1917, Winchester also briefly toyed with the introduction of revolvers — particularly when Colt, its sworn rival, began to market the Burgess-designed lever-action rifle in the early 1880s. The problem was resolved when Winchester threatened to market single-action revolvers, and Colt, which had most to lose, prudently withdrew the Colt-Burgess rifle.

The genesis of the revolvers has been contested. It has been claimed that the development was due to Hugo Borchardt, but it seems that Borchardt's participation was minimal. The bulk of the work seems to have been undertaken by Stephen Wood, to whom patents were granted for improvements in lockwork design from 1864 onward.

One of the few revolvers made by Winchester.

Chambered for the 38-40 or 44-40 WCF rounds, the guns ranged from a solid-frame pattern, with an extractor lever on the frame behind the cylinder, to a swing-cylinder design latched by a sliding sleeve beneath the barrel. They are believed to date from c. 1876-9.

WINFIELD

Winfield Arms Corporation, Los Angeles, California, USA.

This company operated in 1955-65, selling pistols made by the Manufacture d'Armes Bayonne, France (see "Bayonne") under the Winfield name.

WORTHER

E. Worther, Buenos Aires, Argentina.

Pantax This small 22 LR rimfire automatic pistol resembled the Frommer "Stop", with a similar tubular receiver and frame-mounted external hammer. However, the mechanism was pure blowback. The date of production remains unclear, as the design ought to suggest the 1920s, but the condition of the only specimen viewed suggested the 1950s.

WYATT-IMTHURN

In 1959, Kenneth Wyatt and Elmer Imthurn patented a 45-caliber version of the Parabellum (Luger) pistol with an integral butt magazine. The patent was licensed to the Cascade Cartridge Company and the gun was made as the "Target Luger". However, work stopped after no more than 50 had been made.

ZARAGOZA ARMS FACTORY

Fabrica de Armas de Zaragoza, Mexico Pueblo, Mexico.
Little is known of this gunmaking company that manufactured two pistols in 1950-60. Both were 22LR copies of the Colt M1911/A1 so far as the external appearance went, though under the skin they were simple fixed-barrel blowback weapons. The *Corla Model 1* had the curved backstrap and rebated trigger area of the M1911A1 and was about 6 inches long overall; the *Corla Model 2* was somewhat larger and had the straight backstrap of the M1911 pistol, though still with the rebated trigger area. Both had functioning grip safeties, and both were of good quality. About 65 of Model 1 and 400 of Model 2 are said to have been made.

ZASTAVA ARMS

Voini Techniki Zavod ("VTZ"), later Zavodi Crvena Zastava ("ZCZ"); Kragujevac, Yugoslavia/Serbia.
The Serbian state arms factory was created in the early 1900s with assistance from Fabrique Nationale d'Armes de Guerre. It has continued to function ever since, changing ownership with the political shifts of the area. Today it is known as "Zavodi Crvena Zastava" or, since 1989 and in the English-language commercial market, "Zastava Arms". Crvena Zastava has used a "CZ" monogram trademark that is virtually identical to that used by Česká Zbrojovka of Czechoslovakia, which sometimes causes confusion.

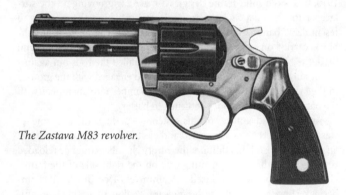

The Zastava M83 revolver.

∼ REVOLVER ∼

Magnum Model 83 This 1983-vintage gun that was broadly based on Smith & Wesson lines was a solid-frame double action with a side-opening six-chamber cylinder, in 357 Magnum caliber. It can also fire the 38 Special cartridge and, using an adapter, can chamber the 9mm Parabellum rimless round as well.

∼ AUTOMATIC PISTOLS ∼

Yovanovicz (or Yovanovich) This was the factory's first venture into the pistol field, appearing in 1931. It looked like a cross between a Browning 1910 and an Astra, having a thin upright butt and a tapering slide above that. The slide covered the barrel and contained the coaxial recoil spring in place. A screwed cap at the rear of the slide held the separate bolt in position and acted as a slide retention device; removing the cap allowed the slide to be pushed forward after the bolt had been removed.

The standard Yovanovicz was in 9mm Short chambering and was issued to the Yugoslavian army in small numbers. It is believed that it was also made in 7.65mm for use by Police and Frontier Guards. Very few have ever been seen outside Yugoslavia.

Model 57 No more pistol manufacture was undertaken until the early 1950s when, under new management, it produced this gun, the Yugoslav terminology for the Soviet Tokarev TT-33.

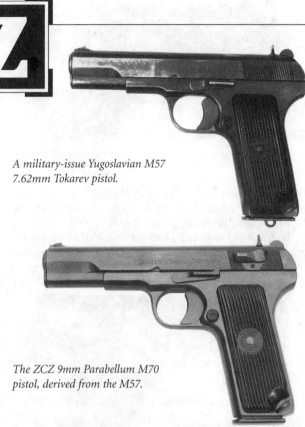

A military-issue Yugoslavian M57 7.62mm Tokarev pistol.

The ZCZ 9mm Parabellum M70 pistol, derived from the M57.

Model 70 (1) When the military requirement was satisfied, the factory converted the design to fire 9mm Parabellum cartridges and placed it on the commercial market as the "Model 70". This was later improved into the Model 70A by adding a manual safety catch on the slide.

Model 70 (2) Next came a downsizing in caliber and, confusingly, another "Model 70", this time a blowback automatic in 7.65mm Auto. Of smaller size, it generally follows the lines of the Tokarev though with a more curved butt.

- *Model 70k* This was a variant of the M70 (2) chambered for the 9mm Short cartridge. Confusion is made worse by the fact that the 7.65mm model had also been seen marked "Model 67" — possibly a factory designation that changed when the gun was adopted by the armed forces.

The ZCZ M88A, another Tokarev-inspired design.

Model 88A The next innovation was a new automatic pistol. This is a reduced-size version of the 9mm Parabellum M70 design and still reflects its Tokarev ancestry, though being much more smooth in outline, with a finger rest on the bottom of the magazine and a slide-mounted safety catch.

The ZCZ 99, a modern double-action design in 9mm Parabellum.

ZCZ99 This, the most recent product, is a 9mm double-action locked-breech automatic pistol that has every appearance of having used the SIG P220 series as its inspiration. It differs in having the slide riding outside the frame and in having a well-curved wooden butt, but the remainder of the outline shows the SIG influence; and it has a similar type of Sauer de-cocking lever beneath the left grip.

The 6.35mm (25 ACP) Zehna pistol.

The 25-caliber Zehna partly dismantled.

ZEHNER
E. Zehner Waffenfabrik, Suhl, Germany.
A 6.35mm blowback pistol developed by Emil Zehner was made in 1921-6. It is sometimes confused with the Haenel-made Schmeisser, but, although the appearance is similar, they are very different in construction.

Zehna The barrel is located in the frame by a cylindrical peg beneath the chamber that goes into a hole in the frame. The peg has a hole bored through it, as does that part of the frame, and the recoil-spring guide rod passes through to lock barrel and frame together. This guide rod ends in a plate beneath the muzzle, with a secondary locating peg fitting into a small hole in the frame. By pulling this plate out, against the pressure of the spring, and turning it so as to rest the peg on the face of the frame, the barrel is freed and can be lifted from the open-top slide.

The second unusual feature is that the backstrap is a separate unit and can be removed, together with the sear and mainspring, by removing the safety catch, hinging the strap backwards and driving out a pivot pin at the heel of the butt. Apart from these features, the design is quite simple.

Early models have "Zehna" on the left side of the slide in flowing script above "D.R.G.M." and were of mediocre quality. The grips have an "EZ" monogram in an oval cartouche. After about 5000 guns had been made, the barrel-attachment system was altered and the slide mark became "… "ZEHNA" CAL. 6,35 D.R.P.a. E. ZENHER SUHL" (in a single line) and quality improved. The grips still had the "EZ" monogram. Total production has been estimated at about 20,000 pistols.

ZOLI
Antonio Zoli, Gardone Val Trompia, Italy.
Marketed in the 1950s under the Zoli name, this pistol was actually the Tanfoglio "Sata" (q.v.) under a sales name.

ZULAICA
M. Zulaica y Cia, Eibar, Spain.
This company began in the early 1900s with the usual Velo-Dog revolvers, but in 1905 patented an unusual automatic revolver of which few were made and even fewer have survived. They then went on to turn out the inevitable "Eibar" automatics during World War I and continued to make them through the 1920s.

∼ AUTOMATIC REVOLVER ∼
Zulaica Patented by Zulaica in 1905 and produced between 1907 and 1910, this was a solid-frame design with zig-zag grooving on the surface of the cylinder and the frame built up behind the cylinder to resemble a "hammerless" design. The extension contained a breech-block, carried on rods, behind the uppermost chamber. When the gun fired, the block was blown backwards and pulled the rods out against springs in the frame. A stud on the lower rod engaged with the grooves in the cylinder, rotating the next loaded chamber into alignment with the barrel as the breechblock returned to battery.

Among the advantages of this system — perhaps the only one — was that the breechblock extracted and ejected the empty case, just like an automatic pistol. In addition, the empty chamber could be reloaded between shots through a pivoting gate on the right side of the frame. Guns of this type were produced in 5.5mm Velo-Dog and 22 LR chamberings. However, though the design was ingenious, it was clumsy compared with the pocket automatics and failed to prosper.

∼ AUTOMATIC PISTOLS ∼
Note: it has been claimed that another "Royal", a copy of the Mauser C/96 in both semi-automatic and selective-fire versions, was also a Zulaica product. However, research has shown that these were made by Beistegui Hermanos (q.v.) and that Zulaica was nothing other than a distributor.

Royal The original pistols of this name, in 6.35mm and 7.65mm, were blowbacks introduced in 1912-14. Though little more than copies of the 1903-type FN-Browning, they did have some original features. The 6.35mm had a sliding latch on the left side of the frame immediately ahead of the grip and a trigger guard that was almost circular. The 7.65mm pattern had a short butt that was raked much more sharply than most guns of this genre. The safety catch lay on the left rear side of the frame.

Markings on the left side of the slide usually included "THE "ROYAL" PATENT" over "— AUTOMATIC PISTOL — CAL. 6,35", with a trademark of "Z" on a crowned shield on the left rear, accompanied by "TRADE MARK" (above) and "NOVELTY" (below). The Royal name and the trademark were repeated on the grips.

The guns made during World War I (see "Zulaica", below) were commonplace 7.65mm-caliber "Eibars" of the so-called Ruby pattern

The 7.65mm (32-caliber) Zulaica Royal pistol, with an unusually long barrel and an elongated butt accepting an 11-round single-column magazine.

but were offered for sale commercially after 1918 in cosmetically improved forms. The most obvious change concerned the retraction grips, which were milled vertically, and greater attention was paid to finish. One post-war long-barrel/long-slide version even had a 12-round magazine. The blowback Royals of Ruby type were usually marked "CAL. 7^{65} MODEL AUTOMATIC PISTOL" over "ROYAL" on the left side of the slide, with "ROYAL" on the grips. The safety catch lies on the left side of the frame above and behind the trigger.

Vincitor Offered in 6.35mm and 7.65mm, these guns were based on Browning designs: the 6.35mm version on the FN-Browning of 1906 and the 7.65mm gun on the FN-Browning of 1903. They were apparently put on the market in 1914 but had soon been supplanted by the wartime "Zulaica" pattern. Some 6.35mm Auto guns have been seen marked "SA ROYAL VINCITOR" but most are marked simply "AUTOMATIC PISTOL CAL. 6^{35} "VINCITOR"…" on the left side of the slide, and may have the safety-catch surround marked in French. One of the larger examples reportedly displays "<7^{65} 1914 MODEL AUTOMATIC PISTOL>" over "<"VINCITOR" PATENT>" on the left side of the slide and has the Vincitor name repeated on the grips. However, it also bears what appears to be an encircled "AV" monogram on the grips, and the attribution to Zulaica needs to be satisfactorily authenticated.

Zulaica This name will be found on standard "Eibar" 7.65mm pistols with nine-round magazines, made for French and Italian army contracts in 1915-16. They have wood grips, lanyard rings on the left side of the butt-heel and prominent fixed sights. The retraction grooves are usually milled radially, and the left side of the slide is usually marked "<7^{65} 1914 MODEL AUTOMATIC PISTOL>" over "M. ZULAICA & Co • EIBAR". A small "ZC" in an oval, for "ZULAICA Y CIA", will be found on the left rear of the frame; the safety catch above the trigger may be marked in French or English.

APPENDIX I
The Pistol Databank

Name or model. The databank in the previous edition was organized on strictly alphabetical lines, which listed, for example, the Smith & Wesson Model 10 under "S". This made it difficult to use and also duplicated the alphabetical layout of the pistol directory. This new version has attempted to extract (for example) all guns known as "Model" — usually, but not invariably military — in the hope that this makes service-issue pistols and revolvers easier to locate. Many were made by more than one manufacturer, confusing identification.

Maker/entry/origin. This usually refers to the entry in which information will be found and <u>not</u> necessarily the actual manufacturer. It should be used in conjunction with the page number in the last column.

Type. A brief indication of construction: <u>A</u>, automatic pistol, <u>M</u>, repeating or multi-shot pistol; <u>R</u>, revolver; <u>S</u>, single-shot pistol.

Caliber/chambering. Some guns are naturally available in a variety of calibers or chamberings, and the Databank may contain information about only a single variant.

Dimensions. Handguns are often made over a period of years, and tolerances (weight, particularly) may vary. This is often true of guns made in wartime by a variety of contractors, when raw material may be scarce. It must be remembered that virtually all automatic pistols can accept an extra cartridge in the chamber and that their capacities are actually "7+1" instead of "7".

Name or Model	Maker/entry/origin	Type	Caliber, chambering	Length in	Weight oz	Barrel in	Rifling	Ctg Cap	Remarks	Page
A25	Sundance Industries	A	25ACP	4.88	13.90	2.00		7		N/A
A50	Astra-Unceta	A	380ACP	6.61	22.90	3.50	6R	7	also 8-shot 32ACP	23
A60	Astra-Unceta	A	380ACP	6.61	24.70	3.50	6R	13	also 12-shot 32ACP	23
A70	Astra-Unceta	A	9Par	6.54	29.63	3.50	6R	7		24
A75	Astra-Unceta	A	9Par	6.54	31.0	3.50	5T	8	also 40 S&W	24
A80	Astra-Unceta	A	9Par	7.10	34.75	3.92	6R	15	double action	24
A90	Astra-Unceta	A	9Par	7.10	34.75	3.92	6R	15	also 45ACP	24
A100	Astra-Unceta	A	9Par	7.10	35.0	3.80	6R	15	also 9-shot 45ACP	24
AA	Azanza y Arrizabalaga	A	32ACP	6.10	20.63	3.42	5R	9	"M1916"	26
AAA	A Aldazabal	A	32ACP	5.92	20.11	3.45	5R	7	"M1919"	11
Ace	Colt	A	22LR	8.5	38.97	4.7		10		85
Acha	D. Acha	A	32ACP	6.1	20.1	3.35		7	"M1916"	10
Acme	Hopkins & Allen	R	32	6.3		2.75	5R	5	"No. 1", hammerless	171
Acme	Hopkins & Allen	R	38	6.77		3.0	6R	5		171
Action	M. Santos	A	25ACP	4.33	10.4	1.96		6	"M1920"	274
Action No 2	M. Santos	A	32ACP	5.83	19.4	3.27		7	"M1915"	274
Adams	Adams	R	450cf	10.03	37.07	6.0	6R	6	representative specimen	10
Adler	Adlerwaffenwerke	A	7Adl	8.19	24.16	3.35	6R	8		10
Aetna	Aetna	R	22rf	6.5		3		7	S&W No 1 copy.	11
Aetna	Harrington & Richardson	R	32rf	5.51		2.36		5	"No.1"; S&W No 1 copy	153
Aetna	Harrington & Richardson	R	32rf	6.70		2.50	5R	5	"No. 2"; S&W No 1? copy	153
Aetna	Harrington & Richardson	R	32rf	6.60		2.43	5R	5	"No. 2?"; saw-handle grip	153
Agent	Colt	R	38Spl	6.73	14.46	2.125		6		78
Agent Lightweight	Colt	R	38Spl	6.75	17.0	2.125		6	variant of Detective Special	78
Aircrewman	Colt	R	38Spl	6.73	14.0	2.125		6	variant of Cobra	78
Aircrew Model	Kimball	A	30Crb	8.0	28.92	3.5		7		189
Airweight	Smith & Wesson	R	38	6.89	18.00	2.125		6	M&P Airweight or "Model 12"	297
A.J. Aubrey	Meriden Arms	R	32				5R	5	top break, DA, also in 38	227
Alamo Ranger	Spanish	R	38	10.47	29.10	5.36	6R	6	"M1929"; Colt-type	354
Alaska	Hood	R	22rf					7		170
Aldazabal	Aldazabal, Leturondo	A	32ACP	6.10	20.81	3.46		7		11
Alert	Hood	R	22rf	5.31	13.58	2.24	5L	7	"M1874"	170
Alfa	A.L. Frank	M	22rf					4	four superposed barrels	129
Alfa	Armas Especialistas	R	38	9.64	28.57	4.7		6	Colt Police Positive copy	19
Alfa	Armas Especialistas	R	38	8.86	21.35	4.66		6	S&W M&P copy	19
Alfa	Armas Especialistas	R	44	8.85	29.10	4.0		5	S&W top-break copy	19
Alkar	Alkartasuna	A	25ACP	4.40	10.58	2.16		7	"M1914"	11
Alkar	Alkartasuna	A	25ACP	4.84	11.64	2.09		7	"M1924"	11
Alkar	Alkartasuna	A	32ACP	6.30	20.63	3.26		9	"M1914"	11
Alkartasuna	Armas de Fuego	A	32ACP	5.90	23.45	3.30		7		19
All American	Colt	A	9Par	7.48	29.00	4.50	6R	15	"M2000"	86
Allies	Bersaluze, Arieto-Aurtena	A	25ACP	4.41	10.75	2.16		6		48
American Bulldog	Johnson, Bye	R	22rf			2.45		5	other barrel lengths	186
American Bulldog	Johnson, Bye	R	32rf			3.0		5	other barrel lengths	186
American Bulldog	Johnson, Bye	R	38rf			4.40		5	also in center-fire	186
American Model	Smith & Wesson	R	44	13.40	41.00	8.00		6	1st Model, SA	288
American Model	Smith & Wesson	R	44	11.88	39.85	6.50		6	2nd Model, SA	288
AMR	Bernardelli	A	380ACP	8.98	25.40	6.9	6R	7	long-barrel M60l	46
Anaconda	Colt	R	44 Mag	11.61	52.40	6.0		6		81
AP	Fegyver	A	32ACP	6.8	21	3.93	6R	8	commercial PA-63	123
AP	Walther Waffenfabrik	A	9Par	8.50	27.80	4.50	6R	8	"Armee-Pistole"	364

Name or Model	Maker/entry/origin	Type	Caliber, chambering	Length in	Weight oz	Barrel in	Rifling	Ctg Cap	Remarks	Page
AP66	Fegyver	A	32ACP	7.10	20.80	3.93		8	"Hege AP66"	N/A
Apache	Ojanguren y Vidosa	A	25ACP	4.40	13.60	2.12		7		243
Apache	Garantazada	R	38	10.0	30.33	4.92		6	Colt Police Positive copy	114
Apache	Dolne	R	7pf	8.0	12.52	0		5	with knife and knuckleduster	102
Apaolozo	Apaolozo	R	38	9.65	28.92	4.70		6	Colt Police Positive copy	15
Arico	N. Pieper	A	25ACP	4.61	13.22	2.55		6	Pieper 1909 type	251
Arizaga	G. Arizaga	A	32ACP	6.50	21.87	3.75		8		16
Arizmendi	F. Arizmendi	R	32ACP	5.90	21.34	2.16		5	folding trigger	17
Arminius	Pickert (Arminius)	R							see under model numbers	
Arminius	Pickert (Arminius)	S	22XLrf	13.77	31.75	10.0		1	"TP-1"	248
Arminius	Pickert (Arminius)	S	22XLrf	15.75	33.50	11.80		1	"TP-2"; set trigger	248
Armscor	Arms Corp. of Philippines	R	38Spl	7.36	22.0	2.50		6	"M200D"; also 22LR, 22WMR	20
Armscor	Arms Corp. of Philippines	R	38Spl	8.85	25.90	4.0		6	"M200P"	20
Army Belt Model	Hopkins & Allen	R	44	11.00	47.25	7.00		6	DA; "Merwin & Hulbert"	228
Army Express	Webley	R	476	10.62	35.50	5.50	7R	6	SA	375
Army Express	Webley	R	450	11.00	34.00	6.00	7R	6	DA	378
Army Model	Langenhan	A	32ACP	6.61	23.65	4.13		8	or "FL-Selbstlader"	197
Army Pocket Model	Hopkins & Allen	R	44	8.00	37.40	3.94		6	DA; "Merwin & Hulbert"	228
Army Special	Colt	R	38	9.85	34.0	4.50		6	also in 32 caliber	77
Army Target	Webley	R	455	13.50	40.75	7.50	7R	6		380
Ariola	Arriola	R	38	10.40	30.15	4.70		6	Colt Police Positive copy	20
Arrizabalaga	Arrizabalaga	A	32ACP	6.0	21.70	3.45		7		20
Arsena Makarov	Arsenal (Bulgaria)	A	9Mak	6.34	25.74	3.66	4R	8	Russian Makarov copy	N/A
Ascaso	Spanish Republican	A	9BB	9.25	31.05	5.90		8	Astra 400 copy	21
Asiatic	Spanish	A	25ACP	4.48	10.58	1.96		6		354
AT9	Accutek	A	9Par	6.33	28.0	3.18		7		9
AT25SS	Accutek	A	25ACP		11.0					9
AT32SS	Accutek	A	32ACP							9
AT380SS	Accutek	A	380ACP	5.61	19.9	2.75		5	based on Walther TPH	9
AT40SS	Accutek	A	40S&W							9
ATCSA	Arnas de Tiro y Casa	R	38	9.84	29.27	4.70	6R	5		N/A
Atlas	D. Acha	A	25ACP	4.52	13.0	2.28		6		10
Audax	MAPF/Unique	A	25ACP	4.48	10.22	2.17		6	or "Unique Model 11"	205,206
Audax	MAPF/Unique	A	32ACP	6.10	20.10	3.82		7	or "Unique Model 19"	205,207
Aurora	Spanish	A	25ACP	4.33	10.22	1.97		6	Browning 1906 copy	354
Aussie Model	American Arms	A	9Par					10	Polymer frame; also 40S&W	13
Autogarde	Société Française des Munitions	R	32ACP					5	hammerless, folding trigger	315
Auto-Mag	Various	A	44AMag	11.50	57.0	6.50	8L	7	various barrels, calibers	N/A
Auto-Mag II	Arcadia Machine & Tool	A	22WMR	9.33	23.0	6.0	8R	10	also 3.2in and 4.5in barrels	16
Auto-Mag III	Arcadia Machine & Tool	A	30Crb	10.52	43.0	6.34	6R	8		16
Auto-Mag IV	Arcadia Machine & Tool	A	10Mag		46.0	6.5		6	Also in 45WinMag	16
Automaster	Sokolovsky	A	45ACP	9.50	57.50	6.0		6		315
Automatic Model	Hopkins & Allen	R	32	6.50		3.00		5		171
Automatic Model	Smith & Wesson	A	32ACP	6.50	22.00	3.50		7	1913; based on Clément	306
Automatic Model	Smith & Wesson	A	35SW	6.50	22.00	3.50		7		306
Automatique Francaise	Soc. Française des Armes…	A	25ACP	4.70	11.11	2.60		6		315
Auto Stand	Manufrance	S	22LR					1	bolt action	210
Avion	Azpiri	A	25ACP	4.50	10.58	2.12	4R	6		26
Azul	E. Arostegui	A	7.63Msr	12.40	43.48	5.50	6R	10	Mauser C/96 copy	20
Azul	E. Arostegui	A	7.63Msr	11.22	43.90	5.12	6R	10	"MM31"; selective fire	20
Azul	E. Arostegui	A	25ACP	4.50	10.75	2.0	4R	6	Eibar type; also 32ACP	20
Azul	E. Arostegui	A	25ACP	4.70	11.30	2.17	4R	7	external hammer; also 32ACP	20
B-76	Benelli	A	9Par	8.08	34.22	4.25		8	also in 7.65Para	30
Baby	Fémáru	A	32ACP	4.70	17.63	2.17		5	"Frommer Baby"	125
Baby Browning	Fabrique Nationale	A	25ACP	4.0	9.70	1.96	6R	6		115
Baby Hammerless	Kolb	R	22rf	5.03		1.75		5	1896 pattern; also 5-shot 32	192
Baby Hammerless	Kolb	R	22rf	4.70		1.5		5	1910 pattern	192
Bany Hammerless	Kolb	R	22rf	4.57		1.5		5	1918 pattern	192
Baby Hammerless	Kolb	R	22rf	4.13		1.5		5	1921 pattern	192
Baby Hammerless	Kolb	R	22rf			1.5		5	1924 pattern	192
Back-Up	Arcadia Machine & Tool	A	380ACP	4.25	17.98	2.52	6L	5		16
Bacon Gem	Bacon	R	22rf			1.25		5	ca 1878	27
Ballester Molina	Hafdasa	A	45ACP	8.98	40.21	5.0	6L	7	Colt M1911A1 copy	169
Bang Up	Bacon	R	22rf	6.41		2.63	3L	5	also in 32rf	27
Banker's Special	Colt	R	38Spl	6.89	22.92	2.12		6		77
Banker's Special	Colt	R	22LR	6.89	19.0	2.12		6		77
Bär	Sauer	P	7Bär	5.90	12.20	2.36	4R	2	two-barrel rotating block	274
Barracuda	Fabrique Nationale	R	357 Mag	8.0	36.15	2.95		6	optional 9Par cylinder	115
Barrenechea	Barrenechea y Gallastegui	R	38	10.43	28.57	4.88		6	S&W M&P copy	28
Basculant	Aguirre	A	25ACP	4.52	10.92	2.4		7		11
Basque	Echave y Arizmendi	A	32ACP	6.29	24.00	3.19		7	also sold as "Echasa"	104
Bauer	Bauer	A	25ACP	4.0	10.0	2.12		6	Baby Browning copy	29
Bayard	H. Pieper (AÉP)	A	25ACP	4.84	14.80	2.16		6	1908 type	250
Bayard	H. Pieper (AÉP)	A	32ACP	4.92	16.57	2.24		5	1910 type	250
Bayard	H. Pieper (AÉP)	A	380ACP	4.92	15.87	2.24		5	1911 type	250

Name or Model	Maker/entry/origin	Type	Caliber, chambering	Length in	Weight oz	Barrel in	Rifling	Ctg Cap	Remarks	Page
Bayard	H. Pieper (AÉP)	A	25ACP	4.80	12.0	2.20		5	1912 type	250
Bayard	H. Pieper (AÉP)	A	32ACP	5.75	19.92	2.20		6	1923 type	250
Bayard	H. Pieper (AÉP)	A	32ACP	5.70	12.0	2.20		6	1930 type	250
BC	Bernedo	A	25ACP	4.49	13.0	2.12		6		47
BDA9	Fabrique Nationale	A	9Par	7.87	32.28	4.65	6R	14	replaced earlier BDA9	115
BDA9C	Fabrique Nationale	A	9Par	7.00	23.45	3.78		7	DA, short frame	115
BDA9M	Fabrique Nationale	A	9Par	7.00	26.28	3.78		14	DA, short barrel	115
BDA9S	Fabrique Nationale	A	9Par	7.87	29.45	4.65		14	DA version of GP35	116
BDAO	Fabrique Nationale	A	9Par	7.87	30.68	4.65	6R	14	DAO	116
Bearcat	Sturm, Ruger	R	22LR	8.86	17.0	4.0		6		329
Beholla	Becker & Hollander	A	32ACP	5.51	22.5	2.88	6R	7		29
Beistegui	Beistegui	A	32ACP	6.14	18.34	3.5		9	"M1914"	30
Bekeart Model	Smith & Wesson	R	22LR	11.02	26.75	6.00		6	Hand Ejector; "K22/32"	289
Benemerita	Ortega de Seija	A	25ACP	4.48	10.58	2.12		6	"M1916"; by Aldazabal?	244
Bergmann-Bayard	H. Pieper (AÉP)	A	9 B-B	9.84	35.80	4.02	6R	6	"M1908"	250
Bergmann-Bayard	H. Pieper (AÉP)	A	9 B-B	9.84	35.80	4.02	6R	10	"M1910"	250
Bergmann	Bergmann	A	25ACP	4.65	14.76	2.17	6R	6	"Model 2"	42
Bergmann	Bergmann	A	25ACP	4.72	16.75	2.17	6R	9	"Model 3"	42
Bergmann-Erben	Bergmann	A	32ACP	6.22	26.20	3.35	6R	8	rebadged Menz PB Special	43
Bergmann-Erben	Bergmann	A	25ACP	4.88	14.50	2.60	6R	7		43
Bernadon-Martin	Bernadon-Martin	A	32ACP	6.0	23.98	3.54		7	or "Hermetic"	45
Bernedo	Bernedo	A	25ACP	4.52	8.88	1.96		7		47
Bernedo	Bernedo	A	32ACP	6.10	20.63	3.39		7		47
BH	Bestegui	R	38	10.63	30.0	5.75		6	S&W M&P copy	30
Big Deuce	Safari Arms	A	45ACP	9.68		6.00		7	M1911A1 clone	272
Bijou	Debouxtay	R	25ACP					5	Velo-Dog pattern	95
Bijou	Menz	A	25ACP	4.10	10.23	2.0	6R	6	or "Liliput"	226
Bisley	Colt	R	38-40WCF	12.52	40.56	7.50		6	many calibers, barrel lengths	72
Bisley Dakota	EMF	R	45LColt	10.50	37.00	5.50	6R	6	Colt Bisley replica	105
Bisley Target	Webley	R	450cf	13.50	39.00	7.50	7R	6	Bisley Target	380
Bittner	Bittner	M	7.7Bitt	11.81	30.16	6.02		6	representative specimen	49
BL9	Accutek	A	9Par	5.63	22.0	3.0		5	XL9 is similar	9
Blackhawk	Sturm, Ruger	R	357Mag	12.25	42.0	6.50		6		330
Bland	Bland	R	577	10.63	49.0	5.50		5	representative specimen	49
Bloodhound	Hopkins & Allen	R	22rf	5.20		2.20		7		171
Blue Jackett	Hopkins & Allen	R	22rf	5.20		2.20	3L, 5L	5	"No. 1"; "No 2" in 32rf	171
Bodyguard	Smith & Wesson	R	38	6.30	20.45`	2.12		5	or "Model 49"	301
Bodyguard Airweight	Smith & Wesson	R	38	6.30	15.0	2.12		5	or "Model 38"	300
Bodyguard Stainless	Smith & Wesson	R	38Spl	6.25	19.92	2.12		5	or "Model 649"	305
Boix	Spanish	A	32ACP	5.90	20.81	3.35	4T	7	Eibar-type blowback	N/A
Boltun	F. Arizmendi	A	25ACP	5.12	12.52	2.44	6R	6	resembles Pieper pistol	17
Boltun	F. Arizmendi	A	32ACP	5.83	20.46	2.55	6R	6	resembles Pieper pistol	17
Boltun	Bolumburu	A	32ACP	5.97	34.40	3.50	4R	9	Eibar-type blowback	N/A
Bonanza	Bacon	R	22rf					7		27
Boot Gun	Freedom Arms	R	22WMR	5.90	5.0	3.0		4		130
Borchardt	DWM; Loewe	A	7.65Bor	10.98	41.60	6.50	4R	8	"C/93"	97
Border Patrol	Colt	R	38	8.86	39.0	4.0		6		78
Boston Bulldog	Johnson, Bye	R	22rf			2.50		7	DA; also 32, 38 calibers	186
Brigadier	Beretta	A	9Par	8.00	31.39	4.53	6R	8	or "Model 951"	38
Brigadier	North American Arms Corp.	A	45NAA	9.65	66.85	5.50		8	special chambering	235
Bristol	Bolumburu	A	32ACP	6.10	21.52	3.46		9	Eibar-type blowback	50
British Bulldog	Forehand & Wadsworth	R	32	6.50		2.52	5R	7	also 6-shot 38, 5-shot 44.	128
British Bulldog	Johnson, Bye	R	38					5		186
British Bulldog	Belgian	R	500cf	5.75	24.50	2.68		5	also 44S&W, 450cf	353
Brixia	Metallurgica Bresciana	A	9Gli	7.68	28.75	3.54		7	or "M1912"	228
Brompetier	Retolaza	R	25ACP	4.10		1.50		5	Velo-Dog type; also 32ACP	260
Bronco	Echave & Arizmendi	R	25ACP	4.41	13.40	2.16		6	"M1918"; also 32ACP	104
Broncho	Errasti	A	32ACP	5.51	20.63	2.75		6	Browning 1906 copy	110
Bron Grand	Ormachea	R	5VD	6.50		2.75		5	Velo-Dog type	244
Brong Petit	Crucelegui	R	25ACP	4.33		1.41		5	Velo-Dog type	92
Bron Sport	Crucelegui	R	25ACP	4.33		1.65		5	Velo-Dog type	92
Brow	Ojanguren y Marcaiso	R	25ACP	4.70		1.85		5	Velo-Dog type	242
Brownie	Mossberg	M	22rf	4.50	10.00	2.50		4	four barrels	231
Browning 380	Fabrique Nationale	A	380ACP	7.48	22.93	4.40		9	improved M1910/22	122
Browreduit	Arostegui	R	25ACP	5.31		1.88		5	Velo-Dog type	20
Brunswig	Unceta	A	32ACP	5.70	21.26	3.23	6R	9	sales name for early Astra	112
Brutus	Hood	R	22rf					7		170
Bryco Model 38	Jennings	A	380ACP	5.31	15.0	2.80	6R	6	"M38"; also 22LR, 32ACP	183
Bryco Model 48	Jennings	A	380ACP	6.70	19.0	3.97	6R	6	"M48"; also 22LR , 32ACP	183
BSA	BSA	A	40BSA	6.34		3.54		7	prototypes only	54
BSW	Berlin-Suhler-Werke	A	9Par	8.27	27.69	4.92		8	prototypes only	43
Buckhorn	Uberti	R	357 Mag	11.22	43.91	5.75		6	many variations	352
Buck Mark	Browning	A	22LR	9.49	31.92	5.50	6R	10		52
Budischwsky TP-70	Korriphila	A	25ACP	4.65	12.34	2.60		6		194
Bufalo	Gabilondo y Urresti	A	25ACP	4.70	13.75	2.28	4R	6	"M1920"	132
Bufalo	Gabilondo y Urresti	A	32ACP	6.73	22.33	3.35	4T	7	also 380ACP	132

Name or Model	Maker/entry/origin	Type	Caliber, chambering	Length in	Weight oz	Barrel in	Rifling	Ctg Cap	Remarks	Page
Buffalo Stand	Manufrance	S	22rf	16.54	43.85	11.81		-	bolt-action	210
Buhag	Buchsenmacher…	A	22rf	11.81	29.27	7.87		5	"Olympiamodell"	55
Bul Standard	Transmark	A	45ACP	8.75	340.00	4.25		13	also 18-shot 9Par	347
Bulldog	Charter Arms	R	44 Spl	7.48	19.0	3.0		5	also in 357 Mag	63
Bulldog	I. Johnson	R	22LR	7.00	26.10	2.50		8	also in 38Spl	183
Bull Dog	Webley	R	442			4.25		6	"No. 1? Bull Dog"	374
Bulldog Pug	Charter Arms	R	44 Spl	7.25	19.0	2.55		5		63
Bulldog Tracker	Charter Arms	R	357 Mag	8.70		4.0		5	also with 2.5 or 6in barrels	63
Bull Dozer	Norwich Pistol Co.	R	44rf	7.00		2.96	5R	5	also 22rf, 38rf and 41rf	237
Bullfighter	Belgian	R	7.62Nag	5.31		1.96		5		353
Bullseye	USA	R	22rf	6.0		2.25		7	typical "Suicide Special"	353
Bulwark	Beistegui	A	25ACP	4.52	10.58	2.0		6	Eibar-type blowbck	30
Bulwark	Beistegui	A	25ACP	4.65		2.40		6	copy of early Star design	30
Bulwark	Beistegui	A	32ACP	6.88	30.51	4.33		8		30
Bulwark	Grande Précision	A	25ACP	4.53	10.23	2.0		6	made by Beistegui	30
Buntline Special	Colt	R	45 Colt	17.52	44.10	12.0		6	10in and 16in barrels	79
Burgham Superior	MAPF/Unique	A	25ACP	4.13	12.87	2.08		7	or "Unique Model 10"	206
Burgham Superior	Spanish	A	25ACP	4.53	10.23	2.00		8	Eibar-type blowback	354
Burgo	Burgsmüller	R	22LR	6.10	11.65	2.25	8R	6	actually Röhm RG-10	55
C/06-08	Mauser	A	9MsrE	11.61		4.33		6		217
C/78	Mauser	R	9cf	10.63	26.45	5.35		6	"Zig-Zag"; also 10.6Ger	214
C/96	Mauser	A	7.63Msr	11.00	39.86	4.76		10	many variants	215
C/96	Mauser	A	7.63Msr	9.88	36.68	3.93		10	1912 type	215
C/96	Mauser	A	9Par	11.65	39.50	5.51		10	1916 type; or "Red Nine"	215
C/96	Mauser	A	7.63Msr	9.88	36.85	3.89		10	1920 type	215
C/96	Mauser	A	7.63Msr	11.26	40.56	5.24		10	1930 type	215
C/96	Mauser	A	7.63Msr	11.34	45.33	5.24		10	1932 type; also 20-shot	215
Cadet	Colt	A	22LR	8.58	32.80	4.48		11		87
Cadet	Coonan Arms	A	357Mag	6.81	38.80	3.46		6	based on Colt M1911A1	91
Cadix	Astra-Unceta	R	22LR	8.94	25.94	4.00		8		21
Cadix	Astra-Unceta	R	32	8.94	25.05	4.00		6		21
Cadix	Astra-Unceta	R	38	8.94	23.98	4.00		6		21
Caminal	Spanish	A	32ACP	5.51	21.0	3.38		7	Eibar-type blowback	N/A
Campeon	Arrizabalaga	A	32ACP	4.70	20.80	2.48		7	also 25ACP.	20
Camper	Astra-Unceta	A	22LR	4.53	15.87	3.97		6	long-barreled Astra 2000	23
Campo-Giro	Esperanza y Unceta	A	9BB	9.33	33.51	6.50		9	M1913; M1913/16 is similar	112
Camp Perry	Colt	S	22LR	14.0	34.56	10.0		1		69
Cantabria	Garate Brothers	A	25ACP	4.40	10.58	2.05		5	Eibar-type blowback	138
Cantabria	Garate Brothers	R	32ACP	5.12		2.16		5	and other calibers	138
Capitain	MAPF/Unique	A	25ACP	4.10	12.52	2.12		7	various Unique models	206
Captain Jack	Hopkins & Allen	R	22rf	5.12		2.20	3 or 5	5	rifling may be left or right	171
Ca-Si	Spanish	A	32ACP	5.31	20.63	2.75		7	Eibar-type blowback	146
Casull	Freedom Arms	R	454 Cas	14.0	49.91	7.5		5	also 45LColt, 44Mag	130
Category 9	Intratec	A	9Par	5.75	17.65	3.00		8		176
Cattleman	Uberti	R	357Mag	13.0	40.92	7.48		6	also 44Mag	352
Cebra	Arizmendi, Zulaica	A	32ACP	6.10	21.34	3.35		9	Eibar-type blowback	18
Cebra	Arizmendi, Zulaica	R	38	8.74	20.28	3.94		6	Colt Police Positive copy	18
Celta	Urizar	A	25ACP	4.53	10.76	2.05		6	or "J.Cesar"	357
Centaur	Réunies	A	25ACP	4.70	14.28	2.25		6	or "Dictator"	261
Centennial	Smith & Wesson	R	38	6.50	19.05	2.125		5	or "Model 40"	300
Centennial	Deringer Rifle & Pistol	R	22rf					7	"1876"; also 5-shot 32RF, 38RF	96
Centennial Airweight	Smith & Wesson	R	38	6.50	13.05	2.125		5	or "Model 42"	301
Cesar	MAPF/Unique	A	25ACP	4.13	12.70	2.08		7	or "Unique Mle 10"	206
Cesar	Urizar	A	25ACP	4.52	10.75	2.05		7	Eibar-type blowback	357
CH	Crucelegui	R	38	8.86	20.45	4.13		6	Colt Police Positive copy	92
Challenger	Norwich Falls	R	32rf	6.50		2.75		5		237
Challenger	Fabrique Nationale	A	22LR	8.86	31.92	6.77		10		116
Champion	USA	R	22RF	6.70		2.36		7	also 5-shot 32rf	N/A
Chantecler	MAPF/Unique	A	25ACP	4.13	12.70	2.06		7	or "Unique Model 10"	206
Chanticler	I. Charola	A	25ACP	4.52	10.40	1.97		6	Eibar-type blowback	62
Charola y Anitua	Garate, Anitua	A	5CyA	9.05	20.11	4.09		6	also 7mm CyA	138
Chicago Cub	Reck	R	22LR	4.92		1.89		6	or "Recky"	256
Chicago Protector	Ames	M	32	4.70		1.77		7	US-made Protector	14
Chichester	Hopkins & Allen	R	38rf	14.56		9.85		5		171
Chief Marshal	Hawes	R	44	11.81	44.10	5.90		6	made by Sauer & Sohn	157
Chieftain	Norwich Falls	R	32rf	6.50		2.75		5	also with 2.36in barrel	237
Chief's Special	Smith & Wesson	R	38	6.50	19.05	2.125		5	or "Model 36"	307
Chief's Special Airweight	Smith & Wesson	R	38	6.50	13.93	2.125		5	or "Model 37"	307
Chief's Special Stainless	Smith & Wesson	R	38	6.50	19.05	2.0		5	or "Model 60"	307
Chimère Renoir	MAPF/Unique	A	25ACP	4.13	12.70	2.08		7	or "Unique Model 10"	206
Chuchu	Chuchu	M	22LR					4	four-barrelled block	66
Chylewski	SIG	A	25ACP	4.61	13.27	2.24		6	one-hand cocker	280
Clair	Clair	A	7.7cf	17.32	45.85	6.30		6	c. 1893-95	67
Classic	Wichita Arms	S	308		80.00	11.25		1	bolt action	388
Clément	Neumann	R	38	9.84	29.10	4.70		6	Colt Police Positive copy	234

Name or Model	Maker/entry/origin	Type	Caliber, chambering	Length in	Weight oz	Barrel in	Rifling	Ctg Cap	Remarks	Page
Clément	Clément	A	32ACP	5.90	20.63	2.95		6	1907 type	67
Clément	Clément	A	25ACP	4.52	13.40	2.00		6	1909 type; 1912 similar	67
Clément Fulgor	Neumann	A	32ACP	7.08	25.22	4.33		7	based on Browning M1903	67
Cloverleaf	Colt	R	41rf	6.73	14.46	3.00		4		70
Cobold	Henrion, Dassy & Heuschen	R	9.4cf	7.48		3.15		5	also in 450cf	163
Cobolt	Ancion-Marx	R	450cf					5	also in 320cf	15
Cobra	Colt	R	22LR	7.68	16.93	3.98		6		78
Cobra	Colt	R	38	6.88	15.00	2.125		6		78
Cobra	Spanish	A	32ACP	6.46	29.98	3.35		9	Eibar-type blowback	354
Cody	Cody	A	22LR	7.28		2.45		6		68
Colon	Orbea	R	32	9.25	15.42	4.13		6	"M1925"; Police Positive copy	243
Colon	Azpiri	A	25ACP	4.52	13.23	2.20		8	Eibar-type blowback	26
Colonial	MAPF/Unique	A	25ACP	4.13	12.70	2.08		7	or "Unique Model 10"	206
Colonial	Grande Précision	A	25ACP	4.53	13.75	2.17		6	Eibar-type blowback	146
Colonial	Grande Précision	A	32ACP	6.89	21.34	4.02		9	FN-Browning 1910 copy	146
Columbia(n)	Columbia Armory	R	32	7.28		3.15		5	"New Safety Hammerless"	90
Columbian Automatic	Foehl & Weeks	R	32	7.08		3.38		5	top break, auto-ejecting	127
Columbian DA	New York Arms	R	38	6.91		3.00		5	also in 32	N/A
Comanche	Gabilondo	R	357M	9.25	28.05	4.01		6	"Llama"; also 6in barrel	131
Combat Commander	Colt	A	45ACP	8.00	33.00	4.25		7	also in 38Sup and 9Par	87
CombatMaster	Detonics	A	45ACP	7.75	28.92	4.49		6	M1911A1 adaptation	96
CombatMaster	Detonics	A	45ACP	6.77	25.75	3.50		6	Series II; also 38Sup, 9Par	96
Commando	Colt	R	38	9.25	32.00	4.00		6		78
Concept VII	Baer Custom	A	45ACP	7.75	27.7	4.25		7	many other versions	27
Conqueror	Bacon	R	32rf	6.22		2.36		5	also 7-shot 22rf	27
Constable	Astra-Unceta	A	32ACP	6.60	25.0	3.50	6R	8	or "M5000"; 22LR, 380ACP	23
Constabulary	Ancion-Marx	R	8cf	6.50		3.00		6	and other calibers	15
Constabulary	Raick	R	320	4.02		2.00		5	"Kobold" pattern	255
Contender	Thompson/Center	S	222Rem	13.50	43.00	10.00		1	other calibers and barrels	346
Continental	Bertrand	A	25ACP	4.56	15.00	2.20		7	or "Le Rapide"	49
Continental	Rheinische W&M	A	25ACP	4.72	14.10	2.08		7	Spanish made	264
Continental	Rheinische W&M	A	32ACP	6.69	22.22	3.94		7	Webley & Scott clone	264
Continental	Great Western	R	32rf					5	also 7-shot 22rf	N/A
Continental	Hood	R	32rf			2.83		5	also 7-shot 22rf	170
Continental	Urizar	A	25ACP	4.45	10.93	2.00		5	also 9-shot 32ACP	357
Continental	Urizar	A	25ACP	4.65	11.11	2.00		6	also 32ACP, 380ACP	357
Cop 4 Shot	American Derringer	M	357Mag					4	four barrels in a cluster	13
Corla	Zaragoza	A	22LR	5.90	21.87	3.82		8	"Model 1"	391
Corla	Zaragoza	A	22LR	6.61	23.10	4.52		8	"Model 2"	391
Corrientes	M. Santos	A	32ACP	5.83	20.64	3.30		7	Eibar-type blowback	274
Cosmopolite Oscillatory	Garate, Anitua	R	38	8.46	28.57	4.13		6	Colt Police Positive copy	138
Courier	Colt	R	32	7.75	13.40	3.00		6		78
Courier	Colt	R	22LR	7.75	19.57	3.00		6		78
Courier	Galesi	A	25ACP	4.52	10.05	1.97		6	name used in USA	136
Cow Boy	Spanish	A	25ACP	4.49	10.23	2.16		7	French markings	354
Cowboy Ranger	Unies	R	38					6	Frontier-style SA	356
Crescent	Norwich Pistol Co.	R	32			2.50		5	Also 6-shot	237
Crest Renegade	Safari Arms	A	9Par	8.66	39.50	5.00	6R	9	other calibers	272
Criolla	Hispano-Argentina	A	22LR	8.46	39.15	4.70		10	Colt Ace copy	169
Crucelegui	Crucelegui	A	32ACP	5.90	21.16	3.35		7		20
Crucero	Ojanguren y Vidosa	R	32	9.28	20.28	4.53		5	Colt Police Positive copy	243
Crucero	Ojanguren y Vidosa	A	32ACP	5.43	20.81	2.56		7	Eibar-type blowback	243
CX-22A	American Arms	A	22LR	6.3	22	3.25		8	Based on Walther PPK	13
CZ99	Zastava	A	9Par	6.69	29.45	3.96	6R	15	later became KSN Golan	392
Czar	Hood	R	22rf	7.48		3.15		7	also in 32rf	170
Czar	Hopkins & Allen	R	22rf	7.48		3.15		7		171
DA	Hopkins & Allen	R	32	8.00		4.00		5	"DA No. 6"; solid frame	171
DA38	American Derringer	M	357Mag					2	Also 9Par, 38Spl, 40S&W	13
Dakota Bisley	EMF	R	45LColt	10.50	37.00	5.50	6R	6	Colt Bisley replica	105
Dakota Outlaw	EMF	R	45LColt	13.50	45.00	7.50		6	Remington M1873 replica	106
Dakota Police	EMF	R	45LColt	13.50	45.00	7.50		6	Remington M1890 replica	106
Dakota Single Action	EMF	R	45Colt	10.50	36.15	5.50		6	Colt M1873 replica	106
Danton	Gabilondo	A	32ACP	6.15	24.00	3.38		8	FN-Browning M1910 copy	132
Danton	Gabilondo	A	25ACP	4.53	13.90	2.08		6	"M1925": Eibar blowback	132
Danton	Gabilondo	A	25ACP	4.60	14.46	2.12		6	"M1929": also in 32ACP	132
Dan Wesson	Wesson Firearms	A	45ACP	8.58	38.80	5.00		7	"M1911"	385
Dan Wesson	Wesson Firearms	A	45ACP	8.70	38.80	5.00		7	"Match"; target pistol	385
Dan Wesson	D. Wesson Arms	R	357Mag	9.25	34.00	4.00		6	"Model 14"; other barrels	385
Dan Wesson	D. Wesson Arms	R	357Mag	9.25	36.00	4.00		6	"Model 15"; also 38 Spl	385
Dan Wesson	D. Wesson Arms	R	357Mag	14.30	64.00	8.00		6	"Model 40"	386
Davis	Davis Industries	A	32ACP	5.40	22.05	2.80		6	"P-32"	94
Decker	Decker	R	25ACP	4.65	9.00	1.96		5		95
Deer Gun	USA	S	9Par	5.00	12.00	2.60	4	1	Also smooth-bored	353
Defender	Johnson, Bye	R	32rf	6.23		2.52	5R	6	also 7-shot 22rf	186
Defender	I. Johnson	R	32rf	6.30		2.50	5R	5	"Defender 89"; also 7-shot 22rf	184

Name or Model	Maker/entry/origin	Type	Caliber, chambering	Length in	Weight oz	Barrel in	Rifling	Ctg Cap	Remarks	Page
Defender	Echaniz	A	32ACP	5.75	20.10	3.43		8	Eibar-type blowback	104
Defense	Spanish	A	25ACP	4.37	12.52	2.08		6	Eibar-type blowback	354
Defiance	Norwich Falls	R	22rf	5.31		2.25		7		237
Dek-Du	Urizar	R	25ACP	4.70	13.93	2.20		12	also in 5.5VD	357
Delta Elite	Colt	A	10Auto	8.50	37.75	5.00		8		88
Delta Gold Cup	Colt	A	10Auto	8.50	38.80	5.00		8		88
Delu	Delu	A	25ACP	4.60	11.65	2.12		7	FN-Browning M1906 copy	95
Deluxe	Bolumburu	A	32ACP	5.90	22.93	3.27		7		50
Demon	MAPF/Unique	A	25ACP	4.13	12.52	2.08		7	or "Unique Mle 10"	206
Demon	Demon	A	32ACP	5.90		3.35		8	Also 20-shot	95
Demon Marine	MAPF/Unique	A	25ACP	4.13	12.52	2.08		7	or "Unique Mle 10"	206
Deputy Marshal	Hawes	R	22LR	11.02	34.00	5.50		6	made by Sauer & Sohn	157
Deringer	Deringer	R	22rf			3.00		7	"Model 1"; also 32rf	96
Deringer	Deringer	R	22rf			3.00		7	"Model 2"; also 32rf, round brl.	96
Derringer	Colt	S	41rf	4.92		2.48		1	"First Model"	68
Derringer	Colt	S	41rf	4.92		2.48		1	"Second Model"	69
Derringer	Colt	S	41rf	4.88	6.52	2.52		1	"Third" or "Thuer" model	69
Derringer	Colt	S	22LR			2.48		1	"Fourth Model"	69
Derringer	Colt	S	22FR			2.48		1	"Lord & Lady Model"	69
Desert Eagle	IMI	A	357Mag	10.25	60.00	6.00	6R	9	also 44Mag, 41AE, 50AE	177
Destroyer	I. Gaztañaga	A	25ACP	4.41	10.92	2.17		6	"M1913"; "M1918" similar	141
Destroyer	I. Gaztañaga	A	32ACP	6.13	20.80	3.30		7	"M1919"	141
Destructor	Salaverria	A	32ACP	5.12	19.92	2.48		7	Eibar-type blowback	274
Detective Special	Colt	R	38	6.75	21.00	2.125		6		77
DH40	Daewoo	A	40SW	7.48	30.33	4.13	6R	11	DP40 has steel frame	93
DH45	Daewoo	A	45ACP	8.15	34.92	4.84	6R	13		93
DH380	Daewoo	A	380ACP	6.70	23.60	3.81	6R	6		93
Diamondback	Colt	R	22LR	9.00	28.60	4.00		6		80
Diamondback	Colt	R	38	9.00	28.60	4.00		6		80
Diana	Spanish	A	25ACP	4.52	13.05	2.16		6	Eibar-type blowback	N/A
Diana	Erquiaga, Muguruzu	A	25ACP	4.57	13.23	1.57		5	or "Fiel"	110
Diane	Wilkinson Arms	A	25ACP					6		389
Dickinson	Dickinson	R	32	6.65		2.80		5	Ranger No 2	101
Dickson Bulldog	Weihrauch	R	22LR	6.93	23.98	2.76		5	US name for HW-3	383
Dickson Special Agent	Echave y Arizmendi	A	32ACP	6.30	24.00	3.19		7	or "Echasa"	104
Dictator	Réunies	A	25ACP	4.70	14.28	2.24		6	also sold as "Centaure"	261
Dictator	Hopkins & Allen	R	32	6.89		2.87		5		171
Dimancea	Gatling	R	450cf	11.22	32.45	5.50		5		140
Diplomat	Hawes	A	380ACP	6.38	23.45	3.15		5	maker unknown	157
Dolne	Dolne	R	6pf	8.00	12.52			5	Apache-type; also in 7pf	102
Domino	Fabbrica Armi Sportive	A	22RF	11.22	40.56	5.60		5	"OP-601" competition pistol	114
Domino	Fabbrica Armi Sportive	A	22LR	11.02	44.10	5.51		5	"SP-602" competition pistol	114
Double Action Army Model	Colt	R	45LColt	9.84	36.00	4.77		6	"M1878"; or "Frontier"	73
Double Action Model	Smith & Wesson	R	32	6.50		3.00		5	four models	289
Double Action Model	Smith & Wesson	R	38	7.50	17.80	3.23		5	five models	289
Double Action Model	Smith & Wesson	R	38	7.50	17.80	3.23		5	"Perfected Model"	289
Double Action Model	Smith & Wesson	R	44	11.25	24.70	6.00		6		289
Double Deuce	Steel City	A	25ACP	5.50	18.00	2.50		6	also 7-shot 22LR	325
Double Eagle	Colt	A	45ACP	8.50	37.75	5.00		8	DA	88
Double Eagle	Colt	A	45ACP	7.75	35.60	4.48		8	"Combat Commander" type	88
Douglas	Lasagabaster	A	25ACP	4.49	10.40	2.00		6	"M1914"; Eibar-type blowback	198
DP40	Daewoo	A	40SW	7.48	44.00	4.21	6R	10		93
DP51	Daewoo	A	9Par	7.48	44.00	4.21	6R	10	As DP40 but for caliber	93
DP51C	Daewoo	A	9Par	7.00	25.75	3.68	6R	10	compact version	93
DP52	Daewoo	A	22LR	6.70	22.92	3.82	6R	10	resembles Walther PP	93
Dreyse	Rheinische M&M	A	25ACP	4.50	14.11	2.00		6	M1907	262
Dreyse	Rheinische M&M	A	32ACP	6.30	25.05	3.66		7	M1907	262
Dreyse	Rheinische M&M	A	9Par	8.11	31.04	4.96		8	military pattern	262
Drulov 70	Drulov	S	22LR	14.76	44.00	9.84		1	"M70"; bolt action	102
Drulov 75	Drulov	S	22LR	14.76	44.00	9.84		1	"M75"; bolt actiom	103
Duan	Ormachea	A	25ACP	4.50	15.00	2.125		6		244
Duplex	Osgood	R	22/32rf	5.75		2.56		8+1	8 x 22rf, 1 x 32rf	245
Durabel	Warnant	A	25ACP	4.33	10.05	1.70		6		372
DWM	DWM	A	32ACP	6.00	20.10	3.46		7	FN-Browning M1910 copy	100
EA	Arostegui	A	24ACP	4.40	10.58	2.00	4T	6	Eibar-type blowback	20
EA	Echave y Arizmendi	A	25ACP	4.52	11.11	2.00		5	FN-Browning M1906 copy	104
EA	Echave y Arizmendi	A	32ACP	5.51	20.63	3.43		7	Eibar-type blowback	104
Eagle	Johnson, Bye	R	22rf					7	also 5-shot 32rf, 38rf, 44rf	186
Eagle	Phelps	R	444Mar	19.50	88.00	12.00	6R	6	also 45LColt, 45-70Gvt	248
Earthquake	Dickinson	R	32rf					5		101
Eastern Arms Co	Meriden	R	32	6.38		3.23		5	for Biffar & Co, Chicago	227
Eastern Arms Co	Meriden	R	38	6.38	10.23	3.23		5	for Biffar & Co, Chicago	227
EBAC	MAPF/Unique	A	25ACP	4.13	12.52	2.08		7	or "Unique Mle 10"	205
Echasa	Echave y Arizmendi	A	22LR	6.22	22.92	3.15		9	based on Walther PP	104

Name or Model	Maker/entry/origin	Type	Caliber, chambering	Length in	Weight oz	Barrel in	Rifling	Ctg Cap	Remarks	Page
Echasa	Echave y Arizmendi	A	32ACP	6.30	24.00	3.19		7	Eibar-type blowback	104
Echeverria	Star	A	32ACP	5.83	20.45	3.27		9	Eibar-type blowback	322
Eclipse	Johnson, Bye	S	22rf	4.70		2.45		1	also in 32rf	185
EIG	EIG Corp	R	22LR	5.90	11.46	2.48		6	"Model 7"; or Röhm RG10	105
Einhand	Lignose AG	A	25ACP	4.75	14.45	2.12		6	or "Model 2A"	199
Einhand	Lignose AG	A	25ACP	4.68	14.28	2.125		9	or "Model 3A"	199
El Cano	Arana	R	32	10.51		5.90		5	S&W M&P copy	16
El Cid	C. Santos	A	25ACP	4.52	10.58	2.16		6	"M1915"; Eibar blowback	274
Eles	Spanish	A	25ACP	4.65	11.80	2.16		6	Eibar-type blowback	354
Eley	Spanish	A	25ACP	4.60	12.70	2.00		7	Eibar-type blowback	354
Elite	Bernardelli	A	9IMI	11.02	45.95	6.7	6R	17	Competition pistol	46
Elite	MAPF/Unique	A	25ACP	4.13	12.52	2.08		7	or "Unique Mle 10"	206
El Lunar	Garate, Anitua	R	8Leb					6	"Lebel Rapide" model	138
El Perro	Lascauren y Olasola	A	25CP	4.56	10.30	1.98		6	Eibar-type blowback	N/A
Em-Ge	Gerstenberger	A	22LR	6.69	15.87	2.48		6	"Model 220K"	142
Em-Ge	Gerstenberger	R	22LR	7.87	27.16	2.95		6	"Model 223"	142
Em-Ge	Gerstenberger	R	32	10.62	34.21	5.90		6	"Model 300"; target pistol	142
Empire	Rupertus	R	22rf					7	also 32rf, 41rff	271
Empire Automatic	Meriden	R	32					5	also in 38; auto-ejecting	227
Empire Arms Co.	Meriden	R	32					5	also in 38.	227
Empire State	Meriden	R	32	6.38		3.23		5	hammerless; also in 38	227
Empire State	Meriden Firearms	R	38	7.55		3.23		5	external hammer	227
Encore	Johnson, Bye	R	22rf					7	similar to "Favorite"	186
Enfield	Enfield	R	476	11.45	40.56	5.86	7R	6	"Pistol, Revolver, BL, Mk 1"	106
Enfield	Enfield	R	38	10.25	27.50	5.00	7R	6	"Pistol, Revolver, No 2 Mk 1"	106
Enforcer	Safari Arms	A	45ACP	7.72	40.00	3.78		6	short version of MatchMaster	N/A
Enterprise	Enterprise	R	22rf					5	solid frame; as in 32rf	107
EP22	Erma-Werke GmbH	A	22LR	7.20	35.60	3.26	6R	8	Luger look-alike	108
EP25	Erma-Werke GmbH	A	25ACP	5.31	18.30	2.75	6R	7		109
EP65A	Erma-Werke GmbH	A	22LR	10.00	45.78	6.00	6R	8		109
EP85A	Erma-Werke GmbH	A	22LR	10.00	40.92	5.90	6R	8	also in 32S&W Long WC	109
EP452	Erma-Werke GmbH	A	22LR	6.30	21.52	3.15	6R	8	blackened steel	108
EP457	Erma-Werke GmbH	A	32ACP	6.30	21.87	3.23	6R	8	stainless steel	108
EP459	Erma-Werke GmbH	A	380ACP	6.30	21.34	3.23	6R	7	stainless steel	108
EP552	Erma-Werke GmbH	A	22LR	5.40	14.46	2.87	6R	7		109
EP555	Erma-Werke GmbH	A	25ACP	5.39	13.93	2.95	6R	7		109
EP652	Erma-Werke GmbH	A	22LR	5.31	13.75	2.87	6R	7		109
EP655	Erma-Werke GmbH	A	25ASCP	5.31	13.40	2.87	6R	7		109
EP882	Erma-Werke GmbH	A	22LR	7.95	26.80	4.92	6R	8	P38 lookalike	109
EP882S	Erma-Werke GmbH	A	22LR	8.94	27.86	5.98	6R	8	and longer barrels	109
ER422	Erma-Werke GmbH	R	22LR	7.28	21.16	2.96	6R	6	ER 423 same, but 22WMR	108
ER432	Erma-Werke GmbH	R	32	7.28	20.63	2.95	6R	6	also with 2in barrel	108
ER438	Erma-Werke GmbH	R	38Spl	7.05	21.87	2.98	6R	5	ER440 in stainless steel	108
ER777	Erma-Werke GmbH	R	357Mag	9.49	42.91	3.94	6R	6	also with 4.7in barrel	108
Erika	Franz Pfannl	A	4.25	3.94	9.00	1.65		6		248
Erma	Erma	A	22LR	8.66	34.92	4.25	6R	10	Old Model target pistol	107
Erma	Erma	A	22LR	12.40	38.80	7.87	6R	10	New Model target pistol	107
Errasti	Errasti	A	25ACP	4.37	10.44	2.08		7	Eibar blowback; also 32ACP	110
Errasti	Errasti	R	38	9.65	28.57	4.70		6	S&W M&P copy; also 32, 44	110
Escodin	Escodin	R	32	8.25	27.70	4.05		6	"M1926"; S&W M&P copy	110
Escodin	Escodin	R	38	9.85	29.27	4.92		6	"M1924"; S&W M&P copy	110
Escort	American Arms	A	380ACP	6.1	19.0			7		13
Esmit	J. Arrizabalaga	R	38	8.97	22.00	4.33		6	Colt Police Positive copy	N/A
Especial	C.Arrizabalaga	A	32ACP	4.70	20.80	2.48		7	or "Campeon"	20
Estrella	Echeverria; Star	A	32ACP	6.10	20.63	3.27		7		322
Etna	Spanish	A	25ACP	4.41	10.58	1.98		6	Eibar-type blowback	N/A
Etna	Salaberrin	A	25ACP	4.53	10.60	2.00		6	Eibar-type blowback	273
Eureka	Johnson, Bye	R	22rf	5.79		2.25		7		185
Euskaro	Esprin	R	38	7.87	19.04	3.94		5	"M1909"	113
Euskaro	Esprin Hermanos	R	44	9.85	25.00	4.92		6	M1914	113
Excelsior	Norwich Pistol Co.	R	32rf			2.25		5		237
Exemplar	J.G. Anschütz	S	22LR			10.0		5	bolt-action; also 22WMR	15
Express	Bacon	R	22rf			2.25		7		27
Express	Garate, Anitua	A	25ACP	4.25	12.35	1.98		6	FN-Browning M1906 copy	138
Express	Urizar	A	25ACP	4.60	10.75	2.05		8	original design	357
Express	Urizar	A	25ACP	4.33	10.22	1.81		6	Eibar-type blowback	357
Express	Urizar	A	25ACP	4.33	12.35	1.98		5	Eibar-type blowback	357
Express	Urizar	A	25ACP	4.68	14.82	2.20		6	external hammer	357
Express	Urizar	A	32ACP	6.00	23.63	3.30		7	Eibar-type blowback	357
Express	Urizar	A	32ACP	6.00	20.80	3.38		8		357
Express	Urizar	A	32ACP	6.10	21.16	3.38		7	"Model 21"; Eibar blowback	357
Express	Webley	R	360cf	7.60	19.00	3.00	7R	6	"No. 5 Express"; also 4.5in brl	375
Extracteur	Ancion-Marx	R	8Leb					5	also other calibers	15
FA	F. Arizmendi	R	320cf					5	Velo-Dog type	17

Name or Model	Maker/entry/origin	Type	Caliber, chambering	Length in	Weight oz	Barrel in	Rifling	Ctg Cap	Remarks	Page
FAG	Arizmendi y Goenaga	R	8Leb					7	Velo-Dog type	18
FAG	Arizmendi y Goenaga	R	7.62Nag	9.06	29.26	4.13		7		18
Fagnus	Fagnus	R	450	10.55	36.15	5.63		6	tip-up, patent extractor	123
Falcon	Astra-Unceta	A	32ACP	6.50	23.96	3.86		8	also 22LR, 380ACP	22
Falcon	Spesco	A	25ACP	4.52	9.52	2.16		5	or "Reck M11"	316
FAMAE	Fabricaciones Militares	R	32	8.18	20.31	4.10		6	Colt Police Positive copy	123
Fast	Echave y Arizmendi	A	22LR	6.10	25.75	3.15		10	"M221"; based on Walther PP	104
Fast	Echave y Arizmendi	A	25ACP	6.10	25.22	3.15		9	"M633"; based on Walther PP	104
Fast	Echave y Arizmendi	A	32ACP	6.10	25.05	3.15		8	"M761"; based on Walther PP	104
Fast	Echave y Arizmendi	A	380ACP	6.10	24.70	3.15		7	"M901"; based on Walther PP	104
Favorite	Spanish	A	25ACP	4.40	12.87	2.05		7	Eibar-type blowback	354
Favorite	Johnson, Bye	R	22rf					7	"No. 1"; sheath trigger	186
Favorite	Johnson, Bye	R	32rf					5	"No. 2"; sheath trigger	186
Favorite	Johnson, Bye	R	38rf					5	"No. 3"; sheath trigger	186
Favorite	Johnson, Bye	R	41rf					5	"No. 4"; sheath trigger	186
Federal Arms	Meriden	R	32	7.28		3.15		5	also in 38 caliber	227
Federal Marshal	Hawes	R	357Mag	11.75	43.90	6.00		6	made by Sauer	157
FI	Firearms International	A	380ACP	6.10	19.75	3.11		6	or "Star Model D"	N/A
Fiala	Fiala	S	22LR	11.22	31.00	7.48		10		127
Fiel	Erquiaga, Muguruzu	A	24ACP	4.57	13.22	1.57		5	original design	110
Fiel	Erquiaga, Muguruzu	A	25ACP	4.33	11.28	2.08		6	"No. 1"; Eibar-type blowback	110
Fiel	Erquiaga, Muguruzu	A	32ACP	5.82	21.00	3.30		7	"No. 1"; Eibar-type blowback	110
Fireball	Remington Arms	S	221	16.73	60.00	10.43		1	"XP-100 Fireball", bolt action	258
Firecat	Astra-Unceta	A	25ACP	4.33	12.92	2.20		6	or "Model 200"	N/A
Firestar Plus	Star–Echeverria	A	9Par	6.50	24.70	3.38	6R	15	also 40S&W, 45ACP	324
Five-SeveN	Fabrique Nationale	A	5.7	8.20	21.80	4.82		20		116
FL-Selbstlader	Langenhan	A	32ACP	6.61	23.65	4.13		8	or "Armee-Model"	197
FME	Fabricaciones Militares	A	25ACP	4.49	12.70	2.125		6	FN-Browning M1906 copy	123
FMG	Fabricacioned Militares	R	32	6.50	17.10	2.56		6	Colt Police Positive copy	123
Forehand	Forehand & Wadsworth	R	32	6.30		2.48		5	solid-frame pattern	128
Forehand	Forehand & Wadsworth	R	38	7.00		2.68		5	solid-frame pattern	128
Forehand	Forehand & Wadsworth	R	38	6.50		3.15		5	top-break pattern	128
Forehand	Forehand & Wadsworth	R	32					6	"Pocket Model"; solid frame	128
Forehand	Forehand & Wadsworth	R	38	7.00		2.68		5	as above	128
Forehand	Hopkins & Allen	R	32RF	7.25		3.25		5	"Forehand M1891"	172
Fortune	Astra-Unceta	A	32ACP	4.56		2.125		6	copy of "Victoria"; also 25ACP	N/A
Forty-Niner	Harrington & Richardson	R	22LR	10.40	31.00	5.50		9	or "Model 949"	154
Forty-Nine	Fabrique Nationale	A	40S&W	7.75	26.30	4.25		14	also 9Par	116
Fosbery	Webley	R	455Bri	10.50	40.75	6.00	7R	6	"Webley-Fosbery", 1901 type	380
Fosbery	Webley	R	455Bri	12.00	41.80	7.50	7R	6	"Webley-Fosbery", 1902 target	380
Fosbery	Webley	R	455Bri	10.50	44.45	6.00	7R	6	"Webley-Fosbery", 1902 type	380
Fosbery	Webley	R	38Sup	10.20	38.00	6.00	7R	8	"Webley-Fosbery", 1902 type	380
Fosbery	Webley	R	455Bri	10.75	44.00	6.00	6/7R	6	"Webley-Fosbery", 1903 type	380
Fosbery	Webley	R	455Bri	10.44	40.50	6.00	6/7R	6	"Webley-Fosbery", 1903 small	380
Fosbery	Webley	R	455Bri	10.50	38.00	6.00	7R	6	"Webley-Fosbery", 1914 pattern	380
Fosbery	Webley	R	455Bri	12.00	40.25	7.50	7R	6	"Webley-Fosbery", 1914 target	380
Fox	Česká Zbrojovka	A	25ACP	4.95	20.63	2.60		7		61
FP	Steyr	S	22LR	18.30	44.62	9.25		1	Free Pistol	328
FP	Walther Sportwaffenfabrik	A	22LR	17.30	47.60	11.80	6R	1	Martini-type free pistol	366
Française	Société Française des Armes	A	25ACP	4.70		2.60		6		315
Franco	Manufrance	A	25ACP	6.00	12.70	3.35		6	or Le Françcais Police	210
Francotte	Francotte	M	8cf	8.85		5.31		7	prototypes only	128
Francotte	Francotte	A	25ACP	4.25	14.46	2.17		6	many minor variants	128
Frommer	Fémáru	A	8Roth	7.08	22.92	3.93		10	1901 type	125
Frommer	Fémáru	A	7.65Roth	7.28	22.57	3.93		9	1906 type	125
Frommer	Fémáru	A	32ACP	7.28	22.40	3.93		8	1910 type; also in 7.65 Roth	125
Frommer	Fémáru	A	32ACP	6.50	21.50	3.93		7	"Stop M1912"; also in 380ACP	125
Frommer	Fémáru	A	32ACP	4.70	17.63	2.17		5	"Baby"; smaller "Stop"	125
Frommer	Fémáru	A	25ACP	4.33	10.58	2.16		6	"Liliput" blowback	125
Frontier	Ronge	R	41cf	9.25	37.38	4.65		6	solid frame	268
Frontier Army	Ronge	R	44cf	10.83	39.00	5.60		5	solid frame	268
Frontier Model	Smith & Wesson	R	44-40	11.88	39.85	6.50		6		294
Frontier Scout	Colt	R	22LR	9.33	24.00	4.70		6		79
Furia	Ojanguren y Vidosa	A	32ACP	5.70	21.35	3.15		8		243
Furor	MAPF/Unique	A	25ACP	4.13	12.52	2.08		7	or "Unique Mle 10"	205
Fyrberg	Fyrberg	R	32	6.30		3.00		5	also in 38 caliber	130
Gabilondo	Gabilondo	A	32ACP	6.10	21.87	3.54		8	Eibar-type blowback	132
GAC	Garate, Anitua	R	32	9.65	29.80	5.04		6	marked "G.A.C. Firearms Co"	138
Galand	Galand	R	9cf	7.95	38.80	3.15		6	representative specimen	135
Galesi	Galesi	A	25ACP						"M1914"	136
Galesi	Galesi	A	25ACP	4.70		2.29		7	"M1922"	136
Galesi	Galesi	A	25ACP	4.70		2.40		7	"M1930"; also in 32ACP	136
Galesi	Galesi	A	380ACP						"M1936"	136
Galesi	Galesi	A	32ACP	6.30		3.54		7	"Model 5"	136

Name or Model	Maker/entry/origin	Type	Caliber, chambering	Length in	Weight oz	Barrel in	Rifling	Ctg Cap	Remarks	Page
Galesi	Galesi	A	25ACP	4.65		2.32		7	"Model 6"	136
Galesi	Galesi	A	32ACP	6.30		3.50		7	"Model 9"	136
Galesi	Rigarmi	A	25ACP	6.30		3.35		7	"Model 1953"; also in 22LR	265
Gallia	MAPF/Unique	A	25ACP	4.13	12.52	2.08		7	or "Unique Model 10"	206
Gallus	Retolaza	A	25ACP	4.52	12.55	2.16	6R	6	Eibar-type blowback	260
Garantazada	Garantazada	R	38	9.30	29.62	4.92		6	"M1924"; also 32-20WCF	137
Garate	Garate, Anitua	A	32ACP	5.90	21.70	3.15		9	Eibar-type blowback	138
Garate	Garate, Anitua	R	455Bri	11.03	24.33	5.12		6	British "Pistol OP Mk 1 No 1"	138
Gasser	L. Gasser	R	11.75cf	14.75	51.15	9.00		6	"Montenegrin"; representative	139
Gasser-Kropatschek	L. Gasser	R	9cf	9.21	27.16	4.56		6	M1878 or officers" model	139
Gasser-Kropatschek	L. Gasser	R	9cf	8.94	28..20	4.65		6	commercial version M1878	139
Gaulois	Manufrance	M	8cf	5.16	10.00	2.20		5	or "La Mitrailleuse"	210
Gavage	Gavage	A	32ACP	5.94	21.15	2.96		7		140
Gaztañaga	I. Gaztañaga	R	32	8.26	18.70	4.33		6	S&W M&P copy	140
GB	Steyr	A	9Par	6.30	29.80	5.35		18	improved Pi-18	328
G&E	Gerstenberger & Eberwein	R	22LR	5.90	14.75	2.36		6	or "Omega"	142
Gecado	Weihrauch	R	22LR	6.89	24.00	2.75		8	Arminius HW-3	383
Gecado	Dornheim	A	25ACP	4.56	11.45	2.20		6	or "Union 1" by SEAM	102
Gecado	Dornheim	A	25ACP	4.57	15.00	2.24	6R	6	Reck Model 11	102
Gecado	Dornheim	A	32ACP	5.19	20.70	2.57	4R	7	"Silesia" by SEAM	102
Geco	Gustav Genschow	A	25ACP	4.65	11.29	2.16		7	made by F.Arizmendi.	142
Geco	Gustav Genschow	R	25ACP	4.70		1.73		5	hammerless	142
Geco	Gustav Genschow	R	32ACP	6.70		2.45		5	hammerless	142
General Officer's Model	Rock Island Arsenal	A	45ACP	7.87	36.00	3.94	6L	7	rebuilt M1911A1; or "M15"	89
German Bulldog	Genschow	R	320cf	6.90	24.35	2.68		6	also in 380cf, 450cf	142
GH	Guisasola	R	38	10.03	18.35	5.00		6	S&W M&P copy	147
Gilon	Fabrique d"Armes Gilon	R	5.5VD	6.50		2.36		5	typical Velo-Dog	N/A
Giralda	Bolumburu	A	32ACP	5.90	20.63	3.35		7	Eibar-type blowback	50
Glisenti	Glisenti	A	9G	8.15	30.00	4.00		7	"M1910"	142
Glock 17	Glock	A	9Par	8.00	22.00	4.49	6R	17	"Model 17"; basic model	144
Glock 17L	Glock	A	9Par	9.52	25.63	6.02	6R	17	"Model 17L"; sport model	144
Glock 18C	Glock	A	9Par	8.00	20.60	4.48	6R	33	"Model 18C"; selective fire	144
Glock 19	Glock	A	9Par	7.40	20.98	4.00	6R	15	"Model 19"; compact 17	144
Glock 20	Glock	A	10mm	8.35	27.65	4.60	6R	15	"Model 20"	144
Glock 21	Glock	A	45ACP	8.35	26.27	4.60	6R	13	"Model 21"	144
Glock 22	Glock	A	40S&W	8.00	22.75	4.48	6R	15	"Model 22"	144
Glock 23	Glock	A	40S&W	7.40	21.06	4.00	6R	13	"Model 23"; compact 22	144
Glock 24	Glock	A	40S&W	8.86	26.45	6.00	6R	15	"Model 24"; 24C has vent. brl.	144
Glock 25	Glock	A	380ACP	6.85	20.10	4.00	6R	15	"Model 25"	145
Glock 26	Glock	A	9Par	6.29	19.75	3.46	6R	10	"Model 26"; sub-compact	145
Glock 27	Glock	A	40S&W	6.29	19.75	3.46	6R	9	"Model 27"; sub-compact	145
Gloria	Bolumburu	A	25ACP	4.41	11.46	2.16		6	Eibar-type blowback	50
Gloria	Bolumburu	A	32ACP	5.35	19.15	2.75		7	Eibar-type blowback	50
Gold Cup National Match	Colt	A	45ACP	8.58	37.00	5.00		7	"M1915"	88
Golden Bison	Super Six	R	45-70Gvt	13.00	92.00	6.00		6	also with 8in barrel	337
Governor	Bacon	R	22RF	5.51		2.25		5		27
Grand	Československá Zbrojovka	R	357Mag	9.05	34.56	4.00		6	other barrel lengths	61
Grande Précision	Grande Précision	A	25ACP	4.56	11.65	2.20		6	Eibar-type blowback	146
Grant-Hammond	Hammond; H&R	A	45ACP	11.25	42.00	6.73		8	1915 patent	153
Green	Green	R	450cf	10.62	35.45	5.50	6R	6	representative specimen	146
Green	Webley	R	455Bri	11.25	40.75	6.00	7R	6	"Webley-Green", first type	377
Green	Webley	R	455Bri	13.25	40.25	6.00	7r	6	"Webley-Green", second type	377
Green	Webley	R	455Bri	13.22	41.80	7.50	7R	6	"Webley-Green", 1892 type	377
Green	Webley	R	476Bri	11.50		6.00	6R	6	"Webley-Green", 1892 Army	378
Green	Webley	R	450Bri	13.25	44.10	7.50	7R	6	"Webley-Green", 1893 target	378
Green	Webley	R	455Bri	13.25	41.25	7.60	7R	6	"Webley-Green", 1896 target	378
Grendel P-10	Grendel	A	380ACP	5.31	15.00	3.00		10	"P-10"	147
Griffon	Safari Arms	A	45ACP	8.70		5.00		10		272
Grizzly WinMag	LAR	A	45WinMg	10.47	51.00	5.40		7	other calibers, barrels	198
GSP	Walther Sportwaffenfabrik	A	22LR	11.50	41.60	4.21	6R	5	also 32S&W	369
GT-22T	G. Tanfoglio	A	22LR	8.97	30.00	6.00		12		339
GT-27	G. Tantoglio	A	25ACP	4.52	12.00	2.44		6	or "Titan"	339
GT-32	G. Tanfoglio	A	32ACP	7.36	27.00	4.88		6		339
GT-380 XE	G. Tanfoglio	A	380ACP	7.35	27.68	3.70		11		339
Guardian	Bacon	R	32rf	6.70		2.75		5	also in 22rf	27
Guardsman	Harrington & Richardson	R	32	7.00	23.10	2.50		6	"Model 732"; also 4in barrel	154
Guerre	F. Arizmendi	A	32ACP	5.70	20.80	2.75		7	Eibar-type blowback	17
Guisasola	Guisasola	R	38	9.85	28.60	4.92		6	Colt Police Positive copy	147
Guisasola	Guisasola	R	38	10.43	29.80	5.50		6	S&W M&P copy	147
Guisasola	Guisasola	A	25ACP	4.33	10.90	2.12		7	made by Gabilondo	147
Gunfighter	Harrington & Richardson	R	22LR	10.40	28.92	5.50		6	"Model 660"	154
Gustloff	Gustloff-Werke	A	32ACP	6.61	25.90	3.74	6R	8	prototypes only	147
Gyrojet	MBA	A	12Gyr	9.75	17.00	8.25		6	rocket launcher	225
Gyurza	Tsinntochmash	A	9Rus	7.68	35.00			18	or "P-9"	349

Name or Model	Maker/entry/origin	Type	Caliber, chambering	Length in	Weight oz	Barrel in	Rifling	Ctg Cap	Remarks	Page
H&A	Hopkins & Allen	R	22RF	9.00		5.90		7	solid frame, single action	171
H&A	Hopkins & Allen	R	32	8.00		4.00		5	"DA No. 6"; solid frame	171
H&A	Hopkins & Allen	R	32	6.50		3.00		5	"Automatic Model"	172
H&A	Hopkins & Allen	R	32RF	7.25		3.25		5	"Forehand M1891"	172
H&A	Hopkins & Allen	R	32	7.70		3.00		6	"Safety Police"	172
Hafdasa	Hispano-Argentina	A	22LR	6.50		2.36		8	"Model A"	169
Hafdasa	Hispano-Argentina	A	22LR	8.50		4.70		10	"Model B"; Colt M1911 copy	169
Hamada	Japan Gun Co.	A	32ACP	6.26	23.80	3.46	6R	9	Type 1	183
Hamada	Japan Gun Co.	A	8Nam	6.97	26.00	3.74	6R	6	Type 2	183
Hammerless Model	Harrington & Richardson	R	32		18.00	4.00		6	also in 22LR	154
Hammerless Model	Harrington & Richardson	R	32	6.50	11.50	2.87		5		154
Hammerless Model	Harrington & Richardson	R	38	8.25	16.90	4.00		5		154
Hammer Model	Harrington & Richardson	R	32	6.92	10.75	3.15		5		153
Hammerli Dakota	Hammerli	R	357Mag	11.10	40.00	5.50		6		151
Hamilton	Thorssin	A	6.5Bgm	10.51	43.20	4.13		6	prototypes only	346
Handy	Spanish	A	380ACP	5.90	23.63	3.30		7	"M1917"; Browning 1910 copy	N/A
Hand Ejector	Smith & Wesson	R	32	8.45	18.00	4.25		6	eight models	290
Hand Ejector	Smith & Wesson	R	32-20WCF	8.25		5.00		6	eight models	290
Hand Ejector	Smith & Wesson	R	22LR	11.02	26.75	6.00		6	Bekeart Model; "K22/32"	290
Hand Ejector	Smith & Wesson	R	44	11.73	37.90	6.50		6	1st or New Century Model	291
Hand Ejector	Smith & Wesson	R	44	11.73	37.38	6.50		6	2nd Model	292
Hand Ejector	Smith & Wesson	R	44	10.24	37.90	5.00		6	3rd Model	292
Hand Ejector Magnum	Smith & Wesson	R	357Mag	11.90	47.00	6.00		6		291
Hard Pan	Hood	R	32rf			2.50		5	solid frame; also 22rf	170
Hartford	Hartford Arms & Equipment	A	22LR	11.00		6.70		10	became High Standard	157
Hartford	Hartford Arms & Equipment	M	22LR	8.26		4.33		10	also as single shot pistol	157
Hartford Arms Co	Norwich Falls	R	32rf					6	a misleading sales name	237
Hawk	STI International	A	45ACP	8.00	26.45	4.33		10	"Hawk 4.3"	N/A
Hawkeye	Sturm, Ruger	S	256WinMg	14.00	44.80	8.50		1		329
H&D	Henrion, Dassy & Heuschen	A	25ACP	4.33	10.90	2.56		6		164
HDH	Henrion, Dassy & Heuschen	A	25ACP	6.89		3.54		20		163
HDH	Henrion, Dassy & Heuschen	A	32ACP	8.10		4.13		16		163
HDH	Henrion, Dassy & Heuschen	R	8Leb	7.28		2.83		5	and other calibers	163
Heavy Duty Police	Smith & Wesson	R	38Spl	10.82	42.00	5.50		6	or "Model 20"	298
Hege	Fegyver	A	32ACP	7.10	20.80	3.93		8	"AP66"	123
Heim	Heinzelmann	A	25ACP	4.25	10.95	2.16		6		163
Hei-Mo	Moritz	A	32ACP	5.50	22.20	2.95		8		230
Helfricht	Krauser	A	25ACP	4.33	10.60	1.96		6	"Model 1"	194
Helfricht	Krauser	A	25ACP	4.33	10.60	1.96		6	"Model 2"	194
Helfricht	Krauser	A	25ACP	4.33	10.60	1.96		6	"Model 3"	194
Helfricht	Krauser	A	25ACP	4.29	12..00	1.81		6	"Model 4"	194
Helkra	Krauser	A	25ACP	4.29	12..00	1.81		6	or "Helfricht Model 4"	194
Helvece	Grande Précision	A	25ACP	4.65	12.50	2.20		6		146
Helwan	Egyptian State Factory	A	9Par	8.00	31.92	4.49		8	Beretta 951 copy	105
Heritage	Phelps	R	45-70Gvt	19.50	88.00	12.00		6	also 444 caliber	248
Herman	Belgian	A	25ACP	4.92	15.16	2.55		6		N/A
Heritage Rough Rider	Heritage Arms	R	22LR	10.00	30.65	4.75		6	Also 22WMR, longer barrels	164
Heritage Sentry	Heritage Arms	R	38Spl	6.30	23.00	2.00		6	also 22LR, 22WMR	164
Hermetic	Bernadon-Martin	A	32ACP	6.00	24.00	3.54		7		45
Heym	F.W. Heym	R	22LR	6.70		1.96		6	"Detective Model"	164
High Velocity	Webley	A	9BL	8.00	33.50	5.00	6R	8		382
Highway Patrolman	Smith & Wesson	R	357Mag	11.25	44.00	6.00		6	or "Model 28"	299
Hijo	Galesi	A	25ACP	6.30		3.35		7	or "Galesi Model 5"	136
Hijo Quickbreak	Iver Johnson	R	22LR	10.75	28.75	5.00		8		184
Hino Komuro	Komuro	A	32ACP	10.00	29.00	8.03		8	blow-forward	193
Hi-Point	Hi-Point	A	45ACP	7.70	41.65	4.50		9	"45"; also 40SW, 9Par	169
Hi-Point	Hi-Point	A	380ACP	6.75	30.00	3.50		8	"380P"; hammerless	169
Hi-Point	Hi-Point	A	9Par	6.75	34.55	3.50		8	compact, steel frame	169
Hi-Point	Hi-Point	A	9Par	6.75	31.75	3.50		8	compact, polymer frame	169
HK4	Heckler & Koch	A	25ACP	6.18	16.90	3.35		8	also 22LR, 32ACP, 380ACP	158
Hood	Hood	R	32	5.50		2.50		5	smooth-bore	170
Horse Destroyer	I. Gaztañaga	R	38	11.00	32.00	6.00		6		140
Howard Arms	Meriden	R	38	7.32		3.00		5	also in 32 caliber	227
HP	Walther	A	9Par	8.38	29.50	5.00	6T	8	"Heeres-Pistole"	365
HP Mark 2	Fabrique Nationale	A	9Par	7.87	31.05	4.65	6R	13	"Mark 2"; improved GP-35l	119
HP Mark 3	Fabrique Nationale	A	9Par	7.87	31.05	4.65	6R	13	"Mark 3"; improved Mark 2	119
HP Mark 3S	Fabrique Nationale	A	9Par	7.87	31.05	4.65	6R	13	"Mark 3S"; improved Mark 3	119
HP40	Fabrique Nationale	A	40S&W	7.87	34.56	4.68	6R	13	improved Mk 3 in 40-caliber	119
H&R Self-loading	Harrington & Richardson	A	25ACP	4.52	12.17	2.125	6R	6	Webley & Scott design	156
H&R Self-loading	Harrington & Richardson	A	32ACP	6.50	20.00	3.35	6R	8	Webley & Scott design	156
H&R Special	Harrington & Richardson	R	22LR	10.25	25.00	6.00		9		155
HS	H. Schmidt	R	22LR	6.10		1.98		7	or "Liberty"	279
HS	H. Schmidt	R	22LR	6.30		1.98		7	"Model 11" or EIG M11	279
HS95	RH-Alan	A	9Par	7.28	35.00	4.05	6R	15	SIG P-226 copy	261
HSc	Mauser	A	32ACP	6.38	22.57	3.38		8	DA lock-work	220
HsP	Mauser-Jagdwaffen	A	9Par	6.50	26.50	3.30	4R	8	prototypes only	224

Name or Model	Maker/entry/origin	Type	Caliber, chambering	Length in	Weight oz	Barrel in	Rifling	Ctg Cap	Remarks	Page
HSP701	Korriphila	A	9Par	7.16	34.92	4.00		9	delayed blowback	194
Hudson	Spanish	A	25ACP	4.48	13.20	2.17		6	Eibar-type blowback	N/A
Hunter	Harrington & Richardson	R	22LR	14.00		10.00		7		153
Huntsman	Colt	A	22LR	8.65	29.45	4.00		10		90
HV	Hourat et Vie	A	25ACP	4.56	10.58	2.04		6	FN-Browning M1906 copy	172
HW-3	Weihrauch	R	22RF	6.88	23.98	2.75		8	also 6-shot 32-cal., 24.5oz	383
HW-5	Weihrauch	R	22LR	8.70	25.60	4.0		8	also 7-shot 32 version	383
HW-7	Weihrauch	R	22LR	10.40	30.90	6.0		8	also 7-shot 32 version	383
HW-9	Weihrauch	R	22LR	10.43	36.68	5.90		6		383
HW-38	Weihrauch	R	38	8.80	30.86	4.02		6		384
HW-38	Weihrauch	R	38 Spl	8.86	30.86	3.94		6	also 2.5 or 6in barrels	384
HW-68	Weihrauch	R	22RF	6.70	17.63	2.5		8	also 22WMR or 32S&W	384
HW-357	Weihrauch	R	357 Mag	9.05	35.30	3.93		6	also 3in or 6in barrels	384
Hy-Score	Röhm	R	22LR	5.90		2.36		6	"Model 108"	266
IAG	Galesi	A	32ACP						several models	136
Ideal	Dušek	A	25ACP	4.48	10.75	2.125		7		103
Illinois Arms	Pickert	R	various						general sales name	248
Imbel	Imbel	A	45ACP	8.50	36.50	5.03	8L	7	"M1911A1" Colt-Browning	175
Imbel	Imbel	A	9Par	8.50	35.60	5.03	6R	8	"M973" Colt-Browning	175
Imbel	Imbel	A	380ACP	7.55	37.12	4.10	6R	7	"MD1" Colt-Browning	175
Imbel	Imbel	A	38Sup	8.62	38.00	5.03	6L	8	"MD1" Colt-Browning	175
Imbel	Imbel	A	32ACP	7.55	32.25	4.10	6R	9	"MD1" Colt-Browning	175
Imperator	Heckler & Koch	A	32ACP	6.18	16.90	3.35		8	US name for HK-4	158
Imperial	Urizar	A	25ACP	4.40	11.00	2.125		7	Eibar-type blowback	357
Imperial	J. Aldazabal	A	32ACP	5.90	21.16	3.35		7	Eibar-type blowback	11
Imperial Arms Co.	Hopkins & Allen	R	38	7.28		3.15		5	also hammerless version	172
INA	Industria Nacional	R	32	6.88	29.80	2.16		6		175
Indian	I. Gaztañaga	A	32ACP	6.30	21.30	3.46		9	Eibar-type blowback	141
Infallible	Davis-Warner	A	32ACP	6.61	24.70	3.22		7		94
International	Hood	R	32rf					5	also 7-shot 22rf	170
Intratec	Intratec	A	9Par	5.75	17.65	3.00		7	"TEC9"; also 380ACP	176
Intratec	Intratec	A	40S&W	6.30	18.00	3.25		6	"TEC40"; also 45ACP	176
Invicta	S. Salaberrin	A	25ACP	4.40	11.11	2.18		6	FN-Browning M1906 copy	273
Iraola	Iraola y Salaverria	A	32ACP	5.90	24.16	3.38		9	FN-Browning M1906 copy	176
Iroquois	Remington	R	22rf	5.90		2.25		7	Smoot pattern	259
Iris	Orbea	R	32-20WCF	9.45	28.22	4.70		6		243
Italia Militar	Rigarmi	A	32ACP	5.95	23.80	3.54		7		265
Ithaca	Ithaca	S	22LR			10.00		1	"Model 20"; also 12in barrel	178
Iver Johnson	I. Johnson	R	22LR	7.00	26.10	2.50		8	"Bulldog"; also in 38Spl	183
Iver Johnson	I. Johnson	R	22LR	7.28	24.00	2.50		8	"Model 55SA"	184
Iver Johnson	I. Johnson	R	38	6.50		2.50		5	"M1900"; various barrels	184
Iver Johnson	I. Johnson	R	22LR	4.13		1.00		7	"Petite"	184
Iver Johnson	I. Johnson	R	22LR	10.75	34.00	6.00		8	"Target" or "Model 57A"	184
Iver Johnson	I. Johnson	A	380ACP	6.10	20.00	3.00		6	"X300" or "Pony"	185
Ixor	MAPF/Unique	A	25ACP	4.13	12.70	2.12		7	or "Unique M10"	206
Izarra	Echeverria	A	32ACP	6.13	23.80	3.46		9	Eibar type blowback	104
IZh70	Izhevsk								Baikal	181
IZh70N	Izhevsk								Baikal	181
Jaga	Dušek	A	25ACP	4.50	15.00	2.125		6	or "Duo"	103
Jäger	Jäeger	A	32ACP	6.13	22.57	3.11		7		182
Japanese 26th Year	Koishikawa	R	9Jap	8.50	31.00	4.70	6L	6	"26th year Type", "M1893"	190
Japanese Nambu	Koishikawa	A	8Nam	8.97	31.75	4.72		8	"Type A", "Papa Nambu"	191
Japanese Type 14	Nagoya	A	8Nam	8.94	32.00	4.72		8	"14th Year Type", "M1925"	233
Japanese Nambu	Koishikawa	A	7Nam	6.73	22.90	3.27		7	"Type B", "Baby Nambu"	191
Japanese Type 94	Nambu/Chuo Kogyo	A	8Nam	7.08	27.00	3.77	6R	6	"Type 94", "M1934"	234
Javelina	Irwindale	A	10Auto	10.50	40.00	7.00		8		
J. Cesar	Urizar	A	25ACP	4.52	10.75	2.05		7	Eibar-type blowback	357
J.C. Higgins	High Standard	A	22LR	10.86	40.90	6.50		10	"Model 80"; "Duramatic" type	165
J.C. Higgins	MAPF/Unique	A	22LR	7.20	21.70	4.33		10	"Model 85"; "Unique" type	208
J.C. Higgins	High Standard	A	22LR	9.25	22.90	3.93		9	"Model 88"; "Sentinel" type	165
J.C. Higgins	High Standard	R	22LR	9.45	27.00	4.50		7	"Model 90"; "Double Nine" type	165
J.C. Higgins	High Standard	R	22LR	10.75	28.00	5.50		9	"Ranger"; "Double Nine" type	165
Jericho	Israeli Military Industries	A	9Par	8.68	39.15	4.41	6R	16	"F"; "R" similar; also 40S&W	178
Jericho	Israeli Military Industries	A	9Par	7.25	31.75	3.54	6R	18	"FS"; also in 40S&W	178
Jericho	Israeli Military Industries	A	9Par	7.25	31.00	3.54	6R	12	"FB"; also in 40S&W	178
Jetfire	Beretta	A	22LR	4.70	11.28	2.36	6R	7	or "Model 950", "Minx"	38
Jewel	Hood	R	22rf	6.00		3.50		7		170
Jieffeco	Janssen	A	32ACP	6.30	22.90	3.54		8	and see "Melior"	182
Joha	Spanish	A	25ACP	4.56	14.10	2.20		6	FN-Browning M1906 copy	354
Jo-Lo-Ar	Arrizabalaga	A	380ACP	8.55	25.40	5.90			also 25ACP and 32ACP, 9BL	21
Jubala	Larranaga y Elartza	A	25ACP	4.33	12.35	2.08		6	Eibar-type blowback	198
Junior	Pretoria Arms Factory	A	25ACP	4.52	13.40	2.16		6		253
Jupiter	Grande Précision	A	25ACP	4.52	13.93	2.28		7	Eibar-type blowback	146
Jupiter	Grande Précision	A	32ACP	6.00	21.70	3.35		9	Eibar-type blowback	146

Name or Model	Maker/entry/origin	Type	Caliber, chambering	Length in	Weight oz	Barrel in	Rifling	Ctg Cap	Remarks	Page
K9	Kahr	A	9Par	6.00	26.80	3.50		7		188
K22/32	Smith & Wesson	R	22LR	11.02	26.75	6.00		6	Hand Ejector, "Bekeart Model"	290
Kaba Spezial	Menz	A	25ACP	4.56	13.58	2.28		6	also in 32ACP	226
Kaba Spezial	Arizmendi	A	25ACP	4.33	13.25	2.125		6	also in 32ACP	17,18
Kahr	Kahr	A	9Par	6.00	26.80	3.50		7	"K9"	188
Kappora	Spanish	A	32ACP	5.70	20.80	3.15		7		N/A
Kareen	KSN Industries	A	9Par	7.80	33.90	4.65		15	"Mark 2"; also 13-shot 40S&W	N/A
Kaufman	Webley	R	450Bri	1.00	40.00	5.75	6R	6	also in 455Bri, 476Bri	377
KGP68A	Erma-Werke	A	32ACP	7.36	22.60	3.46	6R	6	also in 380ACP	109
KGP69	Erma-Werke	A	22LR	7.72	29.60	3.93	6R	8	"blowback Luger"	109
Kel-Tec	Kel-Tec	A	9Par	5.78	17.00	3.07		10	"P-11"	188
Kessler	Kessler	A	32ACP	6.50	22.76	3.75		7	made by Pickert	188
Kimball	Kimball	A	30Crb	9.45	40.00	5.00		7	also 22Hnt	189
Kimball	Kimball	A	30Crb	8.00	29.00	3.50		7	"Aircrew Model"	189
Kirrikale	MKE	A	32ACP	6.61	24.70	3.74		7	also in 380ACP	203
Kittemaug	Norwich Falls	R	32rf	6.61		2.75	5R	5	or "Monarch"	237
Klesesewski	Spanish	A	25ACP	4.33	11.46	2.16		7		N/A
Knockabout	Sheridan	S	22LR	6.77	24.00	5.00		1		285
Kobold	Raick	R	320	4.02		2.00		5	"Constabulary" pattern	255
Kobra	German	A	25ACP	4.56	22.40	2.36		6		354
Kolb	Kolb	R	22rf	5.03		1.75		5	see "Baby Hammerless"	192
Kolibri	Gräbner	A	3Kol	2.55	7.76	1.18		6	also made by Pfannl	145
Kommer	Kommer	A	25ACP	4.13	13.05	2.00		7	"Model 1"; "2" and "3" similar	192
Kommer	Kommer	A	32ACP	5.50	20.10	3.00		7	"Model 4"	192
Korriphila	Korriphila	A	25ACP	4.65	12.70	2.60		6	"TP-70;" "Norton TP-70" in USA	194
Korriphila	Korriphila	A	9Par	7.16	34.92	4.00		9	"HSP-701"; delayed blowback	194
Krnka	Krnka	A	8cf	10.43	34.57	6.70		10?	1895 model	195
Kynoch	Kynoch	R	450	11.50	48.50	6.00		6	and other calibers	196
L9	Lorcin	A	9Par	7.48	30.70	4.48		13		201
L25	Lorcin	A	25ACP	4.70	13.33	2.32		6		201
L35	Jyväskylä Arms Factory	A	9Par	9.25	43.20	4.65		8	"Lahti", "M1935 Finnish army	186
Ladies Escort	Detonics	A	45ACP	6.77	25.75	3.50		6		96
Lady Rossi	Rossi	R	38Spl	7.50	23.00	3.00	6R	5	also 2in barrel	268
Ladysmith	Smith & Wesson	R	22rf	6.50		3.00		7	three models	292
Ladysmith	Smith & Wesson	R	38Spl	6.22	20.00	2.00		5	Models 36LS and 60LS	300
Ladysmith	Smith & Wesson	R								302
La Industria	Orbea	A	32ACP	6.10	22.00	3.38		9	Eibar-type blowback	244
Lahti	Jyväskylä arms factory	A	9Par	9.25	43.20	4.65		8	"L-35", "M1935 Finnish army	186
Lahti	Husqvarna	A	9Par	9.52	44.62	4.70		8	M1940, Swedish army	173
La Lira	Garate, Anitua	A	32ACP	7.48	25.63	4.52		9	Mannlicher 1901 copy	139
Lampo	Tribuzio	M	8cf	4.85		2.16		5	palm-squeezer	348
Lancaster	Lancaster	M	450cf	9.75		6.00		2,4	2 or 4 barrels	197
Landstad	Landstad	R	7.5Swi	9.25	36.00	4.52		7	automatic revolver	197
Langenhan	Langenhan	A	32ACP	6.61	23.65	4.13		8	"Army Model", "FL-Selbstlader"	197
Langenhan	Langenhan	A	25ACP	5.75	17.63	2.28		5	Model II	197
Langenhan	Langenhan	A	25ACP	4.70	16.55	2.28		5	Model III	197
Laumann	Laumann	M	7.7cf	10.20	33.68	4.70		5		198
Lawman	Colt	R	357Mag	9.25	36.00	4.00		6	Mark 2; other barrel lengths	80
LE	Larranaga y Elartza	A	25ACP	4.52	10.95	2.125		6	Eibar-type blowback	198
Leader	USA	R	32rf	6.37		2.36		5	also 7-shot 22rf	353
L'Agent	Manufrance	R	8Leb	5.0		2.16		5	hammerless	210
Le Basque	Urizar	A	32ACP	5.90	21.50	3.23		9	Eibar-type blowback	357
Le Brong	Crucelegui	R	8Leb	6.13		2.16		5	Velo-Dog pattern	92
Le Cavalier	Mre d'Armes de Bayonne	A	32ACP	6.00	22.90	3.23		8	US sales name	205
Le Chasseur	Mre d'Armes de Bayonne	A	22LR	7.28	28.00	4.52		9	external hammer	205
Le Colonial	Manufrance	R	8cf	5.70		2,16		5	hammerless	210
Le Dragon	Aguirre	A	25ACP	4.52	12.52	2.16		7	Eiber-type blowback	11
L'Eclair	Garate, Anitua	R	5.5VD	5.90		2.08		6	hammerless Velo-Dog	138
Lee	Lee	R	22rf	5.70		1.75		5		198
Lefaucheux-Francotte	Francotte	R	11pf/cf	12.20	41.26	5.90		6	Swedish army M1871	129
Le Français	Manufrance	A	25ACP	4.40	10.58	2.36		8	"Pocket Model"	211
Le Français	Manufrance	A	32ACP	6.00	22.20	3.27				210
Le Français	Manufrance	A	9BL	8.00	38.44	5.00			"M1928" or "Military Model"	211
Le Gendarme	Mre d'Armes de Bayonne	A	32ACP	7.08	24.70	3.94		9	or "MAB Modèle D"	205
Legia	H. Pieper (AÉP)	A	25ACP	4.53	12.35	2.16		6		250
Le Majestic	MAPF/Unique	A	25ACP	4.10	12.53	2.16		7	or "Unique M10"	206
Le Martigny	Belgian	A	25ACP	4.45	13.23	2.16		6	FN-Browning M1906 copy	353
Le Meteor	Spanish	A	25ACP	4.65	14.45	2.13		7	FN-Browning M1906 copy	N/A
Le Militaire	Mre d'Armes de Bayonne	A	9Par	7.68	37.00	4.70		8	or "MAB Para"	205
Le Monobloc	Jacquemart	A	25ACP	4.48	13.75	2.08		6		182
Le Novo	Galand	R	25ACP	4.33		1.18		5	folding butt, open frame	136
Leonhardt	Gering	A	32ACP	5.51	22.90	2.95		7	same as "Beholla"	142
Le Page	Le Page	A	380ACP	6.38	25.22	3.78		8	also 12-shot 9BL	199
Le Page	Le Page	A	32ACP	5.75	23.45	3.15		8		199

Name or Model	Maker/entry/origin	Type	Caliber, chambering	Length in	Weight oz	Barrel in	Rifling	Ctg Cap	Remarks	Page
Le Page	Le Page	A	25ACP	4.50	12.15	2.10		6	FN-Browning M1906 copy	199
Le Page	Le Page	R	8Leb	9.45		4.52		8	representative specimen	199
Le Petit Formidable	Manufrance	R	25ACP	4.80		1.77		5		210
Le Protecteur	Turbiaux	M	6cf	4.70		1.65		10	palm-squeezer	351
Le Rapide	Bertrand	A	25ACP	4.70	14.45	1.96		6		49
Lercker	Lercker	A	25ACP	7.25	35.65	4.00		20	selective fire	199
Le Sanspareil	MAPF/Unique	A	25ACP	4.10	12.53	2.16		7	or "Unique M10"	205
Le Secours	Urizar	A	32ACP	5.31	22.20	2.55		7	Eibar-type blowback	358
Le Steph	Bergeron	A	25ACP	4.33	13.00	2.00		6		41
Leston	Unceta	A	25ACP	4.33	11.45	2.16		7	or "Victoria"	112
Le Terrible	Manufrance	R	32ACP					16		210
Le Tout Acier	MAPF/Unique	A	25ACP	4.10	12.53	2.16		7	or "Unique M10"	205
Liberator	Guide Lamp	S	45ACP	5.55	15.70	3.97		1		N/A
Liberty	Retolaza	A	25ACP	4.92	13.00	2.44		6	Eibar-type blowback	260
Liberty	Retolaza	A	32ACP	5.90	26.45	3.22		9	"M1914"; Eibar-type blowback	260
Liberty	Hood	R	32rf	6.50		2.50	5R	5	also 7-shot 22rf	170
Liberty 11	H. Schmidt	R	22LR	5.90	11.46	2.48		6	or "EIG E11"	279
Liberty 12	Röhm	R	22LR	5.90		2.00		6	US sales name	266
Liberty Chief	Miroku	R	38Spl	7.50	17.65	2.50		6		229
Libia	Beistegui	A	25ACP	4.30	12.85	1.89		6		30
Libia	Beistegui	A	32ACP	5.12	25.40	2.36		6		30
Liége	Robar	A	25ACP	4.52	12.70	2.36		6	or "New Model Melior"	265
Liégeoise	Robar	A	25ACP	4.52	12.70	2.36		6	or "New Model Melior"	265
Liégeoise	Esperanza	A	32ACP	5.70	21.35	3.22		6	"Victoria" sold by Robar	112
Lightning	Arcadia Machine & Tool	A	22LR			6.5		10	5in-12.5in barrels	16
Lightning	Echave y Arizmendi	A	25ACP	4.41	13.40	2.16		6	or "Bronco"	104
Lightning	Colt	R	38	9.05	22.90	4.50		6	also 32 caliber	73
Lightning	Whitney Arms Co.	A	22LR	8.98	22.50	4.60		10		388
Lignose	Lignose AG	A	25ACP	4.48	14.10	2.08		6	"Model 2"	199
Lignose	Lignose AG	A	25ACP	4.75	14.45	2.12		6	"Model 2A", "Einhand 2A"	200
Lignose	Lignose AG	A	25ACP	4.70	14.28	2.125		9	"Model 3"	200
Lignose	Lignose AG	A	25ACP	4.68	14.28	2.125		9	"Model 3A", "Einhand 3A"	200
Liliput	Fémáru	A	25ACP	4.33	10.58	2.16		6	"Frommer Liliput" blowback	125
Liliput	Menz	A	4.25cf	3.46	7.95	1.73		6		226
Liliput	Menz	A	25ACP	4.00	10.23	2.00		6	"Liliput"	226
Lincoln	Belgian	R	320	6.10	24.16	2.16		5	representative specimen	N/A
Lion	Johnson, Bye	R	38			2.87		5	also 22, 41, 44	186
Little All Right	Little All Right	R	22Srf	3.93		1.77		5		200
Little Giant	Bacon	R	22rf	4.92		2.25		7		27
Little John	Hood	R	22rf			2.125		7		170
Little Joker	Marlin	R	22rf			2.25		7		212
Little Tom	Tomiška	A	25ACP	4.53	13.23	2.36		6	double action	347
Little Tom	Tomiška	A	32ACP	5.90	20.63	3.54		8		347
Little Tom	Wiener Waffenfabrik	A	32ACP	5.51	20.45	3.15		7		388
Llama Especial	Gabilondo	A	32ACP	6.53		3.75		8		134
Llama series	Gabilondo	A							many different	133
LM-4	American Derringer	M	45ACP	5.2	22.0	2.5		5		13
LM-4	Semmerling and others	M	45ACP	5.20	24.00	3.62		5	also 7-shot 9Par	284
LM-5	American Derringer	M	32Mag	4.0	15.0	2.25		4	Also 25ACP	13
Longines	Cooperativa Obrera	A	32ACP	6.89	21.35	3.82		8	FN-Browning M1910 copy	91
Looking Glass	Acha Hermanos	A	25ACP	4.53	14.46	2.04		6	also in 32ACP	10
Loewe	Loewe	R	44Rus	12.00	40.00	6.50		6	copy S&W Russian	200
Lorcin	Lorcin	A	9Par	7.48	30.70	4.48		13	"L-9"	201
Lorcin	Lorcin	A	25ACP	4.70	13.33	2.32		6	"L-25"	201
Lord & Lady Model	Colt	S	22FR			2.48		1	"Lord & Lady Model"	69
Lone Eagle	Magnum Research	S	various	15.10	67.00	14.00		1	silhouette pistol	202
LS-25	Seecamp	A	25ACP	4.25	12.00	2.00		7	"LS-25"; also LS-32 in 32ACP	284
Luciano	Giacosa	R	38	6.50		2.36		5	sold under EIG name	142
Luger	Stoeger	A	22LR	9.05	29.98	4.50		11	also with 5.5in barrel	329
Luna	Büchel	S	22RF	18.30	40.00	12.00		1	target pistol	54
Lur-Panzer	Echave y Arizmendi	A	22LR	8.78	28.20	4.13		10	Erma EP-22 copy	104
Lusitania	Spanish	A	32ACP	5.90	28.60	3.23		9	Eibar-type blowback	355
MAC 1950	St Etienne, Châtellerault	A	9Par	7.67	30.33	4.40		9	French army pistol	65
Magnum	Smith & Wesson	R	44Mag	11.89	46.90	6.50		6	"Model 29"; 4in, 8in barrels	299
Magnum	Smith & Wesson	R	41 Mag	11.37	48.00	6.00		6	"Model 57"	301
Magnum B	Coonan Arms	A	357Mag	8.31	42.00	5.00		7	based on Colt M1911A1	91
Magnum Massada	IMI	A	357Mag	10.50	61.35	6.13		9	also 41AE, 44,50 Magnum	177
Makarov	Izhevsk	A	9Mak	6.30	23.63	3.56		8	Russian service pistol	180
Maltby & Henley	Norwich Falls	R	32	7.28		3.27		5		237
Maltby & Henley	Norwich Falls	R	38	7.50		3.00		5	hammerless	237
Mamba	Navy Arms	A	9Par	8.50	38.00	4.94	6R	14		234
Mann	Mann	A	32ACP	4.70	12.70	2.36		5		203
Mann	Mann	A	25ACP	4.13	9.20	1.65		5	vest-pocket model	203
Mann	Mann	A	380ACP	4.76	13.40	2.36		5		203
Manurhin	Manurhin	R	357Mag	7.67	31.00	2.48		6	"MR-73"; also 9Par	208

Name or Model	Maker/entry/origin	Type	Caliber, chambering	Length in	Weight oz	Barrel in	Rifling	Ctg Cap	Remarks	Page
Manurhin	Manurhin	R	38Spl	6.42	22.00	2.00		5	"Remora"; other barrels	208
Manurhin	Manurhin	R	357Mag	7.67	32.00	2.48		6	"F-1"; also 9Par, 38Spl	209
Marina	Bolumburu	A	25ACP	4.40	13.40	2.125		6	Eibar-type blowback	50
Marine Corps Model	Colt	R	38	11.00	34.50	6.00		6		75
Mark I	Sturm, Ruger	A	22LR	10.85	42.00	6.89		9	"Mk 1Target"	334
Mark I	Sturm, Ruger	A	22LR	9.50	42.00	5.59		9	"Mk I Bull Barrel"	334
Mark I	Webley	A	455Web	8.50	39.00	5.00	6R	7	Royal Navy issue	382
Mark I	Webley	R	442Bri	9.25	35.00	4.00	7R	6	British issue; Mk I* similar	378
Mark I No. 2	Webley	A	455Web	8.50	39.15	6.00	6R	7	RFC, RHA issue	382
Mark II	Sturm, Ruger	A	22LR	8.82	36.00	4.80		10	"Mk 2 Standard"	334
Mark II	Sturm, Ruger	A	22LR	10.82	42.00	6.89		10	"Mk 2 Target"	334
Mark II	Sturm, Ruger	A	22LR	11.14	42.92	6.89		10	"Mk 2 Government Target"	334
Mark II	Webley	R	455Bri	9.25	35.10	4.00	7R	6	British issue; II*, II** similar	379
Mark III	Webley	R	455Bri	9.50	37.00	4.00	7R	6	British issue	379
Mark IV	Webley	R	320cf	9.00	29.00	4.00	7R	6		380
Mark IV	Webley	R	380cf	10.10	25.75	4.00	7R	6		380
Mark IV	Webley	R	380cf	9.25	26.25	4.00	7R	6	target pattern	380
Mark IV	Webley	R	22LR	10.50	33.33	6.00		6	target pattern	380
Mark IV	Webley	R	320cf	7.00	22.00	3.00	7R	6	pocket pattern; also 380	380
Mark IV	Webley	R	455Bri	9.25	35.00	4.00	7R	6	British issue	380
Mark V	Webley	R	455Bri	9.25	35.50	4.00	7R	6	British issue	379
Mark V	Webley	R	455Bri	11.30	37.50	6.00	7R	6	British issue	379
Mark VI	Webley	R	455Bri	11.33	38.00	6.00	7R	6	British issue; "No. 1 Mk VI"	379
Mark 40	Wichita Arms	S	308	19.40	72.00	13.00		-	bolt action	388
Marke	J. Bascaran	A	25ACP	4.48	14.50	2.24		6	Eibar-type blowback	28
Marlin	Marlin	R	22RF	6.50		3.00		7	"XX Standard"; tip-barrel	212
Marlin	Marlin	R	30RF	6.89		3.00		5	"XXX Standard"; tip-barrel	212
Marlin	Marlin	R	32RF	6.89		3.00		5	"No. 32 Standard"; tip-barrel	212
Marlin	Marlin	R	38	7.48		3.25		5	"No. 38 Standard"; tip-barrel	212
Marlin	Marlin	R	38	7.50		3.25		5	"M1887 DA"; also 6-shot 32	212
Marquis of Lorne	Hood	R	32rf	6.50		2.75		5	also 7-shot 22rf	170
Mars	Bergmann	A	9Bgm	10.00	36.00	4.00		6		42
Mars	Kohout	A	25ACP	4.25	13.20	1.97		6		190
Mars	Kohout	A	32ACP	6.50	22.90	3.78		6		190
Mars	Mars; Webley	A	8.5cf	11.80	49.00	8.75		10	many variants	381
Mars	Mars; Webley	A	9cf	11.80	52.00	8.75		10	or "360 Mars"	381
Mars	Mars; Webley	A	450cf	11.50	50.00	8.45		8		381
Mars	MAPF/Uniques	A	25ACP	4.10	12.53	2.16		7	or "Unique M10"	206
Marshall	Colt	R	38	9.25	31.00	4.00		6		78
Marte	Urquiaga y Muguruzu	A	25ACP	4.48	14.10	2.125		6	Eibar type blowback	110
Martian	M. Bascaran	A	25ACP	4.13	11.21	1.70		6	original; also 32ACP	29
Martian	M. Bascaran	A	32ACP	6.10	22.00	3.46		8	Eibar type blowback	29
Martigny	J. Bascaran	A	25ACP	4.49	11.65	2.16		6	Eibar type blowback	28
Martin-Marres-Braendlin	Braendlin Armoury	M	450	9.25		5.12		4	other calibers	51
MAS 35S	Saint-Étienne	A	7,65L	7.40	27.15	4.16		8		273
Match Model	Wesson Firearms	A	45ACP	8.70	38.80	5.00		7	M1911-type target pistol	386
Matchmaster	Safari Arms	A	45ACP	8.70	39.85	5.00		7	M1911A1 clone	272
Mateba	Macchine termo Ballistiche	R	38Spl	10.43	43.38	3.00		8	"MTR-8"; also 357 Mag	202
Mateba	Macchine termo Ballistiche	R	38Spl	11.42	51.14	3.93		12	"MTR-12"; also 357 Mag	202
Mateba	Macchine termo Ballistiche	R	22LR	10.82	45.85	3.93		20	"MTR-20"	202
Mateba	Macchine termo Ballistiche	R	357 Mag	7.28	37.75	3.07		6	"M2006M"; 6.2, 8.35in barrels	202
Mateba	Macchine termo Ballistiche	R	38 Spl	8.35		4.02		7	"M2007S"	202
Mauser	Mauser-Jagdwaffen	R	38Spl	6.89	23.20	2.50	6R	8	"M38SP"; made by Gamba	222
Mauser-Parabellum	Mauser-Jagdwaffen	A	9Par	8.46	32.00	4.00	4 or 6R	8	"29/70"; Swiss 06/29 copy	222
Mauser-Parabellum	Mauser-Jagdwaffen	A	9Par	9.15	32.00	4.70		8	"06/73"	223
Max-I	Gabilondo	A	45ACP	8.50	35.60	5.11	6R	7		134
Max-I	Gabilondo	A	9Par	7.87	33.50	4.25	6R	9		134
Maxim	Rigarmi	A	25ACP	4.71	13.90	2.28		6	or Rigarmi M1953	265
Maximum	MOA Corporation	S	22LR		56.00	8.50		-	infinity of calibers	230
Mayer	Mayer	R	32	7.68	20.70	3.00	6R	5	also 6-shot 22LR	N/A
Mayor	Mayor	A	25ACP	4.65	11.55	2.16		5		225
MC5	Victory Arms Co	A	9Par	8.60	45.00	4.37	6R	17	"Victory MC-5"; multi-caliber	359
MD1	Imbel	A	380ACP	7.55	37.12	4.10	6R	7	Colt-Browning	175
MD1	Imbel	A	38Sup	8.62	38.00	5.03	6L	8	Colt-Browning	175
MD1	Imbel	A	32ACP	7.55	32.25	4.10	6R	9	Colt-Browning	175
Medusa	Phillips & Rodgers	R	357Mag			6.00	6R	6	"Model 47"; various calibers	248
Meiji 26th Year Type	Koishikawa	R	9mm	8.50	31.00	4.70	6L	6	Japanese army "M1893"	190
Melior	Robar	A	25ACP	4.33	14.10	2.09		6	"Old Model"	265
Melior	Robar	A	32ACP	6.38	22.90	3.54		8	"Old Model"	265
Melior	Robar	A	25ACP	4.53	12.70	2.36		6	"New Model"	265
Melior	Robar	A	32ACP	5.90	22.40	3.54		6	"New Model"; also 380ACP	265
Mendoza	Mendoza	S	22LR	8.07	14.80	4.33		1		226
Menta	Menz	A	32ACP	5.51	22.57	2.95		7	"Beholla" copy	226
Menta	Menz	S	25ACP	4.65	13.50	2.48	6T	6	scaled-down "Beholla"	226
Mercury	Robar	A	22LR	5.90	22.40	3.54		7	"Model 222"; US "Melior"	265
Meriden	Meriden	R	38	7.28		3.25		5	top break	227

Name or Model	Maker/entry/origin	Type	Caliber, chambering	Length in	Weight oz	Barrel in	Rifling	Ctg Cap	Remarks	Page
Merke	Ormachea	A	25ACP	4.48	12.70	2.16		6	Eibar-type blowback	244
Merwin & Hulbert	Hopkins & Allen	R	44	11.00	47.25	7.00		6	DA; "Army Belt Model"	172
Merwin & Hulbert	Hopkins & Allen	R	44	8.00	37.40	3.94		6	DA; "Army Pocket"	172
Merwin & Hulbert	Hopkins & Allen	R	38			3.50		5	DA; "Pocket Model"	172
Merwin & Hulbert	Hopkins & Allen	R	32	6.41		3.50		5	DA; "Pocket Model"	172
Merwin & Hulbert	Hopkins & Alen	R	32			5.50		7	DA; target Model	172
Metropolitan Police	Norwich Pistol Co.	R	32RF			3.0		5	DA	237
Metropolitan Police	Webley	R	450	7.00	27.00	2.50	7R	6		374
Mikros	MAPF/Unique	A	25ACP	4.45	12.34	2.32		7		206
Mikros	MAPF/Unique	A	25ACP	4.40	12.35	2.25		6	"Model 58"	206
Milady	Ancion-Marx	R	25ACP					5		15
Military	Retolaza	A	25ACP	4.92	13.00	2.44		6	Eibar type blowback	260
Military Model	Manufrance	A	9BL	8.00	38.44	5.00		8	"Le Français M1928"	211
Military & Police	Smith & Wesson	R	38	9.25	34.00	4.00		6	or Model 10	296
Military & Police	Smith & Wesson	R	38	6.89	18.00	2.125		6	"M&P Airweight" or "Model 12"	297
Military & Police	Smith & Wesson	R	41 Mag	9.25	38.80	4.00		6	"M&P Magnum" or "Model 58"	301
Military & Police	Smith & Wesson	R	38	9.25	34.00	4.00		6	"M&P Stainless" or "Model 64"	302
Mililary & Police	Smith & Wesson	R	9Par	7.87	31.75	3.00		6	or "Model 547"	303
Militar y Policia	Ojanguren y Vidosa	R	38	10.00	31.20	5.00		6	copy S&W M&P	243
Millennium Series	American Derringer	M	38Spl	9.25	23.0	8.0		2	Also 44-40WCF, 45LColt	14
Minerva	Grande Précision	A	25ACP	4.52	12.85	2.16		7	Eibar-type blowback	146
Mini Massada	IMI	A	9Par	8.20	37.75	4.92		10	also 40SW, 45ACP	178
Mini-Revolver	North American Arms	R	22LR	3.27		1.00		5		236
Miroku Model 6	Miroku Firearms Cio	R	38	5.90	30.35	1.97		6		229
Miroku Special Police	Miroku Firearms Co	R	38	7.68	32.00	2.52		5		229
Mitchell	Mitchell	R	357Mag	9.75	36.50	5.50		6	Yugoslavian; also 44 Mag	229
Mitchell	Mitchell	A	22LR	11.25	39.50	6.73		10	"Olympic ISU"	229
Mitchell	Mitchell	A	22LR	9.72	44.45	5.50		9	"Trophy 2"	229
Mitchell	Mitchell	A	22LR	8.86	43.50	4.52		10	"Victor 2"	229
Mitrailleuse	Manufrance	M	8cf	5.15	10.00	2.20		5	or "Gaulois"	210
MKE	MKE	A	380ACP	6.70	24.00	3.86		7	also 32CP	203
MM31	E. Arostegui	A	7.63Msr	11.22	43.90	5.12	6R	10	Azul; selective fire	20
MNZ-75	Norinco	A	9Par	7.20		3.58		12	compact version of NZ-75	236
Model I	Gabilondo	A	32ACP	6.30		3.74		8	"Llama"	133
Model II	Langenhan	A	25ACP	5.75	17.63	2.28		5		197
Model II	Gabilondo	A	380ACP						"Llama"	133
Model III	Langenhan	A	25ACP	4.70	16.55	2.28		5		198
Model III	Gabilondo	A	380ACP	6.30	19.40	3.62		7	"Llama"	133
Model IV	Gabilondo	A	9BB						"Llama"	133
Model V	Gabilondo	A	38Sup						"Llama"	133
Model VI	Gabilondo	A	380ACP						"Llama"	133
Model VII	Gabilondo	A	38Sup						"Llama"	133
Model VIII	Gabilondo	A	38Sup	8.46	38.80	5.00		9	"Llama"	133
Model IX	Gabilondo	A	45ACP	8.46	37.90	5.00		7	"Llama"	133
Model IX	Gabilondo	A	9BB	8.46	30.70	5.00		8	"Llama"	133
Model IX-C	Gabilondo	A	45ACP	8.50	40.55	5.12	6R	10	"Llama"	134
Model IX-D	Gabilondo	A	45ACP	7.80	35.60	4.25	6R	10	"Llama"	134
Model X	Gabilondo	A	32ACP	6.10		3.54		8	"Llama"	134
Model X-A	Gabilondo	A	32ACP	6.50	22.90	3.66		8	"Llama"	134
Model XI	Gabilondo	A	9Par	8.46	37.90	5.00		8	"Llama"	134
Model XII-B	Gabilondo	A	40S&W	7.91	35.60	4.33	6R	8	1995; "Llama"; M1911 type	134
Model XV	Gabilondo	A	22LR	6.50	21.00	3.62		9	"Llama"	134
Model XVI	Gabilondo	A	22LR	6.50	17.10	3.62		9	"Llama"	134
Model XVII	Gabilondo	A	22LR	4.80	13.00	2.36		6	"Llama"	134
Model XVIII	Gabilondo	A	25ACP	4.70	13.93	2.28		6	"Llama"	134
Model XX	Gabilondo	A	32ACP	6.50	15.87	3.66		8	"Llama"	134
Model XXII	Gabilondo	R	38Spl					6	"Llama"	131
Model XXVI	Gabilondo	R	38Spl	9.25	33.00	4.00		6	"Llama", "Martial"; also 357M	131
Model XXVII	Gabilondo	R	32			2.16		6	"Llama"	131
Model XXVIII	Gabilondo	R	22LR						"Llama"; target model	131
Model 1	American Derringer	M	38Spl	4.75	15.6	3.0		2	also 22LR to 45-70Gvt	13
Model 1	Deringer	R	22rf			3.00		7	also 32rf	96
Model 1	Haenel	A	25ACP	4.70	13.40	2.48		6	"Haenel-Schmeisser"	149
Model 1	Kommer	A	25ACP	4.13	13.05	2.00		7	Models 2, 3 similar	192
Model 1	Krauser	A	25ACP	4.33	10.60	1.96		6	"Helfricht Model 1"	194
Model 1	Pickert (Arminius)	R	22RF	5.341	7.76	1.96		7		248
Model 1	Echeverria	A	32ACP	6.50	32.25	3.86		8	"Star"	104
Model 1	Walther	A	25ACP	4.50	13.00	2.05	4R	6		360
Model 1	Zaragoza	A	22LR	5.90	21.87	3.82		8	"Corla"	391
Model 2	American Derringer	S	22LR	5.5	5.7	2.0		1	also 25ACP, 32ACP	13
Model 2	Bergmann	A	25ACP	4.65	14.76	2.17	6R	6		42
Model 2	Deringer	R	22rf			3.00		7	also 32rf, round barrel	96
Model 2	Haenel	A	25ACP	3.93	11.80	2.04		6	"Haenel-Schmeisser"	149
Model 2	Krauser	A	25ACP	4.33	10.60	1.96		6	"Helfricht Model 2"	194
Model 2	Lignose	A	25ACP	4.48	14.10	2.08		6		200

Name or Model	Maker/entry/origin	Type	Caliber, chambering	Length in	Weight oz	Barrel in	Rifling	Ctg Cap	Remarks	Page
Model 2	Menz	A	32ACP	5.12	15.34	2.67	6R	6	"Model 2", enlarged Liliput	227
Model 2	Pickert (Arminius)	R	22RF	8.26	8.64	5.9		7		249
Model 2	Walther	A	25ACP	4.30	9.70	2.12	6R	6		360
Model 2	Zaragoza	A	22LR	6.61	23.10	4.52		8	"Corla"	391
Model 2A	Lignose	A	25ACP	4.75	14.45	2.12		6	"Einhand 2A"	200
Model 3	American Derringer	S	32Mag	5.0	8.0	1.8		1	also 38Spl	13
Model 3	Bergmann	A	25ACP	4.72	16.75	2.17	6R	9		42
Model 3	Krauser	A	25ACP	4.33	10.60	1.96		6	"Helfricht Model 3"	194
Model 3	Lignose	A	25ACP	4.70	14.28	2.125		9		200
Model 3	Pickert (Arminius)	R	25ACP	5.31	8.81	1.96		5	hammerless	249
Model 3	Trejo	A	380ACP	6.60	23.65	3.54		8	selective fire	348
Model 3	Walther	A	32ACP	5.00	16.50	2.62	6R	6		361
Model 3A	Lignose	A	25ACP	4.68	14.28	2.125		9	"Einhand 3A"	200
Model 4	American Derringer	M	357Mag	6.5	16.7	4.75		2	also 41Mag, 410shot, 45LColt	14
Model 4	Kommer	A	32ACP	5.50	20.10	3.00		7		192
Model 4	Krauser	A	25ACP	4.29	12..00	1.81		6	"Helfricht Model 4"	194
Model 4	Pickert (Arminius)	R	5.5VD	5.12	10.58	1.96		5		249
Model 4	Walther	A	32ACP	6.00	19.50	3.36	4R	8		361
Model 5	Galesi	A	32ACP	6.30		3.54		7	"Model 5"	136
Model 5	Walther	A	25ACP	4.25	9.75	2.12	4R	6		361
Model 5/1	Pickert (Arminius)	R	7.5 Nag	6.89	13.40	2.55		5		249
Model 5/2	Pickert (Arminius)	R	7.62Rus	6.89	14.11	3.15		5		249
Model 6	American Derringer	M	357Mag	7.22	20.0	6.0		2	also 410shot, 45LColt 45ACP	14
Model 6	Galesi	A	25ACP	4.65		2.32		7	"Model 6"	136
Model 6	Walther	A	9Par	8.25	34.00	4.75	4R	8		361
Model 7	EIG Corp	R	22LR	5.90	11.46	2.48		6	US name for Röhm RG10	105
Model 7	Pickert (Arminius)	R	320	5.84	14.11	2.52		5	folding trigger	249
Model 7	Walther	A	25ACP	5.25	12.00	3.03	4R	8		361
Model 8	American Derringer	M	45LColt	9.25	23.0	8.0		2	also 410shot	14
Model 8	Pickert (Arminius)	R	320	5.31	14./10	2.5		5	hammerless, folding trigger	249
Model 8	Walther	A	25ACP	5.13	13.00	2.83	6R	8		361
Model 9	Galesi	A	32ACP	6.30		3.50		7	"Model 9"	136
Model 9	Pickert (Arminius)	R	32ACP	6.61	15.87	3.0		6		249
Model 9	Walther	A	25ACP	4.02	9.25	2.01	6R	6		362
Model 9A	Pickert (Arminius)	R	32ACP	5.90	14.81	2.51		6		249
Model 9*	Steyr	A	9IMI	6.93	23.39	4.01	6R	14	sold in Italy only	328
Model 10	American Derringer	M	38Spl	4.75	12.5	3.0		2	Also 45LColt, 45ACP	14
Model 10	MAPF/Unique	A	25ACP	4.13	12.87	2.08		7	appears under many names	206
Model 10	Pickert (Arminius)	R	32ACP	5.70	14.10	2.5		5	hammerless	249
Model 10	Star–Echeverria	A	10Auto	8.35	44.27	4.60		14	or "Model Ten"	322
Model 10	Stevens	S	22rf	9.45		8.00		1	target pistol; also 6in	328
Model 11	Dornheim	A	25ACP	4.57	15.00	2.24	6R	6	"Gecado" (Reck Model 11)	102
Model 11	MAPF/Unique	A	25ACP	4.10	12.70	2.10		6		206
Model 11/2	Smith & Wesson	R	32rf		12.52	3.50		5	tip-up	287
Model 12	MAPF/Unique	A	25ACP	4.10	12.70	2.10		6		206
Model 13	MAPF/Unique	A	25ACP	4.10	13.60	2.10		7		206
Model 13	Pickert (Arminius)	R	38			2.5		5		249
Model 13	Rossi	R	22LR		11.65	3.00		7	"Princess Model"	268
Model 13A	Pickert (Arminius)	R	22rf			5.31		8		249
Model 14	MAPF/Unique	A	25ACP	4.40	14.10	2.125		9		206
Model 14	Pickert (Arminius)	R	38			2.5		5		249
Model 14	Smith & Wesson	R	38	11.25	38.45	6.00		6	"K-38 Masterpiece"	297
Model 14	D. Wesson Arms	R	357Mag	9.25	34.00	4.00		6	other barrels	385
Model 15	MAPF/Unique	A	32ACP	4.96	20.10	2.60		6		206
Model 15	Rock Island Arsenal	A	45ACP	7.87	36.00	3.94	6L	7	"General Officer's Model"	N/A
Model 15	Smith & Wesson	R	38	9.00	34.00	4.00		6	"Combat Masterpiece"	297
Model 15	D. Wesson Arms	R	357Mag	9.25	36.00	4.00		6	also in 38Spl	385
Model 16	MAPF/Unique	A	32ACP	4.96	21.50	2.60		7		206
Model 16	Smith & Wesson	R	32	11.20	38.45	6.00		6	"K-32 Masterpiece"	297
Model 17	Glock	A	9Par	8.00	22.00	4.49	6R	17	"Glock 17"; basic model	144
Model 17	MAPF/Unique	A	32ACP	5.90	27.65	3.35		9		206
Model 17	Smith & Wesson	R	22LR	11.25	38.45	6.00		8	"K-22 Masterpiece"	297
Model 17L	Glock	A	9Par	9.52	25.63	6.02	6R	17	"Glock 17L"; sport model	144
Model 18	MAPF/Unique	A	32ACP	5.70	21.15	1.97		6		207
Model 18	Smith & Wesson	R	22LR	9.15	36.50	4.00		6		298
Model 18C	Glock	A	9Par	8.00	20.60	4.48	6R	33	"Glock 18C"; selective fire	144
Model 19	Glock	A	9Par	7.40	20.98	4.00	6R	15	"Glock 19"; compact 17	144
Model 19	MAPF/Unique	A	32ACP	5.70	21.70	3.15		7		207
Model 19	Smith & Wesson	R	357Mag	7.50	31.00	2.52		6	"Combat Magnum"	298
Model 20	Beretta	A	25ACP	4.92	10.93	2.36		8		31
Model 20	Glock	A	10mm	8.35	27.65	4.60	6R	15	"Glock 20"	144
Model 20	Ithaca	S	22LR			10.00		1	also 12in barrel	178
Model 20	MAPF/Unique	A	32ACP	5.70	22.90	3.46		9		207
Model 21	Glock	A	45ACP	8.35	26.27	4.60	6R	13	"Glock 21"	144
Model 21	MAPF/Unique	A	380ACP	5.70	21.70	3.45		6		207
Model 21	Smith & Wesson	R	44	11.75	36.00	6.50		6	"M1950 Military"	298

Name or Model	Maker/entry/origin	Type	Caliber, chambering	Length in	Weight oz	Barrel in	Rifling	Ctg Cap	Remarks	Page
Model 22	Česká Zbrojovka	A	25ACP	4.65	14.81	2.125		6	improved Fox	56
Model 22	Glock	A	40S&W	8.00	22.75	4.48	6R	15	"Glock 22"	144
Model 22	Rossi	R	32	6.30	19.75	1.97		6	"Ranger Model"	268
Model 22	Smith & Wesson	R	45ACP	10.63	36.35	5.50		6	"M1950 Army"	298
Model 23	Bersa	A	22LR	6.57	24,.33	3.50	6R	10		47
Model 23	Glock	A	40S&W	7.40	21.06	4.00	6R	13	"Glock 23"; compact 22	144
Model 23	Smith & Wesson	R	38	11.75	41.80	6.50		6	"Outdoorsman" or "38/44"	298
Model 24	Bersa	A	22LR	7.20	25.0	4.0	6R	10	also with 5 & 6in barrels	47
Model 24	Česká Zbrojovka	A	380ACP	6.00	23.97	3.54		8		56
Model 24	Glock	A	40S&W	8.86	26.45	6.00	6R	15	"Glock 24"; 24C has vent. brl.	144
Model 24	Smith & Wesson	R	44	11.75	39.50	6.50		6	"Target Model"	298
Model 25	Glock	A	380ACP	6.85	20.10	4.00	6R	15	"Glock 25"	145
Model 25	Smith & Wesson	R	44	11.88	45.00	6.50		6	"Target Model 1955"	298
Model 26	Glock	A	9Par	6.29	19.75	3.46	6R	10	"Glock 26"; sub-compact	145
Model 27	Česká Zbrojovka	A	32ACP	6.46	25.05	3.82		8	Also in 380ACP	57
Model 27	Glock	A	40S&W	6.29	19.75	3.46	6R	9	"Glock 27"; sub-compact	145
Model 27	Phillips & Rodgers	R	357Mag			6.00	6R	6	"Medusa 47"; various calibers	248
Model 27	Rossi	R	38Spl	6.30	20.15	2.00		5		269
Model 27	Smith & Wesson	R	357Mag	12.10	44.00	5.90		6	variant barrels	299
Model 30	Smith & Wesson	R	32	8.00	18.00	4.00		6	"K-32 Hand Ejector"	299
Model 30M	Echeverria	A	9Par	8.07	40.20	4.33		15	"Star 30M"; all steel	323
Model 30P	Echeverria	A	9Par	7.60	38.80	3.86		15	"Star 30P"; all steel	323
Model 30PK	Echeverria	A	9Par	7.60	30.33	3.86		15	"Star 30PK"; alloy frame	323
Model 30 Match	Echeverria	A	9Par	8.07	40.20	4.33		15	"Star 30 Match"	323
Model 31	Smith & Wesson	R	32	8.50	18.85	4.00		6	"Regulation Police"	299
Model 32	Smith & Wesson	R	38	6.30	15.20	2.125		5	"Terrier"	299
Model 33	Smith & Wesson	R	38	8.50	18.00	4.00		6	"Regulation Police"	299
Model 34	Smith & Wesson	R	22LR	8.00	24.35	4.00		6	or "Kit Gun", "22/32"	300
Model 35	Smith & Wesson	R	22LR	10.50	25.00	6.00		6	or "Target Model 1953"	300
Model 36	Česká Zbrojovka	A	25ACP	5.04	13.75	2.12		7	self-cocking action	57
Model 36LS	Smith & Wesson	R	38Spl	6.22	20.00	2.00		5	"Ladysmith"	300
Model 38	Česká Zbrojovka	A	380ACP	8.11	32.10	4.65		8	self-cocking action	57
Model 38	Jennings	A	380ACP	5.31	15.0	2.80	6R	6	Bryco; also 22LR, 32ACP	53
Model 38	Rossi	R	22LR	10.23	25.75	6.00		6		269
Model 38/200	Smith & Wesson	R	38	10.12	31.00	5.00		6	British service; also 4, 6in brls	300
Model 38 H	Sauer	A	32ACP	6.73	25.40	3.25		8	double action	277
Model 39	Smith & Wesson	A	9Par	7.40	26.45	4.00		8		307
Model 40	Steyr	A	40S&W	6.93	24.05	4.01	6R	12	Also "M9" 14—shot 9Par	328
Model 40	D. Wesson Arms	R	357Mag	14.30	64.00	8.00		6		386
Model 41	Astra-Unceta	R	41 Mag	11.50	4.49	5.90		5		22
Model 41	Smith & Wesson	A	22LR	12.00	43.55	7.125		10		307
Model 42	Rossi	R	22LR	6.30	20.50	1.97		6	Model 43 has 3in barrel	269
Model 43	Smith & Wesson	R	22LR	7.55	14.28	3.54		6	or Kit Gun Airweight	301
Model 43	Star	A	9Par	6.42	28.20	3.38		7	"Firestar"	323
Model 44	Astra	R	44 Mag	14.0	48.67	8.50		6		22
Model 45	Astra	R	45 Colt	11.53	44.62	6.0		6		22
Model 45	Česká Zbrojovka	A	25ACP	5.04	15.00	2.52		7		58
Model 48	Jennings	A	380ACP	6.70	19.0	3.97	6R	6	Bryco; also 22LR , 32ACP	53
Model 48	Smith & Wesson	R	22WMRF	11.15	39.00	6.00		6	or "K-22 Masterpiece"	301
Model 50	Ceska Zbrojovka	A	32ACP	6.57	25.69	3.77		8		58
Model 51	Remington	A	32ACP	6.61	21.15	3.50		8	also 380ACP	259
Model 52	Česká Zbrojovka	A	7.65Cze	8.70	33.86	4.70		8		58
Model 52	MAPF/Unique	A	22LR	5.70		3.15		8		207
Model 52	Smith & Wesson	A	38	8.66	41.00	5.00		5		308
Model 53	Remington Arms Co.	A	45ACP						developed for US Navy	259
Model 55SA	I. Johnson	R	22LR	7.28	24.00	2.50		8	"Cadet"	184
Model 57	Zastava	A	7.62R	7.87	31.75	4.56		8	copy Tokarev TT-33	391
Model 57A	Shin Chuo Kogyo	A	9Par	7.80	28.20	4.60		8	"New Nambu"	285
Model 57A	I. Johnson	R	22LR	10.75	34.00	6.00		8	"Target"	184
Model 57B	Shin Chuo Kogyo	A	32ACP	6.30	21.00	3.54		8	"New Nambu"	285
Model 58	MAPF/Unique	A	25ACP	4.40	12.35	2.25		6	"Mikros 58"	206
Model 59	Smith & Wesson	A	9Par	7.45	27.68	4.00		14		308
Model 60	V. Bernardelli	A	32ACP	6.50	24.16	3.54	6R	8	also 380ACP, 25ACP, 22LR	46
Model 60LS	Smith & Wesson	R	38Spl	6.22	20.00	2.00		5	"Ladysmith" stainless	302
Model 60	Shin Chuo Kohyo	R	38	7.75	24.00	3.00		5	"New Nambu"	285
Model 63	Smith & Wesson	R	22LR	8.66	24.15	4.00		6	or "Kit Gun Stainless"	302
Model 64P	J.G. Anschütz	S	22LR	18.5	56.0	10.1		1	bolt action	15
Model 65	Taurus	R	357Mag	8.46	32.10	3.00		6	other barrel lengths	340
Model 66	Smith & Wesson	R	357Mag	9.50	35.00	4.00		6	or "357 Mag Stainless"	302
Model 66	Taurus	R	357Mag	8.46	32.45	3.00		6		340
Model 67	Smith & Wesson	R	38	9.00	34.00	4.00		6	"Model 15 stainless"	302
Model 68	Bernardelli	A	22rf	4.23	8.82	2.20	6R	5		46
Model 68	Rossi	R	38Spl	7.32	21.15	3.00		5		269
Model 69	Bernardelli	A	22LR	9.00	38.0	5.90	6R	10	target pistol	46
Model 70	Beretta	A	32ACP	6.30	23.28	3.35		7		31
Model 70	Česká Zbrojovka	A	32CP	6.81	24.00	3.82		8	improved CZ50	58

Name or Model	Maker/entry/origin	Type	Caliber, chambering	Length in	Weight oz	Barrel in	Rifling	Ctg Cap	Remarks	Page
Model 70	Drulov	S	22LR	14.76	44.00	9.84		1	bolt action	102
Model 70	Taurus	R	32	8.62	28.40	2.95		6	also 4in barrel	340
Model 70	Zastava	A	9Par	7.87	31.20	4.56		8	modified TT33 copy	391
Model 70	Zastava	A	32ACP	6.50	26.10	3.70		8	also 380ACP	391
Model 71	Beretta	A	22LR	8.86	18.34	5.90	6R	8		31
Model 71	Taurus	R	32	8.62	33.15	4.00		6	also 5in barrel	340
Model 73	Bersa	A	32ACP	6.57	25.40	3.50	6R	7		47
Model 73	Taurus	R	32	6.25	20.00	1.07		6	also 3in barrel	340
Model 75	Česká Zbrojovka	A	9Par	8.00	34.57	4.70		15	double action	59
Model 75	Drulov	S	22LR	14.76	44.00	9.84		1	bolt actiom	103
Model 75 Auto	Česká Zbrojovka	A	9Par	8.00	36.00	4.82	6R	15,25	selective fire. Also 6in barrel	59
Model 75B	Česká Zbrojovka	A	9Par	8.11	35.27	4.70	6R	15	ČZ75 with firing pin safety	59
Model 75BD	Česká Zbrojovka	A	9Par	8.11	35.27	4.70	6R	10	ČZ75B with de-cocking lever.	59
Model 75 Compact	Česká Zbrojovka	A	9Par	7.32	32.45	3.93	6R	13		59
Model 75 Kadet	Česká Zbrojovka	A	22LR	8.11	37.75	4.88	6R	10	ČZ75 converted to blowback	60
Model 76	Beretta	A	22LR	9.05	34.92	5.90		10	or "Jaguar"	31
Model 76	Taurus	R	32	11.50	38.80	6.00		6	target model	340
Model 80	Beretta	A	22LR	11.42		6.69		10	target model	32
Model 80	High Standard	A	22LR	10.86	40.90	6.50		10	"J.C. Higgins"; Duramatic type	165
Model 80	Taurus	R	38Spl	9.25	34.56	3.93		6	other barrel lengths	340
Model 80SA	Mauser-Jagdwaffen	A	9Par	8.00	31.70	4.64	6R	14	Made in Hungary	225
Model 81	Beretta	A	32ACP	6.77	23.63	3.82		12		32
Model 82	Česká Zbrojovka	A	9Mak	6.77	28.00	3.78	6R	12	double action	60
Model 82BB	Beretta	A	32ACP	6.77	20.10	3.82		8	M81 with smaller magazine	32
Model 82	Gabilondo	A	9Par	8.00	39.00	4.25		15		134
Model 82	Taurus	R	38Spl	9.25	33.00	3.92		6		340
Model 83	Bersa	A	380ACP	6.57	25.10	3.50	6R	7	replaced Mod 383 in 1988	47
Model 83	Česká Zbrojovka	A	32ACP	6.81	22.92	3.77	6R	15	also 9Mak or 380ACP	60
Model 83	Taurus	R	38Spl	9.25	33.00	3.92		6	M82 with adjustable trigger	341
Model 83	Zastava	R	357Mag	7.40	31.75	2.50		6	"M83 Magnum"; also 9Par	391
Model 84	Beretta	A	380ACP	6.77	23.63	3.82		13	similar to M81 except caliber	32
Model 84F	Beretta	A	380ACP	6.77	23.60	3.82		13	M84 with de-cocking lever	32
Model 84BB	Beretta	A	380ACP	6.77	23.28	3.82		8	M84 with smaller magazine	32
Model 85	Bersa	A	380ACP	6.57	25.75	3.50	6R	13	M86 same but matt finish	48
Model 85	Česká Zbrojovka	A	9Par	8.00	34.75	4.70	6R	15	improved ČZ75	60
Model 85	MAPF/Unique	A	22LR	7.20	21.70	4.33		10	J.C. Higgins	208
Model 85	Rossi	R	38Spl	6.80	26.45	1.97		6		269
Model 85	Taurus	R	38Spl	6.80	27.50	1.97		6		341
Model 85BB	Beretta	A	380ACP	6.77	21.86	3.82		8		32
Model 85F	Beretta	A	380ACP	6.77	21.86	3.82	6R	8	M85BB with a de-cocker	32
Model 86	Beretta	A	380ACP	7.28	23.28	4.37	6R	8	tip-up barrel	32
Model 86	Taurus	R	38	10.83	34.90	5.90		6		341
Model 87	Gabilondo	A	9Par	9.49	46.90	6.00		14	competition model	134
Model 87	Rossi	R	38Spl	6.30	29.45	1.97		5		269
Model 87BB	Beretta	A	22LR	6.77	20.10	3.82	6R	8	as 84BB except caliber	32
Model 87BB/LB	Beretta	A	22LR	8.86	23.98	5.90	6R	8	long-barrel version	32
Model 88	High Standard	A	22LR	9.25	22.90	3.93		9	"J.C. Higgins"; Sentinel type	165
Model 88	Rossi	R	38Spl	7.32	21.50	3..00		5		269
Model 88	Taurus	R	38Spl	8.46	33.50	3.00		6	also 4in barrel	341
Model 89	Beretta	A	22LR	9.45	40.92	5.90	6R	8	target pistol	33
Model 89	Rossi	R	32	7.32	21.15	3.00		6		269
Model 90	Beretta	A	32ACP	6.69	31.10	3.54	6R	8	double action trigger	33
Model 90	Bersa	A	9Par	7.87	31.75	4.86	6R	13		48
Model 90	High Standard	R	22LR	9.45	27.00	4.50		7	"J.C. Higgins"; Double Nine	165
Model 90DA	Mauser-Jagdwaffen	A	9Par	8.00	35.20	4.54	6R	14	made by Fegyver	225
Model 90DA C	Mauser-Jagdwaffen	A	9Par	7.40	33.50	4.13	6R	13	"Compact" made by Fegyver	225
Model 90	Taurus	R	22LR	9.45	36.00	3.92		6		341
Model 92	Beretta	A	9Par	8.54	33.51	4.92	6R	15	military, double action	33
Model 92	Česká Zbrojovka	A	25ACP	5.03	15.17	2.50	6R	8		60
Model 92D	Beretta	A	9Par	8.54	32.45	4.92	6R	15	DA only, no manual safety	33
Model 92DS	Beretta	A	9Par	8.54	32.45	4.92	6R	15	DA only, with manual safety	34
Model 92F	Beretta	A	9Par	8.54	32.45	4.92	6R	15	M92 modified for US Army	34
Model 92F C	Beretta	A	9Par	7.75		4.29	6R	13	or "92F Compact"	34
Model 92F CM	Beretta	A	9Par	7.75		4.29	6R	8	M92FC wth smaller magazine	34
Model 92FS	Beretta	A	9Par	8..74	34.57	4.92	6R	15	M92F with slide stop safety	34
Model 92FS C	Beretta	A	9Par	7.75		4.29	6R	13	Improved M92SBC	34
Model 92G	Beretta	A	9Par	8.54	32.45	4.92	6R	15	de-cocker, no manual safety	35
Model 92S	Beretta	A	9Par	8.54	33.51	4.92	6R	15	safety/de-cock on slide	35
Model 92SB	Beretta	A	9Par	8.54	33.50	4.92	6R	15	improved "S"	35
Model 92SB C	Beretta	A	9Par	7.75		4.29	6R	13	compact version of M92SB	35
Model 92SB C Type M	Beretta	A	9Par	7.75		4.29	6R	8	M92SBC with smaller mag	36
Model 93R	Beretta	A	9Par	9.45	39.50	6.15	6R	15,25	selective fire version of M92	36
Model 94	Česká Zbrojovka	A	22LR	8.18		4.65		10		61
Model 94	Rossi	R	38Spl	6.60	26.45	1.97		6		269
Model 94	Taurus	R	22LR	7.48	31.75	3.00		9		341
Model 95	Bersa	A	380ACP	6.57	22.93	3.5	6R	7		48

Name or Model	Maker/entry/origin	Type	Caliber, chambering	Length in	Weight oz	Barrel in	Rifling	Ctg Cap	Remarks	Page
Model 96	Taurus	R	22LR	11.42	42.00	5.90		5	target model	341
Model 97	Bersa	A	380ACP						enlarged M644	48
Model 97	Česká Zbrojovka	A	45ACP	8.35	40.00	4.85	6R	10		61
Model 97	Rossi	R	38SPL	6.80	26.45	1.97		6		270
Model 98	Beretta	A	7.65Par	7.75	31.75	4.29	6R	13	As M92SBC except caliber	37
Model 98F	Beretta	A	9IMI	8.54	32.45	4.92	6R	15	As M92F except caliber	37
Model 98F T	Beretta	A	9IMI	9.53	38.80	5.90	6R	15	Target version of M98F	37
Model 99	Beretta	A	7.65 Par	7.75	31.75	4.29	6R	8	As M92SB-C M except caliber	37
Model 99	Zastava Arms	A	9Par	7.40	29.80	4.25		15	SIG 220 style	392
Model 100	Česká Zbrojovka	A	9Par	6.96	24.00	3.74	6R	13	also 10-shot 40 S&W	61
Model 100	Astra	A	32ACP	6.30	29.28	3.35		8		N/A
Model 100 Special	Astra	A	32ACP	6.0	28.92	3.35		9	post-1915	N/A
Model 101	Beretta	A	22LR	8.76	19.05	5.90	6R	10	replacement for M76	37
Model 101	Česká Zbrojovka	A	9Par	7.00	23.65	3.54	6R	7	hammerless	60
Model 101	Savage Arms	S	22LR	8.97	20.00	5.50		1		277
Model 106	Hämmerli	S	22LR	16.73	45.85	11.06		1	Martini-type breech	150
Model 108	Röhm	R	22LR	5.90		2.36		6	"Hy-Score Model 108"	266
Model 120	Hämmerli	S	22LR	16.15	43.38	10.03		1	bolt action breech	150
Model 122 Sport	Česká Zbrojovka	A	22LR	9.45	29.98	6.00		10		62
Model 122 Hobby	Česká Zbrojovka	A	22LR	8.66	26.84	5.20		10		62
Model 150	Hämmerli	S	22LR	15.35	42.33	11.22		1	many variants	150
Model 200	Astra	A	25ACP	4.33	12.92	2.20		6	or "Firecat"	21
Model 200D	Arms Corp. of Philippines	R	38Spl	7.36	22.0	2.50		6	also 22LR, 22WMR	20
Model 200P	Arms Corp. of Philippines	R	38Spl	8.85	25.90	4.0		6		20
Model 206	Hämmerli	A	22LR	12.50	38.80	7.08		8	many variants	151
Model 208	Hämmerli	A	22LR	10.03	34.75	5.90		8	many variants	151
Model 212	Hämmerli	A	22LR	8.45	31.00	4.92		8		152
Model 220K	Gerstenberger	A	22LR	6.69	15.87	2.48		6	"Em-Ge Model 220K"	142
Model 221	Echave y Arizmendi	A	22LR	6.10	25.75	3.15		10	"M221"; based on Walther PP	104
Model 223	Bersa	A	22LR	6.02	22.40	2.95	6R	10		48
Model 223	Gerstenberger	R	22LR	7.87	27.16	2.95		6	"Em-Ge Model 223"	142
Model 224	Bersa	A	22LR			3.94		6		48
Model 225	Bersa	A	22LR			4.92		6		48
Model 226	Bersa	A	22LR			5.90		6		48
Model 230	Hämmerli	A	22LR	11.61	43.75	6.30		6		152
Model 240	Hämmerli	A	38Spl	10.51	45.85	5.90		5	also in 32	152
Model 250	Astra	R	32	6.60	22.40	2.20	6R	6	also 22LR, 22WMR, 38	22
Model 260	Star	A	9Par	8.11	39.33	4.25	6R	15		322
Model 280	Hammerli	A	22LR	11.02	35.90	4.60		6		153
Model 283	Sterling Arms	A	22LR	10.50	40.55	6.00		10	target model	326
Model 286	Sterling Arms	A	22LR	9.00	36.00	4.53		10	target model	326
Model 300	Gerstenberger	R	32	10.62	34.21	5.90		6	"Em-Ge Model 300"	142
Model 300	Sterling Arms	A	25ACP	4.52	13.00	3.25		6		326
Model 300	Unceta	A	32ACP	6.50	19.75	3.54		7	"Astra"; also in 380ACP	355
Model 302	Sterling Arms	A	22LR	4.52	13.00	2.25		6		326
Model 318	Beretta	A	25ACP	4.53	15.0	2.36	6R	8	sold in USA as "Panther"	37
Model 323	Bersa	A	32ACP			3.50		7		48
Model 357	Astra	R	357Mag	9.25	38.80	4.0		6	other barrel lengths	22
Model 357	Steyr	A	357SIG	6.93	24.44	4.01	6R	12		328
Model 357P	Astra	R	357Mag	8.40	36.70	3.0	6R	6	"M357 Police"; compact 357	22
Model 383	Bersa	A	380ACP			3.50		7	improved M97	48
Model 383DA	Bersa	A	380ACP			3.50		7	DA version of M383	48
Model 400	Sterling Arms	A	380ACP	6.50	24.00	3.75		5	also M402 in 22LR	326
Model 400	Unceta	A	9BB	9.84	31.0	5.90	6R	8	"Astra"; Spanish Army M1921	355
Model 418	Beretta	A	25ACP	4.56	9.95	2.56	6R	9	or "Bantam" or "Puma"	37
Model 448	Česká Zbrojovka	A	22LR					10	target pistol	58
Model 469	Smith & Wesson	A	9Par	6.90	26.00	3.50		12		309
Model 511	Rossi	R	22LR	9.00	30.00	4.00		6		270
Model 600	Unceta	A	9Par	8.10	31.92	5.24	6R	8	"Astra"; also in 32ACP	355
Model 607	Taurus	R	357Mag		43.40	4.00		7		342
Model 622	Bersa	A	22RF	9.0	36.0	6.0	6R	7	long-barrel version of 644	48
Model 622	Harrington & Richardson	R	22LR	10.50	32.25	6.00		6		155
Model 629	Smith & Wesson	R	44Mag	9.60	44.00	4.00		6	or "Mountain Gun"	304
Model 632	Harrington & Richardson	R	32	8.00	18.87	4.00		6		155
Model 633	Echave y Arizmendi	A	25ACP	6.10	25.22	3.15		9	"M633"; based on Walther PP	104
Model 644	Bersa	A	22LR	6.57	28.04	3.50	6R	7		48
Model 645	Smith & Wesson	A	45ACP	8.62	37.55	5.00		8		309
Model 650	Smith & Wesson	R	22WMR	7.25	23.00	3.00		6	"Service Kit Gun Stainless"	305
Model 651	Smith & Wesson	R	22WMR	9.00	24.20	4.00		6	"Target Kit Gun Stainless"	305
Model 660	Harrington & Richardson	R	22LR	10.40	28.92	5.50		6	"Gunfighter"	154
Model 669	Taurus	R	357Mag	9.37	42.30	6.00		6		342
Model 680	Astra	R	32	6.60	22.0	2.20	6R	6	also stainless version	22
Model 686	Smith & Wesson	R	357Mag	11.92	45.85	6.00		6	also "Power Port"	306
Model 700	Unceta	A	32ACP	8.46	25.60	5.90	5T	8	"Astra"	355
Model 700S	Unceta	A	32ACP	6.30	29.10	3.75	6R	12	"Astra Model 700 Special"	355
Model 712	Mauser	A	7.63Msr	11.34	45.33	5.24		10,20	selective fire	220

Name or Model	Maker/entry/origin	Type	Caliber, chambering	Length in	Weight oz	Barrel in	Rifling	Ctg Cap	Remarks	Page
Model 732	Harrington & Richardson	R	32	7.00	23.10	2.50		6	"Guardsman"; also 4in barrel	154
Model 761	Echave y Arizmendi	A	32ACP	6.10	25.05	3.15		8	"M761"; based on Walther PP	104
Model 800	Astra	A	380ACP	8.14	35.27	5.30	6R	8	or "Condor"	22
Model 900	Unceta	A	7.63Msr	12.48	49.0	5.51	6R	10	"Astra"; Mauser C/96 copy	356
Model 900	Harrington & Richardson	R	22LR	10.00	29.00	6.00		9		155
Model 901	Echave y Arizmendi	A	380ACP	6.10	24.70	3.15		7	"M901"; based on Walther PP	104
Model 901	Unceta	A	7.63Msr	12.48	48.0	5.51	6R	10	"Astra"; selective fire 900	356
Model 902	Unceta	A	7.63Msr	12.45	48.0	7.48	6R	20	"Astra"; 901, larger mag.	356
Model 903	Unceta	A	7.63Msr	12.12	45.0	6.30	6R	20,30	"Astra"; 901, removable mag.	356
Model 909	Smith & Wesson	A	9Par	7.36	26.45	4.00	6R	9		310
Model 910	Smith & Wesson	A	9Par	7.36	29.20	4.00	6R	15		310
Model 911A1	Imbel	A	45ACP	8.50	36.50	5.03	8L	7	Colt-Browning	175
Model 922	Harrington & Richardson	R	22LR	10.50	24.00	4.00		9		155
Model 923	Harrington & Richardson	R	22LR	6.37		2.25		9		155
Model 926	Harrington & Richardson	R	22LR		31.00	4.00		9		154
Model 939	Harrington & Richardson	R	22LR	11.00	35.60	6.00		9	"939 Premier"	156
Model 940	Harrington & Richardson	R	22LR		33.00	6.00		9		156
Model 948	Beretta	A	22LR	5.90	16.93	3.30	6R	8	or "Featherweight"	37
Model 949	Beretta	A	22LR	12.52	37.92	8.74	6R	6	or "Tipo Olimpionico"	37
Model 949	Harrington & Richardson	R	22LR	9.92	35.25	5.50		9	"949 Classic Western"	154
Model 950	Beretta	A	22LR	4.70	11.28	2.36	6R	7	or "Jetfire" or "Minx"	38
Model 950	Calico	A	9Par	14.00	35.27	6.00	6R	50/100	Helical magazine	56
Model 951	Beretta	A	9Par	8.00	31.39	4.53	6R	8	or "Brigadier"	38
Model 951	Rossi	R	38Spl	9.00	30.00	4.00		6	also 3in barrel	270
Model 951R	Beretta	A	9Par	8.46	47.62	4.02	6R	10	selective fire version of 951	38
Model 960	Astra	R	38Spl	9.49	40.56	4.)	6R	6	also with 6in barrel	22
Model 971	Rossi	R	357 Mag	9.00	36.00	4.00		6	heavy barrel	270
Model 973	Imbel	A	9Par	8.50	35.60	5.03	6R	8	Brazilian army Colt-Browning	175
Model 999	Harrington & Richardson	R	22LR	10.25	33.50	6.00		9		156
Model 1000	Unceta	A	32ACP	7.87	37.0	5.12	6R	11	"Astra"	356
Model 1006	Smith & Wesson	A	10Auto	8.50	41.80	5.00		9		310
Model 1066	Smith & Wesson	A	10Auto	7.75	39.68	4.25		9		310
Model 1100	Dardick	R	38Dar	6.00	24.70	3.00		11		94
Model 1500	Dardick	R	38Dar	8.97	34.00	6.00		15		94
Model 1870	L. Gasser	R	11cf	12.60	45.85	7.28		6	Austro-Hungarian army	139
Model 1870/74	L. Gasser	R	11cf	12.60	45.85	7.28		6	improved M70	139
Model 1871	Francotte	R	11pf/cf	12.20	41.26	5.90		6	Lefaucheux, Swedish army	129
Model 1871	Remington	S	50	11.10		6.81		1	Army model	257
Model 1873	Saint-Étienne	R	11Fre	9.53	42.08	4.49	4R	6	French army, NCOs and men	272
Model 1874	Saint-Étienne	R	11Fre	8.98	34.88	3.95	4R	6	French army, officers	272
Model 1875	Remington	R	44	12.00		5.50		6	Army model	258
Model 1878	L. Gasser	R	9cf	9.21	27.16	4.56		6	Gasser-Kropatschek, officers	139
Model 1878	L. Gasser	R	9cf	8.94	28..20	4.65		6	commercial version of above	140
Model 1878	Nagant	R	9cf	10.62	38.80	5.51		6	Belgian army	232
Model 1878	Soleil	R	9.1cf	8.57	25.45	4.45		8	Portuguese army; Abadie gate	N/A
Model 1878/86	Nagant	R	9cf	10.62	33.15	5.51		6	Belgian army	232
Model 1879	various German	R	10.6Ger	12.20	36.50	7.20	6R	6	Reichsrevolver, "Troopers"	316
Model 1883	Nagant	R	9cf	10.62	33.50	5.51		6	Belgian army	232
Model 1883	various German	R	10.6Ger	10.25	32.50	4.92	6R	6	Reichsrevolver, "Officers"	316
Model 1883	O. Smith	R	32rf	6.90		3.25		5		287
Model 1886	Soleil	R	9.1cf	9.8	22.4	5.59		6	Portuguese army; Abadie gate	N/A
Model 1887	Marlin	R	38	7.50		3.25		5	DA lock-work; also 6-shot 32	212
Model 1887	Nagant; Husqvarna	R	7.5Swi	9.25	27.16	4.48		6	Swedish army	232
Model 1889	Colt	R	38	11.00	24.00	6.00		6	US Navy; also 41 commercial	74
Model 1890	Pieper	R	7.62Rus	10.43	28.55	4.64		6	gas-seal pattern	249
Model 1890	Remington	R	44-40WCF			5.50		6	or SA Army	258
Model 1891	Beaumont	R	320cf						commercial; variant in 6mm	N/A
Model 1891	Hopkins & Allen	R	32rf	7.25		3.25		5	"Forehand M1891"	171
Model 1891	Ronge	R	9cf	10.30	32.25	5.31		6	Danish navy	268
Model 1892	Saint-Étienne	R	8Leb	9.37	29.60	4.48		6	or "Lebel"	272
Model 1892	O. Smith	R	38	7.30		3.00		5	hammerless	287
Model 1893	Koishikawa	R	9Jap	8.50	31.00	4.70	6L	6	"Meiji 26th Year Type"	190
Model 1893	Nagant	R	7.5Swi	8.98	29.30	4.40		6	Norwegian army	232
Model 1894	SIG	A	7.6Man	9.05	35.25	7.28		5	Mannlicher; blow-forward	280
Model 1895	SIG	A	6.5Man					5	Mannlicher; blow-forward	280
Model 1895	Krnka	A	8cf	10.43	34.57	6.70		10?	Maker unknown (Roth?)	195
Model 1895	Nagant; Tula	R	7.62Rus	9.00	28.90	4.30		7	gas-seal type	233
Model 1896	Steyr	A	7.65Man	8.85	35.20	4.68		7	Mannlicher; blowback	328
Model 1897	Steyr	R	7cf	10.23	37.00	5.35		7	gas-seal type	328
Model 1898	L. Gasser; Rast & Gasser	R	8Aut	8.85	34.58	4.56		8	or "Rast & Gasser"	256
Model 1898	Schwarzlose	A	7.63Msr	10.75	37.00	6.42		7		279
Model 1900	Colt	A	38	9.25	36.00	6.00		7	Browning	81
Model 1900	DWM	A	7.65Par	9.37	31.00	4.80		8	Parabellum (Luger)	98
Model 1900	Dreyse	A	7.63Man	9.60	33.5	6.25		8	Mannlicher; delayed blowbk.	102
Model 1900	Fabrique Nationale	A	32ACP	6.70	22.57	40.15		7		120
Model 1900	I. Johnson	R	38	6.50		2.50		5	various barrels	184

Name or Model	Maker/entry/origin	Type	Caliber, chambering	Length in	Weight oz	Barrel in	Rifling	Ctg Cap	Remarks	Page
Model 1901	Fémáru	A	8Roth	7.08	22.92	3.93		10	Frommer	125
Model 1901	Steyr	A	7.63Man	9.68	35.80	6.30		8	Mannlicher; delayed blowbk.	239
Model 1902	Colt	A	38	8.97	34.92	6.00		7	Browning; Sporting Model	82
Model 1902	Colt	A	38	9.25	36.00	6.00		8	Browning; Military Model	82
Model 1902	DWM	A	9Par	8.54	31.22	4.00		8	Parabellum (Luger)	99
Model 1903	Colt	A	38	7.48	31.05	4.52		7	Browning; hammer	82
Model 1903	Fabrique Nationale	A	9BL	8.0	32.10	5.0		7		121
Model 1903	Steyr	A	7.65Man	10.98	36.00	4.52		6	Mannlicher; locked breech	239
Model 1904	DWM	A	9Par	10.51	35.62	5.90		8	Parabellum; German navy	99
Model 1904	Harrington & Richardson	R	32	8.18	15.85	4.50		6	1905, 1906 patterns similar	155
Model 1904	Harrington & Richardson	R	38	8.50	16.00	4.50		5	1905, 1906 patterns similar	155
Model 1905	Colt	A	45	8.00	33.16	4.48		7	Browning	82
Model 1906	Fémáru	A	7.65Roth	7.28	22.57	3.93		9	Frommer	125
Model 1906	Harrington Richardson	R	22rf	6.00	10.05	2.00		7		155
Model 1906	DWM	A	7.65Par	9.29	31.40	4.80		8	Parabellum (Luger)	99
Model 1906	Fabrique Nationale	A	25ACP	4.53	12.35	2.12		6		121
Model 1906	Webley	A	25ACP	4.72	11.82	2.125	6R	6	external hammer	381
Model 1907	Clément	A	32ACP	5.90	20.63	2.95		6		67
Model 1907	Pieper	A	25ACP	4.92	11.45	2.24		6		250
Model 1907	Savage Arms	A	45	9.00	35.45	5.25		8	or "Model H"; US trials, 1907	277
Model 1907	Savage Arms	A	32ACP	6.60	22.00	3.75		10		277
Model 1907	Savage Arms	A	380ACP	6.53	22.00	3.77		10	or "Model 1913"	277
Model 1907	Steyr; Fémáru	A	8Aut	9.17	36.30	5.16	6R	10	"Roth-Steyr"	126
Model 1908	Colt	A	380ACP	6.77	27.93	3.78		7	Browning; Pocket Model	83
Model 1908	DWM; Erfurt; Mauser	A	9Par	8.77	30.00	4.00		8	German army Parabellum	100
Model 1908	DWM; Erfurt	A	9Par	12.32	37.38	7.87		8	"Artillery Model" Parabellum	100
Model 1908	Pieper (AÉP)	A	9BB	9.84	35.80	4.02	6R	6	Bergmann-Bayard	250
Model 1908	Schwarzlose	A	32ACP	5.50	18.35	4.13		7	blow-forward	280
Model 1908	Star	A	25ACP	4.52	15.70	2.16		7		322
Model 1909	Clément	A	25ACP	4.52	13.40	2.00		6	1912 type similar	67
Model 1909	Remington	S	22rf			10.00		1	also 44cf; target model	258
Model 1909	Steyr	A	32ACP	6.37	22.25	3.62		7	Pieper patent	241
Model 1909	Webley	A	25ACP	4.25	10.25	2.125	6R	6	hammerless	381
Model 1910	Fabrique Nationale	A	32ACP	6.0	21.16	3.46		7	also in 380ACP	122
Model 1910	Fémáru	A	32ACP	7.28	22.40	3.93		8	Frommer; also in 7.65Roth	125
Model 1910	Glisenti	A	9Gli	8.15	30.00	4.00		7	Italian army pistol	142
Model 1910	Mauser	A	32ACP	6.30	21.00	3.42	6R	9		217
Model 1910	Mauser	A	25ACP	5.15	15.00	3.15	6R	9		217
Model 1910	Pieper (AÉP)	A	9BB	9.84	35.80	4.02	6R	10	Bergmann-Bayard	250
Model 1910/22	Fabrique Nationale	A	32ACP	7.0	25.75	4.49		9	also in 380ACP	122
Model 1911	Colt; Springfield Armory	A	45ACP	8.58	38.97	5.00		7	Browning; US Army Model	83; 322
Model 1911	Esperanza y Unceta	A	32ACP	5.71	21.0	3.18		7	"Astra"; also sold as "Victoria"	111
Model 1911	Steyr	A	9Styr	8.50	36.00	5.00		8	or "Steyr-Hahn"	241
Model 1911	Wesson Firearms	A	45ACP	8.58	38.80	5.00		7	"Dan Wesson"	386
Model 1911A1	Colt and others	A	45ACP	8.58	39.68	5.00		7	Browning; improved M1911	84
Model 1911A1	Springfield Armory, Inc.	A	45ACP	8.58	35.60	5.00		7	many versions	319
Model 1912	Fémáru	A	32ACP	6.50	21.50	3.93		7	"Stop"; also in 380ACP	125
Model 1912	Metallurgica Brescia	A	9Gli	7.68	28.75	3.54		7	or "Brixia"	228
Model 1913	Esperanza y Unceta	A	9BB	9.33	33.51	6.50		9	or "Campo-Giro"	112
Model 1913	Sauer	A	32ACP	5.66	20.10	2.95		7	"Old Model"	275
Model 1914	Galesi	A	25ACP						"M1914"	136
Model 1914	Mauser	A	32ACP	6.00	21.15	3.42	6r	8		218
Model 1914	Star	A	32ACP	6.90	30.00	4.40		8		322
Model 1915	Beretta	A	32ACP	5.70	20.11	3.35		7	also 380ACP, 9Gli	38
Model 1915	Esperanza y Unceta	A	32ACP	5.71	21.20	3.22		9	"Astra"; also 3.45in barrel	112
Model 1915	Savage Arms	A	380ACP	6.45	22.00	3.77		10		278
Model 1915/19	Beretta	A	32ACP	5.70	24.16	3.35		7	also in 9Gli	39
Model 1917	Savage Arms	A	32ACP	7.00	24.15	4.20		10	also 380ACP	278
Model 1917	Smith & Wesson	R	45ACP	10.78	36.00	5.50		6	US Army issue	292
Model 1919	Beretta	A	32ACP	5.75	24.16	3.35		7		39
Model 1921	Sauer	A	25ACP	4.02	14.11	2.56		7		275
Model 1921	Unceta	A	9 B-B	9.84	31.0	5.90	6R	8	Spanish Army	355
Model 1922	Galesi	A	25ACP	4.70		2.29		7	"M1922"	136
Model 1923	Beretta	A	9 Gli	5.90	28.22	3.35		8		39
Model 1923	Webley	A	9Str	8.40	36.00	5.00	6R	8	Romanian Army model	N/A
Model 1924	Esperanza y Unceta	A	25ACP	4.33	10.4	3.18		6	"Astra"	112
Model 1925	Orbea Brother	R	32	9.25	15.42	4.13		6	"Colon"; Police Positive copy	243
Model 1925	Sauer	A	25ACP	4.20	11.30	2.16		6	WTM	276
Model 1928	Manufrance	A	9BL	8.00	38.44	5.00		8	"Military Model Le Français"	211
Model 1928	Sauer	A	25ACP	4.00	10.58	1.97		6	WTM	276
Model 1929	Fémáru	A	380ACP	6.77	26.45	3.93		7	or "29.M"; blowback	126
Model 1930	Galesi	A	25ACP	4.70		2.40		7	"M1930"; also in 32ACP	136
Model 1930	Sauer	A	32ACP	5.75	21.85	3.04		7	"Behörden Model"	276
Model 1931	Beretta	A	32ACP	5.98	24.70	3.46		8		39
Model 1931	Zastava	A	32ACP	7.28	28.20	4.25		8	"Yovanovicz"; also 380ACP	391
Model 1934	Beretta	A	380ACP	5.90	26.45	3.39		7	or "Cougar"	39

Name or Model	Maker/entry/origin	Type	Caliber, chambering	Length in	Weight oz	Barrel in	Rifling	Ctg Cap	Remarks	Page
Model 1934	Mauser	A	32ACP	6.00	21.10	3.42	6R	8		220
Model 1935	Beretta	A	32ACP	5.83	25.75	3.35		8		40
Model 1935	Fabrique Nationale	A	9Par	7.75	32.45	4.65	6R	13	or "High-Power", "GP-35" etc	122
Model 1935A	SACM	A	7.65L	7.72	26.45	4.72		8		273
Model 1935S	Saint-Étienne	A	7,65L	7.40	27.15	4.16		8		273
Model 1936	Galesi	A	380ACP						"M1936"	136
Model 1937	Fémáru	A	380ACP	7.17	27.00	4.33	6R	7	or "37.M"; also in 32ACP	126
Model 1940	Husqvarna	A	9Par	9.52	44.62	4.70		8	Lahti, Swedish army	173
Model 1950	St Etienne, Châtellerault	A	9Par	7.67	30.33	4.40		9		273
Model 1953	Rigarmi	A	25ACP	6.30		3.35		7	"Model 1953"; also in 22LR	265
Model 2000	Colt	A	9Par	7.48	29.00	4.50	6R	15	"All American"	86
Model 2000	Astra	A	25ACP	4.40	12.52	2.40	6R	6	"Cub"; external hammer	23
Model 2006M	Macchine termo Ballistiche	R	357 Mag	7.28	37.75	3.07		6	also 6.2, 8.35in barrels	202
Model 2007S	Macchine termo Ballistiche	R	38 Spl	8.35		4.02		7		202
Model 3000	Unceta	A	32ACP	6.30	21.87	3.97	6R	7	"Astra"; also 6-shot 380ACP	356
Model 3904	Smith & Wesson	A	9Par	7.50	25.60	4.00		8	variant 3906 stainless	310
Model 3914	Smith & Wesson	A	9Par	6.80	25.00	3.5		8	variant 3913 stainless	311
Model 4000	Astra	A	32ACP	6.50	24.0	3.86	6R	8	"Falcon"; also 22LR, 380ACP	22
Model 4006	Smith & Wesson	A	40SW	7.50	39.00	4.00		11		311
Model 4506	Smith & Wesson	A	45ACP	8.50	36.70	5,00		8	stainless	312
Model 4516	Smith & Wesson	A	45ACP	7.125	34.57	3.75		7		312
Model 4566	Smith & Wesson	A	45ACP	7.75	39.32	4.25		8		312
Model 5000	Astra	A	32ACP	6.60	25.0	3.50	6R	8	"Constable"; 22LR, 380ACP	23
Model 5904	Smith & Wesson	A	9Par	7.52	25.90	4.00		14	variant 5906 stainless	312
Model 6904	Smith & Wesson	A	9Par	6.89	23.45	3.50		12	variant 6906 stainless	313
Model 7000	Astra	A	22LR	4.90	13.75	3.32	6R	7	variant of the 2000	23
Model 8000	Beretta	A	9Par	7.08	33.50	3.62	6R	15	or "Cougar". Other calibers	40
Model A	High Standard	A	22LR	8.45	32.00	4.50		10	Models B and C similar	167
Model A	Hispano-Argentina	A	22LR	6.50		2.36		8	"Hafdasa"	169
Model A	MAB/Bayonne	A	25ACP	4.57	13.05	2.60		6		204
Model A	Star	A	9B-B	8.46	37.55	5.00		8	"Star A"; also 7.63Msr, 45ACP	324
Model AS	Star	A	38Sup	8.26	37.90	4.80		8	"Star AS"	324
Model B	Hispano-Argentina	A	22LR	8.50		4.70		10	"Hafdasa"; Colt M1911 copy	169
Model B	MAB/Bayonne	A	25ACP	4.13	9.62	1.96		6		204
Model B	Star	A	9Par	8.46	38.25	4.80		9	"Star B"	324
Model Bcf-66	MAPF/Unique	A	32ACP	6.61	25.75	3.93		8	also 380	207
Model B KS	Star	A	9Par	7.17	26.10	4.25		8	or "Starlight"	325
Model BM	Star	A	9Par	7.17	34.00	3.90		8	"Star BM"; steel frame	324
Model BKM	Star	A	9Par	7.17	27.00	3.90		8	"Star BKM"; alloy frame	324
Model C	MAB/Bayonne	A	32ACP	6.00	23.00	3.75		7	also 380ACP	204
Model C	MAPF/Unique	A	32ACP	5.70	22.90	3.15		9		207
Model C	Pieper	A	25ACP	4.72	10.95	2.00		6		251
Model C	Star	A	9BL			4.13		8	"Star C"	324
Model CO	Star	A	25ACP	4.72	14.10	2.24		8	"Star CO"	324
Model CU	Star	A	25ACP	4.80	15.00	2.36		7	"Star CU" or "Starlet"	325
Model CU	Star	A	22LR	4.80	15.00	2.36		10	"Star CU" or "Lancer"	324
Model D	High Standard	A	22LR	11.02	40.00	6.75		10	HD, HD-M, USA-HD similar	167
Model D	MAB/Bayonne	A	32ACP	7.08	24.70	3.94		9	ala "Le Gendarme"	204
Model D	MAPF/Unique	A	22LR	6.05	22.75	3.07		10	many variants	207
Model D	Pieper	A	25ACP	4.52	11.65	2.125		6		251
Model D	Star	A	380ACP	6.12	19.95	3.11		6	"Star D" or "Police & Pocket"	324
Model DES/32U	MAPF/Unique	A	32S&W	11.22	40.22	5.90		5/6	target pistol	207
Model DK	Star	A	380ACP	5.70	14.80	3.15		7	"Star DK"; first "Starfire" model	324
Model DKI	Star	A	32ACP	5.70	14.80	3.15		7	"Star DKI"	324
Model DKL	Star	A	380ACP	5.70	14.80	3.15		6	"Star DKL"; light alloy frame	324
Model E	High Standard	A	22LR	11.02	42.00	6.75		10	Model HE similar	167
Model E	MAB/Bayonne	A	25ACP	6.22	20.00	3.26		10		204
Model E	MAPF/Unique	A	22rf	6.05	21.50	3.07		6		208
Model E	Star	A	25ACP	3.94	9.88	1.97		6	"Star E"	324
Model F	Unceta	A	9BB	13.0	54.0	7.10	6R	10/20	"Astra"; 9mm variant of 903	356
Model F	MAB/Bayonne	A	22LR	10.62	29.10	6.00		10	other barrel lengths	204
Model F	MAPF/Unique	A	380ACP	5.70	22.90	3.15		8		208
Model F	Star	A	22LR	6.12	30.00	4.33		10	"Star F"; several minor variants	325
Model FR Sport	Star	A	22LR	8.85	29.80	5.90		10	"Star FR"	325
Model G	High Standard	A	380ACP	9.25	40.00	5.00		6		167
Model GB	High Standard	A	22LR	8.85	32.60	4.50		10	also with 6.75in barrel	167
Model GZ	MAB/Bayonne	A	25ACP	6.22	18.85	3.15		8	made by Arizmendi	204
Model H	Star	A	32ACP	5.51	20.45	2.87		7	"Star H"	325
Model HA	High Standard	A	22LR	11.02	34.00	6.75		10	Model HB similar	167
Model HF	Star	A	22LR	5.40	20.10	2.76		9	"Star HF"	325
Model HN	Star	A	380ACP			3.93		7	"Star HN"	325
Model I	Star	A	32ACP	7.27	24.35	4.84		9	"Star I"	325
Model L	MAPF/Unique	A	32ACP	5.90	22.75	2.35		7	also 22LR, 380ACP	208
Model M	Star	A	38Sup	8.58	24.50	4.80		9	"Star M"	325
Model MD	Star	A	9BB	8.46	24.50	4.80		8	selective fire; also 16, 25rds	325
Model N	Pieper	A	32ACP	6.06	21.16	3.19		7		251

Name or Model	Maker/entry/origin	Type	Caliber, chambering	Length in	Weight oz	Barrel in	Rifling	Ctg Cap	Remarks	Page
Model O	Pieper	A	32ACP	5.70	20.10	2.87		6		251
Model P	Česká Zbrojovka	S	22LR	13.77	26.45	9.85		1	later became the "Pav"	56
Model P	Pieper	A	25ACP	4.96	10.93	2.28		6		250
Model P	Star	A	45ACP	8.46	24.70	4.80		7	"Star P"	325
Model PA-15	MAB/Bayonne	A	9Par	9.65	38.80	6.00		15		205
Model PD	Star	A	45ACP	7.08	25.00	3.93		6	"Star PD"	325
Model Rd	MAPF/Unique	A	22LR	10.00		7.28		9	or "Ranger"	208
Model R Long	MAB/Bayonne	A	32ACP	7.48	26.45	4.17		9		204
Model R Para	MAB/Bayonne	A	9Par	7.67	37.00	5.90		8	or "Le Militaire"	204
Model Rr-51	MAPF/Unique	A	32ACP	5.70	25.90	3.15		9	or "Police Model"	208
Model R Short	MAB/Bayonne	A	32ACP	6.69	23.60	3.35		9		204
Model S	Star	A	38Auto	6.30	21.85	3.93		8	"Star S"	325
Model SI	Star	A	32ACP	6.30	21.85	3.93		9	"Star SI"	325
Model Super SM	Star	A	380ACP	6.70	22.00	4.00		10	"Star SM"	325
Model USA	Bernardelli	A	380ACP	6.45	24.34	3.54	6R	7	or M 80	47
Model Z	Česká Zbrojovka	A	25ACP	4.52	15.00	2.16		6	formerly known as "Duo"	61
Modèle d'Ordonnance	Saint-Étienne	R	8Leb	9.37	29.60	4.48		6	"M1892" or "Lebel"	272
Modelo Militar	Star	A	9BB	7.87	38.80	4.80		8	also 38Sup, 45ACP	324
Mohegan	Hood	R	32rf	6.45		2.64		5		170
Monarch	Norwich Falls	R	32rf	6.70		2.75	5R	5	or "Kittemaug"	237
Monarch	Hopkins & Allen	R	22rf				5R	7	"No. 1"	172
Monarch	Hopkins & Allen	R	32rf				5R	5	"No. 2"	172
Monarch	Hopkins & Allen	R	38rf				5R	5	"No. 3"	172
Monarch	Hopkins & Allen	R	41rf				5R	5	"No. 4"	172
Mondial	G. Arizaga	A	25ACP	4.72	12.00	2.52		7		16
Montana Marshal	Hawes	R	357Mag	11.75	43.90	6.00		6	Made in Italy	157
Montenegrin Model	L. Gasser	R	11.75cf	14.75	51.15	9.00		6	representative specimen	139
Mosser	Spanish	A	25ACP	4.48	14.37	2.16		6	Eibar-type blowback	355
Mountain Eagle	Hopkins & Allen	R	32rf			2.75				172
Mountain Eagle	Magnum Research	A	22LR	10.63	20.80	6.50		15	"Standard"	202
Mountain Eagle	Magnum Research	A	22LR	12.20	23.00	6.50		15	"Target"	202
MP	Walther	A	9Par	8.07	39.00	5.00	6R	8	blowback	363
MP90S	Benelli	A	22LR			4.40	6R	5	Also in 32S&W	30
MP95E	Benelli	A	32S&W	11.81	41.65	4.33	6R	5	also 6 or 9-shot 22LR	30
MR73	Manurhin	R	357Mag	7.67	31.00	2.48		6	also 9Par	208
MR100	Reck	R	22LR			6.00		6	target model	256
MS	M. Santos	A	25ACP	4.52	12.50	2.16		6	Eibar-type blowback	274
MTR8	Macchine termo Ballistiche	R	38Spl	10.43	43.38	3.00		8	also in 357 Mag	202
MTR12	Macchine termo Ballistiche	R	38Spl	11.42	51.14	3.93		12	also in 357 Mag	202
MTR20	Macchine termo Ballistiche	R	22LR	10.82	45.85	3.93		20		202
MTs	Margolin	A	22LR	12.20	41.60	6.30		6	target pistol	212
Mueller Special	Decker	R	25ACP	4.65	15.56	1.97		5	or "Decker"	95
Müller	Müller	A	7.65Par	9.33	35.25	5.50		8	Prototypes only	231
Museum	Unceta	A	25ACP	4.33	11.45	2.16		7	or "Victoria".	112
Musgrave	Musgrave	A	9Par	8.15	30.85	4.52	6R	15	Limited production	231
Mustang	Colt	A	380ACP	5.50	18.35	2.76		5		89
Mustang 380 Plus 2	Colt	A	380ACP	5.50	19.75	2.76		5	stainless steel	89
Mustang PocketLite	Colt	A	380ACP	5.50	12.35	2.76		5	alloy frame	89
Muxi	Spanish	A	25ACP	4.33	11.45	2.20		5	Eibar-type blowback	N/A
Nambu	Koishikawa	A	8Nam	8.97	31.75	4.72		8	"Type A", "Papa"	191
Nambu	Koishikawa	A	7Nam	6.73	22.90	3.27		7	"Type B", "Baby"	191
Napoleon	T. Ryan	R	32rf			2.50		5	also 7-shot 22rf	271
National Match	Colt	A	45ACP	8.58	39.00	5.00		7	also 38Sup	86
Never Miss	Marlin	S	32rf			2.50		1	also 22rf and 41rf	212
New Army & Navy	Colt	R	38	11.50	33.00	6.00		6	also 32 commercial	74
New Baby Hammerless	Kolb	R	22rf	4.72		1.97		6		192
New Century	Smith & Wesson	R	455Bri	11.75	38.00	6.50		6	British service model	291
New Defender	Harrington & Richardson	R	22LR	5.50		2.125		9		155
New England	New England Firearms	R	22LR	7.00	25.00	2.52		9	also 22 WMR, 32H&R	235
New England Ultra	New England Firearms	R	22LR	8.62	31.90	4.00		9	also 22 WMR, 32H&R	235
New Army Express	Webley	R	450cf	10.50	37.90	5.50		6	also 455Bri	376
New Departure	Smith & Wesson	R	38	7.50	18.00	3.25		5	or "Safety Hammerless"	295
New House Model	Colt	R	38rf	7.00	14.50	2.24		5		74
New House Model	Colt	R	41rf	6.00	13.75	2.24		5		74
New Line	Colt	R	22rf	5.50	7.00	2.24		7		72
New Line	Colt	R	30rf	5.75	6.70	2.24		7		72
New Line	Colt	R	32rf	6.37	10.50	2.24		7		73
New Line	Colt	R	38rf	6.30	13.40	2.24		5		73
New Line	Colt	R	41rf	6.00	12.00	2.24		5		73
New Model	Smith & Wesson	R	44	11.88	39.85	6.50		6	44 Russian cartridge	293
New Model Express	Webley	R	455Bri	10.50	38.37	5.50	7R	6		376
New Pocket Model	Colt	R	32rf	9.56	17.00	4.50		6		75
New Pocket Model	Colt	R	32rf	11.00	19.00	6.00		5	target model	75
New Police Model	Colt	R	38cf	7.28	14.50	2.24		5		74
New Police Model	Colt	R	41rf	7.28	14.10	2.24		5		74

Name or Model	Maker/entry/origin	Type	Caliber, chambering	Length in	Weight oz	Barrel in	Rifling	Ctg Cap	Remarks	Page
New Safety Hammerless	Columbia Armory	R	32	7.28		3.15		5	"Columbian"	90
New Service Model	Colt	R	38	9.45	39.00	4.50		6		75
New Service Model	Colt	R	45	11.00	41.00	5.50		6		75
New York Pistol Co.	Hood	R	22rf	7.00		3.50		7		170
Niva	Kohout	A	25ACP	4.25	13.25	1.97		6		N/A
No. 1	American Arms	R	38	7.0		3.35	5R	5	hinged frame	12
No. 1	Bergmann	A	8Bgm	11.02	36.66	5.31	6R	5	prototype, 1893	41
No. 1	Erquiaga, Muguruzu	A	25ACP	4.33	11.28	2.08		6	"Fiel"; Eibar-type blowback	110
No. 1	Erquiaga, Muguruzu	A	32ACP	5.82	21.00	3.30		7	"Fiel"; Eibar-type blowback	110
No. 1	Harrington & Richardsom	R	32rf	5.51		2.36		5	S&W No. 1 copy	153
No. 1	Hood	R	22rf	4.48		2.36	5R	7	"Robin Hood No. 1"	170
No. 1	Johnson, Bye	R	22rf					7	"Favorite"; sheath trigger	186
No. 1	Remington	R	30rf			2.81		5	or "New Model No 1", Smoot	259
No. 1	Webley	R	455Bri	11.33	38.00	6.00	7R	6	British issue; "No. 1 Mark VI"	379
No. 1	Webley	R	442Bri	9.00	30.00	4.50	5R	6	"RIC No. 1"	374
No. 1	Webley	R	442Bri	9.00	30.00	4.50	7R	6	"RIC No. 1 New Model"	374
No. 1?	Webley	R	442			4.25		6	"No. 1? Bull Dog"	374
No. 2	American Arms Co.	R	38	7.48		3.22	5R	5	auto-extracting	12
No. 2	Bergmann	A	5Bgm	11.02	36.3	5.31	6R	5		42
No. 2	Enfield	R	38	10.25	27.50	5.00	7R	6	"No. 2 Mk 1 Enfield"	106
No. 2	Harrington & Richardson	R	32rf	6.70		2.50	5R	5	S&W No. 1? copy	153
No. 2	Hood	R	32r	6.50		3.00	5R	5	"Robin Hood No. 2"	170
No. 2	Johnson, Bye	R	32rf			2.75		5	"Favorite"; sheath trigger	186
No. 2	Remington	R	32rf			2.75		5	or "New Model No 2", Smoot	259
No. 2	Webley	R	450	6.25	18.00	2.50	7R	5	No. 2 Bull Dog	374
No. 2	Webley	R	442Bri	9.00	29.00	4.00	7R	6	"RIC No. 2"; also 320, 380	374
No. 2 1/2	Harrington & Richardson	R	32rf	6.60		2.43	5R	5	saw-handle grip	153
No. 3	American Arms Co.	R	44	7.48		3.22	5R	5	hinged frame	12
No. 3	Johnson, Bye	R	38rf					5	"Favorite"; sheath trigger	186
No. 3	Bergmann	A	6.5Bgm	10.03	31.0	4.40	6R	5		42
No. 3	Remington	R	38rf			3.75		5	or "New Model No 3", Smoot	259
No. 4	Bergmann	A	8Bgm	10.03	31.40	4.40	6R	5		42
No. 4	Johnson, Bye	R	41rf					5	"Favorite"; sheath trigger	186
No. 4	Remington	R	38rf			2.50		5	also 41rf, 38rf/cf, 41cf	259
No. 5	Bergmann	A	7.8Bgm	10.62	49.75	3.94	6R	5	"Military Model"	42
No. 5	Webley	R	360cf	7.60	19.00	3.00	7R	6	No. 5 Express; also 4.5in brl	375
No. 6	Hopkins & Allen	R	32	8.00		4.00		5	"DA No. 6"; solid frame	171
No. 32	Marlin	R	32rf	6.89		3.00		5	"No. 32 Standard"; tip-barrel	212
No. 38	Marlin	R	38	7.48		3.25		5	"No. 38 Standard"; tip-barrel	212
Nonpareil	Norwich Pistol Co.	R	32rf			2.64		5		237
Nordheim	Nordheim	A	32ACP	6.15	21.00	3.62		7		235
Novelty	Mossberg	M	22rf					4	or Shatuck "Unique"	231
NZ-75	Norinco	A	9Par	8.19	35.27	4.49		14	DA; based on CZ75	236
Obregon	Mexico Arms Factory	A	45ACP	8.50	40.00	5.00	6L	7	Mexican army	228
Oculto	Orueta	R	38	7.50	18.15	3.23		6	S&W New Departure copy	245
Off Hand	Stevens	S	22rf	8.98		5.75		1	target pistol	327
Officers Model	Colt	R	38	11.25	33.50	6.00		6		75
Officers Model ACP	Colt	A	45ACP	7.25	34.00	3.50		6	reduced M1911A1	89
Officers Model Match	Colt	R	38	11.25	39.00	6.00		6	also 43oz 22LR	78
Officers Model Special	Colt	R	38	11.25	39.00	6.00		6	also 43oz 22LR	78
Official Police Model	Colt	R	22LR	9.25	34.40	4.00		6	also with 6in barrel	77
Official Police Model	Colt	R	38	11.25	37.00	6.00		6	also 32, 32-20WCF	77
Official Police Mark 3	Colt	R	38	11.22	35.00	6.00		6		80
OH	Orbea Brothers	R	38	9.75	29.60	4.80		6		243
Oicet	A. Errasti	R	38	8.46	21.70	3.93		6	Colt Police Positive copy	110
Ojanguren	Ojanguren y Vidosa	R	32	9.05	31.00	3.93		6	S&W M&P copy	243
Ojanguren	Ojanguren y Vidosa	R	32	8.85	30.35	3.93		6	"Expulso a Mano"	243
Ojanguren	Ojanguren y Vidosa	R	38	10.00	31.20	5.00		6	"Militar y Policia"	243
Okzet	Menz	A	25ACP	4.00	10.23	2.00		6	sales name for Liliput	227
Olympia Pistole	Walther	A	22LR	7.83	27.00	4.76	6R	10	several variations	363
Olympic ISU	Mitchell	A	22LR	11.25	39.50	6.73		10	High Standard type	229
OM	Ojanguren y Marcaido	R	22LR	10.62		6.00		6	"Modelo el Blanco"	242
OM	Ojanguren y Marcaido	R	38	11.00		6.00		6	"Modelo de Tiro"	242
OM	Ojanguren y Marcaido	R	32	10.00		6.00		6	"Cylindro Ladeable"	242
Omega	Gerstenberger & Eberwein	R	22LR	5.90		2.36		6	or "Em-Ge Model 100"	142
Omega	Weihrauch	R	32	10.43	25.00	3.93		6	or Arminius HW-8	383
Omega	Armero Especialistas	A	25ACP	4.33	13.22	2.09		6	Eibar-type blowback	19
Omega	Armero Especialistas	A	32ACP	4.92	19.00	2.36		6	Eibar-type blowback	19
Omega	Springfield Armory Inc	A	10Auto	8.58	42.85	5.00		8	also 38Sup, 45ACP	320
Omega	Onandia Hermanos	R	38	8.85	30.15	4.33		6		N/A
Onandia										
On-Duty DA	Arcadia Machine & Tool	A	9Par	7.8	32.5	4.5		15	also 40S&W, 45ACP	16
OP601	Fabbrica Armi Sportive	A	22rf	11.22	40.56	5.60		5	or "Domino 601" target pistol	114
Open Top Army Model	Colt	R	44rf			7.50		6	Model 1872	70
Open Top Pocket Model	Colt	R	22rf	5.75	8.80	2.40		7		70
Orbea	Orbea Brothers	R	10.35Ita	9.76	29.25	4.71		6	Italian "Bodeo" type	244

Name or Model	Maker/entry/origin	Type	Caliber, chambering	Length in	Weight oz	Barrel in	Rifling	Ctg Cap	Remarks	Page
Orbea	Orbea y Cia	A	25ACP	4.45	13.40	1.88		6		243
Ortgies	Deutsche Werke	A	25ACP	5.25	14.00	2.72	6R	7		101
Ortgies	Deutsche Werke	A	32ACP	6.50	22.50	3.42	6R	8		101
Ortgies	Deutsche Werke	A	380ACP	6.50	21.00	3.45	6R	7		101
Oscillant-Azul	E. Arostegui	R	38	8.66	30.16	3.93		6		20
Osgood Duplex	Osgood	R	22/32	5.75		2.56		8+1	extra barrel	245
OSP	Walther Sportwaffenfabrik	A	22Short	11.50	39.50	4.25	6R	5	rapid-fire target pistol	369
Outdoorsman	Smith & Wesson	R	22LR	10.75	35.00	6.00		6	or "K-22 Hand Ejector"	290
Outlaw	Uberti	R	45	12.50	37.00	5.50		6	and other calibers	352
Outlaw Dakota	EMF	R	45LColt	13.50	45.00	7.50		6	Remington M1873 replica	106
OWA	Österreichische Werke-Anstalt	A	25ACP	4.72	14.45	1.97		6	resembles Pieper	242
Oyez	Oyez	A	32ACP	5.70	21.87	2.83		7		245
Oyez	Spanish	A	32ACP	5.60	22.40	3.15		7	Eibar type blowback	N/A
P1	Walther Sportwaffenfabrik	A	9Par	8.58	27.20	4.88	6R	8	Bundeswehr issue	367
P1A1	Walther Sportwaffenfabrik	A	9Par	7.05	28.50	3.54	6R	8	modified P1	366
P4	Walther Sportwaffenfabrik	A	9Par	7.87	29.10	4.33	6R	8	modified P1	370
P5	Walther Sportwaffenfabrik	A	9Par	7.05	28.50	3.54	6R	8		370
P5	Walther Sportwaffenfabrik	A	9Par	6.61	27.50	3.11	6R	8	"P5 Compact"	370
P7M13	Heckler & Koch	A	9Par	6.54	28.20	4.13		13	also P7M8 with 8-shot mag	161
P9	Springfield Armory. Inc.	A	9Par	8.11	35.25	4.72		16	CZ75 copy, also 45ACP	320
P9C	Springfield Armory, Inc.	A	9Par	7.25	32.00	3.66		10	compact P9	320
P9	Tsinntochmash	A	9Rus	7.68	35.00			18	or "Gyurza"	349
P9S	Heckler & Koch	A	9Par	7.60	28.05	3.97		9	also in 45ACP	160
P10	Grendel	A	380ACP	5.31	15.00	3.00		10		147
P11	Kel-Tec	A	9Par	5.78	17.00	3.07		10		188
P18	LES	A	9Par	8.50	29.80	5.35		18	US-made Steyr GB	199
P018	Bernardelli	A	9Par	8.39	35.20	4.80	6R	15		46
P018-9	Bernardelli	A	9Par	7.48	33.50	4.02	6R	14	or "P-018 Compact"	47
P018 Tir	Bernardelli	A	7.65Par	8.27	35.27	4.84	6R	14	target sights; also 9Par	47
P32	Davis	A	32ACP	5.40	22.05	2.80		6		94
P38	Mauser; Spreewerke; Walther	A	9Par	8.38	29.50	5.00	6R	8	1938-45 military	221
P38	Walther	A	9Par	8.50	28.20	5.70	6R	8	post-war commercial	365
P38K	Walther Sportwaffenfabrik	A	9Par	6.30	27.90	2.75	6R	8	short version of P38	367
P85	Sturm, Ruger	A	9Par	7.88	31.92	4.48		15	several variants	335
P88	Walther Sportwaffenfabrik	A	9Par	7.36	31.70	4.01	6R	15		371
P88	Walther Sportwaffenfabrik	A	9Par	7.12	29.00	3.12	6R	16	"P88 Compact"	371
P88	Walther Sportwaffenfabrik	A	9Par	8.30	28.20	4.92	6R	14	"P88 Competition"; 3.93in brl	371
P98	American Arms	A	22LR	8.1	25.0	5.0		8	P38 lookalike	13
P99	Walther Sportwaffenfabrik	A	9Par	7.1	21.90	4.0	6R	16	polymer frame	371
P210	Schweizerische Ind.-Ges.	A	9Par	8.45	31.75	4.72		8	minor variants	281
P220	Schweizerische Ind.-Ges.	A	9Par	7.80	26.00	4.41	6R	9		281
P225	Schweizerische Ind.-Ges.	A	9Par	7.09	26.00	3.86	6r	8		282
P226	Schweizerische Ind.-Ges.	A	9Par	7.72	31.00	4.41	6R	15		282
P228	Schweizerische Ind.-Ges.	A	9Par	7.09	29.00	3.86	6R	13		282
P229	Schweizerische Ind.-Ges.	A	40S&W	7.80	31.00	4.41		12	also 357SIG, 9Par	283
P230	Schweizerische Ind.-Ges.	A	380ACP	6.61	16.25	3.58	6R	7	also 9-shot 32ACP	283
P232	Schweizerische Ind.-Ges.	A	380ACP	6.61	17.63	3.58	6R	7	also 8-shot 32ACP	283
P239	Schweizerische Ind.-Ges.	A	357SIG	5.20	29.00	3.58	6R	7	also 9Par, 40S&W	283
P240	Schweizerische Ind.-Ges.	A	32	10.00	41.25	5.90		5	also 22LR, 10-shot	283
PA15	MAB/Bayonne	A	9Par	8.00	38.45	4.48	6R	15	French service pistol	205
P64	Polish state	A	9Mak	6.10	22.40	3.30		6		N/A
PA63	Fegyvergyar	A	9Mak	6.89	21.00	3.93		7	also 32ACP	123
PAF Junior	Pretoria Arms Factory	A	25ACP	4.52	13.40	2.16		6	Baby Browning copy	253
Pallas P1	Gaucher	SS	22LR	15.35	42.32	7.87		1	bolt actiom	140
PAMAS G1	MAS	A	9Par	8.54	37.80	4.92	6R	15	French Beretta M92G	N/A
Pantax	Wörther	A	22LR	5.90	18.35	2.83		8		390
Paramount	Beistegui	A	25ACP	4.48		1.97		5		30
Paramount	Retolaza	A	32ACP	5.90	26.45	3.23		9	also 25ACP version	260
Paramount	Apaolozo	A	25ACP	4.40		2.09		6		15
Paramount	Zumorraga	A	32ACP	6.10		3.38		8		N/A
Pardini	Fiocchi	S	22LR	17.32	35.30	9.45		1		127
Pardini GC	Fiocchi	A	32	11.73	36.80	4.92		5	"Gros Calibre"	127
Pardini S	Fiocchi	A	22LR	11.75	37.00	4.92		5	"Standard"	127
Pardini TO	Fiocchi	A	22rf	12.28	44.10	3.93		5	"Tipo Olimpionico"	127
Pardini VO	Fiocchi	A	22rf	11.73	36.70	5.12		5	"Vitesse Olimpionico"	127
Parker	Columbia Armory	R	32					5	"Safety Hammerless"	90
Parole	Norwich Pistol Co.	R	22rf					7		237
Partner	Safari Arms	A	22LR	9.00	23.00	4.56		8		272
Passler & Seidl	Passler & Seidl	M	7.7cf					6	1887; few made	247
Pathfinder	Echave y Arizmendi	A	25ACP	4.40	13.40	2.16		6	or "Bronco"	104
Pathfinder	Charter Arms	R	22LR	7.40	18.50	3.00		6		64
Patriot	Norwich Pistol Co.	R	32rf			2.50		5		237
Pav	F. Pavlíček	S	22LR			10.00		1	target pistol	247
P&B	Menz	A	32ACP	6.18	24.70	3.48	6R	8	or "P&B Model 3"	227
P&B Special	Menz	A	32ACP	6.22	26.20	3.35	6R	8	"P&B Special"	227

Name or Model	Maker/entry/origin	Type	Caliber, chambering	Length in	Weight oz	Barrel in	Rifling	Ctg Cap	Remarks	Page
Peerless	Hood	R	32rf			2.50		5		N/A
Peerless	Spanish	R	38	10.00	30.75	4.52	6R	6		N/A
Penetrator	Norwich Pistol Co.	R	32	6.50		2.64		5		237
Pequeño Police Positive	Colt	R	32	8.50	20.30	4.00		6		76
Perfect	Foehl & Weeks	R	38	6.88		3.15		5	hammerless	128
Perfect	Gabilondo	A	25ACP	4.56	13.58	2.16		6		135
Perfect	MAPF/Unique	A	32ACP	5.90	19.90	2.95		7		206
Perfect	MAPF/Unique	A	25ACP	4.13	12.52	2.08		7	or "Unique Mle 10"	206
Perfecto	Orbea Brothers	R	38	10.43		4.72		6		243
Perla	Dušek	A	25ACP	4.13	9.20	2.05		6		103
Petite	I. Johnson	R	22LR	4.13		1.00		7		184
Pfannl Miniature	Pfannl	A	4.25	3.93	9.00	1.65		6	or "Erika"	248
Phantom GP	Gaucher	S	22LR	17.32	45.85	11.02		1	bolt action, silenced	140
Phoenix	Robar	A	25ACP	4.33	14.10	2.16		6	or "Jieffeco"	265
Phoenix	Urizar	A	25ACP	4.52	12.35	1.97		6	or "Victoria Arms Co"	355
Pi18	Steyr	A	9Par	8.46	33.505.50			18	gas-delayed blowback	328
PIC	Reck	A	25ACP	4.56	14.80	2.24	6R	7	or "Reck P-8"	256
PIC	Gerstenberger/Em-Ge	R	22LR	6.69	15.90	2.48	6R	6	or "Em-Ge 220KS"	142
Piccola	Bersa	A	22rf	4.10	9.30	1.96	6R	5	or "Baby"	48
Pieper Army Model	Pieper	A	32ACP		21.00	3.04		7	or "Model A"	251
Pieper Army Model	Pieper	A	32ACP		19.40			6	or "Model B"	251
Pilsen	Zbrojovka Plze?	A	32ACP	5.90	20.65	3.35		7		N/A
Pinafore	Norwich Pistol Co.	R	22rf					7		237
Pindad	Pindad	A	9Par	7.71	31.05	4.40	6R	13	Browning GP-35 copy	251
Pinkerton	G. Arizaga	A	25ACP	4.33	11.65	1.85		6		17
Pioneer	USA	R	32	6.70		2.56		5	also in 38	N/A
Pistol N	Československá Zbrojovka	A	380ACP	6.00	21.87	3.43		8	or vz/22, "Nickl Pistol"	61
Pistole M	East German state	A	9Mak	6.30	23.45	3.58		8	Makarov copy	N/A
Pit Bull	Auto Ordnance	A	45ACP	7.25	36.00	3.50		7		26
Pit Bull	Charter Arms	R	9Par	7.50	24.50	2.50		5	also with 3.5in barrel	N/A
PLS	Peters-Stahl	A	9Par	8.46	38.80	5.00		9	also in 45ACP	248
Plus Ultra	Gabilondo	A	32ACP	6.70	34.20	3.66		20		135
Pocket Hammerless	Webley	R	320cf	7.00	18.00	3.00	7R	6	1898-type	378
Pocket Model	Bernardelli	A	32ACP	6.39	25.40	3.35	6R	8	other barrel lengths	47
Pocket Model	Forehand & Wadsworth	R	32					6	"Pocket Model"; solid frame	128
Pocket Model	Forehand & Wadsworth	R	38	7.00		2.68		5	as above	128
Pocket Model	Hopkins & Allen	R	38			3.50		5	DA; "Merwin & Hulbert"	172
Pocket Model	Hopkins & Allen	R	32	6.41		3.50		5	DA; "Merwin & Hulbert"	172
Pocket Model	Manufrance	A	25ACP	4.40	10.58	2.36		8	"Le Français"	211
Pocket Model	Webley	R	320cf	7.00	17.10	3.00	7R	6	1901-type	378
Pocket Positive Model	Colt	R	32	8.45	16.00	4.50		6		76
Police Dakota	EMF	R	45LColt	13.50	45.00	7.50		6	Remington M1890 replica	106
Policeman	Manufrance	A	25ACP	6.00	12.70	3.35		6		211
Police Bulldog	Charter Arms	R	38	8.50	20.45	4.00		6		64
Police Positive	Colt	R	32	8.50	20.20	4.00		6		76
Police Positive	Colt	R	22LR	10.50	25.60	6.00		6	target model	76
Police Positive	Colt	R	38	8.26	20.00	4.00		6		76
Police Positive Special	Colt	R	32	8.75	24.00	4.00		6		77
Police Positive Special	Colt	R	38	8.75	23.10	4.00		6		77
Police Service Six	Ruger	R	357 Mag	10.00	34.00	4.00		6		331
Pony	I. Johnson	A	380ACP	6.10	20.00	3.00		6	or "X300"	185
Populaire	Manufrance	S	22LR	13.58		6.89		1	bolt action	210
Powermaster	Wamo	S	22LR	10.95		4.88		1	target pistol	372
PP	Walther	A	32ACP	6.38	25.00	3.35	6R	8	also 22, 25, 380ACP	362
PP	Manurhin	A	22LR	8.86	24.00	5.90	6R	10	"PP Sport"; also 8.26in barrel	209
PP	Walther Sportwaffenfabrik	A	9Pol	6.92	27.50	3.23	6R	7	"PP Super"	368
PPK	Walther	A	32ACP	5.83	20.50	3.15	6R	7	also 22, 25, 380ACP	363
PPK/S	Walther Sportwaffenfabrik	A	32ACP	6.13	23.00	3.26	6R	7	also 380ACP	368
Practical VB	Bernardelli	A	9 IMI	11.10	38.80	5.43	6R	16	also 9Par, 40S&W	47
Praga	Zbrojovka Praga	A	25ACP	4.21	12.15	1.97		6	folding trigger	252
Praga	Zbrojovka Praga	A	32ACP	6.53	20.10	3.78		7	Czech army handgun	252
Praga	SEAM	A	32ACP	6.22	29.10	3.54		9	Eibar-type blowback	315
Precision	Spanish	A	32ACP	5.31	18.87	2.76	6L	7	identical to "Ca-Si"	N/A
Precision	Spanish	A	25ACP	4.45	10.76	2.16		6	different maker	N/A
Prairie King	Norwich Pistol Co.	R	22RF	5.70		3.00		7		237
Premier	Urizar	A	25ACP	4.48	11.92	2.125		7	Eibar-type blowback	357
Premier	Urizar	A	32ACP	5.60	19.75	3.07		8	"M1913"	357
Premier	T. Ryan	R	36			3.50		6		N/A
Prima	MAPF/Unique	A	25ACP	4.13	12.52	2.08		7	or "Unique Mle 10"	206
Princeps	Urizar	A	32ACP	4.72	20.80	2.36		6	Eibar-type blowback	357
Princess	USA	R	22RF	5.70		2.24		7		N/A
Protector	Norwich Pistol Co.	R	32	6.30		2.44		5		237
Protector	Chicago Firearms	M	32RF	4.72		1.77		7	Turbiaux copy	65
Protector	Echave y Arizmendi	A	25ACP	4.48	10.45	2.16		6	Eibar type; or "Renard"	104
Protector	Salaberrin	A	25ACP	4.52	10.93	2.125		6	Eibar-type blowback	273
PSM	Tula	A	5.45	6.30	16.22	3.35	6R	8		181

Name or Model	Maker/entry/origin	Type	Caliber, chambering	Length in	Weight oz	Barrel in	Rifling	Ctg Cap	Remarks	Page
PSP	Heckler & Koch	A	9Par	6.54	28.20	4.13		8	or "P7M8"	160
PSP07	Peters-Stahl	A	10mm	9.05	41.60	5.51		9	also 45ACP	248
PSP2000	Peters-Stahl	A	10mm	9.45	43.38	5.90		20	also 16-shot 45ACP	248
PSS	Tsinntochmash	A	7.62Spe	6.50	24.70			6	silent piston cartridge	349
PT51	Taurus	A	25ACP	4.52	9.87	2.36		8	licensed Beretta M950	343
PT52	Taurus	A	22LR	10.00	29.60	6.00		10	also 4.5in barrel	343
PT55	Taurus	A	22LR	5.61	12.35	2.76		7	licensed Beretta M20	343
PT57	Taurus	A	32ACP	7.75		4.56		15		344
PT58	Taurus	A	9Par	7.20	33.15	4.13		13		344
PT91	Taurus	A	41AE	8.55	33.85	5.00		10		344
PT92	Taurus	A	9Par	8.54	34.00	4.92		15	licensed Beretta M92	344
PT99	Taurus	A	9Par	8.54	34.00	4.92		15		344
PT908	Taurus	A	9Par	7.00	29.60	3.77		8		345
Pug	Webley	R	41RF	6.14	15.85	2.40		5	or "The Pug"	375
Pug	Webley	R	450	6.18	16.00	2.40		5	or "The Pug"	375
Pug Magnum	Charter Arms	R	357Mag	6.30	17.60	2.20	6R	5		63
Puma	Urizar	A	24ACP	4.56	13.93	2.04		6		358
Puppet	Ojanguren y Vidosa	R	25ACP	5.12		1.77		5	Velo-Dog pattern	243
Puppy	Crucelegui	R	5.5VD	7.48		2.56		5	hammerless Velo-Dog	92
Puppy	I. Gaztañaga	R	22RF	5.31		1.57		5		140
Puppy	Henrion, Dassy & Heischen	R	5.5VD	5.90		2.04		5	solid frame Velo-Dog	164
Puppy	Henrion, Dassy & Heuschen	R	25ACP	7.48		3.24		5	top-break	164
Puppy	Ojanguren y Marcaido	R	22RF	6.50		2.28		5		242
Puppy	Retolaza	R	22RF	7.50		2.36		5		260
PX22	American Arms	A	22LR	5.4	15.0	2.9		7	Based on Walther TPH	13
Python	Colt	R	357Mag	9.25	38.00	4.00		6		78
PZK	Kohout	A	25ACP	4.25	13.22	1.97		6		N/A
R8	Reck	A	25ACP	4.56	14.80	2.24		7		256
R12	Reck	R	22LR	11.10	31.00	5.00		6		256
R15	Reck	R	38	8.66	31.75	3.93		6		256
Radium	Gabilondo y Urresti	A	25ACP	4.52	10.40	2.24		6	side-loading magazine	135
Radom	Polish state	A	9Par	8.30	37.00	4.52		8	or "Vis-35"	N/A
Ranger	Dickinson	R	32	6.60		2.75		5		101
Ranger	Federal Ordnance	A	45ACP	8.58	38.00	5.00		7	"M1911A1"	123
Ranger	High Standard	R	22LR	10.75	28.00	5.50		9	"J.C. Higgins"; "Double 9" type	165
Ranger	Hopkins & Allen	R	22rf	6.50		2.59		7	also 5-shot 32rf	172
Rapid-Maxima	MAPF/Unique	A	25ACP	4.10	12.50	2.10		7	or "Unique M10"	206
Raven	Raven	A	25ACP	4.75	15.00	2.44		6	"P-25"	256
Raven	Spanish	A	25ACP	4.40	10.22	2.125		6	Eibar-type blowback	N/A
R.E.	Spanish	A	9BB	9.25	31.00	5.90		8	Astra 400 copy	N/A
Recky	Reck	R	22LR	4.92		1.88		6	or "Chicago Cub"	256
Red Cloud	USA	R	32RF	6.00		1.75		5		N/A
Redhawk	Ruger	R	41Mag	11.00	52.00	5.50		6	also in 44Mag	332
Red Jacket	Lee Arms	R	22rf			2.64		7	other barrel lengths	198
Red Jacket	Lee Arms	R	32rf	6.00		2.66		5	"No.2"; Nos 3 & 4 similar	198
Reform	Spanish	A	25ACP	4.40	12.52	1.97		6		N/A
Reform	Schuler	M	25ACP	5.43	21.90	2.44	4R	4	four-barrel	279
Regent	Bolumburu	A	25ACP	4.40	13.25	2.16	4R	6	or "Regento"	50
Regent	SEAM	A	25ACP	4.72	13.75	2.16	4R	6		315
Regent	Burgsmüller	R	22LR	10.43		4.00		8	probably Weihrauch	55
Regina	Bolumburu	A	25ACP	4.33	10.60	2.16	4R	7	Eibar type blowback	50
Regina	Bolumburu	A	32ACP	5.70	22.40	3.25		7	Eibar-type blowback	50
Regnum	Menz	M	25ACP	5.00	21.20	2.76	4R	4	four-barrel	226
Regulator	American Arms	R	357Mag						also in 44-40WCF, 45L Colt	13
Reifgraber	Union Arms Co	A	32ACP	6.50		3.00		8		357
Reiger	Reiger	M	7.7Bit	10.47	31.00	5.50		6	representative specimen	257
Reina	MAPF/Unique	A	25ACP	4.13	12.70	2.12		7	or "Unique M10"	206
Reims	Azanza y Arrizabalaga	A	25ACP	4.33	13.60	2.28		6	Eibar-type blowback	26
Reising	Reising	A	22LR	9.45		6.70		10	prototype	257
Rekord-Match	U. Anschütz	S	22LR					1	"Model 1933"; Martini breech	15
Remington	Remington	S	221Rem	16.73	60.00	10.43		1	"XP-100 Fireball", bolt action	258
Remora	Manurhin	R	38Spl	6.42	22.00	2.00		5	other barrel lengths	208
Renard	Echave y Arizmendi	A	25ACP	4.52	11.00	2.125		6	or "Protector"	104
Republic	Spanish	A	32ACP	5.12	21.35	3.15		9		355
Resolver	Sites SpA	A	9Par	6.50	23.00	3.74		8*	"AW-9"	N/A
Resolver	Sites SpA	A	380ACP	5.90	19.40	3.35		7	"AW-38"	N/A
Retolaza	Retolaza	A	32ACP	5.90	26.45	3.23		9	"M1914"	260
Rex	Bolumburu	A	32ACP	5.31	21.50	3.15		8	also 25ACP, 380ACP	50
Rex	Spanish	A	25ACP	4.52	13.00	2.125		6	not by Bolumburu	N/A
RG7	Röhm	R	22LR	4.72		1.38		6		266
RG10	Röhm	R	22LR	5.90	11.50	2.36		6		266
RG11	Röhm	R	22LR	7.88		3.62		8		266
RG12	Röhm	R	22LR	8.26		3.54		6		266
RG14	Röhm	R	22LR	6.89	16.20	3.00		6	also 1.75in barrel	266
RG20	Röhm	R	22LR	6.30		3.00		6		266

Name or Model	Maker/entry/origin	Type	Caliber, chambering	Length in	Weight oz	Barrel in	Rifling	Ctg Cap	Remarks	Page
RG23	Röhm	R	22LR	7.48	7.00	3.35		6		266
RG24	Röhm	R	22LR	8.00	19.22	3.54		6		266
RG26	Röhm	A	25ACP		12.00	2.125		6		266
RG27	Röhm	A	25ACP	5.67	15.10	3.03	6R	7	double action	266
RG30	Röhm	R	32	9.05	30.00	3.93		6		266
RG34	Röhm	R	22LR	10.75	34.55	5.90		7		267
RG38	Röhm	R	38Spl	9.25	33.15	4.00	6R	6		267
RG40	Röhm	R	38Spl			2.00		6		267
RG63	Röhm	R	22LR	10.25	34.00	5.00		8	single action	267
RG66	Röhm	R	22WMR	9.84	31.90	4.72		6	SA, adjustable sights	267
RG66T	Röhm	R	22LR	11.10	34.20	5.90		6	micrometer sights	267
RG88	Röhm	R	357Mag		33.15	3.93		6	other barrel lengths	267
Rheinmetall	Rheinmetall	A	32ACP	6.50	23.50	3.65	4R	8		263
RIC	Webley	R	442Bri	9.00	30.00	4.50	5R	6	"RIC No. 1"	374
RIC	Webley	R	442Bri	9.00	30.00	4.50	7R	6	"RIC No. 1 New Model"	374
RIC	Webley	R	442Bri	9.00	29.00	4.00	7R	6	"RIC No. 2"; also 320, 380	374
RIC	Webley	R	450cf	7.00	18.00	2.50	7R	5	"RIC Model" 1883	374
Rigarmi	R. Galesi	A	22LR	5.12	11.45	2.75		7		136
Rigarmi	R. Galesi	A	25ACP	4.72	14.00	2.28		7	"Model 1953"	136
Rigarmi	R. Galesi	A	32ACP	6.30	23.80	3.54		7	based on Walther PP	136
Rival	Union Fábrica de Armas	A	25ACP	4.48	12.70	2.04		6	"M1913"; Eibar-type blowback	N/A
Robin Hood	Hood	R	22rf	4.48		2.36	5R	7	"No. 1"	170
Robin Hood	Hood	R	32rf	6.50		3.00	5R	5	"No. 2"; "No. 3" similar	170
Roland	F. Arizmendi	A	25ACP	4.65	10.00	2.16		6	several variants	17
Roland	F. Arizmendi	A	32ACP	5.20	21.35	2.56		7	Eibar-type blowback	17
Rome	Rome Revolver Co.	R	32rf	6.50		2.63		5		N/A
Romer	Römerwerke	A	22rf	5.50	11.00	2.50	6R	7	also 6.5in barrel	267
Romo	Röhm	R	22LR	5.90	11.50	2.36		6	or "Röhm RG-10"	267
Roth-Frommer	Fémáru	A	7.65Roth	6.60	25.65	3.93	6R	10	1901 pattern	125
Roth-Sauer	Sauer	A	7.65Roth	6.70	23.15	3.93	6R	7		275
Royal	Zulaica	A	7.63Msr	9.05	43.90	6.70		10	selective fire	392
Royal	Zulaica	A	25ACP	4.56	13.00	2.125		6	original; also 32ACP	392
Royal	Zulaica	A	32ACP	8.08	21.35	5.31		12	Eibar type	392
Royal	USA	R	32rf	6.75		2.25		5		N/A
Royal		R	38	10.65		5.90		6	S&W M&P copy	N/A
Royal	Spanish		22LR	6.33		3.35		9	Galesi copy	137
Rubi	Venturini y Cia	A	32ACP	6.10	23.30	3.46		9	definitive "Eibar"	135
Ruby	Gabilondo	A	32ACP	6.10	23.45	3.35		7	FN-Browning M1910 copy	135
Ruby	Gabilondo	A	25ACP	4.48	11.12	1.97		6	Eibar-type blowback	135
Ruby	Gabilondo	A	45ACP	8.26	37.75	4.72		8		132
Ruby Extra	Gabilondo	R	22LR	5.90	17.65	2.16		6	S&W style	132
Ruby Extra	Gabilondo	R	32	7.67	18.00	3.25		6	S&W style	132
Ruby Extra	Gabilondo	A	22LR	8.75	36.00	4.72		9	also 6in barrel	333
Ruger Standard	Sturm, Ruger	R	22rf			2.75		7	"M1871"	271
Rupertus	Rupertus	R	22rf			2.75		7		271
Rural	Garantazada	R	32	9.65		4.92		6	Colt Police Positive copy	137
Russian Model	Smith & Wesson	R	44	12.00	40.00	6.50		6	single action	294
Ryan	T. Ryan	R	32rf			2.75		5	also 7-shot 22rf	271
S9*	Steyr	A	9IMI	6.54	22.40	3.58	6R	10	sold in Italy only	328
S40	Steyr	A	40S&W	6.54	22.75	3.58	6R	10	also as "S-9" in 9Par	328
SA	Societe d'Armes Francaise	A	25ACP	4.40	13.22	2.125		6	FN-Browning M1906 copy	N/A
S&A	Suinaga y Aramperr	R	38	9.25	28.92	4.25		6	S&W style	337
Sable Baby	unknown Belgium	R	22RF	4.80		2.04		6	folding trigger	N/A
Safety Model	Smith & Wesson	R	32	6.60		3.00		5		295
Safety Model	Smith & Wesson	R	38	7.50	18.00	3.25		5	five models	295
Safety Police	Hopkins & Allen	R	32	7.70		3.00		6		172
Saint-Hubert	Pyrenees	A	25ACP	4.13	12.87	2.08		7	or "Unique Model 10"	206
Salaverria	Iraola Salavarria y Cia	A	32ACP	6.10	19.92	3.34		8	Eibar-type blowback	176
Salso	Unceta y Cia	A	26ACP	4.33	11.46	2.16		7	or "Victoria"	355
Salvaje	Ojanguren y Vidosa	A	25ACP	4.40	10.75	2.04		6	Eibar-type blowback	243
San Paolo	San Paolo	R	38Spl	6.80	24.70	2.00		6	"Compact" model	274
San Paolo	San Paolo	R	38Spl	7.20	28.20	2.00		6	"Service"; also 4in barrel	274
San Paolo	San Paolo	R	38Spl	9.05	31.75	3.93		6	"Service Special"	274
San Paolo	San Paolo	R	38Spl	11.50	37.00	5.90		6	"Competition"; also 22LR	274
Sata	Tanfoglio & Sabotti	A	25ACP	4.52	14.63	2.36		8		N/A
Sata	Tanfoglio & Sabotti	A	22LR	4.65	16.75	2.44		8		N/A
Schall	Schall	S	22LR	11.22	31.00	7.48		10	or "Fiala", "Hartford"	278
Schmeisser	Haenel	A	25ACP	4.70	13.40	2.48		6	"Model 1"	149
Schmeisser	Haenel	A	25ACP	3.93	11.80	2.04		6	"Model 2"	149
Schmidt	Herbert Schmidt	R	22LR	5.90	11.50	2.48		8	many sales names	279
Schofield	Navy Arms	R	44-40WCF	12.50	37.55	7.20	6R	6	S&W replica, also 45LColt	234
Schofield	Smith & Wesson	R	45	12.40	40.26	7.00		6	two models	295
Schönberger	Steyr	A	8Salv	12.00	43.73	5.82	4R	5	blowback	328
Schouboe	Dansk Rekylriffel Syndikat	A	7.65ACP	6.70	19.40	3.54		6		93
Schouboe	Dansk Rekylriffel Syndikat	A	11.35cf	8.00	24.25	5.12		6		93
Schulhof	Austro-Hungarian	M	7.7Bit					5		N/A

Name or Model	Maker/entry/origin	Type	Caliber, chambering	Length in	Weight oz	Barrel in	Rifling	Ctg Cap	Remarks	Page
Scott	Scott	R	32			2.50		5		284
Scout	Hood	R	32			2.85		5		170
SEAM	Sociedad Español	A	25ACP	4.50	13.40	2.60		6	Eibar-type blowback	315
SEAM	Sociedad Español	A	25ACP	4.60	12.70	2.60		6	Walther Model 1 copy	315
Secret Service Special	I. Johnson	R	32	7.25	13.90	3.00		5	sold by Biffard, Chicago	185
Secret Service Special	Meriden	R	38	7.00	14.00	3.07		5	sold by Biffard, Chicago	227
Securitas	French	A	25ACP	4.72	10.75	3.07		5	no trigger; grip-fired	N/A
Security Industries	Security Industries	R	38Spl	6.10	18.00	2.00		5		284
Security Industries	Security Industries	R	357Mag	6.10	18.00	2.00		5		284
Security Six	Ruger	R	357Mag	9.25	33.50	4.00		6		332
Selecta	Pyrenees	A	25ACP	4.13	12.87	2.08		7	or "Unique Model 10"	206
Selecta	Echave y Arizmendi	A	25ACP	4.33	11.35	2.00		6	"M1918"; Eibar-type blowback	104
Selecta	Echave y Arizmendi	A	32ACP	5.70	21.35	3.15		7	"M1919"; Eibar-type blowback	104
Service Mark I	Webley	R	442Bri	9.25	35.00	4.00	7R	6	"Mk I", British; Mk I* similar	378
Service Mark II	Webley	R	455Bri	9.25	35.10	4.00	7R	6	"Mk II, British; II*, II** similar	378
Service Mark III	Webley	R	455Bri	9.50	37.00	4.00	7R	6	or "Mark III"	379
Service Mark IV	Webley	R	455Bri	9.25	35.00	4.00	7R	6	or "Mark IV"	379
Service Mark V	Webley	R	455Bri	9.25	35.50	4.00	7R	6	or "Mark V"	379
Service Mark V	Webley	R	455Bri	11.30	37.50	6.00	7R	6	or "Mark V"	379
Service Mark VI	Webley	R	455Bri	11.33	38.00	6.00	7R	6	or "Mark VI" ("No. 1 Mk VI")	379
Servicemaster	Detonics	A	45ACP	8.00	32.00	4.25		7	based on M1911A1	97
Sharps	Sharps & Hankins	M	32RF	4.62		2.40		4	4-barrel. Also 22rf, 30rf	285
Sharpshooter	C. Arrizabalaga	A	32ACP	6.5	27.00	3.85		7		21
Shatuck	Shatuck	R	32RF	6.50		2.50		5		285
Sherriff	Armi-Jager	R	22LR	10.82	30.00	5.50		6	also 4in, 4.7in barrels	19
Sherry	Wilkinson	A	22LR	4.37	9.20	2.126		8		389
Shooting Master	Colt	R	38	11.00	44.00	6.00		6		76
Shorty Forty	Smith & Wesson	A	40SW	7.67	28.80	3.50		9	"Mk 2"; M4013 TSW	311
Sidekick	Harrington & Richardson	R	22LR	8.50	28.00	4.00		9	or "Model 929"	155
Silesia	Sociedad Español	A	32ACP	5.31	23.00	2.68		7	Eibar-type blownack	315
Silhouette	Wichita Arms	S	308	21.40	72.00	14.88		1	bolt action	388
Silver City Marshal	Hawes	R	22LR	11.75	44.00	5.50		6	made by Sauer	157
Simplex	Bergmann	A	8mm	8.00	21.20	2.76		6		42
Simson	Simson	A	25ACP	4.50	13.00	2.20	6R	6	"M1921", "M1927"	286
Singer	F. Arizmendi	A	25ACP	4.53	13.05	2.16		6	Eibar-type blowback	17,18
Singer	F. Arizmendi	A	32ACP	5.90	24.70	3.23		7	FN-Browning M1910 copy	17,18
Singer	Dušek	A	25ACP	4.65	14.10	2.25		6	or "Duo"	103
Single Action Army	Colt	R	45	10.25	36.00	4.72		6	"M1873", "Peacemaker"	70-72
Single Action Army	Colt	R	45	12.45		7.50		6	"Bisley"; many variants	70-72
Single Action Army	Colt	R	45	17.5	43.20	12.00		6	"Buntline"; other barrels	70-72
Single Action Army	Colt	R	45	12.45	39.50	7.50		6	"Flat-Top Target"	70-72
Single Action Army	Colt	R	45	13.1		8.00		6	"New Frontier"	70-72
Single Action Army	Colt	R	45	10.50	40.00	5.50		6	post-1945 product	78
Single Action Dakota	EMF	R	45Colt	10.50	36.15	5.50		6	Colt M1873 replica	105
Single Action Model	Smith & Wesson	R	38	7.68		3.25		5	1st, 2nd models similar	296
Single Action Model	Smith & Wesson	R	38	8.26		4.00		5	3rd Model	296
Single Shot Model	Smith & Wesson	S	22LR	9.52		6.00		1	1st Model, 1893	288
Single Shot Model	Smith & Wesson	S	22LR	13.90		10.00		1	2nd Model, 1905	288
Single Shot Model	Smith & Wesson	S	22LR	13.90		10.00		1	"Perfected Model", 1909	288
Single Shot Model	Smith & Wesson	S	22LR	11.00		10.00		1	"Straight Line Model", 1925	288
Single Six	Ruger	R	22LR1	1.80	34.60	6.50		6	other barrel lengths	332
Sivispacem	Sociedad Español	A	32ACP	4.52	20.10	2.125		6	Eibar; also 10-shot version	315
Slavia	Vilimec	A	25ACP	4.52	15.87	2.125		7		N/A
SM	Spanish	A	25ACP	4.56	13.58	2.16		6	Eibar-type blowback	N/A
SM	SM Corporation	S	22LR	9.00		4.50		1	"Sporter"	N/A
Smith	O. Smith	R	32RF	6.80		3.00		5		286
Smith	O. Smith	R	41	6.90		2.75		5		286
Smith Americano	A. Errasti	R	38	9.25		4.72		5	also 32, 44 caliber	110
Smok	Nakulski	A	25ACP	3.93	9.17	1.97		6	Walther Model 9 copy	N/A
Smoker	Johnson, Bye	R	32rf			2.45		5	also 22, 38, 41rf	186
Sosso	Fabbrica Nazionale d'Armi	A	9Gli					2	endless-chain magazine	N/A
South African Police	Webley	A	9BL	8.00	34.00	5.00		8		382
SP	Steyr	A	32ACP	6.29	21.85	3.42		7	double action	328
SP602	Fabbrica Armi Sportive	A	22LR	11.02	44.10	5.51		5	or "Domino 602" target pistol	114
SPP	Steyr	A	9Par	11.10	45.85	5.12	6R	15,30		328
SP101	Sturm, Ruger	R	38		27.00	3.00		5	many variants	332
Speed Six	Sturm, Ruger	R	357Mag	7.75	34.55	2.75		5	other barrels	333
Spencer	Columbia Armory	R	38	7.28		3.00		5		90
Sphinx	ITM; Sphinx	A	380ACP	6.15	23.00	3.23		10	".3 AT"; also in 9Pol	316
Sphinx	Sphinx	A	9Par	8.00	36.35	4.52	6R	15	"AT2000S"; other calibers	316
Spirlet	Spirlet	R	380	9.75		5.00		5		N/A
SPP1M	Tsinntochmash	A	4.5spe	9.60	33.50		SB	4	underwater pistol	349
Sprinter	Garate, Anitua	A	25ACP	4.65	15.00	2.20		8		139
Spy	Norwich Pistol Co.	R	22rf					7		237
Squibman	Squires, Bingham	R	38		24.50	4.00		6	"M100D" and others	322
Squibman Thunderchief	Squires, Bingham	R	38			4.00		6		322

Name or Model	Maker/entry/origin	Type	Caliber, chambering	Length in	Weight oz	Barrel in	Rifling	Ctg Cap	Remarks	Page
Stallion	Galef	R	22LR	11.40	37.90	6.50		6	also 45 LColt, 357Mag	136
Standard Model	Bernardelli	A	22LR	6.30	24.16	3.54	6R	8	other barrel lengths	47
Stenda	Stendawerke	A	32ACP	5.70	22.75	3.00		8	improved Beholla	326
Stern	Wahl	A	25ACP	4.91	15.52	2.42	6R	10		360
Stechkin	Izhevsk	A	9Mak	8.85	36.34	5.00	4R	20	selective fire	179
Stingray	Hy Hunter	A	25ACP	4.56	14.80	2.24	10R	7	actually Reck P-8	173
Stock	F. Stock	A	25ACP	4.75	12.50	2.48	4R	7		329
Stock	F. Stock	A	32ACP	6.81	23.50	3.62	4R	8		329
Stop	Fémáru	A	32ACP	6.50	21.50	3.93		7	M1912; also in 380ACP	126
Stosel	Retolaza	A	25ACP	4.56	13.10	2.16		6	FN-Browning M1906 copy	261
Stosel	Retolaza	A	32ACP	6.30	29.00	3.46		7	Eibar-type blowback	261
Sundance	Sundance Industries	A	25ACP	4.88	13.90	2.00		7	"A-25"	N/A
Super Blackhawk	Sturm, Ruger	R	44Mag	13.38	48.00	7.50		6		333
Super Blackhawk	Sturm, Ruger	R	480Rug	15.00	58.00	9.50	6R	6	also with 7.5in barrel	333
Super Blackhawk Hunter	Sturm, Ruger	R	44Mag	13.63	52.00	7.50	6R	6		331
Super Destroyer	Gaztañaga, Trocaola	A	32ACP	5.70	19.90	3.23		8	Walther PP copy	141
Super Match	Bernardelli	A	9Par	9.25	38.80	4.92	6R	14	Competition pistol	47
Super Redhawk	Sturm, Ruger	R	44Mag	13.00	52.90	7.50		6	also 9.5in barrel	333
Surete	I. Gaztañaga	A	32ACP	6.13	21.15	3.35		7	FN-Browning M1910 copy	141
Swamp Angel	Forehand & Wadsworth	R	41rf					5		128
Swift	I. Johnson	R	38					5	hammer or hammerless	185
Sympathique	MAPF/Unique	A	25ACP	4.13	12.87	2.08		7	or "Unique Model 10"	206
Syntech	Ram-Line	A	22LR	9.85	28.20	5.50		15		N/A
TAC	Trocaola y Aranzabal	R	32	10.82		5.90		6	Colt copy; also 32-20WCF	348
TAC	Trocaola y Aranzabal	R	38	9.45	28.20	4.52		6	Colt Police Positive copy	348
TAC	Trocaola y Aranzabal	R	32	10.62		4.23		6	S&W M&P copy; also 38	348
Tala	Talleres Armes Livianas	A	22LR	7.28		3.36		10		338
Tanke	Orueta	R	38	7.48		3.54		5	"Automatic Model 1-A"	244
Tanque	Ojanguren y Vidosa	A	25ACP	4.25	10.95	1.77		6		243
Target	I. Johnson	R	22LR	10.75	34.00	6.00		8	or "Model 57A"	185
Target Bulldog	Charter Arms	R	357Mag	10.00	28.90	5.50		5	also 44Spl and 9Par	64
Tarn	Swift	A	9Par	11.00	34.92	5.00		8	prototypes only; 1945	337
Tatra	Spanish	A	25ACP	4.64	13.40	2.20		6	Eibar-type blowback	N/A
Tauler	Gabilondo	A							Llama models sold by Tauler	135
TEC9	Intratec	A	9Par	5.75	17.65	3.00		7	also in 380ACP	176
TEC40	Intratec	A	40S&W	6.30	18.00	3.25		6	also in 45ACP	176
Tell	Büchel	S	22RF	14.76	40.00	12.00		1	free pistol	55
Terrible	Arrizabalaga	A	25ACP	4.33	12.35	2.09		6	or "Campeon"	21
Terror	Forehard & Wadsworth	R	32RF					5	also 6-shot variant	128
Teuf-Teuf	Belgian	A	25ACP							N/A
Teuf-Teuf	Arizmendi y Goenaga	A	32ACP	4.48	12.52	2.04		6		18
Texas Border Special	Texas Longhorn	R	45			4.72		5	other calibers to order	345
Texas Marshal	Hawes	R	357Mag	11.75	44.00	6.00		6		157
Texas Ranger	Réunies	R	38	10.20		5.20		6		261
Texas Scout	H. Schmidt	R	22LR	10.00		4.75		5		279
Thalco	Röhm GmbH	R	22LR	5.90	11.50	2.36		6	or "Röhm RG-10"	266
Thames	Thames Arms	R	32	6.92		3.15		5		346
Thames	Thames Arms.	R	38	10.62		6.00		5	identical with Thames	346
Thayer	Thayer, Robertson & Carey	R	38	10.62	6.00			5	Eibar-type blowback	346
Thieme & Edeler	Thieme & Edeler	A	32ACP	5.78	21.35	3.23		7	patent extraction system	347
Thomas	Tipping & Lawden	R	320					5	patent extraction; also 450cf	347
Thomas	Tipping & Lawden	R	380	9.80	24.70	4.96		5	or "Third Model"	69
Thuer Model	Colt	S	41RF	4.88	6.52	2.52		1	"M1919"	29
Thunder	M. Bascaran	A	25ACP	4.33	13.22	1.97		6		48
Thunder 9	Bersa	A	9Par	7.87	28.98	4.70	6R	15		48
Thunder 22	Bersa	A	22LR	6.57	24.33	3.50	6R	10		48
Thunder 380	Bersa	A	380ACP	6.57	25.40	3.50	6R	7		48
Tiger	USA	R	32RF	6.00		2.50		5		N/A
Tigre	Garate, Anitua	A	25ACP	4,56	13.75	2.25		6	Eibar-type blowback	138
Tipo Rafaga	Trejo	A	22Lr	6.30	21.85	2.93		10	selective fire	348
Tipo Rafaga Especial	Trejo	A	22LR	7.67	28.00	4.13		15	selective fire	348
Tisa	Salaberrin	A	25ACP	4.65	13.40	2.16		6	FN-Browning M1906 copy	273
Titan	Retolaza	A	25ACP	4.52	12.52	2.1	6R	6	identical with "Gallus"	261
Titan	G. Tanfoglio	A	25ACP	4.60	12.00	2.44		6	external hammer	339
Titanic	Retolaza	A	25ACP	4.52	13.75	2.12	6R	6	FN-Browning M1906 copy	261
Titanic	Retolaza	A	32ACP	5.70	21.50	3.15	6R	7	"M1914"; Eibar-type blowback	261
Tiwa	Spanish	A	25ACP	7.28	15.37	4.92	6R	6	Eibar type, extended barrel	N/A
TK	Tula	A	6.3TK	5.03	14.10	2.68		7	or "TOZ"	350
Tokagypt	Fegyver	A	9Par	7.55	32.00	4.52		7		124
Tokarev	Tula	A	7.62Rus	7.71	32.00	4.52	4R	7		350
Touriste	MAPF/Unique	A	25ACP	4.13	12.87	2.08		7	or "Unique Model 10"	206
Tower Bull Dog	Webley	R	450	6.25	29.00	2.40	7R	5		375
Towers Police Safety	Hopkins & Allen	R	38			2.87		5		172
TOZ	Tula	A	6.3TK	5.03	14.10	2.68		7	or "TK"	350
TP	Walther Sportwaffenfabrik	A	25ACP	5.25	11.00	2.56	6R	6	also in 22LR	369

Name or Model	Maker/entry/origin	Type	Caliber, chambering	Length in	Weight oz	Barrel in	Rifling	Ctg Cap	Remarks	Page
TP1	Pickert (Arminius)	S	22XLrf	13.77	31.75	10.0		1	target pistol	248
TP2	Pickert (Arminius)	S	22XLrf	15.75	33.50	11.80		1	target pistol; set trigger	248
TP70	Korriphila	A	25ACP	4.65	12.70	2.60		6	"Norton TP-70" in USA	194
TPH	Walther Sportwaffenfabrik	A	25ACP	5.31	11.46	2.79	6R	6	also in 22LR	369
Trailblazer	Uberti	R	22LR	11.00	34.00	5.50		6		352
Tramp's Terror	Hood Firearms	R	22RF	5.20		2.50		7		170
Tranter	Tranter	R	450	11.75	37.75	5.75	6R	6	representative; many variants	347
Trapper	Harrington & Richardson	R	22LR	10.00	22.00	6.00		9	or "Model 722"	156
Trifire	Arminex	A	45ACP	8.62	42.45	5.00	6L	7		19
Triomphe	Apaolozo	A	25ACP	4.40	13.00	2.08		6	FN-Browning M1906 copy	16
Triomphe Francaise	MAPF/Unique	A	25ACP	4.13	12.87	2.08		7	or "Unique Model 10"	205
Triplex	D. Acha	A	25ACP	4.13	13.75	1.77		6	FN-Browning M1906 copy	9
Triumph	Garate, Anitua	A	32ACP	7.48	23.80	4.52		9	same as "La Lira"	139
Trocaola	Trocaola y Aranzabal	R	32					6	S&W type; many variants	348
Trocaola	Trocaola y Aranzabal	R	38	10.00		4.78		5	"Modelo de Seguridad"	348
Trocaola	Trocaola y Aranzabal	R	45	11.00	24.00	5.10		5	British OP Mark 1 No 2	348
Trooper	Colt	R	38	9.25	34.00	4.00		6		78
Trooper	Colt	R	357Mag	11.50	42.00	6.00		6	"Mark III"	78
Trophy	Hawes	R	38	10.45	38.45	6.00		6	also 22LR	157
Trophy II	Mitchell	A	22LR	9.72	44.45	5.50		9	High Standard type	229
True Blue	Norwich Pistol Co.	R	32RF					5		237
Trust	Grande Précision	A	25ACP	4.56	13.75	2.16		6	Eibar-type blowback	146
Trust	Grande Précision	A	32ACP	6.15	29.25	3.46		9	Eibar-type blowback	146
Trust Supra	Grande Précision	A	25ACP	4.52	13.55	1.97		6	FN-Browning M1906 copy	146
TS22	Astra	A	22LR	9.25	35.25	5.9	6R	10	target variant of the A-80	24
Ttibar	Industrias SRL	A	22LR	10.00		5.50		10	target pistol	N/A
Tue Tue	Galand	R	22rf					5	also 25ACP version	136
Turbiaux	Turbiaux	M	6cf					10	pinfire palm-squeezer	351
Turbiaux	Turbiaux	M	8cf					7	center-fire version	351
Turkish Model	Smith & Wesson	R	44rf	12.00	40.00	6.50		6	single action	293
Tycoon	Johnson, Bye	R	22rf	5.70		3.50		7	also 32rf	186
Tycoon	Johnson, Bye	R	38rf	6.00		3.50		5	also 41rf	186
Type 1	Japan Gun Co.	A	32ACP	6.26	23.80	3.46	6R	9	Hamada	183
Type 2	Japan Gun Co.	A	8Nam	6.97	26.00	3.74	6R	6	Hamada, Yato	183
Type 51	Chinese State/Norinco	A	7.62Rus	7.68	31.40	45.27		8	TT-33 copy	65
Type 59	Chinese State/Norinco	A	9Mak	6.38	25.75	3.70		8	Makarov copy	65
Type 64	Chinese State/Norinco	A	7.62Chi	6.20	19.70	3.46	4	7	Walther PPK copy	65
Type 64-1	Norinco	A	7.65T64	8.74	62.84	3.74		9	silenced; special cartridge	65
Type 64	North Korean State factories	A	32ACP	6.70	22.90	4.00		7	FN-Browning M1900 copy	237
Type 67	Chinese State/Norinco	A	7.65T64	8.86	35.98	3.50		9	silenced; improved Type 64	65
Type 68	North Korean State factories	A	7.62Rus	7.28	28.00	4.25		8	Tokarev TT33 copy	237
Type 77	Norinco	A	32ACP	5.83	17.64	3.46	4	7	revival of Lignose Einhand	236
Type 77B	Norinco	A	9Mak						new design of Einhand	236
Type 80	Norinco	A	7.62Chi	11.81	38.80			10/20	selective fire	236
Type 84	Norinco	A	7.62Chi	4.76	13.40	2.17		6		236
Type 213	Norinco	A	9Par	7.68	31.39	4.57		8	Type 51 in 9mm Parabellum	236
Type 213A	Norinco	A	9Par	7.68	31.75	4.57		14	Type 213 with bigger mag	236
Type 213B	Norinco	A	9Par	7.68	31.39	4.57		8		236
UAE	Union Armeria Eibaressa	A	25ACP	4.40	12.80	1.97		6	Eibar-type blowback	357
UAZ	U. Anschütz	S	22No7					1	or "Büchel Tell"	15
UC	Urrejola	A	32ACP	5.90	21.15	3.35		7	licensed copy of "Ruby"	358
Ulster Bull Dog	Webley	R	450cf	9.25	30.00	2.38	7R	6	limited number	375
Ultrastar	Star	A	9Par	6.92	26.10	3.50	6R	9	also 40&SW	325
UMC	Norwich Pistol Co.	R	32rf	6.50		2.64		5		237
Undercover	Charter Arms	R	38	6.25	16.00	1.97		5	also 3in barrel	64
Undercoverette	Charter Arms	R	32	6.25	16.40	1.97		6		64
Union	Urizar	A	32ACP	5.50	23.60	2.75		7		357
Union	Unceta	A	25ACP	4.52	13.75	2.16		6	FN-Browning M1906 copy	112
Union	Unceta	A	32ACP	5.70	24.70	2.95		6	variant Models 1-4	112
Union	Seytres	A	25ACP	4.68	10.75	2.36		6	also 10-shot version	284
Union	Seytres	A	32ACP	7.87	20.65	4.52		7	Eibar-type blowback	284
Union	Union Firearms Co.	R	32			3.00		5	Lefever auto-revolver	357
Union	Union Firearms Co.	A	32	6.29	20.10	3.54		8	Riefgraber's patent	357
Union Jack	Hood	R	32rf					5	also 7-shot 22rf	171
Unique	Mossberg; Shatuck	M	32					4	multi-brl; also 22, 30 cal	231,285
Unis	MAPF/Unique	A	various						Unique sales name	206
Unis	Salaberrin	A	25ACP	4.48	12.85	2.16		6	FN-Browning M1906 copy	273
Universal	Hopkins & Allen	R	32rf					6		172
USP	Heckler & Koch	A	40S&W	7.64	27.50	4.25		13	also 9Par, 45ACP	161
Urrejola	Urrejola	A	32ACP	6.29	22.75	3.54		7	Eibar-type blowback	358
US Arms Co.	US Arms	R	32rf	6.50	15.85	2.25		6	also 7-shot 22rf	358
US Arms Co.	US Arms	R	41rf	6.50	18.50	2.25		5	also 38rf	358
US Revolver	I. Johnson	R	22rf	5,30	13.00	2.125		7		185
US Revolver	I. Johnson	R	32rf	6.50	16.40	3.00		5	hammer or hammerless	185
US Revolver	I. Johnson	R	38rf	7.52	17.50	3.25		5	hammer or hammerless	185

Name or Model	Maker/entry/origin	Type	Caliber, chambering	Length in	Weight oz	Barrel in	Rifling	Ctg Cap	Remarks	Page
Uzi	Israeli Military Industries	A	9Par	9.45	58.30	4.52		20	scaled-down Uzi SMG	176
Vainquer	Mendiola	A	25ACP	4.40	13.25	2.125		6	FN-Browning M1906 copy	N/A
Valor	Röhm	R	22RF	5.90	11.50	2.36		6	or "Röhm RG-10"	267
VB	V. Bernardelli	R	32 S&W	10.43	19.93	5.90	6T	6	S&W M&P type	45
VB-MR	V. Bernardelli	R	22LR	12.20	21.86	7.0	6R	6	target version of VB	45
VB Pocket Model	V. Bernardelli	R	32 S&W	5.31	18.87	1.96	6R	6	also in 22LR	45
VEC95CG	Voere	S	6UCC	18.70		12.20		-	caseless cartridge	359
Velo-Brom	Retolaza Hermanos	R	5.5VD					5	also 6mm version	260
Velo-Dog	Galand	R	5.5VD	4.92		1.85		5	innumerable copies exist	136
Velo-Mith	various Spanish	R	25ACP					5,6	many variations	17,92
Velosmith	Spanish	R	25ACP	7.95		4.13		10	hammerless, not Velo-Dog	N/A
Velo-Stark	Garate Brothers	R	25ACP	5.50		1.97		5	hammerless, folding trigger	138
Vencedor	C. Santos	A	32ACP	6.10	22.55	3.35		9	Eibar; also 25ACP	274
Venus	Urizar	A	32ACP	5.70	20.30	3.20		6	Eibar; also 25ACP	357
Venus	Will	A	25ACP	4.72	11.65	1.97		7		389
Verney-Carron	Verney-Carron	A	26ACP	4.68	15.85	2.36		7	actually Star M1912	359
Verney-Carron	Verney-Carron	R	32	5.12		1.85		6	Belgian origin?	359
Vesta	Echeverria	A	25ACP	4.65	11.85	2.16		7	Eibar type; also 380ACP	104
Vestpocket	Röhm	R	22rf	5.90	11.50	2.36		6	or Röhm RG-10	267
Veto	USA	R	32rf	6.30		2.50		5		N/A
Vici	Belgian	A	25ACP	4.57	13.75	2.125		7		N/A
Victor	F. Arizmendi	A	25ACP	4.65	9.35	2.10		6	later renamed "Singer"	17
Victor	F. Arizmendi	A	32ACP	5.90	18.70	3.15		7	later renamed "Singer"	17
Victor	Marlin	R	38rf			2.69		1	Derringer, 1870	212
Victor II	Mitchell	A	22LR	8.86	43.50	4.52		10	High Standard type	229
Victoria	Unceta	A	25ACP	4.33	11.48	2.16		7	Eibar-type blowback	112
Victoria	Unceta	A	32ACP	5.70	21.35	3.23		6	Eibar-type blowback	112
Victory	Victory	A	9Par	8.60	45.00	4.37	6R	17	"MC-5" multi-caliber	359
Victory	Zulaica	A	25ACP	4.40	13.40	2.04		6	FN-Browning M1906 copy	392
Victory Model	Smith & Wesson	R	38	8.45		4.00		6	World War II type	296
Vilar	Spanish	A	32ACP	5.70	21.65	3.15		7	Eibar-type blowback	N/A
Vincitor	Zulaica	A	25ACP	4.40	10.90	3.15		6	"M1914"	393
Vincitor	Zulaica	A	32ACP	6.00	23.76	3.34		7	"M1914 No. 2"	393
Vindex	MAPF/Unique	A	25ACP	4.13	12.87	2.08		7	or "Unique Model 10"	206
Virginian	Hämmerli	R	357Mag	11.00	40.00	5.50		6	also 45LColt; various barrels	151
Virginian Dragoon	Interarms	R	44Mag	13.85	44.00	8.37		6	also 45LColt, 357Mag	176
Vite	Echave y Arizmendi	A	25ACP	4.40	13.55	2.125		8	"1912"; Eibar-type blowback	104
Vite	Echave y Arizmendi	A	25ACP	4.65	14.28	2.16		6	"1913"; Browning 1906 copy	104
Vite	Echave y Arizmendi	A	32ACP	6.00	28.20	3.30		9	"1915"; Eibar-type blowback	104
VP	Bernardelli	A	25ACP	4.10	9.20	1.96	6R	5	or Vest Pocket or Mol PA	47
VP70	Heckler & Koch	A	9Par	8.00	28.92	4.56		18	selective fire	160
Volkspistole	Gustloff	A	9Par	11.25	34.00	5.13	6R	8	prototypes only	148
Vulcain	Spanish	A	25ACP	4.52	10.75	1.97	4R	6	FN-Browning M1906 copy	355
Waco	Sociedad Español	A	25ACP	4.41	10.65	2.04		6	sold by Urizar	315
Walam	Fegyver	A	380ACP	6.90	25.55	3.93		8	also 32ACP	123
Walman	Arizmendi y Goenaga	A	32ACP	6.00	20.15	3.46		8		18
Walman	Arizmendi y Goenaga	A	25ACP	4.40	11.45	2.16		6		18
Walman	Arizmendi y Goenaga	A	32ACP	6.13	19.90	3.26		7		18
Walman	Arizmendi y Goenaga	A	380ACP	5.90	21.85	3.46		7	FN-Browning M1910 copy	18
War Eagle	Steel City Arms	A	9Par			4.00		15		326
Warnant	Warnant	A	25ACP	4.33	10.40	1.65		6		372
Warnant	Warnant	R	32	9.05		3.93		5	folding trigger, top-break	372
Warnant	Warnant	R	38	11.22		5.90		6	top-break	372
Warner	Warner	A	32ACP	5.51	18.35	4.13		7	Schwarzlose M1908	372
Warwinck	G. Arizaga	A	32ACP	6.13	24.15	3.70		7	similar to Pinkerton	17
Webley	Webley	S	22LR	13.75	37.00	9.85		1	"Target Model"; variations	373
Webley	Webley	S	450cf	6.00	15.85	3.00		2	"Turnover"; double-barreled	373
Wegria-Charlier	Charlier	A	25ACP						no trigger, grip-fired	62
Welrod	BSA Ltd	S	32ACP	12.28	39.15	4.37	6R	6	integral silencer	54
Wesson & Harrington	Wesson & Harrington	R	22rf	6.90		2.75		5		N/A
Western Field	MAPF/Unique	A	22rf	6.05	21.50	3.07		6	or "Unique Model E"	208
Western Marshal	Hawes	R	357Mag	11.75	44.00	6.00		6		157
Western Style	Röhm GmbH	R	22LR	5.90	11.50	2.36		6	and "Röhm RG-10"	267
West Texas Flat-top	Texas Longhorn	R	45			7,.50		6	other calibers	345
White-Merrill	White-Merrill	A	45	8.45	38.25	6.00		10	prototypes, 1906-7	387
White Star	USA	R	32rf	6.57		2.45		5		N/A
Whitney	Whitney Arms Co.	R	32rf	6.30		2.50		7		387
Whitneyville	Whitney Arms Co.	R	38RF	5.45		3.28		5		387
Wichita	Wichita Arms	S	308	19.40	72.00	13.00		1	"Mark 40"; bolt action	388
Wichita	Wichita Arms	S	308		80.00	11.25		1	"Classic"; bolt action	388
Wichita	Wichita Arms	S	308	21.40	72.00	14.88		1	"Silhouette"; bolt action	388
Wide Awake	Hood	R	32RD			2.75		5		171
Wildey	Wildey	A	44WMag	11.00	51.00	6.00		8	gas operated; also 9Wmag	389
Winfield Arms	Norwich Pistol Co.	R	32rf	4.90		2.60		5		237
Wolverine	Whitney Firearms	A	22LR	9.00	23.00	4.60		10		388

Name or Model	Maker/entry/origin	Type	Caliber, chambering	Length in	Weight oz	Barrel in	Rifling	Ctg Cap	Remarks	Page
Woodsman	Colt	A	22LR	12.40	28.00	6.50		10		84
Woodsman	Colt	A	22LR	10.50	26.00	4.50		10		84
Woodsman	Colt	A	22LR	12.00	39.00	6.00		10	"Match Target"	84
WTM	Menz	A	25ACP	4.65	15.00	2.35	6R	6	vest-pocket	227
WTM, 1925	Sauer	A	25ACP	4.20	11.30	2.16		6		276
WTM, 1928	Sauer	A	25ACP	4.00	10.58	1.97		6		276
WTP1	Mauser	A	25ACP	4.49	11.65	2.40		6		218
WTP2	Mauser	A	25ACP	4.00	11.64	2.40		6		220
X300	I. Johnson	A	380ACP	6.10	20.00	3.00		6	or "Pony"	185
XL No. 1	Hopkins & Allen	R	22rf					7		172
XL No. 2	Hopkins & Allen	R	32rf	5.70		2.36		5		172
XL No. 2 1/2	Hopkins & Allen	R	32rf	5.82		2.36		5		172
XL No. 3	Hopkins & Allen	R	32rf	6.50		2.50		5		172
XL No. 3DA	Hopkins & Allen	R	32rf,cf	6.13		2.50		5	DA lock-work	172
XL No. 4	Hopkins & Allen	R	38			2.45		5		172
XL No. 5	Hopkins & Allen	R	38	8.85		6.00		5		172
XL No. 6	Hopkins & Allen	R	41rf	5.90		3.00		5		172
XL No. 7	Hopkins & Allen	R	41rf			2.50		5		172
XL Bulldog	Hopkins & Allen	R	38			3.15		5		172
XL Police	Hopkins & Allen	R	38			2.50		5		172
XP-100	Remington	S	221	16.73	60.00	10.43		1	"XP-100 Fireball", bolt action	258
XX Standard	Marlin	R	22rf	6.50		3.00		7	tip-barrel	212
XXX Standard	Marlin	R	30rf	6.89		3.00		5	tip-barrel	212
Ydeal	F. Arizmendi	A	25ACP	4.10	10.30	1.88		6		18
Ydeal	F. Arizmendi	A	32ACP	5.90	21.50	3.15		7	also 380ACP	18
You Bet	USA	R	22rf	5.45		2.35		7		N/A
Young America	Harrington & Richardson	R	32	8.00		4.50		5		156
Yovanovicz	Zastava	A	32ACP	7.28	28.20	4.25		8	"Model 1931"; also 380ACP	391
Z	Česká Zbrojovka	A	25ACP	4.48	15.00	2.125		6	or "Duo"	61
Zaragoza	Zaragoza	A	22LR	7.50	24.85	4.52		10	Colt M1911 style	391
Zehna	Zehner	A	25ACP	4.72	13.25	2.65		6		392
Zentrum	Bühag	S	22LR						free pistol	55
Zephyr	Röhm	R	22LR	5.90	11.50	2.36		6	or "Röhm RG-10"	267
Ziegenhan Model IV	Bühag	A	22LR	11.80	35.27	5.90		5	target pistol	55
ZKP524	Československá Zbrojovka	A	7.62Rus	8.07	31.75			8	also for 7.62Cze	62
ZKR551	Československá Zbrojovka	R	38	11.82	37.00	6.10	6R	6	target revolver	61
Zoli	Tanfoglio & Sabotti	A	25ACP	4.52	14.60	2.36		8		338
Zonda	Hispano-Argentina	A	22LR	8.50		4.72		10	or "Hafdasa"	169
Zulaica	Zulaica	A	32ACP	6.02	21.85	3.35		9	"M1914"; Eibar-type blowback	392
Zwylacka	Spanish	A	25ACP	4.65	13.22	2.05		6	FN-Browning M1906 copy	355

Definitions and technical terms are unavoidable in a book of this nature; to avoid lengthy explanations, most of the important terms (and some less well-known ones) are defined here for ready reference.

accelerator A device that, by using leverage, increases the speed of the recoiling bolt to separate it more positively from a recoiling barrel. It is uncommonly found on pistols, though not unknown. The Finnish Lahti is one example.

ACP "Automatic Colt Pistol"; an abbreviation suffixed to some types of cartridge, indicating their original use with Colt firearms and to distinguish them from other cartridges of the same nominal caliber.

American Eagle A name originally applied to a Hopkins & Allen (q.v.) revolver and, often generically, to any Parabellum (Luger) pistol to be found with the displayed-eagle mark above the chamber. It was first applied by DWM, the manufacturer, to 1000 pistols purchased for US Army field trials in the early 1900s, but it subsequently graced many guns sold commercially by A.F. Stoeger & Co. (q.v.) of New York City. The name has also been applied to 22 rimfire and 9mm centerfire Stoeger-Lugers, to a commemorative 06/73 Mauser-Parabellum (q.v.) made in the 1980s and also to a small quantity of near-copies of the German P08 made by the Mitchell Arms Company in the 1990s.

arbor The axis pin or rod on which the cylinder of a revolver is carried.

automatic pistol Strictly, an automatic weapon is one that, once the trigger is pressed, will fire and continue firing so long as the trigger remains pressed and ammunition remains in the magazine. It is applied colloquially to any form of self-loading pistol.

automatic revolver A revolver (e.g., Webley-Fosbery) that uses the forces of recoil to operate the mechanism and prepare for the next shot. It was also once used to signify an automatic-ejecting pattern, particularly in the period before 1914.

barrel extension A frame attached to the barrel of a weapon to carry the bolt. It also usually carries a means of locking the bolt to the extension, holding the bolt closed during firing.

barrel weights These are attached to the barrel of a target pistol to provide the distribution of weight and the balance that the shooter prefers and also to damp down the rise of the muzzle on firing.

belted A type of cartridge with a raised belt around the body, ahead of the extraction groove, that positively locates the cartridge in the chamber. Ammunition of this type is rarely used in handguns, though the BSA (q.v.) pistol was an exception.

bird's-head butt Popular on revolvers made in the late 19th century, this curves down to a pointed or "beaked" tip.

blowback Also known as "case projection", this is a system of operation in which the breech is kept closed solely by the inertia of the breechblock and pressure from the recoil spring. Pressure generated in the chamber on firing, once it overcomes this inertia, "blows the bolt back". Consequently, the breech is not positively locked at the moment of discharge. The term is also used colloquially for the many types of "blowback pistols" embodying such an action.

blow-forward This is analogous to, but the opposite of blowback (above). The barrel of the weapon is blown forward by the chamber pressure, allowing the empty case to be withdrawn before a spring returns the barrel to chamber a cartridge. The system is rare, being confined to a handful of guns such as the 1894-type Mannlicher, the Hino-Kornuro and the SchwarzIose.

bolt A device that closes the breech of a weapon; it usually suggests a separate component moving within the body of the weapon.

breechblock This is similar to a bolt; the dividing line has never been formally drawn, but in pistols, the inference is that a breechblock is part of the slide or other reciprocating part of the weapon and not an entirely independent unit.

Browning Link Also known as the "Browning Swinging Link", this method of locking a pistol breech was devised by John Browning in the 1890s and patented in Britain in 1897. One end of a link is pinned loosely to the barrel beneath the breech, and the other is pinned loosely to the pistol frame. When ready to fire, the barrel is held forward and lugs on its upper surface engage recesses inside the pistol slide. Slide and barrel recoil together on firing, but the link forces the rear of the barrel to move in an arc and withdraw the lugs from their recesses. Once the lugs are clear, the slide is free to recoil while the barrel is held by the link.

Browning cam An improvement on the swinging-link system and made after the end of World War I, this relies on a piece of metal beneath the breech, which has been formed into a cam path, riding on a transverse pin in the pistol frame. The pin acts on the cam path to force the rear of the barrel down, disconnecting its locking lugs from the slide and then restraining the barrel while the slide continues to run back.

caliber The internal diameter of a gun barrel. Strictly, the diameter of a cylinder that will just fit inside the bore, but more usually, the diameter between two opposite lands. The term is often mistakenly used as a synonym for "chambering" (q.v.).

centerfire A cartridge that carries its percussion cap centrally in the base; thus, by extension, a pistol using centerfire ammunition.

chamber The enlarged and shaped area of the interior of the gun barrel, at the breech, that receives the cartridge.

chambering The act of cutting a chamber (q.v.) in the barrel, but also used to indicate the cartridge a particular gun accepts — e.g., "chambering 9mm Parabellum", "chambered for 45 ACP". It should not be confused with caliber (q.v.), as the cartridge chambered in a 9mm-caliber pistol could be one of several alternatives (i.e., 9mm Short, 9mm Largo, 9mm Parabellum), but one chambering 22 LR rimfire, while still "22-caliber", is much more precisely identified.

charger A method of loading a magazine firearm, more commonly encountered in rifles than pistols, that relies on a metal frame holding several individual cartridges. The gun action is opened, the frame is placed over the entrance to the magazine, and the cartridges are pressed (usually with the thumb) out of the frame and into the magazine. Chargers are confusingly known as "clips" (q.v.) in North America, or sometimes as "stripper clips" to avoid problems of communication. The German C/96 Mauser and the Austro-Hungarian M7 pistol, the "Roth-Steyr", were among the few charger-loaded handguns to see extensive use.

clip A method of loading a magazine firearm with cartridges that are held in a separate metal frame. The action is opened and the *entire frame*, with cartridges, is placed in the magazine. When the action is closed, a spring-loaded arm forces up the cartridge inside the clip so that — as the action is worked — a new one is presented to the chamber. As the last cartridge is loaded, the clip falls (or is ejected) from the weapon. Many of the early Bergmann (q.v.) pistols were clip-loaded, though the additional advantages of the box magazine soon made clip-loading obsolete. The term "clip" is widely used in North America to describe what is more appropriately called a "charger".

compensator A device fitted to the muzzle of a firearm to divert some of the propellant gas that emerges behind the bullet upward, developing a downward thrust to counteract the rise of the muzzle during rapid fire.

Constabulary A name attached to numerous revolvers in the 1875-1900 period, all of which were more or less based upon the Royal Irish Constabulary revolver designed by Webley in 1872. The pattern was that of a large-caliber, short-barreled solid-frame revolver, gate-loaded or with a removable cylinder, and many Belgian and French companies produced them under this generic name.

crane A hinged arm attached to the frame of a revolver, carrying the cylinder arbor and the cylinder, that allows the cylinder to be swung sideways out of the frame. Extraction and unloading can then be undertaken simply by pressing backward on the head of the arbor pin. The crane may also be termed "yoke".

cycle of operation The complete sequence of operations required in an automatic weapon — firing, unlocking the breech, extracting, ejecting, cocking, feeding, chambering and breech-locking. (Not all functions may be present, some may overlap, and the order of occurrence may change from gun to gun.)

cyclic rate The theoretical continuous rate of fire of an automatic weapon, assuming an unlimited supply of ammunition and ignoring the need to change magazines.

cylinder The part of a revolver that contains the ammunition; it revolves to present a loaded chamber behind the barrel for each cycle of the trigger mechanism.

cylinder stop A part of the lockwork that rises from the frame of a revolver and, engaging in a recess in the cylinder, locates the cylinder so that a chamber is aligned with the barrel ready to fire.

de-cocking lever A device that safely lowers the hammer of a cocked automatic pistol, even though the chamber may contain a live round. It allows a loaded pistol to be carried without fear of accidental discharge, and, in individual designs, can be used to re-cock the action when required.

delayed blowback This is a blowback (q.v.) mechanism with an additional restraint or brake placed on the bolt or other breech-closure device to slow the opening movement. There is no positive breech lock. Also listed as "retarded" or "hesitation" blowback.

disconnector The part of the trigger mechanism of a semi-automatic pistol that disconnects the trigger from the remainder of the firing train after each shot. The shooter must release the trigger and take a fresh pressure to fire the next shot, preventing the gun firing continuously.

double action A hammer-type firing mechanism in which the hammer can be retracted to the cocked position by the thumb and then released by the trigger; or, alternatively, can be raised, cocked, and released simply by a longer pull of the trigger lever.

Eibar A town in the province of Guipúzcoa, in the Basque region of Spain, which was virtually the home of Spanish gunmaking prior to the Spanish Civil War (1936-9).

Eibar pistol In the early years of the century, Eibar gunmakers developed a distinctive copy of the Browning pistol pattern, generally offering lower quality and several manufacturing shortcuts. One of the most distinctive features of an Eibar-type pistol is the large safety catch mounted on the frame above the trigger, where it doubles as an aid to stripping. Pulling the slide slightly back allows this catch to be pushed upward, hooking into a recess to hold the slide while the barrel is removed. Another prominent feature is provided by the cocking or retraction grips on the rear of the slide, which have often been cut radially to allow a simple lathe to be used instead of an expensive milling machine.

ejector A device for throwing empty cases out of a pistol. In the case of a revolver, the term usually applies to a star-shaped plate in the center of the cylinder, which, as the action is opened, is forced out by a mechanical linkage until it catches beneath the rims of the cases to push them out of the chambers. It thus extracts and ejects in a single movement. In the case of an automatic pistol, the ejector is usually a fixed metal bar or blade that intercepts the empty case as it is withdrawn from the breech by the extractor, knocking it clear of the gun. There are, however, many variations on this theme.

extractor A device used to pull the cartridge case from the chamber of a revolver cylinder. As noted above, this is usually done by one mechanism that also ejects the case clear of the weapon. In automatic pistols, the extractor is almost always a claw attached to the bolt or breech unit that engages with the cartridge-case rim (or a groove ahead of it) to pull the case from the chamber during recoil, before presenting it to the ejector. Some pistols (e.g., early Bergmanns) were made without an extractor or ejector, relying on residual gas pressure to blow cases from the chamber. This presented problems when trying to unload an unfired round, and most designs of this type were speedily abandoned.

feedway That part of a weapon where a cartridge, taken from the feed system, is positioned ready to be loaded into the chamber. It is rarely seen in pistols, where the distance between the magazine and the chamber is generally very short.

fluted chamber A chamber (q.v.) containing grooves cut parallel with the axis of the barrel. These grooves extend into the bore but do not reach the mouth of the chamber. On firing, some of the propellant gas leaks down these grooves to "float" the case on a layer of high-pressure gas, compensating for the pressure inside the case. It is associated with guns in which the breech begins opening while the pressure is still high. If the chamber wall was plain, internal pressure would cause the body of the cartridge case to stick firmly against the chamber and any rearward movement of the bolt would tear the base off the cartridge. Floating the case ensures that there is less resistance to movement, and the bolt can begin opening without risk of damage. It is rarely seen in pistols other than a few that have chambered rifle ammunition.

folding trigger A lever that is hinged to fold forward beneath the frame, allowing the gun to be carried easily in the pocket without the trigger catching. It is more common on revolvers than automatic pistols, though a few examples of the latter will be found.

Frontier Colt made this name famous with their Model 1873 Single Action Army, though exactly where and when it first acquired the name "Frontier" is far from clear. Since then, almost every maker of a Model 1873 copy has used the name somewhere in the title.

gas-seal revolver A class of revolver in which the cylinder and barrel are mechanically forced together before firing, eliminating the gap that exists between the barrel and chamber-mouth of conventional designs. Only the 1895-pattern Nagant (q.v.) was made in quantity, though Pieper in Herstal-lèz-Liége and Österreichische Waffenfabriks-Gesellschaft in Steyr made comparable guns in small numbers. The system was claimed to prevent leakage of gas and any consequent waste of the power of the cartridge, but tests undertaken prior to 1914 showed that the improvements were comparatively small.

gate loading This method of loading a solid-frame revolver was achieved by hinging part of the recoil shield to give access to one of the chambers. After the empty cases had been removed individually through the open gate, new rounds could be inserted as the cylinder was rotated by hand to expose each chamber in turn.

grip safety A safety device forming part of the grip of a pistol and connected to the firing mechanism. Unless this grip is held tightly and forced inward, the firing mechanism is interrupted and the gun cannot fire. It prevents accidental discharge arising from dropping or mishandling, but, contrary to myth, is not intended to prevent suicide. Among the handguns fitted with grip safeties are most pre-1914 Parabellums, the 1911/1911A1-type Colt-Brownings and the Japanese Nambu. Some systems work better than others!

hammerless Genuinely hammerless pistols use a striker instead of a hammer to fire the cap in the base of the cartridge case; "pseudo-hammerless" pistols may look similar externally, but have a conventional hammer inside the frame. Pseudo-hammerless revolvers have a conventional hammer shrouded or concealed within the frame, though the tip of the hammer spur may be exposed to allow thumb-cocking.

hinged frame This describes a gun in which the barrel (and cylinder in revolvers) forms a separate unit attached to the frame by a hinge bolt, so that by releasing a catch, the barrel — and often also the cylinder of a revolver — can be tipped to expose the rear. The phrase is generally assumed to indicate a barrel that tips downward, but a few designs have opened upward. It is generally applied to single-shot pistols and revolvers, particularly the early Smith & Wessons and the British Webleys, though Beretta and Manufacture Française d'Armes et Cycles ("Manufrance") are among the makers of hinged-frame or "tip-barrel" automatic pistols.

inertia firing pin These firing pins, generally encountered in automatic pistols, are shorter than the tunnel in which they rest. When the hammer is lowered to press on the pin, the pin-tip does not protrude through the bush in the breech face to touch the cartridge cap. Only the violent blow of a properly released hammer will overcome the natural inertia of the pin to drive it forward far enough to strike the cap hard enough to fire the cartridge. An inertia firing pin is invariably accompanied by a small spring, pushing back against a collar to withdraw the pin behind the breech face after the hammer has rebounded. This prevents the pin-tip striking the cap of the new cartridge as it is brought into place.

lands The raised portions of a gun-barrel bore between rifling grooves.

loaded-chamber indicator A pin or other device that gives visual and tactile indication of the presence of a cartridge in the chamber.

lock time The time that elapses between pressing the trigger and the explosion of the cartridge. It is important in target shooting, where the shortest possible lock time is desirable to reduce the chance of a shift in aim. A sensitive trigger is obligatory, but short lock times are also dependent upon the design of the firing mechanism.

lockwork An expression covering the whole of the mechanism necessary to fire a gun, from the trigger through to the hammer or striker.

long recoil A system of operation relying on the barrel and breech recoiling locked together for a distance at least as long as a complete unfired cartridge. At the end of this stroke, the bolt is unlocked and held while the barrel runs back to its forward position. During this movement, the cartridge case is extracted and ejected, and a fresh round is placed in the feedway. The bolt is then released, runs forward to chamber a round, locks, and the gun is ready to fire. Long recoil is not common in any type of firearm, least of all in pistols, but some of the Frommers and several notable designs have employed it successfully.

LR, Long Rifle The identifying title of the most common 22 rimfire cartridge, distinguishing it from 22 Short and 22 Long.

machine pistol An imprecise term that is often applied to submachine guns (particularly German ones); here, it means a pistol, such as the Mauser *Schnellfeuerpistole*, with a firing mechanism that has been adapted to fire fully automatically when required. These guns are rare, but not as rare as they ought to be!

magazine safety A safety system ensuring that the firing mechanism of the pistol will not function if the magazine is absent. The objective is to prevent a common accident where, though the magazine has been removed, a round remains in the chamber to be fired when the owner tries to strip the weapon. Magazine safeties are rarely found on military pistols, as the chambered round could come in useful if the shooter is disturbed during the process of changing magazines.

main spring The spring that propels the hammer.

mechanical repeater A class of pistol, briefly popular in the 1880s, in which the cycle of operation was carried out mechanically. This was usually accomplished by finger operation in a ring trigger. Most guns embodied a rotating bolt (e.g., Bittner). The principal defect was that they worked well enough when clean and well oiled, but became progressively harder to use as the weapon got dirty. They were swept away by the arrival of the automatic pistol.

muzzle brake A muzzle attachment similar to a compensator (q.v.), this is intended to turn the emerging gases and drive them backward to pull on the muzzle and thus reduce the recoil. Devices of this type are rarely seen on pistols, excepting some modern ultra-high power designs.

non-ejecting A class of revolver without the ability to eject spent cartridges — apart from removing the cylinder to punch out the cases with a suitable implement, re-loading the cylinder and then replacing it.

open-topped slide A form of pistol slide in which the front upper surface is removed; a short section may be left at the muzzle end to carry the front sight and generally stiffen the construction, thus giving the effect of a very large ejection opening. Alternatively, the two sides are joined at the front below the barrel. Construction of this type typifies many Beretta pistols and also the "Le Français" series made by Manufacture Française des Armes et Cycles de Saint-Étienne.

open-frame revolver This is simply a comparatively weak construction in which the barrel is held to the frame only in front of the trigger area, without a link or "topstrap" between the top of the barrel and the standing breech; the top of the cylinder is entirely exposed. Most of the caplock Colts typify this class.

Parabellum A word derived from the Latin *si vis pacem, para bellum* ("If you want peace, prepare for war"), which was adopted by Deutsche Waffen- & Munitionsfabriken (q.v.) as a telegraphic address — "Parabellum, Berlin" — and later as a trademark. It is associated with DWM firearms, including the pistol familiarly known as the Luger, and cartridges such as the 9mm Parabellum.

prawl A part of the butt frame that curves back over the web of the thumb to prevent the grip riding down in the hand when firing.

proofmarks These are stamped or pressed into components of firearms (such as the barrel and frame) to certify that it has been tested by an official body and found strong enough to withstand use. Unfortunately, spurious proofmarks are not entirely unknown, particularly on some of the less reputable Spanish products of the 1920s.

recoil shield The round plate, usually forming part of the standing breech, which conceals the rear of a revolver cylinder. It prevents the shock of recoil shaking the cartridges loose in their chambers and (in extreme cases) preventing rotation of the cylinder.

recoil spring The spring in an automatic pistol that returns the bolt or slide after firing. It is often, and perhaps more accurately, called the "return spring".

ribbed barrel A barrel forged with a stiffening top-rib, into which the front sight blade is formed or fixed, this is commonly encountered in revolvers. The object is to give the barrel rigidity without the additional weight greater external diameter would have contributed.

rimfire A cartridge in which the priming composition is distributed around the hollow rim. The firing mechanism must be constructed to crush the cartridge-case rim between the firing pin or striker and the chamber face. The system was very popular in the early days of cartridge weapons, as ammunition was easier to make than the first centerfire designs, but it cannot withstand much internal pressure and is now confined largely to 22-caliber pistols and rifles, as well as a few low-powered 9mm shotguns.

rimless These cartridge cases have an extraction groove in the base, the rim thus created being the same diameter as the head of the case. Such a design makes magazine feed more reliable, owing to the absence of protruding rims.

rimmed These cartridges have a protruding rim at the base of the case, which butts against the chamber face to position the cartridge.

Usually confined to revolvers, ammunition of this type may also be used in automatic pistols destined for target shooting.

rod ejection A system of ejection, used with gate-loaded (q.v.) revolvers, that relied on a rod carried below the barrel or on a swinging arm. The rod could be forced back to expel an empty case from the chamber and then drive it out through the open loading gate.

sear A lever or catch, connected to the trigger, that holds the hammer or firing pin back until released by trigger pressure.

self-cocking A firing mechanism in which the action of cocking and releasing the hammer or firing pin is performed by pulling back the trigger. Sometimes misleadingly called "double action only".

self-loading The proper term for any gun that, through recoil or other firing-induced force, extracts and ejects the empty case, then reloads and re-cocks to leave the mechanism ready to fire when the trigger is next pressed. The common "automatic" is properly called a self-loading pistol.

semi-rimmed A cartridge case with an extraction groove like a rimless (q.v.) pattern but with an exposed rim of slightly greater diameter than the case-head. Consequently, the rim can position the case correctly in the chamber but is small enough to avoid interference with the magazine feed. Invented by John Browning, it was first used with the 32 ACP (7.65mm Auto) cartridge.

set trigger A trigger mechanism, commonly used in target weapons, with a lever or button to "set" the trigger by taking up all the slack in the system. The result is so sensitive that only a very slight pressure on the trigger is sufficient to fire the gun.

sheath(ed) trigger A form of trigger, common on pre-1914 revolvers and very occasionally found on automatic pistols, with a projection formed in the frame to conceal or "sheath" the trigger. When the hammer is cocked, the trigger springs forward far enough to be pressed to fire. Fittings of this type are also, if misleadingly, called a "stud trigger" — which would be more appropriate for a protruding button-trigger.

silencer A device attached to the muzzle of a weapon — or incorporated in its construction — to tap gases emerging from the barrel. These are diverted into a chamber where they are allowed to expand, reducing temperature and pressure, before release to the atmosphere. This prevents, or at least greatly reduces, noise created by muzzle blast.

single-action A popular firing mechanism in which the hammer must be independently cocked, either by hand or by the action of the gun, before being released by the trigger. It is common on pre-1914 revolvers and most automatic pistols, the latter being cocked during recoil.

slide stop A catch in the frame of an automatic pistol that can be used to lock the slide to the rear for cleaning or dismantling. Alternatively, automatically moved by the magazine platform, it may lock the slide open to indicate that the last shot has been fired. Most slide stops must be released manually, though a few disengage automatically when a full magazine has been inserted.

solid frame These revolvers have their frames forged or milled in one piece, with an aperture for a cylinder that may be swung out on a crane (q.v.), gate-loaded or entirely removed to reload.

standing breech A fixed part of the pistol frame that abuts the base of the cartridge in the firing position, carrying the firing pin or the firing-pin bush. It is usually encountered on revolvers and single-shot pistols but may also be found on some odd forms of automatic pistol — particularly those embodying blow-forward (q.v.) action.

stirrup latch Commonly encountered on Webley revolvers, this is a method of securing the topstrap of a hinged-frame revolver to the standing breech, comprising a metal frame with a flat top and curved sides. This is hinged to the standing breech and has a thumb-operated locking arm. The whole thing resembles an inverted stirrup; when the arm is pressed, the top section tips backward to release the end of the topstrap.

striker A firing pin of generous proportions, driven by a spring to acquire sufficient momentum to fire the cartridge cap.

Suicide Special This collective term was coined by Duncan McConnell writing in the *American Rifleman* in 1948 but achieved popularity only after the publication in 1956 of *Suicide Special Revolvers* by Donald B. Webster Jr. It is customarily used to describe a particular type of cheap solid-frame non-ejecting single-action revolver, often with a sheathed trigger, that was made in the USA c. 1865-80. Guns of this type flooded the market after the expiration of the Rollin White patent (see "Smith & Wesson"), selling for as little as 60 cents each.

tip-up revolver This is simply a hinged-frame revolver with the barrel unit connected to the frame in such a way that it rises when opened. The most common form of construction relies on a transverse pivot on the standing breech, immediately in front of the hammer, which receives a topstrap formed integrally with the barrel.

toggle lock A method of locking the bolt or breechblock of an automatic firearm by using a two-lever linkage. One end is attached to the barrel extension, the other to the bolt, and in the middle lies a hinge. With the bolt closed, the two levers lie flat, with the hinge slightly below the centerline, and any thrust is directed downward against the breech, frame or receiver. The central hinge is raised as the gun recoils, breaking the strut-like resistance and allowing the two levers to fold up. The bolt then moves backward to open the breech. First used on the Maxim machinegun and, most famously, on the Parabellum pistol, the system is rarely encountered elsewhere, as it demands fine machining and very consistent ammunition performance.

Tractor Pistol A term peculiar to Britain, referring to double-barreled 410-caliber hammer pistols with barrels 10-15 inches long, that could be conveniently stowed under the seat of a tractor by farm workers. They were used to shoot rabbits or other small game that appeared during the day's work. Outlawed by the minimum-length barrel stipulation of the Shotgun Act of 1967, they disappeared overnight.

ventilated rib This is a form of ribbed barrel (q.v.) in which the rib is held away from the barrel by a series of supports, allowing air to circulate beneath it. The object is to cool the barrel to prevent convection currents of hot air rising from the barrel surface to disturb the sight line.

wadcutter This cartridge is used by target shooters. It is loaded with a flat-faced bullet to punch a very clean hole in the target — thus reducing arguments over shots that lie close to the edge of a scoring ring.

APPENDIX III

Bibliography

Much historical information has been omitted to concentrate on essentials. For those wishing to discover more about handguns, the following books are recommended:

BADY, Donald B.: *Colt Automatic Pistols*, 1896-1955. Borden Publishing Company, Alhambra, California, USA; revised (second) edition, 1973.

BARNES, Frank C. (Stan Skinner, ed.): *Cartridges of the World* ("The Book for Every Shooter, Collector and Handloader"). Krause Publications, Iola, Wisconsin; tenth edition, 2003.

BOOTHROYD, Geoffrey: *The Handgun*. Safari Press, Inc., Huntington Beach, California; 1999.

BREATHED, John W., Jr, and SCHROEDER, Joseph J., Jr: *System Mauser* ("A pictorial history of the Model 1896 self-loading pistol"). Handgun Press, Chicago, Illinois, USA; 1967.

BROWNING, John, and GENTRY, Curt; *John M. Browning American Gunmaker*. Doubleday & Company, New York; 1964.

BRUCE, Gordon, and REINHART, Christian: *Webley Revolvers*. Verlag Stocker-Schmid, Dietikon-Zürich, Switzerland; 1988.

DERBY, Harry: *The Hand Cannons of Imperial Japan*. Derby Publishing Company, Charlotte, North Carolina, USA; 1981.

DOWELL, Williarn C.: *The Webley Story* ("A History of Webley Pistols and Revolvers and the Development of the Pistol Cartridge"). The Skyrac Press, Kirkgate, Leeds, England; 1962.

ERLMEIER, Hans A., and BRANDT, Jacob H.: *Manual of Pistol & Revolver Cartridges*. Journal-Verlag Schwend GmbH, Schwäbisch Hall, Germany; volume 1 (centerfire, metric calibres) 1967, volume 2 (centerfire, Anglo-American calibres) 1980.

EZELL, Edward C.: *Handguns of the World* ("Military revolvers and selfloaders from 1870 to 1945"). Stackpole Books, Harrisburg, Pennsylvania, USA; 1981.

— *Small Arms Today*. Stackpole Books, Harrisburg, Pennsylvania, USA; second edition, 1988.

FORS, Williarn Barlow: *Collector's Handbook of U.S. Cartridge Revolvers*, 1856-1899. Adams Press, Chicago, Illinois, USA; 1973.

GANGAROSA, Gene, Jr.: *Complete Guide to Compact Handguns*. Stoeger Publishing Co, Wayne, New Jersey; 1997.

— *Complete Guide to Service Handguns*. Stoeger Publishing Co., Wayne, New Jersey; 1998.

— *Spanish Handguns*. Stoeger Publishing Co., Wayne, New Jersey; 2001.

GLUCKMAN, Colonel Arcadi: *United States Martial Pistols & Revolvers*. The Stackpole Company, Harrisburg, Pennsylvania, USA; 1956.

GORTZ, Joachim: *Die Pistole 08*. Verlag Stocker-Schmid, Dietikon-Zürich, Switzerland, and Motorbuch-Verlag, Stuttgart, Germany; 1985.

— and WALTER, John D.: *The Navy Luger* ("The 9mm Pistole 1904 and the Imperial German Navy: a concise illustrated history"). The Lyon Press, Eastbourne, England, and Handgun Press, Chicago, Illinois, USA; 1988.

GRENNELL, Dean A.: *The Gun Digest Book of the .45*. DBI Books, Northfield, Illinois; 1989.

HACKLEY, Frank W., WOODIN, Williarn H., and SCRANTON, Edward L.: *History of Modern US Military Small Arms Ammunition*. The Macinillan Company, New York, USA; volume 1 (1880-1939), 1976. The Gun Room Press, Aledo, Illinois, USA; volume 2 (1940-45), 1978.

HARTNIK, A.E.: *Encyclopedia of Pistols and Revolvers*. Knickerbocker Press, New York; 1997.

HATCH, Alden: *Remington Arms in American History*. Remington Arms Company, Inc., Ilion, New York, USA; revised edition, 1972.

HATCHER, Major General Julian S.: *Hatcher's Notebook* ("A Standard Reference Book for Shooters, Gunsmiths, Balisticians, Historians, Hunters and Collectors"). The Stackpole Company, Harrisburg, Pennsylvania, USA; third edition, 1962.

HÄUSLER, Fritz: Schweizer *Fastfeuerwaffen–Armes de poing suisses–Swiss Handguns*. Verlag Häusler, Frauenfeld, Switzerland; 1975.

HAVEN, Charles T., and BELDEN, Frank A.: *A History of the Colt Revolver*. William Morrow & Company, New York, USA; 1940.

HEER, Eugen: *Die Faustfeuerwaffen von 1850 bis zur Gegenwart*. Part of "Geschichte und Entwicklung der Militärhandfeuerwaffen in der Schweiz" ("history and development of military hand weapons in Switzerland"). Akademische Druck- und Verlagsanstalt, Graz, Austria; 1971.

HOGG, Ian V.: *German Handguns, 1871-2001*. Greenhill Books; London, and Stackpole Books, Mechanicsburg, Pennsylvania; 2001.

— *Military Pistols & Revolvers*. Arms & Armour Press, London; 1988.

— (revised by John Walter) *Small Arms. Pistols and Rifles*. Greenhill Books, London, and Stackpole Books, Mechanicsburg, Pennsylvania; revised edition, 2003.

— *The Greenhill Military Small Arms Data Book* ("Essential data, 1870-2000, in one book"). Greenhill Books, London, and Stackpole Books, Mechanicsburg, Pennsylvania; 2000.

— *The Cartridge Guide* ("The Small Arms Ammunition Identification Manual"). Arms & Armour Press, London; 1982.

— and WEEKS, John S.: *Military Small Arms of the Twentieth Century*. Krause Publications, Iola, Wisconsin; seventh edition, 2000.

HONEYCUTT, Fred L., Jr: *Military Pistols of Japan*. Julin Books, Lake Park, Florida, USA; 1982.

JINKS, Roy G.: *History of Smith & Wesson*. Beinfeld Publishing Company, North Hollywood, California, USA; 1977.

KASLER, Peter A.: *Glock: The New Wave in Combat Handguns*. Paladin Press, Boulder, Colorado; 1993.

KÖNIG, Klaus-Peter; *Faustfeuerwaffen*. Motorbuch Verlag GmbH, Stuttgart, Germany; 1980.

KOPEC, John A., GRAHAM, Ron, and MOORE, Kenneth C.: *A Study of the Colt Single Action Army Revolver*. La Puente, California, USA; 1976.

LAW, Clive A.: *Canadian Military Handguns, 1855-1985*. Museum Restoration Service, Bloomfield, Ontario, Canada; 1994.

LONG, Duncan: *Combat Revolvers*. Paladin Press, Boulder, Colorado; 1999.

— *Glock's Handguns*. Desert Publications, El Dorado, Arizona; 1996.

— *Hand Cannons: The World's Most Powerful Handguns*. Paladin Press, Boulder, Colorado; 1995.

MARKHAM, George [John Walter]: *Guns of the Empire* ("Firearms of the British Soldier, 1837-1987"). Arms & Armour Press, London; 1990.

— *Guns of the Reich* ("Firearms of the German Forces, 1939-1945"). Arms & Armour Press, London; 1989.

— *Guns of the Wild West* ("Firearms of the American Frontier, 1849-1917"). Arms & Armour Press, London; 1991.

MATHEWS, J. Howard; *Firearms Identification*. Charles C. Thomas, Springfield, Illinois, USA; three volumes, 1962-73.

NEAL, Robert J., and JINKS, Roy G.: *Smith & Wesson 1857-1945*. A.S. Barnes & Company, Inc., South Brunswick, New Jersey, USA; 1966.

NELSON, Thomas B., and MUSGRAVE, Daniel D.: *The World's Machine Pistols & Submachine Guns*. TBN Enterprises, Alexandria, Virginia; 1980.

PARSONS, John E.: *Smith & Wesson Revolvers: The Pioneer Single Action Models*. William Morrow & Company, New York, USA; 1957.

— *The Peacemaker and its Rivals*. William Morrow & Company, New York, USA; 1950.

RAMOS, J.M.: *The CZ-75 Family: The Ultimate Combat Handgun*. Paladin Press, Boulder, Colorado; 1990.

RECKENDORF, Hans: *Die Militär-Faustfeuerwaffen des Königreiches Preussens und des Deutschen Reiches* ("The military small arms of the Prussian Kingdom and the German Empire"). Published privately, Dortmund-Schönau, Germany; 1978.

— *Die Handwaffen der Königlich Preussischen und der Kaiserliche Marine* ("The small arms of the Royal Prussian and the Imperial Navy"). Published privately, Dortmund-Schönau, Germany; 1983.

REINHART, Christian: *Pistolen und Revolver in der Schweiz* ("Pistols and revolvers in Switzerland"). Verlag Stocker-Schmid, Dietikon-Zürich, Switzerland, and Motor-Buch Verlag, Stuttgart, Germany; 1988.

— and AM RHYN, Michael: *Faustfeuerwaffen II. Selbstladepistolen*. The sixth volume of "Bewaffnung und Ausrüstung der Schweizer Armee seit 1817". Verlag Stocker-Schmid, Dietikon-Zürich, Switzerland; 1976.

ROSA, Joseph G.: *Guns of the American West (1776-1900)*. Arms & Armour Press, London; 1985.

RUBÍ, B. Barceló: *Armamento Portatil Español (1764-1939): una labora artillera*. Libreria Editorial San Martin, Madrid, Spain; 1976.

SCHWING, Ned: *Standard Catalog of Firearms*. Krause Publications, Iola, Wisconsin; fourteenth edition, 2004.

— *Standard Catalog of Military Firearms*. Krause Publications, Iola, Wisconsin; 2001.

SERVEN, James E.: *Colt Firearms from 1836*. The Foundation Press, La Habra, California, USA; seventh printing, 1972.

SIMPSON, Layne: *The Custom Government Model Pistol*. Wolfe Publishing Co., Prescott, Arizona; 1994.

SMITH, Walter H.B.: *Mauser, Walther & Mannlicher Firearms*. The Stackpole Company, Harrisburg, Pennsylvania, USA; 1971.

— *The Book of Pistols & Revolvers*. The Stackpole Company, Harrisburg, Pennsylvania, USA; seventh edition, 1968.

STERN, Daniel K.: *10 Shots Quick* ("The Fascinating Story of the Savage Pocket Automatics"). Globe Printing Company, San Jose, California; 1967.

STEVENS, Blake R.: *The Browning High Power Automatic Pistol* ("Expanded Edition"). Collector Grade Publications, Canada; 1996.

STILL, Jan C.: *Axis Pistols* ("The Pistols of Germany and Her Allies in Two World Wars. Volume II"). Published privately, Douglas, Alaska; 1986.

— *Imperial Lugers and Their Accessories* ("The Pistols of Germany and Her Allies in Two World Wars. Volume IV"). Published privately, Douglas, Alaska; 1991.

— *The Pistols of Germany and Its Allies in Two World Wars* ("Vol. 1, Military Pistols of Imperial Germany and Her World War I Allies, and Postwar Military, Para-military and Police Reworks"). Published privately, Douglas, Alaska; 1982.

— *Third Reich Lugers and Their Accessories* ("The Pistols of Germany and Her Allies in Two World Wars. Volume III"). Published privately, Douglas, Alaska; 1988.

— *Weimar and Early Nazi Lugers and Their Accessories* ("The Pistols of Germany and Her Allies in Two World Wars. Volume V"). Published privately, Douglas, Alaska; 1993.

SUPICA, Jim, and NAHAS, Richard: *Standard Catalog of Smith & Wesson*. Krause Publications, Iola, Wisconsin; second edition, 2001.

TAFFIN, John: *Big Bore Sixguns*. Krause Publications, Iola, Wisconsin; 1997.

TAYLERSON, Anthony W.F. [with R.A.N. ANDREWS and J. FIRTH]: *The Revolver, 1818-1865*. Herbert Jenkins Ltd, London; 1968.

— *The Revolver, 1865-1888*. Herbert Jenkins Ltd, London; 1966.

— *The Revolver, 1889-1914*. Barrie & Jenkins, London; 1970.

WALTER, John D.: *Allied Small Arms of World War One*. The Crowood Press, Ramsbury, Wiltshire, England; 2000.

— *Central Powers' Small Arms of World War One*. The Crowood Press, Ramsbury, Wiltshire, England; 1999.

— *German Military Handguns, 1879-1918*. Arms & Armour Press, London; 1980.

— *Military Handguns of Two World Wars*. Greenhill Books, London, and Stackpole Books, Mechanicsburg, Pennsylvania; 2003.

— *Secret Firearms* ("An illustrated history of Miniature & Concealed Handguns"). Arms & Armour Press, London; 1997.

— *The Greenhill Dictionary of Guns and Gunmakers* ("From Colt's first patent to the present day, 1836-2001. Military small arms, sporting guns and rifles, air and gas guns, designers, manufacturers, inventors, patentees, trademarks, brandnames and monograms"). Greenhill Books, London, and Stackpole Books, Mechanicsburg, Pennsylvania, 2001.

— *The Guns that Won the West* ("Firearms on the American Frontier, 1848-1898"). Greenhill Books, London, and Stackpole Books, Mechanicsburg, Pennsylvania; 1999.

— *The Luger Book* ("The encyclopedia of Borchardt and Borchardt-Luger handguns, 1885-1985"). Arms & Armour Press, London; 1986.

— *The Luger Story* ("The Standard History of the World's Most Famous Handgun"). Greenhill Books, London, and Stackpole Books, Mechanicsburg, Pennsylvania; 1995.

— *The Pistol Book*. Arms & Armour Press, London; second edition, 1988.

— *The World's Elite Forces*. Small Arms & Accessories. Greenhill Books, London, and Stackpole Books, Mechanicsburg, Pennsylvania; 2002.

WHITE, Henry P., MUNHALL, Barton D., and BEARSE, Ray: *Centrefire Pistol & Revolver Cartridges*. A.S.Barnes & Company, New York and South Brunswick, USA; 1967.

WILSON, Lieutenant Colonel Robert K. [ed., Ian V. Hogg]: *Textbook of Automatic Pistols*. Arms & Armour Press, London; 1975.

WILSON, R.L.: *The Colt Heritage* ("The Official History of Colt Firearms from 1836 to the Present"). Simon & Schuster, New York, USA; undated (1979).

— *Colt, An American Legend*. Blacksmith Corporation, Chino Valley; 1991.

WINANT, Lewis: *Firearms Curiosa*. Ray Riling Arms Books Company, Philadelphia, Pennsylvania, USA; 1961.

WOOB, J.B.: *Beretta Automatic Pistols*. Stackpole Books, Harrisburg, Pennsylvania; 1995.

ZHUK, A.B: *The Illustrated Encyclopedia of Handguns* ("Pistols and revolvers of the world, 1870 to the present"). Greenhill Books, London; 1995.